AIA GUIDE TO NEW YORK CITY

This edition is dedicated
to the memory of our friends and colleagues
lost since the fourth edition in 2000:
Raimund Abraham, Max Abramovitz, Edward Larabee Barnes,
Armand Bartos, Robert Bien, Max Bond, Paul Byard, Giorgio Cavaglieri,
Victor Christ-Janer, Lewis Davis, Richard Foster,
Margot Gayle, Harmon Goldstone, Charles Gwathmey,
John Hejduk, Philip Johnson, Stephen A. Kliment, Morris Lapidus,
Jan Pokorny, James Rossant, Paul Rudolph, and Hugh Stubbins.

For Norval, 1926-2009, and Bernard M. Leadon, 1917-2009.

American Institute of Architects
New York Chapter

AIA GUIDE TO NEW YORK CITY

Fifth Edition

Norval White   Elliot Willensky
with Fran Leadon

OXFORD
UNIVERSITY PRESS
2010

OXFORD
UNIVERSITY PRESS

Oxford University Press, Inc., publishes works
that further Oxford University's objective of excellence
in research, scholarship, and education.

Oxford   New York
Auckland   Cape Town   Dar es Salaam   Hong Kong   Karachi
Kuala Lumpur   Madrid   Melbourne   Mexico City   Nairobi
New Delhi   Shanghai   Taipei   Toronto

With offices in
Argentina   Austria   Brazil   Chile   Czech Republic   France   Greece
Guatemala   Hungary   Italy   Japan   Poland   Portugal   Singapore
South Korea   Switzerland   Thailand   Turkey   Ukraine   Vietnam

Originally published, in a different form,
by Macmillan Publishing Company in 1968
and 1978, by Harcourt Brace Publishing
in 1988, and by Three Rivers Press in 2000.

Published by Oxford University Press, Inc.
198 Madison Avenue, New York, New York 10016

www.oup.com

Oxford is a registered trademark of Oxford University Press

Library of Congress Cataloging-in-Publication Data
AIA guide to New York City / Norval White, Elliot Willensky with Fran Leadon. — 5th ed.
p.   cm.
At head of title: New York Chapter, American Institute of Architects
Includes index.
ISBN 978-0-19-538385-0; 978-0-19-538386-7 (pbk.)
1. Architecture—New York (State)—New York—Guidebooks.
2. New York (N.Y.)—Buildings, structures, etc.—Guidebooks.
3. New York (N.Y.)—Guidebooks.
I. White, Norval, 1926-2009.
II. Willensky, Elliot, 1933-1990.
III. Leadon, Fran, 1966-.
IV. American Institute of Architects. New York Chapter. V. Title: American Institute of Architects guide to
New York City. VI. Title: New York Chapter, American Institute of Architects.
NA735.N5A78 2010
720.9747'1—dc22   2010001289

American Institute of Architects, New York Chapter

1 3 5 7 9 8 6 4 2

Printed in the United States of America
on acid-free paper

PREFACE

Since 2000 (and the last edition of this Guide), New York City endured an unspeakable tragedy and a subsequent boom and bust that transformed the City. A swift, cowardly act of terrorism on September 11, 2001, horrific beyond our collective imaginations, took the lives of men, women, and children in the midst of a typical week, devastating lower Manhattan. What seemed permanent was suddenly gone, and as this edition goes to press, the World Trade Center site is still physically a void, with only the first steel shoots of rebirth rising out of the ground. But on that crisp, clear Tuesday morning in 2001, our memories were instantly divided, even as the attacks unfolded, into pre– and post–September 11 New York. Tragedies have a way of making previous disagreements and troubles seem trivial, and suddenly, we were all, first and foremost, New Yorkers, its citizens pulling together as if one.

September 11 was followed by an unprecedented building boom, with myriad luxury condominiums promising a whole new interior world *(Pre-war accents! Exquisitely textured sandstone! Rich walnut! Indoor dog runs! Lap pools! Glass! Glass! Glass!)*. Some serious architecture resulted, much of it included in this new edition. *Richard Meier, Asymptote, Winka Dubbeldam, Diller Scofidio+Renfro*, and *SHoP* get much-deserved accolades for their highly publicized work in Manhattan, but also praised in these pages are *Peter Gluck, George Ranalli, Alexander Gorlin, BKSK, Caples Jefferson, Smith-Miller & Hawkinson*, and *Hanrahan Meyers*, architects toiling quietly away on civic-minded projects in less fashionable fringes of the outer boroughs (East New York, Crotona Park, Flushing, Gowanus).

Meanwhile, to sate the building boom, the international crowd descended in force *(Jean Nouvel, Herzog & Demeuron, Enrique Norten, Norman Foster, Renzo Piano)*, while American stars expanded their base *(Frank Gehry, Michael Graves, Gwathmey Siegel, Robert A.M. Stern)*. And for good civic architecture we've had the continuing works of the *Polshek Partnership, Beyer Blinder Belle, Cook+Fox, Dattner Associates, Davis Brody Bond Aedas, FxFowle, Gruzen Samton, Gluckman Mayner, Pei Cobb Freed & Partners, Perkins Eastman, Platt Byard Dovell White*, and *Rafael Viñoly*.

By the time the boom peaked, much of the City had become a three-dimensional futures market in glass and steel. Advertisements promoted new condominiums as sound investments; unbuilt projects were bought and sold *(flipped*, in the spatially evocative parlance) by virtue of a promisingly graphic website and a gleaming sales office open for business. Projects no further along than a poured foundation were considered done deals, and the units sold out immediately. When boom turned to bust in the fall of 2008, we were left with remnants of stalled projects littering neighborhoods from Carroll Gardens to Williamsburg, Hell's Kitchen to Long Island City: deserted construction sites, half-finished steel frames, tattered safety netting flapping in the breeze.

Over the last decade, rising rents have forced out countless small business owners, and once-ubiquitous neighborhood mainstays (bodegas, hardware stores, drugstores, lunch counters) became endangered species. But the boom had its positive side: new attention was paid to neighborhoods long forgotten (Red Hook, Bedford-Stuyvesant, Bushwick, Brownsville), crime decreased to a level not seen since the early 1960s, neglected buildings were rescued and restored, and thousands of low- and moderate-income housing units were built. Landscape architects, a focus of this new edition, were busy (especially *Michael Van Valkenburgh, James Corner, Lee Weintraub*, and *Thomas Balsley*) and their ambitious new public parks (Brooklyn Bridge Park, Hudson River Park, Teardrop Park, the High Line, Erie Basin Park, Riverside Park South) are new civic jewels, benefiting everyone.

Despite the upheavals of boom and bust, we found much of the rest of the City explored during the making of this edition virtually unchanged since 2000, seemingly frozen in time. We, along with 22 of our energetic students from City College, personally visited and photographed every café, chapel, club, convent, and condominium mentioned in these pages. Amid the City's constant demolition and construction, we found that many neighborhoods (Mariners Harbor, Tottenville, Richmond Hill, Bayside, Gerritsen Beach, City Island) are still very much as they were 40 years ago. We encourage you to take this Guide and a good camera and go see them. Midtown is worth a visit, of course, but so is Canarsie. New York City is still full of these authentic and humble enclaves, as yet unconquered by Whole Foods, Fairway, Ikea, and the Apple Store—places where egg creams can still be swigged without irony and a slice is still a slice.

Norval White
Fran Leadon
2009

CONTENTS

BROOKLYN   577

QUEENS 748

THE BRONX   820

USING THE GUIDE

The Guide is designed to serve a whole spectrum of readers, from the casual wanderer to the serious historian; from the provincial New Yorker who rarely, if ever, ventures west of the Hudson River, to the visitor who wants to see more than the well-touted monuments, musicals, and museums.

Some of you may explore familiar neighborhoods before venturing into unfamiliar places. Braver souls will immediately "go abroad" as tourists in other parts of the City, savoring new and exotic precincts. Some may wish to start at the Battery, working their way geographically or following the chronological development of the City.

For the less athletic, you may leave the Guide on your coffee table to leaf through the pages at your leisure, and enjoy excursions of the City in the mind, without ever stepping outside your door. And you will also be able to use the Guide to show visitors from Paris, Tokyo, San Francisco, or even Hackensack how to view and relish not only New York's major monuments, landmarks, and historic districts but also the richness of its buildings and precincts in every borough.

Organization: The Guide, like the City, is divided into five **boroughs**. Each section is organized to illustrate the complexity and richness of a particular borough and, within that borough, its various **sectors** (Lower Manhattan, Northern Brooklyn, Northeastern Queens, etc.). The sectors, in turn, are divided into neighborhoods, called **precincts** (Financial District, Greenpoint, Fresh Meadows, etc.).

Entries: Each entry in the Guide is numbered—the numbers appear within brackets—and is identified by name in boldface type. (Sometimes there is also a former or original name or names.) This information is followed by the address and/or block location, the date of completion (or projected completion), and finally by the designer's name. When no other title follows a designer's name, it should be assumed that title is architect. Identification lines at the top of left-hand pages indicate the borough and sector being discussed. Right-hand pages show the precinct(s) being dealt with and the map page on which the entries appear.

Security: New York is a vast, busy, and complicated city, with much to see. But at certain times and in certain places, sightseers—gawkers if you will —can inadvertently send out signals of distraction or vulnerability that are cues to those with less than lofty motives. Beware. Remember that there is safety in numbers. Don't walk in desolate areas. Don't tour at night. Do take a friend along—it's more fun that way.

Photography: Increasingly in post–September 11th New York, photography of buildings often invites suspicion. There is no law against photographing buildings, so long as the photographer is shooting from public property (the sidewalk or street, for instance). Homeowners, overly assertive security guards, or construction workers might well tell you to stop photographing. In those instances, while it might be tempting to explain the United States Constitution to the objecting party, we have found it best to put your camera away, smile, and avoid a confrontation.

Officially Designated Landmarks: Individual structures and natural objects, scenic landmarks, and historic districts, officially designated by the N.Y.C. Landmarks Preservation Commission (and confirmed by the City Council), are identified by a solid apple ●ʸ . Designated interior landmarks are noted similarly.

Style Symbols: Symbols printed in color signify that an entry is a notable example of a particular architectural style or stylistic group:

Colonial/Colonial Revival. Literally the architecture of New York as a colony, whether of the Netherlands or Great Britain. It doesn't necessarily imply either white clapboard or shutters and is best exemplified in Manhattan by St. Paul's Chapel (the only "Colonial" building remaining from before 1776) and by some of the Dutch Colonial farmhouses of southeastern Brooklyn. The Revival of the late 19th century provided overblown versions for a romanticized Colonial Revival.

Georgian/Federal/Neo-Georgian/Neo-Federal. The Federal style was the first—and therefore the "modern" (in its day)—architecture of our new republic, a modification of the contemporaneous Georgian architecture of London. Dignified and restrained, it emphasized geometric form and harmonious proportion and was executed in both wood and masonry. The neo-Federal and neo-Georgian are early 20th-century revivals of 18th- and 19th-century originals.

Greek Revival. The product of both political and aesthetic interests. The Greek Revolution made Greece independent of the Turks (the Ottoman Empire) in the 1820s. The newly won independence recalled, to fascinated American intellectuals, the patrician democracy of ancient Greece and its elegant architecture, created more than 400 years before the birth of Christ. In America, Classical columns and orders were used mostly for decoration, often at entrance doorways in otherwise simply designed row houses. Whole buildings, however, sometimes were also recalled: Sailors' Snug Harbor in Staten Island and Federal Hall National Memorial on Wall Street are reincarnations of great Greek temples.

Gothic Revival/Neo-Gothic/Neo-Tudor/Neo-Byzantine. In its purest form Gothic Revival refers to the literary and aesthetic movement of the 1830s and 1840s, coincidental with that in England. Interest in the presumed "goodness" of long-gone medieval times suggested that the emulation of its Gothic architecture would instill a similar goodness among the present wicked. The posture gained enough adherents to inspire a re-revival around 1900 and later, particularly for colleges, urban high schools, and major churches, in styles labeled neo-Gothic and neo-Tudor (with all its Scarsdale suburban-style stockbroker "half-timbering").

Italianate and/or **Villa Style**. Buildings with gently pitched (they seem flat) roofs crowning a boxy volume often with a frieze of tiny attic windows. In its more romantic version, the Villa Style, it utilizes a tall, usually asymmetrically placed tower. Litchfield Villa in Brooklyn's Prospect Park is the City's finest example.

The Picturesque: Romanesque Revival/Stick and/or **Shingle Style/Queen Anne**. The late 19th-century Romanesque Revival is a vigorous style more common in Chicago than in New York and is based on the bold arch-and-vault construction of the early medieval Romanesque. Architect *H.H. Richardson* was its greatest American exponent, but Brooklyn's *Frank Freeman* was not far behind. The wooden architecture that exploited the balloon frame's formal possibilities, and/or exploited exposed timber as a structural-decorative exterior armature (the Stick and/or Shingle Styles) was often designed at the same time by the same architects in the 1870s through 1890s. Both are picturesque.

Renaissance Revival/Anglo-Italianate/Beaux Arts. Drawn from the architecture of 15th- through 17th-century Italy, France, and England. On this side of the Atlantic, Italian palazzi, French chateaux, and English clubs became the stylistic image for banking institutions, super town houses, clubs and government buildings, and even mercantile establishments (cf. the Federal Reserve Bank of New York and many of SoHo's cast-iron loft buildings). Proselytized through the École des Beaux Arts in Paris, the Beaux Arts style, from about 1890 to 1920, inflated Classical allusions to truly supergrandiose proportions, as at Grand Central Terminal, the Custom House at Bowling Green, and The New York Public Library.

Roman Revival/Baroque Revival. Roman Revival was more pompous and posturing than Greek Revival. It brought back some of the histrionics of Classical Rome, particularly through use of domes, columns, pediments, and sculpture of a grandiose nature. Baroque Revival echoed similar elaborations found in the quirkier and even more ornate Baroque era that followed the Renaissance.

Art Deco/Art Moderne. The largely French-inspired styles of the era between World Wars I and II, when cubistic structures were embellished by the use of florid ornament inspired by the Paris Exposition of 1925 (Art Deco) and later by sleek streamlined ornament that also influenced the Paris Exposition of 1937 (Art Moderne). Many polychromed works of *Ely Jacques Kahn* exemplify Art Deco; the corner-windowed "modernistic" apartment houses of the Grand Concourse in the Bronx and the Majestic Apartments at Central Park West and 72nd Street are Art Moderne.

Modern/Postmodern. The breakdown of modern (or modernist) into component styles is a new phenomenon, based on the concept that modern as we know it today has its own internal history: beginning with the works of *Louis Sullivan* (the Condict Building on Bleecker Street) and *Frank Lloyd Wright* (best known here for his much later Guggenheim Museum); followed by Art Deco and Art Moderne (see above) and the Bauhaus and/or International Style as imported by *Walter Gropius*, *Marcel Breuer*, and *Ludwig Mies van der Rohe* (the Seagram Building). Postmodernism, notable for its embrace of ornament, historical quotations, and conservative massing, became a fad in the City beginning in the late 1970s and continues today in recent projects by *Robert A.M. Stern*, *Joseph Pell Lombardi*, and others. Recently renewed interest in early modernism, along with technological innovations allowing more liberal use of glass, has brought a **modern Revival** style to the City in earnest (*Deborah Berke's* 48 Bond Street and the *Polshek Partnership's* Standard Hotel are but two of many examples).

ACKNOWLEDGMENTS

This Fifth Edition is a linear descendant of the original, self-published version feverishly prepared over a nine-month period for the 1967 convention of the American Institute of Architects in New York City. Because its approach profoundly influenced subsequent updatings of the Guide, it seems appropriate to credit once again those who helped the authors to set the first edition's tone: writers *John Morris Dixon, Ann Douglass, Mina Hamilton, Roger Feinstein, Henry Hope Reed, Jr., Sophia Duckworth*, and *Richard Dattner*.

Innumerable individuals have contributed information, ideas, comments, corrections, and considerable moral support. As we have done with previous editions, we wish to recognize our legion of supporters:

Thank you to everyone at the **American Institute of Architects New York Chapter**, including *Rick Bell* FAIA, Executive Director, *Sherida E. Paulsen* FAIA, 2009 President, *Anthony P. Schirripa* AIA, 2010 President, *Margaret Castillo* AIA, 2011 President, Vice President *Illya Azaroff* AIA, *Oculus* editor *Kristen Richards*, and *e-Oculus* editor *Jessica Sheridan*.

At **Oxford University Press**, we wish to thank President *Tim Barton* and Vice President *Niko Pfund* for their enthusiastic support for the Guide, our devoted editor *Timothy Bent*, and *Nancy Hoagland, Christine Dahlin, Sarah Russo, Christian Purdy, Megan Kennedy*, and *Dayne Poshusta*.

We salute the administration of the **Bernard and Ann Spitzer School of Architecture at the City College of New York**, including President *Robert E. Paaswell*, Provost *Zeev Dagan*, Dean *George Ranalli*, Chair *Peter Gisolfi*, Deputy Chair *Gordon Gebert*, and our colleagues including *Jacob Alspector, Carmi Bee, Lance Jay Brown, Judy Connorton, Jerrilynn Dodds, Marta Gutman, Michael Sorkin*, and *Lee Weintraub*.

This Guide would simply not have been possible without the energy and enthusiasm, outdoors and in all kinds of weather, of our exceptional student research assistants from the **Spitzer School of Architecture**. These 22 young architects and landscape architects fanned out across the five boroughs, cameras and notepads in hand, contributing not only many of the photographs for this edition, but substantial research and writing as well: *Andrea Barley, Cinthia Cedeno, Amanda Chen, Glenn DeRoche, Mary Doumas, Christopher Drobny, Katja Dubinsky, William Eng, Jon Fouskaris, Jaimee Gee, Adrian Hayes, Calista Ho, Bradley Kaye, Tiffany Liu, Adrian Lopez, Douglas Moreno, Maria Olmedo, Marina Ovtchinnikova, Ross Pechenyy, Jason Prunty, Billy Schaefer*, and *David Seto*.

Thanks to our meticulous book designer, *Teresa Fox* of FoxPrint, our indexer *Martin Tulic*, copy editors *Angela Starita, Yuliya Ilizarov*, and *Jeremy Reed*, and *Ken Ficara*, who designed our photographic database and helped photograph Bedford-Stuyvesant and Crown Heights.

Thank you to *Marcus* and *Diana Willensky, James Weinberger, Ian Leadon* and *Ben Fraker* for the photography tips, *Tony Jin* for computer assistance, *Charles Puckette* and *Jen Larson* for transportation, navigation, and company on Staten Island, *Sean Wright* for car rides in the Bronx, *Yael Hameiri* for the walking tour of Astor Place, *Jesse Goldstine* for checking up on construction sites in Manhattan, *Claudia Moran* for her hospitality in Bed-Stuy, *Andrew Winters* and *Len Greco* for the High Line tour, *Brendan Coburn* for the Navy Yard tour, *Elliot Gordon* for answering questions in Ditmas Park, *Charles McKinney* at the Parks Department, *Barbara Hunt McLanahan* for being gracious when we accidentally trespassed in *Donald Judd's* house in SoHo, and to *Jim Songer* for a tour of Manhattan at lightning speed on sunny February days (with the top down).

Thank you to *Chairman Robert Tierney and the New York City Landmarks Preservation Commission, Anthony Max Tung, Michael Payton, John Tauranac, Henry Smith-Miller, Lockhart Steele* of *Curbed, Gaynor Wynne Shay, Peter Samton, James Rossant, Constance Rosenbloom, Anthony Robins, Jacob Tilove, Joseph Merz, Peggy Latimer, Christopher Gray, Christabel Gough, Jace Garcia, David Dunlap, Andrew Dolkart, John Cetra, Alex Borja*, and a hundred others.

Thank you to *Howard Morhaim* for encouragement, patience, and fortitude; yet again the perfect agent.

Special thank you to *Ian* and *Stephanie Smith* and especially to *Camilla White* and *Leigh Leadon* for their unfailing love and support.

Norval White and *Fran Leadon*

NORVAL WHITE, 1926-2009

The manuscript for this Fifth Edition was completed and delivered to Oxford University Press on December 15, 2009. Less than two weeks later Norval White was suddenly gone. He died of a heart attack at his home in Roques, France, on December 26. Norval was a practicing architect and well-known professor (at Cooper Union and City College) in addition to his work as a writer and historian. He maintained his own practice, and for years was a design partner at *Gruzen and Partners* (he was the lead architect on notable projects including Essex Terrace in East New York, Brooklyn, and 1 Police Plaza on Park Row, at the foot of the Brooklyn Bridge). A New Yorker through and through, he was born and raised on the Upper East Side but lived in later years on Pierrepont Street, in Brooklyn Heights. He was a leader in the unsuccessful but influential fight to save the original Penn Station (he picketed alongside his friend Elliot Willensky), and while he was a staunch preservationist, he was admirably open to new ideas (he was in recent years a fan of the firms *Herzog & de Meuron* and *SHoP*).

He was, of course, best known as co-author of this Guide. Of the previous four editions (1968, 1978, 1988, and 2000), the first three were co-authored with the indefatigable Willensky, who died in 1990. The two made quite a pair, by all accounts (White, taciturn and tall; Willensky, loquacious and muttonchopped). I never had the pleasure of meeting Mr. Willensky (I was still in college when he passed away) but I have had the great honor of knowing Norval White as collaborator, friend, and mentor.

Norval "retired" to France in 1993, but remained more up-to-date on the architectural goings-on in New York City than just about anyone. He eagerly perused the latest postings on *Curbed* and *Brownstoner* and devoured the *Architect's Newspaper*, compiling meticulous lists of buildings in progress. In January 2009 he flew over and spent a month touring the City, joining me for madcap, careering drives through the five boroughs (one pell-mell dash around Brooklyn featured Constance Rosenblum of the *New York Times* riding shotgun, furiously scribbling away, trying to keep up with Norval's one-liners).

During one drive through lower Manhattan, every street corner and building seemed to prompt a memory for him ("I went to a party there, on the third floor, in 1954") and he would grill me whenever he saw a new building under construction: who designed it, when would it be finished, what did it replace? Full of curiosity and energy, he insisted we cover everything from Battery Park to Chelsea in one day. Exhausted, I finally convinced him to break for lunch at the NoHo Star, where he continued to snap photos at our table: the staff, the food, the light fixtures. There was simply no stopping him. When I told him some months later that my students and I had finally completed all the photographs for Manhattan, his response was "What about Brooklyn?"

Norval constantly told me to stop what I was doing and "Go out! Go out!" He didn't like it when I was editing photos at home or doing research on the Internet. The *AIA Guide* has always been first person, fly-on-the-façade research, conducted on-site by hiking through and hanging around neighborhoods like old-time newspaper reporters on the beat (White and Willensky were both kind of like *Joseph Mitchell* with an architecture license). Architectural research and criticism is always the most accurate, and the most fun, when it is conducted at stoop level, looking hard at the City from its sidewalks, up close. Norval didn't want the Guide's readers sitting at home. He would be happy knowing he inspired a legion of new urban wanderers, off exploring the City, walking New York's streets and rambling through its parks. The Guide has grown in weight and thickness over the years, but it is still portable, so throw it in a backpack with a good camera, and get out there!

Fran Leadon
2010

ELLIOT WILLENSKY, 1933-1990

Our father was a central figure in New York City architecture and preservation when he died suddenly of a heart attack at the age of 56. Though well known, he wasn't easy to know well. Those that knew him professionally often did so compartmentally. They might have bonded or clashed with him in his role as Borough Historian of Brooklyn or as Vice-Chair of the Landmarks Preservation Commission. They might have recognized him as a university lecturer at Brooklyn College, Cornell University, or Columbia University's Graduate School of Architecture and Planning, or through his participation in the Brooklyn Historical Society, the Frederick Law Olmsted Association, or the Municipal Art Society of New York. Still others had read the books he authored, *When Brooklyn Was the World*, a much-loved remembrance of Brooklyn from 1920 to 1957, and of course the *AIA Guide to New York City*, with co-author Norval White.

No matter which Elliot Willensky you knew, two things were almost immediately apparent: his infectious laughter and his passion for New York City. Unabashedly quirky with a balding head and General Burnside–style muttonchops, he wore a ring on his index finger adorned with a stainless steel ball-bearing that he'd spin with his thumb, causing a whizzing sound that brought a smile to his face.

Born in Brooklyn and raised in the Bronx, he was a diehard New Yorker who found delight in the minutiae of life, especially of his beloved city. We were often his companions on his constant ramblings through the City's five boroughs. Walking with him was slow. Every few steps he'd stop, pointing out the faded billboard painted on a building's façade, the remnants of a chimney that signaled a pre-existing coal oven, or the staircase leading seemingly to nowhere. Then he'd pull out a small notebook and his signature black Flair marker to document his discoveries.

He liked to say he coined the term "above ground archaeology" (no disrespect intended to *John L. Cotter*), a study he felt was every bit as important as Classical archaeology. He delighted in information—the more obscure the better—and he collected it 365 days a year. Armed with a flashlight and a combination slot- and Phillips'-head screwdriver, he pushed past closed doors and locked gates, venturing deep into remote neighborhoods. He had a burning desire to know each building's raison d'être, and we were his accomplices. Weekends together meant exploring the outer reaches of New York City by subway, bus, ferry, or cable car to find oddball things in oddball places. While our friends were playing stickball or hopscotch, we were touring "Bohack Square," in Queens, or visiting a vacant, yet highly evocative Ellis Island before it re-opened to the public.

He met Norval White at an architecture firm in the 1950s. Their friendship was solidified, at least as far as our father was concerned, when Norval agreed to help him hang a *Bridge-on-the-River-Kwai*-inspired "Be Happy In Your Work" banner in their office. This was a reflection, no doubt, on what these two young architects thought about their work conditions. The sarcastic humor they shared laid a foundation for a lifelong friendship that translated neatly into their collaboration on three editions of the *AIA Guide to New York City*.

Then before the publication of the Fourth Edition, our father died, though his contribution made it into the manuscript in the form of notes and photographs found after his death. With this new Fifth Edition, the Guide is moving forward for a new generation, and with the collaboration of a new author, Fran Leadon, but sadly, without our father. Those that knew our father best remember his joy and exuberance for life. In a characteristic move as Deputy Administrator of Parks and Recreation and Director of Design under Mayor Lindsay, he revamped the huge black and white "No" signs that adorned many city parks warning of all the activities that you could not do. Instead, he created bright blue and orange signs emblazoned with a large "Enjoy!" listing all the things you *could* do, and merely striking out the verboten activities. It is this joyful take on life, combined with an unparalleled knowledge of city history, that we believe has cemented the *AIA Guide to New York City*'s position as a classic and revered architectural reference. As you turn the pages of this new edition, we encourage you to follow his advice: Enjoy!

Marcus Willensky
Diana Willensky Thompson
2009

GLOSSARY

Air Rights: the rights, under zoning laws, to add additional airspace to a building volume by borrowing (for a fee) the air above a shorter, neighboring building. A 19th-century church, for example, might sell the rights to its unused air to a planned office building next door.

Antefix: anthemion-ornamented finials that embellish the edge of a Greek temple above the entablature, covering the open ends of its roof tiles and forming a serrated silhouette.

Anthemion: a stylized honeysuckle ornament in Greek and Greek revival architecture.

Arched Corbel Tables: a sequence of mini-arches that step across corbeled masonry, usually brick, and common in northern Italian Lombardian Romanesque architecture.

Architrave: the "chief beam" of a Classical entablature, spanning directly above and between columns, and, in turn, supporting frieze and cornice.

Archivolt: the decorated band around an arch.

Arcuated: composed of arches.

Art Deco: a modern style first presented at the Paris Exposition Internationale des Arts Décoratifs of 1925 and re-discovered in the late 1970s.

Articulate: to set off and/or emphasize by means of a joint, as a brick is articulated by deeply incised mortar, or a building's wing is articulated by the link that connects it with its parent.

Art Moderne: a modern style characterized by streamlined stucco and chromium, as if buildings traveled at the speed of automobiles. Inspired by the Paris International Exposition of 1937.

Art Nouveau: when *Samuel Bing* opened his shop, "art nouveau," in Pans (1898), little did he know that the sinuous style that we have inherited would be so named. Vegetative ornament that not only became the surface decoration of the then "modern" architecture but also contributed to form, particularly in *Hector Guimard's* entrances to the Paris Metro.

Ashlar: stone cut for a wall; either regular and in courses, or "random."

Atrium: a center courtyard (open or covered) within a house or public building.

Balustrade: the assemblage of railing, balusters, and newels that leads you and your hand up and down the staircase.

Baroque: the exuberant late Renaissance style supported by the Jesuits in their attempt to lure the flock back to Rome in the face of Luther's reformation; extravagant architectural stagecraft for the counter-reformation.

Battered: a wall that is thick at its bottom, thinner at the top.

Bauhaus: the German school led by *Walter Gropius*, where occurred the blending of art and architecture with industrial techniques.

Bay Window: a glassed alcove projecting from a space or building, catching oblique views for its residents and serving as an important punctuation of the building's façade.

Beaux Arts: literally "fine arts," from the Parisian architectural school (École des Beaux Arts) that served as fountainhead for formal American architectural education. The progeny of the school produced grand (sometimes pompous) public architecture: the Paris Opera, the Chicago World's Fair of 1893, the New York Public Library, Grand Central Station, and so forth.

Berm: a linear mound of earth; a common landscape architect's device used for both drainage and design.

Board and Batten: flat boards with square trim covering their joints that gave "verticality" to the Gothic Revival and Stick Style wood cottage.

Bollard: a short fat, round concrete, masonry, or iron pier, set freestanding into the street, that constrains wheeled traffic but allows pedestrians to pass.

Boss: a round, decorative, sometimes sculpted ornament, as at a Gothic or neo-Gothic intersection of vaulting ribs.

Bow Window: a single curved projecting space/form, rather than the bay window's square or angled box.

Brick: usually a unit of kiln-baked clay, but concrete brick also exists as well as the sun-dried adobe of America's southwest, Mexico, and other pre-industrial countries. Some common brick sizes, from thinnest to thickest, include Roman, Standard, Jumbo, Double, and Imperial.

Broken Pediments: pediments broken apart "explosively" as in Baroque and neo-Baroque architecture.

Brown Decades: so dubbed by critic *Lewis Mumford*; the "autumn period of american art" before the classical Columbian Exposition of 1893 introduced America to the "White City."

Brownstone: brown sandstone from the Connecticut river valley or the banks of the Hackensack River; soft, porous, and perishable.

Brutalism: the bold concrete architecture inspired by *Le Corbusier* and brought to fuller realization by *Paul Rudolph*.

Butted Glass: glass sheets, as in a store front, where there is no mullion and the glass, necessarily thicker, meets its neighbor with a joint filled with silicone; a common modernist detail.

Campanile: the freestanding bell tower of an Italian church.

Cantilever: a stationary lever, the arm of which supports a load, as in a fishing pole.

Carpenter Gothic: the jigsaw and lathe allowed carpenters to capture quickly and inexpensively an idea of Gothic in wood. The ogees and finials decorated windows, porches, and cornices.

Caryatid: at the Erectheum on Athens' Acropolis, erect ladies serve as the columns of its porch (now replaced with concrete copies due to deterioration from pollution); nowadays any such female figures used as architectural supports.

Casement: a hinged window that opens out like a door. Originally made of steel, they are usually aluminum these days. Too bad.

Cast Iron: liquid iron poured into a shapely mold and thence cast; fragile in comparison to wrought iron or steel.

Catenary: the natural curve of a hanging string (or a cable, or a suspension bridge), supported at both ends.

Chamfer: a mitered edge given to a frame, gable, column, etc.

Château: a French country castle, with or without fortifications.

Chicago School: the early modern style of *Louis Sullivan, John Wellborn Root, William Le Baron Jenney,* and company; the birthplace of the skyscraper.

Clapboard: linear shingles that clad (clap) each other in courses, common in Federal, Greek Revival, and early American styles. Pronounced "clabberd."

Classical: of and/or relating to the Classical period of architecture and civilization, i.e., Greek and Roman.

Classical Revival: a literal revival of Greek and Roman architecture, rather than the Renaissance re-arrangement of Classical detail into new forms.

Clinker Bricks: bricks over-burned in the kiln and then used decoratively in counterpoint to the rest of the normal brick wall that they share.

Close: the lawn and landscape around an English cathedral or church, usually with other religious buildings defining its limits.

Collegiate Gothic: the Ivy League contribution to American architectural history; an Oxbridge simulation for higher education.

Colonial: the architecture of, particularly, America when it was a colony (strictly speaking before July 4, 1776). In Manhattan, only one extant building can claim the true Colonial title: St. Paul's Chapel of 1766.

Colonial Revival: the late 19th-century revival of America's early architecture. Sometimes also called neo-Federal.

Colonnade: a row of columns usually supporting a beam, architrave, or series of arches.

Colonnettes: little columns for decorative purposes.

Column: the thin, vertical supports of a building or structure as opposed to the fatter "pier" or the archaic "pillar." Columns may range from matter-of-fact supports, such as the modern steel column, to those participating in ornate orders of Classical architecture: Doric, Ionic, Corinthian.

Commissioners Plan of 1811: the surveyed grid that defines Manhattan, mostly intact today.

Composite (columns): mixed orders, where Doric and Ionic might share the same column.

Concrete: a chemical bonding of materials (cement, sand, water, and gravel) into a pourable artificial stone, reinforced with internal steel bars.

Concrete Block: an alternative to brick, made from concrete poured into modular, stackable forms, reinforced with steel bars placed vertically within cavities.

Console Bracket: the scrolled bracket that supports many a Renaissance and neo-Renaissance cornice. Also, cornice bracket. See modillion.

Corbeled: succeeding layers (courses) of bricks, each projecting slightly over the one below; slabs of stone can also be corbeled.

Corbel Table: a series of corbeled bricks or stones supporting a string of small decorative arches, frequently following the gabled end of an Italian Lombardian Romanesque church or its revival.

Corinthian: the late Greek and early Roman order of architecture that produced acanthus-leaved capitals (as opposed to Ionic "ram's horns" and Doric austerity).

Cornice: the crown of a building or room, its edge against the sky, particularly part of a Classical order's entablature. New York has more amazing cornices than any other city!

Course: one layer of wood, brick, block, board, or stone.

Crenellated: crowned with a cornice of solid teeth (merlons) that protect the warrior, interrupted by voids that allow him to shoot.

Cresting: the cast-iron filigreed crest atop a Victorian mansard roof.

Crocket: the teat on a Gothic finial.

Cul-de-sac: a dead-end street, alley, or road.

Deconstructivism: a style borrowed from French philosophy that insists on a gap between form and meaning. In architecture, that difference has been boiled down to a simplistic fracturing of form.

Dentil: the toothy blocks under the cornice of a Greek or Roman entablature, reminiscent of the wood joinery in earlier temples from which Greek architecture in marble was derived.

De Stijl: the design movement and its style, born in Holland, in 1917. Among those involved were *Gerrit Rietveld,* and *Piet Mondrian*; the venerated object is Rietveld's Schröder House (1924, Utrecht); the holy object, the Rietveld chair.

Distyle: with two columns, as in a temple.

Distyle in Antis: two columns flanked by two blank walls.

Doric: the austere and elegant order developed in the sixth and fifth centuries B.C. in Greek architecture (particularly Athenian, and of Athenian colonies).

Dormer: an upright window projecting from a sloping roof, it makes usable a sloping attic space, as well as those myriad mansard roofs of Paris.

Dressed: stone is dressed when cut to size, with leveled horizontals.

Dutch Colonial: the simple house style of New Amsterdam and environs, including those deep-caved gambrel-roofed rural farmhouses (see Brooklyn's various Wyckoff Houses) and the stepped gables of town houses at the tip of Manhattan. The former are numerous; the latter have totally vanished. One needs to view Curaçao to see their equivalents built in the same 17th-century period.

Eclectic: in architecture, the borrowing of assorted styles and stylistic details for a single building.

Egyptian: of or relating to Egypt from approximately 3000 B.C. to its conquest by Alexander the Great, 332 B.C.

Entablature: the set of roof parts in a Classical building that the columns support, i.e., architrave (or first beam over the columns), frieze, and cornice.

Entasis: the slight swelling of a Classical column that reinforces the visual impression of strength. The best (i.e., the Parthenon) are so subtle that one is aware of it only after conscious intellectual effort.

Esplanade: a linear walking part along the water's edge, like that at Brooklyn Heights or Battery Park City.

Exedra: a large semicircular alcove (annex) to a central space (particularly in Classical architecture).

Face Brick: brick with (at least) one side with a weather and visual finish. Common brick, on the other hand, is used as a backup and for internal invisible structural walls.

Faience: a fine pottery glaze adapted to architectural decor.

Fasces: bundle of rods bound up with an axe in the middle and its blade projecting, a symbol of roman authority.

Federal: the first "American" style of architecture, based on English Georgian. Surviving examples of the style are endangered species in New York City.

Festoon: a pendant wreath; it also describes any exuberant decoration.

Fillet: the flat ribbon separating the flutes of an Ionic column.

Finial: the ultimate end of a Gothic pinnacle decorated with crockets, a finger in silhouette against the sky.

Flamboyant: used to describe the flame-like tracery of late French Gothic; later, to describe anything that is ostentatiously ornate.

French Flats: the original term for New York's apartment houses, circa *Edith Wharton's The Age of Innocence*.

Frieze: the bas-relief (or painting) in a band that decorates the top of a room or Classical entablature. The frieze is an opportunity for cartoon graphics, as in the animal frieze at the Parthenon (the zoophorus) or that at Brooklyn's Prospect Park Zoo (also animals).

Fritted Glass: a technique for sandwiching tiny ceramic dots between sheets of glass to form a translucent façade, the better to regulate heat gain (see *Frank Gehry's* IAC Building).

Gable: the triangular ending of a two-way pitched roof.

Gambrel Roof: the double-pitched roofs employed by Dutch and later Victorian architects.

Garland: a collection of flowers, as in a wreath, or festoon.

General Grant: the good General was a passive participant in this mid-Victorian eclectic melange— usually ornate wood houses with mansard roofs that otherwise might be termed "Charles Addams."

Georgian: of the Georges, those imported German kings of England who were in charge when the best of English urban design was around. Simple but elegant brick and limestone.

Gneiss: hard volcanic rock found near Fordham in the Bronx.

Gothic Revival: the romantic revival of largely Gothic detail in the 1840s. Some felt (like John Ruskin) that the Medieval period was filled with good people, and a revival of that architecture might make citizens of the 1840s equally good. Bad psychology, but it left some smashing architecture.

Gothick: an English-style neo-Gothic building.

Granite: the hard, fine-textured igneous (solidified from a liquid state) stone of mixed quartz, mica, and other ingredients. Sedimentary stones (limestone, brownstone) erode, wear out; granite is forever.

Greek Revival: The revival was long-lived in the 19th century, and resulted in untold numbers of American houses decorated with Greek parts (columns, entablatures). Occasionally whole buildings (notably banks and city halls) took the form of Greek temples. The style is ubiquitous in much of New York City, especially in brownstone Brooklyn.

Hammer Beam: the bracketed wood structure of a Gothic or neo-Gothic hall: a kind of wood super-corbeling.

Headers: the short ends of bricks in a wall used as ties to connect (bond) two thicknesses (wythes) of brick.

Hip Roof: a roof without a gable and with eaves all around.

Hood Molds: moldings crowning and enveloping the head (top) of a window particularly in neo-Gothic architecture.

Imbricated: bearing overlapping shingles or plates arranged as in the scales of a fish. Victorian roofs, both mansard and single-gabled, frequently were imbricated in several colors. The more recent mega-cinema on Court Street in Brooklyn by *Hugh Hardy* is severely imbricated.

Impost Block: a block that bears the load, as in those corbeled limestone blocks bearing the ribs or timbers of a Gothic or neo-Gothic vault.

Incunabulum: a precocious affair. Strictly speaking, a book printed from movable type before 1501, but implying equivalent childlike precocity in any activity, including architecture and architects (see the work of *SHoP*).

Intaglio: an incised pattern or decoration, or a printing plate incised to create printed relief.

Intrados: the armpit of an arch.

Ionic: the elegant voluted order of Greek architecture. Its capitals are sometimes compared to ram's horns.

IRT: Interborough Rapid Transit (company), the original privately operated Lexington and Seventh Avenue/Broadway lines.

Italianate: of an Italian character, particularly in mid 19th-century villas copied from Italian prototypes. Row housing in New York is also sometimes of the same style.

Jerkinhead Roof: a gabled roof with a chamfered, or sliced off, plane at its ends.

Jack Arch: a brick arch with an almost flat, subtle parabola. Often handsomely employed in Romanesque style buildings.

Landmark: any notable building, monument, or place. In New York, it's a legal and cultural designation made by the New York City Landmarks Preservation Commission in order to protect significant buildings, parks, neighborhoods (in the form of Landmark Districts), and even trees.

Lantern: at a grand scale, it's the glassy cupola that brings light to the building's central interior space.

Light: a windowpane or, technically, the compartment in which it fits.

Limestone: sedimentary stone, the silted and pressed product of sand and ancient seashells; soft, workable, and subject to erosion over time.

Lombardian Romanesque: the Romanesque style of northern Italy.

Machicolation: the stepped-out cornice of a Gothic structure (frequently in corbeled brick) that allows the protected to pour boiling oil on an enemy attempting to scale the walls. The form, if not the practice, continued in 19th-century New York.

Maisonette: an English term for duplex apartments within an apartment house, like a "little house."

Mannerist: the late Renaissance architecture that infused decorative elements, stylistic exaggeration, and unusual effects into Classical orders, predating the Baroque.

Mansard: the steep roofs developed by the French 17th-century architect *François Mansart*, co-opted by Victorian architects of the 19th century (particularly in Paris where they squeezed in an extra illegal floor).

Marble: pressed and heated (metamorphized) limestone, pressed for extra eons to a harder, finer texture. It can be polished to bring out its striations, and in its purest form it is without veins.

Mastaba: the battered (sloped walled) tomb buildings of early Egyptian nobles subordinate to the pyramids that they surrounded.

Merlon: the tooth of a crenellated wall; a solid between two voids.

Modillion: the horizontal scrolled bracket that supports many a Renaissance and neo-Renaissance cornice. See also console bracket.

Mullion: the vertical member supporting a glass wall, as in a storefront, or between repetitive windows.

Muntin: a small bar that divides a window's sash into panes: the little sticks that make up the framing of six-over-six double-hung sash and so forth.

Nave: the central space of a Christian church; the space for people, as opposed to the space for clergy (chancel) or monastic brethren (transepts).

Neo-Grec: the late 19th-century style that brought back Greece for a second time (Greek Revival in the 1820s, 1830s, and 1840s was the first). Here it was a more decorative and less columnar affair.

Neo-Renaissance: a revival of Renaissance buildings and parts, in New York mostly those of England and Italy with an occasional French example—the New York County Lawyers' association, the Metropolitan Club, and the Polhemus Clinic, respectively.

Nosing: the projecting edge of a stair tread.

Oculus: an eyelike round window.

Ogee: the double-curved arch of both Moorish and French Flamboyant Gothic architecture. S-shaped.

Ogival: having a pointed arch or vault, as in the nave of a Gothic church.

Order: the base, columns, and entablature in Classical architecture: Doric, Ionic, Corinthian, Tuscan, or Composite orders.

Oriel: a bay window up high, usually in Medieval architecture, propped by a projecting corbeled stone from below: a place to catch a special view. See also bay window.

Palazzo: the super town house of Italian nobility (i.e., palace), later a description of any big, urbane building in an Italian town.

Palimpsest: literally a surface that has been reused for writing, symbols, or carving, only partly obliterating a previous message underneath. In architecture and urban studies, it often refers to a previous building, sign, or detail that is still legible beneath newer construction. New York itself is one big palimpsest!

Palladian: of or relating to the 16th-century Italian architect *Andrea Palladio* (*Jefferson* went bananas over him), particularly used in reference to paired columns flanking an arch, as at the basilica of Vicenza.

Parapet: the wall around a building's roof (literally a "breast guard").

Parge: to weatherproof a surface by coating it, as with stucco, but with a lighter cement wash; usually where unseen, below grade, or on the rear of a building.

Pediment: the triangular gable end of a Classical temple and part of that architecture's order, later used separately as a decorative part of Renaissance architecture.

Pepper Pots: see poivrières.

Pergola: a trellised walkway, usually festooned with vines; with grapevines it would be termed an arbor.

Piano Nobile: the principal or most important, but not ground (or American first) floor of a house, as in an Italian palazzo. The piano nobile is equivalent to the brownstone or town house parlor floor. Its literal translation is "noble floor," implying that the space contained and expressed is for noble architectural purposes (no social nobility implied).

Piazza: the Italian word for plaza, and sometimes an American word for porch (particularly in the midwest).

Pilaster: the flat remembrance of a column that articulates a wall, and frequently repeats the rhythm and parts of an adjacent colonnade. Usually decorative and nonstructural.

Pillowed Rustication: Baroque architects gave stone the imagery of wormwood marshmallows, and other fantasies. In the neo-Baroque, pillows take over. See the New York Police Museum.

Pinnacle: the tower atop a Gothic buttress.

Plaza: the English (and now American) version of the Italian Piazza; an outdoor space contained by surrounding buildings.

Plinth: the base that holds it all up, as at a column or a wall.

Point Block: an English term for an apartment tower.

Poivrières: pepper pots, and hence, the corner cylindrical towers on apartment buildings and houses, often sited where streets arrive and leave at acute angles. Park Slope is teaming with them.

Polychromy: of many colors, particularly in architecture.

Postmodern: the movement that began in the 1960s as an expressive, often humorous, response to modernism. *Charles Moore* and *Robert Venturi* were early proponents. *Robert A.M. Stern* is perhaps New York's primary postmodernist today.

Porte Cochère: the covered portal to a house or public building, meant originally for the horse and carriage but now just as useful for a stretch limo.

Proud: a carpenter's term for a piece of wood that projects beyond its neighboring elements. (Also see its opposite, "shy.")

Putti: the cherubs floating on Renaissance ceilings, or carved or cast into decorative sculpture.

Queen Anne: originally the pre-Georgian style of Anne's reign (1702-1714); in 19th-century American architecture the style is that of a mixture of Medieval and Classical parts: Tudor, Federal, and Greek Revival grown fat, bulbous, rich, and encrusted. Eclectic extravaganzas.

Quoins: cornerstones of a building that articulate that corner, frequently in a different material, as in the limestone quoins of a brick Georgian building (pronounced "coins").

Range: the color of brick, where the natural baking process in a kiln produces (from the bricks stacked within) some darker, some lighter, depending on the individual brick's placement in the kiln's stacks.

Rectory: the dwelling of a priest (usually Catholic or Episcopalian).

Renaissance: the rebirth or revival of the Classical Greek and Roman worlds, their humanism, individual creativity. In architecture, the adaptation of the Classical vocabulary to new building types, such as churches and palazzi.

Reredos: a background screen behind an altar and, occasionally, a major art object itself, like the reredos by *Frank Freeman* in Brooklyn Heights' Holy Trinity Church.

Retardataire: laggard, behind the times, a johnny-come-lately to the art or architecture of the moment; but mostly a pejorative for the avant-garde putting down the architecture of what went before.

Reveal: the sides of a window or door opening that "reveal" the thickness of the encompassing walls.

Richardsonian Romanesque: is a full-blown American style drawn from *H.H. Richardson's* fascination with utilitarian use of Roman arches, with rough rock-faced stone details.

Rock-faced: rock made more rocky by artful sculpture; neat stones faced with hewn-rock forms.

Roman: the imperial organizers of the Classical world who brought engineering to architecture, creating great public works: vaulted, domed baths and temples, arched aqueducts, all decorated and ordered with the parts developed by 5th-century B.C. Greece.

Romanesque: the round-arched and round-vaulted sturdy early Medieval architecture of Europe that was succeeded by the more elegant and sinuous Gothic. Its revived forms were highly popular in the late 19th century (see Frank Freeman's City of Brooklyn Fire Headquarters).

Row House: houses that share common walls and form a row, or what the English call "terraces." A "town house" is the elegant social promotion of the same physical place.

Ruskinian: relating to the ideas of the 19th-century English writer, art critic, social theorist, and historian *John Ruskin*. See Gothic Revival.

Rusticated: a Renaissance device. Stones that have deeply incised joints to exaggerate their weight and scale. In New York, rustication expresses the base of many a row house, fire station, and armory.

Sash: the sub-frame carrying a pane of glass in a window, as in one of two double-hung window sashes, or one of two halves of a casement window.

Schist: laminations of rock, the product of hot geology, as a napoleon or baklava has layers of pastry. Manhattan's skyscrapers rest on schist.

Second Empire: the period of Napoleon III in France (1852-1870) that brought to fruition *Baron Haussmann's* plans of mansard roofs and neo-Renaissance detail. In America this style was aped in the 1870s and 1880s.

Sgraffito: the polite antecedent of graffiti, here enhancing architecture with an elegance of writing rather than defacing it.

Shingle Style, Stick Style: the romantic and picturesque styles of the 1880s and 1890s that brought the freestanding architecture of America to its apogee, (predominantly) wood taken to its most fluid, plastic form.

Shy: a carpenter's term for a piece of wood that is recessed behind its neighboring elements (also see "proud").

Sliver: a tower built on a tiny site, not intended, but permissible, under old zoning, forbidden under a revised law, then newly popular again (see *Ismael Leyva's* 785 Eighth Avenue).

Soffit: the underside of an architectural part, as the soffit of a balcony, commonly misused to describe the infill vertical panels to the ceiling above kitchen cabinets.

Spandrel: the space between the window head of one floor and the window sill of the floor above; opaque masonry or paneling that conceals the floor construction behind. In Renaissance or revival architecture it is the triangular space between two adjacent arches.

Star Anchors: the decorative cap on tie rods (internal steel tension rods) that stabilized early 19th-century buildings by tying together the front and rear walls. See tie rod.

Stele: the memorial finial or slab set in the ground that remembers persons, places, or events. A tombstone is a stele, as are the Druidic remains of Stonehenge.

Stepped Gable: a Dutch device. The masonry end (usually) that covers the triangular profile of a pitched roof, rising above it in rectilinear steps, that presents itself to the street.

Strapwork: a 16th-century northern European decoration similar to leather or fretwork.

Surround: that framing material which surrounds an opening, window, door, or whatever.

Swag: a draping of cloth, frequently remembered in stone at a building's cornice; also called a "festoon."

Taxpayer: a low (one- or two-story) modest building where many stories might be permitted by zoning but where the owner, because of limited finances (particularly during the Great Depression), wished only to have sufficient income to pay the expenses and taxes until better times arrived.

Tempietto: a little temple (in Italian).

Tenement: a 19th-century, low-rise (four or five stories) walk-up apartment house that covers most of its site; now a pejorative term.

Terra Cotta: literally "cooked earth" in Italian, terra cotta is baked clay. A hard, red-brown material used for pottery, paving, shingles, statuary, and, in late 19th-century New York, for fireproofing steel (by encasing it in often wonderfully decorative blocks).

Tesserae: the tiny mosaic tiles (originally of marble) that created roman floors. Nowadays they may be of glass.

Tetrastyle: having four columns, usually in the Greek temple manner.

Thermal Granite: sawn slabs of granite the surface of which has been treated under intense flames, producing a roughened texture, as at *Eero Saarinen's* CBS Building.

Tie Rod: internal steel tension rods that stabilize early 19th-century buildings by tying together the front and rear walls. The caps of tie rods were often used as decorative elements on the façade, in the form of stars, shells, or flowers.

Torchère: a simulated torch powered by gas or electricity.

Torus: a convex, half-round molding, in Classical architecture at the base of an Ionic column, also used in the Renaissance and neo-Renaissance.

Tuscan: the Roman version of Doric with a simplified capital and (usually) no flutes.

Tympanum: the vertical recessed face of a pediment, often adorned with sculpture.

Verandah: the airy porch imported from India, partially screened for outdoor living, not just rocking.

Verdigris: the green patina (oxide) on weathered copper, brass, or bronze. It is the handsome equivalent on copper of iron's rust, both resulting from oxidation.

Vergeboard: a board trimming the underside edge of a gabled roof, sometimes called a bargeboard.

Vermiculated: the apparent worm tracks tracing some of the rusticated stonework of Renaissance buildings; naturalistic imagery, but far-fetched for worms.

Vernacular: the ordinary architecture of a culture without benefit of architect, as in the stuccoed houses of the Mediterranean's rim (Greece, Capri, North Africa) or farmhouses of 19th-century America.

Viaduct: an elevated roadway that is the trafficked equivalent of an aqueduct, supported on many columns or piers as opposed to a bridge that spans the space in question.

Victorian: a loosely defined catchall term for the architecture of the Industrial Revolution largely coincidental with the reign of Queen Victoria (1837-1901), which includes multiple styles, from Stick to Shingle to Gothic Revival to Greek Revival to Italianate.

Victorian Baroque: the flamboyant forms and sculpture of an elaborated late 19th-century architecture.

Villa: an (Italian-style) country house for a well-to-do city dweller's escape.

Volutes: the scroll-like cresting of, for example, an Ionic capital.

Voussoir: the wedge-shaped stones or radial backs of an arch, cut to fit its shape, whether circle, ellipse, or ogee.

Wedding Cake: in New York, the ubiquitous tall building profile of the early 20th century, marked by stepped back terraces, which allow light and air to reach lower floors (and the street). Governed by a zoning law passed in 1916.

Wrightian: design inspired by or copied from *Frank Lloyd Wright*, often using forms adapted from the Shingle Style, and possessing *Wright's* characteristic low, horizontal rooflines, and geometric detail.

WPA: Works Progress Administration of *Franklin Roosevelt's* New Deal in the 1930s and 1940s.

Wrought Iron: more easily formed and less brittle than cast iron, it now is used chiefly for railings and decoration. It once served as structural beams and railroad rails, before the more refined steel was invented.

Wythe: a single plane of brick (usually four inches); part of a wall composed of two or more wythes bonded by metal tics or brick "headers." A cavity wall is composed of two wythes with an air space between.

Zoning: the legal constraints governing new construction, intended to protect one's neighbors and oneself from noxious uses, to preserve or ensure one's quota of light and air, and to control density of land use.

AIA GUIDE TO NEW YORK CITY

MANHATTAN
Borough of Manhattan / New York County

 Colonial

 Georgian / Federal

 Greek Revival

 Gothic Revival

 Villa

 Romanesque Revival

 Renaissance Revival

 Roman Revival

 Art Deco / Art Moderne

 Modern / Postmodern

 Designated Landmark

Manhattan *is* New York, unless you happen to be standing in the vast expanses of Brooklyn, Queens, the Bronx, or Staten Island. Manhattan accepts swelling crowds of businessmen and women from New Jersey, Connecticut, and Long Island every morning and expels them during the legendary afternoon rush. Then there are the legions of tourists, overwhelming Times Square, Greenwich Village, the United Nations, SoHo, Battery Park, and now (poignantly) the World Trade Center site. And people **live** in Manhattan too, in every tall building and clapboard cottage, in every nook and cranny of every neighborhood and, down on their luck, in

The canyons of William Street

parks, on roofs, in doorways, in railroad tunnels. Those who live, visit, or work here may linger late into the evening, but most of them eventually go home and fall asleep, contrary to urban myth.

Distinguished architecture is everywhere on the island, and not just in the obvious places: the Financial District, the Village, SoHo, Midtown, and the Upper West and East Sides. Harlem will delight as well, as will the Lower East Side, Chinatown, Little Italy, Yorkville, and the far reaches of hilly Upper Manhattan.

We will begin in **Manhattan's toe**, where the harbor's waves pound the Battery, where seagulls hover and ships ply, where tourists from all over the world mix with lunching Wallstreeters. From the toe the whole of Manhattan unfolds in an unrelenting northward march.

Upper
Manhattan

The Heights
and the Harlems

Upper
West Side

Central
Park

Upper
East Side

Midtown
Manhattan

The Villages

Lower Manhattan

4

Lower Manhattan

MANHATTAN'S TOE

Manhattan's toe, that 1-1/2-square-mile triangle pulsating south of Canal Street and contained by the confluence of the **Hudson** and **East Rivers**, is where **Manhattan**—all of New York for that matter—began. Here lay **Nieuw Amsterdam**, founded in 1625, the first permanent settlement of Europeans in this area, the first fortifications, the first business district, the first community.

Where once all of the settlement's activities—even farming—took place in the toe, population growth and urbanization divined that specialization would take command. For Manhattan's tip the specialties would become shipping and warehousing, and the necessary backup of accounting, banking, and speculation that inevitably followed. Now shipping and warehousing have left for more spacious docks and cheaper land, though finance still reigns. But finance now shares its dominance with habitation, innumerable venerable (and less-venerable) office buildings of small stature and modest floor areas have been converted to condominium housing, and the life of the tip is now vibrant 24 hours a day, and even, good gracious, on Sundays.

Exploring the toe:
Routes for visiting the area's architecture have been turned into a series of walking tours that radiate outward from the Battery to create armatures for exploration. The walks take convenient pathways; Lower Manhattan's development over time has taken more complex routes.
Note: *For the Staten Island Ferry and the Ferry Terminal, see Water Street Corridor.*

FINANCIAL DISTRICT

The Financial District's twisted streets, varying both in direction and width, occupy that part of Manhattan's tip originally laid out by early colonists, vividly recalling the irregular medieval street patterns of northern European settlements. It is this part of the toe, the original part, that became the foundation for the slender skyscrapers built between the turn of the century and the Great Depression of the 1930s. It is also the part abundantly served by the three subway systems whose stations dot the area.

Surrounding the district's early core on the waterside are a later series of concentric landfills. They support the successive waves of warehouses, counting houses, and wharves that would serve the water-oriented enterprises that gave New York its early profits, power, and fame. In time these activities faded even as the core prospered, giving birth to the Financial District's canyons. Yet the 20th century did not saturate the perimeter of the toe until after World War II, when large-scale skyscraper development bulldozed what had become outlying, seedy, low-scale areas, still abundant with architectural significance but marginal economically. The special visual character of these late 18th- and 19th-century commercial precincts is evident today only in the South Street Seaport Historic District.

Walking Tour A—Lower Manhattan's Medieval Street Plan: *From Battery Park to the vicinity of Cass Gilbert's 90 West Street Building, near the World Trade Center site. Start at Castle Clinton National Monument. The IRT Seventh Avenue local (No. 1 train) and BMT Broadway Line local (R and W trains) to the beautiful new Whitehall Street/South Ferry Station (note the botanical motif—roots and branches) will deposit you at Battery Park. The IRT Lexington Avenue Line express (Nos. 4 and 5 trains) to Bowling Green Station leave you a short walk away.*

Battery Park and its perimeter:

[F1] Battery Park
The **Battery** signals the bottom of Manhattan to most New Yorkers, where tourists are borne by ferry to the **Statue of Liberty**, and "provincial" Staten Islanders start their homeward trek to that distant island, which turns out to be, surprisingly, part of New York City. The Battery was the namesake of a row of guns along the old shorefront line now approximated by State Street between Bowling Green and Whitehall. During the War of 1812, the status of the gunnery was elevated: **Castle Clinton**, erected on a pile of rock some 300 feet offshore, was known as **West Battery**, while **Castle Williams**, on

LOWER MANHATTAN KEY MAP

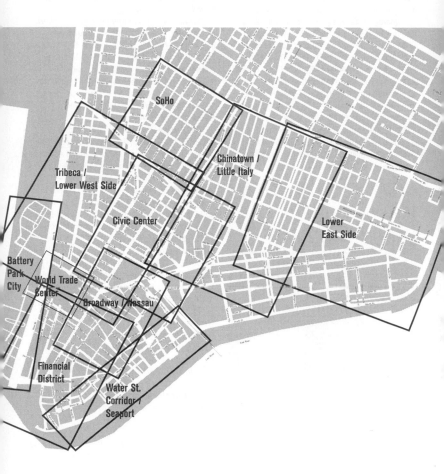

Governors Island, became **East Battery**. The intervening years have seen landfill entirely envelop **Castle Clinton** (and its various trans-mogrifications), forming **Battery Park**, a flat and somewhat originally confused stretch of *Robert Moses* landscaping that provides greenery and summer delight to New Yorkers from nearby offices. A fresh, if sometimes pungent, breeze from the Upper Bay is an antidote for the doldrums or any bad mood aggravated by heat.

Nearby, a statue of *Giovanni da Verrazano* (the first explorer to actually enter the harbor while sailing the east coast) gazes out at the harbor, perhaps admiring his bridge. (1909, *Ettore Ximenes*, sculptor). The buff, bland **Coast Guard Building** at the east edge of the park's bay front is an unfortunate structure in a prominent location.

[F2] **Castle Clinton National Monument**/earlier **New York Aquarium** (1896-1941)/earlier **Emigrant Landing Depot** (1855-1890)/earlier **Castle Garden** (1824-1855)/originally **West Battery** (1807-1811,

F2

renamed **Castle Clinton**, 1815). *Lt. Col. Jonathan Williams and John McComb, Jr.* ♿ Open to the public: 8:30-5 daily. 212-344-7220. Renovations 2010, *Beyer Blinder Belle & Thomas Phifer*.

Until recently, one of the most vitally involved structures in the City's life and history. Built as **West Battery** for the War of 1812 to complement Castle Williams across the waters on Governors Island (it never fired a shot in anger), it was originally an island fortification some 300 feet offshore, connected to Manhattan by a combination causeway bridge. Twelve years after the war it was ceded to the City. As a civic monument it served for the reception of distinguished visitors at the very edge of the nation (*General Lafayette, Louis Kossuth, President Jackson, Prince Albert*). Remodeled as a concert hall and renamed Castle Garden, it enjoyed a moment of supreme glory in 1850 as the much ballyhooed, *P.T. Barnum*–promoted American debut of the Swedish soprano *Jenny Lind*. Only five years later it was transformed into the **Emigrant Landing Depot**, run by N.Y. State, where some

7.7 million new Americans were processed, some into the Union army, others into the Lower East Side. Scandal led to its closure, and the processing of immigrants was transferred to federal control, at the Barge Office in 1890 and at Ellis Island in 1892. Not to be forgotten, its innards were juggled and its decor changed by *McKim, Mead & White*, and it reentered the fray as the **Aquarium**, the much beloved grotto of New Yorkers until 1941.

It was then apparently doomed by *Robert Moses'* call for its demolition to build approaches for his ill-fated harbor bridge to Brooklyn—today's Brooklyn-Battery Tunnel. A loud civic clamor and the reported intervention of *Eleanor Roosevelt* miraculously saved it though it languished inside a construction fence for decades. In 1946 the ruin was belatedly dubbed a National Historic Monument.

With its sea life displays removed to makeshift quarters at the Bronx Zoo, and then permanently installed in new facilities at Coney Island, the fort awaited a new purpose. Urged on by the 1976 Bicentennial, the National Park Service schmaltzified this once lusty place into a tame tourist attraction, a neat lawn surrounded by a shingle roof within its rock-faced brownstone shell. In 1986 it lost out to commerce, reduced to service as a ticket office for the boats to National Park Service attractions in the harbor. But the exhilarating **River to River Festival** summer concert series has enlivened the old fort in recent years. Bluegrass on the battlements? Yee-haw!

The Statue of Liberty and *Ellis Island* [see *The Other Islands]* are must-visit attractions only a short, privately operated boat ride away, sitting in the Upper Bay near the New Jersey shore but in plain view of visitors to Battery Park. Liberty Island was closed for several years after **September 11**, and new airport-style security screening at the Battery is, while necessary, a headache.

Miss Liberty: Perhaps three times the height of the Colossus of Rhodes, which was one of the "Seven Wonders of the World." Liberty, until the 1986 centennial, was considered corny, but corn was a necessary ingredient here. Like an old shoe to New Yorkers, she is always there and continues to wear well, particularly since the restoration on the occasion of her birthday. Take the special boat out to her, stand at her base (there's a museum inside), and look back on one of the romantic glories of the world: the New York skyline. She, still doing her own thing, is meanwhile saluting the rising sun of France.

[F3] **Battery Bosque Park Reconstruction**, East of Castle Clinton, 2005. *Weisz + Yoes*, architects. *Starr Whitehouse*, landscape architects.

A delightful enclave to sit and meditate upon the City's history, where one can enjoy gentle sea breezes, refreshments, a fountain, and lots of shade; then launch a walking trip north into the City. Note *Luis Sanguino's* bronze sculpture, *The Immigrants* (1973).

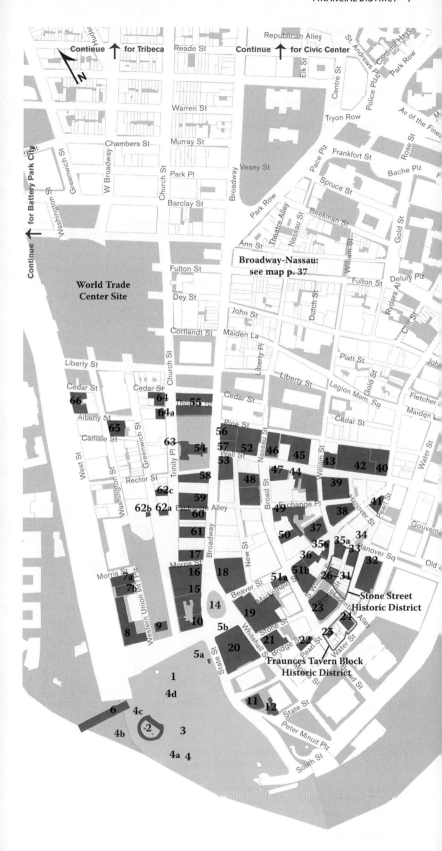

Continue ↑ for Tribeca

Continue → for Civic Center

Continue ← for Battery Park City

N

Republican Alley

Reade St

Warren St

Murray St

Chambers St

Park Pl

Barclay St

Vesey St

Fulton St

Dey St

Cortlandt St

Maiden La

World Trade
Center Site

Liberty St

Cedar St

Cedar St

Cedar St

Cedar St

Albany St

Carlisle St

Rector St

Morris St

St Andrews Plz

Cardinal Hay

Park Row

Police Plz

Centre St

Elk St

Tryon Row

Av of the Fine

Pace Plz

Frankfort St

Rose St

Bache Plz

Spruce St

Park Row

Beekman St

Gold St

Theatre Alley

Ann St

Nassau St

William St

**Broadway-Nassau:
see map p. 37**

Fulton St

Delury Plz

John St

Dutch St

Cliff

Maiden Pl

Platt St

Liberty St

Liberty Pl

Legion Mem. Sq

Gold St

Joh

Cedar St

Fletcher

Maiden Lu

Pine St

Water St

Wall St

Broad St

New St

Exchange Alley

Beaver St

Marketfield St

Stone St

Bridge St

Whitehall St

State St

Pearl St

Hanover St

Pearl St

Hanover Sq

Gouverne

Old

Coenties Alley

S William St

**Stone Street
Historic District**

**Fraunces Tavern Block
Historic District**

State St

Peter Minuit Plz

South St

Western Union Plz

Hudson

[F4] **East Coast Memorial**, Battery Park. 1960. *Gehron & Seltzer*, architects. Sculpture, 1963, *Albino Manca.*

Eight stolid sawn-granite monoliths (steles) form a mall, with rolls of those merchant mariners who died at sea off this coast in World War II. An aggressive basalt eagle stands guard.

[F4a] **Wireless Operators Memorial**, just west of East Coast Memorial. 1915.

Remembering *Jack Phillips*, radio operator of the *Titanic*, and his peers.

[F4b] **Merchant Mariners' Memorial**, just off-shore bet. Castle Clinton and Liberty Gateway. 1991. *Marisol*, sculptor.

[F4c] **New York Korean War Veterans Memorial**, bet. Castle Clinton and Liberty Gateway. 1991. *Mac Adams*, artist.

Two worthy attempts to memorialize brave souls. As art they are both inscrutable. The former is graphic and unsettling: three mariners in dire straits (one figure is eerily submerged in the harbor), calling for help. The latter is more stylized: the soldier as metallic void, framing the City or the harbor, depending on which side you're looking through.

[F4d] **Sphere**, in Hope Garden, between the Old Control House and Castle Clinton. *Fritz Koenig*. 1971. Installed in present site, 2002.

Koenig's abstract metal globe was originally installed in the plaza between the towers of the World Trade Center. Lost on September 11, it was extracted from the rubble and moved here, pur-

Company (IRT). Only one cast-iron version exists, a replica at Astor Place.

[F5b] **The Glass Canopy**, in front of Alexander Hamilton Custom House. 2003-2007. *Dattner Associates.*

Modern curved steel and glass rising from the subterranean world below. A gracious addition to the landscape of Bowling Green, but unfortunate that the elegance did not continue underground. Once below, it's still the same old station (MTA, 1975), tiled in bright, bright red.

From the park savor the wall of buildings that defines its space:

[F6] **Liberty Gateway, Pier A**, NYC Department of Docks & Ferries, onetime **Fireboat House**, off Battery Park, Battery Place SW cor. West St. 1884-1886. *George Sears Greene, Jr.*, engineer. Additions, 1900, 1904, 1919. ✍ Reconstruction master plan, 1991, *Beyer Blinder Belle*. Project architect, 1999, *Ehrenkrantz & Eckstut* with *Allenbrook Benic Czajka*, architects.

Both the pier, built atop granite arches sunk to river bottom, and the pier building are venerable survivors of underwater construction contemporary with that of the Brooklyn Bridge. At the pier's tip the tower clock was the nation's first **World War I memorial** (1919). Recent work toward converting the pier to a visitors' center and ferryboat terminal to the Statue of Liberty and elsewhere have foundered. Scaffolding still reigns.

F4   F5a   F5b   F7a

posely left in its damaged state, where it now serves as a memorial to those lost in the attacks.

The Battery Park Coast Guard site had been successively occupied in earlier years by two richly conceived U.S. Government Barge Offices designed by the Supervising Architect of the Treasury Department, James G. Hill (1880) and James Knox Taylor (1914).

If you're sick of walking and are in need of the 4 or 5 lines to speed things up a bit, you can pick from two distinct architectural styles as your point of entry into the Bowling Green Subway Station:

[F5a] **The Old Control House**, Battery Park, State St., SW cor. Battery Place. 1904-1905. *Heins & La Farge*. ✍

A **Flemish Revival** masonry station entry, companion piece to the same firm's cast-iron kiosks, which once dotted Manhattan's street corners along the route of the City's first subway system: the Interborough Rapid Transit

A short diversion to the north along West Street, then back again:

[F7a] **21 West Street**, SE cor. Morris St. 1929-1931. *Starrett & Van Vleck*. ✍

Formerly offices, now apartments, 21 West bears a chromatic range of salt-glazed tile, from burnt oranges to brown. This is the material of which silos are frequently made: a natural glaze, resistant to urban "fallout," without the crassness of the popular white glazed brick of the 1950s and 1960s. The arcade sports corbeled arches, reminiscent of Moorish architecture. Corners are cantilevered—making corner windows a natural **Art Deco** delight.

[F7b] **Downtown Club**/formerly **Downtown Athletic Club**, 20 West St., bet. Morris St. and Battery Place. 1929-1930. *Starrett & Van Vleck*. ✍

Here was the home of the fabled **Heisman Trophy**, given annually to college football's best athlete. The building was damaged on September 11 and the Athletic Club went bankrupt soon after. It is now (what else?) a condo.

F8

F11

The following three structures on the north side of Battery Place define the southern edge of the Financial District against Battery Park:

[F8] **Whitehall Building**, 17 Battery Place, NE cor. West St. 1902. *Henry J. Hardenbergh.* Rear addition, 1910, *Clinton & Russell.* 🔎

This colossal bulk offers the best views of the harbor from any of the Battery's older buildings. Now offering "luxury rentals." How much for the whole building?

[F9] **Brooklyn-Battery Tunnel Ventilation Building**, Battery Place bet. Washington and Greenwich Sts. N side. 1950. *Aymar Embury II.*

The windowless ventilator is one of three constipated Classico/modern necessities for the tunnel, but was appropriated in the science-fiction movie, *Men in Black*, as a command center (underground, of course) to manage the aliens in our society. Appropriate.

[F10] **International Merchant Marine Company Building** (United States Lines)/originally **Washington Building**, 1 Broadway, NW cor. Battery Place at Bowling Green. 1882-1884. *Edward H. Kendall.* Refaced in limestone, 1919-1921, *Walter B. Chambers.* 🔎

No. 1 Broadway, having come to see a second life in 1922, was again redone in the 1980s. A bank occupies the ground floor space that once served as the U.S. Lines booking hall.

Along Battery Park's eastern boundary, State Street:

Note: *For the U.S. Custom House, the northernmost structure on State Street, see below:*

[F11] **17 State Street**, on former site of **Seamen's Church Institute**, SE cor. Pearl St. 1987-1989. *Emery Roth & Sons.*

A sleek columnar mirror from the park, No. 17 replaced the Seaman's Church Institute hostel for mariners after only 16 years (see

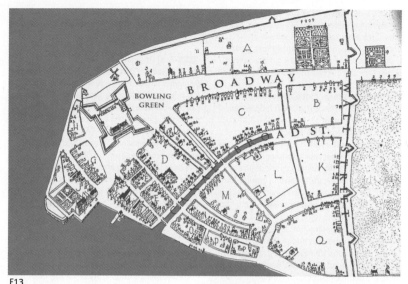

F13

Necrology section). In 1819, *Herman Melville* was born in a house on this site. The understructure displays cross-bracing and glazed elevator shafts for technitecture fans.

[F12] **Rectory of the Shrine of St. Elizabeth Ann Bayley Seton** (Roman Catholic)/ originally **James Watson House**, 7 State St., bet. Pearl and Water Sts. NE side. 1793-1806. Attributed to *John McComb, Jr.* ● Restoration and additions, 1965, *Shanley & Sturges.*

A single survivor of the first great era of mansions; the façade is original. **Federal**, both in the archaeological and political senses, it was built in the fifth year of *George Washington's* presidency of the **federal republic** in a style that is separately considered **Federal**. Slender, elegant, freestanding Ionic columns and delicate late Georgian detailing.

Mother Seton, born on Staten Island, baptized Episcopalian, and converted to Roman Catholicism, was canonized as America's first saint in 1975.

*Peter Stuyvesant's mansion, at 1 State Street, NW cor. Whitehall Street (ca. 1657), was renamed **Whitehall** by the first English governor and occupied a tiny peninsula projecting from the east end of the Battery at this point. Robert Fulton resided in a different building on the same site a century later.*

Leave the Battery Park area and enter the space of Bowling Green, the widening of Lower Broadway in front of the Custom House:

Bowling Green:

[F13] **Street Plan of New Amsterdam and Colonial New York,** the full width of all street beds lying within an irregular curved triangle bounded by (and including the street beds of) Wall St. on the N, Broadway, Bowling Green, and Whitehall Street on the W, and Pearl Street on the E. ●

F12

With the demapping of a part of Stone Street for the construction of No. **85 Broad Street,** the Landmarks Preservation Commission in 1983 designated as a landmark the old boundary lines of the streets that still mark the paths of the City's venerable Dutch and English colonial thoroughfares, many of which date from the 1600s. The officially designated irregular street pattern, in vivid contrast to later gridiron layouts, reflects the organic approach found in medieval European city building quite familiar to those who settled Manhattan in the 17th and early 18th centuries.

Naming of Streets: The early streets of New Amsterdam and New York were often named for their pioneering functions, rather than more abstract sources (numbers, plants, trees, heroes, et alia). **Pearl** *Street was once the edge of the island where mother-of-pearl (oyster shells) littered the beach,* **Bridge** *street served the first bridge to span the old Dutch canal at* **Broad** *Street. Broad Street was broad as it was laid out to have the canal at its center and service roads* *on each side. **Water** Street was under water when the mother-of-pearl defined Pearl Street. **Wall** Street, the most famous, was the site of the northern boundary of New Amsterdam, where a wall (palisades of sharpened logs) was erected against the English and the Indians. And so forth.*

[F14] **Bowling Green**, foot of Broadway. 1733. Altered, various years. Restored, redesigned, reconstructed, 1978, *M. Paul Friedberg & Assocs.*, landscape architects.

Adjacent to the Dutch cattle market, this oval open space became a "parade," then leased from 1733 for an annual fee of one peppercorn as a quasi-public bowling ground (or green), for the "Beauty & Ornament of the Said Street as well as for the Recreation & delight of the Inhabitants."

The 1978 reconstruction removed an atrocious subway entrance, added the fountain, and relocated the 1896 *de Peyster* statue, thereby restoring the simplicity of this patch of green amid the district's sunless canyons.

F14

[F14a] **Bowling Green Fence.** 🔲
The fence remaining today was erected in 1771-1772, although its decorative crowns were snapped off by exuberant patriots after the reading of the Declaration of Independence on July 9, 1776. The same patriots pulled down the gilded lead statue of *George III*, within the fence's bounds, much of which was then reportedly melted down into bullets used against the redcoats.

Clockwise, enclosing Bowling Green, from the west (see above for No. 1 Broadway):

[F15] **Bowling Green Offices**, 5-11 Broadway, at Bowling Green. W side. 1895-1898. *W. & G. Audsley.* Altered, 1920, *Ludlow & Peabody.* 🔲
"Eclectic" was invented for stylistic collections such as this (the architects described it as "**Hellenic Renaissance**"). The battered **Egyptian** pylons framing the entrance are bizarre imports. Above the 3rd floor, however, the spirit changes: strong glazed-brick piers with articulated spandrels have much of the bold verticality of the

Chicago School. Built by financier *Spencer Trask*, founder of **Yaddo**, the writers' colony in Saratoga Springs, N.Y.

[F16] Originally **Cunard Building**, 25 Broadway, SW cor. Morris St. 1917-1921. *Benjamin Wistar Morris*, architect; *Carrère & Hastings*, consulting architects. 🔲 **Great Hall**: ceiling sculpture, *C. Paul Jennewein*; ceiling paintings, *Ezra Winter*; iron gates, *Samuel Yellin*. Interior. 🔲
This "Renaissance" façade and its neighbors handsomely surround Bowling Green with a high order of group architecture. What matters most at No. 25, however, is its great booking hall, with its elaborately decorated groined and conical vaults. It was in this grand setting that passage on such liners as the **Queen Mary** and the two **Queen Elizabeths** was purchased.

[F17] **29 Broadway**, NW cor. Morris St. to Trinity Place. 1929-1931. *Sloan & Robertson.*
The tower's slim 31-story Broadway face widens to a broad Trinity Place backside, but what a wonderfully ornamented **Art Deco** experience it all is—except for the 6-story Broadway annex (where once was Schrafft's Restaurant), clad with a timid refacing. Survey the tower's lobby.

[F18] **26 Broadway**/originally **Standard Oil Building**, NE cor. Beaver St. Expanded from 1884-1885 Standard Oil Building, 1920-1928. *Carrère & Hastings and Shreve, Lamb & Blake.* 🔲
This curving façade reinforces the street's group architecture, working particularly well

F15

with its friend, **No.25**, across the green. Begun as The **Standard Oil Building**, built by the Standard Oil Trust Organization, the earlier structure on the site (1884-1886 *Ebenezer L. Roberts*) was only 10 stories tall. Enveloped and enlarged over the years, it served until *John D. Rockefeller's* trust was broken up, in 1911. Then, one of the trust's five offspring, Standard Oil Company of New York, Socony (later called Socony-Vacuum, Socony-Mobil, and now Mobil), lived here until it removed to its new building on East 42nd Street in 1956.

A circular Classical "temple" scratches the sky (thank you, **Mausoleum at Halicarnassus**), making one ponder the myriad classical toppings of the Wall Street World, with monuments of Rome and Greece crowning capitalism: gods within? The funerary monuments of *Rockefellers* and *Morgans* and their peers?

[F19] **2 Broadway**, bet. Stone and Beaver Sts. E side. 1958-1959. *Emery Roth & Sons.* Remodeled and reskinned, 1999, *Skidmore, Owings & Merrill.*

Sleek glass and elegant metal skins a banal 1950s office building at the hand of corporate America's sometime couturier, **SOM** (they tailored another elegant skin on an ordinary bank and office structure at 410 Park Avenue): Brooks Brothers styling for the man who had never worn suits.

F18

Skidmore, Owings & Merrill, a.k.a. SOM, has graced New York with many early modernisms: Lever House, Manufacturer's Hanover at 43rd and Fifth, Chase Manhattan. These days, SOM's vast offices mostly reach for a higher sky with branded projects: Freedom Tower, still rising a few blocks away. The 160-story Burj stands unreasonably high in Dubai (2,600+ feet). But they have also been the preferred designers for upscale (shorter) corporate America, sometimes merely dressing another's frame (as here at 2 Broadway, and Chase Manhattan on Park Avenue at East 55th Street).

The commanding site south of Bowling Green was successively occupied by forts: Fort Amsterdam for New Amsterdam, later for New York, Fort James, a variety of name changes until finally Fort George. Government House followed, built in 1790 to be George Washington's executive mansion (except that the nation's capital removed to Philadelphia after one year). It then became the Governor's Mansion (until the state capital moved to Albany in 1797), was briefly

leased as John Avery's tavern; then used as temporary Custom House until lost to a fire in 1815.

A row of fine town houses, later occupied by the world's leading shipping companies, (and so dubbed Steamship Row) pre-dated the current structure, built as the U.S. Custom House.

[F20] **Alexander Hamilton Custom House (National Museum of the American Indian** and **Federal Bankruptcy Court)**/originally **United States Custom House**, 1 Bowling Green, bet. State and Whitehall Sts. to Bridge St. 1899-1907. *Cass Gilbert.* ● Sculptures, "Four Continents": E to W: Asia, America, Europe, Africa, *Daniel Chester French, Adolph A. Weinman*, associate. Cartouche at seventh-story attic, *Karl Bitter.* Rotunda ceiling paintings, 1936-1937, *Reginald Marsh.* Partial interior. ● Alterations for the National Museum of the American Indian, 1994, *Ehrenkrantz & Ekstut.* Museum open 10-5, except Thursdays till 8 pm. 212-514-3700. Free.

Until the establishment of a federal income

F20

tax in 1913, the primary means of financing the national government was through customs duties. New York being the busiest point of entry for foreign goods, this **Custom House** became the nation's largest collector. It's no accident that this structure is so grand, one of the City's most splendid Beaux Arts buildings, now re-loved by modernists searching for fresh meaning in the history of architecture. The monumental sculptures by *French* (better known for his seated **Lincoln** at the memorial in Washington) are very much part of the architecture of the façade, their whiteness—and that of those at the attic by other sculptors—provide a rich counterpoint to the structure's gray granite, both in form and color.

No less grand is the interior, where the **giant oval rotunda**, embellished by *Reginald Marsh's* WPA-commissioned murals, is the majestic public space, now serving the **National Museum of the American Indian:** centerpiece, for sure, but curiously the exhibits occupy smaller rooms to the sides. The rotunda is grand but empty; a bit like a train station waiting room with no trains.

Unfortunately for museum visitors, Federal offices sharing the entry necessitate airport-style security screening: please place all items (keys, cellphone, belt, loose change) in the plastic bin. A pain.

Walk south down the Custom House's left (western) flank, Whitehall Street, and turn left (west) on Pearl Street:

F21

Pearl Street:

[F21] **Broad Financial Center**, 33 Whitehall St., NE cor. Pearl St. to Bridge St. 1986. *Fox & Fowle.*
BFC's developers wanted to link its name to Broad Street, a block away from the main entrance. Thus a deal was struck whereby the pale blue, mirrored office tower bought the air rights from the intervening, low, surrealist limestone **Clearing House Association** (see below), overhung its low neighbor, and obtained a tenuous tie to Broad.

[F22] **New York Clearing House Association**, 100 Broad St., bet. Pearl and Bridge Sts. W side. 1962. *Rogers & Butler.*
The awkward little building whose occupants provide a vital financial service, making certain that banks observe a coherent system of clearing checks. Slight buildings like this inspire lust in developers: at first it seems amazing that a glass tower named "The Clearing House" was not superimposed during the Boom of 2003-2008. But BFC next door bought the air rights first.

[F23] **85 Broad Street**, bet. Pearl and S. William Sts. to Coenties Alley. 1983. *Skidmore, Owings & Merrill.*
The structure's enormous and ungainly bulk (close to a million square feet) was drawn from the purchase and transfer of air rights from the **Fraunces Tavern Block** across the street. Its tan cast-stone wall surfaces resulted from an interpretation of the Zoning Law's mandate to harmonize with the Historic District's protected façades. Harmony? Certainly not in scale, and the relationship of materials is a joke.
Although arcaded No. 85 excised part of ancient **Stone Street's** curving route, it pays homage to that thoroughfare's path via a curved elevator lobby and the introduction of vestigial curbs where Stone Street once intersected Broad. With eyes already directed to the ground, turn the Pearl Street corner and view evidence of the 17th century in two glassed-in displays below the sidewalk surface, discovered in an archaeological survey required of the developer by the Landmarks Preservation Commission.

*Broad Street was in Dutch times de **Heere Gracht** [The Gentleman's Canal], a drainage and shipping canal that reached today's Exchange Place, where a ferry to Long Island docked. The canal was filled in 100 years before the Revolution, but its path remains in the street's extraordinary width—at least for this part of town. Manhattan's oldest streets cross Broad: **Bridge Street** was at the first bridge immediately adjacent to the waterfront at **Pearl Street**; Pearl should be "Mother of Pearl," in fact, for the glistening shells that once lined its shore— and its pavement; **Stone Street** was the first to be cobbled. The geometry of the space has not greatly changed, except that **Broad's** meeting with the shoreline is some 600 feet farther into the harbor than at the time of the canal's fill, making **Water, Front,** and **South Streets** on landfill of later dates.*

*The **Stadt Huys**, seat of Dutch colonial government, stood on the north side of Pearl St. (No.71) between Broad Street and Coenties Alley. During preliminary explorations for foundations for an office building on this site, archaeologists turned up a number of colonial artifacts. Here, the old shoreline was so close that tides at times lapped against the Stadt Huys steps.*

Proceed north along Pearl Street, as it curves parallel to today's East River shoreline; remember that Pearl Street once marked the edge of Nieuw Amsterdam and was earlier called the Wal (embankment) by the Dutch and The Strand by the English:

[F24] **Fraunces Tavern Block Historic District**, bounded by Pearl, Broad, and Water Sts., and Coenties Slip. Block created on landfill, ca. 1689. Structures (including Fraunces Tavern), 1719-1883 with 20th-century additions, restorations, alterations, reconstructions, *Stephen B. Jacobs & Assocs., Samuel S. Arlen & Frederick B. Fox, Jr.,* and others. 🖐
Faced with the rapid loss of Lower Manhattan's stock of Federal style and other early buildings, a circumstance prominently

decried in *Ada Louise Huxtable's* 1964 book *Classic New York,* this block was singled out for historic designation. It is regrettable that *no two sides of any street* were included, denying future visitors a sense of the true scale and environment of contained space of that era. But to savor such space, visit the nearby **South Street Seaport Historic District.**

[F25] Fraunces Tavern, 54 Pearl St., SE cor. Broad St. 1904-1907. *William Mersereau.* Museum open to the public: Mo-Sa 12-5 pm; 212-425-1778.

The Queen's Head Tavern of *Samuel Fraunces* (1719) occupied this plot and achieved great historic note in the Revolution: for ten days in 1783 it served as *Washington's* last residence as general. On December 4 he bade farewell to his officers and withdrew to his estate at Mount Vernon. He returned six years later and five blocks away to Broad Street's head, to take office as president of the United States at old City Hall, by then renamed Federal Hall.

F25

Colonial Revival in the dress of **Georgian** architecture. The present building is a highly conjectural construction—not a restoration—based on "typical" buildings of "the period," parts of remaining walls, and a lot of guess-work. With enthusiasm more harmless when attached to genealogy than to wishful archaeology, today's tavern has been billed as the Real McCoy. Such charades enabled **George Washington Slept Here Architecture** to strangle reality in much of suburban America.

[F26] Stone Street Historic District, bounded by Pearl St., Hanover Square, South William St., and Coenties Alley. Block totally rebuilt after the fire of 1835. 1835-1929.

Push-me-pull-you buildings had first pre-sented façades to both Pearl and Stone Streets in Greek Revival brick and granite followed by the grand Italianate brownstone of the **Hanover Bank (India House).**

[F27a] Stone Street Master Plan. 2001. *Beyer Blinder Belle.*

The plan provided a new pedestrian urban space, Stone Street itself, between Coenties Alley and William Street, drawing flocks of Wallstreeters for lunch, transforming the street into a series of **packed-to-the-gills open-air restaurants**. At its most crowded it basically ceases to function as a public street, so if you intend to hang out, it's best to reserve a table. The façades lining the street are lovingly restored, and it's festive and hectic and fun, waiters artfully scrambling for your pasta, your chocolate mousse, your hamburger.

[F27b] New façades, **13-15 South William St.** and **57 Stone St.**, bet. Coenties Alley and Hanover Sq. *C.P.H. Gilbert.* No.13, 1903. No.15, 1908.

Stepped gables ape, at a larger scale, the gabled old houses of **New Amsterdam**, none of which have survived. Street-front gables allowed those 17th-century buildings to hoist goods to a storage attic, necessary in cellar-less Amsterdam, with its canals and high water table. Here it might have been just for fun; more likely portable culture, building a city to mimic the one they came from (see contemporary **Curaçao**, where the architecture is still that of 17th century Amsterdam).

[F28] 17 South William St., new façade, bet. Coenties Alley and Mill Lane. 1906. *Edward L. Tilton.*

Vaguely Dutch.

F27a   F27b

[F29] 21-23 South William St., Neo-Tudor Club, bet. Coenties Alley and Mill Lane. 1927-1928. *William Neil Smith.*

Ornate, mock half-timbering here provided a different cultural stage set for its original club members.

[F30] 54 Stone St., Chubb & Sons, bet. Coenties Alley and Hanover Sq. 1919. *Arthur C. Jackson.*

Steel and rivets append a modern cornice in scale with its neighbors.

[F31] 9-11 South William St., William H. McGee & Co., bet. Coenties Alley and Mill Lane. 1929. *William Neil Smith.*

Crisp limestone offices with some neo-Gothic gestures.

At Hanover Square, look to No. 7, to the right, then turn left (westerly):

[F32] **7 Hanover Square**, bet. Water and Pearl Sts. S side. 1982. *Norman Jaffe*, design architect. *Emery Roth & Sons*, architects.

Twenty-six stories of "Georgian" red brick and limestone-like lintels over 1,000+ windows, squatting atop an overscaled reinterpretation of *Frank Lloyd Wright's* **Midway Gardens**. All of this claimed harmony with the architecture of tiny, three-story brownstone India House (whose air rights were transferred), quietly minding its own business across narrow Pearl Street.

[F33] **India House**/originally **Hanover Bank**/later New York Cotton Exchange and W. R. Grace & Company, 1 Hanover Sq., bet. Pearl and Stone Sts. 1851-1853. *Richard F. Carman*, carpenter. 👁

With the character of a London club (**Italian Renaissance Revival** version), India House remains a vestige of commercial buildings that once dotted this area, replaced by newer and denser construction. Unfluted Corinthian columns and pedimented windows

F33

give an understated enrichment to the dour brownstone. *Carman* (listed as a carpenter in the city directory) was later responsible for Carmansville, a village that stretched along Broadway between today's West 142nd to West 158th Streets.

[F34] **Hanover Square**, along Pearl St. bet. William and Hanover Sts. 1976.

Until the 1970s, ancient Stone Street, both curb lines intact, ran through this space. Now it is a pleasant paved area, happy home to the seated bronze figure of **Abraham de Peyster**, a wealthy Dutch goldsmith (1896, *George E Bissel*).

The Square was originally **Printing House Square**. At **81 Pearl**, *William Bradford* established the first printing press in the colonies in 1693. The great fire of 1835 substantially destroyed all buildings in an area of which this square was the center: the area between Coenties Slip, Broad, Wall, and South Streets, excepting the row facing Broad, and those facing Wall between William and Broad.

Five Corners: intersection of William, South William, Beaver Sts:

[F35a] **Banca Commerciale Italiana**/originally **J.W. Seligman & Co. Building**/later **Lehman Brothers Building**, 1 William St., SW cor. Hanover Sq. 1906-1907. *Francis H. Kimball & Julian C. Levi*. Alterations, 1929, *Harry R. Allen*. 👁 Alteration and addition, 1982-1986, *Gino Valle*.

A **Renaissance Revival** structure in stone, rusticated from sidewalk to cornice. Although regrettably divorced from its original windows, it is now happily married to a brilliant modernist addition that subtly harmonizes with many of its venerable architectural nuances.

[F35b] **Delmonico's**, 56 Beaver St., SW cor. South William St. 1890-1891. *James Brown Lord*. Converted to condominiums, 1996, *Mark Kemeny*. 👁

Occupying, like the Flatiron Building uptown, a valuable but awkward triangular space left between two converging streets. A distinguished restaurant for more than a century, this palatial **Renaissance Revival** headquarters was designed by *Lord* at the height of Delmonico's prestige and popularity: in orange terra cotta and brick, with porch columns reputedly brought from Pompeii by the *Delmonico brothers* themselves for their previous location (consumed in the great fire of 1835).

[F36] **New York City Department of Sanitation**/ originally the **Kerr Steamship Company Building**,

F32   F37

42-44 Beaver St. bet. Broad and William Sts. 1920. *Warren & Wetmore*.

No way to treat a building! This gracious **Neo-Classical** red brick pile surmounts a limestone base. Note the neat entablature depicting a Viking ship upon the waves. Originally home to the Kerr Steamship Company, their ship, the *Rochester,* during the worst days of World War I, became the first vessel to run unarmed through the German blockade, safely reaching Bordeaux. Today the façade's first two floors are covered in dirty, worn, cracked corrugated sheet metal. You would think the Sanitation Department would be more tidy.

[F37] **William Beaver House**, 15 William Street, NW cor. Beaver St. 2009. *Tsao & McKown Architects*.

The Post-it Note building: 47 stories of apartments clad in distinctive alternating swatches of black and bright yellow glazed brick. Daring amidst the financial district's monochromatic canyons, the idea here was to create an entire interior world, a luxurious buffer against the hustle and bustle of the City's street life. Some perks on the inside: 24-hour room service, private movie theater, indoor dog run (*come again?*), on-site auto mechanic. The views are great; why ever leave? But Delmonico's is way across the street. Do they deliver?

Bear right (north) on William Street:

[F38] **20 Exchange Place**/originally the **City Bank Farmers Trust Company,** or 22 William St., bet. Beaver St., Exchange Place, and Hanover St. 1930-1931. *Cross & Cross.* ☛

A slender 57-story tower of limestone, from the awkward period of architectural history between buildings-as-columns and steel-cage construction: **neo-Renaissance** vs. **Art Moderne.** Look up to see the Gulliver-sized coins—not quoins—that ring the building's limestone base. One of the authors' first jobs was as messenger

F35b

boy (for the bank) in the summer of '42.

Naming Wall Street: The Dutch wall of 1653 (a palisade of wood palings) was built as protection against attack from English colonies to the north. The English took it down, but the name remains.

Turn right (east) on Wall Street's south side to Pearl Street, make a U-turn, and return (west) on Wall Street's north side:

[F39] **Cipriani Wall Street** (restaurant), **Cipriani Club Residences** (apartments)/ formerly **National City Bank**/lower portion onetime **U.S. Custom House** (1863-1899)/originally **Merchants' Exchange,** 55 Wall St., bet. William and Hanover Sts, and Exchange Pl. 1836-1841. *Isaiah Rogers.* Converted to Custom House, 1863, *William A. Potter.* Remodeled and doubled in height, 1907-1910, *Charles F. McKim of McKim, Mead & White with William S. Richardson.* Converted to apartments, 2009, *Tsao & McKown.* ☛

Smoked granite. After the destruction of the first Merchants' Exchange in the great fire of 1835, *Rogers* erected on the same site a three-story Greek Revival "temple" (the 12 Ionic columns are monolithic) with a central domed trading hall. Later used as the **Custom House,** it was remodeled in 1907 (after the Fed's removal to Bowling Green) as the head office of the **National City Bank:** another tier of columns, this time Corinthian, was superimposed to double the cubic content. The great hall of *McKim, Mead & White's* First National City Bank has become the grand ballroom of the gourmand, sometimes the gourmet.

[F40] Originally **Seamen's Bank for Savings Headquarters,** 74 Wall St., NW cor. Pearl St. 1926. *Benjamin Wistar Morris.*

Craggy ashlar with a tall round-arched opening into the banking room. A friendly, romantic addition to the cold Wall Street canyon.

[F41] **Beaver Building**/originally Munson Steamship Co./later New York Cocoa Exchange

F39

Building, 82-92 Beaver St./1 Wall St. Court, at Pearl St. (just south of Wall St.). 1903-1904. *Clinton & Russell.* ☛

Glazed terra cotta and brick above, and an early neo-Renaissance polychromatic glazed terra-cotta cartouches below.

[F42] **Morgan Bank Headquarters,** 60 Wall St., bet. Pearl and William Sts. N side to Pine St. 1988. *Kevin Roche John Dinkeloo & Assocs.*

Planted on 1-1/4 acres, this massive 1.7 million-square-foot, 52-story tower not only reinterprets in contemporary terms the Classical column elements of base, shaft, and capital but almost literally replicates the column itself. The result is a hulk, out of step with the gracefully air-cooled slender-spired skyscrapers nearby (their air comes from windows). The transfer of **55**'s air rights from across the street made possible the bulky result.

[F43] **Bank of New York Building**, 48 Wall St., NE cor. William St. 1927-1929. *Benjamin Wistar Morris*. Conversion to condominiums, 1999, *Frank Williams & Associates*. **Museum of American Finance** within. 👁

The banking room, seen through large arched windows on both Wall and William Streets, is a special, serene space. You can enjoy the building's crowning Corinthian-columned temple and mounted bronze eagle only from afar (walk a bit down William Street). *Morris'* grandest New York effort was at the **Cunard Building**: again that shelters a magnificent interior behind a subdued façade.

[F44] **Tiffany's**/old **Morgan Guaranty Building**, 37 Wall St. Bet. William and Broad Sts. ca. 1900.

A Beaux Arts façade of some pomp. In Paris it would be classed as pompier (or fireman) style, the dying extravagance of the late 19th century. Now merely full of diamonds.

[F46] **Federal Hall National Memorial**/formerly **U.S. Subtreasury Building** (1862-1925)/originally **United States Custom House** (1842-1862), 28 Wall St., NE cor. Nassau St. 1833-1842. *Town & Davis*, architects. *Samuel Thompson*, builder, succeeded by *William Ross and John Frazee*. 👁 Interior. 👁 Open to the public: Mo-Fr 9-5; closed Sa & Su. 212-264-8711.

No, *George Washington* did not take his oath of office in front of this building but, rather, its predecessor, the former city hall, renamed Federal Hall. It had been remodeled by *Pierre L' Enfant* from the old shell, to which local government had been removed in 1701 from the **Dutch Stadt Huys** on Pearl Street. The current name, **Federal Hall National Memorial**, commemorates the earlier structure.

This Doric-columned temple and **Staten Island's Sailors' Snug Harbor** are the institutional stars of New York's Greek Revival. The Wall Street façade is a simplified **Parthenon**, without the sculptured frieze or pediment. Carved from marble quarried in Westchester

F42

F43

F44

F45

[F45] **The Trump Building**/originally **Manhattan Company**, 40 Wall St., bet. William and Broad Sts. 1929-1930. *H. Craig Severance,* architect. *Yasuo Matsui,* associate architect. *Shreve & Lamb,* consulting architects. 👁 Lobby and storefront alterations, 1997, *Der Scutt.*

A skyline bank building, now best observed from an upper floor of the composite bank to which it has moved its quarters: the Chase Manhattan on Chase Manhattan Plaza to the north. The pyramidal crown was symbol of the original bank. Chartered first as a water company (the **Manhattan Company**) and the City's first quasi-public utility, it sold its waterworks to the city in 1808. Always permitted by a clause in its charter to engage in banking, it continued solely as the **Bank of the Manhattan Company**, the latter, parent organization becoming incidental to its offshoot.

The Building claimed a higher observation deck than that of the Chrysler Building (836 feet; Chrysler Building, 783 feet); but, in fact, neither is now open to the public.

County, it is raised on a high base to handle the change in grade from Pine to Wall. Inside the rectangular volume is a very non-Greek rotunda, the principal, and startling, space—rather like finding a cubical space in a helical conch shell.

The old **Assay Office** (1823, *Martin Thompson*) stood to the east until the building was demolished to make room for bigger things. **Assay's** façade was rescued and is currently to be seen at the Metropolitan Museum's American Wing.

J(ohn) Q(uincy) A(dams) Ward's statue of **Washington** (1883) stands on the approximate spot in space where the man himself took the oath, in 1789.

Broad Street: South of Wall Street:

[F47] **Downtown by Philippe Starck**/formerly Morgan Guaranty Trust Company/originally **J. P. Morgan & Company,** 23 Wall St., SE cor. Broad St. 1913. *Trowbridge & Livingston.* **15 Wall Street** (formerly **Equitable Trust Building**) adjacent, also by *Trowbridge and Livingston.* ✷ Conversion by *Philippe Starck.*

Luxury residences within the first ground zero attack on capitalism. *J. Pierpont Morgan* epitomized Wall Street to capitalists, communists, radicals, and conservatives alike. And, of course, when Wall Street was to be bombed, this was considered its sensitive center of control: on September 16, 1920, an anarchist ignited a wagon load of explosives next to the Wall Street flank. Thirty-three persons were killed, and 400 were injured. The scars remain visible in the stonework. It has been said that "the great financiers of the turn of the century identified themselves with the merchant princes of the Italian Renaissance."

F46

[F48] **New York Stock Exchange,** 8 Broad St., bet. Wall St. and Exchange Pl. W side. 1901-1903. *George B. Post.* Addition, 1923, *Trowbridge & Livingston.* Pediment sculpture, *J.Q.A. Ward and Paul Bartlett.* ✷

One of the few great architectural spaces accessible to the public in this city. The original Roman temple façade by *Post* is a far cry from his **Queen Anne** style **Brooklyn Historical Society** 22 years before. The Columbian Exposition of 1893 had swept such earth-colored picturesque architecture under the rug. The rage for neo-Classical architecture and cities was compelling even to those who had been the Goths of architecture. The original mythological figures of the pediment became so deteriorated that their stone was replaced, secretively, with sheet metal.

The **Trading Floor Center** (1998, *Asymptote*) is a marvel of both the technology in action and the technological architecture surrounding the action. September 11 resulted in the cordoning off of the Exchange behind ugly barriers.

[F49] **25 Broad Street**/originally the **Broad Exchange Building,** SE cor. Exchange Pl. 1899. *Robert Maynicke.* Revised, 1900-1902, *Clinton & Russell.* ✷ Condominium conversion, 1998, *Costas Kondylis.*

Worthy of the best on Park Avenue, this stalwart housing for finance (once headquarters of the City Investing Company) now houses the apartments of Wallstreeters.

[F50] Claremont Preparatory School/former **Bank of America International**/originally **Lee-Higginson Bank,** 37-41 Broad St., bet. Exchange

F52

Pl. and Beaver St. E side. 1929. *Cross & Cross.* Frieze, *Leo Friedlander,* sculptor.

This chaste convex bow that follows Broad Street's curve is a comforting gesture. Contrary to what usually transpires during a building boom, this nine-story structure replaced the 26-story **Trust Company of America Building** (1907, *Francis H. Kimball*).

[F51a] Originally **American Bank Note Company Headquarters,** 70 Broad St., bet. Marketfield and Beaver Sts. W side. 1907-1908. *Kirby, Petit & Green.* ✷ Restoration of exterior, 1996, *Joseph Pell Lombardi.*

Look up to see the true swelling of **Classical Corinthian** columns. It's an elegant small palazzo designed with a compressed monumentality, as if it were a beginning excerpt of a monumental palace (to be continued north and south).

Transcendental Meditation, by the *Maharishi Mahesh Yogi,* now owns the building. A little meditation now and then might be appropriate for Wall Street.

[F51b] Originally **International Telephone Building**, 75 Broad St. bet. S. William and Beaver Sts. 1930. *Louis S. Weeks.*

A stolid Art Deco tower built by once mighty ITT, with the requisite hyperbole: a majestic top, featuring what looks like an entire **Art Deco village**, best viewed from a few blocks to the east, at the intersection of Pearl and Hanover. Up close, winged cherubs on the Broad Street façade deliver lightning bolts of energy.

Broadway, at the head of Wall Street:

[F53] **Bank of New York Mellon**/originally **Irving Trust Company** (offices), 1 Wall St., SE cor. Broadway. 1928-1932. *Ralph Walker of Voorhees, Gmelin & Walker.* South Addition, 1965, *Smith, Smith, Haines, Lundberg & Waehler.* ☀

Ralph Walker's experiments in the plastic molding of skyscraper form, both in massing and in detail, culminate in this shimmering limestone

F53

F54

Back up Broad Street's hill—its wide part was the site of the Curb Exchange, meeting indoors on Trinity Place since 1921 as the American Stock Exchange. The Curb's brokers literally met on the curb, out of doors, between 1865 and 1921.

Take a left (west) back on Wall Street:

[F52] **Bankers Trust Company Building** (offices), 14 Wall St., NW cor. Nassau St. 1910-1912. *Trowbridge & Livingston.* Addition, 1931-1933, *Shreve, Lamb & Harmon.* ☀

The stepped pyramid, later logo of the resident bank, tops one of the grand skyline finials of the City. When built, it was called the world's tallest structure (540 feet) on the smallest plot (94 X 97 feet). The pyramid is invisible from the neighboring sidewalk, but walk back down Broad for a skyline look.

tower, a fitting companion of quality to Trinity Church across Broadway. Don't miss the lobby, which resonates to the same Art Deco melodies. As for the annex, that's another matter.

[F54] **Trinity Church** (Episcopal), Broadway at the head of Wall St. W side. 1839-1846. *Richard Upjohn.* **William Backhouse Astor Memorial Altar and Reredos,** 1876-1877, *Frederick Clarke Withers.* **All Saints Chapel,** 1911-1913, *Thomas Nash.* **Bishop William T. Manning Memorial Wing,** 1965, *Adams & Woodbridge.* Churchyard, 1681. ☀

Nestled in the canyons of Broadway and Trinity Place, Trinity's form is totally comprehensible to the pedestrian: on the axis of Wall Street the canyon walls read as surfaces, while Trinity sits importantly, a crisp brownstone, bedded in a green baize cemetery. The cemetery offers retreat for summer-tired office workers at noontime. Bronze doors designed by *Richard Morris Hunt* (donated in memory of *John Jacob Astor III*) were executed by *Charles Niehaus, Karl Bitter,* and *J. Massey Rhind* (left entrance, main entrance, and right entrance, respectively) from 1890 to 1896. Cemetery monuments of particular note include the pyramid of *Alexander Hamilton, Robert Fulton's* bronze bas-relief, and that of *William Bradford.*

The attached chapel must not be confused with Trinity's "colonial" chapels, which were separate and remotely located church buildings serving this immense Episcopal parish. Typical of the latter is **St. Paul's Chapel** at Fulton and Broadway. The parish is an enormous landowner

F55

(Fulton to Christopher Streets, Broadway west to the river was its original grant from *Queen Anne* in 1705). Thus, the proselytizing of the faith through missionary activities could be financed comfortably (**St. Augustine's** and **St. Christopher's Chapels** on the Lower East Side are further examples). The original **Trinity Church** was founded in 1696, erected in 1698, enlarged and "beautified" in 1737, and burned to the ground in 1776. A second building, constructed in 1788-1790, was demolished in 1839.

[F55] **Trinity and U.S. Realty Buildings** (offices), 111 and 115 Broadway, straddling Thames St. W. side. 1904-1907. Both by *Francis H. Kimball*. Renovated, 1988-1989, *Swanke Hayden Connell.* 🍎

Rich buildings from top to bottom, their narrow ends at Broadway are broken **Gothic** forms with strongly scaled details. They have a great deal of personality vis-à-vis the passing pedestrian. Unlike the blank austerity of 1 Wall, the

temple entrance of 100 Broadway, or the modern openness of Chase Manhattan's vast transparent lobby for bureaucrats en masse, these are buildings for individual people. Many feel possessive about them.

[F56] Onetime **Bank of Tokyo**/originally **American Surety Company**, 100 Broadway, SE cor. Pine St. 1894-1896. *Bruce Price*. Additions 1920-1922, *Herman Lee Meader*. 1975, *Kajima International*, designers. *Welton Becket Assocs.*, architects. 🍎

Kajima, through designer *Nobutaka Ashihara*, recycled *Price's* "rusticated pillar" into modern and economic elegance. The Italians excelled at this in the 1950s (as at the Castello Sforzesco in Milan, converted to a museum); the Japanese now equal the Italians' best in New York. The ladies above, by sculptor *J. Massey Rhind,* are a stern Athenian octet. Tenancy in flux.

F58

[F57] **Wall Street Subway Station**, IRT Lexington Avenue Line, under Broadway at Wall St. 1905. *Heins & La Farge*. Redesigned, 1979, *NYC Transit Authority Architectural Staff*.

A restrained *Heins & La Farge* design upgraded by the MTA in full height, ultramarine blue glazed brick. (If you're feeling blue, don't venture here.) The restored, golden oak and bronze change booth on the downtown side is a minor bow to the past.

[F58] **Empire Apartments**/originally **Empire Building**, 71 Broadway, SW cor. Rector St. to Trinity Pl. 1895-1898. *Francis Kimball of Kimball & Thompson.* 🍎

An ornate wall, it forms a backdrop to Trinity Churchyard to the north. U.S. Steel managed its empire from here, 1901-1976. Now its resident Wallstreeters can savor the Trinity greensward to the north. The entrance is a triumphant **Roman** ensemble.

*Financier Russell Sage was almost assassinated in 1891 in an older Empire Building that occupied this spot before replacement by this **Empire Building**. He quickly threw his male secretary at the bomber, muffling the intended damage to himself but almost killing his secretary. Sage withstood his assistant's lawsuit and died very rich. His widow later established the Russell Sage philanthropies, among them **Forest Hills Gardens**.*

[F59] Now **J.J. Kenny/Standard & Poor's** Building/originally **American Railway Express Company Building** (offices), 65 Broadway, bet. Exchange Alley and Rector St. W side to Trinity Pl. 1916-1917. *James L.Aspinwall* of *Renwick Aspinwall & Tucker.* ● Altered, 1979, *Carl J. Petrilli.*

An H-plan results in a pair of slender 23-story wings, embracing (and arching over) light courts fore and aft. Note the asymmetric eagle on the lower arch and the symmetric one on the arch atop the building.

F59

[F60] **One Exchange Plaza** (offices), Broadway SW cor. Exchange Alley to Trinity Pl. 1982-1984. *Fox & Fowle.*
[F61] **45 Broadway Atrium** (offices), bet. Exchange Alley and Morris St. W side to Trinity Pl. 1983. *Fox & Fowle.*

A pair of sleek, exquisitely detailed, brick and glass towers built simultaneously by the same developer (HRO International) and architects; separate structures due to the exorbitant price asked by the tiny fast-food holdout between. Note the brickwork mural on the wall facing the Atrium's windows—to appease those whose view is north.

Take a right (west) down the narrow, repaved brick Exchange Alley to Trinity Place, and turn right (north):

[F62a] **Robert and Anne Dickey House,** 67 Greenwich St., between Trinity Pl., Edgar St., and Greenwich St. 1809-1810. Altered, 1872, *Dietlef Lienau.* ●

The only remaining Federal (style) town house in Manhattan with a bowed façade (on the Trinity Place side). A shadow of once gracious architecture, it would be nicer stripped of its layers of gray paint.

[F62b] **3-legged Dog Theater,** 80 Greenwich St. at Rector St. 2006. *Thomas Lesser.*

A new experimental theater in the ground floor of an existing parking garage delights the passing pedestrian: one of its stages behind a 90-foot glass wall brings theater to the street. Cleanly and futuristically modern, like walking onto the set of *Battlestar Galactica*. Take me to the bridge!

[F62c] Originally **American Railway Express Company** (warehouse), 46 Trinity Pl., bet. Exchange Alley and Rector St. W side. ca. 1880. ●

F62b

Note the terra-cotta seal with the company emblem, *avec bulldog*, in relief. A façade of brick arches redolent of pre-skyscraper New York, now scrubbed (freed of paint) back to its 1880s glow. Also see [T25] p. 65.

[F63] **Trinity Place Bridge,** Trinity Parish, linking Trinity Churchyard and 74 Trinity Pl. Trinity Pl. bet. Rector and Thames Sts. 1987. *Lee Harris Pomeroy Assocs.*

As Trinity's congregation grew older and traffic on Trinity Place greater, the church felt a need to separate its aging parishioners commuting to their activity rooms across the street at No.74 from the danger of cars, trucks, and bicycles. This 80-foot-long bridge is the answer.

[F64] **High School of Economics and Finance/** originally **Nichols Hall, NYU Graduate School of Business Administration**, 100 Trinity Place bet. Thames and Cedar Sts. W side. 1959. *Skidmore, Owings & Merrill.*

[F64a] **High School for Leadership & Public Service**/originally **Charles E. Merrill Hall, NYU Graduate School of Business Administration**, 90 Trinity Place, SW cor. Thames St. 1975. *Skidmore, Owings & Merrill.*

A pair, connected by an enclosed bridge high over Thames Street. Stylish in 1959, the northerly building has, in retrospect, become a dull, white-speckled brick ancestor to the sleek off-black *Merrill* monolith to the south, a classic background modernist monument.

Turn into Thames Street and walk west; zigzag left on Greenwich and right (west) again on Albany Street to the last stops on the tour:

[F65] **W New York Downtown (Hotel),** 123 Washington St., bet. Albany and Carlisle Sts. 2010. *Gwathmey Siegel.*

Charles Gwathmey (1938-2009) did not live to see the completion of this glassy high-rise. Here is *Gwathmey* sans the usual curves and undulations that made him famous. Tall but restrained.

[F66] **90 West Street Building** (offices), bet. Albany and Cedar Sts. E side. 1905-1908. *Cass Gilbert.* ●⌁

Limestone and cast terra cotta. Increasingly interesting and complex the higher you raise

F62c   F66

your eyes: designed for a view from the harbor or the eyries of an adjacent skyscraper, rather than the ordinary West Street pedestrian. A similar, but less successful, use of terra cotta than *Gilbert's* spectacular **Woolworth Building**.

*The **Hudson-Fulton Celebration** (1909), as part of the fall festivities, illuminated many of the City's prominent buildings and bridges— not with floodlights but with necklaces of bare electric bulbs, then a relatively new technique. For the 400th anniversary of Hudson's arrival, autumn 2009, the City was illuminated by light bulbs strung aloft in the bare concrete skeletons of unfinished condominiums.*

END of Tour A. The nearest subways are the old BMT Broadway Line (R and W trains) or the old IND Eighth Avenue Line (E train).

NECROLOGY

Seamen's Church Institute, 15 State St., SE cor. Pearl St. 1969. *Eggers & Higgins.*

The picturesque, plastic, and romantic red brick structure that had replaced its 1907 predecessor at Coenties Slip lasted less than 20 years. The institute, which began as a Gothic Revival chapel on a barge in 1834 to serve the spiritual and social needs of mariners, now occupies an elegant new building at the South Street Seaport (**241 Water Street,** *Polshek Partnership*).

The Produce Exchange (1882-1884. *George B. Post*) was one of the City's greatest architectural losses in the post–World War II years. That enormous red terra-cotta and brick Romanesque Revival construction is echoed today only in miniature by *Post's* extant **Brooklyn Historical Society.** The ruddy Exchange contrasted vividly with its newer, paler, limestone and granite neighbors until its demolition in 1957.

F64a

71 Pearl Street (commercial building), bet. Broad St. and Coenties Alley. N side. Foundations, 1641. Walls, 1700. Façade, 1826. ●⌁

The façade of this official landmark, whose foundations were claimed to be those of the Dutch Stadt Huys, New York's first city hall, was carefully dismantled to be reerected at South Street Seaport. Be patient—there is some question as to whether all its parts were located.

60 Wall Street, bet. William and Nassau Sts. N side through to Pine St. 1905. *Clinton & Russell.*

The 27-story structure that for a time (via an overhead connecting bridge) gave a Wall Street address (60 Wall Tower) to the old Cities Service Building at 70 Pine Street. After demolition the enormous site was for almost a decade most notable as a sprawling asphalt-paved pedestrian space, not a parking field. Then came Morgan (see p. 17).

WATER STREET CORRIDOR

Lower Manhattan's Street of Million-Square-Foot Towers.

Under *Mayor Robert F. Wagner*, City Planning Commission chairman *William F. R. Ballard* commissioned the Lower Manhattan Plan of 1966, prepared by *Wallace McHarg Associates and Whittlesey, Conklin & Rossant*. It promised a lively and handsome pedestrian world south of Canal Street, foot-eased by small and unnoxious electric buses and enlarged through landfill to the pierhead line. New residential communities surrounding riverside plazas—"windows on the waterfront"—would be provided. With some adjustments, detours, and compromises we have a new Lower Manhattan skyline of million-square-foot, flat-topped boxes that line the Water Street Corridor.

From the harbor and the Brooklyn Heights Promenade it is these towers, the ones along

W1

Water Street and others, that have come to encircle the Financial District's heart. They have muffled from view the constellation of tall, slender 1920s and 1930s **Art Deco** office buildings and the flamboyant pinnacles of their earlier, shorter, neo-Classical cousins, the structures that made up the inspired—if unplanned—Lower Manhattan skyline that was once the world-renowned symbol of New York City.

Walking Tour B: A Water Street walk northward from the Staten Island Ferry Terminal to South Street Seaport, at Fulton and Water Streets. START in Peter Minuit Plaza in front of the ferry terminal. No.1, R, or W train to Whitehall Street/South Ferry Station. Alternates: A short walk from the start are the 4 and 5 trains at the Bowling Green Station or the 2 and 3 trains at the Wall Street Station.

Or just forget it and get on the Ferry!

[W1] **Whitehall Ferry Terminal**, City of New York, South St. foot of Whitehall St. 1954. *Roberts & Schaefer*, consulting engineers. New building, 2005, *Schwartz Architects with Ron Evitts and TAMS.*

The old terminal, described in previous editions of this Guide as bile-colored, and where "Kafka would have had the shivers" burned in 1991. After two controversial design competitions and much stumbling, its replacement is an airy, cinematic building. Interior walls are inscribed with supergraphics: **PHONES**. Outside an even bigger neon sign, **STATEN ISLAND FERRY**, beckons commuters, gently curving around a driveway and new Whitehall/ South Ferry subway station. Modest, compared to the monumental clock that won the original competition (*Venturi and Scott-Brown, with Schwartz*) but a clean, spacious, light-filled place to catch the ferry.

*The Staten Island Ferry not only ranks as a tourist mecca of great delight but also explains the overall arrangement of the water-bound city quickly, clearly, and with pleasure. You will experience, for free, one of the world's greatest (and shortest) water voyages, through the richly endowed harbor, past buoys, the **West Bank Light House**, **Governors** and **Liberty Islands**, and the U.S. Army Military Ocean Terminal (the old Bayonne naval base), to the community of **St. George** at Staten Island's northeastern shore. (If you decide to stay, turn to the Staten Island section of this Guide. Otherwise, just travel the ferry route in reverse.) This is the low-income substitute for a glamorous arrival in New York by transatlantic liner, receiving first Liberty's salute and then the dramatic silhouette of Lower Manhattan's skyline. On a lucky day you will surge through the wake of freighters, container ships, tankers, tugs, sludge boats, pleasure craft, and the few extant liners used for cruises—and maybe even an occasional warship. Pity the poor daily commuter who spends the ride with nose in book, long ago bored by the routine sounds and sights of the harbor. For the occasional ferry rider, though, it never ceases to amaze: salt spray rising on New York's inland sea.*

Upstream from the ferry terminal is another, older one:

[W2] **Battery Maritime Building**, NYC Department of Ports International Trade & Commerce, originally Whitehall Ferry Terminal, 11 South St., foot of Whitehall St. S side. 1906-1909. *Walker & Morris*. ☛ Restoration, *Jan Hird Pokorny*.

Viewed from a ferry, the monumental arches of the Terminal appear like tunnels opening into the canyons of the City. The ferry slips within, in turn, present a monumental porch to Whitehall. Green paint over sheet metal and 40-foot structural columns simulates verdigris copper. The columns, of no historical style, are original, and rise from the nature of the material. Especially savor the Guastavino tile vaults under the porch roof. Restored and in use: catch the free ferry here to **Governors Island**.

W2

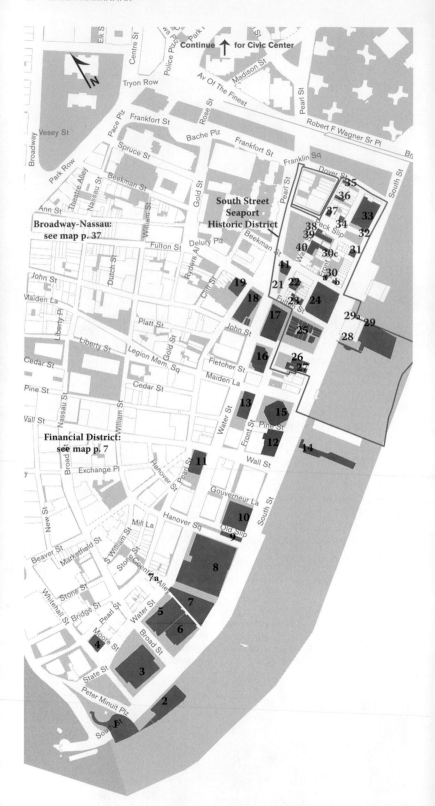

Continue ↑ for Civic Center

Broadway-Nassau:
see map p. 37

South Street
Seaport
Historic District

Financial District:
see map p. 7

Find Water Street in the leaky open space that bears the Peter Minuit name, and proceed northeasterly. It's the wide street one full block inland from the river, a curving version (towers cheek by jowl) of midtown's Avenue of the Americas (Sixth Avenue).

[W3] 1 New York Plaza, Whitehall St. bet. South, Water and Broad Sts. 1969. *William Lescaze & Assocs.*, design architects. *Kahn & Jacobs*, architects. Plaza reconfiguration, 1990s.

A **behemoth**. Thousands of interior decorators' picture frames form an unhappy façade on this all too prominent, dark, brooding office tower. Some aggressive light standards have recently been added to guard the occupants.

[W4] 3 New York Plaza/originally **U.S. Army Building**, 39 Whitehall St., bet. Water, Pearl, and Moore Sts. 1886. *S. D. Hatch.* Reconstructed and reclad, 1986, *Wechsler, Grasso & Menziuso*.

Concealed inches behind that slick green-and-white graph paper curtain wall is the

Coenties Slip: As the landfill crept seaward, this "slip," a tiny artificial bay for wharfing ships, was created with a diagonal breakwater paralleling the present west boundary. Eventually the breakwater was absorbed, as land projected even beyond its former tip.

[W7] New York Vietnam Veterans Memorial/originally **Jeanette Park**, on the bed of Coenties Slip bet. Water and South Sts. **Jeanette Plaza**, 1972, *M. Paul Friedberg & Assocs.* Memorial added, 1985, *William Britt Fellows, Peter Wormser*, architects, *Joseph Ferrandino*, writer.

A 70-foot-long, 14-foot-high rectangular prism surfaced in 12-inch-square glass blocks, lined with a granite shelf for visitors' offerings, and penetrated by two unadorned portals. The glass blocks, made luminescent by night, are etched with excerpts from speeches, news dispatches, and letters written home by those who were fighting in *Nam*. Chosen in a national competition, the winner is simple, thoughtful,

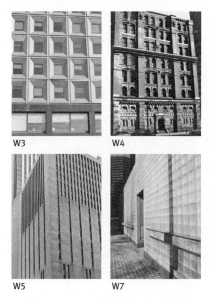

W3   W4

W5   W7

W8

masonry ghost of the building where hundreds of thousands of army inductees took their physical for World War II and Korea. Occupying an entire (small) city block, it rests on the original foundations of the 1861 **Produce Exchange**, by *Leopold Eidlitz*.

[W5] 4 New York Plaza, Water St. bet. Broad St. and Vietnam Veterans Memorial Plaza (old Coenties Slip). S side. 1968. *Carson, Lundin & Shaw*. **[W6] 2 New York Plaza**/briefly **American Express Plaza**, 125 Broad St. NW cor. South St. 1970. *Kahn & Jacobs*.

Twenty-two-story No.4, Manufacturers Hanover Trust's handsomely carved monolith of rich earth-toned salt-and-pepper speckled brick, is the earliest of the **New York Plaza** giants. Its careful choice of materials and details was meant to harmonize in quality, if not in scale, with the tiny **Federal** and **Greek Revival** survivors that were still its neighbors in the 1960s. Those survivors (except the **Fraunces Tavern Block**) and the color scheme rapidly gave way to heavy-handed intruders like the 40-story **No.2**.

carefully detailed, and neatly executed. But in sharp contrast to the emotionally powerful **Vietnam Memorial** in Washington (also a national competition winner), New York's memorial fails to touch the heart.

[W7a] Coenties Slip Park, Coenties Alley, bet. Water and Pearl Sts. 2006. *George Vellonakis*, landscape architect.

Continues Jeanette Plaza west across Water Street, until it narrows to a point and ends. Dominated by a torpedo-like stainless steel sculpture by *Bryan Hunt* (*Coenties Ship*, 2006). A minor park, it's a pleasant place for a short break and a quick sandwich.

[W8] 55 Water Street, bet. Coenties and Old Slips. SE side to South St. 1972. *Emery Roth & Sons*, architects. Terrace over South St., *M. Paul Friedberg & Assocs.*, landscape architects. **Elevated Acre**, 2006, *Rogers Marvel*.

At 3.68 million square feet, it was the world's largest private office building when opened. But awkward. The deal for its bulk, arrived at through zoning modifications, also financed the redesigned **Jeanette Plaza**. Later added, a 1990s canopy swoops out and up, providing a new entrance identity for the taxiing executive.

Take the up-escalator between its south and north wings to visit a strange public park, the **Elevated Acre**, dominated by an AstroTurf lawn and an inscrutable prism that lights up pink and blue at night, but during the day looks like a complicated cell phone tower.

At Old Slip, turn right (southeasterly):

[W9] **New York City Police Museum**/one-time **Landmarks Preservation Commission**, originally **1st Precinct, NYC Police Department.** 100 Old Slip, bet. Front and South Sts. N side. 1909-1911. *Hunt & Hunt.* 🐾

A rusticated **Renaissance Revival** palazzo, miniature in size, majestic in scale. It's considered the City's first modern police station. Now a museum where "exhibits describe law enforcement's evolution from the **Dutch Rattle**

W9

A deep, generous entrance arch through a flamed granite base offers a promise, but the flat detailing above doesn't deliver. The park provides the obligatory waterfall, but little to promote pedestrian serenity. Now transformed into a hotel and apartments.

A peek at the foot of Wall Street:

[W12] **120 Wall Street**, NW cor. South St. to Pine St. 1930. *Office of Ely Jacques Kahn.*

A powerful, symmetric, wedding cake silhouette. Very early for a large commercial building to brave a relatively inaccessible East River site. A Wall Street address and the nearby Second and Third Avenue elevated trains on Pearl Street, still operating in the 1930s, helped. Today it's amid new finance construction.

R.M.S. Queen Elizabeth Monument: Bronze letters from the majestic British ocean liner that sank in Hong Kong waters on January 9, 1972, are preserved in the plaza south of Wall Street

W12

Watch to the NYPD's post–September 11 transformation into a proactive intelligence agency."

[W10] **1 Financial Square**, Front St. bet. Old Slip and Gouverneur Lane to South St. 1987. *Edward Durell Stone Assocs.*

One million square feet. Trading on the transfer of development rights from two low-rise neighbors, a demolished fire station (whose functions are now enveloped within the skyscraper) and **100 Old Slip** [see above], this 36-story high rise is built on the former site of the **U.S. Assay Building** [see **Necrology**]. **Financial Square's** stone-clad base was supposed to harmonize with the stonework of the old **1st Precinct** next door.

Back to Water Street:

[W11] **75 Wall Street Apartments Condominiums & Hyatt Andaz Hotel**/originally **Barclay Bank Building and Park**, 75 Wall St., bet. Water and Pearl Sts. S side. 1987. *Welton Becket Assocs.* 2008. *The Rockwell Group,* interiors.

*Plaza. The adjoining sculpture is **Disk and Slab** (1973, Yu Yu Yang).*

[W13] **Wall Street Plaza**/originally **88 Pine Street Building**, bet. Water St., Maiden Lane and Front St. 1973. *James Ingo Freed of I. M. Pei & Assocs.*

A white, crisp elegance of aluminum and glass (no mullions: one of the earliest examples here of butted glass that fills whole structural bays). Water Street's classiest building: a powerful understatement that belittles, by default, much of the overstriving new architecture nearby.

[W14] **Wall Street Ferry Terminal**, Pier 11: South St. bet. Wall St. & Gouverneur Ln. 1999. *Smith-Miller + Hawkinson Architects. Judith Heintz,* landscape architect. *Community Island Pond,* sculpture, *Carl Cheng* (2000).

A self-confident shed asserts itself as Wall Street's ferry terminal. The back wall is sheet metal, festively painted orange. The front façade is crisp glass and steel, and, best of all, hinged: on a nice day it swings open and you join the great outdoors. *Heintz's* pier and catwalks surrounding the terminal form a nice public space, even when you're not looking for a water taxi. At the pier's tip is an aquarium-like "installation" by *Cheng*, but the stunning view back towards the skyline is the real art here.

A detour of a short block to the right (east) along Maiden Lane will reveal:

[W15] **Continental Center,** 180 Maiden Lane to Pine St., Front to South Sts. 1983. *Swanke Hayden Connell & Partners.*

One million square feet. A deceptively suave, but actually tacky, green monster with a greenhouse base, a project of the Rockefeller Center Development Corporation. (The resemblance to Rockefeller Center ends with the developer's name.)

[W16] Originally **National Westminster Bank USA,** 175 Water St., bet. Fletcher St. and John St. S side to Front St. 1983. *Fox & Fowle.*

Half a million square feet. Mirrored glass cylinders (there are two) are embraced by brick-and-glass horizontal-strip-windows. Neither fox nor fowl.

*During excavation for **National Westminster** the remains of a mid-1700s ship were found buried in the landfill. It had been scuttled to act as a cofferdam for late 18th-century earthmoving operations. The prow was successfully salvaged and removed to **Mariners' Museum** in Newport News, Va.*

The **Edison Electric Illuminating Company's** *first large-scale, permanent commercial power and incandescent lighting system began operations on Monday, September 4, 1882, from a generating station located at 255-257 Pearl Street, between John and Fulton Streets. The area serviced included nearly a square mile, enclosed by Wall, Nassau, Spruce, and Ferry Streets, Peck Slip, and the East River. The generator ran until 1890, when it was partially destroyed by fire.*

[W19] **Seaport Tower,** 40 Fulton St. bet. Pearl and Cliff Sts. 1989. *Fox & Fowle.*

A slender articulated office tower that erased a one-story McDonald's. A lively neighbor to many bland buildings surrounding.

***END** of Tour B. For refreshments, you couldn't be in a better place, at the gateway to South Street Seaport. And if you're in the mood for more touring see the South Street section, below. Otherwise, the closest subways are along Fulton Street in a complex, interconnected Fulton Street/Broadway-Nassau Station: including A, C, J, M, Z, 2, 3, 4, 5 trains.*

NECROLOGY

U.S. Army Building, 39 Whitehall St., bet. Water and Pearl Sts. E side. 1886. *Stephen D. Hatch.*

The mirrored recladding—not a demolition—marks the second reconstruction here. Hatch's Victorian, fortlike hollowed brick doughnut rose from the foundations of *Leopold Eidlitz's* 1861 New York Produce Exchange. The Army facility

W10   W15

W14

[W17] **1 Seaport Plaza,** 199 Water St., to Front St. bet. John and Fulton Sts. 1983. *Swanke Hayden Connell & Partners.*

One million square feet. Developer *Jack Resnick & Sons'* first "contextual" office building, its main façades were designed to differ from one another, ostensibly to address the glitzier obligations of a Water Street frontage on the inland side, while granting low-scale **Schermerhorn Row** its due on Front Street. The height of 1 Seaport Plaza: 34 stories; the height of **Schermerhorn Row**: four stories plus. Contextual?

[W18] **127 John Street Building,** NW cor. Water St. to Fulton and Pearl Sts. 1969. *Emery Roth & Sons.* Lobby, plaza, street level, and mechanical floor elements, *Corchia de Harak Assocs.,* designers.

A no-nonsense building with a happy non-sense-filled lobby and sidewalk. Outside, pipe and canvas structures play with light and shelter pedestrians. An adjacent electric display clock is a building in its own right. Developer *Mel Kaufman* is the person to thank.

was best remembered by the countless thousands who came here with fear and trembling to undergo preinduction physicals.

55, 57, 61 Front Street, bet. Cuylers Alley and Old Slip. S side. 54, 56, 62, 64 Front Street, bet. Coenties and Old Slips. N side. 96-110 Front Street, bet. Gouverneur Lane and Wall St. N side. 142 Front Street, NE cor. Depeyster St. All 1830s.

Such warehouses, almost entirely gone from the scene, formed the core of commercial Lower Manhattan in the early 19th century. Even the most utilitarian structures were done in Greek Revival.

U.S. Assay Building, Old Slip bet. South and Front Sts. E side. 1930. *James A. Wetmore,* Acting Supervising Architect, U.S. Treasury.

A massively sculptural granite monolith low rise with a high-rise smokestack. The Feds auctioned the site off for $27 million, an astronomical sum for the early 1980s.

SOUTH STREET SEAPORT

*South Street Seaport nods on the banks of the East River, lurking in the shadows of FDR Drive and the approaches to the Brooklyn Bridge, at the north end of Water Street, adjacent to the abandoned Fulton Fish Market. A restored enclave of low-rise, small-scale structures—some dating to the 18th century, others new—owes its survival to a number of events: the establishment of the **South Street Seaport Museum**, spearheaded by Peter Stanford, in 1967; the subsequent banking of the area's air-rights development potential, later to be purchased by property owners to the south, where whopping office towers now stand; the State of New York's purchase of **Schermerhorn Row** in 1974; a series of official landmark designations; and the establishment, in cooperation with the City's Public Development Corporation, of a **"festival marketplace"** by the Rouse Company.*

Entry to the Seaport area is best achieved by walking toward the East River on Fulton Street. (The nearest subway stop is the rabbit warren of interconnected Fulton Street/Broadway-Nassau Stations of the A, C, J, M, Z, 2, 3, 4, 5 trains).

Orientation: *The thoroughfare called South Street is literally at the south flank of Manhattan Island, where the adjacent (and parallel) East River runs very roughly an east-west course (more pronounced above the Brooklyn Bridge). Logically, streets in this area that are perpendicular to perimeter South Street have (very roughly) east and west sides. For our purposes, and to tie this grid to the remainder, South Street will be considered running north and south, according to popular, but mildly inaccurate, convention.*

W22a

The Seaport's theme-park quality is at odds with the true grit that the waterfront and fish market once had. Like its Rouse clones in Boston (Faneuil Hall) and Baltimore (Inner Harbor), the Seaport caters primarily to tourists, plus the overflow lunchtime crowd from Wall Street. It has been cleaned up so much that it feels only tangentially like New York. And even worse, the interior of the Pier Pavilion 17 feels like any shopping mall from Maine to Florida. What a shame!

The consensus seems to be that the "festival marketplace" movement has passed. Ironically, what was intended as a time capsule of the early 1800s has become an inadvertent time capsule of the early 1980s. A new master plan by the hipster firm SHoP got some good marks from critics but was shot down, Ancient Mariner–style, by the Landmarks Preservation Commission. Among the plan's controversial features: demolishing Pier Pavilion 17 in favor of a modern tower with a façade like a giant humidifier filter, and moving the "historic" Tin Building to the far end of a new pier. The fish and grit are long gone, so why not?

[W20] South Street Seaport Historic District, An irregular L-shaped area including parts of both sides of South St. from the East River waters below Pier 15 (including Piers 15, 16, and 17); then on a line W to Front St. bet. the S frontage of John St./Burling Slip and Fletcher St., N on Front St. to Fulton St., W along Fulton to Water then Pearl Sts. and on to Dover St. 🍎

Ada Louise Huxtable's **Classic New York** warned in 1964 of the rapid demise of the physical vestiges of the City's 18th- and 19th-century waterfront heritage, much of which was still visible on South Street, the wide thoroughfare along the sheltered, narrow (relative to the Hudson) East River. This area, radiating out from the intersection of Fulton and South Streets, became the City's last holdout against mass demolition; its survivors evoke that period of commercial development that was generated by the City's role as a great domestic and international port.

Manhattan ever widening: The mucky shore became hard-edged and then was pushed outward, the new profile delicately balancing the needs of ships with those of shippers. Wild hills were tamed, and the earth from early cellar holes—and, much later, from deeper skyscraper excavations—was carted to the island's edge. Early on, Pearl Street marked the East River shore. As water lots were filled, the names of newly created streets reflected their succession to the perimeter: first Water Street, then Front, and finally—at least for now—South Street.

[W21] **Titanic Memorial Lighthouse**, in Titanic Memorial Park, Fulton St. bet. Pearl and Water Sts. N side. Installed, 1976, *Charles Evans Hughes III.* 🌢

Originally installed in 1913, by public subscription, atop the **Seamen's Church Institute Building** overlooking the East River at South Street and what was then **Jeanette Park**. Visible from the river, it signaled noon to ships in the harbor with the falling of a black ball, at a signal received from Washington.

For the building it topped, see the Necrology section.

South Street Seaport Museum Block: Water to Front Streets, between Fulton and Beekman Streets:

[W22a] **207-211 Water Street**, bet. Beekman and Fulton Sts. E side. 1835-1837.

Greek Revival granite piers support austere, but elegant, brick bearing walls, with granite

[W23] **The "Bogardus" Building**, 15-19 Fulton St., NE cor. Front St. 1977-1983. *Beyer Blinder Belle.*

Chosen as site for the re-erection of ironmonger *James Bogardus'* demountable cast-iron façade (that had stood at Washington and Murray Streets). Later purloined from the safekeeping of the *Landmarks Preservation Commission*, it was melted down by the perpetrators. With the façade elements gone, the architects attempted to suggest its color, texture, rhythms, and proportions, using similar—but not identical—iron and/or steel materials.

A reincarnation for the first building **ever** physically stolen.

[W24] **Fulton Market Building**, 11 Fulton St., bet. Front and South Sts. N side to Beekman St. 1983. *Benjamin Thompson & Assocs.*

Hoping to echo the vivacious spirit of the original 1883 Fulton Market Building, which stood on this block until razed in 1948, stands this essay of marketplace architecture. Its exterior, wrapped with a massive suspended iron canopy redolent of its predecessors, is intricate without being fussy.

Streetscape: A particularly satisfying aspect of the Seaport Historic District is the use of substantial materials underfoot: Belgian block street pavement modulated by slabs of granite that evoke the horsedrawn era, with bluestone sidewalks and recreations of varying lamppost designs of 19th-century Manhattan.

W23

W25

lintels and slender muntined double-hung sashes. They are adaptively reused storehouses: **No.207** the **Museum Visitors' Center; No.209** the Museum Books and Charts Store; **No.211** is **Bowne & Co. Stationers**, the Museum's 19th-century print shop, where old techniques and equipment are still employed, to visitors' delight.

[W22b] Originally **A. A. Thompson & Company**, 213-215 Water St., bet. Beekman and Fulton Sts. E side. 1868. *Stephen D. Hatch.* Restored, *Beyer Blinder Belle*, 1983.

Nos.213-215, large-scaled and glassy, contains the **Melville Gallery**, an exhibition space.

Cannon's Walk: A passageway between 19 Fulton Street, W of Front to 206 Front Street, N of Fulton:

[W25] **Schermerhorn Row Block**, 2-18 Fulton St., 189-195 Front St., 159-171 John Sts., 91-92 South St. 1811-1849. Variously altered and expanded. 🌢

[W25a] **Schermerhorn Row** (east part), 2-12 Fulton St., SW cor. South St., and 92-93 South St., bet. Fulton and John Sts. W side. 1811. Altered and expanded.

No.92 was immortalized by *Joseph Mitchell* in his 1952 *New Yorker* essay *Up in the Old Hotel*. According to *Mitchell*, this was at one time the **Fulton Ferry Hotel**. By the time *Mitchell* discovered it, the upper floors were blocked up and the thriving restaurant **Sloppy Louie's**, named for owner *Louis Morino*, was on the ground floor. *Mitchell's* essay was a haunting excavation of the City's memory, as he accompanied *Louis* in an urban archaeological expedition up into the dusty, dark upper floors. Sloppy Louie's survived until 1998. Now it's a chain restaurant.

[W25b] Schermerhorn Row (west part), 14-18 Fulton St., SE cor. Front St. 1812. 191 Front St., bet. Fulton and John Sts. E side. 1812. Variously altered and expanded. Both parts restored, 1983, *Jan Hird Pokorny. Cabrera-Barricklo,* storefront consultants. ●

Peter Schermerhorn filled the land on these, his "water lots," to a point 600 feet out from the original shoreline and built his row in two stages a year apart. Served by these buildings, among many others, South Street was lined with ships, parked bowsprits in, oversailing the wheeled, hoofed, and pedestrian traffic below. (The bulkhead was at approximately the line of the west, or inner, row of columns supporting the highway viaduct.)

These were originally **Georgian-Federal** ware- and counting-houses, with high-pitched, loft-enclosing roofs, built as an investment by the *Schermerhorn* family. No storefronts at first: arched business entries of brownstone, quoined, and double-hung windows for light and air; only later did show windows appear at street level. Soon **Greek Revival** granite and cast-iron shopfronts brought a merchandising cast to serve the great crowds brought here, beginning in 1814, by the steam-powered Fulton Ferry from Brooklyn.

[W25c] 191 and 193 Front Street (lofts), bet. Fulton and John Sts. E side. 1793. Altered and expanded upward, 19th century. Restored, 1983, *Jan Hird Pokorny.*

The oldest on the block chronologically, but not visibly so, since their fronts were drastically altered in the mid- and late 19th century.

W27

John Street between Front and South Streets widens to twice its normal dimension as a result of its earlier configuration as Burling Slip, an inlet for ships off the East River. In 1835 the slip was filled in:

[W25d] Originally **Josiah Macy & Son**, 189 Front St., bet. John and Fulton Sts. E side. (also known as 159-165 John St.) ●
[W25e] Originally **Mackle, Oakley & Jennison**, 181 Front St., NE cor. John St. (also known as 159-163 John St.). Both behind Schermerhorn Row. **No.181** expanded upward, 1917. Restored, 1983, *Jan Hird Pokorny.*

A pair of Greek Revival commercial structures built when Burling Slip was filled in, their façades offering the pattern on which easterly neighbor No.165 was refaced.

[W25f] 165 John Street, N side bet. Front and South Sts., behind Schermerhorn Row. 1811. Rebuilt, late 1830s-1840s. Restored, 1983, *Jan Hird Pokorny.* ●

Following its reconstruction, it assumed a Greek Revival façade like its western neighbor. But, unlike its neighbor, it was never increased in height, so the original fascia, cornice, and roof line are all there.

[W25g] The **A. A. Low Building**, South Street Seaport Museum/originally **A. A. Low & Brothers**/later **Baltimore Copper Paint Company**, 167-171 John St. N side (behind Schermerhorn Row), bet. Front and South Sts. 1849. Altered and restored, 1983, *Jan Hird Pokorny.* ●

The youngest of Schermerhorn Row block's treasures, built by traders whose China clippers parked across South Street. Merchant *Abiel Abbot Low* (father of sometime mayor and Columbia University president *Seth Low*) lived only a ferryboat ride away at **No.3 Pierrepont Place.** Restored brownstone honors the original brownstone, revealed after years of stucco and paint were removed.

[W25h] South Street Seaport Museum, 12 Fulton St., bet. Water & Front Sts. 2001. *Beyer Blinder Belle.* Open Tu-Su 10-6 (Apr-Oct), Fr-Mo 10-5 (Nov-Mar). 212-748-8600. *www.southstseaport.org*

A glassy foil to the brickwork of **Schermerhorn Row**, this airy pavilion provides access to multiple exhibits, buried high and deep within the body of the Schermerhorn Row block.

[W26] Originally **Hickson W. Field Stores**/formerly Baker, Carver & Morrell (ship chandlery), 170-176 John St., bet. Front and South Sts. S side. 1840. Expanded upward, 1981-1982. *Buttrick, White & Burtis.* ●

The last survivor of a commercial building type first imported from Boston by *Town & Davis* in 1829. The austere granite blocks and piers offer a dour face to the street.

To the south, along South Street:

[W27] Originally **Maximilian Morgenthau Tobacco Warehouse**, 84-85 South St., bet. Fletcher and John Sts. W side. 1902. *G. Curtis Gillespie.*

Despite the brutal surgery on its base this is one of South Street's—and the City's—unique treasures: terra-cotta Art Nouveau tobacco leaf motifs applied to a late Romanesque Revival storehouse.

Across South Street and onto the piers:

[W28] South Street Seaport **Museum Ships**, anchored along Piers 15, 16, 17, East River. **Maritime Crafts Center,** Pier 15. Piers open to the public.

The great glories of the Museum are the ships moored at the wharves and those, like the tall ships, which periodically tie up for brief visits. Floating architecture is honored here by the **Wavertree** and **Peking** (1885 and 1911. Steel bathtub square-riggers: bathtubs to keep the water out rather than in); the old humanoid **Ambrose Lightship** (1908: Its successor is an electronic rig on stilts); the **Lettie G. Howard** (1893, a venerable oysterman from Gloucester), the **Maj. Gen. William H. Hart** (1925, one of the

W30b

city's smaller ferryboats); and others. In addition there are sometime excursions on the **Andrew Fletcher** and the 1885 schooner, **Pioneer. The Maritime Crafts Center** was constructed in 1983 from two shipping containers. Inside, ye olde craftsmen make ships in bottles as tourists watch: ships inside containers inside containers. Open Mo-Su 8-2:30.

[W29] **Pier Pavilion 17,** East River, at South Street, bet. Fulton & Beekman Sts. 1984. *Benjamin Thompson & Assocs.,* design architects. *The Eggers Group,* consulting architects.

Good intentions gone awry: a "festival marketplace" by serious architects and developers degenerated into a soulless shopping mall, full of cheap novelties and fried food. The best thing about it is the East River lapping cheerfully about the foundations and the cry of gulls overhead. The worst thing about it is everything inside.

[W29a] **The Tin Building,** Pier 17, at South Street, bet. Fulton & Beekman Sts. 1907. *Berlin Construction Co.*

The epicenter for the departed Fulton Fish Market (see Necrology). Recent plans by the architects *SHoP* to push it closer to the water met with protests from preservationists, but little of this "historic" building is original: a suspicious fire in 1995 destroyed much of the structure. It was rebuilt, but with fiberglass cornices. Its future is up in the air, but for now it still peaks above the FDR. Say hello if you drive by.

North of the festival marketplace:

[W30a] **142-144 Beekman Street,** NE cor. Front St. 1885. *George B. Post.*

Built for a Schermerhorn descendant, *Ellen S. Auchmuty.* Particularly note the whimsical terra-cotta maritime ornament: decorative fish motifs, cockleshells, and starfish.

[W30b] **146-148 Beekman Street**, bet. Front and South Sts. N side. 1885. *George B. Post.* **150-152 Beekman Street**, bet. Front and South Sts. N side. 1883. *David & John Jardine.*

Colorful giant signs hawking wholesale seafood—fresh, salt and smoked fish/oysters and clams—cross the brick street façades, are what count here. An advertising stratagem growing increasingly rare, and in this case, fading away. Read it while it's still legible.

Peck Slip, a hundred feet wide and two blocks long, from the East River to Water Street, is a great unused public space, currently a parking lot. A thoughtful landscape architect could turn it into

W30c

*a nice place. But everything designed in this neighborhood seems to become a stage set (see below). Could we have a simple urbane space, or would it have to be the **Piazza San Peck**?*

▌ [W30c] **Front Street Redevelopment**, between Beekman St. and Peck Slip. New buildings: 24 & 36 Peck Slip, 213 & 214 Front St. Renovated buildings: 220, 225 & 229 Front St. 2005. *Cook + Fox.*

A little slice of SoHo! Two blocks of glistening new buildings: four new ones and eleven old ones (meticulously restored). The new buildings, in a kind of modern Fish-Market-Federal style, blend in harmlessly. The biggest one, **24 Peck Slip**, gets too fussy in its details, with wooden slats rigging its façade. Around the corner, **214 Front Street** is handled with more dexterity: the stone slab over the door, featuring a quotation from *Moby Dick*, is one of the few lighter details. (Nautical! We get it!) United by (private) courtyards, all have shops on the ground floor.

Developments like these would have been unthinkable only a few years ago, but the removal to the Bronx of the Fish Market changed everything: the smell and commotion of the fish-mongers at 4 AM wasn't romantic to the Wall Streeters who wanted to move in. Clean, quiet, and expensive ($2.50 for a tiny cup of drip coffee?), it's as much of a **theme park**, in its own way, as its South Street Seaport neighbors.

[W31] **Formerly Meyer's Hotel**, 116-119 South St., SW cor. Peck Slip. 1873. *John B. Snook.*

Its original use is unknown, but it became **Meyer's Hotel** in 1881. The building and its street-front corner bar and restaurant (**Paris Café**) make perfect backgrounds for Hollywood nostalgia.

[W32] Originally **Jasper Ward House**; 45 Peck Slip, NW cor. South St. 1807. Restored, 1983, *Robert E. Meadows.*

Built on a water lot on landfill and impaired by time and unequal settlement. Thoughtful restoration, keeping the unevenness of decades, adds to the visible integrity of this doughty survivor.

[W33] **Consolidated Edison electrical substation**, 237-257 Front St., bet. Peck Slip and Dover St. E side to South St. 1975. *Edward Larrabee Barnes*, design architect. Mural, *Richard Haas,* artist.

An attempt by the City's electrical utility to be a harmonious neighbor to the Seaport, in the days before the historic district was enacted. (The Seaport's Restoration and Development Committee approved the design.) A mural on

W32   W35

Peck Slip was a happy idea, but depicting the Brooklyn Bridge—with the real thing looming in the background—was silly.

[W34] **Best Western Seaport Inn**, Peck Slip, NW cor. Front St. 1840s.

A much-needed facility has recycled some local vernacular architecture: a shell to house a modern hotel within.

[W35] **Bridge Café**, 279 Water St., SW cor. Dover St. Building, 1794.

The district's only extant wood-frame building, built for grocer *Peter Loring,* has remained a commercial structure for more than 200 years. In 1888 it lost its peaked roof and was sheathed in novelty siding and other ornament of the era. Today, a good place for a drink and a repast. At midday politicians used to abound. Painted maroon with black trim, it crouches in the shadows of the Great Bridge.

[W36] Originally **Captain Joseph Rose House** and shop/onetime **Sports' Man's Hall,** 273 Water St., bet. Peck Slip and Dover St. E side. As early as 1773/no later than 1781. Reconstructed, 1998, *Oliver Lundquist.*

A phoenix from what was, 10 years ago, a ruin. Fires in 1904 and 1976 compromised this structure, the South Street District's oldest and Manhattan's third oldest (after the **Morris-Jumel Mansion** and **St. Paul's Chapel**). The reconstructed result is worthy of **Williamsburg** (Virginia, that is, where the squeaky clean modern reconstructions miss the lusty vitality of the original buildings). *Rose* was in the business of shipping Honduras mahogany to the New York market.

Christopher (Kit) Burns, tavern keeper at 273 in the 1860s, put on dog and rat fights to divert patrons. In **The Secrets of the Great City** *(1868) Edward Winslow Martin declared that "It is simply sickening. Most of our readers have witnessed a dog fight in the streets. Let them imagine the animals surrounded by a crowd of brutal wretches whose conduct stamps them as beneath the struggling beasts, and they will haved a fair idea of the scene at Kit Burns." Rentals now $4,000 a month? Kit would have been impressed.*

[W37] **21-23 Peck Slip,** NE cor. Water St. 1873. *Richard Morris Hunt.*

Six wonderful stories of polychromed brick with carefully modulated windows and, on the Front Street façade, 45 neatly spaced star anchors tying in the timber floors to the masonry street wall. This structure was built for the trustees of

W36   W38

Roosevelt Hospital, at the same time as *Hunt's* **Roosevelt Building** was under construction.

[W38] **251 Water Street,** SE cor. Peck Slip. 1888. *Carl F. Eisenach.*

Even a tenement design was infused by South Street fervor: the tympanum over the ornately framed apartment entrance is a joyous explosion of terra-cotta sunflowers. At the 4th-story windows, terra-cotta keystones carry faces surveying the streetlife below.

[W39] **247 Water Street,** bet. Peck Slip and Beekman St. E side. 1840s.

The offices of *Frank Sciame,* the builder of the **Seamen's Church Institute,** were here and left it in elegance.

[W40] **Seamen's Church Institute,** 241 Water St., bet. Beekman St. and Peck Slip. E side. 1989-1991. *Polshek Partnership.*

A stylish understatement that provides a textbook example of the best of modernist architecture, while complementing its 19th-century context.

[W41] **Seaport Park**/in part originally **Volunteer Hospital**/later **Beekman Street Hospital,** 117 Beekman St., bet. Water and Pearl Sts. S side. 1918. *Adolph Mertin.* Conversion and extension, 1981, *Rafael Viñoly Architects.*

Long after its service as a hospital, the original building was part of a notorious nursing home scandal. Converted, the combination of old and new is a handsome neighbor to the Seaport.

NECROLOGY

Seamen's Church Institute, 25 South St., SW cor. Coenties Slip. 1907. Additions, 1919, 1929, *Warren & Wetmore.*

The only part preserved when the Institute built its 1969 tower at 55 Water Street was the verdigris "lighthouse" memorializing the sinking of the Titanic. Then 55 was sold and demolished for greater mammon, and the Institute returned to the neighborhood, building its elegant *Polshek* building further down Water Street.

Fulton Fish Market

Immortalized in the essays of *New Yorker* staff writer *Joseph Mitchell,* the gritty, aromatic Fish Market survived into the 21st century, just to the north of its theme park neighbor South Street Seaport. Here a drama unfolded each night in the wee, wee hours: the arrival of mountains of haddock, flounder, swordfish, shrimp, pompano, clams, oysters, mussels (by truck; the final fish arriving directly by ship was in 1979). Fishmongers hawked, restaurateurs scrutinized and bought, and assorted sketchy types looked on, as did the occasional hipster in search of "authenticity." The most recent version of the market consisted of the "new" building, a straightforward sheet metal shed on the east side of South Street and the "Tin Building" just to the north, their backs to the river, and a collection of ramshackle Federal buildings on the west side of the street, with the FDR overhead. Trucks would begin arriving around 2 AM, and forklifts would scurry to and fro across South Street in a frenzy of activity until the sun came up. It all moved to cleaner, modern facilities in the South Bronx in 2005.

BROADWAY-NASSAU

Lying between Wall Street and the southern tip of City Hall Park, from Church Street to South Street Seaport, is one of Lower Manhattan's least recognized—and therefore most intriguing—areas. Since it bestrides Fulton Street, under which lies the IND Eighth Avenue Line's Broadway-Nassau Station, this area has been dubbed after that station's name. It includes Chase Manhattan Plaza, the Nassau Street pedestrian mall, the Federal Reserve Bank of New York, and the old AT&T Building. But, more important, it includes many minor but delicious background buildings from the days of the earliest skyscrapers.

Entries begin at Pearl and Pine Streets, one block north of Wall Street. (The closest subway stop to the first entry is the Wall Street Station of the IRT Seventh Avenue Line express: Nos.2 and 3 trains.)

[N2] **Down Town Association**, 60 Pine St., bet. Pearl and William Sts. N side. 1886-1887. *Charles C. Haight.* Addition, 1910-1911, *Charles Wetmore of Warren & Wetmore.* 🍎

Sober, anonymous, and understated in contrast to the exuberance of 56 next door, this appropriately conservative club serves

N2

N4

N3a

N5

⊞ [N1] **American International Building**/earlier **60 Wall Tower**/originally **Cities Service Building**, 70 Pine St., NW cor. Pearl St. to Cedar St. 1931-1932. *Clinton & Russell and Holton & George.*

One of the Financial District's most slender towers, it sports **Art Deco** details everywhere—including its "Gothic" crown, unseen from the canyons in which the tower sits and therefore best appreciated as part of the skyline or from a neighboring eyrie. (To help passersby comprehend what they cannot fully see from the street, the architects provided three-dimensional stone replicas of the building at the Pine and Cedar Street entrances.)

Double-decker elevators, serving two floors of the tower at a time, such as those in the Citicorp Tower uptown, were first used here, but proved unpopular, and were later changed.

many distinguished financial executives and lawyers, principally at lunchtime.

🏠 [N3a] **56 Pine Street**/originally **Wallace Building**, bet. Pearl and William Sts. N side. 1893-1894. *Oswald Wirz.* 🍎

Romanesque Revival in stone, brick, and terra cotta. Carved decoration surrounds arched openings, in which, windows, deeply revealed, are flanked by Byzantine colonnettes. A distant leaf from the work of *H.H. Richardson* and his peers.

[N3b] **54 Pine Street**/originally **A.G. Becker & Co.**, bet. Pearl and William Sts. N side. 1907. *Friedrich Schluter.*

Tan brick and terra cotta, missing its original cornice. But the wide arch framing the entry and the frowning sun motifs in the frieze are intact.

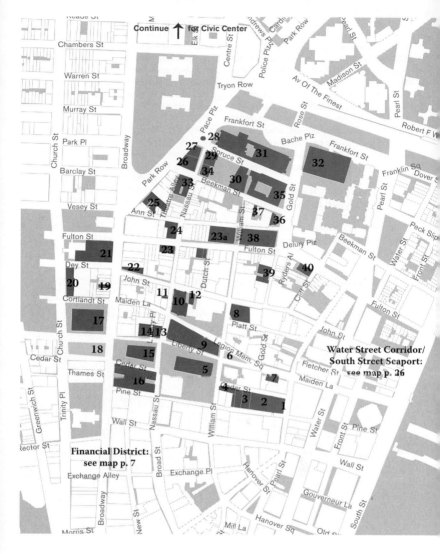

Continue ↑ for Civic Center

[N3c] **50-52 Pine Street**/originally **Caledonian Insurance Company,** bet. Pearl and William Sts. N side. 1905. *Virgil Schönfeld.*

A slender Renaissance Revival palazzo, with horizontally banded floors and a flying cornice. Twin entries are topped with round windows: one is ruined, the other retains its frothy classical details.

[N4] **Banco Atlantico**, 62 William St., SE cor. Cedar St. 1896.

Neo-Romanesque brickwork and limestone supports a tier of grand arches, another of triplet arches, and finally, a grandiloquent cornice.

[N5] **Chase Manhattan Bank Tower** and Plaza, 1 Chase Manhattan Plaza, bet. Pine and Liberty Sts., from William to Nassau Sts. 1960. *Skidmore, Owings & Merrill.*

David Rockefeller and his fellow board members, in their 1950s act of faith in building this Gargantua cried "Excelsior," and the flagging spirit of the Financial District took courage. Architecturally less successful than the later and more sophisticated Marine Midland by the same

firm, it provides the first gratuitous plaza hereabouts. Eight hundred feet of aluminum and glass rise from the paved plaza surface, accessible from both Nassau and Pine Streets. The topography unfortunately forces down the Liberty and William Street sides, detaching them from participation in the plaza's space.

A sunken circular courtyard is paved with undulating forms of granite blocks, crowned with sculpture, and caressed in summer by a fountain and pools, all by sculptor *Isamu Noguchi*. Goldfish were resident at first, but the urban fallout and sentimentalists' "coins in the fountain" destroyed even those resilient carp.

The plaza sculpture **Group of Four Trees** (1972. *Jean Dubuffet*), on the axis of Cedar Street, looks like papier-mâché but isn't: it has a temporary, expendable feeling.

[N6] **Louise Nevelson Plaza/Legion Memorial Square**, Maiden Lane, Liberty St., William St. 1978. Shadows and Flags, 1978, *Louise Nevelson,* sculptor. Renovation, 2009, *Smith-Miller & Hawkinson,* architects.

A unique public space devoted to a single sculptor and named after her. Sit down and measure her work against the rich rustications of the Federal Reserve Bank.

[N7] **90-94 Maiden Lane**, bet. William and Pearl Sts. S side, at Louise Nevelson Plaza. 1815. Cast-iron front, 1870-1871. *Charles Wright.* ◆

A remarkably preserved cast-iron survivor owned by a branch of the *Roosevelt* family. At only four stories, it's amazing that it survived the Great Condo Rush of 2003-2008, when every low building in town made developers salivate. But it holds on, with a variety of tenants, including Gristedes, the Brooks Brothers of groceries.

[N8] **100 William Street**, bet. Platt and John Sts. E side. 1972-1973. *Davis, Brody & Assocs.*

Green schist (split from natural geological strata) slate. A diagonal passage for pedestrians elegantly bisects the form, creating a vista ter-

N9

elevators, couldn't imagine such large-scale grandeur.)

Nassau Street Pedestrian Mall: From John Street to Beekman Street, Nassau serves as a most active local shopping strip: medium-to modest-priced chain stores, discount houses, and small, specialized shops. Panty hose, radio equipment, dresses, shoes, all of the personal and portable items that a lunch-hour shopper would be most inclined to inspect and purchase. The ground-floor activity and clutter of show windows and signs keep the eye at street level. The form and detail of buildings above, no matter how tall, are rarely noticed, almost never observed. The street is officially "closed to traffic" in order to fulfill its promise as a pedestrian-friendly mall. But (walkers beware) there is a lot of traffic. The decision to remove the curbs was a bad one: the brick pavers that replaced the curbs have not worn well, giving the street edge a shabby, down-and-out feel.

N11

minating at the plaza in front of the Home Insurance Group's offices.

[N9] **Federal Reserve Bank of New York**, 33 Liberty St., NE cor. Nassau St. to Maiden Lane. 1919-1924. Extension E to William St., 1935. All by *York & Sawyer. Samuel Yellin,* decorative ironwork. ◆ Open to the public by advance reservation.

A Florentine palazzo conserves within its dungeons more money than Fort Knox. A great neo-Renaissance building of rusticated Indiana limestone, Ohio sandstone, and elegant ironwork. A bank for banks, this is the great stabilizer and equalizer of their separately erratic activities. In the five levels below the street, the gold of many nations is stored—and moved, in the balance of trade, from nation to nation—without ever leaving the building.

The stony south wall, on Liberty Street, is a magnificent foil to the crystalline glass and aluminum of Chase Manhattan Bank Tower. We hope that the Federal Reserve will live forever. (Florence, not having the luxury of 15th-century

[N10] **33 Maiden Lane**, NE cor. Nassau St. to John St. 1984-1986. *Philip Johnson/John Burgee.*

A site once intended for an annex to the Federal Reserve Bank across Maiden Lane, a powerful *Kevin Roche* design. The substitute is a building suspended between a group of giant buff-brick crenellated (to the ramparts, men!) tubes (which permitted the developer to offer seven "corner" offices per floor). The interior street connecting to the Fulton Street subway station is cool in summer and generally peaceful and urbane.

[N11] **63 Nassau Street**, bet. Maiden Lane and John St. W side. ca. 1844. Cast-iron façade ca. 1857-1859. Probably *James Bogardus.* ◆

A venerable façade distinguished by three-story, fluted cast-iron columns sitting on bases that bear "rondels," originally with relief portraits of *George Washington* and *Benjamin Franklin*. Franklin is still there. Indefatigable *Margot Gayle*, founder of **Friends of Cast Iron Architecture**, rediscovered this elegant expatriate from the Civic Center's cast iron district.

[N12] **John Street United Methodist Church**, 44 John St., bet. Nassau and William Sts. 1841. Attributed to *William Hurry and/or Philip Embury.* 🌳

Irish Wesleyans built their first church in America here in 1768: this, however, is the third building on the site. The congregation is, therefore, the oldest Methodist Society in America.

[N13] **Liberty Tower**/onetime **Sinclair Oil Building**, 55 Liberty St., NW cor. Nassau

N10   N13

N14

St. 1909-1910. *Henry Ives Cobb.* Restored and converted to apartments, 1981, *Joseph Pell Lombardi.* 🌳

Glorious terra cotta (similar to *Cass Gilbert's* gothicized 90 West Street) over limestone as high as a person can reach. Wonderfully, humorously detailed: check out the twin alligators beginning to crawl up the façade at either side of the main entrance. The **Hotel Reserve** is entered through a 51 Nassau Street portal.

[N14] Originally **Chamber of Commerce of the State of New York**/now **International Commercial Bank of China**, 65 Liberty St., bet. Nassau St. and Broadway at NW cor. Liberty Place 1900-1901. *James B. Baker.* Restored and converted, 1990-1991, *Haines Lundberg Waehler.* 🌳

Rich, ornate Beaux Arts; a minor palace of imposing scale and rich detail. Rusticated, Ionic columns, mansard roof, oval porthole windows.

[N15] **Marine Midland Bank Building**, 140 Broadway, bet. Liberty and Cedar Sts. E side to Nassau St. 1967. *Skidmore, Owings & Merrill.*

A taut skin stretched over bare bones. The sleek, flush façade is a melodramatic contrast to the ornamented masonry environment surrounding it. The matteness of black spandrels breaks up reflections of the neighbors into more random, mysterious parts. The plaza at Broadway had a major impact on the scale of this neighborhood until the plaza across Broadway deprived it of its enclosing street walls.

Cube (1973. *Isamu Noguchi*) sits on the plaza's lap at Broadway, teetering 28 feet tall and vermilion, gored by a cylindrical punch.

[N16] **Equitable Building**, 120 Broadway, bet. Pine and Cedar Sts. E side to Nassau St. 1913-1915. *Ernest R. Graham,* successor to *D. H. Burnham & Co.,* with *Peirce Anderson.* Restoration, 1983-1990, *Ehrenkrantz, Eckstut & Whitelaw.* 🌳

N15

More famous for what it caused than what it is. An immense volume, it exploited the site as no building had before: 1.2 million square feet of floor area on a plot of just under an acre, or a floor area of almost 30 times the site's area. The hue and cry after Equitable's completion led to the adoption of the nation's first comprehensive zoning resolution, in 1916.

[N17] **1 Liberty Plaza**/briefly **Merrill Lynch Plaza**, Broadway, Liberty, Church and Cortlandt Sts. 1971-1974. *Skidmore, Owings & Merrill.*
[N18] **Liberty Plaza**, Broadway, Cedar, Church, and Liberty Sts. 1974. SE corner holdout, 1980, *Skidmore Owings & Merrill.*

A gloomy, articulate extravaganza of steel, this handsome but somber modernist tower was damaged on September 11. It replaced the great **Singer Tower** (1908-1968) by *Ernest Flagg,* an eclectic palace-tower and the tallest building ever demolished.

N26

Across Liberty Street to the south is a large, bleak, red granite plaza with spindly trees, the result of zoning calculations that allowed added bulk to the behemoth. The plaza may be unimaginative, but real life occurs at the edges, where festive wheeled vending carts form a lunchtime perimeter, serving cheap and generally nutritious fare (lamb over rice with salad: $5).

[N19] **Germania Building**, 175 Broadway, bet. Cortlandt and Dey Sts. W side. 1865.
A tiny miraculous survivor from the City's Reconstruction days: grand Corinthian columns and segmental arches.

A good spot to view the Germania Building is at the NE corner of Broadway and Maiden Lane.

N21   N23

Look down, too; you may be standing on a beautiful relic from 1884, the William Barthman Jewelers clock, inset with precision into the sidewalk, its brass smoothed by billions of feet.

[N20] **Century 21**/originally **East River Savings Bank**, 26 Cortlandt St., NE cor. Church St. to Dey St. 1931-1934. *Walker & Gillette.* Expanded upward.
Cool neo-Classical Art Deco with marvelous stainless steel winged eagles over both entrances, in the spirit of the Chrysler Building but nowhere near as daring.

[N21] Originally **American Telephone & Telegraph Company Building**/now 195 Broadway Building, bet. Dey and Fulton Sts. W side. Built in three sections: 1912-1922. All by *Welles Bosworth.* ● Ground floor interior. ● Addition to W, 1989, *Eli Attia.*
The square-topped layer cake of New York: a deep-set façade of eight Ionic colonnades (embracing three stories within each set) is stacked on a Doric order: handsome parts

assembled into a bizarre and wonderful whole: more Classical columns than any façade in the world, the columns within the lobby extending that record. All was surmounted by *Evelyn Beatrice Longman's* **Genius of the Telegraph**

N24

until that colossal gilded sculpture was moved to *Philip Johnson's* then new AT&T Building at 56th Street, and thence to New Jersey.

[N22] **Corbin Building**, 13 John St., NE cor. Broadway. ca. 1888-1889. *Francis H. Kimball.*
Romanesque Revival arches with ornate voussoirs asserting strong individuality above a tawdry commercial corner.

Note: For St Paul's Chapel and northward, see Civic Center/Chinatown.

East on Fulton Street:

[N23] Originally **Fulton Building**, 87 Nassau St., SW cor. Fulton St. 1893. *De Lemos & Cordes.* [N23a] Originally **Keuffel & Esser Building**, 127 Fulton St., bet. Nassau and William Sts. N side. 1892-1893. *De Lemos & Cordes.* ●
Richly ornamented masonry façades from the architects who later brought you **Siegel-Cooper** and **Macy's** department stores. Tools for

architectural and engineering drafting adorn the cast iron storefront. Divert your eyes from the tawdry addition on top of 87 Nassau.

[N24] Originally **Bennett Building** (lofts), 93-99 Nassau St. and 139 Fulton St., with a third façade on Ann St. 1872-1873. *Arthur D. Gilman*. Mansard roof removed and upper four floors added, 1890-1892, *James M. Farnsworth*. Ann Street extension, 1894, *James M. Farnsworth*. ●⟋

A glassy building with a lavish, deeply three-dimensional, cast-iron structural grid. The building's name, incidentally, is that of *James Gordon Bennett, Jr., New York Herald* publisher, and its developer, who, in 1969, had sent the Herald journalist, *Sir Henry Morton Stanley*, to find the missing explorer, *David Livingstone*.

An aside to Park Row, the east boundary of City Hall Park, from south to north:

[N25] Originally **Park Row Building**/also known as **Park Row Syndicate Building, Ivins**

N30

Syndicate Building, 15 Park Row, bet. Ann and Beekman Sts. E side. 1899. *R. H. Robertson*. ●⟋

Twin towers for the romantic business-man—guarded by four caryatids (*J. Massey Rhind*, sculptor) on the fourth floor. From 1899 to 1908 it was the world's tallest building, at 386 feet.

[N26] **Potter Building**, 38 Park Row, NE cor. Beekman St. 1883-1886. *Norris G. Starkweather*. Converted to apartments, 1979-1981. ●⟋

An elaborately ornate confection in cast and pressed terra cotta, an early use in New York of a material that was to become the rage, producing repetitive elaboration economically. The hidden structural steel of this building is the first in New York to be fireproofed by terra cotta.

Jack Finney's marvelous literary redolence, Time and Again, *takes place in and around the burning of the first Potter Building. Within its pages you can conjure up the sensory flavors of 1882.*

[N27] **Pace University**/originally **The New York Times Building**, 41 Park Row, bet. Beekman and Spruce Sts. 1889. *George B. Post*. Expanded upward, 1905, *Robert Maynicke*. ●⟋

Rusticated granite that would have been exemplary in any hands other than *Post's* (see the **Long Island Historical Society** in Brooklyn for vintage *Post*). The Times left here for what was to become Times Square.

[N28] **Benjamin Franklin**, Printing House Sq. at the intersection of Park Row, Nassau, and Spruce Sts. 1872. *Ernst Plassman*, sculptor.

Here, where the *Times, Tribune, Herald, World,* and *Sun* were once published, is a square commemorating Newspaper Row plus the many job printers who worked hereabouts. A beneficent bronze *Franklin* holds a copy of his *Pennsylvania Gazette*.

[N29] Originally **American Tract Society Building**, 150 Nassau St., SE cor. Spruce St. 1894-1895. *R. H. Robertson*. ●⟋

Fascination is at the roof, where giant "Romanesque" arches provide a geometry of architecture separate from the 20 floors below. *Robertson* left the earliest (extant) steel skeletal-frame skyscraper in New York, with rusticated granite, Roman brick, and buff-colored terra cotta: Romanesque and Renaissance Revival styles melded.

[N30] **Beekman Tower**, bet. Gold and Nassau Sts. 2010. *Frank Gehry*.

Shiny. Here is *Gehry* relatively restrained, his usual geometrical gymnastics tempered by more

N29

traditional skyscraping aspirations. The dented façade (pummeled by a jealous **Chrysler Building**?) seems to hang from the structural frame like supple metal drapes, and is dynamic in the changing light. Its computer-aided skin design was realized by the same software that helped fabricate **Guggenheim Bilbao** and the sculpture of *Richard Serra*. Within resides a 76-story stack of apartments, plus a school on the (less exciting) street level.

[N31] **Pace University**, New Building, Nassau, Frankfort, Gold, and Spruce Sts. 1970. *Eggers & Higgins*. Expanded upward, 1984, *The Eggers Partnership*.

Limestone and bronze-anodized aluminum trying to look modern. Benign.

[N32] New York City **Department of Housing, Planning & Development** (HPD)/formerly **Bache Plaza**, 100 Gold St., SE cor. Frankfort St. 1969. *Gruzen & Partners*.

A delicate concrete cage reminiscent of *Alvar Aalto*. A pleasant and glassy understatement.

N34

[N33] **Temple Court**, 119-129 Nassau St., and 5 Beekman St. to Theater Alley. S part, 1881-1883, *Silliman & Farnsworth*. N part, 1890-1892, *Benjamin Silliman, Jr.* ●

Two mighty, pointed steeples cap this purply-red painted brick office building whose name (lifted from its London counterpart) suggests that it originally catered to the City's legal profession way before Foley Square. Within, a nine-story atrium with cast-iron balustrades awaits, still walled off from view.

[N34] Originally **Morse Building**/later **Nassau-Beekman Building**/now **12 Beekman Street**, NE cor. Nassau St. 1878-1880. *Silliman & Farnsworth*. Addition, 1901-1902, *Bannister & Schell*. Converted, 1980, *Hurley & Farinella*. ●

A hearty red-brick many-arched loft structure, understated but powerful. Described as Victorian Gothic, neo-Grec, and/or *Rundbogenstil*, deep red and glazed black enrich the façade. Eclectic, certainly, and wonderful.

[N35] **Wiggin Pavilion, New York University Downtown Hospital**/originally **Beekman Downtown Hospital**, 170 William St., bet. Beekman and Spruce Sts. E side to Gold St. 1971. *Skidmore, Owings & Merrill*.

A block of serious modernist architecture, a bit forbidding on the Gold Street side due to its high base, unintentionally giving a humane institution an inhumane posture.

[N36] **Staff Residence**, New York Infirmary Beekman Downtown Hospital, 69 Gold St., bet. Beekman and Ann Sts. W side. 1972. *The Gruzen Partnership*.

A vigorous work in reinforced concrete and brick masonry units responding to a simple set of programmatic requirements on a tiny site.

N39

[N37] **Engine Company 6, NYC Fire Department,** 49 Beekman St. bet. Gold and William Sts. S side. 1903. *Horgan & Slattery.*

A Beaux Arts façade with ornate cornice and swags enlivens this stripped modernist street-frontage. The expressive tiger recently painted on the door is interesting; a reminder of the days, mid-19th century, when the fire brigades were entwined politically and culturally with Tammany Hall.

[N38] Originally **Royal Insurance Company Building**/later **Royal Globe Insurance Company Building,** 150 William St., bet. Fulton and Ann Sts. E side to Gold St. 1927. *Starrett & Van Vleck.*

A stately occupant of a full-block site. The gentle setbacks on all four façades terminate in a pedimented Classical temple at the roof.

[N39] Originally **Excelsior Power Company**/now apartments), 33-48 Gold St., bet. Fulton and John Sts. W side. 1888. *William Milne Grinnell.* Converted, 1979, *Wechsler, Grasso & Menziuso.*

Coal-fired electrical generators once occupied this lusty Romanesque Revival brick monolith. Now, yuppies do.

[N40] **Marlo Towers Garage,** 56 Fulton St. bet. Cliff St. and Ryders Alley.

Delirious New York, from a *Winsor MacKay* comic strip: nine floors split in two sections, the gantry between moving swiftly in both the vertical and horizontal directions, placing and retrieving cars as if the whole thing were a display for Gargantua's Matchbox collection. Riveting.

NECROLOGY

Originally German-American Insurance Company, 1 Liberty St., at Maiden Lane. N side. 1907. *Hill & Stout.*

A critical element in one of Lower Manhattan's most cavernous streetscapes, this magnificently corniced, wonderfully proportioned, appropriately triangulated structure was wasted by the City for a street widening—just to accommodate more cars!

Necrology: Singer Building

The Singer Building and Tower, 149 Broadway, NW cor. Liberty St. 1908. *Ernest Flagg.*

The tallest building ever demolished (47 stories, 612 feet). One of the City's great monuments—demolished in 1968 for I Liberty Plaza. The ornate Beaux Arts lobby alone was worth the price of 10,000 sewing machines. Torn down in broad daylight—after the Landmarks Preservation Commission came into existence—this has to be the City's greatest loss since Penn Station.

Girard Building, 198 Broadway, bet. John and Fulton Sts. E side. 1902. *Walter H. Wickes.*

Assyrian Revival on a rampage (above the sleazy commercial chaos below). Its demolition has left the **Corbin Building** as a slender bookend at the corner, with no books to hold up.

B2

BATTERY PARK CITY

Once upon a time, perhaps a century will do, Lower Manhattan's Hudson River shoreline was crammed—like teeth in a comb—with piers, wharves, and ferry slips. With the end of labor-intensive break-bulk cargo in favor of efficient containerization and an increasing need to dispose of enormous volumes of earthen fill from excavations (in this case, mostly from the World Trade Center—but who knows from how many others?), a symbiotic opportunity arose to create a 92-acre add-on to Manhattan Island: **Battery Park City.**

Blossoming in the late 1960s under *Governor Nelson Rockefeller* (riparian rights make the river's landfill State-owned), the **Battery Park City Authority** commissioned *Harrison & Abramovitz* to design a development isolated from Manhattan's existing urban fabric. (It would be prophetic of their later Albany Mall, named for *Nelson*, isolated from the

Quadrant looks like "instant past." The commercial area, the **World Financial Center**—developed according to guidelines by *Alexander Cooper*—was a totally private effort by Canadian developers *Olympia & York.* It lay immediately west of the World Trade Center site, embracing the earlier Gateway Plaza towers and largely concealing them from Lower Manhattan streets. To the south and north are a string of high-density residential communities with structures allocated to different developer-architect teams. Each team was beholden to the design guidelines' tenets, but still exercised its own design and economic initiatives, later reviewed and approved by the Authority. As the financial center and the southerly residential complexes emerged, the fundamental wisdom of the master plan made itself evident.

Today, Battery Park City still seems divided into its constituent parts: the **southern** end

L to R: the Ritz (B4a), Millennium Tower (B5), Visionaire (B7)

urban fabric of the state capital.) After many enthusiastic announcements, but no demonstrated capacity to sell the necessary revenue bonds, **BPCA** finally began its first aboveground project, **Gateway Plaza.**

The real beginning came in 1979, with a master plan by *Cooper, Eckstut Associates* proposing development of the area as an extension of Lower Manhattan, rather than as an isolated futuristic "project." The lines of existing east-west streets would be integrated into the project, and new north-south avenues would be oriented to Manhattan's street grid north of Houston Street. A public waterfront esplanade and other public park space were envisioned. Not only were specific land uses proposed—a mix of commercial, residential, recreational, and arterial—but the visual character of the various developments was also defined in design guidelines. The southern residential areas—guidelines by *Stanton Eckstut*—were to resemble such desirable Manhattan neighborhoods as **Gramercy Park, Tudor City,** and **Riverside Drive.** It is no accident that the South Residential

(dense but squat housing blocks, with rather deserted shopping colonnades on street level), the busier **middle** area (dominated by the World Financial Center and Gateway Plaza), and the well-heeled **northern** end (newer, slicker, taller housing). A series of **public parks** successfully unites all of it, and those green spaces, notably **South Cove, Rockefeller,** and **Teardrop Parks,** as well as the **Irish Hunger Memorial,** are by far the most successful aspect of the whole development. The possibility of a connection to the still-developing **Hudson River Park** to the north is an exciting prospect for the near future.

The Esplanade, entire W edge of site. 1983-1990. *Stanton Eckstut of Cooper, Eckstut Assocs.,* architects. *Hanna/Olin, Ltd.,* landscape consultants.

Seventy-five feet wide, 1.2 miles long, and admittedly derivative—but it works. The design vocabulary draws from the best of the City's existing park design, particularly the Carl Schurz Park promenade atop FDR Drive, the City's traditional "B-pole" park lampposts and Victorian-replica cast-iron and wood benches used in (of all places) the Art Moderne 1939-1940 New York World's Fair.

Entries begin beyond Pier A in the northwestern corner of Battery Park and proceed uptown through Battery Park City.

Battery Place residential neighborhood, southern area:

[B1] **Robert F. Wagner, Jr., Park**, N of Pier A. 1989. *Olin Partnership, Machado & Silvetti, and Lynden Miller.*

A series of interlinked gardens, in the midst of which is:

[B2] **Wagner Park Café and Viewing Platform**, in Robert F. Wagner, Jr., Park, N of Pier A. 1996. *Machado and Silvetti.*

A grand brick sculpture serving as viewing platform, café, and rest rooms. The stairs to the top are monumental: a stairway, not to heaven, but to a panorama of the harbor.

doesn't live up) and face-to-face dealing is in order. Brown, iron-spot brick, and a gray-tinted glass and aluminum curtain wall.

[B4b] **Skyscraper Museum**, within the Ritz, 39 Battery Place, SE cor. 1st Pl., 2004. *Skidmore Owings & Merrill.* Open to the public We-Su 12-6. *www.skyscraper.org*

Tucked into a cramped ground-floor space in the Ritz, on an opposite corner from the hotel entrance. Dedicated to New York's lofty spires, this museum is a grand idea; too bad it can't be perched *on top* of the Ritz, or in a neighboring aerie. Liberal use of mirrors on the floors and ceilings makes the tiny space seem to float, but the museum would be wondrous if perched on high.

[B5] **Millennium Tower Residences**, 30 Little West St., bet. 1st and 2nd Pls. 2007. *Gary Edward Handel & Associates.*

Indistinguishable from the Ritz next door. How about putting the **Skyscraper Museum** on its roof?

B4a

B7

[B3] **Museum of Jewish Heritage**, 36 Battery Place, SW cor. 1st Place. 1996.

Robert M. Morgenthau Wing. 2002. Both by *Kevin Roche, John Dinkleloo & Assocs.* Open to the public Su-Tu, Th, 10-5:45; We 10-8; closed Sat., Jewish holidays, Thanksgiving. Wed. evenings free. *www.mjhnyc.org*

Roche has augmented his original 1996 ziggurat with a large new wing, essentially doubling the museum's size. The Battery Place façade is staid, but the dynamic southern tip, facing the Esplanade and harbor, is sharp and avian. A linear exhibition of Jewish history unrolls within, as well as a memorial to the victims of the Holocaust.

[B4a] **Ritz Carlton**, 2 Little West St. bet. Battery Pl. and 1st Pl., condominiums, 10 Little West St. bet. Battery Pl. and 1st Pl. 2001. *Polshek Partnership and Gary Edward Handel & Associates.*

Another chic hotel for Wall Street's peripatetic traveling investors and out-of-town gurus: when the Internet breaks down (or

[B6] **P.S./I.S. 276**, 55 Battery Place bet, 1st and 2nd Pls. 2010. *Richard Dattner & Partners.*

Eight stories of classrooms curve gently as Battery Place bends north. For all its formal dexterity, Battery Park City can seem lifeless and isolated, so it's heartening to hear the screams of joyful children in the neighborhood.

[B7] The **Visionaire**, 70 Little West St. bet. 2nd and 3rd Places. 2008. *Pelli Clarke Pelli.*

Pelli, architect of the World Financial Center, has been busy in Battery Park City lately, with two other residential towers, both with sci-fi names, farther north on Murray Street: the **Verdesian** and the **Solaire**. Orange ceramic baffles, curvy glass, and meticulous detailing deliver a welcome lightness lacking in most other new Battery Park City construction. Astride the Battery Park Composting Center (2008. *Dattner Architects*).

B3

Tribeca:
see map p. 61

World Trade
Center Site

Continue for Financial District

[B8] **River Watch and South Cove Plaza,** 50 and 70 Battery Place, N and S of 2nd Place. 1999. Both by *Hardy Holzman Pfeiffer.*

Low-rise housing facing the delights of South Cove Park.

[B9] **South Cove Park,** surrounding South Cove bet. 1st and 3rd Place. 1988. *Mary Miss*, artist. *Stanton Eckstut, The Ehrenkranz Group & Eckstut,* architects. *Susan Child, Child Assocs.*, landscape architects. *Howard Brandston Lighting Design, Inc.*, lighting.

An effort to bring the changing character of the seasons, tides, and the river itself into an artful interplay with the southern terminus of the Esplanade, the end of 1st Place, and the Museum of the Jewish Heritage. Not gritty like much of the City, but even hardened New Yorkers need a break from their habitat once in a while. Coming here for an hour is much cheaper than a round-trip ticket to California.

[B13] **Liberty Court** (apartments), 200 Rector Pl., SW cor. West St. 1987. *Ulrich Franzen.*
[B14] **The Soundings** (apartments), 280 Rector Pl., SE cor. South End Ave. 1987. *Bond Ryder James.*
[B15] **Battery Pointe** (apartments), 300 Rector Pl., SW cor. South End Ave. 1987. *Bond Ryder James.*
[B16] **Liberty Terrace** (apartments), 380 Rector Pl., SE cor. The Esplanade. 1987. *Ulrich Franzen/The Vilkas Group.*

Good character actors but the performance is getting a little tired.

[B17] **Rector Park,** within the Rector Place loop, W and E of South End Ave. 1986. *Innocenti-Webel with Vollmer Assocs.*, landscape architects. **Gateway**, 1987, *R. M. Fischer*, sculptor.

Silent greenswardery: the kind of park where you're told not to step on the grass. Here the buildings are the thing, the park the void. For the opposite effect, see the more recent **Teardrop Park**, on River Terrace between Murray and Warren Streets, a park so well designed that the buildings around it almost disappear.

B9

B10

B12

B17

B18

[B10] **Liberty View** (apartments), 99 Battery Pl. bet. 3rd Place and W. Thames St. E side. 1990. *Ehrenkranz, Eckstut & Whitelaw and Costas Kondylis.*
[B11] **Cove Club** (apartments), 2 South End Ave. bet. W. Thames St. and 3rd Pl., through to Battery Pl. 1990. *James Stewart Polshek & Partners.*
[B12] **The Regatta Condominiums**, 21 South End Ave., bet. W. Thames St. and 3rd Pl. 1989. *Gruzen Samton Steinglass.*

Bland developments, part of the initial inventory of Battery Park City's south end, yet adhering to its original design guidelines. Less constrained than the Rector Place ensemble, they have their moments, especially at Cove Club's bay-windowed façade. The Regatta's residents are the clear winners here, hugging the Esplanade.

Rector Place residential neighborhood:
The first residential quarter built under Eckstut's residential design guidelines. To comment at length on any individual group is to forget what was intended by the design guidelines and what, in the end, really counts: the totality of the complex.

[B18] **Liberty House** (apartments), 377 Rector Place, NE cor. The Esplanade. 1986. *James Stewart Polshek & Partners.* [B19] **One Rector Park** /formerly **River Rose** (apartments), 333 Rector Place, NW cor. South End Ave. 1986. *Charles Moore and Rothzeid, Kaiserman, Thomson & Bee.*

The most mannered and exuberant of the Rector Park group, a prime example of 1980s Postmodernist design that has not aged well.

[B20] **Rector Square**/formerly **Parc Place** (apartments), 225 Rector Place, NE cor. South End Ave. 1986. *Gruzen Samton Steinglass.*
Understated with appropriate detailing.

[B21] **320-340 Albany Street** (town house apartments), bet. The Esplanade and South End Ave. S side. 1986. *Davis, Brody & Assocs.*

Six five-story apartment buildings meant to echo the forms and organization of the City's brownstones, with bays and well-modulated stoops. Unlike much 1980s architecture, this has aged well.

B21

[B22] **Hudson Tower** (apartments), 350 Albany St., SE cor. The Esplanade. 1986. *Davis, Brody & Assocs.*

Above a limestone base, the brick body offers bay windows and cantilevered corner windows to capture the harbor view. A happy building.

[B23] **"Upper Room,"** Albany Street Park, E of the Esplanade at foot of Albany St. *Ned Smyth,* sculptor.

No need to voyage up the Nile. Smyth's evocative, eclectic, open-to-the-sky forms offer a cartoon of both Egypt's dynasties and Rome's empire.

Gateway Plaza
[B24] **Gateway Plaza** (apartments), 345, 355, 365, 375, 385, 395 South End Ave. 1982-1983. *Jack Brown and Irving E. Gershon,* associate architects. Interior plaza, *Abel, Bainnson & Assocs.,* landscape architects.

Sam Lefrak in Manhattan: 1,712 units divided among three 34-story lackluster towers and other containers; the scullery maids of Battery Park City residences. Now offering "luxury" rentals.

[B25] **Monsignor John J. Kowsky Plaza**/formerly **Pumphouse Park**, E. of Esplanade, N of Gateway Plaza. 2005. *Weisz & Yoes,* architects. *Mathews Nielsen,* landscape architects.

Two 66-inch-diameter river water intake and outfall tubes for the World Trade Center were relocated to make possible the Liberty Street vehicular entry between the twin Gatehouses. These tubes, together with the required pumping apparatus, are under this park.

[B25a] **New York City Police Memorial**, E. end of Kowsky Plaza, N of Gateway Plaza. 1997. *Stuart Crawford.*

At the edge of the renovated Park, this subtle memorial forms a corner: an understated fountain and channel (patterned after *Louis Kahn's* **Salk Institute** in La Jolla, California), deliver water to a pool before a granite wall bearing the names of officers killed in the line of duty.

A chunk of the Berlin Wall: Just to the east of the Police Memorial, at the entrance to St. Joseph's Chapel (inside Gateway Plaza), is a fragment of the notorious concrete barrier, donated by the city of Berlin in 2004. This piece was originally part of the wall in the area between Potsdamer Platz and Leipziger Platz. It was erected in a spot designed to keep East Germans from entering the heavily guarded "death strip" between the inner and outer wall. Imprisoned within a low iron enclosure, painted with a comically catatonic face, the fragment seems harmless now.

World Financial Center:
The seven-million-square-foot commercial center (not including Goldman Sachs) encompassed in a group of towers sheathed in reflective glass and thermal granite. Towers vary in height from 33 to 51 stories, and each wears a different hat—mastaba, dome, pyramid, stepped pyramid. As bulky as the towers are, they began, in Pelli's irregular placement (dictated by landfill

B30

B25a

B31

configurations), to soften the impact of the then-neighboring World Trade Center's raw, 110-story prisms.

[B26] **1 World Financial Center**/formerly Dow Jones & Company Building and Oppenheimer & Company Tower, West St. opp. Cedar St. W side. 1985. *Cesar Pelli*, design architect. *Adamson Assocs.*, architects.

Mastaba-topped, 40 stories high.

[B27] **North and South Gatehouses**, West St. W side framing Liberty St. 1986. *Cesar Pelli*, design architect. *Adamson Assocs.*, architects.

The marbled interiors of these bulky octagonal pavilions are spacious, lavishly clad, fussily detailed, and embarrassingly devoid of purpose.

[B28] **2 World Financial Center**/Merrill Lynch World Headquarters, South Tower, West St. bet. Liberty and Vesey Sts. W side. 1987. *Cesar Pelli*, design architect. *Haines Lundberg Waehler*, architects.

Dome-topped, perhaps a derby for the tallest tower of 51 floors.

[B29] **The Wintergarden**, opp. North Bridge. 1988. *Cesar Pelli*, design architect. *Adamson Assocs.*, architects. *Lev Zetlin & Assocs. and Thornton Thomasetti*, structural engineers. *M. Paul Friedberg & Partners*, landscape architects. *Balmori Associates,* landscape designers.

Why was London's 19th-century **Crystal Palace** framed in so gossamer a structure, while this is encased in heavy steel-pipe framing? Nevertheless, it's welcome, a sunny, barrel-vaulted, palm-filled interior public space measuring 130 X 230 feet, roughly the size of Grand Central's concourse. (The 90-foot-tall palms are *Washingtonia robusta*, specially chosen for heartiness from among the world's 2,780 species.)

[B30] **World Financial Center Plaza**, W of 2 World Financial Center and the Wintergarden. 1988. *Siah Armajani and Scott Burton*, artists. *Cesar Pelli*, architect. *M. Paul Friedberg & Partners*, landscape architects.

Poised around the indented North Cove, the Plaza comprises the Terrace, the Court, Summer Park, and West Park. The **Belvedere** (1995. *Mitchell/Giurgola*) comprises a platform with a bosquet of trees. **Stainless steel pylons** (1995. *Martin Puryear*) provide welcome symbols to arriving ferryboaters.

[B31] **Goldman Sachs Tower**, 200 West St. bet. Vesey and Murray Sts. 2009. *Henry N. Cobb of Pei Cobb Freed & Partners and Adamson Assocs. International.*

A shiny shield of curved glass faces the river, peering over the shoulder of the World Financial Center. Its best feature is the way it

B35

sidles up to the Embassy Suites Hotel next door, creating a dynamic new public space between, covered with a swooping metal canopy.

[B32] **3 World Financial Center**: American Express Headquarters, West St. SW cor. Vesey St. 1985. *Cesar Pelli*, design architect. *Adamson Assocs.*, architects.
Pyramid-topped.

[B33] **4 World Financial Center**: Merrill Lynch World Headquarters, North Tower, Vesey St. SE cor. North End Ave. 1986. *Cesar Pelli*, design architect. *Haines Lundberg Waehler*, architects.
Step pyramid-topped.

[B34] **5 World Financial Center**: New York Mercantile Exchange, Vesey St. and North End Ave. 1997. *Skidmore, Owings & Merrill.*
No hat this time, but cool views of the Hudson reward its traders. *David Dunlap* (in *The New York Times*) described the trading floor: "...nothing about its gray-flannel façade betrays the sheer pandemonium within....clad in the

eye-popping colors of a medieval pageant, shouting and gesturing wildly, they buy and sell futures and options in crude oil,...platinum, copper, silver and gold."

[B35] **New York Waterways Ferry Terminal**, anchored on the Hudson River opposite Murray Street. 2001. *FTL Happold.*
Happily reinstituted, New York Waterways wafts you to Hoboken/Colgate, and Jersey City. The ride is more important than getting there. But the terminal is wonderful: a floating concourse, with ticket booth and slips, sheltered by a festive tensile roof; the perfect threshold between land and sea.

[B36] **Irish Hunger Memorial**, North End Avenue bet. Vesey & Barclay Sts. 2002. *Brian Tolle*, artist, with *1100:Architect, Gail Wittwer-Laird*, landscape architect, and *Maureen O'Rourke*, historian.
An extraordinary diorama pays tribute to the 1-1/2 million victims of the **Great Potato**

B36

Famine (1845-1852), a collaboration between the historicist sculptor *Tolle* and a team of historians, architects, and landscape architects. An elaborate evocation of a swath of Irish countryside, complete with a cottage (moved from Ireland's County Mayo and rebuilt stone by stone) plus native plants (foxglove, gorse): an **authentic replica** that makes its corporate neighbors seem fake.

[B37] **Riverhouse**, One Rockefeller Park, bet. Barclay and Murray Sts. 2009. *Polshek Partnership, Ismael Leyva, David Rockwell.*
Huge, its pleasantly swooping façade along River Terrace matching the curve of the neighboring Solaire. Sustainably speaking, Riverhouse features the first "green" (LEED* Platinum) double curtain wall in the United States, providing a pocket of insulating air between the layers of glass. Check the courtyard entrance portal on Barclay Street, lit with fluorescent bands of colors reflected on the pavement: trippy!

B43

B39

22 River Terrace, and **Tribeca Green**, into the **frame** for its picture.

The four corners of the frame:

[B40] **Solaire**, 20 River Terrace, bet. Murray St. and Park Pl. 2003. *Pelli Clarke Pelli,* architects, with *SLCE. Balmori Associates*, landscape designers.

"Sustainable" before its neighbors, self-proclaimed as the first "green" tower in the City (LEED* Gold).

[B41] **Verdesian**. 211 North End Avenue. 2006. *Pelli Clarke Pelli*, design architects, with *SLCE.*

Even more sustainable (LEED* Platinum) than its older brother Solaire. *Pelli's* newer Battery Park City towers all have vaguely utopian names (*Solaire! Visionaire! Verdesian!*) but at heart they are sleek glass affairs with pleasant masonry details.

*(*LEED – Leadership in Energy and Everything Designed.)*

[B38] **Embassy Suites Hotel and Regal Cinemas,** North End Ave. at Vesey St. 2000. *Perkins Eastman.*

Contiguous with, and convenient to, the cluster of World Financial Towers, Embassy's dull monolith supplies rooms and movies to business travelers.

[B39] **Teardrop Park,** River Terrace bet. Warren & Murray Sts. 2004. *Michael Van Valkenburgh,* landscape architect.

A shady and mysterious glen filled with switchbacks, secret paths, and surprises; more *Frederick Law Olmsted* than *Robert Moses*. A place for contemplation, not baseball (a long slide for kids is the only programmed activity).

Bluestone and granite form miniature hills and valleys planted with native shrubs and trees. At the center is a massive bluestone wall, a limestone doorway cut through its middle. Not just the leftover void between buildings, this lovely place is the neighborhood star, turning the four surrounding towers, **Solaire, Verdesian,**

[B42] **22 River Terrace**, SE cor. Warren St. 2001. *Gruzen Samton.*

More than 300 apartments. Unremarkable on its own, but here part of a larger whole that forms a swooping edge along **Rockefeller Park**, visually joining *Polshek's* **Riverhouse** to *Stern* and *Kondylis'* **Tribeca Park.**

[B43] **Tribeca Green**, 325 North End Ave., SW cor. Warren St. 2005. *Robert A.M. Stern Architects.*

Good proportions in brick and glass from *Stern* form a strong corner at Warren Street and North End Avenue. Meanwhile its rear façade frames the northeast corner of Teardrop Park.

[B44] **Tribeca Park,** 400 Chambers St, SE cor. River Terrace, 1999. *Robert A. M. Stern,* with *Costas Kondylis.*

A three-dimensional collage of parts simulating a group of buildings.

[B45] **The Hallmark, Brookdale Senior Living**, 455 North End Ave., bet. Warren and Chambers Sts. W side. 2000. *Lucien Lagrange* and *Schuman Lichtenstein Claman Efron*.

Housing for the elderly that, together with its neighbors to the east and south, provide background massing for the bolder **Stuyvesant High School**.

[B46] **Tribeca Bridge Tower/P.S./I.S. 89**, 450 North End Ave., bet. Warren and Chambers Sts.

ment for the original school on East 15th Street. It's multistory volume anticipated the new apartment buildings that now surround it: both urban and urbane, its umbilical cord to the older city across West Street is an overbearing bow-string trussed bridge: too self-absorbed in its own form.

[B49] **Gov. Nelson A. Rockefeller Park and Park House**. 1992. *Carr, Lynch, Hack & Sandell*, landscape architects. Kiosk, 1992, *Demetri Porphyrios*.

B48

1999. *Pasanella + Klein Stolzman + Berg* (school) with *Costas Kondylis* (apartments) and *Richard Cook*.

A 151-unit apartment tower rises over a public school and retail space. With that many chefs (among the architects), no wonder that the whole fails to be greater than the sum of the parts.

[B47] **Tribeca Pointe Tower**, 41 River Terrace, NE cor. Chambers St. (W of Stuyvesant High School). 1999. *Gruzen Samton*.

The base matches the Chambers Street grid across West Street, the tower that of Battery Park City to the south. Unlike the four projects just to the south, this is an object, unto itself. But who doesn't like orange and blue?

[B48] **Stuyvesant High School**, West St. NW cor. Chambers St. 1992. *Cooper Robertson & Partners and Gruzen Samton Steinglass*. Connecting Tribeca Bridge, 1993, *Skidmore, Owings & Merrill*.

One of the City's magnet — admission by competitive test only — high schools, a replace-

Seven acres echo *Olmsted & Vaux's* Riverside Park, which adjoins the Hudson opposite the Upper West Side. Children's playground, handball, and volleyball courts supply active areas. For contemplation, a Greek temple pavilion.

NECROLOGY

Museum of Jewish Heritage Visitor Center and security checkpoint. 1997. *Claire Weisz and Mark Yoes*.

Wonderful, and where did it go? Obliterated by the Morgenthau addition.

North End Avenue Mall. 1989. *Weintraub & di Domenico*.

The antecedents of this central green space inhabit Boston's Back Bay, not our Park Avenue or upper Broadway. Replaced by a new greensward by *Rogers Marvel*.

WORLD TRADE CENTER AREA

Within days of September 11 urgent pleas were heard to rebuild the **Twin Towers**. The impulse lay apart from economics or urban planning; **"build!"** was a necessary, fortifying rallying cry of a country and city under attack. And with so many groups demanding a voice in rebuilding efforts, delays were unavoidable. But more importantly, *Daniel Libeskind's* much-debated master plan has not been realized, stalled first by squabbling and indecision, then by the economic downturn in 2008 that abruptly stalled construction, and dreams of renewal, everywhere.

Thankfully, after years spent clearing and stabilizing the difficult site (the World Trade Center rose from a structurally complex base called the "bathtub," a deep excavation lined with concrete that holds back both the surrounding earth and the waters of the Hudson River only a few blocks to the west), real

WTC1, Sphere

progress has been made, especially on the new, controversial and much-anticipated **1 World Trade Center** (also known as "The Freedom Tower"). A completed **September 11 Memorial** is promised to be open to the public in time for the tenth anniversary of the attacks, in 2011. But other proposed buildings, including a phalanx of **new towers**, an **arts center**, a **transportation hub**, and a **church**, seem to be distant dreams.

Here is a look at what was, what is, and what is proposed.

WHAT WAS:

[WTC1] **1 and 2 World Trade Center** (north and south "twin towers"), **4, 5, and 6 World Trade Center** (plaza structures), Church to West Sts., Liberty to Vesey Sts. **WTC 1**, 1973. **WTC 2**, 1972. **WTC 4**, 1977. **WTC 5**, 1972. **WTC 6**, 1974. *Minoru Yamasaki & Assocs.*, design architects. *Emery Roth & Sons*, architects. Plaza sculptures: **Sphere**, *Fritz Koenig* (rescued and relocated to

Battery Park). **Ideogram**, *James Rosati*. **Unnamed granite**, *Masayuki Nagare*.

Most New Yorkers thought of the twin towers as symbols of success, power, strength, ingenuity, grace, greed, waste. How could two identical corporate towers embody so many conflicting messages? Never ambiguous was scale: each tower was 1,350 feet tall; 110 stories

WTC1

of stainless steel joined by four lower buildings and a vast plaza. The towers included ten million square feet of office space: seven times the area of the **Empire State Building**, four times that of the **Pan Am Building.**

So who could have imagined, in the end, that the towers were so fragile? In the wake of the attack, the towers became American lore, symbols of courage and tragedy. There were initially calls to build exact replicas as soon as possible. Others said the towers should never have been built in the first place; that they were out of scale, cold, bleak.

The World Trade Center did have problems: the windows were narrow and inoperable. Huge consumers of energy, these were no "green" buildings. The plaza between the towers was often desolate. And forgotten amid the post-tragedy eulogies was the fact that even during the economic boom of the late 1990s, much of the World Trade Center lay unused; entire floors were vacant. Just prior to September 11 the Port Authority had even started a program to loan office space to artists for use as studios, free.

Skyline from Brooklyn, circa 1980s

But despite their shortcomings the twin towers were wondrous, majestic at sunrise and sunset, catching morning and evening light, one tower casting its shadow on the other. Storm clouds would roll in off the harbor and divide, cut in two by the towers: they were *that tall*.

WTC2

Upon emerging from a subway downtown, you could always orient yourself by simply looking up and finding them. And the towers, no scrimpy modernist boxes, were well built: beautifully detailed, with classically symmetrical proportions and delicately mitered corners at the top.

Regardless of what anyone thought of the towers as architecture, they have become a sacred memory in the consciousness of millions around the world, and New Yorkers will keep a special place for them in their hearts because of the unspeakable tragedy that happened there.

[WTC2] **Marriott Hotel**/originally **Vista International Hotel**/3 World Trade Center, SW cor. WTC Plaza. 1981. *Skidmore, Owings & Merrill.*

With its elegant, horizontal-striped aluminum-and-glass curtain wall and diagonal orientation, this sleek hotel looked out of place next to its enormous neighbors. The looming canopy was just one of those that proliferated in the City's hotels in the 1990s. Destroyed on September 11 when the twin towers fell.

WTC 1-6 connected to WTC 7 via a pair of 2nd-story pedestrian viaducts (one cocooned against wind and rain by a Star Wars transparent cylindrical container) that threw much of the sidewalks along Vesey Street into shadow.

[WTC3] **Deutsche Bank Building**/originally **Bankers Trust Plaza**, 130 Liberty bet. Washington & Greenwich Sts. 1974. *Shreve, Lamb and Harmon.*

Irreparably damaged on September 11, the demolition of this black 40-story glass box (by the same firm that designed the Empire State Building) has been painfully slow and erratic, marred by a devastating fire in 2007 that killed two firefighters.

Viaduct

[WTC4] **St. Nicholas Greek Orthodox Church**, Cedar Street bet. Washington St. and West Side Highway. Original building ca. 1830. Converted to church, 1919.

A **gem amid giants**, this four-story whitewashed church was destroyed as the twin towers fell. The congregation is raising funds for a new church next door.

[WTC5] **Fiterman Hall**, Borough of Manhattan Community College, 30 West Broadway bet. Barclay St. and Park Pl. 1959.

Originally an office building built by *Miles Fiterman*, he donated it to the College in 1993. Damaged by falling debris when 7 World Trade collapsed on September 11, demolition wasn't completed until 2009. A new building by *Pei Cobb Freed & Partners* is promised by 2012.

[WTC6] **7 World Trade Center** (office tower), Vesey to Barclay Sts., Washington St. to West Broadway. 1987. *Emery Roth & Sons.*

Contrasting with a 25-foot-tall, bright red *Alexander Calder* stabile, *Three Red Wings*, were the sheer 47-story walls of polished red granite veneer that corseted this 1980s addition to the original WTC project. The tower caught fire on the morning of September 11 and collapsed late in the afternoon.

Tribute in Light, World Trade Center site, Julian LaVerdiere and Paul Myoda, designers, Richard Nash Gould, architect.

Eighty-eight searchlights beamed skywards from the World Trade Center site, creating two vertical columns of eerie bluish light. Installed in the spring of 2002, again in 2003 on the second anniversary of the attacks, and once again in 2008.

Visible from everywhere in the five boroughs and far beyond, from New Jersey to Long Island, the lights were a great comfort to those wanting to see something tangible at the suddenly empty tip of Manhattan. There has been talk of making the lights permanent, or at least a more regular feature of the World Trade Center site.

WHAT IS:

[WTC7] **7 World Trade Center**, 250 Greenwich Street, bet. Barclay and Vesey Sts. 2006. *Skidmore, Owings & Merrill*. Public artwork, *Jeff Koons, Jenny Holzer*.

The replacement for the former 7 World Trade Center destroyed on September 11, this shimmering, mirage-like tower rose relatively quickly on the same site and is, notably, the first certifiably "green" skyscraper in the City. Up close it's beautifully detailed, its façade a double layer of thin stainless steel slats.

[WTC8] **World Trade Center Path Station** (temporary). 2003. Port Authority of New York and New Jersey staff.

Temporary place-holder until *Santiago Calatrava's* futurist extravaganza is completed. Nevertheless, this critical transit hub occupies a refreshing and functional shed, airy, full of light.

[WTC9] **Ten House (Ladder Co. 10, Engine Co. 10) Firehouse**, 124 Liberty St. bet. Church and Greenwich Sts.

Ten House, adjacent to the World Trade Center, was among the first responders to the attacks, losing five firefighters on September 11. The building, a sturdy 1970s modernist brick container, was heavily damaged but rebuilt and ultimately re-opened in 2003.

[WTC9a] **Firefighter's Memorial**, west wall of Ten House, 124 Liberty St. bet. Church and Greenwich Sts. 2006. *Viggo Bech Rambusch*, designer. *Joseph A. Oddi*, artist. *Joseph Petrovics*, sculptor. *James Hasler*, lighting designer.

A 56-foot-long bronze bas-relief narrative of the tragic events and dauntless courage of the 343 firefighters killed on September 11.

[WTC10] **Pedestrian Bridges**, spanning the West Side Highway. 2002-2003. *SHoP*.

Kudos to *SHoP* for keeping it simple. Pedestrian links across the West Side Highway at Vesey and Rector Streets were desperately needed in the aftermath of September 11; these handsome steel viaducts are sturdy and functional. Intended as expedients, they are good enough to stay.

WHAT IS PROPOSED:

National September 11 Memorial, World Trade Center site, bet. Greenwich, Liberty, Vesey Streets and West Side Highway. 2011 (predicted). *Michael Arad*, architect. *Peter Walker and Partners*, landscape architect.

Winner of an international competition, *Arad* and *Walker's* plan calls for an eight-acre plaza forested with oak trees, reflecting pools delineating the footprints of the twin towers. Names of

WTC7

the **2,981 victims** (including the 1993 World Trade Center bombing that killed six people) will be inscribed on walls surrounding the pools.

September 11 Memorial Museum, World Trade Center site, bet. Greenwich, Liberty, Vesey Streets and West Side Highway. 2013 (predicted). *Davis Brody Bond Aedas* (museum), *Snøhetta* (entry pavilion).

The Museum, adjacent to the Memorial, will contain artifacts, oral histories, a research center and, at a subterranean level, preserved vestiges of the twin tower's foundations. An entry pavilion will incorporate two "tridents" from the façades.

1 World Trade Center, SE cor. Vesey Street and West Side Highway. 2013 (predicted). *David Childs of Skidmore Owings & Merrill*.

Scrutinized in public perhaps more than any building ever planned in the City (at least since the original twin towers), this prismatic tower would be the City's tallest at 1,776 feet high (including antenna). Curiously, much of the

LEGEND:

- COMMERCIAL BUILDING
- WTC HUB / PLAZA
- MEMORIAL / CULTURAL SITES
- SIDEWALK
- PARK
- PLAZA
- CORTLANDT STREET R.O.W.
- DEY STREET R.O.W.
- EXTENT OF POSSIBLE/POTENTIAL SUB-SURFACE TIE-BACKS ON PRIVATELY OWNED PROPERTY
- INCLUDES CERTAIN PORTIONS OF FORMER GREENWICH STREET * FUTURE DIMENSIONS AND USE OF THIS AREA ARE STILL BEING STUDIED. *
- PROJECT LOCATION

0'   100'   200'   400'

WORLD TRADE CENTER
MEMORIAL AND REDEVELOPMENT PLAN

PROPOSED SITE PLAN AS OF NOVEMBER, 2006

debate over this building mirrors the discussion surrounding the original towers in 1973: does the neighborhood really need 69 more floors of offices?

Tower 2, 200 Greenwich Street, NE cor. Vesey St. 2014 (predicted). *Norman Foster.*

Foster's proposed tower incorporates master planner *Libeskind's* "wedge of light," and would be the third tallest building in the City.

Transportation Hub, Greenwich Street bet. Tower 2 and Tower 3. *Santiago Calatrava.* 2013 (predicted).

Two hundred thousand commuters will pass daily through *Calatrava*'s soaring white steel **Stegosaurus**, providing shops and connections to the PATH, No.1, and N and R trains.

Tower 3, 175 Greenwich Street, bet. Liberty and Vesey Sts. 2014 (predicted). *Richard Rogers.*

Its visible structure cross-braced like the **Hancock Tower** in Chicago, this would be the fourth tallest building in the City.

Tower 4, 150 Greenwich Street, bet. Liberty and Vesey Sts. 2011 (predicted). *Fumihiko Maki.*

Minimal compared to *Rogers* and *Foster's* proposals, with a better chance for reality, since it has a reliable tenant lined up: the **Port Authority.**

Tower 5, 130 Liberty Street, bet. Washington and Greenwich Sts. 2014 (predicted). *Kohn Pederson Fox.*

Planned for the **Deutsche Bank Building** site, Tower 5 is the least likely to see the light of day, as tenant J.P. Morgan Chase backed out in favor of moving to the former Bear Stearns headquarters at 383 Madison Avenue.

*A **Performing Arts Center**, still in the planning stages, would be the new home to the Joyce Theater. But will it happen?*

TRIBECA / LOWER WEST SIDE

Lower West Side

A bit of history: After the Civil War, shipping shifted from the East River to the North (Hudson) River. Bowspritted South Street on Manhattan's southeast flank [see South Street Seaport] was abandoned for the longer, many-berthed piers of steam-powered shipping on this, the west flank. Later, Washington Market, a venue for produce, expanded from the market buildings and spread throughout the local streets, reusing the area's Federal and Greek Revival houses and warehouses as storage for fruits and vegetables.

Much later, truckers to the market and the then still active piers brought street congestion that forced the building of the West Side (Miller) Elevated Highway atop West Street to accommodate through automobile traffic. The elevated highway was demolished in the early 1980s when "deferred maintenance" finally caused a partial

Trade Center site, when the surplus stores of **Radio Row** *were demolished to clear the required super superblock for the WTC super supertowers. Greenwich Street was wiped out entirely between Liberty and Barclay Streets, and as new projects were okayed by the authorities (after a 100-foot-high lid was zoned between Reade and Murray Streets), the narrow roadway north of WTC was widened to near-boulevard width. Happily, Greenwich Street will be reintroduced with the re-building of the WTC complex.*

[T1] **Verizon Building**/formerly **New York Telephone Company** (office building) also known as The **Barclay-Vesey Building**, 140 West St., bet. Barclay and Vesey Sts. to (now demapped) Washington St. 1923-1927. *Ralph Walker of McKenzie, Voorhees & Gmelin.* 👆

T1

T2

collapse; its planned replacement, Westway, a multibillion-dollar underground superhighway (some called it a "boondoggle") yielded to the needs of the Hudson's striped bass population in a notable court ruling. A smaller west side highway has replaced it. After the produce market moved to new city-built facilities at Hunts Point in the Bronx, the Lower West Side (a term less and less used) became Tribeca.

Greenwich Street Corridor

Charles Harvey's experimental cable elevated railway began operation astride Greenwich Street' s eastern curb in 1870 and soon evolved into the Ninth Avenue Elevated Line. In the interim Greenwich Street remained a narrow, dark, noisy thoroughfare lined with three-, four-, and five-story commercial and residential structures along its two-and-a-half-mile length, from the Battery to Gansevoort Street. Though the street' s share of light improved when the el structure was taken down just before World War II, it retained its threadbare character at the southern end until the assemblage of the World

Architect *Ralph Walker*, ceding the sidewalk for a widening of narrow Vesey Street, replaced that pedestrianism with a widely heralded, *Guastavino*-vaulted arcade. More importantly, above, he created a brilliant solution for massing of bulky buildings' required zoning setbacks (legislated after the public outcry over the old **Equitable Building's** consumption of light and air of its neighbors).

"(This) pile of steel and masonry becomes a **brooding sphinx**. It is a ten-strike. Even the inhabitants of New Jersey admit they like it." *Critic Chappell "T-Square," The New Yorker.* November 27, 1926.

Directly across Vesey Street from the twin towers of the World Trade Center, it was damaged on September 11, but miraculously survived.

[T2] **101 Barclay Street** (offices), NW cor. Greenwich St. to Murray St. 1983. *Skidmore, Owings & Merrill.*

A Jordan almond, green graph-papered monolith. Functionally two linked towers sandwiching part of Washington Street, the building defines the path of the missing thoroughfare by creating a light-washed 23-story atrium over the street's 60-foot-wide ghost. At one end, the space is pierced by the elevator's half cylinder. (On entering, it's not unlike entering Cape Canaveral's **Vertical Assembly Building** and gazing up at a Saturn rocket ready for launch. The only thing missing is a cloud forming under the roof.)

[T3] **75 Park Place**, bet. Greenwich St. and West Broadway. N side to Murray St. 1987. *Emery Roth & Sons.*

A block-square silvery structure, somewhat squat in these parts at only 14 stories, but debonair with **thin blue stripes** alternating with strip windows.

[T4] **75 Murray Street Building**/originally *Hopkins Store*/now residential, bet. W Broadway and Greenwich St. N side. 1857-1858. *James Bogardus.*

Another grand *James Bogardus* cast-iron

T9

T4

façade, here remembering the **Venetian Renaissance** (those glassy buildings along the Grand Canal). Early *Bogardus*; things soon became lighter and more elegant as confidence in glass and iron technology grew.

[T5] **St. John's University**/formerly **The College of Insurance,** 101 Murray St., bet. Greenwich and West Sts. N side. 1983. *Haines Lundberg Waehler.*

A complicated polygonal layercake of pink precast panels. The designers excelled in their class in descriptive geometry, but as a free-standing building it fails as a good neighbor, rupturing the area's street-fronted context.

[T6] **101 Warren Street Apartments**, SW cor. Greenwich St., to West St. 2008. *Skidmore, Owings & Merrill with Ismael Leyva Architects.*

Big Box architecture, combining a tower of housing (above) with retail (below). Massive, consuming almost the whole block, it's a welcome sign of life two blocks from the World Trade Center site. The façade is slickly handled, with alternating limestone panels seeming to

slide to and fro, revealing black windows behind. Frozen dynamics?

[T7] **Greenwich Court I and II** (apartments), 275 and 295 Greenwich St., bet. Murray and Chambers St. E side. 1987-1988. *Gruzen Samton Steinglass.*

Large red brick in a red field, generous, rounded corners that ease the turning of odd-angled streets, and green-framed sliding sash that add depth to the façade. **Labored.**

[T8] **Public School 234**, Manhattan, Greenwich St., bet. Warren and Chambers Sts. W side. 1988. *Richard Dattner.*

A fanciful mix of eclectic architectural elements drawn in the architect's imagination from the daydreams of kids who study here: watchtowers, sentry boxes, walled courtyards, arches from Historic Williamsburg, and Starship Enterprise classroom wings. **Excellent.**

[T9] **Dalton on Greenwich** (apartments), 303 Greenwich St., NE cor. Chambers St. 1987. *Beyer Blinder Belle.*

A muted design vocabulary and a subtle palette of grays echoes, but doesn't mimic, the BBB's "Bogardus" Building at **South Street Seaport**. What worked for four stories at the **Seaport** doesn't work for 11 here. The flatness compromises the design.

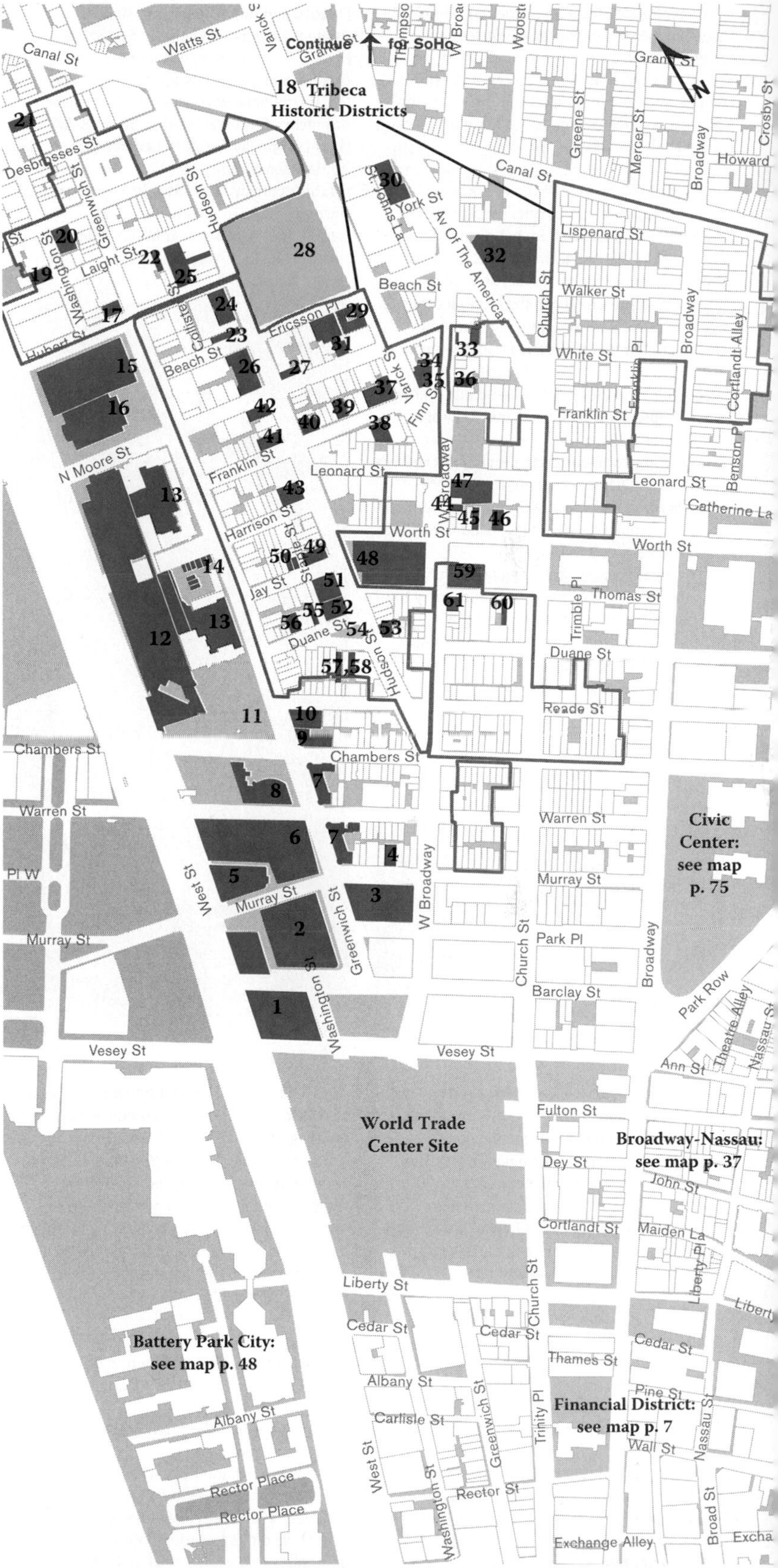

Continue for SoHo
18 Tribeca Historic Districts
Canal St
Watts St
Desbrosses St
Hudson St
Laight St
Washington St
Greenwich St
Hubert St
Beach St
Collister St
Ericsson Pl
York St
St Johns La
Av Of The Americas
Beach St
Lispenard St
Walker St
White St
Franklin St
Leonard St
Worth St
Thomas St
Duane St
Reade St
Chambers St
Warren St
Murray St
Park Pl
Barclay St
Vesey St
N Moore St
Harrison St
Staple St
Jay St
Varick St
Finn Sq
W Broadway
Church St
Broadway
Greene St
Mercer St
Howard
Crosby St
Trimble Pl
Benson Pl
Cortlandt Alley
Catherine La
West St
Pl W
Civic Center: see map p. 75
World Trade Center Site
Fulton St
Dey St
John St
Broadway-Nassau: see map p. 37
Cortlandt St
Maiden La
Liberty St
Liberty Pl
Cedar St
Thames St
Albany St
Carlisle St
Pine St
Financial District: see map p. 7
Wall St
Trinity Pl
Rector St
Rector Place
Battery Park City: see map p. 48
Exchange Alley
Broad St
Nassau St
Park Row
Theatre Alley
Ann St

[T10] **311 Reade Street** (apartments), SE cor. Greenwich St. 1989. *Rothzeid, Kaiserman, Thomson & Bee.*

Hard on the heels of its three downstream neighbors rose this simpler red-brick development. Up a floor or two, the corner glazed prows make choice aeries.

[T11] **Washington Market Park**, NYC Department of Housing, Preservation & Development, Greenwich St. bet. Chambers and Duane Sts. W side. 1983. *Weintraub & di Domenico.*

Honoring the former market area, this spirited amalgam of the natural and the artificial continues the spirit of *Olmsted & Vaux*. Voluptuous landforms, a witty **neo-Gothic** enclosing fence, a gazebo, even a few relocated granite **Art Deco** ornaments from the erstwhile West Side Highway entry ramps, combine to make this a city star.

[T12] **Borough of Manhattan Community College** (CUNY), 199 Chambers St., NE cor. West St., along West St. to N. Moore St. Construction halted 1976, completed 1980. *CRS (Caudill Rowlett Scott Partnership).*

A megastructure, stretching north from Chambers Street, over what were once more than five blocks (Reade, Duane, Jay, Harrison, Franklin, North Moore). A curiosity from that brief era when architects told us that megastructures would cure all urban ills. Damaged on September 11, it has had a refreshing renaissance.

[T13] **Independence Plaza North**, Greenwich St. bet. Duane and North Moore Sts. 1975.

T12

T14

Oppenheimer, Brady & Vogelstein. John Pruyn, associated architect.

Forty-story middle-income blockbusters of brick and striated concrete block. The design, intended to minimize their *Brobdingnagian* bulk (cantilevers and toothiness) nevertheless throws shadows on a flock of exquisite Federal houses that *Oppenheimer* and partners had magnificently restored. Unfortunate.

[T14] **Harrison Street Houses**, 25-41 Harrison St. SW cor. Greenwich St. Partly relocated and restored, 1975, *Oppenheimer, Brady & Vogelstein.* 🍎
[T14a] **23 Harrison Street House.** Originally **Jonas Wood House**, originally at 314 Washington St. 1804. 🍎
[T14b] **25 Harrison Street.** Originally 315 Washington Street (town house). 1819. *John MComb, Jr.* 🍎
[T14c] **27 Harrison Street.** Originally **John McComb, Jr., House**, originally at 317 Washington St. 1796. *John McComb, Jr.* 🍎

[T14d] Originally **Wilson Hunt House**, originally at 327 Washington St. 1828. 🍎
[T14e] Originally **Joseph Randolph House**, originally at 329 Washington St. 1828. 🍎
[T14f] Originally **William B. Nichols House**, originally at 331 Washington St. 1828. 🍎
[T14g] Originally **Sarah R. Lambert House**, 29 Harrison St. 1827. 🍎
[T14h] Originally **Jacob Ruckle House**, 31 Harrison St. (original site). 1827. 🍎
[T14i] Originally **Ebenezer Miller House**, 33 Harrison St. (original site). 1827.

These elegant **Federal** houses, were recycled (and later rejected) as produce market buildings: two on Harrison Street and a group from a now extinct part of Washington Street. Their reincarnation included moving the Washington Street group two blocks to this enclave. They have been lovingly restored—perhaps too lovingly: the patina from the passage of time has been totally erased. Note that *John McComb*, City Hall's co-architect, lived in one!

[T15] **Citigroup Building**/originally **Shearson Lehman Plaza**/**Travellers Group**, 390 Greenwich St., SW cor. Hubert St. to West St. 1986. *Skidmore, Owings & Merrill.*
[T16] **388 Greenwich St.** NW cor. N. Moore St. 1989. *Kohn Pedersen Fox.*

Modern Jeff and Postmodern Mutt. Medium-rise Mutt, 390, serene and understated, stands confidently at Tribeca's edge, while exuberant Jeff shows off its towering bulk, buttressed penthouse and gabled clock to New Jersey (with a side glance at Battery Park City).

T17

[T17] **408 Greenwich Street** Lofts, bet. Hubert and Laight Sts. 2008. *Morris Adjmi.*

A postmodernly neo-Classical condominium, inspired by Italian architect *Aldo Rossi*, with rugged pre-cast arches attached to a steel frame. The exaggerated façade is a caricature of the plain, functional buildings (factories, warehouses) that were here first. It might have worked best on a site a few blocks east, nestled between extant warehouses, or in SoHo, next to *Rossi's* **Scholastic Books** building at 557 Broadway (bet. Prince and Spring Sts). Standing solo here, it needs playmates.

Tribeca
The acronym for the Triangle Below Canal (say Try-BECK-a) was developed in the 1970s, when an imaginative realtor, sensing a displacement of manufacturing and warehousing and an influx of artists from places like SoHo, decided to dub the area with an ear-catching identity (better than Lower West Side) to promote momentum. It did.

Around these corners at Greenwich and Harrison are some of those immense granite slabs that served 19th-century New York as both sidewalk and curb in a single piece. How about 4-1/2 X 7 feet and almost a foot thick? Can you find some bigger? Tell us.

[T19] **Pearline Soap Atelier**, 414 Washington St., NW cor. Laight St.
[T20] **Fairchild and Foster Atelier**, 415 Washington St., SE cor, Vestry St. Both 2008. *Joseph Pell Lombardi.*

Two convincing re-enactments of the past (**Romanesque Revival Revival?**) that will leave you wondering where to catch your time machine back to the 21st century. No, these are not old factory conversions. Yes, these came off *Lombardi's* drawing board. No, you do not have to wear period dress when you walk by.

[T21] Originally **Fleming Smith Warehouse**, 451-453 Washington St., SE cor. Watts St. 1891-1892. *Stephen Decatur Hatch.* ●̆

T21   T22

T25

T24

[T18] **Tribeca Historic Districts** (Tribeca South and Extension, Tribeca East, Tribeca West, and Tribeca North. 1992 & 2002, 1992, 1991, 1992), generally (but following their own distinctive courses) embraced by Broadway, Canal, Greenwich and Chambers Streets, with bump-outs at the northwestern and northeastern corners, and indents where the Holland tunnel erupts, and on some parts of Leonard, Worth, Thomas and Duane Streets. ●̆

Land development by both Trinity Church and the *Lispenard* family provided grids in these precincts for industrial and commercial architecture that retain exemplary examples from the second half of the 19th century; buildings now converted to more gracious uses: up-scale housing, restaurants, and offices. Architects included *Samuel Warner, John B. Snook, James H. Giles, Henry Fernbach, and Isaac Duckworth.*

Fanciful Flemish. As much a surprise in **Tribeca** as it would be anywhere in the City: a golden-hued, gabled, and dormered fantasy with weathered copper details at its picturesquely silhouetted roof. The ground floor has housed the **Capsouto Frères** bistro since 1980.

[T22] **57 Laight Street**, SW cor. Collister St. 1893. *Horgan & Slattery.*

Smooth Roman Brick and brownstone provide elegance missing in its more lusty neighbors. The cornice is spectacular.

[T23] **135 Hudson St.** (warehouse), NW cor. Beach St. 1886-1887. *Kimball & Inhen.*

A laid-back masonry warehouse, now occupied by laid-back artists who appreciate true grit in architecture. As a sample of what to look for, note the cast-iron impost blocks at the top of the street-floor brick piers. And be on the lookout for more. And what of the sign (fading palimpsest) painted across the Beach Street façade?

[T24] **145 Hudson Street**/originally **Hudson Square Building**, bet. Hubert and Beach Sts. W side. 1929. *Renwick, Aspinwall & Guard.* Remodeled for residential lofts, 2000, *Joseph Pell Lombardi.*

Art Deco for the unexhausted lofters seeking an ambience redolent of an earlier Manhattan.

[T25] Originally **American Express Horse Stables**, NE cor. Collister St. through block to Laight St., ca. 1880. Converted to apartments, 2008. *Kevin Kennon.*

Three stories of draft horses were stabled here. Express, of course, is a relative term, here the modest pace of horse and wagon. But those tight wide-voussoired arches are elegant.

See also the **American Express warehouse**, *46 Trinity Place in the Financial District, and compare the company emblem atop in relief. Woof!*

T30

[T26a] **Northmoore** (condominium apartments) including Castree Building, 53 N. Moore, NW cor. North Moore and Hudson Sts. 1891. *Thomas R. Jackson.* Supporting buildings along Hudson, 1890s, *Charles C. Haight.*

In 2000 this Guide whined: "Why don't we build lofts anew? From scratch. With high ceilings and open plans." We have. At least *Messrs Lombardi* and *Adjmi* have, here in Tribeca. More elsewhere: see West Chelsea.

[T26b] **55 North Moore Street** (lofts), bet. Hudson and Greenwich Sts. 1891. *Thomas R. Jackson.*

Roman Revival arches consort with a Classical cornice in this vigorous brick and terracotta warehouse.

[T27] **Bendheim Building**, 122 Hudson St., NE cor. N. Moore St. 1890s.

Creamy brick, terra-cotta capitals, grand arches, a rusticated rock-face granite base, and a festive green cornice: the powerful vocabulary/palette of late 19th-century New York warehousing.

[T28] **St. John's Park**, Hudson to Varick Sts., Ericsson Pl. to Laight St.

The **circular wasteland** within the **Holland Tunnel Exit Rotary** is still called "St. John's Park," but bears no resemblance to the original genteel square that first bore the name. Public in use but privately owned by Trinity Church, it was considered the most urbane space in the City, with trim Georgian row housing defining its perimeter. **St. John's Chapel** (1807. *John McComb, Jr.*), a convincing copy of St. Martin-in-the-Fields in London, faced the park on its eastern flank. The park was sold in 1867, amid howls of protest, to *Cornelius Vanderbilt*, who replaced the park with a huge storage shed for his Hudson River Railroad.

The second blow came in 1918, when the chapel was demolished; again, over cries of anguish from the public. By then, what had been a fashionable neighborhood on par with Washington Square and Gramercy Park had mostly become a warehousing district. The final blow came in 1927, when *Vanderbilt's* shed was razed to make way for the tunnel exit. Today the scene is one of speeding trucks, exhaust, and screeching brakes. But try to superimpose this image: gents in top hats and elegant women in long skirts strolling in a gracefully quiet park lined with staid houses, the chapel bells tolling in the evening. All gone. Our ancestors preserved many a New York treasure, but blew it here.

[T29] Originally **4th Precinct, NYC Police Department**/now **1st Precinct**, 16 Ericsson Place (originally Beach St.), SW cor. Varick St. 1912. *Hoppin & Koen.*

T31

A limestone **Renaissance Revival** palazzetto whose public interior in no way reflects the opulence of the exterior—except for the stable on the Varick Street side. The paddocks and other equine accoutrements have a quality that exceeds that provided for the officers.

[T30] **1 York Street Apartments**, SW cor. Sixth Ave. at Canal St. 2008. *Enrique Norten.*

Enrique Norton has entered the condominium fray. His dark glass chrysalis erupts uncomfortably from the grasp of two old factory buildings. *Norten* is from Mexico City but this seems more like **Miami**.

[T31] **The Ice House**/originally *Merchants' Refrigerating Co.*, 35-37 N. Moore St., 30-32 Ericsson Pl., bet. Hudson and Varick Sts. 1905. *William H. Bickmire.* Renovations, 1998, *Joseph Pell Lombardi.*

Grand terra-cotta capitals top the entrance façades on North Moore and the vast ghost of St. John's Park (now the tunnel exit ramps). Would that the park were still there. Façades on both N. Moore and Ericsson Place. Worth seeing both.

T41

[T32] **Verizon Building**/ originally **AT&T Long Lines Building**, 32 Sixth Ave., bet. Walker and Lispenard Sts. to Church St. Originally 24 Walker Street Building. 1918. *McKenzie, Voorhees, & Gmelin*. Vast expansion, 1930-1932, *Voorhees, Gmelin & Walker.* Interior (lobby).

High **Art Deco** on an irregular site by one of its New York masters, architect *Ralph Walker,* responsible for New York Telephone's sprinkling of office towers during this period and for nearby Western Union's building as well. The lobbies are worth a special visit.

Tribeca Grand Hotel, 2 Sixth Ave., bet. White and Walker Sts. 2001. John Prince of Hartz Mountain Industries. Built on the long vacant site south of Ralph Walker's old AT&T Longlines Building by an unlikely developer; the Hartz Mountain (birdseed-financed real estate) Architectural Staff did the honors. Las Vegas in Manhattan.

[T33] **White Street**, W. Broadway to Sixth Ave:

No.2. 1808-1809. A **Federal** house (for *Gideon Tucker*), now merely a store propped up by a steel pipe-column. The long-time liquor store became a bar/restaurant called The Liquor Store, and now it's a men's clothing store called, of all things, **The Liquor Store.**

Nos.8-10. 1869-1870. *Henry Fernbach.* Elaborated **Tuscan** columns. Watch for the

T33

T34

neo-Renaissance trick of foreshortening each floor to increase the apparent height.

[T34] Originally **High Pressure Service Headquarters**, NYC Fire Department/later Department of Water Supply, Gas & Electricity, 226 W. Broadway, bet. Franklin and White Sts. W side. 1912. *Augustus D. Shepard, Jr.*

A small gem, sculpted, with a cream-glazed terra-cotta galaxy of Fire Department icons that remind of society's need for water under pressure: hydrants, pipe couplings, valves, and the City's seal. Next door at **228** the eclectic façade rises over **The Bubble Lounge.**

[T35] **218-224 West Broadway** (lofts), NW cor. Franklin St. to Varick St. 1881-1882. *George W. DaCunha.*

The battered rusticated base distinguishes this bold, red brick behemoth, cousin to the **Mohawk Atelier** (see p. 69), and other members of their family, in the great late 19th-century masonry tradition.

[T36] **217-219 West Broadway**, opp. Franklin St. E. Side. 2007. *Cook + Fox.*

Gone is **El Teddy's** restaurant and its giant Statue of Liberty crown perched on the roof, replaced by this six-story condominium. It's sedate and composed, another sign that Tribeca has moved well past both its functional era (factories and warehouses) and its weird era (El Teddy's). But why the fussy, redundant sheets of glass hanging from the window railings? The same architects did great things with glass on their new **Bank of America Tower** at Bryant Park, with shimmering facets and soaring spires.

[T37] **140 Franklin Street**, NW cor. Varick St. 1887. *Albert Wagner.* Altered to condominiums, 1999, *Sanba Inc.*

Cream-colored **Romanesque Revival**. Built for the Walton Company, a manufacturer of wrapping papers. *Wagner's* more famous work was the **Puck Building** at Houston Street.

T37

[T38] **143 Franklin Street** (lofts), bet. Hudson and Varick Sts. 1897-1898. *Henry Anderson.*

An eclectic melange of multicolored brick, limestone, arched and banded. The current tenant is **Urban Archaeology,** an upscale distributor of lighting and bathroom fixtures that are recycled or, sometimes, merely copies.

[T39] **152 Franklin Street** (lofts), bet. Hudson and Varick Sts. N side. 1891. *John B. Snook & Sons.*

Ruddy Romanesque Revival with a grand scale of piers and arches.

[T40] **110 Hudson Street/166 Franklin Street** (lofts), NE cor. Franklin St. 1902-1904. *George Howard Chamberlin.* Converted to residential, ca. 1980.

Savor those rusticated marshmallow columns at the entrance portico of this marvelous **Victorian Baroque** heap.

[T41] Originally **Pierce Building** (lofts)/later **Powell Building**, 105 Hudson St., NW cor. Franklin St. 1892. *Carrère & Hastings*. Extension to N and upward, 1905, *Henri Fouchaux*. Restoration, 2002, *Bone/Levine Architects*.

Renaissance Revival, as triggered by Chicago's 1893 World Columbian Exposition. Actually it's a seven-story, 50-foot-wide corner building, later expanded 25 feet in width and four stories in height. Find the joints in this

Staple Street: T43, T49, T50

Renaissance Revival brick and terra-cotta façade? *New York Times* columnist *Christopher Gray* said: "More engaged columns, giant-order pilasters and other classical details than appear altogether for blocks around."

[T42] **119 Hudson Street**, SW cor. N. Moore St. 1888.

Tasty terra-cotta floral inlays and a sturdy cast iron base with Corinthian capitals.

[T43] Originally **New York Mercantile Exchange**, 6 Harrison St., NW cor. Hudson St. 1884. *Thomas R. Jackson*. Converted to office condominium, 1987, *R. M. Kliment & Frances Halsband*.

An eclectic tower dominates this polychromatic and picturesque ensemble of pressed brick and contrasting granite. Voussoirs of alternating color bring to mind neo-Gothicisms promoted by England's *John Ruskin* or France's *Viollet-le-Duc*.

[T44] **175 West Broadway Building**, between Leonard and Worth Sts. E side. 1877. *Scott & Umbach*. 👁

Corbeled brick, polychromy, and the architects were from Newark?

[T45] **39-41 Worth Street** (lofts), bet. W. Broadway and Church St. N side. 1860. *Samuel A. Warner*.

The first floor has been castrated by a banal "modernization."

[T46] **47 Worth Street** (lofts)/now **New York Law School, Broad Student Center**, bet. W. Broadway and Church St. N side. ca. 1860.

Recently restored to its Corinthian columned cast-iron grandeur. And behind, its new 2009 glassiness opens to Leonard Street through the addition:
[T47] **New York Law School Addition**. 2009. *SmithGroup*, architects.

Facing Con Ed's electrical jungle compound: five stories above ground and four (!) below, with a new library, classrooms, and student center. A glassy tail that seems to wag the Worth Street Dog.

[T48] **Verizon Headquarters**/originally **Western Union Building**, 60 Hudson St., bet. Thomas and Worth Sts., E side to W. Broadway. 1928-1930. *Ralph Walker of Voorhees, Gmelin & Walker*. 👁 Interior (lobby) 👁 Remodeled 2001.

Nineteen shades of brick from brown to salmon form a subtly shaded palette, pierced by

T47   T48

a lobby luxuriant with the undulations of vaulting brickwork. From the deft palette of *Ralph Walker*, little appreciated in the modernist era of the 1950s and 1960s, but with a body of work now re-savored.

[T49] Originally **House of Relief, New York Hospital**/later **U.S. Marine Hospital No.70**, 67 Hudson St., NW cor. Jay St. to Staple St. 1893. *Cady, Berg & See*. Converted to residential, 1985. New entry, 1999. *Audrey Matlock*.
[T50] Originally **Ambulance Annex**, 9 Jay St., NW cor. Staple St. 1907-1908. *Robertson & Potter*.

Originally the Lower Manhattan emergency room of **New York Hospital** (then on West 15th Street near Fifth Avenue). The small building to the west, with the hospital's **NYH** monogram, was the ambulance quarters. There is a charming view of the **Mercantile Exchange** up Staple Street under the bridge. Take a walk up and under.

T55

[T51] **55 Hudson Street** (lofts)/**Washington Market School**, SW cor. Jay St. 1890. *McKim, Mead & White.*

[T52] **165 Duane Street** (lofts), NW cor. Hudson St. overlooking Duane Park. 1881. *Stephen D. Hatch.*

A grand pair of eight- to ten-story bold, red-brick warehouses, cousins to the old **Federal Archives** Building in the West Village. Here gentle segmental arches cap 200 windows.

[T53] **The Mohawk Atelier,** 161 Duane St. NE cor. Hudson St. (or 36 Hudson St.) 1891-1892. *Babcock and Morgan.* Renovated for apartments, 2007, *Joseph Pell Lombardi.*

A handsome **Romanesque Revival** brick and brownstone warehouse with an offbeat cornice and odd new name. Stand on Hudson and note how the façade dips along with the street. Joined to a small 1845 neighbor, the latter originally a whalebone-cutting establishment, which has had its sign repainted: WHALEBONE. Old signs left to fade are more romantic.

[T54] **Duane Park**, bet. Hudson, Duane, and Staple Sts. 1795. Reconstructed, 1940. Reconstructed once more, 1999.

Annetje Jans' farm was near here in 1636, despite WPA carvings on the flagpole base, and included family farmer *Roeloff Jans*, whose widow married a *Bogardus* (one *Bogardus* eventually became the great builder of cast-iron New York). The farm later was sold to *Governor Lovelace*, but the *Duke of York* confiscated it and gave it to Trinity Church. The City purchased it as a public park in 1797 for $5! During the last century or so, the area was a **butter, eggs, and cheese market**.

North (odd) side:

[T55] **171 Duane Street** (lofts), NW cor. Staple St. ca. 1859.

Seemingly monolithic, offbeat cast-iron grey-painted façade for a canopied market building, without a market. Condominiums within, neatness without.

T57

 [T56] **173 Duane Street** (lofts), bet. Greenwich and Staple Sts. N side. 1880. *Babb & Cook.*

A grand brick and terra-cotta **Romanesque Revival** monolith. Note the naturalistic incised terra-cotta archivolts banding its great arches.

South (even) side:

[T57] **Lovinger Cohn Associates**/formerly **World Cheese Co.**, 172 Duane St., bet. Greenwich and Hudson Sts. S side. 1871-1872. *Jacob Weber*, designer. Remodeled, 1994, *V. Polsinelli*.

A modern elegance implanted behind the preserved semi-elliptical cast-iron arches. *Brunelleschi* was handsomely remembered here but so was *Pierre Chareau*, whose **Maison de Verre** in Paris (1931) gave the world its first modernist monument in glass block. Note the curved triangles in the spandrel space between the arches.

[T58] **168 Duane Street** (warehouse), W of Hudson St. opp. Duane Park. S side. 1886. *Stephen D. Hatch.* Converted to residential, 1986, *John T. Fifield Assocs.*

Before commissioning his more flamboyant Washington Street warehouse, developer *Fleming Smith* commissioned *Hatch* for this one, perhaps as a trial run in the neo-Flemish style. After years as an eggpacking and cheese-making plant, it was converted into condominiums.

[T59] **New York City Supreme Court**/formerly lofts, 71 Thomas St., NE cor. W. Broadway. 1865. *Jardine, Hill & Murdock.*

Two-faced and wonderful: noble **Anglo-Italianate** high style on wide West Broadway, austere, minimalist, brick-plain, on industrial, narrow, side street Thomas.

Nestled among a row of houses on the south side of Thomas St., between W.Broadway and Hudson St., was a brothel, wherein occurred the 1836 murder of prostitute Helen Jewett. The trial gripped the City and provoked a frenzy in the newspapers.

[T60] **62 Thomas Street** (lofts), bet. W. Broadway and Church St. S side. 1864.

An unusual **neo-Gothic** cast-iron building happily painted cream (it once was dark brown). We had said (in 1988) that brown was a suitable medieval color. Is white less medieval? Note the polygonal columns. As for the rest, glass and class.

[T61] **The Odeon Restaurant**/originally **The Tower Cafeteria**, 145 W. Broadway, SE cor. Thomas St. 1888. *William Kuhles.* Cafeteria, ca. 1935. Altered into restaurant, 1980, *Lynn Wagenknecht, Brian McNaily, Keith McNally, owner-designers.* **145-147** West Broadway (lofts above Odeon). 1869. *John J. O'Neil.*

A vestige of New York's once ubiquitous streamlined, chrome, wood-paneled, and terrazzo self-service cafeterias, gentrified as a popular, and **pricey**, place. "Interesting enough for NYC historians, sceney enough for the hipsters, and edible enough for gastro-snobs," saith *Dining Out in New York City.* The building above merits a glance: cast iron replicates a quoined stone

T53

wall. And peek around the corner at 70 Thomas Street; an old storefront, with gilded lettering on glass: *rope, yarn, twine.*

PROBABLE: 31-33 Vestry Street Apartments, bet. Greenwich and Hudson Sts. *Winka Dubbeldam of Archi-Tectonics.*

A "luminous" curtain wall, inlaid with bands of light-emitting stone that glow at night, will provide a bit of melodrama amid the masonry lanes of Tribeca.

DOUBTFUL: 56 Leonard Street, bet. Church St. and West Broadway. *Herzog and DeMeuron.*

Fifty-seven stories of stacked cubes, cantilevered lofts that would teeter over the low-rise cast-iron neighborhood. If completed, it would be another step in the transformation of Tribeca into Yuppie Heaven, and a third act in the drama "Manhattan, a Stage Set." Foundations poured, the project is stalled in its tracks. Better H&D at **40 Bond Street** and, for the long-range traveler, the **Birdcage** in Beijing.

NECROLOGY

Originally **Morgan Laing Stores** (warehouses), 258-262 Washington St. and 97 Murray St. NW cor. 1848. *James Bogardus.* Stolen, 1974, 1977. ◆

Landmark for a day. Designated a Landmark in 1970, the Laing Stores, one of the country's earliest prefabricated cast-iron buildings, were carefully dismantled, to be reerected as part of the local Renewal Project. Waiting, someone stole the parts. (They were not trivial items but weighed more than six tons.)

T61

Necrology: El Teddy's

Early examples of building prefabrication, they were stored in a nearby vacant lot to be later re-erected at Borough of Manhattan Community College's new campus. In the dead of a 1974 night, two-thirds of the cast-iron pieces were spirited away. Three years later much of the remainder vanished, this time from a city storehouse. ◆

El Teddy's (restaurant)/formerly **Teddy's Restaurant**, 219 W. Broadway, opp. Franklin St. E side. 1956. *Louis A. Bellini.* Redesigned, 1985, *Antonio Miralda.* Remodeled, 1989, *Christopher Chesmutt.*

The earlier, pinkie-ring Teddy's (reputedly for the gravel-voiced set) reopened as El Internacional while the Statue of Liberty was briefly closed for repair, perhaps explaining artist *Miralda's* 1-1/4-ton replica crown on its roof. The seeming apparition was particularly startling from Franklin Street, as it poked out from above the restaurant's painted, Dalmatian-patterned stone veneer wall (also the artist's idea). Whew!

CIVIC CENTER

Flavor in city life sometimes flowers in the sharp juxtaposition of disparate activities: government, commerce, industry, housing, entertainment; activities populated and managed by differing ethnic and economic groups. The Civic Center's flavor comes from such a bouillabaisse; spreading out from City Hall, its heart, are government offices (federal, state, and city), middle-income and public housing, warehousing, edges of the financial district, **Chinatown**, and that ancient viaduct which made possible New York's consolidation with the City of Brooklyn: the **Brooklyn Bridge**. Here are some of New York's most venerable streets, but only a smattering of the structures that originally formed them remain. Blocks have been consolidated, and larger and larger single projects have consolidated their respective turfs.

Civic Center Walking Tour: From St. Paul's Chapel to Chambers Street and West Broadway,

C2

C3

C4

encompassing City Hall, the old newspaper publishing district, the Municipal Building and Foley Square, and the other cast-iron district (as contrasted with SoHo). START at Broadway and Fulton Street: IRT Lexington Avenue express (Nos.4 or 5 trains) to Fulton Street Station, or any train to Fulton Street or Broadway-Nassau Stations (2, 3, 4, 5, A, C, J, M, N, R, or Z).

[C1] St. Paul's Chapel (Episcopal) and **Churchyard**, Broadway bet. Fulton and Vesey Sts. W side to Church St. 1764-1766. Porch, 1767-1768. Maybe *Thomas McBean.* Tower and steeple, 1794-1796, *James Crommelin Lawrence.*

Manhattan's only extant pre-Revolutionary building. Although the City's present territory contains a dozen older structures, they were isolated farmhouses or country seats that bear no more relation to the City than do still-rural 18th-century houses in outlands surrounding today's metropolis. Unlike **Fraunces Tavern**, St. Paul's is as close to the original as any building

requiring maintenance over 200 years could be. Stone from the site (Manhattan schist) forms walls that are quoined, columned, parapeted, pedimented, porched, and towered in Manhattan's favorite 18th- and 19th-century masonry, brownstone. A gilt weather vane forms a finial to the finial of a tower crowning a "Choragic Monument of Lysicrates" (Hellenistic Greek monument for Renaissance and neo-Renaissance copycats). The graveyard is a green oasis, dappled with sunlight, an umbrella of trees over somber gravestones. Ivy. Squirrels. Lovely. It is rumored that *Pierre L' Enfant*, the soldier-architect who designed the **Federal Hall**, America's first capitol, and laid out the plan for Washington, D.C., designed the golden sunburst (gloire) over the high altar. *Governor Clinton's* and *President Washington's* pews are within.

[C2] New York County Lawyers' Association, 14 Vesey St., bet. Church St. and Broadway. 1929-1930. *Cass Gilbert.*

Subdued white limestone in *Gilbert's* late, fainthearted years. Built almost two decades after he completed the **Woolworth Building** nearby, it is the wimp of the neighborhood, but forms a neutral backdrop for some views of St. Paul's.

[C3] Originally **New York Evening Post Building** (offices)/later Garrison Building, 20 Vesey St., bet. Church St. and Broadway. 1906-1907. *Robert D. Kohn. Gutzon Borglum and Estelle Rumbold Kohn*, sculptors.

The interest here is at the top. *Kohn*, his wife, *Estelle Rumbold Kohn*, and *Borglum* collaborated to create sculptured limestone and copper **Art Nouveau**.

[C4] Federal Office Building, 90 Church St., bet. Vesey and Barclay Sts. W side to W. Broadway. 1935. *Cross & Cross and Pennington, Lewis & Mills, Inc. Lewis A. Simon*, Supervising Architect of the Treasury.

C1

A boring limestone monolith that has trouble deciding between a heritage of stripped-down **neo-Classical** and a new breath of **Art Deco**.

🏛 [C5] **St. Peter's Church (Roman Catholic)**, 22 Barclay St., SE cor. Church St. 1836-1840. *John R. Haggerty and Thomas Thomas.* 📷
A granite **Greek Revival** temple with smooth Ionic columns. The wood-framed pediment and roof structure are sheathed in sheet

metal molded to the appropriate profiles. The oldest site of Catholic worship in New York.

Columbia College (originally King's College) occupied the blocks between West Broadway, Barclay, Church, and Murray Streets. The river's edge was then 250 feet away, approximately at Greenwich Street. In 1857 the college moved north, occupying the former buildings of the deaf and dumb asylum between 49th and 50th Streets, Madison and Park Avenues.

[C6] See "Postponed Births," p.85.

🏛 [C7] **Woolworth Building** (offices), 233 Broadway, bet. Park Place and Barclay St. W side. 1910-1913. *Cass Gilbert.* 📷 Partial interior. 📷 Façade restored, 1977-1981, *Ehrenkrantz Group.*
Once much maligned for its eclectic **Gothic** detail and onetime charcoal Gothic crown, this sheer shaft is one of New York's most imposingly sited skyscrapers. Rising 792 feet without setback, it soars; only the **Seagram** and **CBS**

Buildings have the combination of articulate architecture and massing to achieve similar drama. The lobby is clothed in Skyros veined marble. *Horace Walpole*, who built a Gothic "castle" at "Strawberry Hill" and wrote *The Castle of Otranto* (1765), could have set his action here. The lobby sculpture includes *Woolworth* counting nickels, *Gilbert* holding a model of the building, *Gunwald Aus*, the structural engineer, measuring a girder.

[C8a] **23 Park Place Building** (aka 20 Murray Street), bet. Broadway and Church St. N side. 1856-1857. *Samuel Adams Warner.* 📷
A double store-and-loft building typical of **Tribeca**. Seven bays on Park Place and five bays on Murray.

[C8b] **25 Park Place Building** (aka 22 Murray Street), bet. Broadway and Church St. N side. 1856-1857. *Samuel Adams Warner.* 📷
More *Warner*, here four bays wide instead of three at **No.23**.

C5

C9b

C9a

[C9a] **Home Life Insurance Building annex**/ originally *Postal Telegraph Building*, 253 Broadway, bet. Murray and Warren Sts. W side. 1892-1894. *Harding & Gooch.* 📷
[C9b] Originally **Home Life Insurance Building** (offices), 256-257 Broadway, bet. Murray and Warren Sts. W side. 1892-1894. *Napoleon Le Brun & Son.* 📷
Home Life is a lordly midblock building, with a steep pyramidal top, that was among the world's tallest when it opened. *Pierre*, son of *Napoleon*, was the son-in-charge. **No.253** is a pallid brick annex to the vigorous **No.256**.

[C10] **African Burial Ground and the Commons Historic District.** 📷
The **Commons** served eclectically as pasture, parade ground, and place for celebrations and executions. It harbored at various times powder magazines, an almshouse, and a jail: a venerable palimpsest for what became **New York's first park** (1780s), setting for the new **City Hall** (1802+), and, between Chambers and Duane Streets, the **burial ground** for both slaves and freed Africans.

C7

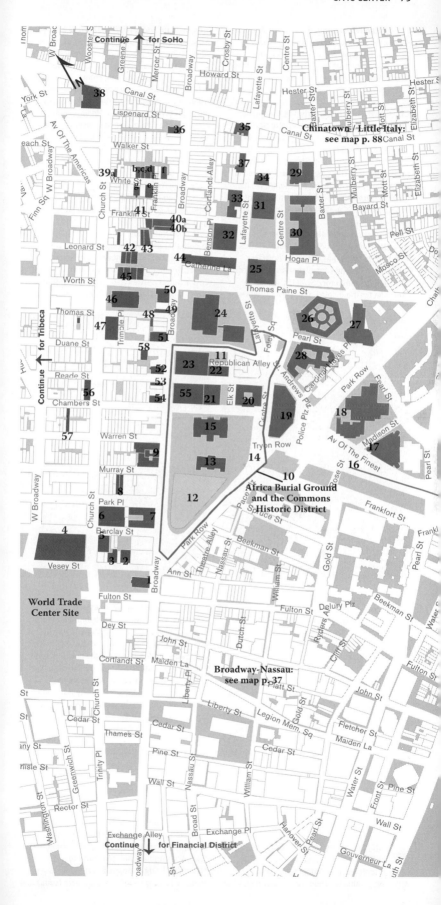

Continue ↑ for SoHo

N

Chinatown / Little Italy:
see map p. 88

Continue ← for Tribeca

Africa Burial Ground
and the Commons
Historic District

World Trade
Center Site

Broadway-Nassau:
see map p. 37

Continue ↓ for Financial District

[C11] **African Burial Ground National Monument**, SW cor. Duane and Elk Sts. 2007. *Rodney Léon.*

Léon's design, chosen in a national competition, is a spiral that evokes the memory of the 20,000 Africans buried in this vicinity in the 17th and 18th centuries.

[C12] **City Hall Park**/formerly **The Commons**, bet. Broadway and Park Row/Centre St., from Vesey/Ann St. to Chambers St. ca. 1730. 🍎

In the early 18th century the City itself extended barely to Fulton Street, when the eastern boundary of The Common was determined by the Boston (or Eastern) Post Road. On its northward trek it spawned other thoroughfares that linked the island's scattered villages and settlements.

Buildings, seemingly for random purposes at random locations, occupied pieces of this turf from time to time. One of special note was **Vanderlyn's Rotunda** (near the southwest corner of Chambers and Centre Streets), a mini-Pantheon for the display of panoramic views,

John Duncan; 1903, *William Martin Aiken*; 1907, 1915, 1917, *Grosvenor Atterbury*; 1956, *Shreve, Lamb & Harmon*; 1998, *Cabrera Barricklo.* 🍎 Interior: entrance, stairs, rotunda and dome. 🍎

A mini-palace, crossing **French Renaissance** detail with **Federal** form, perhaps inevitable where the competition-winning scheme was the product of French architect *Mangin,* and *McComb,* the first native-born New York City architect. *Mangin* (who had worked in Paris with *Gabriel* on the Place de la Concorde) was the principal preliminary designer and theorist; *McComb* supervised construction and determined much of the detailing.

The central domed space leads past the offices of mayor and city councilmen, up twin spiral, self-supporting marble stairs to the Corinthian-columned rotunda serving as entry to both the **City Council Chamber** and the old **Board of Estimate** chambers. The **Governor's Room**, originally for his use when in New York City, is now a portrait gallery replete with portraits by *Sully, Inman, Jarvis, Trumbull,* and

C11   C13

such as that of Versailles, which, in a pre-photography, pre-electronic world simulated the experience of being there very nicely. The biggest guest building was the **Post Office** by *Alfred Mullett,* much maligned at the time; in retrospect it was a rich building inspired by *Napoleon III's* Paris. *Mullett's* more famous, and preserved, building is the **Executive Office Building** in Washington.

Assorted sculpture is also present: **Nathan Hale** (1893. *Frederick MacMonnies,* sculptor; *Stanford White,* architect of the base) is looking into the BMT for his tardy date. **Horace Greeley** (1890. *J. Q. A. Ward*) is grandly seated before the Surrogate's Court.

New events include the replacement of the 1871 *Jacob Wrey Mould* fountain exiled to Crotona Park, and a new fence cast from the one removed to a Bloomingburg, N.Y., cemetery.

[C13] **City Hall**, City Hall Park, bet. Broadway and Park Row. 1802-1812. *Joseph François Mangin* and *John McComb, Jr.* Altered, 1860, *Leopold Eidlitz;* 1898,

others. Interiors have been restored and refurbished, and the exterior peeled off and reproduced in new Alabama limestone (piece by piece). The original soft Massachusetts marble was badly eroded by joint attacks of pollution and pigeons (and the rear of the building had been built in brownstone to save money!).

A bronze tablet in front of City Hall commemorates the construction of the first viable subway system in America: the **IRT** (Interborough Rapid Transit) in 1900.

[C14] **City Hall Station**, IRT Lexington Avenue Line local, below City Hall Park. 1904. *Heins & La Farge.* Not open to the public. 🍎 **Tours in the offing?**

Under City Hall Park, sealed like **King Tut's** tomb, is New York's first, and the world's most beautiful, (former) subway station marking the south edge of the loop that turns the Lexington Avenue IRT locals around from "Brooklyn Bridge" pointed south to "Brooklyn Bridge" pointed north.

Heins & La Farge were the architects (1904) and

no expense was spared for what was, at the time, a highly experimental form of transportation: the station originally included crystal chandeliers and a grand piano! Serious citizens have proposed using these vaulted spaces for a new transit museum. If successful, they will return a glorious civic place to the public.

[C15] Old **New York County Courthouse** ("Tweed" Courthouse)/now **Municipal Offices**, 52 Chambers St., bet. Broadway and Centre St. S side. 1861-1872. *John Kellum and Thomas Little*. Enlarged, 1877-1891, *Leopold Eidlitz*. Interior restorations, 1990s, *John Waite*.

A building both maligned and praised: maligned mostly because of the great scandal in its construction (the **Tweed Ring** apparently made off with $10 million of the $14 million construction "cost"); praised because of a new understanding of, and interest in, **Victorian** architecture: perhaps a late **Victorian** version of an English Renaissance country house.

C15

[C16] **Brooklyn Bridge**/originally New York & Brooklyn Bridge, Park Row, Manhattan, to Adams St., Brooklyn. 1867-1883. *John A., Washington and Emily Roebling*.

A saunter across the raised central boardwalk to **Brooklyn Heights** is one of the great dramatic strolls of New York. As a side tour from City Hall, it is a unique experience, viewing Brooklyn, Manhattan, their skylines, and the harbor through a filigree of cables. The steel and cables have been repainted their original sprightly colors—beige and light brown—instead of the somber battleship gray that gloomed for a misguided generation.

Required reading before, during, or after a stroll over the bridge: *David McCullough's* **The Great Bridge** (1972). Never have the ins and outs of design, construction, client meetings, and materials specifications (an entire chapter devoted to the selection of No.8 gauge wire!) been written with such urgency and all the page-turning drama of a suspense (or suspension) thriller.

"Brooklyn Bridge, which is old, . . . is as strong and rugged as a gladiator, while George Washington Bridge, built yesterday, smiles like a young athlete. In this case the two large Gothic towers of stone are very handsome because they are American and not ' Beaux-Arts.' They are full of native sap . . ."
—*Charles Edouard Jeanneret (Le Corbusier)* **When the Cathedrals Were White**, 1947

[C17] **Murry Bergtraum High School**, 411 Pearl St., S cor. Madison St. to Avenue of the Finest. 1976. *Gruzen & Partners*.

A sleek, purple-brown triangular "fort," complete with corner turrets, financed through the **Educational Construction Fund** (a sometime experiment in school financing, now defunct), by the overwhelming telephone building next door. (The air rights of the school provide zoning credit for the telephone building; the latter, in return, pays off the bonds that built the school.)

[C18] **NYC Police Headquarters**, bet. Park Row, Pearl St., and Avenue of the Finest. 1973. *Gruzen & Partners*, architects. *M. Paul Friedberg*, landscape architect.

One of New York's most urbane civic buildings since the City Hall of 1812, largely because

C16

of its elegant—but ill-maintained—plaza, stepped pedestrian passageways, and terraces that form an interlock for pedestrians in this otherwise car-infested area. An orange/brown brick cube of office space hovers over special police facilities below. **Five in One**, a sculpture by *Bernard (Tony) Rosenthal* in self-weathering (consciously rusty) steel, looms over the Municipal Building end.

[C19] **Municipal Building**, Centre St., opp. Chambers St. E side. 1907-1914. *William M. Kendall and Burt Fenner of McKim, Mead & White*. Façade restoration, 1990, *Wank Adams Slavin*.

This is urbane architecture, boldly straddling a city street. In those days the ways of traffic were entwined with architecture (see *Warren & Wetmore's* **Grand Central Terminal** of 1913). The "Choragic Monument" atop this composition is, in turn, surmounted by Civic Fame by *Adolph A. Weinman*. For *Guastavino* tile fans, move under the arcaded south wing (over the subway entrance). Look up.

[C20] **Surrogate's Court**/originally Hall of Records, 31 Chambers St., bet. Centre and Elk Sts. N side. 1899-1907. *John Rochester Thomas and Horgan & Slattery.* ☛ Interior. ☛

Civic monuments were designed to impress the citizen in those days—not merely humor him, as is most often the case today. Therefore his records were kept in a place of splendor. Go in. The central hall, in a small way, is worthy of *Charles Garnier's* earlier **Paris Opera**.

[C21] Originally **Emigrant Industrial Savings Bank Building**, 51 Chambers St., bet. Broadway and Elk St. N side to Reade St. 1908-1912. *Raymond F. Almirall.* ☛ Interior. ☛

Emigrant (originally founded for Irish-Americans) was once America's wealthiest savings bank: **Beaux Arts** and **Art Nouveau**, it is now used by the City's bureaucracy. Ranks of copper oriels line the light courts and spirited sculptures top each wing. *Almirall*'s ornament came from **Vienna**, not **Dublin**.

C23

C22

C25

[C22] **NYC Department of City Planning**, 22 (formerly 14, 16, 18, 20, 22) Reade St., bet. Elk St. and Broadway. N side. No.14, 1878. Nos.16, 18, 20, 22, ca. 1858. Restored, 1987, *NYC Department of General Services Architectural Division.* ☛

The **Department of City Planning** and its commissioners moved in 1987 to this landmarked row of six-story, 19th-century business buildings. Preservation prevailed.

[C23] **Federal Offices**, 290 Broadway, NE corner Reade St. 1994. *Hellmuth, Obata & Kassabaum (HOK).*

The **postmodernists** have quietly arrived: quietly, as most of the spectacle is at the top, to be seen from afar, and the streetscape seems a pleasant reprise of the Rockefeller Center era with polished brass and granite.

Foley Square

Big Tom's Square: This once chaotic irregular subdivided excuse for a public space has been graciously upgraded, its center space delivered to the pedestrian as **Thomas Paine Park**. An installation, **Garden for the Accused**, (2006. *Dennis Oppenheim*) was resident from 2006 to the present.

Named for *Thomas F. ("Big Tom") Foley* (1852-1925), an alderman, sheriff, saloonkeeper, Tammany Hall district leader, and political mentor of Governor *Alfred E. Smith*. The square, site of Big Tom's last saloon, was named for him by his successors on the Board of Aldermen (1926).

Around the unsquare square are gathered many noble Civic Center structures. Clockwise around the square from the west:

[C24] **Jacob K. Javits Federal Office Building and Court of International Trade** (Customs Court), 26 Federal Plaza, Foley Sq. bet. Duane and Worth Sts. W side. 1963-1969. *Alfred Easton Poor, Kahn & Jacobs, Eggers & Higgins*, associate architects. Western addition on Broadway 1975-1977, *Kahn & Jacobs, The Eggers Partnership, Poor & Swanke*. New plaza landscaping, 1997, *Martha Schwartz*.

The building: an ungainly checkerboard of granite and glass built along Foley Square, was later extended westward to Broadway with a continuing heavy hand. The tranquil work of *Martha Schwartz* has succeeded the vibrant sculpture of *Richard Serra*. Fortunately the benches and sculpted mounds of grass are a happy event. Serenity replaces passion.

C26

[C25] **Health, Hospitals, and Sanitation Departments Building**/originally **NYC Department of Health Building**, 125 Worth St., bet. Lafayette and Center Sts. N side to Leonard St. 1935. *Charles B. Meyers.*

Aside from intriguing spandrel ornament and bas-reliefs on this boxy **neo-Classical/Art Deco** cube, the connoisseur can inspect the finely crafted pairs of anthropomorphic bronze Art Deco torchères flanking the main entrance. Mmmmm, luscious!

[C26] **New York State Supreme Court**/ originally **New York County Courthouse**, 60 Centre St., bet. Pearl St., Hamill Place, and Worth St. in Foley Sq. E side. 1913-1927. *Guy Lowell.* ☛ Interior. ☛

Lowell's hexagon won a 1912 competition (WWI put off completion until 1927). The imposing **Corinthian** portico is handsome **Roman** archaeology, but doesn't measure up to the vigorous forms of the building in plan. Grand to view from above, its circular central space is surrounded by the hexagon, light courts intervening between.

[C27] **U.S. Courthouse Annex**, behind New York County Courthouse, 500 Pearl St. bet. Worth St. and Park Row. 1995. *Kohn Pedersen Fox Associates.*

Concave and convex, recessed and bellied out: two mannerisms of the current crop of new Federal Buildings that fall short of the urbane **Rockefeller Center** crowd.

[C28] **Thurgood Marshall United States Courthouse**, 40 Centre St., SE cor. Pearl St., in Foley Sq. E side. 1933-1936. *Cass Gilbert and Cass Gilbert, Jr.* 🍎

Giant **Corinthian** columns stand at attention in this dour granite Roman façade fronting Foley Square. Above, the tower is capped by a *Gilbert* gold pyramid in the manner of his **New York Life Insurance Company Building**; this was *Gilbert, Sr.'s* last building.

C27

Critic *Lewis Mumford* (in a 1934 *New Yorker*) deemed it "the supreme example of pretentiousness, mediocrity, bad design and fake grandeur." Now a major landmark. How times change.

The Northern Civic Center:

[C29] **White Street Correctional Facility**, NYC Department of Correction, bet. Centre and Baxter Sts. N side to Walker St. 1989. *Urbahn Assocs., Inc.* and *Litchfield-Grosfeld Assocs.*, joint venture.

High-rise maximum-security detention for 500 inmates, rising from a base of little shops, a community clock, and a bridge of sighs connecting to the **Tombs**. Tootsie Rolls?

[C30] **"The Tombs," NYC Criminal Courts Building and Men's House of Detention**, 100 Centre St., bet. Leonard and White Sts. E side to Baxter St. 1939. *Harvey Wiley Corbett and Charles B. Meyers.* House of Detention redesigned, 1986, *The Gruzen Partnership.*

The **Tombs**, was named after its Egyptian Revival, long-gone, twice-over ancestor (that lived across the street). This is a ziggurated construction overlaid with stylish detail of the 1930s: **Art Moderne**, as at the Paris Exposition of 1937. The redesign is largely within.

[C31] **Civil Courthouse, City of New York**, 111 Centre St., SW cor. White St. 1960. *William Lescaze and Matthew Del Gaudio.*

Late *Lescaze* (see his uptown house): a sleek, but dull, cube fills the site facing an open plaza, site of the old Tombs building, and under which the City has concealed the area's air-conditioning equipment. Bas-reliefs by *William Zorach.*

C28

[C32] **Family Court, City of New York**, 60 Lafayette St., bet. Leonard and Franklin Sts. 1975. *Haines, Lundberg & Waehler.* Remodeled and reclad, 2006, *Mitchell Giurgola.*

Upgrading and rebirth: it was black granite, polished and pretentious, more than somber. What message did this building send to families entering with problems? But **Death Star** has been reborn, its new light granite cladding providing a relief so great that we can forgive the heavy handed forms inherited.

[C33] **Ahrens Building**, 70 Lafayette St., bet. Franklin and White Sts. W side. 1894-1896. *George H. Griebel.* 🍎

Smooth and stylish Romanesque Revival brick archwork, counterpointed with metal-clad polygonal oriels. And with polychromy à la *John Ruskin*, akin to his mode of **"modern medievalism."**

[C34] Originally **Engine Company No.31**, NYC Fire Department/now **Downtown Community Television Center**, 87 Lafayette St., NE cor. White St. 1895. *Napoleon LeBrun & Sons.* ●🍎

A house for fire engines, disguised as a **Loire Valley château**, now reincarnated as a civic center, it remains in its ball costume.

Cast-Iron District 1 (South of Canal Street)
Cast iron gave an inexpensive means of reproducing elaborate detail, previously possible

C30

only as carving in stone. More Corinthian, Ionic, Doric, Composite, Egyptian, and Lord-knows-what-else columns were cast for New York façades of the 1850s and 1860s than Greece and Rome turned out in a millenium. The two great centers were between Broadway and West Broadway, Canal to Duane (here and in **Tribeca** *described), and in* **SoHo** *to the north from Crosby Street to West Broadway, and Canal to Houston Streets.*

These handsome loft spaces have been used by assorted commercialdom, principally for warehousing, sometimes for light manufacturing, often for studios by the neighborhood's many real or would-be artists, and finally by only those wealthy enough to afford them.

[C35] **254-260 Canal Street** (lofts), SW cor. Lafayette St. 1857. Cast-iron façades attributed to *James Bogardus.* Converted to offices, 1987, *Jack L. Gordon.* ●🍎

One of the City's earliest surviving cast-iron façades. If in fact the castings are by *Bogardus*, this would be the largest and most important of his extant works. **Breathtaking!**

[C36] **415 Broadway**/originally **National City Bank of New York**, bet. Canal and Lispenard Streets. 1927. *Walker & Gillette.* Remodeled, 1998, *Joseph Pell Lombardi.*

Art Moderne. 1812 on the upper façade is not the date of construction (good grief!), but when the Bank was founded. Critic *Lewis Mumford* noted, in a 1928 *New Yorker*: "The note of modernism pervades this structure... and is splendidly successful."

[C37] **Avildsen Building**, 94-100 Lafayette Street, SW cor. Walker St. 1907-1910. *Howells & Stokes.* ●🍎

Howells and Stokes again. When did *Stokes* (*Isaac Newton Phelps Stokes*) have time for his *Iconography of Manhattan Island*, those six magnificent volumes of the history of New York before the 1898 consolidation with Brooklyn, and expansion?

[C38] **Canal Street Post Office**, 350 Canal St., SW cor. Canal and Church Sts. 1937. *Alan Balch Mills.*

C32   C33

C35

Art Moderne. The articulated inset bay-windows on Church Street are a wonderful mannerism (often used in late 19th-century architecture). They give the illusion of scanning the street north and south, and add plasticity to the building.

White Street, bet. Church St. and Broadway:

[C39a] **"Let There Be Neon."** No.36. Formerly on West Broadway, a shop that elevates neon to an art form. [C39b] Formerly **Woods Mercantile Building**. Nos.46-50. 1865. ●🍎 A set of marble buildings organized by their pediment.
[C39c] **No.52.** Tuscan columns, segmental arches.
[C39d] **Nos.54-56.** Italianate brownstone over the cast-iron ground floor.
[C39e] **Condict Store** (saddlery). Nos.55-57. 1861. *John Kellum & Son.* ●🍎 Another **Daniel D. Badger** Architectural Iron Works project, unhappily with a mutilated ground floor.
[C39f] **Nos.60-66.** 1869. Crisp white piers and cornices.

C39f

C39e

C40a, No.362

[C39g] **Congregation Shaare Zedek** (Civic Center Synagogue), 49 White St., bet. Church St. and Broadway. S side. 1965-1967. *William N. Breger Assocs.*

Interrupting the street frontage, **Shaare Zedek** unrolls a ribbon of undulating marble tiles to reveal a garden behind: unhappily (due to modern security needs) barred from the passerby by wrought-iron fencing.

[C40a] Originally **James S. White Building**, 361 Broadway, SW cor. Franklin St. 1881-1882. *W. Wheeler Smith*. Renovations, 2000, *Joseph Pell Lombardi*. 🍎

A corner building with two intersecting late cast-iron façades. Catercorner, across the street at **362**, are some resident stern-eyed **Classical** caryatids (breastplates attached) holding up the third floor.

[C40b] Originally **Thompson's Saloon,** 359 Broadway, between Franklin and Leonard Sts. W side. 1852. *Field & Correja.* 🍎

Brady's Gallery occupied the upper three floors. *Abraham Lincoln* came here to be photographed the morning after his famed Cooper Union speech, which many believe won him the presidency. **Italianate**.

[C41] **Franklin Street**, bet. Church St. and Broadway. 1860s.

More white, brown, and simulated (cast-iron) stone. Savor the **Corinthian** capitals, the glassy windows, the rich and variegated variations on a theme. Until recently a tired but elegant block, it is now blossoming with paint and washed windows. It is said that *Renwick and Co.* did **No.71** (not much glory for *Renwick* here). **Nos.86-88** make a rich stone and cast-iron set.

[C42] **Leonard Street**, bet. Church St. and Broadway. 1860s.

Limestone (white), brownstone, and cast iron. The game is to look to separate them: the iron tends to be more slender than the brittle stone. For cast iron at **No.85**, see below; **Nos.87-89** (1860-1863) are similar but simpler, and of stone, matching *Bogardus'* cast iron; **Nos.80-82**. 1860-1862. *James H. Giles*; **Nos.74-78** Leonard. 1860s. Grand **Corinthian** capitals; **No.73**. 1864. *James F. Duckworth*; **No.71**. 1860. *Samuel A. Warner*.

[C43] Originally **Kitchen, Montross & Wilcox Store**, 85 Leonard St., bet. Church St. and Broadway. 1861. *James Bogardus.* 🍎

Sperm-candle style (a new classification for the cocktail-party preservationist) provides two-story cast-iron columns emulating candles. The fire escapes mask much of the guts of this rare *Bogardus* remnant.

C40b

C42

[C44] Originally **New York Life Insurance Company Building**/now **New York City Municipal Offices**, 346 Broadway, bet. Catherine Lane and Leonard St. E side to Lafayette St. (originally Elm St.) Also known as 108 Leonard St. E end, 1894-1899. *Stephen D. Hatch with McKim, Mead & White*. Broadway end, *Stanford White of McKim, Mead & White*. Various interior spaces. 🍎

New York Life occupied the Broadway end of this block from 1870. *Hatch*, engaged to design an eastern addition, died (1894) before construction was completed. *MM&W* joined in the completion of the addition, and went on to demolish the Broadway structure and design its successor; especially noteworthy is its wonderful **Classical** clock overlooking Broadway.

[C45] **65-85 Worth Street** (lofts), bet. Church St. and Broadway. N side. ca. 1865.

This handsome remnant row of **neo-Renaissance** whitestone buildings once faced a fabulous cast-iron row, replaced by **AT&T** below.

[C46] Originally **American Telephone & Telegraph Company Long Lines Building**, Church St. bet. Thomas and Worth Sts. E side. 1974. *John Carl Warnecke & Assocs.*

A giant electronic complex in the guise of a building. Pink, textured (flame-treated) Swedish granite sheathes a stylish leviathan that looms over the City with architectural eyebrows. The only bow to the neighboring humanity is a bleak plaza to the east. Ma Bell, why didn't you leave the air for people and place your electrons underground?

[C47] **NYS Insurance Fund** (offices), 199 Church St., bet. Thomas and Duane Sts. E side to Trimble Place. 1955. *Lorimer Rich Assocs.*

A white glazed-brick monolith atop a polished red granite base. The funky flaring stainless-steel entrance canopy is a dated 1950s relic. Retro-unchic?

[C48] **8 Thomas Street Building**/formerly *David S. Brown Store*, bet. Broadway and Church St. S side. 1875-1876. *J. Morgan Slade.* 🍎

C43

C45

An elaborate confection of **Romanesque, Venetian Gothic**, brick, sandstone, granite, and cast-iron parts, worthy of *John Ruskin*, whose medieval-revival polemics inspired such delicacies as this and the Jefferson Market Courthouse.

[C49] Originally **Metropolitan Life Insurance Company Home Office**, 319 Broadway, NW cor. Thomas St. 1869-1870. *David & John Jardine.* 🍎

More of the Daniel D. Badger Architectural Iron Works, "Good Works" stands as a sentinel marking the entrance of Thomas Street. Very elaborate, this is a cast-iron building with grand style. The **New York Life Insurance Company** began in rented rooms in this structure before graduating to 346 Broadway above.

[C50] **325-333 Broadway**, SW cor. Worth St. 1863-1864. 🍎

Marble Renaissance-revival for a conservative developer who cared not for the radical cast-iron.

C49

[C54] **Broadway Chambers Building** (offices), 277 Broadway, NW cor. Chambers St. 1899-1900. *Cass Gilbert.* 🖤

Renaissance Revival in granite, brick, and limestone. Crowned with an arcade and cornice including heads of ladies and lions. Gilbert was fascinated with architectural sculpture. (His own image is in the Woolworth Building lobby and the Supreme Court pediment in Washington.)

[C55] **NYC Department of Building Offices**/280 Broadway/onetime **Sun Building**/originally **A. T. Stewart Dry Goods Store No.1**, NE cor. Chambers St. 1845-1846. *John B. Snook of Joseph Trench & Co.* Additions: 1850-1851, 1852-1853, *Trench & Snook*; 1872, *Frederick Schmidt*; 1884, *Edward D.Harris.* 🖤 Rehabilitation, 1999, *Beyer Blinder Belle.*

Here *Stewart* founded America's first great department store, later to occupy grand premises at Broadway between 9th and 10th Streets (known to recent generations as **Wanamaker's**, who bought out all of *Stewart*'s enterprises).

C51   C52

C53

🏠 [C51] **Langdon Building** (lofts), 305 Broadway, NW cor. Duane St. 1892-1894. *William H. Hume.*

Clustered **Romanesque Revival** piers embrace colonnettes with ornamented capitals, equal to the natural incised bas-reliefs of *Louis Sullivan.*

[C52] **East River Savings Institution Building**, 291 Broadway, NW cor. Reade St. 1910-1911. *Clinton & Russell.*

Corinthian pilasters support an impressive entablature, the frieze alternating windows and cartouches, in the space where metopes and triglyphs were placed in Classical temples.

[C53] **287 Broadway** (lofts), SW cor. Reade St. 1871-1872. *John B. Snook.* 🖤 The most succulent cast-iron street-show in all New York: a glassy, mansarded, wrought-iron-crested, **Ionic**- and **Corinthian**-columned delight. Lovely! 51 Corinthians, 17 Doric. Count them.

Henry James and *Anthony Trollope* both lavished words of wonder on these premises. Later the **Sun** (newspaper) was published here. The corner **clock**, long frozen, was brought to life by the indefatigable campaigning of the late *Margot Gayle.*

[C56] **Cary Building** (lofts), 105-107 Chambers St., NW cor. Church St. to Reade St. 1856-1857. *King & Kellum.* Cast-iron façade by *D.D. Badger's Architectural Ironworks.* Storefronts altered, 1985, *Grandesign Architects.* 🖤

This **Anglo-Italianate** palazzo reflects the talents of *John Kellum*, who later designed some of the City's finest cast-iron structures, including the full-block **A. T. Stewart Store** (at its end called **Wanamaker's**, destroyed by fire in 1960?). Construction of the **Cary** heralded establishment of a commercial center north and west of City Hall in the mid-19th century. Once a mid-block structure, it has boasted an inadvertent east façade ever since Church Street was widened for the IND subway in the late 1920s.

[C57] **Swift, Seaman & Company Building**, 122 Chambers St., 52 Warren St. bet. Broadway and Church Sts. 1857-1858. 🍎

Extraordinary carvings float above window cornices, swags and shells, all in pale sandstone.

[C58] Formerly **Fire Engine Company No.7/Hook & Ladder Company No.1**/now **Hook & Ladder Company No.1 and Fire Department Bureau of Fire Communication,**

C55

C57

C56

100 Duane St., bet. Church St. and Broadway. 1904-1905. *Trowbridge & Livingston.* 🍎

An Anglicized palazzo in banded brick and rusticated limestone; a stylish stable for fire engines.

Colonnaded block: Look carefully at the storefronts surrounding the block bounded by West Broadway and Reade, Duane, and Church Streets, and you'll discover along the ground floor a series of fluted Corinthian cast-iron columns carrying the masonry façades of the upper floors. Some are asphyxiated with modern materials or just hidden behind unwashed show windows, but they are there. What a wonderful contribution to the urbanity of this rediscovered district as they become revealed!

POSTPONED BIRTHS

[C6] **99 Church Street Tower**, bet. Barclay St. and Park Place. *Robert A.M. Stern.*

Buddying up to and peering over the neighboring Woolworth Building, *Stern's* slender tower dreamed of being the tallest tower of housing (80 stories) in New York. Delayed, with only the foundation completed.

5 Franklin Place, 369-371 Broadway, bet. Franklin and White Sts. 2009. *Ben van Berkel of UN Studio.*

The Dutch were here first on this crazy little island, but the talented *van Berkel* has had little luck in getting projects built here. This mid-block glowing red wine bottle of a building was heavily advertised, but only a few steel columns were erected before the weakening economy put the cork back in the project.

NECROLOGY

"Tilted Arc," 1981, *Richard Serra*, sculptor. Removed 1990s.

The sculpture: a pre-rusted 75-ton steel work rested on the building's Foley Square plaza, becoming the subject of contention when added as part of a federal 5% set-aside-for-art program. *Opponents* cried: "A symbol of artistic noblesse oblige." *Serra:* "This newly created concave volume has a silent amplitude which amplifies your awareness of yourself and the sculptural field of the space." A great work, but the philistines won that round.

Moody's Office Building, 99 Church Street, bet. Barclay St. & Park Pl. 1930s.

Demolished for "greater things," a soaring tower by *Robert A.M. Stern* that will be back-to-back with *Frank W. Woolworth's* grand gesture.

Suerken's Restaurant, 27 Park Place, NE cor. Church St.

Fordham University, City Hall Division/formerly **Vincent [Astor] Building,** 302 Broadway, SE cor. Duane St. 1899. *George B. Post.*

Sixteen terra-cotta-trimmed stories demolished to make way for an ill-fated project: a gargantuan municipal office building to accommodate the ever expanding bureaucracy.

H. Bowker & Company (lofts), 101-103 Duane St., bet. Broadway and Church Sts. N side. 1870. *Thomas Little.*
317 Broadway (lofts), SW cor. Thomas St. 1865.
10-12 Thomas Street (lofts), bet. Broadway and Church Sts. S side. 1870. *Thomas Little.*
64-66 Thomas Street (lofts), bet. Church St. and W. Broadway. S side. 1867.
43-45 Worth Street (lofts), bet., Church St. and W. Broadway. N side. 1860. *S. A Warner.*
54 Worth Street (lofts), bet. Broadway and Church Sts. S side ca. 1860. *William Field & Son.*
58-60 Worth Street (lofts), bet. Broadway and Church Sts. S side. 1869. *Griffith Thomas.* Rebuilt, 1879, *J. Morgan Slade.*

L3

L4

While the cast-iron columned façade remains behind a layer of 1980s glitz, the old-fashioned German eatery itself, of darkened wood, stained glass, and tiled floor, is no more. Gone also are the hearty sauerbraten and dumplings, the bauernwurst, sauerkraut, and hot mustards, and those steins of beer . . . lots of beer.

Pedestrian walkway, Brooklyn Bridge, City Hall Park, Manhattan, to Cadman Plaza, Brooklyn. 1883. *Washington Roebling.*

The original pedestrian walks, at the bridge's edge, were relocated to the center, where originally there had been a Manhattan to Brooklyn trolley. The walkway, interrupted at the pairs of anchorages and towers by stairs, provided one of the most carefully modulated, peacefully exhilarating, and spiritually invigorating walks in the City. It has been replaced by a predictable, continuous ramp that often becomes a high-speed bikeway, courtesy of the New York City Department of Transportation.

66-68 Worth Street (lofts), bet. Broadway and Church Sts. S side. ca. 1870.

Cast-iron "gray ghosts" that are now truly ghosts: the ones on Worth and Thomas Streets lost to AT&T's Long Lines tower.

END of Civic Center Tour. The nearest subways are along Chambers Street: IRT Seventh Avenue Line at West Broadway, and IND Eighth Avenue Line at Church Street.

CHINATOWN / LITTLE ITALY

In most large American cities Chinese have formed enclaves that are sought by tourists and relished by city dwellers with an appetite for China's diverting cuisines. Since the 1840s New York's Chinatown has traditionally been centered in the eight blocks encircled by Canal, Worth, and Mulberry Streets and the Bowery/Chatham Square. In the early 1970s Chinese began to push out the enclave's historic boundaries, although Mott Street below Canal, lined with popular places to dine and shop, remains Chinatown's Main Street. Chinese expansion is evident in every direction, dissipating the Italianness of Little Italy and replacing with Chinese ideographs the Yiddish signs that were once ubiquitous along East Broadway to the Forward Building and beyond. Except for Confucius Plaza and the Manhattan Bridge, the area east of Chatham Square and the Bowery is covered in the Lower East Side.

The Five Points

The 19th century's most notorious enclave, named from the multi-intersection at Worth and Baxter Streets (still there) with Park Street (covered over long ago). Five Points was cradled in a natural bowl of land, built largely on quagmire where the fetid Collect Pond had been filled in with dirt from leveled Bunker Hill (just to the north of what is now Bayard Street).

By the 1850s Five Points had become a crossroads for an emerging African-American community and epicenter of Irish and Italian immigrant populations. Also the most dangerous city precinct, it was rife with murder and mayhem. The Democratic Tammany Hall machine was born here, and here Catholics first gained a foothold in politics and commerce.

The infamous old neighborhood was nearly erased in the early 20th century, as Centre Street became the center of city government, but

L1

Park Row: *Toward Chatham Square*

[L1] **Chatham Towers** (apartments), 170 Park Row, bet. Park Row and Worth St. N side. 1965. *Kelly & Gruzen*.
  Sculpted concrete: as with all strong architectural statements, Chatham Towers rouses great admiration and great criticism.

[L2] **Chatham Green** (apartments), 185 Park Row, bet. Pearl St. and St. James Place. S side to Madison St. 1961. *Kelly & Gruzen*.
  A great undulating wall: open-access galleries served by vertical circulation towers were designed after *Barney Gruzen* visited *Alfonso Reidy's* undulating slabs at Pedregulho in Rio de Janeiro. But *Reidy's* slabs undulated to follow contours. Here lay a pancake. Did we say it was flat?

enticing fragments remain, especially northeast of the intersection of Worth and Baxter:

[L3] **Columbus Park**, bounded by Worth, Mulberry, Baxter, and Bayard Sts.
  This park and playground replaced shadowy and decrepit **Mulberry Bend**, the most notorious block in the Five Points. *Jacob Riis* drew public attention to the deplorable conditions here in his groundbreaking book, *How the Other Half Lives*, and lobbied long and hard to convince the City to raze the block. They finally did, in 1895.

[L4] Originally **Banca A. Cuneo & Co.**, 28 Mulberry St, SE corner of Mosco St. 1888.
  Currently a funeral parlor, this was one of the principal banks forming "Italian Wall Street" along Mulberry in the hey day of the Five Points. Of the dozens of banks, or *padroni*, only two remain: this and **Banca Stabile** at Mulberry and Grand.
  The **padroni** were much more than cash depositories. Immigrants could send and

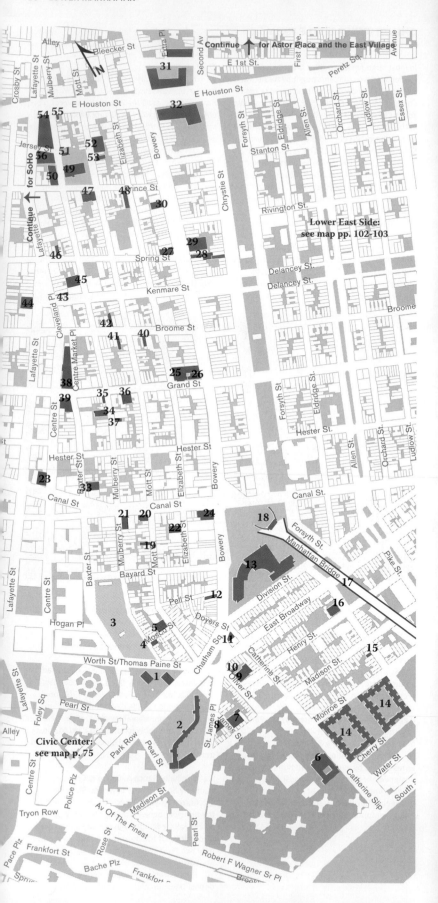

Alley
Bleecker St
N
Crosby St
Lafayette St
Mulberry St
Mott St
Extra Pl
31
Second Av
First Ave.
Avenue
Continue ↑ for Astor Place and the East Village
E 1st St.
Peretz Sq.

E Houston St
E Houston St

54 55
32
Jersey St
51 52
56
53
50 49
Lafayette St
for SoHo
47
48
Prince St
30
Contique ← for SoHo
Lafayette St
46
27 29
Spring St 28
45
Cleveland Pl
43
44
Centre Market Pl
42
41 40
Broome St
38
25 26
Grand St
39
35 36
Centre St
34
37
Hester St
Hester St
23
Baxter St
33
Mulberry St
Mott St
Elizabeth St
Bowery
Canal St
Canal St
Canal St
21 20
24
22
19
18
Mulberry St
Mott St
Elizabeth St
Bowery
Forsyth St
Manhattan Bridge
13
17
Bayard St
12
Pell St
Division St
16
3
5
Doyers St
East Broadway
15
4
Chatham Sq
11
10 9
Catherine St
Henry St
Madison St
14
Worth St/Thomas Paine St
1
10 9
Oliver St
Monroe St
Civic Center:
see map p. 75
2
8 7
St. James Pl
James St
14
Cherry St
Pearl St
Foley Sq
6
Catherine Slip
Alley
Park Row
Madison St
Water St
South S
Lafayette St
Centre St
Police Plz
Tryon Row
Av Of The Finest
Pace Plz
Frankfort St
Rose St
Robert F Wagner Sr Pl
Bache Plz
Frankfort
Broadway

Forsyth St
Chrystie St
Stanton St
Eldridge St
Allen St.
Orchard St
Ludlow St
Essex St.
Rivington St.
Delancey St.
Delancey St.
Broome
Lower East Side:
see map pp. 102-103
Forsyth St.
Eldridge St.
Hester St.
Allen St.
Orchard St.
Ludlow St.
Canal St.
Pike St.

receive mail from back home, buy railroad tickets, and find work. *Antonio Cuneo* was one of the most prominent of these bankers, and it is a small miracle that his bank (and home) survives. Unremarkable overall architecturally, **except — what an entrance**: a miniature Greek temple at the corner, complete with columns, pediments, cherubs, plaques, and a crouching eagle! That doorway, and the sound of Italian voices within, were irresistible to the lonesome immigrant.

Walk up tiny Mosco Street, the last remaining fragment of former Park Street, one of the three intersecting streets that formed the Five Points. Note that you are walking uphill. The depression that the Five Points nestled within is still very much there, topographically if not economically.

[L5] **Church of the Transfiguration (Roman Catholic)**/originally **Zion English Lutheran Church**, 25 Mott St., NW cor. Mosco St. 1801. 🍎

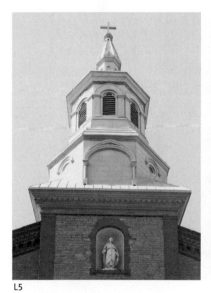

L5

Like **Sea and Land**, a Georgian church with Gothic (small-paned double-hung) windows; here they are composed with Gothic tracery. Dressed Manhattan schist makes neat building blocks, with brownstone detail. The octagonal tower, copper sheathed, is from the 1860s. Transfiguration became a Catholic parish in 1853, and served the Five Points neighborhood throughout its most infamous decades. Thousands of Irish and Italian immigrants were married, baptized, and eulogized here. Today it serves a mostly Chinese congregation, and mass is said in Mandarin, Cantonese, and English.

East of St. James Place (formerly New Bowery):

[L6] **Public School 126, The Jacob Riis School**, and Alfred E. Smith Recreation Center, 80 Catherine St., bet. Cherry and Monroe Sts. W side. 1966. *Percival Goodman.*

A neatly articulated school and community recreation center, within the **Governor Smith Houses** site. Both are aging prematurely.

[L7] **St. James Church (Roman Catholic)**, 32 James St., bet. St. James Place and Madison St. E side. 1835-1837. Maybe *Minard Lafever.* 🍎

Brownstone Greek Revival Doric saved by the Ancient Order of Hibernians (Catholic Irish in America). Distyle (two columns) in antis (between flanking blank walls). Compare it with Mariners' Temple below, built almost a decade later.

[L8] **First Shearith Israel Graveyard**, 55 St. James Place, bet. Oliver and James Sts. S side. 1656-1833. 🍎

The only man-made remnant of Manhattan's 17th century, this bears the remains of Sephardic Jews (of Spanish-Portuguese extraction) who emigrated from Brazil in the mid-1600s.

[L9] **Mariners' Temple** (Baptist)/formerly **Oliver Street Baptist Church**, 12 Oliver St., NE cor. Henry St. 1844-1845. Perhaps *Isaac Lucas.* 🍎

L7

A stone, Greek Revival Ionic temple. Black and Chinese communicants worship in a one-time sailors' church that might have been, in another time, a temple to Athena.

[L10] **St. Margaret's House**/originally *Robert Dodge House*, 2 Oliver St., bet. St. James Place and Henry St. E side. 1820. *James O'Donnell.* Third floor added, 1850.

A Federal house, its roof raised, dormers removed, and pitch flattened, now part of adjacent Mariners' Temple's work. Nice to preserve, but sad in its lost Federal-ness.

[L11] **HSBC**/originally **Manhattan Savings Bank branch**, 17 Chatham Sq., SW cor. Catherine St. 1977. *George W. Clark Assocs.*

A virtuoso mock-Chinese temple naively commissioned to serve as a branch bank for Chinatown. Like the former pagoda telephone booths, it's harmless, amusing kitsch.

[L12] Metro Communications Center/ originally **Edward Mooney House**, 18 Bowery, SW cor. Pell St. 1785-1789. Alterations, 1807. Restoration, 1971. 🍎

Built after the Revolution but before *Washington's* inauguration, this is presumably Manhattan's oldest row house, combining Georgian elements with the incoming Federal style. Ignore the later portal and all that paint.

L12

[L15] 51 Market Street /originally *William Clark House*, bet. Monroe and Madison Sts. W side. 1824. 🍎

A lovely Federal two-story gambrel-roof house, later elevated to four floors. Its leaded glass fanlit entranceway is **Federal** at its most superb.

[L16] The First Chinese Presbyterian Church/onetime **Sea and Land Church**/originally **Market Street Reformed Church**, 61 Henry St., NW cor. Market St. 1817-1819. 🍎

A Georgian-Federal body punched with Gothic Revival windows of dressed Manhattan schist, with brownstone surrounds (enframement) and trim. The triple-hung windows have 35 panes in each of their sashes: 35 over 35 over 35.

[L17] Manhattan Bridge, bet. Canal St. and the Bowery in Manhattan and Flatbush Ave. Ext. in Brooklyn. 1903-1910. *Gustav Lindenthal*, engi-

L16

[L13] Confucius Plaza (apartments) and **Public School 124, The Yung Wing School**, bet. the Bowery, Division St., Chatham Sq. and the Manhattan Bridge approaches. 1976. *Horowitz & Chun.*

Housing looms over the school, integrated in a city program. Its curved slab is arbitrary, and seems to **seek some skyline credit**. Not urbane, or even friendly, as a street-smart New Yorker, this might be anywhere.

[L14] Knickerbocker Village (apartments), Catherine to Market Sts., Monroe to Cherry Sts. 1934. *Van Wart & Ackerman.*

A blockbuster, with **1,600 apartments on 3 acres** (New York City public housing averages 80 to 100 units per acre). The central courtyards, reached through gated tunnels, seem a welcome relief by contrast with their dense and massive surroundings. This was the first major housing project even partially aided by public funds. It maintains its well-kept modest air today.

neer *Henry Hornbostel*, architect (1903-1904), *Carrère & Hastings*, architects (1904-1910).

The Hornbostel fillips are little known or observed, but provide entrancing details on what seems ordinary engineering (after Brooklyn Bridge's spectacular breakthrough a generation before).

[L18] Manhattan Bridge Arch and Colonnade, at entrance to bridge. 1910-1915. *Carrère & Hastings.* 🍎

This regal horseshoe-shaped colonnade survived past attempts by highway engineers to remove it; now, to clear the record, the Department of Transportation restored it: a giant exedra triumphantly marking your entrance (or exit). A nice diversion when your cab is stuck in traffic.

Mott Street, west across the Bowery:

[L19] 67 Mott Street Cornice, between Bayard and Canal Sts. W Side. 1890s.

Long before the ground floor became Chinatown shopping, this **regal cornice** crowned a simple tenement, one of thousands that garnished these "warehouses" for immigrants. Architecture was an essential to marketing space then, like a rose in your lapel.

[L23] Hong Kong Bank Building (offices)/originally **Golden Pacific National Bank Headquarters,** 241 Canal St., NW cor. Centre St. 1983. Ornament and tiles, from Taiwan artisans.

A red lacquer, polychromed, embellished, Pagoda style, Chinese confection. Not a building: an event. It again brings the Hollywood version of China on stage.

"The Bloody Angle": The unexpected sharp turn midway down blocklong Doyers Street was

L18   L20   L23

L19

[L20] Chinese Merchant's Association, 85 Mott St., SW cor. Canal St. 1958.

Grauman's Chinese Theater architecture. On this both Beijing and Taipei might once have agreed. Now Beijing has the **Birdcage,** and Taipei has **Taipei 101,** the tallest existing skyscraper (until Burj Dubai confesses its true height).

[L21] Bank of East Asia, SE cor. Canal and Mulberry Sts. 1980s.

A cool modernist building more in tune with the economics of Hong Kong and Shanghai than the gimcracks of Chinatown.

[L22] 5th Precinct, NYC Police Department/originally 6th Precinct, 19-21 Elizabeth St., bet. Bayard and Canal Sts. W side. 1881. *Nathaniel D. Bush.*

A dignified Italianate station house. The department's house architect, *Bush,* designed a fleet of them during this period of rapid constabularial growth.

named for the tong (gang) wars fought there between 1880 and 1926 by the On Leong Tong and the Hip Sing Tong for control of local gambling and opium trafficking.

The Bowery, Old and New
Beginning at Canal Street, in the heart of Chinatown, take a hike north on the Bowery. Virtually synonymous since the mid-19th century with skid row, mythologized in films, comics, and dime novels, historically a row of cheap flop houses, brothels, vaudeville houses, and pawn shops, it was under the shadows of the Third Avenue El, demolished in 1955. Little of old skid row Bowery remains. The southern end is discount jewelry exchanges, Chinese bus lines (Fung Wah Bus at 139 Canal), and cheap novelties.

The Lighting District starts as Bowery crosses Grand Street, and the Restaurant Supply District begins in earnest just north of Kenmare Street (Chairs! Tables! Stools! Dishes! Pots! Pans!). Colorful, wordy signs are the main

L29

feature here, but there are some architectural treasures as well, notably two landmarked banks: Stanford White's **Bowery Savings Bank**, just north of Grand, and Robert Maynicke's **Germania Bank**, at Spring Street.

Bowery flophouses, cheap hotels that sheltered unfortunate souls who were skidding to the bottom of skid row, began disappearing years ago, but there are still a few here and there: the **Sunshine Hotel**, at 241 Bowery, the **Grand Hotel** (formerly the Delevan Hotel), at 143 Bowery, and the **Bowery Lodge** (formerly the Mascot Hotel) at 81 Bowery. Meanwhile, the **World Hotel**, at 101 Bowery, looks the part from the street, but the rates ($65 per night for a room with no bathroom, $95 with) don't seem so floppy.

Hipsters appear in droves north of Kenmare, and recently built sleek modern buildings follow in quick succession: a skinny condo at **195 Bowery**, the stacked mesh boxes of the **New Museum** just to the north, and the perfectly tidy glass boxes of the massive **Avalon** development at East Houston Street. In the midst of all the new glass and steel, the **Bowery Mission**, at 227, soldiers on, helping the homeless with soup and salvation since 1879.

[L24] **HSBC**/formerly **Republic National Bank**/originally **Citizen's Savings Bank**, 58 Bowery, SW cor. Canal St. 1924. *Clarence W. Brazer.*

An enormous bronze dome, saluting the Manhattan Bridge across the street, anchors the corner of Canal Street and the Bowery. Finally

L25

HSBC has arrived, bringing in its own Asian flavor (Hongkong and Shanghai Banking Corporation).

[L25] **Bowery Savings Bank**, 130 Bowery, bet. Grand and Broome Sts. 1893-1895. *Stanford White of McKim, Mead & White.* Pediments sculptor, *Frederick MacMonnies.* 💣 Interior. 💣

Roman pomp wraps around Renaissance luster, on the Bowery at the edge of Little Italy. Pass through the triumphal arch into an interior that is one of the great spaces of New York. Enter.

[L26] **Grand St. Branch, Citibank**, 124 Bowery, NW cor. Grand St. 1902. *York & Sawyer.*

This and the Bowery Savings have served as architectural and economic anchors through the Bowery's years of hard times.

[L27] Former **Germania Bank Building**, 190 Bowery, NW cor. Spring St. 1898-1899. *Robert Maynicke.* 💣

It may look abandoned, with its festoons of graffiti, but in fact this grand granite and limestone banking palace is a single-family house. Photographer *Jay Maisel* has maintained his home and studio within since 1966. Within are 75 rooms and (rumored) a basketball court in the former banking hall. Take that, yuppies with your puny $15 million penthouses!

L27

[L28] **195 Bowery Apartments**, opp. Spring St. 2008. *Keith Strand.*

A handsome five-story affair, in pleasant tan Roman brick, with an additional 11 stories in modern grays and whites sutured to its top. *Look at me! I'm the biggest thing on the Bowery!* (for now).

[L29] The **New Museum of Contemporary Art**, 235 Bowery, bet. Spring and Prince Sts. 2007. *Kazuyo Sejima and Ryue Nishizawa aka SANAA.* Open We, Sa, Su, 12-6; Th, Fr, 12-9. Closed Mo-Tu. *www.newmuseum.org*

A stack of boxes, seemingly left over from an afternoon's play (*"clean up your toys, Kazuyo!"*). Its skin casts a quiet steel veil over its rich contents, and at night the rooms glow behind the mesh with a haunting intensity. But the pizzazz is all on the exterior: inside, the galleries are serviceable, not remarkable, and the circulation (by stair) is confusing and claustrophobic. Stick to the elevators.

[L30] Originally **Young Men's Institute Building**, YMCA, 222-224 Bowery, bet. Spring and Prince Sts. W side. 1885. *Bradford L. Gilbert.* 🍎 Converted.

Brooding sandstone Queen Anne on Reformer's Row, when the Bowery was the wasteland of humanity and where the gauntlet of reform (read: sober up) was thrown down by this brave institution and several others. The Y decamped in 1932 (prohibition and automatic salvation?). Art, written and visual, replaced it; *Fernand Léger* painted here in 1940, later, merchandise was stored. After 1958, *William S. Burroughs, Mark Rothko*, and others shared living and studio space.

[L31] **Avalon Bowery Place** (apartments), 22 E. 1st St. bet. Bowery & Chrystie St., N side, and 11 E. 1st St., bet. Bowery & Chrystie St., S side; [L32] **Avalon Chrystie Place** (apartments), 229 Chrystie St., bet. E. Houston & Stanton Sts.; **Houston Street Center (YMCA)**, 273 Bowery bet. E. Houston & Stanton Sts.; **Whole Foods** (grocery), 95 E. Houston St., bet. Bowery & Chrystie Sts. 2006. *Arquitectonica.*

Both north and south of East Houston Street on three city blocks, with over 700 housing units, 85,000 square feet of retail space, a vast grocery store, and a YMCA.

Those who fear New York has become more than a bit homogenized during the recent **Boom** need look no further than this sprawling housing collective/retail center that obliterated a seedy but colorful chunk of the Bowery. The infamous **McGurk's Suicide Hall**, at 295 Bowery,

L30

was razed to make way for Avalon Bowery Place (see **Necrology** in the East Village section). New, clean, flat, cold.

NECROLOGY

The Music Palace, SE cor. Bowery and Hester Sts. *McKim, Mead & White.*

Recently demolished, this was the last Chinese language cinema: Chinatown's **Chuan Kung Theater.** Covered with sheet metal and murals, who knew a *McKim, Mead & White* building lurked underneath?

Turn left (west) from Bowery into the heart of Little Italy:

LITTLE ITALY

Canal to Houston Streets, Lafayette Street to the Bowery, is still, in large part, the most important old Italian center of New York—but now with old Italians, as the newest generation has made the move to suburbia. They return, however, for festivals and family festivities: marriages, funerals, feasts, and holy days. Meanwhile, the Chinese have rapidly moved north across the former cultural moat of Canal Street and partially share this turf, and yuppies have arrived from all directions.

The northern part of the neighborhood, from Kenmare Street to East Houston, has annoyingly been dubbed **NoLita**, even though it's not really *"north of Little Italy."* Developers enjoy new labels, the better to sell condominiums.

Here, the old label **Little Italy** is fine.

L33

L35

Besides, if we call part of the neighborhood **NoLita**, must we start calling SoHo **LoLita** (*"Left of Little Italy?"*).

[L33] **Most Precious Blood Church**, 113 Baxter St. bet. Canal and Hester Sts. E side. ca. 1890.

The façade of the church that harbors the shrine of **Saint Gennaro**. At its rear, opening on Mulberry St., is a tacky brick suburban house that manages the festival of this gourmand saint each September.

[L34] Originally **Stephen van Rensselaer House**/onetime **Paolucci's Restaurant**, 149 Mulberry St., bet. Hester and Grand Sts. W side. 1816. 🍎

A Federal two-story, dormered brick house, a surprising remnant in these tenemented streets (but it was moved from the corner of Mulberry and Grand in 1841). The gambrel roof and dormer windows join with incised stone lintels as signals of its **Federal** ancestry.

L38

[L35] **Banca Stabile** (former bank), 189 Grand St., SW cor. Mulberry St. 1885.

A onetime Italian family bank *(padroni)* totally bypassed by time. Tin ceilings, terrazzo floors, oscillating electric fans, bare-bulb incandescent fixtures. One of the brass teller's cages still offers steamship tickets (at least that's what the gilt lettering reads).

The **Italian-American Museum** moved here in 2008, incorporating two adjoining houses. Open to the public We-Su 11-6, Fr 11-8, closed Mo-Tu. 212-965-5000. *www.italianamericanmuseum.org*

[L36] **Ferrara's** (pastry and coffee shop), 195 Grand St., bet. Mulberry and Mott Sts. S side. Altered, 1980, *Sidney P. Gilbert & Assocs.*

While the family has been making dolci since 1892, this is a new departure, a modern building in which to serve its devoted public. Very different, very flat, a flock of windows.

[L38] **Police Building Apartments**/originally *NYC Police Headquarters*, 240 Centre St., bet. Grand and Broome Sts., and Centre Market Place. 1905-1909. *Hoppin & Koen + Franklin B. Huntington.* 🍎 Converted to residential use, 1988, *Ehrenkranz Group & Eckstut.*

In the manner of a French **hôtel de ville** (town hall), this is tightly arranged within the City's street system, not isolated palatially (as is City Hall or almost any state capitol). Ornate **Renaissance Revival** architecture is laced with bits of Baroque. The shape of the building even follows that of the wedge-shaped plot it occupies.

[L39] **165-171 Grand Street**/originally **Odd Fellows Hall**, SE cor. Centre St. 1847-1848. *Trench & Snook.* Roof addition, 1881-1882, *John Buckingham.* 🍎

The Corinthian pilastered palace of the **Odd Fellows,** a high-rise brownstone second only to the Cooper Union. *Snook* contributed many cast-iron buildings in the SoHo district to the west.

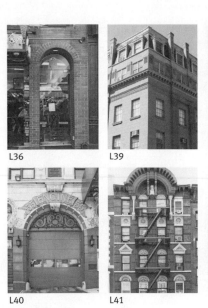

L36   L39

L43

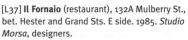

L40   L41

L46

[L37] **Il Fornaio** (restaurant), 132A Mulberry St., bet. Hester and Grand Sts. E side. 1985. *Studio Morsa,* designers.

An evocation of an old-time Italian restaurant, residing hectically in the midst of Little Italy's restaurant row. No sentimentality, only good design sense, with tables on the sidewalk in nice weather, loud waiters beckoning prospective dining parties: *"Quanti? Quanti?!"*

The Feast of San Gennaro fills Mulberry Street from Columbus Park to Spring Streets in the middle of September. Happily, autos are exiled. Arcaded with a filigree of electric lights, the street becomes a vast al fresco restaurant, interspersed with games of chance, for the benefit of this venerable Neapolitan saint. Fried pastries and sausages steam the air, and for one evening you may become part of the gregarious Italian public life (are those vendors really Italian? Greek? Jewish?).

[L40] **Engine Company No.55,** NYC Fire Department, 363 Broome St., bet. Mott and Elizabeth Sts. S side. 1898. *R.H. Robertson.* 🍎

Ornate, eclectic Renaissance Revival, dominated by a grand arched vomitory for the engines within. Triumphal fire fighters.

[L41] **375 Broome Street** (tenement), bet. Mott and Mulberry Sts. S side. ca. 1880. *Peter and Francis Herter.*

Who is that figure peering out of the deep sheet metal cornice? *Jupiter, Michelangelo, Mazzini, Garibaldi*—or is it *Moses?* Note the terra-cotta stars of David (commonly found in turn-of-the-century architectural ornament with no Jewish connection).

[L42] **Most Holy Crucifix Church (Roman Catholic),** 378 Broome St., bet. Mott and Mulberry Sts. N side. 1926. *Robert J. Reiley.*

A vest-pocket church, occupying just one lot in this crowded precinct. Everything is arrayed one above the other, as in the adjacent tenements.

L44

[L43] **Storefront for Art and Architecture**, NE cor. Kenmare and Centre Sts. 1993. *Stephen Holl and Vito Acconci*. Restored, 2008, *Pernilla Ohrstedt*.

A sliver of a slice in plan: the building is only five feet wide at its Centre Street end. The Storefront is, however, an offbeat and exciting venue for exhibitions. The original façade, which swings open in nice weather, had become frayed over the last decade and has been restored by *Ohrstedt*.

L45   L47

[L44] **1 Kenmare Square,** 210 Lafayette St. through to Crosby St. 2006. *Gluckman Mayner Architects*.

At the western terminus of Kenmare Street, behind an expanse of concrete and traffic euphemistically called Kenmare Square, waves *André Balasz's* undulating flag of charcoal masonry and glass. Inscrutable and vaguely suburban, like an office park in Houston, it seems more a corporate headquarters than a residence.

[L45] Originally **14th Precinct, NYC Police Department**/later **Police Department Storehouse,** 205 Mulberry St., bet. Kenmare and Spring Sts. W side. ca. 1870. *Nathaniel D. Bush*.

An Italianate station house with mansard roof, somehow spared from both demolition and "modernization." The old "house of detention" is at the left.

[L46] **Ceci-Cela Patisserie,** 55 Spring St., bet. Mulberry and Lafayette Sts. N side.

An elegant pastry shop.

[L47] Old **St. Patrick's Convent and Girls' School**/originally *Roman Catholic Orphan Asylum*, 32 Prince St., SW cor. Mott St. 1825-1826.

A Georgian-Federal building with a classy Federal entryway. Here the vocabulary of a Federal house was merely inflated to the program requirements of a parish school (originally an orphan asylum).

[L48] **211 Elizabeth Street,** SW cor. Prince St. 2009. *Roman & Williams*.

A convincing reenactment of the past, with brick forming a heavy wall against the street, with enough modulation to cast pleasing shadows. For an interesting comparison, see *SHoP's* apartment house at 290 Mulberry Street (p. 99). While *Roman & Williams* laboriously stacked their brick by hand (a lost art) to create a sense of weight, *SHoP* hung their brick in panels to create a sense of lightness. But the **Puck Building** (p. 99) still has them both beat.

[L49] **St. Patrick's Old Cathedral** (Roman Catholic), 260-264 Mulberry St., bet. Prince and E. Houston Sts. E side. 1809-1815. *Joseph Mangin*. Restored after fire in 1868, *Henry Engelbert*.

The original Roman Catholic cathedral of New York; the present **St. Patrick's Cathedral** uptown replaced it after a disastrous fire. Restored, this building was demoted to parish church status. The interior is a grand, murky brown "Gothicized" space, with cast-iron columns supporting a timber roof. The original

L55

(prefire) shell is in the Gothic-decorated Georgian tradition of **Sea and Land** or the **Church of the Transfiguration**, both in the Chinatown area.

[L50] **Old St. Patrick's Cathedral Rectory**, 263 Mulberry St., opp. church.
    Eclectic, and very well maintained. Fine ironwork.

[L51] **Saint Michael's Russian Catholic Byzantine Church**/formerly St. Michael's Chapel/originally **Saint Patrick's Chancery Office**, 266 Mulberry St., bet. Prince and E. Houston Sts. 1858-1859. *James Renwick, Jr., and William Rodrigue.*
    Neo-Gothic sandstone and painted brick, built in a shape and location as if it replaced a tenement.

[L52] **262 Mott Street**/onetime **Ciao Bella Ice Cream Factory**, bet. Prince and E. Houston Sts. E side. ca. 1885.
    The softly rounded corners framing window openings in this brick Romanesque Revival industrial building suggest a fluid sense of masonry, where its shape follows intent, rather than being constrained by brick as a rectangular box.

[L53] **256-258 Mott Street apartments**/ originally **14th Ward Industrial School**/ Astor Memorial Building, bet. Prince and E. Houston Sts. E side. 1888-1889. *Vaux & Radford.*
    Gothic Revival buttresses, colonnettes, and

L49

some **Louis Sullivanesque** terra-cotta ornament give this somber relic substantial panache. The central bay window (perhaps oriel here) rests on a Classical corbel. Way above its stepped gable hopes to recall that the Dutch were here first.

[L54] **Puck Building** (originally printing plant), 295-309 Lafayette St., bet. Jersey and E. Houston Sts. E side to Mulberry St. N part, 1885-1886. S addition, 1892-1893. Both by *Albert Wagner*. Relocated W front to accommodate widened Elm Place (now Lafayette St.), 1899, *Herman Wagner*. Rehabilitated, 1983-1984. Further restoration, 1995, *Beyer Blinder Belle*.
    A colossal gold-leafed **Puck** holds forth from a third-story perch at the corner of Mulberry and Houston (*Casper Buberl*, sculptor); a smaller version welcomes those who enter on Lafayette

Street (*Henry Baerer*, sculptor). Built by the publishers and chromolithographer of the color cartoons that distinguished *Puck,* the nationally renowned satirical magazine published in both German- (1876-1896) and English-language (1877-1918) editions, between the publication's founding and its demise. After years of neglect as a marginal structure in the printing trades, the rich red-brick building has now been resurrected and sensitively restored.

[L55] **290 Mulberry Street Apartments**, SE cor. E. Houston St. 2009. *SHoP.*
    A building is sometimes best viewed from the rear. Here the building's front, on busy Houston Street, can't help but be compared to the wondrous **Puck Building** across Mulberry. Not surprisingly, it loses (in a rout). But when viewed from behind, a few yards south on Mulberry, the building's modernist concrete innards are revealed, its undulating purple brick panels hung like a masonry billboard, pulled away from the structure.

L54

[L56] **New York Public Library, Mulberry Street Branch**, 10 Jersey Street, SW cor. Mulberry St. 2008. *Rogers Marvel.*
    Back to back with *Puck*, here is the conversion of an old chocolate factory into a branch library serving SoHo and Little Italy. Tucked in tiny, dark Jersey Street (really not so much a street as an alley), the library is a convincing combination of old (cast-iron columns, brick walls) and new (steel, drywall).

LOWER EAST SIDE

Far more significant historically than architecturally, this area harbors the legions of **tenement buildings** that warehoused the wave of homeless, tempest-tost immigrants who arrived from the 1880s up to World War I.

Six-story masonry blocks covered 90 percent of the lots in question, offering no light and air except at the 90-foot-distant ends of these railroad flats and through minuscule sidewall air shafts. (Rooms strung end to end like railroad cars gave rise to the term "railroad flats.")

On a 25- by 100-foot lot, at four families per floor, 24 families (not including boarders, in-laws, and double-ups), living with bathtubs in the kitchen and toilets in the hall, were the standard. Post-1930s reaction against overcrowding has produced an unhappy overcompensation. The density per acre remains the same or greater, but the edges of the Lower East Side have become dominated by high-rise, freestanding structures (it seems the taller and farther apart the better). Project dwellers are supposed to yearn for light and air, or at least the apparent virtues of light and air. In that cause they sacrifice the urbanity that exists, say, in **Brooklyn Heights** or **Greenwich Village**, in the name of great sweeping lawns (that you can't touch or cavort upon).

If there is a significant building type in this precinct it is the synagogue. In the years before World War I, some 500 Jewish houses of worship and talmud torahs (religious schools) were

Katz's Delicatessen, 205 E.Houston St.

built here. Few remain and fewer still are in use. A sampling follows, together with other landmarks of the community.

For our purposes the **Lower East Side** lies E of The Bowery, NE of the Manhattan Bridge and its approaches, and S of East Houston Street. The area N of Houston and E of The Bowery up to 14th Street is sometimes also referred to as part of the L.E.S. We (and most of its residents) call it the **East Village.**

South of Canal Street and Seward Park:

[E1] **Intermediate School 131,** The Dr. Sun Yat-Sen School, 100 Hester St., bet. Forsyth and Eldridge Sts. 1983. *Warner, Burns, Toan & Lundy.*
Curvilinear, extroverted, expansive—it burst forth and wiped out a block of Forsyth Street's street-bed.

[E2] **St. Barbara Greek Orthodox Church**/originally **Congregation Kol Israel Anshe Poland**, 27 Forsyth St., S of Canal St. E side. ca. 1895.
A proud temple that found new life as a church. However, its false dome would seem more appropriate in *Blazing Saddles* than on Forsyth Street.

[E3] **Museum at Eldridge Street**/ **Eldridge Street Synagogue**, 12 Eldridge St., bet. Forsyth and Canal Sts. E side. 1886-1887. *Herter Brothers.* ☛ Restoration, 1998, *Giorgio Cavaglieri.* Restoration, 2007, *Walter Sedovic.* (Congregation K'hal Adath Jeshurun), *212-219-0888.* Su-Th 10-4. *contact@eldridgestreet.org*
Vigorously Eclectic: some Flamboyant Moorish embellishment and a Gothic wheel window join together in the ornate façade of this first grand temple of worship built by Eastern

E2

European Jews. Vandalism took its toll on the stained glass, deterioration lasted a generation, but restoration brought it back. Aided by the steadfast *Roberta Gratz*, this brilliant star of New York's immigrant Jewish history (more than a million and a half Jews migrated to this part of Manhattan), now has become a museum of its own history.

The unfolding of the immigrant experience in the Lower East Side became the focus of an effort, beginning in 1984, to establish a historic/ cultural enclave in which that experience could be commemorated and interpreted. The single block of Eldridge Street between Forsyth and Canal, filled as it is with Old Law tenements, the K' hal synagogue, and other remnants of 19th- and early 20th-century life, emerged as the center of the effort by the **Lower East Side Jewish Conservancy,** *a private not-for-profit group (www.nycjewishtours.org).*

E3

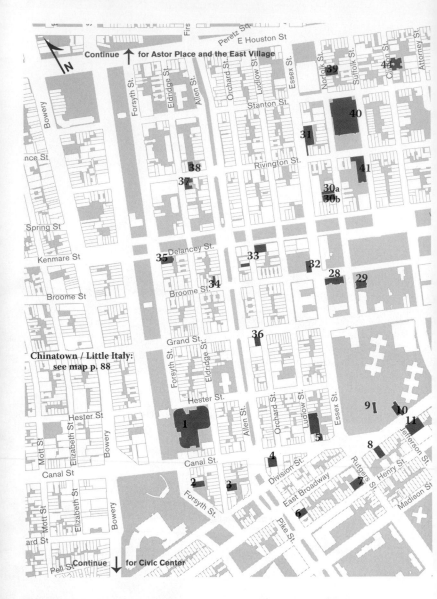

Continue ↑ for Astor Place and the East Village

Chinatown / Little Italy:
see map p. 88

Continue ↓ for Civic Center

[E4] Originally **Sender Jarmulovsky Bank Building**, 54-58 Canal St., SW cor. Orchard St. 1912. *Rouse & Goldstone*.

Lafayette Goldstone, father of *Harmon Goldstone*, the first Chairman of the Landmarks Preservation Commission, designed this **Renaissance Revival** banking house for the immigrant poor. Some uptown architecture brought confidence to the depositors, with a domed, columned "temple" once capping its 12 stories. For sale!

*The saga of **Jarmulovsky**'s bank makes the building a historical, rather than architectural landmark. Jarmulovsky's, established in 1873, was a local bank catering to the flood of non-English-speaking immigrants drawn to the area. With the coming of World War I many sought to withdraw deposits to aid relatives caught in Europe. Runs on this and other local banks soon*

*developed, and then actual riots. For the Lower East Side, **Black Tuesday** was August 4, 1914, when this bank and another were closed as being "in an unsound and unsatisfactory condition." Thousands lost their savings; the Jarmulovskys received a suspended sentence.*

[E5] Originally **Loew's Canal Street Theatre**, 31 Canal St., bet. Ludlow and Essex Sts. N side. ca. 1920.

The lobby's ornate glazed terra-cotta and glass façade remains (as does the theater's brick auditorium box behind), the marquee is long gone. Needs more than a wash.

[E6] **Sung Tak Buddhist Temple**/originally *Pike Street Synagogue* (Congregation Sons of Israel Kalware), 15 Pike St., bet. E. Broadway and Henry St. E side. 1903-1904. *Alfred E. Badt.* 💣

Rundbogenstil (German round-arched neo-Romanesque) in limestone, rounded sash

echoing the framing arches. The Temple occupies most of the old sanctuary, with stores below and apartments above.

[E7] St. Teresa's Roman Catholic Church/originally **First Presbyterian Church of New York**, 16-18 Rutgers St., NW cor. Henry St. 1841.

An ashlar Gothic Revival church that served a rural Presbyterian congregation long before the great flux of immigration. Manhattan schist, it's the local stone for many early ashlar buildings.

[E8] Originally **Forward Building**, 173-175 E. Broadway, bet. Rutgers and Jefferson Sts. S side. 1912. *George A. Boehm*. Conversion to condominiums, 1999, *Alfred Wen*. 🍎

A grand portal greets the present-day condoliers, and atop, a coronation of Corinthian columns fronts a Roman temple. The *Jewish Daily Forward* (newspaper) was once housed in this citadel of Yiddish thought and culture. The building's 12 stories sheltered not only the editorial offices of the newspaper, but also the main headquarters of the Arbiter Ring (Workmen's Circle), a distinguished social organization, which relocated uptown with the *Forward*.

Seward Park: A bit of green (three acres) at the intersection of East Broadway, Canal and Essex Streets seems less rare today than it did before urban renewal, when tenements were cleared and towers were placed on lawns. The park was named for Lincoln's secretary of state, William H. Seward (1801-1872).

[E9] **Recreation Building**, in Seward Park. 1939. *NYC Department of Parks & Recreation*.

A Greek temple updated in the style of the Paris Exposition of 1937. Limestone with an ultramarine blue terra-cotta frieze (and lots of calligraphic graffiti—added later).

[E10] **Seward Park Branch**, New York Public Library, 192 E. Broadway, opp. Jefferson St. W side. 1909. *Babb, Cook & Welch.*

A brick and rusticated limestone palazzo for book (and now computer) users. When built, the area was bulging with people and land was scarce, so the roof was planned as an outdoor reading area. Note the powerful piers, balusters, and verdigris beginnings of a trellis.

[E11] **David Sarnoff Building**, Educational Alliance, 197 E. Broadway SE cor. Jefferson St. 1889. *Brunner & Tryon.* Remodeled, 1969, *David Kenneth Specter.*

A **Roman-Romanesque Revival** brick and terra-cotta settlement house with its new *Sarnoff* identity emphasized by a wide new entrance arch. Round arches above say Romanesque, the cornice says Renaissance.

[E12] **Bialystoker Center Home for the Aged**, 228 E. Broadway, E of Clinton St. N side. 1930.

Surviving amid acres of adjacent post–

E10

World War II projects, an amusing Moorish Art Deco product of the Roaring Twenties. Two families vying for recognition are represented in two cornerstones, at the façade's far ends: *Lutenberg* (west), and *Marcus* (east). Shrubbery conceals the rivalry (both).

[E13a] **Isaac Ludlum House**, 281 E. Broadway, just E of the SE cor. of Montgomery St. 1829.

A Henry Street settlement annex, backing up to the original Settlement headquarters below. A Federal house with intact dormers, but the entrance has lost its Federal details. No.279 next door should see an equal revival as a house in private hands.

[E13b] **Martin Luther King, Jr., Community Garden.** Adjacent to the Henry Street Settlement. 1993.

A mini-park, festive, with brightly painted murals.

[E14] **Henry Street Settlement**/ originally **Nurses Settlement**, 263 and 265 Henry St., bet. Montgomery and Gouverneur Sts. N side. 1827. 267 Henry Street. 1834. New façade, ca. 1910, *Buchman and Fox.* Restorations, 1996, *J. Lawrence Jones Associates.*

Federal and Greek Revival town houses now happily preserved (in altered form) by a distinguished private social agency, founded by *Lillian Wald* (1867-1940), who is personally memorialized in the public housing bearing her name between East Houston and East 6th Streets on the river. No.265 is the Federal star. Greek Revival No.267 was "updated" to Colonial Revival around 1910, a curious reversion from the early 19th century to the mid-18th.

[E15] **Engine Company No.15, NYC Fire Department**, 269 Henry St., bet. Montgomery and Gouverneur Sts. 1883. *Napoleon LeBrun & Sons.*

A virtuoso façade of brick over a cast-iron ground floor. Particularly enlivening are the pair of corbeled cornice brackets and marvelous, brick-textured spandrels.

[E16] **St. Augustine's Episcopal Chapel**/originally *All Saints' Free Church*, 290 Henry St., bet. Montgomery and Jackson Sts. S side. 1827-1829. Attributed to *John Heath.*

Georgian body with Gothic Revival windows. Compare the similar duality of Chinatown's **Church of the Transfiguration** or the **Sea and**

E11   E16

Land Church. Built with Manhattan schist and crisp white pediments.

[E17] Formerly **Gouverneur Hospital**, Franklin D. Roosevelt Drive bet. Gouverneur Slips E. and W. N side. 1901. Attributed to *McKim, Mead & White.* Converted to treatment center, 1997, *Thanhauser & Esterson.*

The tiers of curved, screened verandas that jut out toward the Drive are familiar to the thousands of motorists who have passed this old City hospital daily.

Banana boat piers: With the advent of containerization and its need for enormous backup space, Manhattan in the 1970s and 1980s lost its shorefront piers, docks, and wharves. The last active freight operations were those of the Netumar Line at Piers 35 and 36, East River, at Clinton Street. Until 1987, bananas were offloaded here, giving motorists on the elevated FDR Drive a last glimpse of one of the City's former glories. In writing of the demise in the New York Times, *Sam Roberts described it as "the ultimate banana split."*

E17

[E18] **East River Houses**/Cooperative Village (International Ladies Garment Workers Union)/originally called *Corlear's Hook Houses*, N and S of Grand St., bet. Lewis and Jackson Sts. to Franklin D. Roosevelt Dr. 1956. *Herman Jessor.*

Five thousand people dwell in these carven brick monoliths that excel their descendants at **Co-op City** (perhaps 55,000 people) in cost, architecture, and views. *Herman Jessor*, not widely known to the public, was the Union's architect for both projects.

[E19] **Hillman Housing**, 500, 530, and 550 Grand St., bet. Abraham Kazan Place and Lewis St. 1951. *Springsteen & Goldhammer.*

[E20] **Amalgamated Dwellings**, 504-520 Grand St., NW cor. Abraham Kazan St. (formerly Columbia St.), to Broome St. 1930. *Springsteen & Goldhammer.*

Abraham Kazan, longtime president of the United Housing Foundation, here explored mass housing for the Amalgamated Clothing Workers, creating, in concert with his architects, these pioneer projects.

Amalgamated Dwellings (236 units) is a hollow rectangular doughnut, heavily influenced by the work of *Michel de Klerk* (1884-1923), founder of the Amsterdam school, and *Karl Ehn's* **Karl Marx Hof** in Vienna. The parabolic arched opening from Broome Street offers a view into the fine central courtyard. **Hillman Housing** (807 units) begins to reflect the tower-on-lawn approach. It comes off poorly in comparison.

[E21a] **511 Grand Street**, bet. East Broadway and Henry St. ca.1827-1828.

The requisite hints for **Federal** (style) are there; its two-story height, peaked roof, pedimented dormers, and brick chimney: but it's a sorry survivor stripped of its original glory. Perhaps the original owners ate on Chinese dishware, brought back by clipper ships remembered at South Street Seaport. Doubtful that **Wing Hing** (the Chinese restaurant on the ground floor) has such place settings.

[E21b] **513 Grand Street**, bet. East Broadway and Henry St. ca.1827-1828.

Remodeled in the 1940s when the building, in commercial use, was converted back into a single-family dwelling. Members of the *Picerno* family resided there until 2003.

[E22] **Ritual Bathhouse** (mikveh)/formerly **Young Men's Benevolent Association**, 311-313 E. Broadway, W of Grand St. 1904.

This ornate façade clads a building now used for the ritual baths that Orthodox Jewish women are required to take prior to the marriage ceremony and monthly thereafter. According to the Scriptures the water must be unadulterated—when possible it is rainwater captured in cisterns.

[E23] **Louis Abrons Arts for Living Center**, Henry Street Settlement and Neighborhood Playhouse, 466 Grand St., bet. Pitt St. and Bialystoker Place (formerly Willett St.). N side. 1975. *Prentice & Chan Ohlhausen*. Gallery open 12-6 daily. 212-598-0400.

[E25] **St. Mary's Roman Catholic Church**, 438 Grand St., W of Pitt St. N side. 1833. Enlarged, present façade added, 1871, *Patrick Charles Keely*.

The second-oldest Roman Catholic church structure in all of the City (**old St. Patrick's** was first: 1815)—the somber gray ashlar rear portion, that is. The amusing red brick front and its twin spires are by the prolific church architect *Keely*.

[E26] **7th Precinct Station House, NYC Police Department**, and **Engine Company No.17, Ladder Company No.18, NYC Fire Department**, 19-25 Pitt St., NW cor. Broome St. 1975. *William F. Pedersen & Assocs*.

Sculpted massing, each function with its special shape and view, the antithesis of the universal spaces of modern commercial America (or *Mies van der Rohe*). A bit labored, but less dated than some of its contemporaries. Clinker bricks provide subtle texture up close.

E23

E22

E24   E26

An urban exedra, these buildings make a civic space in this wasteland of amorphous streets. A high moment of architecture that brings a suggestion of urbane Manhattan (cf. Greenwich Village, Gramercy Park) to this Rego Park–styled area.

*Mmm...doughnuts.... **The Doughnut Plant**, 379 Grand St. between Essex and Clinton, makes exotic glazed (Meyer lemon!) and cake doughnuts and traditional Mexican churros. A great place for a sugar rush as you hike the streets.*

[E24] **Bialystoker Synagogue**/originally **Willett Street Methodist Episcopal Church**, 7-13 Bialystoker Place (formerly Willett St.), bet. Grand and Broome Sts. W side. 1826.

Manhattan schist, brownstone, and whitestone. Shifting ethnic populations create changing uses for venerable buildings such as this. Originally a rural Protestant church, it became a synagogue when the neighborhood became the center for a burgeoning Jewish population.

[E27] **Seward Park Extension West, NYC Housing Authority**, 154-156 Broome St., E of Clinton St. N side. 1973. *William F. Pederson & Assocs*.

The sibling of Seward Park West below, minus a community facility annex. This slab's richly modeled façade faces east to the river.

B'nai B'rith: A plaque on the courtyard wall of the public housing calls attention to the birth at that site of B' nai B' rith, the nation's first national service agency, on October 13, 1843.

[E28] **Seward Park Extension West, NYC Housing Authority**, 64-66 Essex St., bet. Grand and Broome Sts. E side. 1973. *William F. Pedersen & Assocs*.

One of the pair of tall tan slabs whose design is concentrated on one rich, plastic, three-dimensional, balconied façade, this one facing south. Adjacent is an outdoor court and low recreation building.

The Pickle District: *for generations the Lower East Side Jewish community was home to great kosher pickles. A few hang on: Pickle Guys, 49 Essex, and **Essex Street Pickles**, 35 Essex, both between Grand & Hester Streets, and **Guss' Pickles**, 87 Orchard between Broome and Grand. At Guss' they still sell the pickles from barrels on the sidewalk, and they will pickle anything that sprouts. Old New York!*

[E29] **Congregation Beth Hamedrash Hagodol**/ originally **Norfolk Street Baptist Church**, 60-64 Norfolk St., bet. Grand and Broome Sts. E side. 1850. ☙

The Methodists bought it from the Baptists in 1860; the Orthodox congregation from the Methodists in 1885: social, religious and architectural mobility with the moving tide of immigrants. The most recent congregation was the oldest of the Russian Orthodox in America. Slated for new uses by the Lower East Side Conservancy.

E30a

▌ [E30a] **The Switch Building**, 109 Norfolk St., bet. Delancey and Rivington Sts. 2008. *nArchitects.*

Modest in scale compared to the many luxurious apartments built in the most recent Building Boom, when architects and developers seemed keenly interested in lots of glass, lots of square footage, and not much else. This neat stack of units, off-set at each floor, is a welcome, restrained exception.

▌ [E30b] **Blue Tower**, 105 Norfolk St., bet. Delancey and Rivington Sts. 2007. *Bernard Tschumi.*

A 1916 zoning law dictated that taller buildings should **step back** as they rise, in order to give the sun a fighting chance to reach the street. The resulting silhouette, or "wedding cake," became the ubiquitous apartment and office building profile that has collectively defined much of the borough.

Tschumi's tower does the opposite, **swelling** as it rises. But with low-rise buildings around it, it doesn't block much sun, so what's the harm? When viewed from Delancey Street, it seems to be on the move, like a commuter pushing its way south through rush hour traffic. (The black and white photo included here captures its shape, but not its hue: it is indeed **blue**, top to bottom.)

[E31] **Essex Street Market**, City of New York (originally **NYC Department of Markets**), Essex St. bet. Broome, Delancey, Rivington, and Stanton Sts. E side. 1940.

The **Department of Markets** no longer exists in the City's table of organization (a result no doubt of the preservatives in junk food), but this indoor market does. Art Moderne in red brick and industrial steel sash. Other markets of this LaGuardia-era genre include First Avenue and East 10th Street, Arthur Avenue in the Bronx, and 13th Avenue and 40th Street in Brooklyn.

E32

*Ludlow Street, bet. East Houston and Delancey Streets, has become a kind of epicenter for hipsters. Heading south, the street begins at the front door of **Katz's Delicatessen** (est. 1888), 205 E.Houston St., where the pastrami on rye reaches vertical heights best measured with an architect's scale. Southward, forgettable new condominiums have been wedged in everywhere amid the original, lower-scale brick tenements. Live music is the street's main attraction, notably at the **Living Room**, 154 Ludlow St. (its original, cozier location was at the NE corner of Stanton and Allen Sts.), and at **Piano's**, 158 Ludlow St., both bet. Stanton and Rivington Sts. On Saturday nights, the street is a madhouse.*

[E32] Originally **Eastern Dispensary**/later **Good Samaritan Dispensary**, 75 Essex St., NW cor. Broome St. ca. 1895.

Once the eastern outpost of a dispensary system for Lower Manhattan. Stately golden brown and salmon brick.

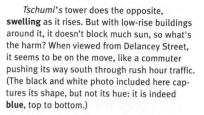

E30b

E39

[E33] **Lower East Side Tenement Museum,**
108 Orchard St., bet. Broome and Delancey Sts.
1863. Tours Mo-Su, 11-5. Museum Shop open
Mo-Su, 11-6. *212-431-0233. www.tenement.org*
97 Orchard is a time capsule, with living units
that were sealed off from 1935 to 1988. Its life-
time graduates include more than 7,000, some of
whom had lived in tight quarters: as many as 13
to an apartment. A National Trust Historic Site.

[E34] **Kehila Kadosha Janina Synagogue**, 280
Broome St., bet. Allen and Eldridge Sts. N side.
1926-1927. *Sydney Daub.* ●
    Built for Romaniote Jews who emigrated
from Ioannina in northwestern Greece, this simple brick façade is enlivened with stained glass
windows and mild banded brick relief.

[E35] **Seventh-Day Adventist Church of Union
Square**/originally **Congregation Poel Zedek
Anshe Ileya,** 128-130 Forsyth St., SE cor.
Delancey St. ca. 1895.
    This house of worship is reached by sym-
metrical flights of steps on Forsyth Street, permitting retail establishments to occupy the
ground floor on Delancey. The combination of
worship (sacred) and business (profane) did
well. Good cornice.

[E36] **319-321 Grand Street,** (Originally dry
goods store), SW cor. Orchard St. ca. 1870.
    Around the Civil War, Grand Street east of
the Bowery was center of the City's women's
fashions. *Lord & Taylor,* at Grand and Chrystie
Streets, and *Edward Ridley's,* at Allen Street,
were the two most popular dry goods stores.
(Pink) iron and glass.

[E37] **University Settlement House,** 184 Eldridge
St., SE cor. Rivington St. 1901. *Howells & Stokes.*
    A neighborhood institution by a team of
architects better known for their later accomplishments. *Howells,* son of author *William
Dean Howells,* won the Chicago Tribune Tower
competition with *Raymond Hood. Stokes (Isaac
Newton Phelps Stokes)* wrote the definitive
architectural historical work: *The Iconography
of Manhattan Island.* Another good cornice.

[E38] **Originally Congregation Adath Jeshurun
of Jassy**/later **First Warsaw Congregation**, 58-60
Rivington St., bet. Eldridge and Allen Sts. N
side. 1903.

E36

A magnificent eclectic façade with bits and
pieces from a variety of styles and influences.
Fading away.

▥ [E39] **Angel Orensanz Foundation**/origi-
nally **Congregation Anshe Chesed** /one-
time **Ohab Zedek**/later **Anshe Slonim,** 172- 176
Norfolk St., bet. Stanton and E. Houston Sts. E
side. 1849-1850. *Alexander Saeltzer.*
    With this exception, all Lower East Side
Jewish congregations before 1850 had purchased and converted existing churches. This
edifice, the City's oldest (and for a time its
largest) synagogue (and its first Reform temple), was built by an established Jewish community whose members subsequently moved
northward, together with their Christian neighbors, as the area became a refuge for Eastern
European immigrants. Congregation **Anshe
Chesed** is today on the Upper West Side.
Spanish sculptor *Angel Orensanz* bought the
fading building in 1986 for art shows and theatrical events. A small orthodox congregation
still worships in the basement.

[E40] **Intermediate School 25**, 145 Stanton St., bet. Norfolk and Suffolk Sts. S side. 1977. *David Todd & Assocs.*

A successful combination of creamy white concrete horizontals with dark red, giant brick infill—all embraced by the strong forms of the stair towers at the corners.

Streit's Matzoth Company, 148 Rivington St., NE cor. Suffolk St.

Matzos (flatbread) made on the premises. Go in and watch the bread come off the rotating roller and the workers stack and sort it into baskets running by overhead. A last vestige of the old Jewish Lower East Side, but for how long? The building has been for sale several times in the last few years.

[E41] **Clemente Soto Velez Cultural and Educational Center**, originally **Public School 160**, Manhattan, 107 Suffolk St., SW cor. Rivington St. ca. 1898. *C. B. J. Snyder.*

It looks abandoned, with broken windows, graffiti, and a thick layer of grime, but it's not. Lack of exterior maintenance aside, this former public school is, in fact, site of a thriving arts community, with experimental theater, artist's studios, a cafe, and a bar. "Fame" on the Lower East Side.

[E42] **Williamsburg Bridge**, from Delancey and Clinton Sts. in Manhattan to Washington Plaza in Brooklyn. 1903. *Leffert L. Buck*, chief engineer. Rehabilitation, 1993, *Beyer Blinder Belle.*

To the former City of Williamsburgh, now

E41

part of Brooklyn. The unusual (straight) cables on the land side of the towers result from the fact that support is by truss and pier, rather than pendant cable as in the Brooklyn Bridge. The latter's landside cables hang in a catenary curve, in contrast.

[E43] **Public School 142**, Manhattan, 100 Attorney St., SE cor. Rivington St. 1975. *Michael Radoslavitch.*

A fashionable form in plan, a banjo, fails to come to life as architecture.

[E44] **Congregation Chasam Sofer** (synagogue)/originally **Congregation Rodeph Sholom**, 8-10 Clinton St., bet. Stanton and E. Houston Sts. E side. 1853.

The second-oldest surviving synagogue in the City. **Rodeph Sholom** left these parts in 1886. Today its temple is on West 83rd Street.

[E45] **Our Lady of Sorrows Roman Catholic Church**, 101 Pitt St. bet. Rivington and Stanton Sts. W side. ca. 1867. **Our Lady of Sorrows School**, 219 Stanton St., SW cor. Pitt St. ca. 1890. **Rectory**/originally **Capuchin Monastery**, 213 Stanton St., bet. Ridge and Pitt Sts. S side. ca. 1890.

A spectacular religious complex run by the Capuchin Order, once down at the heels, resuscitated in recent years by the Latino community.

[E46] **Hamilton Fish Park Play Center**, NYC Department of Parks, NYC Department of Parks & Recreation/originally Hamilton Fish Park Gymnasium and Public Baths, in Hamilton Fish Park, 130 Pitt St., bet. Stanton and E. Houston Sts. E side. 1898-1900. *Carrère & Hastings.* Restored, 1985, *John Ciardullo Assocs.* Park, 1898-1900, *Carrère & Hastings.* Park altered, 1903. Swimming pool added, 1936, *Aymar Embury II.*

The play center's design is a miniaturization of *Charles Girault's* widely acclaimed Petit Palais in Paris, designed in 1895 for the Paris Exposition of 1900, this copy is an oompah Beaux Arts pavilion built to serve the recreation and bathing needs of immigrants drawn to this precinct before the turn of the century. Though monumental in scale, it failed to be adequate in size. (Almost immediately after completion, C&H's formal park was totally in ruins "owing, it is said, to the radical defects of the original plan and to the strenuous nature of the youth of the neighborhood"; it was redone in three years.)

[E47] **DeWitt Reformed Church**, 280 Rivington St., NE cor. Columbia St. 1957. *Edgar Tafel.*

A simple brick box that contains a sanctuary faced in reused brick and a cross of tree trunks: rustic and humane charm amid overpowering housing.

NECROLOGY

Originally **Olive Branch Baptist Church**/later **Congregation Beth Haknesseth Anshe Sineer** (synagogue), 290 Madison St., SW cor. Montgomery St. 1856.

The pink synagogue, isolated amid low- and middle-income housing, was destroyed by fire.

Congregation Shaarai Shomoyim First Roumanian American Congregation (synagogue)/ originally **Allen Street Methodist Church**, 83-93 Rivington St., bet. Orchard and Ludlow Sts. S side. ca. 1890.

In 2000, it was "solid, stolid Romanesque Revival, flattened by paint and soot." In January 2006 it collapsed, and was demolished two months later. A doorway at 95 Rivington is the only remnant.

Mills House No.2 (hotel), 16 Rivington St., NW cor. Chrystie St. 1897. *Ernest Flagg.*

A lesser-known *Flagg* work built as a hostel for low-income guests. It is survived by a larger cousin, now The Atrium in Greenwich Village.

SOHO

SoHo (or South of Houston), as an acronym, is stretching it, recalling the "Greenwich Village" of London: Soho. These 20-odd blocks between Canal and Houston (How-stun) Streets, West Broadway and Broadway, contain the City's quintessential stock of cast-iron-fronted buildings, a high point in urban commercial architectural history. They are, largely, to be noticed not as individual monuments but as parties to whole streets and blocks that, together, make the most glorious urban commercial groupings that New York has ever seen. Mostly Italianate, some might be termed Palladian: they are sur-

Confusion: SoHo, being south of Houston, is also south of Manhattan's street grid established by the **Commissioners' Plan of 1811**. **SoHo** is arranged on a grid in which the long blocks stretch north-south, their axes exactly perpendicular to those above Houston Street. Similarly, in contrast to Manhattan's main grid, the wide streets in SoHo (except for Broadway, West Broadway, and the much later Sixth Avenue) run east-west, and are all called streets, none avenues. Not unsurprisingly, the direction and placement of house numbers vary from thoroughfare to thoroughfare. So

H3

prising precursors of modern exposed structural expression in another material—concrete—seen at Kips Bay Plaza and the American Bible Society.

Once these were called **Hell's Hundred Acres** because of the many fires in overcrowded, untended warehouses filled with flammables. Then given over in large part to artists' (and would-be artists') studios and housing, the once-empty streets and buildings became a lively, urbane place, much tended and loved, and hence no longer a potential lonely inferno. Huge lofts here give possibility of great space for large paintings or sculptures and equally great space for living. Initially rediscovered by artists, it has since been invaded by those with deep pockets. Prices for lofts have skyrocketed. The richest single street is Greene, then Broome—but wander throughout. Not only the revived architecture but also shops, stores, galleries, and boutiques of elegance and delight abound.

watch carefully and make no rash assumptions about **SoHo**.

SoHo entries appropriately begin south of Houston Street along Broadway (below Astor Place & Environs). They sequentially snake around, first south, then north, moving generally to the west. Feel free to break the sequence—we did.

Before your travels, you might want to check which/what store/restaurant is where. A website that helps: www.artseensoho.com/map.html.

[H1] **SoHo Cast-Iron Historic District**, irregular area E of W. Broadway's center line bet. center lines of W. Houston and Canal Sts. to Broadway, and E of Broadway bet. center lines of E. Houston and Howard Sts. on center line of Crosby St. ●

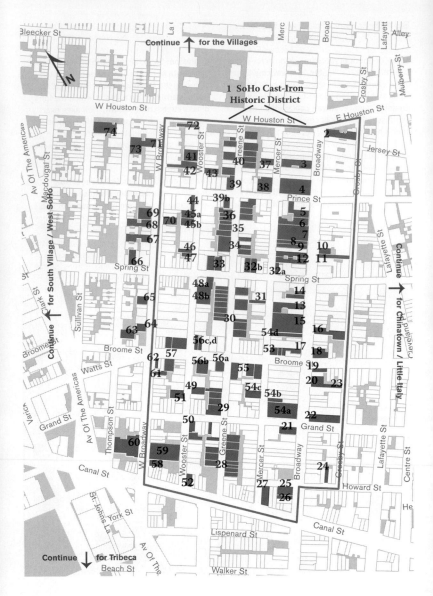

Continue ↑ for the Villages

1 SoHo Cast-Iron Historic District

Continue ← for South Village / West SoHo

Continue → for Chinatown / Little Italy

Continue ↓ for Tribeca

Within the 26 blocks of this Historic District are arrayed, according to the official designation report, "the largest concentration of full and partial cast-iron façades anywhere in the world." Their protection under law in 1973, after having been saved in the late 1960s from destruction for the ill-fated Lower Manhattan Expressway, was a great victory for preservation activists. Cast iron and other bountiful structures from the City's late 19th-century business boom abound on these streets. Remember, **SoHo's** festooned fire escapes and its bumpety Belgian block pavements are also part of this wonderfully gritty scene.

SoHo's north edge is bounded by the expressway-scaled Houston Street which, having been widened for the IND Sixth Avenue Subway, caused the body of SoHo to offer a ragged edge to Greenwich Village on the north. Gas stations, lots, and unkempt buildings' sides are all that SoHo here reveals of its inner splendors. Later roadwork widened the asphalt pavement itself and inserted the slender traffic island down the middle. More recent projects such as the former University Village and NYU's sports center disguise the gash, but the little two-story polychrome taxpayer [H72] between Wooster and West Broadway emphasizes it by its shallow depth.

Broadway between Houston and Prince Streets:

[H2] **600 Broadway** (loft building). E side. 1883-1884. *Samuel A. Warner.*

Corinthian columns of descending height support each successively ascending floor. Abercrombie & Fitch's Hollister store replaced the departing Pottery Barn in 2009.

[H3] Originally **Astor Building**/onetime **New Museum of Contemporary Art,** 583 Broadway. W side. 1896-1897. *Cleverdon & Putzel.*

Outside, the carapace that shelters this hermit crab is magnificent: **Corinthian** columns and reentrant bay windows join to present a lush **Classical** ensemble.

[H4] **Prada Soho**/onetime **Guggenheim SoHo**/ originally **Rogers Peet Store**, 575 Broadway, NW cor. Prince St. 1881-1882. *Thomas Stent.* Remodeled, 1996, *Arata Isozaki.*

▌▊ Remodeled interior for Prada, 2001, ▬▬ *Rem Koolhaas.*

In the *Ruskinian* manner, exuberant cast-iron **Corinthian-Victorian** columns support a stone and brick volume; and it is a choice location, it would seem. **Rogers Peet** was no slouch as a preppy store of the 1940s and 1950s, and *Isosaki's* **Guggenheim SoHo** (1996-2002) was a serious event.

Today's **Prada** store, by *Koolhaas,* is a whimsical wonderland: a "wave" of steps cascading downward from the street. At one side you can step down; at the other you can slide (no, don't do it!). For the handicapped, or those too shy to enter stage center, there is an exquisitely designed, excruciatingly slow, round glass elevator. Downstairs, it's all smoke and mirrors (well, mirrors anyway). Try on a suit; changing rooms are under Broadway's sidewalk, and

H4

H5   H6

being walked on by SoHo's well-heeled never felt so cool.

Broadway between Prince and Spring Streets:

▌▊ [H5] **Singer Building**/onetime **Paul** ▬▬ **Building**/ originally **The Singer Manufacturing Company**, 561 Broadway, bet. Prince and Spring Sts. Secondary façade on Prince St. S side. 1902-1904. *Ernest Flagg.* Restoration, 2008, *Bone/Levine Architects.*

"The Little Singer Building," to distinguish it from the demolished **Singer Tower** [see Necrology]. Curled steel, recessed glass, and textured terra cotta—all avant-garde for their time. The façade foretells the curtain wall, that delicate metal-and-glass skin in which much of Manhattan of the 1950s and 1960s is clad—grossly it seems, when compared to this post-turn-of-the-century charmer. Its original name can still be seen cast in iron on the Prince Street store transom of this L-shaped structure. Painstakingly restored by *Kevin Bone* and *Joseph Levine.*

▌▊ [H6] **Scholastic Books**, 557 Broadway, ▬▬ bet. Prince and Spring Sts. W side. 2001. *Aldo Rossi and Gensler Associates.*

These boldly columned offices seemed a first foothold in New York for the Italian architect and urban theorist *Aldo Rossi*; unfortunately it's a lone, posthumous construction (he died at 66 in 1997). *Rossi* approached architecture in a traditional manner, understanding that urban form is imbedded with memory. But his Italian memory scale is an inflated one in the world of delicate cast-iron SoHo.

[H7] Originally **Charles Broadway Rouss Building** (lofts), 555 Broadway. 1889-1890. *Alfred Zucker.* Attic pediments added, 1900.

A tribute to a debt-ridden Virginian whose name mightily adorns this through-block behemoth. *Rouss*'s construction sign modestly stated: "He who builds, owns, and will occupy this marvel of brick, iron, and granite, thirteen years ago walked these streets penniless and $50,000 in debt." The tale far more interesting than the building.

[H8] **547 Broadway** (lofts). W side. 1888. *O.P. Hatfield.*

Strongly patterned brick and stone, bearing tiers of lacey wrought iron fire escapes, bowing (in two senses of the word) graciously over the sidewalks of Broadway.

[H9] **545 Broadway** (lofts). W side. 1885. *Samuel A. Warner.*

Freestanding cast-iron colonnettes, stacked.

H12

[H10] **542-544 Broadway**, E side. 1864.

Composite **Corinthian** columns support, in their turn, draped women, their heads barely touching the cornice; if they were working with more structural conviction, they would be **Classical caryatids**.

[H11] **540 Broadway**, E side. 1867. *David & John Jardine.*

Neighbors in its time were already employing cast iron, but this out-of-the-ordinary dour façade is very two-dimensional: intaglioed sheets of marble.

[H12] **537-541 Broadway** (lofts). W side. 1868-1869. *Charles Mettam.*

Beautifully cast and articulated **Corinthian** cast-iron with colossal windows. A particular winner.

Broadway between Spring and Broome Streets:

[H13] **Originally De Forest Building**, 513-517 Broadway (lofts). W side. 1884. *Lamb & Rich.*

Six stories of floriated, polychromed somber red brick with terra-cotta detail, make a magnificent, rich, deeply modeled **Queen Anne** façade. More of these, please (not to be built, but a retroactive wish).

[H14] **St. Nicholas Hotel**. 521-523 Broadway. W side. 1851-1853. *John B. Snook* or *Griffith Thomas.*

The only remaining part of a much larger 1,000-bed hotel complex, which, with **Astor House**, were Broadway's most prominent hostelries before the Civil War. During the War the hotel became the headquarters of the War Department.

[H15] Originally **Loubat Stores**, 503-511 Broadway. W side. 1878-1879. *John B. Snook.*

H15

A generous composition of three warehouses with demure (and grave) cast-iron façades produced at the **Cornell Iron Works**. The capitals were never installed, giving a more austere, modern look to this *Snook* work.

[H16] Originally **C. G. Gunther's Sons Store**, 502 Broadway. E side. 1860. *John Kellum & Son.*

Slender, two-story arches exquisitely worked, in stone, not cast iron. When new, smooth, and pristine white, the tall, graceful columns (with original capitals) gave rise to the term **"Sperm Candle Style,"** after those slender 'torches' cast from spermaceti wax drawn from whale oil.

[H17] Originally **New Era Building** (lofts). 491 Broadway. W side. 1896-1897. *Buchman & Deisler.*

An **Art Nouveau** marvel: from the squat street-level **Doric** columns, fairly bulging from the weight of the masonry walls above, to the colossal multistory verdigris copper mansard, six floors up.

[H18] Originally **E. V. Haughwout & Co. Store**, 488-492 Broadway, NE cor. Broome St. 1856-1857. *John P. Gaynor.* Cast-iron façade by *Daniel D. Badger* Architectural Iron Works. Restored, 1995, *Joseph Pell Lombardi.* 🍎

A cast-iron magnificence, drawn by *Gaynor*, built by *Badger*: proud, handsome, not egocentric, refining the relationship between structure and glass in this then new technology. A classic example with Classical parts.

Those Classical parts are the arches and **Corinthian** columns that flank them, termed **Serlian**, after the works of *Sebastiano Serlio* (1475-1554), later lifted by *Andrea Palladio* (1508-1580) and most elegantly displayed at the latter's **Basilica** in Vicenza, near Venice. 300 years later their great-great-grandchildren marched around *Gaynor's* façade.

Built for *Eder V. Haughwout*, a merchant in china, cut glass, silverware, and chandeliers, it also housed the first practical safety elevator, installed by *Elisha Graves Otis*, founder of that ubiquitous elevator company.

H16

Broadway between Broome and Grand Streets:

[H19] Formerly **Mechanics & Traders Bank** (lofts), 486 Broadway, SE cor. Broome St. (also known as 437-441 Broome St.) 1885. *Lamb & Rich.*

The Broome Street façade of this **Romanesque** and **Moorish Revival** bank building has long been enriched with a glorious appliqué of fire escapes.

[H20] Originally **Roosevelt Building**. 478-482 Broadway. E side. 1873-1874. *Richard Morris Hunt.*

Filigreed cast iron, with **Composite** columns on a huge scale, built for the trustees of Roosevelt Hospital. Relish particularly openwork brackets that bear the flat cornice and curved cast-iron screens atop the fourth-floor windows. A very different style of *Hunt* (20+ years later) can be seen at the Metropolitan Museum's Fifth Avenue entrance. (One bay of the Roosevelt Building continues through the block to become **No.40 Crosby** Street, with an abbreviated form of façade).

Next door, at **476**, great Ionic columns foreshadow the **Classical Revival** after 1893, the direction that *Hunt* would follow in those years.

[H21] Originally **D. Devlin & Co. Store**, 459-461 Broadway, SW cor. Grand St. (also known as 115-119 Grand St.). 1860-1861.

A late **Italianate** temple of commerce whose beautifully weathered stone surfaces are pierced with ranks of finely proportioned round-arched windows.

[H22] Originally **Mills & Gibb Building**, 462 Broadway, NE cor. Grand St. to Crosby St. 1879-1880. *John Correja.*

This mammoth cast-iron commercial palace evokes memories of the **French Renaissance**. The ground floor has been mutilated by suffocation from polished red granite, a malady often reversible in cast-iron buildings. Let's hope.

H25

Detour: Crosby Street/Mercer Street:
Twin streets with Belgian block street pavers and an abundance of fire escapes and loading docks that reveal the rear of the large structures that line Broadway's originally prestigious flanks.

[H23] Originally **Roosevelt Building** (lofts), 40 Crosby St., bet. Grand and Broome Sts. 1874. *Richard Morris Hunt.*

The single-bay rear of 478-482 Broadway [H20].

Broadway between Grand and Howard Streets:

[H24] **34 Howard Street** (lofts), bet. Broadway and Crosby St. N side. 1868. *Renwick & Sands.*

Unusually distinguished (more in the sense of the unusual than excellence) — but no surprise since its architects were *James Renwick, Jr.,* and his then partner, *Joseph Sands.*

Broadway between Howard and Canal Streets:

[H25] **Broadway Portfolio**/originally **A.J. Ditenhoffer Warehouse**, 429 Broadway, SW cor. Howard St. 1870-1871. *Thomas R. Jackson.* Converted to residential lofts, 2000, *Joseph Pell Lombardi.*

Two dozen cadaverous arches spring from **Corinthian** columns facing Broadway in this lusty, glassy place. Gloriously repetitive.

H18

[H26] Originally **Le Boutillier Brothers Store**, 425 Broadway. W side. 1869. *Griffith Thomas.*

A small neighbor to No.429, with a monumental broken pediment silhouetted against the sky.

Canal Street:

[H27] Originally **Arnold Constable & Company** (dry goods store), 307-311 Canal St., NE cor. Mercer St. to Howard St. Corner, Nos.309-311, 1856. No.307, 1862. Fifth-story addition, 1862.

Years of Canal Street déclassé retailing numb most viewers to the lyrical architecture of this once elegant block-long bazaar. Here the wall dominates, with windows subordinate, in contrast to the cast iron of SoHo, where the columnar structure acts in concert with huge glass areas. Success and changing land-use fashions propelled **Arnold Constable** to a new location uptown in Ladies Mile. Later, economics in retailing sent it to oblivion.

Greene Street:

🏢 **[H28] Greene Street, bet. Canal and Grand Sts.** [a] **10-14 Greene St.** 1869. *John B. Snook.* **Tuscan** columns and pilasters. [b] **15-17 Greene St.** 1895. *John A. Warner.* Delicate **Corinthian** pilasters. [c] **16-18 Greene St.** 1880. *Samuel A. Warner.* Fire escapes have become the new façade. [d] **19-21 Greene St.** 1872. *Henry Fernbach.* Bold **Tuscan** columns by the architect of Central Synagogue. [e] **20-26 Greene St.** 1880. *Samuel A. Warner.* Two buildings in grand **Corinthian.** [f] **23-25 Greene St.** 1873. *Isaac F. Duckworth.* Sparsely leaved **Corinthian.** [g] **28-30 Greene St.** Fat Corinthian, with a magnificent **Second Empire** roof. [h] **31 Greene St.** 1876. *George W. DaCunha.* Extraordinarily ornate. [i] **32 Greene St.** 1873. *Charles Wright.* Leafless **Corinthian.** [j] **34 Greene St.** 1873. *Charles Wright.* **Tuscan.** [k] **83-87 Grand St.,** SW cor. Greene St. 1872. *William Hume.* Serene **Tuscan** over elaborate **Corinthian.**

The creamy king of this block: a magnificently fashioned, projecting-pedimented porch of **Corinthian** columns and pilasters. [g] **80 Greene St.** 1873. *Griffith Thomas.* Tuscan.

An aside to Mercer Street:

🍴 **[H31] Bar 89** (restaurant), 89 Mercer Street, bet. Spring and Broome Sts. 1995. *Ogawa/Depardon.*

89's two stories of crisp steel and glass reveal a double height dining space (a mezzanine in the far corner). The skylight overhead, a parabola, washes the space with natural light, the curve of the bar repeating the geometry above. *Oh, bartender!*

Spring Street:

[H32a] **Donald Judd House and Museum,** 101 Spring Street, NE cor. Mercer St. 1870. *Nicholas Whyte.* Renovation architect, *Architecture Research Office.* www.juddfoundation.org

H27   H28e   H29a

🏢 **[H29] Greene Street, bet. Grand and Broome Sts.** [a] **33 Greene St.,** NW cor. Grand St. 1873. *Benjamin W. Warner.* Composite columns above, **Tuscan** below. [b] **37-43 Greene St.** 1884. *Richard Berger.* Green composite columns over a **Corinthian** base. Lehmann Maupin Gallery at [c] **No.39.** 1996. *Rem Koolhaas.* The author of *Delirious New York* came to earth here for his first New York City architectural adventure. [d] **45 Greene St.** 1882. *J. Morgan Slade.* Crisp white **Composite** columns.

🏢 **[H30] Greene Street, bet. Broome and Spring Sts.** [a] **60 Greene St.** 1871. *Henry Fernbach.* Bold **Corinthian.** [b] **62 Greene St.** 1872. *Henry Fernbach.* Bulky **Composites.** [c] **66 Greene St.** 1873. *John B. Snook.* More fire-escape architecture. [d] **65 Greene St.** 1873. *John B. Snook.* Bold **Tuscan.** [e] **67, 69, 71, 75, 77, 81 Greene St.** 1873. *Henry Fernbach.* All bold **Tuscan.** [f] **72-76 Greene St.** 1873. *Isaac F. Duckworth.*

A profound project: the preservation of minimalist artist *Judd's* home and studio. When completed, the whole building will be open to the public. Meanwhile its (minimalist) cast-iron façade is being replaced, piece by piece, not with synthetics, but with actual cast iron. A labor of love, true to *Judd's* work. Projected completion date: 2013.

[H32b] **113, 115 Spring Street** (lofts), bet. Greene and Mercer Sts. N side. 1878. *Henry Fernbach.*

Freestanding **Tuscan** columns enliven a pair of cast-iron fronts: strapwork fire escapes added later suggest woven basketry.

[H33] **131-135 Spring Street** (lofts), bet. Greene and Wooster Sts. N side. 1891-1893. *Franklin Baylies.*

Rose pressed brick, sturdy granite piers, and limestone trim spruced up with pink-painted columns. **Sounds awful.** Looks great.

[H34] **SoHo Hotel**, 101-111 Greene St., bet. Spring and Prince Sts. 103-105 (1880s. *Henry Fernbach*), New buildings, 101 and 107-111, 2000. *Joseph Pell Lombardi*.

Fernbach's pair are replicated at 101, but *Lombardi* turns to riveted steel at 107-111, contrasting with neighboring cast iron.

[H35] **Sidewalk Subway Map**: On the east side-walk of Greene Street is "Subway Map Floating on a New York Sidewalk" (1986) by artist *Françoise Schein*, an abstracted map of subway systems in Manhattan.

Set into a black-on-black matrix, the routes are of stainless steel bars with the individual stations represented by glass roundels. Curiously, *Schein* and colleague *Petar Gevremov* reversed the design: "uptown" is "downtown," difficult to comprehend, as the map shows no other geography: no street grid, no shorelines, no Central Park. Obscurantism.

H30

[H36] **Greene Street, bet. Spring and Prince Sts.** [a] **92-94 Greene Street** 2004. *Joseph Pell Lombardi*. New pressed steel façades (on both Greene and Mercer Streets) for 20th-century infill into its 19th-century cast-iron context.
[b] **93-99 Greene St.** 1881. *Henry Fernbach*. Three buildings sporting Composite **Ionic**, now spruced up.
[c] **96 Greene St.** 1879. *Henry Fernbach*. **Tuscan**.
[d] **100 Greene St.** 1881. *Charles Mettam*. "**Corinthionic!**"
[e] **105 Greene St.** 1879. *Henry Fernbach*. Modified **Corinthian**.
[f] **112 Greene St.** 1884. *Henry Fernbach*. Slender brown **Ionic**.
[g] **113 Greene St.** *Henry Fernbach*. Attenuated abstract colonnettes and lintels of wrought iron.
[h] **114-120 Greene St.** 1882. *Henry Fernbach*. Two in Composite Ionic with stylized acanthus leaf antefixa atop the cornice. **Very grand**.

Mercer Street:

Like Crosby Street on the other side of Broadway, a service thoroughfare.

[H37] Originally **Firemen's Hall**/later **Hook & Ladder No.20, N.Y.C. Fire Department**, 155 Mercer St., bet. W. Houston and Prince Sts. 1854. *Field & Correja*. Altered.

When this was built, the City's fire laddies were volunteers. Most of the original ornate trim and moldings are gone, but some of its early form is visible in the quoins. Look for what was there in the **Necrology** section.

[H38] **Hotel Mercer**, 99 Prince St., NW cor. Mercer St. 1887-1888. *William Schickel & Co.* Renovations, 1986-1994, *Harman Jablin*. Façade restoration, *Marc Markowitz*.

A brick **Romanesque Revival** masonry exception in this cast-iron precinct, it once housed *John Jacob Astor's* fur coat fabrications. Now such high style is partially replaced by a preppie J.Crew store.

[H39] **Prince Street, bet. Greene and Wooster Sts.** [a] **109 Prince St.**, NW cor. Greene St. (also known as **119 Greene St.**). 1889. *J. Morgan Slade*. Composite pilasters. [b] **112-114 Prince St.** 1890. *Richard Berger*. Altered, 1975, *Hanford Yang*. A City Walls, Inc. photo-realistic painted façade by *Richard Haas* brings the image of rich cast-iron architecture to the side wall. Note the trompe l'oeil cat at the "open" window.

H36d   H38

[H40] **Greene Street, bet. Prince and Houston Sts.** [a] **121 Greene St.** 1883. *Henry Fernbach*. A cream-colored and classy **Corinthian**. Savor the monolithic granite side-walks, self-curbed, an old and fast disappearing local amenity.
[b] **129 Greene St.** 1881. *Detlef Lienau*. Lienau's only work in the district: brick with enormous windows.
[c] **132-140 Greene St.** 1885. *Alfred Zucker*. Three buildings wear a free-spirited **Ionic** façade (capitals turned sideways).
[d] **135 Greene St.** 1883. *Henry Fernbach*. A delicate **Tuscan**-ordered building. Originally Anthony Arnoux House.
[e] **139 Greene St.** 1824-1825. A lonely but rare and elegant brick **Federal** holdout. In a state of renovation without end.
[f] **142 Greene St.** 1871. *Henry Fernbach*. Bulky **Tuscan**.
[g] **148 Greene St.** 1884. *William Worthen*. Magnificent brick with light and elegant ironwork.

[H40h] **Alessi**, 130 Greene St., bet. Prince & W. Houston Sts. 2006. *Asymptote* (interiors).

Patisserie in the front, knick-knacks and housewares in the back (please don't laugh when they tell you the price of the dog food dish...$80). The exterior is nothing, but *Asymptote's* inside is reflective, spacey, wonderful.

[H41] **141-145 Wooster Street** (loft building), bet. W. Houston and Prince Sts. W side. 1897. *Louis Korn.*

Bland **Renaissance Revival**: a latecomer to SoHo, a building more comfortable around Washington Square East. (Chalk & Vermilion Gallery used to be here, 1987, *Smith-Miller & Hawkinson*). Good granite piers, however.

[H42] **139 Wooster Street**, bet. W. Houston and Prince Sts. 2008. *Beyer Blinder Belle.*

Block through to West Broadway. Masonry on West Broadway, Iron and glass on Wooster. Understated, with nice details.

H40d

H48b

[H43] **Adidas Store**/formerly **Gagosian Gallery**, 136 Wooster St., bet. W. Houston and Prince Sts. E side. 1992. *Gluckman Mayner.*

A glazed garage door, when opened, used to display monumental sculpture to the street. Now the displays are of "superstars" and "samba sleeks."

[H44] **130 Prince Street** (office buildings), SW cor. Wooster St. 1988. *Lee Manners & Assocs.*, designer. *Walter B. Melvin*, associate architect.

A pair: the corner in **neo–Art Deco**, the mid-block a former commercial bakery reconfigured. Clunky revivalism.

[H45a] **Room & Board**/formerly **Knoll International Design Center**, 105 Wooster St., bet. Prince and Spring Sts. W side. 1892. *Charles Behrens.* Altered, 1982, *Paul Haigh*, designer.

Hard brick and granite on the outside; soft pillows and couches on the inside.

[H45b] **115 Wooster Street**, bet. Prince and Spring Sts. W side. Circa 1890s.

Subtle: piers change profile at each floor as they rise, and don't always line up vertically, either. The effect is pleasing; a reminder that not everything has to adhere to an imaginary grid.

[H46] Originally **Engine Company No.13, NYC Fire Department**/now **Peter Blum Gallery**, 99 Wooster St., bet. Prince and Spring Sts. W side. 1881. *Napoleon LeBrun.* Altered, 1987.

A cast-iron bottom supporting a masonry top. The piers carry shields that once contained the engine company's insignia.

[H47] **97 Wooster Street** (lofts), bet. Prince and Spring Sts. W side. 1897. *George F. Pelham.*

Powerful corbels, each with a stern face, support bold attached columns; incised ornament embellishes both a mid-height band and the cornice.

H40h

[H48a] **84 Wooster Street** (warehouse), bet. Spring and Broome Sts., E side. 1896. *Albert Wagner.*
[H48b] **80 Wooster Street** (warehouse). E side. 1894. *G. A. Schellenger.*
[H48c] **64 Wooster Street** (warehouse), E side. 1899. *E.H. Kendall.*

Arches and cornices here creep into these cast-iron precincts: seven- and eight-story **Renaissance Revival** depositories, larger and more pretentious than their neighbors.

[H49] **42-46 Wooster Street** (lofts), bet. Broome and Grand Sts. E side. 1895. *F.S. Baldwin.* Reconfigured (together with 50 next door) with central atrium, 1999, *Bogdanow Partners.*

Brick **Romanesque Revival**, with rock-faced brownstone and cast iron in concert. Here the attempt is at grandeur, more than the spartan elegance of cast iron alone.

H54a

🏛 [H50] **26-28 Wooster Street**, SE cor.
Grand St., also known as 71 Grand St.
Wooster St. brick façade, 1879. Grand St. cast-
iron façade, 1888. Both, *Mortimer C. Merritt.*
  Two wonderful façades in different materials,
at a different time, but by the same architect.

[H51] **The Drawing Center**, 35 Wooster St.,
bet. Broome and Grand Sts. W side. Gallery
open: Tu-Fr 10-6; Sa 11-6. 212-219-2166.
www.drawingcenter.org
  The contents here, not the 1860s building,
are the pearl in the oyster, although there are
some lovely Corinthians, and atop, a broken
pediment, with **Lyall** inscribed. *Inigo Jones'*
"complete architectural drawings" were once
displayed here. You can't beat that.

[H52] **2 Wooster Street**, NE cor. Canal St. 1872.
W. H. Gaylor.
  Monumental. A phoenix of restoration and
maintenance since 2000.

*Canal Street becomes a Casbah between the
Avenue of the Americas (Sixth Avenue to everyone) and Centre Street. Here shops spill into the
street; their wares—"bargains" real or apparent—abound: cameras, batteries, fake Louis
Vuitton bags, watches, sheet metal, plastic —
you name it. A great place for the browsing gad-
geteer, do-it-yourselfer, or the serious bargain
hunter familiar with his or her needs. Rumor has
it that secret escape tunnels connect some of
the shops to each other, in case of a police raid.*

looks better up close than from afar. Usually,
these days, it's the opposite: the image is
the most important thing, the actual construction an afterthought. This one is well built and
has **weight**.

[H54b] **44 Mercer Street Apartments**, bet.
Broome and Grand Sts. 2009. *TRA Studio.*
  A shy little brother to **Nouvel's Big Grid** next
door, it's clad in trendy panels of stainless steel
(see *Gwathmey Siegel's* **SoHo Mews**, p.122, for
comparison). The façade's bowed glass "shield"
is a fussy, unnecessary detail.

[H54c] **47-49 Mercer Street** (lofts), bet. Broome
and Grand Sts. W side. 1873. *Joseph M. Dunn.*
  Crisp and lusty white cast-iron **Roman
Tuscans**. These Tuscans have ribbed bands
below the **echinus**. (That which supports the
weight: look it up.) Keep your eye out for Tuscan
variations.

[H54d] **72 Mercer Street/501 Broadway**, bet.
Broome and Spring Sts. 2008. *TRA Studio.*
  A cast-iron stalwart, consumed by fire in the
1960s, gave *TRA* this opening. Hooray for a **simple new building** with nice details, fitting into
the background in this historic district. Façades
face both Mercer and Broadway.

[H55] **Broome Street, bet. Mercer and Greene Sts.**
[a] Originally **Hitchcock Silk Building**,
453-455 Broome St. 1873. *Griffith Thomas.*
Corinthian, with a **wow of a cornice**, supported
by pairs of console brackets.

H50   H52   H56a

*Broome Street from Broadway to West
Broadway:*
  *Four blocks of SoHo at its most idiosyn-
cratic and hectic, a mixture of delightful cast-
iron façades, previously decayed, now restored
to glory. Traffic-choked. Walk it on an early
Sunday morning.*

[H53] **448 Broome Street**, bet. Broadway and
Mercer St. 1871-1872. *Vaux & Withers.*
  Eccentric and laden with fire escapes: nevertheless, the bas-reliefs within the pilasters,
emboldening friezes, window enframements
and the underbelly of the cornice are **extraordinary**. But, of course, *Vaux* passed by here.

📋 [H54a] **40 Mercer Street**, NE cor. Grand
St., through the block to Broadway. 2006.
Jean Nouvel and SLCE.
  Shimmering apartments above, and offices
below, all adhering strictly to **the Nouvel grid**!
Full of meticulously detailed steel connections,
it is the rare contemporary building that actually

[b] **461 Broome St.** 1871. *Griffith Thomas.*
Another decorated **Tuscan**.
[c] **467 Broome St.** 1873. *Isaac F. Duckworth.*
Decorated **Tuscan** encore.

🏛 [H56] **Broome Street, bet. Greene and
Wooster Sts.** [a] **The Gunther Building**,
469 Broome St., SW cor. Greene St. 1873.
Griffith Thomas. Rich **Corinthian** foliage and the
elegant curved glass corner.
[b] **477-479 Broome St.** 1885. *Elisha Sniffern.*
Corinthian below, plain pilasters above.
[c] **476-478 Broome St.** 1873. *Griffith Thomas.*
They were green-painted **Corinthian**.
[d] **480 Broome St.** 1885. *Richard Berger.*
Composite **Ionic** columns.

H55

H57

[H57] **Broome Street, bet. Wooster St. and West Broadway.** [a] **484 Broome St.,** NW cor. Wooster St. 1890. *Alfred Zucker*. Grand Monumental **Romanesque Revival** brick and rock-face brownstone. Entwined serpents form corbel arch supports in sandstone. No cast iron, but one of SoHo's stars. [b] **489-493 Broome St.** 1873. *J. Morgan Slade*. Note the similarity to *Griffith Thomas'* Gunther Building [above]. [c] **492-494 Broome St.** 1892. *Alfred Zucker*. While it lost three floors in 1938, it didn't lose the foliate ornament up the sides.

West Broadway:
  *In originally designating the **SoHo Cast-Iron District**, the Landmarks Preservation Commission did not include the **west** side of West Broadway.*

[H58] **307 West Broadway** (lofts), bet. Canal and Grand Sts. E side. 1892. *Douglas Smyth*.
  A still powerful **Ionic** capital anchors the façade.

[H59] **Soho Mews,** 311 West Broadway, bet. Canal and Grand Sts. E side. 2009. *Gwathmey Siegel*.
  A strict grid of steel (columns and beams), clad in stainless steel panels and varying panes of glass, frosted here, clear there. A block-through lot with a pleasant courtyard in the middle. This is sober and serene *Gwathmey*, in contrast to his 2005 **Astor Place Tower**, next to Cooper Union. Apparently content to be a well-behaved background building, it makes its next door neighbor, *Smyth's* **307 West Broadway**, seem like a riot of exuberant form and detail.

H59

[H60] **SoHo Grand Hotel**, 310 W. Broadway, bet. Canal and Grand Sts. W. side. 1990s. *Helpern Architects*.

Some nice contextual detailing (brick and stone courses alternate) at street level, but higher up it's banal boxes, stacked.

[H61] **357 West Broadway**, bet. Grand and Broome Sts., E side. 1820s.

Yet another rescued **Federal** house. Good incised lintels upstairs.

[H62] **Kenn's Broome Street Bar** (restaurant), 363 West Broadway, SE cor. Broome St. ca. 1825.

This too was a **Federal** house, its present occupation advertised with elegant Victorian gilt lettering, and home to a pleasant pseudo-vintage eating and drinking place. Plants. Ceiling fans. Stained glass.

Broome Street, West of SoHo:

The once seemingly forgotten paved triangle between Broome, Watts, and Thompson Streets was for decades an outdoor display for the rusted steel delights of welder-sculptor Robert S. Bolles (known locally but inaccurately as Bob Steel). Now it's a nice little sliver park, with benches and trees, and three of the remaining sculptures.

[H63] **54 Thompson Street** (lofts), NE cor. Broome St. ca. 1900. Converted, 1999.

Some modest rock-faced granite and brick, embellished with a private garden contained within an articulated sheet-steel wall (**Sculpture Garden Fence**. 1995. *Architecture Research Office*).

West Broadway between Broome and Spring Streets:

[H64] **380 West Broadway** (lofts). W side. ca. 1870.

Prosperous cast-iron front: a renovation done neatly but without pizzazz.

Name change: Between 1870 and 1899 West Broadway assumed the name South Fifth Avenue (a name change later promoted — unsuccessfully — by Robert Moses). During that period house numbers ascended southward from Washington Square to Canal Street. The number 159, cast into the iron pilaster of today's 383 West Broadway, dates from that period.

[H65] **392-394 West Broadway**, W side. 1872. *John H. Whitenack.*

Cast-iron elegance, with somber gray and green **Tuscan** columns.

[H66] **Metropolitan Lumber & Mill Works**/originally **Metropolitan Railway Company electrical substation**, 175 Spring St., bet. West Broadway and Thompson Sts. N side. ca. 1885.

A satisfyingly monumental granite **Romanesque Revival** arch is a portal to do-it-yourself lumber et al. So what's behind the mural? Once upon a time the Sixth Avenue El

H64

H66

H74

trundled up West Broadway before turning at West 3rd Street to find Sixth Avenue. This robust brick and granite structure served the El's electrical needs.

West Broadway between Spring and Prince Streets:

[H67] **420 West Broadway**. W side. ca. 1890.

Cut granite over black **Tuscan** stone; cool composition: somber elegance, housing art galleries.

[H68] **426 West Broadway**, W side. 1870s.

The exposed steel girders and decorated columns that embrace the façade give an engineering counterpoint to the brick and banded limestone above.

[H69] **430-434 West Broadway**, W side. 1988. *Arpad Baksa & Assocs.*, architects.

Five levels of **glitz** that serve merchants: out of place on West Broadway (but Landmarks did not designate the west side of W. Broadway).

[H70] **429 and 431 West Broadway**, E side. 1872. *Robert Mook.*

Two **Corinthians** freely stand at 431, and a sea of Tuscans populate the upper four façade floors.

[H71] **468 West Broadway**, W side. 1890s. Magnificent maroon painted brick arches, the black spandrels wearing swags, are decorated with iron strapwork and punctuated with granite rock-faced blocks. A major **Romanesque Revival** citizen.

[H72] **65-77 West Houston Street**, bet. West Broadway and Wooster St. S side. 1984. *Beyer Blinder Belle.*

Horizontal slivering to consume space, rather than squeeze in. The widening of Houston (Street) left the raw edge of SoHo unfinished. This is a bandaid on the block. Clad in colorful tile, it resembles a large Indian headband, two stories high.

H72

Thompson Street, south of West Houston Street:

[H73] **138-144 Thompson Street**, bet. Prince and W. Houston Sts. E side. 1883. *Oscar Seale.*

This former warehouse, off the beaten track, presents tall brick arches worthy of a **Roman** aqueduct, and carries a "cornice" of small, windowed spaces. Now used to store yuppies. Actually they enter through West Broadway, as this is, in fact, the tail of **468**!

Sullivan Street, south of West Houston Street:

[H74] **St. Anthony of Padua Roman Catholic Church**, 155 Sullivan St. E side. ca. 1888. St. Anthony's Pious League, 151 Thompson St. W side. ca. 1880.

A hard **neo-Romanesque** church where rough rock-faced ashlar contrasts with cut limestone pediments and arches. It is the parish of the South Village's dwindling Italian community.

H71

NECROLOGY

A neo-Georgian "suburban" bank building (originally **Franklin National Bank**) provided a tree-canopied plaza at the northwest corner of Broadway and Howard Streets (1967. *Eggers & Higgins*, architects. *Zion & Breen*, landscape architects.).

The impulse to provide amenities was commendable, but the result strange and inappropriate in this virile cast-iron environment. Incidentally, the Georges never used the hexagon for building: that is a later, Greek Revival game.

St. Alphonsus Church (Roman Catholic)/originally **Church of St. Alphonsus Liguori,** 312 W. Broadway, bet. Canal and Grand Sts. W side. 1872. **Rectory,** 308 W. Broadway. ca. 1878. **Church Hall,** 320 W. Broadway. ca. 1885.

The lively combination of fronts was dominated by the asymmetric **Lombardian Romanesque** façade of the church. Conveniently, as the community's Roman Catholic population began to sag, so did the buildings' foundations, resulting apparently from settlement into a long-forgotten underground stream. Closed in 1980 because of danger of collapse, the church and its companions were soon demolished. Site of the **SoHo Grand** Hotel.

The Villages

GREENWICH VILLAGE

Nonconformist in its street grids (they differ from each other as well as from those of the rest of Manhattan), open to the lifestyles it tolerated, and rich in its remarkable variety of architecture, **Greenwich Village** was a concentration of contrasts in a city of contrasts. But in the Village's case, these contrasts were long synonymous with its onetime identity: bohemia. That fading persona is largely gone today (as opposed to the days when most aspiring and successful artists and writers gravitated to its charm, and its onetime low-rents). The artists those observers have, in turn, been swept back to the City's outer boroughs as the cost of real estate has risen astronomically. The people of the visible Village changed—leaving West Village families, such as those written about by urbanist *Jane Jacobs*, and those of the South Village (the Italian community), to go about their own business, largely unnoticed.

As nostalgia fades, however, the Village continues to fulfill a variety of seemingly conflicting roles, although mostly to a much more affluent clientele: a genteel place to live, a

Washington Mews

have now migrated to Greenpoint, Williamsburg and Long Island City, leaving families, stockbrokers, movie stars, wallstreeters and mid-town bankers, with myriad children, in their places.

Since 1900 the **Village** had been not only a proving ground for new ideas among its creative residents but also a symbol of the forbidden, the free life—the closest thing to Paris that we had in this country. But with the opening up of Sixth and Seventh Avenues and the subways beneath them, the area became more accessible. After the hiatus caused by the Depression and World War II, the Village once again attracted interest, this time from high-rise housing developers, from smaller entrepreneurs who created little studio apartments with mini-spaces inversely proportional to their high rents, and from tenants who left the "duller" (meaning the outer) parts of the City to taste forbidden fruit. **Creators** were swept out by **observers** (middle-class doctors, dentists, cloak and suiters, and other vicarious residents). And

fashionable step up the professional ladder. Curiously, because the Village continues to attract tourists still half-expecting to run into *Bob Dylan* or *Allen Ginsberg*, the neighborhood's nightclubs and theaters remain proving grounds for local musicians and thespians. Few of the old coffeehouses, bakeries, and restaurants that gave the Village its character survive, however, and New York University remains a startlingly land-hungry and tone-deaf neighbor.

Heritage: Always a village, the first one was an **Algonquin** community, **Sapokanikan**. The Dutch, upon their arrival in 1626, quickly kicked out the natives, taking over the fertile rolling farmland for their own profit and pleasure.

Growth was leisurely since the village was completely separated from the bustling community concentrated at the lower tip of the island; but its stature rose suddenly in the 1730s with the land purchases of socially prominent naval *Captain Peter Warren*. When *Captain Warren* bought a large parcel in 1731, he was the first of

THE VILLAGES KEY MAP

West Village

Washington Square
& Environs

Astor
Place,
NoHo
& Environs

South Village/
West SoHo

East Village

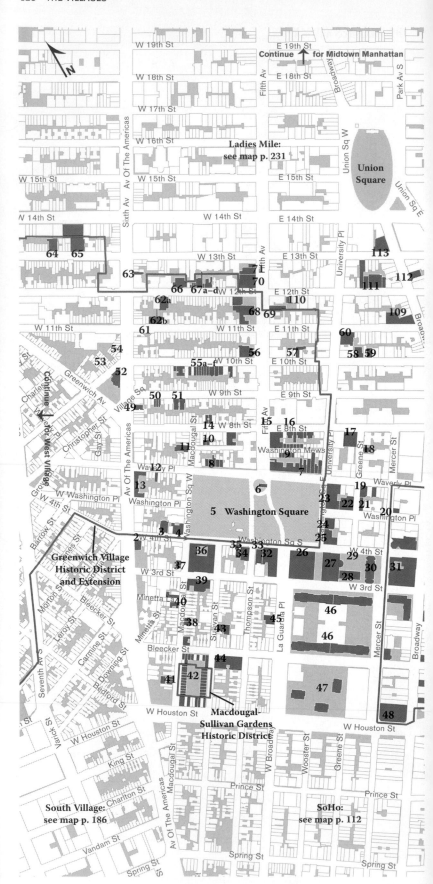

N

W 19th St
W 18th St
W 17th St
W 16th St
W 15th St
W 14th St
W 13th St

E 19th St
Continue ↑ for Midtown Manhattan
E 18th St
Fifth Av
Broadway
Park Av S

Ladies Mile:
see map p. 231

Union Sq W
Union
Square
Union Sq E

E 15th St
E 14th St
E 13th St

Av Of The Americas
Sixth Av
Sixth Av

64 65
63
62a
62b
61

W 13th St
W 12th St
71
70
66 67a–d
68 69

University Pl
E 12th St
110
109
113
112
111

54
53 52
49

Greenwich Av
Village Sq
Charles St

W 11th St
W 10th St
56
55a–f

E 11th St
57
E 10th St

60
58 59
Broadway

50 51
49

W 9th St
W 8th St
E 9th St
Fifth Av
E 8th St

17
18
Greene St
Mercer St

14
10
11
8

15 16
Washington Mews
9
7

Gay St
Christopher St
Continue for West Village

12
13

Waverly Pl
Washington Pl

6

19
23
22 21
20
Waverly Pl
Washington Pl

Grove St
W 4th St
W Washington Pl

5 Washington Square

24
25

Greenwich Village
Historic District
and Extension

3 4
W 4th St

35 33
34 32
36
37
39

26
27
28
29
30 31
W 3rd St

Barrow St
Commerce St

Bleecker St
Leroy St
Carmine St
Downing St
Bedford St

Minetta La
40
38 43
45
Macdougal St
Minetta St
Sullivan St
Thompson St
La Guardia Pl

46
46
47

Mercer St
Broadway

Seventh Av S
Varick St

Bleecker St
44
41 42

W Houston St
Macdougal–
Sullivan Gardens
Historic District

W Broadway
Wooster St
Greene St

48

W Houston St

South Village:
see map p. 186

Macdougal St
Av Of The Americas

Prince St

SoHo:
see map p. 112

Prince St

Charlton St
King St
Vandam St

Spring St

Spring St

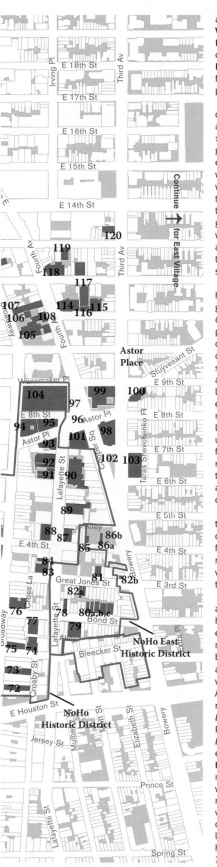

a long line of affluent individuals to settle in the **Village**. His mansion was soon followed by **Richmond Hill** (owned by *Aaron Burr*, among others) and the *Brevoort* homestead. **Richmond Hill** was the best known of these homes, which for nearly 100 years gave the Village an unsurpassed social status.

The City commissioners, having already contemplated the future growth of Manhattan, appointed *John Randel, Jr.,* who from 1808 to 1811 prepared maps and plans for the present gridiron of Manhattan's streets. The **Village** escaped most of this layout, however, since it was simply too difficult to impose it over the well-established pattern. The commissioners, though, had their way with the hills, leveling them all by 1811 and taking with them the grandeur of the old estates. These properties were then easily divisible into small city lots, and by 1822 the community was densely settled, many of the settlers "refugees" from a series of "downtown" epidemics.

Sailors' Snug Harbor and Trinity Parish have both had leading roles in the Village's growth. The **Harbor** was founded in 1801, when *Captain Robert Richard Randall* deeded in perpetual lease 21 acres of land (around and north of Washington Square), together with a modest cash grant, for the support of a home for aged seamen. It was moved to Staten Island in 1833, and since then has received its income from its leased **Village** land. Prior to the 1920s, its property had been divided into small lots, rented mainly for individual residences. Since then, land values have skyrocketed, and the **Harbor** understandably sought to increase its income from its holdings. In doing so, however, it leased rather indiscriminately, permitting the demolition of many historic and architectural treasures and their replacement by mediocre works, to the detriment of the area.

Trinity Parish made great contributions to the development of the **West Village** in the 19th century, encouraging respectful care and beautification of its leased land. In 1822 it developed a residential settlement around **St. Luke's Church**, which to this day is a positive influence upon the neighborhood.

Residents: Perhaps as important as the architectural heritage are the people the Village has attracted: the artists and writers, entertainers, intellectuals, and bohemians who have made their homes alongside long-established but less conspicuous **Village** families. But the artist in his garret is today mere legend. The well-established Hollywood actor, "Madison Avenue gallery" painter, and copywriter have replaced the struggling painter and writer. *Eugene O' Neill* and his group at the Provincetown Playhouse, *Maxwell Bodenheim, Edna St. Vincent Millay*, the delightful, "spirited" *Dylan Thomas* at Hudson Street's **White Horse Tavern**, and quiet *Joe Gould* accumulating material for his "oral history" at the **Minetta**—it was such as these who once made the **Village's** reputation international. Their forerunners were writers of the 19th century who took up residence here, attracted by modest rents, the leisurely pace and the delightful streets and houses. They included *Poe and Melville, Mark Twain, and Henry James*.

WASHINGTON SQUARE & ENVIRONS

The Village, though no longer bohemian, still represents the unconventional, a reputation supported by its winding streets, its tiny houses sandwiched between impersonal behemoths, and its charming shops and eateries.

[V1] **Greenwich Village Historic District and Extension** See maps. 👌

It took more than four years and seven public hearings to decide upon one contiguous **Historic District** for the Village—at one point 18 separate districts were considered—and the enormous irregular shape of the 100-plus-block area resulted in a two-volume designation report divided into nine sub-areas stretching from **NYU's** borders (the university successfully fought inclusion of much of its real estate) to the West Village's Washington Street with its adjacent, then functioning **High Line**. Since

Torn down in 1928, the lot was weedy and forgotten until 1999, its subsequent renovation a delightful example of what a small garden can contribute to the City. Cut the corner, hurry down its single path on the hypotenuse, or sit for a spell. This is a garden for enjoying a ten-minute coffee break; humble, perfect.

[V3] **Washington Square Methodist Church**, 135-139 W.4th St., bet. Washington Sq. W and 6th Ave. 1859-1860. *Gamaliel King*. Converted to apartments, 2006, *Flank Architects*.

Romanesque Revival marble. See **Brooklyn's Borough Hall** for more of this poorly remembered architect. Unfortunately, the outer shell is all that's left: a carapace for the swank condo conversion lurking inside, consuming the nave volume.

V4

V6

then, a **2006** extension, **Greenwich Village East,** has been added.

Walking Tour A: Washington Square, its four edges, and NYU from West 4th Street and Sixth Avenue, south to West Houston Street and Sixth Avenue. START at West 4th Street Station (A, B, C, D, E, F, and V trains of the former IND Sixth and Eighth Avenue Lines).
Note: *Only some of the entries on this tour lie within the Greenwich Village Historic District. See map.*

Walk east on West 4th Street, towards Washington Square Park. Visit these three on the way:

[V2] **Golden Swan Garden**, SE cor. W. 4th St. & Sixth Avenue. 1999. *New York Parks Dept.*

A shady spot at one of the busiest corners of the Village, formerly inhabited by the infamous **Golden Swan Cafe**, a dive known locally as the Hell Hole, upon which (and from within which) **Eugene O'Neill** based many of his plays.

[V4] **37 Washington Square West** (apartments), NW cor. W. 4th St. 1928. *Gronenberg & Leuchtag.*

Some comely glazed terra cotta enriches an otherwise banal façade.

Enter the park from the south:

[V5] **Washington Square Park**, at the foot of Fifth Ave. Redesigned, 1971, *John J. Kassner & Co.*, engineers. *Robert Nichols*, landscape architect. Service buildings, 1971, *Edgar Tafel & Assocs.* Patchwork mosaic plaza, 1971, *Cityarts Workshop.* Redesigned, 2008-2009, *George Vellonakis*, landscape architect, New York Parks Dept.

Originally marshland, Minetta Brook meandering through, then a potter's field, and later the site of the hanging gallows. In the 1820s a less sadistic citizenry converted it to a public park and parade ground for the military. With this change, building quickly began on all sides of the park, the north side with its "Row," and the east, which became the site of the first NYU building in 1837.

In 1964 local and citywide groups achieved a victory in their battle to keep an underpass from being built beneath the park. They later managed to free the park entirely of vehicular traffic—Fifth Avenue buses had for years used the space around the fountain as a turnaround, idling their engines there between runs. These accomplishments were later escalated into a full-blown redesign of the park, which kept the canopy of trees and added a circular pedestrian plaza ringing the old central fountain, a fresh interpretation of the European plaza. Despite substantial involvement of the community in the redesign, the physical changes have been the subject of great controversy. Some of this is the result of major demographic population shifts in the adjunct community—an outflow of families and an influx of outcasts.

A new design by *Vellonakis*, unveiled in phases during 2008-09, amid some controversy from neighborhood critics, includes more trees, benches, and lights, and moves the fountain slightly east so it lines up with **Washington Arch**. Not drastic, but a necessary sprucing up.

[V6] **Washington Arch**, 1889-1895. *Stanford White of McKim, Mead & White*. Winged figures, *Frederick MacMonnies*. West pier, **Washington in Peace**, 1918, *A. Stirling Calder*. East pier, **Washington in War**, 1916, *Herman A. MacNeil*. ●

The **Memorial Arch** (1895) was first erected in wood in 1889 for the centennial celebration of *George Washington's* inauguration by *McKim, Mead & White*. It was so well liked that pianist *Jan Paderewski* gave a benefit concert to help

According to the district's Landmarks Preservation Commission report, **Nos.1-13** are "the most important and imposing block front of early Nineteenth Century town houses in the City [sic]." **Nos.19-26**, a Greek Revival group that includes an unusual large town house in the Federal style (**No.20**), is not far behind. When built, they housed New York's most prominent merchant and banking families and, over time, other distinguished individuals. Architect *Richard Morris Hunt* lived at **No.2** between 1887 and 1895. Novelist *Henry James*, who was to immortalize the western part of the row in his novel *Washington Square*, paid many visits to his grandmother, *Elizabeth Walsh*, at No.18, demolished in favor of **2 Fifth Avenue's** low wing. In this century *John Dos Passos* wrote *Manhattan Transfer* at **No.3**; others living there have been *Edward Hopper* and *Rockwell Kent*. **No.8** was once the official residence of the mayor.

Over the years community pressure and artful illusion have maintained **The Row** in a fairly whole condition. Those from **Nos.7 to 13**, to the east of Fifth Avenue, retain the shell of their front and side façades only: **Sailors' Snug Harbor** gutted them for multiple-dwelling housing, and entrance to these now NYU-owned apartments is via a pergola facing Fifth Avenue. On the west side of Fifth, when the huge **No.2 Fifth Avenue** apartment tower was being planned, citizens put up an outcry, and a neo-neo-Georgian wing was designed for the Washington Square frontage, conspicuously lower than the adjacent real Greek Revival row houses.

V3

V7

finance construction of the permanent arch. The statue on the west pier of *Washington* as a civilian was sculpted by *Alexander Stirling Calder* (1870-1945), father of mobilemaker *Alexander Calder*.

Along the north edge, best seen from the park:

[V7] **"The Row."** 1-13 Washington Square North (town houses), bet. University Place and Fifth Ave. 1832-1833. **No.3**, new façade added, 1884, *J.E. Terhune*. **Nos.7-13**, converted to apartment house, Fifth Ave. pergola added, 1939, *Scott & Prescott*. [V8] **19-26 Washington Square North** (town houses), bet. Fifth Ave. and MacDougal St. **No.20**, 1829; altered, 1880, *Henry J. Hardenbergh*. Others, 1836-1839. (**No.14**, the southern wing of **No.2 Fifth Avenue**, 1950, *Emery Roth & Sons*).

Walk north on Fifth for a short block, and hiding behind "The Row," is a delightful urban passage: Washington Mews.

[V9] **Washington Mews**, from University Place to Fifth Ave., bet. E.8th St. and Washington Sq. N. North stables remodeled, 1916, *Maynicke & Franke*. South buildings constructed, 1939.

A 19th-century mews lined on its uptown side with converted stables that once served the brownstones on 8th Street and Washington Square and that now, in the case of many, serve New York University. **Nos.1-10**, on the south side, were built in 1939, and almost all were stuccoed in concert, causing an unfortunate regimentation. A walk through this Belgian-block-paved alley (private, but pedestrians are not discouraged) is the best way to sense its space.

V10

Back towards the Arch, then right (west) along Waverly Place, then right (north) on MacDougal Street:

[V10] **MacDougal Alley,** off MacDougal St., bet. W.8th St. and Washington Sq. N. E side.

This charming cul-de-sac (less charming when filled with residents' cars) is jointly owned by property holders on Washington Square North and on the south side of 8th Street. The 20-story bulk of **No.2 Fifth Avenue** looms over it, overwhelming its space and diminishing its small-scaled delight.

Now, south on MacDougal Street:

[V11] **Tenth Church of Christ, Scientist**/originally factory and store. 171 MacDougal St., bet. W.8th St. and Waverly Place. W side. 1891. *Renwick, Aspinwall & Russell.* Converted to church, 1967, *Victor Christ-Janer.* Conversion to apartments, new chapel, restoration of 1891 façade, 2009, *Hanrahan Meyers* and *TRA Studio.*

In 2006 Landmarks Commissioners said *Mr. Christ-Janer's* "severe modern brick façade detracts from the scale and architectural character of the streetscape." It did not mention that in its own 1969 report, the spare, moody work was described as "handsome." Be that as it may be, the *Renwick and Partners* façade is returning, with "improvements," and Christian Scientists will be gathering in their own new *Hanrahan Meyers* **Chapel** within.

Go back to Waverly, turn right (west), then take a left (south) on Sixth Avenue:

V12

[V12] **108 Waverly Place** (house), bet. Sixth Ave. and Washington Sq. W./MacDougal St. S side. 1826. Altered, 1906, *Charles C. Haight.* Garage entrance removed, 1927.

In this pleasantly Classical street, this eccentric and dour granite house wears crenellations (presumably to protect the skylight against insurrection).

Left on Sixth Avenue, briefly:

[V13] **Washington Court** (apartments), 360-374 Avenue of the Americas, bet. Waverly and Washington Places. E side. 1986. *James Stewart Polshek & Partners.*

A brilliantly conceived, designed, detailed, and executed **postmodern** apartment house (with stores on Sixth Avenue) that captures the scale, rhythms, and some of the accretive quality of many a Village street. Yet it was built only six stories high in the rapidly boiling 1980s Manhattan real estate market—chalk up the low-rise character to the IND subway running

under part of the plot, local hyperactive citizen watchdog groups, and a vigilant Landmarks Preservation Commission.

North on Sixth Avenue, right on West 8th Street:

Frederick J. Kiesler's Film Guild Playhouse (52 West 8th Street) has vanished, its succession of owners having failed to value the Viennese architect-stage designer's visionary designs, though they were applauded and applied by theater architects throughout the world. But here, in 1928, Kiesler (1892-1965) made provisions for simultaneous slide projections on the side walls and created a main screen where the projection surface area could be altered in size—film projection concepts that are still considered avant-garde. The exterior bears no trace of his hand.

[V14a] **24, 26 West 8th Street**, bet. MacDougal St. and Fifth Ave. 1838.

Town houses built (together with **No.28**) as an investment by merchant *Joseph W. Alsop, Jr.*

V13

Their subsequent conversion into studios to enjoy north light has given them distinctive—and not inharmonious—window patterns.

[V14b] **New York Studio School of Drawing, Painting & Sculpture**/ the original **Whitney Museum of American Art**/earlier **Gertrude Vanderbilt Whitney House** and private art gallery/originally 8, 10, 12 West 8th Street (houses), bet. MacDougal St. and Fifth Ave. Houses, 1838. Converted into House and gallery, 1931, *Auguste L. Noël* of *Noël & Miller.* Converted into Whitney Museum, 1936, *Auguste L. Noël.*

The 1930s neo-**Classical** entranceway remains the single hallmark of the Whitney when it opened at the onset of the Great Depression. The museum moved to a new structure next to the **Museum of Modern Art** garden, with *Noël* as architect (but with the MoMA garden façade by *Philip Johnson*), then left for its monumental Upper East Side *Breuer* building. Soon to come is the new **Gansevoort Street** satellite Whitney.

[V15] **1 Fifth Avenue** (apartments), SE cor. E.8th St. 1929. *Helmle, Corbett & Harrison and Sugarman & Berger.*

A stepped-back pinnacle of cool brown brick that has been a visual landmark on lower Fifth Avenue and Washington Square ever since it was built.

A "real kick in this super-castle. There are battlements, machiciolations, pointed buttresses and various medieval suggestions...." *T-Square, The New Yorker.* October 1, 1927.

V15

[V16] **4-26 East 8th Street**, bet. University Place and Fifth Ave. 1834-1836. Remodeled, 1916, *Harvey Wiley Corbett.*

Stuccoed apartment buildings made picturesque by the addition of bold decorative eaves, brickwork inlaid in a stucco ground, and bits of wrought ironwork. A stage set, symbolic of the "village" of a bohemian artist but not typical of its Federal/Greek Revival architectural reality.

[V17] **Iris and B. Gerald Cantor Film Center**, Tisch School of the Arts, SW cor. E.8th and Greene Sts. 1998. *Davis Brody Bond.*

A sleek banded house for film. The superlettering attempts some modest modernist graphic enrichment of the façade; and the sidewalk marquee provides elegant shelter for theoretical window shopping. But the architecture is overwhelmed by a subsequent arrival of ground floor fast food.

Turn right (south) into Greene Street:

*New York University: NYU's avaricious landgrabbing has created an empire larger than the Village holdings of Sailors' Snug Harbor, consisting of loft buildings, apartment houses, and Greek Revival rows on and around Washington Square. Once the bane of Villagers' existence, NYU's empire building was tamed in the 1970s by economic realities. Philip Johnson and Richard Foster had been commissioned to create a unified urban campus where none had existed before. Their plans called for rebuilding and refacing buildings around the east side of Washington Square with the vivid red sandstone visible in the master plan's only fruits: the **Bobst Library**, the **Tisch Building**, and the **Meyer Physics Building**. Happily, the rest of this grandiose scheme was abandoned.*

[V18] Originally **Sailors' Snug Harbor Headquarters**, 262 Greene St., bet. E.8th St. and Waverly Place.

Once the administrative center of the compact real estate empire (within a short walk of this building), funded by *Capt. Robert Richard Randall* in 1801 to endow a home for aged seamen. The sailors' home for many years, **Snug Harbor**, an elegant Greek Revival landmark on Staten Island, was vacated by them in 1976 in favor of new facilities in North Carolina. Its Headquarters has taken off as well.

[V19a] **Kimball Hall, NYU**, 246 Greene St., SE cor. Waverly Place. 1891. *Alfred Zucker.*

V16   V19b

Gloomy brown and beige brick, patterned to simulate a larger scale of stone coursing at its base.

[V19b] **Torch Club**, 18 Waverly Place (in Kimball Hall), bet. Washington Sq. East and Greene St. 2000. *Beyer Blinder Belle.*

A private club for faculty and alumni. A candy factory from 1937 until 1986, Kopper's Chocolates, created chocolate mints served at the **Torch Club** today.

From Greene Street turn left (east) into Washington Place to Mercer, then backtrack to Washington Square East:

[V20] **3-5 Washington Place, NYU**. NE cor. Mercer St. 1890s.

The bas-relief of the incised pier capitals are an exotic, but glorious detail. Higher up, brick with banded brownstone and terra-cotta colonnettes frame the many-windowed façade. Understated, but rich.

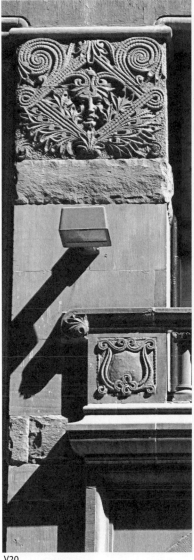

V20

V22

[V22] Brown Building, NYU/originally **Asch Building**, 23-29 Washington Place, NW cor. Greene St. 1900-1901. *John Wooley.* ●

Rich limestone piers with terra-cotta capitals support a stolid, modestly detailed brick façade, topped with a strong projecting cornice over an arcade of small Romanesque-Revival windows. Handsome.

[V23] Silver Center for Arts and Science, Hemmerdinger Hall NYU/earlier **NYU Law School**, 100 Washington Sq. E., bet. Waverly and Washington Places. 1895. *Alfred Zucker.* Remodeled, 1990s, *Polshek Partnership.*

NYU originally built this to accommodate a paying tenant, **The American Bank Note Company**, on the lower seven floors (hence the façade division at that point) and the Schools of Commerce, Law, and Pedagogy above. By the end of World War I the increase in students caused a takeover of the entire building for classes.

In the building: **Grey Art Gallery**. Open to the public: Tu,Th,Fr 11-6; We 11-8:30; Sa 11-5; closed Mo. 212-998-6780.

One of NYU's bright spots: an offbeat gallery with high standards of quality. Note the grid of white-painted Doric columns on the interior, around which the exhibitions are arranged.

[V24] Pless Building, NYU, 82 Washington Sq. E. & 26 Washington Pl. 1890s.

At the fifth floor, clustered brick and terra-cotta colonnettes support limestone ellipses that parade around the corner to Washington Place. Atop, a modest cornice hovers over trios of Romanesque-Revival windows.

[V25] Paulette Goddard Hall, NYU, 79 Washington Sq. E., NE cor. W. 4th St. 1890s.

If you don't remember, *Paulette Goddard* was the The Gamine in *Modern Times, Charlie Chaplin's* greatest film. (And *Chaplin's* third wife). Hardly gamine, the building is of brick, limestone, and terra cotta, providing lusty

[V21] Carter Hall, NYU, 10 Washington Place, bet. Greene and Mercer Sts. 1891. *Richard Berger.* Façade restored, 1972.

The loss of its cornice has diminished (but not destroyed) this loft building's orange terracotta, black cast-iron, and granite façade: renovated (the original windows were removed) by NYU on the advice of master planners *Philip Johnson and Richard Foster.*

The Triangle Shirtwaist Fire: A polite bronze plaque at the northwest corner of Washington Place and Greene Street refers discreetly to "the site" of the Triangle Shirtwaist Company fire, a tragedy which took 146 lives, mostly those of young women, on the Saturday afternoon of March 25, 1911. The Brown Building (NYU), originally called the Asch Building, is the very building in which the disaster took place; Triangle occupied the upper three floors of the 10-story building:

V25

pilasters, their composite capitals supporting arches that spring across the façade. Dour and delightful. **New York University Welcome Center,** in Paulette Goddard Hall. 2009. *Rogers Marvel.*

Along Washington Square South:

[V26] Elmer Holmes Bobst Library, NYU, 70 Washington Sq. S., bet. La Guardia Pl. and Washington Sq. E. S side. 1965-1972. *Philip Johnson and Richard Foster.*

Johnson as a **Mannerist** (the "columns" are concave rather than convex): from a late-Renaissance game using Classical parts in a sometimes illogical, but startling manner. But the produced red sandstone façade is bulky and heavy-handed. Inside, a great atrium brings light and grand space to its users. Outside it shades the park.

[V27] Tisch Hall, Stern School of Business, NYU, 40 W.4th St., bet. Washington Sq. E. and Greene St. 1972. *Philip Johnson and Richard Foster.*

V26

V28

V30

Another ruddy **Johnsonian,** this time without a meaningful inner space.

[V28] Henry Kaufman Management Center, Stern School of Business, NYU, 44 W. 4th St., bet. Washington Sq. E. and Greene St. 1990s.

A crisp counterpoint to the brownstone surrounding; a white body entered through a cylindrical pavilion. **Concourse Project, Stern School of Business,** 2008-2010. *Perkins & Will.* Connecting the business worlds of NYU Graduate Teaching.

[V29] NYU, lacking a traditional campus quad, uses city streets and passageways as surrogates. As a true urban campus, a central public node could be its Piazza San Marco, serving both university and neighborhood. Tisch and Weaver Halls and the Kaufman Center form three sides of a slightly elevated paved plaza, bounded on the north by W. 4th St. Aside from a boring

modernist sculpture and a few uncomfortable benches, it's a wasteland. It could be, in the hands of a thoughtful architect/landscape architect, a magnificent complement to adjacent Washington Square Park.

*For **Meyer Hall** and other **NYU** and related buildings continue east here to Mercer Street and Broadway beyond. Resume tour at [V32].*

[V30] Warren Weaver Hall, NYU, 251 Mercer St., bet. W.3rd and W.4th Sts. W side. 1966. *Warner, Burns, Toan & Lunde.*

An early **NYU** attempt at creating architectural identity through a new, modern building—now dated. The *Johnson-Foster* master plan followed, for better, or for worse.

[V31] 250 Mercer Street (lofts), SE cor. W. 4th St. 1890s.

Cast iron, brownstone, brick, and terra cotta combine to corner West 4th and Mercer with this rich eclecticism.

V31

V32

V33

From Bobst Library and Tisch Hall walk west along Washington Square South:

[V32] Helen and Martin Kimmel Center for University Life (student center), 566-576 LaGuardia Pl., SW cor. Washington Sq. S. 2001. *Kevin Roche John Dinkeloo & Assocs.*

Kimmel stands on the site of its predecessor, the demolished **Loeb,** providing twice the student space in a volume that matches Bobst's bulk to the East. The atrium and lobby, with their light-filled grand stairway, form space for lively indoor student interchange.

[V33] Holy Trinity Chapel, Generoso Pope Catholic Center at NYU, 58 Washington Sq. S., SE cor. Thompson St. 1964. *Eggers & Higgins.*

Awkward modernism from a time when the search for form preoccupied American architects.

*A peek south on Thompson Street reveals the tiny but lovable **Chess District: The Village Chess Club**, 219 Thompson, and **Chess Forum**, 230 Thompson, both between W. 3rd and Bleecker Streets. Rainy day addendums to the famous chess tables in Washington Square Park, the clubs are scruffy, with pick-up games (pay by the hour) at worn tables. They don't mind people watching and hanging out; the late-night scenes within, players hunkered over boards in great concentration, are wonderful to behold. Both clubs sell chess sets and supplies.*

[V34a] **Judson Memorial Baptist Church**, 54-57 Washington Sq. S., SW cor. Thompson St. 1888-1893. *Stanford White of McKim, Mead & White.* Stained glass, *John La Farge.* Marble relief, S wall of chancel (after *Saint-Gaudens'* plans), *Herbert Adams.* 🌿
[V34b] **Judson Hall and Tower**, 51-54 Washington Sq. S., bet. Thompson and Sullivan Sts. S side. **Tower, Nos.52-54.** 1895-1896. *McKim, Mead & White.*

F35

Hall, No.51. 1877. *John G. Prague.* 🌿
[V34c] **King Juan Carlos of Spain Center**, 53 Washington Sq. S. 1997. *Polshek Partnership.*
　　An eclectic **Early Christian** (Roman) church and tower of yellow roman brick, limestone, and terra cotta that once dominated Washington Square but is now dwarfed by many cacophonous neighbors. Its ornate and pompous detail, en masse, recalls such inflated Roman churches as **St. Paul's Outside-the-Walls** (rebuilt at the same time after a fire, from the ground up). Look inside these walls. And within is the King Juan Carlos of Spain Center.

[V35] **Hagop Kevorkian Center for Near Eastern Studies, NYU**, 50 Washington Sq. S., SE cor. Sullivan St. 1972. *Philip Johnson* and *Richard Foster.*
　　A classy but overscaled polished granite building matching in size the adjacent "town house." It would have been a happier neighbor to the Judson complex were it in brick.

[V36] **Vanderbilt Law School, NYU**, 40 Washington Sq. S., bet. Sullivan and MacDougal Sts. 1951. *Eggers & Higgins.*
　　A blockful of **neo-Georgian** building, built much in advance of the current historicist fashions, trying to be neighborly and offering a pleasant arcaded and contained forecourt to the street.

Left (south) on MacDougal Street (Washington Square West).

　　MacDougal Street, *between West 3rd and Bleecker: MacDougal is the most colorful and magnetic venue for tourists on an evening outing in the Village. With the advent of the drug scene in the late 1960s its activities took a turn to the bizarre, and many of its restaurants, coffeehouses, jewelry boutiques, and folk song emporia disappeared. Some still remain, some replaced, some reincarnated. The Grizzly Pear, at No.107, between Bleecker Street and Minetta Lane, features a boisterous bluegrass jam session every Wednesday night until the wee, wee*

"Chess District"

hours, led by the legendary "Uncle Bob, the Sheriff of Good Times."

[V37] **127-131 MacDougal Street**, bet. W.3rd and W.4th Sts. W side. 1828-1829. 🌿
　　These **Federal** houses were built on land owned by *Alonzo Alwyn Alvord.* The pineapple ironwork newel posts at **No.129** are one of the few surviving pairs remaining in the Village.

[V38] **130-132 MacDougal Street**, bet. W.3rd and Bleecker Sts. E side. 1852.
　　Twinned entrances and an ironwork portico.

Peek left on West 3rd Street, then back to MacDougal:

[V39] **Filomen D'Agostino Residence Hall, NYU Law School**, 110 W.3rd St., bet. Sullivan and MacDougal Sts. 1986. *Benjamin Thompson & Assocs.*
　　Twelve stories, detailed to seem in scale with its smaller neighbors. Standard, not jumbo brick, laid in Flemish bond, like the **Law School**;

V34a

deep window reveals and weighty window frames further emphasize the heft of the masonry walls. Substantial ironwork shows learning from lessons of the past. A fine work.

[V40] **Minetta Tavern**, 113 MacDougal St., SW cor. Minetta Lane.

A sorry 1950s exterior masks a drinking person's museum of Greenwich Village. The walls are crammed with photographs and other mementos of the famed characters who claimed the **Minetta** as a second home during the heyday of the Village. Note especially the *Joe Gould* memorabilia.

Coffeehouses: The Village has been associated with coffeehouses for generations, but they have been steadily disappearing in recent years. The oldest (since 1927) and most authentic is **Caffe Reggio,** *119 MacDougal St., north of Minetta Lane, on the west side, with a nickel-plated brass macchina spewing forth steamed espresso and various coffee, cocoa, or milk*

V40

combinations. **Caffe Dante,** *81 MacDougal St., south of Bleecker Street on the west side, has a giant sepia photo mural of Florence from San Miniato. Both Reggio and Dante have pastries, hot and cold beverages, and conviviality.* **Le Figaro,** *at the southeast corner of MacDougal & Bleecker, was a fixture for eons, but recently went the way of the sandaled folk singer.* **Café Borgia,** *on the opposite corner, also has bitten the dust. Will future generations lament the closing of Starbucks?*

[V41] **Tiro a Segno/New York Rifle Club,** 77 MacDougal St., bet. W. Houston and Bleecker Sts.

An Italian club where the shooting described is off-premises. Handsome brickwork scaled to the **"Gardens"** ensemble across the street.

[V42] **MacDougal-Sullivan Gardens Historic District,** bet. MacDougal and Sullivan Sts., W. Houston and Bleecker Sts. ca. 1923. 170-188 Sullivan St., W side. 1850. 74-96 MacDougal St., E side. 1844. Altered, 1921, *Francis Y. Joannes and Maxwell Hyde.* 🍎

The whole-block renovation started as an idea from *William Sloane Coffin* (then a director of the family business, the W. & J. Sloane furniture house) to develop a pleasing residence for middle-income professionals from a slum neighborhood. He formed the **Hearth and Home Corporation,** bought the block, renovated it, and by 1921, the following year, had rented nearly all the houses. *Coffin's* dream of a private community garden was realized around 1923; each house has its own low-walled garden that opens onto a central mall with grouped seating for adults and, at one end, a small playground. The garden is for residents only.

Circle the harmoniously painted Gardens, worth a gaze from all sides, then south to W. Houston and then back north on Sullivan, continuing momentarily across Bleecker:

[V43] **Philip Coltoff Center, Children's Aid Society**/originally **Sullivan Street Industrial School,** 209-219 Sullivan St., bet. Bleecker and W.3rd Sts. E side. 1892. *Vaux & Radford.*

A rich interplay of brick and brownstone (now simulated in stucco), solid and void, arches and angles; its renovated details have been smoothed by less skilled craftsmen than those of 1892.

Then back to Bleecker and continue east, where things gradually get more modern:

[V44] **The Atrium**/originally **Mills House No.1,** 160 Bleecker St., bet. Sullivan and Thompson

V42

Sts. S side. 1896. *Ernest Flagg.* Converted, 1976.

Reclaimed by the middle class as apartments, the structure was built originally as a hostel for poor "gentlemen" (*the room rate was only 20¢ a night, but the expenses were covered by profits on the 10¢ and 25¢ meals*). The building was a milestone in concept and plan: 1,500 tiny bedrooms either on the outside or overlooking the two grassed interior courts open to the sky. Eventually the courts were skylighted and paved, and the structure became a seedy hotel, **The Greenwich.** The courts, now neatly rebuilt with access balconies to the apartments which ring them, are the inspiration for the project's new name.

[V45] **Center for Architecture,** 536 LaGuardia Place, bet. W. 3rd & Bleecker Sts. Loft building, 1911. Storefront, 2003, *Andrew Berman,* architect. Galleries open to the public, Mo-Fr 9-8, Sa 11-5. *www.aiany.org*

The home base of the **AIA** (American Institute of Architects) New York chapter; a delightful, light-filled space filling three levels with galleries, lecture halls, and meeting rooms.

The Center, open to the public, is host to count-less informative exhibits and lectures behind a meticulously designed aluminum and glass storefront. Lively.

[V46] **Washington Square Village**, W.3rd to Bleecker Sts., LaGuardia Pl. to Mercer St. 1956-1958. *S. J. Kessler*, architects. *Paul Lester Weiner*, consultant for design and site planning.

Superbuildings on superblocks. These crisp gargantuas are the antithesis of **Village** scale and charm. Spanning what were University Place and Greene Street, they come from architects' fantasies of ideal city planning, now much discredited.

[V47] Originally **University Village**, 100 and 110 Bleecker St., and 505 LaGuardia Pl. Bleecker to W. Houston Sts., bet. Mercer St. and LaGuardia Pl. 1966. *I. M. Pei & Partners*. Central sculpture, 1970, *Pablo Picasso* (large-scale concrete trans-lation, *Carl Nesjar*).

Three pinwheel-plan towers visible for miles. What is exceptional for this high-rise housing is that the size of individual apartments can be grasped because of their articulated form. Inside, corridors are short—not the usual labyrinth—and handsomely lit and carpeted. Outside, the advances in the technology of cast-in-place concrete were remarkable to behold; the smooth surfaces and intricate curved fillets of the deeply formed concrete façade could be achieved despite the vicissitudes of on-site cast-ing. The two Bleecker Street units (Silver Towers) are NYU owned; the third is a private co-op. NYU has proposed a fourth tower.

V46

At the center is the 36-foot-high enlarge-ment, in concrete and stone, of *Pablo Picasso's* small cubist sculpture **Portrait of Sylvette**. Despite sensitive craftsmanship, the work loses much in translation.

Turn right (south) into Mercer Street:

Mercer Street Books, 206 Mercer St. bet. W. Houston & Bleecker Streets, has been a book-store in one form or another since the 1970s, a holdout from New York's funkier past. Enter through its tiny portal and it seems to expand and go on forever. There are thousands of excel-lent, cheap used books and vinyl records; a refreshing reminder of an era when bookstores didn't sell cappuccino.

[V48] **Cable Building**, 611 Broadway, NW cor. Houston St. 1892-1894. *McKim, Mead & White*.

The name reflects its original role as head-quarters for, and one of the power stations of, Manhattan's **not inconsiderable cable car empire**. Over the entrance, an oculus, flanked by two elegantly draped Classical ladies, announces that the architects were staunchly in the **American Renaissance** world of the Great Columbian Exposition of 1893.

Around the corner the **Angelika Film Center** within (Mercer Street entry. 1989. *Igor Josza and Don Schimenti*), offers art and offbeat film fare. At the end of a tour, sit down in the café with pastry and coffee, and plan which movie to see, then and there.

END of Tour A. For Tour B, head back to West 4th Street and Sixth Avenue. For Astor Place tour, head one block east to the corner of Broadway and E. Houston Street and turn to that section of the Guide (p. 151).

Necrology: Broadway Central Hotel

The nearest subways are at W. Houston Street and Broadway (Broadway-Lafayette Street Station of the former IND Sixth Avenue Line, B, D, and F trains) or Bleecker and Lafayette Streets (No.6 local of the old IRT Lexington Avenue Line local, Bleecker Street Station).

NECROLOGY

Eighth Street Bookshop: When Greenwich Village was the intellectual center of New York, West 8th Street was its main commercial strip. One of the street's great institutions was a real bookshop, founded by two brothers, *Eli and Ted Wilentz*. It opened at No.30, at the corner of MacDougal Street, until success caused it to move to a much larger multistory space across the street at No.17 (1965. *Elliot Willensky*). The genial shop not only attracted casual customers but was a haven for writers and poets as well.

V45

Broadway Central Hotel, originally **Southern Hotel**/later **Grand Central Hotel**, 673 Broadway, bet. Bleecker and W. 3rd Sts. W side. 1871. *Henry Engelbert*.

When this great Beaux Arts lady went, she did so in dramatic fashion—not so much a peaceful demise as a mighty—and deadly— collapse into the center of Broadway's pavement. Its replacement, the **Mercer St. Residence Hall NYU** (1981. *Benjamin Thompson & Assocs.*) is a pale replacement.

Loeb Student Center, 566 Laguardia Place, SW cor. Washington Sq. S. 1959. *Harrison & Ambramovitz. Reuben Nakian*, sculptor.

Demolished for the huger Kimmel Center.

AS GOOD AS DEAD

Originally **Mori's Restaurant**, 146 Bleecker St., bet. LaGuardia Pl. and Thompson St. S side. Restaurant alteration and façade, 1920. *Raymond Hood*.

Hood, soon to gain recognition for his firm's winning entry in the **Chicago Tribune Tower** competition, converted a pair of old row houses to one of the Village's best-known Italian restaurants of the period, **Mori's**. He and his wife lived briefly in a tiny apartment over the premises. History lost out to tawdry maintenance and economics.

Walking Tour B: From West 8th Street and Sixth Avenue, north to East 12th Street near Union Square. START at West 4th Street Station (A, B, C, D, E, F, and V trains of the former IND Sixth and Eighth Avenue Lines) and walk north three blocks to West 8th Street.

Note: The map district boundary lines show which entries lie within the Greenwich Village Historic District.

[V49] **Bigelow Building**, 412 Sixth Ave., bet. W.8th and W.9th Sts. E side. 1902. *John E. Nitchie.*

Still occupied by **C. O. Bigelow, Chemists, Inc.**, culture lag is evident: still transitional Romanesque Revival moving toward neo-Classical, more than a decade after it had affected others.The terra-cotta arched enframements wear magnificent cartouches at their keystones and where the arches spring.

[V50] **54, 56, and 58 West 9th Street**, bet. Fifth and Sixth Aves. 1853. *Reuben R. Wood*, builder.

V49

A mock **Neuschwansteinian** assemblage (after *King Ludwig II* of Bavaria's castle, **Neuschwanstein**) of leaded glass, steeply sloping roofs, gables, pinnacles, Venetian Gothic embellishments, and an intricate tower and clock; one of the City's most remarkable buildings. Endangered when no use could be found for it—it had remained vacant since 1945—local residents went into action. Led by indefatigable *Margot Gayle*, they first repaired and lighted the clock and eventually persuaded city fathers to restore the entire structure as a regional branch library. Budgetary limitations meant the loss of the polychrome slate roof shingles, but the exterior did get a thorough cleaning and repair.

Today's prominent tower served originally as a fire lookout, replacing a tall clapboard version, around which the **Jefferson Market's** sheds, dating from 1833, clustered. In 1877 the courthouse and its adjoining jail along 10th Street were completed from *Frederick Clarke Withers'* designs. In 1883 a masonry market building designed by *Douglas Smyth* filled the

V52

A distinguished group: pairs of half-round arched windows set within segmental arched openings.

[V51a] **The Portsmouth**, 38-44 W.9th St., bet. Fifth and Sixth Aves. 1882.
[V51b] **The Hampshire**, 46-50 W.9th St. 1883. Both by *Ralph S. Townsend.*

Lusty Victorian flats embellished with rich terra-cotta spandrels and, in the case of The Hampshire, diminished by festoons of fire escapes.

Back to Sixth Avenue:

[V52] **Jefferson Market Branch**, New York Public Library/originally Third Judicial District or **(Jefferson Market) Courthouse**, 425 Sixth Ave., SW cor. W.10th St. 1874-1877. *Vaux & Withers.* Exterior restoration, interior remodeling, 1967, *Giorgio Cavaglieri*. Further restoration, 1994, *Joseph Pell Lombardi.*

remainder of the site, replacing the market's old sheds. Both jail and market were demolished in 1927 in favor of the high-rise **Women's House of Detention** (1931. *Sloan & Robertson*), in turn demolished in 1974.

The trial of *Harry Thaw*, the assassin of *Stanford White*, took place in these halls.

*The **Jefferson Market Greening**, on Greenwich Avenue between Christopher and West 10th Streets, is the official name for the fenced formal park that occupies the site of the old market and of the more recent **Women's House of Detention**. The greening was started (and is maintained, with help from the Vincent Astor Foundation) by members of the local community. It forms a verdant foreground to the amusing forms of the Jefferson Market Library.*

Behind the Market, continue briefly on West 10th Street where it has now joined an earlier, diagonal street grid, first to Patchin Place, on your right, and then retracing your steps back, and to the left (north) onto Sixth Avenue, Milligan Place.

[V53] **Patchin Place**, off W.10th St., bet. Greenwich and Sixth Aves. NW side. 1848.
[V54] **Milligan Place**, Sixth Ave. bet. W.10th and W.11th Sts. W side. 1852.

In 1848 and 1852, respectively, **Patchin** and **Milligan Places** were built as second-class boarding houses for Basque waiters and workers at the old **Brevoort House** on Fifth Avenue. Today they are charming, not for the quality of their architecture, but rather as peaceful pedestrian cul-de-sacs that contrast with the agitated ebb and flow of Village Square crowds only a block to the south.

In the 1920s **Patchin Place** became famous for its writer residents. Its most renowned tenant was *e. e. cummings*, who lived at No.4. Others: *John Reed, Theodore Dreiser, Padraic Colum, Jane Bowles, and Djuna Barnes.*

Back (east) across Sixth Avenue again, continuing on West 10th Street:

[V55d] **"The English Terrace Row"** (row houses), 20-38 West 10th St., bet. Fifth and Sixth Aves. 1856-1858.

The first row houses in the City to abandon the high **"stoop,"** placing the entry floor only two or three steps up from the street in the English manner. Terrace does not refer to the handsome balcony that runs the length of these houses; it is the English term for rows of houses, such as found in the Kensington and Paddington districts of London of the 1840s, 1850s, and 1860s. New Yorkers visiting England were impressed with this style and saw good reason to adopt it upon their return. Sculptor *Frederick MacMonnies* lived in **No.20** during the 1930s; painters *Louis Bouche* and *Guy Pène du Bois* lived there some years afterward.

[V55e] **14, 16, and 18 West 10th Street** (town houses), bet. Fifth and Sixth Aves. 1855-1856.

Grand mansions for the small-scaled Village. **No.14** maintains the crust of its original brownstone detail. **No.18** is more serene. **No.16**, in the middle, was neatly stripped.

V54

V55a

[V55a] **56 West 10th Street** (house), bet. Fifth and Sixth Aves. 1832.

Among the oldest houses in this part of the Village, it has much of its original detail: pineapple newel posts (indicating welcome) with segmented ironwork in mint condition, and a door with fluted Ionic colonnettes and leaded lights. The cornice and dormer trim came later.

[V55b] **50 West 10th Street** (originally stable), bet. Fifth and Sixth Aves. 1863-1869.

The upper stories of this former stable use brick in a bold, straightforward fashion to ornament as well as to support and enclose (in contrast with the smooth nondecorative planes of brickwork elsewhere on the block). This became the residence of playwright *Edward Albee.*

[V55c] **40 West 10th Street** (apartments), bet. Fifth and Sixth Aves. 1890s. Altered, 1980s.

A modest house surmounted by modern penthouse terraces. Look up.

[V55f] **12 West 10th Street**, bet. Fifth and Sixth Aves. 1846. Extensive renovations, 1895, *Bruce Price.*

Unique after several renovations: an important one divided it into four apartments—one for each daughter—by owner-architect *Bruce Price*. One of those daughters, *Emily Post,* tells of having *President Wilson* to Thanksgiving dinner (it is rumored that he proposed to his second wife here).

[V56] **Church of the Ascension** (Episcopal), 36-38 Fifth Ave., NW cor. W.10th St. 1840-1841. *Richard Upjohn.* Interior remodeled, 1885-1889, *Stanford White of McKim, Mead & White.* Altar mural and stained glass, *John La Farge.* Altar relief, *Augustus Saint-Gaudens.* Pulpit, *Charles McKim.* Parish House, 12 W.11th St., bet. Fifth and Sixth Aves. 1844. Altered to present appearance, 1889, *McKim, Mead & White.*

Random brownstone ashlar in Gothic Revival dress. One of the few churches that lights up its stained glass at night, allowing evening strollers on lower Fifth Avenue to enjoy the colors. If you're wondering about the inconsistent quality of the stained glass, you're correct: not all the windows are *La Farge's*.

[V57a] Originally **Lockwood De Forest House**/ now New York University, **Edgar M. Bronfman Center for Jewish Student Life**, 7 E.10th St., bet. University Place and Fifth Ave. 1887. *Van Campen Taylor*. Restored, 1994-1997, *Helpern Associates*.
[V57b] **9 E.10th Street Apartments**, bet. University Place and Fifth Ave. 1888. *Renwick, Aspinwall & Russell*.

Unique in New York is the exotic, unpainted, and intricately carved teakwood bay window that adorns **No.7**. Its infectious forms influence the other East Indian details of this town house as well as those of the apartment building to the east, designed the following year.

V62a

Note that the exterior teakwood here has withstood the rigors of the City's atmosphere better than the brownstone of neighboring row houses. *De Forest* (1850-1932) was an artist who worked in the Middle East and India and founded workshops in Ahmadabad to revive the art of woodcarving.

[V58] **The Lancaster**, 39-41 E.10th St., bet. Broadway and University Place. 1887. *Renwick, Aspinwall & Russell*.

Like No.9, above, an early apartment house from the era when those who could afford a town house still weren't in a rush to move. Beautiful terra cotta and a fine **Queen Anne** entrance.

[V59] **43 East 10th Street**, bet. Broadway and University Place. 1890s.

Grand terra-cotta, brick, and cast iron complex, straddling aspects of the Classical Revival, a bit of **Richardsonian Romanesque**.

North on University Place one block to West 11th Street:

[V60] Originally **Hotel Albert**/now **Albert Apartments**, University Place SE cor. E.11th St. 1883. *Henry J. Hardenbergh*.

Dark red brick and black-painted wrought-iron trim distinguish this work of architect *Hardenbergh* (contemporary with his **Dakota**).

*Then left (west) on 11th for a short detour to an ancient cemetery. But first, **an explosion on memory lane:***

For years a tall wooden fence enclosed the property at 18 West 11th Street. Between 1845 and 1970 a Greek Revival row house stood here, similar to its neighbors on either side. On March 6, 1970, the street was rocked by an explosion. When the smoke cleared, little was left of the house—its cellar, it turned out, was being used by the terrorist group the **Weathermen** as a bomb manufactory. The bombs were allegedly intended for Fort Dix in New Jersey and for

V57b

Columbia University, a plot that fortunately only resulted in the destruction of one house and three of the terrorists themselves.

[V61] **Second Cemetery of the Spanish and Portuguese Synagogue**, Shearith Israel, in the City of New York, 72-76 W.11th St., bet. Fifth and Sixth Aves. 1805-1829.

The original **Shearith Israel** cemetery is at Chatham Square. Burials began here in 1805, in what was a much larger, square plot extending into the present street. The commissioners' plan had established the City's grid in 1811, but West 11th Street was not cut through until 1830, reducing the cemetery to its present tiny triangle. The disturbed plots were moved farther uptown to the **Third Cemetery** on West 21st Street. After City law forbade burial within Manhattan, subsequent interments have been made in Queens. West 11th between Sixth and Seventh Avenues is a mixed bag of ridiculous (institutional) and sublime (residential) architecture.

V56

[V62a] The **New School for Social Research**, 66 W.12th St., bet. Fifth and Sixth Aves. 1929-1931. *Joseph Urban.* 🕏 Interior (**Tishman auditorium** and **Orozco Room**) restored, 1992, *Rolf Ohlhausen of Prentice & Chan, Ohlhausen.* 🕏

[V62b] **Jacob M. Kaplan Building,** 11th Street Building, and Interior Court, additions to the W and SW. 1958. *William J. Conklin of Mayer, Whittlesey & Glass.* **Vera List Courtyard** (renovation of courtyard and two lobbies), 1997. *Mitchell/Giurgola; Ohlhausen Dubois; Micheal Van Valkenburgh* (landscape); *Martin Puryear* (sculptor).

The **New School** became the "university in exile" for the intelligentsia fleeing Nazi Germany in the 1930s. The original (east) building is a precocious modern design (for New York) with its restrained use of strip windows and spandrels where brick coursing sets back slightly from the street as it rises. These subtleties make it appear shorter, less imposing, more in scale with adjacent row houses. The auditorium

The best **Greek Revival church** in the City, modeled after the **Theseum** in Athens. Columns and pediment resemble stone, but are actually wood; walls are brick and stucco. The porch is most inviting, as was the light and airy interior with its clear glass windows. But, alas, no longer a church, the entry porch serves merely as a latter-day false front. Duplex apartments and flats fill the volume.

Rum, Romanism, and Rebellion: The characterization of Grover Cleveland's Democratic Party as one of rum, Romanism, and rebellion cost Republican candidate James G. Blaine the presidency in 1884. The fiery speech, containing the phrase that antagonized the (Roman) Catholic Irish in New York City, was delivered by Dr. Samuel D. Burchard, long minister of what is today Portico Place. The adjacent row house at 139 West 13th Street was built in 1846 as the manse for Dr. Burchard when he became the church's first rector.

V63

V65

V66

V68, Church House

within is a dramatic example of *Urban's* theatrical talents and was the "model" for **Radio City Music Hall**; its 1992 renovation by *Rolf Ohlhausen* has restored its original glory. The school's additions to the south are linked across a rear sculpture court by an impressive glassed-in two-story-high bridge. This has been remodeled as the Vera List Courtyard to provide accessibility for the disabled through the whole block, with new paving, planting, and sculpture.

[V63] **496 Sixth Avenue** (tenement), bet. W.12th and W.13th Sts. E side. 1889.

Architecture for the masses in brickwork, terra cotta, and a sheet metal cornice.

Tangent to West 13th Street, across Sixth Avenue:

[V64] **Portico Place** (apartments)/earlier **Village Community Church**/originally **13th Street Presbyterian Church**, 143 W.13th St., bet. Sixth and Seventh Aves. 1847. Attributed to *Samuel Thomson.* Rebuilt after fires, 1855, 1902. Converted, 1982, *Stephen B. Jacobs & Assocs.*

[V65] **John and Mary R. Markle Memorial Residence/ Evangeline Residence,** Salvation Army, 123-131 W.13th St., bet. Sixth and Seventh Aves. 1929. *Voorhees, Gmelin & Walker.*

A mildly ornamented **Art Deco** work (check the window grill) of great charm and understatement. At the skyline Art Deco massing takes hold.

Then back across Sixth and east on West 12th:

[V66] **59 West 12th Street** (apartments), bet. Fifth and Sixth Aves. 1931. *Emery Roth.*

Art Deco motifs are particularly evident on the elevator and water tank penthouses atop this 14-story box.

[V67a] **45 West 12th Street**, bet. Fifth and Sixth Aves. 1846.

Look carefully at the east side of this building for the acute angle. The side wall slants back because it originally faced the once aboveground Minetta Brook. *Frank Lloyd Wright's sister, Mrs. William Pope Barney,* owned and lived in the house.

[V67b] **Butterfield House** (apartments), 37 W.12th St., bet. Fifth and Sixth Aves. 1962. *Mayer, Whittlesey & Glass; William J. Conklin,* associate partner in charge of design, and *James S. Rossant.*

The **friendly neighborhood** high rise. On residential 12th Street, this cooperative apart-

V67b

character, like this one, were designed by many distinguished firms. And *Snook* was no minor player: he designed the original 1871 **Grand Central Depot**. The client here was *George A. Hearn,* the department store magnate, whose dry goods emporium was once a showplace nearby on 14th Street.

Turn right (south) on Fifth Avenue, briefly:

[V68] **First Presbyterian Church**, 48 Fifth Ave., bet. W.11th and W.12th Sts. W side. 1846. *Joseph C. Wells*. Chapel, 1893-1894, *McKim, Mead & White*. Chancel added, 1919. **Church House**. 1958-1960. *Edgar Tafel.*

With a stately, crenellated, dressed brownstone ashlar central tower, set well back from Fifth Avenue, First Presbyterian presents bold form. Embellishing its walls are **Gothic Revival** quatrefoils that form the motif for the adjacent, properly reticent, Church House, built more than a century later. Set back from Fifth Avenue on a greensward, the House is by *Tafel,* a long-

V71

ment rises only seven stories; varied windows, projecting bays and balconies, break up the façade and relate it to the prevailing 19th-century residential scale of the street. A glazed courtyard passage to the north wing shares its neighbors' backyard charm. On 13th Street, though, with numerous neighboring lofts and 20th-century apartment towers, the building's flat wall rises agreeably (and economically) to 13 stories.

[V67c] **35 West 12th Street**, bet. Fifth and Sixth Aves. 1840. Altered 1868; right half removed, 1893.

Originally about 25 feet wide; the building of **Nos.31-33** consumed half of this house, leaving a curious but not unpleasing reminder.

[V67d] **The Ardea**, 31-33 W.12th St., bet. Fifth and Sixth Aves. 1895, 1901. *John B. Snook & Sons.*

This dark crusty façade, lyrically set off by delicate ironwork balconies, is one of many structures in the City wrongfully attributed to *McKim, Mead & White.* Buildings of great

time disciple of *Frank Lloyd Wright,* and its copper-clad structure shares *Wright's* sense of materials and proportion.

[V69] **Salmagundi Club**/originally *Irad Hawley House,* 47 Fifth Ave., bet. E.11th and E.12th Sts. E side. 1852-1853. ● Exterior restoration, 1997, *Platt Byard Dovell.* Exhibitions open to the public: 1-5 daily.

The Salmagundi Club, America's oldest artists' club (founded in 1870), moved to Fifth Avenue in 1917; members included *John La Farge, Louis C. Tiffany,* and *Stanford White.* Painting exhibitions open to the public are sometimes installed on the parlor floor, a superbly preserved interior of the period.

Then back north on Fifth:

[V70] **Forbes Magazine Building**/originally **Macmillan Company Building**, 60-62 Fifth Ave., NW cor. W.12th St. 1925. *Carrère & Hastings and Shreve & Lamb.* Galleries open to the public: Tu, We, Fr, Sa 10-4; closed Su, Th, Mo. 212-206-5548. *www.forbesgalleries.com*

For some four decades, Macmillan conducted its publishing business from this pompous limestone cube embellished with echoes of Rome's glories. Following Macmillan's relocation to an anonymous midtown tower, *Forbes* magazine assumed ownership. *Malcolm Forbes*' various collectibles are displayed within.

[V71] **Sheila C. Johnson Design Center, Parsons The New School for Design**, 66 Fifth Avenue, SW cor. W. 13th St. 2008. *Lyn Rice.*

The skylit center unites four existing buildings that form the "campus" of Parsons. *Rice's* storefront windows are adjusted "proud" of the existing façade, like rearview mirrors, while

Rhinelander Gardens: In 1955, P. S. 41, Manhattan—with its garish yellow-glazed auditorium—on the south side of West 11th Street, just west of Sixth Avenue, replaced *James Renwick, Jr.'s*, Rhinelander Gardens. These were a one-of-a-kind group of eight wrought-iron balconied row houses, in the manner of New Orleans' Bourbon Street. For nostalgia's sake a bit of the wrought iron was saved and applied to the school's rear façade—barely visible across the bleak asphalt play area from Greenwich Avenue.

Elizabeth Bayley Seton Building, St. Vincent's Hospital, 157 W. 11th St., NE cor. Seventh Ave. 1899. *Schickel & Ditmars.*

Its dark red brick set off by bold rows of light-colored limestone trim, the hospital's main building was the most distinguished element in the complex. Demolished for the state of the art George Link, Jr., Pavilion.

V69

V70

metallic signs on both Fifth and 13th (legible only if you lie on the sidewalk and look up), form dynamic entrance canopies.

END of Tour B. The nearest subways are two blocks north at Union Square, along East 14th Street, between University Place and Fourth Avenue: 14th Street/Union Square Station (Nos.4, 5, 6, L, N, Q, R, W trains).

NECROLOGY

Women's House of Detention, 10 Greenwich Ave., bet. Christopher and W. 10th Sts. E side. 1931. *Sloan & Robertson.*

Not the architecture—Art Deco—but its ungainly bulk and earpiercing conversations (screamed from barred windows to friends in the street below) led to this jail's demise.

Plaque, Greta Garbo Home for Wayward Boys and Girls, 146 W. 11th St., bet. Sixth and Greenwich Aves.

The strange brass plaque on the door of this Victorian row house briefly announced the reclusive star's (perhaps imaginary) philanthropic bent and always evoked a double take from passersby. A hoax?

Uprooted: When the huge **Loew's Sheridan Theater** was demolished in the 1970s by St. Vincent's to make way for expansion, the West Village Committee took advantage of a hiatus in the building schedule to create a charming English garden, along with a recycling center for refuse, in the **Village Green**, bounded by Seventh and Greenwich Avenues and West 12th Street. The hospital eventually undid the greenery for its Materials Handling Center.

ASTOR PLACE, NOHO, & ENVIRONS

For one brief generation in the changing fashions of New York, Lafayette Street (then Lafayette Place) was its most wealthy and elegant residential avenue. Then running only from Great Jones Street to Astor Place, it was a short, tree-lined boulevard, flanked by town houses of the Astors, Vanderbilts, and Delanos. Now the trees are gone, and only a piece of **Colonnade Row** (LaGrange Terrace) remains. Although in shoddy condition, its character is so strong that it still suggests the urbane qualities present up until the Civil War. Mostly developed in 1832-1833, the street cut through Sperry's Botanic Gardens, later Vauxhall Gardens, a summer entertainment enclave where music and theatrical performances were presented in the open air. *John Lambert*, an English traveler of 1807, noted it as a "neat plantation . . . the theatrical corps of New York is chiefly engaged at Vauxhall during summer." Only 20 years after this resi-

Astor Place Walking Tour: A walk northbound along Broadway/Lafayette Street/Astor Place/Fourth Avenue past the Public Theater, the Cooper Union, Grace Church and lesser, but still intriguing, wonders: START at Broadway and Houston Street (No.6 local of the old IRT Lexington Avenue local to Bleecker Street Station or B, D, or F trains of the old IND Sixth Avenue to Broadway-Lafayette Station).

[V72] **NoHo Historic District**, along Broadway, most of both sides of Lafayette Street, bet. E. Houston and 8th Sts. See map. ● **NoHo East Historic District**, 1-49 Bleecker St. bet. Lafayette St. and the Bowery with 309-321 & 288-320 Elizabeth St. and 307-321 & 308-320 Mott St., and 300-324 Bowery. ●

A cadre of Federal row houses (endangered species) hold on at 7 to 13 and 21 to 25 Bleecker St., 300 Elizabeth St., and 306 to 310 Bowery.

V72

dential development in the 1830s did the street's principal families move away to Fifth Avenue. At the same time the **Astor Library** (later to become a major part of New York's Public Library) and the **Cooper Union Foundation Building** were built (started in 1850 and 1853, respectively), seeding the precinct with different uses: Lafayette became primarily a light manufacturing and warehousing street, with erratic or isolated physical remnants of its varied history. The Astor Library was bought by HIAS (Hebrew Immigrant Aid Society), but beginning in the late 1960s it was converted into a clutch of indoor theaters for **Joseph Papp's New York Shakespeare Festival**.

[V73a] **Little Cary Building**, 620 Broadway, bet. E. Houston and Bleecker Sts. E side. 1858. *John B. Snook.*

The *Daniel D. Badger Co.* constructed the vigorous **Corinthian** cast-iron frames, now contrasted with thoughtless, lifeless, flat, bronze-anodized aluminum windows.

[V73b] Originally **The New York Mercantile Exchange**, 628 Broadway, E. Houston and Bleecker Sts. E side. 1882. *Herman J. Schwarzmann, with Buchman & Deisler.*

Delicate cast-iron columns and deep—very deep—window reveals, by the chief architect of Philadelphia's **1876 Centennial Exhibition**. Note the name appliquéed to the third- and fifth-floor span.

Left on Bleecker Street, and then back across Broadway to Crosby:

[V74] Originally **Condict Building** (lofts)/later **Bayard Building**, 65 Bleecker St., bet. Broadway and Lafayette St., opp. Crosby St. N side. 1897-1899. *Louis Sullivan*, architect. *Lyndon P. Smith*, associate architect. Original storefronts recreated, 2003. 🖋

This was a radical building in its time, a direct confrontation with the architectural establishment that had embraced American Renaissance architecture after the **Columbian Exposition** (Chicago World's Fair) of 1893. *Sullivan*, the principal philosopher and leading designer of the **Chicago School** (the antithesis of the **American Renaissance**), was the employer and teacher of *Frank Lloyd Wright* (who referred to him romantically as *lieber Meister*). The sextet of angels supporting the cornice was added at the request of his client, *Silas Alden Condict*. The building had little influence in New York for, as *Carl Condit*

Turn right on Bond Street:

[V77] **1-5 Bond Street**/originally **Robbins & Appleton Building**, SE cor. Shinbone Alley, bet. Broadway and Lafayette St. 1879-1880. *Stephen D. Hatch.* 🖋

Magnificent north-light. Capped by a great **Second Empire** mansard roof and dormers are five generous stories of creamy, elegant Corinthian cast iron and glass. The building was originally used for the manufacture of watch cases. Now the **Breitlings** are on the arms of its tenants.

[V78] **26 Bond Street**, bet. Lafayette St. and the Bowery. 1830s.

Greek Revival presenting "battered majesty," said *New York Times* columnist *Christopher Gray*. The last piece of the ancient Bond Street, before it was paved with gold.

[V79] **25 Bond Street**, bet. Lafayette St. and Broadway. 2008. *George Schieferdecker of BKSK Architects.*

V74

V75

V73b

V76

V77

wondered, "Who would expect an aesthetic experience on Bleecker Street?"

Return to Broadway:

[V75] Originally **Manhattan Savings Institution Building**/now residential lofts, 644 Broadway, NE cor. Bleecker St. 1889-1890. *Stephen D. Hatch.* Restored, 1987.

A great rock-cut brownstone, terra-cotta, and brick heap (with cast-iron trim) finally recognized for its quality—and restored—after many years of neglect. Check out the cast-iron and marble floor system exposed on the underside in both the lobby and the corner store.

[V76] **670 Broadway**/originally **Brooks Brothers**, NE cor. Bond St. 1873-1874. *George E. Harney.*

A romantic rose brick and granite commercial structure at the third of five sequential locations of **Brooks Brothers**. Eastlakian (after *Charles Eastlake*, one of the 19th century's most ornate designers).

Classical materials and proportions within a lively modernist composition. Limestone and steel slip past each other like two IRT trains passing from opposite directions. Cohesive, kinetic, expensive.

[V80a] **40 Bond Street**, bet. Lafayette St. and Bowery. 2008. *Herzog & DeMeuron, with Handel Architects.*

Herzog & DeMeuron gave us the Birdcage in Beijing. On Bond, they remain cool; all swirling shiny surfaces in vivid aquamarine. Three layers compose the façade: setback penthouses on top, a proud mid-section in cast Coca Cola-green glass and, at the street, a rampant graffiti-esque aluminum screen growing upward like morning glory vines.

[V80b] **42 Bond Street**, bet. Lafayette St. and Bowery. ca. 1880.

Romanesque arches provide a little sobering history, sandwiched between *Berke* and *Herzog*.

V80a

[V80c] **48 Bond Street**, bet. Lafayette St. and Bowery. 2008. *Deborah Berke*.

Charcoal granite and glass. Dour (especially when seen near its wild child neighbor at No.40) and elegant, a thoughtful meditation on the awning window, frozen in mid-swing, from the accomplished minimalist *Berke*.

Back to Lafayette Street. Take a quick detour on Great Jones Street, and then resume your northerly walk on Lafayette:

[V81] **Engine Company No.33, NYC Fire Department**, 44 Great Jones St., bet. the Bowery and Lafayette St. N side. 1898-1899. *Flagg & Chambers*. 👁️‍🗨️

A huge concave **Beaux Arts** arch, drawn from the architecture of *Louis XV*, forms the heart of this flamboyant *Ernest Flagg* façade.

[V82a] **31-33 Great Jones Street**, bet. the Bowery and Lafayette Sts. 1870.

Twin former stables now restored for people. Note the entablatures in the cornice: *Jos. Scott*

Tkgn. Corp. Stables (No.31) and *Bienecke & Co.'s Stables* (No.33). What does "Tkgn." stand for? On today's stock market it stands for *Tekoil and Gas* but it's unlikely Mr. Scott was using these humble stables for off-shore oil exploration. *Or was he?*

[V82b] **Downtown Auto and Tire**, 348 Bowery, NW cor. Great Jones St.

Architectural humility itself: a courtyard enclosed by a façade composed of posters, signs, tires, and graffiti, with a billboard on top to complete the picture. A lively ensemble! *Architects of sterile glass boxes, take heed!*

[V83] **376-380 Lafayette Street**/also known as the **Schermerhorn Building**, NW cor. Great Jones St. 1888-1889. *Henry J. Hardenbergh*. 👁️‍🗨️

Created by the architect of the **Dakota** and the **Plaza Hotel**, this free-swinging **Romanesque Revival** work is a rich addition to the area's architecture. From bottom (the monumental polished granite dwarf columns) to top (the richly decorative cornice), it's a gem: sandstone, terra cotta, and brick. *William C. Schermerhorn* built this

V82a

V85

V86a

lusty stonework on the site of his family mansion. Look below to the *Seabury Tredwell House* to find a typical neighbor from *Schermerhorn*'s time.

Lamented: the now vanished **Fez**, a mysterious subterranean jazz and folk club (1992-2005) in the cellar.

[V84] **382 Lafayette Street**, bet. Great Jones and E. 4th Sts. W side. 1896. *Cleverdon & Putzel.*

Delicate incised ornamentation near the sky, atop an arcade.

Turn right (east) on East 4th for an interesting detour:

[V85] **Merchant's House Museum**/formerly **Seabury Tredwell House**/originally **Joseph Brewster House**, 29 E.4th St., bet. the Bowery and Lafayette St. 1832. Restored, *Joseph Roberto.* Tea Room Restoration, 2007, *Jan Hird Pokorny Associates.* ● Interior Open to the public: Th-Mo, Noon-5pm. 212-777-1089. *merchantshouse.com.*

A relic from New York's **Federal** past, when the blocks surrounding were lined with similar houses. This house and its early interior furnishings derive from *Tredwell*'s daughter, *Gertrude*, who lived here for 93 years, until 1933. The parlor floor furnishings reflect the period of Gertrude's youth, when it was refurbished with wall-to-wall custom carpeting. It has been open to the public since 1936.

[V86a] Originally **Samuel Tredwell Skidmore House**, 37 E.4th St., bet. the Bowery and Lafayette St. 1845. ●

Greek Revival. Ionic columns unequaled of this vintage. But with each edition of this Guide less remained, a tragic example of death by conscious negligence. The new 15-story **2 Cooper Square** next door dwarfs the little house but offers a structural shoulder to lean upon, and a **complete restoration is promised**. Really?

[V86b] **2 Cooper Square**, NW cor. Bowery and E. 4th St. 2009. *Gerner Kronick & Valcarcel Architects.*

"Contextual" say architects, whenever they

need to justify something that's much, much larger than its tiny neighbors. Here the real context is the cubist brick **Bowery Hotel** one block south, in every way the slightly older twin.

Lafayette Street between East 4th Street and Astor Place:

[V87] Originally **DeVinne Press Building**, 393-399 Lafayette St., NE cor. E.4th St. 1885-1886.

V89

[V89] **411 Lafayette Street**, bet. East 4th St. and Astor Place E side. 1891. *Alfred Zucker.* Restored, 1987.

Ornate cast-iron and brick Romanesque Revival. The three freestanding columns—interspersed with those engaged—form a virile base.

[V90] **Joseph Papp Public Theater**, onetime **HIAS Hebrew Immigrant Aid Society**/originally **Astor Library**, 425 Lafayette St., bet. E.4th St. and Astor Place. E side. 1853-1881. **South wing**, 1849-1853, *Alexander Saeltzer.* **Center section**, 1856-1869, *Griffith Thomas.* **North wing**, 1879-1881, *Thomas Stent.* **Conversion** into theater complex, 1967-1976, *Giorgio Cavaglieri.* **Lobby**, stair addition, 2009, *Polshek Partnership.* 212-539-8500. *www.publictheater.org*

A funky, generously scaled red brick and brownstone building considered by some to be the finest American example of **Rundbogenstil**, a German variant of Romanesque Revival. *John Jacob Astor* here contributed New York's first

V91, in days gone by

Babb, Cook & Willard. Addition, 1892, *Theodore de Vinne.*

Roman arches in brickwork worthy of the Forum's **Basilica of Constantine**. The waterfront of Brooklyn is graced with poor country cousins (the **Empire Stores**) of this magnificent pile. Certainly this is a sample of "less is more"—especially when considered with **Nos.376-380** down the block. But that extravagance is equally worthy in more self-indulgent circles. Don't ever say 'more is more.'

[V88] **401 Lafayette Street**. bet. East 4th Street and Astor Place. E side. ca. 1893.
400 Lafayette Street, NW cor. E.4th St. ca. 1887-1888. *Cleverdon & Putzel.*

Two different, very wonderful loft structures from the great era of Lafayette Street's expansion.

free library, later combined with its peers (**Lenox Library**, which was sited where the Frick Collection is today, and the **Tilden Foundation**) to form the central branch of The New York Public Library at 42nd Street. These are the theaters of the late *Joseph Papp*, whose outdoor Shakespeare Festival in Central Park used these as its indoor habitat. "Hair" debuted here in 1967. At least one of the authors was there.

Tucked into the first floor, and approached through a side alley, is **Joe's Pub**, a dark, intimate dinner theatre featuring cozy (mostly acoustic) concerts. Both the sound system and the orrechiette are excellent.

[V91] Originally **Colonnade Row**/also known as **LaGrange Terrace**, 428-434 Lafayette St., bet. E. 4th St. and Astor Place. W side. 1832-1833. Attributed to *Seth Geer.*

Four of nine houses built speculatively by *Seth Geer* in 1833. Five at the south end were demolished for the still existing Wanamaker Annex next door. An elegant urban arrangement of private structures subordinated to an imposing Corinthian colonnade (compare the **Place de la Concorde** in Paris). *Delanos, Astors*, and *Vanderbilts* lived here, until their game of social musical chairs sent them uptown. The Astor Place Theatre presents off-Broadway at **No.434.**

[V92] **436 Lafayette Street**, bet. E. 4th St. and Astor Place. W side. 1870-1871. *Edward H. Kendall.*

Vigorous architecture of the 19th century's last quarter. Note the nice old brass clock over the door: *Mann Refrigeration.*

Along Astor Place on the left; then return:

[V93] Originally **Astor Place Building, O. B. Potter Trust**, 444 Lafayette St., SW cor. Astor Place. 1876. *Griffith Thomas.*

Brick and painted cast-iron eclectic Eastlake.

[V94] **Astor Place Building**, 750 Broadway, NE cor. Astor Place (also known as 1 Astor Place). 1881. *Starkweather & Gibbs.*

Intricate brickwork framed with grand terra-

In the large open space crisscrossed by traffic and frequently the center of a sidewalk flea market.

[V96] **Alamo,** on traffic island, Astor Place/E.8th St./Lafayette St./Fourth Ave. 1966, installed 1967. *Bernard "Tony" Rosenthal,* sculptor.

Installed as part of a giant but temporary citywide exhibition, "Sculpture in the Environment," **Alamo** was made permanent through a gift to the City by a private donor. A giant steel cube "en pointe," it pivots (with some difficulty) and has become a beloved fixture in these parts.

[V97] **Astor Place Subway Station**, IRT Lexington Avenue Line, below Lafayette St. and Fourth Ave. at Astor Place. 1904. *Heins & La Farge.* Restored, 1986, *Prentice & Chan, Ohlhausen. Milton Glaser,* artist. **Astor Place Subway Kiosk.** Replica, 1985, *Prentice & Chan, Ohlhausen.*

Architect *Rolf Ohlhausen's* 1985 kiosk, a

V93

V96

V97

V94

V95

V98

cotta Corinthian pilasters. Its façade curves leisurely along Astor Place to meet Broadway.

[V95] **Astor Place Hotel**/originally **Mercantile Library Building**/onetime **District 65 Building (Distributive Workers of America),** 13 Astor Place, NW cor. Lafayette St. to E.8th St. 1890. *George E. Harney.* Remodeled as hotel, *David Chipperfield*, design architect. *William B. Tabler*, architect of record.

Harney's ode to *Ruskin* at 670 Broadway, 16 years earlier, is here replaced by establishment *Harney.* The new **American Renaissance** of the 1890s overwhelmed the more picturesque recent years.

The District 65 Building rests on the site of the Astor Place Opera House, where in May 1849 rioting between competing claques of the American actor Edwin Forrest and the English actor William Macready caused the death of 34 stalwarts. The Seventh Regiment National Guard, quartered in an armory then on the present site of Cooper Union's Hewitt building, quelled the passions forcibly.

palliative remembrance of the IRT past (kiosks occurred at most stations): remembrance from the Transit Authority's disastrous decision to scrap all IRT kiosks. The new kiosk was cast using new wood patterns developed from *Heins & La Farge* drawings submitted to the *Hecla Iron Works* in Williamsburg, Brooklyn, the original fabricators. (Both *Ohlhausen* and *Glaser* are graduates of Cooper Union across the street.)

The Cooper Union for the Advancement of Science and Art:

[V98] **Cooper Union Foundation Building**, E.7th St. to Astor Place, Fourth Ave. to Third Ave., at Cooper Sq. 1853-1859. *Frederick A. Peterson.* Second-floor window alterations, 1886, *Leopold Eidlitz.* ☞ Interior reconstructed, 1975, *John Hejduk.* Exterior restorations, 1999, *Platt Byard Dovell.* Galleries open Mo-Fr 11-7; Sa 12-5; closed Su. 212-353-4195.

A high-rise brownstone, Cooper Union is the oldest extant building framed with steel beams in America. *Peter Cooper*, its founder and a benefactor in the great Victorian paternalistic tradition (he gave presents to Cooper Union on his birthday), was partner of *Samuel F. B. Morse* in laying the first **trans-Atlantic Cable** and builder of the Tom Thumb steam locomotive; also an iron maker, he rolled the first steel railroad rails. Such rails were used by *Cooper* as beams, spanning brick bearing walls. In turn, brick floor arches jumped between rail and rail. The façade is in the Italianate brownstone tradition popular at the time with cast-iron designers, but heavier-handed, as it is in masonry except at the ground floor. The remodeling was almost entirely internal, with simultaneous fulfillment of one of *Cooper's* original designs: a round elevator finally rides in his clairvoyantly round shaft. The *Platt Byard Dovell* exterior restoration avoids the pastiness of artificial brownstone, and delivers a new, but real, texture to the façades.

ENDANGERED

[V99] Formerly **Pasqua's Coffee Pavilion**, in the Cooper Union School of Engineering colonnade,

[V101] **Astor Place Tower**, 445 Lafayette St., at Astor Place. 2005. *Gwathmey Siegel*.

A sinuous sky-blue glass tower from the noted modernist *Charles Gwathmey* (1938-2009). This is a great and hectic site, where Astor Place, Fourth Avenue, the Bowery, and Lafayette Street converge at Cooper's doorstep, but *Gwathmey's* tower seems aloof to the wonderful commotion below. It might be more at home on the skyline of some other town: Stamford, Charlotte, Tampa all come to mind.

Gwathmey's father, *Bob,* taught painting to a generation of New York artists across the street, and was *Charles's* client for a wonderful 1967 weekend house in Amagansett (L.I.), widely published and widely honored.

[V102] **Peter Cooper Memorial**, in Cooper Sq. S of E.7th St. 1897. *Augustus Saint-Gaudens,* sculptor; *Stanford White*, architect of the base.

Cooper seated in front of his benefaction. His eyes are winging left to see what the 21st century has wrought. "What the —?" he gasps.

V100

V101

NW cor. Third Ave. at Astor Pl. 1997. *Smith-Miller + Hawkinson*.

The deadly space enclosed by Engineering's colonnade had been translated into a lively humanistic center of urbane activity. Tear it down, and make way for *Maki* (see p. 165), or fix it up? Please decide.

[V100] **Undergraduate Dormitory, Cooper Union**, 29-31 Third Ave., SE cor. E. 9th St. 1995. *Prentice & Chan, Ohlhausen*.

Ohlhausen's understated, yet powerful, contribution to the urban campus of Cooper Union. His celebration of the everyday rooftop water tower has been copied in more recent, lesser works.

The ground floor is occupied by **St. Mark's Book Shop**, a hip little den, with a predictably large *Critical Theory* section, and (often) *Patti Smith* records blaring. *Gloria!*

[V103] **Arthur Nerken School of Engineering, Cooper Union**, Cooper Sq., between E.6th and E.7th Sts. 2009. *Thom Mayne of Morphosis* with *Gruzen Samton*.

Bare bones stylishly clad in a cloud of mesh that hovers overhead and wraps your route into the heart of this staid engineers' habitat. Sacrificed in passing was Cooper's **Hewitt Building** (see Necrology).

"*Cooper Union's intention (is) to create an academic building that will have the same impact that the Foundation Building had on higher education in 1859 and that our Chrysler Building had on New York architecture in the 1930s*" said Cooper Union President Dr. George Campbell.

Another verdict will come from the students cocooned within, from Cooper's architecture faculty and students across the street in the original 1859 Foundation Building.

V103

V102   V104   V105   V106

*East Village: For the area to the east, beginning at Third Avenue, including the St Mark's Place corridor, **McSorley's**, and Alphabet City, see the next section, East Village.*

Resume the northward walk this time along Fourth Avenue:

[V104] Originally **Wanamaker Department Store Annex**, Fourth Ave. bet. E.8th and E.9th Sts. to Broadway. 1904. Addition, 1907-1910. Both by *D. H. Burnham & Co.* Expanded, 1926.

The annex, a stolid 15-story monolith, considerably larger than its parent (demolished) main store to the north, contains as much space as the 102 floors of the Empire State Building.

A left on East 10th Street to Broadway, and then a right:

[V105] **Grace Church** (Episcopal) and Rectory, 800 and 804 Broadway, at E.10th St. E side. 1843-1846. *James Renwick, Jr.* Rectory, 1846-1847. *James Renwick, Jr.* Original wood steeple replaced in marble, 1888, *James Renwick, Jr.* Chancel extension, 1903, *Heins & La Farge.* Other alterations, 1910, *William W. Renwick.* 💜

A magnificent **Gothic Revival** church in Sing Sing marble, designed by an engineer who studied the copybooks of the Pugins, the great English Gothic Revival theorists and detailers. At the bend of Broadway, its tower dominates, and punctuates, the vista from the south. One of the City's greatest treasures, together with its outreach 'Houses' on Broadway and Fourth Avenue (below).

[V106] **The Renwick**, 808 Broadway, opp. E.11th St. 1887-1888. *Renwick, Aspinwall & Russell.* Converted to residential use.

A Gothic Revival wall forms a visual backdrop for **Grace Church**, built 41 years after the church's completion by *Renwick's* successor firm. Terra cotta from the fourth floor up, eroding stone below. Originally offices, now apartments. For more on fictional doings here read *Caleb Carr* conjure marvelous doings within in *The Alienist.*

[V107] **810 Broadway**, opp. E.11th St. E side. 1907. *Rouse & Stone*.

Next door to **The Renwick**, and slightly younger, 810 is a showcase for the turn-of-the-century effort to combine a metal and glass wall and a masonry carapace.

Retrace your steps to Fourth Avenue to see the Houses of Grace Church. The tour continues up Broadway:

[V108] **Grace Church School**, originally **Grace Church Houses**, including: **Clergy House**, 92 Fourth Ave., bet. E.10th and E.12th Sts. W side. 1902-1903. *Heins & La Farge*. ● **Memorial House**, 94-96 Fourth Ave. 1881-1883. *James Renwick, Jr.* ● **Neighborhood House**, 98 Fourth Ave. 1906-1907. *Renwick, Aspinwall & Tucker*. ● **Addition to School**, 2007, *Jacob Alspector*.

A trio in **Gothic Revival**, a tradition established by the elder *Renwick* at Grace Church around the corner. Endangered in the 1970s for

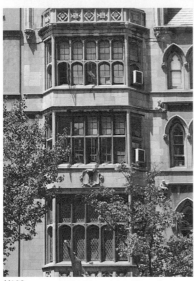
V108

improvements to the school, the façades were finally saved. In this case landmark designation *followed* the threat of loss. *Alspector's* addition amazingly fits classrooms and an entire new gymnasium underground, with no great loss of the charm of the original.

[V109] **The Cast Iron Building** /originally *James McCreery Dry Goods Store*, 67 E.11th St., NW cor. Broadway. 1868-1870. *John Kellum*. Converted and extended upward, 1971, *Stephen B. Jacobs*.

The old **McCreery's** cast-iron Corinthian columns and almost endless arches both enrich and discipline the façade—though concern for historic preservation waned at the upper stories. One of the earliest cast-iron upscale residential conversions.

[V110] **Police Athletic League Building**/ onetime Girls' High School/ originally **Grammar School 47**, 341/2 E.12th St., S side. 1855. *Thomas R. Jackson*. ●

Beautifully preserved Italianate painted brownstone and painted brick from an era when most public buildings—whether school, police station, or hospital—were styled the same way. Proper but gloomy. *Lydia Wadleigh*, for whom the high school (now intermediate school) in Harlem was named, was principal

V111d   V111e

V109

here, where she fought effectively for free education for girls.

[V111a] **43 East 12th Street** (converted lofts), 1894. *Cleverdon & Putzel*. [V111b] **42 East 12th Street** (converted lofts). 1894. *Cleverdon & Putzel*. [V111c] **39 East 12th Street** (converted lofts). 1896. [V111d] **37 East 12th Street** (converted lofts). 1896. *Cleverdon & Putzel*. [V111e] **36 East 12th Street** (converted lofts). 1895. *Cleverdon & Putzel*. [V111f] **35 East 12th Street** (converted lofts). 1897. *Albert Wagner*.

A big and bold "Beaux Arts meets 1890s High-Tech" row, each multistory loft competitively outdoing the other. Look up at rich stone and brickwork. Much of the Rue Réaumur in Paris, of the same vintage, displays masonry and steel with similar integration, an effort by conservative Beaux Arts architects to enter the new mainstream.

Booksellers' Row, along Fourth Avenue and Broadway from Astor Place to Union Square: Once upon a time—and well into the 1960s—both sides of Fourth Avenue and parts of Broadway and the side streets were lined with used bookshops of all descriptions, beginning at Bible House (which occupied the site of Cooper Union's Engineering Building) and stretching almost all the way to S. Klein's on the Square (the cut-rate department store whose site is now occupied by Zeckendorf Towers). Books were displayed both within the shops and on racks along the street—a browser's delight, particularly in balmy weather. Alas, the number of shops today is reduced to a sparse handful, dominated by giant Strand Book Store, at 828 Broadway, on the northeast corner of East 12th Street, where books are displayed on shelves that stretch on street, floor and basement (and for aficionados elsewhere) for miles.

[V112] **827-831 Broadway**, bet. E.12th and E.13th Sts. 1866.

V115

V112

V116

A magnificent pair of **Italianate** business buildings fashioned in marble, patterns for the later cast-iron structures that picked up this elegant neo-Renaissance style, imported from England.

[V113] **Roosevelt Building**, 839-841 Broadway, NW cor. E.13th St. 1893. *Stephen D. Hatch*. Restorations, 2009, *Israel Berger Architects.*
This sandstone and brick edifice offers a majestic expression of **Romanesque Revival**. Named *Roosevelt* after *Cornelius, Teddy's* grandfather, who lived on the block in midcentury, when Union Square was the place to reside. *Berger* has enticed a lovely copper cornice to make a resilient comeback.

Turn east on East 13th Street and south on Fourth Avenue to East 11th Street, then left:

[V114] **U.S. Post Office, Cooper Station**, NE cor. Fourth Ave. and 11th St. 1937.
Art Moderne fluted columns without capitals swoop around this neo-Classical corner: the height of 1930s Worlds' Fair style.

East 11th Street between Third and Fourth Avenues: A gold mine of public buildings:

[V115] **Webster Hall**, 119 E.11th St., bet. Third and Fourth Aves. N side. 1886. *Charles Rentz.* ◖
An 1880s dance hall, then a 1930s ballroom, then a 1980s rock and roll club called **The Ritz**, then DJ's and raves in the 1990s, now returned to rock and roll. Labyrinthian inside, with multiple stages. Good luck.

V117

[V116] Originally **St. Ann's Parochial School**/ later **Delehanty Institute**, 117 E.11th St., bet. Third and Fourth Aves. N side. 1870.

A dignified dark red-brick and terra-cotta institutional building that has seen many uses, and now houses the adventurous.

Left on Third Avenue and left again on East 12th Street; And lo, not Necrology, but Necro-Taxidermy unfolds:

[V117] The shell of **St. Ann's Shrine Armenian Catholic Cathedral**/originally **12th Street Baptist Church**, 120 E.12th St., bet. Third and Fourth Aves. ca. 1847.

Preserve or demolish? Or preserve **and** demolish? Here **St. Ann's Shrine** is gone, excepting bell tower and façade, recast as a folly behind which lurks yet another dorm for **NYU** (2009. *Perkins Eastman*). The exercise is futile: no connection is made, or even attempted, between the old church and the new 26-story hulk, save some pavers laid between. The effect is of a majestic elk, shot and stuffed.

Right on Fourth Avenue:

[V118] **Hancock Building**, 127 Fourth Ave., bet. E.12th and E.13th Sts. E side. 1897. *Marsh, Israels & Harder.*

Once the home of **Hammacher Schlemmer**, the gadget store. The apartments upstairs have an added balcony escape route around a grand Composite column. What a delight!

Right on East 13th Street:

[V119] Originally **Kearney & Van Tassel Auction Stables**, 130 E.13th St., bet. Third and Fourth Aves. 1889. *David & John Jardine.* Annex, 128 E.13th St. 1904. *Jardine, Kent & Jardine.*

Old horse-auction rooms—the ornament makes references. Inside, an enormous space that would hold a blimp. A recent stroll-by revealed a gut renovation in progress. Wild guess: condos?

V118

[V120] **One Ten Third** (apartments), 110 Third Avenue bet. E. 13th and E. 14th Sts. 2008. *Greenberg Farrow Architects.*

Another **Blue Tower**? Scarcely. More an incoherent construction of glass. The **Variety Arts Theater** lived here, showing, in the 1960s, triple features to the movie-starved penurious. 110's cousin, **Blue**, by *Bernard Tschumi*, was last seen headed south near Delancey.

END of Tour. The nearest subways are at Union Square, at East 14th Street, between Fourth Avenue and Broadway: 14th Street/Union Square Station (IRT Lexington Avenue Line (Nos.4, 5, and 6 trains) and BMT Broadway Line (N and R trains).

NECROLOGY AND LONG SHOTS

Cooper Union Hewitt Building, Cooper Sq. bet. E.6th and E.7th Sts. 1914. *Lemuel Haffenreffer.* The sacrificed lamb of Cooper Union's history, replaced by *Morphosis's*

Variety Arts Theatre/originally **Variety Photoplays,** 110 Third Ave., bet. E.13th and E.14th Sts. W side. ca. 1900.

Some say this was the City's oldest movie house. Its marquee of both neon and incandescent lights was a cultural monument of another time and is irreplaceable.

Long Shot: 51 Astor Place Apartments, bet. Fourth Ave. and the Bowery. 2015? *Fumihiko Maki.*

V119

V120

Arthur Nerken School of Engineering. Hewitt's offbeat entry lobby was impaled by an Ionic column inspiring postmodern thoughts to the freshmen architects within. *Hewitt* married *Cooper's* daughter, and hence the Cooper-Hewitt Museum (once in the Foundation Building, now in the Carnegie Mansion at 91st Street).
The main **Wanamaker** store (originally **A. T. Stewart & Company** (*John Kellum*, 1862) on the block to the north) occupied a full block in Italianate cast iron, was arranged around a skylighted central court, and offered the most gracious shopping space in New York, very much in the European tradition. The only **Ladies Mile** survivor to continue in business, it finally closed in 1954 and was consumed in a conflagration two years later.

Minskoff Equities contracted with Cooper Union to purchase the engineering building as site for a new 13-story mixed-use tower by *Fumihiko Maki.* An exterior of black granite with clear and ribbed glass. Face to face with Cooper's 1859 **Foundation Building**. Mano a mano?

WEST VILLAGE

Walking Tour C: A loop through northern West Village, starting along Christopher Street, to the neo-modernists Meier and Asymptote at West Street, north to a point just south of Gansevoort Market, and back through Greek Revival blocks to the start. START at what is commonly referred to (though not with great accuracy) as Sheridan Square (No.1 train of the old IRT Seventh

[W2] **95 Christopher Street**, NW cor. Bleecker St. 1931. *H. I. Feldman.*

Using a palette of browns, these banded brick **Art Deco** apartments stand in forceful contrast to the typical 19th-century Village scale.

Take a right (north) on Bleecker Street for three blocks past all sorts of chic antiquaries and

W1

Avenue Line local to the Christopher Street/ Sheridan Square Station). It is, in fact, Christopher Park.

Note: Only some of the entries on this tour lie within the Greenwich Village Historic District; the district lines are shown on the maps.

Proceed southwesterly from Seventh Avenue South along Christopher Street:

[W1] **St. John's Evangelical Lutheran Church**/formerly **St. Matthew's Church** (Episcopal)/originally **The Eighth Presbyterian Church**, 81 Christopher St., bet. Seventh Ave. S. and Bleecker St. N side. 1821-1822. Altered, 1886, *Berg & Clark.*

A **Federal** cupola rises over a Romanesque body of painted brownstone and sheet metal. The parish house to the west, next door, is stolid brick **Romanesque Revival**. Eclectic!

such, and then a right (northeasterly) onto Perry Street for a brief look:

[W3] **The Hampton**. 80-82 Perry St., bet. W.4th and Bleecker Sts. S side. 1887. *Thom & Wilson.*

A red brick and brownstone upscale supertenement eyes the street through Moorish "keyholes" at its ground-floor windows and entry.

[W4] **70 Perry Street**, bet. W.4th and Bleecker Sts. S side. 1867. *Walter Jones,* builder.

The architectural winner on this block, impressively in a superb state of repair. Tooled brownstone and stately proportions give it a grand scale in the style of the **French Second Empire**. As a result, it seems larger than its neighbors. It isn't.

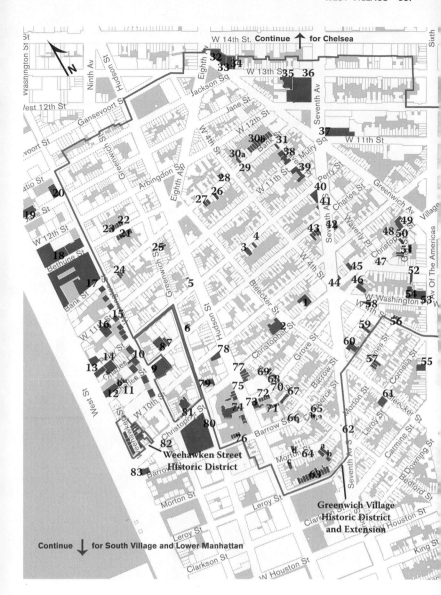

W 14th St. **Continue** ↑ for Chelsea

Continue ↓ for South Village and Lower Manhattan

Weehawken Street
Historic District

Greenwich Village
Historic District
and Extension

Now, back on Perry southwesterly to Hudson Street:

[W5] **Jane Jacobs House**, 555 Hudson St., NW cor. Perry St. 1842. 🔴

The urban activist and writer *Jane Jacobs* (1916-2006) lived in this simple brick house with her family from the late 1940s to 1968. Her *Death and Life of Great American Cities* (1961) remains one of the great urban design treatises for New York, and cities everywhere. They should be reading it in Dubai and Beijing.

South on Hudson one block, then right (southwesterly) onto Charles Street:

[W6] Onetime **Sven Bernhard House**, 121 Charles St., NE cor. Greenwich St. Relocated, 1968. *William Shopsin.*

As a mongrel mutt, out for a walk, claims its territory, this white-framed eccentricity rested at two other sites before stopping here. Its provenance is unknown, but it served as a

backhouse at York and 71st Street in the 19th century. When threatened with demolition in the 1960s, the *Bernhards* rolled it here: five miles through city streets.

[W7] **131 Charles Street**, bet. Greenwich and Washington Sts. N side. 1834. *David Christie*, builder. 🔴

A **Federal** gem whose delicate scale contrasts—in a not unpleasant way—with the oompah details of the old police station adjacent. Note the blind oval window over the second descending doorway leading to **No.131**, a backhouse.

[W8] **Le Gendarme**/originally **9th Precinct, NYC Police Department**, 135 Charles St., bet. Greenwich and Washington Sts. N side. 1895-1897. *John Du Fais.* Converted, 1978, *Hurley & Farinella.*

Now apartments, this ungainly mélange of styles served as the Village police station until 1971, when operations moved to a new, bland

W7

W9

W11b

Robert Moses, then the City's urban renewal czar. A pyrrhic victory for David: the five- and six-story red-brick products are dumpy, dull, and for their time, expensive. Scale simply isn't enough!

[W11a] **159 Charles Street**, bet. Washington and West Sts. Ca. 1838. *Henry Wyckoff*, owner. 🍒
Gracious **Greek Revival** topped with a Renaissance cornice. A survivor almost surrounded by the 21st century.

[W11b] **163 Charles Street**, bet. West & Washington Sts. 2007. *Daniel Goldner.*
Folks in the neighborhood took to calling this balcony-happy glass box the **Mini-Meier.** But *Goldner* is more of a constructivist than *Meier*: see his confident **Ironworkers Training Center** in the South Astoria, Queens, section of this Guide.

Continue westward to West Street. Here, the neo-modernists have been busy:

low-rise replacement at 233 West 10th Street, a visual catastrophe that houses today's 6th Precinct. Revealed by the conversion: *premium vertutis honis* [sic] (loosely from *Cicero's* Philippics).

[W9] **The Memphis Downtown**, 140 Charles St., SE cor. Washington St. 1986. *Rothzeid, Kaiserman, Thomson & Bee.*
A slender aerie that looms over its neighbors. We said, in 2000, that this dated postmodernism was more appropriate to the Upper East Side than to these low-rise high-density blocks. It still is an urbanistic lone wolf.

[W10] **West Village Houses** (apartments), along Washington St. bet. W.10th and Bank Sts. W side. Also along Christopher and Morton Sts. and side streets. 1974. *Perkins & Will.*
Scene of the great war between defenders of "Greenwich Village scale" and the Establishment, the latter having proposed another high-rise housing project. The **David** in this case was critic *Jane Jacobs*, the **Goliath,**

[W12] **165 Charles Street**, NE cor. West St. 2006. *Richard Meier & Assocs.*
173 and 176 Perry Street act here as doting parents to their overgrown offspring next door. *Meier's* sequel to 173/176 seems younger, thinner, lighter, and sharper, the details handled with more economy (of moves, not materials). It's cooler than its parents, with their heavy steel frames, but the kid also has slightly (just slightly) less personality.

*Turn right into cobble-stoned **Charles Lane**, and you are backstage among neo-modernist heroes: Meier, Asymptote, and Goldner. But the real gem here is at **No.12**, a beautiful glass carriage house by Christoff:Finio (2007):*

[W13] **173/176 Perry Street apartments**, NE and SE cors. West St. 2002. *Richard Meier & Assocs.*
Credited, and sometimes blamed, for initiating the glass condominium revolution that spread up and down the Hudson (and even to Brooklyn) from 2002 until the Downturn of '08

(see the **Glass Box District**, just south of here). *Meier's* rationalist towers of laminated glass and white steel made modernism palatable again for the masses (the wealthy masses). They look crisp and glamorous when viewed from **Hudson River Park**, and we imagine the Park looks wonderful when viewed from them.

Briefly walk up Perry Street to look beyond Meier's 176 Perry:

[W14] **166 Perry Street**, bet. West and Washington Sts. 2009. *Asymptote.*
   On a quiet side street, a waterfall of blue glass panels beckons. *Wikipedia* tells us that "a curve may cross its asymptote repeatedly or may never actually coincide with it." Sounds fun, but where's the front door?

Back to West Street and right on West 11th toward the Palazzo Chupi:

W14

[W15] **354 West 11th Street**, bet. West and Washington Sts. ca. 1841-1842. ●✶
   A superb example of Greek Revival row houses (1830s-1840s) hereabouts. Rare, but not extinct. You can even find some in Brooklyn.

[W16] **Palazzo Chupi**, 360 W. 11th St., bet. Washington and West Sts. 2007. *Julian Schnabel,* designer.
   This 12-story eruption is a mess of competing balconies, arched windows, faux-Venetian details, and hot pink stucco. At a smaller scale it might be funny, but it's too big to be a good joke.
   Schnabel, well-known painter and filmmaker, superimposed this bizarre aerie on his studio warehouse. Perhaps he perceives himself as the 21st-century New York Renaissance man. *Michelangelo* created great sculpture, painting, poetry and architecture. Et tu, *Julian?*

Backtrack to West Street and head north again. At Bank Street, a half-block detour to the right (easterly) will reveal the entrance and light courts of the 13-building Westbeth complex:

[W17] **Westbeth**/earlier **Bell Labs, American Telephone & Telegraph Company**, 155 Bank St., bet. Washington and West Sts. N side through to Bethune St. ca. 1861-1898. *Cyrus W. Eidlitz and others.* Converted to housing, 1969, *Richard Meier & Assocs.*
   A block filler, reincarnated with major assistance from the J. M. Kaplan Fund as artists' loft housing. The exterior is a 40-year mélange of loft buildings embracing a bleak entrance court on Bank. The inner court, closer to Bethune, is a dark canyon festooned with fire-egress balconies. A severed fragment of the **High Line** ran through the building along Washington: Westbeth's co-operators missed that train.

Back to West Street and North past Superior Ink:

W12   W18

W15

[W18] **Superior Ink Condominiums**, 469 West St. and 70 Bethune St. 2009. *Robert A.M. Stern Architects.*
   Fifteen stories replacing, and yet mimicking, the Superior Ink Factory, with an additional seven brick town houses along Bethune Street. The big building took its cue from Superior's architecture, while the town houses are meant to look as if built over time (their cornices don't quite line up). A handsomely detailed, urban stage set. Action!

*STOP! Here's a great place to step into **Hudson River Park** (see p. 224), or continue walking northerly on West Street, up to Jane Street, and hang a right:*

W22

W21, No.27

W27

[W21] **19-29 Bethune Street**, bet. Greenwich and Washington Sts. S side. 1837. *Henry S. Forman and Alexander Douglass,* builders.
[W22] **24-34 Bethune Street**, bet. Greenwich and Washington Sts. N side. 1845. *Alexander R. Holden,* builder.
[W23] **36 Bethune Street**, bet. Greenwich and Washington Sts. N side. 1837. Altered, 1928.

Small-scaled and handsome mongrels. Note the diminutive windows at the third floor (servants' rooms), typical of early Greek Revival.

[W19] **Jane Hotel**/formerly **Hotel Riverview**/ originally **American Seamen's Friend Society Sailors' Home & Institute**, 113 Jane St., NE cor. West St. 1907-1908. *William A. Boring.* ●

The ships, sailors, longshoremen, wicked women, and gin mills have disappeared from the Hudson's shore. But this reformers' safe haven for merchant mariners now enjoys new life. In 1912 it housed the survivors of the **Titantic's** sinking. Now the ship's cabin rooms are inexpensive. *Boring* was the architect of **Ellis Island.**

[W20] **99 Jane Street**, NW cor. Washington St. 1999. *Fox & Fowle.*

Rockrose Development constructed new lofts as available buildings suitable for recycling diminished, a building type that flourished in the first decade of the 21st century: look at *Adjmi* or *Lombardi* new lofts in the index.

Turn right (south) onto Washington and, after two blocks, left at Bethune Street:

Back to Washington and turn left (south), then left again (easterly) on Bank Street for a leisurely stroll on this, one of the West Village's most wonderful streets:

[W24] **128 and 130 Bank Street**, bet. Greenwich and Washington Sts. S side. 1837.

Two Greek Revival houses, attic windows in the frieze; perfect moments in a motley row.

Turn right briefly onto Greenwich for a peak at the 767 Greenwich Street House, then back to Bank, turn right, and proceed in a northeasterly direction:

[W25] Originally **Helmut Jacoby House**, 767 Greenwich St., bet. Bank and W.11th Sts. E side. 1965. *Helmut Jacoby,* designer. *Leonard Feldman,* architect.

A modernist single-family town house, one of fewer than a dozen in Manhattan. As crisp as a rendering but lacking passion. *Jacoby* was the star architectural renderer of

W30a

the 1960s. (Renderings are realistic, usually perspective, presentation drawings.)

Auntie Mame: *Beginning in 1927, at 72 Bank Street, Marion Tanner, the self-described "ultimate Greenwich Village eccentric," created a haven and salon for a wide spectrum of bohemian types. Her nephew, Edward Everett Tanner III—under the pen name Patrick Dennis— immortalized her in his best-selling novel* **Auntie Mame** *(1955), which became a play, then a film, and then a Broadway musical—which resulted in another film. She died nearby in 1985, aged 94, at the Village Nursing Home, 607 Hudson Street.*

[W26] **68 Bank Street**, bet. W.4th and Bleecker Sts. S side. 1863. *Jacob C. Bogert,* builder.
[W27] **74 and 76 Bank Street**, bet. W.4th and Bleecker Sts. S side. 1839-1842. *Andrew Lockwood,* builder.

[W28] **55 and 57 Bank Street**, bet. W.4th and Bleecker Sts. N side. 1842. *Aaron Marsh,* builder.

A charming group: Greek, save for No.68, almost a generation later than the other three, exhibiting the Renaissance Revival and crisp dour brownstone details of its time.

[W29] **48 Bank Street**/originally stable, bet. Waverly Place and W.4th St. 1910. Converted, 1969, *Claude Samton & Assocs.*

Sober and serious in brown brick and linseed-oil-brushed copper, a rare modern town house among Federal and Victorian neighbors.

[W30a] **37 Bank Street**, bet. Waverly Place and W.4th St. N side. 1837.

A Village winner in the Greek Revival sweepstakes. The block is striking, despite curious lintels at [W30b] **Nos.16-34,** and some ghastly refacing across the street.

W32

[W31] **Ye Waverly Inn**, 16 Bank St., SW cor. Waverly Place. 1845.

Tucked away in basement nooks and crannies: *New York Magazine* noted "*Graydon Carter's* much-hyped, much-publicized restaurant... [is] decorated like a kind of modest,

[W34] Formerly the **Great Building Crack-Up** and **International Headquarters of the First National Church of the Exquisite Panic, Inc.**/originally **Jackson Square Branch, New York Free Circulating Library**/later **New York Public Library**, 251 West 13th St., bet. Greenwich and

W31

W34

Anglophile dining society." Paparrazzis abound. You've been warned.

Left (northwest) on Greenwich Avenue up to the shady confines of Jackson Square, popular with the boxed-lunch set:

[W32] **1 Jackson Square Residences** (aka 122 Greenwich Ave.), NE cor. Greenwich Ave. and E. 13th St. 2009. *Kohn Pedersen Fox.*

Undulations bound to produce joyous ululations from many a strolling architecture critic. *KPF* delivers the glass goods here, in rippling horizontal bands that seem on the verge of melting and flowing south on Greenwich Avenue.

[W33] **IND Electrical Substation**, 253 W.13th St., NE cor. Greenwich Ave. 1930.

The City's own subway system, the Independent (independent of the then privately owned **IRT** and **BMT**), arrived on the scene at the time of **Art Deco**. Homely civic structures hopped on the Deco ornamental bandwagon.

Seventh Aves. N side. 1888. *Richard Morris Hunt*. Altered, 1970, *Paul Rudolph*.

A benefaction of *George W. Vanderbilt*, this former library building resembles an old Dutch guildhall. The artist *Robert Delford Brown (1930-2009)* founded the **First National Church of the Exquisite Panic, Inc.** in 1964, moved the Church to this headquarters in 1970, and lived here until he sold the building in 1997. He considered this to be his greatest work of art, a dadaist gesture, an "architectural doodle," a collision of the 19th (*Hunt*) and 20th (*Rudolph*) centuries. Despite its comically violent name, *Brown* and *Rudolph's* conversion was a thoughtful, subtle endeavor, carving light-filled spaces from the dark masonry rooms within the old library.

Most of *Rudolph's* work has been ripped out in a recent conversion back to more conventional apartments, although his airy entrance portico remains.

[W35] **Lesbian and Gay Community Services Center**/formerly **Food and Maritime Trades Vocational High School**/earlier **Public School 16**, 208 W.13th St., bet. Seventh and Greenwich Aves. Center portion, 1844, *Thomas R. Jackson*? Extensions, ca. 1859, ca. 1899, *C.B.J. Snyder*. Conversion to Community Center, 1997, *Françoise Bollack*.

An excellent example of New York's many Italianate school buildings built and expanded by *Jackson* and/or *Snyder* in the late 19th century.

Turn right (south) on Seventh Avenue:

[W36] **New Building, St. Vincent's Hospital**, 36 Seventh Ave., bet. W.12th & W.13th Sts., W side. 2012 predicted. *Pei Cobb Freed*.

When the Landmarks Preservation Commission OK'd the storied hospital's proposed new medical building in the Greenwich Village Historic District (the centerpiece of a multi-building hospital/residential redevelopment), it **green-lit a slightly smaller version** of

Then right (southwest) onto West 11th Street, and left on Waverly Place:

[W38] **St. John's-in-the-Village Church** (Episcopal), 216-222 W.11th St., SW cor. Waverly Place. 1974. *Edgar Tafel*.
[W39] **Parish House**/originally South Baptist Church, 224 Waverly Place, bet. Perry and W.11th Sts. W side. Early 1850s.

An austere red brick box elaborated with a pediment and a brow of giant quasi-Greek details. It replaced a lovely Greek Revival 'temple' destroyed by fire. Its predecessor's style is visible in the parish house.

Bear right (south) back onto Seventh Avenue South:

Seventh Avenue South: *Before construction of the West Side IRT Subway below Times Square, around World War I, Seventh Avenue began its northward journey at Greenwich Avenue and West 11th Street. The building of the Seventh*

W40   W41

the *Pei Cobb Freed*-designed elliptical tower. Originally, the building was 329 feet tall, but that was trimmed to 299 feet following some initial LPC concerns.

[W37] **George Link, Jr., Pavilion, St. Vincent's Hospital & Medical Center of New York**, 165 W.11th St., NE cor. Seventh Ave. 1984-1987. *Ferrenz, Taylor, Clark & Assocs.*

The **Link Pavilion**, with a lower 11th Street wing closer in height to row house neighbors, replaced the venerable **Elizabeth Bayley Seton Building**, (*Schickel & Ditmars*). *Link's* cubistic brick architecture, however handsome in its own right, fails to harmonize with more intricately detailed brownstones.

Avenue subway to connect with Varick Street and the creation of Seventh Avenue South as a surface thoroughfare made huge scars through these West Village blocks, leaving the backs and sides of many buildings crudely exposed. Isolated triangles of land once filled with dingy gas stations and parking lots are now seeing reuse as building sites. Seventh Avenue South opened for traffic in 1919.

[W40] **22 Perry Street**, SW cor. Seventh Ave. S. 1987. *Architects Design Group*.

A "witch's hat" over the squat pepper-pot corner make this a not-unappealing novelty. With more careful detailing it could have been much more.

[W41] Originally **Duane Colglazier House**, 156 Seventh Avenue S., bet. Perry and Charles Sts. W side. 1983. *Smith & Thompson*.

An unabashedly personal statement that apes no Greenwich Village sentimentality, yet fits surprisingly well into the context of this odd-site-filled Seventh Avenue South corridor. A breath of fresh air. The retail space is occupied by *The Pleasure Chest*, a store vending sex appliances.

[W42] **137 Seventh Avenue South**, bet. Charles and W.10th Sts. 1998. *Platt Byard Dovell.*
    An unassuming constructivist infill, continuing the cosmetic surgery needed when Seventh Avenue South was slashed through this neighborhood. Stylish.

A peek into Charles Street again, then back to Seventh Avenue:

[W43] **48, 50, 52-54 Charles Street**, bet. Seventh Ave. S. and W.4th St. 1840.
    Among the Village's most riotous and picturesque groupings of brick row houses. What makes them wonderful is their spirited conversion to studios, involving major changes in window size and placement. *Emerson* was right: a foolish consistency can be the hobgoblin of little minds!

W44

W43

[W44] **59-61 Christopher Street**, NE cor. Seventh Avenue S. 1987. *Norval White and William Fegan of Levien DeLiso White Songer.*
    An essay on contemporary reuse of early 19th-century architecture motifs, built on a triangular 750-square-foot site.

END of Tour C. To continue into Tour D, walk around the corner and rest on a Christopher Park bench. For the nearest subway, Christopher Park is on a block ending at 7th Avenue South, with entry to the No.1 train (former/old IRT Seventh Avenue Line local), the Christopher Street/Sheridan Square Station).

NECROLOGY

Church of St. John's-in-the-Village
(Episcopal)/originally Hammond Street Presbyterian Church, 220 W. 11th St., SW cor. Waverly Place. 1846.
    The original Greek Revival church was destroyed by fire in 1971 and then replaced by *Edgar Tafel's* 1974 building.

Soon to GO: Edward and Theresa O'Toole Medical Services Building, St. Vincent's Hospital & Medical Center of New York/originally **National Maritime Union of America**, AFL-CIO, 36 Seventh Ave., bet. W. 12th & W. 13th Sts., W side. 1964. *Albert C. Ledner & Assocs.* Altered, 1977, *Ferrenz & Taylor.*
    Plans are underway to give this the wrecking ball in favor of a **new building** by *Pei Cobb Freed.* Some would cheer, some would mourn, but this huge, white double-dentured modernist monument was without precedent.

Walking Tour D: A continuation from Walking Tour C, or a fresh start. BEGIN at what is commonly referred to (though erroneously) as Sheridan Square. It is, in fact, Christopher Park. For Sheridan Square see No.58.

There are so many early 19th-century houses in this precinct that one is tempted to say "when you've seen one, you've seen 'em all." Not so. There are always surprises; some are squashed between six-story lofts, others tucked away in backyards, often bedecked with nostalgic but destructive wisteria vines. It's this rich texture that makes them such a valuable contribution to the Village—take away the contrasts and it would be a dull place indeed.

Only some of the entries on this tour lie within the Greenwich Village Historic District; the district lines are shown on the maps.

Across from Christopher Park:

W47

[W45] **Stonewall Inn**, 53 Christopher St., bet. Seventh Avenue and Waverly.

Facing **Christopher Park,** this non-descript tavern was the scene (June 1969) of a brick- and bottle-throwing rampage that followed a police raid (a landmark in the gay rights movement). The melée is celebrated in an annual parade and 53's inclusion in the National Register of Historic Places.

And on the other side of Christopher Park:

[W46] **88 and 90 Grove Street**, bet. W. Washington and Waverly Pls. 1827. **No.88** altered with mansard, 1860s. **No.90** remodeled, 1893, *Carrère & Hastings.*

Two personalities facing Christopher Park. Painter *Robert Blum* commissioned the studio alteration of **No.90** in 1893, then lived and worked there until his death in 1903. New owner *Howard Reed* can enjoy the chrysanthemums *Blum* painted on the dining room wall. Seventeen years later architects *Carrère & Hastings* built the grand New York Public Library at 42nd Street.

[W47] **Hostel for the Disabled**/formerly **Northern Dispensary**/originally **Northern Dispensary Institute,** 165 Waverly Place, on triangle with Waverly Place and Christopher St. 1831. *Henry Bayard,* carpenter; *John C. Tucker,* mason. Third floor added, 1854. Restored, 1977, *H. Dickson McKenna.* Remodeled into apartments, 1997, *John Ellis & Assocs.*

An austere vernacular Georgian building with sheet metal lintels and cornice of a later period. Remarkable for having continuously

W49

operated as a public clinic from its founding in 1827. *Edgar Allan Poe* was treated here for a head cold in 1837—without charge. Closed 1989. Reopened as a hostel, 1997.

For the Guinness Book of Records: *triangular Northern Dispensary is the only building in New York with one side on two streets (Grove and Christopher where they join) and two sides on one street (Waverly Place, where it forks to go off in two directions).*

[W48] **18 and 20 Christopher Street,** bet. Gay St. and Waverly Place. SE side. 1827. *Daniel Simonson,* builder. Alterations: storefronts.

A once Federal pair with later superdormers. Lintels still in place upstairs.

W50

[W49] **11 Christopher Street**, bet. Greenwich Ave. and Gay St. 2000. *Richard Cook of Cook + Fox.*

A mini-modernist Parisian with French doors and steel garde-corps elegantly punctuate this classic façade, bottomed in crisp steel for a fashionable shop. The microbuilding next door (complete with faux-mansard roof) is the entry.

[W50] **14 Christopher Street**, SW cor. Gay St. 1903. *Jardine, Kent & Jardine.* Altered, 1939, 1975.

W53

Alterations to this turn-of-the-century tenement gave it a modernist facelift, but happily retained its eloquent cornice cum frieze, supported by Corinthian pilasters. It contrasts graciously with the tiny houses on Gay Street, where its back wall curves to match the bend in Gay.

[W51] **Gay Street**, bet. Christopher St. and Waverly Place. Houses, 1827-1860.

My Sister Eileen territory. A handful of little Federal houses, delightful for hugging the street. More superdormers.

*Circle around the delightful sliver of **Christopher Park** and head back north along Grove Street. Then right on Waverly Place:*

[W52] **Residence of the Graymore Friars**/formerly **St. Joseph's Church Rectory**, 138 Waverly Place, bet. Sixth Ave. and Grove St. S side. 1895. *George H. Streeton.*

Austere brick and brownstone with neo-Gothic arched window openings next to the parent church in very Greek dress.

Turn right (south) on Sixth Avenue, left on Washington Place:

[W53] **St. Joseph's Roman Catholic Church**, 365 Sixth Ave., NW cor. Washington Place. 1833-1834. *John Doran.* Rebuilt after fire, 1885, *Arthur Crooks.*

This church is one of New York's dwindling flock of **Greek Revival** "temples." Its recent repainting in gray and white is elegant.

W54

[W54] **St. Joseph's Washington Place School**, 111 Washington Place, bet. Sixth Ave. and Grove St. N side. 1897. *George H. Streeton.*

A five-story façade embellished with cornices and window enframements borrowed from Italian Renaissance palazzi and Baroque country houses.

Back to Sixth Avenue:

[W55] **IFC Center** (cinema)/formerly **Waverly Theater**, 323 Sixth Ave. bet. W. 3rd and W. 4th Sts. 2005. *Larry Bogdanow.*

Closed for years, this onetime church then movie theater, recently re-opened as an art-house cinema. Short films before the main feature are an old-fashioned (1950s) treat.

Turn around and head back north a few paces, turning at an angle left on W. 4th St.:

[W56] **175-179 West 4th Street**, at Jones St. N side. 1833-1834.

Three Federal houses, parlor floors and basements rented for shops. Look up at the exquisite dormers—No.175 had them too, until altered.

*"Folk Scare" memories: West 4th Street was a main avenue during the folk music revival of the early 1960s. **Bob Dylan** lived at No.161. **The Music Inn**, at No.169, sold and lent instruments of every kind to folkies and is still holding on against all odds. **Allan Block's Sandal Shop**, famous for its Saturday afternoon jam sessions, was at No.171 and survived well into the 1970s.*

A glance down Jones Street:

[W57] **26, 28, 30 Jones Street,** bet. Bleecker and W.4th Sts. S side. 1844. *Henry Hoople Mott.* ●
Severely simple, late Greek Revival: three prim stories top a low basement, low stoops.

Back to West 4th, one block to Sheridan Square:

Sheridan Square, between Washington Place and W. 4th, Barrow, and Grove Streets, was scarcely a square, but an abandoned stretch of asphalt, defined by stripes on the pavement and guarded by NO PARKING signs. Today. magnificent greenery flourishes (eyes only), created and maintained by neighborhood volunteers.

[W60] **Greenwich House**, 29 Barrow St., bet. W.4th St. and Seventh Ave. S. SE side. 1917. *Delano & Aldrich.*

The building, an ill-kept Georgian Revival, is most significant for its work: social reform. In 1901, when **Greenwich House** was founded (by *Mary Kingsbury Simkhovitch*, daughter of an old patrician family), Jones Street, a block to the east, was home to 1,400 people—975 to the acre—then the highest density in this part of Manhattan. These were first-generation Italian, second-generation Irish, some black, some French. From Greenwich House came the **Greenwich Village Improvement Society**, the first neighborhood association in the City.

Gently left (south) at Seventh Avenue, briefly, then gently left down Bleecker Street to Father Demo Square (at Sixth Avenue), a colorful Italian-American shopping street, now gradually submerging under the rising tides of yuppiedom:

*Gastronomical holdouts: **Faicco's** (sausages), 260 Bleecker St. SW side. Homemade sausage since 1927. Tipico italiano. **Rocco's Pastry Shop**, 243 Bleecker St., opp. Leroy St. NE side. Great Italian ices for a summer stroll. The Italian rum cake (with luscious frosting!) is not to be believed. **John's Pizzeria**, 278 Bleecker St, SW side. Authentic brick oven pizza in a dark den divided by wooden booths carved with generations of initials that seem to date from the Middle Ages. Actually, it's only been here since 1929.*

*Lamented is the recently vanished **A. Zito &***

W60

W57

W61

*Before this greening the Square was frequently confused with **Christopher Park** around the corner, where, confusingly, a statue of Civil War general Philip Sheridan stands. This identity crisis frequently caused havoc in emergencies, when ambulances and fire equipment rushed to the wrong place.*

[W58] **Sheridan Square Triangle Association Viewing Garden**, Sheridan Sq. 1983. *Pamela Berdan*, landscape designer. *David Gurin*, planner, NYC Department of Transportation.
If only the City had more such delights; this one courtesy of the Department of Transportation, not the Department of Parks.

Turn left (southwest) at Barrow Street:

[W59] **15 Barrow Street** (originally **Conrad Schaper's stable**), bet. W.4th St. and Seventh Ave. S. SE side. 1896. *H. Hasenstein.*
Originally a four-story stable; and to press the point, a horse's head protrudes from just below the cornice.

Sons, 259 Bleecker, at Cornelia St., and its long, round, crusty loaves.

[W61] **1 Leroy Street,** SW cor. Bleecker St. 1999. *Stephen B. Jacobs Group.*
A six-story infill providing duplexes and triplexes for the super-rich to live among the exoticism of Greenwich Village. How could one resist, with Rocco's Pastry Shop just across the street?

Left on Leroy Street, and continuing southwesterly across Seventh Avenue:

[W62] **28 Seventh Avenue South**, bet. Leroy St./St. Luke's Place and Bedford St. W side. Building, 1921. Store redesign and residential addition, 1988, *Matthew Gotsegen.*
Serendipitous architecture for a serendipitous location, an interruption in an earlier, pre-subway grid.

W64b

W68

Changing street names in midstream: St. Luke's Place assumes its name (and a sequential, rather than odd-even, house numbering system) halfway between Seventh Avenue South and Hudson Street—at the bend to be precise. The eastern portion is officially Leroy Street, a lesser thoroughfare to those who are snobbish about such things.

[W63] **5-16 St. Luke's Place**, bet. Leroy and Hudson Sts. N side. 1852-1853.

This impressive row of handsome brick and brownstone Italianate residences seems an eerie stage set in this world of converted industrial lofts visible across **James J. Walker Park**— named for the colorful mayor who lived at **No.6**. Fortunately, when the street's two rows of gingko trees green they form a graceful arbor, giving form to a streetscape one-sided in winter.

Between 1834 and 1898 the land occupied by then titled **Hudson Park** (*Carrère & Hastings*, 1898), was part of Trinity Parish's cemetery until that cemetery moved to 155th Street. A relic

from the cemetery is the marble monument to members of *Eagle Fire Engine Company No.13*, retained at the St. Luke's Place entrance. No traces of *Carrère and Hastings* remain.

The block's latest resident, *Nat Rothschild*, has gutted the interior of No.8, preserving a façade that now fronts remarkable innards (2007. *David Chipperfield*). Just how much of the Village is masking other worlds?

Turn right (northerly) on Hudson Street and right again (east) on Morton (which echoes the Leroy Street/St. Luke's Place bend in the middle):

[W64] **Morton Street**, from Hudson to Bedford Sts.

If there is a typical Village block, this is it. It bends. It has a private court with its own, out-of-whack numbers [W64a] **Nos.44A, 44B**. It is full of surprising changes of scale, setbacks, façade treatments. [W64b] **No.42**, 1889, presents a bottomless caryatid of some charm. [W64c] **No.66**, 1852, has a bold bay; [W64d] **No.59,** 1828, has one of the finest **Federal** doorways in the Village. Old Law tenements interrupt the street, greedily consuming their property right out to the building line. In them live staunch Italian and Irish holdouts, groups that remind their more affluent neighbors of an earlier, less moneyed Village.

Take a sharp left (northwesterly) into narrow Bedford Street:

[W65a] **"Narrowest house in the Village,"** 75 Bedford St., bet. Morton and Commerce Sts. W side. 1873.

It's nine feet wide; originally built to span an alley to the rear. Though narrow by any standards, it was wide enough for carriages to pass below. One of several sequential village residences of poet *Edna St. Vincent Millay* (1923-1924).

Edna St. Vincent Millay (1892-1950): This poet, closely identified with the Village in the 1920s, was middle named for St. Vincent's Hospital, even though she was born in Rockland, Maine. It seems that the hospital had saved the life of a relative.

W63

W66

[W65b] **Isaacs-Hendricks House**, 77 Bedford St., SW cor. Commerce St. 1799. Alterations, 1836, 1928, 1985.

Significant for its early date, but it's a reconstruction rather than a restoration. This reborn Federal house seems more part of a diorama than Village nitty-gritty survival. Clapboard walls, visible to the side and rear, were an economy for an ending row house, cheaper than brick.

Take a left (southwest) on Commerce Street to see the next pair and then circle around to the right (northeast) via Barrow Street:

[W66] **39 and 41 Commerce Street**, at Barrow St. E side. 1831 and 1832, respectively. Mansard roofs, 1873, *D.T. Atwood*.

This extraordinary dour mansarded pair remembers the elegance once surrounding and on neighboring **St. Luke's Place**. A local legend holds that they were built by a sea captain for his two daughters — one each, because they could not live together. The records show they were actually built for a milkman, one *Peter Huyler*.

Having doubled back, take a left (northerly) to resume on Bedford Street:

[W67] Originally **J. Goebel & Company**, 95 Bedford St., bet. Barrow and Grove Sts. W side. 1894. *Kurzer & Kohl.*

Once the end of the century (19th) stable of a wine distributor, as lettering on the façade indicates; converted into apartments in 1927.

[W68] **17 Grove Street**, NE cor. Bedford St. 1822. third floor added, 1870. **100 Bedford Street**, bet. Grove and Christopher Sts. 1833.

William Hyde built this imposing wood house for himself, the best preserved of the few remaining wood-frame houses in the Village. Trim and crisp with a renewed and serious repainting. His shop was around the corner at 100 Bedford.

[W69] **Twin Peaks**, 102 Bedford St., bet. Grove and Christopher Sts. E side. ca. 1830. Renovation, 1925, *Clifford Reed Daily.*

W69

The renovation was the work of *Daily*, a local resident, financed by the wealthy financier and art patron *Otto Kahn*, whose daughter lived here for some time. *Daily* considered the surrounding buildings "unfit for inspiring the minds of creative Villagers" and set out to give them this "island growing in a desert of mediocrity." Great fun for the kids — pure *Hansel and Gretel.*

Turn around, make a right on Grove Street:

[W70] **14-16 Grove Street**, bet. Bedford and Hudson Sts. S side. 1840. *Samuel Winant and John Degraw,* builders.

A pair of vine-clad pristine Greek Revival houses. Until altered in 1966, **No.14** was believed to have been the last completely untouched Greek Revival residence in the City.

[W71] **Grove Court**, viewed bet. 10 and 12 Grove St., bet. Bedford and Hudson Sts. S side. 1853-1854. Alterations.

A pedestrian cul-de-sac lined with story-book brick-fronted houses, their position remembering the irregularity of early 19th-century property lines. Evidence of similar holdings can be glimpsed throughout the West Village. These were built for workingmen; the court was once known as **Mixed Ale Alley**.

Cross Hudson Street for the St. Luke's church complex:

■■■■ [W74] **Church of St. Luke-in-the-Fields**
■ 🛈 (Episcopal)/formerly **St. Luke's Episcopal Chapel** of Trinity Parish, 485 Hudson St., bet. Barrow and Christopher Sts. opp. Barrow St. W side. 1821-1822. Attributed to *Clement Clarke Moore. John Heath*, builder. Interior remodeling, 1875, 1886. Fire, 1981. Restoration and expansion to W and S, 1985, *Hardy Holzman Pfeiffer Assocs.*

W72

W73

W77

W76

■■■■ [W72] **4-10 Grove Street**, bet. Bedford and
■ 🛈 Hudson Sts. S side. 1827-1834. *James N. Wells,* builder.

Honest and humble. The Federal houses at **4-10 Grove Street** represent the prevailing style of the 1820s. Americans had few architects then; instead, the local carpenters and masons copied and adapted plans and details from builders' copybooks. In translation, the detailing is less pretentious, adapting to the needs of American merchant and craftsman clients; nonetheless, there is a faint, pleasant echo of London's Bloomsbury.

▬▬ [W73] **2 Grove Street**, SE cor. Hudson St.
🔲 1938. *Irving Margon.*

A modest Art Deco apartment block, counterpoint to first-class Federal architecture next door.

An austere country church from the time when this was countryside to New Yorkers living on the southern tip of Manhattan. The original church was founded independently by local residents, with financial help from wealthy, downtown **Trinity Parish**. With the influx of immigrants to the area, the carriage-trade congregation moved uptown to Convent Avenue to found a St. Luke's there. After an 1886 fire, this St. Luke's reopened and, from 1891-1976, was a chapel of Trinity Parish.

The additions following the 1981 fire, visible within the church property, are handsomely conceived, detailed, and executed brick masonry volumes. Emitting rich overtones of the past, they are fresh in spirit, while harmonious to the older structures. Visit the yard and church interior, too. On leaving **St. Luke's**, scan the small houses along Hudson and Barrow Streets, and then proceed northward on Hudson.

[W75] **473-477, 487-491 Hudson Street,** flanking St. Luke's Chapel, bet. Barrow and Christopher Sts. W side. 1825.

[W76] **90-96 Barrow Street,** bet. Hudson and Greenwich Sts. N side. 1827. *James N. Wells,* builder.

Only six houses remain of 14 originally symmetrically arrayed, seven to the north of the church and seven to the south. Such development was possible because the entire tract of land was developed under a lease from the

W78

Trinity Church Corporation. All in an austere Federal mode.

Back north on Hudson, just a glance north of Christopher:

[W77] **510-518 Hudson Street,** bet. Christopher and W.10th Sts. E side. 1826. *Isaac Hatfield,* carpenter and builder.

Five Federal houses, of which only 510 and 512 maintain their original dormered silhouettes.

[W78] **248 West 10th Street,** SW cor. Hudson St. 1988. *Norval White,* design architect.

Modernist sensibility brought to the stolid forms of the masonry vernacular buildings along Hudson Street. Here the Village begins to open up as the Hudson River beckons.

Turn left (southwesterly) on Christopher Street:

[W79] **PATH/Port Authority Trans-Hudson Christopher Street Station** /originally **Hudson & Manhattan Railroad** entrance, 137 Christopher St., bet. Hudson and Greenwich Sts. N side. 1912. *John Oakman.* Restored, 1985, *Port Authority of N.Y. & N.J. Architectural Design Team.*

A wondrous restoration of this sadly neglected amenity. The scene captures one — figuratively—at a London tube entrance.

[W80] **The Archives Apartments**/originally **U.S. Appraiser's Stores** (warehouse)/then **U.S. Federal Archives Building**, 666 Greenwich St., bet. Christopher and Barrow Sts. to Washington St. W side. 1892-1899. *Willoughby J. Edbrooke, William Martin Aiken, James Knox Taylor.* Conversion, 1988, *Avinash K. Malhotra.* Street-level and lobby design, *Judith Stockman & Assocs.,* designers. 🖌

A block-filling, 10-story monolith of smooth brick in the **Romanesque Revival** style of

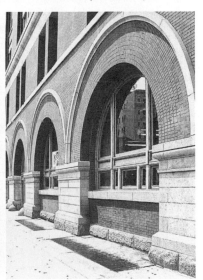

W80

H.H. Richardson. Great brick arches form a virile base, and arched corbel tables march across the cornice against the sky.

The structure was sold for a mixed residential-commercial-retail facility, some income from which will benefit historic preservation activities through the New York Landmarks Conservancy.

[W81] **St. Veronica's Roman Catholic Church**, 153 Christopher St., bet. Greenwich and Washington Sts. N side. 1889-1890. *John J. Deery.*

Here are squat towers worthy of Prague's Old City.

*Continue towards the water and the fresh breezes of **Hudson River Park**, but inspect these two en route:*

[W82] Weehawken Street Historic District, 1-13 & 2-14 Weehawken St., 177 & 185-187 Christopher St., 304-308 & 305 West 10th St., 388-398 West St. ca. 1830s-1840s. 🍎

A charmingly wee historic district (one street, 14 buildings), hard against the roar of traffic on West Street. Here was the site of the **Weehawken Market** (1830s), and vestiges remain: the highlight is a memorably ram-shackle shingled house with two faces: **No.6** on Weehawken Street and **No.392** on West Street.

W82

W83

W79

The only remnant of the original houses, it was purchased by boatbuilder *George M. Munson* and functioned as a saloon until 1867. A rare survivor indeed, especially considering all the recent glass and steel concoctions in the neighborhood. Stand outside and the shouts of drunken sailors and squawking parrots are not hard to imagine.

🏨 **[W83] Keller Hotel,** 150 Barrow St., NE cor. West St. 1897-1898. *Julius Munckwitz.* 🍎 **Renaissance Revival** with Corinthian columns, cast-iron storefronts. Originally a cheap hotel for sailors (one can imagine a lonely seafarer carving "mother" into the plaster with a knife), then a flop house, and then, for the last 15 years, vacant. Gentrification has so far missed this ghost, with its mournful Hopperesque vertical sign: **HOTEL.**

Unclear fate: Chumley's, 86 Bedford Street, bet. Barrow and Grove Sts. E side.

Opened in 1922 as a speakeasy, the dim lights of Chumley's shone for years on famous writers, allegedly including *Cather, Fitzgerald,* and *Hemingway,* and their dusty books lined the walls. More recently, tourists gathered in search of that authentic New York smell of stale beer and old wood and to peer into the side alley, accessed by a secret door in a bookcase that (in theory, anyway) allowed Prohibition-era patrons a chance to flee during police raids. A wall collapsed in the spring of 2007, however, and subsequent reconstruction revealed more structural problems.

END *of Tour D. The nearest subway stations are quite a distance back along Seventh Avenue South or Sixth Avenue. A convenient but unusual route to midtown is via the PATH system (uptown to West 33rd Street and Broadway—extra fare to NYC subway connections—via Sixth Avenue, or to Jersey City, Hoboken, or Newark, N.J.). The PATH Christopher Street Station can be found beneath the marquee on Christopher Street, between Greenwich and Hudson Streets, N side.*

SOUTH VILLAGE / WEST SOHO / THE GLASS BOX DISTRICT

An intersection of brick and glass, searching for an identity. Developers keep trying to dub this area "Hudson Square," but we don't buy it. Trump tries to pass it off as SoHo. **HoTunA** ("Holland Tunnel Approach") anyone?

Walking Tour E: a perambulation through the less well known parts of the south Village, West SoHo, and the Glass Box District, ending up near Tribeca and SoHo proper. START at Sixth Avenue and Spring Street. The IND subway will take you right to the spot (IND Eighth Avenue Line local, C or E train, Spring Street Station).

Amble south on Sixth Avenue for one block, and make almost a complete U-turn (north) onto acutely intersecting Sullivan Street. Across the way to the east:

S2

S3b

[S1] **57 Sullivan Street**, bet. Broome and Spring Sts. E side. 1817. *Frederick Youmans,* builder. Expanded upward, before 1858.

Once two stories with attic, the originally dormered house was increased in height to accommodate a full third floor. Later, over-zealous restoration provided brick joints too wide for the Federal period, and **dubious shutters** for exterior decoration, that don't shut.

[S2] **83 and 85 Sullivan Street**, bet. Broome and Spring Sts. E side. 1819. Expanded upward.

A pair of well-bred **Federal** houses, survivors from a longer row displaced by more recent construction; their cornices added later, on occasion of their upward expansion. The same brick jointing problems as No.57, fat mortar joints from the "restoration" (in the early 18th century lime mortar allowed slim jointery).

[S3a] **114 Sullivan Street**, ca. 1820. Expanded upward.

[S3b] **116 Sullivan Street** (row house). 1832. Expanded upward, 1872. Both bet. Spring and Prince Sts.

Another eloquent pair of **Federal** houses in this unprepossessing block. The glory of **No.116** is the unique enframement of the front door within a simple round-arched masonry opening. Here are benchmark brick joints.

Left on Prince:

[S4] **203 Prince Street**, bet. Sullivan and MacDougal Sts. N side. 1834. Expanded upward, 1888.

The almost-perfection of the restoration makes the neighbors seem shabby in contrast. Crisply elegant **Federal** details (the entryway) have been inflated to **Greek Revival** proportions. Next door at 205, a much altered compatriot.

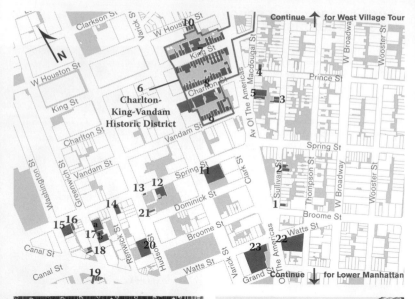

S13

S10

Turn left (south) briefly at MacDougal and peek at:

[S5] Onetime **Quartermaster Storehouse**, NYC Police Department/originally **10th Precinct Station House**, 194 Sixth Ave. (originally 24 MacDougal St.) bet. Prince and Spring Sts. E side. 1893. *Nathaniel D. Bush.* Converted, 1987, *Terrance R. Williams.*

The old station house was a stately, if dour, pressed brick and granite structure with rusticated voussoirs around an arched entrance portal, and about all that remains; nearly everything above the ground floor is new. Nowhere near original quality.

Richmond Hill, a country mansion built in 1767, once enjoyed magnificent views from its 100-foot-high mound near today's intersection of Charlton and Varick Streets. George Washington briefly used it as his headquarters during the Revolution, John Adams occupied it as vice-president later when the City was the nation's

capital. In 1797 Aaron Burr acquired the elegant structure to lavish entertainment upon those who might further his political ambitions. It was John Jacob Astor who recognized the value of the surrounding 26 acres. He had them mapped into 25- by 100-foot lots beginning in 1817, after this and other Village hills were leveled by the Commissioners' Plan of 1811 to their present flatness, and saw the development of the row houses still extant in the Charlton-King-Vandam district. Meanwhile the mansion itself, literally knocked off its "pedestal," was moved across the street. After losing its status, it served as a theater and amusement garden and was finally demolished in 1849.

At **Father Fagan Park,** *a sliver formed by the intersection of Sixth Avenue, MacDougal and Charlton/Prince (the names are different on the two sides of the avenue), follow Sixth Avenue north, one block into the **Charlton-King-Vandam Historic District.***

By crossing Sixth (west) you have a choice of walking through any (or all) of the three east-west blocks that make up much of the Historic District:

[S6] **Charlton-King-Vandam Historic District**. Early row houses, 1820-1829; later row houses, 1840-1849. From N to S: [S7] **1-49, 16-54 King Street**. [S8] **9-43, 20-42 Charlton Street**. [S9] **9-29 Vandam Street**. ●

This Historic District, minute in size when compared with that of Greenwich Village to the north, is New York's greatest display of Federal style row houses. The two best (and best preserved) examples are **Nos.37** and **39 Charlton**, whose exquisitely detailed entrances with original doors and leaded glass sidelights convey many of the style's most distinctive qualities. The later Greek Revival rows, like the ones at **Nos.20, 40, 42, 44 King Street**, almost perfectly preserved, are impressive, too. Check **29 King Street** (Public School 8; *David I. Stagg*. 1886. "A lively Queen Anne").

[S12] **NYC Fire Department Museum**/originally **Rescue Company No.1**, 278 Spring St., bet. Hudson and Varick Sts. S side. Open to the public: Tu-Sa 10-5; Su 10-4. closed Mo & major holidays. 212-691-1303.

A retired specialized firehouse now filled with artifacts for fire buffs of all ages and with old equipment, photos, and other goodies.

Jerome L. Greene Performance Space, WNYC, 44 Charlton St., SE cor. Varick St. 2009. Kostow Greenwood Architects. www.thegreenespace.org
Public radio, with live broadcasts, before an audience. What could be better?

[S13] **Greenhouse**, 286 Spring St. bet. Hudson and Varick. 2008. *Antonio Di Oronzo of bluarch.*

The first "LEED*-certified" nightclub in the City, constructed with environmentally friendly materials. Unlike many velvet-roped clubs, Greenhouse is not cold or austere; it's botanically lush and cozy. Fake moss grows up the wall, tiny crystal balls hang from the ceiling in a

S8

Take a moment just to the north, outside the boundaries of the Historic District:

[S10] **197-203 West Houston Street**, bet. Bedford and Varick Sts. S side. ca. 1820.

Four once Federal houses, all raised to a Greek Revival flat roof. Note the lintels retained over a picture window intrusion on **No.201.**

Walk south on Varick, and then west on Spring Street:

[S11] **Trump Soho**, SE cor. Spring and Varick Sts. 2008. *David Rockwell and Handel & Assocs.*

The neighborhood's controversial hot spot: too tall to meet zoning codes for a residential project, it transmogrified (same building) as a "hotel." Legally residents can only inhabit it for part of the year. After successfully skirting that issue, *Trump* proceeded to build, higher, yet higher! When the shouting subsided, the neighborhood was left with this tall, banal glass box.

standing wave formation, and in the downstairs lounge the entire ceiling is covered in faux fall foliage. Environmentally sustainable, but are clubs by nature sustainable? In New York, they come and go like autumn leaves.
Leadership in Energy and Environmental Design.

THE GLASS BOX DISTRICT

*Although the glass curtain-wall skyscraper or its squatter compatriots have been around since Lever House triggered the explosion (Park Avenue, SOM, 1952), early 21st-century New York may be marked as the **Glass Decade**, when serious architects strove to add cool, frequently frivolous, and sometimes seemingly unimaginable glazed objects to skyline and streetscape. Searching for the trendy, rather than the merely good, many contracted a fever for the sinuous, the serrated, and/or the crystalline. The trick*

S17b

was to bring reality to what seemed awesome on a computer, often leaving the results stiff and inert in the cold harsh light of a New York afternoon.

A neighborhood smorgasbord of such glassery, packed together with masonry padding in between:

[S14] **304 Spring St**. SE cor. Spring & Renwick Sts. 2006. *Zakrzweski & Hyde.*

A bland box compared to its neighbors, it's partially redeemed by a "Japanese" entry courtyard: serene (until the doorman kicks you out).

[S15] **The Urban Glass House**, 330 Spring St., SE cor. Washington St. 2006. *Philip Johnson & Alan Ritchie.* Interiors by *Annabelle Selldorf.*

Johnson's last project (he died at 98 in 2005) takes the name, if not the spirit, from his own **Glass House** in New Canaan, Connecticut. The original was a floating frame for the landscape, but this clunky cube cares not for its

Around the corner on Greenwich:

[S17a] **505 Greenwich Street** bet. Canal and Spring Sts. 2006. *Handel Architects.*

Two buildings separated by a central courtyard. Both stern, with brownish flat glass façades, they sport curious copper "light box" protrusions. Inscrutable by day, inscrutable by night.

S15

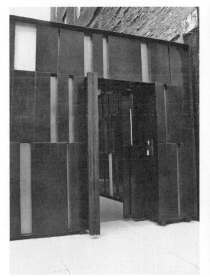

S14

S16

decidedly quirky surroundings, nor for the elegance of its New Canaan precedent. Tone-deaf, it tunes out the historic **Ear Inn** next door (a socially inconvenient neighbor), while striving to measure up to this **Glass Decade's** neighborhood pioneer, *Richard Meier*, on Perry Street eight blocks north.

Amid the glass, a Federalist holdout, with more lurking just to the south:

[S16] **Ear Inn**/originally **James Brown House**, 326 Spring St., bet. Greenwich and Washington Sts. S side. 1817. 🍺

A treasure. Gambrel roof, dormers, and Flemish-bonded brick reveal an ill-maintained **Federal** house now simultaneously propped up and shoved aside by the **Urban Glass House** next door. Lively inside and out (in nice weather patrons can sip their pints on sidewalk benches), it used to be in a backwater known only to a few stalwarts; now it's surrounded by the Glass Box District. The neon sign: "BAR" became "EAR" when its "B" burned out.

[S17b] **497 Greenwich Street Apartments**, bet. Canal and Spring Sts. 2008. *Winka Dubbeldam.*

Dubbeldam is better at crinkling her façades than most of her contemporaries. Retaining kinetic energy in the finished product, the façade buckles and cascades as promised, meanwhile embracing a stolid masonry building smartly absorbed into the project. Carefully detailed, this is glass without the box.

[S18a] **486 Greenwich Street**, bet. Canal and Spring Sts. ca.1823. Perhaps *John Rohr*, mason. 🍺

A much-altered Federal shell. Nothing remains except the pitched roof and a lamentable dormer.

[S18b] **488 Greenwich Street**, bet. Canal and Spring Sts. ca.1823. Perhaps *John Rohr*, mason. ●

Federal to a T, much of its detail lost in the period when this neighborhood was at its nadir.

A row on the south side of Canal Street:

[S19a] **John Y. Smith House**, 502 Canal Street SW cor. Greenwich St. 1818-1819. ●

S19a

S20

S21

Smith commissioned it, operating his starch and hair powder business at street level, his family quarters upstairs.

[S19b] **504 Canal Street**, bet. Greenwich and Washington Sts. ca. 1841. ●

Greek Revival, granite beamed storefront, sloping roof.

[S19c] **506 Canal Street** (John Rohr House), bet. Greenwich and Washington Sts. 1826. ●

Rohr, a merchant tailor, developed property on both sides of Canal Street and worked in a building at the northwest corner of Canal and Greenwich.

[19d] **508 Canal Street**, bet. Greenwich and Washington Sts. 1826. ●

Federal, Flemish brick bond and a peaked roof.

Then east along Canal, left on Hudson, past industrial behemoths that once housed the City's great printing industry now converted for back-office use for the financial industry:

[S20] **255 Hudson Street**, bet. Canal and Spring Sts. 2004. *Handel Architects.*

A glassy condominium with lively pre-cast concrete work, patterned with subtle ripples on the two end walls.

[S21] **284 Hudson Street**, bet. Dominick and Spring Sts. E side. ca. 1820.

A Federal remnant in which some early American middle-class citizens once lived: a classic form (simple body with pitched roof and dormer windows) that now shelters **Tauro's**, a charmingly unpretentious lunch spot. No.288 next door has disappeared since the previous edition of this Guide.

Back to and east on Watts Street. At the NE corner of Varick St., glimpse the ghost of a Federal style house (the former No.66: see Necrology below) imprinted on No.64, and then continue on the far side of Sixth—worth the wide crossing—to admire some nice bas-reliefs up close:

[S22] **100 Avenue of the Americas** (lofts)/earlier 100 Sixth Avenue/originally Green Sixth Avenue Building, SE cor. Watts St. to Thompson St. 1928. *Ely Jacques Kahn.*

S23

Three street façades are industrial window-filled Art Deco. Even the fourth, a barren lot-line wall, still lets in gobs of sunlight since expected high-rise neighbors to the south never materialized. Particularly note the strongly characterized bas-reliefs of artisans and workers in the second-floor pilasters and other two- and three-dimensional masonry ornament.

[S23] **Building Services Employees International Union Headquarters,** 101 Ave. of the Americas (Sixth Ave.), bet. Watts and Grand Sts. W side. 1992. *Fox & Fowle.*
A huge, loft-like schematic hulk, in the postmodern style popular in the early 1990s, that fails to resolve its participation in the pedestrian world at street level. Impressive but awkward.

END of Tour E. If you are ready for more, cross the humongous Canal Street intersection and stroll through Tribeca, to the south. And to the northeast lies another fascinating area, SoHo. If you're calling it a day, the nearest subways are also here (IRT Seventh Avenue Line local (1 train), or IND Eighth Avenue Line local or express (A, C, or E train), both at their respective Canal Street Stations (no interchange available).

NECROLOGY

Formerly **Barney Rosset House**, 196 W. Houston St., bet. Bedford and Varick Sts. N side. Altered for Rosset, 1969, *Eugene Futterman.*
The publisher of the Grove Press (cf., *Tropic of Cancer* by *Henry Miller*) commissioned a harsh vision: the original brown-purple vitreous-tile structural blocks have been defaced with a shroud of beige paint, the reveals at the two ribbon windows filled in, and tacky faux balconies and topiary added. Might as well tear it down and put it out of its misery. Cacophony.

Necrology: the ghost of 66 Watts Street

66 Watts Street, bet. Avenue of the Americas and Varick St. 1820.
The Federal style form described at 284 Hudson has been here recently demolished, and the site is now a vacant lot. The building's **ghostly profile** is visible, for now, on the wall of No.64 to the east. A shame.

EAST VILLAGE

The East Village is an area of vivid contrasts. Around St. Mark's-in-the-Bowery there are traces of an 18th- and 19th-century aristocracy. But elsewhere the area reveals quite a different social history.

Along St. Mark's Place, 7th, and 6th Streets is evidence of a 19th-century German community. Late in that century, population from the crowded Lower East Side was squeezed northward into the precinct generally lying between East Houston and East 14th Streets, assuming the name Lower East Side (as an extension of the already established neighborhood to the south). The area blossomed with eastern European populations, both Jewish and Gentile. To this day, favored Ukrainian and Polish dishes are still to be found in local restaurants. (On the other hand, most of the kosher delicatessens are gone.) Around First Avenue and East 11th Street the gustatorial remnants of an Italian community are evident and are being rediscovered. And McSorley's recalls the day of many other Irish saloons.

In the 1960s the area assumed the name East Village as a result of the incursion of hippies and flower children from the relatively expensive (and Establishment bohemian) Greenwich Village. The major point of entry was through the St. Mark's Place corridor, which led to Tompkins Square Park, to cheap tenement apartments, and to crash pads as far east as Alphabet City, where Manhattan's north-south avenues assume letters, rather than numbers. This area today, between Avenues A and D, is heavily Latino in population and has been dubbed **Loisaida** (pronounced low-ees-SIDE-ah), the local pronunciation of Lower East Side. Sketchy as recently as 2000, the area has been further transformed along with the rest of Manhattan by the Boom of 2003-2008. Lower and middle-income housing remain, but rubble strewn vacant lots are mostly a thing of the past. Today there are soaring rents, crowds of well-educated hipsters, and trendy, pricey restaurants where dive bars, laundromats, and hardware stores used to be. Still, the East Village remains a beautiful, less precious version of its namesake to the west, full of willow trees, community gardens, and music venues where musicians pass the tip bucket.

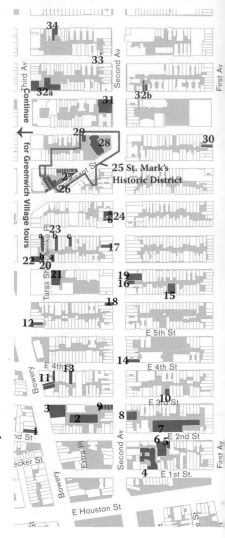

[E1] **Bouwerie Lane Theatre**/first opened as the **Bond Street Savings Bank**, 330 Bowery, NW cor. Bond St. 1873-1874. *Henry Engelbert.* ●

An intricate columnar interplay in a most sophisticated cast-iron building. The cornice is a proper tiara for two tiers of Roman Doric and three of Ionic Composite cast-iron columns.

Odds and evens: *Here, in these single-digit precincts of Manhattan's grid, the customary placement of odd and even house numbers is reversed. On both 1st and 2nd Streets the even numbers are on the north side; the odd numbers on the south—contrary to the pattern followed elsewhere in the grid.*

[E2] **New York Marble Cemetery**, interior of the block bet. E.2nd and E.3rd Sts., Second Ave., and the Bowery. Entrance on Second Ave. bet. E.2nd and E.3rd Sts. W side. 1830-now. ● *Not open to the public.*

One of the earliest sophistications of burial practices, anticipating (and therefore preventing) a marble orchard: those interred are noted by tablets inlaid in the perimeter brick wall.

[E3] **Bowery Hotel,** 335 Bowery, SE cor. E. 3rd St. 2007. Original bones, *Robert Scarano.*

A confusing provenance. Originally built in 2003 amid allegations of zoning violations, and designed by *Scarano.* Sold in 2004 to new developers who peeled off the façade and gutted all but the bones, later adding a brick exterior and swank interiors for marketing as a "boutique" (read: *expensive*) hotel. Despite its painful birth, it's twice too tall but not half-bad.

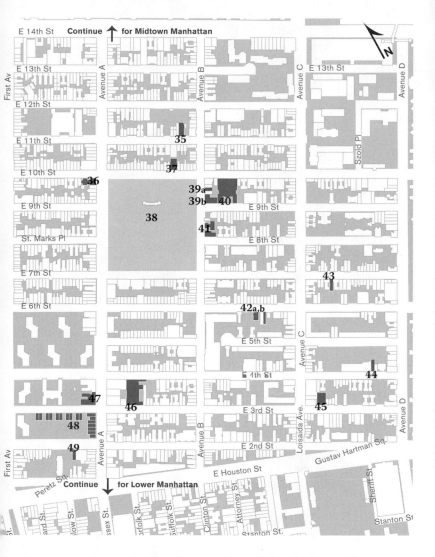

[E4] Originally **Public School 79**, 40 E.1st St., bet. First and Second Aves. N side. ca. 1886.

Like so many of the nearby tenements whose occupants it once served (it is no longer a school) this is a somber ornamented red-brick and terra-cotta "high-rise" walk-up. Our legs hurt.

[E5] **65 East 2nd Street**, bet. First and Second Aves. S side. ca. 1860.

Mt. Olivet's Italianate church rectory now converted to apartments. The billowing wrought-iron fire escapes echo the generous proportions of Victorian matrons.

[E6] **Protection of the Holy Virgin Cathedral** (Russian Orthodox Church in America)/originally **Mt. Olivet Memorial Church,** 59 E.2nd St., bet. First and Second Aves. S side.

Russian Orthodox only since 1943. Mushy rock-cut limestone.

[E7] **New York City Marble Cemetery,** 52-74 E.2nd St., bet. First and Second Aves. N side. 1830-now. ☛ *Not open to the public.*

President *James Monroe* was briefly interred in this, one of two remaining cemeteries in a part of town that contained many in the 1830s and 1840s. Also interred: Mayor *Isaac Varian*, shipping merchant *Preserved Fish*, financier *Moses Taylor*, book collector *James Lenox*, *James Henry Roosevelt*, founder of Roosevelt Hospital, and *Rebecca Ogilvie*, wife of *Andrew S. Norwood*: see the latter's house at 241 West 14th Street.

[E8] **Church of the Nativity** (Roman Catholic), 46 Second Ave., bet. E.2nd and E.3rd Sts. E side. 1970. *Genovese & Maddalene.*

Catholicism and modernism often intersected in the first decade following Vatican II. Replaced an elegant 1832 Greek Revival church by *Town & Davis.*

E3

E5

E8

A striking silhouette for the 21st-century Bowery. *Zapata*, the New York architect who turned the stately classicism of **Soldier Field** in Chicago into a football stadium from Mars, has here designed a luxury hotel with similar disregard for its neighbors. The hotel, 23 stories of trendy white fritted glass, rises in a vertical arc that emphasizes its haughty stance. For a better mix of Bowery Modernism check the **New Museum**, eight blocks south.

E12

[E9] **30-38 East 3rd Street**, SW cor. Second Ave. ca. 1830.

Five convincing remembrances of old New York in this neighborhood, particularly No.36.

[E10] **67 East 3rd Street**, bet. First and Second Aves. 1987. *Ted Reeds Assocs.*

Clear postmodern evidence of early (1987) gentrification in these once poorer parts. (This is the Hell's Angels' block, incidentally.)

[E11] **52 East 4th Street/351 Bowery**, E side of Bowery, bet. E.3rd and E.4th St. 2009. *Robert Scarano.*

A slim steel and glass apartment tower with two entrances: one on the Bowery, another by alley on East 4th Street. Festooned vertically with X-bracing, it seems to be playing a losing game of tic-tac-toe with itself.

[E12] **Cooper Square Hotel**, 25 Cooper Sq., bet 5th and 6th St. on the Bowery. E side. 2008. *Carlos Zapata with Perkins Eastman.*

Forming the "International" (ILGU): 64 East 4th Street, between the Bowery and Second Avenue, is the site of the former Labor Lyceum. It was here on June 3, 1900, that the United Brotherhood of Cloakmakers of New York and Vicinity convened with their far-flung brethren (from Philadelphia, Baltimore, Newark, and Brownsville) to form the International Ladies' Garment Workers Union.

[E13] **Rod Rogers Dance Theater/Duo Theater**, 62 E.4th St., bet. The Bowery and Second Ave. 1889.

An imposing fire exit spirals down from the fourth floor loggia, amid an array of Tuscan columns and Renaissance arches.

[E14] Formerly **Industrial National Bank Building**, 72 Second Ave., NE cor. E.4th St. ca. 1926.

Polychromatic Art Deco terra-cotta detail with the original name still evident atop the south wall.

[E15] **Community Synagogue, Max D. Raiskin Center**/originally *St. Mark's Lutheran Evangelical Church*, 323 E.6th St., bet. 1st and 2nd Aves. 1848.

It was the German immigrant parishioners of St. Mark's who boarded the General Slocum in June 1904 for that ill-fated excursion which cost over 1,000 lives as the ship caught fire just after passing through the Hell Gate. A plaque placed on the site in 2004 notes that the **General Slocum Disaster** was the worst tragedy in the City until September 11. It has been a synagogue since 1940.

Between First and Second Avenues, the south side of East 6th Street is lined with a phalanx of restaurants serving different versions of the cuisine of the Indian subcontinent. Reading from W to E: Brick Lane, Taj, Taj Mahal, Angon, Raj Mahal, Calcutta, Spice Cove, Sonar Gaow, Mitali East, Banjora, and all by himself across East 6th, Gandhi. (Some say that despite the many entrances there's only one kitchen.)

E13

E16   E22

E20a

[E16] Formerly **Isaac T. Hopper House**, 110 Second Ave., bet. E.6th and E.7th Sts. E side. 1839.

A grand Greek Revival town house. Once a home for "wayward" girls (as *Horatio Alger* would have called them).

Old neighborhood treasures, still thriving!

[E17] **B&H Dairy**, 127 Second Ave., bet. St. Mark's Pl. & E. 7th St.

A narrow classic Jewish lunch counter from the old days, with a menu not much varied for generations. Of special note is the **challah with jam** ($1) or "with a shmear" ($2). Also not to be missed are the borscht and matzo ball soups, not to mention the smoked white fish sandwich. For a brief time in the early 1990's urban chronicler/cartoonist *Ben Katchor* displayed a new comic strip each week in the front window.

[E18] **Block Drugstore**, 101 Second Ave., SW cor. E. 6th St. 1885.

In this age of big, homogeneous chain drugstores, it's rare to find one family-owned, especially one holding on since 1885. Get a load of the vintage sign wrapping the façade, especially when the sun goes down and bright red neon shines.

[E19] **Middle Collegiate Church** (Reform), 112-114 Second Ave., bet. E 6th and E 7th Sts. E side. 1892. *S. B. Reed*. Originally Middle Collegiate Church, Church House, 50 E.7th St., bet. First and Second Aves. ca. 1910.

A granite rock-faced hulk, from the sidewalk to the very tip of the spire, with window surrounds in smooth granite, and windows by *Tiffany*. The old church house is neo-Romanesque.

[E20a] **McSorley's Old Ale House**/formerly **McSorley's Saloon**, 15 E.7th St., bet. Cooper Sq. and Second Ave. N side.

Opened in the early 1860s shortly after the new Cooper Union's completion, it was made famous by painter *John Sloan* and *The New Yorker* stories by *Joseph Mitchell*. Ale, brewed to their own formula, is sold in pairs of steins. The unisex toilet facilities date back to when this was a male-only retreat. The sign says 1854, but bar researcher *Richard McDermott* discovered that the site was still an empty lot in 1861.

[E20b] **The Surma Book and Music Company**, 11 E.7th St., bet. Cooper Sq. and Second Ave. N side.

A fascinating Ukrainian store (books, records, **decorated Easter eggs**) retains the flavor of this old neighborhood's Eastern European society.

[E21] **St. George's Ukrainian Catholic Church**, 16-20 E.7th St., SE cor. Taras Shevchenko Place. 1977. *Apollinaire Osadca*.

A domed polychromed symbol of the parish's wealth and burgeoning membership: Atlantic City on 7th Street. It replaced the real thing—the humbler **Greek Revival** St. George's Ruthenian Greek Church.

[E22] **First Ukrainian Evangelical Pentecostal Church**/originally **The Metropolitan Savings Bank,** 59 Third Ave., NE cor. E.7th St. 1867. *Carl Pfeiffer.* ●

Marble at the time of the then-current cast-iron world: marble denoted class (cast iron was used to gain elaboration inexpensively). The church use is a happy solution to the problem of preserving a grand old neighborhood friend. Not too old, however: **McSorley**'s (wonderful) **Saloon** down the block is 13 years its senior.

*The **St. Mark's Place** corridor: St. Mark's Place, although the standard width (60 feet between building lines) in theory, is actually wider, as most of the buildings are built back from their respective property lines (unusual for Manhattan). Cast-iron stairs once modulated the space, jumping from street to parlor floors as matter-of-fact pop sculpture; scarcely any remain. Basement shops now line both sides of the street, including those for dresses, jewelry, beads, buttons, and posters. Record stores (a*

E23b

E24a

dying breed) still survive here, and there seems to be ten tattoo parlors per capita.

[E23a] **Hamilton-Holly House,** 4 St.Mark's Place, bet. Second and Third Aves. S side. 1831. ●

If you've wondered what a **Gibbs surround** was, you've found it (varied width of quoins). Here marble is also vermiculated (as if worm eaten). English-born real estate developer *Thomas E. Davis* sold this house in 1833 to *Col. Alexander Hamilton,* son of the first U.S. Secretary of the Treasury.

[E23b] **German-American Shooting Society Clubhous**e (Deutsch-Amerikanische Schuetzen Gesellschaft), 12 St. Mark's Place, bet. Second and Third Aves. S side. 1885. *William C. Frohne.* ●

A German marksmen's club reveled here and shot elsewhere. A symbolic target with crossed rifles marks the fourth floor, under a steep, dormered mansard roof.

[E23c] Originally **Daniel LeRoy House,** 20 St. Mark's Place, bet. Second and Third Aves. S side. 1832. *Thomas E. Davis,* builder. ●

St. Mark's Place in the 1830s (originally E. 8th Street), was an elegant residential block. No.20's arched limestone portal still shouts Greek Revival with its vermiculated voussoirs. Swinging again as the Grassroots Tavern.

[E24a] Originally **Deutsches Dispensary/** onetime **Stuyvesant Polyclinic,** 137 Second Ave., bet. St. Mark's Place and E.9th St. W side. 1883-1884. *William Schickel.* ● Restored, 2009, *David Mayerfield.*

Built as the downtown dispensary of the German Hospital (today's Lenox Hill at Park Avenue and 77th), it lost its "German" appellation as a result of rampant patriotism during World War I. Simultaneously somber and exuberant in its rich moulded red-brick and terra-cotta dress, the façade bears busts of Roman and Greek physicians over those of the 19th century: including *Harvey, Humbolt, Lavoisier.*

E24b

[E24b] **Ottendorfer Branch, New York Public Library**/originally **Freie Bibliothek und Lesehalle,** 135 Second Ave., bet. St. Mark's Place and E.9th St. W side. 1883-1884. *William Schickel.* ● Interior. ●

Built as a free German public library during the period of heavy German immigration to the surrounding streets. Another architectural confection next to its medical soul-mate.

St. Mark's-in-the-Bowery and northward:

[E25] **St. Mark's Historic District,** 21-35 and 42-46 Stuyvesant St., 102-128 and 109-129 E.10th St., 232 E.11th St. and St. Mark's-in-the-Bowery Church. ●

The District, an area subdivided and partly developed by *Governor Peter Stuyvesant's* grandson, includes two individual landmarks established earlier, **St. Mark's Church** and the **Stuyvesant-Fish House,** as well as the "Renwick" Triangle.

[E26] Stuyvesant-Fish House/ formally the **Nicholas and Elizabeth Stuyvesant Fish House**, 21 Stuyvesant St., bet. Second and Third Aves. NW side. 1803-1804. 🍎

A fat Federal house, of width unusual for its time, five years younger than the body of **St. Mark's** down the block. Built by *Governor Stuyvesant's* great-grandson, it was a wedding gift for his daughter, who married *Nicholas Fish*, hence its hyphenated name. Over-restoration has given it a bland cast.

[E27] "Renwick" Triangle, 114-128 E.10th St., 23-35 Stuyvesant St., bet. Second and Third Aves. 1861. Attributed to *James Renwick, Jr.*

Buildings with differing plans but uniform façades (within, buildings vary in depth from 16 to 48 feet, in width from 16 to 32 feet) make a handsome grouping, carefully restored by new owners as one- and two-family houses.

[E28] St. Mark's-in-the-Bowery Church (Episcopal), Second Ave. NW cor. E.10th

E26

St. 1799. Steeple, 1826-1828. *Ithiel Town (Town & Thompson)*. Cast-iron portico, 1854. 🍎 Restored, 1975-1978, *The Edelman Partnership*. Fire, 1978. Restored, 1978-1984, *The Edelman Partnership*.

This **Federal** body, **Greek Revival** steeple, and pre-Civil War portico stand on the site of the garden chapel of *Peter Stuyvesant's* estate. The graveyard, containing *Stuyvesant's* vault, is now remodeled in undulating cobblestones for play purposes. *Harold Edelman* not only was architect of the restoration (after a tragic fire) but also designed the new stained-glass windows.

In 1927 Frank Lloyd Wright designed a cluster of three apartment towers (one at 18 stories, two at 14 stories) that presaged his later **Price Tower** *in Bartlesville, Oklahoma. Commissioned by the rector of St. Mark's-in-the-Bowery, they were to have been shoehorned into the space on either side of and behind the diminutive church—and would have totally overwhelmed it. The onset of the Great Depression scuttled the project . . . thankfully.*

[E29] Neighborhood Preservation Center/originally **Rectory, St. Mark's-in-the-Bowery Church**, 232 E.11th St., bet. Second and Third Aves. 1900. *Ernest R. Flagg*. Restoration, 1999, *Harold Edelman of the Edelman Partnership*.

A lesser-known work of a great architect. Note the cast-iron entrance stair. Now the home to the **Historic Districts Council**, the **Greenwich Village Society for Historic Preservation**, and the **St. Mark's Historic Landmarks Fund**. Drop in.

Governor Peter (Petrus) Stuyvesant's country house sat roughly at the intersection of Tenth and Stuyvesant Streets, just west of Second Avenue. The Bowery was then the Bouwerie (Dutch for "plantation") Road, bounding the southwest flank of the Stuyvesant estate (which extended north to 23rd Street, east to Avenue C, and south to 3rd Street). Stuyvesant Street was the driveway from the Bouwerie Road to the mansion, subsequently destroyed by fire in 1778. There's a plaque from 1890 on the NE corner of 3rd Avenue and E. 12th St. where

E29

Stuyvesant's prize pear tree stood for 200 years (until the late 19th century).

[E30] 171 First Avenue, bet. E.10th and E.11th Sts. W side. ca. 1880.

Outcast four-story cast-iron in exile from SoHo? A wonderful surprise. We could use more throughout the City to invigorate bland blocks.

[E31] Originally The Yiddish Art Theatre/later **The Phoenix**/later **Louis N. Jaffe Art Theater**/now **Village East City Cinemas**, 189 Second Ave., SW cor. E.12th St. 1925-1926. *Harrison G. Wiseman*. 🍎 Interior. 🍎 Converted to cinema multiplex, 1991.

In the mid 1920s, this part of Second Avenue (known as the **Jewish Rialto**) supported 20 theaters staging Yiddish performances. Developer *Louis N. Jaffe*, a devotee of actor *Maurice Schwartz* (Mr. Second Avenue), built this one for him. Like many synagogues searching for an architectural style, the theater alludes to the neo-Moorish. In 1932 *I.J. Singer's* "Yoshe Kalb" ran for a record 300 performances.

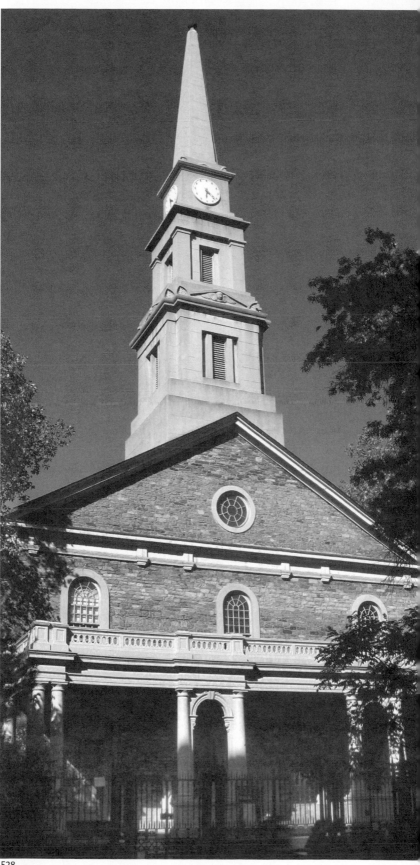

Café Royal, on the SE corner of Second and East 12th, was, until it closed in 1953, in the words of New York Times writer Richard F. Shepard, "the uncontested artistic and intellectual center of the Yiddish-speaking world in America . . . an enclave where artists, actors and writers came to debate, over endless glasses of tea, the great questions of art that have gone unanswered in every civilized language." Now a dry cleaner dispenses clean clothes, if not much wisdom.

E36

[E32a] **201-213 East 12th Street**, bet. Second and Third Aves. ca. 1880. Converted, 1981, *Mullen Palandrani Grossberg.*

A beautifully detailed brick mill building (graceful decorative brick arched lintels), now defaced with unfortunate glass enclosures at each apartment entrance.

Butch Cassidy of Same & Sundance Kid fame lived (1901) in a boardinghouse run by Mrs. Catherine Taylor at 234 East 12th Street, between Second and Third Avenues.

[E32b] Originally **Elizabeth Home for Girls, Children's Aid Society,** 307 E. 12th St. bet. First and Second Aves. 1892. *Vaux & Radford.* ●

Now cut into apartments, originally a home for homeless, orphaned, and wayward girls. *Calvert Vaux* designed at least a dozen such refuges in the City for the Children's Aid Society. This one is typical: handsome Victorian Gothic red brick, its façade expressed in two parts; the right half with a merry Dutch gable, the left with two dormers. Great chimney. (More *Vaux* below...)

[E33] Formerly **Karl Bitter Studio**, 249-1/2 E.13th St., bet. Second and Third Aves.

Bitter (1867-1915) was sculptor of the figures of Architecture, Sculpture, Painting, and Music on the **Metropolitan Museum's** entrance façade, and the figure **"Pomona"** atop the Plaza's Pulitzer fountain, as well as many well-known works. Note his (and a partner's) name carved in stone: *bitter & moretti sculptors.*

[E34] **224 E. 14th Street**, bet. Second and Third Aves. 1869. Renovation, 2006, *Bill Peterson.*

A brownstone drastically re-imagined by *Peterson*. The entire second-floor wall hinges and opens like a garage door! The lucky inhabitants can thus gaze upon 14th Street in all its unfettered glory.

East Village/Far East: the eastern reaches of these precincts:

[E35] **The Father's Heart Ministry Center**/originally **People's Home Church and Settlement** (Methodist Episcopal), 545 E.11th St., bet Avenues A and B. 1868.

Italianate brick, Gothic hooded window moldings, and an ogive arched corbel-table that may be unique. Dignified eclecticism.

[E36] **St. Nicholas Carpatho-Russian Orthodox Greek Catholic Church**/originally **St. Mark's Memorial Chapel**, 288 E.10th St., SW cor. Avenue A. 1883. *James Renwick, Jr., and W.H. Russell.*

Gothic Revival in exuberant red brick and matching terra cotta. A bit too smooth for English neo-Gothic, but heaven knows what was going on in Carpathia at the time.

[E37] **Tompkins Square Branch, New York Public Library**, 331 E. 10th St., bet. Aves. A and B, north side of Tompkins Sq. 1904. *Charles McKim of McKim, Mead & White.* ●

Modest *McKim*, who had Pennsylvania Station (in the works) on his mind. Austere flush Renaissance façade wth a delicate frieze, pleasant dentils, and bas-relief spandrel panels within the arches at the second floor.

[E38] **Tompkins Square Park**/originally **Tompkins Square**, E.7th to E.10th Sts., Avenue A to Avenue B. 1834.

Another London (**Bloomsbury**) park surrounded by high-density, low-rise housing: 16 blessed acres in these tight and dense streets. The *Charlie Parker Jazz Festival* happens in the park each summer (*Parker* lived adjacent to the park: see next page).

The park is generally much quieter than it was 20 years ago, when the clearance of homeless encampments and a city-imposed curfew led to protests and an all-night riot on August 6, 1988. The skirmish resulted in the official reprimand of 14 police officers who beat the living daylights out of protestors and bystanders alike. That riot was largely the result of neighborhood tension over gentrification, basically a moot point today.

E40

Elm trees: Tompkins Square Park is notable for its stand of beautiful elm trees that somehow have avoided Dutch Elm Disease. Under one elm in the park's center, on October 9, 1966, A.C. Bhaktivedanta Swami Prabhupada, founder of the International Society for Krishna Consciousness, held the first recorded outdoor chanting session of the Hare Krishna mantra

[E40] **Public School 64**, 605 East 9th St., bet. Ave. B and Ave. C. N side. 1904-1906. *C.B.J. Snyder.* 💣🔭

The H-plan, developed by *Snyder* provided airy courtyards front and back bathing classrooms with light and air. All in French Renaissance dress.

E39b

E42b

outside of the Indian subcontinent; participants included beat poet Allen Ginsberg. Maybe the chanting has kept the elms alive? Or is it all the spilled beer that has seeped into the roots over the years?

[E39a] **Charlie Parker Residence**, 151 Avenue B bet. E. 9th and E. 10th Sts. ca. 1849. 💣🔭
Bird lived in this Gothic Revival row house from 1950-54. *Crazy, man!*

[E39b] Originally **Christodora House**/now **Christodora House Apartments**, 1 Tompkins Sq. also known as 145 Avenue B, NE cor. E.9th St. 1928. *Henry C. Pelton.* Conversion, 1987, *John T. Fifeld Assocs.*

George Gershwin gave his first public recital in the original third-floor concert hall. Beautifully detailed brick and stone in a transition between neo-Classical and Art Deco.

[E41] Originally **Tompkins Square Lodging House for Boys and Industrial School**/aka **Children's Aid Society Newsboys and Bootblacks Lodging House**/onetime **Talmud Torah Darch Moam**, 127 Ave. B, NE cor. E.8th Sts. also known as 295 E.8th St. 1887. *Vaux & Radford.* 💣🔭 Restoration, 2006, *Roland Legiardi-Laura.*

One of the series of industrial schools/lodging houses to which *Calvert Vaux* turned his attention and considerable talent after his Central Park-Prospect Park days were behind him. Its polychromy, muted with paint, was stripped in 2003, and the façade restored to its former exuberant brick and terra-cotta glory.

[E42a] Originally **6th Street Industrial School**, Children's Aid Society/ later **Sloane Children's Center**/now **Trinity Lower East Side Parish and Shelter (Lutheran)**, 630 E.6th St., bet. Avenues B and C. 1890. *Vaux & Radford.*
Magnificent and stately.

[E42b] Originally **Congregation Ahavath Yeshurun Shara Torah** /now **Sixth Street Community Center**, 638 E.6th St., bet. Aves. B and C. 1898.

Built in the space module normally occupied by a tenement, this and Beth Hamedrash Hagodol Anshe below were each *shtiblech*—tiny synagogues. The intricate brickwork of **No.638** recalls the **Moorish** decorative scale of Jewish non-representational art.

[E43] Originally **Congregation Beth Hamedrash Hagadol Anshe Ungarn**, 242 E.7th St., bet. Aves. C and D. 1908. *Gross & Kleinberger*. Converted to apartments, 1985. ●

A miniature Renaissance palazzo served the same religious purposes as 42b.

[E44] **San Isidro y San Leandro Orthodox Catholic Church of the Hispanic Rite**/originally **Russian Orthodox Church**, 345 E.4th St., bet. Aves. C and D. ca. 1895.

Painted polychromy in the spirit of *John*

[E47] **Ageloff Towers**, 141 E.3rd St., NW cor. Ave. A. 180 East 4th St. SW cor. Ave. A. 1929. *Shampan & Shampan*.

This massive apartment pair suggests that some developers may have thought the Roaring Twenties would make a silk purse even out of the Lower East Side. Needless to say, it didn't. Some charming **Art Deco** detail remains.

[E48] **First Houses, NYC Housing Authority**, 29-41 Ave. A, SW cor. E.3rd St., 112-138 E.3rd St., bet. First Ave. and Ave. A. Reconstructed into public housing, 1935-1936, *Frederick L. Ackerman*. ●

The first houses built, or rather, rebuilt, in this instance by the City's Housing Authority. In a block of tenements every third was demolished, allowing the remaining pairs light and air on three sides. This, as a remodeling, and **Williamsburg Houses**, as new construction, are still the brightest lights in the history of this city's early public housing. Walk through the urbane cobbled and tree-filled space behind.

E43   E49

E45   E48

Ruskin (except that the palette, chocolate and white, is hardly **Ruskinian**).

[E45] **Ryan/NENA Comprehensive Health Service Center**, Northeast Neighborhood Association, 279 E.3rd St., bet. Ave. C and Ave. D. 1976. *Edelman & Salzman*.

The façade of this multistory health center enjoys a monumentality once reserved for cathedrals. Within, the spaces (and the muted color scheme) establish a scale more appropriate to community health care.

[E46] **Most Holy Redeemer Roman Catholic Church and Rectory**, 161-165 E.3rd St., bet. Ave. A and Ave. B. 1870s.

A powerful, deeply modeled, limestone pile, one of the tallest structures (except for the "projects") in the community. **Eclectic**, of course, it might be classified as Baroque Romanesque.

[E49] Originally **Rectory, St. Nicholas Roman Catholic Church**, 135 E.2nd St., bet. First Ave. and Ave. A. 1867.

An essay in late Gothic Revival mannerism, with swell stone trim around the tiers of pointed arch windows. Note the silhouette of the demolished church on the old rectory's west wall: **palimpsest**.

NECROLOGY

Old Church of the Nativity (Roman Catholic), 46 Second Ave., bet. E.2nd and E.3rd Sts. E side. 1832. *Town & Davis (A.J. Davis, J.H. Dakin, and James Gallier)*.

By a most distinguished firm, this Greek Revival, Doric-columned, white painted wood church grew very old and very decayed. It was finally replaced in 1970 by a modern edifice.

E46

Old St. George's Ukrainian Catholic Church, 26 E.7th St., bet. Second Ave. and Hall Place. 1840.

This **Greek Revival** temple in stucco with a mini-onion dome was demolished in 1976 to provide off-street parking for the congregation's new building next door.

The Old Bowery

Transformed, for better or worse, from flop houses to glass boxes. For a fuller explanation see the Chinatown/Little Italy section.

CBGB & OMFUG ("Country Blue Grass Blues and Other Music For Uplifting Gormandizers"), 315 Bowery bet. E.2nd St. & E.1st Pl., opened in 1973 and closed in 2006.

The birthplace of the loud bands **Television, Ramones, Talking Heads, Patti Smith Group,** and **Blondie,** it is remembered here for its music, not its architecture, which had all the charm of a claustrophobic, dark urinal.

ENDANGERED

Extra Place, north side of E.1st St., bet. the Bowery & Second Avenue.

A little alley, described this way by *Brendan Gill* in *The New Yorker*, November 8, 1952: "Extra Place is a narrow little dead-end street, dark even by day and marked off by rusty iron warehouse doors and shuttered windows, with week-old newspapers blowing along the gutters." It may not be much, but it's a last vestige of **old New York.** The City doesn't seem to want it. Developers do.

McGurk's Suicide Hall, 295 Bowery bet. E.Houston & E.1st Sts.

Razed in 2005 in favor of the larger, rather bland **Avalon** development by *Arquitectonica*. McGurk's was infamous in the mid-19th century for its knife fights, flying ale glasses, and high patron mortality rate. Dangerous, to be sure, but definitely not bland.

Midtown Manhattan

L18, Rubin Museum of Art

If Manhattan is the center of the City, midtown is the center of the center. Here are most of the elements one expects to find in a city core: the major railroad and bus stations, the vast majority of hotel rooms, the biggest stores, the main public library and post office. Of the four principal activities that have traditionally sustained New York, two—nationwide corporations and the garment industry—are concentrated in Midtown. Another of the four, shipping—also historically centered in Midtown—has declined to a point where freight, largely in the form of container shipping, has sought available space elsewhere, in Staten Island and Brooklyn. Transatlantic passenger travel, once almost extinct, has made a comeback in the luxury cruise market, with the *Queen Mary 2*, *Norwegian Dawn*, *Caribbean Princess*, and others making regular stops at Piers 89 and 90. Only one of Manhattan's major commercial activities—the financial center—is concentrated in lower Manhattan, although following September 11, much of that industry moved to Midtown as well.

Social status in Midtown once followed a clear-cut pattern: all the fashionable shops and living quarters ran up a central spine along Fifth and Park Avenues and Broadway. But Central Park, by driving a cleft between this spine and the Upper West Side, diverted fashionable Manhattan a bit to the east, and the purposeful development of Park Avenue in the 1920s shifted the weight a bit farther, encouraging some colonies of high society to move far to the east, particularly after the demolition of that psychological barrier, the Third Avenue el, in 1956. With the construction of the United Nations Headquarters on the East River and its many ancillary and quasi-official satellites and delegations' structures, a whole new profile took shape.

MIDTOWN KEY MAP

N

Clinton

Times
Square to
Columbus
Circle

Fifth Avenue/
Swath

West
Chelsea

Grande Central/
Park Avenue

Madison Square Garden
to the Javits Center

Madison
Square
Garden to
Bryant Park

United Nations /
Turtle Bay

Murray Hill

Chelsea

Rose Hill

Ladies Mile

Kips Bay

Gansevoort
Market

Union Square to
Gramercy Park

Stuyvesant
Square
& North

CHELSEA

More than two and a half centuries of ups and downs have left **Chelsea** a patchwork of town houses, tenements, factories, and housing projects. The name was originally given by *Captain Thomas Clarke* to his estate, staked out in 1750, which extended roughly from the present 19th to 28th Streets, from Eighth Avenue west to the Hudson. The modern place-name covers approximately a similar area, with its eastern boundary at Seventh Avenue and its southern one at 14th Street.

Captain Clarke's grandson, *Clement Clarke Moore* (1779-1863) grew up in the family mansion near the present 23rd Street west of Ninth Avenue, dividing the estate into lots around 1830. *Moore*, noted in his time as a scholar of languages, is remembered now mainly for his poem "A Visit from Saint Nicholas," which sealed the unscholarly but indestructible connection between Saint Nick and Christmas. *Moore* donated one choice block for the **General Theological Seminary**, which is still there, and the surrounding blocks prospered as a desirable suburb. Then the Hudson River Railroad opened along Eleventh Avenue in 1851, attracting slaughterhouses, breweries, and the like, followed quickly by the shanties and tenements of workers.

In 1871 the dignity of town-house blocks, still unaffected by the railroad, was shattered by the steam locomotives of New York's first elevated railroad, which ran up Ninth Avenue. In the 1870s a declining Chelsea was brightened

H24   General Theological Seminary

by the blossoming of the City's theater district along West 23rd Street. For a decade or so, these blocks were ideally convenient to both the high society of Madison Square and the flourishing vice district along Sixth Avenue in the upper 20s and 30s. When the theater world moved uptown, artists and literati stayed on to make Chelsea New York's bohemia; early in the 20th century bohemia moved south to Greenwich Village, but the writers never quite deserted 23rd Street.

Around 1905-1915 a new art form, the motion picture, was sheltered in Chelsea, where old lofts and theaters made economical studios until the sunshine of Hollywood lured the industry away. In the 1920s and 1930s Chelsea got a lift from some impressive new industrial buildings near the piers and some luxury apartments inland. But the greatest improvements were on the grade-level freight line, long since part of the New York Central, which ran along Eleventh Avenue (there was a Death Avenue Cowboy on horseback, carrying a red flag of warning ahead of each train); it was replaced in 1934 by an "inconspicuous" through-the-block elevated line just west of Tenth Avenue, now a phoenix risen from the ashes of its neglect: converted into the **High Line** park, a spine for many branches of experimental architecture that are clinging to its trunk.

In the 1950s and 1960s public housing and urban renewal uprooted large chunks of slum housing, and rehabilitation of Chelsea's many fine town houses followed a slow upward trend. Before 2000, gentrification had reclaimed the brick and brownstone town houses, spurred in part by the migration of art galleries from SoHo.

A new wave of luxury housing in the millenium's first decade has spread north from the scouting party (*Richard Meier's* elegant glass boxes and their star-tenant owners at Perry Street) to Chelsea proper, and into the emerging enclave of West Chelsea, anchored at its Hudson River edge by *Jean Nouvel* and *Frank Gehry*. In between are small and bigger apartments designed by an impressive roster of emerging architects, notably *Deborah Berke, Audrey*

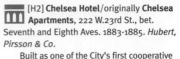 **[H2]** **Chelsea Hotel**/originally **Chelsea Apartments**, 222 W.23rd St., bet. Seventh and Eighth Aves. 1883-1885. *Hubert, Pirsson & Co.*

Built as one of the City's first cooperative apartment houses, the Chelsea became a hotel in 1905, but has a high ratio of permanent tenants, even today. The 12-story brick bearing-wall structure has been called **Queen Anne** or **Victorian Gothic**, but its style is hard to pin down. The most prominent exterior features are the delicate iron balconies (made by *J. B.* and *J. M. Cornell*) that screen the hefty brickwork. Plaques at the entrance honor writers who have lived here: *Thomas Wolfe, Dylan Thomas,* and *Brendan Behan*, three of a long list that runs from *Mark Twain* and *O. Henry* to *Tennessee Williams, Yevgeni Yevtushenko,* and *Arthur Miller*. Guests from other arts have included *Sarah Bernhardt, Virgil Thomson, John Sloan,* and *Jackson Pollock. Edgar Lee Masters* wrote a poem about the Chelsea, and *Andy Warhol* made it the scene of his 1966 movie **The Chelsea Girls**.

H1   H2   H3   H4

H5   H7

Matlock, Annabelle Selldorf, and *Winka Dubbeldam*, to name a few. These western reaches of Chelsea are in the proceeding sections: pp. 215-223.

For the heart of Chelsea. START at West 23rd Street W of Seventh Avenue. Take the No.1 train or the C or E train to their respective 23rd Street Stations:

[H1] Muhlenberg Branch, New York Public Library, 209 W.23rd St., bet. Seventh and Eighth Aves. 1906. *Carrère & Hastings.* Renovations, 1999, *R. M. Kliment & Frances Halsband.*

A modest neo-Renaissance library overwhelmed by the powerful architecture of the Chelsea Hotel across the street.

*Name change: **Philip G. Hubert** (1830-1911), partner in the firm of Hubert, Pirsson & Company, was the son of Charles Antoine Colomb Gengembre, whose children adopted the surname of their mother, Hubert, since their father's was so difficult for Americans to pronounce.*

[H3] McBurney YMCA, 215 W.23rd St., bet. Seventh and Eighth Aves. 1914.

A stoic portico: its grand granite Roman Doric columns confront the Chelsea Hotel across the street. The door handles put it in a class by itself: bronze skulls? Avast, matey!

[H4] 240 West 23rd Street, bet. Seventh and Eighth Aves. 1880s.

Golden rams overlook those entering the bank below. A restrained and elegant eclectic building.

[H5] 244 West 23rd Street, bet. Seventh and Eighth Avenues. 1890s.

Romanesque Revival (above a sullied commercial ground floor) in a rich fabric of arcuated limestone, brick, terra cotta, and granite.

*The **Grand Opera House** stood on the northwest corner of 23rd Street and Eighth Avenue until 1960, when land was cleared for the surrounding **Penn Station South**. Bought by the notorious financier, impresario, and bon vivant "Jubilee" Jim Fisk in the late 1860s, it did double service as head office of his **Erie Railroad**. It withstood repeated assaults by irate Erie stockholders (with steel doors reputedly 12 inches thick) and was the scene of Fisk's funeral in 1872, after he was shot by Edward S. Stokes, hot-blooded third party of a triangle whose apex was the famous actress Josie Mansfield, Fisk's onetime mistress. Fisk's demise was a preview of a similar tragedy in the assassination of Stanford White 34 years later.*

[H6] **Chelsea Historic District**, generally both sides of. W.20th, W.21st and W.22nd Sts. bet. Ninth and Tenth Aves. with irregular legs E of Ninth Ave.

This Historic District forms the kernel displaying a condensation of the best qualities of Chelsea, with architecture from all its periods: Greek and Gothic Revival, Italianate, and 1890s apartment buildings by such firms as *C.P.H. Gilbert* and *Neville & Bagge*. Chelsea in this Guide goes beyond the Historic District to selected old and new outposts of interest and/or great quality.

[H7] **305-313 West 22nd Street**, bet. Eighth and Ninth Aves. 1873. ● Extended and altered upward, 1986, *Weinberg, Kirschenbaum & Tambasco*, with *Jay Almour Assocs.*

H9

Here venerable mansard roofs crested with cast iron are beautifully restored, and a modern entry tower at the west end stands sulkily to one side.

[H8] **260 West 22nd Street**, bet. Seventh and Eighth Aves. Converted, 1969, *Robert Ostrow*.

This 1960s reconstructed row house was rebuilt from a shell by owner-architect Ostrow. His exterior modeling of dark brick, glass, and ribbed metal roofing reflects equally intricate interior spaces.

[H9] **Joyce Theatre**/originally **Elgin** (movie theater), 175 Eighth Ave., SW cor. W.19th St. 1942. *Simon Zelnik*. Converted to dance theater, 1982, *Hardy Holzman Pfeiffer Assocs.*

A onetime neighborhood movie house, then a revival showcase, now lovingly updated to honor its Art Moderne beginnings. A refreshing renaissance of streamlining.

[H10] **Yves Chelsea** (apartments), 166 W. 18th St., SE cor. Seventh Ave. 2008. *Ismael Leyva*.

Glassy housing akin to many similar projects sprouted along the High Line and westward.

[H10a] **145 and 147 Eighth Avenue**, bet. 17th and 18th Sts. W side. 1827-28. ●

A pair of rare, wonderfully intact Federal-style houses, both recently landmarked.

[H11] Originally **Port of New York Authority Commerce Building/Union Inland Terminal No.1**, 111 Eighth Ave., bet. W.15th and W.16th Sts. to Ninth Ave. 1932. *Abbott, Merkt & Co., Lusby Simpson*, designer.

An enormous inner-city warehousing facility occupying a full city block, a whale of a structure but a little brother to the **Starrett-Lehigh Building** (p. 223). Art Moderne bronzework articulates the entries.

H10   H11

H12   H13

[H12] Originally **Andrew Norwood House**, 241 W.14th St., bet. Seventh and Eighth Aves. 1845-1847. ●

An Italianate brownstone with late Greek Revival detail. It, and its two defaced neighbors, were the first masonry houses on the block. Next door, at **243**, was the speakeasy **Tammany Tough Club**. Note the railings: *cast*-iron, not wrought.

[H13] **Iglesia Católica Guadalupe (Roman Catholic)**, 229 W.14th St., bet. Seventh and Eighth Aves.

An extraordinary brownstone conversion from row house to humble Spanish Catholic church. Its Iberian ancestry is expressed both in the language of its services and in its Spanish Colonial Baroque façade.

[H14] Onetime **Manufacturers Hanover Trust Company** branch/originally **New York County National Bank**, now **Nickel Spa for Men**, 75-79 Eighth Ave., SW cor. W.14th St. 1906-1907. *DeLemos & Cordes*, succeeded by *Rudolph L. Daus.* 🍎 Later addition to S. Renovations and addition, 1999, *Lee Harris of Hudson River Studios and John Reimnitz.*

[H15] Originally **New York Savings Bank**/later Goldome Bank branch/now **Balducci's** (groceries), 81 Eighth Ave., NW cor. W.14th St. 1897. *R. H. Robertson.* 🍎

A rare occurrence for this city: a pair of classically inspired **sentinels** guarding the western corridor of 14th Street. The two have lately given way to less mammon-inspired activities: a men's health club on one corner and gourmet groceries on the other (what do they keep in the old bank vault, mahi mahi fillets?), hardly a typical case for the enlightened reuse of landmarks, but happy preservation events nevertheless. The seven-story addition to the old **New York County National**

Ninth Avenue Improvements: Amid the hurtling panel trucks, a new bike lane extends from 23rd Street south to Bleecker, sandwiched ingeniously between buildings and parked cars. Why didn' t they think of that before? And at 14th Street, where Ninth widens, a new plaza has been installed. Lo, and behold: a few slabs of granite to sit on, some tables, chairs, umbrellas, and robust potted flowers. Voilà! A tiny, but public, park! (The same strategy is being replicated elsewhere, notably along Broadway in the Flatiron District.) But why not go a step farther and jackhammer the concrete and expose some actual earth?

[H18] **The Porter House**, 366 West 15th St., bet. Eighth and Ninth Aves. 2003. *SHoP.*

The Boom (2003-2008) encouraged adding square feet to desirable sites by hook or crook. Nice buildings were sacrificed in the process (see the tragic mangling of the historic **Society for the Prevention of Cruelty to Animals** at

H15

H17

H14   H16

Bank mimics the spirit of *DeLemos & Cordes'* original architecture.

[H16] **The Church of St. Bernard (Roman Catholic)**, 330 W.14th St., bet. Eighth and Ninth Aves. 1875. *Patrick Charles Keely.*

Dour two-tone brownstone Ruskinian Gothic Revival, its pointed portals a gabled staccato trio, its blue-glazed wheel window overglowing the dark of 14th Street.

[H17] **The Apple Store**, 401 W.14th St. bet. Ninth and Tenth Aves. 2007. *Cook + Fox.*

Cook + Fox restored the old Western Beef meatpacking plant, and *Bohlin Cywinski Jackson* reconfigured the interior for Apple's design aesthetics. The original shell is somber brick, but inside it's bright, sleek and modern, the center piece a trendy circular glass stair. At the edges, windowsills are deep enough for two to sit together, encouraging a therapist/patient relationship between salesperson and customer.

Madison Square Park). Here, in what crime novelist *V.P. Johns* called "...a juicy porterhouse neighborhood," the clever partners of *SHoP* thoughtfully join old and new. A black box attached off-center to an old brick warehouse creates a cantilever on one side and a corresponding terrace on the other. Things are most interesting in the details, especially on the north façade, where new and old materials join in an elegant slit: brick to zinc to glass.

[H19] **Maritime Hotel**/originally **National Maritime Union of America, Joseph Curran Annex**, 346 W.17th St., bet. Eighth and Ninth Aves. 1966. Originally **Joseph Curran Plaza**. Both by *Albert C. Ledner & Assocs.*

A startling white tile-faced, porthole-pierced front wall sloping 8-1/2 degrees from vertical was the architect's way of meeting the setback requirements of the 1961 zoning resolution. The plaza then created has been obliterated by its new owner's heavy-handed hotel/restaurant facilities.

H18

[H20a] **Chelsea Modern**, 447 W.18th St., bet. Ninth and Tenth Avenues. 2008. *Audrey Matlock.* [H20b] **459 West 18th Street**, bet. Ninth and Tenth Avenues. 2008. *Della Valle Bernheimer.*

Two young apartment buildings standing arm in arm, cheek to cheek, dancing the *Chelsea Waltz* around the corner from the High Line. Unless you really knew you might think they're the same building, they get along so well. In fact, *Matlock's* wavy blue box is the building to the east and *Della Valle Bernheimer's* sibling is the slightly taller fellow to the west. Both share a profusion, protrusion and confusion of glass.

[H20c] **456 West 19th/140 Tenth Ave**, SE cor. 10th Avenue. 2009. *Cary Tamarkin & H. Thomas O'Hara.*

A black brick box with warehouse windows and curves up high. *Tarmarkin's* insight was in foreseeing yuppies moving to West Chelsea with an insatiable desire for raw space: 6,500 square foot apartments cloaked in a faux-industrial aesthetic, allowing wealthy investors to act the part of urban pioneers.

[H21] **365 West 19th Street**, bet. Eighth and Ninth Aves. Converted, 1970, *Robert Ostrow.*

Another special event among Chelsea's converted row houses by an architect who followed *Horace Greeley's* (much earlier) advice: he went west.

[H22] **Avant Chelsea**, 245 W.19th St., bet. Eighth and Ninth Aves. 2008. *1100 Architects.*

A glassy high-rise offering five-star hotel living, but the floor to ceiling glass and chiseled blue shell has nothing to do with the street to which it belongs. The sales pitch is "Your Life Here." Is that an offer or a threat?

[H23a] **St. Peter's Church (Episcopal)**, 344 W.20th St., bet. Eighth and Ninth Aves. 1836-1838. *James W. Smith, builder,* after designs by *Clement Clarke Moore.* 🔵
[H23b] **Rectory**. 1832. [H23c] **Church Hall**/now **Atlantic Theater**, 336 W.20th St. 1854-1871. 🔵 Addition to theater, 2011, *Coburn Architecture*.

These buildings form a remarkable study in popular adaptation of styles. The rectory, which first served as the church, is austere Greek Revival, and its fine proportions give it dignity. By the time the much larger church was built, the congregation was ready to make it one of New York's earliest ventures into the Gothic Revival. Its massively buttressed fieldstone walls are articulated with spare limestone trim. The third building in the group, the hall east of the church, is an example of later common brick Gothic; started in 1854, it was given its strangely churchlike front in 1871. Now the **Atlantic Theater** lives here. The wrought-iron fence along the street is older than any of the buildings. It dates from about 1790, a hand-me-

H19

down from venerable Trinity Church, then (in the 1830s) building its third incarnation.

[H24] **General Theological Seminary**, Ninth Ave., bet. W.20th and W.21st Sts., to Tenth Ave. Main buildings, 1883-1900. *Charles C. Haight.* 🔵
[H24a] **West Building**, Nos.5 and 6 Chelsea Sq., W.20th St., bet. Ninth and Tenth Aves. N side. 1836. 🔵
[H24b] **Chapel** on the green within. ca. 1900. [H24c] **Desmond Tutu Center**, along 10th Ave. bet. 20th and 21st Sts. 2007. *Beyer Blinder Belle.* 🔵

The **West Building**, one of the City's oldest examples of Gothic Revival, was modeled after an even earlier, matching **East Building** (built 1827; razed 1892). *Haight's* surrounding dour collegiate Gothic red brick and brownstone structures are a delightful and convincing stage set for the resident Episcopalians.

A renovation and reconstruction of brown-stone buildings along Tenth Avenue created the **Tutu Center**, providing meeting rooms, guest rooms and dining facilities.

[H24d] **Chelsea Enclave**, 177 Ninth Ave., bet. W.20th and W.21st Sts. 2009. *Polshek Partnership*.

The seminary tore down its bland building along Ninth Avenue (1960, *O'Connor & Kilham*), leasing the valuable land to developers who built this bland luxury condominium. The new building includes some space for the seminary's theological pursuits, and has helped the seminary financially, but architecturally it's a real intrusion. What had been a secret, and sacred, garden is now the shared back yard of yuppies.

[H25] **The Cushman Row**, 406-418 W.20th St.; bet. Ninth and Tenth Aves. 1840. 🔵
Built by dry goods merchant *Don Alonzo Cushman* (*Don* was his first name), a friend of *Clement Moore's* who became a millionaire developing Chelsea. The fine **Greek Revival** detail, except for losses here and there, is intact: tiny, wreath-encircled attic windows; deeply recessed doorways with brownstone

H20a   H22

H24a   H24c

frames, handsome iron balustrades newels, and fences. The dormers are a later addition.

[H26a] **446-450 West 20th Street**, bet. Ninth and Tenth Aves. 1855.
[H26b] **465-473 West 21st Street**, NE cor. Tenth Ave. 1853. 🔵

Eight exceptional Italianate houses facing, respectively, the austere side walls (West 21st Street) and the gardens (West 20th Street) of the seminary across the streets.

[H27] **Clement Clarke Moore Park**, W.22nd St. SE cor. Tenth Ave. 1968. *Coffey, Levine & Blumberg, architects/landscape architects.* 🔵
A friendly, understated canopy of trees is an adjunct to this row house district. A place to be, not to inspect.

H26a

[H28] **Empire Diner**, 210 Tenth Ave., NE cor. W.22nd St. 1943. Altered, 1976, *Carl Laanes*, designer. 🍎

Sleek and Streamlined, it is the reincarnation of, and ultimate homage to, the American diner. Stainless steel never looked better, set off by black and chrome furnishings.

[H29] **428-450 West 23rd Street**, bet. Ninth and Tenth Aves. ca. 1860. 🍎

A phalanx of **Anglo-Italianate** brownstones opposite the bulk of London Terrace. Here is a "terrace" remnant that gives a taste of what were once almost endless and uniform blocks

[H31] **437-459 West 24th Street** (row houses), bet. Ninth and Tenth Aves. 1849-1850. *Philo Beebe,* builder. 🍎

A row of late Italianate brick houses unusual in their large setback from the street. **No.461** next door is an earlier Federal house. The front gardens are a refreshing pause in the streetscape.

[H32] **242-258 Tenth Avenue**, bet. W.24th and W.25th Sts. E side.

An Italianate commercial row provides an old New York image seemingly from an *Edward Hopper* painting.

H25

H28

H29

H30

[H30] **London Terrace**, W.23rd to W.24th Sts., Ninth to Tenth Aves. 1930. *Farrar & Watmaugh.*

This vast brick pile, in **Proto-Modern Planar** style, with some Romanesque Revival details, comprises two rows of connected apartment buildings enclosing a blocklong private garden, invisible from the street. All in all it contains 1,670 units. Massive blocks like these are excellent examples of eco-building, clustered modern apartments allowing minimal heat losses compared to the free-standing house. Cheap fuel, vast freeways, and cheap mortgages turned America into an auto-dependent society long before the millennium. The pedestrian and transity city (here New York) is far more energy efficient than suburbia: less gas, less electricity, much less energy per capita.

[H33] **Church of the Holy Apostles** (Episcopal), 300 Ninth Ave., SE cor. W.28th St. 1845-1848 and 1853-1854. *Minard Lafever.* Transepts, 1858. *Richard Upjohn & Son.* Restored after 1990 fire. 🍎

A remarkably independent work that fits no stylistic slot: sometimes called an early effort at Romanesque Revival. Its brick details, bracketed eaves, and unique copper and slate octagonal spire completely dominate a low nave, enriched by stained glass by *William Jay Bolton,* (some were lost in a 1990 fire).

[H34] **The Onyx**, 261 W.28th St., NE cor. Eighth Ave. 2008. *FxFowle.*

A touch of class, but with no serious difference from myriad boxy apartment buildings recently sprouted around town. Black panels are laboriously screwed "proud" of the façade, creating a gap between cladding and structure: an elegant detail. Nevertheless, the overall effect is of an expensive **Lego set.**

[H35] **Fashion Institute of Technology,** W.26th to W.28th Sts., bet. Seventh and Eighth Aves.
[H35a] **Administration and Technology Building,** and
[H35b] **Morris W. & Fannie B. Haft Auditorium,** both on W.27th St. N Side. 1958.
[H35c] **Nagler Hall** (dormitory), W.27th St. S side. 1962.
[H35d] **Shirley Goodman Resource Center,** Seventh Ave., bet. W.26th and W.27th Sts. W side. 1977.

H34

H33

H35

[H35e] **Fred R. Pomerantz Art and Design Center,** Seventh Ave., bet. W.27th and W.28th Sts. W side. 1977.
[H35f] **David Dubinsky Student Center,** Eighth Ave., bet. W.27th and W.28th Sts. E side. 1977. *All by DeYoung & Moscowitz.*
[H35g] **Dormitories,** W.27th St. S side. 1988. *Henry George Greene.*
[H35h] **Center for Design Innovation,** W.27th St. 2001. *Kevin Hom + Andrew Goldman.*
    This complex was planned as the training ground for interns for New York's garment industry. Fashions in dresses, coats, and suits change every season; so did the Institute's style of architecture over the 30 years this campus took to complete.

***END** of Chelsea. Nearby trains are at Seventh Avenue and 28th Street (IRT No.1 train).*

GANSEVOORT MARKET

H38

[H36] **Gansevoort Market Historic District**, generally between Hudson Street and the High Line, mid-block between Horatio Street and Gansevoort Street on the south to mid-block between West 14th and West 15th Streets on the north. 🍎

Gansevoort Market, also known locally as the **Meatpacking District**, lies roughly between Ninth Avenue and the Hudson River, from Gansevoort Street north to 14th. From these wholesale meat markets came the beef for many of Manhattan's restaurants and institutions. Until recently it was busy, chaotic, and earthy from before sunrise well into the day, and empty, eerie, and scary at night. Not anymore: today it's high-end shops and restaurants, right next door to the remaining meat wholesalers. You're as likely to spot a supermodel wearing a Yamamoto dress and high heels as a butcher wearing a bloody smock and hip-waders. The cobblestone streets remain, but no longer run as deeply with the blood of sectioned livestock, although you may still encounter cattle carcasses hanging out to dry. Gentrification has been happening for at least a decade here, but the adaptation of the **High Line** from a freight line to a linear park promises to preserve its melancholy vistas while connecting the area to West Chelsea and spurring even more development. Countless interesting characters have passed through, including *Herman Melville* (1819-1891), who worked here on what was then the Gansevoort Dock as an outdoor customs inspector for 19 years. He came to this job, discouraged and unable to earn a living as a writer. It was during these years that he began *Billy Budd,* his last novel.

[H37] **The West Coast**, originally **Manhattan Refrigerating Company Warehouse/Peter J. Carey & Son,** 95 Horatio St., NW cor. Washington St. to Gansevoort St. 1898-1900. *George P. Chappell.* Converted to apartments, 1984, *Rothzeid, Kaiserman & Thomson.* 🖐️

The eight once-open bays of the second-story arcade of the corner structure formerly welcomed slow-moving **New York Central** electric switch engines shunting produce-laden reefers (refrigerator cars) to and fro.

[H38] **40 Gansevoort Street** (retail), SE cor. Greenwich St. 2006. *Morris Adjmi with Rogers Marvel.* 🖐️

Gansevoort Market boasts unique vernacular architecture: block buildings with loading docks, canopies pendant over the sidewalk, their steel joists and translucent vinyl panels cabled to the façade. Here *Adjmi*, a disciple of the late, great Italian architect *Aldo Rossi,* attempts new canopies, using the same vocabulary. But try as he might, the old ones, often

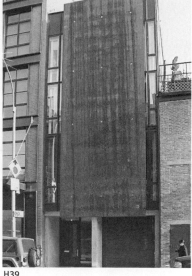

H39

mangled from countless trucks backing into them, are more funky and authentic. The rest of the building channels vintage *Rossi:* Classical and industrial, with an emphasis on horizontal steel beams that divide the façade into clearly defined floors.

[H39] **829 Greenwich Street** (town house), bet. Horatio and Gansevoort Sts. 2005. *Matthew Baird.* 🖐️

A small but uncompromising exercise in **weight and weightlessness** from the modernist *Baird*. Impossible to miss is the 40-foot-high rusted steel "billboard" bolted to the façade. A funny take on privacy: the residents can peek out, barely. Don't feel bad for them, though: the entire back of the building, not visible from the street, is glass. *Baird's* billboard, obsessed with the vertical, works surprisingly well with *Adjmi's* horizontally obsessed building next door.

[H40] **Gansevoort Square,** intersection of Gansevoort, Little W.12th Sts. & Ninth Ave. 2008. D.O.T.(Dept. of Traffic)/Project for Public Spaces.

Trucks, taxis, and pedestrians have converged here for years with reckless abandon, creating comical but dangerous scenes of riotous honking, cursing, and startled pigeons—just like Rome! Recent additions of granite blocks for sitting and stone bollards shaped like stuffed olives for traffic-taming have formed a unique little piazza, with a more permanent plan promised. A work in progress.

[H41] **Yamamoto** (clothing boutique), 1 Gansevoort St. at crossing of W.13th & Hudson Sts. 2008. *Junya Ishigami.*

A drastic, but ingenious, approach to the adaptive re-use of old buildings. Japanese architect *Ishigami* has performed invasive but beautiful surgery on an existing brick shed, removing layers of green paint, punching big openings in the façade, and last but not least, slicing the building into two parts. One half is now a light-filled showroom and the other half provides storage and office space. The showroom gleams like a lantern at night, and comes to a razor-sharp point where Gansevoort and West 13th meet.

Unbuilt: Whitney Museum of American Art, Gansevoort St. bet. Washington and Eleventh Ave. 2015? *Renzo Piano Building Workshop with Cooper, Robertson & Partners.*

Piano's expansive downtown location for

H40   H41

the Whitney, with almost twice the space as its *Marcel Breuer* building at 945 Madison (at E. 75th St.), promises tiered outdoor galleries overlooking the High Line, and a large public gathering space at street level. The High Line needs an anchor. Will it happen?

PLANNED NECROLOGY

Wholesale Meat Market Building/ formerly **Gansevoort pumping station, High Pressure Fire Service,** NYC Fire Department/originally **Gansevoort Market House,** 555 West St., NE cor. Gansevoort St. 1906-1908. *Bernstein & Bernstein.*

This clumsily altered Romanesque Revival structure had been originally built to serve as a market house, later converted into a pumping stations, then returned to the meat business as a beef wholesaler, its façade painted festively with livestock. But the building is set to meet the same fate as its slaughtered cattle: cut up and hauled away to make room for the new Whitney Museum.

THE HIGH LINE
AND WEST CHELSEA

It seems like yesterday that the old elevated New York Central freight line, the now-beloved **High Line,** was a rusty ghost, too massive to pilfer for scrap and too strong to fall down on its own, silently weaving in silhouette in and out through abandoned factories and warehouses from Gansevoort Street to 34th Street, just west of Tenth Avenue. After the last train

Starting at Gansevoort Street and following north along the High Line:

[H42] **The High Line,** Gansevoort St. to 34th St., mostly bet. Tenth & Eleventh Aves. 1929-1934. Renovated as a linear park, 2009 (Phase One), 2011 (Phase Two). *James Corner of Field Operations* (landscape architect), *Diller*

H42

rattled through in 1980 (reportedly carrying frozen turkeys) the viaduct, thirty feet above street level, began its inevitable conversion back to wilderness, as prairie grasses, wildflowers, sumac, and ever larger trees took root.

Photographers, artists, and urban adventurers were attracted to the beautiful desolation of what gradually became a 1.45-mile-long elevated meadow, and visions of a linear park began to form in earnest during the 1990s. A community group, **Friends of the High Line**, ultimately saved the winding trestle through lobbying and fundraising. Now, improbably, the High Line has become one of the most unique public parks in the world.

Where once the High Line was a wasteland amid vacant lots, parking garages, and derelict storefronts, now trendy condos and hotels with names like **The Caledonia** and **The Standard** are sprouting up everywhere. "You're only steps from the High Line!" is these days a sales pitch, not a warning. Who'da thunk it?

Scofidio & Renfro (master plan).

Major access points to ascend the High Line occur at Gansevoort and Washington Streets, at 14th Street, and at 16th Street & Tenth Avenue.

Built by the New York Central Railroad as a freight spur from 1929 to 1934, designed to accept the weight of two freight trains, this massive steel viaduct was abandoned in 1980. But devotees said it was a beautiful, melancholy place; that it should be saved and reinterpreted as a linear park, and so it has come to pass. Construction is scheduled in phases: Gansevoort Street north to 20th Street opened in 2009, and the section continuing north to 30th Street will open in 2011. The fate of a compelling third section that wraps around the Hudson Yards to 34th Street is not yet determined.

As a linear park, The High Line is meticulously thoughtful, perhaps even a bit overdesigned. Many of the original rails were preserved as *Donald Judd*–style artifacts, and native plant species have been arranged in beds with considerable care. The trail bed is a series

H43

of interlocking concrete strips that seem to grow and dissolve as needed, with grasses allowed to grow between; occasionally they curve upward to form a bench. There are also wooden lounge chairs that roll on tracks (only vaguely like freight cars, but we get the idea), a plunging amphitheater where the High Line briefly widens at 17th Street, and the inevitable "water feature" next to Chelsea Market.

It's all extremely well done, but the wonder of the High Line isn't the design work, but in seeing the familiar landscape of Chelsea from a brand new vantage point, sailing along above, beside, and through the neighboring buildings. It remains to be seen how *Corner's* rather delicate details will endure trampling by millions of human feet. The High Line, worn and frayed by use, may find its most natural and profound beauty in ten or twenty years.

[H43] The Standard Hotel, 848 Washington St. bet. Little W.12th & 13th Sts. 2009. *Polshek Partnership.*

H42

Boldly straddling the **High Line** on massive piers, Standard's folded form is like an open cocktail cabinet in concrete. *Polshek* has embraced both the High Line and the best of modernism; strong form taking advantage of a unique site with an unabashed expression of structure and materials. If too many buildings were built this way, it would be a mistake; most buildings in the City need to fit it and behave themselves. Here, with no adjacent buildings to relate to, what could have been a dull program (yet another luxury hotel) turns into real architecture. *Polshek's* recent forays into massive industrial projects (see his **Newtown Creek Water Treatment Plant** in Greenpoint, Brooklyn) must have influenced him here, bringing clarity and substantial boldness.

[H44] The **High Line Building**, 450 W.14th Street, bet. Washington St. & Tenth Ave. 2011. *Morris Adjmi Architects.*

A train runs through it (or rather, once did). *Adjmi* strikes again (see [H38], p. 216), this time with a block of glass telescoping out of an old

brick warehouse. A surgical procedure that forms a nice diptych with *Polshek's* Standard Hotel up the line: the High Line runs through *Polshek*'s legs and then pierces *Adjmi*'s heart before crossing 14th Street and plunging into Chelsea Market. *Ah, to see the trains pass through one more time!*

[H45] DVF Studios, 440 W.14th St., SW cor. Washington St. 2008. *WORK Architecture Company.*

H46   H47

H45

Diane Von Furstenberg moves into the meatpacking district. Stand at the corner of 13th and Washington and look northwest to see the crystalline crown erupting from the old brick shell.

[H46] **Chelsea Market**/originally **Nabisco Bakery**, 75 Ninth Ave., NW cor. W.15th St. 1898. Remodeled 1990s, again in 2008.

Chain mail and aggressive steel form a grand entrance to this upscale market. But the rear is more interesting: at the intersection of 15th Street and Tenth Avenue, The High Line pierces the building, slicing its back corner, creating a brooding industrial stage set right out of *Detective Comics*. An art-filled colonnade is promised as part of the new High Line master plan.

[H47] **The Caledonia**, 450 W.17th St. bet. Ninth & Tenth Aves. 2007. *Handel Architects.*

Large-scale housing in brick and glass, looking shiny and corporate, promising both "zen luxury" (says the developer, swear to God) and a small percentage of affordable housing. It's a bland box on the north, east, and south sides, but its western edge curves and sweeps gently along with the High Line, making it interesting up close, if not from afar.

At 18th Street, turn left and take a side trip to the far western edge of West Chelsea, to Eleventh Avenue, the West Side Highway, and the Hudson River beyond, where a funhouse called Chelsea Piers collects basketball players, yachting types, and the tuxedoed banquet set, all under one roof (in theory). Way out there, where winds blow off the Hudson, is a startling collection of cutting-edge architecture (ouch! the building cut me!):

[H48] **IAC Building,** 555 W. 18th St., at 11th Ave., to 19th St. E side. 2007. *Frank Gehry with Adamson Associates.*

Gehry's first building in New York, for media mogul *Barry Diller,* is notable for its use of fritted glass (which regulates solar gain but also

[H50] **Metal Shutter Houses,** 524 W.19th St. bet. Tenth & Eleventh Aves. 2010. *Shigeru Ban & Dean Maltz.*

What does it say about the 21st-century city when an entire residential building is clad, from sidewalk to roof, in roll-down doors? Is this a comment on the nature of privacy in modern New York? Regardless, this is as far as you can get from the shared social space of the old neighborhood stoop.

[H51] **520 West Chelsea,** 520 West 19th St., bet. Tenth & Eleventh Aves. 2008. *Annabelle Selldorf Associates.*

An 11-story understated and crisply-detailed glass box with floor-to-ceiling ribbon windows and waves of midnight-blue glazed terra cotta. Quietly behaving itself in the shadows of *Nouvel* and *Gehry*; as mum as *Mies*.

The Kitchen, the media center at 512 West 19th Street, began as a reuse of the old Broadway Central Hotel's food preparation area (hence

H50

H52

H49

H48

H55

makes it look spray-painted white), and for its billowy façade. Much has been made of *Gehry's* use of the computer to transform the instant gesture into architecture, but here the gesture is static. For kinetic *Gehry,* see his **Beekman Tower** (p. 41), with its shiny façade hung like a soft metal curtain.

[H49] **100 Eleventh Avenue,** NE cor. W.19th St. 2009. *Jean Nouvel with Beyer Blinder Belle.*

Nouvel's works do wander from elegance to wry experiment. His sleek **Institut du Monde Arabe** in Paris is a taut machine, his **Museum of the Quai Branly,** an awkward construction. In New York at **40 Mercer** (p. 120), *Nouvel* the strict machinist surfaced. Here, next to *Gehry* and the Hudson, the search for originality trumped precision.

its name). For years it occupied space in SoHo, but rising rents made it an expatriate to Chelsea's west edge. The place for avant-garde video, music, dance, performance, and film.

Return east along 19th Street back to the High Line and turn left, north along 10th Avenue:

[H52] **Church of the Guardian Angel (Roman Catholic),** 193 Tenth Ave., NW cor. W.21st St. 1930. *John Van Pelt.*

Lush brick and limestone, Italian Romanesque, backed up snug against the **High Line.** Despite the obvious difference in style and materials, the two were built around the same time.

H53d

[H53a] **555 W. 23rd Street** bet. Tenth & Eleventh Aves. 2007. *Steven B. Jacobs.*
[H53b] **The Tate**, 535 West 23rd Street bet. Tenth and Eleventh Aves. 2007. *The Rockwell Group.*

Massive, rather dull background buildings, but necessary uncompetitive support for the flashy new stars in the neighborhood.

[H53c] **High Line 519** at W.23rd St. bet. Tenth & Eleventh Aves. 2008. *Lindy Roy.*

[H53d] **HL23** Residential Tower, 517 W.23rd St. 2010. *Neil Denari.*

Two thin paperback books at the end of a row of heavy encyclopedias. Two narrower lots would be hard to find, yet *Roy* and *Denari* have managed to squirm in tight against the spine. *Roy's* is a simple glass "sliver," decorative screens guarding french doors (open to the floor). **HL23**, pressed like a panini against **519**, expands as it gets higher, revealing an innovative structural system (it's basically a giant truss) through transparent sides. Rippling panels of stainless steel face **The High Line**.

[H54] **245 Tenth Avenue Apartments**, bet.24th & 25th Sts. W side. 2009. *Della Valle Bernheimer.*

A gleaming container, swollen with square footage, its skin reminiscent of an airplane fuselage clad in perforated steel panels and glass. Both this and *Denari's* adjacent **HL23** have the same attitude toward the High Line: they dance, cautiously. Their flirtation with the High Line is laudable, but compared to the original industrial buildings that the railroad unapologetically pierced (see Chelsea Market), the relationship between building and park is not as daring as it could have been.

Beautiful people in black: *West Chelsea has gradually turned into an art mecca over the last few decades. Several blocks, notably 22nd and 24th between Tenth and Eleventh Avenues, are gallery rows, with a dozen or more snazzy emporia lined up on each side. Architecturally, most are blank statements within and without: an industrial exterior with white walls inside that quietly support painting and sculpture. But two stand out as inventive architecture:*

[H55] **Jim Kempner Gallery**, NW cor. W.23rd St. & Tenth Ave. 1999. *Smith & Thompson*.

Steel plates embrace a serene courtyard. Modernism with a sensitivity to urbane urban space. Bring a rubber hammer... the enclosing wall is a steel drum in waiting.

[H56] **Marianne Boesky Gallery**, 509 W. 24th St., bet. Tenth & Eleventh Aves. 2008. *Deborah Berke & Partners*.

A subtle endeavor from *Berke* in glazed

appropriate at the river's edge, where the historic scale of industrial buildings expands. Here, however, we are only four blocks from *Nouvel-Gehry* land. The "sky garage" (an elevator that lifts cars directly into the apartments) sounds **exhausting**.

[H58] Originally **H. Wolff Book Bindery**, 259-273 Tenth Ave., bet. W.25th & W.26th Sts. W side. ca.1900. Addition, 1926, *Frank Parker*. 🐦

Notable for its technology—not its aesthet-

H57   H60

H56

H59

white brick and corrugated metal siding, with gently receding geometric planes at the entrance. *Berke* practices a kind of exaggerated industrial contextualism; here, inexpensive materials house expensive art.

Famous Players in Famous Plays: *Adolph Zukor, who originated this title, produced a number of old films in Chelsea. Nor was his the only studio, others being Kalem, Charles O. Bauman & Adam Kessel Films, Reliance, Majestic, etc. The Famous Players Studios was at 221 West 26th Street, its roster of stars contained such names as* **Mary Pickford** *and* **John Barrymore***.*

[H57] **200 Eleventh Avenue** (apartments), SE cor. 24th St. 2009. *Annabelle Selldorf.*

Hollywood returns to Chelsea! *Pickford* and *Barrymore*, were they alive during the condo craze of the early 2000s, might have bought a piece of this luxury behemoth, another step in the trend toward housing that mimics luxury hotels. The glassy faux-factory façades are

ics: here was an early poured-in-place concrete (in situ) building, an industrial monument.

[H59] **Chelsea Arts Tower** (offices and art galleries), 545 W. 25th St., bet. Tenth & Eleventh Aves. 2007. *Kossar & Garry with Gluckman Mayner Architects.*

A slick totem pole for the 21st-century arts scene, corporate and drab, clad in glass and charcoal panels. The everyday water tank at the top is framed like a picture.

[H60] **520 W. 27th Street**, bet. Tenth & Eleventh Aves. 2008. *Flank Architects.*

Apartments in two parts, with an outdoor recreation space between. The base is black block with white window frames flush to the façade. The upper stories, steel frame with translucent glass block, is reminiscent of the **Brooklyn Men's House of Detention** (p. 589). Can the residents leave on the weekends?

H62

[H63] **260 Eleventh Avenue**/originally **Otis Elevator Building**, bet. 26th & 27th Sts., 1911-1912. *Clinton & Russell.* 🍎

A massive romanesque brick cliff. Look up to the glorious copper cornice, hovering on high, cantilevering a good 10 feet. That's sobriety: the building halts, duly crowned: none of your sky-scraping.

[H64] **261-273 Eleventh Avenue**/originally **Central Stores, Terminal Warehouse Company**, bet. W.27th to W.28th Sts., to Twelfth Ave. 1890-1891. *George B. Mallory, Otto M. Beck.* Further alterations by *D'Oench & Yost.* 🍎

Twenty-four acres of warehousing within a brick fortress composing 25 separate buildings crowned with a Tuscan arched corbel-table. Stripped of its paint job (still there in 2000) it achieves a somber monumentality worthy of a *Piranesi* etching.

H63

H64

[H61] **548 West 28th Street**, bet. Tenth & Eleventh Aves. 1899-1900. *William Higginson.* 🍎

Monumental industrial, from its corbeled cornice down.

▌ [H62] **Starrett-Lehigh Building** (lofts),
▆▆ 601-625 W.26th to W.27th Sts., Eleventh to Twelfth Aves. 1930-1931. *Russell G.and Walter M. Cory. Yasuo Matsui,* associated architect. *Purdy & Henderson,* consulting engineers. 🍎

Nine miles of strip windows and brick-banded spandrels streak, then swerve around this block-square, 19-story, factory-warehouse structure, a landmark of modern architecture from the moment it rose (through air rights) over the Lehigh Valley Railroad freight yards. The office section, crowning the north façade, is astonishingly heavy-handed, the architects withdrawing to safer (and ponderous) ground from the perilous radicalism of the engineered warehouse.

NECROLOGY

The Tunnel, 220 Twelfth Avenue, a mid-1980s dance club, occupied the vaulted tunnel where, in the Terminal's heyday, whole box cars delivered bulk goods to the building. It milked mystery of the onetime warehouse for all it's worth. "Opulence inside a stone fortress. Golden chambers and heavy machinery. Dungeons below ivory towers." Now just a memory.

HUDSON RIVER PARK

The great river's past of shipping and industry is now just a memory, for better or worse. (Better: less pollution. Worse: less romantic.) The majestic Hudson has lately become a riparian canvas for teams of talented architects, landscape architects, and artists upon which to collaboratively design the biggest, boldest new city park since *Frederick Law Olmsted's* vast

Segment 3, Tribeca

Segment 3, Tribeca

Segment 4, Greenwich Village

greensward that keeps the Upper West and East Sides safely apart. **Hudson River Park** and **Riverside Park South** together connect **Battery Park** all the way north to *Olmsted's* **Riverside Park**, providing (in theory) an uninterrupted waterfront for recreation and contemplation. Hovering over all this furious design and construction are the ghosts of *Olmsted* and *Robert Moses*, arguing. *Olmsted: "More trees!" Moses: "More volleyball courts!"*

The goal is for one continuous swath of green space, but that hasn't yet happened. The park is interrupted over and over again by existing facilities that obstruct the park's flow: Pier 40's athletic fields at W. Houston Street, the huge Sanitation Department facility at Gansevoort Street (oh, the smell!), the Chelsea Piers complex at West 19th, helicopter pads at West 28th Street. Designing around those obstructions is the main challenge here, and right now the landscape feels more like a series of parks, each serving a different neighborhood, with its own character (and characters). But that's not necessarily a bad thing.

The segments (for segments 1 and 2 see Battery Park City section):

Segment 3 (Tribeca), between West Street and the Hudson River, from Harrison St. north to Leroy Street. 2008. *Mathews Nielsen*, landscape architects. *Weisz + Yoes*, architects.

Terrific: recreation can be had here (tennis, basketball), but those activities are secondary to the lush swath of native grasses and flowers, with an elegant wooden boardwalk passing through. New, gently swelling topography provides just enough rise and fall to make it feel like you're momentarily leaving the traffic and noise of West Street behind. This is the best strategy for a park: plant, plant, plant!

The existing Pier 40, at the foot of West Houston Street, provides more sports fields. Piers 25 and 26, near North Moore Street, are planned as future parkland conversions (miniature golf, snack bars, boathouse). Pier 32 will remain in its beautiful, decayed state (a matrix of piles).

Pier 66a, Frying Pan

Segment 5, Chelsea

Segment 4 (Greenwich Village), between West Street and the Hudson River, from Leroy Street north to Jane Street. 1999-2003. *Abel Bainnson Butz*, landscape architects.

At Pier 45, tensile structures form shelters that frame a large expanse of grass, and sunbathing is the main activity. The first segment of the park to open, in 1999, it remains extremely popular with the Village crowd. Festive.

Segment 5 (Chelsea), between West Street and the Hudson River, from Jane Street north to W. 26th Street. 2008-2010. *Michael Van Valkenburgh*, landscape architect.

He had to design around the hulking Chelsea Piers complex, but the design is unmistakably *Van Valkenburgh* (see his **Brooklyn Bridge Park** and the Olmstedian **Teardrop Park** in Battery Park City). Here groves of trees incongruously grow on Pier 64, framing a lawn. A carousel and gardens by artists *Lynden Miller* and *Meg Webster* are planned for a newly constructed Pier 63. Pier 57, the former terminal of the Cunard lines, is in development for a future project.

Pier 66a: Lackawanna Railroad Barge, with Ships, at W. 26th Street. The barge, with tracks running down its center, was used to transport trains across the Hudson to the Lackawanna terminal on the Jersey side. What a brilliant idea to moor it here, tie historic ships to its sides, and build a clam shack in the middle! Ships include the lightship **Frying Pan**, built in 1929. Originally stationed off Cape Fear, North Carolina, it was raised from the bottom of Chesapeake Bay, refurbished, and sailed here in 1989. It is on the National Register of Historic Places. Relaxing here with a beer and a peck of clams on a summer night, under haphazardly strung lights, is serene, urban perfection.

The historic tugs **Hackensack** (1954) and **Pegasus** (1907) are also moored here. A red caboose from the Erie Lackawanna Railroad is on display mid-barge. Open to the public, boats included. For more information see *www.fryingpan.com*

Segment 4, Greenwich Village, with *Richard Meier's* towers as backdrop (see p. 168)

Segment 6, Clinton, Pier 66

Pier 66a

Segment 4, Greenwich Village

Segment 6, Kayak Club, Pier 66

Hudson River Park Segments 6 and 7 (Midtown and Clinton), between West St. and the Hudson River, from W.26th St. north to W. 59th St. 2000-2007. *Richard Dattner Architects, Miceli Kulik Williams,* landscape architects.

Dattner and Co. had the biggest challenge of all the designers. Their segments are constantly interrupted by existing facilities: the **USS Intrepid Museum,** water taxi and cruise line terminals, Department of Sanitation buildings, helicopter pads, and NYPD mounted unit stables (the horses get a river view!) and vehicle tow pound. The main parts of the scheme are at Clinton Cove, at W.56th Street, and further south in the vicinity of Pier 66. All feature crisp modernist buildings (boathouses, bathrooms and the like) that successfully allude to the river's vibrant industrial history. Popular with the midtown office crowd (during lunch hour) and tourists, but stretches have a lonely, unpopulated feel, unlike the more neighborhood-centered segments to the south.

NECROLOGY

Piers 62 and 63. Demolished and rebuilt as part of the river's conversion to parkland, the piers were already one of the most vibrant, culturally diverse waterfront spaces in the City. Basketball City and the Manhattan Kayak Company were both evicted, as was the irrepressible **Frying Pan,** an historic lightship with a colorful backstory. The kayaks and the lightship have been reinstalled just south, happily, on Piers 66a and 66. But where's Basketball City?

*For **Riverside Park South** (north of 59th Street) see the Riverside South section (Upper West Side) of this Guide.*

L10, Hugh O'Neill Dry Goods Store

LADIES MILE

[L1] **Ladies Mile Historic District**, West of Park Avenue South to West of 6th Avenue; 15th to 24th streets, with wandering connections. See map. ●

*Sixth Avenue Emporia: The old **Stern's** dry goods store on West 23rd Street and other blocklong ghosts lining what is officially Avenue of the Americas recall the latter part of the 19th century, when this was the precinct termed **Fashion Row**. Now used again for big box stores and office space, their splendor is still evident, and reincarnations have slowly made these long-seedy skeletons glisten once again. In their heyday, it was quite a different avenue, with the clatter of the Sixth Avenue El bringing the middle class to this segment of what came to be a far-ranging, ready-to-wear clothing district.*

L2

[L2] Originally **Stern's Dry Goods Store**, 32-36 W.23rd St., bet. Fifth and Sixth Aves. 1878. *Henry Fernbach.* 38-46 W.23rd St. 1892. *William Schickel.* Altered, 1986, *Rothzeid, Kaiserman, Thompson & Bee.*

A resplendent cast-iron emporium for "New York's first merchandising family." It reeks of birthday cake with vanilla icing. The glass and iron canopy added note of elegant entry, but the glazed curtain wall floors atop Nos.32-36 are out of context. **Home Depot** now enthroned in a cast-iron palazzo! Do they sell DIY casting equipment?

*Edith Wharton, author of such revealing New York novels as **The Age of Innocence**, was born in 1862 at 14 West 23rd Street, in a three-story brownstone altered into a store by H. J. Hardenbergh in 1882. The cast-iron columns date from yet another alteration in 1892. As a signal of the migrating social geography of her own early years, Mrs. Wharton noted that her*

hero, Newland Archer, in reflecting on his father-in-law to be, "knew that he already had his eye on a newly built house in East Thirty-ninth Street. The neighborhood was thought remote, and the house was built in a ghastly greenish-yellow stone that the younger architects were beginning to employ as a protest against the brownstone of which the uniform hue coated New York like a cold chocolate sauce; but the plumbing was perfect."

[L3] **61 West 23rd Street**, bet. Fifth and Sixth Aves. 1886. *John Butler Snook.*

A powerful cast-iron remnant of the Ladies Mile. Five tiers of **Composite Corinthian** columns support smaller-scaled piers and arches on the sixth and seventh levels.

[L4] **The Traffic Building**, 163 W.23rd St., bet. Sixth and Seventh Aves. 1920s.

L3   L4

L6

A tapestry of brick and terra cotta, slung from the steel frame of the building behind, in sharp contrast to the self-supporting cast-iron grillage at No.61. An early modernist was here, who (40 years after No.61) yearned to show the brick to be not load-bearing, but a skin.

[L5] **167 West 23rd Street**, bet. Sixth and Seventh Aves. Altered, 1898, *P. F. Brogan.*

Painted sheet metal and cast iron make ten naive Ionic columns; nevertheless it's a simple, elegant façade.

[L6] **The Caroline**, 60 W. 23rd St., SE cor. Sixth Ave. 2001. *Cook + Fox.*

Massive brick, with flying pergolas cribbed from *Frank Lloyd Wright* at the top in place of a more traditional cornice. Retro-chic, it tries for some of the monumentality of the neighboring Sixth Avenue emporia.

[L7] Originally **Ehrich Brothers Emporium**, 695-709 Sixth Ave., bet. W.22nd and W.23rd Sts. W side. 1889. *William Schickel*. Expansions, 1894-1911, *Buchman & Deisler, Buchman & Fox, Taylor & Levy*.

More Classical history reformed in cast-iron, for a columned and corniced Renaissance Revival palazzo of merchandising.

[L8] Originally **Adams Dry Goods Store**/now **Mattel Toys**, 675-691 Sixth Ave., bet. W.21 St and W.22nd Sts. W side. 1900-1902. *DeLemos & Cordes*.

A splendid American Renaissance building, its **Composite Roman** columns in terra cotta supporting a steel cornice. Note the **ADG** monograms among the ornament.

[L9] **Third Cemetery of the Spanish-Portuguese Synagogue, Shearith Israel**, 98-110 W.21st St., bet. Sixth and Seventh Aves. 1829-1851. 💣

A private haven sheltered by a venerable ailanthus tree. This is the youngest of three

L8

Shearith Israel cemeteries on Manhattan Island. The oldest is just south of Chatham Square (Chinatown), the other in Greenwich Village.

[L10] Originally **Hugh O'Neill Dry Goods Store**, 655-671 Sixth Ave., bet. W.20th and W.21st Sts. W side. 1887-1890. *Mortimer C. Merritt*. Fifth story, 1895. Cupola and dome reconstruction and addition, 2006, *CetraRuddy*.

"Neo-Grec" to the Landmarks Commission, the cast-iron Corinthian columned and pilastered façade, with almost full cylindrical towers, is once again crowned with golden domes at its two corners, courtesy of a meticulous reconstruction by *John Cetra* and *Nancy Ruddy*. The name remains in bold relief at the pediment. Gutsy.

[L11a] **Rectory, Church of the Holy Communion**, 47 W.20th St., bet. Fifth and Sixth Aves. 💣

A distinguished Gothic Revival town house, the onetime home of *William Muhlenberg*, the Scholarly Rector, whose library later formed the basis of the Muhlenberg Branch Library.

[L11b] Originally **Church of the Holy Communion** (Episcopal)/onetime **Limelight Disco**, 49 W.20th St., NE cor. Sixth Ave. 1844-1853. Chapel, 1879, *Charles C. Haight*. 💣

More notable because *Upjohn* did it than because of its intrinsic architectural quality. A stylish disco in the 1980s and 1990s. Churches can become lustily secular in this city when organized religion withdraws.

[L12] **The Westminster**, 180 W. 20th St., along Seventh Ave. to 21st St. 2002. *Robert A.M. Stern Architects*.

The **Old Shoe** approach, bringing historical contextualism (in this case an inflated Art Deco) to a precinct that doesn't have one. It worked for *Ralph Lauren*. The entrance canopy is the secret weapon that signals its retro intents.

[L13] Originally **Simpson Crawford & Simpson**/ later **Simpson Crawford**, 641 Sixth Ave., bet. W.19th and W.20th Sts. W side. 1900-1902. *William H. Hume & Son*.

L10

Seven stories of sober limestone, perhaps too sober, with the more gutsy plasticity of Ladies Mile's *Siegel-Cooper, Ehrich's and Adams* competing for visual attention.

[L14] **The Emory**, 27 W.19th St., bet. Fifth and Sixth Aves. 2009. *Morris Adjmi Architects*.

The return of the Sliver Building, now in Retro-dress, brownstones flanking.

[L15] Originally **B. Altman Dry Goods Store**, 621 Sixth Ave., bet. W.18th and W.19th Sts. W side. 1876-1877. 1880. *David & John Jardine*. Addition to S, 1887, *William H. Hume*. Addition on W.18th St., 1909–1910, *Buchman & Fox*.

Altman's forsook this cast-iron emporium in 1906 for its more imposing limestone columned palace at Fifth Avenue and 34th Street.

"To have the Altman name on your coat or muff or seal collar was equivalent to the hallmark on sterling silver," said Valentine's Manual of 1921. Did Altman's grand palace at 34th

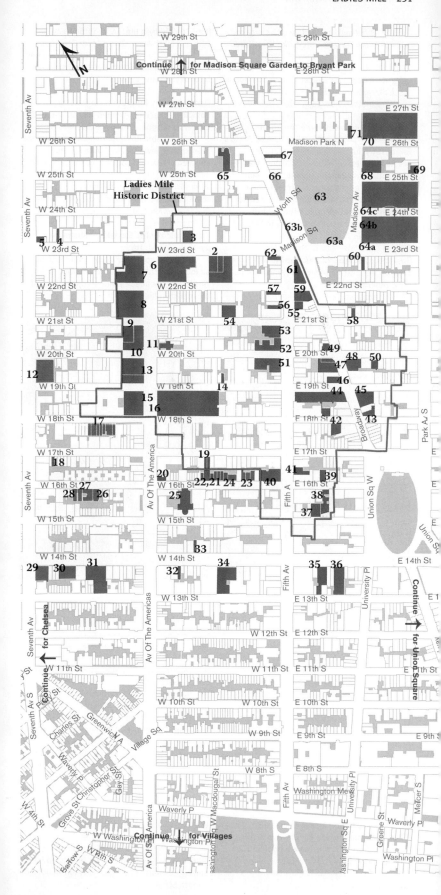

transfer its hallmark to the City University and N.Y. Public Library when they (like hermit crabs in a conch shell) occupy the premises?

[L16] Originally **Siegel-Cooper Dry Goods Store**, 616-632 Sixth Ave., bet. W.18th and W.19th Sts. E side. 1895-1897. *DeLemos & Cordes.*

A clear outgrowth of the "American Renaissance" promoted by the **Chicago World's Fair of 1893,** its 15-1/2 acres of space are enveloped in elaborately embellished glazed terra cotta. The Roman columned and vaulted entryway led at one time to a fountain and the figure of **The Republic** by *Daniel Chester French* (now reposing at California's Forest Lawn Cemetery) giving rise to proposals to "*Meet you at the fountain!*"

[L17] **126, 128, 130-132, 136, 140 W.18th Street Stables,** bet. Sixth and Seventh Aves. S side. 1864-1865. 🍎

Romanesque Revival housing for the horse-

L16   L24

L23, No.23

and carriage trade north of 14th Street. Currently small-scale retail.

[L18] **Rubin Museum of Art,** 150 West 17th Street, bet. Sixth and Seventh Aves. 2004. *Beyer Blinder Belle* (project architects) *and Atelier Imrey Culbert* (façade and gallery design) Stair, *Andrée Putnam.* Hours: Mo/Th 11 AM – 5 PM, We 11 AM – 7 PM, Fr 11–10, Sa/Su 11-6, closed Tu. Adults $10. Free Fri, 7–10. 2 12-620-5000. *www.rmanyc.org*

A formidable collection of art of the Himalayas. Understated, the Rubin occupies an annex to the former Barney's department store. Outside it's brownstone-contextual, save for a three-story stepped figure sliced from the masonry, evoking a Buddhist shrine. Inside, a swooping steel-and-marble spiral stair unites seven gallery floors. Also in-house are a theater, restaurant, and the inevitable gift shop. The free Friday nights are popular with younger wine-sipping mandala lovers.

[L19] **The Chelsea Inn**, 46 W. 17th Street, bet. Fifth and Sixth Aves. 1890. *Henry Congdon.*

Romanesque Revival with Queen Anne bay-windows, dressed in terra cotta and molded brick. A charming survivor.

[L20] Originally **Knickerbocker Jewelry Company,** 574 Sixth Avenue, NE cor. W.16th St. E side. 1903-1904. *Simeon B. Eisendrath.*

A formidable upswept neo-Baroque cornice for erstwhile level-looking Sixth Avenue Elevated riders. But you can look *up.* It hovers.

West 16th Street between Fifth and Sixth Avenues: a wealth of architectural styles and building types:

[L21] Originally **IRT Electrical Substation No.41,** 27-29 W.16th St. 1917.

A chaste tapestry of brick embellished by an intricate verdigris cornice. The New York Health and Racquet Club now enjoys some of those high ceilings.

L20

[L22] **31 West 16th Street**. Altered, 1971, *Stephen B. Jacobs.*

Syncopated rhythms mark the window place-ment in this re-dressed modernist row house.

[L23] **5, 7, 9, 17, 19, 21, and 23 West 16th Street** (originally row houses). ca. 1846. 🍎

No.17 is the **Greek Revival** House where *Margaret Sanger* maintained her Birth Control Clinical Research Bureau from 1930 to 1973. Its bow front (and those of its neighbors at **Nos.5-9**) was a common characteristic of Boston's Greek Revival (as around Louisburg Square) but rare in New York. **Nos.19, 21,** and **23** complete an ensemble with simpler detailing but match-ing scale; **No.23** presents magnificent ironwork.

[L24] **The Center for Jewish History,** 15 and 17 W.16th St. Remodeled with additions on 17th St. 2000. *Beyer Blinder Belle.* 🍎

Two **neo-Georgian** buildings, amid the landmark cluster from 5 to 23, lead to an inner and bigger world mid-block, and loft buildings on 17th Street.

[L25] **Church of St. Francis Xavier (Roman Catholic)**, 40 W.16th St. 1882. *Patrick Charles Keely.*

The monumental porch of this neo-Baroque church spills onto the sidewalk. Inside is an equally monumental Baroque space. Historian Christopher Gray queried: is this "a lugubrious assemblage of wildly contrasting elements by an untutored designer, or a deft collation of historical references by a master?"

[L26] **Young Adults Institute**/originally **New York House and School of Industry**, 120 W.16th St., bet. Sixth and Seventh Aves. 1878. *Sidney V. Stratton.* 🖋

Strong Queen Anne in red brick. The *Picturesque Style* was currently flowering, abetted by romantic landscape painting and the architecture of recently completed Central Park. This institution was founded in 1851 to teach poor women "plain and fine" sewing.

L24   L26

L25

[L27] **French Evangelical Church**/originally **Catholic Apostolic Church**/later **Eglise Evangelique Française de New-York**, 126 W.16th St., bet. Sixth and Seventh Aves. ca. 1835. Current façade, 1886, *Alfred D. F. Hamlin.*

A robust example of what the Germans called Rundbogenstil. The dour dark paint almost smothers form and detail.

[L28] **136-40 West 16th Street**, bet. Sixth and Seventh Aves. 1870s.

Rich brickwork and cast-iron balconies provide a much grander tenement façade.

[L29] **154-160 West 14th Street**, SE cor. Seventh Ave. 1913. *Herman Lee Meader.*

A lavish display of glazed and colored terra-cotta decoration with a flavor of the older **Art Nouveau** (the frieze at the second floor), and yet anticipating the later **Art Deco** at its cornice.

[L30] **Pratt Institute Manhattan Campus**, 138- 146 W.14th Street, bet. Sixth and Seventh Aves. 1896. *Brunner & Tryon.* Restored and rehabilitated for Pratt, 2002, *Ehrenkrantz & Eckstut.*

Eight monumental arches, 16 small ones, and a strong cornice keep to the new Classical architectural model of Burnham's 1893 Chicago World's Fair.

14th Street: In days gone by, the magnetism of Wanamaker's department store radiated from

L30

Broadway and East 9th Street throughout the area. As recently as the mid-1990s 14th Street (east and west) was sketchy. Today, much of the street from Seventh Avenue to Union Square is again crowded with shoppers, and the broad thoroughfare is increasingly chic and pricey. But 14th Street remains a weird, wonderful place to stroll and people-watch. Recent sightings: a weary fast-food employee dressed as a chicken passing out flyers, a woman selling box turtles on the corner ("turtles! get your turtles here!"), an open-topped truck precariously loaded with watermelons idling at the curb. Above the bustle is the grander architecture of an earlier era, well worth considering and enjoying.

[L31a] **Salvation Army Centennial Memorial Temple and Executive Offices**, 120 W.14th St., bet. Sixth and Seventh Aves. 1930. [L31b] **John and Mary R. Markle Memorial Residence**/**Evangeline Residence**, Salvation Army, 123-131 W.13th St. 1929. All by *Voorhees, Gmelin & Walker.*

Art Deco on a monumental scale gives entrance to the Centennial Memorial Temple. The interior is as splashy. To the west and south (on 13th Street) are related but more subdued adjuncts.

[L32] **56 West 14th Street**/once **Macy's Drygoods Store,** bet. Fifth and Sixth Aves. ca. 1894.

This nine-story sliver, deliciously laden with **Beaux Arts** eclectic detail, was once part of R. H. Macy's many holdings in the vicinity of 14th

L33   L34

L36

Street and Sixth Avenue before the store consolidated at Herald Square.

 [L33] **Painters and Paperhangers District Council 9 Headquarters, Painting Industry Welfare Building,** 45 W.14th St., bet. Fifth and Sixth Aves. 1960. *Mayer, Whittlesey & Glass, William J. Conklin,* associate partner in charge.

Bronze and glass, paper and trash. In 1967, this Guide said: "Hopefully, this witty and elegant refacing of a tired façade will inspire its neighbors to follow." They didn't.

[L34] Originally **Ludwig Brothers Dry Goods Store,** 34-42 W.14th St., bet. Fifth and Sixth Aves. 1878. *W. Wheeler Smith.* Enlarged, 1899, *Louis Korn.*

A subdued cast-iron office building above, retail below.

[L35] Originally **Le Boutillier Brothers,** 12-16 E.14th St. 1891. *D'Oench & Simon.*

A pioneering retailer in women's fashions. The grand Corinthian pilastered original façade is evident above the street-level storefront.

[L36] **The New School**/originally **Baumann's Carpet Store,** 22-26 E.14th St., bet. Fifth Ave. and Union Sq. W. 1880. *David & John Jardine.*

A rich embroidery of cast iron: Composite columns, anthemia garlands, festoons, floral bas-reliefs embrace four tiers of enormous double-hung windows.

[L37] Originally **YWCA** (Young Women's Christian Association)/formerly **Rand School,** 7 E.15th St., bet. Union Sq. W. and Fifth Ave. 1885-1887. *R. H. Robertson.*

Romanesque Revival in granite, brick, and brownstone. The grand bay windows give the entrance portal a stronger stature.

L40

[L38] **Sidney Hillman Health Center**/originally **Margaret Louisa Home,** YWCA (lodging house), 16 E.16th St., bet. Union Sq. W. and Fifth Ave. 1890. *R. H. Robertson.*

Rock-face brownstone (with some interspersed brick) in Romanesque Revival, with a charming colonnade at the top floor. A benefaction of *Mrs. Elliott F. Shepard, Cornelius Vanderbilt's* eldest daughter.

[L39] **9-11 East 16th Street,** bet. Union Sq. W. and Fifth Ave. 1895-1896. *Louis Korn.*

Sullivanesque limestone for the first two floors, terra-cotta candy cane above.

[L40] Originally **Judge Building,** 110 Fifth Ave., NW cor. W.16th St. 1888. *McKim, Mead & White.* Remodeled, 1988, *Davis, Brody & Assocs.*

Early *McKim, Mead & White*: a powerful brick and granite Roman Revival monolith, now happily restored up to the cornice. Magnificent.

[L41] **91 Fifth Avenue**, bet. E.16th and E.17th Sts., E side. 1894. *Louis Korn.*

Six busty caryatids bearing up under the weight of four Corinthian columns and two matching pilasters.

[L42] **Engine Co. NYC Fire Department**, 14 E. 18th St., bet. Broadway and Fifth Ave. 1890s. *Napoleon Lebrun.*

A delicate Italian Renaissance town house for fire engines, arches at the third floor support-

L42

ed by composite-capitaled columns and sheltering terra-cotta fans. High above, the frieze and cornice are rich in far-out, far-east detail.

Broadway between Union and Madison Squares
The upper-class dowagers (socially, not architecturally) of Ladies Mile congregated in this area of Broadway. Here the elite shopped, and hence this was a precinct of the carriage trade—a shopping strip of somewhat more elevated snobbery than that enjoyed by Fashion Row, the great Sixth Avenue emporiums originally in the shadows of an El (but also included in the Ladies Mile Historic District). The latter might be termed, in contrast, the transit trade, serving in vast department stores great hordes of the middle class. Here along Broadway the shined hooves of curried horses drew the glistening black enamel and leather carriages of Society, traveling from their town houses nearby, past Lord & Taylor, W. & J. Sloane, and their equals, from Union Square to Madison Square. Sadly, these once grand partici-

pants show their ill-cared-for forms only above the street level, where "modern" alterations have mostly defaced what were once grand doorman-guarded entries.

[L43] **MacIntyre Building** (lofts), 874 Broadway, NE cor. E.18th St. 1890-1892. *R. H. Robertson.*

Unspeakable eclectic: a murmuration of Byzantine columns, Romanesque arches, Gothic finials and crockets—the designer used the whole arsenal of history in one shot. And then the renovation.

[L44] Originally **Arnold Constable Dry Goods Store**/now **ABC Carpet Store**, 881-887 Broadway, SW cor. E.19th St., through to Fifth Ave., with a later entry and address at 115 Fifth Ave. 1868-1869. Extended, 1873, 1877. All by *Griffith Thomas.*

Lovers of marble walls, cast-iron façades, and mansard roofs, rejoice! There is something here for each of you. The Broadway façade, the oldest, is of marble. The extension to Fifth

L44

Avenue, the youngest, is of cast iron, an economical simulation of its adjacent parent. In between, the two-story miraculous mansard crown rises over the original body and the Fifth Avenue extension.

[L45] Originally **W. & J. Sloane Store**/now **ABC Carpet**, 884 Broadway, SE cor. E.19th St. 1881-1882. Expanded, 1898. All by *W. Wheeler Smith.*

Located on Broadway opposite City Hall since 1843, Sloane's moved here (temporarily) before settling on Fifth Avenue and 45th Street. In this ornate brick and terra-cotta structure the firm sold carpeting, oriental rugs, lace curtains, and upholstery fabric. They later expanded to furniture. Now a carpeter has returned.

[L46] Originally **Gorham Silver Manufacturing Company Building**/now **cooperative apartments**, 889-891 Broadway, NW cor. E.19th St. 1883-1884. *Edward H. Kendall.* Alterations, 1912, *John H. Duncan.*

The Queen Anne skyline labors desperately to achieve a varying picturesque profile, as bits and pieces of roof interlock at random with the brick façade. Gorham, of course, manufactured silverware. The show windows are elegant billows onto the street. The 1884 building originally provided two floors for Gorham surmounted by bachelor apartments! Renovations, 2009.

[L47] Originally **Lord & Taylor Dry Goods Store**, 901 Broadway, SW cor. E.20th St. 1869-1870. *James H. Giles*. Façade restored, 1990s, *Kutnicki Bernstein*. 👁️

An exuberant cast-iron façade, capped with a dormered mansard roof. The corner pavilion is reminiscent of the Renaissance architecture of Prague. Windows explode everywhere, a time when merchandisers sought natural light. Now, the opposite is true; Lord & Taylor and its peers want a sealed box, with controlled artificial lighting.

L46

Mumford was talking about: a building overloaded with rich detail in contrast to Goelet's simple surfaces and bold form. Nevertheless, *White* went on to greater and better works until his assassination in 1906.

[L50] **Theodore Roosevelt Birthplace National Historic Site**, 28 E.20th St., bet. Broadway and Park Ave. S. Original building, 1848, demolished. Replicated, 1923, *Theodate Pope Riddle*. 👁️ Open to the public: We-Su 9-5; closed Mo & Tu. 212-260-1616.

After the property was recaptured by the **Women's Roosevelt Memorial Association**, this reproduction was built to copy the one *Roosevelt* knew (he was born here in 1858 and died elsewhere in 1919). The restoration remembered the house as of 1865, not the much altered building that was demolished in 1916.

🏛️[L51] Originally **The Methodist Book Concern**, 150 Fifth Ave., SW cor. W.20th St. 1888-1890. *Edward H. Kendall*. 👁️ **Romanesque Revival** in brick, and the ground-floor entrance has been modernized with misunderstanding. Nevertheless, the brick on top still rests on a rock-face granite podium.

[L52] Originally **Presbyterian Building**, 154-158 Fifth Ave., NW cor. W.20th St. 1894-1895. *James B. Baker*. 👁️

Baker created this Romanesque Revival building while a neo-Classical counterrevolution was gathering steam at the Chicago World's Fair of 1893. He hopped on board that

L47   L52

[L48] Originally **Goelet Building**, 900 Broadway, SE cor. E.20th St. 1886-1887. *Stanford White of McKim, Mead & White*. Enlarged, 1905-1906, *Maynicke & Franke*. 👁️

Bricksmiths were here, their brick mounted on a grand set of polychromatic brown- and limestone Romanesque Revival arches, in turn, supported by rough granite piers and polished granite columns. Vandals have removed the cornice and defaced the ground floor for dubious commercial enterprises, but *Lewis Mumford* in *The Brown Decades* had described it as "a building above fashion." Renovations, 2009.

[L49] Originally **Warren Building**, 907 Broadway., NW cor. 20th St. 1890. *Stanford White of McKim, Mead & White*. 👁️

White trumpeted his Renaissance Revival horn less than five years after lusty Goelet, and did it cater-corner across the intersection. *Lewis Mumford* had dismissed subsequent *MM&W* architecture (after the Goelet), as "learned eclecticism." Here is the evidence of what

American Renaissance express and later produced the wondrous Chamber of Commerce of the State of New York in 1901.

[L53] Onetime **Merchants' Bank**/originally **Mohawk Building**, 160 Fifth Ave., SW cor. W.21st St. 1891. *R. H. Robertson*. 👁️

This Renaissance Revival pile becomes increasingly complex as it approaches its domical corner tower. Nicely cleaned and restored.

[L54] **Spero Building**, 19 W.21st St., bet. Fifth and Sixth Aves. N side. 1907-1908. *Robert Kohn*. 👁️

Boldly scaled Art Nouveau.

🏛️[L55] **United Synagogue of Conservative Judaism**/originally **Scribner Building**, 153-157 Fifth Ave., bet. E.21st and E.22nd Sts. E side. 1893-1894. *Ernest Flagg*. 👁️

The first headquarters built for publishers Charles Scribner's Sons by a soon-to-be-great architect (and *Charles Scribner's* brother-in-law), who would later build the *Scribners* a bookstore and headquarters uptown, a printing plant, and a family residence. This chaste façade was once enriched by a broad, semi-ellipsoidal cast-iron and glass canopy, in the Parisian mode.

[L56] **166 Fifth Avenue**, bet. E.21st and E.22nd Sts. W side. 1899-1900. *Parfitt Bros.*
Terra-cotta Eclectic.

[L57] **Sohmer Piano Building**, 170 Fifth Ave., SW cor. E.22nd Sts. 1897. *Robert Maynicke.* Restored, 2005, *Bone/Levine Architects.*
A thin palazzo in sliver form, with a jaunty gold cupola on top. Sliver buildings are all the rage today, and tend to be made with angular glass panels, but hip young architects should see this for themselves and take notes. Educational.

[L58] **Originally Hotel 21**, 21 E.21st St., bet. Broadway and Park Ave. S. 1878. *Bruce Price.*
A socialite architect, *Price* planned the wealthy suburban private community of Tuxedo Park, N.Y., and designed many of its Shingle Style houses. His daughter, *Emily Post*, dictated social manners to the flock that wanted to join the elite. **No.21** is an example of **American Queen Anne**, a picturesque composition ornamented with its original metalwork. The corbeled column supporting the bay window is a marvelous example of late Victorian structural whimsy.

L56   L58

[L59] **Albert Building**/originally **Glenham Hotel**, 935 Broadway, SW cor. E.22nd St. to Fifth Ave. 1861-1862. *Griffith Thomas.* ●
A dignified neo-Renaissance structure, saved by the new Restoration Hardware shop that, with its projecting clock, make noteworthy statements of restored gentility.

[L60] **1 Madison Park**, 22 E. 23rd St., bet. Broadway and Park Ave. South. 2009. *CetraRuddy.*
A pencil-thin 60-story tower with an intriguing structural off-set that allows the apartments, arranged in stacked cubes, to cantilever slightly beyond the supporting columns. Because it's so much taller than anything around it, and almost all glass, the views from within are astonishing. Plans are on hold for a companion tower, an engineering marvel that would sprout from a tiny footprint and lean south over its next-door neighbor (*CetraRuddy with Rem Koolhaas and Shohei Shigematsu of OMA*AMO*).

[L61] **Flatiron Building**/originally **Fuller Building**, 175 Fifth Ave., E.22nd St. to E.23rd St., Fifth Ave. to Broadway. 1901-1903. *Daniel H. Burnham & Co.* ● Façade restored, 1991, *Hurley & Farinella.*

L60, under construction

The diagonal line of Broadway formed pivotal triangular buildings here and at Times Square. *Burnham* was master of architectural ceremonies at the *World's Columbian Exposition* in 1893, which changed the course of civic architecture for a generation, diverting attention from Romanesque and Romantic Revival to a revival of the Classical Architecture of Rome and the Renaissance.

Here rustications are uniformly detailed from ground to sky, as if the Flatiron were an elevatored palazzo: limestone at the bottom, giving way to brick and terra cotta as the floors rise. The acutely chamfered corners contribute to an exaggerated and dramatic perspective. It is sometimes (incorrectly) thought to be the first (or at least an early sample) steel-skeletoned skyscraper; dozens of New York commercial buildings had been steel-framed in the 1890s, including the tallest at the time, the 391-foot Park Row Building.

[L62] Originally **Western Union Telegraph Building**, 186 Fifth Ave., SW cor. W.23rd St. 1884. *Henry J. Hardenbergh.* 🍎

A dour survivor from *Hardenbergh*'s **Dakota Apartments** period, completed that same year. This is one of Fifth Avenue's earliest commercial buildings, from a time when the fashionable were fleeing to residences farther north. The glowing, but somber, brickwork with its terra-cotta banding, with the sky punctuated by six homely dormers, conjure together images out of Victorian London.

Madison Square and Environs

[L63] **Madison Square Park**/earlier **Madison Square**/formerly part of The Parade/originally a potter's field, Fifth to Madison Aves., E.23rd to E.26th Sts. Opened, 1847. *Ignatz Pilat* (former assistant to *Frederick Law Olmsted*). Refurbished, 1999-2000, *City Parks Foundation.*

The City crept past this point just prior to the Civil War. Madison Avenue springs from

assassinated (1906) in the roof garden restaurant of the original Madison Square Garden (1892-1925) that he had designed, a hundred yards away (on the site of the present New York Life building).

[L63a] **The Shake Shack**, within Madison Square Park. 2004. *James Wines and Denise M.C. Lee of SITE Environmental Design.*

Wines, the brains behind the wacky firm **SITE**, has taken his cues here from post-war roadside architecture (remember *Robert Venturi & Denise Scott-Brown*?), with a little **Flatiron Building** thrown in. It fits into the park so well it seems to have been there forever. One of the best new buildings in recent memory because of what it creates: a place. A kit of adaptable parts, the Shack is being replicated in other locations: Upper West Side, CitiField, Little Italy. Hungry New Yorkers happily wait in long lines for the best burgers, hot dogs, milk shakes and frozen custard in the City.

L61

L63a

23rd Street on the east flank of the square, bisecting the block from Fifth to Fourth (or Park Avenue South in its 1959 renaming). The commissioners plan of 1811 had shown a Parade from Third to Seventh Avenues, 23rd to 34th Streets, a pleasant void in the surveyor's grid. The present space (6.23 acres) is all that remains of that intention, replaced in scale by Central Park (which had never been a part of the commissioners' scheme).

Statuary: **Chester Allen Arthur**, 1898. *George Bissell.* An accidental president (he was vice president to the assassinated *James Garfield*). **Roscoe Conkling**, 1893. *John Quincy Adams Ward.* Republican political leader. **William H. Seward**, 1876. *Randolph Rogers. Lincoln's* secretary of state. The **Eternal Light Flagpole** base, 1924. *Carrère & Hastings.*

Madison Square's greatest work is the melancholy Art Nouveau memorial to **Admiral David G. Farragut**, 1880-1881. *Augustus Saint-Gaudens,* sculptor. *Stanford White,* architect. *White,* the contributing architect, was

*The Four Squares: The laying out of **Union, Gramercy, Stuyvesant,** and **Madison Squares** in the 1830s and 1840s gave promise of urbane residential precincts for wealthy New Yorkers. All four squares were speculative developments in the spirit of London's Bloomsbury and Covent Garden (where the Dukes of Bedford had developed farmland into a grand neighborhood of Georgian architecture and garden squares).*

[L63b] **Sidewalk clock**, in front of 200 Fifth Ave., bet. W.23rd and W.24th Sts. W side. 1909. *Hecla Iron Works.* 🍎

A shopper's clock from the era when these blocks marked the end of Ladies Mile, an area of mercantile elegance. Its Ionic column signals the Classical allusions of those Edwardian years.

[L64a] **Metropolitan Life Insurance Company**, 1 Madison Ave. in NE cor. E.23rd St. to Park Ave. S. 1893. Altered. [L64b] **Tower**, SE cor. E.24th St. 1909. Both by *Pierre Le Brun of Napoleon Le Brun & Sons.* 🍎 Tower altered, 1964, *Lloyd Morgan.*

[L64c] **North Building**, 11-25 Madison Ave., bet. E.24th and E.25th Sts. E side. 1932. *Harvey Wiley Corbett and D. Everett Waid.*

Retained as a symbol when its adjacent base was rebuilt, the tower was stripped of its ornament and became a warehouse for company records—in effect the insured world's attic: now rental offices. At the **North Building** the polygonal modeling of the upper bulk became an experiment in sinuous plasticity, a step in the search for form by *Corbett* in his early mod-

[L66] **Worth Monument**, W.24th to W.25th Sts., Fifth Ave. to Broadway. 1857. *James G. Batterson.*

General William J. Worth, hero of the Seminole and Mexican wars, is buried here, one of the City's few interments that is actually under the memorial monument (*General Grant* is entombed in his own mausoleum as well). Here, one noted for subduing Native and Hispanic Americans rests under a Renaissance Revival obelisk. A cultural mismatch at the least.

L64b, as seen from L60

ernist architecture. For we mere pedestrians there are wondrous vaulted entrance spaces at each of the four corners.

[L65a] **Serbian Orthodox Cathedral of St. Sava**/originally **Trinity Chapel** (Episcopal), 15 W.25th St., bet. Fifth and Sixth Aves. 1850-1855. *Richard Upjohn.* ✪
[L65b] **Clergy House**, 16 W.26th St. 1866. *Richard and Richard M. Upjohn.* ✪
[L65c] **Parish House**/originally **Trinity Chapel School**, 13 W.25th St. 1860. *Wrey Mould.* ✪
In the church: Swope Memorial reredos, 1892, and altar, 1897, both by *Frederick Clarke Withers.*

A somber brownstone church (and clergy house) is paired with a playful polychromatic Ruskinian Gothic parish house to its east. An unexpected pedestrian shortcut results, from 25th to 26th Streets.

A century of grime conceals the detailing and multicolor of the ensemble. *Edith Wharton*, born nearby, was married here in 1885. *Michael Pupin* (1858-1935), a noted physicist of Serbian background, stands, frozen in time, in the walkway.

[L67] Originally **Cross Chambers**, 210 Fifth Ave., bet. W.25th and W.26th Sts. W side. ca. 1895.

A **Belle Epoque** extravagance with balconies and bay windows. Look up—the riches are on high. In 19th- and early 20th-century New York, that's where the "riches" are. Helicopter?

[L68] **Appellate Division, New York State Supreme Court**, 35 E.25th St., NE cor. Madison Ave. 1896-1899. *James Brown Lord.* ✪ Interior. ✪ Restorations, 2000, *Platt Byard Dovell White.*

This small marble palace is the reincarnation of an 18th-century English country house: Corinthian columned and elaborately crowned with sculpture: **Wisdom and Force** by *Frederick Ruckstuhl* flank the portal, **Peace** by *Karl Bitter* is the central figure on the balustrade facing the Square. **Justice** (fourth from left on 25th Street) is by *Daniel Chester French*, whose seated **Lincoln** chairs the Lincoln Memorial. *T-Square, The New Yorker* critic in 1928, referred to "the rather pleasant little Appellate Court House with its ridiculous adornment of mortuary statuary."

[L69] **Provident Loan Society of New York,** 346 Park Ave. S., NW cor. E.25th St. 1909.

Three stories of limestone atop a granite base: an English club dispensing credit. It followed in the footsteps of *MM&W's* nearby bank.

North of Madison Square:

[L70] **New York Life Insurance Company,** 51 Madison Ave., E.26th to E.27th St., Madison to Park Ave. S. 1928. *Cass Gilbert.*

Limestone Renaissance at the bottom, birthday cake at the top. *Gilbert* was obsessed with pyramidal hats for his buildings: compare the **Woolworth Building** (1913) and the **Federal Courthouse** at Foley Square (1936). Among *Gilbert's* iconic heirs, and utilizing the license of Post Moderism, *Cesar Pelli, Kevin Roche, David Childs* (of SOM), *Helmut Jahn,* and others have recently crowned many new towers all over the island.

This site has a rich history. It was originally

L70

occupied by the **Union Depot,** the New York terminal of the New York and Harlem Railroad. After 1871, when the first **Grand Central Station** opened at 42nd Street, the Depot was converted to house *Gilmore's* Garden and then *P.T. Barnum's* Hippodrome; it was later refinanced and renamed (1879) **Madison Square Garden.** *Stanford White* then designed a lavish replacement, complete with a tower copied from the **Giralda** in Seville, which opened in 1892. *White* was shot on its roof garden in 1906 by *Harry Thaw,* whose wife, the actress *Evelyn Nesbit,* had reputedly been *White's* mistress before her marriage. One added irony: Madison Square Garden's quarters (two buildings later) are on the site of the demolished **Pennsylvania Station,** *McKim, Mead & White's* greatest New York work.

[L71] **50 Madison Avenue Apartments,** NW cor. E. 26th St. *Platt Byard Dovell White.*

It swallowed Renwick & Cos.' ASPCA building almost whole. A grand, historic (though sadly not landmarked), Renaissance Revival palazzo has been sur-elevated: the top floor and cornice were surgically removed, a mundane tower mounted on what remained. An attempt at "dovetailing old and new" (in the words of the project architect) only points to how much better the old was than the new.

NECROLOGY

42nd Division Armory N.Y. National Guard, 125 W.14th St., bet. Sixth and Seventh Aves.1971. N.Y.S. General Services Administration, *Charles S. Kawecki,* State Architect. R.I.P. 1971-1995

A gross and overbearing modern drill hall that replaced a 19th-century fantasy fort of rich detail.

Xavier Apartments, 30 W.16th St. bet. Fifth and Sixth Aves. S side. 1890s.

Some flamboyant limestone for those seeking apartment grandeur. The replacement is a mere banality.

Originally **Leonard Jerome House**/later **Union League, University,** and **Manhattan Clubs,** 32 East 26th St., SE cor. Madison Ave. 1859. *Thomas R. Jackson.*

Famous as the mansion of *Winston Churchill's* grandfather, this Second Empire structure later served as transitory homes for

L71   Xavier Apartments

several of New York's elite clubs. The building achieved questionable notoriety as one of New York's few officially designated landmarks to be demolished.

Originally American Society for the Prevention of Cruelty to Animals, 50 Madison Ave., NW cor. E.26th St. 1896. *Renwick, Aspinwall & Owen.*

A proper London club in delicately tooled limestone. Even stray mongrels and alley cats deserved distinguished architecture in the 1890s. The elaborately modeled cornice and fourth floor were cut off in a recent apartment conversion/lobotomy.

END *of Ladies Mile Walking Tour. The IRT Lexington Avenue line (No.6 train) is at Park Avenue South and 23rd Street.*

UNION SQUARE TO GRAMERCY PARK

A ramble around Union Square, then a saunter up Irving Place to Gramercy Park. START at Union Square. (Take the IRT Lexington Avenue Line [4, 5, and 6 trains], the BMT Broadway Line [N, R, W trains], or the 14th Street-Canarsie Line [L train] to the Union Square/14th Street Station.)

Union Square/originally **Union Place**: The crotch between Broadway from the southwest and the Bowery (Fourth Avenue at this point) from the southeast, nicknamed **The Forks**. Before the Civil War it was a grand residential square, with an iron-fenced public park, primarily for the fashionable town-house residents surrounding it, much as **Gramercy Park** (fenced and locked) still is today. In 1854 it blossomed as a new "uptown" theatrical district with the opening of the Academy of Music. That venerable house was on the site of the present Con Edison Building, opposite a later,

W1

namesake Academy, (briefly the **Palladium**), now the site of another NYU dormitory.

Union Square later became the center of the political left: here, in August 1927, protestors awaited news of the execution of *Sacco* and *Vanzetti*. May Day, the annual celebration of socialism, brought a million to this mecca where the *Daily Worker* and many other radical publications and organizations abounded.

[W1] **Union Square Park**, E.14th to E.17th Sts., Union Sq. W. to Union Sq. E. Laid out, 1830. Opened to public, 1839. Rebuilt, 1986, *Bronson Binger*, architect; *Hui Mei Grove*, landscape architect; N.Y.C. Department of Parks & Recreation, Capital Projects Division. Newsstand, Union Sq. E. opp. E.15th St. 1986. *Kuo Ming Tsu.*

The park's raised topography is a latter-day event, allowing the subway to snake through its underworld: the original street-level park with romantically curving pathways was then totally rebuilt as a more formal public place. In those early subway times crowds gathered around

their favorite debater to heckle, support, or berate him or her. This was **New York's Speakers' Corner**; it became a sacred precinct for soapbox orators and other agitators after police excesses in repressing unemployment rallies in the 1930s.

Drug traffickers in the 1960s and 1970s controlled the scene, but the 1986 renovation removed the perimeter screens of green, making all activities within visible and returning the park to a civilized population. The renovation, designed by the Parks Department's own staff, is the best in memory: replanning of the entry areas, stone detailing, railings in scale (for once!) with a public place (using bulbous malleable iron fittings at joints), punctuated with steel and glass kiosks over the subway entrances and for the newsstand, and lighted with ornate multiglobed lamps. The park abounds in sculpture: **Washington** (*Henry Kirke Brown,* with *J. Q. A. Ward*, sculptors; pedestal by *Richard Upjohn*), a copy of *Houdon's* original horseback eulogy, arrived in 1856. *Brown* also contributed **Lincoln**. In 1876, *Bartholdi*, sculptor of the **Statue of Libert**y, left **Lafayette** as a token of Franco-American relations at a point early in his unceasing campaign to raise funds for the base of Liberty. The flagpole base is by *Anthony de Francisi*, sculptor, in 1866. **Mohandas Karamchand Gandhi** (*Kantilal B. Patel*, 1986) stands amid the shrubbery.

W3   W4

[W2] **Greenmarket**, along W.17th St. bet. Broadway and Park Ave. S. at the N edge of Union Sq.

Architect/planner *Barry Benepe* brought back urban farmers' markets to New York City in 1976: a resounding success. Similar markets have since proliferated, with *Benepe's* guiding hand, in all the boroughs: concerned with the serious architecture of cheese, tomatoes, legumes, and other edibles.

 [W3] Originally **Lincoln Building**, 1 Union Sq. W., NW cor. E.14th St. 1889-1890. *R. H. Robertson.*

Romanesque Revival granite arches large and small. Inside, the structure is steel framing, then new. But outside walls bear their load, and offer Byzantine capitals and carved lions.

[W4a] **Spingler Building**, 5-9 Union Sq. W., bet. E.14th and E.15th Sts. W side. 1890s.

Tan brick and terra cotta clothe another **Romanesque Revival**, arched on high, pilastered at street level.

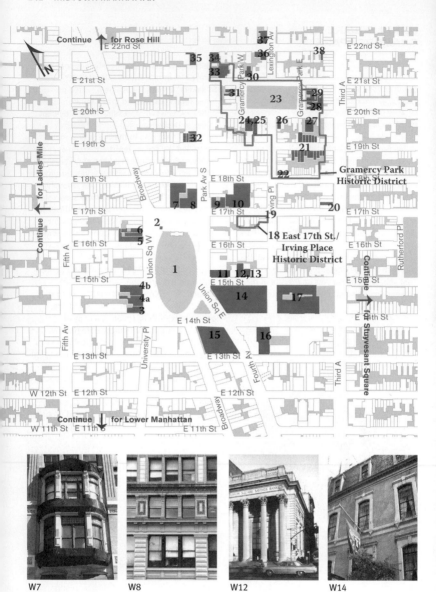

W7   W8   W12   W14

[W4b] **15 Union Square West,** SW cor. W.15th St. 2009. *Perkins Eastman.*

The 1870 cast-iron façade of **Tiffany's** 'Palace of Jewels' was for years hidden behind brick veneer. Now there are seven more stories, stacked like Christmas boxes, and a glass curtain, wrapping the cast-iron arches.

[W5] **31 Union Square West**/originally **Bank of the Metropolis** Building, NW cor. 16th St. 1902-1903. *Bruce Price.* ●

This slender neo-Renaissance slab now houses a restaurant in its original banking rooms, a place for *Superman's* lunch. For the office renter a grand bowed entry portico with giant granite Ionic columns provides a sense of status. High above, a luscious copper cornice hovers.

[W6] **Union Building** (condominiums)/originally **Decker Building,** 33 Union Sq. W., bet. 16th and 17th Sts. 1892-1893. *John Edelmann,*

designer. *Alfred Zucker,* architect. Renovated for condominiums, 1990s, *Joseph Pell Lombardi & Assocs.* ●

Edelman was both mentor to and friend of *Louis Sullivan* (and gave him his first "architectural" opportunity: decoration for Sinai Synagogue and frescoes for Moody Tabernacle, both in Chicago). He later introduced him to *Dankmar Adler.* In 1881, the new partnership of *Adler & Sullivan* was born (**Auditorium Building,** Chicago. 1886. **Condict Building,** New York. 1897-1898). Here the incised decoration shows what *Edelman*, in turn, may have learned from *Sullivan.*

[W7] Originally **Century Building**/now **Barnes & Noble Bookstore,** 33 E.17th St., bet. Park Ave. S. and Broadway to W.18th St. 1880-1881. *William Schickel.* Façade restoration, 1994-1995, *Li-Saltzman Architects.* ●

This red-brick, terra-cotta, and whitestone charmer is where the popular *Century* magazine (for grown-ups) and *St. Nicholas* (for boys and girls) were published before the century turned.

[W8] **Everett Building**, 200 Park Ave. S., NW cor. 17th St. 1908. *Goldwin Starrett & Van Vleck.* 🐦

Goldwin Starrett had worked for four years in the Chicago office of *Daniel Burnham*. Careful, but bland, the *Burnham* touch (elegantly evident at the **Flatiron Building**) did not rub off here.

[W9] **W New York Hotel**/onetime Guardian Life Insurance Company/originally **Germania Life Insurance Company Building**, 201 Park Ave. S., NE cor. E.17th St. 1910-1911. *D'Oench & Yost.* Hotel conversion, 2001, *The Rockwell Group.* 🐦
[W10] **Annex**, 105 E.17th St., bet. Park Ave. S. and Irving Pl. 1961. *Skidmore, Owings & Merrill.*

The mansarded bulk of this **Renaissance Revival** marvel (and its early electric supersign)

W6

is best seen from a distance, down 17th Street or from the adjacent Union Square Park. The name Germania Life became a millstone at the advent of World War I. The board of directors renamed it with the largest number of reusable letters that they could find. Guardian still crowns the roof against its mansard backdrop. But a rearrangement of Guardian is no help to **W New York**!

Next door a sleek annex is composed of a simple grid of aluminum and glass. As an accessory, it is a graceful annex to the proud parent, unabashedly "modernist," an articulated annex.

[W11] **Daryl Roth Theater**/formerly **American Savings Bank**/originally **Union Square Savings Bank**, 20 Union Sq. E., NE cor. E.15th St. 1905-1907. *Henry Bacon.* 🐦

A classy Corinthian colonnade seems somewhat forlorn in this neighborhood. *Bacon's* best remembrance is the **Lincoln Memorial**. Now a space for spectacular off-Broadway theater.

[W12] **105 East 15th Street**, bet. Union Sq. E. and Irving Pl. ca. 1900.

Granite shafts support terra-cotta **Corinthian** capitals, with gray brick and terra cotta articulating the bayed façade above. Sophisticated form.

[W13] **Trinity Broadcasting Theater**/formerly **Century Association Building**/onetime **Century Center for the Performing Arts**, 109-111 E.15th St. bet. Union Sq. E. and Irving Pl. 1869. *Gambrill & Richardson*. Richardson Room converted to theater, 1996-1997, *Beyer Blinder Belle.* 🐦

H. H. Richardson in New York? He joined *Gambrill* as partner, and the **Century** as a **Centurion** (member: 1866-1867), after *Gambrill* had begun the design. Then what happened? Not too much: red brick and a mansard roof. But **H.H.** went on to great glories elsewhere.

[W14] **Zeckendorf Towers** (mixed use), 1 Irving Place, bet. W.14th and W.15th Sts. to Union Sq. E. 1987. *Davis, Brody & Assocs.*

W16

Four mega-finials, each with an illuminated, levitating, pyramidal yarmulka, crown a massive commercial bottom. Each finial is a separate apartment tower: a colossal project that blocks the once familiar view of Con Edison's clock tower for users of the park. But well done.

From 1921, until they were demolished in 1985, this was the site of a clutch of small 19th-century buildings that were the home of S. Klein's-on-the-Square, the original discount department store. Above them stood a Times Square-scale neon sign that advertised Klein's name to hordes of shoppers. The modest budget was served there not only with bargains but also occasional high style . . . the latter for those stalwarts with energy and sharp eyes who combed the sea of clothes racks with vigor. (Klein's closed in August 1975.)

[W15] **Union Square South**, 14th St. bet. Fourth Avenue and Broadway. 1999. *Davis Brody Bond and Schuman Lichtenstein Claman & Efron.* **Artwall**, *Kristin Jones and Andrew Ginzel.*

W14

Careful, but bulky, urban architecture: a mixed-use complex at a major nexus of mixed uses (within are a Circuit City, Regal Cinemas, and 240 apartments). Unbelievably crowded, especially on weekends. *Artwall*, on the building's north façade facing the square, is cryptic: suggestions?

[W16] **University Hall (N.Y.U. Dormitory)**, 110 E.14th St., bet. Third and Fourth Aves. 1998 and 2008. *Davis Brody Bond.*

Precast concrete echoes the limestone of Con Ed across the street. But upstairs, higher tech reigns. An atrium space within is covered by a sloped, tensile-structured skylight.

[W17] **Consolidated Edison Company**/originally **Consolidated Gas Company**, 4 Irving Place, NE cor. E.14th St. 1915. *Henry J. Hardenbergh.* **Tower**, 1926. *Warren & Wetmore.*

Hardenbergh, who gave us the **Dakota**, the **Plaza**, and the **Art Students League**, here delivered a dull swan song for an establishment

paid (and highly paid) interior decorator. Later, as *Lady Mendl*, she gave parties with as much élan as her décor.

Where TIME *began: In an upstairs room at 141 East 17th Street in 1922, Briton Hadden and Henry Luce wrote the prospectus for what was to become* TIME *magazine. The rent was $55 a month.*

 [W20] Originally **Scheffel Hall**/ later Joe King's Rathskeller, or **The German-American**/recently **Fat Tuesday's Jazz Club**/190 Third Ave., bet. E.17th and E.18th Sts. W side. 1894. *Henry Adam Weber & Hubert Drosser.*

Eclectic Renaissance Revival, inspired by the **Friedrichbau** in Heidelberg. The jazz was cool downstairs, where collegians of an earlier generation merely drank beer and made out. Later, in **Fat Tuesday's** days, youth of all ages did the same—to jazz rhythms. The once massive local immigrant German population centered its recreation here. An early (for New York) terra-cotta

W17

W16   W19

W20   W22

client—profitable no doubt, but a far cry from his earlier glories. A landmark clock tops it, Con Ed's GHQ, on the site of the original **Academy of Music**. The academy's namesake across the street, an aging movie palace, became The Palladium, now demolished for another NYU dormitory.

[W18] **East 17th Street/Irving Place Historic District** 104-122 East 17th Street and 47-49 Irving Place.

A clutch of houses reflecting old Irving Place character, modest, but gracious, with or without the slippery trail of *Washington Irving*.

[W19] **"Washington Irving House,"** 122 E.17th St., SW cor. Irving Place. 1845.

Irving's connection with this house is the wishful thinking of an ancient owner; this is one *Washington* who never slept here. In the real world, *Elsie de Wolfe* and *Elisabeth Marbury* lived here from 1894 to 1911, maintaining a salon where notables from all walks of life gathered amid *Elsie's* "white decor," the stylistic statement that launched her career as America's first

façade joins a cast-iron storefront for a strong, but pleasant architectural simulation. Fun.

Gramercy Park and Environs:

[W21] **The Block Beautiful**, E.19th St. bet. Irving Place and Third Ave. Remodeled as a group, 1909, *Frederick J. Sterner.*

This block, where the sum of the parts rather than its architectural actors creates one of the best places in New York. Treelined, with limited traffic, it's quiet, serene, and urbane. *Sterner* first bought and lived at No.138.

[W22] **Pete's Tavern**/once **Portman Hotel**/later **Tom Healy's**, 129 E.18th St., NE cor. Irving Place. 1829.

A social landmark since 1903 in a corner tavern with the patina of age. The shallow sidewalk café bounds two sides, and bare brick brings a vintage experience: good Italian food and burgers. One apocrypha states that *O. Henry* wrote "The Gift of the Magi" in the second booth, but it's a comforting story.

[W23] **Gramercy Park Historic District**, Gramercy Park E. and W., Gramercy Park N. and S., with axis on Lexington Ave. to the N, Irving Place to the S. 1831. *Samuel Ruggles.*

Enlightened self-interest graced the neighborhood with this lovely park. Private and restricted to tenants occupying the original surrounding plots, it is, nevertheless, a handsome space for all strollers to enjoy. Built under the same principles employed by the *Dukes of Bedford* in London, it shared with Union Square this gracious urban-design approach (speculative housing at **Bloomsbury** and **Covent Garden** were made not only more delightful but also more profitable by the addition of parks and squares).

Edwin Booth, brother of *Lincoln's* assassin *John Wilkes,* lived at 16 Gramercy Park South. His statue stands within the park. (*Edmond T. Quinn,* sculptor. 1916).

[W24] **The Players**, 16 Gramercy Park South, bet. Park Ave. S. and Irving Place.

security in a time of riots, *Tilden* had rolling steel doors built into the Gramercy Park façade (behind the windows), and a tunnel to 19th Street for a speedy exit in case the doors failed. **Gothic Revival** in the manner of *John Ruskin.* Polychromatic, brownstone and polished black granite trim. Transformed into the National Arts Club in 1906.

[W26] Onetime **Benjamin Sonnenberg** House/ formerly **Stuyvesant Fish House**, 19 Gramercy Park S., SE cor. Irving Place. 1845. Altered for *Stuyvesant Fish.*

In 1900, *Fish* moved north to grander *Stanford White* digs at 78th Street, recently acquired (2007) by the **Bloomberg Foundation**: a step in the inexorable movement of "society" as commerce and living space reshaped Manhattan's demographics. *Sonnenberg* was an old-fashioned publicist as renowned as *Edward L. Bernays*, the advisor to *John D. Rockefeller, Sr.*, who persuaded him to give dimes prolifically to small children.

W24

W25

W27

W29

W30

S side. 1845. Remodeled, 1888-1889, *Stanford White of McKim, Mead & White.*

Edwin Booth bought this **Gothic Revival** town house to found a club for those in the theater (as loosely defined). He was a star in a sense not easily conceivable today, when stars are not so rare. A super brownstone, with *White's* two-story Tuscan-columned **Renaissance** porch bracketed by great wrought-iron lanterns.

[W25] **National Arts Club**/originally *Samuel Tilden House*, 15 Gramercy Park S., bet. Park Ave. S. and Irving Place. S side. 1881-1884. *Vaux & Radford.*

Here *Calvert Vaux* of Vaux & Radford, once of Central Park's Olmsted & Vaux, reverted to a single architectural commission for *Samuel J. Tilden*, outspoken opponent of the Tweed Ring, who was elected governor of New York in 1874. In 1876 *Tilden* ran for president against *Rutherford B. Hayes*, won the popular vote by almost 250,000 but lost in the electoral college (too bad the sands of time prevented a quick drink with *Al Gore*). Fearful of his personal

[W27] **The Brotherhood Synagogue**/originally **Friends Meeting House**, 28 Gramercy Park S., bet. Irving Place and Third Ave. S side. 1857-1869. *King & Kellum.* Remodeled as synagogue, 1975, *James Stewart Polshek & Partners.*

An appropriately chaste brownstone box built for the Quakers and now converted to a synagogue.

[W28] **The Gramercy**/originally **Gramercy Park Hotel**, 34 Gramercy Park E., NE cor. E.20th St. 1883. *George W. da Cunha.*

A craggy, mysterious red-brick and red terra-cotta pile whose Queen Anne forms are among the City's most spectacular. Look up to terra-cotta Indians, eagles, and geometry.

[W29] **36 Gramercy Park East** (apartments), bet. E.20th and E.21st Sts. E side. 1908-1910. *James Riely Gordon.*

None shall pass! Knights in armor guard the doors, plus lots of gargoyles, shields, and neo-Gothic arches in white terra cotta. The uptown brethren of this bay-windowed white terra-cotta apartment house have mostly been demolished to build anew with more floors and lower ceilings. For its office tower equivalent see the **Woolworth Building**.

[W30] **50 Gramercy Park North** (apartments), bet. Gramercy Pk. East and West. 2007. *John Pawson.*

"But it's easy to mess it up. Architecturally, it's more what you don't do than what you do." **Minimalist** *John Pawson*, speaking of his understated hotel on Gramercy North. Sleek, but not sexy.

[W31] **3 and 4 Gramercy Park West**, bet. E.20th and E.21st Sts. W side. 1846. Ironwork attributed to *Alexander Jackson Davis.*

Intricate ironwork over plain brick bodies. *Davis* was one of America's most versatile 19th-century architects, his other New York City work ranging from the Italianate **Litchfield Villa** in Prospect Park to that transported **Parthenon**, the Federal Hall National Memorial on Wall Street.

[W32] **2forty**, 240 Park Avenue South, NW cor. E.19th St. 2008. *Gwathmey Siegel.*

A heavy hand was here: *Gwathmey Siegel's* wide spectrum of noted postmodern New York works range from the Astor Place Tower to the new U.S. Mission to the U.N., all staunch statements. **2forty,** however, mumbles its presence, probably suffering from developer's lockjaw, where the architect hired to be brand-name on the sales brochure, loses, unwittingly, to the vagaries of real estate commerce.

[W35] **Gramercy Place** (apartments)/originally **New York Bank for Savings,** 280 Park Ave. S., SW cor E.22nd St. 1894. *C. L. W. Eidlitz.* Alterations to bank building and new apartment tower, 1987, *Beyer Blinder Belle.*

The shell of the old **Bank for Savings** presents a historical street-fronted corner entrance to better-than-average apartment tower—maintaining a link with lower Fourth Avenue history.

[W36] **Sage House** (apartments)/originally *Russell Sage Foundation Building & Annex*, 4 Lexington Ave., SW cor. E.22nd St. 1912-1913 & 1922-1923. *Grosvenor Atterbury with John A. Tompkins II. Annex, 1930-1931.*

Converted to apartments in 1975, this lovingly detailed Renaissance Revival rockface, rusticated sandstone building continues to bear traces of its original mission, e.g., the frieze by *Rene Chambellan* illustrating the Foundation's work for the improvement of social and living conditions. Among early works of this philanthropic foundation was **Forest Hills Gardens.**

W35

W32

W33a

W36   W37

[W33a] **Calvary Church** (Episcopal), 273 Park Ave. S., NE cor. E.21st St. 1848. *James Renwick, Jr.*
[W33b] **The Sunday School Building,** to N on Park Ave. S. 1867. *James Renwick, Jr.*

Second-echelon *Renwick*, its wooden towers long since removed because of deterioration. The adjacent Sunday school pavilion is now rented as offices.

[W34] **Protestant Welfare Agencies Building**/originally **Church Missions' House,** 281 Park Ave. S., SE cor. E.22nd St. 1892-1894. *Robert W. Gibson and Edward J.N. Stent.* Restored, 1990s, *Kapell & Kastow.*
Cadaverous, deeply coffered, and filled with glass creating offices filled with natural light. From the **Flemish/Dutch Renaissance**.

[W37] **Mabel Dean Bacon Vocational High School**/originally **Manhattan Trade School For Girls,** 127-129 E.22nd St., NW cor. Lexington Ave. 1915. *C.B.J. Snyder.*

No nonsense here: 10 stories of loft space for vocational education. The exterior, however, displays some handsome terra-cotta detailing.

[W38] **150 East 22nd Street** (carriage house), bet. Lexington and Third Aves. 1893. *S.V. Stratton.*

A Dutch gable presents its stepped brickwork to the street, while behind a glass eruption sails skyward, bearing apartments. Nice deal for the developer's bank account; lousy deal for landmarks preservation.

STUYVESANT SQUARE
AND NORTH

[S1] **Stuyvesant Square Historic District**, generally including the Square, its entire frontage on
Rutherford Place, partial frontages on E.15th &
E.17th Sts., and parts of E.15th, E.16th, E.17th.,
and E.18th Sts., bet. Second & Third Aves. ☙

A complex area of widely mixed uses: row
houses on the side streets, churches on the
blocks facing the Square, hospitals outside the
district.

[S2] **Stuyvesant Square Park**/originally
Stuyvesant Square, Second Ave. bet. E.15th
and E.17th Sts., Rutherford and Nathan D.
Perlman Places. 1836. Reconstructed, 1936,
N.Y.C. Department of Parks.

A park in the London tradition of fenced
greenswards, here bisected by Second Avenue.
Note the statuary: **Peter G. Stuyvesant** (1936,
Gertrude Vanderbilt Whitney).

S3

[S3] **David B. Kriser Psychiatric Day
Treatment Program**/originally **Sidney
Webster House**, 245 E.17th St., bet. Second and
Third Aves. 1883. *Richard Morris Hunt.*

A brick and brownstone bow to an austere
phase of the **French Renaissance**. A beautifully
crafted understatement; old money well spent?

[S4] **Hazelden New York**/formerly **Salvation
Army**/originally **St. John the Baptist House**,
231-235 E.17th St., bet. Second and Third Aves.
E part, 1877, *Emlen T. Littel.* W part, 1883,
Charles C. Haight.

Picturesque, asymmetrical polychromatic
Victorian Gothic, pressing its case with pointed
arches.

[S5] **St. George's Church (Episcopal)**,
Rutherford Place, NW cor. E.16th St., facing
Stuyvesant Sq. 1846-1856. *Blesch & Eidlitz.* ☙
[S6] Originally **St.George Memorial House**, 207
E.16th St. 1886. *Cyrus L. W. Eidlitz.*

[S7] **St. George's Chapel**, 4 Rutherford
Place. 1911-1912. *Matthew Lansing Emery
and Henry George Emery.*
[S8] **Henry Hill Pierce House**/originally *St.
George's Rectory*, 209 E.16th St. Early 1850s.
Leopold Eidlitz.

J. P. Morgan's church: stolid brownstone
Romanesque Revival, bald and bold, cut and

S6

dressed. The adjacent chapel, outclassed by its
parent, is in an overdressed Eclectic-
Romanesque Revival. And around the corner
on 16th Street, Pierce House (now a condominium), a late medieval Germanic tower,
walled in rock-faced brownstone, punctuates
the streetscape.

[S9] **Friends Meeting House and Seminary**, 221
E.15th St. NW cor. Rutherford Place, facing
Stuyvesant Sq. 1860. *Charles T. Bunting.* ☙

Appropriately austere Quaker architecture, a
spartan image that spoke well to the era of austere modernist architecture. Here packaged in
red brick, brownstone quoins, and white trim.

[S10] **St. Mary's Catholic Church of the
Byzantine Rite**, 246 E.15th St., SW cor.
Second Ave. 1964. *Brother Cajetan J. B.
Baumann.*

A concrete and stained-glass box that glows
polychromatically on the nights it is lit within.

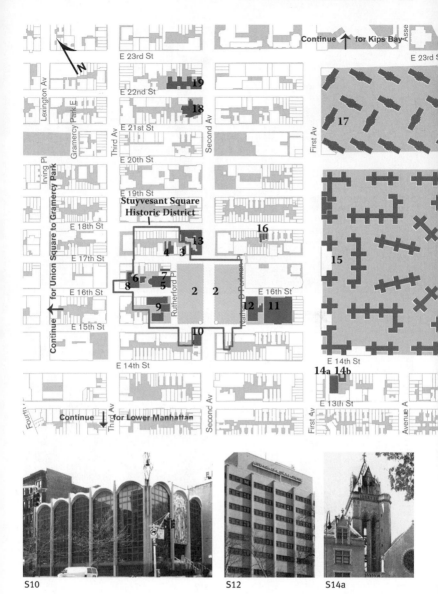

S10

S12   S14a

[S11] Former **Stuyvesant High School**, 345
E.15th St., bet. First and Second Aves. N side.
1905-1907. *C.B.J. Snyder.* 🌂
  Built for the City's prestige academic high
school, its admission by examination, its halls
are now filled with three independently operated special city schools.

[S12] Originally **New York Infirmary**/now
Bernstein Pavilion, Beth Israel Hospital,
Nathan D. Perlman Place, bet. E.15th and E.16th
Sts. E side. 1950. *Skidmore, Owings & Merrill.*
  Modernist architecture has become dated
more rapidly than that of any other period. Here
a bold 1950 "statement" seems a bore in retrospect. Alterations, of course, have dimmed its
elegant detailing: clunky windows have
replaced those of considerable style.

[S13] **305 Second Avenue**/originally **Lying-In
Hospital**, bet. E.17th and E.18th Sts. W side.
1902. *R. H. Robertson.* Converted, 1985, *Beyer
Blinder Belle.*

  Swaddled babies lurk in laurel wreaths in
the spandrels. Otherwise this bland **neo-
Renaissance** block is boring until the top, where
a Palladian crown surmounts it all. Architects at
the turn of the 20th century, concerned about
the idea of a New York skyline, often neglected
the pedestrian, spending all their efforts and
money against the sky. *Robertson* did it often:
compare his **American Tract Society** and **Park
Row** buildings in Civic Center.

[S14a] **Immaculate Conception Church**
(Roman Catholic)/originally **Grace Chapel
and Dispensary** (Episcopal), 406-412 E.14th St.,
bet. First Ave. and Avenue A. 1894-1896. *Barney
& Chapman.* 🌂
  These François I–style buildings, built as an
outpost of **Grace Church**, were purchased by
the Roman Catholic archdiocese in 1943. Their
picturesque forms might be found in the Loire
Valley as well as those of their uptown descendant, **Holy Trinity**, in Yorkville.

S9

S18

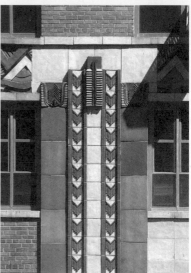

S19

[S14b] **Clergy Houses of the Church of the Immaculate Conception**/originally **Grace Hospital**, 414 E. 14th St. 1894-1896. *Barney and Chapman.* 🍎

Six brick and stone clergy houses in French Renaissance Eclectic with an air of refined elegance resembling a small French château.

[S15] **Stuyvesant Town**, E.14th to E.20th Sts., First Ave. to FDR Drive/Avenue C. 1947. *Irwin Clavan and Gilmore Clarke.* Altered, 2008, *CetraRuddy.*

Tax abatement allowed this Metropolitan Life Insurance Company project to supply middle-income housing to servicemen returning from World War II. The early brutality of this huge, dense (8,755 families) project is now softened by trees. Innocuous architecture, but, nevertheless, landscaping has made it a pleasant place.

[S16] **326, 328, and 330 East 18th Street**, bet. First and Second Aves. 1853. 🍎

Deep front yards have caused this tiny trio to be overlooked but certainly not neglected;

the charming original cast-iron work is reminiscent of New Orleans. An early development for land east of Third Avenue here leased from *Cornelia Stuyvesant Ten Broeck.*

[S17] **Peter Cooper Village**, E.20th to E.23rd Sts., First Ave. to FDR Drive. 1947. *Irwin Clavan and Gilmore Clarke.*

More space and more rent make this the rich stepbrother of Stuyvesant Town.

[S18] **Church of the Epiphany**, 373 Second Ave., bet. E.21st and E.22nd Sts. W side. 1967. *Belfatto & Pavarini.*

Highly styled brown brick: this is the phoenix of a 19th-century church on this site destroyed by fire. A positive modern religious statement for Manhattan.

[S19] **Gramercy House**, 235 E.22nd St., NW cor. Second Ave. 1929-1930. *George & Edward Blum.*

An **Art Deco** frieze bands this early modern apartment house in glazed terra cotta.

ROSE HILL

A precinct seeking a name; 23rd to 32nd Street, Madison to Third.

[B1] Madison Square Station, U. S. Post Office, 149 E.23rd St., bet. Lexington and Third Aves. 1937. *Lorimer Rich,* architect. *Louis A. Simon,* Supervising Architect of the Treasury.

A cool, stripped **Classical** building in polished dark red granite that was, surprisingly, the idiom of 1930s Washington, *Albert Speer's* 1939 Berlin, and the revived memory of the mortuary temple of *Queen Hatshepsut* at Deir el Bahari (1500 B.C.). Plus ça change.

[B2] William and Anita Newman Vertical Campus, Baruch College, E.24th to E.25th St., Lexington Ave. E side. 2000. *Kohn Pedersen Fox.*

A mega-mammoth for the complex functions of an urban college; another unit of the City University keeping up with City College's **North Academic Center** (which *Pedersen* designed in the offices of *John Carl Warnecke*) and *Ulrich Franzen's* East and West Buildings for **Hunter College.** A colossal cruise ship beached, its mini-city components stashed in a dizzying and magnificent interplay of vertical interlocking spaces flooded with light (a 10-story atrium).

|B3| **William and Anita Newman Library and Conference Center,** Newman Library and

B3   B4

Technology Center, Baruch College/originally **Lexington Building** (cable-car power station), 151 E. 25th St., bet. Lexington and Third Aves. 1895. *G.B. Waite.* Remodeled as library, 1994, *Davis Brody Bond.*

Roman brick and grand arches present Baruch's books in a properly monumental container. *DBB* has inserted a high-tech interior that has become the resident hermit crab with a five-story atrium, illuminated by a great skylight.

[B4] Originally B.W. Mayer Building/ now **Friends House,** 130 E.25th St. SW cor. Lexington Ave. 1915-1916. *Herman Lee Meader.* Restored, 1995-1996, *Cindy Harden & Jan Van Arnam.*

A rich terra-cotta façade by the architect of the amazing **Cliff Dwellers' Apartments** on Riverside Drive at West 96th Street. Now a Quaker-sponsored community for people living with AIDS. Coiled snakes and cattle skulls lurk about the second floor.

[B5] Originally **"I Love You Kathy" Apartments,** 160 E.26th St., SW cor. Third Ave. Altered, 1975, *Stephen B. Jacobs.*

Stuccoed sculpture. Here what are normally visually negative ideas—open metal fire escapes—are translated into form that enriches the building.

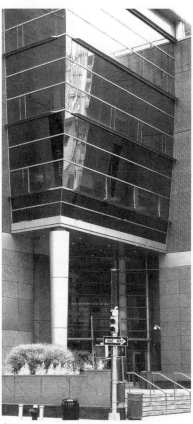

B2

[B6] Originally **69th Regiment Armory, N. Y. National Guard,** 68 Lexington Ave., bet. E.25th and E.26th Sts. W side. 1904-1906. *Richard Howland Hunt and Joseph Howland Hunt.* 🍎

The armory of the **Armory Show of 1913,** the bombshell entry of cubist painting to America (*Picasso, Cézanne, Braque, Gaugin, Van Gogh, Matisse* were all there, but the show was stolen by *Marcel Duchamp's* "Nude Descending a Staircase;" *President Roosevelt* called the show's exhibitors "a bunch of lunatics"). A brick, mansarded palace with gun bays surveying Lexington. The drill hall behind the Lexington Avenue façade shows its barrel form to the street, ribbed and buttressed with an exposed, articulated structure.

[B7] St. Stephen's Church (Roman Catholic), 149 E.28th St., bet. Lexington and Third Aves. 1854. *James Renwick, Jr.* Extended to N, 1865, *Patrick Charles Keely.* Restored, 1949. **School,** ca. 1902, *Elliott Lynch.*

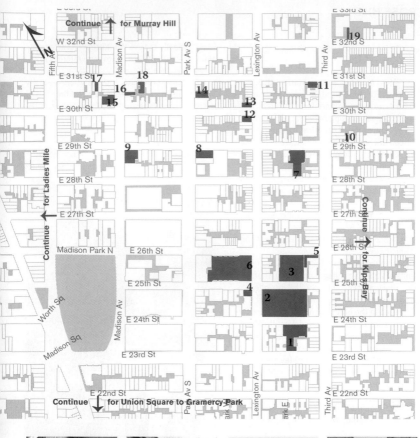

B5

B6

B9

B10

Brownstone **Romanesque Revival** and within, an airy hall, its slender cast-iron (plaster encased) columns with elaborate foliated capitals support multiribbed vaulting. There is a mural by *Constantino Brumidi,* "decorator" of the **Capitol** in Washington. Unfortunately, the whole has been smoothed over in brownstone-colored stucco. Too smooth.

[B8] **Bowker Building,** 419 Park Ave. S., SE cor. E.29th St. 1927. *Walter Haefli* in the office of *Ely Jacques Kahn.*

A strange multihued, almost phosphorescent, terra-cotta-clad building. Its dark polychromy suggests an unknown Islamic Industrial style. In fact, it is but one of *Kahn's* office's broad-ranging experiments into **Art Deco** cum modernism. See, elsewhere in this book, contrasting stylistic experiments: the **Film Center** and former **Squibb Buildings**.

[B9] **Emmet Building,** 89-95 Madison Ave., SE cor. E.29th St. 1912. *J. Stewart Barney and Stockton B. Colt, associated architects.*

A terra-cotta **neo-Renaissance** confection, perhaps inspired by the **Woolworth Building**. Note particularly the canopied cavaliers and courtesans atop the first floor. Atop the top, where detail has gone wild and window bays are vast, *Dr. Emmet*, its gynecologist-owner, maintained an apartment.

[B10] **203 East 29th Street,** bet. Second and Third Aves. ca. 1790. (carriage house). 1870 (house*)*. *James Cali,* architect. *John Sanguiliano,* restoration architect.

Connecticut in Manhattan. A rare wood framed house in the Manhattan streetscape—not hidden in some out-of-the-way backyard, a grand island to inhabit, like a landed craft of Litchfield County aliens.

[B11] **Kips Bay Branch, New York Public Library,** 446 Third Ave., SW cor. E.31st St. 1971. *Giorgio Cavaglieri.*

Sculptured architecture as a corner-turner on Third Avenue. Just enough of a widened

B7

[B12] **First Moravian Church**/originally **Rose Hill Baptist Church**, 154 Lexington Ave., SW cor. E.30th St. 1849.

This self-assured plain brick box presents tall, narrow, half-round arched windows to the street, its gable end reinforced by arched corbel tables, from the **Lombardian Romanesque** . A noted early organ, by *Henry Erben* (1840) built for the French Episcopal Church of St. Esprit, is the prize within.

[B13] Formerly **Touro College**, Lexington Avenue Campus/onetime **Pratt-New York Phoenix School of Design**/originally **New York School of Applied Design for Women**, 160 Lexington Ave., NW cor. E.30th St. 1908-1909. *Harvey Wiley Corbett.*

In 1892, *Ellen Dunlap Hopkins*, an affluent painter, founded a school to train women for careers in art and architecture. *Corbett*, an instructor, and partner in the firm of *Pell & Corbett*, designed this tour de force for it, a **neo-Roman** design, a veritable 20th-century

B13

B15

sidewalk to invite its users to enter. The late *Cavaglieri* here showed his modern thoughts in contrast to his brilliant historic preservations (cf., **Jefferson Market Library**, for example.).

Curry Hill: from Lexington to Third Avenue, between approximately 28th and 31st Streets, is a mini-bazaar of foods, fabrics, and other delicacies from the Far East. **Kalustyan's Orient Trading**, *123 Lexington bet. 28th & 29th, with an upstairs deli and Manhattan's most diverse spice store on the first floor, is famous among epicureans. Other cheap, aromatic nooks include* **Tibetan Kitchen**, *444 Third Ave bet. 30th & 31st, and* **Jaiya**, *396 Third bet. 28th & 29th.*

Old Print Shop, 150 Lexington Ave., bet. E.29th and E.30th Sts. W side.

Appropriately humble, like the rich wearing old clothes (or is it reverse snobbery?), a mine of maps and prints, from modest to very expensive. See some old **New York buildings**, *in print, if not in place.*

temple to the arts. Note the witty, single polished gray marble column (in antis) on the Lexington Avenue façade.

[B14] **Raymond R. Corbett Building**/originally **Iron Workers Security Funds**, 451 Park Ave. S., bet. E.30th and E.31st Sts. E side. Altered, 1978. Addition, 1988, *Susana Torre of Wank, Adams, Slavin & Assocs.*

This **Cor-Ten** building (rusty steel meant to be rusty) expanded upward, with a new façade worthy of the union leader for whom it was renamed.

[B15] **American Academy of Dramatic Arts**/originally **The Colony Club**, 120 Madison Ave., bet. E.30th and E.31st Sts. W side. 1904-1908. *Stanford White of McKim, Mead & White.* Original interiors, *Elsie de Wolfe*, designer.

Georgian-Federal Revival seems appropriately not-so-fancy dress for venerably connected and socially prominent ladies. The brickwork is unusual, with the headers (short ends) facing out. *Stanford White*, its designer, succumbed to an assassin during its construction—only three blocks away, and it certainly wasn't one of these ladies who was the assassin's wife.

[B16] **m127 Apartments**, 127 Madison Ave, bet. 30th and 31st Sts. E side. 2007. *SHoP architects.*

SHoP is becoming known for interesting, well-detailed blending of old (masonry) and new (glass). Here the glass protrudes from the old façade like rearview mirrors on a Maserati. See also their **Porter House**, at 366 15th Street, in Chelsea, and for façade comparisons, the **Switch Building**, 109 Norfolk Street, bet. Broome and Delancey, by *nArchitects.* (nNot a typo.)

[B17] **22 East 31st Street**, bet. Fifth and Madison Aves. 1914. *Israels & Harder.*

A mannered **Georgian Revival** town house with—surprise!—seven stories, and extra-

B16

ordinary lintels, composed of dramatically radiating voussoirs.

[B18] **Madison Avenue Baptist Church Parish House**, 30 E.31st St., bet. Madison Ave. and Park Ave. S. 1906.

An offbeat gem in brick and limestone. Middle Eastern motifs decorate the spandrels of its **Romanesque Revival** body. Atop it all a copper cornice forms an overhanging eave supported by exotic brackets.

[B19] **Milton Glaser, Inc.** (design studio)/ originally **Tammany Central Association Clubhouse**, 207 E.32nd St., bet. Second and Third Aves. ca. 1910.

Beaux Arts pomp and circumstance, orphaned when its row-house neighbors were removed for an apartment house plaza and schoolyard. Sophisticated modern graphic design evolves within.

*Baseball's beginnings: A plaque once affixed at the southeast corner of Lexington Avenue and 34th Street stated that at this site **Alexander Joy Cartwright, Jr.**, organized the first baseball game played in America using most of the rules governing today.*

B18

Stables on site of Baruch Vertical Campus

NECROLOGY

Stables on the site of the Baruch Vertical Campus: Bowstring arches cleared spanning space for horses and their maneuvers.

UNBUILT

400 Park Avenue South, cor. 28th St. 2011. *Christian de Portzamparc & Gary E. Handel.*

Ephemeral shapes from *de Portzamparc's* drawings promised some Park Avenue fantasies, but the recession has cut them short. They might blossom if the developers could only find some of that **ephemeral capital** that vanished in the recession.

KIPS BAY

From 23rd to 34th Streets between Second Avenue and the East River.

[K1] **East Midtown Plaza**, E.23rd to E.25th Sts., bet. First and Second Aves. 1972, 1974. All by *Davis, Brody & Assocs.*

Urbane street architecture, with the terraces of Babylon. This is an ode to brick, cut, carved, notched, and molded. The balcony-terraces are containers of architectural space and givers of form, rather than the common "luxury apartment" paste-ons. Powerful, with great style, rather than stylish. The best of what is now called *Davis Brody Bond*.

[K2] **Public Baths**, City of New York, E.23rd St., NE cor. Asser Levy Place, bet. First Ave. and FDR Drive. 1904-1906. *Arnold W. Brunner and William Martin Aiken*. Restored, 1989-1990, Department of Parks.

K1

[K4] **Waterside**, FDR Drive bet. E.25th and E.30th Sts. E side. 1974. *Davis, Brody & Assocs.*

Brown towers of **cut and carved cubism** mounted on a platform tucked in a notch of the East River. Sixteen hundred units, shopping, restaurants, and pedestrian plazas give a share of Manhattan's glorious waterfront back to the people. Wander about, and to the water's edge.

K4

K2

K3

Roman pomp was particularly appropriate for a public bath, a Roman building type we reproduced indiscriminately for other functions (cf. the now demolished Pennsylvania Station modeled on the Baths of Caracalla). These public baths are, in that sense, our **Baths of Roosevelt** (Teddy) or, on a local level, **Baths of McClellan** (mayor of New York). Free-standing columns flank two entrances—one for each sex—surmounted by a full entablature, frieze and urns.

[K3] **United Nations International School**, 24-50 FDR Drive, opp. E.25th St. S of Waterside. 1973. *Harrison, Abramovitz & Harris.*

A heavy-handed, precast-concrete construction hugging the East River shore and Waterside; an illogical site for students in need of large-volume public transportation.

[K5] **The Water Club**, 500 E.30th St. at the East River. 1982. *Michael O' Keeffe*, owner-designer; *Clement J. Benvenga and Mullen Palandrani*, architects. *M. Paul Friedberg*, landscape architect.

A pseudo-nautical structure using traditional bent-metal materials from which its wharf predecessors—alas, largely demolished—were often crafted. Popular with the "enjoy dinner with a view of Newtown Creek across the river" set. But Newtown Creek, since the Fourth Edition of this Guide, has become a center of handsome architecture and environmental design. See *Polshek's* **Newtown Creek Wastewater Treatment Plant** and its park surroundings.

[K6] **Bellevue Hospital Center**, E.26th to E.28th Sts., First Ave. to FDR Drive. 1908-1939. *McKim, Mead & White.* [K6a] **Psychiatric Hospital**, *Charles B. Meyers and Thompson, Holmes & Converse.*

Its original brick hulk is now squeezed between the parking garage addition on First Avenue and a monster 22-story "wing" facing the river. The top floors and roof contain its only serious architectural embellishments: Roman brick, Corinthian columns, and pitched tile roofs. "**Belle Vue**" was the name of *Peter Keteltas'* farm, which occupied this site in the 18th century.

K14

[K7a] **Bellevue Hospital Ambulatory Care Facility**, First Avenue bet. E.27th and E. 28th Sts. 2005. *Pei Cobb Freed & Partners.*
  Sleek. A glassy 300-foot-long atrium connects this new facility to the *McKim, Mead and White* façade beyond. The original **Bellevue** entrance arch, built in 1736, is visible from the street. That arch briefly stood guard on First Avenue during construction. (1995, *Lee Harris Pomeroy.*)

[K7b] **ACS Children's Center,** 492 First Ave. SE cor. E.29th St. 1907-1912. *McKim, Mead & White.* Renovated for ACS, 2001, *Dattner Architects.*

K10

K7b

K8

Vacant for 20 years, this *McKim, Mead and White* unit was part of the original **Bellevue** complex. Rebuilt within, and newly canopied without, it is a facility of New York City's Administration for Children's Services (**ACS**).

[K8] **New Building, Bellevue Hospital**, E.27th to E.28th Sts. 1974. *Katz, Waisman, Weber, Strauss; Joseph Blumenkranz; Pomerance & Breines; Feld & Timoney.* Parking garage, 1965.
  New? It was, in 1974, but retains that title as the **behemoth**. Each floor is 1-1/2 acres of loft space served by 20 elevators. A tall beige cube when you drive by on the FDR Drive. No pomp and circumstance here, but, as a pedestrian, you enter through the 2005 "new" *Pei Cobb Fried* entrance above.

[K9] Original **Mount Sinai-N.Y.U Medical Center**/now **Langone Medical Center**, behind Skirball Institute, bet. E.30th and E.34th Sts. E side to FDR Drive. 1950. *Skidmore, Owings & Merrill.* Additions through 1977.

A teaching hospital can attract staff and faculty of the highest stature. They are provided for here in a facility complementing Bellevue Hospital, designed in a single master plan by **SOM**, and constructed over more than 25 years. White glazed brick and aluminum sash.

[K10] **Skirball Institute of Biomolecular Medicine**, part of **Langone** (formerly Mount Sinai-N.Y.U.) **Medical Center,** 540 First Ave., bet. 32nd and 33rd Sts. 1992. *Polshek Partnership.*
  The multipurpose slab that serves as entrance to the whole medical complex. Above the vast lobby are five floors of bio-molecular research topped by 20 floors of faculty offices and staff apartments. Behind, the various elder components of the complex unfold.

[K11] **Kips Bay Plaza**, E.30th to E.33rd Sts., First to Second Aves. S Building, 1960. N Building, 1965. *I.M. Pei & Assocs. and S.J. Kessler.*

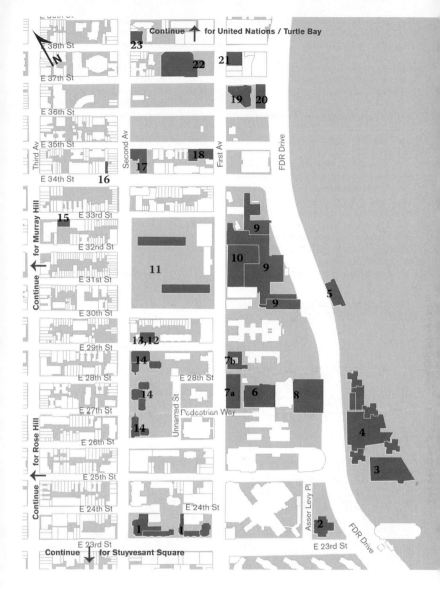

Continue ↑ for United Nations / Turtle Bay

Stepchildren of *Le Corbusier's* **Marseilles Block**, giant and beautifully detailed concrete buildings in a park. New York's first exposed concrete apartment houses, joined soon after by **Chatham Towers** (1965. *Kelly & Gruzen*) and Pei's own **University Plaza** (1966). Concrete was a common building material in the postwar era, but was replaced by stone, usually granite, in the buildings of the 1980s and 1990s, and then by fritted glass, aluminum, and steel in the 2000s. Compared to the thinness and transparency of a typical 21st-century apartment tower, these look rooted, confident, and permanent.

[K12] **Churchill School and Center,** originally **Madison Square Boys and Girls Club,** 30 E. 29th St., bet. First and Second Aves. 1940. *Holden, McLaughlin & Assocs.* Expansion and sur-elevation, 2000, *Paul Segal Associates.*

A handsome, no-nonsense early modern building in salmon brick, with a dado of shining black-glazed tile, now expanded and sur-elevated for the Churchill School. It was nicer smaller.

[K13] **Churchill School and Center Garden**/former **Pinkerton Environmental Center,** Madison Square Boys & Girls Club, 524-528 Second Ave., NE cor. E.29th St. 1979. *Wank, Adams & Slavin,* architects. *Zion & Breen,* landscape architects.

A lovely garden that used to be public. Not anymore.

[K14] **Phipps Plaza**, Second Ave. bet. E.26th and E.29th Sts. E side. 1976. *Frost Assocs.*

High-rise red brick that caught some styling from East Midtown Plaza to the south. Polygonal diagonal. But it fails to honor any street, as does East Midtown's glorious bow to 23rd.

[K15] **Public School 116,** 210 E.33rd St., bet. Second and Third Aves. 1925. *William H. Gompert.*

Neo-Romanesque brick, terra cotta, and sandstone. A lovely cornice hovers over multiple arches, both in terra cotta. Whimsical figures support arches over the "Boy's" and "Girl's" entrances.

[K16] Originally **Civic Club**/now **Estonian House**, 243 E.34th St., bet. Second and Third Aves. 1898-1899. *Thomas A. Gray.* ●

A lonely limestone and terra-cotta Beaux Arts town house commissioned by philanthropist *F. Norton Goddard.* The bull's-eye windows at the mansard roof almost ogle.

[K17] **St. Vartan Cathedral of the Armenian Orthodox Church** in America, 630 Second Ave., bet. E.34th and E.35th Sts. E side. 1967. *Steinmann & Cain.*

A very large (to accommodate cathedral-sized congregations) and simplified version of early Romanesque Armenian churches in Asia Minor. Its austere exterior makes it seem without scale: huge close up, puny in the distance.

[K18] **Permanent Mission of the People's Republic of China to the U.N.**, 350 E.35th St., SW cor. First Ave. 1990s.

Chinese modern in two-tone polished

K21

granite. The canopy is an elegant modern version of the 19th-century Parisian marquise.

[K19] **Manhattan Place**, 630 First Ave., bet. E.36th and E.37th St. E side. 1984. *Costas Kondylis of Philip Birnbaum & Assocs.* Plaza, 1984, *Thomas Balsley Assocs.*, landscape architects.

A giant bay-windowed brick winged-slab forcefully turned on the bias, creating a triangular fountained plaza. Glitzy polished brass adorns the first few floors; dark anodized aluminum clads the penthouse level (as though the budget for glitz ran out).

[K20] **The Horizon**, 415 E.37th St., bet. First Ave. and FDR Drive, to E.38th St. 1988. *Costas Kondylis of Philip Birnbaum & Assocs.*

A hard-edged neighbor to the Corinthian, but even closer to the river.

[K21] Originally **Kips Bay Brewing Company**, 660 First Ave., bet. E.37th and E.38th Sts. E side. ca. 1895. Additions.

Its colorful posters once boasted of lager beer, ales, and porter with views of the curious mansarded cupolas that corner the roof. Brewing has disappeared here; substantial floors once meant for mash cookers and brew kettles now serve as outposts of the Medical Center.

The East Midtown Leviathans
Not a rock group, but apartment towers gone wild: taller, wider, overwhelming the streets and the river's edge. Their awkward entities seem to have evolved from real estate accounting confronting zoning and building laws, rather than good urban and building design with a plaza thrown in to assuage the slavering citizens. The Corinthian, however, stands above the fray, with style, rather than its neighbors frumpery.

▇ [K22] **The Corinthian**, 645 First Ave., bet. E.37th and E.38th Sts. W side. 1987. *Der Scutt,* design architect. *Michael Schimenti,* architect.

A fluted tower presents myriad round bay windows. Here *Scutt* has excelled his neighbors and brought high style to the riverside.

And further west:

[K23] **The Whitney** (apartments), 311 E.38th St., bet. Second Ave. and the Queens-Midtown Tunnel access road. 1986. *Liebman Liebman Assoc.*

K16   K23

Smoothly syncopated balconies with alternating curved and straight edges give this yellow brick slab style.

UNBUILT, BUT INEVITABLE

Con Ed Development Site. 30th to 41st Street, bet. First Ave, and FDR Drive. 2015? *SOM + Richard Meier.*

Developer **Sheldon Solow's** ambitious plan proposes to build seven towers south of the United Nations along the East River, with over five million square feet of residential, commercial, and retail space.

K22

Diamond and Jewelry Way

Continue ↑ for Times Square / Columbus Circle   Continue ↑ for Fifth Avenue Swath

Duffy Sq

N

W 47th St
E 47th St
W 46th St
E 46th St
W 45th St
E 45th St
Times Sq
72
65 71 70
W 44th St
E 44th St
Vanderbilt Av
66 69 60
67 68
64 63 62
W 43rd St
E 43rd St
55 61 58 59
54 56 57
W 42nd St
E 42nd St
Broadway
52 51
W 41st St
E 41st St
Madison Av
50 45
W 40th St
E 40th St
44
53 49 48 47 46 b
43
a
W 39th St
E 39th St
42
40
41
W 38th St
E 38th St
W 37th St
E 37th St
38 39
36 37
35
W 36th St
E 36th St
Seventh Av / Fashion Av
Sixth Av
34
W 35th St
E 35th St
Fifth Av
Continue
29 26 33
W 34th St
E 34th St
Herald Sq
for Murray Hill
30 28 32
27 31
W 33rd St
Greely Sq
24
25 23 22
E 33rd St
W 32nd St
Broadway
21
20
W 32nd St
19 18
17
W 31st St
16 15 E 31st St
13
W 30th St
14 12 10 11
W 29th St E 29th St
8
7
6
Seventh Av
5 9
1 Madison Square North
Historic District
E 27th St
4 3
2a 2b
W 26th St Madison Park N E 26th St
W 25th St E 25th St
Seventh Av
W 25th St
Madison
Square
W 24th St Park
Madison Av
E 24th St
Continue ↓ for Ladies Mile W 24th St
Worth Sq
Madison Sq
E 23rd St

MADISON SQUARE TO BRYANT PARK

Starting at the north side of Madison Square. The N and R (old BMT) trains dock at 28th Street and Broadway; the former IRT line (No.6 train) at 28th and Park Avenue South.

[Q1] **Madison Square North Historic District**, a wandering boundary including much of Fifth Avenue and Broadway between much of 26th and 28th Streets, and those streets themselves. ☙

[Q2a] **Croisic Building**, 220 Fifth Ave., NW cor. W.26th St. 1905-1907. *Frederick C. Browne. Rudolph H. Almiroty*, associate architect.

At the top a richly ornamented brick and terra-cotta neo-Gothic confection—watch those architectural calories: dormered, arched, with thrusting dragon gargoyles. It stands on the site of another earlier Croisic apartment hotel.

Q2a

[Q2b] **Brunswick Building**, 225 Fifth Avenue, bet. W.26th and W.27th Sts. E side. 1906-1907. *Francis H. Kimball.*

The new marquise (canopy in the French Belle Epoque fashion) brings attention back to this Renaissance Revival block; the bracketed balconies at the 11th floor join with a powerful projecting cornice to sturdily crown it all.

[Q3] **222 Fifth Avenue** (lofts), bet. W.26th and W.27th Sts. W side. New façade, 1912. *John C. Westervelt.*

Originally a house, converted to a store and dwelling in 1883. *Westervelt's* new façade provided a bayed blend of metal and glass with a Classical limestone enframement.

An aside to Sixth Avenue:

[Q4] **Coogan Building**/originally Racket Court Club, 776 Sixth Ave., NE cor. W.26th St. 1876. *Alfred H. Thorp.*

Dour eclectic Romanesque Revival with a cornice supported by filigreed iron brackets. *Coogan*, incidentally, is the *Coogan* of **Coogan's Bluff,** the escarpment that overlooked the old New York Giants' Polo Grounds (now replaced by housing projects).

Back to Fifth:

[Q5] **242 Fifth Avenue,** bet. W.27th and W.28th Sts. W side. Cast-iron front, 1885. *George Harding.*

A triumphant pediment crowns this glass and sheet-metal precursor of the post–World War II curtain wall. The ground floor succumbed to "renovation." Look up at the intact *Harding* design of 1885.

[Q6] **Baudouine Building**, 1181 Broadway, SW cor. W.28th St. 1895-1896. *Alfred Zucker.*

A sliver with a meticulous Ionic-columned Roman temple on top. Peer upward.

[Q7] **Broadway National Bank**/originally **Second National Bank**/then **National City Bank of New York**, 250 Fifth Avenue, NW cor. W.28th St. 1908. *W.S. Richardson of McKim, Mead & White.*

One of the few *McKim, Mead & White* small banking buildings (compare with the one at 55 Wall Street). No great shakes, it is in naively proportioned limestone, but with a jolly cornice. *Stanford White*, not involved in this one, had been assassinated in 1906.

Q6   Q3   Q5

[Q8] **256 Fifth Avenue**, bet. W.28th and W.29th Sts. W side. 1893. *Alfred Zucker and John Edelman.* ☙

A Venetian-Gothic phantasmagoria in terra cotta, with Moorish overtones, but way above the commercialized ground floor.

[Q9] **Prince George Hotel and Ballroom**, 14 E.28th St., bet. Fifth and Madison Aves. 1904-1905, 1912-1913. *Howard Greenley.* ☙ Renovations, 2000, *Beyer Blinder Belle.*

Elliptical arched windows punctuate the rusticated limestone base. Within, its colossal ballroom dazzles with a blinding polychromy of gold, red and blue. Ballroom columns are of *Mr. Greenley's* own bizarre order, where the lower part of the shafts have been said to look suspiciously like radiators.

Q14, former Gilsey House Hotel

[Q10] **Church of the Transfiguration** (Episcopal)/**"The Little Church around the Corner"** (Episcopal), 1 E.29th St., bet. Fifth and Madison Aves. Church, Rectory, 1849-1850. Guildhall, 1852. 1849-1850. Unknown architect(s). Lych Gate, 1896, *Frederick Clarke Withers.* Lady Chapel, 1906, Mortuary Chapel, 1908. ●⚲

A picturesque English village church, reincarnated in the Manhattan grid, now crushed by Skyhouse next door. Its notorious nickname has stuck since 1870, when a fashionable local pastor declined to officiate at the funeral of *George Holland*, an actor, and suggested that the obsequies be held at the "little church around the corner." It has been a church for those in the theater ever since. Of a charming small scale, it has a delightful garden.

[Q11] **Skyhouse**, 11 E. 29th St., bet. Fifth and Madison Aves. 2009. *FxFowle.*

A sleek 55 stories overwhelming the gentle architecture and landscape of the adjacent "Little Church around the Corner." *FxFowle*

Q10

used brick of a similar violet hue in an effort to "blend in" with the church. Agree?

[Q12] **Marble Collegiate Church** (Dutch Reformed), 1 W.29th St., NW cor. Fifth Ave. 1851-1854. *Samuel A. Warner.* ●⚲

Sharp-edged limestone Gothic Revival, contemporary with Grace and Trinity Churches. Clean planes give elegant shade and shadow to the street. Architecturally modest, Marble Collegiate is most remembered for its former pastor, *Norman Vincent Peale*, whose many books tried to meld popular religion with popular psychology. *Richard Nixon* attended this church in his lawyer days, between his roles as vice president and president.

*Holland House: The loft building at the southwest corner of Fifth Avenue and West 30th Street is the old and famous **Holland House Hotel**, spruced up in the early 1920s for use as a mercantile establishment. In its original*

*incarnation (1891, Harding & Gooch) its opulent interior was adorned with marble, brocade, and lace, and the hotel was considered the peer of any in the world. Its suites were patterned on those of **Lord Holland's mansion** in London.*

[Q13] **835 Sixth Avenue**, bet. 29th and 30th Sts., W side. 2010. *Perkins Eastman.*

A sleek new hotel/condominium.

[Q14] Originally **Gilsey House Hotel**, 1200 Broadway, NE cor. W.29th St. 1869-1871. *Stephen D. Hatch.* ●⚲

A *General Grant* Second Empire eclectic extravaganza, columned and mansarded, with the vigor that only the waning years of the 19th century could muster. Cast iron (*Daniel Badger Iron Works*) and stone. O happy the day it was in 1992 when the façade was restored and painted cream!

[Q15] Originally **S.J.M. Building**/now **The Cass Gilbert**, 130 W.30th St., bet. Sixth and Seventh Aves. 1927. *Cass Gilbert.* ●⚲

Q12

Q16

Assyrian Revival? An early bronze and glass curtain wall embraced by a pair of masonry elevator towers. Figures in Mesopotanian friezes race around the walls of the building at each setback. And, over the two entrances, stylized symmetrical lions glare in polychromed terra-cotta bas-relief. *Gilbert*, architect of the Woolworth Building, is here remembered for a minor work (necessary for those pesky monthly bills).

[Q16] Originally **23rd Precinct, N.Y.C. Police Department**/now **Traffic Control Division**, 134-138 W.30th St., bet. Sixth and Seventh Aves. 1907-1908. *R. Thomas Short.* ●⚲

Battlements, merlons, embrasures, crenellations—a fortress out of place among loft buildings but serving the area by contribution of wit to a midtown canyon.

[Q17] **Wilbraham Building**, 1 W.30th St. and 284 Fifth Ave., NW cor. W.30th St. 1890. *D. & J. Jardine*. 🌣

Brownstone and brick, with a bit of cast iron: Belle Epoque crowned with a verdigris copper roof, it is one of the earliest settlers on Fifth Avenue. Here the Brown Decades that preceded the Great White City of the 1893 Chicago World's Fair were still exuding their somewhat murky medievalism, but propped up by Classical composite cast-iron columns and limestone piers. Lovely and lusty.

[Q18] **Wolcott Hotel**, 4-10 W.31st St., bet. Fifth Ave. and Broadway. 1904. *John Duncan*.

A lavish French Empire bay-windowed façade—carved, corniced, and mansard-roofed; the style conceals a white and gilt lobby that is both flamboyant and sad.

[Q19] Originally **Grand Hotel**, 1232-1238 Broadway, SE cor. W.31st St. 1868. *Henry Engelbert*. 🌣

[Q20] **Herald Square Hotel**/originally **Life Building**, 19 W.31st St., bet. Fifth Ave. and Broadway. 1894. *Carrère & Hastings*.

This ornate Classical façade once enclosed the offices of the very literate humor magazine *Life* (from which the present Time-Life organization bought the name in 1936). Visible mementos include the inscriptions "wit" and "humor" and a pattern of L's back to back on handsome iron balconies. Some gross alterations mar the cornice and windows.

[Q21] **Kaskel & Kaskel Building**, 316 Fifth Ave., SW cor. W.32nd St. 1903. *Charles L. Berg*.

Crusty old **Beaux Arts**, in the process of being devoured by its crummy commercial occupants. But a copper-clad mansard roof keeps a hat on what is deteriorating at street level.

[Q22] **Best Western Hotel**/originally **Hotel Aberdeen**, 17 W.32nd St., bet. Fifth Ave. and Broadway. 1902-1904. *Harry B. Mulliken*. 🌣

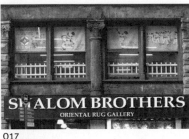

Q17

Q18

Q19

Q22

Two blocks from **Gilsey**, this renewed neighbor is simpler, but its mansarded hat gives it a strong posture on this street. See above.

In the 1870s and 1880s the whole section of the W.20s and W.30s between the respectability of Fifth Avenue and the slums of **Hell's Kitchen** *(west of Seventh Avenue), was anointed as New York's* **"Tenderloin."** *Present Herald Square was at its center. Dance halls and cafés lined up under the El along Sixth Avenue, with bordellos on the shady side streets, all flourishing under Tammany Hall's political machine. A brief period of reform in the 1890s dimmed the gaiety of the Tenderloin, and its lush facilities slowly faded away. Both the theater and the press (such as James Gordon Bennett's New York Herald) made brief stops at Herald Square in the 1890s on their way north—leaving behind one of two squares with newspaper names.*

The Parisians would call it **Pompier** (or Fireman Style), after the ornate boulevard façades of the 1890s: neo-Baroque Composite columns support carving worthy of (but different from) **Churrigueresque Spanish Colonial America** (South, that is).

[Q23] **Radisson Hotel**/formerly **Hotel Martinique**, 53 W.32nd St. (also known as 1260-1266 Broadway), NE cor. Broadway. 1897-1898, 1901-1903. Enlarged with annex, 1907-1911. All by *Henry J. Hardenbergh*. 🌣

An opulent French Renaissance pile, topped with several stories of mansards; the south façade is the real front. For years a notorious shelter for the homeless, now reclaimed for the middle-class tourist.

[Q24] **Wilson Building**, 1270-1280 Broadway, bet. 32nd and 33rd Sts. E side. 1911-1912. *Rouse & Goldstone*.

The arcade and cornice at the roof are an elegant crown for the rusticated body below.

[Q25] **Greeley Square**, intersection of Sixth Ave. and Broadway, bet. W.32nd and W.33rd Sts. Established as Greeley Square, 1894.

Horace Greeley, founder of the **New York Tribune**, is remembered by this island triangle and a statue (1890, *Alexander Doyle*). His newspaper later combined with the *Herald*, remembered two blocks north.

[Q26] **Herald Square**, intersection of Sixth Ave. and Broadway bet. W.34th and W.35th Sts.

Q24

Minerva, the Bellringers, and Owls, 1895. *Antonin Jean Carles,* sculptor. Plaza, 1939-1940, *Aymar Embury II.*

Namesake of the **New York Herald**, whose two-story palazzo (1893, *McKim, Mead & White*) stood just to the north, this small triangular park is dominated by the newspaper's once crowning clock. Every hour *Stuff* and *Guff*, the bronze mannequins, pretend to strike the big bell as *Minerva* supervises from above. Don't confuse this square with Greeley Square to the south.

[Q27] **Manhattan Mall**/originally **Gimbel Brothers Department Store**, 1275 Broadway, bet. W.32nd and W.33rd Sts. opp. Greeley Sq. W side. 1908-1912. *D.H. Burnham & Co.* Converted to mall, 1987-1989, *RTKL Assocs.*

A neo-Classical box by Chicago's *Burnham* was hollowed out, then enveloped in glass, for a galleria. But high above 32nd Street flies a multistory connecting bridge (look up!), a copper-clad *Art Deco* sleeper (1925) by *Shreve, Lamb & Harmon*, of Empire State Building fame.

[Q28] **Herald Center**/originally **Saks & Company**, later **Saks-34th Street**, 1311 Broadway, bet. W. 33rd and W.34th Sts. 1901-1902. *Buchman & Fox.* Rebuilt, 1982-1985, *Copeland Novak, & Israel and Schuman Lichtenstein Claman & Efron.*

A bulbous blue whale swallowed *Buchman & Fox.*

[Q29] **Macy's**, W.34th to W.35th Sts., Broadway to Seventh Aves. Original Broadway building, 1901-1902, *De Lemos & Cordes.* Successive additions to W, 1924, 1928, 1931, by *Robert D. Kohn.*

The oldest (eastern) part of "the world's largest store" is sheathed in a dignified Palladian façade. The newer (western) parts grew increasingly Art Deco in style. The Broadway entrance and show windows have been remodeled, but the 34th Street side shows original details; note the canopy, clock, and the hefty turn-of-the-century lettering. A quartet of older caryatids guards the 34th Street entrance (*J. Massey Rhind*, sculptor).

Q29

At the southeast corner of Macy's there once was the world's busiest hot dog stand with a Macy's sign on top. It's actually a five-story 19th-century building bought around 1900 for an outrageous $375,000 by Robert S. Smith, Macy's neighbor at its old locations at 14th and Sixth. Smith was thought to be acting as a spoiler on behalf of the owners of Siegel-Cooper, who had completed what they believed to be the world's largest store in 1896. Macy's imperiously built around the corner holdout by creating a right-angled arcade so its window shoppers could traverse the department store's perimeter without passing Smith's frontage. The arcade is gone and Macy's went on to lease the façade for a monster sign with Smith's heirs and their successors, the Rockaway Company.

Q31

[Q30] Originally **Spear & Company**, 22 W.34th St., bet. Fifth and Sixth Aves. 1934. *DeYoung & Moscowitz.*

Now decrepit and ill-loved, it was a startling modern work for Midtown when completed during the Great Depression. Its antecedents in the work of *Willem Dudok* in the Netherlands and in Great Britain's cinema designs of the 1930s are evident behind the mascara.

[Q31] **A.T. Demarest & Co.**, 336 Fifth Ave., NE cor. 5th Ave. and 33rd St. 1890. *Renwick, Aspinwall & Russell.* 🍎

Iron-spot bricks form monumental archways for glass, glass, glass. Never a department store, these were offices and showrooms for carriages built in the interregnum between

Q33

the sway of the carriage trade and the seduction of the automobile. The brickwork and terra cotta join to make a grand frieze in high relief and a hovering cornice.

[Q32] **Empire State Building**, 350 Fifth Ave., bet. W.33rd and W.34th Sts. W side. 1929-1931. *Shreve, Lamb & Harmon.* 🍎 Partial interior. 🍎

Once the world's tallest building, originally 1,250 feet high to the top of its mooring mast for apocryphal dirigibles. Planned during the booming 1920s, it went up during the Depression and remained largely vacant in its early years, it was said that the building relied on the stream of sightseers to the observation decks to pay its taxes. The monumental Fifth Avenue entrance is less interesting than the modernistic stainless steel canopies of the two sidestreet entrances. All of them lead to two-story-high corridors around the elevator core (with 67 elevators in it), which is crossed here and there by sleek stainless-steel-and-glass-enclosed bridges.

Empire State site: This pivotal spot has been occupied by two previous sets of landmarks. From 1857 to 1893 it was the site of two mansions belonging to the Astor family. Mrs. William Astor's place, on the corner of 34th Street, was for years the undisputed center of New York social life, and the capacity of her ballroom gave the name "The 400" to the City's elite. But in the early 1890s a feud developed between Mrs. Astor and her nephew, William Waldorf Astor, who had the house across the garden, on 33rd Street. He and his wife moved to Europe and had an 11-story hotel built on his property, naming it the Waldorf (the first John Jacob Astor's native village in Germany). Within a year after it opened in 1893, Mrs. Astor wisely decided to move out of its ominous shadow (up to 65th Street and

Q35

Fifth Avenue) and put a connecting hotel, the Astoria, on her property. When the 16-story structure was completed in 1897, the hyphenated hotel immediately became a social mecca. The requirement of full formal dress (tails) in the Palm Room created a sensation even then, but made it the place to be seen. Successful as it was, the old Waldorf-Astoria operated under a curious agreement that the elder Mrs. Astor could have all connections between the buildings walled up at any time on demand.

[Q33] Originally **B. Altman & Company Department Store**, now **B. Altman Advanced Learning Super Block** (New York Public Library, Science, Industry and Business Library; Oxford University Press; and City University of New York, Graduate School and University Center) 355-371 Fifth Ave., bet. E 34th and E.35th Sts. E side. 1905-1913. *Trowbridge & Livingston.* Exterior restored, *Hardy, Holzman Pfeiffer.* Interior reconfigured for the three institutions, 1996, *Gwathmey Siegel & Associates.* 🍎

Even after the first Waldorf-Astoria opened in 1897, Fifth Avenue from the 30s north remained solidly residential. *Benjamin Altman* made a prophetic breach by moving his department store from Sixth Avenue and 18th Street to this corner. To make the change less painful, it was designed (on its Fifth Avenue frontage) as a dignified eight-story Italian Renaissance Revival block; the Fifth Avenue entrance shows the atmosphere *Altman* was trying for. Altman's set off a rush of fashionable stores to Fifth Avenue above 34th Street. Many of them made a second jump, to the 50s, leaving Altman's behind and, ironically, isolated.

[Q34] Originally **Gorham Building**/formerly **Russek's Furs**, 390 Fifth Avenue, SW cor. W.36th St. 1904-1906. *Stanford White of McKim, Mead & White*. Alterations. 🍎

When Altman's opened at 34th Street, Gorham's, then famous jewelers, had just completed its Italian Renaissance palace. Russek's kept the fine architecture largely intact. The lower floors have been grossly altered, but the original columns and arches are visible on the 36th Street side. A monumental crowning cornice hovers at the sky.

The Garment Center: The West 30s have been the center of sewing fabrics, ruffles, and lace since entrepreneurs discovered the wealth of labor in vast pools of urban immigrants—once Eastern European, now Latino and Asian. Fashion designers still hover around these needle-trade blocks, where the hand-sewer still vies with the machin-

Q36

Q32

ing needle. Nowadays, however, uptowners in other businesses (architects, lawyers, for example) have moved in, and condominium residences are rife.

[Q35] originally **Greenwich Savings Bank**/now **The Haier Building**, 1352-1362 Broadway, NW cor. W.36th St. and Sixth Ave. 1922-1924. *York & Sawyer.* 🍎 Interior 🍎

Giant Corinthian columns march around three sides of the trapezoid that shapes this temple-like bank; inside, more Corinthians define a grand elliptical rotunda with a central skylight.

[Q36] **Church of the Holy Innocents** (Roman Catholic), 128 W.37th St., bet. Seventh Ave. and Broadway. S side. 1870. *Patrick Charles Keely.*

Light sandstone and darker brownstone intermingle in this Gothic Revival church, more elegantly detailed than the prolific *Keely's* usual red brick models. Savor the ceiling within.

[Q37] **400 Fifth Avenue Hotel and Apartments**, NW cor. 36th St. 2010. *Gwathmey Siegel & Assocs.*

Surrounded by designated landmarks: old Tiffany's (diagonally across Fifth) and Gorham (South across 36th), both by *Stanford White*, and Stewart & Company, next door, by *Warren & Wetmore*. Classy company for an up-and-coming hotel.

[Q38] **Stewart & Company Building**, 402-404 Fifth Ave., SW cor. 37th St. 1914. *Warren & Wetmore.* 🍎

Sullivan's Chicago is remembered here (*Louis Sullivan* was the radical early modernist Chicagoan of the 1890s whom *Frank Lloyd Wright* called his "lieber meister"). A magnificence in tile by the New York Architectural Terra-Cotta Company, but a startling aside by *Warren & Wetmore*, architects of Grand Central Station.

[Q39] Originally **Tiffany's**, 409 Fifth Avenue, SE cor. E.37th St. 1903-1906. *Stanford White of McKim, Mead & White.* Altered. ☞

Finished within the year after the Gorham Building by the same architects, this more massive structure was drawn from the Palazzo Grimani in Venice. The 37th Street side retains the original ranks of giant paired Corinthian columns shouldering a broad cornice. Eyes raised, the ensemble is breathtaking.

[Q40] **Lord & Taylor**, 424-434 Fifth Ave., NW cor. W.38th St. 1913-1914. *Starrett & Van Vleck.* ☞

This and the old W.&J. Sloane store on the block to the south (now replaced by an office building) were the first along the Avenue to dispense with Italian Renaissance colonnades and look frankly commercial. Pleasantly uncomplicated in the middle floors, but a grand palazzo cornice stands on high.

Q41

[Q41] **425 Fifth Avenue** (apartments), NE cor. 38th St. 2003. *Michael Graves and Thomas O' Hara.*

A neo-Art Deco tower mounts a boxy base, the spire drawn from memories of the spirited punctuations of Central Park West, as at the Century or the Majestic. But *Chanin* and *Delamarre* had a lighter hand.

A few notions: The side streets between Fifth and Sixth Avenues in the upper 30s are full of suppliers of trimmings for garments and millinery, and their windows are a great show. Beads, rhinestones, spangles, and laces predominate on West 37th Street; milliners' flowers and feathers, on West 38th.

[Q42] **Keppel Building**, 4 E.39th St., bet. Fifth and Madison Aves. 1905. *George B. Post & Sons.*

The gargoyles on this small side-street building's cornice will watch you intently as you examine the sculpted heads of *Whistler* and *Rembrandt*.

[Q43a] **HSBC Bank**/originally **Republic National Bank Tower**, also incorporating the former **Knox Hat Building**, 452 Fifth Ave. SW cor. W.40th Sts. W side. 1981-1983. *Attia & Perkins.*

[Q43b] **HSBC Bank**/onetime **Republic National Bank Building**/originally **Knox Hat Building**, 452 Fifth Ave., SW cor. W.40th St. 1902. *John H. Duncan.* ☞

Overhead, the new digital tidal wave swells over the old **Knox Building**, the latter built as an exuberant Classical showcase for *Col. Edward M. Knox*, hatter to Presidents. *Knox's* grandiosity comes from the day when men were valued by their hats, or used them as a badge of social station and power. No wonder *Duncan's* edifice claimed the corner of Fifth Avenue and Fortieth Street.

[Q44] **461 Fifth Avenue**, NE cor. E.40th St. 1988. *Skidmore, Owings & Merrill.*

The modernists who brought us Lever House switched to high-tech in the 1980s, with

Q43a   Q46

Q45

exposed, "pedimented" trusswork for wind bracing decorating the building form. The innovative and ultra-refined precast-concrete curtain wall was a refreshing note, but hasn't aged well: it was stylish without style. *SOM*, happily, has since returned to sleek modernism (for example, see their **Mortimer B. Zuckerman Research Center** in Hospitalia).

[Q45] **The New York Public Library**, Fifth Ave. bet. W.40th and W.42nd Sts. W side. 1898-1911. *Carrère & Hastings.* Lions, *E. C. Potter*, sculptor. Figures over fountains, *Frederick MacMonnies*, sculptor. ☞ Partial interior. ☞ Restoration and renovations: Periodicals Reading Rooms, 1985, *Giorgio Cavaglieri and Davis, Brody & Assocs.* Murals, *Richard Haas*. Gottesman Exhibition Hall, 1986; Celeste Bartos Forum, 1987; and other spaces, all by *Davis, Brody & Assocs.* Rose Main Reading Room Restoration, 1998, *Lewis Davis*

Q39

of Davis Brody Bond. Restructured stacks & Reading Rooms under the Rose Reading Room, 2009-2012, *Norman Foster*. Open to the public: Mo & Th-Sa 11-6; Tu & We 11-7:30, Su. 1-5. 917-275-6975. *www.nypl.org*

The apogee of Beaux Arts for New York, a white marble "temple" magnificently detailed inside and out, entered over extravagant terraces, imposing stairs, and post-flamboyant fountains, all now happily restored. Here knowledge is stored in a place worthy of aspiration—a far cry from one's local library-supermarket. The Roman Renaissance detailing is superb.

The 1980s restorations gave back public spaces claimed by librarydom's bureaucracy. Some are breathtaking; others, divorced from posters, prints, and paintings on the walls, produce a shadowless *Last Year at Marienbad* surrealism.

Lewis Davis's 1998 renovation of the Main Reading Room is, in the words of critic *Carter Wiseman*, an event "that makes one not only proud to be a New Yorker, but an American... The oak gleams, the brass shines, and the baroque clouds of the freshly painted ceiling soar heavenward beyond the surrounding office towers."

Speaking of *Foster's* appointment: "We had to have someone as good as *Carrère & Hastings*," said *Paul LeClerc*, president of the library. "We had to create a second masterpiece."

[Q46] **The Columns**/originally **The Engineers Club**, 32 W.40th St., bet. Fifth and Sixth Aves. 1906. *Whitfield & King*.

Brick and limestone Georgian and Renaissance Revival. Giant Corinthian pilasters give this a scale appropriate to the New York Public Library opposite.

[Q47] Originally **American Standard-American Radiator Building**/now **The Bryant Park Hotel**, 40 W.40th St., bet. Fifth and Sixth Aves. 1923-1924. *Hood & Fouilhoux*. Addition, 1937, *André Fouilhoux*. Hotel conversion, 2001, *David Chipperfield and William Tabler*. 🍎

The centerpiece in a row of Renaissance club façades is designer *Hood's* black brick and gold terra-cotta, Gothic-inspired tower. The first-floor façade, of bronze and polished black granite, and the black marble and mirror-clad lobby are worth a close look. Poetic and artistic allusions include *Georgia O' Keeffe's* Radiator Building—*Night, New York*, and in words: *Architecture* (magazine. 1925) "the black...suggesting a huge coal pile, and the gold and yellow of its higher points the glow of flames of an unbanked fire." Wow!

Not to be outdone, famed renderer *Hugh Ferriss* declaimed in 1929: "It has probably provoked more arguments among laymen on the

Avenue side (site of the New York Public Library) in 1842. The locale was still at the northern fringe of the City in 1853 when New York's imitation of London's Crystal Palace opened on the park site; it burned down in 1858. The park was established in 1871 and in 1884 was named for William Cullen Bryant, well-known poet and journalist; in 1899-1901 the reservoir was razed to make way for the library.

[Q50] **Bryant Park**/originally **Reservoir Square**, Sixth Ave., bet. W.40th and W.42nd Sts. E side. 1871. Redesigned, 1934, *Lusby Simpson*. 🍎 **Scenic landmark**. Library stacks extended beneath park, 1989, *Davis, Brody & Assocs.* Surface reconfigured, 1988-1991, *Hannai Olin*, landscape architects, *Lynden B. Miller*, garden designer. Bryant Park Grill and Café, 1995, *Hardy Holzman Pfeiffer*.

Midtown's only large greenspace. A serene and formal garden redesigned (in its 1924-1989 state) through a competition among unemployed architects. Ringed by allées of trees and

Q47

Q52

Q53

Q50

subject of architectural values than any other structure in the country." Now a boutique hotel.

[Q48] Originally **Republican Club**/now **Daytop Village**, 54-56 W.40th St., bet. Fifth and Sixth Aves. 1904. *York & Sawyer.*

Monumental Tuscan columns ennoble the grand portal of this rehabilitation center.

[Q49] **Bryant Park Studios**/originally **Beaux Arts Studios**, 80 W.40th St., SE cor. Sixth Ave. 1901-1902. *Charles A. Rich.* 🍎

A Beaux Arts extravaganza. Double-height studios gather north light from across Bryant Park via double-height windows. Artists who worked here included *Edward Steichen* and *Fernand Leger.*

The land of Bryant Park and the Public Library was set aside in 1823 by the City as a potter's field. The Egyptian-style Croton Reservoir, with walls 50 feet high and 25 feet thick around a four-acre lake, was completed on the Fifth

filled with statues of **William Cullen Bryant** (1911, *Herbert Adams*), Phelps-Dodge copper magnate **William E. Dodge** (1885, *J.Q.A. Ward*), **Goethe** (1932, *Karl Fischer*), and **Jose de Andrada**, father of Brazil's independence (1954, *Jose Lima*), **Josephine Shaw Lowell Fountain** (west end, 1912, *Charles Platt*), and formerly, a convention of drug pushers. The druggers moved out as New Yorkers regained the turf, one step behind the *Hardy Holzman Pfeiffer/Hannai Olin*–designed renaissance.

[Q51] **1095 Sixth Avenue**, formerly **Bell Atlantic**, bet. W.41st and W.42nd Sts. W side. 1970. *Kahn & Jacobs*. New glass façade, 2008, *Moed de Armas & Shannon.*

The previous heavy, stone façade has disappeared and it's been re-clad in aquamarine glass.

[Q52] **Bush Tower**, 130-132 W.42nd St., and 133-137 W.41st St., bet. Sixth Avenue and Broadway. 1916-1918, 1921. *Helmle & Corbett*. 🍎

This building rises 480 feet from a base only 50 by 200 feet, built by the developers of Brooklyn's vast industrial complex, Bush Terminal. Note the trompe l'oeil brickwork on its east flank.

[Q53] **World's Tower Building**, 110 W.40th St., bet. Sixth Ave. and Broadway. 1915. *Buchman & Fox.*

An elaborate and unique terra-cotta prism in the Beaux Arts mode. Sandwiched between two lower adjacent buildings, it presents four ornate façades.

[Q54] **One Bryant Park, Bank of America Tower**, 113 W. 42nd St., NW cor. Sixth Ave. and 42nd St. 2009. *Cook + Fox.*

Don't scrape the sky, *be* the sky. A sleek, chamfered glass prism, now the City's second tallest building, surpassing the venerable **Chrysler Building**. The multifaceted glass makes it seem much shorter than those aging champions. Whereas the Empire State and

[Q56] **W. R. Grace Building**, 1114 Sixth Avenue, SE cor. W.43rd St., also known as 41 W.42nd St., bet. Fifth and Sixth Aves. 1974. *Skidmore, Owings & Merrill.*

Anarchist in the streetscape. Bowing to that era's zoning requirements for setbacks produced an excuse to develop the swooping form that interrupts the street wall that contains the space of Bryant Park.

Under Bryant Park: Connecting the 42nd Street Station of the Sixth Avenue IND (B, D, F, V) and the Fifth Avenue Station of the IRT Flushing Line (7) is an underground passageway previously enhanced by a group of photographic enlargements of nearby street scenes, old and new, transferred to porcelain enamel panels. The photos were replaced in 2002 by a neat art installation, a rootsy mosaic in glass, stone, and marble, by Samm Kunce.

Q56

Q57

Chrysler were graceful Art Deco soldiers with spires atop, *Cook + Fox's* entry is all spire, disappearing as it rises while anchoring the corner of Bryant Park at its base.

There is an intriguing new pedestrian passage from 42nd to 43rd Street, connecting to a restored and expanded Henry Miller's Theater.

[Q55] **Henry Miller's Theater**, 124 W.43rd St., bet. Sixth and Seventh Aves. 1917-1918. *Allen, Ingalls & Hoffman.* Rebuilt and expanded, 2008, *Cook + Fox.*

Neo-Georgian, with brick pilasters and limestone capitals. Here we were *Born Yesterday*, attended *The Cocktail Party*, and wandered *Under Milk Wood*. The *Kit Kat Club* was also on the premises during the run of *Cabaret*. Gutted and completely rebuilt, with only elements of the façade remaining.

[Q57] **500 Fifth Avenue**, NW cor. W.42nd St. 1931. *Shreve, Lamb & Harmon.*

A 699-foot-high phallic pivot that once balanced a great tin can marked "500." Designed concurrently with their Empire State Building, this one was spared an iconic tower.

[Q58] **Manufacturers Hanover Trust Company**, 510 Fifth Ave., SW cor. W.43rd St. 1954. *Charles Evans Hughes III and Gordon Bunshaft of Skidmore, Owings & Merrill.*

The building that led the banking profession out of the cellar and onto the street; a glass-sheathed supermarket of dollars. The safe in the window is a symbolic descendent of *Edgar Allan Poe's* purloined letter. *Hughes* won an internal *SOM* design competition.

[Q59] **Israel Discount Bank**/originally **Postal Life Insurance Building**, 511 Fifth Ave., SE cor. E.43rd St. 1917. *York & Sawyer*. Remodeled, 1962, *Luss, Kaplan & Assocs., Ltd.*, designer.

Superb renovation of a Renaissance Revival bank interior. All the old fittings that could be kept have been; everything added is 1960s vintage.

[Q60] **Sidewalk Clock**, in front of 522 Fifth Ave., SW cor. W.44th St. 1907. *Seth Thomas Company*. ☀

As the European church signaled the hour to the town dweller, here the minutes are displayed for the more time-conscious American. The pair of harmonizing bollards are happy post-landmark designation additions.

[Q61] **Unification Church Headquarters**/formerly **Columbia University Club**/originally **Hotel Renaissance**, 4 W.43rd St., bet. Fifth and Sixth Aves. 1900. *Howard, Cauldwell & Morgan, with Bruce Price*.

A simplified **Renaissance Revival** palazzo, less elegant than the Century across the

[Q64] **Fire Engine Company No.65,** 33 W.43rd St., bet Fifth and Sixth Aves. 1897-1898. *Hoppin & Koen*. ☀

Italian renaissance fire-house, keeping company with the Century Association down the block.

[Q65] **Algonquin Hotel**/originally **The Puritan Hotel**, 59 W.44th St., bet. Fifth and Sixth Aves. 1902. *Goldwin Starrett*. ☀

The hotel/restaurant has a bay-windowed neo-Renaissance façade like many others, but it has long been a rendezvous for theater and literary figures. In the 1920s its Oak Room housed America's most famous luncheon club, the Round Table, around which *Franklin P. Adams, Robert Benchley, Harold Ross, Dorothy Parker*, and others sat (and ate, and talked, and drank, and drank, and drank).

1903 Algonquin prices: sitting room, library, dining room, 3 bedrooms, 3 baths, private hall— $10.00/day. Bedroom and bath—$2.00/day.

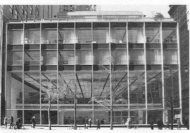

Q58

Q65

Q59

Q62

Q67

street—and inflated. *John Galen Howard* eventually became the architect of the University of California at Berkeley.

[Q62] **The Century Association**, 7 W.43rd St., bet. Fifth and Sixth Aves. 1889-1891. *Stanford White and Joseph Wells of McKim, Mead & White*. ☀

A delicate Palladian rusticated limestone façade for a private club of artists, professionals, and intellectuals. The arched window above the entrance was originally an open loggia.

[Q63] **25 West 43rd Street**, bet. Fifth and Sixth Aves. 1920s.

Several floors of this building were occupied from 1925 to 1991 by The *New Yorker* magazine; lurking about were such luminaries as *E.B. White, James Thurber, John Cheever, John Updike, Brendan Gill, A.J. Liebling, Calvin Trillin, Peter Arno,* and *Saul Steinberg.* Read the plaque. If you couldn't find them here, maybe they were at the **Algonquin** Round Table, across 44th Street.

[Q66] **Association of the Bar of the City of New York**, 37 W.43rd St. and 42 W.44th St., bet. Fifth and Sixth Aves. 1895-1896. *Cyrus L. W. Eidlitz*. ☀

A Classical limestone structure with the massive sobriety of the law. Doric, Ionic, and Corinthian orders are all there. But as an ensemble, it has the austere elegance of Greek architecture of the 5th century B.C.

[Q67] **Royalton Hotel**, 44 W.44th St. bet. Fifth and Sixth Aves. Interiors, 1988, *Philippe Starck and Gruzen Samton*.

High French style brought to the public spaces and rooms of what then became a "boutique" hotel.

[Q68] **University of Pennsylvania (Penn) Club**/ originally the **Yale Club**, 30 W.44th St., bet. Fifth and Sixth Aves. 1900. *Tracy & Swartwout*.

A brick and limestone clubhouse in inflated and flamboyant neo-Georgian. George IV with elevators?

[Q69] **General Society of Mechanics and Tradesmen**/originally **Berkeley Preparatory School**, 20 W.44th St., bet. Fifth and Sixth Aves. 1891. Lamb & Rich. Extension, 1903-1905, *Ralph S. Townsend*. ● Open to the public.

A free evening technical school founded in 1820 is housed in this dour Classical structure. The interior is a surprise: a three-story gallery-ringed drill hall housing a library and exhibits of old locks, the John H. Mossmann Collection. Savor particularly "A Very Complicated Lock."

[Q70] **Harvard Club**, 27 W.44th St., bet. Fifth and Sixth Aves. 1893-1894. Major additions, 1900-1905, 1913-1916, *Charles McKim of McKim, Mead & White*. Addition, 1989, *Edward Larrabee Barnes Assocs*. Extension, 2003, *Max Bond of Davis Brody Bond*. ●

Behind the modest but elegant neo-Georgian exterior are some imposing spaces; their large scale can be seen on the 45th Street rear façade. *Barnes* has designed an addition that enhances the facilities without competing

Q66   Q71

Q72

with *MM&W*. It is rumored that sometimes applicants seek Harvard admission just for the future opportunity of joining here. The late *Max Bond* said that "the design mediates between the existing Harvard Club to the east and the robust limestone and glass Beaux-Arts landmark New York Yacht Club to the west."

[Q71] **New York Yacht Club**, 37 W.44th St., bet. Fifth and Sixth Aves. 1900. *Warren & Wetmore*. ●

A fanciful example of Beaux Arts design, neo-Baroque division, with windows that bear the sterns of old ships drooling pendant waves, and worked in among the columns. The **America's Cup** was born here. *Warren & Wetmore's* first building.

[Q72] **Club Quarters Hotel**/formerly **Hotel Webster**/originally **Webster Apartments**, 38-42 W.45th St., bet. Fifth and Sixth Aves. 1904. *Tracy & Swartwout*.

A wonderful rusticated base supports a simple brick body.

The closest subways (B, D, F, and V trains) are at 47th-50th Street/Rockefeller Center Station of the IND Sixth Avenue Line.

NECROLOGY

Belmore Cafeteria, 407 Park Ave. S., bet. E.28th and E.29th Sts. E side.

An East Side landmark: the long line of yellow cabs parked outside signaled a taxi drivers' haven. Once filled with Formica, cigar smoke, and cabbies' tales of woe, this local institution succumbed to a condo apartment tower after half a century.

Wendell L. Willkie Building of Freedom House/originally **The New York Club**, 20 W.40th St., bet. Fifth and Sixth Aves. 1907. *Henry J. Hardenbergh*.

It was home to a gentlemen's club that from the late 1840s had slowly made its way uptown. Its upper floors later housed the New York chapters of the City's architects' and planners' organ-

Q70

izations, just beneath the colossal brick gable. Defaced in advance of consideration by the Landmarks Preservation Commission and eventually demolished. It is now a parking lot, although the front gates survive.

Aeolian Hall, 33 W.42nd St. 1912. *Warren & Wetmore*.

What was once a concert hall and then a five-and-ten was briefly a bluestone-floored pedestrian arcade forming an elegant shortcut (and art gallery) between 42nd and 43rd Streets. It also afforded access to the CUNY's Graduate Center above and library and an auditorium below. *George Gershwin* introduced "Rhapsody in Blue" in **Aeolian Hall** with *Paul Whiteman's* orchestra in 1924. Now the passage has been filled in, with the floors above the State University College of Optometry.

MADISON SQUARE TO THE JAVITS CENTER

In 1904 the Pennsylvania Railroad opened its tunnel under the Hudson and cut a broad swath to its monumental two-block-square station (opened 1910), erasing some of the Hell's Kitchen tenements. (In the 1930s Lincoln Tunnel approaches cut down more.) The new station quickly attracted the equally monumental General Post Office, some major hotels, and a cluster of middle-class department stores, which found the precinct an ideally convenient goal for their march up Sixth Avenue from 14th Street. By the 1920s garment manufacturing had moved from the Lower East Side into the streets surrounding these pivot points. Today's garment industry is concentrated in the West 30s and 40s between Sixth and Eighth Avenues, with suppliers of fabrics, trimmings, and such located to the east as far as Madison Avenue.

In the 1980s the precinct was reactivated,

a 20,000-seat "garden," a 1,000-seat "forum," a 500-seat cinema, a 48-lane bowling center, a 29-story office building, an exposition "rotunda," an art gallery, and the usual dining, drinking, and shopping areas—all above the railroad station, which was underground to begin with, but had a ceiling 150 feet high. The present "Garden," the third one and closer to Madison Square than the second, is housed in a precast concrete-clad cylinder and roofed by a 425-foot-diameter cable structure that only physically replaces its magnificent noble predecessor.

A successor station within the body of the old General Post Office across Eighth Avenue awaits, perhaps, the injection of 2009 stimulus dollars. And then the building that developer *Irving Felt* claimed as a future monument (to justify, at least in his mind, the demolition of *Charles McKim's* great portal to arrival), would be assigned to the dustbins.

J1

with, most prominently, the Javits Center as its economic if not spiritual leader.

[J1] **Hotel Pennsylvania**/sometime **New York Penta**/onetime **Statler**/originally **Hotel Pennsylvania**, 401 Seventh Ave., bet. W.32nd and W.33rd Sts. W side. 1918. *McKim, Mead & White.*

Its sober Ionic sextet is set back 15 feet from the building line in response to the great colonnade of old Pennsylvania Station facing it. A center for 1930s big bands, *Glenn Miller* wrote a tune called "Pennsylvania 6-5000," still the hotel's phone number, now converted to all digits.

[J2] **Madison Square Garden Center**, W.31st to W.33rd St., Seventh to Eighth Aves. 1968. *Charles Luckman Assocs.*

Anybody who remembers the vast Roman Revival waiting room and even vaster iron-and-glass train shed of *Charles McKim's* (*McKim, Mead & White*) 1910 **Penn Station** will feel bereaved here.

The complex covers two blocks and includes

The Underground Pennsylvania Station occupies little more than a rabbit warren under the two-square-block Penn Plaza office building and Garden.

On August 2, 1962, a band of architects picketed—alas, unsuccessfully — against the demolition of the McKim, Mead & White's grand Roman cum modern glass-and-steel train shed Penn Station. Organized by **AGBANY***, the Action Group for Better Architecture in New York, a group of young New York architects including Norval White, Jim Burns, Jordan Gruzen, Norman Jaffe, Diana Kirsch, Jan Rowan, Peter Samton, and Elliot Willensky, among others, picketed with posters prepared by students at all of the City's architectural schools. Among the architectural notables it attracted for picketing and television interviews were Philip Johnson, Peter Blake, Aline Saarinen, John Johansen, and board members of the Museum of Modern Art.*

J4

[J3] **Long Island Railroad Entrance Pavilion**, W.34th St. bet. Seventh and Eighth Aves. 1990-1994. *R. M. Kliment & Frances Halsband*, in association with *TAMS*.

An ethereal cage of metal and glass signals the entrance to Long Island transit. Elegant. Wonderful.

[J4] Originally **General Post Office**/now **James A. Farley Building**, Eighth Ave. bet. W.31st and W.33rd Sts. W side. 1913. *William M. Kendall of McKim, Mead & White*. Annex to W, 1935.

The two-block row of 20 53-foot Corinthian columns, and what is probably the world's longest inscription, once faced the equally long, somewhat stubbier row of Penn Station's Doric columns.

The near future may reincarnate Pennsylvania Station within these *McKim, Mead & White* folds (but entered on the side streets), a block west from where *Charles McKim* originally planted it, and within yet another embrace of Roman splendor. The proposed **Moynihan Station** is a great idea on precarious life support. Political CPR is needed, immediately!

[J5] Originally **New Yorker Hotel**, 481 Eighth Avenue, bet. W.34th and W.35th Sts. W side. 1930. *Sugarman & Berger*.

An Art Deco relic, and a popular economy-priced hotel. In its heyday it boasted 92 "telephone girls" at the 41st-floor switchboards, and a 42-chair barber shop with 20 manicurists. In

J3

J5

1976 it became a property of *Rev. Sun Myung Moon's* **World Unification Church**. Check the cubistic compositions of its setbacks. Better from afar.

[J6] **Manhattan Center Studios**/formerly **Manhattan Center**/originally **Manhattan Opera House**, 311 W.34th St., bet. Eighth and Ninth Aves. 1906. Altered.

A traditional gathering place for union-contract debates and votes. And what about the incised lettering: Ancient Accepted Scottish Rite? Masons? When were they here?

Sound films were still experimental when Warner Brothers, collaborating with Bell Laboratories, exhibited them at the Manhattan Center in 1926, when it was still known as the Manhattan Opera House. Warner created elsewhere, but here was a vast auditorium that preceded by several years Radio City, the Roxy, and other mass places of mesmerization.

For the Hungry:

[J7] **Manganaro's Grosseria**/originally **Ernest Petrucci's**, 488-492 Ninth Ave., bet. W.37th and W.38th Sts. E side. 1893.

The architecture of food: pendant, stacked, glazed, bottled, canned—a symphony of color, texture, patina, and aroma. If you pass through, you will reach the Old World (self-service) restaurant. A special place.

Hell's Kitchen Flea Market: A stretch of 39th Street, between 9th and 10th Avenues, was for almost 50 years full of pushcart food venders, banished by Mayor La Guardia in the late 1930s. The market soon revived however, as indoor shops with big outdoor displays featuring fresh fruit and vegetables, Italian, Greek, Polish, Spanish, and Philippine products. Open weekends 9-6.

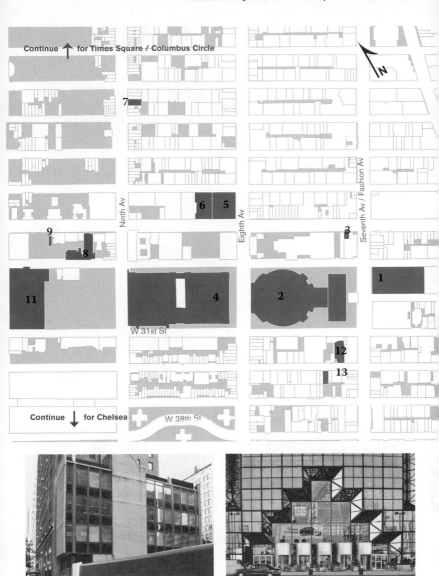

Continue ↑ for Times Square / Columbus Circle

Continue ↓ for Chelsea

J9

J10

[J8] **St. Michael's Church**, 424 W.34th St., bet. Ninth and Tenth Aves. 1892. Rectory, 1906.

Romanesque Revival limestone, its wall in rock-face ashlar, the arches and details smoothly contrasting, the column capitals richly carved in the spirit of 11th-century France.

[J9] **Spearin Preston & Burrows**, 446 W.34th St. bet. Ninth and Tenth Aves. 1967. *Edelman & Salzman.*

A diminutive, now dated, modernist office block occupying a curious sliver of land left over to one side of the Lincoln Tunnel approaches.

[J10] **Jacob Javits Convention Center**, Eleventh to Twelfth Aves. bet. W.34th and W.37th Sts. 1986. *James Ingo Freed of I.M. Pei & Partners. Lewis Turner Assocs.*, associate architects. Renovation and expansion, 2014 (estimated), *FxFowle Epstein.*

Vast. Within lies an entire world between the City and the Hudson River, but seemingly distant from both. The Javits is a complex with a complex: it aspires to be the heir to *Joseph Paxton's* **Crystal Palace** (1851) but has never lived up to that pioneering pavilion's structural delicacy. A planned renovation will replace the Center's opaque black glass with the transparent variety, which should help open it up to the City. But more civic ambition is required here: why not link the Center to both the river and to the forlorn and endangered terminus of the **High Line** just to the south?

[J10a] Originally **Hill Publishing Co. Lofts**, 475 Tenth Ave., NW cor. W.36th St. 1914. *Goldwin Starrett & Van Vleck.*

Extremely modern for its time, this handsome loft building features a steel frame and a façade made mostly of glass, but with the requisite Romanesque Revival cornice and arches up top. Such confections would soon be left on the drafting room floor as architects embraced the spare functionalism of the International Style.

J11

[J11] Originally **Westyard Distribution Center,** Tenth Ave. bet. W.31st and W.33rd Sts. E side. (aka 450 West 33rd Street). 1970. *Davis, Brody & Assocs.* Lobby upgrade, 1990, *Der Scutt.*

A gutsy concrete structure that spans the Penn-Central tracks below. Its penthouse once sheltered ice skating—Sky Rink—since removed to sea level at the Chelsea Piers.

[J12] **St. John the Baptist Church** (Roman Catholic), 211 W.30th St., bet. Seventh and Eighth Aves. 1872. *Napoleon LeBrun.*

Lost in the Fur District is this exquisite single-spired brownstone church, a Roman Catholic midtown Trinity. The interior, of white marble, radiates light. Worth a special visit.

[J13] **Fire Patrol No.1,** W.30th St., bet. Seventh and Eighth Aves. 1874.

A mildly ornate eclectic "row house" for the Insurance Company funded patrols that attend major fires, protecting the goods that might potentially be damaged by smoke and, particularly, water.

NECROLOGY

Pennsylvania Station, Seventh Ave. bet. W. 31st and W. 33rd Sts. W side to Eighth Ave. 1910. *McKim, Mead & White.*

An imperial neo-Roman monument built for ordinary people, its much protested demolition in 1963 spurred the permanent establishment of New York City's Landmarks Preservation Commission. Mourning the station's demise, an editorial in the October 30, 1963, *New York Times* observed: "We will probably be judged not by the monuments we build but by those we have destroyed."

MURRAY HILL

During the Revolutionary War, *Robert Murray's* 18th-century country estate served as headquarters for a day for alternately *General George Washington* and the British commander *General Sir William Howe.*

It was here that Murray's wife entertained Howe and his staff while Revolutionary troops escaped to the northwest. In the late 19th century, social status on this fashionable hill was highest near the great mansions of Fifth Avenue, dropping off toward the east, where carriage houses gave way to tenements at El-shaded Third Avenue. When commerce moved up Fifth Avenue in the early 1900s, Murray Hill became an isolated but vigorous patch of elegance, centered about Park Avenue, where through traffic (first horsecars, then trolleys, now cars) was diverted into the old railroad tunnel from 33rd to 40th Streets. Fashionable **Murray Hill** then gradually shifted to the east, (the El down in the 1950s) where carriage houses have become residences, as commerce has made slow but steady inroads on the north, west and south.

[M1] **Murray Hill Historic District & Extensions** ● See the district perimeters on the map.

A world of, mostly, town houses, that are, in turn, mostly brownstones. But you will see below the wide range of public architecture that lends the neighborhood to a distinguished level. And nice trees.

M2

Murray Hill Walking Tour: START at Park Avenue and East 34th Street (IRT Lexington Avenue Line "No.6 train," 33rd Street Station).

[M2] **10 Park Avenue**, NW cor. E.34th St. 1931. *Helmle, Corbett & Harrison.*
The massing of this apartment hotel resembles a larger-than-life crystalline outcropping of some exotic mineral. Its golden-hued brick and expansive windows (divided into tiny panes) provide an appropriate domestic scale: look up to cubism: that scale is in the sky.

[M3] Originally **Della Robbia Bar** (also known as The Crypt), 4 Park Ave. NW cor. E.33rd St. 1910-1913. *Warren & Wetmore. R. Guastavino Co. and Rookwood Pottery Co.,* builders. ●
Contained in the **Vanderbilt Hotel** originally. 1976. *Shreve, Lamb & Harmon Assocs.* ●

The old **Hotel**'s vaulted crypt sheltered, until recently, what might be termed an Italian rathskeller, its *Guastavino* vaults similar to those at Grand Central's Oyster Bar, but embellished by Rookwood's ornaments. Here architecture conquers interior decoration.

[M4] **2 Park Avenue**, bet. E.32nd and E.33rd Sts. W side. 1926-1928. *Ely Jacques Kahn of Buchman & Kahn.* ●
A very neat pier-and-spandrel pattern on the walls of this office block bursts into **Art Deco** angular terra-cotta decoration in primary colors on its upper floor setbacks. *Lewis Mumford* wrote in 1928 that the building "...strikes the boldest and clearest note among all our recent achievements in skyscraper architecture." But the most fun for the pedestrian is the lobby ceiling, a sparkling Art Deco tapestry.

[M5] **The Madison**/originally **Grolier Club**, 29 E.32nd St., bet. Madison and Park Aves. 1889. *Charles W. Romeyn & Co.* ●
Superb *Richardsonian Romanesque* with brownstone—smooth, rough, and carved. An unlikely and powerful interruption in a street of loft buildings.

[M6] **Remsen Building**, 148 Madison Ave., SW cor. E.32nd St. 1917. Altered ca. 1930, *Frank Goodwillie.*
A modest pattern of Art Moderne terra cotta

M3   M5

at the base is interrupted, at the entry, by extraordinary neo-Gothic tri-partite windows, hooded and the hood finialed, a macabre portal.

[M7] *The Complete Traveller (bookshop), at 199 Madison Avenue. Travelers and tourists—and otherwise serious people—should mine this lode of guidebooks, maps, and other nuggets for those of a wandering bent. In addition to a clutch of New Yorkiana, those more brave will discover literature on Mongolia, Montparnasse, and even Montana.*

[M8] Originally **Thomas and Fanny Clarke House**/now **Collectors' Club**, 22 E.35th St., bet. Madison and Park Aves. 1901-1902. *Stanford White of McKim, Mead & White.* ●
A neo-Georgian town house with extravagant small-paned bay windows, reminiscent of the late 19th-century avant-garde work of the talented Briton, *Richard Norman Shaw.* Savor the elegant Composite-columned portal.

[Map of Midtown Manhattan showing Murray Hill Historic District with numbered locations from E 31st St to E 42nd St, bounded by Fifth Av, Madison Av, Park Av, Lexington Av, and Third Av. Navigation notes: "Continue for Grand Central / Park Ave.", "Continue for Kips Bay", "for Madison Square Garden to Bryant Park", "Continue", "Continue for Rose Hill".]

M8

M10

M13

M16

[M9] The New Church (Swedenborgian), 112-114 E.35th St., bet. Park and Lexington Aves. 1858.

A modest Renaissance Revival building and garden provides spatial punctuation to the block. Rusticated, powerful brackets make monumental its wide cornice and pediment.

[M10] Originally **James F. D. Lanier House**, 123 E.35th St., bet. Park and Lexington Aves. 1901-1903. *Hoppin & Koen.* ●

Giant limestone Composite pilasters and red brick infill are superposed on a rusticated limestone base. A **Beaux Arts** town house pulls out all stops to wear the tiara on a block of brownstones. Copper roof and dormers crown it all.

[M11] Originally **James Hampden and Cornelia Van Rensselaer Robb House**/now **23 Park Avenue Apartments**/sometime **Advertising Club of New York**, NE cor. E.35th St. 1888-1892. *Stanford White of McKim, Mead & White.* ●

Stately. An Italian Renaissance palazzo dressed in ironspot brick and brownstone, the latter switching to terra cotta above the ground floor. Once a place to appropriately disguise flamboyant advertising account executives, it now merely shelters condominiums for the more than affluent. *Russel Sturgis*, a prominent critic at the time of its construction, said that it was "not a palace, but a fit dwelling house for a first-rate citizen." Now, his first-rate citizens have removed to penthouse aeries, and the ordinary affluent share its subdivided condominia.

[M12] **Church of the Incarnation** (Episcopal), 205 Madison Ave., NE cor. E.35th St. 1864. *Emlen T. Littel.* Restoration and enlargement, 1882. *D. & J. Jardine.* ●

[M13] The **H. Percy Silver Parish House**, 209 Madison Ave., bet. E.35th and E.36th Sts. E side. 1868. *Robert Mook.* New façade, 1905-1906, *Edward P. Casey*

Two orphans from Madison Avenue's earlier

elite years: a dour Gothic church and a Renaissance Revival town house named for a rector of the adjacent church. Murals by *John La Farge*, stained glass by Tiffany Studios. Light sandstone frames openings, and vermiculated brownstone abounds.

[M14] **Morgan Court**, 211 Madison Ave., bet. E.35th and E.36th Sts. E side. 1985. *Liebman Liebman & Assocs.*

The local sliver, with gusto, shields a garden court behind. Peek.

[M15a] **The Morgan Library & Museum**, 225 Madison Ave., at 36th St. **Addition.** 2006. *Renzo Piano Building Workshop and Beyer Blinder Belle.* Open to the public: Su 11-6; Tu-Thu 10:30-5; Sat 10-6; closed Mo. 212-685-0008. *www.themorgan.org*

Piano's new façade on Madison provides bland entry to this rich complex, perhaps consciously avoiding any sense of competition with *Charles McKim* and *Benjamin Wistar Morris.* But

[M16] Onetime (1904-1943) **J.P. Morgan, Jr., House**/originally **Isaac N. Phelps House**/later **Anson Phelps Stokes House**/, 231 Madison Ave., SE cor. E.37th St. 1853. 🍎

A Classical block that has suffered from additions to and restoration of its brownstone. The sinuous iron balustrades on the entry stoop first-floor windows are outstanding. Now a part of the Library/Museum.

[M17] **Consulate General of Poland**/sometime the **National Democratic Club** originally **Joseph R. De Lamar** House, 233 Madison Ave., NE cor. E.37th St. 1905-1906. *C. P. H. Gilbert.* 🍎

Heavily rusticated and surmounted by the most formidable mansard roof in New York, this was to be *DeLamar's* means of entry into the "society" of Murray Hill. (The interiors are even more opulent, and largely intact.) *DeLamar* was a Dutch-born merchant seaman who made his fortune in mining and metallurgy.

M15b

the internal links are gracious organizers of this building triad.

[M15b] **J. Pierrepont's Private Library**, 33 E.36th St., bet. Madison and Park Aves. 1906. *Charles McKim of McKim, Mead & White.* Addition at 29 E.36th St., NE cor. Madison Ave. 1928. *Benjamin Wistar Morris.* 🍎 Interior. 🍎

Brunelleschi would be pleased by Morgan's Private Library, an elegantly understated palazzo, offspring of the Florentine Renaissance via *Charles McKim.* Constructed of dry marble masonry, the joined surfaces are set without mortar. The addition, built on the site of the *J. Pierpont Morgan, Sr.* mansion after his death, modestly defers to its master. The interior of the complex is notable not only for its exhibits of rare prints and manuscripts but also for *Morgan's* opulent Private Library, maintained just as he left it. Outside is marble, whitestone, brownstone, bronze, and wrought iron.

[M18] **19 and 21 East 37th Street**, bet. Madison and Park Aves.

Surviving town houses. Enjoy the Composite capitals on the porch of **No.19** (ca. 1900), the sinuous wrought iron gateway and balustrades of **No.21** (ca. 1885).

[M19] **Union League Club**, 38 E.37th St., SW cor. Park Ave. 1931. *Morris & O'Connor.*

This effete neo-Georgian pile is the red brick home of a club founded by Republicans who left the Union Club in 1863, incensed by its failure to expel Confederate sympathizers. It was on the right side politically, but architecturally its club-house is no competition for Union's 69th Street Classical elegance.

M17

[M20] **Scandinavia House**, 56 Park Ave., bet. E.37th and E.38th Sts. W side. 2001. *Polshek Partnership.*

Zinc and spruce on Park Avenue? More than 60 years ago, when two United Nations council chambers were constructed with interiors and furniture by Scandinavian architects (*Sven Markelius*, Sweden; *Fin Juhl*, Denmark), Swedish and Danish modern design swept into New York (1948). Here the cool hand of *Polshek* brings back some of those memories.

[M21] Originally **Adelaide L.T. Douglas House**/now **Guatemalan Mission to the United Nations**, 57 Park Ave., bet. E.37th and E.38th Sts. E side. 1909-1911. *Horace Trumbauer.*

An impressive cornice crowns the third floor surmounted by Tuscan columns where French doors open to narrow balconies. But basically more limestone Beaux Arts, now used by a Central American mission that can savor its ebullience more lustily than could its original Protestant tenant.

[M24] **The Library**, 299 Madison Ave., NE cor. E. 41st St. 1912. *Hill & Stout.* Remodeled into hotel, 1999, *The Stephen Jacobs Group.*

An early sliver building in brick and terra cotta (only 25 feet wide), its grand copper-clad bays give travelers a grand view down 41st to the main façade of the real New York Public Library.

[M25] **285 Madison Ave.**, NE cor. E. 40th St. 1926. *William L. Rouse and Lafayette A. Goldstone.*

An unremarkable block of brick at the corner, but the details bear a closer look: dozens of whimsical stone figures ring the shop windows.

[M26] **275 Madison Ave.**, SE cor. E. 40th St. 1931. *Kenneth Franzheim.*

The City's many fine Art Deco structures have recently caught the attention of the Landmarks Commission, including this joyful tower in streamlined stone. Construction began in 1930, only one year after the Crash of '29. Here's to optimism!

M18

M24

M22

[M22] **Church of Our Saviour** (Roman Catholic), 59 Park Ave., SE cor. E.38th St. 1959. *Paul W. Reilly.*

Somewhat convincing neo-Romanesque archaeology. Among its inconsistencies, however, is air-conditioning equipment where, in a true Romanesque church, a carillon would be. Look up within at the neo-Baroque ceiling. Outside, the carved Gallery of Kings has all the expression of a flock of Barbie dolls.

[M23] **The Towne House**, 108 E.38th St., bet. Park and Lexington Aves. S side. 1930. *Bowden & Russell.*

An unsung **Art Moderne** apartment house in a reddish-black brick that sports rippling brick spandrels. The cubistic composition is crowned with brilliant glazed terra-cotta panels in a broad and wondrous spectrum that can be enjoyed as a special colorful cresting from a distant skyline view.

[M27] **The Ritzy Canine**/originally **Jonathan W. Allen Stable**, 148 E.40th Street, bet. Lexington and Third Aves. 1871. *Charles Hadden*, builder.

A distinguished mansard-roofed emissary in miniature from France's Second Empire, languishing amid characterless high-rises on all sides. Napoléon III is going to the dogs.

[M28] **150-152 East 38th Street** (house), bet. Lexington and Third Aves. 1858. Remodeled, 1934-1935, *Robertson Ward.*

Ward, the architect, was the out-of-wedlock son of sculptor *Frederick William MacMonnies*, whose work adorns many buildings cited in this book. A walled front garden breaks the block-front: a happy urban design gift. The three story neo-Federal house stands at the back of the garden, accessible via a covered walkway.

[M29] **Carriage House Center for the Arts** / originally **George S. Bowdoin Stable**, 149 East 38th Street (carriage house), bet. Lexington and Third Aves. 1902. *Ralph S. Townsend.* ●

A Dutch Renaissance stepped limestone and brick gable displays carved heads of bulldogs and wreathed horses. An exuberant gift to the block.

[M30] **Sniffen Court Historic District**, 150-158 E.36th St., bet. Lexington and Third Aves. 1863-1864. ●

Ten **Romanesque Revival** brick carriage houses make a mews, a tasteful oasis, and an urbane lesson for those developing dense streets. Here urban style could be replicated with whole blocks of such mews at intervals in the cityscape.

[M31] **157 and 159 East 35th Street**, bet. Lexington and Third Aves. ca. 1890.

Two conversions to modern use. **No.157** is restrained and successful. **No.159**, the more ebullient architectural statement upstairs (note

J.P. Morgan Carriage House, 211 Madison Ave., bet. E. 35th and E. 36th Sts. E side.

A rare remnant from Madison Avenue's early elite era later housed the Anthroposophical Society in America. Now Morgan Court slivers upward.

Pierpont Morgan Library Garden courtyard, 29-33 E.36th St., bet. Madison and Park Aves. 1993. *Voorsanger & Mills.*

This delightfully urbane greenhouse garden court linked the library and its addition to *Morgan's* onetime house, reclaimed as part of this gracious complex. Replaced by the new *Renzo Piano* alterations and expansion.

Architects Building, 101 Park Ave., NE cor. E. 40th St. 1912. *Ewing & Chappell and La Farge & Morris.*

In this building, built by architects for architects, scores of the profession's offices filled the floors above the Architects' Samples Corporation exhibition space, which snaked

M29

M32

the terra-cotta garlands at the cornice), suffers from a stuffy ground-floor reconstruction.

[M32] **Armenian Evangelical Church of America**, 152 E. 34th St., bet. Lexington and Third Aves. 1840s.

A **Doric** temple, adjacent to Dumont Plaza (public), sharing space with the neighboring Barking Dog Cafe.

END *of Murray Hill Tour: The 33rd Street IRT Local (No.6 train at Park Avenue South) is the nearest rapid transit.*

NECROLOGY

71st Regiment Armory, New York National Guard, Park Ave. bet. E. 33rd and E. 34th Sts. E side. 1905. *Clinton & Russell.*

The first edition of the *AIA Guide* called it a "burly brick mass topped by a medieval Italian tower." It is now replaced by **3 Park Avenue** and the **Norman Thomas High School** (1976. *Shreve, Lamb & Harmon Assocs.*)

through the lobby level and mezzanine. Now, this and the two below have been replaced by an ego event: a skewed glass office shaft (1985. *Eli Attia*).

Ernest Flagg House/later **Chess and Athletic Club**, 109 E. 40th St., bet. Park and Lexington Aves. 1905. *Ernest Flagg.*

Flagg (1857-1947), who resided here until his death, included in his palatial city house an intriguing tiled entrance for his auto, which would be lowered by elevator to a garage below street level. The entrance opened onto an opulent multilevel interior space.

113 and 115 East 40th Street (houses)/formerly **The Architectural League of New York**, bet. Park and Lexington Aves.

For decades these interconnected buildings, one a carriage house, sheltered the **New York Chapter of the AIA**, the **Architectural League**, and other art and architectural organizations.

CLINTON

From Ninth Avenue westward to the Hudson, roughly parallel to the Times Square theater district, lies the area known since the 1970s as Clinton, after DeWitt Clinton Park (1905) at its western edge between West 52nd and West 54th Streets. Like Cobble Hill, Carroll Gardens, and Boerum Hill in Brooklyn, Clinton is a new moniker for a community trying to live down its infamous past. From the Civil War to World War II the area south to about West 30th Street was better known as Hell's Kitchen, one of the City's most notorious precincts. Gangster rule in its early years and the abundance of slaughterhouses, freight yards, factories, and tenements (to house those whose meager livings these industries provided) established the area's physical character. It is a quality the current inhabitants wish to upgrade, and the area boasts substantial improvements toward that end. But the ubiquitous lofts, repair shops, and taxi garages and the disappearance of pier activity (as well as piers) have made this stretch unfamiliar to all except those who live, work, or play here. It remains an enigma why Clinton, so close to the heart of Manhattan's central business district, is still a relative backwater. Change has come to western parts around 42nd Street, and in a new boom, after the present recession, the proposed apartment complex by Enrique Norten at DeWitt Clinton Park might bring a giant boost to the neighborhood.

L1   L7

To begin: The nearest subways are not close, which helps to explain Clinton's sluggishness in being redeveloped. (Take the IND Eighth Avenue Line (A, C, and E trains), the closest, to the 42nd Street Station.)

[L1] **St. Raphael's Croatian Catholic Church,** 41st St. bet. 10th and 11th Aves. 1890s.

Granite ashlar, limestone trim, slated and copper-crested twin towers all serve to enrich this eclectic outpost of the Balkans.

[L2] **440 West 42nd Street** bet. Tenth and Dyer Aves. 2011. *Arquitectonica.*

A 60-story mixed use tower by the architects of the W Hotel two blocks east. Currently "Hell's Swimming Hole" (foundations in Hell's Kitchen waiting for the economy).

[L3] **Model Tenements for New York Fireproof Tenement Association,** 500 W.42nd St., SW cor. Tenth Ave. and 569 Tenth Ave., bet. W.41st and W.42nd Sts. ca. 1900. *Ernest Flagg.*

Their fireproof qualities may have been a step forward for tenements, but having lost their ironwork embellishments, they are grim.

Hell's Kitchen Redux: a new frontier for desperate affluent luxury invaders, pioneered by Riverbank West, invaded by the unmentionable hulk of River Place, relieved mildly by the relative spare glassiness of River Place 2 and the Atelier.

[L4] **Riverbank West** (apartments), 555 W.42nd St., NE cor. Eleventh Ave. 1987. *Hardy Holzman Pfeiffer Assocs.,* design architects. *Schuman, Lichtenstein, Claman & Efron,* architects.

Polychromatic brickwork and staggered bal-

L5

conies make a lively if not graceful façade. The syncopated top is where most of the action is.

[L5] **River Place 2,** 600 W. 42nd St., SW cor. Eleventh Ave. 2009. *Costas Kondylis.*

Twin glasseries that join the Atelier in gorging on the river views.

[L6] **Atelier,** 635 W. 42nd St., bet. 11th & 12th Aves. 2007. *Costas Kondylis.*

Sleek glass with projecting "hashmarks," like the sleeve of a venerable sergeant.

[L7] **Manhattan Plaza** (apartment complex), W.42nd to W.43rd Sts., Ninth to Tenth Aves. 1977. *David Todd & Assocs.*

Two 45-story red brick balconied towers anchor this block-square project, built for performing artists and intended to spur redevelopment of the Clinton community. Between the towers, on the garage deck, are recreational buildings for residents of the 1,688 apartments.

[L8] **Actors Studio**/originally **Seventh Associate Presbyterian Church**, 432 W.44th St., bet. Ninth and Tenth Aves. 1859. Restored 1995, *Davis Brody & Associates.* 🍎

Lee Strasberg held forth after 1955 in this simple, late Greek Revival brick church. Here was the cradle of thespians such as *Marlon Brando*.

[L9] **New Dramatists**/originally Church, 424 W.44th St., bet. Ninth and Tenth Aves. 1880s.

A free-spirited Gothic Revival fitted gracefully into a continuous row house and apartment blockfront façade. The **New Dramatists** enjoy another happily recycled found space.

[L10] **Film Center Building**, 630 Ninth Ave., bet. W.44th and W.45th Sts. E side. 1928-1929. *Ely Jacques Kahn of Buchman & Kahn.* 🍎 1982. Lobby interior.

Typical of 1920s **Art Deco**-influenced loft buildings where design is just skin deep. This one, however, has a glorious polychromatic

L8

L12

L10

elevator lobby (and an asymmetric, Moderne bronze tenants' directory).

[L11] **Film Center Café**, 635 Ninth Ave., bet. W.44th and W.45th Sts. W side. 1940s.

A small and stylish Art Moderne café frequented by the movie/video clan that works across the street in the Film Center.

428 West 44th Street, the former home of actress June Havoc, is also the scene of mysterious tapping sounds. Perhaps its resident tapper was a friend of Peter Stuyvesant and afforded him temporary digs during the 1978 fire that gutted his home. Seances have been conducted to determine who the noisy ghost is. Two spirits are said to have been contacted so far.

[L12] **Playground, N.Y.C. Department of Parks & Recreation**, W.45th to W.46th Sts., midblock bet. Ninth and Tenth Aves. Reconstructed, 1977, *Michael J. Altschuler,* architect. Outdoor mural, 1973, *Arnold Belkin*, Cityarts Workshop. Mosaics, 1974, *Philip Danzig,* with community participants.

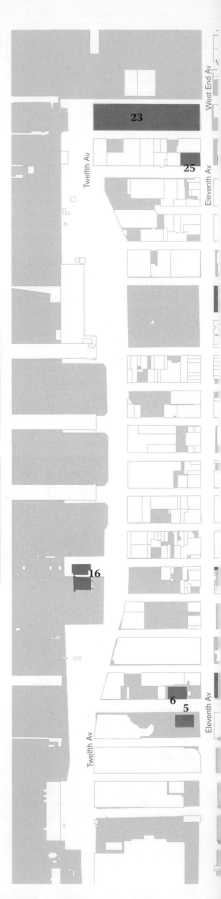

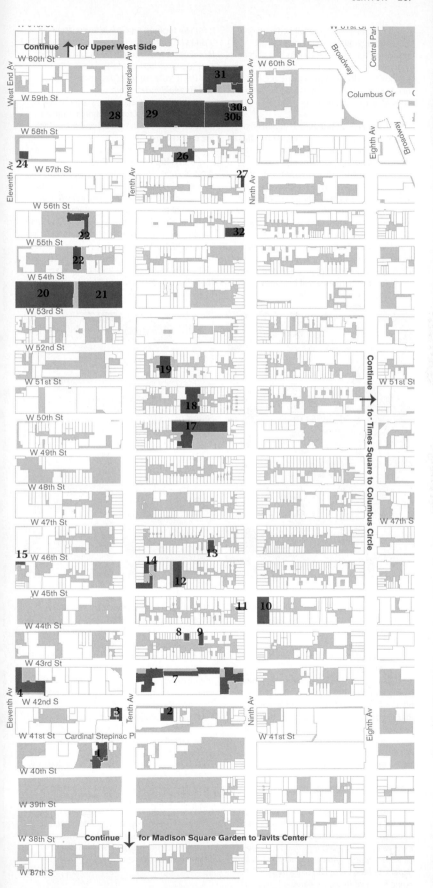

Continue ↑ for Upper West Side

W 60th St

Continue → to Times Square to Columbus Circle

Continue ↓ for Madison Square Garden to Javits Center

An unusual reconstruction of the ubiquitous city playground: community-crafted mosaics on the walls, reflections and distortions from polished stainless-steel mirrors, all beneath a Mexican-inspired outdoor mural of social commentary. The train is a late but well-received arrival. Get aboard.

[L13] **St. Clement's Church** (Episcopal)/originally **Faith Chapel, West Presbyterian Church,** 423 W.46th St., bet. Ninth and Tenth Aves. 1870. *Edward D. Lindsey.* Altered 1882.

Picturesque Gothic Revival, with Victorian brickwork, fish-scale slate shingles, and very-pointed window arches. It has also served for many years as home for Playhouse 46 and many noteworthy dance and dramatic productions.

[L14] **The Piano Factory**/originally **Wessell, Nickel & Gross Company,** 454 W.46th St., bet. Ninth and Tenth Aves. 1888. Converted, 1980.

A New England-style mill building (complete with mill yard entered through a

[L16] **The Intrepid Sea, Air & Space Museum,** a World War II aircraft carrier, moored at Pier 86, foot of West 46th Street. Open to the public: April 1-September 30, Mo-Fr 10-5, Sa-Su 10-6. Oct 1-Mar 31 Tu-Su 10-5.
www.intrepidmuseum.org

It is both a museum where one can climb into the cockpit of a torpedo bomber (or see films of fighting in the 1940s) and **giant floating architecture.**

[L17] **High School of Graphic Communication Arts**/originally **High School of Printing,** 439 W.49th and W.50th Sts., bet. Ninth and Tenth Aves. 1959. *Kelly & Gruzen.*

One of the most vigorous International Style buildings in town, overlooked in its isolation in the west reaches of Clinton (its style has worn well). Here glass block presents a façade of style, with a sinuous articulated auditorium umbilically connected as a specially shaped form. The interior sports escalators are the first to be used in a local high school.

L14

L13

L15

L18

robust Romanesque Revival arch) squeezed onto an urban site. The factory made the innards for pianos.

[L15] **Landmark Tavern,** 626 Eleventh Ave., SE cor. W.46th St.

It dates from 1868 and looks every minute of it: dark wood, dusty mirrors, floors of two-bit-sized round white tiles, and Franklin stoves for heat on cold days. There's even a paneled and stained-glass "Gentlemen's" off the bar.

N.Y.C. Cruise Terminal, Port Authority of New York and New Jersey, Hudson River at W.48th, W.50th, and W.52nd Sts. along Twelfth Ave. W side. 1976. When the Liberté, Queen Mary, United States, *or* Andrea Doria *were still plying the oceans, it was said that what New York City needed to dignify transatlantic arrivals and departures was modern superliner piers. The piers were finally built; the superliners, however, were scrapped: now cruise ships dock and depart, but the* Queen Mary II's *new New York home is in Red Hook, Brooklyn.*

[L18] Originally **New York Telephone Company,** now **AT&T,** 425-437 W.50th St., and 430 W.51st St. bet. Ninth and Tenth Aves. 1930. *Voorhees, Gmelin & Walker.*

A telephone building from the era when people were still needed to complete your phone call (thus requiring windows), and the image of a company in the community was a high priority (thus justifying the willow leaf **Art Deco** and **Art Moderne** ornament).

[L19] **Sacred Heart of Jesus Church** (Roman Catholic), 457 W.51st St., bet. Ninth and Tenth Aves. 1884. *Napoleon LeBrun & Sons.* **Rectory,** 1881, *Arthur Crooks.*

A symmetric confection of deep red brick and matching terra cotta frosted with light-colored stone arches, band courses, and copings: a sober, if not sturdy, Victorian Romanesque. Inside, the Romanesque (still Victorian) opts for Italian, lighter and airier colonnades, rather than the stolid masonry of France and Spain.

STALLED: [L20] **Clinton Park Apartments**, 770 Eleventh Ave., bet. 53rd and 54th Sts. *Enrique Norten of TEN Arquitectos.*

A tall, swiveling wall of apartments is promised; space for people above and horses (from the Times Square mounted police unit) and cars (for sale) at ground level. What an intriguing mix! Horses in the paddock, cars in the garage, yuppies in glass. But the project, foundations poured, is stalled.

[L21] Originally **Switching Center, New York Telephone Company/American Telephone & Telegraph Company**, 811 Tenth Ave., bet. W.53rd and W.54th Sts. W side. 1964. Exterior, *Kahn & Jacobs.* Interior, *Smith, Smith, Haines, Lundberg & Waehler.*

A tall windowless colossus that looks, from a distance, as though covered with glistening mattress ticking. No long distance operators here—only electronic robotry.

L17

[L22] **Harbor View Terrace, N.Y.C. Housing Authority**, W.54th and W.55th, and W.55th and W.56th Sts., bet. Tenth and Eleventh Aves. 1977. *Herbert L. Mandel.*

The Authority's best in Manhattan. The combination of cast-in-place concrete and deep terra-cotta-colored giant brick (for walls) and bronze anodized aluminum (for balcony railings) promotes a domestic and urbane scale. The project is built over the air rights of the depressed West Side freight line.

[L23] Originally **Interborough Rapid Transit Company (IRT) Powerhouse**/now **Consolidated Edison**, W.58th to W.59th Sts., bet. Eleventh and Twelfth Aves. 1904. *Stanford White of McKim, Mead & White.*

A brick and terra-cotta temple to power with a *Stanford White* exterior, that once boasted six tall smokestacks belching gas from enormous coal furnaces. The coal was received at an adjacent dock on the Hudson and transport-

ed to bunkers on electric conveyor belts; ashes were removed the same way. All the electricity for the original IRT subway, opened in 1904, was generated here.

[L24] **BMW Manhattan Showroom**, NE cor. Eleventh Ave. and 57th St. 1990s.

A hi-tech glass skirt shields the Beemers with cables, clips, and struts: merchandising architecture worthy of the products on sale?

[L25] **The Helena (apartments)**, 601 West 57th Street, NW cor. Eleventh Ave. 2007. *FxFowle.*

A 38-story luxury pioneer at the west edge of Clinton. A notch above most of the fervored glasseries of 21st-century Manhattan. Located "beyond the pale," it's sleek, but not sassy.

[L26] **Catholic Apostolic Church**, 417 W.57th St., bet. Ninth and Tenth Aves. 1885-1886. *Francis H. Kimball.* 🍎

A superior work of urban architecture, three-dimensional—not merely a façade—now almost forgotten because of bulky nonentities that squeeze against but fail to conceal it. Its restrained coloring of russet brick and terra cotta adds to its power.

[L27] **The Windermere**, 400-406 W. 57th St., SW cor. Ninth Ave. 1880-1881. *Theophilus G. Smith.* 🍎

Somber brick and brownstone clads this venerable apartment block from the era of the Dakota. Apartment living came to the West Side

L24

earlier that to the East. Corbeled and polychromatic brick patterning enriches the façade planes.

[L28] **John Jay College of Criminal Justice**/formerly **Haaren High School**/originally **DeWitt Clinton High School**, 899 Tenth Ave., bet. W.58th and W.59th Sts. 1903-1906. *C.B.J. Snyder.* Rebuilt and expanded, 1988, *Rafael Viñoly Architects.*

Flemish Renaissance Revival encrustations enliven the façades of this old high school. John Jay, the City University unit for police and ancillary criminal justice, inherited this as their central building, expanded elegantly and gracefully by *Rafael Viñoly.*

[L29] **St. Luke's/Roosevelt Hospital Center**, Tenth Ave. bet. W.58th and W.59th Sts., E side. 1990. *Skidmore, Owings & Merrill.*

Grandiosity without grace, this 13-story cube brought the old Roosevelt block into the late 20th century: a technological set of tubes, wires, computers, and other hard assets are encapsulated in this bland external fancy dress.

[L30a] **Entrance lobby, Roosevelt East,** 925 Ninth Ave./originally **William J. Syms Operating Theater,** Roosevelt Hospital, 400 W.59th St., SW cor. Ninth Ave. 1890-1892. *W. Wheeler Smith.* 👁

[L30b] **Roosevelt East,** 925 Ninth Ave. bet. 58th and 59th Sts. 1997. *Buck/Cane and Schuman Lichtenstein Claman & Efron.*

Originally Roosevelt Hospital's teaching amphitheater, where spectators, on concentric, stepped seating rings oversaw the master medics at work. Now the affluent mingle with ghosts of surgeons past as they trundle through to their 49 stories of condos.

[L31] **Church of St. Paul the Apostle** (Roman Catholic), Columbus Ave., SW cor. W.60th St. 1876, 1885. *Jeremiah O' Rourke.* Altar and baldachino, 1887-1890, *Stanford White.* Ceiling and windows. *John La Farge.*

The largest **un-cathedral** in America. An unadorned fort on the outside, except for the awkward bas-relief over the entrance; a Roman

L28

basilica inside, embellished with the works of *Augustus Saint-Gaudens, Frederick MacMonnies,* and *John La Farge,* with the advice of *Stanford White* and *Bertram Goodhue.* All of their efforts are lost in the thick atmosphere. *O' Rourke* died before the plans were complete. *Paulist Father George Deshon, U.S. Grant's* roommate at the U.S. Military Academy, took over.

The former **Henry Hudson Hotel**/once the **Clubhouse of the American Women's Association,** 353 W.57th St., bet. Eighth and Ninth Aves. 1929. Benjamin Wistar Morris. Remodeled, 1999, Philippe Starck. A social, rather than architectural landmark on San Juan Hill; it began as a club for young women, served as bachelor officers' quarters in World War II, and once housed Channel 13. Note the bridge in the sky connecting the roof gardens of the two wings.

[L32] **Joan Weill Center for Dance,** 405 W.55th St., NE cor. 9th Ave. 2004. *Iu and Biblowitz.*

The new home for the Alvin Ailey Dance Foundation. A brick core divides the building into two glass volumes. The transparent façade is animated by the sight of troupes of dancers going through their routines on each of the six stories. A sympathetic addition to the neighborhood, both in scale and materials.

San Juan Hill: The rise in topography near Ninth Avenue and West 57th Street was, around 1900, a black community dubbed San Juan Hill after the heroic exploits of a black unit in the Spanish-American War. This stretch of West 57th Street between Eighth and Ninth Avenues bears a curiously European look in its architectural scale.

END of Clinton Tour: The nearest subways are along Eighth Avenue between 57th Street and Columbus Circle: the IND Sixth and Eighth Avenue Lines (A, B, C, and D trains) and the IRT Broadway-Seventh Avenue local (1 train).

NECROLOGY

Miller Elevated Highway/better known as **The West Side Highway,** Rector St. to W.72nd St., over West St., Eleventh and Twelfth Aves. Canal to W.22nd Sts., 1931. W.59th to W.82nd Sts., 1932. W.22nd to W. 38th Sts., 1933. W.38th to W.46th Sts., 1934. W.46th to W.59th Sts., 1937. *Sloan & Robertson,* architects for these sec-

L30a

tions. Canal St. bridge, 1939. Rector to Canal Sts., 1948.

Potholes, rust, and many other indications of the impact of rock salt, heavy traffic, and deferred maintenance were visible along the elevated West Side Highway before December 15, 1973, when the combined weight of an asphalt- laden dump truck and a car finally caused a major collapse—near the Gansevoort Market—thus sealing its doom. For a time, the abandoned roadway attracted bicyclists and artists eager to exploit its huge concrete canvas. The elegant steel arch that suspended the highway across Canal Street spent its last days gaily decorated with 140 gallons of pink, purple, and blue paint, a composition called "Hudson Summer Sunset" by its creator, *A. Eric Arctander.*

TIMES SQUARE TO
COLUMBUS CIRCLE

Up to the 1890s, much of the 40s and 50s west of Seventh Avenue were written off as Hell's Kitchen, a seething mixture of factories and tenements where even the cops moved in pairs. The rich ventured in only as far west as Broadway in the upper 40s, an area of carriage shops for the horsey set called Long Acre, after a similar district in London. In 1883 the Metropolitan Opera House opened on Broadway between 39th and 40th Streets. Some said the 3,700-seat theater looked like a yellow brick brewery on the outside, but inside the City's nouveaux riches could observe each other in red and gold-encrusted splendor. They had built their very own opera house when the Old Guard denied them boxes in their Academy of Music downtown. The tide turned quickly as the moneyed classes soon flocked uptown, and three years later the Academy closed. The whole center of social gravity had now shifted from points south to the 50s on Fifth Avenue.

Then big things happened quickly. Charles Frohman ventured to open his Empire Theatre, directly across Broadway from the Metropolitan Opera, in 1893; Oscar Hammerstein did him one better in 1895 by opening the Olympia, a block-long palace on Broadway between 44th and 45th Streets (then a muddy stretch) with a concert hall, a music hall, a theater, and a roof garden. Soon lavish restaurants like Rector's, Shanley's, and Café de l'Opera were dispensing lobster and champagne to Diamond Jim Brady, "Bet a Million" Gates, George M. Cohan, and other luminaries of the theater, financial, and sporting world. When the City decided to route its first subway west from Grand Central along 42nd Street, then north on Broadway, New York Times publisher Adolph Ochs saw a chance to outdo his competitors by erecting an imposing tower at Broadway and 42nd. He got the station there officially named Times Square in April 1904.

By then the area was becoming established as the theater district, and the evening crowds and broad vistas attracted the early electric sign makers; the 1916 Zoning Resolution made specific allowances for vast signs in the area. In the 1920s, neon and movies took over. In Hollywood's heyday, movie and variety palaces preempted the valuable Broadway frontier, and legitimate theater retreated to the side streets. The signs got bigger as the crowds got bigger, and began to feature things like rooftop waterfalls and real smoke rings. As bigtime movies waned in the 1950s and 1960s, most of the palatial movie theaters were razed, and Times Square was on the verge of an office-building boom.

The banishing of sexual enterprise and the commercial renaissance of Times Square have rapidly changed its flavor: not squeaky clean, but sanitized, at least superficially. New and imposing skyscrapers have brought a daytime weekday crowd to the area. Best of all are the reconstructions of live theaters on 42nd Street. Design and use guidelines developed by the 42nd Street Development Project's advisors, *Robert A.M. Stern* and *Tibor Kalman*, encouraged eclectic tourist and entertainment uses, exuber-ant design, and dazzling signage on façades and rooftops. See the results for yourself.

For Times Square: IRT Broadway-Seventh Avenue Line (Nos.1, 2, and 3 trains), Flushing Line (No.7 train), the Shuttle from Grand Central, or the BMT Broadway Line (N and R trains) to the interconnected Times Square Station.

[T1] **Parsons Center, New School University**/ originally **Brotherhood in Action Building**, 560 Seventh Ave., NW cor. W.40th St. 1950s. *William Lescaze.*

Lescaze (with *George Howe*) designed the noted PSFS Building (Philadelphia Savings Fund Society) included in the MoMA 1932 International Style exhibition. Where did he go? To see *Lescaze* in his most fertile time, visit his house on East 48th Street.

T1a

▌[T1a] **Times Tower**, The New York Times
═ Building, Eighth Ave., bet. 40th and 41st Sts. 2007. *Renzo Piano Building Workshop and FxFowle.*

A tense tower obsessed with its own fussy connections, its glass façade bracketed by steel columns, X-bracing for lateral support, and horizontal bars that act as a sun screen (and ladder: lunatics have been climbing it). As grey and dour as a rain-soaked copy of the Sunday Style section. But venture inside to see the light-filled atrium (open to the public), where bright orange walls accent a maple floor and birch trees and mosses enrich a nice glazed garden.

[T2] **Port Authority Bus Terminal**, W.40th to W.42nd Sts., bet. Eighth and Ninth Aves. 1950. Decks added, 1963. Expansion to W.42nd St. 1980. All by *Port Authority of N.Y. & N.J. Architectural Design Team*.

Glorious **Pennsylvania Station** is only a memory; **Grand Central Terminal** basks in its glorious reconstruction. The **Port Authority Bus Terminal** only grows in popularity. Twenty years ago this was one of the scariest places in the City. Now it's a shopping mall where you can catch a bus.

In 2009 Richard Rodgers designed 42 stories of shiny steel and glass for the top of the bus termi-nal, the better to go tower-to-tower with Renzo Piano across Eighth Avenue. Or did we dream it?

 [T3] **330 West 42nd Street Building**, originally **McGraw-Hill Building**, bet. Eighth and Ninth Aves. 1930-1931. *Raymond Hood, Godley & Fouilhoux.* 🍎
Hood's tower with continuous horizontal

octagonal drum, dome, lantern, and crucifix over the crossing. This was the parish church of *Father Duffy* of World War I fame (see his statue at Duffy Square). The school, on West 43rd Street, has a rich Romanesque Revival façade of red brick and matching terra cotta.

[T5] **11 Times Square Tower**, SE cor. 42nd St. and Eighth Ave. 2009. *FxFowle.*

Chiseled glass? Facets of glass tilted and shimmering play for lively reflections on this bulky block. A stretch for the Times Square address, and a hulk of a building: but aren't they all these days, some cleverly disguised by slots and shapes to diminish their apparent bulk. Some make it that way, some don't.

[T6] **Second Stage Theater**/originally **Manufacturers Hanover Bank**, 681 Eighth Ave., NW cor. W.43rd St. 1927. Converted to theater, 1999. *Rem Koolhaas and Richard Gluckman.*

An austere bank, its multicolored column cap-itals a rich abstraction of Art Deco variations on a

T2

T3   T5

T8

bands of blue-green terra-cotta rose simultane-ously with his vertically striped News Building at the other end of 42nd Street. *Lewis Mumford*, an early fan of modern architecture, wrote that the building was just a "stunt," and that the colors were "heavy and unbeautiful." Critic *Arthur North* (in the *American Architect*, 1932) called it a "storm center" that showed "disregard for every accepted principle of archi-tectural designing in the most flagrant man-ner." Yet it was the only New York building shown at *Hitchcock* and *Johnson's* epochal MoMA exhibition, The International Style, in 1932. The details, however, are Art Deco/Art Moderne: the lobby an extraordinary remem-brance of Carrera (opaque) glass, stainless steel, and elegant lights.

[T4] **Holy Cross Church** (Roman Catholic), 333 W.42nd St., bet. Eighth and Ninth Aves. 1870. *Henry Engelbert.* [T4a] Holy Cross School, 332 W.43rd St. 1887. *Lawrence J. O'Connor.*

Dubbed "Byzantine style" when built, the brick façade conceals the verdigris copper-clad

Classical theme. The *Koolhaas/Gluckman* interior is appropriately spartan (no 1920s retro flamboy-ance here), but the bathrooms are orange.

[T7] Originally **Charles Scribner's Sons** printing plant, 311 W. 43rd St., bet. Eighth and Ninth Aves. 1907. *Ernest Flagg.*

Flagg, architect of **Scribner's** headquarters, stores, and town houses, was, predictably, also architect for this straightforward industrial facili-ty. Its iron curtain wall is marred by a thoughtless ground-floor "improvement and replacement of the gutsy, industrial steel, sash windows." See the faded *Scribner's* on the west wall.

42nd Street, Eighth Avenue to Broadway:

[T8] **Westin New York at Times Square** (hotel), Eighth Ave., SE cor. 43rd St. 2002. *Arquitectonica.*

An extravagance delivering histrionic archi-tectural form, sadly banal, and missing an opportunity for the renaissance Times Square's old world of light bulbs and neon. Meant as a bit of Florida color and Las Vegas fantasy imported to Manhattan's strict blocks, it's not an inside joke.

[T9] **E-Walk Complex**, NE cor. W.42nd St. and Eighth Ave. 1999. *D'Agostino Izzo Quirk and Gensler Associates.* Signage, *Kupiec Koutsomitis Architects.* Within: Vegas! (restaurant), *The Cunningham Group.* 13-screen SONY theater complex, *The Rockwell Group.*

Controlled **visual cacophony** here hoped to outperform the traditional image of Times Square lights and action: all based on the schematic criteria developed by *Robert A.M. Stern* for a renaissance of vitality on what had become a bleak (and sex-oriented) block. The attempt to bring extravagance to the streetscape has succeeded as a "wax museum" of childish architecture, save for the New Victory reconstruction and the 42nd Street studios. Unlike a stage set, it can't merely be put aside for another scene designer.

The trendy **Hilton** hotel straddles wide entertainment and merchandising spaces below, astride massive trusses.

History: **Harris Theater**. 226 W.42nd St. 1914. *Thomas W. Lamb.* **Liberty Theater**, 234 W.42nd St. 1904. *Herts & Tallant.* **Empire Theater**, 236 W.42nd St. 1912. *Thomas W. Lamb.*

[T11] **Candler Building**, 220 W.42nd St., bet. Seventh and Eighth Aves. 1914. *Willauer, Shape & Bready.* Renovations, 1999, *Swanke Hayden Connell.*

The nationwide success of **Coca-Cola** persuaded *Asa Candler*, its supersalesman, to build this gleaming white terra-cotta-clad tower off Times Square; but now, with an overpowering marquee, it seems to be the McDonald's building. Above, its skin, long begrimed, shines once more and its innards have been equally modernized. Look up, and skyward there are lurking dragons. Telescope?

T9   T17

T11

T12

[T10] **Forest City Ratner Theater & Store Complex**, including the former **Harris, Liberty,** and **Empire Theaters**, between the Candler Building and Eighth Ave., S side of 42nd St. 2000. *Beyer Blinder Belle and The Rockwell Group.* **AMC** (movie) **Theaters**, *Benjamin Thompson & Assocs.* [T10a] **Hilton Hotel**, above and behind the theater and store complex. 2001. *Beyer Blinder Belle.*

The relocated **Empire Theater façade** (170 feet west of its birthplace) screens the lobby of a 25-screen movie house. The façades of its classmates, **Harris** and **Liberty**, punctuate the length of this all-new mega-merchandising and movie complex. **Liberty** leads to a merchant of athletic shoes, Just for Feet (*Lawrence M. Rosenbloom Architects*), and **Harris** to *Madame Tussaud* (she does get around; *Ohlhausen Dubois*, architects with *Architecture IMG*).

[T12] **The New 42nd Street Studios**, 229 W. 42nd St., bet. Eighth and Seventh Aves. 2001. *Platt Byard Dovell.*

A glassy set of studios for actors and dancers that plugs the gap between E-Walk and a venerable but renewed theater row. Stainless-steel sun grilles shield the south façade, but at night the action within becomes part of street theater, more alive than the tawdry E-Walk complex to the west. 229's reality outscores that theme park.

[T13] **Times Square Theater**, 215 W.42nd St., bet. Eighth and Seventh Aves. 1920. *DeRosa and Pereira.*

Once a 1,056-seat theater, the grand colonnade leads to a clothing store—four stories of stuff within the theater's old volume—balconies and domes lurking within the retail space as ghostly representatives of past patronage.

[T14] **Hilton Theater**/originally **site of Lyric and Apollo Theaters**, 213 W.42nd St., bet. Eighth and Seventh Aves. **Lyric**, 1903, *Victor Hugo Koehler*. **Apollo**, 1920, *DeRosa & Pereira*. Blended and reconstructed, 1998, *Beyer Blinder Belle*.

Behind all those signs and lightbulbs lurks a tiny but ornate façade leading to the bulky body of the theater on 43rd. Inside, reincarnations provide a massive three-dimensional collage of recycled parts, incorporating elements of the **Lyric** and **Apollo** theaters (domes, arches, vaults, boxes). (Alternately enter on 43rd to a façade of terra cotta: snakes, rams, a deer.)

[T15] **New Victory Theater**/originally **Republic Theater**/sometime **Belasco Theater**/onetime **Minsky's**, 209-211 W.42nd St., bet. Eighth and Seventh Aves. 1899. *Albert Westover*. Restored and remodeled, 1995, *Hardy Holzman Pfeiffer*.

A glorious robust restoration redolent of this turn-of-the-century theater's whole district (*Oscar Hammerstein* built this one). One ascends the theatrical stoop to the perform-

TIMES SQUARE

A state of mind as much as a physical location, this is the center of circulation to a much larger area of theaters and restaurants—a vast vestibule to entertainment. Gaudy signs are its nighttime architecture, their exuberant vulgarity the marquee that proclaims the theatrical wonders in the surrounding streets. Zoning and Landmarks laws have teamed up to require brilliant and pervasive signs within viewing of the central spaces created by the crossing of Seventh Avenue and Broadway.

[T17] **1 Times Square**/formerly **Allied Chemical Tower**/originally **Times Tower**, W.42nd St. bet. Broadway and Seventh Ave., N to W.43rd St. 1903-1905. *Cyrus L.W. Eidlitz* and *Andrew C. MacKenzie*. Reconstructed, 1966, *Smith, Smith, Haines, Lundberg & Waehler*.

The **New York Times** moved into its 25-story tower with dramatic timing on December 31, 1904, marking the occasion with a fireworks

T15

ance as one did to a great museum. The interior is breathtaking. And there is a bit of **Minsky's** in its exuberance. (Minsky's was a famed burlesque house 1931-1938.)

[T16] **New Amsterdam Theatre**, 214 W.42nd St., bet. Seventh and Eighth Ave. 1902-1903. *Herts & Tallant*. ● Interior. ● Elaborately restored, 1995-1997, *Hardy Holzman Pfeiffer and Walt Disney Imagineering*. [T16a] **New Amsterdam Roof Theatre**/originally **New Amsterdam Aerial Gardens**. 1904. *Herts & Tallant*.

The sliver office tower on 42nd Street houses the lobby of the theater on 41st. Rare for New York: Art Nouveau. But what a miracle the Disney Renaissance has produced within, through *Hugh Hardy's* extraordinary heightened restoration of *Herts & Tallant* ideas; and the ideas of artists *Robert Blum, George Peixotto*, and *Henry Mercer*. The **Ziegfield Follies** and *George White's* **"Scandals"** were both staged here.

display at midnight that made Times Square the place to see in the New Year ever since. The paper moved a decade later (1913) to larger quarters on West 43rd Street, but the name remained. New owners stripped off the original Italian Renaissance terra-cotta skin and replaced it with Miami Beach marble. More recent Times Square "renewal" has relegated it to a role as a supersignboard, though offices still survive within.

World's first "moving" sign: First to electrify passers-by along the Great White Way were the election returns of 1928 delivered along the Motogram, a five-foot-high, 360-foot-long sign flasher that wrapped around the old Times Tower's four sides and utilized 14,800 lamps to convey its constantly changing messages. The tower has changed its face; a much revised and restored Motogram remains.

[T18] **Ernst & Young National Headquarters**, 5 Times Square, Seventh Ave. bet. 41st and 42nd Sts. W side. (or SW cor. 42nd St.) 2002. *Kohn Pedersen Fox.*

Big and bulky, it flaunts its CPA (accounting) brand name on a great Broadway sign (but, of course, the signs are required by the Zoning District). And, at the base, it's a riot of other signage. From a good distance a fin flashes reflections: architecture is up here.

[T19] **Times Square Tower,** 7 Times Square, bet. Broadway and Seventh Ave. 2002-2004. *David Childs (Skidmore, Owings and Merrill).*

An elusive building to the Times Square stroller: behind the old Times Building at No.1, it looms, but seems almost part of its smaller ancestor. And, as part of its costume, it presents different faces to different streets. Broadway is the most interesting: trying too hard doesn't make the grade (e for effort?).

[T21] **Condé Nast Building**, 4 Times Sq., NE cor. Broadway. 1999. *Fox & Fowle.*

[T22] **Reuters Building**, 3 Times Sq., bet. W.42nd and W.43rd Sts. 2001. *Fox & Fowle.*

The complicated skyscraper has replaced the skyline skyscraper to contend, and perhaps compete, with the coordinated chaos of Times Square. Here two buildings supply visual cacophony at the street, morphing into different shapes and materials as they rise, veneered, then crowned, with an armature of signs and finials. Each one provides a microcosm of Times Square's spirit. Condé Nast offers a further sophisticated step, providing a sedate elevation to the east.

Fowle speaks of his "cues from **Nathan's**" harking back to one of **SOM's** earliest buildings on the SE corner of Broadway and 43rd (originally **Toffenetti's**, lastly **Nathan's** of hot dog fame. 1939-1940. *Skidmore, Owings & Merrill with Walker & Gillette).* Built for World's Fair crowds, **Toffenetti's** was a sleek streamlined place of curving blue panels.

T19   T21

T20   T26

[T20] **6 Times Square**/onetime **Newsweek Building**/originally **Knickerbocker Hotel**, 1462-1470 Broadway, SE cor. Broadway. 1901-1906. *Marvin & Davis,* architects. *Bruce Price,* consultant. Annex, 143 W.41st St. 1907. *Trowbridge & Livingston.* Altered, 1980, *Libby, Ross & Whitehouse.* 🍎

An import from Napoleon III and his **Second Empire** inflated to New York scale. Three of its 21 floors are harbored within the mansard, their dormers cascading down the slopes. Knickerbocker, originally built for John Jacob Astor, was home to many Broadway elite: stars such as *Enrico Caruso* and *George M. Cohan* once lived here. A gold service for 60 and a bar so fashionable in its heyday made it known known as the 42nd Street Country Club.

[T23] **U.S. Armed Forces Recruiting Station**, on an island in Times Sq. bet. Seventh Ave. and Broadway. 1999. *Parsons Brinckerhoff and Architecture Research Office.*

An electronic flag? For electronic warfare?

[T24] **Town Hall**, 113-123 W.43rd St., bet. Sixth Ave. and Broadway 1919-1921. *McKim, Mead & White.* 🍎 Interior. 🍎

Bland Georgian Revival on the outside shelters a large but intimate, acoustically distinguished, concert hall within. Citizens of the world who have spoken here include *Winston Churchill, Theodore Roosevelt, Margaret Sanger,* and *Henry James.*

[T25] Onetime **New York Times Building**/originally the **Times Annex**, 217-247 W. 43rd St. 1912-1913. *Buchman & Fox.* 1922-1924. *Ludlow & Peabody.* 1930-1932. *Albert Kahn.* 🍎

The annex child (complete with printing plant) became the parent *New York Times* headquarters; later the plant was exiled, to an

T22

elegant new building in College Point, Queens (1997, *Polshek Partnership*). The ultimate move brought *Times* staff to the new *Renzo Piano*-designed Times Tower on Eighth Avenue.

[T26] **Paramount Building**/originally **Paramount Theatre Building**, 1501 Broadway, bet. W.43rd and W.44th Sts. W side. 1926-1927. *C. W. Rapp & George L. Rapp*. 🗝

The tower, clocks, and globe (once illuminated) are sensational. In the early days there was even an observation deck.

T-Square, the first **New Yorker Magazine** architectural critic, ranted that "the design... (was) likely to knock the layman for a loop, while leaving the instructed critic more than cold... (there is) gargantuan rudeness in the huge clock at the top, over which perches something like an incense-burner or incinerator for the ashes of departed films...". We hardly notice it today, our eyes at street level, glutted with flashing and shifting light.

[T27] Originally **The Lambs Club**/now **Manhattan Church of the Nazarene**, 130 W.44th St., bet. Sixth Ave. and Broadway. 1905. *Stanford White of McKim, Mead & White*. Doubled westerly, 1915, *George A. Freeman*. 🗝

A neo-Federal clubhouse built for a still-lively assembly of the elite in theater and its arts; now relocated to 51st Street at Fifth Avenue. *McKim Mead & White* were all Lambs. "Floreant Agni 1874-1904." Doric columns with full entablatures mark entries at the ground floor; upstairs Flemish bonded brickwork, limestone-quoined, takes over.

[T28] **Belasco Theater**/originally **Belasco's Stuyvesant Theater**, 111 W.44th St., bet. Sixth Ave. and Broadway. 1906-1907. *George Keister*. 🗝 Interior. 🗝

Red brick Colonial Revival; limestone pilasters supporting Composite capitals embrace a trio of monumental arched window openings. *David Belasco* was catalyst (producer or director) to more than 100 plays, including both *Madame Butterfly* and *The Girl of the Golden West*, both later adapted as operas by Puccini.

[T29] **Aka Hotel Residences** / formerly **Gerard Apartments**/onetime **1-2-3 Hotel**/originally **Hotel Gerard**, 123 W.44th St., bet. Sixth Ave. and Broadway. 1893-1894. *George Keister.* 🍎

A tan brick and limestone pile—one of many that once filled Times Square's side streets—extravagantly decked out with German Renaissance gables and dormers and undulating bow windows (beaux bows). Look up...and further up.

[T30] **Hudson Theater of the Millenium Hotel**/originally **Hudson Theater**/once **Savoy Theater**, 139-141 W.44th St., bet. Sixth and Seventh Aves. 1902-1904. *J. B. McElfatrick & Son and Israels & Harder.* 🍎 Interior. 🍎 Restored, 1990, *Stonehill & Taylor.*

A dour survivor between two wings of the **Millenium**. But that's where its air rights went. Beaux Arts out, exuberant in.

T29

Mid-Block Pedestrianism: *lengthy blocks between Sixth and Eighth Avenues offer mid-block shortcuts that honor pedestrianism in this densely packed section of the City.* **Shubert Alley** *(44th-45th, bet. 7th and 8th) has been around "forever," but modern buildings often offer (sometimes a zoning-bonus requirement) air conditioned tunnels through the block.* **Minskoff Alley**, *east of Shubert, is nearby. Others include the* **Millenium Hotel** *(44th-45th, bet. 6th and 7th), the* **Bertelsmann Building**

T31

(45th-46th, bet. 6th and 7th), the **Marriott Hotel** *(45th-46th, bet. Broadway and 8th),* **Crowne Plaza** *(48th-49th, bet. Broadway and 8th),* **Rockefeller Center West's** *backsides (48th-50th Sts., W of 6th),* **Gershwin Alley** *(50th –51st, Broadway to 8th),* **Equitable Life** *(51st-52nd, 6th to 7th), and* **Flatotel** *(52nd-53rd, 6th to 7th). Look for the black and white diamond pattern and yellow arrows marking the sidewalks (thanks to the Times Square Business Improvement District).*

[T31] **Astor Plaza**, 1515 Broadway, bet. W.44th and W.45th Sts. W side. 1968-1970. *Kahn & Jacobs. Der Scutt, designer.*

A 50-story office tower that replaced one of Times Square's most beloved landmarks, the **Astor Hotel**. From afar its finial fins look like the tail of an impaled spaceship. This was the first building to exploit the special Times Square Theater District zoning bonuses that allowed developers to erect buildings of greater than normal bulk in return for constructing a new "legitimate" theater.

[T32] **Shubert Alley**, from W.44th St. to W.45th St., bet. Broadway and Eighth Aves.

Now a convenience for theatergoers, this private alley was once a magnet for aspiring actors, who gathered in front of the offices of *J.J. and Lee Shubert* when plays were being cast.

[T33] **Sam S. Shubert Theatre**, 225 W.44th St., bet. Broadway and Eighth Ave. at Shubert Alley. 1912-1913. *Henry B. Herts.* 🍎 Interior 🍎
[T34] **Booth Theatre**, 222 W.45th St. 1913. *Henry B. Herts.* 🍎 Interior. 🍎

The pair of richly ornamented theaters—the large Shubert and the smaller Booth—that forms the west "wall" of Shubert Alley. The Shubert is the heart (cum theater and offices) of the Shubert theater empire. *A Chorus Line* showed that empire's lasting power. And the Booth was home to *You Can' t Take It with You* and *Sunday in the Park with George.* The light-bulbed sign is a good remembrance of 1930s Broadway: no LCD computer simulation here.

*[T35] **Sardi's**: The restaurant at 234 West 44th Street, strategically located among theaters and at the back door to the New York Times, has for decades been the place for actors to be seen—except during performance hours.*

[T36] **Helen Hayes Theater**/formerly **Little Theater**/onetime **Anne Nichol's Little Times Hall**, 240 W.44th St., bet. Broadway and Eighth Ave. 1912. *Ingalls & Hoffman.* Interior rebuilt 1917-1920. *Herbert J. Krapp.* 👁 Interior. 👁

Bland Georgian Revival with awful pseudo-shutters that, of course, don't shut. Producer *Winthrop Ames* sought a context for "intimate" theater.

[T37] **St. James Theater**/formerly **Erlanger Theater**, 246-256 W.44th St., bet. Broadway and Eighth Ave. 1926-1927. *Warren & Wetmore.* 👁 Interior. 👁

T40

The fire escape offers the street a rich **Moorarabic** balcony set in an austere brick wall. Here were sung *Oklahoma!, Hello Dolly,* and *The King and I.*

[T38] **Broadhurst Theater**, 235-243 W.44th St., bet. Broadway and Eighth Ave. 1917-1918. *Herbert J. Krapp.* 👁 Interior 👁
[T39] **Majestic Theater**, 247 W.44th St., bet. Broadway and Eighth Ave. 1926-1927. *Herbert J. Krapp.* Interior. 👁

Two subdued, understated, but functional playhouses. The **Majestic** was home to *South Pacific* and *The Phantom of the Opera,* the longest running play in Broadway history. The **Broadhurst's** stars includes *Leslie Howard, Katherine Hepburn* and *Dustin Hoffman.*

[T40] **Marriott Marquis Hotel**, 1531-1549 Broadway, bet. W.45th and W.46th Sts. W side. 1981-1985. *John Portman, Jr.*

A spectacular lobby with glassed-in rocket ship elevators starts at the eighth floor, a super-atrium here squeezed into Broadway real estate (*Portman's* earlier attempts in Atlanta, Chicago, and San Francisco allowed for more horizontal dimension). Inside, it is glitzy in a way developers think appropriate to Broadway.

[T41] **Lyceum Theatre**, 149-157 W.45th St., bet. Sixth Ave. and Broadway. 1902-1903. *Herts & Tallant.* 👁 Interior. 👁

Powerful neo-Baroque columns articulate the grandest of Beaux Arts façades. Saved from demolition in 1939, it survived to become the oldest New York theater still used for legitimate productions and the first to be landmarked. Magnificent.

[T42] **Music Box Theater**, 239-247 W.45th St., bet. Broadway and Eighth Ave. 1920. *C. Howard Crane and E. George Kiehler.* 👁 Interior. 👁

Irving Berlin built this intimate theater for his own productions. A porch with slender

T41

Federal Revival columns articulates the façade. Within some have seen *The Man Who Came to Dinner* and *Dinner at Eight.*

For the Booth Theater, see above.

[T43] **Schoenfeld Theater** / formerly **Plymouth Theater**, 236 W.45th St., Bet. Broadway and Eighth Ave. 1917-1918. *Herbert J. Krapp.* 👁 Interior. 👁 [T44] **Bernard B. Jacobs Theater**/ formerly Royale Theater, 242 W.45th St. 1926-1927. *Herbert J. Krapp.* 👁 Interior. 👁 [T45] **Golden Theater**/originally **Theatre Masque**, 252-256 W.45th St. 1926-1927. *Herbert J. Krapp.* 👁 Interior. 👁 [T46] **Imperial Theater**, 249 W.45th St. 1923. *Herbert J. Krapp.* Interior only. 👁

Unassuming except for the **Golden,** where tall arches relieve a façade crowned with a colonnaded gallery. *Ethel Barrymore* receiving adulation from her fans? *Tobacco Road* began here. The **Plymouth** housed *The Odd Couple,* and the **Royale** was home to *The Night of the Iguana.* The **Imperial** *Gypsy, Cabaret,* and *Les Misérables.*

[T47] **Al Hirschfeld Theater**/originally **Martin Beck Theater**, 302 W.45th St., bet. Eighth and Ninth Aves. 1923-1924. *C. Albert Lansburgh.* ● Interior. ●

Producer *Martin Beck* commissioned *Lansburgh* and painter *Albert Herter* to create this fantasy of Romanesque histrionics. What better place to play *Man of La Mancha*?

[T48] **The Platinum**, 247 W. 46th St., bet. Broadway and Eighth Ave. 2008. *Costas Kondylis.*

More glass, another 43 stories. Ho, and two hums.

[T49] **Paramount Hotel**, 245 W.46th St., bet. Broadway and Eighth Ave. Interiors remodeled, 1980s. *Philippe Starck.*

A boutique hotel wearing the high style of French designer and motorcyclist *Philippe Starck*. Much ado on its façade, swathed in concealing drapery; when whipped off, perhaps the style of *Starck* will have oozed out by osmosis.

T47

Brick and brownstone Romanesque Revival: a sober Protestant foil to St. Mary's quasi-Catholic façade opposite. It was *C.B.J. Snyder*'s first school, the beginning of his 30-year career as Superintendent of School Buildings.

[T52] **I. Miller Building**, 1522-1554 Broadway, NE cor. 46th St. 1926. *Louis H. Freeland.* ●

"The Show Folks Shoe Shop." Great women of the theater are honored in sculpture on the façade of the former I. Miller Building: Mary Pickford (as the title in Little Lord Fauntleroy), Rosa Ponselle (in the title role in Norma), Ethel Barrymore (as Ophelia), and Marilyn Miller (in the title role of the musical, Sunny). They are all by A(lexander) Stirling Calder, father of the late, famed inventor of mobiles, Alexander Calder. 1929.

[T53] **Richard Rodgers Theater**/originally **Chanin's Forty-sixth Street Theater**, 226 W.46th St., bet. Broadway and Eighth Ave. 1924. *Herbert J. Krapp.* ● Interior. ●

Giant white terra-cotta Corinthian pilasters and arches suggest a style that could be coined as Broadway Renaissance. Within played *Guys and Dolls*.

[T54] **Lunt-Fontanne Theater**/originally **Globe Theater**, 205 W.46th St. 1909-1910. *Carrère & Hastings*. Rebuilt, 1957-1958. *Roche & Roche*. ●

A mannerist Spanish or Italian Rococo palazzo of the first order. Home to a long run of *The Sound of Music*.

T51   T52

T53

🏛 [T50] **Church of St. Mary the Virgin** (Episcopal); Rectory, Clergy House, Mission House, 145 W.46th St., bet. Sixth and Seventh Aves. 1894-1895. *Pierre Le Brun of Napoleon Le Brun & Sons*, architects. *J. Massey Rhind*, sculptor. ●

A rich liturgical oasis in this precinct of Mammon, booze, and pornography—incense and liturgy here often exceed that of the Catholic Counter-Reformation. The first church in the world to be erected on a steel frame (but concealed; many before, particularly in France, were of cast- and/or wrought-iron, but there exposed).

⌂ [T51] **Jacqueline Kennedy Onassis High School for International Careers**/formerly **Public School 67**/later **High School of the Performing Arts**, 120 W.46th St., bet. Sixth and Seventh Aves. 1893-1894. *C.B.J. Snyder.* ● Restored, 1991-1993, *Jack L. Gordon.*

Duffy Square: The northern triangle of Times Square is dedicated to Father Francis P. Duffy (1871-1932. Charles Keck.) Facing the back of one representing George M. Cohan (1878-1942), another Times Square hero (1959. George Lober). Duffy became a national hero in World War I as "Fighting Chaplain" of New York's 69th Regiment, later as friend of actors, writers, and mayors while pastor of Holy Cross Church on West 42nd Street. Is this an unwritten Bing Crosby story?

▮ [T55] **tkts**, W.47th St., bet. Seventh Ave. and Broadway. S side. 2008. *Nicolas Leahy* of *Perkins Eastman*, architects, & *Choi Ropiha,* designer.

An elegant replacement for the previous "temporary" pipe-and-canvas structure discount ticket stand by the firm of *Mayers & Shiff*, on Duffy Square, 1973-1999. A row of glowing red bleachers doubles as the roof for the ticket stand. *Father Duffy* turns his back, though. What's wrong, Father?

[T56] **Times Square Visitors Center**/originally **Embassy Theater**, 1556-1560 Broadway, bet. W.46th and W.47th Sts. 1925. *Thomas W. Lamb and the Rambusch Studio*. Interior only. ☛ Remodeled as visitors' center, 1998, *Ronette Riley*.

Outside, McDonald's dominates. Inside, a stylish (and tiny) movie house, it became the consummate newsreel theater. The grand foyer now leads to the auditorium space Visitors' Center, where booths will inform you.

[T57] **Doubletree Suites Times Square Hotel**/ originally **Embassy Suites Times Square Hotel**, over the **Palace Theater**, 1564 Broadway, SE cor. W.47th Sts. E side. Theater, 1912-1913. *Kirchoff & Rose*. Renovated, 1965-1966. *Ralph Alswang & John J. McNamara*. ☛ **Palace Theater Interior**. New superimposed and surrounding hotel, 1990-1991, *Fox & Fowle*.

Stacked signs, required by zoning, seem to support the sleek new tower above. The old building, the Carnegie Hall of vaudeville, is now

[T60] **Barrymore Theater**, 243-251 W.47th St., bet. Broadway and Eighth Ave. 1928. *Herbert J. Krapp*. ☛ Interior. ☛

Wondrous ironmongery supports the marquee and modulates the pedestrianway. Here played *A Streetcar Named Desire*.

[T61] **Brooks Atkinson Theater**/originally **Mansfield Theater**, 256-262 W.47th St., bet. Broadway and Eighth Ave. 1925-1926. *Herbert J. Krapp*. ☛ Interior. ☛

Theatrical architecture here delivered a "Spanish" palazzo, Mozarabic columns, and Palladian windows. *Green Pastures* and *Noises Off* played here.

[T62] **Renaissance Hotel** (and offices), 1580 Broadway, on the island at Times Square's north end, between W.47th and W.48th Sts., Broadway to Seventh Ave. 1989. *Mayers & Schiff.*

Here a building is as much a carriage for signs as it is a useful hotel tower. But here again it has been difficult to capture the

T60

T64

enveloped by the new hotel and commercial construction. Before its immersion in this larger project the Palace had already been obliterated by signs.

[T58] **W Times Square**, 1567 Broadway, SW cor. W.47th St. 2001. *Frank Williams & Associates*.

Giant projection screens bring video as an architectural element on this 54-story newcomer to Times Square. **The Central** (later, **Holiday**) Theater (*Herbert J. Krapp*, 1918), was here, converted to a cinema and nightclub, before being sold.

[T59] **Samuel J. Friedman Theater**/formerly **Manhattan Theater Club**/originally **Biltmore Theater**, 261-265 W.47th St., bet. Broadway and Eighth Ave. 1925-1926. *Herbert J. Krapp*. 1987 Interior only. ☛

A simple French palace: perhaps a cut-rate Grand Trianon. *Hair* in the Trianon?

Broadway serendipity of yore. A pure black crystalline form stands behind the display.

[T63] **49th Street BMT Subway Station**, below Seventh Ave. bet. W.47th and W.49th Sts. 1919. Renovated, 1973, *Johnson/Burgee*.

Brilliant glazed vermilion brick set the tone for this early reconstructed subway station.

[T64] Onetime **Morgan Stanley Dean Witter Building**, 1585 Broadway, bet. W.47th and W.48th St. 1995. *Gwathmey Siegel Assocs. & Emery Roth & Sons*. **MSDW'S Investment/ Information Center**. 1998. *Brennan Beer Gorman Monk*.

A talented partnership here designed its first major office building—a jump in scale difficult for all, no matter how gifted. See their addition to the Guggenheim Museum, and their new U.S. Delegation to the United Nations building.

The zipper stock signs have enlivened 1585's early austerity.

[T65] **Longacre Theater,** 220-228 W.48th St. 1912-1913. *Henry B. Herts.* Interior.

An imposing neo-Classical terra-cotta façade, Corinthian pilasters organizing its rand scale. Here we might have seen *Ain' t Misbehavin'* and *Children of a Lesser God.*

[T66] **Walter Kerr Theater**/originally **Ritz Theater,** 218 W. 48th St., bet. Seventh and Eighth Aves. 1921. *Herbert J. Krapp.*

T70

[T69] **Engine Company No.54, Ladder Company No.4, Battalion 9,** N.Y.C. Fire Department, 782 Eighth Ave., SE cor. W.48th St. 1974. *Department of Public Works.*

Even the City's avenue of streetwalkers needs fire protection. This muted brown brick cubist exercise provides it. Congratulations to the D.P.W.

[T70] **785 Eighth Avenue Sliver,** bet. 47th and 48th sts. W.side. 2009. *Ismael Leyva.*

Sliver was an *Ira Levin* novel and a steamy stinker of a movie. But the sliver as building type has made a big comeback, even if *Sharon Stone* hasn't. In the hands of architect *Ismael Leyva* this sliver is higher (556 feet), slimmer (24 feet) and sharper (we assume) than other recent perilously thin condo projects. Viewed from several blocks south, *Leyva's* icy blue needle contrasts nicely with the bulky Worldwide Center just to its west. But seen at street level, with no other towers visible to give it a sense of context and visual support, the

T66

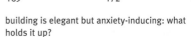

T69   T72

Here we took *The Piano Lesson,* later saw visions of *Angels in America,* and considered *Doubt.*

[T67] **Cort Theater,** 138-146 W.48th St., bet. Sixth and Seventh Aves. 1912-1913. *Thomas W. Lamb.* Interior.

Step back. The marquee masks its grand image as a **Petit Trianon** off Broadway. *The Diary of Anne Frank* played here.

[T68] **Broadway 49 Hotel**/formerly **Crowne Plaza Hotel,** 1601 Broadway, bet. W.48th and W.49th Sts. W side. 1987-1989. *The Alan Lapidus Group.*

The Marriott opened the door for the return of hotels to Times Square. *Alan Lapidus,* son and sometime partner of his father, *Morris* (who created the Miami Beach hotel architecture of the 1940s and 1950s), brings a second dollop of glitz to this precinct. The bottom is in the cluttered Times Square style; the top could be from Hong Kong.

building is elegant but anxiety-inducing: what holds it up?

[T71] **Worldwide Plaza,** Eighth to Ninth Aves., W.49th to W.50th Sts. Apartment towers, 1989, *Frank Williams.* Office tower, 1989, *Skidmore, Owings & Merrill.*

This giant complex occupies the site of the second **Madison Square Garden** (1925-1966), which had been in turn replaced by the present Garden that consumed *McKim's* **Pennsylvania Station**. Zoning changes have encouraged this western migration of both offices and residences, allowing more construction here than can now be erected in East Midtown.

Heavy-handed, the office tower aspires to the serene solidity of **Rockefeller Center,** but lacks that center's graceful slenderness, setbacks and elegant understated urban space: Rockefeller Plaza and its skating rink.

[T72] **St. Malachy's Roman Catholic Church,**
239-245 W.49th St., bet. Broadway and Eighth
Ave. 1903. *Joseph H. McGuire.*

Brick and limestone neo-Gothic, best known
as Broadway's chapel cum offices for Catholic
actors, where a mass could be interwoven with
their matinee and evening schedules.

[T73] **Eugene O'Neill Theater**/formerly **Coronet
Theater**/originally **Forrest Theater**, 230-238
W.49th St. 1925-1926. *Herbert J. Krapp.* ❧
Interior. ❧ Interior restoration, 1994,
Campagna & Russo.

A delicate iron balcony suggests New
Orleans. *Tobacco Road* survived 3,182 perform-
ances here (1934-1941) after opening at the
Theater Masque.

[T74] **Ambassador Theater**, 219 W.49th St., bet.
Seventh Ave. and Broadway. 1919-1921. *Herbert
J. Krapp.* Interior only. ❧

An austere exterior with subtle brick relieving arches and updated machicolations. *Bring*

floors, but the entrancement for most New
Yorkers happens thirty feet above sidewalk
level: In 1999, the City Planning Commission
decreed that new construction in Times Square
must feature large electronic displays. KPF
hired Imaginary Forces, Hollywood experts, to
wow the tourists. Three strips of LED screens
stacked 2-1/2 stories high (alternating politely
with the window grid) sweep across the
Seventh Avenue façade and around the corners.
Images include a sunrise sequence in the morning, abstract swirls during lunch hour, and
moons rising in the evening.

[T77] **Times Square Church**/originally
Hollywood Theater/sometime **Mark Hellinger
Theater**, 217-239 W.51st St., bet. Broadway and
Eighth Ave. 1929-1930. *Thomas W. Lamb* and
the *Rambusch Studio.* ❧ Interior. ❧

Lamb blended *Frank Lloyd Wright, Eliel
Saarinen* outside and Hollywood Baroque
within. Steamy. But the new marquee demeans
it all.

T71

T75

T76

T77

In 'Da Noise, Bring in 'Da Funk has played
here. Inside the delicate plasterwork is reminiscent of the *Adam Brothers*. Outside, Dark. Dour.

[T75] Originally **Morgan Stanley
Building**, 750 Seventh Avenue, bet.
W.49th and W.50th Sts., Broadway and Seventh
Ave. 1988-1990. *Kevin Roche John Dinkeloo &
Assocs.*

Here the heirs of *Eero Saarinen* bring high
style to the blocks north of Times Square proper. The finial finger points accusingly at the sky.
Elsewhere see their **Morgan Bank Headquarters**
at 60 Wall Street, the new Central Park Zoo, and
United Nations Plaza, Nos.1, 2, and 3.

[T76] **Barclay's Capital**/originally **Lehman
Brothers Building**, 745 Seventh Ave. bet.
W.49th and W.50th Sts. E side. 2002. *Kohn
Pederson Fox.*

Students of architecture lift their gaze to
the upper floors to admire intertwined towers
and a glass cage housing the mechanical

[T78] **Winter Garden Theater**/originally
American Horse Exchange, 1634-1646
Broadway, bet. W.50th and W.51st Sts. 1881-
1883. *David & John Jardine*. Rebuilt after fire,
1897, *A.V. Porter*. Remodeled into theater, 1910-
1911, *W. Albert Swasey*. Again remodeled, 1922-
1923, *Herbert J. Krapp.* ❧ New 50th Street
façade, 1997, *Menz & Cook*. Interior. ❧

A horse exchange? There was a horse ring
80 by 160 feet, spanned by trusses, that
became the volume of the future theater. *Cats*
was entrenched here for years. And its première
show was *La Belle Paree*, introducing *Al Jolson.*

[T79] **Equitable Center**, 787 Seventh Ave., bet.
W.51st and W.52nd St. E side. 1986. *Edward
Larrabee Barnes Assocs.*

A through-block galleria (with *Barry
Flanagan*'s elephant) modulates the bulk of
polished rose granite. *Roy Lichtenstein's* monumental mural dominates the lobby's central
atrium space. From afar one can see the great
arch of the boardroom at the top, but up close
the building skin is bland and smooth, without

articulated detail, a kind of Asia Society times ten. Less successful *Barnes* than IBM, where there is at least the tension of a hovering corner entrance; but the best of *Barnes* has always been at a smaller scale.

[T80] **1675 Broadway**, NW cor. W.52nd St. 1986-1989. *Fox & Fowle.*

A green granite slab, its cubistic modeling reminiscent of the **RCA Building** in Rockefeller Center. It yearns for a solidity of masonry (reflections) that 1950s and 1960s modern rejected in favor of glass (but daytime glass is visually solid, and nighttime glass a see-through negligee). Enveloped within is the old **Broadway Theater** (1924. *Eugene De Rosa*).

[T81] Gallagher's Restaurant: 228 West 52nd Street. Slaughterhouse on Seventh Avenue, its windows a refrigerator displaying meat that is an encyclopedia of beef's possibilities. The restaurant within offers a sauce that makes the simplest sliced steak a mouth-watering proposition.

T80   T83

T90   T94

[T82] **Neil Simon Theater**/originally **Alvin Theater**, 250 W.52nd St., bet. Broadway and Eighth Ave. 1926-1927. *Herbert J. Krapp.* Interior.

Georgian run amok. *Porgy and Bess* and *Funny Face* (with *Fred* and *Adele Astaire*) played here.

[T83] **August Wilson Theater**/formerly **Virginia Theater**/once **ANTA Theater**/originally **Guild Theater**, 245 W.52nd St., bet. Broadway and Eighth Ave. 1924-1925. *Crane & Franzheim.*

A top-of-the line Tuscan villa? Rusticated brownstone quoins and pediments overlay a half-hearted north Italian vocabulary on the otherwise bland stucco façade. *Much Ado About Nothing, Mourning Becomes Electra,* and *Ah, Wilderness!* played here.

Dining and dancing, Times Square style: With venerable Lindy's gone from Times Square, Jewish-American delicatessen-style food, long-favored by entertainers, reaches its peak at the [T84] Stage Delicatessen, a small, crowded

place at 834 Seventh Avenue between West 53rd and West 54th Streets, and the [T85] Carnegie Delicatessen, a block north at No.854. Each has partisans who claim theirs is better. Try both and decide. Big dance halls, once common around the square, survive only in the sedate Roseland, in a former ice skating palace at 239 West 52nd Street (between Broadway and Eighth Avenue).

[T86] **St. Benedict's Church** (Roman Catholic)/ formerly **Church of St. Benedict, the Moor,** 342 W.53rd St., bet. Eighth and Ninth Aves. 1869. *R.C. McLane & Sons.*

This church for black Catholics was founded in 1883 at 210 Bleecker Street. In the mid 1890s the congregation moved to this brick Italianate building, built by an earlier Protestant Evangelical congregation, at the edge of what was then a middle-class black community.

[T87] **Ed Sullivan Theater**/originally **Hammerstein's Theater,** 1697-1699 Broadway, bet. W.53rd and W.54th Sts. 1925-1927. *Herbert J. Krapp.* Interior.

Home to the *Late Show with David Letterman*. From 1945 *Ed Sullivan* produced his long lasting television show here, and from here *the Beatles* conquered America one evening in 1964.

[T88] **Midtown North Precinct, N.Y.C. Police Department**/originally **18th Precinct,** 306 W.54th St. 1939. *Department of Public Works.*

A serene **Art Moderne** limestone cube contrasts with the chaos of entertainment district police business flowing into and out of its doors. Note the freestanding lanterns of stainless steel that flank the entrances, and the moss growing under the air conditioners.

[T89] **St. George Tropoforos Hellenic Orthodox Church**/formerly **New Amsterdam Building,** 307 W.54th St. 1886.

This **Romanesque Revival** building began as small offices and now, in sandblasted natural brick, serves as a church. The joyous ornament is still evident.

[T90] **Midtown Community Court**/originally **11th District Municipal Court,** 314 W.54th St., bet. Eighth and Ninth Aves. 1894-1896. *John H. Duncan.* Altered, 1993, *Davis Brody Bond.*

A quartet of banded Corinthian columns in terra-cotta frames the principle floor (piano nobile) of this **Renaissance Revival** courthouse. The **Art Moderne** police station next door is a stern neighbor, ascetic in comparison.

[T91] **Hilton Hotel**, 1335 Sixth Ave., bet. W.53rd and W.54th Sts. 1963. *William B. Tabler Architects.*

The architecture is forgettable, but the lobby's carnival atmosphere, with hordes of tourists and business types checking in and out simultaneously, is worth a gander.

[T92] **154 West 55th Street**/formerly **55th Street Playhouse**/originally stables and **Holbein Studio**, bet. Sixth and Seventh Aves. 1888. *E. Bassett Jones.*

A **Romanesque Revival** stable, once a movie theater, now **endangered**.

[T93] **City Center 55th Street Theater**/originally **Mecca Temple**, 135 W.55th St., bet. Sixth and Seventh Aves. 1922-1924. *Harry P. Knowles* (d. 1923), succeeded by *Clinton & Russell.* 🍎

Tile faced and tile-domed, the City Center has served for decades as a performing arts center, dressed in architecture delightfully absurd, as might be expected from members of

[T97] **Metropolitan Tower**, 142 W.57th St., bet. Sixth and Seventh Aves. 1987. *Schuman, Lichtenstein, Claman & Efron.*

Harry Macklowe, the developer, says that he designed this himself. If so, he can take the blame for a gross and insensitive intrusion into these blocks. Its knife-edged glass form is impressive but inappropriate. But the rock star tenants and their peers will savor its parvenu glitz.

[T98] **The Russian Tea Room**, 150 West 57th St., bet. Sixth and Seventh Aves. 1927 (original building, 1875). New interiors, 1999, *Harman Jablin Architects.*

The spacer that allowed (some) light and air to the competing Carnegie and Metropolitan towers. Closed and gutted from 1995-99, the new Tea Room seats 140 on the ground floor in a décor that matches the 1927 original. It closed in 2002, reopened yet again in 2006.

T95

T100

the **Ancient and Accepted Order of the Mystic Shrine**, its original builders. The Muslim rulers who ruled from the Alhambra would shudder at this naive attempt at their architecture. But it's a nice place inside for performers from *Charles Aznavour* to the Paul Taylor Dance Company.

[T94] Originally **Steinway Hall**/now The Economist Building, 109-113 W.57th St., bet. Sixth and Seventh Aves. 1924-1925. *Warren & Wetmore.* 🍎

A sober Classical tower built by one of many music concerns clustered around Carnegie Hall. The Ionic temple on top enriches the skyline, but, unfortunately, has little influence at street level.

[T95] **130 West 57th Street** (studios), bet. Sixth and Seventh Aves. 1907-1908. *Pollard & Steinam.* 🍎
[T96] **140 W.57th St.** (studios), bet. Sixth and Seventh Aves. 1907-1908. *Pollard & Steinem.* 🍎

Bay windows in great tiers seem reminiscent of a never-before-achieved high-rise Oxbridge Gothic. Double height living rooms stand behind them.

[T99] **Carnegie Hall Tower** (mixed use), 152 W.57th St., bet. Sixth and Seventh Aves. 1986-1990. *Cesar Pelli & Assocs.*

In the venerable slot between Carnegie Hall and the Russian Tea Room ("slightly to the left of Carnegie Hall"), rises a slender tower that defers to the Renaissance Revival architecture of its parent next door. Highrise Medici?

[T100] **Carnegie Hall**, 156 W.57th St., SE cor. Seventh Ave. to W.56th St. 1889-1891. *William B. Tuthill.* Office Wing, 1892-1895, *William B. Tuthill.* Studio wing, 1896-1897, *Henry J. Hardenbergh. Richard Morris Hunt, Dankmar Adler*, consultants. 🍎 Reconfigured and restored, 1986, *James Stewart Polshek & Partners.* Zankel Hall, 1990s, *Polshek Partnership.*

Dour Renaissance Revival engulfed in studios and other appendices bristling above and around it. World-famous more for its acoustics than its architectural envelope, it was threatened in the early 1960s when Lincoln Center's Avery Fisher Hall rose up. Violinist *Isaac Stern*

T102

and others, raising a public outcry, saved it. It is now solidly booked.

Lovingly restored, grander than ever, its familiar form is re-appreciated (urban architectural tastes are sometimes fickle: see the story of the Jefferson Market Courthouse). And for the sound, book a seat.

Now turn around and discover (across the street) some hearty survivors from 57th Street's past:

[T101] **Columbia Artists Management**/originally **Louis H. Chalif's School of Dancing,** 165 W.57th St., bet. Sixth and Seventh Aves. 1916. *George and Henry Boehm.* ●'

Italian Mannerist with Tuscan overtones make it a distinctive neighbor to Carnegie Hall across the street. The colonnaded gallery on top would make a magnificent apartment. *Christopher Gray* quotes *Louis Chalif* denouncing modern music as "barbarians banging on human skulls in a cannibalistic orgy." Sounds like fun.

[T102] **Alwyn Court Apartments,** 180 W.58th St., SE cor. Seventh Ave. 1907-1909. *Harde & Short.* ●' Restoration, 1980-1981, *Beyer Blinder Belle*; murals by *Richard Haas.*

A French Renaissance exterior, every square foot literally encrusted with terra-cotta decorations: crowns and dragons abound. Within the courtyard is a painted architectural façade by *Richard Haas.* Fantastic!

[T103] **Brooklyn Diner and Plaza Pergola,** 212 W.57th st. entry to 888 Seventh Ave.

What sculpture provided for the elegant tower (say *Noguchi* at 140 Broadway), razmatazz supplies in these more theatrical precincts. There have been the Hard Rock Café and Planet Hollywood. The Brooklyn Diner hoped to draw some of the more affluent members of those crowds. Affluent? New York City diners don't come cheap, and they won't blink while charging you 12 bucks for a burger.

[T104] **200 W.57th St Office Building**/formerly **Rodin Studios**, bet. Seventh Ave, and Broadway. 1916-1917. *Cass Gilbert.* ● Restoration, 2008, *Zaskorski & Notaro Architects.*

Neo-Gothic filigree hovers over each alternate floor capping the original two-story studio spaces. An award-winning restoration effort by *Zaskorski & Notaro* returned it to its former glory.

monuments: the Plaza (Hotel), and the Dakota (Apartments), and several runners up. Now a venerable art school, it has the air of the old Parisian École des Beaux Arts, but the spirit of New York now.

[T107] **A.T. Demarest & Company** and **Peerless Motor Car Company Buildings** (later **General Motors Corporation Building**), 224 W.57th St., SE cor. Broadway. 1909. *Francis H. Kimball.* ●

T105

[T105] **Osborne Apartments**, 205 W.57th St., NW cor. Seventh Ave. 1883-1885. Enlargement of top story, 1889. *James E.Ware.* Extension to west, 1906, *Alfred S. G. Taylor.* ●

The dour matriarch of 57th Street,its muted exterior of Classical and Chicago School stonework hiding magnificent interiors (including many duplex apartments), foreshadowed by the extravagant marble vestibule and lobby. In the manner of a Florentine palazzo, it is stark and ascetic without, lush, luscious and luxurious within.

[T106] **Art Students League**/originally **American Fine Arts Society**, 215 W.57th St., bet. Seventh Ave. and Broadway. 1891-1892. *Henry J. Hardenbergh.* ● Gallery open Su 9-5 (Sept-Dec); Mo-Fr 9-8:30; Sa 9-5. 212-247-4510. *www.theartstudentsleague.org*

A stately French Renaissance pile, grand without being grandiloquent. *Hardenburgh* honored New York with two other extraordinary

Nothing much in architectural history, save for its modest moulded white terra-cotta sculpture that once related to the monumental Broadway Tabernacle next door. The latter, demolished, has been replaced by an unsympathetic and gawky condominium.

[T108] **3 Columbus Circle**/former **General Motors Building**, 1769-1787 Broadway, bet. 57th and 58th St., to Eighth Ave. originally **Colonnade Building** (first three floors), 1923. *W. Welles Bosworth.* Upper stories of building, 1927-1928, *Shreve & Lamb.* Sheathed in glass, 2009, *Gensler.*

A bizarre glass masque on the old General Motors Building (see Necrology) is the pretense for a trendy new name (the ubiquitous 3 Something), via new feathers on an old duck. The old punched openings still (mournfully) show through the glass (as if all of GM was wallowing in Gargantua's fish tank).

[T109] **Hearst Magazine Building**, 951-969 Eighth Ave., bet. W.56th and W.57th Sts. W side. 1927-1928. *Joseph Urban and George B. Post & Sons.* ●

With shades of the Austrian Secession movement, this sculpted extravaganza was commissioned by the Hearst publishing empire. It was a base for a skyscraper aborted due to the Depression. The foundations were still there, waiting...when, in the 21st century, lo and behold, a tower sprouted:

[T110] **Hearst Tower**, 300 W. 57th St. or 951-969 Eighth Ave., bet. W.56th and W.57th Sts. W side. 2006. *Norman Foster and Partners.*

A multifaceted glazed cage that treats the *Joseph Urban* base as a burdensome relic. Out of "respect" for the original 1926 landmark, *Sir Norman Foster* instead cremated the interior and preserved only the façade, a shell from which 46 stories suddenly erupt *Alien*-like in triangular facets of glass and steel. The resulting clash of styles and eras is (from the exterior, at least) about as strange and abrupt as one could imagine in a single building. Formal awkwardness aside, it's laudable that the tower uses the latest in "green" technology, including rooftop rainwater collection, recycled steel, non-toxic paints and carpets, and Forest Stewardship Council-certified wood. Woodsy Foster? An oxymoron.

[T111] **St. Thomas Choir School**, 202 W.58th St., bet. Seventh and Eighth Aves. 1987. *Buttrick, White & Burtis.*

T112

1930s Georgian revived. Boy sopranos here study, dwell, and sing in preparation for magnificent *Bach* chorales at the parent St. Thomas Church. A background building for frontline St. Thomas's.

[T112] Originally **Helen Miller Gould Carriage House**/now the **Unity Center of Practical Christianity**, 213 W.58th St., bet. Seventh Ave. and Broadway. 1902-1903. *York & Sawyer.* ●

A grand mansarded brick and limestone stable that would be at home on Henry IV's **Place des Vosges** in Paris. Check the stone hitching rings, lovely ironwork above.

[T113] **Engine Company No.23**, N.Y.C. Fire Department, 215 W.58th St., bet. Seventh Ave and Broadway. 1905-1906. *Alexander H. Stevens.* ●

A grand fraternal twin to the Gould Carriage House (above). The lions, both sculpted and pictured, come from someone else's palette.

[T114] **United States Rubber Building**, 1790 Broadway, SE cor. 58th St. 1911-1912. *Carrère & Hastings.* ●

The grandiloquent copper cornice seems to hold up the sky, sheathed in Vermont marble. Vermont?

[T115] **Gainsborough Studios**, 222 Central Park South, bet. Broadway and Seventh Ave. 1907-1908. *Charles W. Buckham.* Frieze, *Isidore Konti.* ●

The eponymous painter surveys the park from his second-floor perch. Two-story glazing, seeking the open park's wondrous north light, shields the real or would-be artists within. But what artist can afford it?

Central Park South east of No.222 is an impressive cliff, including luxury hotels and apartments, but except for the Gainsborough Studios (above), there is little that calls for a close look. Essex House, Hampshire House, the New York Athletic Club, and the St. Moritz are all distinguished by their opulence and opulent

T116

residents. Architecturally they form a bland wall (perhaps appropriately) for the lush parkland opposite.

The **St. Moritz** *of 1929 was threatened with a strip tease and rebuilding by the ubiquitous Donald Trump as a retardataire design of, say, 1929. Beyer Blinder Belle might have created a class act. But a leveler head prevailed: now re-furbished as a Ritz-Carlton.*

[T116] **240 Central Park South Apartments**, SE cor. Broadway. 1939-1940. *Mayer & Whittlesey.* ●

Two distinguished apartment towers with cubistic modeling, rise from a one-story, garden-topped podium, and give almost everyone within a good view. Relish the Art Moderne zigzag storefronts on Broadway.

T109, 110

that Manhattan's tower mania has so subverted the attitudes of developers that the firm that produced East Midtown Plaza finally had to play the 1980s urban finial game. Nicely done, but it's not **San Gimignano**.

[T119] **Time Warner Center**, Columbus Circle, W.58th to W.60th Sts. W side. 2003. *David Childs of Skidmore, Owings & Merrill.*

A behemoth of glass prisms, replacing the old **New York Coliseum**. Much hand-wringing preceded it and critics decried it when finished (*Paul Goldberger* said it belonged in Chicago, not New York: ouch). But it fits in the City and the Circle of Columbus much better than anyone thought it might. The interior shopping mall provides a cheerful, light-filled semi-public gathering space (with overpriced chocolates, clothes, and kitchen utensils for sale). Not Paris, but not bad; a pleasant arcade that many pedestrians use as a short cut.

T117

T119

[T117] **Museum of Arts and Design, The Chazen Building**/originally **Gallery of Modern Art**, 2 Columbus Circle, bet. Broadway and Eighth Ave. to W.58th St. 1964-1965. *Edward Durell Stone.* Reconstructed, 2008, *Brad Cloepfil of Allied Works Architecture.*

Inside, with preconceptions left at the coat check downstairs, it's a beautiful jewel box: full of light, coherently planned, with elegant details, including a grand wood and steel-cabled stair that rises to the second level (and would have been neater if it continued all the way to the top).

Its façade is inscrutable; stylish, the new building still has the old bones, but it wears a fancy gown for another ball.

[T118] **1 Central Park Place** NW cor. W.57th St. and Eighth Ave. 1988. *Davis, Brody & Assocs.*

A very tall, very slender luxury tower by the architects who gave us the City's most distinguished publicly assisted housing. It seems sad

[T120] **Columbus Circle**, Broadway/Eighth Ave./Central Park W./Central Park S. New plan, *Laurie Olin.*

This focal point, where Broadway glances the corner of Central Park, was the obvious place for monumental treatment, but it resulted only in a few sculptures in a tangle of traffic. *Gaetano Russo's* statue of **Columbus** (1892) is at the hub: architect *H. Van Buren Magonigle's* **Maine Memorial** (1913) wallows in from the park corner, with a boatload of figures by sculptor *Attilio Piccirilli*. The **Museum of Arts and Design** and the **Time Warner Center** have given definition that this rond-point always yearned for, and *Laurie Olin's* new landscaping includes granite amphitheater seating, wood benches, trees and fountains that help reduce noise and provide more spatial definition. With traffic hurtling pell-mell, the circle is unbroken.

Columbus Circle's IND and IRT subways (IND A, B, C, and D trains; IRT 1 train).

NECROLOGY

Playpen Theater, 693 Eighth Ave., bet. W.43rd and W.44th Sts. W side. ca. 1900.

It might be termed Times Square Beaux Arts: an exuberant building that might have been recaptured during the uplifting of Times Square's neighborhood.

The site of the **Reuters Building** had been a largely unnoticed architectural orphan, the old **Rialto Building** (1935. *Thomas W. Lamb and Rosario Candela*); the ground floor tawdry with shops. Upstairs however a swan song of Art Deco was still singing to a small group of fans.

Helen Hayes Theatre/originally **Folies Bergère Theatre**/later **Fulton Theatre**, 210 W. 46th St., bet. Broadway and Eighth Ave. 1911. *Herts & Tallant*.

One of the finest of Broadway's theaters to disappear, it opened originally as a theater-restaurant. The previous *AIA Guide* called its lavish blue and cream terra-cotta façade

T120

"worked by a crochet hook." Obliterated by the Marriott Marquis.

B. Smith's Restaurant, 771 Eighth Ave., NW cor. W.47th St. 1986. *Anderson/Schwartz*.

A supersleek Italo-new wave restaurant topped with a penthouse of corrugated steel in the fashion of *Frank Gehry*. The painted stucco and simple detailing of the exterior give way to elegance inside. Gold chains brighten the terrazzo within, while bottle caps inlay the asphalt street without. Now succeeded by a more than banal Duane Reade Pharmacy.

Broadway Tabernacle (Congregational)/later **Broadway United Church of Christ**, 1750 Broadway, NE cor. W.56th St. 1905. *Barney & Chapman*.

Pale buff brick and pale gray terra cotta and very big, it was extolled by architecture critic *Montgomery Schuyler* (1843-1914) as "The Best of Modern Gothic."

Originally **Horn & Hardart's Automat**, 104 W.57th St., bet. Sixth and Seventh Aves. 1938. *Ralph B. Bencker*.

One in a seductive chain of technocratic restaurants where a nickel could buy not only a cup of coffee, but a magnificent sticky bun. Drop the nickel in a slot and one could open a brass-framed glass door and "win" the sandwich or dessert behind. For a live rerun, rent *That Touch of Mink to* see the nickels and glass doors in action. A Hilton Hotel has taken its place.

Row houses, 147-153 W.57th St., bet. Sixth and Seventh Aves. **147-151**, 1886. *Douglas and John Jardine*.

No.153's brick and limestone Renaissance Revival was cheek by jowl with two heavily made-up Queen Annes. Demolished.

General Motors Building, 1769-1787 Broadway, bet. 57th and 58th St., to Eighth Ave. originally **Colonnade Building** (first three floors), 1923. *W. Welles Bosworth*. Upper stories of building, 1927-1928. *Shreve & Lamb*.

After his extraordinary columnar wedding cake for **AT&T** on lower Broadway, Bosworth created a three-story Ionic colonnade for this site that served, shortly after, as the plinth for the 26-story General Motors building. Slickly and sadly re-packaged for the transient trade. Modified beyond recognition as 3 Columbus Circle.

Originally **Gallery of Modern Art**, 2 Columbus Circle, bet. Broadway and Eighth Ave. to W.58th

2 Columbus Circle   104 W.57th St.

St. 1964-1965. *Edward Durell Stone*.
A compact white marble confection with vaguely Middle Eastern motifs, commissioned by A&P heir *Huntington Hartford* and shaped to the constricted site. It showed off well when seen from the north, on Broadway, gleaming among larger, darker structures. Although disliked by many, it delivered professional reinforcement to the circling streetscape of Columbus; a bit of Hollywood at Central Park.

New York Coliseum, 10 Columbus Circle, bet. W.58th and`W.6oth Sts. W side. 1956. *Leon and Lionel Levy*.

One of *Robert Moses*' early manipulations of the federal Title I urban renewal program produced this dreary white brick, white elephant. Long before it was outclassed by the Javits Convention Center, it had been relegated to the has-been stage: obsolete the minute it opened. Its footprint lies beneath Time-Warner.

P6, Chrysler Building

GRAND CENTRAL /
PARK AVENUE

Grand Central Terminal to East 57th Street:

"As a bullet seeks its target, shining rails in every part of our great country are aimed at Grand Central Station, heart of the nation's greatest city. Drawn by the magnetic force of the fantastic metropolis, day and night great trains rush toward the Hudson River, sweep

locomotives were later banned below 23rd Street, then 42nd Street, as the socially prominent residential areas moved north. At 42nd Street the original, cupolaed **Grand Central Depot**, with a vast iron-and-glass train shed, was opened in 1871 (*John B. Snook*, architect; *R. G. Hatfield*, shed engineer. Remodeled, 1892, *Bradford L. Gilbert*).

P1

down its eastern bank for 140 miles, flash briefly by the long red row of tenement houses south of 125th Street, dive with a roar into the 2-1/2-mile tunnel which burrows beneath the glitter and swank of Park Avenue and then... Grand Central Station! Crossroads of a million private lives! Gigantic stage on which are played a thousand dramas daily."
 – Opening from "Grand Central Station," broadcast over the NBC Radio Blue Network, beginning 1937.

The one-mile stretch from **Grand Central Terminal** to East 59th Street—the busiest portion of Park Avenue—is a uniquely successful integration of railroad and city. The avenue itself was built over the New York Central lines (now Amtrak and Metro-North); up to 50th Street the buildings along it rise on columns sprinkled among the fan-shaped yards.

The railroad's right-of-way, down what was originally Fourth Avenue, dates to 1832, when the New York and Harlem Railroad terminated at Chambers Street. The smoke and noise of

In the early 1900s, when electric locomotives were introduced, the railroad took audacious steps that not only increased the value of its property many times over but also gave the City a three-dimensional composition that was a major achievement of the **City Beautiful** era. The terminal itself was made more efficient and compact by dividing its 67 tracks between two subterranean levels, and Park Avenue north and south of the terminal was joined in 1919 by a system of automobile viaducts wrapping around the station.

New engineering techniques for shielding tall buildings from railroad vibrations made possible a complex of offices and hotels around the station and extending north above the yards and tracks. By the onset of the Great Depression the avenue through the 50s was lined with remarkably uniform rows of apartments and hotels, all solid blocks 12 to 16 stories high, punctuated by the divergent form of a church or club. Although some of the buildings had handsome central courtyards, their dense ground coverage must have made summer living unbearable in pre-air-conditioning times (merely luxury tenements)—but, then, people who lived here never summered in the City. Firm as these palaces appeared, most of them lasted only a few decades. Their loss, as a result of the office building boom of the 1950s and 1960s ("convenient to Grand Central"), eliminated much of Park Avenue's air of elegance on these 17 blocks.

Park Avenue Walking Tour: From Grand Central Terminal to 60th Street. (Take a subway to the terminal itself: the IRT Lexington Avenue Line (4, 5, or 6 trains), the IRT Flushing Line (7 train), or the IRT Shuttle from Times Square.)

[P1] **Grand Central Terminal**, E.42nd St. at Park Ave. N side. 1903-1913. *Reed & Stem and Warren & Wetmore*. Painted ceiling over main concourse, *Whitney Warren with Paul Helleu and Charles Basing*. 👞 Partial interior. 👞 Restoration and addition of East Stair, 1998, *Beyer Blinder Belle*. Pershing Square Viaduct, 1919. 👞

This remarkably functional scheme (termi-

P2

nal and approaches) is housed in an imposing **Beaux Arts Classical** structure. Its main façade, facing south down Park Avenue, is a grand symmetrical composition of triumphal arches, filled with steel and glass, surmounted by a colossal clock and sculpture group (by *Jules Coutan*) in which Roman deities fraternize with an American eagle. The symbolism may be confusing, but the scale and composition are powerful.

A superb restoration by the current landlord, Metro-North (and its architects, *Beyer Blinder Belle*) gave rise to critic *Carter Wiseman*: "Led by *John Belle*...the architects redefined an aging transportation facility as a center for the city's social interaction."

The simple ceiling vault, restored to its original cerulean blue, 125 feet across, decorated with the constellations of the zodiac, is actually hung from steel trusses. (The zodiac is here seen as if viewed from the point of view of God; or, for the atheist, a mirror image). Smaller spaces are structurally spanned by Guastavino tile vaulting left exposed, with handsome effect, in parts of the lower level, as at the Oyster Bar.

All in all, breathtaking. The outside is a grand 19th-century civic building (although built in the 20th), but the inside: in descending those **"Spanish Steps"** (from a taxi on Vanderbilt Avenue), one overlooks, then slides into, encapsulated city life, bounded and sheltered by grand, but not grandiose, Classical architecture. Look Ma, no Ads.

Grand Central Oyster Bar: World-renowned for its shellfish stews and pan roasts. The oyster bar and its equipment are worth seeing under exposed tan tile vaulting low enough to touch.

[P2] Originally **Philip Morris Headquarters**, 120 Park Ave., SW cor. E.42nd St. (Pershing Sq.). 1982. *Ulrich Franzen & Assocs.*

A sober granite slab, somewhat schizophrenic in its elevations, housed the offices of Philip Morris, now relocated to Virginia. Those long legs give a friendly reception to the pedestrian, a deep alcove off the street.

P3

P4

[P3] **Cipriani's 42nd Street**/originally **Bowery Savings Bank**, 110 E.42nd St., bet. Park and Lexington Aves. 1921-1923, 1931-1933. *Louis Ayres of York & Sawyer*. 👞 Interior. 👞

Once through its monumental arched entrance, one enjoys one of the great interior spaces of New York. But what is on the menu? *Giuseppe Cipriani*, together with *Harry Pickering*, opened **Harry's Bar** in Venice in 1931. Now they have expanded operations from their restaurant in the Sherry Netherland to this Italo-Romano-Byzantine basilica.

[P4] **Chanin Building**, 122 E.42nd St., SW cor. Lexington Ave. to E.41st St. 1927-1929. *Irwin S. Chanin with Sloan & Robertson*. Frieze, *René Chambellan*. Lobby, *Jacques Delamarre*. 👞

Surprising combinations of angular and floral decoration—even Gothic buttresses—sprout on this exuberant office tower. Don't miss the lobby, (including extraordinary convector grilles). Outside, an **Art Deco** bas-relief by *Edward Trumbull* belts the façades. The *Chanin*

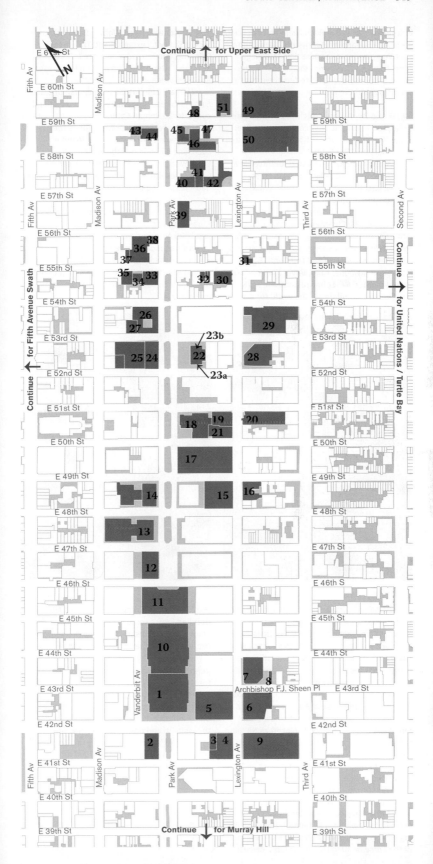

brothers began in Brooklyn, went on to develop the Times Square theater district, then Central Park West, and, at the same time this elegant spire. Classic style, rather than stylish ephemera. Such distinguished self-improvement seems beyond the grasp of current developers.

[P5] **Grand Hyatt Hotel**/originally **Commodore Hotel**, 125 E.42nd St., NW cor. Lexington Ave. 1920. *Warren & Wetmore*. Rebuilt, 1980, *Gruzen & Partners and Der Scutt*.

A dowager hotel building re-outfitted in a somewhat rumpled reflective glass dress. Within, past the 3-D lobby, old walls lurk behind all that glitter.

[P6] **Chrysler Building**, 405 Lexington Ave., NE cor. E.42nd St. 1930. *William Van Alen*. ☛ *JCS Design Assocs.*, designers, and *Joseph Pell Lombardi*. Further interior renovations, 1999, *Beyer Blinder Belle*. Partial interior. ☛ Lobby restoration, 1978.

The tallest building in the world for a few

P7

[P8] **St. Agnes Church** (Roman Catholic), 145 E.43rd St., bet. Lexington and Third Aves. Original church. 1876. *Lawrence J. O'Connor*. Replaced after fire with a new building. 1997. *Acheson Doyle*.

The late building was the church of *Bishop Fulton J. Sheen*, popular television priest and converter to Roman Catholicism of such notables as *Claire Booth Luce*, author of The Women, wife of *Time* magazine founder *Henry Luce*, and sometime ambassador to Italy. Destroyed by fire, it has been replaced by a vaguely Jesuitical façade in cool and very crisp neo-Classical postmodern limestone.

[P9] Formerly **Mobil Building**/originally **Socony Mobil Building**, 150 E.42nd St. bet. Lexington and Third Aves. 1955. *Harrison & Abramovitz*. ☛

A 1.6-million-square-foot building sheathed with embossed stainless-steel panels. A previous edition of this Guide called it a "tin can." But it's much better than many recent cans made of glass.

P9

months before completion of the **Empire State Building**: 1,048 feet to the top of its spire. Stainless steel not only burnished the lancelike spire and the cowl that forms its supporting crown, but formed the gargantuan radiator cap gargoyles (look for photographer *Margaret Bourke-White's* widely published image at work, sitting on one). And don't miss the lobby, an **Art Deco** confection of African marble and chrome steel. And at night that lancet crown glows in the skyline. Now displaced as No.2 in the sky scraping contest by **One Bryant Park**.

[P7] **425 Lexington Avenue**, bet. E.43rd and E.44th Sts. E side. 1988. *Murphy/Jahn*.

A flamboyant, top-heavy, skyline building, that seems an ugly dwarf next to the venerable reality of the adjacent Chrysler Building. The entranceway suggests a stage set from a terrifying 1930s movie, perhaps the portal to the lair of the *Emperor Ming* (*Flash Gordon's* nemesis).

[P10] **Met Life Building**/originally **Pan Am Building** (office complex), 200 Park Ave. 1963. *Emery Roth & Sons, Pietro Belluschi, and Walter Gropius*. Lobby alterations, 1987, *Warren Platner*.

This latter-day addition to the Grand Central complex was purely a speculative venture. The building aroused protest both for its enormous volume of office space—2.4 million square feet, the most in any single commercial office building at the time—and for blocking the vista up and down Park Avenue, previously punctuated but not stopped by the Helmsley (originally New York Central) Building tower. The precast-concrete curtain wall was one of the first in New York.

*Note the staid, neo-Classical **Yale Club** (identified in letters only one inch high) across Vanderbilt Avenue from the Pan Am at East 44th Street (1901. Tracy & Swartwout.) It was once part of an understated neo-Renaissance group, severely compromised with the closing and recladding of the Biltmore Hotel, between 43rd and 44th.*

[P11] Helmsley Building (offices) / originally **New York Central Building**, 230 Park Ave., bet. E.45th and E.46th Sts. 1929. *Warren & Wetmore.* ☛ Partial interior. ☛

Once visible for miles along Park Avenue, symbol of the then-prosperous railroad. Its fanciful cupola and opulent but impeccably detailed lobby departed from the sobriety of the terminal and the surrounding buildings.

The north façade, once a remarkably successful molding of urban space, maintained the cornice line of buildings flanking the avenue, carrying it in small curves to create an apse of grand proportions, crowned by the tower. Only a fragment of the original composition remains: in

P10

the relation of the building to 250 Park Avenue. Carved into this façade are two tall portals for automobile traffic, clearly differentiated from the central lobby entrance and the open pedestrian passages to the east and west.

As for the elevators; *"You won't believe me when I tell you...the architect has succeeded in cramming into the lifts all the best features of the Chicago Post Office Rotunda, the Palmer House Barbershop, the Hoffman House Bar, and the late mansion of the late Senator Clark."* New Yorker. March 30, 1920. (*T-Square* quoted a friend.) It's true.

[P12] Originally **Postum Building, 250 Park Ave., bet. E.46th and E.47th Sts. W side to Vanderbilt Ave. 1925. *Cross & Cross,* architects. *Phelps Barnum,* assoc. architect.

Saved miraculously (by its small full-block site) from being demolished and replaced by a grotesquely larger occupant, **No.250** is one of Park Avenue's few between-the-wars neo-Classical office structures that revere the idea of *Warren & Wetmore* creating a **Terminal City** to surround—and enhance—their Grand Central Terminal complex.

[P13] Chase Bank Offices / originally **Union Carbide Building**, 270 Park Ave., bet. E.47th and E.48th Sts. W side to Madison Ave. 1960. Remodeled, 1983. All by *Skidmore, Owings & Merrill.*

The 53-story sheer tower is articulated with bright stainless-steel mullions against a background of gray glass and blackmatte-finished steel panels. The 13-story wing to the rear (well related in scale to Madison Avenue) is linked to the tower by a narrow transparent bridge, dramatically placed at the north end of Vanderbilt Avenue. The site of the building over railroad yards made it necessary to start elevators at the second floor, reached by escalators. In charge was SOM's *Natalie DuBois,* one of modern architecture's early prominent women.

"The new buildings on Park Avenue...have not so much arrived as seeped through, and they hover on their thin stilts, slightly darker than the sky, like boxy clouds that, the next moment, may shrug and be gone." – John Updike.

P11   P14

P15

[P14] Bankers Trust Building, 280 Park Ave., bet. E.48th and E.49th Sts. W side. 1963. *Emery Roth & Sons. Henry Dreyfuss,* designer. Addition to W, 1971, *Emery Roth & Sons. Oppenheimer, Brady & Lehrecke,* associated architects.

A rare example of an industrial designer (*Dreyfuss*) playing a major role in the design of a large building, most obvious in the very neat concrete curtain wall. The effort to fit into the **1916 Zoning Resolution** envelope without producing a stepped-back wedding-cake silhouette produced two rectangular masses that simply coexist.

[P15] Hotel Inter-Continental/Barclay Hotel, 111 E.48th St., NW cor. Lexington Ave. 1927. *Cross & Cross.*

An elegant survivor of 1920s residential Park Avenue, built in concert with Grand Central, now replaced by office buildings south of 59th street. For magnificent *Cross & Cross* see the Canadian Imperial Bank of Commerce on William Street.

[P16] **New York Marriott East Side**/formerly **Halloran House**/originally **Shelton Towers Hotel,** 525 Lexington Ave., bet. E.48th and E.49th Sts. 1924. *Arthur Loomis Harmon.*

Look up. *Harmon* created brick cubism at Shelton Towers from the new 1916 required setbacks for light and air. A powerful influence on architects and artists in the 1920s, it's embellished with Romanesque Revival fillips.

[P17] **Waldorf-Astoria Hotel,** 301 Park Ave., bet. E.49th and E.50th Sts. E side. 1929-1931. *Schultze & Weaver.* ●

Due to the changing social geography of Manhattan, this icon for travelers of power and wealth had migrated, in stylish new trappings, to where it's visitors would be in the precinct of their peers. *Schultze & Weaver's* new, grand and sedate, Art Deco Waldorf checked into Park Avenue (a then-20-year-old City Beautiful residential avenue dressed in Renaissance Revival). The Empire State Building, almost simultaneously, consumed the Hotel's former site.

P18

The Waldorf Hotel opened in 1893, built by William Waldorf Astor on the site of his own mansion at the NE corner of Fifth Avenue and 33rd Streets. Within a year, Mrs. Caroline Schermerhorn Astor, next door on the SW corner of 34th Street, moved from the Waldorf's shadow to 65th Street and Fifth Avenue, to a mansion where Temple Emmanuel now stands. She built a connecting hotel, the Astoria, on the site of her former house. When completed in 1897, the hyphenated hotel immediately became a social mecca.

Completion of the 1910 Grand Central Station, its face to the north the New York Central Building (later Helmsley Building), and the covering of the tracks that fed the Station down 4th Avenue (Park's original name), triggered a wave of uniform corniced residential building, eventually up to 96th Street.

The 625-foot Waldorf Towers, with a separate entrance on East 50th Street, have been temporary home to such notables as Herbert Hoover, Douglas MacArthur, the Duke of Windsor, and John F. Kennedy.

[P18] **St. Bartholomew's Church** (Episcopal), Park Ave. bet. E.50th and E.51st Sts. (109 E. 50th St.) E side. 1914-1919. *Bertram G. Goodhue.* ● Entrances relocated from old St. Bartholomew's, Madison Ave. SW cor. E.24th St. 1902. *Stanford White of McKim, Mead & White.* **Community House,** 109 E.50th St., bet. Park and Lexington Aves. 1926-1928. *Mayers, Murray & Philip.* **Sallie Franklin Cheatham Memorial Garden.** 1971. *Hamby, Kennerly, Slomanson & Smith,* architects. *Paschall Campbell,* landscape architect.

St. Bartholomew's, and buildings behind it, gave Park Avenue what it desperately needed: open space, color, variety of form and detail. Around its open terrace at the 50th Street corner are arrayed picturesque polychrome forms that rise to the ample dome of the church, dip, and then soar to the 570-foot pinnacles of the **General Electric tower.**

Critics at the time: "They compare it frequently with St. Thomas's...[St.Bart's] lacks the romantic, theatricality...of the Gothic, the tortured silhouette of gargoyle, pinnacle and buttress..." T-Square, New Yorker, 1927.

[P19] **General Electric Building**/originally **RCA Victor Building,** 570 Lexington Ave., SW cor. E.51st St. 1929-1931. *Cross & Cross.* ● Restored, 1995, *Ernest de Castro of WCA Design Group.*

Built to be contextual with St. Bart's, its neighbor, long before that word entered the City's development vocabulary. Art Deco details

P17   P19

at both street and sky are both sumptuous and exuberant.

[P20] **Doubletree Metropolitan Hotel** (originally **Summit Hotel**) 569-573 Lexington Ave., SE cor. 51st St. 1959-1961. *Morris Lapidus, Harle & Liebman.* ●

The Second Edition of this Guide described it as "a sleek supermotel that offers characterless but efficient quarters for the traveller. For character or class go to The Plaza or St.Regis." The winds of changing fashion have brought *Lapidus* to Landmark status, an impossible thought for many.

[P21] **560 Lexington Avenue** (offices), NW cor. E.50th St. 1981. *The Eggers Group.* Brick sculpture, *Aleksandra Kasuba.*

A latter-day addition to the **St. Bart's block,** this reserved tower attempted consciously (with *Landmarks Preservation Commission* prodding) to integrate itself into the total composition. The entrance to the subway is the most serious architectural gesture.

Fire down below. What lies beneath New York's streets is often as intriguing as the buildings and monuments that adorn them—at least for Hollywood. In the 1946 fantasy Angel on My Shoulder, set in New York, Claude Rains, as the devil, commuted between his world and ours via a rising sidewalk freight elevator. Marilyn Monroe, in The Seven Year Itch, *enjoyed a world-famous burst of subway-blown air, raising Tom Ewell's eyebrows (and hopes) as her skirt billowed over an IRT subway grating. The grating is still there, in Lexington Avenue's west sidewalk, just south of 52nd Street—the buildings have changed.*

| [P22] **Seagram Building,** 375 Park Ave., bet. E.52nd and E.53rd Sts. E side. 1955-1958. *Ludwig Mies van der Rohe* with *Philip Johnson*, design architects. *Kahn & Jacobs*, associate architects. 🍎

The bronze and bronze-glass tower that reintroduced the idea of plaza to New York. *Mies van der Rohe* brought reality to the fantasies he had proposed for Berlin in the 1920s, *Philip Johnson*, his biographer and acolyte designed its interiors. *Phyllis Lambert*, daughter of the Seagram board chairman, the late *Samuel Bronfman*, was the catalyst for it all, bringing architectural standards learned at Vassar. *Lambert* went on to become a planner and founded, in 1979, the CCA (Canadian Center for Architecture).

The plaza, daring in that it was proposed at all (considering real estate values), seems, when devoid of people and active fountains, a bit of a bore. In summer, with fountains flower-

P21   P22

ing and lounging lunchers, it's lively; and at Christmastime the trees and lights are like a great piling of bridal veil—a delight.

| [P23a] **The Four Seasons** (restaurant), 99 E.52nd St. (in the Seagram Building), bet. Park and Lexington Aves. 1958-1959. *Philip Johnson.* 🍎

An entrance dominated by *Picasso's* backdrop for the ballet **The Three-Cornered Hat** (1919) leads from the Seagram lobby into the restaurant (to the north) and the bar (to the south). The walnut-paneled dining room is laid out around a square pool, the other room around the square bar, over which is a quivering brass rod sculpture by *Richard Lippold*. Both rooms are impeccably designed down to the last napkin, with tableware by *L. Garth Huxtable*.

[P23b] **The Brasserie,** 100 E.53rd St., bet. Park and Lexington Aves. S side (within Seagram; enter from E.53rd). 2000. *Diller + Scofidio.*

The new Brasserie, replacing Philip Johnson's 1959 original, is a subterranean time machine

with the cool detachment of a 1960s airport lounge. *Diller + Scofidio's* trademark translucency rules here, with a "wall of wine" in silhouette. This being a *D+S* project, the inevitable bank of video screens hover. For exterior *Diller + Scofidio* see the **High Line** (p. 217).

🏢 [P24] **Racquet and Tennis Club,** 370 Park Ave., bet. E.52nd and E.53rd Sts. W side. 1918. *William S. Richardson of McKim, Mead & White.* 🍎

P24

An elegant Brunelleschian foil for the Seagram's plaza, this Florentine Renaissance palazzo is a wealthy male chauvinist's club housing squash (both lemon and racquets) and one of the few extant court tennis courts (the game of Louis XIV). The deep loggia provides strong counterpoint to Seagram's plaza across the street. Check the crossed racquets in the frieze.

[P25] **Park Avenue Plaza,** E.52nd to E.53rd Sts., bet. Madison and Park Aves. 1981. *Skidmore, Owings & Merrill.*

A bulky glass prism lurking behind the **Racquet and Tennis Club,** enjoying its purchased air rights that provided more heft. **The Club,** in turn, will in all likelihood remain unchanged forever by virtue of its landmark designation, the impossibility of replacing it with something bigger, and the implacability of its members.

The atrium within has a subtle waterfall and sometime restaurant service, but feel free to sit without ordering – mandated by the zoning concessions obtained. It is a public place and once had remarkably clean public toilets!

P29

‖ [P26] **Lever House**, 390 Park Ave., bet.
E.53rd and E.54th Sts. W side. 1950-1952.
*Gordon Bunshaft of Skidmore, Owings &
Merrill.* Curtain wall replaced, 2003, *Skidmore,
Owings & Merrill.* 🍎

This slender, hovering elegance, its prismatic forms small-scaled for Park Avenue, was
clad in avant-garde (for 1950) metal and glass
curtain walls. At first it received the reflections
of ornate neo-Renaissance stonework from the
Racquet Club next door and lush brick and
stone buildings to the north and east. In itself,
it was a class act. Now it's a lonesome, but
dated, modern memento, demeaned by

P26   P27

dozens of gross boxes glassed without grace.

[P27] **Banco Santander**, 45 E.53rd St., bet.
Park and Madison Aves. 1994. *Rogers, Burgun,
Shahine and Deschler.*

The new kid on the block capitalized on the
open space of Lever House next door to reveal
two aggressive elevations.

[P28] **599 Lexington Avenue**, SE cor. E.53rd St.
1987. *Edward Larrabee Barnes Assocs.*

A *Barnes*-corner, chamfered here, overhung
elsewhere (see **IBM** at 57th and Madison),
pulls back the street façade to reveal more of
Citicorp next door. The sleek gray skin also
classes it as Citicorp's daughter, with a similar
fabric, but with a different couturier arranging
the folds.

*The subway kiosk is a wonderful entry to two
formerly disconnected lines: the IND Lexington
Avenue Station (E and V trains) and the IRT 51st
Street Station (6 train), coupled as part of a
zoning bonus that gave the tower more bulk.*

‖ [P29] **Citicorp Center**, Lexington Ave.
bet. E.53rd and E.54th Sts. E side. 1978.
Hugh Stubbins & Assocs., design architects.
Emery Roth & Sons, architects. Plaza and atrium
upgrading, 1997, *Gwathmey Siegel & Associates.*
[P29b] **St. Peter's Church** (Lutheran). 1977.
Hugh Stubbins & Assocs. **Erol Beker Chapel of
the Good Shepherd**. *Louise Nevelson*, designer-
sculptor. Interior, *Massimo Vignelli*, designer.

This tour de force brought a stylish silhouette to the sky and, for the earthbound eye, a
hovering cantilevered hulk under which nests
St. Peter's Church. The smooth aluminum
façade lacks the rich austerity of 140 Broadway

P33

(a flush, but black, predecessor by *Skidmore,
Owings & Merrill*). The raked profile at its crest
was a gesture to the idea of a sloping sun
collector but now is just a vestigial form, like a
Rolls-Royce radiator ornament. The central atrium within, skylit, is urbane.

[P30] **Central Synagogue** (Congregation
Ahawath Chesed Shaar Hashomayim), 652
Lexington Ave., SW cor. E.55th St. 1871-1872.
Henry Fernbach. 🍎 Restored after fire, 1886,
Ely Lacques Kahn. Restored again, 2000, *Hardy
Holzman Pfeiffer.* Tours: Wednesdays, 12:30.
212-838-5122. *www.centralsynagogue.com*

Fernbach, America's first prominent Jewish
architect, built this, the oldest building in continuous use as a synagogue in New York. Dour on
the exterior, except for star-studded bronze
cupolas, the synagogue wore an interior gaily
stenciled with rich blues, earthy reds, ocher, and
gilt – Moorish, but distinctly American 19th-cen-
tury. A 1998 fire caused the need for substantial
restorations, and gave opportunity to *Hugh
Hardy* to re-introduce detail that *Ely Lacques*

Kahn had removed after the 1886 fire. *Hardy* said "What we have done is much more exuberant than what people here are used to, but it is original to the building.... as raucous as ever."

[P31] Originally **Babies' Hospital**, now offices, NE cor. Lexington Ave. and East 55th St. 1902, 1910. *York & Sawyer.*

Rusticated limestone and brick, belted with a frieze honoring its original clients. A quiet but strong background building.

[P32a] **124 East 55th Street**/originally Mary Hale Cunningham House, bet. Park and Lexington Aves. 1880-1881. New façade, 1906-1910, *Harrie T. Lindeberg of Albro & Lindeberg.* 🍎

Neo-Tudor? 120 is neo-Georgian with neo-Regency spunk. 122 is Brownstone Palladian.

[P32b] **The Levins Institute (SUNY)**/originally **William and Helen Ziegler, Jr., House,** 116-118 East 55th St., bet. Park and Lexington Aves. 1926-1927. *William L. Bottomley.* 🍎

[P34] **Heron Tower,** 70 E.55th St., bet. Madison and Park Aves. 1987. *Kohn Pedersen Fox.*

Postmodern, 1930s division. Gray granite, rock-face blocks punctuating the façade. It inspires thoughts of a possible unfinished 1930s movie: *Prince Kong.* But savor the lobby!

[P35] **Park Avenue Place,** 60 E. 55th Street, bet. Madison and Park Aves. 2005. *Kohn Pedersen Fox.*

This block supported trial runs of postmodernism, and here, in concert, a clunky lot. Here KPF returns to a modernist vocabulary, next to their 1987 *Prince Kong.* It has a civilized feature that more glass boxes might consider: operable windows.

[P36] **Park Avenue Tower,** 65 E.55th St., bet. Madison and Park Aves., through to E.56th St. 1987. *Murphy/Jahn.*

Sleek and sassy, the skin below is wrapped in planes, then articulated with stainless-steel

P30

P36

Flemish-bond brickwork with burnt headers face a bland but pleasant neo-Georgian town house. Upgraded with Eagle-capped entry pilasters.

[P33] **Chase Manhattan Bank,** 410 Park Ave., SW cor. E.55th St. 1959. Bank and curtain wall, *Skidmore, Owings & Merrill.* Building, *Emery Roth & Sons.*

A wedding cake, common in its time, with an elegant metal and glass curtain wall, designed to fulfill the self-image of the bank on the lower two floors. The high second-floor banking room is an impressive setting for an *Alexander Calder* mobile. Drop into the sleek Ferrari showroom on the ground floor. What better place to keep your Ferraris than in a bank?

tori, those half-round horizontal projections typical in Renaissance architecture. Although this would generally be classified as postmodern, it has many modernist mannerisms.

[P37] **The Friar's Club,** 57 E.55th St., bet. Madison and Park Aves. 1920s.

A bit of frivolity with Tuscan columns below, Ionic pilasters above. See if you can find the time capsule from 2004, sealed behind a plaque on the façade. 2004? We remember 2004... seems like only a few years ago...

[P38] **Mercedes-Benz Showroom**/originally **Jaguar Showroom,** 430 Park Ave., SW cor. E.56th St. 1955. *Frank Lloyd Wright.* Altered, 1982, *Taliesin Associated Architects.*

In the "Master's" first New York City work, his creativity seems to have been smothered by the cramped space. More notable in that he did it (and that it's still there), rather than for what he did.

[P39] **Universal Pictures Building**, 445 Park Ave., bet. E.56th and E.57th Sts. E side. 1947. *Kahn & Jacobs.*

The first office building built on this once-residential portion of Park Avenue, it achieved an additional distinction as the first evenly stepped-back "wedding cake" form—precisely prescribed by the zoning law. Prismatic, Crisp.

[P40] **Ritz Tower**, 465 Park Ave. NE cor. 57th St. 1925-1927. *Emery Roth with Thomas Hastings.* 🏛

A 42-story tower, a stepped obelisk (with supporting obelisks on the set-backs), conspicuous on the skyline. Rich details around the street-level walls now struggle with the egalitarian issues of the Bookstore within.

On the 19th and 20th floors, at the terraced setback, an 18-room duplex apartment was constructed for *Arthur Brisbane* (1927. *Thomas Hastings*).

[P42] **135 East 57th Street**, NW cor. Lexington Ave. 1987. *Kohn Pedersen Fox.*

New York's response to the French architecture of Spaniard *Ricardo Bofill* and his arcuated neo-Classical housing in Paris. Here the corner is king, an exedra opening to the intersection of Lexington and 57th. Within that space stands a tempietto marking what the sponsors termed the **Place des Antiquaires**. Silly.

P43   P44

P41

P45

At 111 East 57th Street (in the side flank of the Ritz Tower) stood France's greatest restaurant in America, Le Pavillon, founded by Henri Soulé at the New York World's Fair of 1939, then moved here to fulfill the wildest dreams of both gourmands and gourmets. After Soulé died (in 1966), the space became the home of the short lived First Women's Bank (1975. Stockman & Manners Assocs., designers). Now chain store America has arrived in the form of Borders Bookstore. Go in. Pick out a ritzy book. Sit down and read it.

▌[P41] **The Galleria**, 119 E.57th St., bet. Park and Lexington Aves. 1975. *David Kenneth Specter*, design architect. *Philip Birnbaum*, associated architect.

Luxury apartments stacked over offices and a club, embracing a balconied seven-story public galleria (cf. La Galleria, Milan). The skylit balconied space penetrates the block to 58th Street, affording pedestrians delight in passing through. Pretentious, but it has some grounds to be so.

▌[P43] **500 Park Tower**, annexed to the **Amro Bank Building**, on E.59th St., bet. Madison and Park Aves. 1986. *James Stewart Polshek & Partners*, design architects. *Schuman, Lichtenstein, Claman & Efron*, associated architects.

A residential condominium annexed both legally and architecturally to the elegant heirs of Pepsi-Cola. At the lower levels it matches Pepsi's sleekness. In between, deeply incised granite openings provide a strong and handsome foil.

▌[P44] **ABN-Amro Bank Building**/sometime **Olivetti Building**/originally **Pepsi-Cola Building**, 500 Park Ave., SW cor. E.59th St. 1958-1960. 🏛 *Gordon Bunshaft and Natalie DuBois of Skidmore, Owings & Merrill.*

An understated elegance that bowed to the scale of its Park Avenue neighbors rather than advertising itself as the newest (in its time) local modern monument. Large bays of glass are enlivened by the seemingly random arrangements of partitions (that kiss the glass with rubber gaskets), and vertical blinds.

[P45] Banque de Paris Building, 499 Park Ave., SE cor. E.59th St. 1981. *Pei Cobb Freed & Partners.*

This obsidian prism, blackly marking its Park Avenue corner, is so subtle externally as to be boring. Its lobby, however, presents a wondrous—and wondrously lit—tree to the passer-through (diagonally, from Park to 59th, and vice versa).

[P46] 110 East 59th Street, bet. Park and Lexington Aves. 1968. *William Lescaze.*

This simple, understated, and unpretentious tower is a notch above its speculative competition. The sculpture (1973. *Tony Rosenthal*) in the south plaza (on 58th Street) is a rich, carved piece of a bronze cylinder.

[P47] Argosy Print and Book Store, 116 E.59th St., bet. Park and Lexington Aves. 1966. *Kramer & Kramer.*

An elegant shop that replaces the long-gone streetstands along this block; used books, maps, and prints filled the sidewalk to the

that saloon-bespotted boulevard inspired Bloomie's to shed its bargain basement image. The castle of consumerism that emerged became, for many, and for a while, the source from which all upscale, total lifestyle statements flowed.

[P50] Bloomberg Tower and One Beacon Court, 731 Lexington Ave., and 151 E.78th St., bet. E.58th and E.59th Sts., through to Third Ave. 2005. *Pelli Clarke Pelli, with Schuman, Lichtenstein, Claman & Efron (SLCE).*

This grand towered complex, a multi-use base at its feet, is named for its anchor tenant, Bloomberg LP (*Mayor Bloomberg's* own), and ranks as one of New York City's tallest skyscrapers (868 feet). Its footprint consumes a full city block (formerly the site of Alexander's Department Store). A 55-story office and apartment tower stands on the Lexington side, an 11 story tower on Third Avenue, with a horseshoe-shaped, mid-block courtyard uniting the two sectors in a public open space dubbed One

P42

delight of browsers, as on the Left Bank of the Seine. Upstairs (by elevator) are floors devoted to old prints, painting, and specialized books.

[P48] The Lighthouse: New York Association for the Blind, 111 E.59th St., bet. Park and Lexington Aves. New building, 1994. *Mitchell/Giurgola.*

Rational modern, its logic expressed clearly in its understated massing and elevations. It replaces the charming 1964 *Kahn & Jacobs* effort with a much bigger building (partially using the old steel skeleton), hence providing necessary office and residential extras.

[P49] Bloomingdale's/originally **Bloomingdale Brothers**, E.59th to E.60th Sts. bet. Lexington and Third Aves. Main Lexington Avenue Building, 740 Lexington Ave. 1930. *Starrett & Van Vleck.*

An aggregation of Victorian and Art Deco structures, completely interlocking on the interior, houses one of America's most comprehensive and sophisticated stores. Demolition of the Third Avenue El and the 1960s renaissance of

Beacon Court. Cloaked in a curtain wall of floor-to-ceiling glass and stainless steel, the top five floors light up each night to form a crown. Hail Hizzoner!

[P51] 750 Lexington Avenue, bet. E.59th and E.60th Sts. W side. 1988. *Murphy/Jahn.*

Chicago's *Helmut Jahn* has provided New York with its most exotic skyline elements since those slender finialed towers of the 1930s from the Chrysler Building to the Canadian Imperial Bank of Commerce. The catch is that these new vast office structures have the waistline of a Dutch burgher rather than a Chanel model. Air-conditioning, virtually nonexistent in the 1930s, now allows buildings to be deep and mechanically ventilated. The slim Chrysler Building was provided with air-conditioning (and light) by windows. Environmentally friendly "green" buildings are suddenly all the rage; this one ain't.

NECROLOGY

There at **120**, in the days of **Philip Morris**, was a satellite of the wondrous **Whitney Museum**. This oasis not only allowed contemplation of art but also provides a dry and warm resting place for the harried midtown traveler: a small café lurked within. Rats.

P50

Airlines Terminal Building (ticket office/bus terminal), 80 E.42nd St., SW cor. Park Ave. 1940. *John B. Peterkin*.

The low but powerful limestone Art Deco airline ticket and airport transit center was from the beginning dwarfed by its neighbors, the Lincoln and Pershing Square Buildings. Replaced by the Philip Morris Building, the massive eagles now grace a facility of the cigarette manufacturer in Richmond, Va.

Hotel Biltmore, Madison to Vanderbilt Aves., E.43rd to E.44th Sts. 1914. *Warren & Wetmore*.

The ornate lobby clock (or rather, under it) was a favorite meeting place for college students in the days between World War II and the Biltmore's demise. In the early 1980s, as soon as the preservation community got wind of the Biltmore's impending recladding, the developers quickly stripped the building to its steel frame. Strangely the clock survives.

Acquavella Building, 119 E. 57th St., bet. Park and Lexington Aves.

An enchanting Tudor jewel replaced by an even more enchanting baguette.

137 East 57th Street (offices), NW cor. Lexington Ave. 1930. *Thompson & Churchill*, architects. *Charles Mayer*, consulting engineer.

As a previous edition of this Guide put it, "a pioneering piece of structural virtuosity: the columns are recessed nine feet from the skin. Steel tensile straps hang the perimeter floors and walls from roof girders." All this apparently to avoid a stream bed beneath the building's corner. But its inclusion in the Museum of Modern Art's modern architecture exhibition of 1932 was not sufficient to justify landmarking.

Alexander's Department Store, 731 Lexington Ave., NE cor. E.58th St. to Third Ave. 1965. *Emery Roth & Sons*.

The container is innocuous commercial modern pretending to be more. Designed along a

Airlines Terminal Building

Alexander's Department Store

module with intentions of expansion to fill the entire block, Alexander's was in danger of replacement by a high rise, reflecting the enormous desire for space in this area. Ergo: Bloomberg Tower.

The nearest subways are at 59th and Lexington: the IRT Lexington Avenue (59th Street Station: 4, 5, and 6 trains) or the BMT Broadway Line (Lexington Avenue Station: N, R, and W trains).

THE FIFTH AVENUE SWATH

East 46th to East 60th Streets, Sixth to Madison:

This stretch of the avenue, where fashionable shops were concentrated since the 1920s, had been a solid line of mansions, churches, and clubs two decades before. Two factors sustained the elegance of Fifth Avenue as stores moved north along it: the Fifth Avenue Association (whose members had fought off billboards, bootblacks, parking lots, projecting signs—even funeral parlors), and the absence of Els or subways. To provide a genteel alternative for rapid transit, the **Fifth Avenue Transportation Company** was established in 1885, using horse-drawn omnibuses until 1907, followed by the fondly remembered double-deck buses. Once upon a time even the traffic lights were special: bronze standards with a neo-Grec Mercury atop, subsidized by the Fifth Avenue Association concerned with style. One can still go to **Cartier's** for an occasional diamond or to the **St. Regis' King Cole Bar** for a drink below Maxfield Parrish's famous mural; but much of the Fifth Avenue style has gone.

Fat—or merely avaricious—cats abounded hereabouts, although the best work was done through the enlightened self-interest of old-line, hard-nosed capitalists. This precinct enjoyed the families Rockefeller, Scribner, Saks, Villard, Onassis, Heckscher, and others more modest, who gave some wonderful moments of class through buildings and shops to this sequence of blocks. Here looking up is as important as looking in; for above the luxurious, or interesting, or even sometimes tawdry shopfront, rises architecture of consequence.

Rockefeller Center

*The waves of elegant construction that rolled up Fifth Avenue never reached as far west as Sixth. **Rockefeller Center** was expected to trigger renewal in the 1930s, but the Sixth Avenue El, rumbling up to 53rd Street until 1938, was too grim an obstacle. It was not until an enormous new **Time & Life Building** went up at West 50th Street in 1959 that a Sixth Avenue building boom started, resulting in the glitzy canyon we see today. All these blocks were formerly, and almost uniformly, seas of brownstones before the glitz: middle-class dwellings that declined in elegance and opulence with each increment of their distance from Fifth Avenue. Rockefeller Center proper had erased hundreds of them, but its later annexes, and the other commercial development they inspired, were the crowning blows.*

The numbering starts at Rockefeller Center, moves south along Fifth Avenue to 45th Street, then north again.

[F1] **Rockefeller Center**, originally W.48th to W.51st Sts. bet. Fifth and Sixth Aves. 1932-1940. *The Associated Architects: Reinhard & Hofmeister, Corbett, Harrison & MacMurray; Raymond Hood, Godley & Fouilhoux.* Expanded, 1947-1973. 🍎

An island of architectural excellence, this is the greatest urban complex of the 20th century: an understated and urbane place that has become a classic lesson in the point and counterpoint of space, form, and circulation. Its campanile is the **GE** (formerly **RCA**) **Building**, a slender, stepped slab rising precipitously from Rockefeller Plaza proper, that many-leveled

F1

pedestrian space surrounding and overlooking the ice skating rink in winter, outdoor cafés in summer, all overseen by **Prometheus** (1934, *Paul Manship*). Opposite, **Channel Gardens** rises on a flower-boxed slope to Fifth Avenue between the low-scaled French and British Pavilions; the foliage here is changed with the seasons.

Limestone, now-grayed cast aluminum, and glass clad these towers and their lower neighbors. The skin is straightforward, modern, and unencumbered by the need for stylishness—but stylish nevertheless. Perhaps the most undated modern monument that New York enjoys.

[F1a] **1270 Sixth Avenue Building**/ originally **RKO Building**. 1932.
[F1b] **Radio City Music Hall**. 1931-1932. *Edward Durrell Stone*, design architect; *Donald Deskey*, interior design coordinator. 🍎 Interior 🍎 Renovation, 1999, *Hardy Holzman Pfeiffer and The Rockwell Group.*

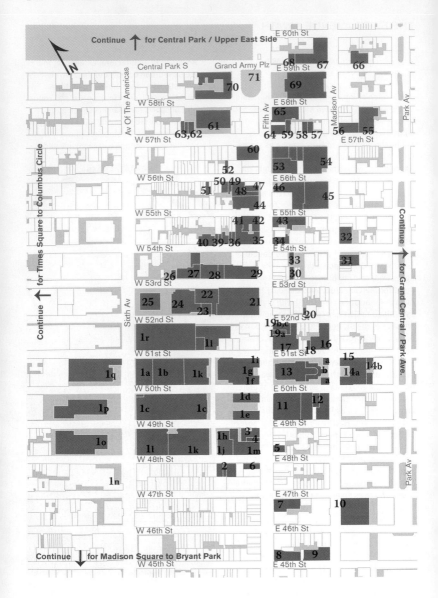

Continue ↑ for Central Park / Upper East Side

N

Continue ← for Times Square to Columbus Circle

Continue → for Grand Central / Park Ave.

Continue ↓ for Madison Square to Bryant Park

Critic *Chapell* in a 1933 **New Yorker Magazine** review dubbed the new Music Hall: "The dashing piece of architecture (at Rockefeller Center)... one has the feeling that the atmosphere of the place will be gay... (especially) *Donald Deskey's* dizzily mirrored women's powder-room." In 1998 the owners (Cablevision) hired *Hardy* to renovate Radio City's grand spaces so that they would look, in *Hardy's* words, "like I hadn't done anything at all." It's true.

[F1c] **GE Building**/formerly **RCA Building**, 30 Rockefeller Plaza. 1932-1933. Partial interior. 🖐

The **Rainbow Room** (at the top), a restaurant cum dancing of great elegance (Hugh Hardy redid this one as well), seems to close every ten years, then miraculously reopen under new management. Most recently the Cipriani family has been in charge.

[F1d] **British Building**/originally **British Empire Building**, 620 Fifth Ave. 1932-1933.

The Channel Gardens (or Promenade): The gently sloped and fountained space, which takes you from Fifth Avenue to the stairway leading into the sunken plaza, is called Channel Gardens since it is, like the English Channel, the separation between France (La Maison Française to the south) and the United Kingdom (the British Building to the north).

[F1e] **La Maison Française**. 610 Fifth Ave. 1933.
[F1f] **Palazzo d'Italia**. 626 Fifth Ave. 1933-1934.
[F1g] **International Building**, 630 Fifth Ave. 1933-1934. 🖐 Partial interior. 🖐
[F1h] **1 Rockefeller Plaza**/originally **Time & Life Building**. 1936-1937.
[F1i] **Associated Press Building**, 45 Rockefeller Plaza. 1938.
[F1j] **10 Rockefeller Plaza**/originally **Eastern Airlines Building**. 1939.

[F1k] **Simon & Schuster Building**/originally **U.S. Rubber Company Building** and **Addition** (on site of Center Theater), 1230 Sixth Ave. 1939. 🍎
All the above, A through K, excepting the Radio City interiors, by *Associated Architects*.

Additions since the original complex (1932-1940):

These assorted annexes to the Center along the Avenue of the Americas (Sixth Avenue) are of lesser stuff: posturing, bulbous boxes built in the 1960s and 1970s, grabbing onto the Rockefeller Center name, organization, and underground passages but sorry neighbors to their parent buildings. Included here are the **Time & Life**, *the old* **Sperry-Rand, McGraw-Hill, Exxon, Celanese** *buildings and others. In concert with the Zoning Resolution of 1961, they brought barren plazas to the Avenue of the Americas: good intentions misdirected those present lifeless places, without the people who would populate an Italian piazza, windswept*

The Landmarks Commission designation referred to "the elevator core, wrapped in shimmering stainless steel panels which contrast and complement the gray and white terrazzo floor laid in a playful serpentine pattern: a rare, intact, example of mid-century modernism."

[F1r] **Sperry Corporation Building**/originally **Sperry Rand Building**, 1290 Sixth Ave., bet. W.51st and W.52nd Sts. E side. 1961. *Emery Roth & Sons.*

[F2] **The Centria Apartments**, 18 W. 48th St., bet. Fifth and Sixth Aves. S side. 2008. *Perkins Eastman.*

The reflections of Rockefeller Center give some pause. As Lever House, the original modernist glass curtain wall once reflected the stone renaissance around it (now gone). This sleek building inspires hope that Rock Center will be there for an eternity. Said to be "corporate housing" (business travelers who tend to pass through, not make it a home). Will the Rock get sick of its own reflection?

F1q

F2

and dull. The midblock open-air arcades to the west of the three southernmost towers are more successful.

[F1l] **Warner Communications Building**/originally **Esso Building**, 15 W.51st St., bet. Fifth and Sixth Aves. to W.52nd St. 1946-1947. *Carson & Lundin.*

[F1m] **600 Fifth Avenue Building**/originally **Sinclair Oil Building**, NW cor. W.48th St. (purchased by Rockefeller Center, 1963). 1952. *Carson & Lundin.*

[F1n] **Celanese Building**, 1211 Sixth Ave., bet. W.47th and W.48th Sts. W side. 1973. *Harrison, Abramovitz & Harris.*

[F1o] **McGraw-Hill Building**, 1221 Sixth Ave., bet. W.48th and W.49th Sts. W side. 1972. *Harrison, Abramovitz & Harris.*

[F1p] **Exxon Building**, 1251 Sixth Ave., bet. W.49th and W.50th Sts. W side. 1971. *Harrison, Abramovitz & Harris.*

[F1q] **Time & Life Building**, 1271 Sixth Ave., bet. W.50th and W.51st Sts. W side. 1956-1960. *Harrison & Abramovitz.* Ground floor interior. 🍎

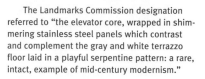 [F3] **Swiss Center Building**/originally **Goelet Building**, 608 Fifth Ave., SW cor. W.49th St. 1930-1932. *Edward Hall Faile & Co. and Victor L. F. Hafner.* Lower façade altered, 1998, *Garrison & Siegel*. 🍎

Above a new base, the original crisp cubist office building survives with a rich geometry of contrasting materials: marble, limestone, and stainless steel. Savor the **Art Deco** lobby.

[F4] **TGI Fridays**/originally **Childs Restaurant Building**, 604 Fifth Ave., bet. W.48th and W.49 Sts. W side. 1925. *William Van Alen.*

A lesser work by the architect of the **Chrysler Building**. A onetime church garden next door permitted the curved glass-block corner. The brilliant blue on Fifth Avenue is a sign of desperate marketing.

[F5] **Benetton**/originally **Charles Scribner's Sons**, 597 Fifth Ave., bet. E.48th and E.49th Sts. E side. 1912-1913. *Ernest Flagg.* 🍎 Interior. 🍎 Restored and remodeled, 1996, *Phillips Janson Group.*

An ornate black iron and glass storefront, crowned by a shallow elliptical arch, opens to a grand, two-story, plaster-vaulted mezzanined space: an almost-basilica. *Benetton* has preserved the interior volume, though all those books were part of the architecture too.

[F6] **Bank of America**/onetime **Fleet Bank**/originally **Black, Starr & Frost** (jewelers), 592 Fifth Ave., SW cor. W.48th St. *Carrère & Hastings.* 1912. Totally reclad, 1964, *Hausman & Rosenberg.*

Elongated black ports are the windows of this stark white marble-veneered prism. The *Carrère & Hastings* neo-Classical façade of *Black, Starr & Frost* was considered "old-fashioned" in the 1960s, therefore "modernized."

[F7] **575 Fifth Avenue**, SE cor. E.47th St. 1985. *Emery Roth & Sons.*

W & J Sloane was sited here, then **Korvette's** in the swinging sixties. Now the remnant body has been absorbed into this 40-story granite veneered galleria cum offices. Go in.

F7   F8

F11

[F8] **Fred F. French Building**, 551 Fifth Ave., NE cor. 45th St. 1927. *Fred F. French Co., H. Douglas Ives and Sloan & Robertson.* Partial interior.

The headquarters of the former designer-builder company has exotic multicolored faience at the upper-floor setbacks and a rich **Art Deco** lobby. From the days when even the greediest developer owed serious and intricate architectural detail and materials to the tenant and public.

[F9] **360 Madison Avenue**, NW cor. 45th St. 2003. *Cook + Fox.*

Those mysterious lines recount the historic profile of the old **Abercrombie & Fitch** building, home of the most venerable sporting goods store of the 20th century. The skeleton mostly remains within, while what we see is an understated skin (curtain wall) in tune wth our memories of A. & F.'s understated sportswear. A great urban sight, circa 1999: *James Prosek*, author of *Trout*, fly fishing on Madison Avenue.

[F10] Originally **Bear Stearns World Headquarters**, 383 Madison Ave., bet. 46th & 47th Sts. E side. 2002. *SOM (Skidmore, Owings & Merrill) + Gerner Kronick & Valcarcel Architects.*

A bulky octagonal hulk for the mighty Wall Streeter felled in the 2009 financial crash. Stolid, not graceful; a dour banker in a bespoke suit.

[F11] **Saks Fifth Avenue** (department store), 611 Fifth Ave., bet. W.49th and W.50th Sts. E side. 1922-1924. *Starrett & Van Vleck.*

A stately department store as a low-key foil to St. Patrick's to the north and the **GE Building** to the west, visible on axis through the Channel Gardens. A landmark more for its background role in counterpoint to rich neighbors, nevertheless its façade reeks of style rather than stylishness.

[F12] **Cohen Brothers Tower**/formerly **Swiss Bank Tower**, and **Saks Fifth Avenue Expansion**, 10 E.50th St., bet. Fifth and Madison Aves.

F13

through to E.49th St. (also called 623 Fifth Ave). 1989. *Lee Harris Pomeroy Assocs. and Abramovitz Kingsland Schiff.*

A midblock event, using the air rights of the landmark Saks store. (*Abramovitz* was the latter-day partner of *Wallace Harrison*, who had been party to Rockefeller Center's creation). *Pomeroy* was the new boy on this team.

[F13] **St. Patrick's Cathedral Complex** (Roman Catholic), E.50th to E.51st Sts., bet. Fifth and Madison Aves. 1853-1879. Towers, 1888, *James Renwick, Jr., William Rodrigue.*
[F13a] **Cardinal's Residence**, 452 Madison Ave., NW cor. E.50th St. and **Rectory**, 460 Madison Ave., SW cor. E.51st St. 1880. Both by *James Renwick, Jr.* [F13b] **Lady Chapel**, 1901-1906. *Charles T. Mathews.*

Renwick's adaptation of French Gothic was, seemingly, trivialized by his use of unyielding granite and his deletion of the flying buttresses (without deleting their pinnacle counterweights). But the cathedral, with its twin 330-

foot towers, is a richly carved counterfoil to Rockefeller Center, across Fifth Avenue. Go in. **The Lady Chapel**, added behind the altar, is in more academically correct French Gothic.

[F14a] Originally **Villard Houses**, 451-457 Madison Ave., bet. E.50th , and E.51st Sts. E side. 1882-1886. Façades by *Joseph Wells*, interiors by *Stanford White*, both of *McKim, Mead & White*. ● Restoration, 1981, *James Rhodes*, restoration architect. [F14b] **New York Palace Hotel** (behind), 1980. *Emery Roth & Sons.*

Once there were six brownstone mansions, built as if they were a single great Renaissance palazzo: two of them—and parts of the third, fourth, and fifth—were severed from the grand Madison Avenue forecourt to create the Palace Hotel. That tall, bulky, but essentially innocuous structure can be entered grandly through the courtyard, or banally under its glitzy 50th or 51st Street canopies. The price for preservation was greater height and bulk for the hotel. Journalist, railway promoter, and financier *Henry Villard* (born *Ferdinand Heinrich Hilgard* in Bavaria) built the surviving Madison Avenue remnants first; they were extended down the side streets immediately thereafter (all loosely based by *Wells* on the **Palazzo della Cancelleria** in Rome). After the collapse of his railroad empire, the south wing was bought by *Whitelaw* and *Elizabeth Mills Reid*, who brought *Stanford White* back to enrich the interiors. Now the hotel occupies that south wing, preserving the Gold Room. The north wing is the Urban Center:

F14b   F17

[F15] **The Urban Center**, 457 Madison Ave., SE cor. E.51st St. entry, through the New York Palace Madison Ave. forecourt. 1980. Open to the public. [F15a] **The Urban Center Bookstore**, within the Urban Center. 1980. Galleries open to the public: Mo-Fr. 10am-6:30pm. Sat. 12noon-5:30pm. 212-935-3595. *www.mas.org*

The Municipal Art Society negotiated a lease for the Villard mansion's north wing, creating space for a cluster of concerned professional organizations in addition to itself, a venerable and sometimes feisty civic organization with a largely lay membership. **The Urban Center Bookstore** and the **Architectural League** share common exhibition and lecture facilities with the Society. The Bookstore is a matchless source of books and periodicals on architecture, planning, and urban history.

[F16] **488 Madison Avenue**/originally **Look Building**, NW cor. 51st Street. 1950. *Emery Roth & Sons.* Building Renovated, 1997, *Hardy Holzman Pfeiffer.* Lobby renovated, 1997, *Fox & Fowle.*

Staccato setbacks and rounded corners make this one of the high-style office buildings of the 1950s. Little appreciated in the time of Lever House and the Seagram Building, such streetfronted setback architecture has made a comeback. The new "retro" lobby is onto another tack.

[F17] **Olympic Tower** (mixed use), 645 Fifth Avenue, NE cor. 51st St. 1976. *Skidmore, Owings & Merrill.* Olympic Place, from E.51st to E.52nd Sts. 1977. *Chermayeff, Geismar & Assocs.* with *Zion & Breen.*

An elegant urban idea for multiple uses (apartments over offices over shops) in a sleek but dull skin. To the pedestrian its attractions were its elegant shops and its arcade, **Olympic Place**, that penetrates the building mid-block

F16

F19a

from St. Patrick's to 52nd Street; a skylit, treed, and waterfalled public space of gray granite. Its dedication to public use allowed the owner to build a bigger building than normally permitted.

[F18] Originally **John Peirce House**, 11 E. 51st St., bet. Fifth and Madison Aves. 1904. *John H. Duncan.* ●

Rampant rustication from the architect of **Grant's tomb**. Not strictly by the books (Renaissance books, that is; only the ground floor is usually rusticated). *Duncan* counters the high granite relief below with a flat plane above, and a grand cornice.

[F19a] **Versace**/originally **George W. Vanderbilt House**, 647 Fifth Ave., bet. E.51st and E.52nd Sts. E side. 1902-1905. *Richard Howland Hunt & Joseph Howland Hunt.* Addition, 1917, *Charles L. Fraser.* Façade restored, 1995-1996. ●

Biltmore, near Asheville, North Carolina, was *George's* main house, designed by the *Hunt* brothers' father, *Richard Morris Hunt*. This was his sometime pied-à-terre in New York. *Hunt* designed **Biltmore** for *George* in the vocabulary of **Blois** and neighboring French Renaissance Chateaux along the Loire River Valley. A vast house, the largest ever built in America, sitting on 125,000 acres (50,600 hectares).

 [F19b] **Cartier, Inc.**/originally **Morton and Nellie Plant House**, 651-653 Fifth Ave., SE cor. E.52nd St. 1903-1905. *Robert W. Gibson.* Con-verted to shop, 1917, *William Welles Bosworth.* ✦ Restored, 1990s, *Joseph Pell Lombardi.*

On the 52nd Street façade four fluted **Doric** pilasters rise from an ornate stone balcony.

[F19c] **Cartier, Inc. extension**/originally **Edward and Frances Holbrook House**, 4 E.52nd St., bet. Fifth and Madison Aves. *C.P.H. Gilbert.* 1904-1905. Absorbed into **Cartier** shop, 1917, *William Welles Bosworth.* ✦

At one time both sides of Fifth Avenue were lined with American Renaissance mansions.

F19b　　　　　　F25

F23

These two, for *Plant* and a *Vanderbilt*, were a free interpretation of 16th- and 17th-century palazzi.

F26

DEATH WATCH

[F22] **Donnell Library**, 20 W.53rd St., bet. Fifth and Sixth Aves. 1955. *Edgar I. Williams and Aymar Embury II.*

Mayhem on the Orient-Express: The New York Public Library sold their Donnell Library to the Orient-Express Hotel for $59 million, planning to use the cash to fund *Norman Foster's* underground addition to their main branch at Bryant Park. The hotel promised to build a **new Donnell** within their new digs, backed out of the deal in 2009, then came back. Check our next edition to see what happened, or just stroll by.

*The **21 Club**: "Jack and Charlie's place" at 21 West 52nd Street (1872. Duggin & Crossman) was only one of several Prohibition-era clubs on its block that became fashionable in the 1930s. But it alone remains, having become successor to **Delmonico's** and **Sherry's** as café society's dining room.*

[F23] **The Museum of Television and Radio**, William S. Paley Building, 23 W.52nd St., bet. Fifth and Sixth Aves. 1989. *John Burgee with Philip Johnson.* Open to the public: Tu-Su 12-6; Th til 8. closed Mo. 212-621-6800. *www.mtr.org*

Paley, chairman of the museum, contributed land for this new facility, to replace the one at 1 East 53rd Street (1976. *Beyer Blinder Belle*). The arched entrance is a Johnsonian variation on one of the 1789 Parisian tollgates of *Claude-Nicolas Ledoux.*

[F24] **Paramount Group Building**/originally E.F. Hutton Building, 31 W.52nd St., bet. Fifth and Sixth Aves., through to W.53rd St. 1987. *Kevin Roche John Dinkeloo & Assocs.*

Granite neo-Assyrian polygonal columns straddle an allée through the block, punctuating a small plaza between this and the adjacent **CBS Building**. The thin skin of granite balloons over a steel armature. Way up there, a serrated Halloween crazy hat crowns it all, breaching the skyline.

[F20] **Austrian Cultural Institute**, 11 E.52nd St., bet. Fifth and Madison Aves. 2000. *Raimund Abraham.*

A sliver of Vienna steps back from mundane 52nd Street with a powerful presence. *Abraham*, a teaching theorist, here enters the hard world of New York architecture.

[F21] **666 Fifth Avenue**, bet. W.52nd and W.53rd Sts. W side. 1957. *Carson & Lundin.* First- and second-floor façade and lobby, 1999, *Nobutaka Ashihara Associates.*

A million square feet of office space wrapped in embossed aluminum. Note the sinuous lobby waterfall by sculptor *Isamu Noguchi.* The recent exterior "upgrading" is heavy-handed.

F20

[F25] **CBS Building** (Columbia Broadcasting System), 51 W.52nd St., NE cor. Sixth Ave. 1965. *Eero Saarinen & Assocs.* ●

"Black Rock," *Saarinen's* only high-rise building, is a sheer, freestanding 38-story, concrete-framed tower clad in dark gray honed granite: a somber and striking understatement. Here lawyers and money managers sit in splendor, while creativity is rampant in lesser facilities elsewhere. Elegant, austere.

[F26] **American Folk Art Museum**, 45 W.53rd. St. bet. Fifth and Sixth Aves. 2001. *Tod Williams & Billie Tsien.* Tu-Su 10:30-5:30, Fr 'til 7:30. 212-265-1040. *www.folkartmuseum.org.*

An often dizzying pretzel of spaces behind a timeless somber patina mask. "Folk art" has also embraced "outsider art." Here *Williams and Tsien*, well-regarded insiders, have designed a space for outsiders to get "inside." Compelling.

[F27] **Museum Tower**, 21 W.53rd St., bet. Fifth and Sixth Aves. 1985. *Cesar Pelli & Assocs.*

Sleek and subtly polychromatic, the Tower leaves architectural histrionics to the **E.F. Hutton Building** down the block. In the reconstruction of the museum complex the tower's edge was laid bare to the Museum Garden, a slit skirt revealing a lithe leg. A compliment.

[F28] **Museum of Modern Art (MoMA)**, 11 W.53rd St., bet. Fifth and Sixth Aves. 1939. *Philip Goodwin and Edward Durrell Stone.* Additions and alterations, 1951 and 1964. *Philip Johnson*, architect. *James Fanning*, landscape architect. Further additions and alterations, 1985, *Cesar Pelli & Assocs.*, design architects. *Edward Durrell Stone Assocs.*, associate architects. **New building**, 2004. *Yoshio Taniguchi.* Open to the public: Sa-Mo & We-Th 10:30-5:30, Fr 10:30-8. Closed Tu. 212-708-9400. *www.moma.org*

The history of modern art, more than its current events, is here enshrined. The 1939 building was a catechism of the **International Style** (a

F28: MoMa, pre-*Taniguchi*

F29

F30

style so dubbed by MoMA's 1932 exhibition, presented by *Henry-Russell Hitchcock* and *Philip Johnson*): an austere streetfront of marble veneer, tile, and opaque and transparent glass, with a pleasant rooftop garden worthy of a *Le Corbusier* acolyte. *Johnson's* east wing departed radically from the original flat International Style surfaces, with deeply three-dimensional grids of painted steel standing free of the wall. His finest contribution was the 1964 garden along 54th Street, where stone, plantings, pools, and fountains were composed into a serene and urbane oasis, one of the great urban gardens.

The guts of the museum were vastly altered and expanded (in part into *Johnson's* garden) by *Cesar Pelli*. The multileveled galleried and escalated interior seemed more like a shopping center of packaged aesthetics than a true museum, where the visitor could selectively inhabit the history of modern art. Happily, *Taniguchi's* **new building** brought back the original design intentions of the museum's various architects, complementing their work: *Stone's* canopy, *Pelli's* tower, *Johnson's* garden.

 [F29] St. Thomas' Church and Parish House (episcopal), 1 W.53rd St., NW cor. Fifth Ave. 1906-1913. *Cram, Goodhue & Ferguson*. Reredos, *Bertram G. Goodhue*, architect; *Lee Lawrie*, sculptor. ● Façade restoration, 1997, *Beyer Blinder Belle*. 7-6 weekdays, Sa 10-3:30, Su 7-3:30. *www.saint-thomaschurch.org*

One of New York's finest essays in picturesque Medieval massing and detail, built on a constricted corner. Is it by the hand of *Goodhue*, or is it *Cram's*? The powerful **French Gothic** interior culminates in the shimmering white, richly carved reredos behind the altar. Windows by *Whitefriars* of London.

[F30] Samuel Paley Plaza, also known as **Paley Park,** 3 E.53rd St., bet. Fifth and Madison Aves. 1967. *Zion & Breen*, landscape architects. *Albert Preston Moore*, consulting architect.

A parklet on the former site of the **Stork Club** contributed by *William S. Paley*, founder of CBS, and named for his father (1875-1963). A great oasis in good weather to refresh in the spray of the waterfall and to have a snack. The fall's white noise masks the cacophony of the City.

[F31] **527 Madison Avenue**, SE cor. E.54th St. 1987. *Fox & Fowle.*

Pleated glass and two-toned granite modulate an otherwise simple Madison Avenue façade. Along 54th Street stretches a great glass-sheeted skylight to its entrance atrium, tilted assuredly to make **Continental Illinois**, across Madison, feel less out of place.

[F32] **535 Madison Avenue**, NE cor. 54th St. 1986. *Edward Larrabee Barnes Assocs.*

Barnes again overpowers the pedestrian as he did at IBM. Here, however, the giant cantilever is supported by a Brobdingnagian column. The bonus plaza is overwhelmed.

[F33] Originally **William H. Moore House**, 4 E.54th St., bet. Fifth and Madison Aves. 1898-1900. *McKim, Mead & White.* ●

When Fifth Avenue's flanks were lined with residential palaces, fortresses, and châteaux, side streets were littered with the runners-up. A modest Italian Renaissance façade.

[F34] **Aeolian Building**/later **Elizabeth Arden Building**, 689-691 Fifth Ave., NE cor. 54th St. 1925-1927. *Warren & Wetmore.* ●

A small turreted château crowns this gracious neo-Renaissance cornering, its spirit

[F37] Originally **Philip Lehman House**, 7 W.54th St., bet. Fifth and Sixth Aves. 1900. *John H. Duncan.* Renovated as office building, 2008, *Belmont Freeman.* ●

Not only was *Robert Lehman's* private collection of paintings removed to the Metropolitan's Lehman Wing, but so were this town house's interiors (although remodeled much after 1900). The oculi, perforating the crowning mansard roof, are the best part of this neo-Baroque façade.

Renovation for a hedge fund included the restoration of the façade and interiors, and a glazed penthouse addition.

[F38] **U.S. Trust Company**/originally **James J. & Josephine Goodwin House**, 9-11 W.54th St., bet. Fifth and Sixth Aves. 1896-1898. *Charles F. McKim and William Mead* of *McKim, Mead & White.* Restoration for bank, 1981, *Haines Lundberg Waehler.* ●

Sober **neo-Georgian** limestone and brick from the blossoming of the Colonial Revival

F35

F34   F38

F37

mildly influenced by the **Art Deco** of its years: with a rounded corner of the same era as the old Child's restaurant (TGI Friday's) just south of 49th Street.

[F35] **University Club**, 1 W.54th St., NW cor. Fifth Ave. 1896-1900. *Charles McKim* of *McKim, Mead & White.* ●

A Florentine super-palazzo beyond the *Medicis'* wildest dreams; only if they had had elevators to make this 10-story equivalent. Monumental bronze railings offer overview of the Avenue. The greatest neo-Renaissance American palazzo.

[F36] **5 West 54th Street**, originally **Moses Allen and Alice Dunning Starr House**, bet. Fifth and Sixth Aves. N side. 1897-1899. *R.H. Robertson.* ●

A modest town house (by Fifth Avenue Swath standards) with gracious fluted Ionic pilasters flanking its entry.

movement: inspired by *Charles Bulfinch's* third Harrison Gray Otis House (Beacon Street, Boston. 1806).

[F39] **13-15 West 54th Street**, bet. Fifth and Sixth Aves. 1896-1897. *Henry J. Hardenbergh.* ●

Neo-Renaissance limestone outpomps the modesty of Nos.9-11. *John D. Rockefeller, Jr.,* lived in No.13 from 1906-1918. His son, *Nelson*, sometime Governor, used it as an office (and died there). *Nelson* also purchased No.15 for the Museum of Primitive Art (now the *Michael Rockefeller* collection at the Metropolitan Museum).

[F40] **Rockefeller Apartments**, 17 W.54th St., bet. Fifth and Sixth Aves. 1936. *Harrison & Fouilhoux.* Interior alterations, 1982, *Hobart Betts.* Window Renovation, 1997, *William Leggio.* ●

Elegant cylindrical bay windows overview the Museum of Modern Art Garden—on part of a midblock strip of land acquired by the

Rockefellers when their Center was assembled. The leftovers included the **Donnell Library** on West 53rd Street, the Museum of Modern Art, and this urbane place. One of the great modernist apartment blocks in Manhattan, its garden within a pleasant private oasis.

 [F41] **Privatbanken Building**, 20 West 55th Street, bet. Fifth and Sixth Aves. 1985. *Emery Roth & Sons and Hobart Betts.*

The Bank of Denmark's toehold in New

F41

F42   F44

F48   F49

York. But that toe cascades skyward to a barrel vaulted penthouse.

[F42] **The Peninsula**/originally **The Gotham Hotel**, 2 W.55th St., SW cor. Fifth Ave. 1902-1905. *Hiss & Weekes.* Partly altered, 1984, *Stephen B. Jacobs & Assocs.* Altered, 1987, *Hirsch/Bender, designers; AiGroup Architects,* architects. ●

Soul-mate of the **St. Regis** across the street, old **Gotham's** cornice is regal, its entry grand (fluted, banded Mannerist columns flanking), but not grandiose. Designed with its next-door neighbor, the University Club, in mind.

[F43] **St. Regis Hotel**, 2 E.55th St., SE cor. Fifth Ave. 1901-1904. *Trowbridge & Livingston.* Addition to E, 1927, *Sloan & Robertson.* ●

An opulent **Beaux Arts** mass that gets richer toward the sky. Second only to the Waldorf-Astoria in prominent guests, it is especially popular with foreign diplomats. The **King Cole**

Bar is designed around the monumental *Maxfield Parrish* mural that once graced Times Square's old **Knickerbocker Hotel** bar. Outside the brass and glass doorman's kiosk greets you with magnificence.

[F44] **Fifth Avenue Presbyterian Church**, 705 Fifth Ave., NW cor. W.55th St. 1875. *Carl Pfeiffer.*

A somber brownstone neo-Gothic remnant of early days on Fifth Avenue, long before it became a boulevard of fashionable mansions.

[F45] **SONY Building**/originally **AT&T Headquarters**, 550 Madison Ave., bet. E.55th and E.56th Sts. W side. 1984. *Philip Johnson/John Burgee.* Atrium and underspaces altered into Sony Entertainment Center, 1994, *Gwathmey Siegel & Associates.*

Dubbed by the press the **"Chippendale"** skyscraper, this granite hulk turned the market around among developers in New York. Glass modern was replaced with stone postmodern, and a building's profile against the sky became

F45

a competition to create the most unique silhouette. The atrium is smashing, its quarter-arched glass roof truly reminiscent in scale of the ancestral Milan Galleria, by *Giuseppe Mengoni. Gwathmey Siegel's* renovations have activated the ensemble.

[F46] Originally **Corning Glass Building**, 717 Fifth Ave., SE cor. 56th St. 1959. *Harrison & Abramovitz & Abbe.* Entrance altered, 1994, *Gwathmey Siegel & Assocs.*

Mirror-smooth walls of green glass. *Gwathmey Siegel's* vigorous new entry has brought distinction to its street-level architecture. What was once a pool has become a plaza planter, and more recently, the ground floor space a prismatic **Armani** store by *Maximiliano Fuksas.*

F40

[F47] **Henri Bendel Building**, consolidating and expanding the sometime **Rizzoli Building**, old 712 Fifth Avenue. 1908. *Adolph S. Gottlieb*; and the former **Coty Building**, 714 Fifth Ave. 1907-1908. *Woodruff Leeming*. Window glass, 1912, *René Lalique*. Both bet. W.55th and W.56th Sts. W side. **Rizzoli** and **Coty**, now restored and redesigned, 1989-1990, *Beyer Blinder Belle*.

Here two early (first growth) commercial buildings replaced town mansions of the latter 19th century. **712's** giant **Corinthian** pilasters surmount some modesty below. **714**, resplendent in **Lalique** glass, sparkles. And *Henri Bendel* is the beneficiary.

[F48] **712 Fifth Avenue Building**, behind. 1989. *Kohn Pederson Fox with Beyer Blinder Belle*.

The address is by proximity, not position. The two tails (**Rizzoli** and **Coty**) wag this architectural dog, internally related to the fifth avenue charmers, but externally isolated by *Harry Winston's* heavy handed folly at the corner. But a crisp tower rises from it all.

[F49] Originally **Frederick C. and Birdsall Otis Edey House**/now **Felissimo**, 10 W.56th St., bet. Fifth and Sixth Aves. 1901. *Warren & Wetmore*.

An exuberant Beaux Arts town house,with a grand Palladian window over its ground floor. The arch, supported with Roman Tuscan columns, is enrichened by a grand cartouche and dentils.

[F50] Originally **Harry B. and Evelina Hollins House**/now **Consulate of Argentina**, 12-14 W.56th St., bet. Fifth and Sixth Aves. 1899-1901. *Stanford White of McKim, Mead & White*. Alterations, 1924, *J.E.R. Carpenter*.

A wide **neo-Federal-Georgian** town house, elegant limestone bas reliefs capping its second floor arched windows. The bold cornice comes more from *White's* sketchbooks, than Georgian England.

[F51] **Omo Norma Kamali**, 11 W.56th St., bet. Fifth and Sixth Aves. 1978. *Rothzeid Kaiserman Thompson & Bee*, architects. *Peter Marino*, designer.

A framed façade. The horizontal slots suggest a fortified function, but the flags, a major element in this architecture, give golden motion to the street.

[F52] Originally **Henry Seligman House**, 30 W. 56th Street, bet. Fifth and Sixth Aves. S side. 1899-1901. *C.P.H. Gilbert.* 🍎

An orphaned **Renaissance-Revival** town house a bit far from its Fifth Avenue soulmates, and in the midst of:

Eat Street: The columnist Earl Wilson's name for West 56th Street between Fifth and Sixth Avenues. It held the record for a single block, with about two dozen restaurants—from French and Italian to Japanese and Korean. Above the close ranks of canopies are some interesting old house fronts. Among the stars are some Venetian Gothic, a replication of detail from the Grand Canal's Ca' d'Oro.

[F55] **Four Seasons Hotel**, 57 E.57th St., bet. Madison and Park Aves. 1990s. *I.M.Pei, Pei Cobb Freed & Partners/Frank Williams & Assocs.*, associated architects.

A brawny insertion into this low-key block of art galleries: the Chinese "moon gate" hovers between "buttresses" surmounted by finials. Pompous.

[F56] **Fuller Building**, 41 E.57th St., NE cor. Madison Ave. 1929. *Walker & Gillette*, architects. *Elie Nadelman*, sculptor. 🍎 Interior. 🍎

The Brooks Brothers of **Art Deco**: black, gray, and white. This was the successor headquarters of Fuller after they moved uptown from the vaunted Flatiron Building. Check the bronze elevator doors.

[F57] **LVMH** (Louis Vuitton, Moët Hennessy) Offices, 19 E.57th St., bet. Fifth and Madison Aves. N side. 1999. Design architect, *Christian de Portzamparc*.

F52

F57

F53

F54

F55

[F53] **Trump Tower**, 725 Fifth Ave., NE cor. 56th St. 1983. *Der Scutt*, design architect, with *Swanke Hayden Connell.*

Folded glass conceals a fantasyland for the affluent shopper. Within, the multilevel space houses a café with waterfalls and moving stairways to shoppers' heaven: flamboyant, exciting, and emblematic of the American Dream. *Donald Trump* entered here stage left and has since delivered the Trump brand everywhere: his aesthetics, however, are still more akin to malt liquor than to Veuve Clicquot.

[F54] Originally **IBM Building**, 590 Madison Ave., bet. E.56th and E.57th Sts. W side. 1983. *Edward Larrabee Barnes Assocs.*

This polished monolith is a cut prism, its faceted form skewing the street. Most obvious to the pedestrian is the looming cantilevered corner at 57th and Madison.

Construction documents, *The Hillier Group.*

Folded planes create a sleek but aggressive glass curtain wall punctuating dour 57th Street. Its high style may soon be last year's. French champagne does those things.

[F58] **The Chanel Building**, 15 E.57th St., bet. Fifth and Madison Aves. N side. 1996. *Platt Byard Dovell.*

A sober façade in contrast to French exuberance at **LVMH** next door. Perfume versus champagne.

[F59] Former **L.P. Hollander & Company Building**, 3 East 57th St., bet. Fifth and Madison Aves. N side. 1929-1930. *Shreve, Lamb & Harmon.* 🍎

A foretaste of the Empire States's embossed aluminum panels. More an interesting experiment than an important building. Crisp, though.

Tiffany's: One of the world's oldest and most famous jewelers came to the corner of Fifth Avenue and 57th Street in 1940. The show windows in the massive polished granite façade (727 Fifth Avenue) are famous for their miniature stage-setting displays. Holly Golightly found it comforting, and it's comforting knowing it hasn't changed since she gazed at its window displays in 1961. See their original palace at 409 Fifth Avenue.

[F60] **The Crown Building**/originally **Heckscher Building**, 730 Fifth Ave., SW cor W.57th St. 1921. *Warren & Wetmore.*

Although one of the first office buildings erected after passage of the City's 1916 Zoning Resolution, it reveals no radical change in massing, but is crowned with an elegant octagonal hat rich in copper roofing and gilded detail. In spite of its redolence of the Beaux Arts, the Museum of Modern Art opened its first gallery here on the 12th floor in November 1929.

[F61a] **9 West 57th Street**, bet. Fifth and Sixth Aves. to E.58th St. *Skidmore, Owings & Merrill.*

A black-and-white swooping form, destructive of the street wall as its sibling overlooking Bryant Park. Wind bracing here is proudly displayed (way up there at each end) like a pair of new suspenders. And down below savor *Hugh Hardy's* **8-1/2 Restaurant.**

[F61b] **Brasserie 8-1/2 Restaurant**, 9 W. 57th St., bet. Fifth and Sixth Aves. 2000. *Hardy3.*

F60   F61b

Ivan Chermayeff vermilion-red **"9"** marks the building, and his **"8-1/2"** alerts you to the brasserie's entrance. The stairs peel through a cylinder painted the same shade of red as *Chermayeff's* famous 9. Want a staircase just made for those dramatic entrances? This is it. *Hugh Hardy* unleashed.

[F62] Originally **Ampico Building**/later **Curtiss-Wright Building**, 29 W.57th St., bet. Fifth and Sixth Aves. N side. 1923. *Cross & Cross.*

Ampico pianos were the pseudo-Légion d'Honneur medallions on the tower flanks (*Napoleon*, Empereur des Francais). For heroic pianos?

[F63] **Rizzoli Bookshop**, 31 W.57th St., bet. Fifth and Sixth Aves. N side. ca. 1905. Restored, 1986, *Hardy Holzman Pfeiffer Assocs.*

A bookshop that feels like a library in a baronial mansion, designed by the multitalented firm that restored the *Carnegie* mansion for use as the Cooper-Hewitt Museum.

[F64] **Louis Vuitton**/originally **New York Trust Company Building** (offices)/onetime **Manufacturers Hanover Trust Company**, 1 E.57th St., NE cor. Fifth Ave. 1930. *Cross & Cross.* Store design. 2004. *Jun Aoki.*

A light conversion from the heavy-handed Warner Brothers Store to a sleeker replacement. It's a classy building. Look to the top where the original neo-Classical details have been blended with elegant marble cubism.

[F65] **745 Fifth Avenue**/originally **Squibb Building**, SE cor. E.58th St. 1931. *Office of Ely Jacques Kahn.* Upgraded, 1988, *Hammond, Beebe & Babka.*

Kahn remains one of the grand old men of New York Art Deco. Here his talent remains at the entry and in the building's overall massing. The storefronts are another matter.

[F66] **Delmonico Plaza**, 55 E.59th St., bet. Madison and Park Aves. 1986. *Davis, Brody & Assocs.*

F64   F66

Slate and granite. The ground-floor colonnade is a lusty break in the streetfront architecture, and its matte finish contrasts well with the glitter opposite.

[F67] **650 Madison Avenue**/originally **C.I.T. Building**, bet E.59th and E.60th Sts. W side. 1957. *Harrison & Abramovitz.* Reclad and tower added, 1987, *Fox & Fowle.*

The original black granite and stainless steel eight-story building has been overcome by its new tower and skin. The crowning floors are the most impressive sight, with a stainless-steel logo against the sky between incessant panels of green glass.

[F68] **5 East 59th Street**/ formerly **Hong Kong and Shanghai Banking Corporation**/onetime **Playboy Club**, bet. Fifth and Madison Aves. Altered, 1984, *Der Scutt.*

This modest building has passed through serial incarnations. Once the Savoy Art Galleries, it was remodeled into the Playboy Club (1962. *Oppenheimer, Brady & Lehrecke*) and, later, remodeled again (1976. *Paul K. Y. Chen*). Now sexy dining has given way to serious business.

F71

[F69] **General Motors Building**, 767 Fifth Ave., bet. E.58th and E.59th Sts. to Madison Ave. 1968. *Edward Durell Stone, Emery Roth & Sons,* associated architects. **Apple cube and store**. 2007. *Bohlin Cywinski Jackson.*

Here stood the **Savoy Plaza** (hotel) and a miscellany of others, none particularly distinguished. The hue and cry over the new tower was based not on building design but on the creation of a redundant plaza that weakened the definition of The Plaza as an urban space.

A crystal cube crowns the new **Apple store**, a delightful urban presence shimmering by day, glistening at night; the store, below, occupies the space of the banal sunken plaza that preceded it.

[F70] **Plaza Hotel**, 768 Fifth Ave. and 2 Central Park South, between W.58th to W.59th Sts. facing Grand Army Plaza. 1905-1907. *Henry J. Hardenbergh.* Addition, 1921, *Warren & Wetmo*re. 🍎 Renovation 2005-2008, *Costas Kondylis & Partners.* New interiors, *Annabelle Selldorf.*

A vestige of Edwardian elegance. *Hardenbergh*, its designer, graced New York with another, and equal, social and architectural monument: **The Dakota**. The white glazed brick and the verdigris copper and slate mansard roof have been returned to their pristine splendor. One of the most exciting views of New York (*Eloise-style*) is from any room on the north side from the third to the fifth floors. From there eyes can skim the trees in a dramatic perspective of Central Park and Fifth Avenue. *Frank Lloyd Wright* was a devotee of the Plaza and used it as his headquarters while he was designing, and re-designing, the Guggenheim. His room, or at least a simulation of it, is still there. The extensive three-year renovation by *Kondylis* converted 181 units to condos and added a shopping corridor.

The **Oak Room** and adjoining **Oak Bar**, tastefully renovated by *Annabelle Selldorf*, is a great, though pricey, place for lunch. *Selldorf* designed new furniture but kept the oak paneling and murals intact. It's a quiet retreat from the City, and despite what happened to *Cary Grant* there in the opening scene of *North by Northwest*, it's highly unlikely you will be abducted by foreign agents. The Bar faces Central Park with an entry on 59th, but enter through the hotel lobby and wind your way back to the bar; it's more fun that way.

The Paris Theater, 4 W.58th St. bet. Fifth & Sixth Aves. (adjacent to the Plaza), 1948. Emery Roth & Sons, *interiors by* Warner-Leeds Assocs. Roth's *theater opened in 1948, has only one screen and thus shows only one movie at a time. A suggestion for a rainy day: lunch at the Oak Bar followed by a matinee at the Paris. What could be better?*

[F71] **The Plaza**/officially **Grand Army Plaza Scenic Landmark,** Fifth Ave. bet. W.58th and W.60th Sts. W side. Central Park. 1913-1916. *Thomas Hastings of Carrère & Hastings.* 🍎

Formally called Grand Army Plaza, this is *The* Plaza to New Yorkers; until 1973 it was New York's only public urban plaza for people. The Police Plaza is number two (chronologically). Plazas at Rockefeller Center, and the World Financial Center, are parts of private building complexes; but here, in the European tradition, is an outdoor room contained by buildings of varied architecture and function, an island of urbane repose. The more significant half (the area is bisected by 59th Street) to the south is centered on the Plaza Hotel on the west and the General Motors Building across Fifth Avenue.

The Plaza is ornamented by varied paving and trees enclosing the **Pulitzer Fountain**, surmounted by **Pomona**, a lithe lady by *Karl Bitter* on a cascade of pools by *Carrère and Hastings*. To the south are the seemingly separate seven buildings of **Bergdorf-Goodman** (It was one building trying to look like a row of seven. 1928. *Buchman & Kahn*. Façades reorganized, 1980s, *Allan Greenberg*) and the **Paris Theater**. Looming high in the local skyline is 9 West 57th Street.

General Sherman occupies the Plaza's northern half, which is more of a traffic turn-around than a pedestrian enclave. The General (*William Tecumseh*) is here marching, not through Georgia but, rather, in allegory.

Augustus Saint-Gaudens presented this casting at the Paris Exposition of 1900, and the good General mounted his present pedestal in 1903. Now the oldest resident of this place, he antedates the Plaza Hotel by four years.

NECROLOGY

Olivetti-Underwood Showroom, 584 Fifth Ave., bet. W. 47th and W. 48th Sts. W side. 1954. *Belgiojoso, Peressutti & Rogers,* architects. Wall relief, *Constantino Nivola,* sculptor.

Olivetti's elegant office equipment roosted on green marble pedestals growing out of the green marble floor.

Gotham Book Mart, at 41 West 47th Street, in the heart of the City's jewelry district, was a great, though cramped and cluttered, bookshop. Its strengths were literature, poetry, dance, and esoterica. Its loyal customers were the literati of the City and the world. Upstairs, in the gallery (clubhouse for the James Joyce Society), were changing exhibitions including—in the summer—those on postcards, its owner's passion. (The sign: wise men fish here.)

La Fonda del Sol (restaurant), 123 W.50th St., bet. Sixth and Seventh Aves., in the Time & Life Building. 1960. *Alexander Girard.*

An exuberant design in which the forms, spaces, and materials were impeccably controlled. A very special place. A recent incarnation on Park Avenue has the same name but little of the same style.

Schrafft's (restaurant)/originally **Knoedler Gallery**, 558 Fifth Ave., bet. E. 45th and E. 46th Sts. W side. 1911. *Carrère & Hastings.*

Its façade was cosmetized via radical plastic surgery into the Philippine Center (1974. *Augusto Comacho*).

The Webb & Knapp Building at 383 Madison. 1922-1923. *Cross & Cross.* Demolished May 1998.

In 1952 *I.M. Pei* and *William Lescaze,* the former acting as the head of *Webb & Knapp's* architectural division, designed a critically acclaimed duplex penthouse office for the company owner, developer *William Zeckendorf* and his design team, topped with a cantilevered turret-like private lounge.

The Ground Floor (restaurant), 51 W.52nd St., NE cor. Sixth Ave., in the CBS Building. 1965. *Eero Saarinen & Assocs.*

The elegant, dark, sleek interior, replaced by a series of redesigns, was planned by the *Saarinen* firm down to the table settings.

The Museum of Modern Art's annex at No.23, the former **George Blumenthal House** of 1904 by *Hunt & Hunt,* was converted into offices, and the ground floor was transformed in 1973 and 1975 by *Abraham Rothenberg Assocs. and Thomas Lowrie.* **MoMA's** own original canopy and penthouse terrace restaurant by *Philip L. Goodwin* and *Edward Durell Stone,* and the 1951 west addition by *Philip Johnson & Assocs.,* were removed to accommodate the vast expansion of

1985, which had claimed the **Blumenthal** annex for one of the museum's shops, always leaving the grand Beaux Arts façade intact, until the end. Demolished for the Museum Tower of 1985.

IBM Showroom, 590 Madison Ave., SW cor. E. 57th St. Altered, 1959, *Eliot Noyes.*

The architecture of display par excellence and the pure pleasure of viewing exhibits (some by *Charles Eames*) from the street; the showroom enabled anyone to participate in an experience without actually having to enter. Replaced by the hovering cantilever of the IBM tower.

Bonniers (gift shop)/later **Georg Jensen Specials**, 605 Madison Ave., bet. E. 57th and E. 58th Sts. E side. 1949. *Warner-Leeds Assocs.*

Originally commissioned as a bookstore for the Swedish publishing house, the store broadened, selling exquisitely tasteful household and gift items. Its elegantly understated yet unmannered interior and its gangplank stair were considered a scripture for modern design.

Olivetti-Underwood Showroom

D/R Design Research (home furnishings)/formerly **Galerie Norval**, 53 E.57th St., bet. Fifth and Madison Aves. Altered, 1965, *Benjamin Thompson.*

The New York branch of the store that Boston architects *Ben and Jane Thompson* opened on Brattle Street in Cambridge. New York's four-story primer of good contemporary design was filled with furniture, kitchen gadgets, clothes, and toys—all of good contemporary design.

The Savoy Plaza Hotel, Fifth Avenue, bet. 58th and 59th Sts. 1927. *McKim, Mead & White.*
Stomped.

UNITED NATIONS / TURTLE BAY

The tract known by the mid-18th century as **Turtle Bay Farm** extended roughly from East 40th to East 48th Streets, from Third Avenue to the East River. The little cove that gave it its name is now covered by the gardens on the northern half of the United Nations grounds. Bucolic in the early 19th century, the area was invaded around 1850 by riverfront industry, with shantytowns inland that were soon replaced by tenements. By 1880, El trains were rumbling along both Second and Third Avenues. Town houses on the **Beekman tract** along the river around East 50th Street remained respectable (due to deed restrictions against industry) until about 1900 and were among the first in the area to be rehabilitated. There was much ambitious building and renovation in the 1920s, but it was not until six city blocks of slaughterhouses along the river were razed in 1946 for the **United Nations**, and the **Third Avenue El** (the

U3

U1   U4

last one to operate in Manhattan) closed down in 1955 that Turtle Bay was ready for thorough rehabilitation.

Begin at Grand Central, *where IRT subways abound (4, 5, 6, and 7 trains).*

*New York's last **automat** expired in 1991 at 200 East 42nd Street, in the office building at the southeast corner of Third Avenue. A cafeteria in which food was dispensed in individual portions through the doors of little glazed compartments, the automat was born just before World War I, when technology was believed capable of solving all ills. Most of its siblings elsewhere were housed in delightful 1930s Art Deco/Art Moderne architecture, the most spectacular at 104 West 57th Street. A thousand little glass doors displayed the goodies within (baked beans, macaroni en casserole), and opened to the magic of your coins. Once upon a time a nickel or two could buy almost anything in the Automat.*

▌ **[U1] Daily News Building** 220 E.42nd St., bet. Second and Third Aves. 1929-1930. *Raymond Hood.* Lobby. Addition SW cor. Second Ave. 1958. *Harrison & Abramovitz.*
Hood abandoned the Gothic sources with which he won the *Chicago Tribune* tower competition in 1922, and here used a bold, striped verticality: patterned red and black brick spandrels and russet window shades alternating with white brick piers—the whole effect to minimize the appearance of windows in the prism. The 1958 addition wisely repeated the same stripes, but in different proportions, to yield wider windows. The street floor, outside and in, is ornamented in Art Deco abstractions. See the enormous revolving globe and weather instruments in the (mostly) original old lobby. The newspaper is gone, but its artifacts remain.

An aside to 43rd Street:

▌ **[U2] Permanent Mission of India to the United Nations,** 235 E.43rd St., bet. Second and Third Aves. 1991. *Charles Correa. Bond Ryder & Assocs.,* associated architects.
A modest polished granite tower with a disciplined composition of large and small square openings. At the street the grand balcony is where a Bombay movie star might appear (too grand for the likes of *Gandhi*). *Correa* is one of India's most noted modern architects.

Back to 42nd Street:

▌ **[U3] Ford Foundation Building,** 321 E.42nd St., bet. First and Second Aves. to E.43rd St. 1963-1967. *Kevin Roche John Dinkeloo & Assocs.* Original landscape, *Dan Kiley.*
People and plants share a leafy world worthy of Kew, elegantly contained in masses of brick and stretches of glass. An avant-garde work that respects the street and enhances the urban fabric of the City. Best of all, the garden is **open to the public** and the generally cheerful security guards will not threaten to confiscate your camera, unlike in many "public" spaces in post–September 11th New York. Enjoy.

[U4] United Presbyterian Church of the Covenant, 310 E.42nd St. bet. First and Second Aves. 1871. *J. C. Cady.*
A lonely leftover from other times; perhaps a piece of Tudor Scarsdale floated into town.

[U5] Tudor City, E.40th St. to E.43rd St., bet. First and Second Aves. 1925-1928. Fred F. French Co., *H. Douglas Ives.*
An ambitious private renewal effort that included 12 buildings (3,000 apartments and 600 hotel rooms) along its own street (**Tudor City Place**), hovering over abutments over First Avenue. Everything faced in, toward the private open space and away from the surrounding tenements, slaughterhouses, and generating plants. As a result, almost windowless walls faced the United Nations.

Continue ↑ for Upper East Side

E 62nd S
E 61st St
E 60th St
York Av
30
E 59th St
34
E 59th St
35
32
Sutton
E 58th St 33
29
31 E 57th St
Sutton Pl S
Second Av
First Av
E 56th St
28
E 56t
Lexington Av
Third Av
36
E 55th St
38 37
E 54th St 26
27
39
E 53rd St
40
45
41
42
24
44
E 52nd St
43
25
46
23
Gen D. Macarthur Plz
47
E 51st St
E 50th St
22
Beekman Pl
53
21
48 50
52
20
E 49th St
18 Mitchell Pl
49
19
55
51
51
E 48th St
51
Turtle Bay Gardens
Historic District
17
16
E 47th St
15
E 46th S
14
E 45th St
13
9
12
10 9 7
11 10 8
United Nations Pl
E 44th St
2
6
Archbishop F.J. Sheen Pl E 43rd St
3
5
6a
E 42nd St
1
4 5
E 41st St
Tudor City Pl
5a Tudor City
Historic District
Continue ↓ for Murray Hill or Kips Bay

E 40th St
E 39th St

for Grand Central / Park Ave.

Lexington Av

U5, Tudor City

[U5a] **Tudor City Historic District**, Tudor City Place and both sides of 42nd and 43rd Sts., from First Ave. halfway to Second Ave. 🍎

▌ [U6] **United Nations Headquarters**, United Nations Plaza (First Ave.), bet. E.42nd and E.48th Sts. E side. 1947-1953. *International Committee of Architects, Wallace K. Harrison, chairman.* Partially open to the public.
[U6a] **Library Addition**, NE cor. E.42nd St. 1963. *Harrison, Abramovitz & Harris.*

John D. Rockefeller, Jr.'s donation of the $8.5 million site, already assembled by real estate tyro *William Zeckendorf* for a private development, decided the location of the headquarters. The team of architects included *Le Corbusier* of France, *Oscar Niemeyer* of Brazil, *Sven Markelius* of Sweden, and representatives from ten other countries. The final massing is clearly a concept from *Le Corbusier* (seconded by *Niemeyer*), but the details are largely *Harrison's.*

The 544-foot-high slab of the **Secretariat** (only 72 feet thick) dominates the group, with the **Library** to the south, the **General Assembly** to the north—its form played against the Secretariat's size—and the **Conference Building** extending to the east over Franklin D. Roosevelt Drive, out of sight from U.N. Plaza. Every major nation donated some work of art to the headquarters. Immediately noticeable is England's gift, a *Barbara Hepworth* sculpture standing in the pool (a gift from U.S. schoolchildren) in front of the Secretariat. Probably the most interesting are the three **Council Chambers** donated by three Scandinavian countries.

U8

The City, under *Robert Moses'* direction, made way for the U.N. by diverting First Avenue's through traffic into a tunnel under United Nations Plaza and opening up a half-block-wide landscaped park, **Dag Hammarskjold Plaza**, along East 47th Street—a meager space in the shadow of tall buildings, with no view at all of the U.N. Headquarters. The General Assembly lobby and gardens are open to the public, and tours of the conference spaces are available. Enter at East 46th Street.

▌ [U7] **1 and 2 United Nations Plaza**, NW cor. E.44th St. 1976 and 1983. *Kevin Roche John Dinkeloo & Assocs.*

Folded graph paper—elegant scaleless envelopes of aluminum and glass, one form sliced at its corner and sheltering the pedestrian at the street with an overhead glass apron. The public spaces within are some of the best in New York's modern architecture.

▌ [U8] **UNICEF** (United Nations International Children's Emergency Fund), 3 United Nations Plaza (E.44th St. S side), bet. First and Second Aves. 1987. *Kevin Roche John Dinkleloo & Assocs.*

Two tones of granite clad this architectural cousin of the E.F. Hutton Building. Here the columns are more restrained, and the building fits more serenely into its blockfront.

[U9] **Kuwait Mission to the United Nations**, 321 E.44th St., bet. First and Second Aves. 1986. *Swanke Hayden Connell.*

A melange of Gulf States fantasies and New York State postmodern.

[U10] **Beaux Arts Apartments**, 307 and 310 E.44th St., bet. First and Second Aves. 1929-1930. *Kenneth Murchison and Raymond Hood, of Hood,Godley & Fouilhoux.* 🍎

Named for the adjacent (to 310) old **Beaux Arts Institute** building, this pair of cubistic Art Moderne compositions in light and dark tan brick

U12, under construction

faces each other across the street; both with streamlined metal railings and corner windows.

[U11] **Permanent Mission of Egypt to the United Nations**/originally **Beaux Arts Institute of Design**, 304 E.44th St., between First and Second Aves. 1928. *Frederic C. Hirons of Dennison & Hirons.* 🍎

The fantasies of Beaux Arts (cf. École des Beaux Arts, Paris) architectural education are here incorporated, built when that educational system was on the wane. The style is, of course, Art Deco, now reloved by the profession that rejected it for so long. But how is Egypt going to cope with that monumental lettering? Contestants in the competition for its design included *Raymond Hood, Philip Goodwin, Ralph Walker,* and *Harvey Wiley Corbett.*

[U12] **United States Mission to the United Nations**, 799 United Nations Plaza, SW cor. E. 45th Street. 2010. *Gwathmey Siegel & Assocs.*

A crisp and sturdy (bombproof?) replacement for the 1961 egg-crate by *Kelly & Gruzen* and *Kahn & Jacobs.* The new monolith merely provides blank walls for the possible attacker, but gives notion of an austere memorial to the free exchange of ideas. Is there a tunnel to the U.N.? The wavy-roofed glass box at its foot makes a gesture to the Assembly building across the street, but the posture would be more steely-eyed if it weren't there and its contents were in the stele proper.

[U13] Originally **Institute of International Education**, 809 United Nations Plaza, bet. E.45th and E.46th Sts. W side. 1964. *Harrison, Abramovitz & Harris.* **Kaufmann Conference Rooms**, 1965, *Alvar Aalto.*

Important for an interior space—the penthouse Edgar J. Kaufmann Conference Rooms, one of only two U.S. works of the Finnish architect *Aalto.*

JUST DEMOLISHED!
[U14] **Anti-Defamation League, B'nai B'rith**, originally **Carnegie Endowment for International Peace**, 823 United Nations Plaza, NW cor. 46th St. 1953. *Harrison & Abramovitz.* Renovated for B'nai B'rith, 1991, *Der Scutt.*

A modest, but dated, modernist building, recently given the wrecking ball.

U16

U20

[U15] **Dag Hammarskjold Tower**, 240 E.47th St., SW cor. Second Ave. to E.46th St. 1984. *Gruzen & Partners.*

An understated tower with simple, faceted balconies, built of preassembled brick panels, the joints of which give a second design rhythm to the façade.

[U16] **Japan Society**, 333 E.47th St., bet. First and Second Aves. 1971. *Junzo Yoshimura and George Shimamoto.* Additions and Expansion, 2002, *Beyer Blinder Belle.* Open to the public: Tu-Th 11-6; Fr, 11-9; weekends, 11-5. 212-715-1258. *www.japansociety.org*

Japan's public architectural emissary to the City of New York. Delicately detailed, inside and out, it stages cultural exhibitions often worth seeing. A somber black building with delicate sun grilles, it has been gracefully expanded by *Beyer Blinder Belle.*

[U17] **Trump World Tower**, 845 United Nations Plaza, NW cor. First Ave. and E.47th St. 2001. *Costas Kondylis.*

The tallest residential building in America? No more. Does *Donald* care? But he does, for the extreme projects he promotes are marketing tools that bring in maximum dollars. $1,000 a square foot? $2,000? "The top houses a duplex penthouse of 20,000 sq.feet with 19-foot ceilings."

[U18] **German House,** Permanent Mission of the Federal Republic of Germany to the United Nations. 871 First Ave., bet. E.48th and E.49th Sts. W side. 1990s. *SLCE.*

The heavy-handed side of German design: picture-framed postmodern with labored details. Where was *Egon Eiermann* (architect of Germany's lovely Washington embassy) when we needed him?

[U19] **860 and 870 United Nations Plaza**, bet. E.48th and E.49th Sts. E side. 1966. *Harrison, Abramovitz & Harris.*

Desirable for views and its ostensible social snobbery, not for its banal architecture. But *Truman Capote* lived here.

[U20] **Beekman Tower** (apartments)/originally **Panhellenic Tower**, 3 Mitchell Pl. (E.49th St.), NE cor. First Ave. 1927-1928; annex 1928-1930, *John Mead Howells*. Sculptured relief, *René Chambellan*. 🗡

A miniature reprise of *Eliel Saarinen's* second-prize "styleless" design in the 1922 Chicago Tribune tower competition. *Howells* (with *Raymond Hood* as partner) took first prize there with a free **neo-Gothic** entry. Originally a hotel for women members of Greek letter societies (sororities).

U22

[U22] **Paul Rudolph House**, 23 Beekman Place, bet. E.50th and E.51st Sts. E side. 1983-1987. *Paul Rudolph*. Renovated, 2006, *Della Valle Bernheimer*.

Look up. Crowning the town house, a steel-framed cage of balconies gives a strong, radical presence to the local skyline. Never quite finished, *Rudolph* (1918-1997) used the space as an ongoing spatial experiment for both his apartment and studio. Full of transparencies and layers, and well worth a look, but tours are infrequent.

[U23] Formerly **Public School 135**/later **United Nations School**, 931 First Ave., NW cor. E.51st St. 1892. *George W. Debevoise*. Addition, 1904. Conversion, 2000, *Conklin & Rossant*.

Brick and brownstone **Romanesque Revival** multistory schoolhouse, **crushed** visually by a super ziggurat of apartments. Stand close to enjoy the old school.

[U24] **River House**, 435 E.52nd St., E of First Ave. 1931. *Bottomley, Wagner, & White*.

U23

U24   U25

A walk along FDR Drive: At the east end of East 51st Street, Peter Detmold Park steps lead down to a footbridge over the Franklin D. Roosevelt Drive. Cross the bridge for a back view of Beekman Place and a view of the drive disappearing at East 52nd Street under a Sutton Place South apartment house. From the walk along the river there is a good view of the waterside of Beekman Place, one of those affluent bluffs that defied industrial expansion at the commercial waterfronted edge of the City:

[U21] Beekman Place

Along with Sutton Place and, to an extent, Gracie Square, an elegant social enclave atop a river-fronted bluff. Here, on two blocks, were once the town houses and understated apartment houses of WASPS, diplomats, movie stars, and others who savor low-key luxury. Among them is the former home of the late Paul Rudolph, architectural hero of the 1950s and 1960s, one-time dean of the Yale School of Architecture and the controversial designer of the School's building.

A palatial **Art Deco** 26-story cooperative apartment house with a gated, cobbled entrance court. The River Club, on its lower floors, includes squash and tennis courts, a swimming pool, and a ballroom. Prior to construction of the FDR Drive, there was even a private dock where the best yachts tied up.

[U25] **400, 414, 424, and 434 East 52nd Street**, E of First Ave. 1929. *Emery Roth*.

Park Avenue style on far east 52nd Street, an understated wall for the upper middle class, ornamented with handsome Art Deco details.

[U26] **Recreation Center and Indoor Pool**, N.Y.C. Department of Parks & Recreation/originally 54th Street Public Bath and Gymnasium, 348 E.54th St., bet. First and Second Aves. 1906. *Werner & Windolph*.

A minor building with a major façade. For once the screened roof space is part of the overall design, heralded by colossal brick Classical columns.

[U27] **Le Mondrian**/originally **Le Grand Palais**, 254 E.54th St. (apartments), SW cor. Second Ave. 1992. *Fox & Fowle.*

Some class, compared to its East Side peers of the 1980s and 1990s.

[U28] **400 East 57th Street** (apartments), SE cor. First Ave. to E.56th St. 1931. *Roger H. Bullard, Philip L. Goodwin, and Kenneth Franzheim.*

An Art Moderne apartment building in the style of Central Park West's Century and Majestic, single towered.

Sutton Place

[U29] **Sutton Place Town Houses**, Sutton Place bet. E.57th and E.58th Sts. E side, Sutton Sq. (E.58th St.), and Riverview Terr. (a private street bet. Sutton Sq. and E.59th St.).

An enclave of wealth and elegance from the early 1920s, when factories and tenements largely shared the banks of the East River. The

[U30] **Bridgemarket**, under the Queensboro Bridge, along E.59th St. to E.60th St., E of First Ave. **Vaulted underbridge space**, 1914, *Henry Hornbostel.* 🖝 Conversion to shops and restaurant, 1999, *Hardy Holzman Pfeiffer Assocs.*

Here grand *Guastavino* tile-vaulted space was converted to an elegant marketplace, one of the grand found spaces formerly wasted on casual storage by City agencies. Others that should be recaptured include the vast volume under the **Riverside Drive viaduct** in the West 150s and those beneath the **Brooklyn Bridge**.

The grand vaults are somewhat diminished by a restaurant mezzanine, and the view of it all by the conning-tower glass entry to the basement Conran's store.

[U31] **322 East 57th Street**, bet. First and Second Aves. 1930. *Harry M. Clawson of Caughey & Evans.*

A simple **Park Avenue** façade, rusticated at the base, houses studios with dramatic two-story windows.

U26

U30

U28

U34

Dead End Kids were the denizens of these blocks which dead-ended in piers on the river and where summer fun included diving into that not yet fetid tidal waterway. (Construction of the East River Drive and the toiletization of the river itself ended all that.)

This group was started as an experimental enclave of private houses at a time when most of those who could afford a private house were moving to (or already living in) Park and Fifth Avenue apartments. Architects here included *Mott Schmidt* (Nos.**1, 3, 13**, and **17 Sutton Place**), *H. Page Cross* (No.**9**), *William Lescaze* (No.**21**), *Delano & Aldrich* (No.**12 Sutton Square**), and *Ely Jacques Kahn* (**6 Riverview Terrace**). Nothing is spectacular in itself, but the whole is an intact block and a half, with riverfront private gardens that jointly provide an urbane architectural grouping.

Sutton Square, the short section along the E.58th Street cul-de-sac comprises ex-brownstones upscaled for the wealthy in 1920 by *Webb & Knapp.*

[U32] **311 and 313 East 58th Street Houses**, bet. Second Ave. and the Queensboro Bridge access ramp. 1856-1857. **No.313**. *Hiram G. Disbrow*, builder. 🖝

The 1930 approaches to the bridge partially submerged these modest onetime suburban dwellings, now squeezed by bridge approaches and looming commerce. **Vernacular** of another era.

[U33] **Modulighter Building**, 246 E.58th St., bet. Second and Third Aves., 1989. *Paul Rudolph.*

An almost musically composed, structural steel façade from the under-appreciated *Rudolph*. Originally a pair of duplex apartments above the lighting company founded by *Rudolph* and *Ernst Wagner*, the **Paul Rudolph Foundation** is now housed within.

[U34] **205 East 59th Street**, wrapping around the NE cor. Third Ave. 2007. *Richard Dattner & Assocs.*

Nestling around Cinemas I, II, & III, and the corner deli, 205 soars with bellied bowed balconies. A civilized arrival.

[U35] **Decoration and Design Building**, 979 Third Ave., NE cor. E.58th St. 1965. *David & Earl Levy.*
The zigguratted New York zoning envelope capitalized into a positive architectural statement (if you look skyward). Things are pedestrian for the pedestrian at the street. There are corner windows up there for even the lowliest swatch-bearers.

Here's a chance to take a rest, and continue another day. The nearest subways are at 59th Street and Lexington (IRT Nos.4, 5, 6 trains, and the IND N and R). Or else onward to the south.

[U36] **919 Third Avenue**, bet. E.55th and E.56th Sts. E side. 1970. *Skidmore, Owings & Merrill.*
A sleek but monumental black metal and glass curtain wall that uses P. J. Clarke's as its plaza "sculpture":

U37

U40

P. J.'s: This characteristic but truncated 19th-century relic (at 915 Third Avenue, northeast corner of East 55th Street) has always been known officially as Clarke's Bar. But to generations of collegians it has been P. J.'s, and it is partly responsible for the rash of other places called P. J. "Something." Seen by millions as the set for the 1945 movie Lost Weekend, *it has lots of real stained glass and mahogany, and one of New York's most lavish old-fashioned men's rooms. Clarke's is so economically successful that everything on the block except the first two of its original four floors was demolished for No.919.*

[U37] **909 Third Avenue**, and Franklin D. Roosevelt Station, U.S. Post Office, bet. E.54th and E.55th Sts. E side. 1967. *Max O. Urbahn & Assocs.*
The tower's deeply coffered, cast-concrete window walls seem a honeycomb for the killer bees of Manhattan business. The podium is New York 10022's mail-handling factory. A requisite sculpture punctuates the sidewalk.

[U38] **900 Third Avenue**, NW cor. E.54th St. 1983. *Cesar Pelli and Rafael Viñoly,* design architects. *Emery Roth & Sons,* associate architects.
Another slick shaft with the Citicorp "bolt of cloth" for the Argentine developer *Jacobo Finkielstain.* More elegant gray and silver sleekness.

[U39] **885 Third Avenue**, bet. E.53rd and E.54th Sts. E side. 1986. *John Burgee with Philip Johnson.*

U36, P.J. Clarke's

A bumpy ellipse (in plan) of red-brown and pink, it acquired the sobriquet **Lipstick Building** because of its telescoping tiers. Columns with Turkish capitals saunter around its grand ground floor. A connection to what is one of the more complex (and yet convenient) subway concourses, the IND Lexington Avenue Station, is here provided.

[U40] **312 and 314 East 53rd Street** (houses), bet. First and Second Aves. 1866. Attributed to *Robert & James Cunningham,* builders.
A pair of post–Civil War clapboard town houses with Second Empire inspiration: mansarded. Complex corbeled entrance hoods and round-topped dormers supply special character.

[U41] **875 Third Avenue**, bet. E.52nd and E.53rd Sts. 1982. *Skidmore, Owings & Merrill (Chicago office).*
The ghost of a *Mies van der Rohe* grid appears in this Windy City octapod invention that is about as much New York as pan pizza, or cherry phosphate. Poor *Mies.*

[U42] **Salvation Army Building**, 221 E. 52nd St., bet. Second and Third Aves. 1940s.

Modern for those who considered "modern" to be the distillation of a historical style, here Georgian brick translated into simple modernist forms.

[U43] **The Enclave**, 224 E.52nd St., bet. Second and Third Aves. 1985. *Marvin H. Meltzer.*

A modern eccentric, in glass block and pink stucco, supplies curved balconies.

[U44] **Rockefeller Guest House**/originally **Museum of Modern Art Guesthouse**, 242 E.52nd St., bet. Second and Third Aves. 1949-1950. *Philip Johnson & Assocs.*

Roman brick and painted steel front a house from *Johnson's* period of *Mies van der Rohe*-isms. Built for guests of the *Rockefellers*, they later gave it to the Museum of Modern Art. *Johnson* lived in the house from 1971 to 1979.

U44

[U45] **301 East 52nd Street**/originally **Kips Bay Boys Club**, bet. First and Second Aves. 1931. *Delano & Aldrich.* Converted, 1978.

A handsome, low-key conversion. Note the segmental arched windows and brickwork with alternating headers and stretchers.

[U46] **Greenacre Park,** 217-221 E.51st St., bet. Second and Third Aves. 1971. *Sasaki, Dawson, DeMay Assocs.*, landscape architects. *Goldstone, Dearborn & Hinz*, consulting architects.

An urbane place, larger and lusher than Paley Plaza (but again complete with waterfall), to rest on your rounds in the City. Food and drink available. A gift from the daughter of *John D. Rockefeller, Jr., Mrs. Jean Mauze.*

[U47] **245 East 50th Street**, bet. Second and Third Aves. 1980. *David Kenneth Specter & Assocs.*

A modest eight-story modern apartment house with flower-crested balconies. Look up; the bay windows look down.

[U48] **Instituto Cervantes**/originally **Amster Yard**, 211-215 E.49th St., bet. Second and Third Aves. 1868-1870. Remodeled, 1945, *Harold Sterner.* Demolished and rebuilt, 2002, for the Instituto Cervantes.

Once upon a time, vagaries of early property transfers created an inner-block space. A passage paved in slate, with iron settees, led to a garden, from which the office of *James Amster Associates*, other interior designers, and a few shops were reached. Sculptor *Isamu Noguchi* once did his work here, before discovering Ravenswood (see the **Noguchi Museum**).

Now the Instituto Cervantes (with Landmarks Commission approval) has constructed an updated replica of what was always a refreshing urban event: contained semi-public space reflecting the scale of an older low-rise New York.

[U49] **212 East 49th Street**, bet. Second and Third Aves. 1986. *Mitchell-Giurgola.*

An elegant postmodern town house; marble, granite, and limestone mingling in exquisite detail. The adjacent buildings to the west, with false shutters, and to the east, in a heavy-handed Modern, seem gross by comparison.

[U50] **219 East 49th Street**, between Second and Third Aves. 1935. *Morris Sanders.*

A ground-floor office and two duplexes, all clearly expressed on the façade in the Modernist style of the 1930s. Dark blue glazed brick was used to fend off soot; balconies control sunlight and a sleek modernity, its glistening façade enriched with shade and shadow.

U43

U47

[U51] **Turtle Bay Gardens Historic District**, 226-246 E.49th St., bet. Second and Third Aves. and 227-247 E.48th St. Remodeled, 1920, *Edward C. Dean and William Lawrence Bottomley.*

Two rows of 10 houses each, back to back, assembled by *Mrs.Walton Martin (Charlotte Hunnewell Sorchan* before her marriage). A six-foot strip was taken from the backyard of each house to form a common path and garden. Near a very old willow tree at the center of the group is a fountain copied from the Villa Medici. Low walls and planting mark off the private yards. House interiors were remodeled with living rooms opening to the yard, with lowered front doors set in pastel-painted stucco façades. Such notables as *Katharine Hepburn, Leopold Stokowski, E. B. White, Stephen Sondheim, Garson Kanin, Maggie Smith*, and *Tyrone Power* have lived here. *White* memorialized the block in his marvelous anthology *The Second Tree from the Corner.*

[U52] **Sterling Plaza**, 255 E.49th St., NW cor. Second Ave. 1985. *Schuman, Lichtenstein, Claman & Efron*, architects. *Arquitectonica*, design consultants.

The fins on top are styling added to an otherwise ordinary apartment building. *Arquitectonica*'s normal turf is Miami, where they have created numerous resplendent and/or eccentric structures.

[U53] **303-309 East 49th Street**, bet. First and Second Aves. 1984. *Architects Design Group.*

The sliver wing on Second Avenue is attached to a slab on 49th— all in smooth and striated contrasting concrete block. The curved masonry balcony parapets give a strong modulation to the façade, but they are low enough, with railings atop, to allow those seated to enjoy the view.

[U54] Originally **William Lescaze House**, 211 E.48th St., bet. Second and Third Aves. 1933-1934. *William Lescaze.* 🍎

U54

A pioneering Modern town house by and for a pioneering Modern architect, protected from city atmosphere by glass block and air-conditioning. The office was at the bottom, the house above; the living room occupied the whole top floor.

[U55] Onetime **Wang Building**, 780 Third Ave. bet. E.48th and E.49th Sts. W side. 1984. *Skidmore, Owings & Merrill.*

There is an implicit indication of structure in this red granite monolith: the omitted windows draw blank diagonal lines across the façade where wind bracing lurks.

END of Walking Tour: The nearest subways, at the interwoven IRT/IND stations running from 51st to 53rd Streets on Lexington Avenue are the IRT (No.6 train) and the IND (F train).

NECROLOGY

United States Mission to the United Nations, 799 United Nations Plaza, SW cor. E.45th St. W side. 1961. *Kelly & Gruzen and Kahn & Jacobs.*

A precast-concrete eggcrate "sunscreen" veneered the seat of America's envoys to the U.N. (Its design, of course, catered not at all to sun control—facing, as it did, east and north.) A new replacement building is due in 2010 from *Gwathmey Siegel & Associates.*

United Engineering Center, NW cor. First Ave. & 47th St. 1961. *Shreve, Lamb & Harmon.*

A bland box, replaced by the klunky Trump World Tower.

Originally **The Henry Keep Flower Memorial and Halsey Day Nursery**, St. Thomas' Parish/ later **Alvin Ailey Dance School**, 229 E. 59th St., bet. Second and Third Aves. 1896. *Wolfgang Partridge.*

This Gothic Revival holdout was built by New York Governor *Roswell P. Flower* (1891-1895) in memory of his son. Its replacement: a nondescript three-story taxpayer.

RKO 58th Street Theatre, 964 Third Ave., bet. E.57th and E.58th Sts. W side. ca. 1925.

One of central Manhattan's last movie palaces. While its marquee had been streamlined, its interior was pure *Valentino.*

U52

U.S. Mission to the U.N.

Original **Cinemas 1, 2**, 1001 Third Ave., bet. E.59th and E.60th Sts. 1962. *Abraham W. Geller & Assocs.*

Modern architecture met the movies for the first time (in New York) in 1962. A duplex that has since become a triplex, it was at first a piggyback pair. *Geller* and his wife, who did the interiors, produced a simple elegance with counterpoints of rich paintings and graphics. Now shopworn and somewhat degraded within.

Upper West Side

In a way the Upper West Side is as much a state of mind as a place to live: a successor to Greenwich Village as a magnet for those in the vanguard of cultural or social action and also—particularly today—political action.

Early Manhattan development was confined mostly below and to the east of Central Park; the latecomer West blossomed during a period of substantial immigration of urbane Europeans. That population, culturally crossbred with adventurous local migrants, and served by equally adventurous developers, created a mix of people and buildings with a flavor distinct from that of the East. The West once owed as much to the imported culture of Vienna, Berlin, and Budapest as to the enterprising patronage of those such as Singer Sewing Machine heir *Edward Severin Clark*. His **Dakota Apartments** at 72nd Street became a social outpost so remote from "The 400" that it was considered the geographical equivalent—in New York City terms—of the Dakota Territory.

Whereas Greenwich Village became a bohemian haven and a crucible for the individual painter, sculptor, writer, or poet—a place of rebellion and artistic creativity—the West Side is a nexus of group art concerts, opera, theater, and film—the cultural mecca for national as well as New York audiences. Here live a major portion of those who fill those many stages, intermingled with a locally passionate audience. Perhaps passion is a local character trait, not only of those who perform or savor performance but also of a vast group of political activists who voice their community and national concerns with a vigor unequaled elsewhere in the City.

But how did it all begin?

After the English "conquest" of New Amsterdam in 1664, *Richard Nicolls* was appointed governor by the *Duke of York* to oversee his new proprietary colony. *Nicolls* not only honored Dutch property owners and landlords already in place but also granted vast tracts to new patentees. The **Thousand Acre Tract,** bounded by the Hudson and (roughly) modern 50th Street, 89th Street, and Sixth Avenue, now the heart of the Upper West Side, was divided into ten lots and granted to four Dutchmen and one Englishman.

In its original verdant state the area was known as **Bloomingdale,** honored by its nominal association with a flower-growing region near Harlem named Bloemendael. The **Bloomingdale Road** followed a serpentine Indian trail that also produced the meandering alignment of much of Broadway. As a northern extension of Lower Manhattan's principal street, it was the road to Albany, a commercial route whose scale after widening (1868-1871) allowed its ultimate potential to be planned. And so, it was briefly renamed **The Boulevard** until 1899, when buildings such as The Ansonia, The Belnord, The Apthorp, and The Belleclaire would begin to fulfill these plans.

It was not until public transportation had penetrated these precincts that serious development occurred. Although horsecars had reached West 84th Street by 1864, the Ninth Avenue elevated did not arrive until 1879, with stations at 72nd, 81st, 93rd, and 104th Streets (others were added later). Clark's almost simultaneous construction of the Dakota (1880-1884) was an equal inspiration and stimulus. New buildings centered on these nodes at first, with developers uncertain about the City's intentions to level and grade the streets and to evict squatters and shanty owners. But by 1886, a boom had occurred, as related grandiloquently in the *Times*:

"The West side of the city presents just now a scene of building activity such as was never before witnessed in that section, and which gives promise of the speedy disappearance of all the shanties in the neighborhood and the rapid population of this long neglected part of New York. The huge masses of rock which formerly met the eye usually crowned by a rickety shanty and a browsing goat, are being blasted out of existence. Streets are being graded, and thousands of carpenters and masons are engaged in rearing substantial buildings where a year ago nothing was to be seen but market gardens or barren rocky fields."

*For the purposes of this Guide we have divided the Upper West Side's two square miles into precincts: **Lincoln Center, Riverside Drive, Central Park West,** the old **West Side Urban Renewal Area,** and **Manhattan Valley.** The vital center, loosely termed **Broadway and Environs,** embraces the powerful diagonal thoroughfare where a dual necklace of shops attempts to emulate, admittedly somewhat crassly, the boulevards of Paris. With one exception, the Urban Renewal Area, each precinct is described in an uptown sequence, moving away from the central business district. The Renewal Area, constructed sequentially from north to south, is also described in that direction.*

UPPER WEST SIDE KEY MAP

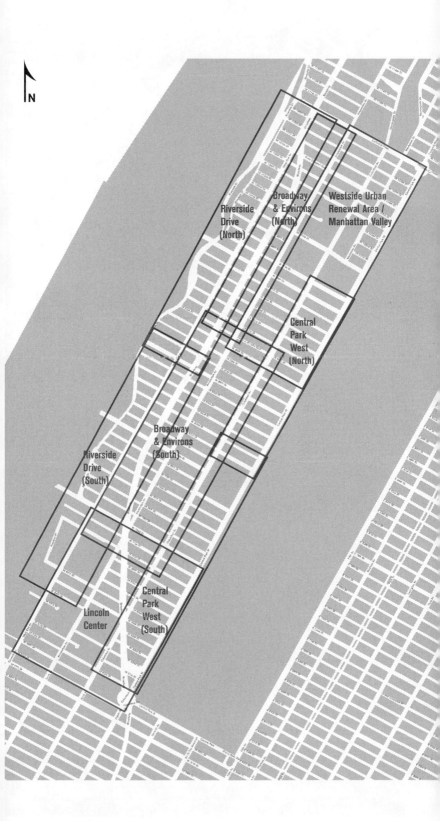

N

Riverside
Drive
(North)

Broadway
& Environs
(North)

Westside Urban
Renewal Area /
Manhattan Valley

Central
Park
West
(North)

Broadway
& Environs
(South)

Riverside
Drive
(South)

Lincoln
Center

Central
Park
West
(South)

L14, Capital Cities ABC Inc. Studios

LINCOLN CENTER

The southern part of the Upper West Side developed quickly in the 1880s along Columbus Avenue, the route of the Ninth Avenue El, which intersected **Lincoln Square** at Broadway and 65th Street. The area was never fashionable except along Central Park. By the late 1940s the part west of Broadway was a slum, fostered by its proximity to the open New York Central railroad yards lying between West End Avenue and the river. This latter area was the subject first of low-rent subsidized apartments and then of a 12-block urban renewal project that cleared the tenements and is now the site of Lincoln Center, Fordham University's in-town campus, many luxury apartments, and public and institutional buildings. The old railroad has proven to be a much more difficult project. **Trump Place** promised to be a man-made escarpment overlooking a new park down to the river. A relocated and submerged West Side Highway was part of the original plan but was eliminated for its expense: the result is an elevated highway traipsing through a park. The area described below lies between West 60th and West 70th Streets from Broadway to the Hudson River.

[L1] **Trump International Hotel and Tower**/originally **Gulf + Western Plaza**, 1 Central Park W., bet. Broadway, Columbus Circle, and W.61st St. 1969. *Thomas E. Stanley*. Reconfigured and reclad, 1990s, *Philip Johnson and Alan Ritchie*.

A reincarnation in glitz for those **Trumpites**

L1

L3

[L3] **Sofia Apartments**/formerly **Sofia Brothers Warehouse**/originally **Kent Automatic Parking Garage**, 43-45 W.61st Street, NE cor. Columbus Ave. 1929-1930. *Jardine, Hill & Murdock*. Converted to apartments, 1983-1985, *Alan Lapidus Assocs., Rothzeid Kaiserman Thompson & Bee,* and *Abraham Rothenberg*. 🍎

Built as an early "automatic" (i.e., "elevatored") parking garage, it was converted to apartments (punched windows) in the wake of Lincoln Center gentrification. Check the former grand auto entrance on Columbus — now **The College Board** [entrance exams] office: **Art Deco** glazed blue and cream terra cotta. Wonderful.

L2

who seek the sleekest and latest arriviste quarters. Gulf+Western was stripped to its bones, reconfigured, and reclad as very expensive pieds-à-terre for the international set with wanderlust. The sunken mini-plaza subway entry (marked by the hovering globe) is the one urbane contribution.

[L2] **American Bible Society Building**, 1865 Broadway, NW cor. W.61st St. 1966. *Skidmore, Owings & Merrill*. New glass entrance, stairs, and **Museum of Biblical Art** (second floor), 1998. *FxFowle*. Museum hours: Tu, We, Fr-Su 10-6; Th 10-8. 212-408-1500. *www.mobia.org*

The neatly cast-in-place concrete of this burly building is exposed, its bridge-sized beams making a giant ladder of the Broadway end. The more recent high-tech steel and glass entry element relieves, at close range, some of its overweighing bulk.

Lincoln Center:

[L4] **Lincoln Center for the Performing Arts**, W.62nd to W.66th Sts. Columbus to Amsterdam Aves. 1962-1968. *Wallace K. Harrison,* director of board of architects (composed of the architects of individual buildings).

This travertine acropolis of music and theater represents an initial investment of more than $165 million of early 1960s dollars—mostly in private contributions—along with federal aid for acquisition of the site and a State contribution toward the New York State Theater. The project aroused dissent on both urbanistic and architectural grounds. The congestion caused by the location of so many large theaters in one cluster (with only meager public transportation) has been an obvious problem, left unsolved by the vast underground garage beneath the project. Making a single impressive group out of structures with such demanding interior requirements has imposed inhibitions on the individual buildings. As a result, former *New York Times* architecture critic *Ada Louise*

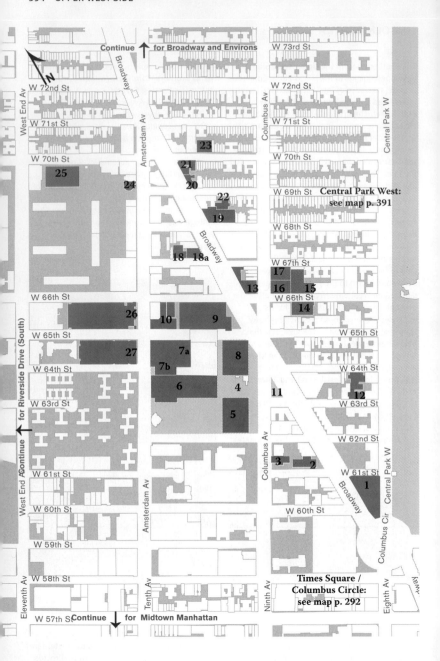

Continue ↑ for Broadway and Environs

Central Park West:
see map p. 391

Times Square /
Columbus Circle:
see map p. 292

Continue ← for Riverside Drive (South)

Continue ↓ for Midtown Manhattan

Huxtable wrote, "Philharmonic Hall, the State Theater, and the Metropolitan Opera are lushly decorated, conservative structures that the public finds pleasing and most professionals consider a failure of nerve, imagination and talent. Fortunately," she continued, "the scale and relationship of the plazas are good, and they can be enjoyed as pedestrian open spaces."

A renovation by *Diller Scofidio + Renfro (DS+R)* with *FXFowle* and additional work by *Tod Williams* and *Billie Tsien* don't do away with the vehicular moat. But the architects hope the revamp will mitigate the "fortress" aspect, turning Lincoln Center into the welcoming public space it was meant to be.

[L5] **New York State Theater**, SE cor. Lincoln Center, Columbus Ave., bet. W.62nd and W.63rd Sts. W side. 1964. *Philip C. Johnson and Richard Foster.* Reconstructed, 1982.

This 2,737-seat hall, designed mainly for ballet and musical theater, boasts a vast four-story foyer used separately for receptions and balls. The most frankly Classical building facing the plaza, its ground-level lobby reads as an under-stated **Baroque** space carved from enveloping travertine. The grand foyer above it, in contrast, is ornate with tiers of busy railings, golden chain drapery, and a velvet ceiling, all dominated by two superb white marble sculptures, enlargements of *Elie Nadelman* works.

After years of trying to remove itself from its garment center location on Broadway between 39th and 40th Streets—negotiating at one point to occupy what eventually became the site of Rockefeller Center's GE (once RCA) Building—the Met finally came here, to Lincoln Center. It is the focal building of the complex and its largest hall.

[L6] **Metropolitan Opera House**, W side of Lincoln Center, bet. W.63rd and W.64th Sts. 1966. *Wallace K. Harrison of Harrison & Abramovitz.* Lobby paintings facing the plaza, *Marc Chagall.*

It's not the **Palais Garnier** (Paris) or Milan's **La Scala**, and will never earn the love that **Carnegie Hall** has captured in musicians' hearts, but it serves dedicated opera lovers with enthralling productions: from *Wagner* to *Puccini*, from *Britten* to *Offenbach*. The enshrouding building is a schmaltzy pastiche of forms (the "arcade"), materials (mostly travertine), and effects, beginning with self-con-

over the Theater below, especially true when the transparent lobby is activated with light and a theater crowd.

[L8] **Avery Fisher Hall**/originally **Philharmonic Hall**, NE cor. Lincoln Center, Columbus Ave. SW cor. W.65th St. 1962. *Max Abramovitz of Harrison & Abramovitz.* Reconstructed, 1976, *Johnson/Burgee,* architects. *Cyril Harris,* acoustical engineer. Stabile suspended from lobby ceiling, 1962, *Richard Lippold,* sculptor.

The most controversial of Lincoln Center's buildings, its hall has been rebuilt a number of times in attempts to solve its well-publicized acoustical deficiencies. The most elaborate change, in 1976, converted the hall into a classic European rectangle (and redesigned the public lobby spaces as well) to wide acclaim from both acoustical and architectural critics. But then?

[L9] **Juilliard School of Music & Alice Tully Hall**, 144 W.66th St., bet. Broadway

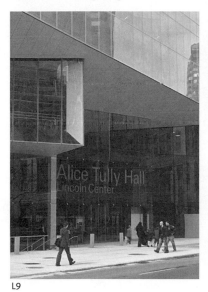

L9

L6

L10

L8

sciously sensuous red-carpeted stairs, and ending with brilliant Austrian crystal chandeliers (which hang in the tall lobby space, as they do in the hall itself until, at the start of a performance, they silently rise to the gold-leafed ceiling). Come listen.

The café at the top of the Met's lobby offers a dazzling view down into the entry area and out across the plaza.

[L7a] **Vivian Beaumont Theater**, NW cor. Lincoln Center, 150 W.65th St., SE cor. Amsterdam Ave. 1965. *Eero Saarinen & Assocs.* [L7b] **Library and Museum of the Performing Arts**, The New York Public Library, 111 Amsterdam Ave. 1965. *Skidmore, Owings & Merrill.* Renovations, 2001, *Polshek Partnership.* Pool sculpture in plaza, **Reclining Figure,** *Henry Moore.* Theater lobbies remodeled, 1997-1998, *Hardy Holzman Pfeiffer.*

An unusual collaboration: bookstacks fill the massive, travertine-clad attic volume looming

and Amsterdam Ave. 1968. *Pietro Belluschi,* with *Eduardo Catalano* and *Westermann & Miller.* Remodeled, 2009, *Diller Scofidio + Renfro.*

Glass and a slash have led the counterattack against this outpost of Lincoln Center travertine. Originally connected to the superblock of Lincoln Center proper by a hovering deck over West 65th Street, light and transparency have arrived. Originally monolithic in appearance, Alice Tully seemed to have been carved from travertine. It has now broken free.

[L10] **Samuel and David Rose Building** and **Wilson Residence Hall**, W.65th St. NE cor. Amsterdam Ave. 1992. *Davis, Brody & Assocs.* and *Abramovitz Kingsland Schiff.*

This multiuse annex to Lincoln Center provides, at its base, an auditorium and rehearsal spaces for the Juilliard School, and in the tower, dormitory space and apartments. The cream and brown stonework is welcome after the sea of travertine next door.

[L11] **Dante Park**, W.63rd to W.64th Sts., bet. Broadway and Columbus Ave. **Dante,** 1920, *Ettore Ximenes*, sculptor.

Here a dour and grumpy *Dante* holds the Commedia, a hard act for all of Lincoln Center's halls to follow.

[L12] **West Side YMCA**, 5 West 63rd St., bet. Central Park W. and Broadway. 1930. *Dwight J. Baum*. Adjacent apartment tower (Park Laurel) on site of McBurney School, 15 W.63rd St. 1990s. *Beyer Blinder Belle*.

A center of athletic culture and cultural athletics, this **Y** is one of two remnants from a time when young urban immigrants (from Omaha or Walla Walla) were housed in Christian or Hebrew hostels (the extant other is the YMHA at East 92nd Street). The Y's are now known more for their cultural and athletic possibilities than their service as caravansaries. This **Y** is a **neo-Romanesque** pile, in limestone and brick, complete with machicolations, arched corbel tables, and other medieval encrustations.

[L15] **Capital Cities/ABC Headquarters**, 77 W.66th St., bet. Central Park W. and Columbus Aves. N side. 1988. *Kohn Pedersen Fox*.

The corporate headquarters, at 23 stories, is mature **postmodern**, but most important—especially to its shadowed neighbors to the north—is the arrogance of the midblock tower's height and bulk.

[L16] **ABC Building**, 147 Columbus Ave., NE cor. W.66th St. 1992. *Kohn Pedersen Fox*.

Postmodern meets high-tech, as the ABC 66th Street parade from **47** to **77** ends a decade at this corner.

[L17] **WABC Channel 7 Building**, 149-155 Columbus Ave., SE cor. W.67th St. 1979. *Kohn Pedersen Fox*.

These TV studios are understated, handsome in their counterpoint of glass and brick, with few mannerisms.

L12

L13   L15   L16

[L13] **Lincoln Triangle**, 1 Lincoln Sq. (144 Columbus Ave.), bet. Columbus Ave. and Broadway, W.66th and W.67th Sts. 1997. *Gary Edward Handel + Assocs.*, design architect. *Schuman Lichtenstein Claman & Efron*, architects of record.

For the casual passerby this is the **Barnes and Noble** Building, but overhead the tower houses residents drawn to this new West Side story.

[L14] Originally **First Battery Armory**, N. Y. National Guard/then **102nd Medical Battalion Armory**/now **Capital Cities ABC, Inc. Studios**, 56 W.66th St., bet. Central Park W. and Columbus Ave. S side. 1900-1903. *Horgan & Slattery*. Altered, 1978, *Kohn Pederson Fox*.

Lots of stylistic bravado here but only in the front ranks (as a sidelong glance from the east will reveal). The reserves are utilitarian and dull (never having been meant to be seen), in contrast with the elegantly attired architectural forces leading the march. The fun-filled façade might as well be one of those intricate European cardboard scale models. A delight!

[L18] **Kaufman Center, Merkin Concert Hall, Lucy Moses School of Music**/originally **Abraham Goodman House**, 129 W.67th St., bet. Broadway and Amsterdam Ave. N side. 1978. *Ashok Bhavnani* of *Johansen & Bhavnani*. Renewed and remodeled, 2008, *Robert A.M. Stern Architects*.

Brutalism spruced up and retailored for suave concertgoers in need of a more glamorous reception. The original *Ashok Bhavnani* façade was, for New York, an early introduction of "brutalist" concrete.

[L18a] **The Apple Store**, 1981 Broadway, NW cor. W.67th St. 2009. *Bohlin Cywinski Jackson*.

New from the ground up, with no messy old building to interfere with Apple's sleekness. Look, Ma! No mullions!

[L19] **The Copley**, 2000 Broadway, NE cor. W.68th St. 1987. *Davis, Brody & Assocs.*

A sleek understated tower among the mess of Broadway. One of the few serene buildings on the old **Boulevard**.

[L20] **The Seminole**, 2020 Broadway, NE cor. W.69th St. 1895-1896. *Ware & Styne-Harde.*

Granite for power; tan brick, limestone, and terra cotta for texture. This ornamented ensemble is typical of upscale tenements at the turn of the century, most receiving a tasteful embellishment. But *tenement*, in modern days a pejorative, was the term for apartment houses before apartment life blossomed.

L19

L23

[L21] **Hotel Embassy**/originally **The Ormonde,** 154 W.70th St, SE cor. Broadway. 1899-1900. *Robert Maynicke.*

A soldier in the battle of Broadway, bringing substance and scale to the boulevard. This brick and limestone palazzo shares blockfront space with the former **Hotel Seminole** to the south, a pair of modest urban twins that match the understated streetscape of Park Avenue.

[L22] **Christ and St. Stephen's Church** (Episcopal)/formerly **St. Stephen's Church**/originally **Chapel (of the Church) of the Transfiguration**, 120 W.69th St., bet. Columbus Ave. and Broadway. S side. 1880. *William H. Day.* Altered, 1887.

Brigadoon? From the days when the West Side was still suburban, its lawn is now a spacial oasis among its Brobdingnagian neighbors.

[L23] Originally **Pythian Temple**/now **Pythian Condominium,** 135 W.70th St., bet. Columbus Ave. and Broadway. N side. 1927. *Thomas W. Lamb.* Renovated, 1986, *David Gura.*

Assyrian sages guard the entry. Hollywood may have had its **Grauman's Chinese Theater,** but New York has its Pythian Temple! Hidden on an anonymous side street, this sober dream is best seen from across the street.

The critic T-Square, in a 1928 **New Yorker:** *"...Lamb scores once more in the new Temple for the Knights of Pythias...the polychrome terra cotta is beautifully done and makes me long for more color in architecture..."*

[L24] **Lincoln Square Synagogue**, 200 Amsterdam Ave., NW cor. W.69th St. 1970. *Hausman & Rosenberg.*

The theaters of nearby **Lincoln Center** set the travertine tone for the area, and this mannered, curvy, articulated synagogue picks up

L25

L26

the cue. The travertine bank to the north actually came first, but the two together seem to be making an inadvertent comment about money changers at the temple.

[L25] **Public School 199**, 270 W.70th St., bet. Amsterdam and West End Aves. S side. 1963. *Edward Durell Stone & Assocs.*

An early example of an urban public school designed by a prominent architect. The hovering roof was brought from his successful **U.S. Embassy Building in New Delhi.** *Stone* was also architect of the lately lamented Gallery of Modern Art at Columbus Circle.

[L26] **Martin Luther King, Jr., High School**, 122 Amsterdam Ave., bet. W.65th and W.66th Sts. W side. 1975. *Frost Assocs.,* architects. *William Tarr,* sculptor.

A glass box of enormous size and scale sits proudly on the busy avenue. A self-weathering steel, **Mayari R**, was employed in both the school's carefully detailed curtain wall and in the boldly fashioned memorial sculpture to the slain civil rights leader that towers over the sidewalk.

█▌ [L27] Fiorello H. LaGuardia High School,
══ 108 Amsterdam Ave., bet. W.64th and W.65th Sts. W side. 1985. *Eduardo Catalano.*

A strongly articulated, poured-in-place concrete building typical of the best of 1960s construction. The cost of achieving such quality in New York soon became prohibitive, and architects switched to mostly brick and metal assemblies. This exception resulted from the halt of all school construction during the City's 1970s financial crisis and completion of the original plans many years later.

NECROLOGY

Goelet Garage, 1926 Broadway, bet. W.64th and W.65th Sts. 1906-1907. *Frank M. Andrews.*
A handsome player from Broadway's past.

Columbia Fireproof Storage Warehouse, 149 Columbus Ave., bet. W. 66th and W. 67th Sts. E side. 1893. *G. A. Schellenger.*

Its ornate brickwork and soaring verticality were emblematic of a time when the financial bottom line was not critical and architects managed to find urbane solutions to even the most mundane problems, such as the blank walls of a warehouse. Replaced by WABC.

Lincoln Square Center for the Arts/originally **26th Precinct, N.Y.C. Police Department**/later **20th Precinct,** 150 W.68th St., bet. Broadway and Amsterdam Ave. ca. 1889. *Nathaniel D. Bush.*

The Second Edition of this Guide (1978) admired its "dignified composition: segmental and semicircular arched openings linteled in neatly carved stone and set into a russet brick field." And, it continued, "Lucky for us that it has found another use." It did—temporarily. Since then it has been replaced by a permanent hole in the ground, the entrance to a below-

L27

Originally **St. Nicholas Skating Rink**/later **St. Nicholas Arena**/finally **American Broadcasting Companies Broadcasting Operations and Engineering,** 57 W. 66th St., bet. Central Park W. and Columbus Ave. 1896. *Ernest Flagg and Walter B. Chambers.*

In spite of the many layers of stucco and different hues of paint—all battleship gray—the gay ornament of the post–Columbian Exposition era came through to the end. Now the site of Capital Cities/ ABC Inc. headquarters.

street parking garage for **Lincoln Square** (1997. *Kohn Pedersen Fox*).

College of Pharmaceutical Science, Columbia University/originally **College of Pharmacy of the City of New York,** 115 W. 68th St., bet. Columbus Ave. and Broadway. 1894. *Little & O' Connor.*

A fuddy-duddy building that seemed nevertheless to scoff at its lesser neighbors.

RIVERSIDE DRIVE / WEST END AVENUE

Terrain that slopes steeply west to the banks of the river, a roller coaster of north-south gradients, the water-level route of the smoke-belching **New York Central and Hudson River Railroad,** and the Palisades across the flowing Hudson River currents—such contrasts made the planning of "the Riverside Park and Avenue" a powerful challenge to landscape architect *Frederick Law Olmsted*. Between 1873 and 1910 *Olmsted*, and his associates and successors, developed a great green waterside edge for the West Side, as he and *Calvert Vaux* had earlier created **"The Central Park"** on the inland site. The style was in the tradition of English landscape architecture: naturalistic and picturesque. Development along Riverside Drive (and straight as an arrow West End Avenue behind it) resulted from the magnetism of this great urban design, now augmented by **Riverside Park South**, by the landscape architect *Thomas Balsley*.

parts is the three-level structure at West 79th Street: traffic circle at the top, masonry arcades and pedestrian paths surrounding a splendid, circular, single-jet fountain at the middle level; and, at the bottom, parking space for frequenters of the 79th Street Boat Basin. Now joined at W. 72nd Street to **Riverside Park South** (see next page).

Riverside South:
Stretching inland from the Hudson River shore between 59th and 72nd Streets and fostering the slums that gave rise to **Lincoln Center's** redevelopment plan was the former freight yard of the New York Central Railroad (and of the Hudson River Railroad before that), a dead-flat expanse worthy of Chicago. The noisy, dusty scene included thousands of freight cars shunted day and night along scores of parallel ladder tracks, some leading to waterfront grain

R11

In the 1930s the **Henry Hudson Parkway Authority,** using **WPA** funds, added a four-lane highway (since expanded to six) to the park area and a host of recreational amenities—essentially the amalgam of asphalt and greenery we see today. This change accomplished two other important results: it covered the freight line, and it built the highway in part on landfill.

Riverside Park and Riverside Drive Scenic Landmark, Riverside Dr. to the Hudson River bet. W.72nd and W.153rd Sts. 1873-1910. Original design, *Frederick Law Olmsted*. New work, 1888, *Calvert Vaux and Samuel Parsons, Jr.* Completion, *Frederick Law Olmsted, Jr.* Reconstruction for Henry Hudson Parkway, 1934-1937, *Clinton F. Loyd.* 🐎
    To the endless relief of stifled West Siders, this green ribbon of hills and hollows, monuments, playgrounds, and sports facilities fringes some 70 blocks of winding Riverside Drive, all the while covering the abandoned rail line in a tunnel below. One of its most complex

elevators, others to wharves projecting diagonally into the river—like half chevrons—accomodating ships and barges that helped interchange freight over the waters of the **Port of New York.** There was even a locomotive roundhouse and turntable. The fallow site, long abandoned by the railroad but traversed by the elevated West Side Highway viaduct, continues to separate the precinct from its nearby Hudson River shoreline. Since the railroad activities began to wind down in the 1950s, the 76-acre waterfront site had been the subject of a number of ill-fated redevelopment proposals until purchased for $95 million in 1983 by *Donald J. Trump,* heir to the Brooklyn residential-development fortune accumulated by his father and grandfather. It is on these idle acres that then-young *Trump* proposed (**Scene 1**) to erect a 150-story tower—the world's tallest—again worthy of Chicago, as well as 7,600 units of housing and a major shopping development, using the skills of a Chicago architect, *Helmut Jahn. Trump's* dream of a relocated NBC media empire (and its attendant City subsidies)

N

Continue ↑ for Riverside Drive / West End Ave. (North) Henry J. Browne Blvd

44

43

W 89th St

41

d c b
42 W 88th St
f e

40

35

37 38

36

Riverside Drive-West End
Historic District

34 33

32

W 87th St

W 86th St

West End Av

Broadway

Amsterdam Av

39

31

30

W 85th St

29

27   28

W 84th St

Riverside Dr

Henry Hudson Parkway

W 83rd St

20

26

W 82nd St

Continue → for Central Park West

W 81st St

19   25

23

21

18 24   22

Riverside Drive-
West 80th-81st Street
Historic District

W 79th St

2

17

W 78th St

16

15

14 W 77th St

12   11

13

W 76th St

West End-Collegiate
Historic District

10

W 75th St

Riverside Dr

W 74th St

W 73rd St

8

7b 5
7a 6

W 72nd St

9

4

3

Broadway and Environs:
see map p. 374

W 70th St

2

1

1

1

Freedom Pl

Continue ↓ for Lincoln Center

W 69th St

W 68th St

W 67th St

evaporated in 1987, as did *Jahn. Alexander Cooper & Assocs.* then took on the challenge (**Scene 2**), which included negotiating with a feisty Upper West Side community that just loves a good fight. **Scene 3** unfolded with a truce worthy of *Netanyahu* and *Arafat: Trump* and his nemesis, the **Municipal Art Society,** joined hands (for how long we don't know), allowing the construction of new apartment blocks along what hoped to be Riverside Drive South. Architect and planner *Paul Willen* suggested an ensemble in his proposed master plan that would combine the character of **Central Park West,** with the undulating serpentry of **Riverside Drive. Scene 4** is the reality of Trump Place (the surrogate street for Riverside Drive South), now serving the edge of this new construction, from 70th Street southward. **What a disaster.**

[R1] **Trump Place**, bet. W.66th and W.70th Sts., W of West End Ave. 1999. *Philip Johnson & Alan Ritchie and Costas Kondylis.*

R3   R5

R4

Brobdingnagia. This phony incarnation of Riverside Drive, south of its historic 72nd Street ending, has sprouted awkward giants, glorious to look out (at the river and palisades) and inglorious to look at. A heavy hand from one-time virtuoso *Johnson*, or rather his partner, *Alan Ritchie*, acting in his name. *Johnson* was 93 when the first buildings were in place (he died at 98 in 2005). An unfortunate valedictory for an eminent and facile architect.

[R2] **Riverside Park South**, bet. W.59th and W.72nd Sts. Phases 1 and 2, 2001-2008. Phases 3 and 4, 2012 (estimated). *Thomas Balsley Associates,* landscape architects.

An ambitious new park takes up where *Olmsted and Vaux* left off. A tricky site if there ever was one, *Balsley* successfully threaded the park underneath the Henry Hudson Parkway (the elevated highway provides the park with shade for the first half of each day), and incorporated reminders of the site's industrial past. Wisely, decaying piers and grain elevators were

left as fragments, recast as rusty sculpture to be admired from shore.

Native grasses and boardwalks were reintroduced to the river's edge, a similar approach to the one taken by the landscape firm *Mathews Nielsen* in their beautifully designed Tribeca segment of Hudson River Park (p. 224).

Back to 70th Street and around the corner on West End Avenue:

[R3] Originally **Forrest Lawther House**/ now **Hineni Heritage Center**/onetime **Abraham Erlanger House**, 232 West End Ave., bet. W.70th and W.71st Sts. E side. 1887. *E.L. Angell.* Altered for *Erlanger*, 1904, *Herts & Tallant.*

At the behest of the new owner, Broadway producer *Erlanger, Herts & Tallant* created a new and robust **Beaux Arts** façade replacing *Angell's* original. The inset stoop on West End Avenue's narrow sidewalk provides a sheltered moment for the ceremony of arrival.

R7a

[R4] **West 71st Street Historic District**, W of West End Ave. Thirty-three row houses in six groups, 1893-1896; and a single 1906 town house.

Neo-Renaissance at the edge of Trumpland? On the south, paint updates most of these columned, swagged, and arcuated brownstones, already struggling through Romanesque Revival toward the American Renaissance of the late 1890s. On the north, however, they arrived: a neo-Renaissance potpourri: freestanding **Corinthian** columns, **Baroque** piers in light brick and terra cotta.

[R5] Originally **Spencer Aldrich House**, 271 W.72nd St. NE cor. West End Avenue. 1897. *Gilbert A. Schellenger.* Altered.

Crass shops and signs at street level serve only to point out the richness of what remains: the complex gabled and towered forms of the upper floors and roof. Much more interesting than *Schellenger*'s work at **No.309.**

[R6] **309 West 72nd Street House**/also known as the **William E. Diller House**, bet. West End Ave. and Riverside Dr. N side. 1899-1901. *Gilbert A. Schellenger.* 🍎

A timid step for *Schellenger* (see **Aldrich House** above) from the **Brown Decades** (of Romanesque Revival, brownstone, and dark brick) into the light palette and limestone of the **American Renaissance**.

[R7a] Originally **John and Mary Sutphen, Jr., House**, 311 W.72nd St. bet. West End Ave. and Riverside Dr. N side. 1901-1902. *C.P.H. Gilbert.* 🍎
[R7b] Originally **Frederick and Lydia Prentiss House**, 1 Riverside Dr., NE cor. W.72nd St. 1899-1901. *C.P.H. Gilbert.* 🍎

An architect more comfortable with Renaissance copybooks, but still muddling the details: the porch **Composite** capitals clash into the cornice console brackets.

[R8] **Philip and Maria Kleeberg House**, 3 Riverside Dr. bet. 72nd and 73rd Sts. 1896-1898. *C.P.H. Gilbert.* 🍎

A freely interpreted **Dutch Renaissance** town house, with stepped gables on its dormer and on its flank.

[R9] **Chatsworth Apartments and Annex**, 344 W.72nd St., SE cor. Henry Hudson Pkwy. and 353 W.71st St. W end of W.71st St. 1902-1904. **Annex**, 340 W.72nd St. S side. 1905-1906. Both by *John E. Scharsmith.* 🍎

Two of the three buildings that compose The Chatsworth face West 72nd and West 71st Streets, gracious russet-colored brick apartment blocks embellished with lavish limestone trim in the tradition of the **Kenilworth** and **Rossleigh Court/Orwell House.** The annex to the east on West 72nd is lower and all limestone. One of the flock of early apartment houses for the wealthy, leaving town houses behind in favor of French Flats.

[R10] **West End-Collegiate Historic District**, generally bet. Riverside Dr. and West End Ave. N side of W.74th to N side of W.78th Sts., with irregular ins and outs. 🍎

A full palette of materials and styles, bow and bay windows, copper-clad cornices and dormers—rich and wonderful. Architects include *Clinton & Russell, C.P.H. Gilbert, Lamb & Rich, Neville & Bagge*, and the endless and marvelous houses of *Clarence F. True.*

[R11] **301-305 W.76th St., 341-357 West End Ave.** W side, and **302-306 W.77th St.** 1891. *Lamb & Rich.*

This witty row enlivens the whole blockfront on West End Avenue. Long may they reign! *Eberhard Faber,* the pencil king, lived at **No.341.** This is what eclecticism is all about: a studied assembly of architectural parts (from varied geography and history) and an equally conscious arrangement of contrasting buildings.

R8

R10

R13

R17

R15

Clarence F. True. *In an 1899 account by local architect and land developer Clarence F. True,* ***Lower Riverside Drive****, the Drive's earliest segment opened for "improvement," was planned for flats. He recognized the higher potential of the area by buying all fronting parcels below West 84th Street and covering them "with beautiful dwellings" of his own design. Hardly typical row houses (though built speculatively and employing party walls), many of these elegant mansion-residences have survived. They are highly idiosyncratic and readily identified as being in the True style (characterized at the time as* ***Elizabethan Renaissance****): ornate roof lines, crow-stepped gables, bay, bow, and three-quarter-round oriels, and so on. Most are concentrated in these groupings:*

[R12] **40-46 Riverside Drive**, bet. 76th and 77th Sts. E side. 1896-1899. *Clarence True.*

An extraordinary ensemble that blends strong **Renaissance Revival** cornices and pilasters, a porch and a colonnade, with Amsterdam stepped gables. An idiosyncratic medley.

[R13] **337 West 76th Street** and [R14] **334-338 West 77th Street**, bet. West End Ave. and Riverside Dr. 1896-1897. *Clarence True.*

At **No.337**, unhappily, the **Baroque** broken pedimented dormers have been erased by an elevation to a banal fifth-floor façade. Insert here one *Shakespearean* line: "More strange than *True.*"

[R15] **West End Collegiate Church and Collegiate School**, West End Ave., NE cor. W.77th St. 1892-1893. *Robert W. Gibson.* Reconstruction after sanctuary fire, 1980s, *The Hall Partnership.* Basement education center, 1990, *Peter W. Charapko.* 👁

It's easy to understand the generous use of Dutch stepped gables on this church façade, since the roots of the **Reformed Church in America** lie in the Netherlands. But along West End Avenue, *McKim, Mead & White* had already built such a Dutch-inspired house as early as 1885 (demolished); another predating the church (but not by *M,M&W*) still remains at the

[R18] **74-77 Riverside Drive**, SE cor. W.80th St., and **320-326 W.80th Street**, bet. West End Ave. and Riverside Dr. 1898-1899. *Clarence F. True.*

Another *True*. The Dutch gable of **No.74** throws a **Baroque** swoop skyward, its bayed façade supported on three limestone arches.

[R19] **81-86 Riverside Drive**, bet. 80th and 81st Sts. and **316-320 W.81st Street**, bet. West End Ave. and Riverside Dr. *Clarence F. True.*

No.86 is a dour and forbidding essay in rock-face granite. But its neighbors south and east bear stepped and serrated gables in brick and/or limestone.

[R20] **103-109 Riverside Drive, 332 W.83rd Street**, 1898-1899. *Clarence F. True.* **103** and **104**, redesigned, 1910-1911, *Clinton & Russell.* **105** and **107-109**, redesigned 1910-1911, *Bosworth & Holden and Tracy, Swartout and Litchfield.* 👁

After a lawsuit, stoops and bow windows were removed that had encroached onto the

R18   R21

R20

R22

northwest corner of West 78th Street. And so do *Clarence True's* **45** and **46 Riverside Drive**. The church presents its steps in a rich palette of orange brick and terra cotta, with Baroque finials in counterpoint.

[R16] **Collegiate School** (annex), 260 W.78th St., bet. Broadway and West End Ave. 1968. S side. *Ballard, Todd & Assocs.*

A highly disciplined modernist façade that, through its varied window patterns, shows what's going on within.

[R17] **301-307 W.78th Street** and **383-389 West End Avenue**. 1886. *Frederick B. White.*

Powerful stuff by an architect who died at the untimely age of **24**, shortly after their completion. The brickwork (and supporting terra cotta) is a work of virtuoso masonry, the great arches monumental. Extraordinary.

public way. **No.109** crosses a crenellated eclectic body with a **Gothic Revival** entry.

[R21] **Riverside Drive–West 80th-81st Street Historic District**, Riverside Dr. to a line north-south midblock bet. Riverside Dr. and West End Ave., including the S side of W.81st St. and both sides of W.80th St. 👁

A group of 32 row houses built between 1892 and 1899 by architects *Charles H. Israels* (**308-314 W.81st St.** and **307-317 W.80th St.**) and *Clarence F. True* (**319-323 W.80th St.** and **316-320 W.81st St.**). The *Israels* houses are crowned with surprising shades of purple/blue/red tile.

[R22] **411 West End Avenue**, SW cor. W.80th St. 1936. *George F. Pelham II.*

Art Deco with touches of *Corbusier*-inspired ships' railings on the balconies and terraces near the top. Note how "drapes" of ornament cascade from some of the parapets (in stainless steel) and over the entrance (in cut stone).

[R23] **307-317 West 80th Street**, bet. West End Ave. and Riverside Dr. N side. 1894. *Charles H. Israels.*

Gothickesque—neither the Gothic Revival of earlier years nor the Collegiate Gothic of the 1920s—and picturesque, but what could be more picturesque than Gothic? Note the stained glass, bearing numbers, over the doors and windows (but No.317 has been painted). The delights of this block.

[R24] **328 West 80th Street**, bet. West End Ave. and Riverside Dr. S side. 1899. *Clarence F. True.*

Articulated voussoirs alternating with lusty vines articulate this arched entryway. Above, windows are framed with quoins, lintels, and voussoirs in simpler cut limestone. A vaguely Georgian enterprise. But you could seldom predict *True*'s next step in architecture.

[R25] **The Calhoun School Learning Center**, 433 West End Ave., SW cor. W.81st St. 1975. *Costas Machlouzarides.* Expansion upward, 2004, *FxFowle.*

R25

A modern-day *Gulliver* must have passed here in 1975 and left behind his giant-sized TV. Not to be outdone (perhaps they are parents, as well) *FXFowle* added four stories to *Maclouzarides*'s existing five. *Christopher Gray* in the *Times* called *Maclouzarides* "Architect of the Audacious."

[R26] **309-315** and **317-325 West 82nd Street**, bet. West End Ave. and Riverside Dr. ca. 1892.

Two groups of **Roman brick** plus brownstone-trimmed residences, the first rich in intricately formed roofs, dormers, chimney pots, finials, and colonnettes; the second more restrained with handsome verdigris-copper cornices. Purples and orange hues abound.

[R27] **Red House**, 350 W.85th St., bet. West End Ave. and Riverside Dr. S Side. 1903-1904. *Harde & Short.* •

A romantic six-story masterpiece, its multi-paned glassiness reminiscent of the work of the English country-house architect, *Robert Smythson,* in the 1590s (**Wollaton Hall/**

Hardwick Hall)! Note the dragon and crown cartouche set up high into the brickwork. These talented architects also designed the **Studio Building** and **Alwyn Court.**

[R28] **316-326 West 85th Street Houses**, bet. West End Ave. and Riverside Dr. S side. 1892. *Clarence F. True.* •

Six dark red sandstone row houses designed as a unit. The banded sills at the second floor are voluptuous examples of the fine stone carving abundant everywhere in the 1890s. Unlike the Hackensack River brownstone used for much of New York earlier in the century, the carving shows little deterioration.

[R29] **329-337 West 85th Street Houses**, bet. West End Ave. and Riverside Dr. N side. 1890-1891. *Ralph Townsend.* •

Brownstone and brick, pyramidal roofs form rhythmic crowns. A face-off between *Townsend* on the north, *True* on the south. *Townsend's* more picturesque, *True's* more stolid.

R27

[R30] **John B. and Isabella Leech House**, 520 West End Avenue, NE cor. W.85th St. 1892. *Clarence F. True.* •

Rock-faced brownstone joins with brick, many gables, and a bold elliptical inset terrace to form the picturesque ensemble of this former town house. Note also the arched doorway with delicate transom ironwork, leading from the strong stoop. **A custom *True*.**

A daring developer proposed to hover an apartment structure on legs above the Leech House (1987, William Gleckman); the bizarre thought elicited thunderous opposition from the neighborhood.

[R31] **530 West End Avenue**, SE cor. W.86th St. 1912. *Mulliken & Moeller.*

The **Spanish Renaissance**, rusticated and iron-grilled at its base, as in a private palace, here adapted to West End high-rise living. The terra-cotta cornice, pilasters, friezes, lintels, and enframements are unique.

R29

[R32] **Church of St. Paul and St. Andrew** (United Methodist)/originally **St. Paul's Methodist Episcopal Church and Parish House**, 540 West End Ave., NE cor. W.86th St. 1895-1897. *R.H. Robertson.* 🍎

A startling work. While other architects (including *Robertson*) were pursuing more or less faithful revival-styles, this is in the imaginative vein of the French neo-Classicist architects *Claude-Nicolas Ledoux* or *Etienne-Louis Boullée.* The bold octagonal corner tower is reminiscent of the fire tower that was once part of the **Jefferson Market**.

[R33] **St. Ignatius Church** (Episcopal), 552 West End Ave., SE cor. W.87th St. 1902. *Charles C.*

R34

Haight. **Shrine** (inside), 1926, *Cram & Ferguson.*

One of *Haight's* less inspired works. Inside it's better, a bit of London. Fortunately, churches and a few remaining row houses combine to keep West End Avenue from being an apartment-house canyon.

[R34] **Cathedral Preparatory Seminary** (Roman Catholic)/formerly **McCaddin-McQuick Memorial, Cathedral College**/originally **St. Agatha's School**, 555 West End Ave., SW cor. W.87th St. 1908. *Boring & Tilton.*

Dignity in Collegiate Gothic red brick and limestone by the architects of **Ellis Island** and the **Brooklyn Heights Casino**.

[R35] **Riverside Drive–West End Historic District**, between Riverside Drive, a north-south line midway between Broadway and West End Avenue, 87th and 94th Streets, with peninsulas north to 95th and south to 85th along Riverside Drive. 🍎

Clarence F. True was here, along with *Thom & Wilson, C.P.H. Gilbert,* and *Ralph Townsend.* Eclectic row houses by these and others abound on **88th** and **89th** Streets, with *True*

R35

R37

dominating the blocks to the north (90th, 91st, and 92nd) between West End Avenue and Riverside Drive.

[R36] **560 West End Avenue**, NE cor. W.87th St. 1890. *Joseph H. Taft.*

This house, among the many West Side projects of *W.E.D. Stokes,* once had nine similar neighbors to the north. *Stokes* was developer of the **Ansonia**.

[R37] **565 West End Avenue**, NW cor. W.87th St. 1937. *H.I. Feldman.*

One anonymous architectural historian: Art Deco, with "corner windows substituting for (the) quoins" necessary in a neo-Renaissance West End apartment house. An upscale version of architecture on the **Grand Concourse**.

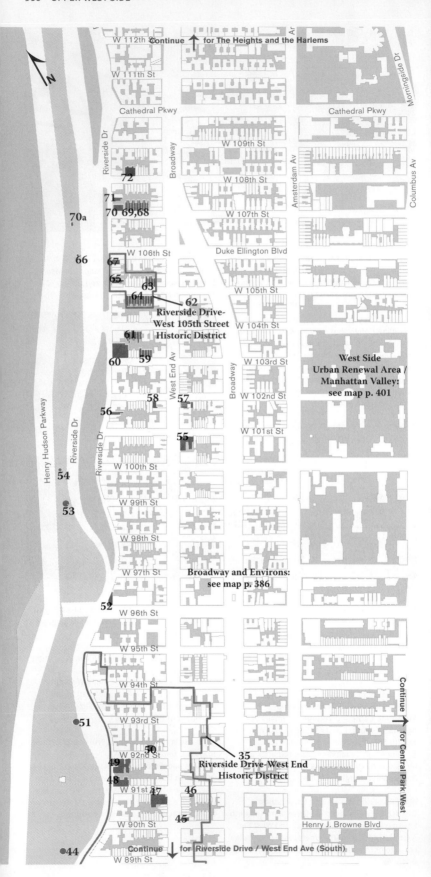

W 112th St
Continue ↑ for The Heights and the Harlems

W 111th St

Cathedral Pkwy

Cathedral Pkwy

W 109th St

Riverside Dr

Broadway

W 108th St

72

W 107th St

71

70 69,68

70a

Duke Ellington Blvd

Amsterdam Av

Columbus Av

66

W 106th St

67

65

63

64

62

Riverside Drive-
West 105th Street
Historic District

W 105th St

W 104th St

61

60   59

West End Av

Broadway

W 103rd St

West Side
Urban Renewal Area /
Manhattan Valley:
see map p. 401

58   57

W 102nd St

56

W 101st St

55

Riverside Dr

W 100th St

W 99th St

54

W 98th St

53

W 97th St

Broadway and Environs:
see map p. 386

52

W 96th St

W 95th St

Henry Hudson Parkway

W 94th St

51

W 93rd St

50

W 92nd St

49

48

47

46

45

35

Riverside Drive-West End
Historic District

Continue → for Central Park West

Henry J. Browne Blvd

44

Continue ↓ for Riverside Drive / West End Ave (South)

W 89th St

N

[R38] **562 West End Avenue**. bet. W.87th and W.88th Sts. E side. 1913. *Walter Haefeli.*

Well-groomed **Doric** columns guard this entry to middle-class apartment life: gargantuan versions of the flanking Ionic and Doric columns that marked the entries of Federal and Greek Revival houses; revived yet again, but in megastyle.

[R39] **Normandy Apartments**, 140 Riverside Drive, NE cor. W.86th St. 1938-1939. *Emery Roth & Sons.* 🍎

Sleek Art Moderne streamlines the corners of Normandy's twin towers on the Hudson, a stylistic advance from an earlier and more eclectic *Roth* (the **Beresford** and the **San Remo** on Central Park West). The water towers on top still hold on to the Renaissance, stripped down from those crowning *Roth*'s **Oliver Cromwell** on West 72nd Street.

[R40] **Congregation B'nai Jeshurun**, 257 W.88th St., bet. Broadway and West End Ave. N side.

R39

R42a

1918. *Henry B. Herts and Walter Schneider.*
[R41] **The Abraham Joshua Herschel School and Community Center**, 270 W.89th St. 1928. *Henry B. Herts. Louis Allan Abramson,* associate. Restorations, 1990s, *Giorgio Cavaglieri.*

The synagogue's façade is an embroidery of brick and terra cotta from the waning days of an era when important Jewish houses of worship were drawn from the **Byzantine/Romanesque.** The School, on 89th, drools "Moorish" tentacles from its entry cornice.

West 88th Street, between West End Avenue and Riverside Drive:

[R42a] **302-338 West 88th Street**, bet. West End Ave. and Riverside Dr. S side. Early 1890s.

Stepped gables, sharply pointed dormers, **bay-** and **bow-**windows, all with Roman brick, adding eclectic touches to this row.

[R42b] **315-323 West 88th Street**. 1896. *Theodore E. Thomson.*

Bow-fronted brown and white stones, panels and bow-soffits carved in bas-relief.

[R42c] **325-327 West 88th Street**. 1894. *Thom & Wilson.*

Bow-fronted Roman brick.

[R42d] **329-341 West 88th Street**. 1894. *Thom & Wilson.*

Great **neo-Baroque** hoods at **Nos.337 & 331**), filled with a young woman before an unfurled fan, cap asymmetrical stoops, the buildings stars of this *Thom & Wilson* terrace.

[R42e] **342-344 West 88th Street**. 1893-1894. *Thom & Wilson.*

More Roman brick, patterned friezes, and some colonnaded bay windows.

[R43] Originally **Isaac L. Rice House "Villa Julia"**/now **Yeshiva Ketana School**/onetime **Solomon Schinasi House**, 346 W.89th St., SE cor. Riverside Drive. 1901-1903. *Herts & Tallant.* Additions and alterations, 1908, *C.P.H. Gilbert.* 🍎

A neo-Renaissance villa and its garden. Although the Drive was once lined with freestanding mansions, only this maroon brick villa and one other survive: named **Villa Julia** for *Rice*'s wife (the prescient founder of the **Society for the Suppression of Unnecessary Noise**). In 1907 the building was sold to *Solomon Schinasi*, a well-known cigarette manufacturer. *Schinasi*'s brother, *Morris*, at the same time, was awaiting

R43

completion of his own villa on the Drive, at West 107th Street. Curiously it is these two *Schinasi* mansions that survive.

[R44] **Soldiers' and Sailors' Monument**, in Riverside Park, Riverside Dr. at W.89th St. 1897-1902. *Stoughton & Stoughton, Paul E.M. Duboy.* 🍎

Monument to the Civil War dead of New York soldiers, taking its form as an inflated **Choragic Monument of Lysicrates** (335 B.C., **Athens**). On axis with the northbound driver or pedestrian, its 12 Corinthian columns rise above a monumental rusticated marble base. *Duboy* was also architect of that other West Side monument, the **Ansonia Hotel.**

[R45] **620 West End Avenue**, NE cor. W.90th St. 1899-1901. *Hugh Lamb.*

An eclectic amalgam of **Georgian** and **Renaissance** parts in a willful **Edwardian** manner. Good brick banding at the fourth floor, and a very nice cornice.

[R46] **272 West 91st Street**, bet. West End Ave. and Broadway. S side. 1899-1901. *Hugh Lamb*.

Salmon brick, a Palladian window, and a quartet of Composite columns in a vocabulary similar to *Lamb's* **620 West End**.

[R47] **Greek Orthodox Cathedral Church of the Annunciation**/originally **Fourth Presbyterian Church**. 635 West End Ave., SW cor. W.91st St. 1893-1894. *Heins & La Farge*.

A very Anglo-American **Gothic Revival** church

R48

[R51] **Joan of Arc Statue**, in Joan of Arc Park, Riverside Dr. at W.93rd St. 1915. *Anna Vaughn Hyatt Huntington*, sculptor. *John V. Van Pelt*, architect.

The *Maid of Orleans,* in full armor, stands in her prancing steed's stirrups, looking heavenward with sword held high. Atop *Van Pelt's* granite pedestal. *Huntington* exhibited a plaster model at the **1910 Paris Salon**, and an American committee, wishing a monument for *Jeanne's* 500th birthday (January 6, 1412),

R50

R52

now transformed for services of a different flock. It serves as a happy punctuation to the Avenue.

[R48] **190 Riverside Drive**, NE cor. W.91st St. 1909-1910. *Townsend, Steinle & Haskell*.

A venerable apartment block, its rusticated limestone base supporting a field of tan brick, quoined at its corners. Bay windows proliferate. At the sky a grand **neo-Renaissance** copper cornice crowns it all.

[R49] **194 Riverside Drive**, bet. W.91st and W.92nd Sts. 1902. *Ralph S. Townsend*.

The deeply slotted entry creates twin forms: each with rusticated limestone and brick, square volumes intersecting **pepper-pot** corners.

[R50] **Montessori School**, 309 W.92nd St., bet. West End Ave. and Riverside Dr. N side. 1905. *Charles A. Rich*.

A **neo-Georgian** mansion, its exaggerated lintels, tiny dormers, and bay windows with stained-glass transoms, from Victorian times.

saw it, and commissioned the bronze that we see here.

[R52] **Cliff Dwellers' Apartments**, 243 Riverside Dr., NE cor. W.96th St. 1914. *Herman Lee Meader*.

An off-beat building predating Art Deco interest in **Mayan motifs**, and known primarily for the frieze of mountain lions, rattlesnakes, and buffalo skulls, symbolizing the life of Arizona cliff dwellers, and contrasting these prehistoric people with Manhattan's modern "cliff dwellers." A long joke. Look up at *this* cliff.

*Woodman, Spare That Tree! In 1837 an old elm on the property of the **Stryker's Bay Mansion**—which then stood on a hill northeast of the 96th Street viaduct—was to be cut down. George Pope Morris, journalist and poet (1802-1864), was inspired to pen the exhortation that saved the tree.*

> *Woodman, spare that tree!*
> *Touch not a single bough!*
> *In youth it sheltered me,*
> *And I'll protect it now.*

O THE MEMORY OF THE B

R57

[R53] **Carrère Memorial**, Riverside Park at W.99th St. 1916. *Thomas Hastings*.

On a small granite-balustered terrace below the park entrance lays a graffitied, barely noticeable, memorial tablet to one of New York's great architects: *John Merven Carrère* (of *Carrère & Hastings*), killed in an automobile accident in 1911.

[R54] **Firemen's Memorial Monument & Plaza**, Riverside Dr. at W.100th St. 1913. *Attilio Piccirilli*, sculptor. *H.Van Buren Magonigle*, architect. Restored, 1987-1992, *Jan Hird Pokorny Associates*.

Piccirilli's **Courage** and **Duty** guard this **neo-Classical** memorial to SOLDIERS IN A WAR THAT NEVER ENDS. Embedded in the plaza is a bronze tablet to the firehorses who also served "in the line of duty."

[R55] **838 West End Avenue**, SE cor. W.101st St. 1914. *George & Edward Blum*.

Intricate vegetal and geometric bas-reliefs

R56

turn terra cotta into damask, both embellishing this apartment house and recalling a *Sullivan-esque* approach to ornament.

[R56] **William and Clara Baumgarten House**, 294 Riverside Drive., bet. W.101st and W.102nd Sts. 1900-1901. *Schickel & Ditmars*. 🍎

Beaux Arts limestone mansion with a remarkable **Art Nouveau** window guard at the ground floor. *Baumgarten* managed *Herter Brothers*, prominent interior architects of the time.

[R57] **854, 856, & 858 West End Avenue,** and **254 West 102nd Street House**. 1892-1893. *Schneider & Herter*. 🍎

A pepper-pot (poivrière) corners this West End complex, clad in brownstone **Queen Anne**. The deep-set terraces articulate it, making the cornering monumental.

[R58] **Ralph Samuel Townsend House**, 302 W.102nd St., bet. West End Ave. and Riverside Dr. 1884. S side. *Ralph S. Townsend*.

Arts and Crafts for *Townsend* chez *Townsend*. Moved from the Avenue, this was early *Townsend*, before he went on to Beaux Arts adventures at the **Hotel Churchill** and the **Kenilworth**. A radiant sun bursts in terra cotta below an upstairs window.

[R59] **303-309 West 103rd Street**, bet. West End Ave. and Riverside Dr. N side. 1895-1896. *George F. Pelham*.

Five well-groomed brownstones with synco-pated bow and bay windows.

The Gershwins and the Bogarts, 103rd Street, 1905-1931.

*The Gershwins lived at **No.316** (1899. Henri Fouchaux) from 1925 to 1931; Morris and Rose Gershwin and their grown children Ira, George, Arthur, and Francis. The Bogarts were at **245**. Bogie was raised here from age six (1905) onward, under the eye of his surgeon father, Belmont Deforest Bogart. A histrionic change from here to **Casablanca**. Then again his name was Humphrey Deforest Bogart. Neither building is interesting.*

[R60] **Master Building**/formerly **Master Institute of United Arts** and **Riverside Museum**/originally **Nicholas Roerich Museum**, 310-312 Riverside Dr., NE cor. W.103rd St. 1928-1929. *Harvey Wiley Corbett of Helmle, Corbett & Harrison and Sugarman & Berger*. 🍎

Built as a residential hotel, the **Master**

R60

Institute also housed artist *Nicholas Roerich*'s museum and a school, now removed elsewhere. *Roerich* was responsible for the idea of shading the building's brickwork from a purplish base to a pale yellow crest. A major **Art Deco** monu-ment in brick and terra cotta, but everything *Corbett* did seemed major. Look up to his **Deco** cubism against the sky.

[R61] **312-322 West 104th Street**, bet. West End Ave. and Riverside Dr. S side. 1890s.

Six mates in brick and brownstone, bay-, bow-, and flat-fronted, many gabled against the sky; terra-cotta panels and parapets enrich them all.

[R62] **Riverside-West 105th Street Historic District**, generally along Riverside Dr. bet. W.105th and W.106th Sts., plus some of both sides of W.105th St. bet. West End Ave. and Riverside Dr. 🖾

Enjoying a magnificent setting overlooking the City's great river is this enclave of English **Edwardian** and French **Beaux Arts** town houses. Executed between 1899 and 1902, they were designed by *Janes & Leo, Mowbray & Uffinger, Hoppin & Koen*, and *Robert D. Kohn*. Of special interest are:

[R63] **301-307 West 105th Street**, bet. West End Ave. and Riverside Dr. N side. 1899-1900. *Janes & Leo.*

Four houses form an Edwardian English terrace: the billowing ironwork at entry portals supported by deeply carved **Victorian Baroque** corbelled terraces.

[R64] **302-320 West 105th Street**, bet. West End Ave. and Riverside Dr. S side. 1899-1900. *Janes & Leo.*

R63

R64

Ten red brick and limestone houses form a more stolid group than the limestone bevy opposite. Here a **heavier hand** (by the same architects) was applied: to bays, parapets, balustrades, and grillwork.

[R65] **New York Buddhist Church and American Buddhist Academy**, 331-332 Riverside Dr., bet. W.105th and W.106th Sts. **No.331,** formerly **Marion Davies House**. 1902. *Janes & Leo.* No.332, 1963. *Kelly & Gruzen.*

The heroic-size bronze statue of *Shinran-Shonin* (1173-1262), founder of a **Buddhist** sect, became a local landmark before the City designated it an official one. Skip the architecture, study *Shinran*.

[R66] **Statue of Franz Sigel,** Riverside Dr. at W.106th St. 1907. *Karl Bitter,* sculptor. *W.Welles Bosworth,* architect of base.

A placid equestrian statue of the **Civil War General**, a favorite of *Lincoln. Sigel* (1824-1902) had immigrated to the U.S. in 1852 after the German revolutionary movement lost to Prussia (he had been Commander-in-Chief of the Baden army and its Secretary of War).

R65

[R67] **River Mansion,** 337 Riverside Dr., SE cor. W.106th St. 1900-1902. *Stewart & Smith.*

An opulent Beaux Arts brick and limestone mansarded mansion, anchoring the corner, and enjoying views of both River and Drive.

[R68] **305-319 West 107th Street**, bet. Broadway and Riverside Dr. N side. 1900s.

Seven bowed bays in light brick and limestone undulate in the streetscape. With a very grand wrought-iron balcony at **No.311**.

[R69] **Nicholas Roerich Museum,** 319 W.107th St., bet. Riverside Dr. and Broadway. N side. 1898. *Clarence F. True.* Open Tu-Su, 2-5; closed Mo. 212-864-7752.

Permanent collection of the work of *Nicholas Roerich,* prolific artist, designer, explorer, philosopher, and collaborator of *Stravinsky* and *Diaghilev.* Architectural landmarks of his native Russia were the subjects of many of *Roerich's* early paintings, and he contributed to the design of **310 Riverside Drive.**

R68

R70a

R72

[R70] **The Children's Mansion**/originally **Morris and Laurette Schinasi House**, 351 Riverside Dr., NE cor. W.107th St. 1907-1909. *William B. Tuthill.* 🍎

A marble freestanding neo-**French Renaissance** château by the architect of Carnegie Hall. Dozens of similar mansions once lined the Drive. Now a school.

[R70a] **Peter J. Sharp Riverside Volunteer House**, in Riverside Park at 107th St. 2006. *Murphy Burnham Buttrick.*

On the site of an existing one-story building, enlarged, a mezzanine and a second story added. Upstairs the Evelyn Sharp Meeting Room gives a park overview to the volunteers. Appropriately understated, with *Wrightian* (*Frank Lloyd*) details.

[R71] **352 Riverside Drive**, bet. W.107th and W.108th Sts. 1900s.

A grand entry portal bears a balcony for savoring *Olmsted's* park.

[R72] **Assumptionist Provincial House**/formerly **America Press Building**, 329 W.108th St., bet. Broadway and Riverside Dr. N side. ca. 1900. *Thomas Graham.* Altered, 1902, *Horgan & Slattery.*

Double-width row houses joined in **Edwardian** confusion forming an internally interlocked Roman Catholic residence. Ornate limestone carving is profuse, set in fields of cool red brick. Freestanding Composite columns at the entry are the most convincing detail.

NECROLOGY

All Angels' Episcopal Church, 428 West End Ave., SE cor. W.81st St. 1890. *Samuel B. Snook of J.B. Snook & Sons.* Altered, 1896, *Karl Bitter Studio*, sculptors.

The delicacy of this church was made even more fragile by the brilliant placement of its axis diagonal to the street grid. Its slow annihilation was all the more painful with the triumphant survival of the giant TV tube across the street.

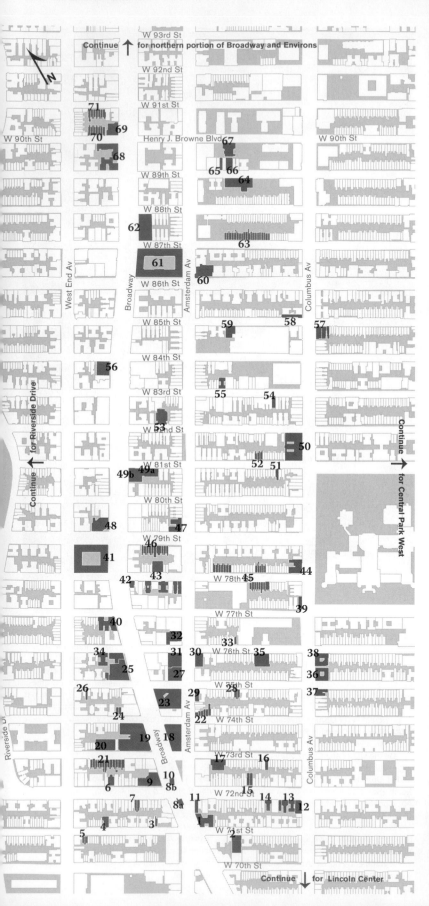

W 93rd St

Continue ↑ for northern portion of Broadway and Environs

W 92nd St

W 91st St

W 90th St

Henry J. Browne Blvd

W 90th St

W 89th St

W 88th St

W 87th St

W 86th St

W 85th St

W 84th St

W 83rd St

W 82nd St

W 81st St

W 80th St

W 79th St

W 78th St

W 77th St

W 76th St

W 75th St

W 74th St

W 73rd St

W 72nd St

W 71st St

W 70th St

West End Av

Broadway

Amsterdam Av

Columbus Av

Riverside Drive

for Riverside Drive

← Continue

Continue → for Central Park West

Continue ↓ for Lincoln Center

BROADWAY AND ENVIRONS

From 70th Street to Cathedral Parkway (110th Street):

Broadway's route dates from 1703: the plotting of the **Bloomingdale Road**. Initially only 33 feet wide, the road increased in width in concert with its growing popularity. By 1871 it was 150 feet wide, its course straightened between 59th and 155th Streets, its name then **The Boulevard**. In 1899 it was renamed **Broadway**, the northern extension of the route from Bowling Green.

[B1] **Dorilton Apartments**, 171 W.71st St., NE cor. Broadway. 1900-1902. *Janes & Leo.* ✿
Walking uptown on Broadway this grandiloquent mansarded **Beaux Arts** pile will prepare you for the even greater **Ansonia** two blocks north: here a cornice-copia. Look up at the frolicking freestanding amazons.

A modernist essay in New York's post-World War II streetscape: streamlined form opens to the light and air of a side yard. The children win.

[B5] **274, 276 West 71st Street**, bet. Amsterdam and West End Aves. S side. ca. 1890.
Shades of Philadelphia architect *Frank Furness* are visible in these dour **Queen Anne** mavericks. The bay window within an arch is a *Furness* gambit.

[B6] **247-249 West 72nd Street**, bet. Broadway and West End Ave. N side. 1890s.
Excellent eclecticisms: **Romanesque Revival** arches and gables, balustraded bow windows; all in brownstone, terra cotta, and brick. The shops below blind most to the charms above.

B1

B4   B5

B2   B3

B6

[B2] **Blessed Sacrament Church** (Roman Catholic), 150 W.71st St., bet. Columbus Ave. and Broadway. S side. 1916-1917. *Gustave Steinback.*
Steinback's brilliantly modeled façades exploit this jam-packed midblock site. The vigorous interplay of limestone through **volume, void, and silhouette**, works well, even in the shallow side street. And the rose window, in striking reds and blues, merits a visit within. Enter.

[B3] Originally **Christ Church Rectory**, 213 W.71st St., bet. Broadway and West End Ave. N side.
A dour tan brick, brownstone, and terracotta **Romanesque Revival** remembrance of the church that used to be next door.

[B4] Originally **The Godmothers League**/now **West End Day School**, 255 W.71st St., bet. Amsterdam and West End Aves. N side. 1950. *Sylvan Bien.*

[B7] **216-218 West 72nd Street**, bet. Broadway and West End Ave. S side. 1890s.
Cousins of 247-249 across the street. As usual the bottom tail of commerce is wagging the top dog.

*Let them eat cake: Named for the family who settled it, the hamlet of **Harsenville** was one of several strung along what is now upper Broadway. Its rustic charm attracted a number of French émigrés fleeing their revolution's Reign of Terror. The statesman **Charles Maurice de Talleyrand-Perigord** sought refuge here in 1795 while heads rolled at home, and the **duc d'Orleans**—later to become **King Louis Philippe**—came here two years later. While on an extended visit he toured much of the newborn republic from Maine to Louisiana, supplementing his meager financial resources by teaching French at the Somerindijk farmhouse, located at what is now the northwest corner of Broadway and West 75th Street. Does his ghost* *hover nearby, savoring the croissants, brioches, and other patisseries françaises once purveyed by Beaudesir, the site's previous occupant? Allons, enfants. . .*

Prediction fulfilled, *from the Fourth Edition of this Guide: "The traffic in and out (of the subway station) is horrendous. Development rights for* **Riverside South** *include financing for a total reconstruction of this station complex. Included is the greening of Broadway to the north, an extended* **Verdi Square** *that caps the new subway facilities."*

[B8a] **72nd Street IRT Subway Kiosk,** Broadway and Amsterdam Ave. S of W.72nd St. 1904. *Heins & La Farge.* ☛ Reconstruction and extension of the station, 1999-2004, *Gruzen Samton and Richard Dattner & Assocs.*

Cartoonist and wit *James Stevenson* termed this a **"Peruvian Cathedral."** And so it has been preserved, in concert with the new, much larger, entrance:

B13

[B8b] **New 72nd Street Subway Entrance,** Broadway and Amsterdam Ave., N of W.72nd St 1999-2004. *Gruzen Samton and Richard Dattner & Assocs.*

Roomy and full of light inside, a welcome addition to the most congested transfer platforms on the IRT. But the old **Peruvian Cathedral** still reigns.

[B9] **The Alexandria,** 201 W.72nd St., NW cor. Broadway. 1990. *Frank Williams & Assocs. and Skidmore, Owings & Merrill.*

Ramses II's mummy may return (*Harrison Ford* has the part) and terminate this insult to ancient Egypt. It took two distinguished firms to consummate schmaltz. Fortunately the dissonance is mostly on high, and ubiquitous chainstores merely bore us at ground level.

[B10] **Verdi Square Scenic Landmark,** Broadway, Amsterdam Ave., and W.73rd St. 1906. Giuseppe Verdi, *Pasquale Civiletti,* sculptor. ☛

This vastly expanded greensward honors

the great Italian composer. At sculpted *Verdi's* feet are life-size figures of characters from **Aida, Falstaff, Otello,** and *La Forza del Destino.* The new park grew to the west, embracing the former northbound lanes of Broadway, hence not only topping the expanded trackspace below, but giving breathing space both visually and physically to the new subway entrance by *Gruzen Samton/Richard Dattner.*

[B11] **Gray's Papaya** *(Let's Be Frank. We Want You to Buy Our Furters), 2090 Broadway, SE cor. 72nd Street, is a local landmark long famous for its cheap hot dogs ($1.25). Here the mustard is* **Dijon** *(Gulden's out of gallon containers). Wash it down with a glass of papaya juice, piña colada, or fresh squeezed oranges. It's all good and based on quality served in great volume. A spin-off from the still existing* **Papaya King,** *there are two other Gray's Papaya locations: 402 Sixth Avenue (at 8th Street) and 539 Eighth Avenue (at 37th Street).*

🏛 [B12] Originally **Park & Tilford Building,** 100 W.72nd St., SW cor. Columbus Ave. 1892-1893. *McKim, Mead & White.*

An *MM&W* rusticated limestone and brick background building, not self-important, but a nice neighbor. Next door, to the west, is a **humdinger:**

🏛 [B13] Originally **Hotel Hargrave,** 112 W.72nd St., bet. Columbus and Amsterdam Aves. S side. 1901-1902/1905-1907. *Frederick C. Browne.*

Belle Epoque bay windows give a rich mod-

B8b   B12

ulation to this rusticated limestone and brick façade. Topped with a double-dormered mansard roof, the ensemble is redolent of Paris, except for its height. In Paris body and mansards would never total more than **eight** floors. Here there are **12.**

[B14] Originally **The Earlton,** 118 W.72nd St., bet. Columbus and Amsterdam Aves. S side. 1914-1915. *Buchman & Fox.*

One of three white glazed terra-cotta studio buildings, tall and narrow, developed by builder *Edward West Browning,* whose initials are entwined in the façade above the second floor.

🏠 [B15] **137-139 West 72nd Street,** bet. Columbus and Amsterdam Aves. 1885-1887. *Thom & Wilson.* Storefronts, 1925.

A grand pair of **Gothic Revival** town houses, towers conically capped in the manner of a Loire valley château. An 1887 critic (quoted by *Christopher Gray*) remarked that "the level of badness is so low and so uniform that it is hard

B9

B15   B17   B18   B19

to pick out the worst" on (this) block of "shocking bad architecture." *Phineas Lounsbury*, governor of Connecticut from 1887 to 1889, lived here after his term in Hartford.

[B16] **126 West 73rd Street**, bet. Columbus and Amsterdam Aves.

Another white-glazed studio building for *Mr. Browning*, in his terra-cotta trilogy.

 [B17] **Sherman Square Studios,** 160 W.73rd St., bet. Columbus and Amsterdam Aves. S side. 1928-1929. *Tillion & Tillion.*

Deco-Gothic brick and sandstone step cubistically down from the water tower and penthouses, each tier punctuated with terra-cotta finials. The original slender steel-muntined casement windows have been replaced by gross aluminum. Reprehensible.

[B18] Originally **Central Savings Bank**/now **Apple Bank for Savings,** 2100 Broadway, NE cor. 73rd St. 1926-1928. *York & Sawyer,* architects. Decorative ironwork, *Samuel Yellin Studio.* ☙ Interior. ☙

A miniature of the **Federal Reserve** on Liberty Street, Central Savings seems a noble palazzo. Thrift at the palace, inspired by *Florentine Medici's,* the first family of banking in the western world, led to 15th-century Florentine-exported architecture, here, and at a myriad of banks nationwide. This one, however, has class. Go in, it gets better.

[B19] **Ansonia Hotel**, 2101-2119 Broadway, bet. W.73rd and W.74th Sts. W side. 1899-1904. *Paul E.M. Duboy.* ☙

Inflated Paris came to Broadway, poivrières and all. The Landmarks Commission described its effect on a viewer as one of "joyous exuberance profiled against the sky." The collaboration between a demanding developer, *W.E.D. Stokes,* and an architect steeped in the forms of Parisian apartment buildings, *Paul E.M. Duboy,* had a magic result: The **Ansonia** is a New York treasure. Judging from the "guest list," a galaxy of important figures thought so too: *Arturo Toscanini, Lily Pons, Florenz Ziegfeld, Sol Hurok,* and *Igor Stravinsky,* to name a musico-theatrical few.

[B20] Originally **The Level Club** (of the Masonic order)/then **Hotel Riverside Plaza**, 253 W.73rd St., bet. Broadway and West End Ave. N side. 1926-1927. *Clinton & Russell.*

This **neo-Romanesque/Art Deco** façade sports the secret signs and symbols required by the original client, a Masonic organization. But level? The façade cascades down to the passerby. Cross the street and look up.

T-Square in the January 21, 1928, New Yorker: the Level Club is "...a vigorous and picturesque design ... devoted to Masonic activities, the emblems of which are cleverly introduced in the strongly-carved Byzantine detail."

counts. Go in, even if you must attend a concert that deafens you—the interior is **Greco-Deco-Empire** with a Tudor palette. It's strange to see such unruly rock-and-roll crowds in such posh digs. At least they can't smoke inside anymore.

[B24] **231 & 233 West 74th Street**, bet. Broadway and West End Ave. 1885-1886. *W.E.D. Stokes.*

Christopher Gray (in his *New York Times* "Streetscapes" column): "Inside, the vestibules' crumbling tiled floors still provide an illusionistic treat worthy of *Piero della Francesca.*"

[B25] **Astor Apartments**, 2141-2157 Broadway, bet. W.75th and W.76th Sts. W side. 1905. *Clinton & Russell.* Addition to N, 1914, *Peabody, Wilson & Brown.*

William Waldorf Astor, a major landowner hereabouts, speculated with this apartment complex. Bland but handsome: the copper cornice, however, is a prize, powerful and elegant.

B21

B20

B25   B27

[B21] **248-272 West 73rd Street**, bet. Broadway and West End Ave. S side. 1887. *Charles T. Mott.*

The crowning copper-sheathed dormers and finials seem ready to combat the secret signs across the street. Architectural critic *Montgomery Schuyler* wrote that the row **"animated the skyline without tormenting it."** Not landmarked and in need of love.

[B22] **161-169 West 74th Street** and **301-309 Amsterdam Avenue**, NE cor. W.74th St. 1886. *Lamb & Rich.*

Early West Side row housing that, happily restored at the corner, conveys a clear sense of the area's early development. No.**161** has been least touched by change. Brick, brownstone, and terra cotta.

[B23] **Beacon Theater**, 2124 Broadway, bet. W.74th and W.75th Sts. E side. 1927-1928. *Walter W. Ahlschlager.* Interior restoration by *Rambusch Studio.* Partial interior.

Skip the exterior. It's the opulent interior, second only to that of Radio City Music Hall, that

[B26] **254 West 75th Street**, bet. Broadway and West End Ave. S side. ca. 1885.

Three exuberant rockface limestone arches in a brick façade. The main arch allows a lovely interplay between its recessed terrace and the projecting bay window below. **Remarkable**.

The blocks between Broadway and West End in the 70s hold many surprises. Take a stroll and keep your eyes peeled.

[B27] **Champion Garage**/originally **The New York Cab Company**, 201 W.75th St., NW cor. Amsterdam Ave. 1888-1890. *C. Abbott French & Company.*

Three monumental **Romanesque Revival** half-round arches on 75th Street trumpeted entrance to the horses and drivers using this onetime multistory stable, crowned with a powerful cornice.

But years of internal pummelling by Suburbans and Range Rovers have taken a toll.

[B28] **140-142 West 75th Street**, bet. Columbus and Amsterdam Aves. S side. 1891. *George A. Bagge.*

The wandering stoop is a West Side specialty, allowing access, rather ceremonially, and an opportunity for communal seating.

[B29] **170 West 75th Street**, SE cor. Amsterdam Ave. 1888-1889. *Edward L. Angell.*

A veteran brick and terra-cotta tenement-apartment house rehabilitated for the modern fray. The cornice is exotic, an **Angellic** special.

B26

[B30] **Riverside Memorial Chapel**, 331 Amsterdam Ave., SE cor. W.76th St. 1925. *Joseph J. Furman and Ralph Segal.* Restored, and ground floor redesigned, 1998, *Belmont Freeman.*

Designed in a somber palette of browns and dull reds: tapestry brick, matte terra cotta, stucco, and a slate roof. **Gothic** windows reveal the chapel proper. The 1998 sheathing in modern granite didn't help.

[B31] **Jewish Community Center**, Samuel Priest Rose Building, 334 Amsterdam Ave., SW cor. W.76th St. 2001. *A.J. Diamond.*

Dark brick walls, slotted for windows, rise to all glass, then more glass — a stylish venue for wide-ranging religious, cultural, and athletic activities.

[B32] **The Harrison**, 206 W.76th St., NW cor. Amsterdam Ave. 2008. *Robert A.M. Stern.*

Massive, and festively bulging with "pre-war accents," but curiously unresolved at the top (compare with the convincing cornice on the old hotel holding out at the corner). The recent trend in naming new apartment blocks is to unleash the definite article: **The Brompton, The Laurel, The Lucida, The Standard,** and on and on. Therefore, The Harrison is just one of many: an indefinite particle of the definite article.

[B33] **153 West 76th Street**, bet. Columbus and Amsterdam Aves. S side. 1885-1886. *William Baker.*

Banded and piered brick and limestone; a solo eclectic eccentricity. The bay window gives it a special posture on the street.

[B34] **Hotel Churchill**, 252 W.76th St., bet. Broadway and West End Ave. S side. 1903. *Ralph Townsend.*

Among the many **Beaux Arts** hotels in the flock around Broadway and West End, this one excels, in superb condition: with bold **Mannerist** broken pediments over bay windows.

B28   B32

B36

[B35] Originally **St. Andrew's Methodist Episcopal Church**/now **West Side Institutional Synagogue**, 120 W.76th St., bet. Columbus and Amsterdam Aves. 1889. *Josiah Cleveland Cady.* Altered, 1958.

After a severe fire, a modernist approach morphed the church into a synagogue. Here the remnant body, desteepled and deroofed, seems to be **architecture astray**, without direction.

[B36] **La Rochelle**, 57 W.75th St., NE cor. Columbus Ave. 1898. *Lamb & Rich.*

Here is a grand entry portal worthy of an **English Renaissance** town house. The powerful columns are repeated along the avenue, fronting the shops, the latter respectfully inserted. A handsome accommodation: much good architecture is mutilated by its commercial street-fronts.

[B37] **The Hartford**, 60 W.75th St., SE cor. Columbus Ave. 1890. *Frederick T. Camp.*

Construction of these **French Flats** spanned the time of name change: Ninth to Columbus

B38

Avenue. The pedimented stone insert at the third-floor corner preserves the old name. But what an entry portal to come home to!

[B38] **The Aylsmere,** 60 W.76th St., SE cor. Columbus Ave. 1894. *Henry Anderson.*

French Flats from the **Brown Decades** of picturesque architecture, but here with some growing neo-Classical influences: note the pedimented columned balconettes at the corner. The verdigris bronze letters are another charming detail.

[B39] **The Shake Shack No.2,** 366 Columbus Ave., NW cor. 77th St. 2008. *James Wines and Denise M.C. Lee of SITE Environmental Design.*

Wines and Lee have taken cues from postwar roadside architecture, duplicating the hit formula of their original Shake Shack in Madison Square Park. Here they get to do what *SITE* does best: crash one building into another (the brick shell was existing). The burgers are heavenly.

[B40] **Belleclaire Hotel,** 250 W.77th St., SW cor. Broadway. 1901-1903. *Emery Roth of Stein, Cohen & Roth.*

Belle Epoque with bay windows, typical of a dozen similar, built hereabouts, exiles from the Rue Réaumur in Paris. Articulating its Beaux Arts body are giant **Art Nouveau** pilasters.

While in New York in 1906 to raise funds for the Bolsheviks, Maxim Gorky and his mistress briefly stayed at the Belleclaire. They were asked to leave when word got out that "Mme. Gorky" was not only not his wife (horrors!) but an actress (shudder!) with whom he had been living for three years.

[B41] **Apthorp Apartments,** 2209 Broadway to West End Ave.,W.78th to W.79th Sts. 1906-1908. *Clinton & Russell.*

Monumental and magnificent, this richly ornamented limestone **Renaissance Revival** building occupies an entire block. The individual entrances are reached through high vaulted

B45

tunnels, then across a huge interior court, a fountain at its center. The best of the surviving Astor apartments in New York.

Triple the height of a Roman palazzo, yet using its vocabulary, the Apthorp **Brobdingnag** makes that model seem Lilliputian.

[B42] **170 West 78th Street**, SE cor. Amsterdam Ave. 1890. *Higgs & Rooke.* Some *Louis Sullivanesque* inscribed

B40

ornament enhances a magnificent limestone **Romanesque Revival** arch. The incised number, itself, is an elegant carving.

[B43] **West 78th Street**, bet. Amsterdam Avenue and Broadway.

An architectural exhibit of stylistic sources—or is it a montage of Hollywood stage sets? Sturdy Romanesque Revival brownstone and brick at **No.202**. Some watered-down Tudor England hangs out at **No.210**. A bit of 1890s Chicago fronts **No.215**. Sedate 19th-century Boston occupies **No.226**. At **Nos.219-223** local row house talents left their own New York West Side marks.

[B44] **The Evelyn**, 101 W.78th St., NW cor. Columbus Ave. 1882-1886. *Emile Gruwe.*

A big, bold symphony in reds: brick with all kinds of wondrous unglazed terra-cotta flourishes.The spandrel putti are glorious. **The Evelyn Lounge**, on the Columbus Avenue side, was a dark, romantic spot but is now, sadly, closed.

[B45] **West 78th Street**, bet. Columbus and Amsterdam Aves. ca. 1883-1892.

A modern public school and other regrettable "improvements" have emasculated what was once one of the most vigorous and spirited streetscapes of the Upper West Side. The spirit was due in part to the works of *Rafael Guastavino*, who designed the idiosyncratic red and white sextet, **Nos.121-131** and **Nos.118-134** across the way (all completed in 1886). The

B41

B44

client for these rows, *Bernard S. Levy*, allowed *Guastavino*, then a recent emigrant from Catalonia, to introduce his system of "cohesive construction" in **No.122**, making it an entirely fireproof row house. (*Levy* himself lived at **No.121** between 1886 and 1904.) Look at the curious stepped balusters along the stoops in front of **Nos.157-167**. Their unusual forms and shadows are a favorite among architectural photography buffs.

[B46] **206-226 West 79th Street**, bet. Amsterdam Ave. and Broadway. 1894. *Thom & Wilson.*

A terrace of **Roman** brick town houses, bowed here and bayed there, based in limestone and decorated with terra cotta. The anchoring end buildings project, in an attempt to meet the line of the corner apartment houses. Sorry, their alleys intervened.

[B47] **Hotel Lucerne**, 201 W.79th St., NW cor. Amsterdam Ave. 1903-1904. *Harry B. Mulliken.*

Distinguished detailing in plum-colored brownstone, brick, and terra cotta. The deeply modeled, banded entrance columns, adopted from the **Baroque**, are luscious. Now gloriously restored as a condominium—an extravagant palace for its cooperators.

[B48] **First Baptist Church**, 265 W.79th St., NW cor. Broadway. 1894. *George Keister.*

Like the life that swirls past it on this busy corner, this church's eclectic façade is restless and polyglot. Overexuberant **Italian Romanesque** (Broadway division)?

[B49a] **The Broadway**, 2250 Broadway, SE cor. W.81st St. 1987. *Beyer Blinder Belle*, behind [B49b] **Staples**/originally **RKO (Radio Keith Orpheum) 81st Street Theatre Lobby & Offices.** 1914. *Thomas W.Lamb.* Converted, 1988, *Beyer Blinder Belle.*

Jewish appetizing store with charcuterie, salumeria, and **Wurstgeschäft**, *adds an array of cheeses, coffees, and breads, and offers an extensive selection of cooking utensils and cookbooks, too.*

[B50] Originally **Hotel Endicott**/now **Endicott Apartments**, Columbus Ave. bet. W.81st and W.82nd Sts. W. side. 1889. *Edward L. Angell.* Converted, 1984, *Stephen B. Jacobs & Assocs.*

Somber red brick with matching terra-cotta ornament produced a monolithic monumentality for this once fashionable hotel. Lovingly restored as a condominium; at the ground floor elegant and understated shops are framed in oak.

Maxilla & Mandible, *"The World's First and Only Osteological Store," 451 Columbus Avenue, established in 1983, designs museum installations and sells supplies to paleontologists, entomologists, and the general public. So if you're still in a paleontological mood after your trip to the* **Museum of Natural History,**

B48

B52

B47

B51

Exuberant glazed white terra-cotta neo-**Palladian** theater offices (now Staples) are the venerable frontispiece of a bland brick tower (**The Broadway** replaced the volume of the theater proper). But still a long-running Broadway show.

Broadway is the quintessential New York street, providing the entire gamut of quality food and shopping. Without the pretentious precincts and prices of the East Side (say upper Madison Avenue) one can find superior fruit and vegetables at **Fairway** *(market) between 74th and 75th Streets, fresh seafood at* **Citarella** *next door, and just about anything at* **Zabar's***. Elaborate cooking is an everyday matter in this cosmopolitan neighborhood, and the raw, canned, pickled, smoked, or whatever materials are conveniently at hand.*

Zabar's, bet. W.80th and W.81st Sts. W side. A larger-than-life horn of plenty: wall-to-wall food and, on weekends, wall-to-wall people as well. What makes Zabar's remarkable is its phenomenal variety of foodstuffs from all over the world. It combines the delights of the

and before you buy your flounder at Citarella, you can head here and pick up a complete spider monkey skeleton, no questions asked.

[B51] **110 West 81st Street**, bet. Columbus and Amsterdam Aves. S side. 1893. *Neville & Bagge.*

Stolid brownstone mansion, rockface and smooth, with incised Sullivanesque detail. The **stoop** is a glorious monument in itself.

[B52] **137-143 West 81st Street**, bet. Columbus and Amsterdam Aves. N side. 1886. *Rossiter & Wright.*

Many-gabled bow-fronted triad: rockfaced limestone bears brick bows, linteled in limestone, corniced in terra cotta. *Times* columnist Christopher Gray said that "the colossal wisteria vine running up the front of...143...nearly swallowed the building...four intertwined trunks so muscular and gnarly that they seem like the serpents that strangled **Laocoön** and his sons in *Virgil*'s 'Aeneid.'" **Wow**.

[B53] **Holy Trinity Roman Catholic Church**, 207 W.82nd St., bet. Amsterdam Ave. and Broadway. N side. 1900. *J.H. McGuire*. Rectory, 1928, *Thomas Dunn*.

Old Rome and the **Italian Renaissance** contributed to this complex façade. The grand congregational space within is shrouded under a dome upon pendentives that bring the circle back to a square plan. Intricate brickwork contrasts with white-glazed terra cotta. Two choragic monuments of Lysicrates once crowned it all: decapitated.

[B54] **Engine Company No.74, N.Y.C. Fire Department**, 120 W.83rd St., bet. Columbus and Amsterdam Aves. S side. 1888. *Napoleon LeBrun & Sons*.

Horses charging out, a steam **red and gold** Fire Engine (pumper) behind. Now they're gone, but the iron jib for hoisting hay remains overhead. Rock-face brownstone and brick; row house-scaled. And red and gold still blaze at the entry portals.

Nevermore: Notwithstanding the two plaques affixed to upscale apartment buildings along West 84th Street, both claiming to be the site where Edgar Allan Poe put the finishing touches to "The Raven," the tenement at No.206 just west of Amsterdam Avenue is the rightful claimant to that distinction. It was here in "the bleak December" of 1844 that Poe and his ailing wife boarded at Patrick and Mary Brennan's farmhouse, which surmounted a promontory later dynamited when the site was graded. Poe would often stroll down the hill to the immense rock outcropping west of Riverside Drive near West 83rd Street that he named Mount Tom after the Brennans' young son. There he would sit alone for hours, gazing across the river. In more sociable moments he would amble up the sylvan Bloomingdale Road to the Striker's Bay

B53

B55

B58

B56

[B55] **167-173 West 83rd Street**, bet. Columbus and Amsterdam Aves. N side. 1885. *McKim, Mead & White*.

McKim, Mead & White? **Italian Renaissance tenements?** The noble firm builds ignoble housing for the masses? Here developer *David H. King, Jr.*, believed that these floor-through apartments were the coming fashion.

[B56] **Broadway Fashion Building**, 2315 Broadway, SW cor. W.84th St. 1930-1931. *Sugarman & Berger*.

Long before curtains of metal and glass wrapped midtown, this stylish cladding of stainless steel, glass, and terra cotta arrived to grace Broadway. The retail signs at street level have happily improved in the past 20 years.

Tavern, located northeast of today's Riverside Drive viaduct over 96th Street. Only one remnant survives from the "home by horror haunted": the mantel upon which Poe scratched his name, now preserved at Columbia University.

[B57] **74, 76, and 78 West 85th Street**, SE cor. Columbus Ave. 1895. *John G. Prague*.

Ordinary façades with extraordinary portals; their foliate carving is ravishing, particularly that of **SUDELEY** at **No.76**. Try to make out the letters incised over **No.74**. Are they a Roman numeral? Do they spell **CLIIION**? Is the word **CLIFTON**? Or is this a rare example of a poor speller turned fine stonecutter?

[B58] **The Brockholst**, 101 W.85th St., NW cor. Columbus Ave. 1890. *John G. Prague*.

Endearingly dark and craggy rock-face stone and brick, these **French Flats** are laced with delicate ironwork fire escapes. It announces its name in floral terra-cotta relief.

B57

[B59] **Mannes College of Music of the New School**/originally **United Order of True Sisters**, 150 W.85th St., bet. Columbus and Amsterdam Aves. 1928. *Bloch & Hesse.*

A simply austere neo-**Georgian** brick and limestone house for music, with a verdigris copper mansard roof, and a mild **Palladian**

B59

window at its portal. But no architect in the time of the Georges would condone such asymmetry.

ENDANGERED!

[B60] **West Park Presbyterian Church**, 165 W.86th St., NW cor. Amsterdam Ave. Chapel, 1884, *Leopold Eidlitz.* Sanctuary, 1890, *Henry F. Kilburn.* 🕊

Although overwhelmed by the grim apartment building to the north, this dour brownstone Romanesque Revival church is one of the area's loveliest landmarks. Expensive to maintain, the church favors demolition. The Landmarks Preservation Commission and neighborhood groups would prefer saving it.

[B61] **Belnord Apartments**, 225 W.86th St., Amsterdam Ave. to Broadway, W.86th to W.87th Sts. 1908-1909. *H.Hobart Weekes* of *Hiss & Weekes.* 🕊

Like its smaller cousin the **Apthorp**, this block-square Renaissance Revival structure is an immense square doughnut. From the street it's brilliant but boring; but savor the low

vaulted entry tunnels that burst the entering traveler into the giant garden court. Apartments accessible only through the court.

[B62] **The Montana**, 247 W.87th St., NE cor. Broadway to W.88th St. 1986. *The Gruzen Partnership.*

B62   B65

B67   B68

Named as if it were godchild of the **Dakota**, whose patron, *Stephen Clark,* bequeathed us that 72nd Street "château" in the then undeveloped territory of the Upper West Side. More than a hundred years later a new developer hopes that twin towers and a western sobriquet will give it equal cachet. Nice place to live, but just a caricature of the **Century** or the **Majestic**.

[B63] **West 87th Street**, bet. Columbus and Amsterdam Aves. 1880s.

Some fine row houses line this block: **No.145** has a fascinating regressed bay window; **Nos.135** through **141** show rockfaced brownstone, brick, with wild cornices; **No.159** has a black, weathered cornice that might be (almost) a *Louise Nevelson* sculpture.

[B64] **Public School 166**, 140 W.89th St., bet. Columbus and Amsterdam Aves. 1898-1899. *C.B.J. Snyder.* 🕊 Upgraded, 1998, *Fox & Fowle.*

B61

A stately, glazed terra-cotta **Collegiate Gothic** school by this prolific architect of schools of the 1890s. Yes, Virginia, schoolchildren do know how to walk up stairs in Manhattan.

[B65] Originally **Claremont Riding Academy**, 175 W.89th St., bet. Columbus and Amsterdam Aves. N side. 1892. *Frank A. Rooke*. 🍎

A grand barn, but the horses and riders have gone: Manhattan's last public stable closed in 2007. Here you could rent a steed for a trot along Olmsted's original dedicated Central Park trails. Plans to turn the barn into a luxury condominium ("Honey, is there a weird smell in here?") didn't pan out; now the **Stephen Gaynor School** has bought the building in hopes of expansion.

[B66] **Ballet Hispanica**, 167 W.89th St., bet. Columbus and Amsterdam Aves. N side. ca. 1890.

One of a series of carriage houses that served the grand mansions nearby, or on Central Park West. Modest, but the arch is

enough. Now a dance school, linked to and sharing space with **Gaynor's** new building on 90th Street.

[B67] **Stephen Gaynor School and Ballet Hispanica**, 148 W.90th St., bet. Columbus and Amsterdam Aves. 2006. *Rogers Marvel.*

The Gaynor School inhabits the first seven floors. The **Ballet Hispanica** on 89th Street has extended space on top: the three floors above Gaynor.

[B68] **Astor Court Apartments**, 205 W.89th St. and 210 W.90th St., along Broadway. E side. 1914-1916. *Charles A. Platt.*

Stolid Park Avenue style: rusticated limestone and self quoined brickwork (with iron window grilles and iron lanterns at the entry) surround a **garden court** in the manner of the **Apthorp** and Belnord. But the pièce de résistance is the hovering cornice, worthy of *Michelangelo*.

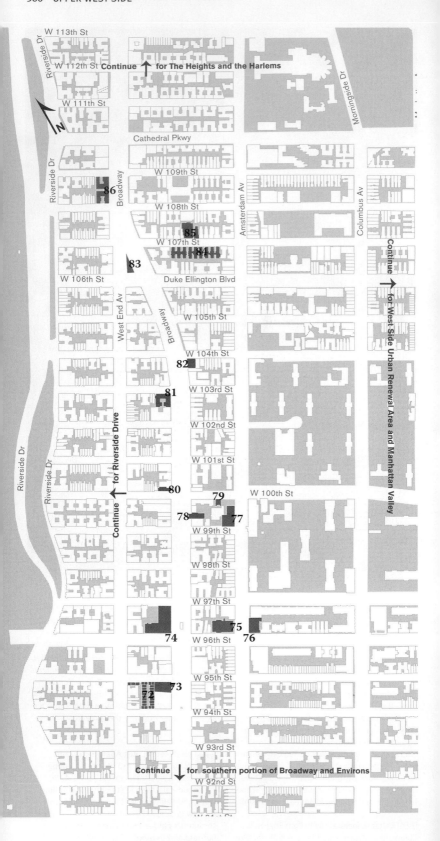

W 113th St

Riverside Dr

W 112th St **Continue** ↑ for The Heights and the Harlems

W 111th St

N

Cathedral Pkwy

Riverside Dr

Broadway

W 109th St

86

W 108th St

W 107th St **85**

83 **84**

W 106th St

Duke Ellington Blvd

West End Av

Broadway

W 105th St

W 104th St

82

81 W 103rd St

W 102nd St

W 101st St

80

W 100th St

79

Riverside Dr

78 **77**

W 99th St

Continue ← for Riverside Drive

W 98th St

W 97th St

74 **75**

W 96th St **76**

W 95th St

73

72 W 94th St

W 93rd St

Continue ↓ for southern portion of Broadway and Environs

W 92nd St

W 91st St

Amsterdam Av

Columbus Av

Morningside Dr

Continue → for West Side Urban Renewal Area and Manhattan Valley

[B69] **The Cornwall**, 255 W.90th St., NW cor. Broadway. 1909-1910. *Neville & Bagge.*

An extraordinary cornice is the place to focus: a **terra-cotta diadem**, modeled and perforated as if on an Indian temple. Under it, the building's body is a normal but nice West Side limestone and brick apartment block, with a grand Corinthian piered entrance.

[B70] **263-273 West 90th Street**, bet. Broadway and West End Ave. N side. Late 1890s.

B77   B78

B69

A terrace of seven houses, **bowed and bayed** in brick, limestone, and terra cotta. The end unit gracefully bows out to meet the line of adjacent avenue blocks.

[B71] **258-270 West 91st Street**, bet. Broadway and West End Aves. S side. 1896-1897. *Alexander M. Welch.*

Seven units form a terrace with bow and bay windows in yellow brick and limestone with **terra-cotta cornice** on high.

The night shift: Soon after her first arrest as a madam, Polly Adler decided to go legit. With $6,000 in savings she and a friend opened a lingerie shop in 1922 at 2487 Broadway near West 92nd Street. Within a year the shop was out of business—and Adler was back to business as usual.

[B72] **Pomander Walk**, 3-22 Pomander Walk, 261-267 W.94th St. and 260-274 W.95th St. bet. Broadway and West End Ave. 1921. *King & Campbell.* 🍎

Pomander Walk first came to New York as a stage play. This charming double row of small town houses arrayed along a private pedestrian byway was modeled by developer *Thomas Healy* on the stage sets used in the New York production. Quaint and homely, its residents on a charming escapade.

[B73] **Peter Norton Symphony Space**, 2537 Broadway, SW cor. W.95th St. 2002. *Polshek Partnership.* Apartment house surrounding, 2002, *Costas Kondylis.*

In addition to preserving the 827-seat Symphony Space theater, the project recreates the Thalia as a flexible venue. See **Necrology**.

*It was here (above at Symphony Space) that Vincent Astor originally built a street-level produce market and, underneath, in the space that later became the **Thalia Theatre**, a fish market—perhaps on the theory that most mammals ride high, while the fish swim below.*

B74

[B74] **The Columbia**, 275 W.96th St., NW cor. Broadway to W.97th St. 1984. *Liebman Williams Ellis.*

This towering hulk was the first adventure in sophisticated modern housing on the Broadway blocks, followed by the **Montana**, two years later. (Central Park West's **Majestic** and **Century** were earlier housing pioneers in a different sort of West Side milieu.) A bit brash, it borrows from the cubistic dreams of *Walter Gropius* in his wonderful but losing scheme for the Chicago Tribune Tower. But overbuilt and overblown.

[B75] **Holy Name of Jesus Church** (Roman Catholic), Amsterdam Ave., NW cor. W.96th St. 1898. *T. H. Poole.*

A forbidding granite ashlar **Gothic Revival** façade. Enter for a more pleasing architectural experience—particularly the hammer-beamed ceiling and roof.

[B76] Originally **East River Savings Bank**/now **CVS Pharmacy**, 743 Amsterdam Ave., NE cor. W.96th St. 1926-1927. Expanded to N, 1931-1932. Both by *Walker & Gillette.* 🍎

A Classical temple inscribed with exhortations to the thrifty. Note how the **Ionic** columns come down to the sidewalk in the Greek (as opposed to Renaissance) fashion, without pedestals. **Temple to cosmetics?**

[B77] **St. Michael's Church (Episcopal)**, 225 W.99th St., NW cor. Amsterdam Ave. 1891. *Robert W. Gibson.*

A tall and slender tower, crowned with doubled tiers of **neo-Romanesque** arcades, a rounded apse, and a quiet garden. Inside are mosaics and Tiffany glass.

[B78] Originally **Midtown Theatre**/ formerly **Metro Theater**, 2626 Broadway, bet. W.99th and W.100th Sts. E side. 1932-1933. *Boak & Paris.* 🍎

[B81] Originally **Hotel Marseilles**, 2689-2693 Broadway, SW cor. W.103rd St. 1902-1905. *Harry Allan Jacobs.* 🍎

Another Broadway hotel springing from the renderings of the Paris École des Beaux Arts; then impatiently waiting for the opening of the 103rd Street subway stop. Banded **Mannerist** columns, broken pediments at the sky.

[B82] Originally **Horn & Hardart Automat**/now **Rite Aid Drugs**, 2712 Broadway, SE cor. W.104th St. 1930. Altered, 1928, *F.P. Platt & Brother.* 🍎

A faint limestone and glazed terra-cotta memory is recycled as an **Art Deco** drugstore. Look up.

[B83] **Straus Park and Memorial Fountain**/originally **Schuyler Square** (1895-1907)/onetime **Bloomingdale Square**, Broadway and West End Ave., at W.106th St. N side. 1919. *H. Augustus Lukeman*, sculptor. *Evarts Tracy*, architect.

Named Bloomingdale Square in 1907, not for the midtown department store (pure coincidence),

B76

B77

B79

B78

B80

B81

B84

The façade in glazed terra cotta maintains its **Art Deco/Art Moderne** freshness, recalling the 1920s and looking forward to the 1939 New York World's Fair.

[B79] Originally **New York Free Circulating Library**/now **Ukrainian Academy of Arts and Sciences**, 206 W.100th St., bet. Amsterdam Ave. and Broadway. 1898. *James Brown Lord.* 🍎

Beaux Arts **Ionic** above, **Tuscan** below. Libraries were obviously intended as temples of learning in the 1890s, rather than supermarkets for checking out books.

[B80] Originally **Henry Grimm Building**/now **Metro Diner**, 2641 Broadway and 225 W.100th St., NW cor. Broadway. 1871. Addition to W, 1900.

Amid the masonry canyons of Broadway, West End Avenue, and the side streets stands this holdout from the West Side's frontier days. Once a saloon, it now offers more substantial provender. Real building, **retro** memories.

but for the old settlement here of Bloemendael (flower valley in Dutch). The Titanic disaster in 1912 claimed the lives of Macy's owners **Isidor and Ida Straus** whose country house, now the site of an apartment block at 924 West End Avenue, overlooked the triangle. *Lukeman's* **"Memory"** gives a poignant note to this oasis of repose.

[B84] **Ivy Court**, 210, 220, and 230 West 107th St., bet. Amsterdam Ave. and Broadway. 1903. *William C. Hazlett.*

This apartment house trio imparts a **town house scale** by use of streetfront courtyards. Two wings in limestone, three in brick, terra cotta, and limestone. The balconies and ironwork would be worthy in Paris.

[B85] **Church of the Ascension (Roman Catholic)**, 221 W.107th St., bet. Amsterdam Ave. and Broadway. 1897.

A dour rock-faced limestone **Romanesque Revival** surprise, and a pleasant one. Go inside. The adjacent rectory, friendlier, presents its glassy bay window to the street.

[B86] **The Manhasset Apartments**, 2801-2825 Broadway, 301 W.108th St. and 300 W.109th St. W side. First eight stories, 1899-1901. *Joseph Wolf*. Surelevated with three stories and a mansard roof, 1901-1905, *Janes & Leo.* 🐦

The surelevated mansard roof gives a **grand if somber crown** to the building once corniced at the eighth floor. At street level four Composite columns flank Manhasset's entry and support its arched pediment.

NECROLOGY

Christ Church (Episcopal)/later **Bible Deliverance Evangelical Church**, 211 W. 71st St., bet. Broadway and West End Ave. 1890. *Charles C. Haight*. Addition, 1925.

Because its entrance was originally on Broadway—until its valuable frontage was sold off in 1925—the nave of the orange brick and terra-cotta **Romanesque Revival** church ran parallel to West 71st Street. An apartment building now fills the site.

Phoenix House/originally **West 80th Street Community Child Day Care Center**, 223 W.80th St., bet. Amsterdam Ave. and Broadway. 1972. *Kaminsky & Shiffer*.

The hoped-for creative plaything on the scale of side-street architecture didn't make it despite good intentions. Once abandoned, it has been replaced by a lesser work with more floors.

B83

Originally **Dakota Stables**/then **Pyramid Garage**, 348-354 Amsterdam Ave., SW cor. W.77th St. 1894. *Bradford L. Gilbert*.

A brownstone and brick "high rise," originally for horses and carriages, sullied at the ground floor by commerce and gross graphics. Demolished for **The Harrison**.

Formerly Mt. Neboh Synagogue/originally **Unity Synagogue**/later **Adventists' Crossroads Church**, 130 W. 79th St., bet. Columbus and Amsterdam Aves. 1928. *Walter S. Schneider*.

The fastest landmark in the West—the West Side, that is. The artificial stone and granite Byzantine-style structure held the record as an officially designated landmark for the shortest time. Designated in February 1982, de-designated for reasons of economic hardship in February 1983, and demolished soon after. It's now the site of an apartment building.

New Yorker Theater/originally **Adelphi Theatre**/later **Yorktown Theatre**, 2409 Broadway, bet. W.88th and W.89th Sts. W side. 1915. *Rouse & Goldstone*. **New Yorker** (bookstore), 250 W.89th St. SW cor. Broadway.

One of the fine movie theaters that ran films from out of our past, the New Yorker Theater and its colleagues were doomed by upper Broadway's new residential developments. The bookshop, around the corner and up the stairs, was a great place to kill time (browse?) and even buy a book or two before the show started.

Thalia Theatre, 258 W. 95th St., bet. Broadway and West End Ave. 1931. *Ben Schlanger and R. Irrera*.

Who doesn't miss the Thalia? You swore you'd never go there again but then couldn't pass up the magnificent flicks—if your seat didn't flip over backward and the old film didn't catch fire at the moment of *Bogart* and *Bergman's* parting. And those weird sloping

Necrology, Phoenix House

floors: up, yet! The perfect ambiance for *Strangers on a Train* or *Marat/Sade*. What, the Thalia's coming back? Oh, no... And is it a new, squeaky clean family affair? The seats don't flip over??

Grace United Methodist Church/originally **Grace Methodist Episcopal Church**, 131 W. 104th St., bet. Columbus and Amsterdam Aves. 1905. *Berg & See*.

This midblock church, with its orange Roman brick façade, provided a pleasing relief from the drab surroundings.

CENTRAL PARK WEST / THE PARK BLOCKS

While the Upper West Side is a place of contrasts and in constant flux, Central Park West, if not the so-called "park blocks," has generally retained its unflaggingly fashionable quality—at least up through 96th Street. The park blocks began to be converted into rooming houses following World War II, a pattern turned around somewhat by the rising desirability of brownstone living among upwardly mobile middle-class families and by the "singles" of the West Side. In the northern stretch the Urban Renewal Act helped save its row house stock on the park blocks above 86th Street; their health can often be seen to fall off the greater their distance from Central Park. *Olmsted* and *Vaux's* great green space, one of the major attractions in the settlement of the West Side, still acts as an important touchstone.

C1

This precinct begins above Columbus Circle and includes Central Park West up to 96th Street and the park block corridor up to 86th Street. North of 86th Street lies the West Side Urban Renewal Area.

Upper West Side/Central Park West Historic District, 62nd to 96th streets bet. Central Park and a line embracing parts of Columbus and Amsterdam Avenues. See map. 🐦

[C1] **15 Central Park West**, bet. 61st and 62nd Sts. 2007. *Robert A.M. Stern.*
   A stage set: an attempted re-incarnation of the spacious, luxurious apartment architecture constructed along Central Park West between the two world wars. Everything's exaggerated, retro and gigantic, from the marble lobby to the bathrooms, from private screening rooms to wine cellars. **The Century**, next door, was a founding father of this Central Park West apartment row, and the real thing.

[C2] **Century Apartments**, 25 Central Park W., bet. W.62nd and W.63rd Sts. 1931. *Irwin S. Chanin with Jacques Delamarre.* 🐦
   An Art Deco icon, more for the form of its crowning fins and ribbery than for decorative detail (American Art Deco concerned itself with mini-cubistic form; in Paris it was more a question of decorated surfaces). The name recalls a lavish and unprofitable Century Theater, designed by *Carrère & Hastings*, that shared this site and survived for only 21 years. Twin towers are a symbol of Central Park West, recurring at the San Remo, Majestic, and Eldorado.

[C3] **Hall, New York Society for Ethical Culture**, 2 W.64th St., SW cor. Central Park W. 1909-1910. *Robert D. Kohn*, architect. *Estelle Rumbold Kohn*, sculptor. 🐦 [C4] **Ethical Culture School**, 33 Central Park W., NW cor. W.63rd St. 1902-1904. *Carrère & Hastings and Robert D. Kohn.*
   The **Hall** is a clear departure from the Beaux Arts, and cited in the architectural press of its

C5

time as the best Art Nouveau building designed in this century. It has since lost prestige. Not as exuberant as *Hector Guimard's* Parisian efforts or those in Brussels by *Victor Horta*. The school is, for *Carrère and Hastings*, a lesser work.

[C5] **The Prasada**, 50 Central Park W., SW cor. W.65th St. 1905-1907. *Charles W. Romeyn and Henry R. Wynne.*
   Wondrous Baroque banded limestone columns and their entablature, both monumental in scale, are the architectural event at an otherwise awkward apartment block. The rest of the show, the cornice, has succumbed to poor maintenance.

[C6] **Holy Trinity Lutheran Church**, 51 Central Park W., NW cor. W.65th St. 1903. *Schickel & Ditmars.*
   Dour rock-face ecclesiastical limestone breaks Central Park West's phalanx of boxy blocks. The kaleidoscope-like rose window and delicate copper verdigris flèche over the crossing are notable.

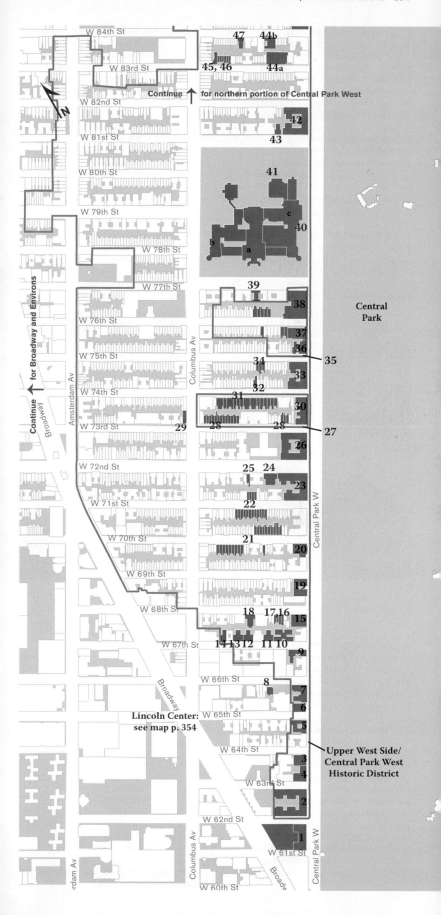

W 84th St
47   44b
45, 46   44a

Continue ↑ for northern portion of Central Park West

W 83rd St
W 82nd St
N
W 81st St
42
W 80th St
43
W 79th St
41
W 78th St   c
40
W 77th St   b   a
W 76th St   39
38
W 75th St   37
36   35
W 74th St   34   33
32
W 73rd St   31
28   28   27
29   30
W 72nd St   26
25 24
23
W 71st St   22
W 70th St   21
20
W 69th St   19
W 68th St   18   17 16
15
W 67th St   14 13 12   11 10
9
W 66th St   8
7
W 65th St   6
5
W 64th St

Lincoln Center:
see map p. 354

Central
Park

Upper West Side/
Central Park West
Historic District

3
4
W 63rd St
2
W 62nd St
1
W 61st St
W 60th St

Amsterdam Av
Broadway
Columbus Av
Central Park W

Continue ← for Broadway and Environs

[C7] **55 Central Park West**, SW cor. W.66th St. 1930. *Schwartz & Gross.*

Art Deco evolved through a carefully studied modulation of colored brick planes and boldly fluted ornament. With this one, if the sun seems brighter at the top than the bottom, it is brighter. A flush of brick from red to yellow rises from the second floor to the sun.

[C8] **Congregation Habonim**, 44 W.66th St., bet. Central Park W. and Columbus Ave. 1957. *Stanley Prowler and Frank Faillance.*

A stained-glass cube set 45 degrees to itself and its neighbors along the street. Its setback permits a better understanding of the old armory next door.

For the **American Broadcasting Company** buildings, see **Lincoln Center**.

Studio Street: The park block of West 67th Street is a haven for those who like studio living or living among artists: there are no fewer

[C11] **Central Park Studios**, 15 West 67th Street, bet. Central Park W. and Columbus Ave. 1904-1905. *B.H. Simonson* and *Pollard & Steinam.*

Neo-Gothic portal and lobby. Apparently, before the First World War, the "Artist" donned Gothic dress for his/her studio building, a cultural signal.

[C12] **67th Street Atelier Building**, 33 W.67th St., bet. Central Park W. and Columbus Ave. 1904-1905. *B.H. Simonson* and *Pollard & Steinam.*

One of the first buildings in the City built as a co-op. The carved limestone detail is lovely.

[C13] **Macaulay Honors College, City University of New York (CUNY)**/originally **Swiss Home of the Swiss Benevolent Society**, 35 W.67th St., bet. Central Park W. and Columbus Ave. 1904-1905. *John E. Scharsmith.*

A Beaux Arts interpretation of the North European Renaissance, but with both pointed and elliptical arches. Swiss cheese.

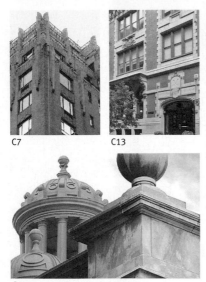

C7   C13

C15   C10

than six studio buildings on the block. Among them:

[C9] **70 Central Park West**, SW cor. W.67th St. 1916-1919. *Rich & Mathesius.*

A bland 15-story studio building, but the two-story industrial sash that illuminates the duplex apartments is spectacular (particularly for those within).

[C10] **Hotel des Artistes**, 1 W.67th St., bet. Central Park W. and Columbus Ave. 1915-1918. *George Mort Pollard.* Café redecorated, 1979, *Judith Stockman & Assocs.*

The Gothicized façade clearly reveals balconied studios within, places of light and spatial volume. An early tenant, *Howard Chandler Christy,* painted a pinup girl (his specialty) to decorate the cozy **Café des Artistes** on the first floor. An all-time roster of tenants of the elaborate (and lavish) spaces would also span from *Isadora Duncan* to congressman-mayor *John V. Lindsay.*

[C14] **39-41 West 67th Street**, bet. Central Park W. and Columbus Ave. 1906-1907. *Pollard & Steinam.*

Four stacks of bay windows zip up the street façade of this tall narrow studio building. Sheet metal, not masonry, here creates an early curtain wall. And the cornice, copper-clad and modilioned, is monumental.

Tavern on the Green: The entrance to this chronically remodeled eating-drinking-dancing spot, built around Central Park's 1870 sheepfold, is at 67th Street and Central Park West. Expensive. (At night the trees, wrapped to their roots in minilights, suggest an invasion of the bulb people.) The flocks that lived here maintained the lawns of the Park, noiselessly.

[C15] **Second Church of Christ, Scientist**, 77 Central Park W., SW cor. W.68th St. 1899-1901. *Frederick R. Comstock.*

Its copper-clad green domes, best seen from the edge of the park, cap a crisp neo-Classical limestone building.

C19

[C16] **14 West 68th Street**, bet. Central Park W. and Columbus Ave. S side. 1895. *Louis Thouvard.*
A somber mansarded brick and brownstone town house entered from its adjacent open green space, the latter serving the whole block in spatial counterpoint.

A wondrous projecting bracketed copper cornice hover, benignly, over brick limestone and terra cotta. Raise your eyes, it gets better as it goes up.

C16

C20

C17

C18

C21, NO.21

[C17] **16-22 West 68th Street**, bet. Central Park W. and Columbus Ave. 1896. *George F. Pelham.*
Roman brick, terra cotta, and limestone bow- and bay-fronted houses, stoop-less, with entries up a step or three.

[C18] Originally **The Free Synagogue**/now **York Preparatory School**/onetime **Hebrew Union College-Jewish Institute of Religion**, 40 W.68th St., bet. Central Park W. and Columbus Ave. 1923. *S.B. Eisendrath & B. Horowitz.*
[C18a] **Stephen Wise Free Synagogue**, 30 W.68th St. 1949. *Bloch & Hesse.*
Wan Collegiate Gothic clad in Manhattan Schist ashlar (cut stone). Today's school (once college) building was the sanctuary until the new one was begotten in 1941. An important center of the Reform Jewish movement.

[C19] **The Brentmore**, 88 Central Park W., SW cor. W.69th St. 1909-1910. *Schwartz & Gross.*

[C20] **Congregation Shearith Israel** (the Spanish and Portuguese Synagogue), 99 Central Park W., SW cor. W.70th St. 1896-1897. *Brunner & Tryon.* ☛
The newest home of New York's oldest Jewish congregation, its temple drew its formal vocabulary from the glittering 1893 Chicago World's Fair; an architectural decision far from the then modish Moorish/Middle Eastern Synagogue architecture elsewhere in America.
Shearith Israel was founded in 1655 in New Amsterdam by Spanish and Portuguese immigrants, mostly moving from Brazil. Three venerable Shearith Israel cemeteries that resisted the march of progress, and remain in Manhattan, belong to this congregation [see index].

[C21] **Row houses, W.70th St., bet. Central Park W. and Columbus Ave.** Early 1890s.
Bay-windowed, **Nos.9-19** intermingle yellow Roman brick with brownstone façades. **Nos.21** and **24** offer grand meandering stoops. **Nos.40-58** again try for individuality within a developer's terrace.

[C22] **Row houses**, W.71st St., bet. Central Park W. and Columbus Ave. Late 1880s/early 1890s.

No.24 is extraordinary, with its unusual stoop, cupids at its cornice, and concave shell-molded lintels over the topmost windows. **Nos.26, 28,** and **30** show that handsome houses come in threes: an elegant russet color scheme (brick, stone, terra cotta, and the cartouches) and wide doors that must certainly have encouraged the purchase of expansive furnishings. On the stoops of **Nos.32-40** a gentle separation of the balusters as they reach the sidewalk subtly signals you to enter. Across the street **Nos.33-39** offer both hungry and satiated lion's-heads to decorate the doorway keystones. An architectural feast.

[C23] **Majestic Apartments**, 115 Central Park W., bet. W.71st and W.72nd Sts. 1930-1931. *Irwin S. Chanin with Jacques Delamarre*. 🍎

This Art Deco masterpiece enjoys wide bands of windows that loop around its sides,

[C25] **42 West 72nd Street**, bet. Central Park W. and Columbus Ave. 1915. *Buchman & Fox*.

Yet another lanky white studio tower by developer *"Daddy" Browning*.

[C26] **Dakota Apartments**, 1 W.72nd St., NW cor. Central Park W. to W.73rd St. 1880-1884. *Henry J. Hardenbergh*. 🍎

The City's first luxury apartment house. Designed for Singer Sewing Machine heir *Edward S. Clark*, it dominated Central Park before the park drives were even paved. A prestige address, particularly for those in the arts, since the days when this part of the City was thought as remote as the Dakota Territory. Note the railings: griffins and Zeuses, Neptunes and sea monsters?

Clark boasted in his prospectus that it is "where persons of ease can find a home equal in every comfort and luxury to a first-class private dwelling house and without the discomforts and inconveniences of the ordinary hotel."

C22

C27

C28, NO.43

C23   C25

C29

C31

brickwork patterns, and futurist forms by sculptor *René Chambellan* and the talents of *Irwin Chanin* developer-architect and his French associate, *Jacques Delamarre*. Its twin towers are one of the five sets (including the Beresford) that make Central Park West's skyline memorable.

[C24] **The Oliver Cromwell**, 12 W.72nd St., bet. Central Park W. and Columbus Ave. 1927. *Emery Roth*.

A monotower among the array of twin-towered Central Park West. A pioneer, for *Chanin's* **Majestic** came later. A tempietto crowns an octagonal drum, perforated with oculi. The crown is better enjoyed from a neighboring penthouse!

[C27] **Central Park West-W.73rd Street-W.74th Street Historic District**. The entire block between W.73rd and W.74th Sts., Central Park W. and Columbus Ave: subsumed within the Upper West Side/Central Park West Historic District. 🍎

[C28] **15A-19 and 41-65 West 73rd Street**, bet. Central Park W. and Columbus Ave. 1882-1885.
[C29] **101 and 103 West 73rd Street**, NW cor. Columbus Ave. 1879-1880. All by *Henry J. Hardenbergh*.

Another collaboration of the client (*Clark*) and architect (*Hardenbergh*) of the **Dakota**. Light brownstone and brick, they lack the flair of the Dakota.

[C30] **The Langham**, 135 Central Park W., bet. W.73rd and W.74th Sts. 1904-1907. *Clinton & Russell*.

A ponderous hulk, dull, except at the roofline, where a simple cornice has been so elaborated with ornament and ornate dormers that it sparkles with light.

C26

[C31] **18-52 West 74th Street**, bet. Central Park W. and Columbus Ave. 1902-1904. *Percy Griffin.*

A phalanx of 18 brick and limestone neo-Georgian speculator's row houses fills the block's south side, each bearing names such as **Park Terrace, Riverside**, and **Hayden Manor**. Built to compete with apartment buildings, then growing in popularity, these 25-foot-wide, 17- to 19-room houses each boasted four or five bathrooms and an electric elevator. Subsequently there was easy conversion to school and other institutional uses. Nice balcony ironwork.

[C32] **37 West 74th Street**, bet. Central Park W. and Columbus Ave. N side. 1889. *Thom & Wilson.*

Belle of the block. Sturdy Ionic pilasters frame the bow window. Below glorious diamond rustications give a special identity and support it all. Lovingly overrestored.

[C33] **San Remo Apartments**, 145-146 Central Park W., bet. W.74th and W.75th Sts. 1929-1930. *Emery Roth.* 🖌

Twin towers surmounted by those ubiquitous Hellenistic temples, finialed, against the sky. A base and bustle of chunky apartments sits below. Classical parts and limestone serenity here rule, in contrast with the Art Deco world of the **Century, Majestic,** and **El Dorado**.

[C34] **34, 36, & 38 West 75th Street**, bet. Central Park W. and Columbus Aves. S side. 1889-1890. *George H. Budlong.*

The gabled streetfronts alternate, colonettes supporting mock-medieval tympanums at **Nos.34** and **38**, dour rusticated brownstone at **No.36**.

[C35] **Central Park West-76th Street Historic District**, Central Park W. bet. W.75th and W.77th Sts., including W.76th St. W to Nos.51 and 56, and 44 W.77th St. Subsumed within the Upper West Side/Central Park West Historic District. 🖌

In addition to the buildings on Central Park

West and West 77th Street, covered below, the Historic District encompasses a variety of row housing along West 76th Street dating from 1889 to 1900. The earliest, **Nos.27-37**, are by architect *George M. Walgrove*, who used alternately smooth stone with neo-Grec incised detail, and the then newly fashionable rock-faced stonework. The most recent, **Nos.8-10**, are flamboyant Upper East Side neo-Baroque town houses by *John H. Duncan*, designer of Grant's Tomb and Brooklyn's Soldiers' and Sailors' Memorial Arch. **No.34** is notable for its contrasting smooth and rockface brownstone. Works by other architects fill in both sides of the block: *Gilbert A. Schellenger, Schickel & Ditmars,* and *Cleverdon & Putzel.* The architecture is decorative, the designation abounding with references to garlanded brackets, Herculean heads, elegant cartouches, and spiral colonnettes.

[C36] **The Kenilworth**, 151 Central Park W., NW cor. W.75th St. 1906-1908. *Townsend, Steinle & Haskell.*

C32, see page 45

An imposing russet-brick and limestone *frosted wedding cake*, topped by a Parisian convex mansard roof. The great sub-cornice at the ninth floor and broken pediments at the fifth floor are the frosted highlights. The entry portal is the best part: Mannerist columns embrace a pedimented doorway.

[C37] Originally **Church of the Divine Paternity, Fourth Universalist Society**/now **Universalist Church of New York and Parish House**, 4 W.76th St., SW cor. Central Park W. 1897-1898. *William A. Potter.*

Oxford University on Central Park West: this church sports a neo-Gothic tower reminiscent of Oxford's Magdalen College. Flush limestone walls enhance, in contrast, the strength of the neo-Gothic detail.

[C38] **New-York Historical Society**, 170 Central Park W., bet. W.76th and W.77th Sts. Central portion, 1903-1908. *York & Sawyer.* N and S wings, 1937-1938. *Walker & Gillette.* ☗

Modifications, 2007, *Platt Byard Dovell White.* Tu-Sa, 10-6; Fr, 10-8; Su, 11-5:45. 212-873-3400; *www.nyhistory.org*

Reminiscent of a Parisian bibliothèque, this neo-Roman museum, library, and exhibition building is an important center for American and local history. An Ionic colonnade frames the great reading room. Among the library's vast holdings are the *McKim, Mead & White* files and the 432 original watercolors of *John James Audubon's Birds of America.*

[C39] **The Studio Building**, 44 W.77th St., bet. Central Park W. and Columbus Ave. 1907-1909. *Harde & Short.*

Several of the adjacent apartments along West 77th Street replaced row housing when abundant and unobstructed north light encouraged redevelopment. Although a great deal of terra cotta was removed in 1944, the lacy tapestry of the Studio building's **neo-Gothic** façade is still breathtaking.

C35

C36

[C40] **American Museum of Natural History**, Manhattan Sq., Central Park W. to Columbus Ave., W.77th to W.81st St. General plan and first wing, 1872-1877. *Calvert Vaux and J. Wrey Mould.* [C40a] **W.77th Street frontage**, and auditorium, 1888-1908. *J.C. Cady & Co. (later Cady, Berg & See).* [C40b] **Southwest wing** (Columbus Ave.), 1905-1908. *Charles Volz.* **Powerhouse**, 1927-1932. **Southeast wing**, 1912-1924. Both by *Trowbridge & Livingston.* ☗ Interior. ☗ [C40c] **Theodore Roosevelt Memorial**, Central Park W., 1931-1934. *John Russell Pope*, architect. Roosevelt statue and heroic figures on attic. *James Earle Fraser*, sculptor. Animal relief, *James L. Clark*, sculptor. **Library**, 1990-1992. *Kevin Roche John Dinkeloo Assocs.* Daily 10-5:45. 212-769-5100. *www.amnh.org*

Conceived by *Vaux and Mould* to be the largest building on the continent. The museum trustees had other thoughts, and *V&M's* wing (the first) is now visible, only barely, from Columbus Avenue. The best parts of the complex are *Cady's* Vermont granite **Romanesque**

Revival façade, towers, and stairs on West 77th Street—though Pope's pompous Central Park West façade, the **Roosevelt Memorial**, gets the publicity photos and therefore **seems** important.

T-Square in the New Yorker, *February 13, 1932, referring to the then new* Roosevelt Memorial: *"This Classic monument, so painfully, so grotesquely inappropriate, so defiantly out of the picture of the Museum itself…"*

[C41] **Frederick Phineas and Sandra Priest Rose Center for Earth and Space,** including: **New Hayden Planetarium,** American Museum of Natural History, W.81st St., bet. Central Park W. and Columbus Ave. S side. 2000. *Polshek Partnership.* Exhibition designer, *Ralph Applebaum Associates.* Landscape architect, *Judith Heintz.* Daily, 10-5:45; till 8:45 for "Starry Nights." 212-769-5100. *www.amnh.org*
An illuminated, glistening 90-foot-diameter sphere "floats" within a glass cube as if a reincarnated *Boullée* (alias *Polshek*), invigorated

[C44a] **Congregation Rodeph Sholom,** 7 W.83rd St., bet. Central Park W. and Columbus Ave. N side. 1928-1930. *Charles B. Meyers.*
[C44b] **Day School,** 12 W.84th St. 1974-1977. *William Roper.*
A stolid synagogue with delicately incised **neo-Romanesque** limestone arches. The school (facing the next block) follows a 1970s fad of deeply recessed windows and sloped brick reveals. It is, in fact, a reconstruction of a group of row houses.

[C45] **65, 67, and 69 West 83rd Street,** and **71 West 83rd Street,** bet. Central Park W. and Columbus Ave. N side. 1884-1885. *George W. DaCunha.*
These exuberant **Queen Anne** row houses were planned so that **No.69** carries their recessed façades out to the building line, where the group curtsies to **No.71,** a restrained and exquisitely detailed apartment house.

C42

C40

C45, NO.69

C47

with hi-tech wisdom, had fulfilled one of his marvelous Revolutionary (French, that is) fantasies. The building adjoins **Theodore Roosevelt Park,** beautifully re-designed by *Heintz.*

[C42] **Beresford Apartments,** 1 and 7 W.81st St. and 211 Central Park W., NW cor. 1928-1929. *Emery Roth.*
Named for the hotel it replaced, the **Beresford** is another of Central Park West's twin-towered luxury apartment buildings, but with a plus: it has a twin-towered silhouette visible not only from the east but also from the south, a result of four Baroquoid tile-roofed projections to the sky.

[C43] **Hayden House,** 11 W.81st St., bet. Central Park W. and Columbus Ave. N side. 1906-1908. *Schickel & Ditmars.*
Here cast-iron balconies modulated the façade, all topped with a mansard roof and dormer windows.

[C46] **59, 61, and 63 West 83rd Street,** bet. Central Park W. and Columbus Ave. 1890s.
The rusticated, alternately smooth- and rock-faced brownstone bays establish a strong rhythm on the streetscape.

[C47] **Church of St. Matthew and St. Timothy,** 26 W.84th St., bet. Central Park W. and Columbus Ave. S side. 1970. *Victor Christ-Janer.*
This radical, cast-in-place concrete church was built after a disastrous fire destroyed its predecessor. The stark exterior does not prepare you for the carefully modulated circum-ambulatory entry and what you find within: a rich combination of white (plaster) and gray (concrete) surfaces set off by warm natural wood pews.

C51

C55

C53

[C48] **241 Central Park West**, NW cor. W.84th St. 1930-1931. *Schwartz & Gross.*
Subtly colored giant glazed terra-cotta ears of corn sprout (literally) from the brickwork of this **Art Deco** structure. The West 84th Street side is beautifully modeled at street level.

[C49] **247-249 Central Park West**, SW cor. 85th St. 1888. *Edward L. Angell.*
Sturdy Queen Anne survivors from an earlier Central Park West. The bay windows are a park-viewers dream. Built in the time of **The Dakota.**

[C50] **53-75 West 85th Street**, bet. Central Park W. and Columbus Ave. N side. 1886-1887. *George H. Griebel.*
Serrated gables against the sky punctuate this long row of brick and limestone **Queen Anne** town houses.

[C51] **32-36 West 85th Street**, bet. Central Park W. and Columbus Ave. S side. 1897. *George F. Pelham.*

Five stories of Roman brickwork, their alternate undulating bays articulated by a quartet of terra-cotta Ionic columns.

[C52] **44 and 46 West 85th Street**, bet. Central Park W. and Columbus Ave. S side. 1886-1887. *Edward L. Angell.*
Offbeat. Multi-paned and multi-sashed bay windows, exuberant dormers, and coats of paint that exaggerate it all.

[C53] **70 West 85th Street**, bet. Central Park W. and Columbus Ave. S side. 1894-1895. *John G. Prague.*
The incised projecting brownstone supporting the bay window and that cresting the stepped entry-step walls recalls foliate vines, much like that in the work of *Louis Sullivan.*

[C54a] **Bard College Graduate Center**, 18 W. 86th St., bet. Central Park W. and Columbus Ave. S side. 1905. Renovated, *Polshek Partnership.* Museum hours: Tu, We, Fr-Su, 11-5; Th 11-8. *www.bgc.bard.edu*

The **Beaux Arts** façade remains, but behind it the body was stripped to its bones, two floors added on top, and all was extended to the rear. A face of a gracious turn-of-the-century town house masks modern innards.

[C54b] **Rossleigh Court**, 1 W.85th St., NW cor. Central Park W. 1906-1907. **Orwell House**/formerly **Hotel Peter Stuyvesant**/originally **Central Park View**, 257 Central Park W., SW cor. W.86th St. 1905-1906. Both by *Mulliken & Moeller*.

Twin **Beaux Arts** apartment buildings occupying the full Central Park West blockfront. They are of a disarming and cheery purplish brick, set off to advantage by elaborate limestone trim.

Renewal Area: Central Park West's frontages between West 87th and 97th Streets and the park blocks in that stretch lay within the official boundaries of the old 1970s West Side Urban Renewal Area. CPW's apartment buildings (with the exception of No.325) did not directly benefit from the designation; but many of the side-street brownstones, converted into single-room occupancy and rooming houses, did. (No.235, slated to be demolished, was saved, upgraded, and turned into a co-op.) For the side streets, therefore, see the precinct called West Side Urban Renewal Area; for the continuation of CPW's buildings uptown to West 97th, see below.

[C55] **279 Central Park West**, NW cor. W.88th St. 1987-1990. *Costas Kondylis*.

Bay windows embraced within the front plane of Central Park West, a subtle trick

C57   C58

borrowed from the late 19th century, and a crowning **ziggurat**.

[C56] **The Walden School/Andrew Goodman Building**, 11-15 W.88th St., bet. Central Park W. and Columbus Ave. N side. 1974. *Edgar Tafel*.

The desire to relate the addition's façade to that of the now-demolished Progress Club, the school's Classical Revival original building, is commendable. The result, on the other hand, **misses the mark**. The demolished parent building (1904. *Louis Korn*) had almost a postmodern look, with its hefty columns supporting thin air. For better *Tafel* see the **First Presbyterian Church House** at Fifth Avenue and West 11th Street.

Moses King, author and publisher of the incomparable King's Handbooks and King's Views of New York City (and the cities of Brooklyn and Boston and even of the United States) lived in The Minnewaska, an eight-story apartment house that once stood at 2 West 88th Street. He died there on June 12, 1909.

[C57] **The St. Urban**, 285 Central Park W., SW cor. W.89th St. 1904-1905. *Robert T. Lyons*.

Central Park West's only single-towered apartment building, its tower splendidly crowned by dome and cupola, gray slate shingles, and verdigris trim. And all is festooned with 16 broken-pediment dormers.

[C58] **The Eldorado**, 300 Central Park W., W.90th to W.91st Sts. 1929-1930. *Margon & Holder*, architect. *Emery Roth*, consultant.

The northernmost of CPW's twin-towered apartment houses. **Art Deco** metalwork embellishes the base (subtle bronze reliefs) and the towers (*Flash Gordon* finials).

[C59] **The Ardsley**, 320 Central Park W., SW cor. W.92nd St. 1930-1931. *Emery Roth*.

Mayan influences appear in this **Art Deco** apartment building, particularly in the modeling of the upper stories. At street level, closest to the eye, are precast exposed-aggregate

C60

terrazzo reliefs in subtle colors and forms. Compare this with the **San Remo**, completed by the same firm the previous year!

[C60] **The Raleigh**, 7 W.92nd St., bet. Central Park W. and Columbus Ave. N side. 1899-1900. *Gilbert A. Schellenger*.

A magnificent tenement that modulates the street with its columnar bays, and displays mannered and luscious rustications at its lower floors.

[C61] **Columbia Grammar and Preparatory School**, 5 W.93rd St., bet. Central Park W. and Columbus Ave. N side. 1907. *Beatty & Stone*. Remodeled, 1987, *Pasanella & Klein*.

Savor the **neo-Classical** frieze (parthenogenesis?) adorning this building below its surprising Classical-Moderne, deep, flat cornice.

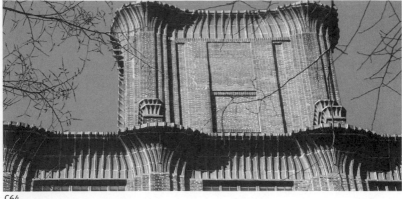

C64

[C62] **Columbia Grammar and Preparatory School**, 4 W.93rd St., bet. Central Park W. and Columbus Ave. S side. 1986. *Pasanella + Klein.*

A **gentle intruder**, scaled for its context, with crossed blue mullions framed within

C62

C63   C66

squares: a lively and elegant neighbor to its 19th-century neighbors.

[C63] **The Turin**, 333 Central Park W., NW cor. W.93rd St. 1909-1910. *Albert J. Bodker.*

Study the Roman medallions in the spandrels, but savor the quarter-sphere marquee over the entry.

[C64] **336 Central Park West**, SW cor. W.94th St. 1928-1929. *Schwartz & Gross.*

This 16-story apartment house is crowned with terra-cotta reminiscences of an Egyptian-styled cavetto cornice (**Art Deco Egyptian**, not the Egyptian Revival of the 1840s). The tapestry brick enriches the viewer's experience closer to eye level.

The West 95th Street park block, a diverting detour, is described below in the West Side Urban Renewal Area.

[C65] **353 Central Park West**, NW cor. W.95th St. 1992. *Yorgancioglu Architects & The Vilkas Group.*

This subsumed **Nos.351, 352**, and **353**, original partners of the designated pair below. The replacement, happily, has enlivening setbacks cascading to the stolid streetface, and modeled

brickwork worthy of the Central Park West landscape. Cigarette baron *Solomon Schinasi* owned the now vanished **No.351** in 1906, before buying the Rice House on Riverside Drive.

[C66] **354 and 355 Central Park West**, bet. W.95th and W.96th Sts. 1892-1893. *Gilbert A. Schellenger.* 🍎

Twin early West Side speculative houses that look as though they belong on a side street, from the era when no one believed Central Park West would be anything else.

[C67] **First Church of Christ, Scientist**, 1 W.96th St., NW cor. Central Park W. 1899-1903. *Carrère & Hastings.* 🍎

The architects of the Beaux Arts-style **New York Public Library** at Fifth Avenue and 42nd Street flirt with the forms of *Nicholas Hawksmoor's* great **Baroque churches** in London. Exciting.

C67

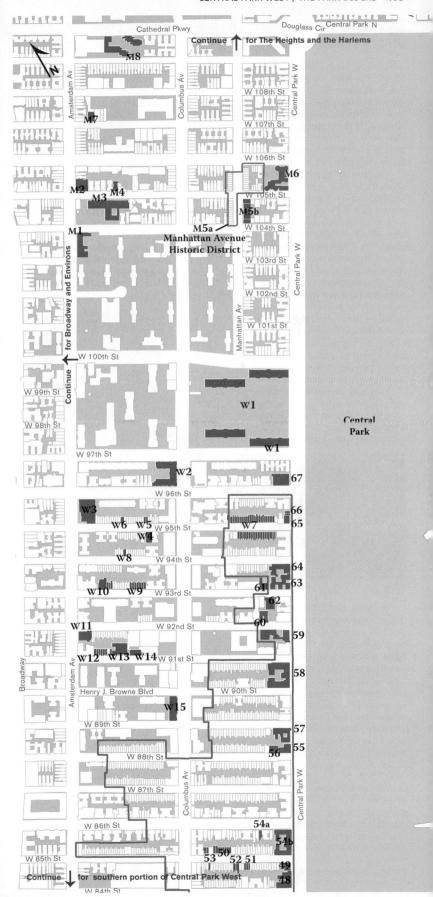

Douglass Cir   Central Park N

Cathedral Pkwy

Continue ↑ for The Heights and the Harlems

N

M8

Amsterdam Av

Columbus Av

Central Park W

W 108th St

M7

W 107th St

W 106th St

M2   M4   M6

M3   W 105th St

M5b

M5a   W 104th St

M1   Manhattan Avenue
Historic District   W 103rd St

W 102nd St

Manhattan Av   W 101st St

for Broadway and Environs

Central Park W

← W 100th St

Continue

W 99th St

W 98th St   W1

Central
Park

W 97th St   W1

W2   67

W 96th St

W3   66

W6   W5   W7   65

W4   W 95th St

W8   W 94th St   64

W10   W9   W 93rd St   63

61   62   60

W11   W 92nd St   59

W12   W13   W14   W 91st St   58

Henry J. Browne Blvd

W15   W 90th St   57

W 89th St   55   56

Broadway

Amsterdam Av   W 88th St

W 87th St

Columbus Av

W 86th St   Central Park W

54a

W 85th St   54b

53   50   52   51   49

Continue ↓ for southern portion of Central Park West   48

W 84th St

WEST SIDE
URBAN RENEWAL AREA

The blocks between West 87th and West 97th Streets, from Amsterdam Avenue to Central Park West, sheltered 40,000 residents in 1956, when this area's acute social and physical decline indicated a need for public action. In a series of moves the district, one of the nation's most densely populated, was designated the West Side Urban Renewal Area, and plans were drawn for change.

The concepts that emerged were radically different from those of earlier renewal efforts. Exploitation of the highest possible rental scales was abandoned. Clearance and rebuilding from scratch, once the only redevelopment tools, were combined with rehabilitation and renovation, particularly of the basically sound side-street brownstone row houses. Steps were taken to ensure an economic and social mix within the district by providing not only separate low-rent projects but also low-rent families within middle-income developments. Finally, the plan provided for phased development from West 97th Street south to encourage the relocation of on-site tenants. The plan as amended called for 2,500 low-income units, 5,421 middle-income units, and 151 luxury units. In addition, 485 brownstones were to be saved and renovated.

The results are most visible architecturally along Columbus Avenue, which is lined with high-rise construction. The side streets have been more subtly upgraded: behind the façades, in backyards, and with added street trees.

W1

spaces. Developers had acquired six blocks of tenements at a reduced price from the City under the federal urban renewal program. Instead of developing the site they sat tight for five years, collecting rents, neglecting repairs, and inventing ingenious schemes to exploit their unhappy tenants. Some say these disclosures marked the beginning of construction czar *Robert Moses'* loss of power.

West Side Urban Renewal Area

[W2] **Key West**, 750 Columbus Ave., bet. W.96th and W.97th Sts. W side. 1987. *Schuman, Lichtenstein, Claman & Efron.*

Bay-windowed and bold, **Key West** forms a happier relationship with its context than do many of the architecturally self-conscious towers of earlier urban renewal.

W6

One thing is clear. The renewal effort, though not without its critics, did much to reverse the decline of this part of the West Side. Unlike other West Side precincts in this Guide, this one proceeds from north to south to reflect the phasing of the redevelopment plan. Although the first project, **Park West Village**, actually predates these plans (it is within another urban renewal area, West Park), we include it first, both as a logical part of the urban renewal story and as an example of the techniques that had been abandoned. Start at West 96th Street and Amsterdam; then continue over to Columbus and proceed south.

[W1] **Park West Village**, 784, 788, 792 Columbus Ave., bet. W.97th to W.100th Sts. 1957-1958. 372, 382, 392, 400 Central Park W., 1958-1961. *S.J. Kessler & Sons.*

This large and banal housing development was built in the aftermath of a 1957 urban renewal scandal, with the then usual slab-and-balcony domino blocks and vast parking

[W3] **New Amsterdam**, 733 Amsterdam Ave., bet. W.95th and W.96th Sts. E side. 1971. *Gruzen & Partners.*

Concrete balconies, private with cheek walls, exposed concrete floor slabs, and floor-to-floor window assemblies, contribute to a better-than-average effort.

[W4] **Congregation Ohab Zedek**, 118 W.95th St., bet. Columbus and Amsterdam Aves. S side. 1926. *Charles B. Meyers.*

Intricate terra-cotta ornament enriches the tall **Byzantine** arch that dominates the façade.

[W5] **123 and 125 West 95th Street**, bet. Columbus and Amsterdam Aves. N side.

Unique three-story brick and brownstone houses.

[W6] **Claude A. Vissani House**, 143 West 95th Street, bet. Columbus and Amsterdam Aves. N side. 1889. *James W. Cole.* ●

W2

W5

W7

W8

Exuberant **neo-Gothicism** as if done in the Renaissance fashion by a student trained at the École des Beaux Arts. It is a grand presence on this handsome block. *Vissani*, a Roman Catholic priest, used this as a base for promoting the preservation of holy places in Jerusalem and Palestine.

[W7] **West 95th Street**, bet. Central Park W.and Columbus Ave.

Diversely styled row houses, luxuriant trees, and lots of care make this one of the loveliest of the park blocks. A leisurely walk will reveal delightful touches: sculpted griffins and cherubs, fine lanterns, simply designed metal guards around the street-tree pits. **Nos.27** and **29** (1887. *Charles T. Mott*) display unique and glassy segmental bay windows, and **No.14** (1889. *George Holiday*, builder) bears the fluted and unfluted pilasters and arches of the American Renaissance. The rhapsodic architectural exercise in circles and arcs at the entrances, balconies, and stoops of **Nos.6** and **8** (1894. *Horace Edgar Hartwell*) is a small delight.

[W8] **141 West 94th Street**, bet. Columbus and Amsterdam Aves. N side. 1900s.

The ornate pressed-metal bay window and cornice give this some personal eccentricity.

[W9] **125-139 and 151-159 West 93rd Street**, bet. Columbus and Amsterdam Aves. N side. ca. 1890.

Two groups of Queen Anne façades in red and gray. Curiously restrained for this style.

[W10] **Templo Adventista del Septimo Dia**/originally **The Nippon Club**, 161 W.93rd St., bet. Columbus and Amsterdam Aves. 1912. *John Van Pelt*.

The **Chicago School** (of Architecture) cross-bred with Florence: the brick frieze alternates with windows, simulating the metopes and triglyphs of a Greek temple (as borrowed for the Italian Renaissance). The cornice is extraordinary; it sails overhead with the assurance of *Lorenzo de' Medici*.

[W11] **Central Baptist Church,** 659 Amsterdam Ave., SE cor. W.92nd St. 1915-1916.

Collegiate Gothic, with a corner tower worthy of *Ralph Adams Cram.* Marvel at the crockets and finials.

[W12] **149-163 West 91st Street,** bet. Columbus and Amsterdam Aves. 1890s.

Soulmates with **Trinity School** next door, some of their spaces have been co-opted by their next-door neighbor. Would you rather live

W14

W11

W15b

W13

in one of these venerable Romanesque brownstones or in **Trinity House** down the block?

[W13] **Trinity School,** Main Building, 121-147 W.91st St., bet. Columbus and Amsterdam Aves. N side. 1893-1894. *Charles C. Haight.* 🍎

[W14] **East Building**/originally **Parish House, St. Agnes Chapel** (Episcopal), adjacent to and east of main building. 1888-1892. *William A. Potter.* Restorations, 1990s, *Buttrick, White & Burtis.* 🍎

Founded in 1709. Among the many interlocking buildings that this school occupies are the **Anglo-Italianate** brownstone Main Building, the wonderful Romanesque Revival remnant of an otherwise demolished Trinity Parish outpost (**St. Agnes Chapel**), and the podium of **Trinity House,** an apartment building.

[W15a] **600 Columbus Avenue** (apartments), bet. W.89th and W.90th Sts. W side. 1987.

[W15b] **103-105 West 89th Street,** bet. Columbus and Amsterdam Aves. 1987.

[W15c] **Community Garden,** bet. W.89th and W.90th St. behind 600 Columbus Ave. 1988. All by *Hoberman & Wasserman,* architects. *The Schnadelbach Partnership,* landscape architect.

The greenhouses along Columbus Avenue make a graceful transition from the setback slab and the streetfront stores below. The **"town houses"** are a pleasant bow to the tradition of the side-streeted West Side. But whereas most of the West Side was originally composed of single-family houses, these were built to be apartment units from the start. This was both designed and developed by *Joe Wasserman.*

M1

MANHATTAN VALLEY

A new event in Manhattan's usually predictable gridiron plan occurs at West 100th Street. It is here, between Central Park West and Columbus Avenue, that a new north-south thoroughfare is born: Manhattan Avenue, which strikes out northward across Cathedral Parkway into Harlem. As it moves north, the topography it covers begins to drop (as does the economic level of the community), and this descent of the terrain has given rise to the area's unofficial name: **Manhattan Valley**. We define it in this Guide as bordered by West 100th Street and Cathedral Parkway (West 110th Street) and by Central Park West and Amsterdam Avenue.

[M1] **Hosteling International-USA**/originally **Association for Respectable Aged Indigent Females**, 891 Amsterdam Ave., bet. W.103rd and W.104th Sts. E side. 1881-1883. *Richard Morris Hunt.* Addition, 1907-1908, *Charles A. Rich.* ●❦ Converted to hostel, 1990, *Larsen Associates.*

Vacated by the **Association** in 1975, this institutional landmark, once open only to women who had not "lived as servants," is now an international youth hostel. Red brick and brownstone, its busy, dormered, gabled roof lines are redolent of Victorian London.

[M2] **West End Presbyterian Church**, 325 Amsterdam Ave., NE cor. 1 W.105th St. 1891. *Henry Kilburn.*

Restrained **Romanesque Revival**—in the subdued north Italian mode, much in contrast to *H. H. Richardson's* lusty works. The tall, delicately striped, brick corner tower anchors this intersection from afar. The pressed terra-cotta ornament reads as incised stone, delicate in its intricate detail.

[M3] **Public School 145**, Manhattan, The Bloomingdale School, 150 W.105th St., bet. Columbus and Amsterdam Aves. S side. 1961. *Unger & Unger.*

M2

Bright vermilion columns, with a concrete entrance canopy reminiscent of angels' wings, highlight this school's façade. A faded outpost of the **modernist** sixties.

[M4] **St. Gerasimos Greek Orthodox Church**, 155 W.105th St., bet. Columbus and Amsterdam Aves. N side. 1951. *Kokkins & Lyons.*

A historicist design that "foresaw the future": a later **postmodernist** might have been pleased to accomplish this exaggerated façade. The **neo-Byzantine** capitals are charming.

[M5a] **Manhattan Avenue Historic District**, 101-137 and 120-159 Manhattan Ave. 10-51 W.105th St. and 34-44 W.106th St. ●❦
Included are 37 three-story row houses, one six-story apartment building and two structures built by General Memorial Hospital for the **New-York Cancer Hospital**. See map.

M4

M5a

M6

[M5b] **Manhattan Valley Town Houses**, Manhattan Ave. bet. W.104th and W.105th Sts. E side. 1986. *Rosenblum/Harb.*

A reductionist row that pales in comparison to the richly detailed 1888 houses across Manhattan Avenue.

[M6] Originally **New-York Cancer Hospital**/later **Towers Nursing Home**/now apartments, 455 Central Park West and 2 W.106th St. 1884-1886. Additions, 1889-1890. *Charles C. Haight.* ☕ Remodeled and adjacent residential tower added, 2001, *Rothzeid Kaiserman Thomson & Bee Architects.*

This castellated emigré from the **Loire Valley** has charmed the Upper West Side for more than a century. The first American hospital devoted exclusively to cancer patients, it is now party to condominiums within and in an adjacent tower. A circular living room overlooking the park would suit us fine.

[M7] **171-173 West 107th Street**/originally **Edison Company substation**, bet. Columbus and Amsterdam Aves. N side. ca. 1916. Remodeled with added tower, 1990s.

The power station as handsome palazzo, clobbered by a newer (and banal) tower stuck to the top.

[M8] **Cathedral Parkway Houses**, 125 W.109th St., bet. Columbus and Amsterdam Aves. to Cathedral Pkwy. N side. 1975. *Davis Brody & Assocs.* and *Roger Glasgow.*

Two zigzag towers occupy opposite corners of this hilly midblock site; between them a private, terraced, open space leaps from level to level, street to street. The towers, cousins to *Davis Brody's* **Waterside**, **Ruppert**, and **Riverpark** ensembles, are more self-consciously articulated in plan and massing to minimize their impact upon the adjacent smaller-scale community. The site was formerly occupied by the **Woman's Hospital.**

M8

Central Park

Central Park Scenic Landmark, Fifth Avenue to Central Park West, 59th Street to 110th Street. 1858-1876. With many later modifications. *Frederick Law Olmsted and Calvert Vaux.* 🍎 *www.centralpark.com*

This great work of art, the granddaddy of America's naturally landscaped parks, was named a National Historic Landmark in 1965. Better still, for the sake of its eternal preservation, it is now a "scenic landmark," so designated by the New York City Landmarks Preservation Commission. This latter designation, happily, has teeth (whereas the national one is largely honorific and hopeful). Many believe that this park, Prospect Park, and the Brooklyn Bridge are the three greatest creations in New York City.

But who made this 840-acre (larger than Monaco) masterpiece possible in the center of New York City? One of the first was the poet and newspaper editor *William Cullen Bryant*, who in 1844 called for a large, public pleasure ground (at that time Washington Square was considered uptown). After landscape architect *Andrew Jackson Downing* appealed for a park, the idea caught on, and both mayoralty contestants made it a promise in the 1850 campaign. The winner, *Ambrose C. Kingsland*, kept his word, and the Common Council took action.

The site was then physically unprepossessing: "A pestilential spot where miasmic odors taint every breath of air," one report concluded.

Greensward construction progressed. It took nearly 20 years but, long before completion, the park became the place for rich and poor alike to promenade, to see and be seen. Today it is even more the playground for New Yorkers: for some a place to enjoy nature, for many the only "country" they have ever seen, for others a magnificently designed Garden of Eden to ease the strains of city living, and most recently a place of amateur gambling, gamboling, and beer drinking for residents of all boroughs. Central Park is the forecourt and front garden to the residential slabs and towers of Central Park South, Central Park West, Central Park North, and Fifth Avenue (otherwise Central Park East). At the southeast corner the surrounding towers cast romantic reflections in its waters (for the postcard maker) and enjoy the Plaza's great space, a happy symbiosis for both.

Invasions: Despite continuing threats of preposterous intrusions, the original plan was closely followed until the advent of the automobile and active sports. In 1912 the gravel drives were paved with asphalt, and two new entrances were cut through on Central Park South. Permanent tennis courts were then constructed. The first paved playground, the Heckscher, appeared in 1926. By the 1950s large structures had sprung up, all partially financed by philanthropists: the Wollman Memorial Rink (www.wollmanskatingrink.com),

But it was available. Land was acquired (1856) for $5.5 million and surveyed by *Egbert L. Viele*. Clearing began the next year: squatters and hogs were forcibly removed, often with the aid of the police, bone-boiling works and swill mills were torn down, swamps were drained, and the omnipresent Manhattan schist was blasted.

The first Board of Park Commissioners, helped by a committee including *Bryant* and the writer *Washington Irving*, decided in 1857 that an open competition should determine the park's design. Greensward, so named by contestants *Frederick Law Olmsted* and *Calvert Vaux*, won out among the 33 designs submitted. It was a simple, uncluttered plan, calling for a picturesque landscape: glade, copse, water, and rock outcroppings. Bridges (each individually designed by *Vaux*) separated footpaths, bridle paths, and the carriage drives—which were curved to prevent racing. The four sunken transverse roads for crosstown traffic were revolutionary.

Ten million cartloads of stone, earth, and topsoil were moved in or out of the site as

the Delacorte Theater, the Children's Zoo, and the Lasker Pool-Rink: some worthy additions, others vulgar and ugly intruders. The establishment of the Central Park Conservancy (www.centralparknyc.org) offers an opportunity to reconstruct the park in an Olmstedian vision adapted to current needs, but only if the well-meaning gifts can be directed toward thoughtful goals.

South and North

By topography and design the park falls into two sections. The large "pastoral" south is by far the more familiar; but the once neglected north is well worth a visit for its contrasting wild picturesqueness—a worthiness best savored in groups by day (avoided totally by dusk or dark) for personal security. The following two tours are meant to serve only as an introduction to these sections.

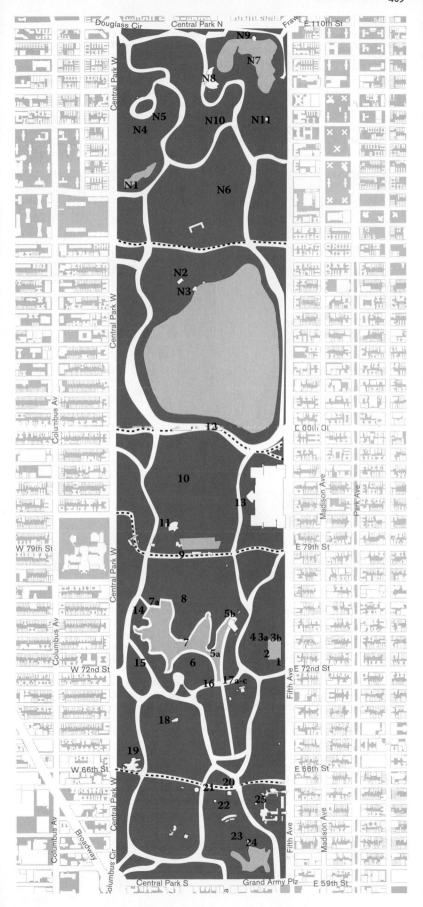

Douglass Cir

Central Park N

Fraw

E.110th St

N9

N7

N8

N5

N4

N10

N11

N1

N6

N2

N3

Central Park W

Columbus Av

E 100th St

11

10

13

Madison Ave

Park Ave

11

9

W 79th St

E 79th St

7a

8

14

5b

7

4 3a 3b

5a

2 1

15

6

W 72nd St

E 72nd St

16 17a-c

18

Fifth Ave

19

W 66th St

E 66th St

20

21

25

22

23 24

Columbus Av

Broadway

Central Park W

Columbus Cir

Central Park S

Grand Army Plz

E 59th St

Fifth Ave

Madison Ave

Walking Tour A, The South: Conservatory Water (at East 72nd Street and Fifth Avenue) to Grand Army Plaza (59th Street and Fifth Avenue) or the Zoo. Arrive via 68th Street Station of the Lexington Avenue IRT subway (No.6 train); Madison or Fifth Avenue buses.

START at Fifth Avenue and 72nd Street (this is **Inventors' Gate**, one of *Vaux's* 18 named gates piercing the park's wall) [S1]. Turn north, cros-

S2, Pilgrim Memorial

sing the park drive, and bear left past the **Pilgrim Memorial** (1885. *John Quincy Adams Ward*, sculptor) [S2]. Note the pilgrim's spectacular bronze boots. Descend Pilgrim Hill to the **Conservatory Water** [S3a], a formal neo-Renaissance concrete basin, named for the conservatory (greenhouse) promised but unbuilt on its eastern shore. Model and toy boats, some of which are stored at the **Alice H. and Edward A. Kerbs Memorial Boathouse** (1954) [S3b], are usually sailing here (races April through October mornings). Two statues overlook this water: **Alice in Wonderland Margarita Delacorte Memorial** (*Jose de Creeft*, sculptor) and **Hans Christian Andersen** (1956. *George J. Lober*, sculptor. *Otto F. Langmann*, architect). Neither is of any great artistic merit, but both are beloved by swarming children (storytelling at Andersen, Saturday mornings, May-September). From here look across the water to enjoy a view of Fifth Avenue through a filigree of branches and/or leaves.

Continue around the western shore to the path leading west to **Trefoil Arch** [S4] (restored, 1985, *Beyer Blinder Belle*), a brownstone tunnel with a wood ceiling, and pass under the East Drive to reach the shore of **The Lake** [S5a], where a gondola accompanies the flotilla of rowboats. The **Loeb Boathouse** (1954. Expanded and upgraded, 2004, *Ehrenkrantz Eckstut & Kuhn*) [S5b]. Note the rowboat sculpture, from a fudgy clay, cast into bronze, in the front court (1967. *Irwin Glusker,* sculptor). The boathouse has a

S6, Bethesda Fountain

S7, Bow Bridge

restaurant and a pleasant terrace overlooking The Lake. The bicycle concession to the right is jammed, particularly on those days and evenings when the park drives, closed to traffic, become the cyclist's province.

The path along the south shore reaches the **Bethesda Terrace** [S6] (The *Ehrenkrantz Group & Eckstut*, architects; *Philip Winslow*, landscape architect). It is the only formal architectural element of the Greensward Plan. *Jacob Wrey Mould* detailed the stonework, but *Vaux* was the conceptual designer. Bethesda Fountain (1870. *Emma Stebbins,* sculptor. *Calvert Vaux,* architect) is the centerpiece, with a bronze winged **Angel of the Waters** crowning vigorous chubby cherubs (Purity, Health, Peace, and Temperance). The terrace is a faded elegance of brick paving, sandstone bordered, walled, and crowned.

S9, Belvedere Castle

Side trips:
Northwest of The Terrace stands **Bow Bridge** *[S7]*
*(1860, Calvert Vaux. Restored, 1974), a cast-iron
elegance spanning the middle of The Lake (the
last vestige of the old reservoir drained in 1929).
The **Oak Bridge** [S7a] (1860, Calvert Vaux) was
replaced with a functional plank in 1935, but has
been rebuilt (2009, Jan Hird Pokorny) according
to Vaux's original, but in steel and aluminum this
time. **The Ramble** [S8], a simulation of Appalachia,
has meandering streams and small, hidden lawns.
The Ramble ascends to **Vista Rock**, topped by
Belvedere Castle [S9], former home of the city's
weather station (restored, 1978, James Lamantia).
The reservoir's dry bed was used by squatters
during the Depression, then filled in, becoming
the **Great Lawn** [S10], today's favored spot for
frisbee, soccer, and softball. The **Delacorte Theater** [S11], with summer Shakespeare performances, hovers over the new lake's western flank.
The **Central Park Precinct, N.Y.C. Police Department** [S12], on the 85th/86th Street Transverse
Road, is another Calvert Vaux building (1871).*

Strawberry Fields *[S15] (1983. Bruce Kelly, landscape architect), a gift from John Lennon's
widow, Yoko Ono, in memory of the legendary
Beatle killed in front of the Dakota, which overlooks the site. Resume tour.*

The Mall [S16], the Park's grand promenade,
lies south of the Terrace Arcade. Pass through,
noting the glazed and decorated tile ceiling.
The Mall's axis points to the Belvedere Castle,
deliberately kept small by architect *Vaux* to
lengthen the perspective, but full-grown trees
have obliterated the vista. Behind the intrusive
limestone half-hemispherical vaulted **Naumburg
Bandshell** [S17a] is **The Pergola** [S17b] (rebuilt,
1987, *Laura Starr,* landscape architect). A low,
light-filtered wood trellis, it is one of the park's
few wisteria-covered arbors. Behind it is
Rumsey Playground [S17c] (redesigned, 1986,
Philip Winslow). **The Mall**, in recent years, has
been a place for action, rather than strolling:
juggling, guitar playing, drug dealing, beer drinking, gambling, hamburger eating, and so forth.

S15, Strawberry Fields

S16, The Mall

*To the east, behind the Metropolitan Museum of
Art, rises* **"Cleopatra's Needle"** *[S13], one of a
pair of red granite obelisks from the reign of
Pharaoh Thutmose III (ca. 1450 B.C.). The pair
spent some time (2,000 years) in Alexandria at
a memorial to Cleopatra's Marc Antony;
ultimately this one was a gift from the khedive
of Egypt, erected in the park in 1881. The oldest
bit of architecture in New York (by millennia).*

*Resting on a promontory on the west side of the
Lake (near the West 77th Street park entrance) is
The Ladies Pavilion [S14] (1871. Vaux & Mould).
It was purportedly moved there from its original
location on the edge of the park at Columbus
Circle, where it had sheltered ladies awaiting
streetcars and was later bumped for the erection
of The Maine Monument. Vandalized and ruined
at the lake shore, it was reincarnated through
the efforts of the Parks Department monuments
officer, Joseph Bresnan, and is now a lacy cast-
iron Victorian delight. To its south, near the West
72nd Street park entrance, is the Italian mosaic
spelling out "Imagine" set in the paving of*

On The Mall are several statues: **Fitzgreene
Halleck** (1877. *J. Wilson MacDonald*), a prissy
and pretentious bronze of a self-styled poet.
Walter Scott (1872. *John Steell*). The 100th
anniversary of Scott's birth is memorialized by
this dour bronze, a copy of *Steell's* original in
the Scott Memorial in Edinburgh. **Robert Burns**
(1880. *John Steell*) is represented as a faraway
and saccharine romantic; **Columbus** (1894.
Jeronimo Suñol): an entranced religious maniac;
Shakespeare (1870. *John Quincy Adams Ward*):
the thoughtful bard in pantaloons.

*Side trip: West of The Mall, past the park's
closed Center Drive, stretches the **Sheep
Meadow** [S18], a sweeping lawn where sheep
could safely graze until banished in 1934 (they
lived in the nearby Sheepfold, now converted to
the pricey, periodically renovated **Tavern-on-
the-Green**) [S19]. From the north end there is a
splendid view of skyscrapers. Resume tour.*

S20, The Dairy

Continue at the southern end of The Mall, cross the drive, and don't blame Olmsted for not providing an underground passage here: the **Marble Arch**, the park's most famous bridge, was **removed** in the 1930s. Take the southeast path along the drive, and while crossing over the 65th Street Transverse Road, notice how little the sunken drive intrudes into the park. To the right, a path leads past **The Dairy** [S20], a sturdy Gothic Revival building provided once again with a copy of its original porch (Restored, 1979, James Lamantia with Weisberg Castro Assocs.). Note Manhattan schist and sandstone neo-Gothic colonnettes. Vaux designed it.

Another side trip: Head west, to the north of the hillsite of the Kinderberg, once a large arbor. It's now replaced by the squat **Chess and Checkers House** [S21], a gift of financier Bernard Baruch, a red and beige brick neo-Ruskinian cum Moses (Robert, that is) octagonal lump. Continue west, under **Playmates Arch** beneath the drive to the **Michael Friedsam Memorial**

Carousel (Building, 1951. Carousel, 1900s), another beige and red brick octagon replacing an earlier one, destroyed by fire. Resume tour.

From **The Dairy**, after dropping down to the left, the path passes east of the Chess and Checkers site. Skirt southeast around the **Wollman Memorial Rink** [S22] and go up the hill along the fence enclosing the **Bird Sanctuary** [S23]. **Gapstow Bridge**, crossing **The Pond** [S24], is a good place to admire the reflections of the City's towers in the water below. A few swans and many ducks are usually swimming around. Swan boats, the same as those still in Boston's Public Garden, sailed here until 1924. Leave the park by the gate across from **Sherman's statue** or, if you want to visit the Zoo, go, via **Inscope Arch** under the East Drive, northeast of the Pond.

END of tour: Nearest transit is the BMT Broadway Line (N, R, W trains) Fifth Avenue Station at East 60th Street or Fifth or Madison Avenue buses.

*Side trip: **The Zoo** [S25], off Fifth Avenue at 64th Street, is a favorite haunt of New Yorkers. It is a formal plaza once surrounded by WPA-built red brick arched buildings now totally redesigned (1988. Kevin Roche John Dinkeloo & Assocs.) to provide glazed arcades and more professional operation by the New York Zoological Garden staff. A constant is the centrally located and much beloved sea lion pool. The Arsenal is a participant in the Zoo plaza by default.*

Walking Tour B, The North: *The Pool to Conservatory Garden (IND Eighth Avenue subway, B or C trains, to 96th Street Station). Start at Central Park West and West 100th Street.*

The Boys' Gate gives access to a path descending to **The Pool** [N1]. It is the start of the waterway that flows east to Harlem Meer and was once the course of Montayne's Rivulet, which led to the East River. Across the West Drive and to the south of the 96th Street Transverse are a group of tennis courts popular with the public

At the eastern end of The Pool, the **Glen Span** carries the West Drive over **The Ravine**. On the other side flows **The Loch**, formerly an abundant body of water, now a trickle. This is very picturesque and completely cut off from the City.

*Side trip: To the south, behind the slope, is the **North Meadow** [N6], scene of hotly contested baseball games: to get there, take Springbanks Arch. Resume tour.*

In wet weather the Loch cascades down before disappearing under the East Drive at Huddlestone Bridge. Through the arch in front of **Harlem Meer** [N7] you can see the park's most disastrous "improvement," the **Loula D. Lasker Pool-Rink** [N8]. New Yorkers have always tried to give things—especially buildings—to their park. Few succeeded until recent generations of park administrators misguidedly began again to encourage large philanthropic bequests.

S25, The Zoo

but an intrusion into the *Olmsted & Vaux* vision. In 1987 plans were offered by the Central Park Conservancy to replace the 1930 **Tennis House** [N2] with a new structure at a higher elevation (1989. *Buttrick White & Burtis*). This area of the park is also the home of cast-iron **Bridge No.28** [N3] (1861. *Calvert Vaux with E.C. Miller*), a Gothic Revival masterpiece.

*Side trip: North of the Pool is the **Great Hill** [N4], where picnickers once enjoyed an unobstructed view of the Hudson and East Rivers. Perched on a cliff to the northeast is a lonely **Blockhouse** [N5], a remnant of the fortifications built during the War of 1812 when the British threatened the City. Resume tour.*

Across Harlem Meer, backing onto Central Park North, is a Central Park Conservancy project to provide quality food service and such amenities as boat rentals to an arriving upscale community at the **Charles A. Dana Discovery Center** [N9] (1993. *Buttrick White & Burtis*).

To the right of **The Loch** find **Lamppost No.0554.** (All the older lampposts, designed by *Henry Bacon* in 1907, bear a street-designating plaque; here, the first two digits indicate that this one stands at 105th Street.) A path goes sharply uphill and then turns east, crossing the East Drive below **McGown's Pass**, which was fortified by the British during the Revolutionary War. **The Mount** [N10], to the right, was for many years the site of a tavern; its chief ornament today is the park's mulch pile.

North Gatehouse

N3, Bridge No.28

The path descends to **Conservatory Garden** [N11], designed by *Thomas D. Price* in 1936. The Greensward Plan called for a large arboretum of native trees and shrubs to be planted here. Instead, a conservatory was built at the turn of the century but torn down in 1934. On the east side the **Vanderbilt Gate** opens on Fifth Avenue (open 8 AM-dusk every day). Nearby is the **Museum of the City of New York**, where historical material about the park is on display.

END of tour. Transportation: IRT Lexington Avenue subway at East 96th Street (No.6 train), and Fifth or Madison Avenue buses.

Upper East Side

The area's first development was not residential but, rather, recreational: Central Park. Toward the middle of the last century, a tremendous influx of Irish and German immigrants, dislocated by economic and political turmoil in their homeland, was straining the City's resources. Reformers were pressuring for a great public park to serve a population expected to grow even further. In the 1850s *Mayor Fernando Wood* and his Tammany Hall cronies foresaw the construction of the park as an opportunity to create enormous numbers of patronage positions among the new electorate. And the park's central site would neatly divide upper Manhattan into twin development opportunities: the

Upper East Side are relatively recent. To those who could afford them, Park Avenue's steam trains provided accessibility but also brought smoke and noise, thus creating an "other side of the tracks" opportunity. Beginning in the 1890s, between Park Avenue and Central Park, a corridor formed that attracted capitalists from downtown residential enclaves, such as lower Fifth Avenue and Gramercy Park, to costly sites along Fifth Avenue—the Gold Coast—and to lesser ones along the side streets and brownstone-lined Madison Avenue. East of Park Avenue huddled a mixture of row houses, stables, and carriage houses—truly the other side of the tracks.

Most of the mansions built at the turn of the

G5

G15

rough terrain of the West Side (to be reserved for later) and the relatively flat East Side. The latter was made more accessible from downtown by cutting through Madison and Lexington Avenues as additions to the original gridiron street plan of 1811.

The first transit connections from downtown were horsecar lines along Second, Third, and Madison Avenues and steam trains (including local service) along today's Park Avenue. Not surprisingly, the first row house development, during the 1860s and until the Panic of 1873, followed these routes of opportunity. The late 1870s brought the Second and Third Avenue elevated lines from downtown—mass transit. With it came the masses, housed in an explosive development of tenements— many of which remain—in the area's eastern flank.

The elegant associations with the term

century along Fifth (except those now used largely as museums) were demolished in two waves of high-rise luxury apartment development, the first in the Roaring Twenties, the second following World War II. In response to the first building boom, Madison Avenue's brownstones were altered to provide neighborhood shops and services for an expanding number of affluent apartment dwellers. Gracie Square and parts of East End Avenue then also saw apartment development. The post–World War II boom, (to the east signaled by the 1956 demolition of the grim Third Avenue El structure) has extended—with gasps for air—to the present day. It transformed practically every Upper East Side development site into a pot of gold and turned Madison Avenue into the ultrachic shopping street for wealthy Americans—and internationals as well.

UPPER EAST SIDE KEY MAP

Carnegie Hill
& Beyond

Metropolitan
Museum
Vicinity

Yorkville /
Gracie Square

Gold Coast

East of Eden /
Hospitalia

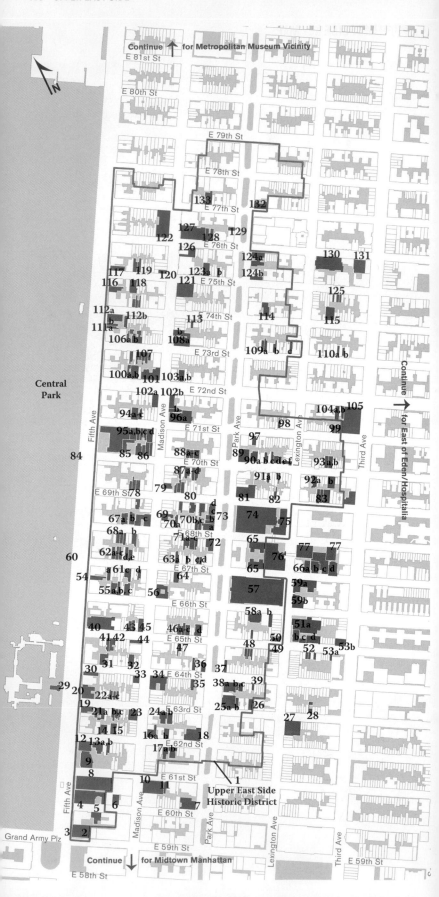

Continue ↑ for Metropolitan Museum Vicinity

E 81st St
E 80th St
E 79th St
E 78th St
133
132
E 77th St
127
128 129
122
126 E 76th St
124a
130 131
117 119 124b
116 118 120 123a b
121 E 75th St
125
112a 112b
b 114 115
111a
106a,b 113
108a E 73rd St
107 109a b
110a,b
100a,b 101 103a,b
102a 102b
b
94a-c 96a 104a,b 105
95a,b,c,d 98 99
85 86 E 71st St 97
88a-c 89
90a b c d e f 93a,b
87a-d 91a b 92a b
79 81 82 83
78 80
d
67a b c 69 c
70b,c b 73
68a b 70a a 74 75
62a-c 63a b c d 65
a 61c d 64 76 77 77
55a,b c 56 66 a b c d
57 59a
58a b 59b
40 43 45 51a
41 42 44 46a,b c d b c d
47 48 50 52 53a 53b
30 31 32 36 49
33 34 35 37
29 38a b,c 39
20 22a-c 25a b 26
19 27 28
21a b,c 23 24a b
14 15 16a b 18
12 13a,b
17a b
9 E 62nd St
8 10 11
1
4 5 6 Upper East Side
3 2 Historic District

Central Park
Grand Army Plz
Fifth Ave
Madison Ave
Park Ave
Lexington Ave
Third Ave

Continue → for East of Eden/Hospitalia

E 69th St
E 70th St
E 72nd St
E 74th St
E 68th St
E 67th St
E 66th St
E 65th St
E 64th St
E 63rd St
E 61st St
E 60th St
E 59th St
E 58th St

84
60
54

Continue ↓ for Midtown Manhattan

THE GOLD COAST

Borrowing a term initially used to denote Fifth Avenue along Central Park, together with its park blocks, the area included is bounded by Fifth and a line east of Lexington, from just above 59th Street to 78th. Much—but not all—is officially designated as the Upper East Side Historic District. The upper reaches of Fifth Avenue are covered in precincts called **Metropolitan Museum Vicinity** and **Carnegie Hill**.

[G1] **Upper East Side Historic District** 📷
In 1981, 16 years after the passage of the City's landmarks law, the unachievable was achieved: the establishment under former Chairman *Kent L. Barwick* of a historic district that stretches along Fifth Avenue's gold coast from 59th to 78th Streets—where it abuts the **Metropolitan Museum Historic District**—and reaches inland in a leg that wraps up to 79th and Park. In between, its boundaries irregularly

G2

G2a

G3

G4

faintly echoing *Chanin* and *Dela Marre's* Central Park West Art Deco.

[G3] **Sidewalk Clock**, in front of 783 Fifth Ave., bet. E.59th and E.60th Sts. E side. 1927. *E. Howard Clock Company.* 📷
General Sherman's timepiece as he gallops through history across the street in **The Plaza**. *William Tecumseh*'s been there since 1903 (*Augustus St. Gaudens*, sculptor), but time is not of his essence.

[G4] **Metropolitan Club**, 1-11 E.60th St., NE cor. Fifth Ave. 1891-1894. *Stanford White of McKim, Mead & White.* E wing, 1912, *Ogden Codman, Jr.* 📷
A monumental Italian palazzo enhanced by a great carriage entrance and courtyard. Smooth limestone walls, the rusticated base, and a hovering, bracketed cornice crowned with

encompass properties beyond Madison and Park Avenues to the east, even crossing Lexington from 69th and 71st.

[G2] **Sherry Netherland Hotel**, 781 Fifth Ave., NE cor. E.59th St. 1926-1927. *Schultze & Weaver and Buchman & Kahn.*
A tower fit for a muezzin crowns its peaked and finialed roof. Inside, old and new money jostle for position. Now for $1,000 a night you can join them. The restaurant and bar along Fifth Avenue, now *Harry Cipriani's*, is one of New York's greatest: venerable elegance.

[G2a] **Dominico Vacca**/originally **Diane von Furstenberg**, 783 Fifth Ave. (in the Sherry-Netherland Hotel). Façade, 1984. *Michael Graves.*
A token, but stylish, presence from *Graves*. In the search for more local *Graves*, he has disappointed us: at the **Impala** (75th and First Avenue), and at **425 Fifth Avenue**, its tower

copper are complemented by the courtyard void that reinforces the building's posture. Tuscan Doric columns and Parisian black and gilt iron grilles keep we plebs at bay.

[G5] **The Harmonie Club**, 4 E.60th St., bet. Fifth and Madison Aves. S side. 1904-1906. *Stanford White of McKim, Mead & White.* Altered upward and inside, 1935, *Benjamin Wistar Morris.*
A high-rise Renaissance palace: giant *Corinthian* pilasters in terra cotta joined by sturdy limestone *Ionic* columns define a rich façade over an austere limestone plinth. It is the second home of the club founded by members of those chronicled in *Our Crowd*.

[G6] **The Grolier Club**, 47 E.60th St., bet. Madison and Park Aves. N side. 1917. *Bertram G. Goodhue*. Exhibitions open Mo-Sa 10-5; closed Su. Closed Aug. 212-838-6690. *www.grolierclub.org*
Named for the 16th-century French bibliophile *Jean Grolier*, this club is for those devoted

to the bookmaking crafts. More *Georgian* than most American neo-Georgian, it boasts the larger windows of its English ancestry. Light for good reading, most likely.

[G7] **Christ Church** (Methodist), 520 Park Ave., NW cor. E.60th St. 1931-1932. *Ralph Adams Cram.*

The marble and granite columns appear to be, in the *Romanesque* and *Byzantine* manner, pillaged from Roman temples. Handsome, and of impeccable taste, they form an archaeological and eclectic stage set for well-to-do parishioners. Look at the mosaic ceiling, especially when lit by blue bulbs. This, of course, is *late Ralph*, long after the Gothicism of **St. John the Divine,** but in tune with a similar vocabulary used by his partner, *Goodhue,* at **St. Bartholomew's** (10 blocks south, and 13 years earlier).

[G8] **Hotel Pierre,** 795 Fifth Ave., SE cor. E.61st St. 1929-1930. *Schultze & Weaver.*

A tall, slender, romantic hotel-apartment house with a mansard-roofed-tower silhouette.

[G11] **36 East 61st Street,** bet. Madison and Park Aves. 1890s.

Beaux Arts grandeur in limestone and brick. Curved glass adds another level of elegance to the bulging bay window. The canvas entrance canopy is demeaning: out of scale with a grand mansion — a flimsy marquee.

East 62nd Street, between Fifth and Madison Avenues:

 [G12] **Knickerbocker Club,** 2 E.62nd St., SE cor. Fifth Ave. 1913-1915. *Delano & Aldrich.* ☙

London Georgian more than American Federal: a **revival** in either case. The renaissance of 18th-century forms in early 20th-century New York opened the door to subtle and diverse architectural options. See the **Grolier Club** around the corner for a more austere version (except the latter's overblown door enframement).

G7   G8

G11

G12

G9   G10

G13a

G13b

17th-century French arched windows flanked by paired flat pilasters enliven a mildly rusticated wall, topped with giant urns on a balustrade.

[G9] **800 Fifth Avenue,** NE cor. E.61st St. 1978. *Ulrich Franzen & Assocs.,* design architects. *Wechsler & Schimenti,* associate architects.

The tower, standing behind a three-story limestone screen wall, the latter responding literally to the Special Zoning District's demands, the wall matching in height—but not in ambience—the **Knickerbocker Club** to the north.

East 61st Street, between Madison and Park Avenues:

[G10] **667 Madison Avenue,** SE cor. E.61st St. 1987. *David Paul Helpern.*

Glass with stone surrounds (as opposed to a stone building with openings), it gracefully turns the corner within the complex rules of the Zoning Resolution. But what a corner.

[G13a] **Curzon House:** Combination of No.4 and No.6 E.62nd St. **No.4.** 1880. *Breen & Nason.* Present façade, 1898, *Clinton & Russell.* Formerly **No.6** E.62nd St. 1901. *Welch, Smith & Provot.* General renovations and addition to W of former 4 E.62nd St., 1985, *Stephen B. Jacobs & Assocs.*

Old Nos.4 and 6 housed the former **York Club** after 1931. The infill addition is respectable in size and materials, but with too much glass to be an appropriate member of this ménage à trois.

[G13b] Originally **Edmund L. Baylies House,** 10 E.62nd St. S side. 1906. *Hoppin, Koen & Huntington.*

The floors above the parlor level decrease in height as they decrease in intricacy. The sinuous transom tracery of French doors at the second floor leads to elegant wrought railings, the archways behind overseen by sculpted-face keystones.

[G14] **The Fifth Avenue Synagogue,** 5 E.62nd St. N side. 1956. *Percival Goodman.*

An urban temple, clad in finely striated cream-colored stone, with sharply incised stained glass windows. In daylight they read as cat's eyes; after dark they glow, once the interior is lit.

[G15] Originally **Edith and Ernesto Fabbri House**/now **Residence of the Permanent Representative of Japan to the United Nations,** 11 E.62nd St. N side. 1898-1900. *Haydel & Shepard.*

Beaux Arts limestone and brick extravaganza for the *Fabbris*. A gift to *Edith Shepard Fabbri*, *William H. Vanderbilt*'s granddaughter, by her mother. See 95th Street for the *Fabbris'* later house. It could be the stage set for an ultimate French embassy, but a far cry from the austere architecture of Japan, home of its present occupants.

East 62nd Street, between Madison and Park Avenues:

[G17a] **The Links Club,** 36 E.62nd St. S side. 1902, *Trowbridge & Livingston.* Façade, 1916-1917. *Cross & Cross.*

Creamy travertine frames rose-red Flemish-bond brickwork, making a *neo-Georgian* swell-fronted façade almost worthy of the real thing. *Christopher Gray* reminded us of the 1917 *Architectural Record* article, describing the club as showing "the effects of quiet breeding, traditional elegance, of considered good taste." Take the *Records'* words with several grains of salt.

[G17b] **40 East 62nd Street,** S side. 1910. *Albert Joseph Bodker.*

An eight-floor studio building borrowing medieval forms: tier upon tier of multipaned casemented bay windows are tucked into the façade with unglazed terra cotta. The two-story base is rich with foliage and griffins. *Henry Hardenburgh* (architect of **The Dakota** and **The Plaza Hotel**) lived here; no greater compliment necessary.

G14

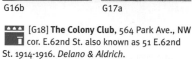

G16a

G16b   G17a

[G16a] **Hermès Madison**/onetime **The Limited**/ originally **Louis Sherry's Restaurant,** 691 Madison Ave., NE cor. E.62nd St. 1928. *McKim, Mead & White.* Altered into stores, 1950. Redesigned for The Limited, 1986, *Beyer Blinder Belle.*

A late *MM&W* neo-Classical/Art Deco ho-hum candy box metamorphosed (and gilded) in the 1980s as flagship of **The Limited**. The boxy skylight gives the building dignity and adds the bulk it needs to effectively compete, architecturally, on Madison Avenue. Hermès has swallowed it, or been swallowed by it, whole, with a few minor decorative flourishes.

[G16b] Originally **Eleanor Keller School,** 35 E.62nd St. N side. 1905. *George Keller.*

Columns and arches in a sextet of brick, terra cotta, and limestone, with a loggia at the summit for a breath of air on a summer's evening. The ground-floor arcade is a prominent presence to those strolling by.

[G18] **The Colony Club,** 564 Park Ave., NW cor. E.62nd St. also known as 51 E.62nd St. 1914-1916. *Delano & Aldrich.*

The **Colony** was founded by the wives of Those Who Mattered, moving here from their original home at 120 Madison Avenue (1904-1908. *Stanford White of McKim, Mead & White*) only 13 years later. Those That Mattered had multiplied, to be housed on Park Avenue in this tasteful and immense neo-Georgian town mansion. (There had been an open railroad cut here in 1908.) *Stanford* did it better for them downtown.

East 63rd Street, between Fifth and Madison Avenues:

[G19] **817 Fifth Avenue**, SE cor. E.63rd St. 1925. *George B. Post & Sons.*
[G20] **820 Fifth Avenue**, NE cor. E.63rd St. 1916. *Starrett & Van Vleck.*

High-rise palazzi of copper-corniced limestone, these are two of the great eclectic apartment houses of New York, although 817 has lost its many-paned windows to sheets of fixed thermal glass. Glass eyes upon the park without pupils or irises.

[G21a] Originally **Mr. and Mrs. William Ziegler, Jr., House**/onetime **New York Academy of Sciences**, 2 E.63rd St. 1920. *Sterner & Wolfe.*

A pasty palace, large but unresolved, its cornice a remnant from the architecture of earlier and lesser row houses. The colossal iron fence is a good lesson in how something necessarily large can be detailed to be in scale with its surroundings.

G19

G21c

G23

[G21b] **14 E.63rd Street**, 1873. *J.G. and R.B. Lynd.*
[G21c] **16, 18 E.63rd Street**, 1876. *Gage Inslee.*

Brownstone mansions, unlike those endless, modest middle-class rows east of Park Avenue; the Composite-columned porches of **No.16** (which has lost its stoop), and **No.18**, are grand for their time.

[G22a] **Edmond J. Safra Synagogue**, 11 E.63rd St., bet. Fifth and Madison Aves. N side. 2002-2003. *Thierry Despont.*

Mildly rusticated Israeli limestone, a London bank by a French architect for a Spanish-Portuguese congregation. The folded planes and cornices at each edge are reminiscent of similar historical gestures: *Despont* may have seen London's National Gallery's **Sainsbury Wing** by *Venturi and Scott-Brown.*

[G22b] Originally **Elias Asiel House**, 15 East 63rd St., 1901. *John H. Duncan.* [G22c] **17 East 63rd Street.** *Welch, Smith & Provot.*

Exquisite, delicately carved, limestone win-

dow enframements enrich the second-floor façade (a level better described in this classy building as the *piano nobile*). *Asiel's* eponymous son-in-law, *Lyman Bloomingdale*, founded that emporium.

No.17, not to be outdone, has grand swags pendant over its deeply inset French windows. A 1990s penthouse addition replaces the mansard roof with a swooping glass wall. Pas mal.

[G23] **The Bank of New York,** 63rd Street Office, 706 Madison Ave., SW cor. E 63rd St. 1921-1922. *Frank Easton Newman.*

A charming *neo-Federal* house that once boasted a garden to the south along Madison, now infilled with ATM machines. The new addition offers subtle *neo-Georgian* detail: white marble window reveals, rather than mere brick returns.

[G24a] **The Lowell,** 28 E.63rd St., bet. Madison and Park Aves. 1925-1926. *Henry Churchill and Herbert Lippman.* Entrance

G24b

mosaic, *Bertram Hartman.* Renovations, 1989, *Gruzen Samton.*

Tapestry brick and steel sash are the background for a startling and stylish glazed terracotta **Art Deco** ground floor. But the canopy belongs to another building. Bronze Greek acroteria? Not from *Churchill, Lipton, Gruzen Samton.*

"There is nothing stereotyped about this building, no hardening of the architectural arteries. Conservatives will look at it askance, and call it freakish. I find it vital, well-studied and successful." —T-Square, New Yorker, *February 5, 1927.*

[G24b] Originally **The Hangar Club**/onetime **Assisium School, Missionary Sisters of the Third Order of St. Francis,** 36 E.63rd St., bet. Madison and Park Aves. 1929-1930. *Cross & Cross.*

A bowfront bay of brick and travertine is set against the flat façade, much as the same architects' work, **Links Club,** on East 62nd. A neo-Georgian composition of contrasting colors and textures. Wonderful. Now a private residence.

[G25a] **Third Church of Christ, Scientist,** 585 Park Ave., NE cor. E.63rd St. 1923-1924. *Delano & Aldrich.*

The lantern rises like a lighthouse over the modest dome, like a bit of *Wren's* London superimposed on the *neo-Georgian* bulk below. Unfluted Doric columns look fondly across Park Avenue toward their **Colony Club** *Corinthian* cousins a block to the south.

[G25b] Originally **Michael J. O'Reilly House**/onetime **Roy H. Frowick (Halston) House,** 101 E.63rd St., bet. Park and Lexington Aves. 1881. *Cornelius O' Reilly.* Altered, 1968, *Paul Rudolph.*

A somber steel grid and dark glass give an understated face to a dramatic set of domestic spaces within. Recast from a former stable-garage. See other *Rudolph* projects in Manhattan: pp. 172, 345, 346.

[G26] **123 East 63rd Street,** bet. Park and Lexington Aves. 1900. *Trowbridge & Livingston.*

The balcony for a *Beaux Arts* emperor: *Napoleons I* and *III* came from more austere architectural times, leaving this lush architecture for a once and future king.

[G27] **Barbizon Hotel**/originally **Barbizon Hotel for Women,** 140 E.63rd St., SE cor. Lexington Ave. 1927. *Murgatroyd & Ogden.* Lobby, restaurants, public spaces altered, 1986, *Judith Stockman & Assocs.,* designers.

G25b   G31   G28

A romantic, tawny brick, eclectic charmer, built originally for young working women in New York far from home, and now lovingly restored.

[G28] Originally **Cyril and Barbara Rutherford Hatch House,** 153 E.63rd St., bet. Lexington and Third Aves. 1917-1919. *Frederick J. Sterner.* ☛

A picturesque loner in well-crafted stucco by the designer of the "Block Beautiful" on 19th Street. A *Spanish Baroque* portal and decorative fence contrast with the austere building plane.

[G29] **The Arsenal,** N.Y.C. Department of Parks & Recreation Headquarters, 821 Fifth Ave., in Central Park opp. E.64th St. 1847-1851. *Martin E. Thompson.* Altered, 1860, *Richard Morris Hunt.* ☛ Gallery open to the public. Gallery open Mo-Fr 9-4:30; closed Sa & Su.

Originally built as principal cache of military explosives for the State of New York, the **Arsenal** stood lonely guard at one side of Fifth

Avenue (Central Park blossomed later, surrounding it from behind). Nine years after completion it served the City as a Police Station and then incubator space for the **American Museum of Natural History** (1869-1877).

Recent renovations have reclaimed the austere but elegant neo-Gothic civic building behind decades of blurring foliage, and have soberly removed it from its role as an ivy-clasped romantic castle, symbolic guardian of the Zoo.

[G30] Originally **Edward J. Berwind House**/later **Institute of Aeronautical Sciences,** 2 E.64th St., SE cor. Fifth Ave. 1893-1896. *Nathan Clark Mellen.* Dormers, 1902, *Horace Trumbauer.*

Berwind's town-house (his country house, **The Elms,** was in Newport). Here is the same pallid eclectic brick and limestone vocabulary used at *Carnegie's* mansion 27 blocks north: indecisive ornament and window openings (perhaps they should have been larger?). However, the cornice is a real winner.

[G31] Originally **Marshall Orme and Caroline Astor Wilson House**/now **New India House,** 3 E.64th St., bet. Fifth and Madison Aves. 1900-1903. *Warren & Wetmore.* Interior altered for Government of India, 1952, *William Lescaze.*

Beaux Arts, dressed in limestone, its plain surface in tense counterpoise with richly sculpted window keystones...but the guts are at the sky: a slate and copper mansarded attic, grand dormers, and eyebrowed oculi. The overblown entrance enframement would have been better, simplified, in tune with the austere monumentality of the windows.

Mrs. Wilson was an Astor, daughter of the Mrs. Astor, whose ballroom, in her earlier house, where the Empire State building now stands, had a capacity that gave the name The 400 to the City's elite. In 1903, she lived around the corner in a mansion on the site of today's Temple Emanu-El.

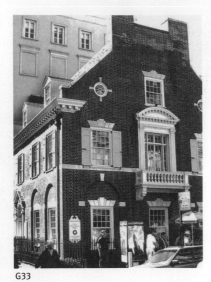

G33

[G32] **Wildenstein & Company**, 19 E.64th St., bet. Fifth and Madison Aves. 1931-1932. *Horace Trumbauer.*

Travertine within and without: an art palace (never a house) that marked, with a ribbon, the end of *Trumbauer's* rich, eclectic career. Beautiful in proportion and patina, with *Trumbauer's* good taste. Founded in Paris in 1875, the gallery had previously been at 647 Fifth Avenue.

[G35] Originally **Robert I. Jenks House**/now **Near East Foundation**, 54 E.64th St., bet. Madison and Park Aves. 1907. *Flagg & Chambers.*

Four stories of delicate but unconvincing *neo-Federal* detail, complete with Flemish-bond brick. Some elegant parts contribute to a bland whole (good entry railing). A minor *Flagg.*

[G36a] **57 East 64th Street**, bet. Madison and Park Aves. 1905. *C.P.H. Gilbert.*

From the *Flemish Renaissance*, with Gothic details hanging on to its finialed dormers and balustrade details. The portly bayed front demands attention.

[G36b] Originally **Jonathan Buckley House**/now **Swedish Consulate and Permanent Mission to the United Nations**, 600 Park Ave., NW cor. E.64th St. 1911. *James Gamble Rogers.* Restored, *Rothzeid Kaiserman Thomson & Bee.*

Small windows, smooth limestone, with a proper London sometimes-colonnaded parapet: neo-English-Regency garb for an American paper manufacturer.

[G37] Originally **Thomas A. and Emilia Howell House**, 603 Park Ave., NE cor. E.64th St. 1920. *Walter Lund and Julius F. Gayler.*

Stupendous *neo-Federal* as though, like *Popeye*, it must have feasted on spinach! The strong twin-columned *Palladian* entry contrasts with lovely understated black-muntined multi-paned windows and flush marble lintels.

G34   G35   G36a   G37

[G33] Originally **Bank of the Manhattan Company**/now **Chase Manhattan Bank**, 726 Madison Ave., SW cor. E.64th St. 1932-1933. *Morrell Smith.*

A charming *neo-Georgian* fantasy built a hundred years after similar houses might have been built anywhere on Manhattan Island. The brick and limestone-keystoned relieving arches improve scale of the smaller-than-Georgian windows.

[G34] **The Verona**, 32 E.64th St., SE cor. Madison Ave. 1907-1908. *William E. Mowbray.* Cornice restoration, 1988, *Jan Hird Pokorny Associates.*

Names were once just as important as addresses, but this high-rise palazzo deserved one from the best of Italy (check that *neo-16th-century cornice*). The lamp standards add extra panache.

[G38a] **Central Presbyterian Church**/originally **Park Avenue Baptist Church**, 593 Park Ave., SE cor. E.64th St. 1920-1922. *Henry C. Pelton and Allen & Collens.*

The original Baptist congregation (previously **Norfolk Street Baptist Church** and later **Fifth Avenue Baptist Church**, where the *Rockefellers* worshipped) left here to build its true monument, **Riverside Church**, with the same architects and *JDR, Jr.'s* money. Collegiate Gothic (comfort for the upper middle class).

[G38b] **110 East 64th Street**, bet. Park and Lexington Aves. 1988. *Agrest & Gandelsonas.*

Captured in conversation between a stony church and a glassy box [see next], as though at tea. This very high-style urbane single house toasts its neighbors while demurely lifting its chin. That fourth-floor inset terrace seems more an appropriate place for a prince to harangue the people, than a stance to enjoy the weather.

G38b

[G38c] Originally **Asia House**/now **Russell Sage Foundation/Robert Sterling Clark Foundation**, 112 E.64th St., bet. Park and Lexington Aves. 1958-1960. *Philip Johnson.*

A decorous curtain of dark glass suspended in a gossamer grid of thin, white-painted steel makes a street wall that accommodates itself to this varied block. The sometimes disturbing opacity of the glass, mirroring the street's opposite side, disappears at night, revealing the volume of interior spaces behind the wall.

[G39] Formerly **Edward Durell Stone House**, 130 E.64th St., bet. Park and Lexington Aves. 1878. *James E. Ware.* Front addition/façade, 1956, *Edward Durell Stone.*

The body was a mate to **No.128.** In 1956 architect-owner *Stone* extended the façade, and hence volume, of the structure to the permissible building line. The precast terrazzo grillage echoed the design of his **American Embassy in New Delhi**, widely acclaimed when it was built. After *Stone's* death, his third wife and son stripped away this orientalism, revealing floor-to-ceiling glass, and themselves, unabashedly. The Landmarks Commission made them put it back.

East 65th Street, between Fifth to Madison Avenues:

[G40] **Temple Emanu-El**, 840 Fifth Ave., NE cor. E.65th St. 1927-1929. *Robert D. Kohn, Charles Butler, Clarence Stein,* and *Mayers, Murray & Philip.* Restored, *Beyer Blinder Belle.*

G38c

G44

The merging in 1927 of **Emanu-El** with **Temple Beth-El** (whose sanctuary then stood at the southeast corner of Fifth and 67th) paved the way for construction of this large, bearing-wall sanctuary on the former site of *Richard Morris Hunt's* double mansion for *the* Mrs. Astor. North of the main space, and set back from the avenue, is the **Beth-El Chapel**, built in memory of the other congregation's structure (1891. *Brunner & Tryon*), which was then demolished.

[G41] Originally **Mrs. William H. Bliss House**/now **Permanent Mission of Pakistan to the United Nations**, 6 and 8 E. 65th St., 1902. *Hiss & Weeks.* [G42] **12 East 65th Street**. 1909. *Walter B. Chambers.*

Two monumental *Beaux Arts* baubles. **No.8**, unusually wide (43-foot) with a generous two-story Parisian mansard pierced by bull's-eye dormers, is visually linked to its neighbor

No.6 by a common second-floor balcony and roof cornice. **No.12**, now **Pakistan House**, also harmonizes.

[G43] Originally **James J. Van Alen House**/now **Kosciuszko Foundation**, 15 E.65th St. 1917. *Harry Allan Jacobs.* Gallery open Mo-Fr 9-5; but call first. 212-734-2130. *www.thekf.org*

Crisp *Regency* limestone with an inset pink marble *Palladian* window. The original owner *Van Alen*, a socialite, was *the* Mrs. Astor's son-in-law. He sold the house in 1919 and moved to Europe in protest over impending Prohibition. The foundation has owned it since 1945.

Madison Avenue, between East 65th and East 66th Streets:

[G44] Originally **Frederic H. Betts House**, 750 Madison Ave. also known as 22 E.65th St., SW cor. Madison Ave. 1897. *Grosvenor Atterbury.* Stores added, 1915, 1936.

G41

Time has had a schizophrenic effect on this corner town house: on Madison it has become a proscenium for a succession of shops, often changing. On 65th its original dour character is sustained.

[G45] **Giorgio Armani**, 760 Madison Ave., NW cor. E.65th St. 1996. *Peter Marino + Assocs.*

Armani's awkward envelope tries for an understated *Miesian* elegance, but fails to turn its end-corners gracefully. Elegant at the center, weak at the ends. Single-stitched?

East 65th Street, between Madison and Park Avenues:

[G46a] Originally **Benson Bennett Sloan House**, 41 E.65th St. 1910. *Trowbridge & Livingston.* Interior remodeling, 1960, *Edward Durell Stone.*

The Tuscan-columned loggia at the top, now glazed in, originally offered an eyrie for sun-sitters.

[G46b] Originally **John M. Bowers House**/now **Albert Ellis Institute**, 45 E.65th St. 1910. *Hoppin & Koen*.

A monumental quoined and corniced neo-Georgian rose brick and limestone town house; attic story dormered in copper, roofed in slate.

[G46c] Originally **Sara Delano Roosevelt and Franklin and Eleanor Roosevelt Houses**/now **Roosevelt House Public Policy Institute, Hunter College CUNY**, 47-49 E.65th St. 1907-1908. *Charles A. Platt.* 🖼

Built as a double town house (with a single entry) by *FDR's* mother: she lived in **No.47** while *Franklin* and *Eleanor* lived in **No.49**. It was here, in a fourth-floor bedroom, that the president-to-be convalesced from his bout with polio in 1921-1922.

The brick and limestone neo-Renaissance façade was an appropriate understated presence for the well-born *Sara Delano*, an understatement matched when her son, as President, drove (himself at the wheel) *King George VI*

*The **IRT**, the City's first subway system, invariably linked to the name of its financier, August Belmont (1853-1924), was actually planned and constructed under the supervision of engineer William Barclay Parsons. Parsons commissioned the double-width, double-scaled neo-Federal house at 121 East 65th Street from architects Welles Bosworth and E. E. Piderson. It was completed in 1923.*

🖼 [G48] **114, 116 & 118 East 65th Street,** bet. Park and Lexington Aves. 1900. *Buchman & Deisler*.

Two in limestone flank their mate in brick and limestone in this inflated-Georgian triad. Heavy Renaissance detailing shows that in *Edwardian* times architects often complicated and embellished their ancestors' simpler styles. But the same thing happened in *Alexander's Greece* as well.

[G49] **The Parge House**, 132a E.65th St., SW cor. Lexington Ave. Altered, 1922, *Frederick J. Sterner*.

G47

G46a

G46c

G46d

G48

and *Queen Elizabeth* about his Hyde Park (country house) surroundings in a mere Ford open touring car.

[G46d] **55 East 65th Street**. 1892. *Thom & Wilson*.

French Flats of roman brick and brownstone for wealthy pioneers in apartment living (for social implications of such life, see *Edith Wharton's The Age of Innocence*). The sheet-metal fire escape covers (added later) were a *Bauhaus*-inspired attempt to sterilize the late 19th-century vigor.

[G47] **44 East 65th Street**. 1877. *John G. Prague*. Present façade, 1912, *J.M.A. Darrach*.

The **Tuscan**-colonnaded ground level provides counterpoint to the street. Above, the brick plane offers a play of arches with flush lintels and keystones, worthy of the best **London Georgian**.

Though compromised by the addition of a Lexington Avenue shop, this picturesque conversion of a row house into *Sterner's* office and apartments remains an unusual work, with decorative stucco relief. *Sterner* is most noted for the "Block Beautiful" on East 19th Street.

[G50] Originally **Michael and John Davis House**, 135 E.65th St., NW cor. Lexington Ave., also known as 868 Lexington Ave. 1904. *Edwin Outwater* (or was it *Alfred E. Barlow*?)

Large and ungainly, as if fearing design enrichment, shying from the grandeur of neighboring **114-118**, this somber brick box offers a bay window over the side street. The unsympathetic **Smallbone** storefront doesn't help.

G49

East 65th Street, between Lexington and Third Avenues:

■■■ [G51a] **Church of St. Vincent Ferrer** (Roman
Catholic), 869 Lexington Ave. SE cor.
E.66th St. 1914-1918. *Bertram G. Goodhue.* ✪
[G51b] **Priory, Dominican Fathers**/originally
Convent, 869 Lexington Ave., NE cor. E.65th St.
1880-1881. *William Schickel.* [G51c] **Holy Name
Society Building**, 141 E.65th St. 1930. *Wilfrid E.
Anthony.* ✪ [G51d] **St. Vincent Ferrer School**,
151 E.65th St. 1948. *Elliot L. Chisling-Ferrenz
& Taylor.* ✪

A fashionable parish church complex built
by the *Dominican Order* (and therefore not

G50

G51b

under the control of the New York Archdiocese).
The *Goodhue*-designed church, in rock-face
granite with limestone trim and sculpture, is,
perhaps, too academically correct, as if restored
by an acolyte of the French neo-Gothicist
Viollet-le-Duc: an "improvement" on Gothic reality. A planned 150-foot steeple was never built.
Well worth a visit within.

While the *Priory* is an older, quite picturesque relic, the two newer structures along 65th
Street pale in comparison to their Lexington
Avenue cousins. (The incised Old English
inscription on the new school gives its date as
1954; the Buildings Department dates it 1948.)

*Across 65th Street from the St. Vincent Ferrer
Church complex is a picturesque set of row
houses, Nos.132-156, of varying quality but
united by trees, ivy, and ironwork that peters
out as it approaches Third Avenue. Among the
houses are:*

[G52a] **136 and 138 East 65th Street**. 1870s.
Copper-clad bay windows give rich, but
understated, character to these brick town
houses. Prominence without posturing.

*The most notorious house (for its occupants) is
No.142:*

[G52b] Originally **Charles C. Pope House**/onetime
Richard M. Nixon House/long-time **Learned
Hand House**, 142 E.65th St. 1871. *Frederick S.
Barus.* Altered, 1961, *Casale & Nowell.*

Following his resignation as president and
unsuccessful attempt to buy a co-op apartment,
Nixon settled for this row house in 1979. Federal

G52a

G52b

Judge *Learned Hand*, perhaps the most
esteemed judge in the Federal system (but
abhorred by *Franklin Roosevelt*, who denied him
a place on the Supreme Court), lived here from
1906 until his death in 1961. A cousin of **Nos.136
and 138**. But did *Nixon* paint the copper?

*Two apartment towers, built 33 years apart on
opposite corners of East 65th and Third Avenue,
regard each other coldly and agree to disagree:*

[G53a] **The Phoenix**, 160 E.65th St., SW cor.
Third Ave. 1968. *Emery Roth & Sons.*

A sober but boring modernist concrete grid.
Some of the exuberance of the original *Emery
Roth* at the **San Remo** could be used here.

[G53b] **The Chatham**, 181 E.65th St., NW cor.
Third Ave. 2001. *Robert A.M. Stern Architects.*

Limestone and brick again prevail on Third
Avenue, embellished with arches and a dentil-

encrusted entablature. The vertical ribbons of bay windows are a nice touch, but things get out of hand at the top, where the building ends in a flourish of over-scaled **Neo-Collegiate** details. This was the site of the most recent **Dove Tavern**.

*One life for my country: **The Dove Tavern**, a landmark for travelers on the Boston Post Road, stood at the northwest corner of what is now Third Avenue and East 66th Street, a block north of its latter-day namesake. It had been established sometime prior to 1763 and flourished for over 30 years. Commemorative plaques and statues elsewhere notwithstanding, **Captain Nathan Hale** was hanged by the British on September 22, 1776, in the Artillery Park near the tavern. Captured while reconnoitering British forces on Long Island, he was executed immediately—denied even the attendance of clergy. Though his last letters to his mother and friends were destroyed, his last words remain familiar to many.*

William H. Vanderbilt's granddaughter from her mother. The **Deutscher Verein** took possession briefly in 1925, the **Lotos** in 1946.

[G55b] Originally **Charles and Louise Flagg Scribner, Jr., House**/now **Permanent Mission of the Republic of Poland to the United Nations**, 9 E.66th St. 1909-1912. *Ernest Flagg*.

A light touch from a sometime exuberant talent. *Flagg* also designed *Scribner's* commercial buildings (he had married into the family). But his remaining chef d'oeuvre in New York is the **Little Singer Building** at Prince Street. The 47-story **Singer Tower** was demolished in 1968.

[G55c] Originally **Harris Fahnestock House**/now **Consular House, Republic of the Philippines**, 15 E.66th St. 1918. *Hoppin & Koen*.

The firm's masterwork was the old **Police Headquarters**. Here they delivered a serene neo-Renaissance town house reminiscent of London's **Covent Garden Piazza**, rusticated limestone below, grand pilasters above.

G55a

G53b

G54

G56

West to Fifth Avenue, then along 66th:

[G54] Originally **R. Livingston and Eleanor T. Beeckman House**/now **Permanent Mission of the Republic of Serbia to the U.N.**, 854 Fifth Ave., bet. E.66th and E.67th St. 1903-1905. *Warren & Wetmore*. ●

One of the few remaining mansions on Fifth Avenue; view the best parts from the Central Park sidewalk: the copper verdigris roof with its ornately framed oculi.

On East 66th Street, between Fifth and Madison Avenues:

[G55a] Originally **Margaret Vanderbilt Shepard House**/now **The Lotos Club**/onetime **William J. and Maria Shepard Schiefflin House**, 5 E.66th St. 1898-1900. *Richard Howland Hunt*.

An architectural *opera buffa*. Rose-colored brick and limestone, its slate- and copper-sheathed mansard punctuated with bulls-eye dormers for the household staff. A present for

[G56] **45 East 66th Street Apartments**, NE cor. Madison Ave. 1906-1908. *Harde & Short*. ●

They hoped for **Perpendicular Gothic**. Two glassy ten-story walls of 12 over 12 large double-hung windows intersect in a magnificent cylinder of even more windows: one of the City's glassiest façades. Monumentally exuberant, and scarcely shy.

East 66th Street, between Park and Lexington Avenues:

[G57] **Seventh Regiment Armory, N.Y. National Guard**, 643 Park Ave. (Park to Lexington Aves. bet. E.66th and E.67th Sts). 1877-1879. *Charles W. Clinton*. ●
Tower removed, Park Ave. façade. **Interiors**, Park Ave. wing, *Louis Comfort Tiffany, Stanford White, Herter Brothers, Alexander Roux & Co., L. Marcotte Co. and Pottier & Stymus*. ●
Renovations, 2009, *Platt Byard Dovell White*.

A friendly brick fortress. New York armories were composed of two distinct elements: a three- or four-story collection of office, meeting, and socializing spaces (Park Avenue) and a vast drill hall (Lexington). The latter, 187 X 270 feet of clear space, is sufficient for maneuvering modern military vehicles—not to mention tennis practice and antiques expositions. The regimental monument stands along Central Park's wall at 67th Street.

The Armory's Park Avenue Building was in large part furnished and detailed on its interior by Louis Comfort Tiffany, son of Charles, founder and owner of Fifth Avenue's **Tiffany & Company***. Louis rejected the business world for that of the applied arts. His studios eventually specialized in decorative crafts ranging from the stained glass for which he is best remembered to stone-carving, metalworking, and casting of bronze—crafts complementing the ornate Late Victorian architecture of his architect-clients. In this case some tables were turned: Stanford White worked*

[G59a] **130-134 East 67th Street**, SE cor. Lexington Ave. 1907. *Rossiter & Wright.* ●
[G59b] **131-135 East 66th Street**, NE cor. Lexington Ave. 1905-1907. *Charles A. Platt of Simonson, Pollard & Steinam.* ●

Two adjacent **neo-Italian Renaissance** apartment blocks, produced by different architects of record, but designed by *Platt*, who left one firm to join the other so that he could create the complement to his first work. The 66th Street side, where the entry is crowned with a glorious broken pediment, rises to a **Florentine** cornice. For an even grander *Platt* cornice see the **Astor Court Apartments** at Broadway and 89th. There the crown seems Michelangeloesque.

From Fifth Avenue along East 67th Street to Madison Avenue:

[G60] **7th Regiment Monument, N.Y. National Guard**, Fifth Ave. at E.67th St. W side, fronting Central Park. 1927. *Karl Illava*, sculptor.
Dynamic bronze; seething bayonets.

G57

G58a

G58b

G60

G59a

G61a

G61b

under Tiffany's direction on this interior work, rather than the later, and more obvious, reversed relationship (but White was then only 24).

[G58a] **The Cosmopolitan Club**, 122 E.66th St., 1932. *Thomas Harlan Elett.*
One of the northernmost outposts of "New Orleans" cast iron. Organized as a club for women professionals and semiprofessionals, the **Cos** contrasts with the **Colony Club**. As much as the **Colony's** architecture is grand, the **Cos's** is frivolous.

[G58b] Originally **Henry O. Havemeyer Stable** (coach house/coachman's residence)/later **John Hay Whitney Garage**, 126 E.66th St. 1895. *W.J. Wallace and S.E. Gage.*
A glorious brick arch, onetime portal for nine *Whitney* cars. Rarely does even consciously monumental architecture achieve such power. The Roman molded brickwork, forming the arch, is breathtaking.

[G61a] Originally **Henri P. Wertheim House**/now **Residence of the Consul General of Japan**, 4 E.67th St. 1902. *John H. Duncan.*
A little brick and a lot of limestone: **Beaux Arts** with a slate, oculi pierced, copper crested, mansard roof. But Japan's U.N. Delegate's residence on 62nd Street is grander still.

[G61b] Formerly **Jules S. Bache House**, 10 E.67th St. 1881. *James E. Ware.* Altered for Bache, 1899, *C.P.H. Gilbert.*
A fashionable, but timid, neo-Classical bow front, guarded with neo-18th-century ironwork.

[G61c] Formerly **Jeremiah Milbank House**, 14-16 E.67th St. (combined houses). **No.14**, 1879, *Lamb & Wheeler*; altered, 1920, *Dodge & Morrison.* **No.16**, 1905, *John H. Duncan.*
Separate structures for *Mr. Milbank* linked within, and harmonized in 1920 with renaissance swaggery, without.

[G61d] Formerly **R. Fulton Cutting House**, 22 E.67th St. 1879. *Lamb & Wheeler*. Altered for Cutting, 1908, *Harry Allan Jacobs*.

Cutting (1852-1934) was known as "first citizen of New York" for his leadership of myriad groups, as well as the **Cooper Union**. He was also the Citizens Union's first president. An understated London limestone façade, as befits a brahmin.

[G62a] Originally **Samuel H. Valentine House**, 5 E.67th St. 1909. *Carrère & Hastings*.

A Neo-Reniassance façade with an ornately ornamented two-story bowed bay with unfluted pilasters bearing French neo-16th-century bas-relief.

[G62b] **7 East 67th Street**. 1882. *Thom & Wilson*. Present façade, 1900, *Clinton & Russell*.

Paired Ionic columns support a wide bay-fronted façade, allowing a shallow porch. Another streetfront counterpoint amongst flatter façades.

A turn-of-the-century **Parisian** town house, rusticated and swagged. The shallow balconies, in front of the French doors, for (mostly psychological) security, enliven the façade.

East 67th Street, between Madison and Park Avenues:

[G63a] Originally **Hugh D. Auchincloss House**/onetime **Histadruth Foundation**/now **Italian Trade Commission**, 33 E.67th St. 1903. *Robertson & Potter*.

Sober neo-Georgian brick and limestone with a cornice of Italian grandeur. It must be the latter that seduced the Trade Commission to move here.

[G63b] Originally **Arthur H. Scribner House**, 39 E.67th St. 1877. *David & John Jardine*. Present façade, 1904, *Ernest Flagg*.

Flagg's swags enliven this limestone confection: *Scribner's* town house. Its relative sobriety contrasts with the both decorative and

G61c

G61d

G62c

G63a

G62a

G62b

G63c

[G62c] Originally **Charles C. Stillman House**, 9 E.67th St. 1882. *Thom & Wilson*. Current façade, 1912, *Hiss & Weeks*.

French Renaissance. At the ground floor a quartered square, stone-mullioned, presents stained glass to the street. Above, three dormers and a carved balcony enrich the plain limestone façade.

[G62d] Originally **Martin Beck House**/sometime **Barbara Sears** (*Bobo*, onetime *Mrs. Winthrop*) **Rockefeller house**, 13 E.67th St. 1921. *Harry Allan Jacobs*.

Martin Beck, a prominent figure of New York's stage commissioned this façade, dominated by a **Palladian** window, that served as *Beck's* point of overview, and symbol of prestige. Later, *Bobo* lived here, from 1955 to 1998, and looked out.

[G62e] Originally **Cortlandt F. Bishop House**/now **The Regency Whist Club**, 15 E.67th St. 1907. *Ernest Flagg*.

spacial exuberance of the **Scribner Store** on Fifth Avenue.

[G63c] Originally **James R. Sheffield House**/later (1964-1973) **Gloria Vanderbilt Cooper House**, 45 E.67th St. 1913. *Walter B. Chambers*.

Modest (in relation to its competing neighborhood peers), but the recessed ground floor offers a rhythm to the street that grander buildings can't match.

[G63d] **47 East 67th Street**. 1878. *J.H. Valentine*. Present façade, 1909, *William A. Bates*.

A neo-Georgian bowed brick façade supported by leggy Doric columns.

[G64] Originally **Elizabeth and Mary Thompson House**, 36-38 E.67th St. 1906. *Henry Bacon*.

Bacon was architect for the **Lincoln Memorial** in Washington. And in New York, the **Union Square Savings Bank** (now a theater).

G62e

East 67th Street, between Park and Lexington Avenues:

[G65] **Milan House**, 115 E.67th St., and 116 E.68th St. 1931. *Andrew J. Thomas.*

Two 11-story secrets, complete with carved monsters, grotesques, florid capitals atop colonnettes, and wonderful multipaned steel casement windows, one of the few distinguished apartment buildings to retain this elegance. The midblock **Italian** garden court between the wings, barely visible through the entry doors, is an urban dream.

East 67th Street, between Lexington and Third Avenues:

G63d

G64

G65

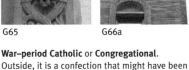

G66a

[G66a] **Kennedy Child Study Center**/originally **Mount Sinai Dispensary**, 149-151 E.67th St. 1889-1890. *Buchman & Deisler and Brunner & Tryon.* 🍎

Built as an adjunct to an earlier **Mt. Sinai Hospital**, this is an eclectic, but dignified, **neo-Renaissance** civic building, in brick and terra cotta, with 15th-century (Italian quattrocento) details: all in sandstone, salmon-colored brick, and white terra cotta.

[G66b] **19th Precinct, N.Y.C. Police Department**/originally **25th Precinct**, 153 E.67th St. 1886-1887. *Nathaniel D. Bush.* 🍎 Altered, 1988, *The Stein Partnership.*

A Victorian palazzo: limestone and red brick borrowing heavily from the **Florentine Renaissance**. The rusticated base supports a mannered Victorian body. A complicated 1980s restoration-reconstruction links it to its neighbor, *Le Brun* (see next).

[G66c] Originally **N.Y.C. Fire Department Headquarters**/later **Engine Company No.39, Ladder Company No.16**, 157 E.67th St. 1886. *Napoleon Le Brun & Sons.* Restored, 1992, *The Stein Partnership.* 🍎

Lusty **Romanesque Revival** in brownstone and brick; the herringbone decoration of the voussoirs is straight from Norman England.

[G66d] **Park East Synagogue/Congregation Zichron Ephraim**, 163 E.67th St. 1889-1890. *Schneider & Herter.*

Inside, a Victorian preaching space, nominally made Jewish through Saracenic detail. Stripped to its essentials, it could be **Civil War–period Catholic** or **Congregational**. Outside, it is a confection that might have been conceived in a Moorish trip on LSD: a wild, vigorous extravaganza.

East 68th Street, between Fifth and Madison Avenues:

[G67a] Originally **John J. Emery House**/now **Consulate General of Indonesia**, 5 E.68th St. 1896. *Peabody & Stearns.*

A bloated mansion, impressive in size, unconvincing in character and detail.

[G67b] Originally **Mrs. George T. Bliss House**, 9 E.68th St. 1907. *Heins & La Farge.*

From the spirit of *Sir John Soane*: known for his radical architecture, *Soane's* mansion (now a museum) at **Lincoln's Inn Fields**, London, is one of the great experiments in **Regency** architecture. Here the great Ionic columns support the sky and form a magnificent stage set.

[G67c] **The Marquand**, 11 E.68th St., NW cor. Madison Ave. 1913. *Herbert Lucas*.

The brick and bow-bay upper floors of this 11-story apartment rest atop a handsome pillow-rusticated limestone base. The structure occupies the site of three brownstones designed by *Richard Morris Hunt* for *Henry G. Marquand* in 1880. Note the incised **M** at various points in the façade.

[G68a] **6 East 68th Street**, 1881. *John G. Prague*. **8, 10 East 68th Street** (houses). 1882. *Lamb & Wheeler*. Linked and altered, 1920, *Harry Allan Jacobs*.

This trio of now-interlinked mansions was owned, in varying combinations, by family members of the *Lehman Brothers* and Kuhn, Loeb & Company banking firms. Among them was *Otto Kahn*, who lived at **No.8** until he commissioned his grand palazzo on 91st Street. The modern alterations and sur-elevation are heavy-handed.

[G68b] Originally **Henry T. Sloane House**, 18 E.68th St. 1905. *C.P.H. Gilbert*.

Don't confuse this **Beaux Arts** *Sloane* House with the one at 9 East 72nd where *Sloane* (1845-1937), of the **W. & J. Sloane Store**, lived with the first *Mrs. Sloane*. After his divorce, he built this limestone hôtel de ville.

[G69] Originally **Dr. Christian A. Herter House**, 817-819 Madison Ave., bet. E.68th and E.69th Sts. E side. 1892. *Carrère & Hastings*. Storefronts added, 1922, *Carrère & Hastings*.

Sadly compromised by commercial claims and the need for fire escapes, this monumental

G67c

G66d

G68a

G70a

G70c

survivor rises deliciously, a bit **frowsy**, behind the modern front of Donna Karan.

East 68th Street, between Madison and Park Avenues:

[G70a] Originally **Mary D. Dunham House**, 35 E.68th St. 1901. *Carrère & Hastings*.

Extravagant ornament on a "modest" *Carrère & Hastings* palace. Note the guard railings at the third-floor French doors (garde-fous).

[G70b] Originally **Ruth Hill Beard House**, 47 E.68th St. 1907. *Adams & Warren*.

A bold stone Italian **Renaissance** cornice, pediments, and balcony.

[G70c] Originally **J. William and Margaretta C. Clark House**/onetime **Automation House**, 49 E.68th St. 1913-1914. *Trowbridge & Livingston*. Restored, 1991, *Buttrick, White & Burtis*. ✴

The muntined French window replacements are a retrofit: fixed glass sheets were fitted in a

previous alteration. At the ground floor, arcaded recessed space provides a pleasant modulation of the streetscape.

[G71a] Formerly **John D. Crimmins House**, 40-42 E.68th St. **No.40**, 1879, *William Schickel*. **No.42**, 1878, architect unknown. Joined, 1898, *Schickel & Ditmars*.

Two houses combine to form a monumental mansarded **Beaux Arts** limestone complex. *Crimmins* was the contractor for some of the City's largest 19th-century public works. The house looks as if the budget of many ended up as this bloated extravagance.

[G71b] Originally **Michael Friedsam House**/now **Dominican Academy**, 44 E.68th St. 1922. *Frederick G. Frost*.

A bland box noted for its historical associations rather than its architecture. Businessman, philanthropist, art collector, and civic leader *Friedsam* succeeded *Benjamin Altman* as that department store's president. Good entry ironwork.

[G71c] **Peter G. Peterson Center for International Studies**, 50 E. 68th Street. 1999. *Bell Larson*.

The entrance to a new complex including 50 through 56 East 68th Street: not **postmodern** or **historicist**, it's the new, offbeat, and eccentric white knight on the block.

[G72] Originally **Harold I. Pratt House**/now **Council on Foreign Relations**, 58 E.68th St., SW cor. Park Ave. 1919-1921. *Delano & Aldrich*. Addition to W, 1954, *Wyeth & King*.

Harold was the youngest son of Brooklyn's 19th-century industrialist *Charles Pratt*, kerosene magnate and later major shareholder in the **Standard Oil** trust. Four sons built minor palaces along Brooklyn's Clinton Avenue (three still stand) near their dad's mansion. When *Harold's* turn came, he was swept by changing fashions to Manhattan's Park Avenue—hence this sober limestone **neo-Renaissance** marvel.

G71a

G71c

G72

G73a

The whole blockfront on the west side of Park Avenue between E.68th and E.69th Sts:
A whole that is much greater than the sum of its parts, although each, separated, would be distinguished in its own right. Georgian architecture's greatest contribution is not only the style of individual structures but a comprehensive attitude toward urban design. Buildings of character, quality, and refinement were integrated in a larger system of designing cities, the blithe basis of this neo-Georgian row.

[G73a] Originally **Percy and Maude H. Pyne House**/now **Americas Society**/one-time **USSR Delegation to the United Nations**, 680 Park Ave., NW cor E.68th St. 1906-1912. *Charles McKim of McKim, Mead & White*. 🍎 Gallery and library open We-Sa 12-6. 212-628-3200.

Rusticated limestone enlivens this crisp neo-Federal town house, supporting red brick in Flemish bond. Client *Percy R. Pyne* (1857-1929) was a New York financier and philanthropist. It was here that *Prime Minister*

Khrushchev, shoe in hand, held forth from the second-floor window in 1960.

[G73b] Originally **Oliver D. and Mary Pyne Filley House**/now **Queen Sofia Spanish Institute**, 684 Park Ave. 1925-1926. *McKim, Mead & White*. 🍎

Built by *Percy Pyne* next door for his daughter and her husband; on the site of *Pyne's* **No.680** garden. Similar to **680**, but note the swagged relief in the lintels.

[G73c] Originally **William and Frances Crocker Sloane House**/now **Istituto Italiano di Cultura**, 686 Park Ave. 1916-1919. *Delano & Aldrich*. 🍎

Perhaps less refined than *M.M.&W.'s* two houses next door, it conforms in scale and materials: note that, when built, it bordered *Pyne's* garden, before **684** filled that space.

[G73d] Originally **Henry P. and Kate T. Davison House**/now **Consulate General**

G73b

of Italy, 690 Park Ave., SW cor. E.69th St. 1916-1917. *Walker & Gillette*. 🍎

Henry P. Davison, a J.P. Morgan partner, commissioned this splendid residence, the northern terminus of this **neo-Federal** block. Like the others, it uses rusticated limestone and brick in Flemish bond; but with especial grandeur at the carved and columned entry.

Marquesa de Cuevas (a Rockefeller gone Spanish) received wide praise in 1965 for buying the endangered structures at 680 and 684 Park Avenue to save them from demolition; she then presented them (and later her own house, 52-54 East 68th Street) to her favorite charities. The Marquesa was the former Margaret Rockefeller Strong, married to the eighth Marquis de Piedrablanca de Guana Cuevas.

Hunter College
Note: Hunter College's buildings straddle the boundary of the Upper East Side Historic District. Those within the district are, like others, so protected.

[G74] **Hunter College, CUNY,** 695 Park Ave., bet. E.68th and E.69th Sts. E side. 1938-1941. *Shreve, Lamb & Harmon, Harrison & Fouilhoux,* associated architects.

An interruption in the pace of Park Avenue: not only modern and glistening with glass, it is also set back 10 feet from the lot line. A proud self-confident monument in the City's early **international modernism:** high style, without being stylish.

[G75] **Thomas Hunter Hall, Hunter College, CUNY**/briefly **Hunter College High School,** 930 Lexington Ave., bet. E.68th and E.69th Sts. W side 1913. *C.B.J. Snyder.*

Like the Ivy League (cf. Princeton, Yale), Hunter commissioned an academic shell in **English Gothic,** suggesting higher learning. The only thing missing is the ivy. But crenellations abound. The prestigious **Hunter High,** a some-time occupant, enrolled the City's most talented young women by competitive examination.

[G76] **South Building and East Building, Hunter College, CUNY,** E.68th St. SW cor. and SE cor. Lexington Ave. Designed 1980, completed 1986 (delayed by City fiscal crisis). *Ulrich Franzen & Assocs.*

Resplendent **modernist** blocks, they are welcome additions to the cityscape. The glassy overpasses on the third and eighth floors over Lexington Avenue provide syncopation to the City's endless street vistas.

[G77] **Sam and Esther Minskoff Cultural Center,** Park East Day School, 164 E.68th St., bet.

[G79] Originally **Isaac and Virginia Stern House,** 835 Madison Ave., bet. E.69th and E.70th Sts. 1885. *William Schickel.* Storefronts added, 1921. Altered, 1930, and recently.

There's great satisfaction in discovering a weather-beaten but largely intact **Queen Anne** brick and limestone row house atop ubiquitous Madison Avenue storefronts.

[G80] **East 69th Street, Madison to Park Aves.**

A rich and changing block of varied architectural styles, all of human scale, and greater than the sum of its parts. Roll call:

No.27/formerly **Lucretia Lord Strauss House**/now **Permanent Mission of the Republic of Cape Verde to the U.N.** 1886. Altered, 1922, *York & Sawyer.* English critic *Osbert Lancaster* might describe this as Stockbrokers' Tudor. But English **neo-Gothic** for the Cape Verde Islands.

No.31/originally **Augustus G. Paine, Jr., House**/now **Consulate General of Austria.** 1918. *C.P.H. Gilbert.* **Neo-Federal,** but the shutters are a joke.

G76   G77

G73d   G75   G78   G79

Lexington and Third Aves. 1974. *John Carl Warnecke & Assocs.*

Creamy brick articulated with granite: a throwback to the streamlined **Art Moderne** architecture displayed at the 1939-1940 New York World's Fair.

[G78] **East 69th Street, Fifth to Madison Aves.** Roll call:

No.7. 1986. *Hobart Betts.* The great banded arch sits on frail Tuscan columns, providing a visually crushing overload for the recessed loggia below.

No.9. 1917. *Grosvenor Atterbury.* Marble and brick **neo-Georgian.**

No.11. 1924. *Delano & Aldrich.* Cool, but not calculating, limestone.

No.12. 1884. Altered, 1913, *William Welles Bosworth.* Denuded and far from its Georgian antecedents.

No.33. 1912. *Howells & Stokes.* Bland. Lightly rusticated limestone.

No.35/now **The Episcopal School.** 1911. *Walker & Gillette.* A monumental mansard roof with oculi; but the charm is in the verdigris bronze railings on the second (parlor) floor.

No.36. ca. 1875. Altered, 1903, *Jardine, Kent & Jardine.* Altered, 1923, *Carrère & Hastings.*

Lesser works by name architects:

No.42/**Jewish National Fund**/originally **Arthur and Alice G. Sachs House.** 1921. *C.P.H. Gilbert. Arthur Sachs* was a descendant of *Sachs* of Goldman, Sachs. Stolid medieval. The flat limestone façade, ornamented only at the openings, gives it bearing.

No.50. 1918. *Henry C. Pelton.* Both grand and bland.

[G81] **The Union Club of New York,** 101 Park Ave., NE cor. E.69th St. also known as 101 E.69th St. 1930-1932. *Delano & Aldrich.*

New York City's oldest social club (founded in 1836) is housed in the style of the **English 18th century**: limestone and granite understated at street level, increasingly enriched above the piano nobile, culminating in a classical frieze (windows are triglyphs, ornate panels serve as metopes, topped with a balustraded cornice).

[G82] **115 East 69th Street,** bet. Park and Lexington Aves. 1903. *Hoppin & Koen.*

Modest **Georgian revival** for these creators of the old Police Headquarters.

[G83] **East 69th Street, Lexington to Third Aves.**

A roll call of idiosyncratic stables/carriage houses/garages:

No.147. 1880. *John Correja.* Present façade, 1913, *Barney & Colt.*

The glassy second floor proffers multi-panes as in **Perpendicular Gothic**. Gutsy.

G80

G81

G82

G83

No.149/for London subway financier *Charles T. Yerkes*/later *Thomas Fortune Ryan.* 1896. *Frank Drischler.* A **Romanesque Revival** personality on the block.

No.153. 1884. *William Schickel.* Dour brick **Romanesque** with terra-cotta and limestone counterpoints.

No.159/for W. & J. Sloane's *John Sloane.* 1882. *Charles W. Romeyn.* Oculi below, arched corbel-tables at the sky.

No.161/for *William Bruce-Brown.* 1916. *Frederick B. Loney.* Note BB in keystone. Using leftovers from a Park Avenue apartment house?

No.167/for the Museum of the American Indian's founder, *George G. Heye.* 1909. *Charles E.Birge.* A diverse collection of 19th-century necessities. Plodding eclectic.

[G84] **Richard Morris Hunt Memorial,** E.70th St. at Fifth Ave., W side, fronting Central Park. 1898. *Daniel Chester French,* sculptor. *Bruce Price,* architect.

A monument to the first American architect trained at the **École des Beaux Arts** who later was founding president of the AIA, American Institute of Architects. A grand classical exedra, *Hunt's* bust at its center, responded to *Hunt's* **Lenox Library** (1877) across the street. See below.

East 70th Street, between Fifth and Madison Avenues:

The north side of this block, through to 71st Street, was developed early in the 20th century, following the demolition of the ***Lenox Library****, which occupied the Fifth Avenue frontage. The library's holdings were transferred to* ***The New York Public Library's Astor, Lenox & Tilden Collections*** *at 42nd Street prior to that building's opening in 1911.*

[G85] Originally **Henry Clay and Adelaide Childs Frick House**/now **Frick Collection,** 1 E.70th St., NE cor. Fifth Ave. to E.71st St. 1913-1914. *Carrère & Hastings.* Altered as a public museum, 1931-1935, *John Russell Pope.* Addition to E, 1977, *Harry Van Dyke, John Barrington Bayley, and G. Frederick Poehler,* architects; *Russell Page,* landscape architect. Museum open to the public: Tu-Sa 10-6; Su 1-6; closed Mo. 212-288-0700. *www.frick.org*

The Collection's garden and open, balustraded stone railing provide a welcome break in the almost endless wall of high-rises along Fifth Avenue. Bland, sometimes fussy, frequently indecisive, the exterior belies a rich interior, both in architecture and contents. The glass-roofed courtyard, entered almost directly, is a delightful transition from the noisy activity of the street. The soothing sound of water from a central fountain makes this a place for pause, utterly relaxing—not surprising in the work of *Pope,* who created similar islands of light, sound, and repose at the **National Gallery** in Washington.

G84

The eastern addition was an anachronism for 1977: not prescient postmodernism, but conscious historicism: a garden court in a Beaux Arts embrace atop a world of underground services. It preceded the historicism of modernist *Kevin Roche* at the **Jewish Museum** (1993) by 16 years. It's a happy addition.

[G86] **East 70th Street, Fifth to Madison Aves**. Roll call, interesting more for their survival as a group than for individual merits:

🔲 **No.11**/sometime **Consuelo Vanderbilt Smith House**. 1909-1910. *John Duncan*. Solemn *Duncan* (of **Grant's Tomb**) limestone. ●

🔲 **No.15**/originally **John Chandler and Corinne DeBébian Moore House**. 1909-1910. *Charles I. Berg*. ●

🔲 **No.17**/originally **Alvin W. and Angeline Krech House**. 1910-1911. *Arthur C. Jackson of Heins & La Farge*. ●

🔲 **No.19**/originally **David Hennen and Alice Morris House**/now **Knoedler Gallery**. 1909-1910. *Thornton Chard*. ● Severity reigns overhead, but arches springing from Tuscan columns reveal spatial modulation that enriches the street.

No.21/originally **Gustav and Virginia Pagenstecher House**/now **Hirschl & Adler Galleries**. 1918-1919. *William J. Rogers*. ● Modern railings form the store's cornice.

[G87c] Originally **Augustus G. Paine, Jr., Garage**. 1918. *C.P.H. Gilbert*. Surelevated, 1990s.

A heavy-handed topping to what was once a graceful garage. The twin Tuscan columns are, perhaps, the necessary structure (or its concealment), but they convert grace into stumbling **Georgian**.

🏛️🔲 [G87d] Originally **Stephen C. Clark House**/now **Lowell Thomas Building, Explorers' Club**, 46 E.70th St. 1912. *Frederick J. Sterner*.

A richly ornamented **neo-Jacobean** work commissioned by a member of the **Singer Sewing Machine** *Clarks*. Unique in this city.

[G88a] Originally **Walter N. and Carola Rothschild House**/now **Twentieth Century Fund**, 41 E.70th St. 1929. *Aymar Embury II*.

An austere façade built for the chairman of the board of Abraham & Straus department store; his wife was *Carola Warburg*, daughter of *Felix M. Warburg*.

G86   G87a

G85   G87c   G87d

East 70th Street, Madison to Park Aves:

[G87a] Originally **Laura K. Bayer House**/then **Clendenin Ryan House**/then **Clendenin Ryan, Jr., House**, 32 E.70th St. 1911. *Taylor & Levi*.

Stately limestone. The dormer façade, buttressed by giant console brackets, grandly elevates the status of the fifth floor. The *Ryans* were son and grandson of financier *Thomas Fortune Ryan*. Both *Clendenin* and son committed suicide here, in 1939 and 1957, respectively.

[G87b] **James P. Warburg House**, 36 E.70th St. 1885. Altered, 1924, *William Lawrence Bottomley*.

A double-width, eclectic two-tone brownstone and sandstone house. *James*, a banker and author, is the son of *Paul M. Warburg*, whose father, *Felix M.*, conveyed the family's 92nd Street mansion to form part of the **Jewish Museum**. A large, but modest, façade.

[G88b] Originally **Walter and Florence Hope House**, 43 E.70th St. 1928-1929. *Mott B. Schmidt*.

Clad in the warm, pocked texture of travertine, rusticated at the base, dormered atop.

[G88c] Originally **Arthur S. and Adele Lewisohn Lehman House**/then **Joseph and Estée Lauder House**, 45 E.70th St. 1928-1929. *Aymar Embury II*.

The cosmetics pioneer *Lauder* died here in 2004 at the age of 97.

Arthur Lehman's brother, Herbert, was Governor of New York, 1933-1942, a time when "old money" took their hands to politics. (Before Lehman there had been Franklin D. Roosevelt; after, Averill Harriman and Nelson Rockefeller.)

[G89] **The Asia Society**, 725 Park Ave., NE cor. E.70th St. 1979-1981. *Edward Larrabee Barnes Assocs.* Remodeled and extended, 2001, *Voorsanger Associates.* Gallery open Su 12-5; Tu, We, Fr, Sa 11-6; closed Mo. 212-288-6400. *www.asiasociety.org*

Open to the public. An austere brooding polished brown granite prism. Only when it flies colorful multistory banners above its Park Avenue entry does it extend a welcome to those who visit its fine exhibitions of Asian art. *Voorsanger's* expansion is lively and less austere than the original, employing a bright color palette, a serene garden courtyard, and a floating, twisting stair leading to the galleries.

East 70th Street, between Park and Lexington Avenues: A block as diverse, friendly, inviting, tactile, dappled, intricate, and surprising as anyone might wish. A masterpiece of the culture rather than of narrow architectural or planning decisions.

G89

[G90a] Originally **Thomas W. and Florence Lamont House**/onetime **Visiting Nurse Service of New York**, 107 E.70th St. 1920-1921. *Walker & Gillette.*

English Gothic—or **Tudor Revival**, if you wish— for the taste of the country parson's son who became head of **J. P. Morgan's**. The ashlar and cut stone, gable-roofed façade is an unexpected— and welcome—break in the rhythms of this block.

[G90b] Originally **I. Townsend Burden House**, 115 E.70th St. 1922. *Patrick J. Murray.* Mansard added, 1935.

A bold **neo-Georgian/Italian Renaissance** blend for the cousin of iron and steel magnate *James A. Burden.*

[G90c] **123 East 70th Street**. 1902-1903. *Trowbridge & Livingston.*

The elliptical arched opening and ironwork at the third floor bring the scent of **Beaux Arts Paris** to the block. The glazing and French doors touch on the **Art Nouveau**.

[G90d] **Paul Mellon House**, 125 E.70th St. 1966. *Page Cross.*

Replacing two 1860s row houses, this is one of the rare row houses built in Manhattan since World War II. Anachronistic: a charming stuccoed confection of **"French Provincial"** that France itself never experienced.

[G90e] Originally **James and Helen Geddes House**, 129 E.70th St. 1863. Stoop removed, 1940.

The oldest survivor in the Upper East Side Historic District, speculatively built as one of five: **Nos.121-129.** (The "white" stone is actually painted brownstone.) **Neo-Gothic** Victorian, bay-windowed, and classically corniced.

[G90f] Formerly **Mr. and Mrs. Charles Lamed Atterbury House**, 131 E.70th St. ca. 1871. Altered and extended, 1911, *Grosvenor Atterbury.* Store, 1940.

A picturesque extravaganza fashioned from an earlier structure by *Atterbury* for his parents—sometimes it pays to send your son to architecture school. Oriels, bay windows, bow windows, light, and eccentric spaces everywhere.

[G91a] **112-114 East 70th Street** (houses). 1869. *James Santon.*

Two late Italianate brownstone survivors of a matching row of five with **English basements. No.112** retains its original double-hung window pattern and detail, **No.114** has been "modernized," its window openings refitted (before landmarks designation) with single sheets of glass. Which do you prefer?

G90c   G90d

[G91b] Originally **Edward A. Norman House**, 124 E.70th St. 1940-1941. *William Lescaze.*

A dated **modernist** house shouting "look at me!" It was included in the *Museum of Modern Art's Built in USA, 1932-1944* exhibition, undoubtedly because it did thumb its nose at its historicist neighbors. *Lescaze's* own house on East 48th Street is far more sophisticated.

East 70th Street, between Lexington and Third Avenues:

[G92a] Originally **Stephen H. Brown House**/now **Manhattan High School for Girls**, 154 E.70th St. 1907. *Edward P. Casey.*

This double-width **Tudor Revival** house was built for a family known as collectors of medieval art. Leaded panes and crenellations validate its **neo-Gothic** yearnings. Since 1932 a series of private institutions have taught within.

[G92b] Originally **Daniel G. Reid stable and groom's apartments**/now **New York School of Interior Design**/onetime **Lenox School**, 170 E.70th St. 1902. *C.P.H. Gilbert*. Converted to school, 1925, *Bradley Delehanty*. Expanded upward, 1939, 1963.

Finely worked **Renaissance Revival** limestone, penetrated by a grand, rusticated arch, must have led to a **fleet** of carriages. Now it leads to a fleet of interior designers.

[G93a] Originally **Jules S. Bache Stable**/later **John D. Rockefeller Garage**, 163 E.70th St. 1902. *C.P.H. Gilbert*.
[G93b] Originally **Henri P. Wertheim Stable**/later **Stephen C. Clark Garage**, 165 E.70th St. 1902. *C.P.H. Gilbert*.

Grand rusticated limestone and brick carriage houses; however, **No.163** and its neighborhood are compromised by the substitution of bland single sheets of glass for the original multi-paned windows.

G91a

East 71st Street, between Fifth and Madison Avenues:
The south side of this block, through to East 70th, was developed after the death (1880) of James Lenox, whose Lenox Library had occupied part of it.

[G94a] Originally **Herbert N. Straus House**/now **Birch Wathen School**, 9 E.71st St. 1932. *Horace Trumbauer*. Roof addition, 1977.

Regal limestone ladies oversee the street from the fourth floor terrace. *Straus*, of the **Macy's** clan, never occupied this mansarded house; work was stopped shortly before his death in 1933.

[G94b] Originally **Mr. and Mrs. Richard M. Hoe House**, 11 E.71st St. 1892. *Carrère & Hastings*.

A town house for the founder of a great printing press manufactory. The hopefully exotic, but merely tacky, column shafts, detract.

[G94c] **13 East 71st Street**. 1891-1892. *R.H. Robertson*.

A remnant from Manhattan's **Brown Decades**: after 1893 (World's Columbian Exposition) **American Renaissance** whitestone, terra cotta, and marble immediately usurped the place of brownstone buildings in Manhattan. To find a trove, travel to Brooklyn's Fort Greene, Clinton Hill, and Bedford-Stuyvesant. Here is *Robertson's* elegant and unique use of that material.

[G95a] **Frick Art Reference Library**, 10 E.71st St. 1931-1935. *John Russell Pope*. 212-547-0641. *www.frick.org*

A grand **Palladian** portal to the verbal annex of the visual Frick Gallery. Open to researchers; no appointment necessary.

[G95b] Originally **William A. Cook House**, 14 E.71st St. 1913. *York & Sawyer*.

Magnificent bronze gates set in a two-story column-embraced portal. A great overhanging

G94a

G94b

G94c

G95a

cornice shelters a Guastavino-vaulted penthouse balcony. Limestone surfaces are subtly worked, as though they were tooled leather.

[G95c] **16, 18 East 71st Street**. 1911. *John H. Duncan*.

Early 20th-century **plain Jane** whitestones which, over the years, have served as town houses, apartments, private hospitals, and private schools.

[G95d] Originally **Julius Forstmann House**/later **Catholic Center for the Blind**, 22 E.71st St. 1923. *C.P.H. Gilbert*. Altered, 1942, *Robert J. Reiley*.

A double-width limestone house with expansive proportions that comfortably fit its broad façade: contented, self-satisfied. *Forstmann* was a well-known manufacturer of wool fabrics.

[G96a] **St. James Episcopal Church**, 861-863 Madison Ave., NE cor. E.71st St. 1884. *R.H. Robertson*. Rebuilt, 1924, *Ralph Adams Cram*. Original tower, 1926, *Ralph Adams Cram*; replacement (smaller) tower, 1950, *Richard Kimball*.

Crisp brownstone and steel produce modern overtones on the reworked **neo-Gothic** body whose intended tower (had it been built) would have been more than twice the height of the main roof peak. The stonework of *Cram's* more modest tower of 1926 began to crumble, and today's basketweave-ornamented replacement is a regrettable addition.

[G96b] **St. James Parish House**, 865 Madison Ave., bet. E.71st and E.72nd St. E side. 1937-1938. *Grosvenor Atterbury*.

A late *Atterbury* work in the **neo-Gothic**, replacing a brownstone purchased by the church in 1920 and subsequently outgrown. Flat stonework emphasizing the projection of the entry surrounds and the recession of the multi-paned windows.

G95b   G95d

G98

East of Madison Avenue:

[G97] **Viscaya**/formerly **New York Society for the Prevention of Cruelty to Children**, 110 E.71st St., bet. Park and Lexington Aves. 1917. *Hill & Stout*. Sliver tower added, 1982, *Architects Design Group*.

A round-cornered 16-story sliver pokes through—and cantilevers over—the midsection of a dignified five-story **neo-Georgian** town house. New Yorkers have "never seen anything like the Tower on top of the Brownstone," said the ads. True enough. Let's not do it again.

[G98] Formerly **Elsie de Wolfe House**, 131 E.71st St., bet. Park and Lexington Aves. 1867. New façade, 1910, *Ogden Codman, Jr.*, architect. *Elsie de Wolfe*, designer.

The original **de-stooped** house. *Miss de Wolfe*, the original "lady decorator" (later *Lady Mendl*, the almost-original great-party-giver), set the pace for brownstone conversions throughout Manhattan's Upper East Side. The few remaining stoops are, in reaction, nostalgically embraced and protected; some have been rebuilt.

[G99] Formerly **Mildred Phelps Stokes Hooker House**, 173-175 E.71st St., bet. Third and Lexington Aves. 1869. *James Fee*. Current façade, 1911, *S.E. Gage*. Altered within, 1920, 1944.

A romantic **neo-Gothic** redesign, pairing and expanding two brownstone row houses, projecting their volume into the former stoop space. The owner from 1910 to 1946 was the sister of the architect and author *Isaac Newton Phelps Stokes*.

G97

East 72nd Street, between Fifth and Madison Avenues:

[G100a] Originally **Oliver Gould and Mary Brewster Jennings House**/onetime **Lycée Français de New York**, 7 E.72nd St. 1898-1899. *Ernest Flagg & Walter B. Chambers.* 🍎

The rich opulence of **Napoleon III's Paris** was imported to New York: vermiculated and rusticated voussoirs, deep-set French windows, gracious ironwork, and a luscious copper and slate roof: a bijou in contrast to the monumentality of **No.9** next door.

[G100b] Originally **Henry T. and Jessie Sloane House**/later **James Stillman House**/sometime **Lycée Français de New York**, 9 E.72nd St. 1894-1896. *Carrère & Hastings.* 🍎

Colonnaded grandeur is on display, in contrast to the more subtle posture next door.

G103b

G99

G100b

G103a

[G101] **19 East 72nd Street**, NW cor. Madison Ave. 1936-1937. *Rosario Candela* with *Mott B. Schmidt*. Entrance enframement, *C. Paul Jennewein*, sculptor.

This timid **Art Moderne** apartment house replaced *Charles Tiffany's* robust Romanesque Revival mansion (an early *McKim, Mead & White* masterpiece), later decorated and occupied by his son, *Louis Comfort Tiffany*. However, 19's Art Moderne cornering is succulent.

[G102a] Originally **Gertrude Rhinelander Waldo House**/now **Polo Ralph Lauren**/ onetime **Olivetti Building**, 867 Madison Ave., SE cor. E.72nd St. 1895-1898. *Kimball & Thompson*. ✲ Altered for shops, 1921.

Every part of this building exudes personality: bay windows, a roof line bristling with dormers and chimneys. This extravagantly ornamented **neo-French Renaissance** limestone palace has captured the imagination of the commercial world since 1921, when it was first occupied by an antiques firm. It has subsequently housed interior decorators, auction houses like

Christie's of London, the **Zabar** family's East Side outpost **E.A.T.**, and now fashion designer *Ralph Lauren's* flagship retail outlet. *Rhinelander Waldo*, socialite, hero of the Spanish-American War, and police commissioner, can be observed "in action" in the novel and movie *Ragtime*.

[G102b] **Ralph Lauren #2**, 888 Madison Ave., SW cor. E.72nd St. 2010. *HS2 (Hut Sachs Studio)*.

Ralph's Faux Beaux (Arts). A five-story palazzo by *McKim, Mead & White* (1894) stood here until 1951, when it was replaced by a two-story taxpayer since demolished by his Laurenship.

[G103a] **Chase Bank**/formerly **Manufacturers Hanover Trust Company**, 35 E.72nd St., bet. Madison and Park Aves. 1931. *Cross & Cross*.

A bank, of all things, in the manner of the *Brothers Adam*, who festooned for the upper classes in **18th-century London** and Edinburgh. Elegant.

[G103b] **Mayer House**, 41 E. 72nd St., bet. Madison and Park Aves. 1881-1882. *Robert B. Lynd.*

A brownstone town house from an earlier 72nd Street, long before brick, white limestone, and marble took over.

[G104a] **176 East 72nd Street**, bet. Lexington and Third Aves. 1996. *Tod Williams Billie Tsien.*

A **collage** of glass, steel, and limestone crowned with a north-facing skylight. Compare with [H39] on p. 216.

[G104b] **Provident Loan Society of America**, 180 E.72nd St. bet. Lexington and Third Aves. ca. 1895.

An exquisite tiny **Doric** temple of finance, in the shadow of Tower East.

[G105] **Tower East**, 190 E.72nd St., SW cor. Third Ave. to E.71st St. 1962. *Emery Roth & Sons.*

A sheer, freestanding tower: four apartments per floor, all with magnificent views. One of Manhattan's earliest excursions into high-rise luxury housing. Built on the site of the **Loew's 72nd Street** movie theater.

East 73rd Street, between Fifth and Madison Avenues:

[G106a] **5 East 73rd Street**. 1901. *Buchman & Fox.*

Freestanding **Beaux Arts** enhanced by the garden next door at **No.11**, once wrapped in a stole of ivy, now bared.

[G108a] **Madison Avenue Presbyterian Church**, 917 Madison Ave., NE cor. E.73rd St. 1899-1901. *James E. Ware & Sons.* Madison Ave. entrance altered, 1960, *Adams & Woodbridge.* [G108b] **Parish House**, 921-923 Madison Ave., bet. E.73rd and E.74th Sts. E side. 1816-1817. *James Gamble Rogers.*

The austerity of the church walls contrasts sharply with its ornate detail, making normal **neo-Gothic** carving, particularly on the tower, appear extravagant. The adjacent nine-story parish house is a regal neo-Renaissance neighbor with Venetian overtones. It crests with a colonnade and cornice far above the entering Presbyterians, who settle in their more dour world at sidewalk level.

[G109a] **105 and 107 East 73rd Street**, bet. Park and Lexington Aves. 1881-1882. *Thom & Wilson.* Present façade, 1903.

Offbeat **Arts and Crafts** in brick with multi-paned sash and (some) leaded glass. The cornice is an active participant in the four-story façade: monumental, projecting, with a strong rhythm of outriggers that activates the ensemble.

[G109b] Originally **Mr. and Mrs. Arthur C. Train House**/now **The Buckley School** addition, 113 E.73rd St., bet. Park and Lexington Aves. 1908. *George B. Post & Sons.* Converted, new façade added, 1962, *Brown, Lawford & Forbes.*

A simple, well-scaled façade for an extension through the block, from 74th Street, for a venerable boys' private primary school.

G106a

G104b

G106b

[G106b] Originally **Joseph and Kate Pulitzer House**, 11 E.73rd St. 1900-1903. *Stanford White of McKim, Mead & White.* Rear extension, 1904, *Foster, Gade & Graham.* Converted to apartments, 1934, *James E. Casale.*

It would be happy on the Grand Canal in Venice like **Palazzo Pesaro, Rezzonico,** or **Labia**: here, paired Ionic composite columns frame a glassy body. Also note the marshmallow rustications at the ground floor columns. It's **Pulitzer's Prize** (to himself), long before those dispensed for literary and journalistic works.

[G107] Originally **Albert Blum House**, 20 E.73rd St. 1911. *George and Edward Blum.*

The best in the row from No.8 to No.26, inclusive. The other façades (1897-1923) are by such architects as *Donn Barber* (**No.8**), *Harry Allan Jacobs* (**Nos.10, 12**), *William A. Boring* (**No.14**), *William Lawrence Bottomley* (**No.18**), and *Alexander M. Welch* (**Nos.24, 26**).

[G109c] Originally **Charles Dana Gibson House**, 127 E.73rd St., bet. Park and Lexington Aves. 1903. *Stanford White of McKim, Mead & White.*

A lovingly restored **Colonial Revival** town house in limestone and red brick for the artist who created the **Gibson Girl** by the architect who dallied with the **Girl in the Red Swing**.

Stables. Manhattan's gridiron plan, unlike those of other cities, didn't provide back alleys for service. Therefore, New York's horsedrawn livery was housed on certain blocks, serving the role of service streets. These smelly, noisy places were often located some distance from the properties of their well-to-do owners. Typically, carriages were housed in the front, horses stabled in the rear, and grooms' quarters were above. Later, garages blossomed as conversions.

East 73rd Street, between Lexington and Third Avenues:

[G110a] **Roll call of carriage houses on S side:**
No.166/originally **Henry G. Marquand's**/later **Joseph Pulitzer's**. 1883-1884, *Richard Morris Hunt*.

Simplified **Romanesque Revival** by the architect of the Metropolitan Museum's main wing, for its President.
Nos.168-182 and 161-179 East 73rd Street, bet.Lexington and Third Aves. ☛ As follows:
No.168/Originally **William Baylis's**/later **Charles Russell Lowell Putnam's**, 1899, *Charles Romeyn*. The stepped gable crowns a **neo-Dutch Renaissance** façade.
No.170/originally **George C. Clausen's**/later **Henry T. Sloane's**/later **James Stillman's**. 1890-1891. *Frank Wennemer*. Dour brownstone and brick.
Nos.172-174/originally **James B. Layng's**, 1889. *Frank Wennemer*. Previously painted white, but the mask has been removed.
No.178/originally **Charles I. Hudson's**, 1902. *John H. Friend*. A more pompous **Beaux Arts** effort.
No.180/originally **Max Nathan's**/later **George D. Widener's**, 1890-1891. *William Schickel & Co.* Naïve **Romanesque Revival** brickwork supported by a rockface granite podium.
No.182/originally **S. Kayton & Company**, 1890. *Andrew Spense Mayer*. Ground floor altered, 1908, *Edward L. Middleton*. Expanded upward, 1938, *James J. Gavigan*. Originally a tenement for horses, now a banal garage. Little to look at, but part of this block's history.

G109b   G112b

[G110b] **Roll call of carriage houses on N side:**
Nos.161 and 163: Originally **William H. Tailer's**, both 1896-1897. Both by *Thomas Rae*.

Sober but lusty arches combine the vigor of the **Romanesque Revival** with detail from the **Colonial Revival**: note that swagged frieze.
Nos.165, 167/originally **Henry H. Benedict's**, both 1903-1904, both *George R. Amoroux*. **Beaux Arts** whimsy at the entries.
[G110c] **171 East 73rd Street**. 1860. Vestibule and garden wall added, 1924, *Electus Litchfield*, architect and owner.

LaPierre, Litchfield & Partners was a distinguished architectural firm in the 1930s and 1940s.
[G110d] **175 East 73rd Street**/onetime **blacksmith shop** on ground floor. 1860. Ground floor altered into smithy, 1896. Restored, 1926, *Francis Livingston Pell*, architect and owner.

Two separated "broken teeth" are all that remain of the block's original group of six Italianate row houses. They reveal the earliest

stage of development, as a modest street for lower-middle-class families. The others were demolished in order to build the adjacent carriage houses.
[G110e] Originally **J. Henry Alexandre** carriage house, 173 E.73rd St. 1893. *Hobart C. Walker*.

Alexandre lived at 35 East 67th Street (extant), whose façade he had altered (by another architect).
[G110f] Originally **Automobile Realty Company Garage**, 177-179 E.73rd St. 1906. *Charles F. Hoppe*.

A proud, exquisitely detailed **Beaux Arts** container for the newly emerging automobile. A rare surviving example of the City's early response to the needs of the horseless carriage.

[G111a] Originally **John W. Simpson House**/formerly **Mary E. W. Terrell House**, 925 Fifth Ave., bet E.73rd and E.74th Sts.
[G111b] **926 Fifth Ave.**, bet. E.73rd and E.74th Sts. Both 1899. Both by *C.P.H. Gilbert*.

A pair of **Beaux Arts** five-story town houses representative of modest Fifth Avenue houses

G109a

at the turn of the century. Of the monumental ones only those that are museums or institutions remain (the **Frick, Stuyvesant, Vanderbilt, Carnegie, Warburg, Straight** mansions).

[G112a] **927 Fifth Avenue**, SE cor. E.74th St. 1917. *Warren & Wetmore*.

A modest—in façade, not rent—**neo-Italian Renaissance** apartment house. A dutiful cornice and requisite rusticated limestone.

[G112b] **4 East 74th Street**, Fifth to Madison Aves. 1899, *Alexander M. Welch*

A **Beaux Arts** beauty, its bay supported by free-standing **Composite** columns, makes another happy punctuation of the streetscape. Local developers, *W.W. and T.M. Hall*, sold it to hatmaker *Stephen L. Stetson*.

G113

G111a

[G113] Originally **Raymond C. and Mildred Kramer House**, 32 E.74th St., bet. Madison and Park Aves. 1934-1935. *William Lescaze*.

A handcrafted version of a machine aesthetic common to most Bauhaus-inspired design and architecture. Its original composition of glass, glass block, and white stucco must have startled its neighbors in the 1930s. Still does.

[G114] **Church of the Resurrection** (Episcopal)/ originally **Church of the Holy Sepulchre** (Episcopal), 115 E.74th St., bet. Park and Lexington Aves. 1869. *Renwick & Sands*.

A shy retiring, side-street retreat of random ashlar bluestone with a steep polychrome slate roof. An ecclesiastical sleeper.

ornate cornice sports a lush frieze under dentils and console brackets.

[G118] Originally **Nathaniel L. McCready House**/later **Thomas J. Watson, Jr., House**/later **Harkness House for Ballet Arts**, 4 E.75th St., bet. Fifth and Madison Aves. 1895-1896. *Trowbridge, Colt & Livingston*. Renovated for **William Hale Harkness Foundation**, 1965, *Rogers, Butler & Burgun*.

Standard Oil heiress *Rebekah Harkness* transformed this chaste neo-French Renaissance double house into an opulent temple of **Terpsichore**, as the home of her very own ballet company. Ten years and $20 million later, she changed her mind and terminated the company. Sic transit...

G111c

G114

G115

[G115] **Saga House**, 157 E.74th, bet. Lexington and Third Aves. 1980s.

A modestly scaled apartment house. The ship-like railings give it a step of style over the competition.

From Fifth Avenue and 74th Street to 75th and Madison:

[G116] Originally **Charles E. Mitchell House**/ now the **French Consulate**, 934 Fifth Ave., bet. E.74th and E.75th Sts. 1926. *Walker & Gillette*.

Rusticated limestone on a timid neo-Renaissance body; a Georgian Composite-columned entry supports a balcony on the grand arcuated Italianate *piano nobile*, overlooking Central Park. Come into France on Fifth.

[G117] Originally **Edward S. and Mary Stillman Harkness House**/now **The Commonwealth Fund**, 1 E.75th St., NE cor. Fifth Ave. 1907-1909. *Hale & Rogers*. ●

A cool limestone neo-Renaissance palace guarded by an intricate wrought-iron fence. The

[G119] **5 and 7 East 75th Street**, bet. Fifth and Madison Aves. 1902. *Welch, Smith & Provot*.

More graceful **Beaux Arts** tooled and rusticated limestone. The marble cartouche bearing the number 5 is exquisite.

[G120] **964 Madison Avenue**, NW cor. E.75th St. also known as 21-27 E.75th St. 1925. *George F. Pelham*. Altered, ca. 1985.

White-glazed terra-cotta modified **Corinthian** pilasters provide elegant neo-Classical dress for this modest commercial temple.

[G121] **Whitney Museum of American Art**, 945 Madison Ave., SE cor. E.75th St. 1963-1966. *Marcel Breuer & Assocs. Hamilton Smith*. Expansion, 1995-1998, *Richard Gluckman of Gluckman Mayner*. Open Sa, Su, We, Th: 11am-6pm. Fr 1-9pm (6-9pm pay-what-you-wish). Closed Mo, Tu. *www.whitney.org*

As independent of the streetscape as the **Guggenheim**, it boasts its wares with a vengeance. Reinforced concrete clad in granite, moated, bridged, cantilevered in progressive steps overshadowing the mere patron, it is a forceful place and series of spaces. At the top of the list of must-be-seen modern objects in New York.

Plans have been drawn for a new downtown satellite on Gansevoort Street in the meat-packing district, designed by the Italian, *Renzo Piano*, who was co-architect of the high-tech Pompidou (or **Centre Beaubourg**) in Paris.

Whitney Museum addition: In the spirit of MoMA's residential tower, the Whitney trustees in 1978 considered building a high-tech, high-rise, 35-story mixed-use tower to the south of the Breuer building by a collaboration of British architects Foster Associates and Derek Walker Associates. This plan was canceled in favor of an expansion to the museum itself, first proposed in 1986 by Michael Graves. The Graves scheme, to many, buried the Breuer under a panoply of postmodern forms, and was, happily, discarded in favor of the more civilized Gluckman proposals.

[G122] **980 Madison Avenue**/originally **Parke-Bernet Galleries**/later **Sotheby, Parke-Bernet,** bet. E.76th and E.77th Sts. W side. 1950. *Walker & Poor*, architects. *Wheeler Williams*, sculptor. Addition upward, 1987, *Weisberg Castro Assocs.* Proposed sur-elevation, 2010? *Norman Foster.*

Parke-Bernet once understood and catered to America's cultural starvation: buy history or at least live vicariously with its remnants. Unfortunately, *Parke-Bernet's* "house" remains a dowdy matron culturally confused. The *Wheeler Williams* sculpture pinned to the

[G124a] **823 and 829 Park Avenue**, bet. E.75th and E.76th Sts. E side. 1911. *Pickering & Walker.*

Floral pilasters bracket windows in gently projecting central bays in these (almost) matching midblock and corner apartment blocks. A lovely touch.

[G124b] **821 Park Avenue**, NE cor. E.75th St. 1891. *Lorenz Weiher.*

A happily preserved façade from **old 4th Avenue,** built before the avenue's upgrade to "Park" status (upon the depression of the railroad and its subsequent covering). When this was built trains traveled in an open cut.

[G125] **168, 170, 172, 174, 176 East 75th Street**, bet. Lexington and Third Aves. ca. 1900.

A **clinker-brick complex** of stables with a very complex and picturesque roof line. A happy punctuation in the blockscape.

[G126] **32 East 76th Street**, bet. Madison and Park Aves. also known as 969 Madison Ave. 1983. *Stephen B. Jacobs & Assocs.*

A stylish **modernist** residential high rise on an L-shaped plot that wraps around to Madison.

[G127] **Hotel Carlyle**, 35 E.76th St., NE cor. Madison Ave. to E.77th St. 1929. *Bien & Prince.*

One of the last gasps of the **Great Boom,** this became, in its latter years, New York headquarters for both *Presidents Truman* and *Kennedy*, who usually stayed here when visiting the City. *Ludwig Bemelmans* was unleashed

G116

G117   G124a

façade acts as a dated gatekeeper. Now *Foster* proposes a boxy crown dressed in crisp bronze grillage for its renewal/revival (and the profit of developers).

[G123a] Originally **Dr. Ernest Stillman House**/now **The Hewitt School**, 45 E.75th St., bet. Madison and Park Aves. 1925. *Cross & Cross.*

A late **neo-Georgian** town house. *Dr. Stillman* was an amateur fire buff (as was then-Mayor *La Guardia*) and had installed an alarm system that would tell him where any current fire was located. He often served, unpaid, those needing medical care.

[G123b] **57 East 75th Street**, bet. Madison and Park Aves. 1979. *William B. Gleckman.*

A curious former row house, transformed into an early "sliver building." As an object it is abstractly handsome. As a citizen of the block, it's inciting a riot.

with delightful success in the bar; even the ceiling was not spared his whimsical brush as airplanes and birds float overhead.

[G128] **The Imperial**, 55 E.76th St., bet. Madison and Park Aves. 1883. *Frederick T. Camp.*

A grand and gracious high-rise brownstone, one of the earliest apartment buildings in the City (**French Flats,** as they were the imported idea of those decadent Parisians). "A simplicity so affected that it becomes mere baldness" producing "a design of real dignity and beauty," saith the 1883 *Real Estate Chronicle.*

[G129] Formerly **Leonard N. Stern House**, 870 Park Ave., bet. E.76th and E.77th Sts. W side. 1898. Altered, 1976, *Robert A.M. Stern and John S. Hagman.*

An altered stable, this bow-fronted faux-limestone early **postmodern** town house produces a staccato blip in Park Avenue's endless façades.

[G130] **St. Jean Baptiste Church** (Roman Catholic), 1067-1071 Lexington Ave., SE cor. E.76th St. 1910-1914. *Nicholas Serracino.* ☛ Restored, 1995-1996, *Hardy Holzman Pfeiffer*.

Pomp but not pompous. Outside, various **Roman** parts are clustered about a nave and transepts, unfortunately with a pasty result. Inside, the **neo-Baroque** reigns, both in space, and a richness of gold and polychromy. The congregation was originally French Canadian, and the bill was paid by *Thomas Fortune Ryan*, who built the streetcar lines that allowed the congregation to get here.

[G131] **The Siena**, 188 E. 76th St., SW cor. Third Ave. 1997. *Hardy Holzman Pfeiffer*.

Air rights from **St. Jean Baptiste** allowed this slender shaft. Punctuated at its apex by belvederes at each of its four corners in the manner of a modern-day *Hawksmoor*.

[G132] **863 Park Avenue**, NE cor. E.77th St. 1908. *Pollard & Steinem*.

A pioneer cooperative. Architectural historian *Christopher Gray* terms it "chaste and classical." He's right.

[G133] **55 East 77th Street**, bet. Madison and Park Aves. 1902. *Charles Brendon*.

Sinuous tracery under a grand arch framed in rusticated limestone. Said to be a "vigorous but untutored design." Vainglorious architecture of its time.

NECROLOGY

Mrs. Marcellus Hartley Dodge House, 800 Fifth Ave., NE cor. E. 61st St. 1923. *R.S. Shapter*.

Although undistinguished and unused—its perpetually shuttered windows provoked many juicy rumors—it was one of the avenue's few remaining freestanding mansions. The shuttered town house, a seldom used and seemingly abandoned home of a Rockefeller kin, was screened from the rabble by a painted wood fence higher than anyone's eyes.

7 East 62nd Street, bet. Fifth and Madison Aves. 1900. *Clinton & Russell*. **9 East 67th Street**, bet. Fifth and Madison Aves. 1913. *Hiss & Weeks*.

A pair of fine residences that were sacrificed to "progress."

Originally **First of August Boutique**, 860 Lexington Ave., bet. E.64th and E.65th Sts. W side. 1978. *George Ranalli*.

A storefront of glass squares set within mini-monkey bars (as in a city playground) that crawled up an old brownstone (as ivy crawls up brick walls). *Ranalli* is now Dean of the School of Architecture at the City College of New York.

M. Sherman M. Fairchild House, 17 E.65th St. 1941. *George Nelson and William Hamby*. New façade, 1981, *Milton Klein*. ☛

A revolutionary plan and façade in its day: two separate functional elements at the front and rear of the lot, separated by an open garden court over which glass ramps sprang, linking living/dining/kitchen (front) with bedrooms (rear). The **1941 façade** included a series of motor-operated wood louvers to control sunlight—*Fairchild* was an aircraft manufacturer.

Klein's new façade was a studied cubistic composition of fired (rough) and highly polished red granite veneer, set off by a polished stain-

G121   G129   G130

less-steel ship's railing, and a lone gingko tree. A **sorry fate** for the *Hamby/Nelson* wonder.

Both demolished for the Asia Society:
Originally **Elihu Root House**, 733 Park Ave., SE cor. E. 71st St. 1905. *Carrère & Hastings*.

This was a **neo-Georgian** manor built for the distinguished statesman.
Formerly **Gerrish H. Milliken House**, 723 Park Ave., NE cor. E.70th St. ca. 1870.

From the **second edition**: "The spiral fire stair at the rear (off 70th Street) is an unconscious architectural highlight of this somber, conservative brownstone townhouse." The new Asia Society building occupies the two sites.

Presbyterian Home, 49 E. 73rd St., bet. Madison and Park Aves. 1869. *Joseph Esterbrook*.

An invigorating Victorian mansard-roofed institution. Replaced by a comfortable (for the residents), but bland block.

METROPOLITAN MUSEUM VICINITY

[M1] **Metropolitan Museum Historic District**, Along the E side of Fifth Ave. from E.78th St. to E.86th St. running irregularly through the Fifth-Madison blocks. ☛ The map district lines embrace all buildings within the district.

[M2] Originally **James B. and Nanaline Duke House**/now **N.Y.U. Institute of Fine Arts**, 1 E.78th St., NE cor. Fifth Ave. 1909-1912. *Horace Trumbauer*. Interior remodeled, 1958, *Robert Venturi, Cope & Lippincott*. ☛

A push here and a pull there, *Trumbauer* modeled this understated but elegant town house on its model, the 18th-century **Château Labottière** near Bordeaux. The *Duke's* resources were those of the American Tobacco Company. Now it serves New York University graciously. *Julian Francis Abele*, *Trumbauer's* chief designer, and an early African-American architect, was probably responsible for the design.

M2

M4

M3

[M3] Originally **Payne and Helen Hay Whitney House**/and originally **Henry Cook House**/now **Cultural Services, Embassy of France**, 972 and 973 Fifth Ave., both bet. E.78th and E.79th Sts. Both 1902-1909. *Stanford White of McKim, Mead & White*. ☛

Pale neighbors to the grand *Dukes* adjacent; anywhere else **No.972's** swell and swelling façade, with its 24 Corinthian pilasters, would be the best act on the block. The French have been in residence since 1952.

[M4] **3 and 5 East 78th Street**, bet. Fifth and Madison Aves. **No.3**, 1897-1899. *C.P.H. Gilbert*. **No.5.** 1902-1904. *C.P.H. Gilbert*.

At **No.3,** *Gilbert* provided a brace of winged griffins to guard his **François I** neo-French-Renaissance town house; later, at **No.5,** he lapsed into generic **"Beaux Arts."**

[M5] **4 East 78th Street**, bet. Fifth and Madison Aves. 1887-1889. *Edward Kilpatrick*.

A soaring elliptical arch shelters a monumental porch. **Rock-faced brownstone**. Wonderful.

[M6] Originally **Albert Morgenstern House**/later **Mr. and Mrs. Andrew J. Miller House**/now **N.Y.U. Institute of Fine Arts Conservation Center**, 14 E.78th St., bet. Madison and Fifth Aves. 1887. Façade altered for the Millers, 1917, *Harry Allan Jacobs*. Altered for N.Y.U., 1983, *Michael Forstl*.

Belying the twinned **Ionic** columns and simple four-story 1917 façade, the innards have

M5

been reconfigured as 15 levels of conservation facilities, including a cascade of floors built atop the old roof. The added structure catches north light but is invisible from the street.

[M7] Originally **Stuyvesant and Marian Fish House**, 25 E.78th St. NW cor. Madison Ave. 1897-1900. *Stanford White of McKim, Mead & White*.

Limestone and yellow **Roman** brick combine for a bland façade. But look up: the monumental copper cornice (surmounted by a balustrade) brings memories of *Michelangelo*.

[M8] **Philip and Beulah Robbins House**, 28 E.78th St., SW cor. Madison Ave. 1899-1902. *William M. Kendall of McKim, Mead & White*.

Comfortable **Protestant Georgian**, unassuming, but hardly timid. Stately, it suggests the affluent home of prestigious residents, homelier than *White's* regal palazzo across the street.

M10

M11

M12

M13

[M9] **Rabbi Joseph Lookstein Ramaz Upper School, The Morris B. and Ida Newman Educational Center,** 60 E.78th St., bet. Madison and Park Aves. 1980. *Conklin & Rossant.*

Five brownstone row houses of Finch College removed, and, in their place, an **Orthodox Jewish** school inserted. Sleekly stylish on its arrival in 1980, dated and eccentric now. Let's pursue style, not the ephemeral stylish.

[M10] **157, 159, 161, 163-165 East 78th Street** (row houses), bet. Lexington and Third Aves. 1861. *Henry Armstrong*, builder. 🍎

Vernacular row houses in the **Italianate** style, popular in the City in the 1850s and 1860s. The tall parlor windows, retained in all five, are rare in these parts.

East 79th Street, between Fifth and Madison Avenues:

▓▓▓ [M11] Originally **Isaac D. and Mary**
▓▓▓ **Fletcher House**/now **Ukrainian Institute of America**/onetime **Harry F. Sinclair House**/followed by **Augustus and Ann van Horn Stuyvesant House**, 2 E.79th St., SE cor. Fifth Ave. 1897-1899. *C.P.H. Gilbert.*

A miniature **French-Gothic** château squeezed into the urban context. The precedents are limited: few in the Middle Ages ever achieved commercial wealth. The classic comparison is the house of *Jacques Coeur* (ca. 1450) at Bourges (France). Finials are profuse, many silhouetted against the steep slate roof and sky.

▓▓▓ [M12] **6 East 79th Street.** 1899-1900.
▓ *Barney & Chapman.*

A sensuous bowed façade converts what was designed for Anglican sobriety into an exotic **Georgian Revival** (or neo-Federal) town house.

The sturdy Doric columns at the base and curved mansard roof add to its notability. Critic *Montgomery Schuyler* praised it as "an exceptional palatial example... with unpretending homeliness."

[M13] Originally **John S. and Catherine C. Rogers House**/now the **New York Society Library**, 53 E.79th St., bet. Madison and Park Aves. 1916-1917. *Trowbridge & Livingston*. 🌃

A limestone **London town house**, now the Library *of* the New York Society (rather than a library *for* members of society). Anyone may join for a yearly membership fee: 225,000 volumes and a quiet reading room. Founded in 1754.

[M14a] Originally **John H. and Catherine Iselin House**, 59 E.79th St., bet. Madison and Park Aves. 1908-1909. *Foster, Gade & Graham*. 🌃 neo-French Renaissance. [M14b] Originally **Thatcher and Frances Adams House**, 63 E.79th St. 1902-1903. *Adams & Warren*. 🌃

Some more tired **neo-Georgian**. But next door, the *Rives* house has class.

modeled setback penthouses and water tower on high produce magnificent cubist modeling.

[M18] **Franklyn and Edna Woolworth Hutton House**, and **houses for her two sisters** 2, 4, and 6 E.80th St., NE cor. Fifth Ave. 1911-1916. *C.P.H. Gilbert*.

F.W. Woolworth built them for his three daughters (an economical assemblage for the 5 & 10 cent store king). Two cool **Italian Renaissance** revivalists flank a late Gothic, Loire Valley château: the latter, wider and more ornate with detail, wants to be the social center of this triple marriage.

[M19] **45 East 80th Street**, NE cor. Madison Ave. 1987. *Liebman Liebman & Assocs*.

Twenty-seven crisp stories, with loft-like windows, faced with Italian granite and Indiana limestone. A **postmodern** plinth continues Madison Avenue's two stories of shops and services. It's a better building than most produced by the recent rash of star architects.

M15

M17

M16

M18

M19

[M15] Originally **George and Sarah Rives House**/now **Consulate of Greece**, 67-69 E.79th St. 1907-1908. *Carrère & Hastings*. Altered and expanded upward, 1962, *Pierre Zannettos*. 🌃

An import from the Place Vendôme; **Tuscan Doric** pilasters support a full entablature crowning the third floor.

[M16] **72-76 East 79th Street**, town houses and apartment tower, bet. Madison and Park Aves. **Nos.72-74**. 1884. *Anson Squires*. **No.76**. 1884. *James E. Ware*. Conversion, 1988, *Conklin & Rossant*.

A strange tower looms over Victorian town houses: **Parisian** Left Bank studios at the top, boredom at the waist, and a rich row of brick and brownstone along the street-front (all part of a zoning package).

[M17] **895 Park Avenue**, SE cor. E.79th St. 1929. *Sloan & Robertson*.

Art Deco hadn't yet been fully embraced by these talented architects, nor had neo-Classicism been given a warm farewell. The

[M20] **Manhattan Church of Christ**, 48 E.80th St., bet. Madison and Park Aves. 1967. *Eggers & Higgins*.

Raw concrete from the "brutalist" years of the 1950s-60s, when *Le Corbusier* created his monastery, **La Tourette**, from similar materials. Here, in the hands of reluctant modernists, a heavy hand has ruled.

[M21] **52 East 80th Street**, bet. Madison and Park Aves. 1890s.

A copper-clad elliptical bay window bellies into the streetscape, a glassy aerie from which to see and be seen. The royal box? Below, a Grecian bust loiters by the stoop.

East 80th Street, Park to Lexington Aves.
Roll call on the south:

[M22] **No.116**/originally **Lewis Spencer and Emily Coster Morris House**. 1922-1923. *Cross & Cross*. 🌃

A large, but modest, **neo-Georgian** residence that suffers from awkward proportions and timid windows (timid windows? Yes, dear reader, in New York they frequently lacked the impressive glassiness of the real English **Georgian** façade).

[M23] No.120/originally **George and Martha Whitney House**. 1929-1930. *Cross & Cross*. 🍎

Cross & Cross showed more self-confidence here than displayed at **116**. Doric columns and pilasters support a marble porch with appropriate ironwork above. And the windows have better scale.

[M24] No.124/originally **Clarence and Anne Douglass Dillon House**. 1930. *Mott B. Schmidt*. 🍎

Neo-Georgian again, but *Mott Schmidt* really knew how to pull it off. The pedimented entry is elegant, the brick quoins a subtler enrichment.

[M25] No.130/originally **Vincent and Helen Astor House**/now **Junior League of the City of New York**. 1927-1928. *Mott B. Schmidt*. 🍎

M20

M28   M21

Most subtle and most powerful of the 80th Street Quartet. Here brick Georgian gives way to travertine **Regency**, taut Ionic pilasters, and an elegant relieving arch in the manner of the *Brothers Adam*. *Schmidt* was a winner.

[M26] Unitarian Church of All Souls, 1157 Lexington Ave. and SE cor. 80th St. 1932. *Hobart Upjohn*.

The tower's brick base is **Regency** in the manner of *John Soane*, the façade less so: the almost baroque broken pedimented entry portal takes away some of the austere power of its surrounding arch.

[M27] 998 Fifth Avenue, NE cor. E.81st St. 1910-1912. *William Richardson of McKim, Mead & White*. 🍎

A landmark, pacing the design of Fifth Avenue. The understated **Italian Renaissance** detail rises to a rich copper cornice and frieze at the sky. *Richardson's* dignified design grew from the work of the original partners, all deceased by this date.

[M28] 14a East 81st Street, bet. Fifth and Madison Aves. 1991. *Buttrick White & Burtis*.

The new kid on the block, with all the parts for town-house success, but appearing to be a party-crasher: too new, perhaps, and too perfect?

[M29] 24 East 81st Street, bet. Fifth and Madison Aves. 1900-1902. *Buchman & Fox*.

Ornate **neo-Renaissance** bayed façade, enriched with some late Gothic detail.

[M30] 26 East 81st Street, SW cor. Madison Ave. 1900s.

A venerable apartment house from the turn of the century, when they were derogated in "Society," as **French Flats** (Parisian sin?). Tan brick and limestone support a glorious cornice, its frieze a continuous garland of swags.

[M31] Grenville Lindall Winthrop House, 15 E.81st St., bet. Fifth and Madison Aves. 1919-1921. *Julius F. Gayler*.

M27

M31   M32

A wide **neo-Federal** house, its brickwork a Flemish-bond, entered through a porch flanked by paired marble Ionic columns. Large, understated: is this the wealthy Protestant aesthetic?

[M32] La Résidence, 1080 Madison Ave., bet. E.81st and E.82nd Sts. W side. 1981. *Thierry W. Despont*, designer. *Emil N. Steo*, architect.

A serene midblock high-rise addition to Madison Avenue that minimizes its tower by a setback from a carefully detailed base. Both bold and subtle, the windows are magnificent.

[M33] 940 and 944 Park Avenue, NW cor. E.81st St. **No.940**, 1926. *George & Edward Blum*. **No.944**, 1929. *George F. Pelham*.

Within Park Avenue's somber urbanism the materials, details, and textures provide an **architecture of surface:** here the vocabulary is Romanesque and Art Deco.

M37

From Fifth Avenue and 82nd Street to Madison Avenue:

[M34] **1001 Fifth Avenue**, bet. E.81st and E.82nd Sts. 1978-1980. *Johnson/Burgee*, design architects. *Philip Birnbaum & Assocs.*, associated architects.

"**Queen Anne** front and **Mary Ann** behind." But here the façade appliqué reveals the behind as the side! The false front continues into the sky, where it is propped up for all to see.

M34

M35

[M35] Originally **Benjamin N. and Sarah Duke House**, 1009 Fifth Ave., SE cor. E.82nd St. 1899-1901. *Welch, Smith & Provot.* ●

Grandiosity on spec! Built by speculative developer brothers *W.W. and T.M. Hall*, and quickly snapped up by a founder of the American Tobacco Company. *Benjamin's* brother, *James*, later bought it and lived here before he built his elegant bit of **18th-century France** at No.1 E.78th Street.

[M36] **East 82nd Street**, Fifth to Madison Aves., on axis of the main entrance of the Metropolitan Museum.

Rich façades as a group frame the **Met's** main entrance, as if they housed the courtiers of the palace of art. Worth a special stroll.
Roll call:

No.2. 1898-1900. *Alexander Welch of Welch, Smith & Provot.* Overblown **Georgian**: those console brackets got out of hand.

Nos.3 and 5. 1900-1901. *Janes & Leo.* ● Bowed bay and bowed front. Gargantuan dentils and florid keystones.
No.14. 1903-1904. *C.P.H. Gilbert.* The powerful bayed façade (imposing rusticated swellfront) is incised with rustication and embellished with concave-surrounded arches.
Nos.17 and 19. 1894-1896. *Henry Andersen.* Look up to tan Roman brick and bowed fronts; the neo-Romanesque of the 1890s is struggling with the **American Renaissance.** Check the cornices.
Nos.20 and 22. 1900-1901. *Richard W. Buckley.* ● Glassy eclecticisms.
No.18: flamboyant eclecticism.
No.22: French **Beaux Arts** with exuberant ornament. ●

[M37] **Metropolitan Museum of Art,** in Central Park facing Fifth Ave. bet. E.80th and E.84th Sts. ●
Rear façade (now visible only within Lehman Wing). 1874-1880. *Calvert Vaux & J. Wrey Mould.*
SW wing and façade, 1888, *Theodore Weston.*
Central Fifth Avenue façade. 1895-1902, *Richard Morris Hunt and Richard Howland Hunt.*
Side wings along Fifth Ave. 1904-1926, *Charles F. McKim of McKim, Mead & White.*
Thomas J. Watson Library. 1965. *Brown, Lawford & Forbes.*
Lehman Wing, front stairs, pools, and **Great Hall** renovations, 1969-1975.
Sackler Wing for the Temple of Dendur, 1979. **American Wing,** 1980. **Michael C. Rockefeller Wing for Primitive Art,** 1981. *Dillon*

M36, no.14

Galleries for Far East Art, 1981. **André Meyer Galleries for European Paintings,** 1981. **Egyptian Wing,** 1982. **Wallace Galleries for 20th Century Art,** 1986. **Iris and B. Gerald Cantor Roof Garden,** 1987. **Tisch Galleries,** 1988. **European Sculpture and Decorative Art Wing,** 1989. All by *Kevin Roche John Dinkeloo & Assocs.* Open to the public. **Partial Interior** (Great Hall and Stair) ● Open Su and Tu-Th 9:30-5:30; Fr and Sa 9:30-9:00; closed Mo. 212-535-7710. *www.metmuseum.org.*

The neo-Renaissance design example for this elegant warehouse of art was revealed at the World's **Columbian Exposition of 1893,** at which the opposing Romanesque Revival style lost its position of pre-eminence. *Vaux's* earlier Ruskinian Gothic kernel is now largely encased: the Fifth Avenue frontage filled in with a **City Beautiful** palace in the manner of **Versailles,** the behind devoured by the Lehman Wing, a flashy glass pyramid flanked by walls designed to screen what *Roche and Co.* considered the vulgar excesses of *Vaux.* It is a rich and confusing mélange—exciting, grand, controversial, often elegant, sometimes banal. The main hall is still one of the great spaces of New York, the City's only suggestion of the visionary **neo-Roman spaces** of the 18th-century Italian draftsman and engraver *Piranesi*.

Since 1969 the museum has undergone a reconstruction and expansion, unrivaled by any museum in America (if not the world), designed by *Roche*. Many are offended by their impact on Central Park. The works within are without peer. Savor them moment by moment, year by year. (Mandatory contribution—an oxymoron—on entry.)

[M38] **25 East 83rd Street**, NW cor. Madison Ave. 1938. *Frederick L. Ackerman, and Ramsey & Sleeper*. Altered, 1986.

A modern monument, not in its external elegance but in its pace-setting technology: the first centrally air-conditioned apartment building in the City (note that there are no grilles penetrating the walls—air is drawn in at the roof and distrib-

M39

M40

M42

uted by interior ductwork). In the 1980s the glass block "windows" thought necessary for economical cooling were removed in favor of clear glass, perhaps giving the building a new lease on life, but losing much of its prescient **modernist** flavor.

[M39] Originally **Jonathan and Harriet Thorne House**/now **Marymount School**, 1028 Fifth Ave., SE cor. E.84th St. 1901-1903. *C.P.H. Gilbert*.

Praise to the Church for preserving this handsome mansion by default. The school also occupies **Nos.1026** and **1027** (1901-1903. *Van Vleck & Goldsmith*.)

No.1026. French Beaux Arts. **No.1027.** The center of three striking Beaux Arts buildings.

[M40] **3 East 84th Street**, bet. Fifth and Madison Aves. 1927-1928. *John Mead Howells & Raymond Hood*.

Cubistic modeling presages *Raymond Hood's* later News and McGraw-Hill Buildings. The glistening spandrels seem to be fashioned of Navajo silver.

The *New Yorker* (magazine) critic *T-Square* wrote (in 1929) that it was "a charming little building in which the contemporary style is handled with fine restraint... worthy of the (AIA) medal for new apartment houses."

[M41] **9 and 11 East 84th Street**, bet. Fifth and Madison Aves. 1902-1903. *Warren & Wetmore*.

Hood's limestone and brick neighbors.

[M42] **1128 Madison Avenue**, SW cor. E.84th St. 1986. *Rosenblum/Harb*.

A clever expansion and re-cladding of a dull two-story taxpayer turns it from a pumpkin into *Cinderella's* coach. Through talent, not magic.

[M43] **Church of St. Ignatius Loyola** (Roman Catholic), 980 Park Ave., SW cor. E.84th St. 1895-1900. *Schickel & Ditmars*.

Inspired by *Vignola* (mannerist Italian architect), here with a German accent. Limestone, super-scaled, air-conditioned, grim, proper, and **Park Avenue-ish**. The chapel downstairs is an

M43

ethnic balancer, dedicated to *St. Lawrence O'Toole*, titular saint of Yorkville's mid-1800s Irish settlers. *St. Lawrence's* church, the foundations of which formed this basement (starting in 1884), was nosed out by *St. Ignatius* for the final building.

[M44] **Regis High School** (Roman Catholic), 55 E.84th St., bet. Madison and Park Aves. 1913-1917. *Maginnis & Walsh*.

A mighty vanguard of grand **Ionic** columns form the armature of this façade; the building goes through the block to 85th Street. Within, a courtyard lights the surrounding classrooms.

[M45] **21 East 84th Street**, bet. Fifth and Madison Aves. and **1132 and 1134 Madison Ave.**, NW cor. E.84th St. 1892. *John H. Duncan*.

A rich and somber brick and terra-cotta **terrace** (English grouping of jointly designed town houses), now sullied by unhappy storefronts on the avenue. But look up, the frieze and cornice are first-rate.

[M46] **16 and 18 East 85th Street**, bet. Fifth and Madison Aves. 1988. *Gwathmey Siegel & Assocs.*

Bold **modernist** façades display a hierarchy of deep-set square windows (with square subdivisions). Snuggled between two apartment blocks, they fit well, no clashing mismatch of scale and proportions.

[M47] Originally **Lewis Gouverneur and Nathalie Bailey Morris House,** 100 E.85th St., SE cor. Park Ave. 1913-1914. *Ernest Flagg.* ●

The radical English architect and urban designer *Richard Norman Shaw* (1831-1912) converted **Georgian** fantasies into such rich and complex places as this. A sprightly collision of quarter-round windows, widow's walks, and dormers, flying in all directions. Among *Flagg's* best. For more monumental *Flagg,* see the **Little Singer Building** (p. 113).

M46

M47

[M48] **Park Avenue Christian Church** (Disciples of Christ)/originally **South Reformed Church,** 1010 Park Ave., SW cor. E.85th St. 1911. *Cram, Goodhue & Ferguson.*

Native materials, here Manhattan schist, were assembled with "inspiration from the **Sainte-Chapelle**" in Paris. Such were the words of *Cram*, but the inspiration seems to have been effective largely for the **flèche**. (Sainte-Chapelle is a glass box with incidental stone supports; this is a stone box with incidental glass.)

[M49] Originally **Reginald and Anna DeKoven House,** 1025 Park Ave., bet. E.85th and E.86th Sts., E side. 1911-1912. *John Russell Pope.* ●

A charming **Tudor Revival** town house that was opportunely overlooked in the serial redevelopment of Park Avenue. The glassy openness of its bay windows contrasts with the rusticated lower floors, defending Park Avenue's apartment dwellers. *DeKoven* (1859-1920) was a composer of popular light opera; his "*O, Promise Me*" is a potboiler that has jerked many tears from many reluctant wedding guests.

[M50] **Neue Galerie New York, Museum for German and Austrian Art**/originally **William Starr Miller House**/onetime **Mrs. Cornelius Vanderbilt House**. 1048 Fifth Ave., SE cor. E.86th St. 1912-1914. *Carrère & Hastings.* Renovated as a museum, 2000, *Annabelle Selldorf.* Open: Th, Fr, Sa, Su, and Mo, 11am-6pm. Closed Tu and We. 212-628-6200. *www.neuegallerie.org*

An elegant émigré — from the **Place des Vosges** without the **Place** — a town palace of

M48

M49

limestone and brick (reinforced with Ionic pilasters), crowned with a slate mansard roof. Now the elegant Museum of German and Austrian culture developed by cosmetics heir *Ronald Lauder* and the late art dealer *Serge Sabarsky.* Go in. Look at the *Klimts.* Check the *Miesian* elevator.

NECROLOGY

Originally **John Sherman Hoyt House**/later **James Stillman House**/sometime **Consulate of the United Arab Republic**, 900 Park Ave., NW cor. E.79th St. 1917. *I.N. Phelps Stokes.*

A richly ornamented **Tudor** mansion by the author of *The Iconography of Manhattan Island.* Replaced by an inappropriate apartment tower that muddles the sweep of Park Avenue.

CARNEGIE HILL AND BEYOND

Carnegie's Hill is most pronounced as you move uptown along Madison Avenue above 86th Street or downtown on Park at 96th Street, where trains bound for Grand Central dive into the 2.5-mile tunnel which burrows beneath the glitter and swank of Park Avenue. The area covered here runs from 87th to 106th Streets east of Fifth, over to Lexington and environs below 96th, over to Park and environs above 96th. Remember, the Carnegie Hill Historic District is just a fraction of this area.

[C1a] Originally **Henry and Annie Phipps House**/ now **Liederkranz Club**, 6 E.87th St., bet. Fifth and Madison Aves. 1902-1904. *Grosvenor Atterbury*.

The relocated sculpture in the eastern side yard (1896. *G. Moretti*, sculptor) commemorates the semicentennial of the **Liederkranz Club**, a German music society. The house is in somber Renaissance Revival dress.

C1c

C1a   C4a

[C1b] Originally **Buttinger House**/now **Phelps-Stokes Fund**, 10 E.87th St., bet. Fifth and Madison Aves. 1958. *Felix Augenfeld & Jan Hird Pokorny*.

Built as a house surrounding a **private library** that occupied a two-story glass-walled space within. Unassuming.

[C1c] **The Capitol**, 12 E.87th St., bet. Fifth and Madison Aves. 1910-1911. *George & Edward Blum*.

White brick and glazed ornamental terra cotta sheathe this early *Blum* apartment block. The cornice has vanished, leaving the "supporting" modillions without their **Classical** load.

[C2] **Park Avenue Synagogue**, 50 E.87th St., SE cor. Madison Ave. 1980. *James Rush Jarrett and Schuman Lichtenstein Claman & Efron*, associated architects.

Offbeat rusticated sandstone provides an **arcaded rhythm** for glazed class and meeting rooms. It seems a stage set more than a religious entity. Lost to demolition was the *Milton Steinberg House*.

[C3] **Solomon R. Guggenheim Museum**, 1071 Fifth Ave. bet. E.88th and E.89th Sts. 1956-1959. *Frank Lloyd Wright*. **Aye Simon Reading Room**, 1978, *Richard Meier & Assocs.* ♿ Interior. ♿ **Addition** along E boundary facing E.89th St. 1992. *Gwathmey Siegel & Assocs*. Renovated, 2008. Open, except Th, 10-8. 212-423-3500. www.guggenheim.org

C2

C3

The Guggenheim's central space is one of the world's great **modern** interiors: a museum important more as architecture than for the contents it displays. To appreciate it, take the elevator (half round) to the skylighted top and descend the helical ramp. *Gwathmey Siegel's* addition is awkwardly connected to *Wright's* spectacle but provides the museum with much-needed backup spaces.

[C4a] **5, 7 and 9 East 88th Street**, bet. Fifth and Madison Aves. 1901-1903. *Turner and Killian*.

Beaux Arts neo-Renaissance in limestone and brick. *Wright* scorned them as "decadent" neighbors, while he was living in 19th-century grandeur at the Plaza. (Only *Wright* would re-design a hotel room to better suit his tastes, but that's what he did at the Plaza.)

Continue ↑ for The Heights and the Harlems

E 107th St
E 106th St
N
E 105th St
60
59
E 104th St
58
E 103rd St
57
E 102nd St
E 101st St
56
E 100th St
d
53a
c
b
E 99th St
52
54
E 98th St
55
51
E 97th St
50
44 45 47
E 96th St
46
49
43
48
E 95th St
39
40
41
E 94th St
42
32
E 93rd St
35 36
33 34
28
37 38
E 92nd St
27
29
31
30
19–22
E 91st St
25
18
23b 24
26
23a
14
15
16
17
13
Carnegie Hill
12
11
Historic District
7
10
E 89th St
8
9
3
4
6
E 88th St
5
1
2 E 87th St
E 86th St

Fifth Ave
Madison Ave
Park Ave
Lexington Ave
Third Ave
Second Ave

E 85th St

Continue ↓ for Metropolitan Museum Vicinity
E 84th St

Continue → for Yorkville / Gracie Square

[C4b] **Fulton and Mary Cutting House**, 15 E.88th St., bet. Fifth and Madison Aves. 1919-1922. *Delano & Aldrich*.

Crisp white reveals in the arcaded **neo-Georgian** brick façade liven the building and the neighborhood, a demonstration of the power of understatement.

[C5] **60 East 88th Street**, bet. Madison and Park Aves. 1987. *Beyer Blinder Belle*.

A restrained midblock handshake between those of the **postmodern** (the giant oculus, and rustication that is only horizontal) and the **1920s** (the French-doored balconettes are stylishly outfitted with flat metal railings).

[C6] **1082 Park Avenue**, bet. E.88th and E.89th Sts. W side. Altered, ca. 1927.

Sicily in terra cotta, a vibrant yellow and whiteglaze, redolent of a simple Baroque.

[C7] Originally **Collis P. Huntington Houses**/ now **National Academy of Design**, 1083

C5

C6

C9

C8

C12   C13a

Fifth Ave., bet. E.89th and E.90th Sts. *Turner & Kilian*; and **3 E.89th St.**, bet. Fifth and Madison Aves. 1913-1915. *Ogden Codman, Jr.* **No.5**, 1957-1959, *William and Geoffrey Platt*. Open to the public: We-Su 12-5; Fr 12-8; closed Mo and Tu. 212-369-4880. *www.nationalacademy.org*

Onetime center of conservatism in the arts, it has become a refreshing venue for imaginative exhibitions. Founded in 1825, it includes architects, painters, and graphic designers.

[C8] Originally **The Cutting Houses**/now **St. David's School**, 12, 14, and 16 E.89th Sts., bet. Fifth and Madison Aves. 1919-1922. *Delano & Aldrich*.

Comely **neo-Georgian** town houses with elegant arched and layered façades at the ground level: designed to read as a single building.

[C9] **Graham House**, 22 E.89th St., SW cor. Madison Ave. 1891-1893. *Thomas Graham*.

The serendipitous entry portal combines **Romanesque** columns with urban fantasies: a portal worthy of entering a Wonderland.

[C10] **45 East 89th Street**, along Madison Ave., bet. E.89th and E.90th Sts. E side. 1969. *Philip Birnbaum* and *Oppenheimer, Brady & Lehrecke*, associated architects.

A notch above its competition, particularly at the lower levels.

[C11] **Church of St. Thomas More** (Roman Catholic)/originally **Beloved Disciple Protestant Episcopal Church**/later **East 89th Street Reformed Church**, 59-63 E.89th St., bet. Madison and Park Aves. 1870. *Hubert & Pirsson*. Chapel to the west, 1879. Rectory, 65 E.89th St. 1880-1893.

A "country" church of **Nova Scotia sandstone** that has survived the percolating real estate cauldron of the Upper East Side. Over the years, its worth has been recognized by the sequential religious denominations that it has sheltered.

East 90th Street, between Fifth and Madison Aves:

[C12] **Church of the Heavenly Rest** (Episcopal), SE cor. Fifth Ave. and E.90th St. 1926-1929. *Hardie Philip of Mayers, Murray & Philip*, architects. Pulpit Madonna, *Malvina Hoffman*, sculptor. Exterior sculpture, *Ulrich Ellerhausen*.

Stripped Gothic, with some stylish **modernist** massing, serving as external dress over more conservative space within.

[C13a] Originally **George L. McAlpin House**/later **Roswell and Margaret Carnegie Miller House**, 9 E.90th St. 1902-1903. *George Keister*.  Connected to 2 E.91st (Cooper-Hewitt) and altered, 1996-1997, *Polshek Partnership*.

Carnegie's daughter and family lived here, abutting her parent's garden. Now an annex to the **Cooper-Hewitt Museum**, it suffers with awkward neo-Federal massing, the pedimented portico at odds with the bowed floors above.

C16

[C13b] Originally **William and Louise McAlpin House**/later **Grafton W. and Anne Minot House**, 11 E.90th St. 1902-1903. *Barney & Chapman*. New façade and alterations, 1929, *A. Wallace McCrea*. 👁

The *Minot's* neo-18th-century façade replaced the *McAlpin's* Beaux Arts neo-19th-century façade: **1929** vs. **1903**, reverting to an earlier era! Oh, we Americans. You didn't know that scores of Gold Coast and Carnegie Hill town houses had facelifts. Check the entries.

[C14a] Originally **Emily Trevor House**, 15 E.90th St. 1927-1928. *Mott B. Schmidt*. 👁
Neo-Federal with Flemish-bond brick, a

C13b   C15

tepid 1920s favorite style in many of these park blocks. The portico has some class, but ho-hum....

[C14b] Originally **Harriet S. Clark House**, 17 E.90th St. 1917-1919. *F. Burrall Hoffman, Jr.* 👁
This **neo-Georgian** house rests on its loggia, arcaded in the manner of London's Covent Garden or the Place des Vosges in Paris. Another pleasant break in the street rhythm.

Sinclair Lewis and Dorothy Thompson, husband and wife, lived in the undistinguished apartment block at 21 East 90th Street in the early 1930s. They maintained two sitting rooms so they could entertain guests separately.

🏛 [C15] **1261 Madison Avenue**, NE cor. E.90th St. 1900-1901. *Buchman & Fox*. 👁
The monumental broken pediment at the entry, wing-like, seems to soar; a monumental, perhaps outrageous, trapping for an otherwise modest building. *We love it.*

[C16] **57-61 East 90th Street**, bet. Madison and Park Aves. 1886-1887. *J.C. Cady & Co.*
A trio of granite and brownstone mansions, with **No.57** showing its original colors: brownstone alternately smooth and rockfaced. Elegant.

[C17] **Carnegie Hill Historic District**. 86th Street to 98th Street, between Madison and Fifth Avenues, with a grand peninsula eastward to Lexington Avenue, varying between 90th and 95th Streets. 👁
A landmark district continuing the spirit and embrace of the Upper East Side and Metropolitan Museum Historic Districts to the south. Expanded 1993.

C18

East 91st Street, between Fifth and Madison Avenues:

🏛 [C18] **Cooper-Hewitt National Design Museum, Smithsonian Institution**/originally **Andrew and Louise Carnegie House**, 2 E.91st St., SE cor. Fifth Ave. to E.90th St. 1899-1903. *Babb, Cook & Willard*. 👁 Converted to museum, 1976, *Hardy Holzman Pfeiffer Assocs*. Renovations, 1996, *Polshek Partnership*. Further renovations, 2008, *Gluckman Mayner with Beyer Blinder Belle Architects*. Open to the public: Mo-Fr 10-5; Sa 10-6; Su 12-6. 212-849-8400. *www.cooperhewitt.org*

When **Carnegie** built this brick and limestone château, squatters were his neighbors. **Louise** and **Andrew Carnegie** lived here from 1901 until the surviving *Louise's* death in 1946. Its new life is as houser and exhibitor of the great collection originally assembled for the Cooper Union by the **Cooper** and **Hewitt** families: the decorative arts, from wallpaper to furniture; and as a stage for imaginative exhibitions in the decorative arts, architecture, graphics, and you-name-it. *Carnegie*, when called to describe it, said "modest and plain."

[C19] Originally **Otto and Addie Kahn House**/now **Duchesne Residence School faculty residence, Convent of the Sacred Heart**, 1 E.91st St., NE cor. Fifth Ave. 1913-1918. J. Armstrong Stenhouse with *C.P.H. Gilbert*. 🍎 Renovations, 2006, *Murphy Burnham & Buttrick*.

A **Leviathan** of a house (145 feet wide): and an American version of an English version of an Italian **Renaissance** palace (cf. Palazzo della Cancelleria in Rome). It is rich, but subdued, as expected in Boston or Florence. A Convent facility since 1934. The renovations within, together with those in the **Burden House** next door, are substantial, but visible to the stroller only in the deeply recessed glass connection between the buildings.

[C20] Originally **James A. and Florence Vanderbilt Sloane Burden, Jr., House**/now **Duchesne Residence School, Convent of the Sacred Heart**, 7 E.91st St. 1902-1905. *Warren, Wetmore & Morgan*. 🍎 Renovations, 2006, *Murphy Burnham & Buttrick*.

Built by the industrializing ironmonger from Troy, N.Y., whose commercial legacy was the American Machine and Foundry Company (AMF). A freestanding mansion with a side court, it has been called "the finest Beaux Arts town house in the City." We'd rather dub it the finest **Renaissance Palazzo**, austere, monumental, and master of the street. Those lucky students.

C20   C23b

[C21] Originally **James Henry and Emily Vanderbilt Sloane Hammond House**/now **Consulate of the Russian Federation**, 9 E.91st St. 1902-1903. *Carrère & Hastings*. 🍎 Alterations, 1976, *William B. Gleckman*.

Fussier in detail than the **Burden House** next door, it lacks its sheer power. *Hammond's* world entered popular history when his daughter *Alice* married *Benny Goodman*, and his son *John* became a legendary record producer, launching the careers of (among others) *Billie Holiday* and *Bob Dylan*. A half-century later the **Soviet government** bought this palazzo for their first New York consulate in 1942; it now houses the consulate of the Russian Federation.

[C22] Originally **John B. and Caroline Trevor House**/now **Consulate of the Russian Federation**, 11 E.91st St. 1909-1911. *Trowbridge & Livingston*. 🍎

A pale mansarded **Beaux Arts** neighbor to the magnificence to the west.

[C23a] **The Spence School**, 22 E.91st St. 1929. *John Russell Pope*. Addition, 1988, *Fox & Fowle*.

High-rise, indecisive, **neo-Georgian** by someone who should have known better. Nevertheless, there are great windows at the second (here the most important) floor. *Pope's* work elsewhere is monumental (**National Gallery, Jefferson Memorial**); perhaps he should have left working public buildings for others. The *Fox & Fowle* addition tries not to compete.

[C23b] **47 East 91st Street**, NE cor. Madison Ave. 2004. *Platt Byard Dovell White* and *Cary Tamarkin*.

Floating façades and crisp limestone. A cool and understated modern neighbor in the streetscape of traditional Upper East Side apartment houses. A taller tower, proposed for the same site in 1999, didn't go over well with neighbors, including *Woody Allen*. This is the shorter compromise.

C19

[C24] **The Dalton School**, the First Program, 61 E.91st St., bet. Madison and Park Aves. 1923-1924. *Mott B. Schmidt*.

With large and well-scaled windows, a convincing **neo-Georgian** town house, eaveless, a **Regency** idea, with the attic roof set back behind the façade wall. *Schmidt*, architect to the *Astors* and the *Dillons*, supplied his thoughtful historicism, penultimately applied in the 1966 *Wagner* wing at Gracie Mansion.

[C25] **Brick Presbyterian Church**, 1140-1144 Park Ave., NW cor. E.91st St. 1938. *York & Sawyer; Lewis Ayres,* designer. Chapel of the Reformed Faith, 1952, *Adams & Woodbridge*.

The safe brick and limestone American academic **neo-Georgian** of the 1930s.

[C26] **115-121 East 91st Street**, bet. Park and Lexington Aves. 1876-1877. *Arthur B. Jennings*.

Bay windows offer pregnant views across town. Simple brownstones raised to a more substantial architectural posture.

[C27] **1107 Fifth Avenue**, SE cor. E.92nd St. 1924-1925. *Rouse & Goldstone.*

Marjorie Merriweather Post (Toasties) sold her town house and its site to a developer who crowned his building with her superb **54-room triplex** vantage point in space. Note the elegant auto entrance on 92nd Street.

[C28] Originally **Felix and Frieda S. Warburg House**/now **The Jewish Museum**, 1109 Fifth Ave., NE cor. E.92nd St. 1907-1908. *C.P.H. Gilbert.* Cloned addition to the north on Fifth, 1990-1993, *Kevin Roche.* ●́
Open to the public: Su, Mo, We, Th 11-5:45; Tu 11-8; closed Fr and Sa. 212-423-3200.

This neo-**Loire Valley château** became the surprising envelope for a museum of Jewish art and history (the hermit crab syndrome: except here a wandering museum found a delightful carapace); but the image was so powerful that, on expansion, modernist *Kevin Roche* chose to replicate precisely the existing architecture as he crept north on Fifth. AIA Guide co-author *Elliot*

Vigorous pioneers from the 1880s, these **Romanesque Revivals** still present strong character over tawdry shops that lie below their brick and brownstone bayfronts.

East 93rd Street, between Madison and Park Avenues:

[C32] **1321 Madison Avenue**, NE cor. E.93rd St. 1890-1891. *James E. Ware.* ●́
Craggy **Queen Anne**: mysterious and so rich in detail that the later Madison Avenue storefront insertions can almost be overlooked. Almost. The survivor of an original row of five.

[C33] Originally **William Goadby and Florence Baker Loew House**/now the **Spence School**, 56 E.93rd St. 1930-1931. *Walker & Gillette.* ●́ Renovations for the Spence School, 2000, *Platt Byard Dovell White.*

New York's penultimate great mansion, it has the manners of *John Soane*, the avant-garde Regency architect who used classic parts, but a

C27   C28   C30

C29   C31   C33   C34

Willensky was a consultant to the Museum in choosing the architect who did these good works.

[C29] **"Night Presence IV,"** on the Island in Park Ave., N of E.92nd St. 1972. *Louise Nevelson*, sculptor.
This purposely rusty (self-weathering) steel construction is a feisty **modern** loner in these neo-Renaissance precincts.

[C30] Originally **John C. and Catherine E. Rennett House and Adam C. Flanigan House**, 120 and 122 East 92nd Street, bet. Park and Lexington Aves. 120, 1871. Maybe *Albro Howell*, builder. 122, 1859. ●́
A homely scale. Wooden houses from rural times. Even in their original 1858/1871 isolation, they were required to conform to the **Commissioners' Plan of 1811.**

[C31] **1283-1293 Madison Avenue**, SE cor. E.92nd St. 1889-1890. *James E. Ware.*

fresh attitude toward form and space. *Florence Loew* chose the site to be near her brother, *George Baker, Jr.* After the *Loews*, ownership passed from *Broadway* to *Rehabilitation*, on route to *Education.* (Billy Rose House, later Smithers Alcoholism Center, now the Spence School).

[C34] Originally **Virginia Graham Fair Vanderbilt House**/sometime **Lycée Français de New York**, 60 E.93rd St. 1930-1931. *John Russell Pope.* ●́ Altered to Lycée, 1976, *William B. Gleckman.*
Another in the onetime flock of grand mansions co-opted for the education of a French-speaking child, this from the time of **Louis XV.** Look at the voussoirs: each has the face of a different woman. Now awaiting other use.

[C35a] **George F. Baker, Sr., House**, 67 E.93rd Street. 1931. *Delano & Aldrich.* ●́
Built by *George F. Baker, Jr.*, to town-house his father, who died, unfortunately, before he could enjoy it.

C36

[C35b] **69 East 93rd Street House**, an addition to, and courtyard for **George F. Baker, Jr., House**. 1928-1929. *Delano & Aldrich.* 🍎

The elegant side façade (a garage and apartment within) completes, together with the earlier ballroom addition, the courtyard of *Baker's* complex, dominated by a great **Ionic** colonnade.

[C36] Originally **Francis F. Palmer House**/later **George F. Baker, Jr., House Complex**/now **The Russian Orthodox Church Outside of Russia**, 75 E.93rd St. 1917-1918; northern ballroom addition, 1928, both by *Delano & Aldrich.* 🍎

A beautifully fashioned **neo-Federal** urban complex. The main building, built by *Francis F. Palmer*, was bought by *George F. Baker, Jr.* (then Chairman of the First National Bank), ten years

C37   C38

after it was begun. *Baker* enlarged the house with a ballroom, garage, and servants' quarters that embraced a newly created courtyard (see 69 E.93rd Street above).

[C37] **1185 Park Avenue**, bet. E.93rd and E.94th Sts. E side. 1928-1929. *Schwartz & Gross.*

A blockbuster with a central interior court (square doughnut) in the manner of the West Side's **Apthorp** and **Belnord**. The ogee-arched pedestrian and carriage entrances and other terra-cotta details are an elegant fantasy. They draw one's attention from the sheer size of it all, making **1185** much better for close study, than a long look down the street.

[C38] **128 East 93rd Street**, bet. Park and Lexington Aves. 1866. *Edmund Waring.*

A restored mansarded frame house: too much "restoration" can put out the flame. An entrance porch originally met the street, but basement space is precious, and the porch gave way to "progress."

[C39] **1130 Fifth Avenue House**/originally **Willard and Dorothy Whitney Straight House**/onetime **International Center of Photography**, NE cor. E.94th St. 1913-1915. *Delano & Aldrich.* 🍎

Elegant, distilled, refined; a studied eclectic **neo-Georgian** house with a homely residential

C40

C39   C41

scale, enriched by an anthemion-patterned marble cornice and balustrade. The **ICP** sold the house to a private householder in 2001. Single family residence: wow.

[C40] **5-25 East 94th Street**, bet. Fifth and Madison Aves. 1892-1894. *Cleverdon & Putzel.*

A speculator's row of brownstone, whitestone, and rock-face ashlar **Romanesque Revival** houses with a variety of detail for individuality. **Nos.15, 17, 21,** and **25** are the most vigorous of the lot.

[C41] **West façade of Squadron A Armory**, 8th Regiment, N.Y. National Guard, Madison Ave., bet. E.94th and E.95th Sts. E side. 1893-1895. *John Rochester Thomas.* 🍎

A fantasy of the brickmason's virtuosity: arches, corbels, crenellations; plastic, neomedieval modeling. Now a play castle, a backdrop for the open space of Hunter's facilities to the east.

[C42] **Hunter College Campus Schools**/formerly **Hunter High School**/originally **Intermediate School 29**, Manhattan, Park Ave. bet. E.94th and E.95th Sts. W side. 1969. *Morris Ketchum, Jr., & Assocs.*

Castellated brick awkwardly complementing its neighbor, the old machicolated west façade of **Squadron A**, preserved as a monument along Madison Avenue. But why didn't they use the same colored mortar?

[C43] Originally **Ernesto and Edith Fabbri House**/now **House of the Redeemer**, 7 E.95th St., bet. Fifth and Madison Aves. 1914-1916. *Egisto Fabri and Grosvenor Atterbury.* ●

Neo-Georgian limestone and brick town house entered through an entrance courtyard in the manner of a **Parisian Hôtel Particulier**. Iron gates flank urn-supporting piers.The product of an amateur architect, *Fabri*, and *Grosvenor Atterbury.*

[C46] Originally **Robert L. and Marie Livingston House**/now **Scuola New York Guglielmo Marconi**/onetime **Emerson School**, 12 E.96th St. 1916. *Ogden Codman, Jr.*

Codman once more, but a lesser *Codman* work. The slate roof and copper-clad dormers are the rich frosting on this dry cake.

[C47] Originally **Lucy Drexel Dahigren House**/later **Pierre Cartier House**, 15 E.96th St. 1915-1916. *Ogden Codman, Jr.* ●

A magisterial (for *Codman*) **French Renaissance** limestone town house, disciplined with gentle rustication and bas-reliefs. The eponymous later owner **Cartier** founded that jeweled empire.

[C48] **New York Public Library**, 126 E. 96th St., bet. Park and Lexington Aves. 1900s.

A simple limestone palazzo for **Carnegie Hill** book-lovers, appropriately constructed with *Andrew Carnegie's* money.

C43

C44

C47

C48

C46

C50

East 96th Street, between Fifth and Madison Avenues:

[C44] Originally **Mrs. Amory S. Carhart House**/onetime **Lycée Français de New York**, 3 E.95th St. 1913-1916. *Horace Trumbauer.* ●

The carriage doors (man-door inset) are a typical **Parisian** division between the public world and the private house and garden. Another surprise from *Trumbauer's* chief drafts-man, African-American architect *Julian Abele*.

[C45] Originally **Ogden Codman, Jr., House**/now **Manhattan Country School**, 7 E.96th St. 1912-1913. *Ogden Codman, Jr.* ●

Limestone, bracketed and swagged, sup-porting **neo-18th-century** iron railings. It has been described as an "airy frivolity." To us it seems a Parisian town house cut down to American "size." Homely. *Codman* and his co-author *Edith Wharton* wrote **The Decoration of Houses.**

[C49] **Saint Francis de Sales** (Roman Catholic), 135 East 96th St., bet. Park and Lexington Aves. 1890s.

A triumphal façade of twinned **Ionic** columns supports a pediment. Rustications below make the unfluted columns and smooth wall above seem even smoother. And check that bronze bay.

[C50] **Islamic Cultural Center** (mosque), 201 E.96th St., NE cor. Third Ave. Mosque, 1991. *Skidmore, Owings & Merrill.* Minaret, 1991. *Swanke Hayden Connell.*

A stolid, domed, stone-clad, modern place of worship, built askew of Manhattan's grid: the mosque is oriented in the traditional fashion toward **Islam's Mecca**, in Saudi Arabia.

[C51] **St. Nicholas Russian Orthodox Cathedral**, 15 E.97th St., bet. Fifth and Madison Aves. 1901-1902. *John Bergesen.* ●

An exotic form among dour surroundings. High **Victorian Baroque**, Ruskinian, eclectic, polychromatic (red brick, blue, and yellow tile), crosses, arches, ornations, and a bunch of delicious onion domes.

[C52] **St. Bernard's School**, 4 E.98th St., bet. Fifth and Madison Aves. 1918. *Delano & Aldrich*.

A block of brick: large, relaxed, much-altered, some-parts-neo-**Georgian**, medium-rise scholastic mélange (medium to indicate where elevators kick in, as they couldn't in Georgian London).

Mt. Sinai Medical Center

[C53a] **Mt. Sinai Medical Center**, E.98th to E.101st Sts., Fifth to Madison Aves. Original buildings, 1904, *Arnold W. Brunner*.
[C53b] **Magdalene and Charles Klingenstein Pavilion**, 1952, *Kahn & Jacobs*.
[C53c] **Annenberg Building**, 1976, *Skidmore, Owings & Merrill*.
[C53d] **Guggenheim Pavilion, Phase 1,** 1989; **Phase 2,** 1991. Both by *I.M. Pei, Pei Cobb Freed & Partners*.

C51

It grew within the grid (absorbing two cross streets), rebuilding itself in the same manner as Roosevelt, Lenox Hill, and so many other hospitals; the body remained and gradually changed its appearance. The high-rise **Annenberg Building** at center block, surrounded by a plaza space, is a great, rusty, cadaverous blockbuster of a building, an incursive hulk that dominates the skyline of East Harlem (to its east). The **Metzger Pavilion** (by *Brunner*) faces **Annenberg** at midblock, a French Baroque Revival delight. But the **Guggenheim Pavilion** brought elegance to the hospital patient. Built surrounding an atrium/skylit court, patients' rooms share this grand space.

Sphere (1967, *Arnaldo Pomodoro*) is a sophisticated punctuation to the plaza space.

[C54] **Icahn Medical Institute**, Mt. Sinai School of Medicine, 1425 Madison Ave., bet. 98th and 99th Sts. E side. 1997. *Davis Brody Bond*.

An austere, but richly modeled, composition, providing multi-purpose research facilities:

oncology, cardiobiology, immunology, molecular genetics, neural aging and structural biology. A **tunnel** under Madison Avenue connects the building with the rest of Mount Sinai.

[C55] **Jane B. Aron Residence Hall**, Mt. Sinai Medical Center, 50 E.98th St., SW cor. Park Ave. 1984. *Davis, Brody & Assocs*.

A composition of rectangular prisms, cylinders, and subtle tapestries of golden-hued brick, interspersed with green-framed windows.

[C56] **New York Academy of Medicine**, 2 E.103rd St., SE cor. Fifth Ave. 1926. *York & Sawyer*. Library open to the public.

Literal eclecticism—a little bit of **Byzantine** detail and mannerism, a pinch of Lombardian Romanesque. Monolithic and massive (windows and doors are tiny apertures), it contains the medical library of the City.

[C57] **Statue of Dr. J. Marion Sims**, M.D., L.L.D., Fifth Ave. along Central Park, opp. E.103rd St.

C54

C56

C53c

Tribute to a surgeon, philanthropist, and founder of Women's Hospital.

[C58] **Museum of the City of New York**, 1220 Fifth Ave., bet. E.103rd and E.104th Sts. 1928-1930. *Joseph Freedlander*. Gallery renovations and new pavilion, 2008, ● *Polshek Partnership*. Tu-Su, 10-5; 212-534-1672. *www.mcny.org*

A bland neo-Georgian building, product of a competition between five invited architects. The contents compensate for any architectural deficiencies: "dioramas" demonstrate the physical form and history of New York. Savor Indians, maps, Dutch and English colonists, antique toys, *Rockefeller* rooms, period rooms, ship models, portraits—a mishmash. Seek out the model (on the first floor) of the *Castello* plan (1660) of New Amsterdam, the best visualization available of that Dutch beaver-trading town. *Alexander Hamilton* and *DeWitt Clinton* face Central Park from niches in the façade (*Adolph A. Weinman*, sculptor).

[C59] **The Reece School**, 25 E. 104th St., bet. Fifth and Madison Aves. 2006. *Platt Byard Dovell White.*

Crisply detailed aluminum, with clear and colored glass, all within a bay projecting modestly from the brick body. It should attract attention and students.

[C60] **El Museo del Barrio**/originally **Heckscher Foundation for Children**, 1230 Fifth Ave., bet. E.104th and E.105th Sts. E side. 1922. Alterations, 2004, *Gruzen Samton.* Open to the public: We-Su 11-6; closed Mo and Tu. 212-831-7272.

The museum of Latin-American (mostly Puerto Rican) art, history, and culture. The 1922 brick fortress has been augmented by some trim modernist revisions by *Gruzen Samton*, including a festive new courtyard.

C59

NECROLOGY

Milton Steinberg House, 50 East 87th St., bet. Madison and Park Aves. 1955. *Kelly & Gruzen.* Stained glass, *Adolf Gottlieb.*

From the Second Edition of this Guide: "A sleek stained-glass façade forms a rich night-time tapestry in front of this activities-and-office building. Friday night (time of **Jewish** Sabbath services) is the best time to savor it." The building was given the wrecking ball, but the stained glass has been reinstalled within the Park Avenue Synagogue next door.

Squadron A (Eighth Regiment) Armory, N.Y. National Guard (east section), Park Ave., bet. E. 94th and E. 95th Sts. 1895. *John Rochester Thomas.*

The east part was removed in favor of a modern echo, I. S. 29, Manhattan, now Hunter High School, the west part survives as a "ruin."

EAST OF EDEN

*If the expanse of the Upper East Side flanking Fifth Avenue seems a social **Eden**, then this precinct, lying between that ultrachic neighborhood and York Avenue's health care and research row, can be called **East of Eden**. It begins at Third Avenue and ranges to just short of York, from the Queensboro Bridge to East 79th Street.*

[E1] **Roosevelt Island Tramway Station**, Second Ave. SW cor. E.60th St. 1976. *Prentice & Chan, Ohlhausen.* Altered, 2010, *BL Companies.*

Spectacular transit. This glassy box, perched high astride, and slightly askew of, Second Avenue, adds to the quasi-ski-slope drama. A beautifully detailed industrial container shelters the wheels and chains (out of *Chaplin's Modern Times*) that propel the cars, those silent, **bird's-eye viewers** of city and river,

E1

moving observation decks. Take a trip! But more is in store: a new building, system, and cars will arrive in 2010.

[E2] **1009 Third Ave.**, SE cor. E.60th St. 1860s.

The body and detail of one brownstone, a **module** of Third Avenue of the mid- to late-19th century. Yellow walls and cream trim supplanted red brick, limestone, and a dark-painted sheet metal cornice. Slowly whole relics like this one are slipping away, altered, de-corniced, buried under signs and shop windows.

[E3] **Evansview** (apartments)/originally **Memphis Uptown**, 305 E.60th St., bet. First and Second Aves. to E.61st St. 1987. *Abraham Rothenberg and Gruzen Samton Steinglass.*

The **penultimate sliver**: lanky, proud, colorful, and witty. A fine addition to a jumbled area if not ultimately lost amid a sea of lesser towers. The route in, under the tentacle of its canopy, is part of the game.

Continue ↑ for Yorkville / Gracie Square

E 80th St

E 79th St

51

E 78th St

47   48 49   50

E 77th St   45   44

43

E 76th St

40   42

E 75th St 39   41

36

35   37

34   38

E 74th St

32   33

30

31

E 73rd St

Third Ave   Second Ave   First Ave   York Ave

26   28

23 24 25   29

E 72nd St

22   27

United Jerusalem Pl   q   r   p

l

E 71st St

k   o

E 70th St

j   i

20 21   m

E 69th St   g f   n

19   e   h   d   Hospitalia

E 68th St

16 17   18

15

E 67th St

14   c

E 66th St

E 65th St

13

E 64th St

E 63rd St

a   b

12

E 62nd St

4   11

6   7   8   10

E 61st St

2   5   3   9

1

Treadwell Farm
Historic District

for The Gold Coast

Third Ave   Second Ave   First Ave   York Ave

E 59th St

E 58th St

Continue ↓ for United Nations / Turtle Bay

Continue ←

[E4] **Day and Meyer, Murray and Young Corporation** (storage warehouse), 1166 Second Ave., bet. E.61st and E.62nd Sts. E side. ca. 1928.

One of a fast disappearing urban form: a largely windowless, high-rise storage warehouse, detailed with a hint of **Art Deco** in brick, limestone, and terra cotta.

[E5] **Treadwell Farm Historic District**, generally both sides of the midblocks of E.61st and

E5   E8

E9

E.62nd Sts. bet. Second and Third Aves. 1868-1876. Much altered. 🍎

Two blocks of brownstone houses on the lands of **Adam Treadwell's** farm: uniform rows of human scale sought by the affluent among surrounding commercial blocks. For another *Tredwell* memory—the family spelled it both with and without the a — this time of *Adam's* brother, see **Seabury Tredwell** and the 1832 **Merchant's House Museum** (see p. 154).

[E6] **206-210 E.61st St.** 1873-1875. *Frederick S. Barus.*

A particularly tasty brownstone trio: original survivors with Roman Tuscan columns holding dentiled pediments.

[E7] **Trinity Baptist Church**/originally Swedish Baptist Church, 250 E.61st St., bet. Second and Third Aves. 1929. *Martin G. Hedmark.*

Sandwiched between the Historic District's brownstones, *Hedmark's* façade is a **celebration** of brick— corbeled, arched, grilled, yellow, brown,

and rust — and a mason's triumph: a brilliant façade that provides monumentality to the church behind, an island of Swedish modern architecture.

[E8] **1114 First Avenue**, NE cor. E.61st St. 1948. *Horace Ginsbern & Assocs.*

A retardataire entry in the **Art Moderne** sweepstakes: banded brick and glass block are a far cry from the glass and metal curtain walls dominating the post–World War II decades.

[E9] **1 Sutton Place North,** 420 East 61st Street, bet. First and York Aves. 2004. *Davis Brody Bond.*

Cousin to *Davis Brody Bond's* earlier **1 East River Place**, up-river at E.72nd Street: sleek, reflective, inscrutable. The work best seen as a set from afar: black knights on the City's chess board.

[E10] **Mount Vernon Hotel Museum and Garden**/longtime **Abigail Adams Smith Museum**, Colonial Dames of America/earlier **Mt. Vernon Hotel** (1826-1833)/originally

E10

E11   E12

William T. Robinson coach house, 421 E.61st St., bet. First and York Aves. 1799. 🍎
Open to the public: Tu-Su 11-4. Closed Mo. 212-838-6878. www.mvhm.org

An unassuming **Federal** ashlar stone building situated on lands of *William and Abigail Adams Smith*, daughter and son-in-law of President *John Adams*. Sold in 1798 to *William T. Robinson*, he built the stable for his new estate, but the memory of *Abigail* is better history than that of *Mr. Robinson*. The stable subsequently became a hotel, its memory retained for the present museum. No manger.

[E11] **East River Waterfront Pavilion**, opposite E.60th St. 1995. *Alice Aycock,* sculptor. *Quennell Rothschild,* landscape architects.

A garbage transfer station transformed into a public pavilion affording one of the most dramatic views in Manhattan: part of New York Hospital's zoning 'payment' for its own new construction over the FDR Drive. Included is a major environmental art installation by sculptor, *Alice Aycock.* **Garbage once had the best views.**

E7

[E12] **Our Lady of Peace Roman Catholic Church**/originally **Presyterian Church of the Redeemer,** 239 E.62nd St. bet. Second and Third Aves. 1886-1887. *Samuel A. Warner.*

An intimate chapel festooned with crystal chandeliers: an oasis amid the tumult surrounding the **Queensboro Bridge** approaches. The marble tablets, just inside the door, honor the (mostly Italian) donors whose contributions built **Our Lady** (back then, for fifty bucks, *your* name was carved in stone!).

[E13] **City and Suburban Homes Company, First Avenue Estate** (model tenements), E.64th to E.65th Sts. bet. First and York Aves: 1168-1190, 1194-1200 First Ave. 1898. *James E. Ware.* 403-423 E.64th St. 1901. *James E. Ware.* 402-416 E.65th St. 1900. *James E. Ware.* 429 E.64th St. and 430 E.65th St. 1915. *City and Suburban Homes Architectural Department: Philip H. Ohm.* ●

Experimental housing for the working classes by a do-good organization in the era before governmental intervention. The apartment groups are six-story walk-ups similar to the ones at 79th Street: straightforward design, successful background buildings. *Ware*, architect of the majority of the structures, won second prize in the **City and Suburban Homes Company Model Tenement Competition** of 1896.

*Anchoring the ground-floor corner of East 65th and First Avenue, is **Goldberger's Pharmacy,** a rare find indeed: a drugstore from 1898 still in its original location. Check out the hard-to-miss neon sign. The old New York, still dispensing.*

E19

Manhattan House and Beyond
   This unnamed hillcrest runs from 66th to 72nd Streets, falling away toward the north, the south, and Second Avenue. Until 1955 its spine was the clanking steel and wood-grilled elevated trestle along Third Avenue, an economic and social wall limiting migration to its east. When the El was scrapped (reducing the convenience of rapid transit for this neighborhood) the eastern blocks blossomed with high-rise luxury.

[E14] **Manhattan House,** 200 E.66th St., bet. Second and Third Aves. through to E.65th St. 1947-1951. *Skidmore, Owings & Merrill* and *Mayer & Whittlesey.* 🍎
   The subtle aesthetic decision to choose pale gray glazed brick and white-painted steel windows by itself **once** raised this block above its coarse new neighbors (white glazed brick + aluminum sash = pasty). The balconies become the principal ornament, but unfortunately small and precarious for those with any trace of vertigo. Sometime in the 1980s the original windows were replaced—with regrettable aesthetic results.

[E18] **St. John Nepomucene Church** (Roman Catholic), 411 E.66th St., NE cor. First Ave. 1925. *John Van Pelt.*
   A romantic paean to the Romanesque style for a Slavic (*St. John of Nepomuk*) congregation. Another version by the same architect, **Guardian Angel**, stands in Chelsea.

[E19] **210 East 68th Street,** SE cor. Third Ave. 1928. *George & Edward Blum.*
   Brutal bulk, lovely detail. An **Art Deco** essay with Kelly green terra-cotta embellishments.

[E20] **340 and 342 East 69th Street,** bet. First and Second Aves. 1865.
   Two in a row of twelve well-preserved brownstones. Another terrace of houses that is large enough to give one a sense of the old city's scale. For a taste of what a well-meaning architect can do to disrupt the block's serenity, look at **No.310.**

[E21] **First Magyar Reformed Church of the City of New York,** 346 E.69th St., bet. First and Second Aves. 1916. *Emery Roth.*
   The founding *Roth* before his **Beresford** and

E14

E15

E17

[E15] **265 East 66th Street,** NW cor. Second Ave. 1978. *Gruzen & Partners.*
   A suave rounded-glass residential tower — the equivalent, in architectural terms, of the gray flannel suit. At ground level is the entrance to the **Beekman Theatre**, a snug little subterranean cinema.

[E16] **222-242 East 67th Street,** bet. Second and Third Avenues. 1984. *Attia & Perkins.*
   These 11 town houses, built in concert with **No.265** above, fail to capture any of the abundant spirit and charm of their linear antecedents. They form a boring block of rich materials and architectural poverty. Directly opposite is a row of gems designed for horses, carriages, and grooms:

[E17] **223, 225, 227 East 67th Street,** bet. Second and Third Aves. 1920. *J.M. Felson.*
   Lusty recollections of the horse-and-carriage era. Their rich façades, articulated with round and **elliptical arches and bull's-eye** windows, shame more recent examples intended for residential purposes.

San Remo fame. Here, white stucco and bright faience vernacular were transported, packed in his memory bank, from his native Hungary to this cramped East Side site.

[E22] **Lenox Hill Station, U.S. Post Office,** 221 E.70th St., bet. Second and Third Aves. 1935.
   Once much maligned by **modernists**, this W.P.A. neo-Georgian post office is now popular among historicists (current architects seeking literal historical styles, as opposed to **postmodernists**, who exaggerate and parody the styles of the past).

East 71st Street, between Second and Third Avenues:

[E23] **203, 207, 209, 211 East 71st Street.** Altered, 1980s.
   Hollywood's East of Eden where the whole, rather than being the sum of the parts, as in most of the Historic Districts, is chaos. Wildly conflicting architectural statements cheek by

jowl. Too bad. **No.213**, next door, retains a largely untouched façade, a foil to its vulgar western show-offs.

[E24] Originally **Junior League**/now **Marymount Manhattan**, 221 E.71st St., bet. Second and Third Aves. 1928. *John Russell Pope*. Altered.

High-rise neo-**Georgian**: a comforting image for those Catholic young women.

[E25] **251 East 71st Street**, bet. Second and Third Aves. Altered, ca. 1975.

Star Trek? Elliptical bubbles in aluminum frames punctuate a white stucco façade. Most serious modernists would use this as an example of the need for extended Historic District coverage.

[E26] **St. John the Martyr Catholic Church**/ originally **Knox Presbyterian Church**, 252 E.72nd St., bet. Second and Third Aves. ca. 1888. Rededicated, 1904.

A congregation Bohemian in origin dressed

(72nd). The small plaza and waterfall are pleasant, but have nothing to do with the building proper. For a recent duplication of the same idea down-river see **1 Sutton Place North**.

[E29] **"Black & Whites,"** 527, 531, 535, 541 E.72nd St., at the end of 72nd St. at the E. River Drive. 1894. Remodeled as apartments, 1938, *Sacchetti & Siegel*.

Tenements, the villains, were replaced by high-rise towers in the 1930s and 1940s, on the principle that light and air bring civilized living to the underprivileged. Partially true. But today city agencies are recycling tenements for that same populace on the principle that keeping the urban streetscape (see the works of *Jane Jacobs*) is better in the long run. The late *George Plimpton*, and the *Paris Review*, resided here, among **tenement affluence**.

[E30] **Buckley School, The Hubball Building**, 210 E.74th St., bet. Second and Third Aves. 1974. *Brown, Lawford & Forbes*.

E21

E23

E27

E28

E24

E25

E29

in rock-faced and smooth brownstone **Romanesque Revival**.

[E27] **Sotheby's**/earlier **Sotheby, Parke-Bernet York Avenue Gallery**/originally **Eastman Kodak Company**, 1334 York Ave., SE cor. E.72nd St. to E.71st St. ca. 1929. Converted to gallery, 1980, *Lundquist & Stonehill*. Expanded, 1999, *Kohn Pedersen Fox*. Top galleries by *Gluckman Mayner*.

An ethereal merchandise mart box for Sotheby's art auctions. Its sheer size is an indication of the speculation that infects the art world. The galleries are open to the public and worth a look. Where else can you see Greek antiquities one month and Johnny Cash's guitars the next? The cafe on the 10th floor is a cool place to relax from sensory overkill.

[E28] **1 East River Place**/**525 E.72nd St**, E of York Ave. through to E.73rd St., bet. York and FDR Drive. 1987. *Davis, Brody & Assocs*.

An elegant tower occupying a back street site (73rd) but with a main-street address

This through-block essay in 1970s concrete, red brick, and freestanding smokestack replaced a **Con Ed** substation.

[E31] **220, 225, 230, 235 East 73rd Street**, bet. Second and Third Aves. 1930-1935. *Emery Roth*.

Four substantial apartment blocks (*Bing & Bing*, developer-owner), each rising 10 sheer stories on opposite sides of the street. Their detail and subtle ornament make them urban grace notes despite their large scale.

[E32] **Bohemian National Hall/Národni Budova**, 321 E.73rd St., bet. First and Second Aves. 1895, 1897. *William C. Frohne*. Restoration, 1990-1994, *Jan Hird Pokorny*. ●'

Lovingly renovated after years of neglect, this distinguished Renaissance Revival hall returns in triumph as a center of Czech culture in New York. Here are the relocated offices of the **Czech Consulate General** and the Czech Center, including a 70-seat, state-of-the-art theater and a library collection focusing on history, art, and literature (in Czech, Slovak, and English).

[E33] **Ronald McDonald House** (children's residential facility), 407 E.73rd St., bet. First and York Aves. 1989. *The Spector Group.*

Handsome, relaxed, it seems to be a large cardboard model on an old street. Not much detail, but folded planes keep it stiff and upright. We faintly praise anything with bay windows.

East 74th Street, between First and Second Avenues:

[E34] **310 East 74th Street**. 1937. *J.M. Felson.*

Art Moderne, unusual in red brick livery (coarsened by poor repointing); orange or cream brick were the 1930s colors of choice, but here an independent statement was made.

[E35] **Greek Orthodox Archdiocesan Cathedral of the Holy Trinity**/Hellenic Eastern Orthodox Church of New York, 319 E.74th St. 1931. *Kerr Rainsford, John A. Thompson, Gerald A. Holmes.*

Neo-Romanesque red brick and limestone by the architects who later designed the vastly different neo-Gothic Hunter College Uptown (now **Lehman College**) in the Bronx, under the name *Thompson, Holmes & Converse.*

[E36] **Jan Hus Presbyterian Church**, 347 E.74th St. 1880. Church House also known as Jan Hus House, 351 E.74th St. 1915.

Jan Hus House is better known, citywide, for the dramatic, musical, and light opera events held in its auditorium, than for the parent church next door. Bohemian Gothic Revival?

[E37] **Memorial Sloane-Kettering International Center**, 1425 First Ave., NW cor. 74th St. 1930s. Remodeled, 1997, *Perkins Eastman.*

Classical Revival bank, **Regency** division.

[E38] **Church of the Epiphany** (Episcopal), 1393-1399 York Ave., NW cor. E.74th St. 1939. *Wyeth & King. Eugene W. Mason,* associated architect.

The distinctive squat spire is a **Scandinavian** romance for Manhattan's streetscapes. Powerful silhouette!

[E39] **310 East 75th Street**, bet. First and Second Aves. 1937. *Sidney L. Strauss.* Altered, 1982, *Stephen B. Jacobs.*

Art Moderne, once appropriately steel-casemented, now demeaned with bronzed double-hung windows; golden yellow, orange, and red brick. The corner windows were not only stylish but also an exciting spatial event for the tenants. The replacements clunk.

[E40] **The Impala**, 1456 First Ave., bet. E.75th and E.76th Sts., 404-408 E.76th St., 411 E.75th St. 2001. *Michael Graves*, design architect. *RFR/Davis*, architects of record.

Not a mere tower, but in fact three buildings embracing a courtyard, the latter two on the 75th and 76th sidestreets. Who could miss the pep rally colors and — whoa, boy — giant, rearing impala (cousin to the antelope) out front?

[E41] **Lycée Française de New York**, 505 E.75th Street, bet. York Ave. and FDR Drive. 2003. *Polshek Partnership.*

Crisp, rationalist modernism in two parts, joined by an interior court. The **Lycée Française**, known for its rigorous, structured curriculum, is perfectly suited to *Polshek's* recent rigorous, structured work, bold and confident in its organization and materials. Here the building facing E. 76th Street is the more interesting of the two, with its façade divided into translucent panels.

E34   E36

E31   E33   E37   E38

[E42] **The Town School**, 540 E.76th St., SW cor. FDR Drive. 1973. *Armand Bartos & Assocs.* Altered, 1978, *R.M. Kliment + Frances Halsband.*

Stylish brickwork is punctuated with incised windows and a splayed entry.

[E43] **430 East 77th Street**, bet. First and York Aves. Converted, 1971.

A stylish conversion from tenements to luxury apartments. Brick piers, arches, and iron railings give this a rich order unmatched by the marble-framed and plastic-plant-festooned lobbies of its vulgar competitors.

[E44] **John Jay Park**, Cherokee Place (E of York Ave.) bet. E.76th and E.78th Sts., to FDR Drive. E side. Bath house, 1908, *Stoughton & Stoughton.*

A small neighborhood park with both a swimming pool and playground intensively used. The pool building is monumental. Its surroundings form a lush parasol of trees.

[E45] Originally **Shively Sanitary Tenements**/later **East River Homes**/now **Cherokee Apartments**, 507-515, 517-523 E.77th St., 508-514, 516-522 E.78th St., W side of Cherokee Place. 1909-1911. *Henry Atterbury Smith.* 🍎

Tuberculosis, rampant and deathly in the early 20th century, was thought, by *Dr. Henry Shively,* to be curable by light and air. His ideas were tested in these model tenements, financed by *Mrs. William Kissam Vanderbilt.*

And, happily, **architecture happened**: the triple-hung windows allow a tenant to step onto a narrow French balcony and view the river; and even without taking that step, one has a dramatic sense of space and view. The units are entered through *Guastavino* tile-vaulted tunnels opening into central courtyards from which, at each corner, stairs rise five flights. Wrought-iron seats and iron-and-glass canopies shelter the stair climber from the rain.

[E46] **City and Suburban Homes Company, York Avenue Estate** (model tenements), E.78th to E.79th

E41

E43

E45

E46

& *Short*) was first-prize winner in the **Charity Organization Society Competition of 1900**. The onetime hotel originally had balconies overlooking the East River and a windswept, wood-trellised roof garden.

York Avenue was originally Avenue A, as the incised street names reveal at the corners of Public School 158, Manhattan, at 1458 York Avenue (between East 77th and East 78th Streets). The thoroughfare was renamed in

E48

Sts. bet. York Ave. and FDR Drive: 1194-1200 York Ave. 1901. *Harde & Short.* 503-509 E.78th St. 1904. *Percy Griffin.* Bishop Henry Codman Potter Memorial Buildings, 510-528 E.79th St. 1912. *City and Suburban Homes Architectural Department: Philip Ohm*, chief architect.519-539 E.78th St. and 536 E.79th St. 1913. *City and Suburban Homes Architectural Department: Philip Ohm.* 🍎
[E63] Originally **Junior League Hotel**/later **East End Hotel for Women**/now apartments, 541 E.78th St. (once 1 East River Drive). 1910-1912. *City and Suburban Homes Architectural Department: Philip Ohm.* 🍎

Experimental housing for the working classes (and a hotel for women once operated by the **Junior League**). The apartment groups are six-story walk-ups but without the charm of the neighboring **Shively** group on Cherokee Place. *Ware*, architect of the earliest group on this site, won second prize in the City and Suburban Homes Company Model Tenement Competition of 1896. *R. Thomas Short* (of Harde

1928 in honor of the nation's greatest World War I hero, Sergeant Alvin C. York. Single-handedly he killed 25 enemy soldiers, took 132 prisoners, and silenced 35 machine guns—all in one morning's skirmish.

East 78th Street, between Second and Third Avenues:

[E47] **208, 210, 212, 214, 216, 218 East 78th Street** (row houses). 1861-1865. *Warren and Ransom Beman, John Buckley*, builders. 🍎
A graceful terrace of brick and painted limestone **Italianate** town houses, each a little over 13 feet wide. The elliptical openings aren't particularly stylish.

[E48] **235 East 78th Street**. ca. 1870. Altered, 1964, *Bruce Campbell Graham.*
Modernized with the addition of a projecting brick wall, separating the architecture and spaces of upper and lower duplex apartments.

E51

[E49] **237-241 East 78th Street**, and **255-261 East 78th Street**. ca. 1870.

Modest vernacular brick row housing.

[E50] **450, 450a, 450b East 78th Street,** bet. First and York Aves. ca. 1855.

Shops below and residence above in this two-story wood frame clapboard-veneered structure. **Manhattan miracle.**

[E51] **Yorkville Branch, New York Public Library,** 222 E.79th St., bet. Second and Third Aves. 1902. *James Brown Lord.* Interior redesigned, 1987, *Gwathmey Siegel & Assocs.* 🍏

A **Regency** neo-Renaissance "London club"—but for the masses, not the classes, with an exquisite interior redesign.

E47

NECROLOGY

Our Lady of Perpetual Help Church/Infant of Prague National Shrine (Roman Catholic). 321 E.61st St., bet. First and Second Aves. 1887.

A **Romanesque Revival** church overshadowed by bridge approach and exit ramps—a sorry bit of luck, but things got worse: it was torn down.

Bethany Memorial Church (Reformed in America), 400 E.67th St., SE cor. First Ave. 1910. *Nelson & Van Wagenen.*

A curiously fashioned church structure, much more demure (Protestant) than St. John of Nepomuk next door (Catholic). Now just a memory, demolished in 2008 in favor of **The Laurel,** a lifeless stone and glass tower.

E50

Cherokee Club, 334 E.79th St., bet. First and Second Aves. ca. 1885.

This **Romanesque Revival** building was once a Democratic Party clubhouse. After losing a tardy battle for landmark designation, the ornately carved façade was first defaced, then mutilated, and finally destroyed. A tacky eight-story apartment building is on the site.

HOSPITALIA

*The **York Avenue** corridor between the Queensboro Bridge and 71st Street, once the land of the tenement but now—cutting off the East River shoreline—the site for more and more facilities for health care and research. The upland area has become increasingly desirable to those seeking housing, and so the gargantuan institutions have had to build their own backup residential facilities here and on Roosevelt Island in order to lure qualified staff and students.*

Rockefeller University

[Ha] **Faculty House, Rockefeller University,** 500 E.63rd St., SE cor. York Ave. 1975. *Horace Ginsbern & Assocs.*

A stylish apartment building, from an era when few high-rise apartments in the Upper East Side were actually designed.

[Hb] **Scholars Building, Rockefeller University,** 510 E.63rd St., over FDR Drive. 1988. *Abramowitz Harris & Kingsland.*

Its architecture, closely keyed to **Faculty House,** is physically linked by a new pedestrian bridge, both an architectural and engineering tour de force (2000. *Wendy Evans Joseph*).

[Hc] **Rockefeller University**/originally **Rockefeller Institute for Medical Research,** 1270 York Ave., bet. E.64th and E.68th Sts. Site

Hc   Hf

acquired, 1901. 1903-1910. *York & Sawyer.*

A campus for research and advanced education occupies a high bluff overlooking the East River, the site once the summer estate of the *Schermerhorn* family of Lafayette Street. The first building opened in 1903.

Caspary Auditorium (1957. *Harrison & Abramovitz)* is the gloomy dome adjacent to York Avenue. It once sparkled with blue tile, but weather problems caused its re-roofing with what might whimsically be thought of as geodesic gutta-percha. The **President's House** (1958. *Harrison & Abramovitz)* is a limestone-and-glass country house tucked in a corner at the bluff's edge.

The Sloane-Kettering Buildings

[Hd] **Memorial Sloane-Kettering Cancer Center,** 1275 York Ave. bet. E.67th and E.68th Sts. W side. Main Building, 444 W.68th St. 1938. *James Gamble Rogers, Inc.* Additions.

1930s virtuoso brickwork defines the building's name in bold letters, and mini-balconies belly out on high.

[He] **Arnold and Marie Schwartz International Hall of Science for Cancer Research**/earlier **James Ewing Memorial Building**/originally **James Ewing Memorial Hospital,** N.Y.C. Department of Hospitals, First Ave. bet. E.67th and E.68th Sts. E side. 1950. *Skidmore, Owings & Merrill.*

The sensible modernism of the 1950s, minimal and institutional. Now hospitals, in fervent competition, seek the grandiose (see, particularly, Roosevelt-St.Luke's entry on Tenth Avenue).

[Hf] **Mortimer B. Zuckerman Research Center, Memorial Sloane-Kettering Cancer Center,** 415-417 E.68th St., 410 E.69th St., bet. First and York Aves. 2008. *Skidmore Owings & Merrill* with *Zimmer Gunsul Frasca.*

Crisp, machined modernism, perfectly sympathetic to its laboratory program. The glass tower is bisected by a thin wall that rises 420

Hn

Hg   Hp

feet, clad in red ceramic strips, and the stair tower is beautifully articulated with horizontal sunscreens. A curious thing happens at ground level, where the tower is connected by a slim glass aperture to **St. Catherine of Siena Church**. The church's new **priory** inhabits the lower level of the cancer center, proving that science and religion can get along, after all.

[Hg] **St. Catherine of Siena Church** (Roman Catholic)/**Shrine of St. Jude Thaddeus,** 411 E.68th St., bet. First and York Aves. 1931. *Wilfred E. Anthony.*

A departure for the architect: bare red-brick neo-Gothic inside and out, revealing the influence of the English Arts and Crafts movement and *William Lethaby* (1857-1931). Now connected at the hip to the Zuckerman Center.

[Hh] **Rockefeller Research Laboratories,** 430 E.68th St., bet. York and First Aves. 1988. *Davis, Brody & Assocs. and Russo+ Sonder.*

A sleek, banded brick-and-glass block shows off only at its spectacular entrance canopy.

[Hi] **Sloane House,** 1233 York Ave., bet. E.66th and E.67th Sts. W side. 1965. *Harrison & Abramovitz.*

A dated dormitory for the medical center's valued nurses.

[Hj] **The Premier,** 333 E.69th St., bet. First and Second Aves. 1963. *Mayer, Whittlesey & Glass; William J. Conklin,* designer.

A simple, crisp, but forceful façade of exposed concrete and pale brick. The contained balconies are far more usable and weather-resistant than the toothy ones punctuating innumerable lesser buildings. It has happily survived the test of time.

[Hk] **Jacob S. Lasdon House, Cornell Medical College,** 420 E.70th St., bet. First and York Aves. 1975. *Conklin & Rossant.*

Concrete and glass, elegant and crisp; a friendly, cool, and handsome neighbor.

[Hl] **Laurence G. Payson House, New York Hospital,** 435 E.70th St., NW cor. York Ave. to E.71st St. 1966. *Frederick G. Frost, Jr., & Assocs.*

Three staggered slabs straddle two service corridors: a dramatic freestanding form.

Hm

[Hm] **New York Hospital-Cornell Medical Center,** York Ave. bet. E.68th and E.71st Sts. to FDR Drive. 1933. *Coolidge, Shepley, Bullfinch & Abbott.* Altered and expanded.

The word "massing" could have been invented to describe the original structures of this great medical complex. It has steadily expanded upland and is now growing, extending, and replacing itself on a platform over the drive (to the river's edge, in the same manner that Carl Schurz Park covers the drive in the 80s, and Rockefeller University and apartment buildings bestride it to the south).

[Hn] **William and Mildred Lasdon Biomedical Research Center,** York Ave. bet. E.68th and E.69th Sts. 1988. *Payette Assocs.,* architects. *Rogers, Burgun, Shahine & Deschler, Inc.,* associated architects.

An earlier **Art Deco** jazz age is added to the Gothic cubism handed down from the parent hospital next door.

[Ho] **Weill Greenberg Center of Weill Cornell Medical College,** 1305 York Ave., at 70th St. 2007. *Polshek Partnership.*

Faceted glass planes capture reflections of old Cornell Medical Center across the street. Both this and *Frank Gehry's* **IAC Center** (see p. 220), completed around the same time, use white fritted glass. Compare.

[Hp] **Hospital for Special Surgery,** 535 E.70th St., bet. 70th and 71st Sts. *Rogers & Butler.* Operating room addition and portico, 1981. Extension over the East River Drive, 1990s. *AHSC (Architects for Health, Science and Commerce).* Addition, 2010, *Smith-Miller+ Hawkinson* with *Cannon Design* and *R.A. Heintges & Associates.*

A hard-to-find adjunct to Cornell-New York enjoying river views. Almost invisible from Manhattan streets, it is a bland stacking of limestone and glass when seen from Roosevelt Island, but enlivened by *Smith-Miller + Hawkinson's* crisp rooftop addition.

Ho

[Hq] **Helmsley Medical Tower,** 1320 York Ave., bet. E.70th and E.71st St. E side. 1987. *Schuman, Lichtenstein, Claman & Efron.*

A smooth and very busy reinterpretation of the medical center's already smoothed neo-Gothic originals, but at the 1980s superheated scale: tall. Staff apartments and, at street level, administrative and retail space.

[Hr] **Hamad Bin Khalfia Biomedical Building**/originally **Institute for Muscle Diseases, Muscular Dystrophy Association of America,** 515 E.71st St., bet. York Ave. and FDR Drive. 1961. *Skidmore, Owings & Merrill.*

A classic modern antidote to some sloppy new architecture around here. Details are impeccable, if unimaginative.

YORKVILLE

This northeastern quadrant of the Upper East Side was named for the village originally centered on 86th Street and Third Avenue. 86th Street later became the City's German-American **Hauptstrasse** (Main Street). In the distant 1930s *Fritz Kuhn* led parades of the German-American Bund until Pearl Harbor finally put an end to such antics. Other Central European groups also found this area to their liking: there is still evidence in church names, settlement houses, and the vanishing restaurants of the former Hungarian and Czech communities. Architectural interest is scattered: because wealthy latecomers at first migrated only to the upper riverside near Carl Schurz Park (see the Gracie Square section), the bulk of the area's building became, until the late 20th century, housing for the lower middle class. In the new millennium it is overrun with scores of new towers for the newly rich, and gentrification is

[Y2] **Lexington House**, 1190-1192 Lexington Ave., NW cor. E.81st St. 1983. *Noah Greenberg.*

One of the early wave of sliver buildings: this one turns the corner (later slivers were outlawed in midblock locations). Some mini-scaled set-backs recall the early modeling of the RCA/GE Building.

Y2

Y1

Y3

Y4

rampant in the shops and restaurants along the avenues.

For the purposes of this Guide **Yorkville** *begins above 79th Street and runs to 96th, from Lexington Avenue to the East River, except for the area around East End Avenue, described in the next section,* **Gracie Square and Environs**. *Generally the entry numbers run from south to north.*

[Y1] **Hungarian Baptist Church**, 225 E.80th St., bet. Second and Third Aves. ca. 1890.

A crisp, somber, brick, and terra-cotta Romanesque Revival palazzo. The cornice and radial bi-color brick voussoirs could be Italian, the arches *Richardsonian.* A cultural mélange.

[Y3] **1220, 1222, 1224 Lexington Ave.**, bet. E.82nd and E.83rd Sts. W side. 1880.

A gray marble Italianate trio, **1880** carved in the central pediment. Its streetfront shops join it to its neighbors, causing most people to overlook the quality overhead. Crane your neck: the original is from the third floor up.

[Y4] **J. Leon Lascoff Pharmacy**, 1209 Lexington Ave. SE cor. E.82nd St. Building, 1870s. Pharmacy, 1899.

A neighborhood anchor and landmark that dresses its façade with a faux-Gothic canopy and shop windows. The canopy makes a strong cornering for the neighborhood.

[Y5] **American Federation for Hungarian Education & Literature, Ltd.**, 213-215 E.82nd St., bet. Second and Third Aves. 1860s.

A pair of painted brick houses set back from the street (they were here first!) and later unified with a wrought-iron balcony. A plaque marks the visit of *Cardinal Mindszenty* of Hungary in 1973.

Continue ↑ for East Harlem

E.97th St

E 96th St

E 95th St

E 94th St

E 93rd St

E 92nd St

E 91st St

E 90th St

E 89th St

E 88th St

E 87th St

E 86th St

E 85th St

E 84th St

E 83rd St

E 82nd St

E 81st St

E 80th St

E 79th St

E 78th St

E 77th St

E 76th St

E 75th St

Lexington Ave

Third Ave

Second Ave

First Ave

York Ave

East End Ave

York Ave

Third Ave

Lexington Ave

Second Ave

First Ave

Third Ave

N

← Continue for Carnegie Hill

← Continue for Metropolitan Museum & Vicinity

Hardenburgh/ Rhinelander Historic District

Henderson Place Historic District

East of Eden / Hospitalia: see map p. 465

[Y6] **312 East 82nd Street**, bet. First and Second Aves. 1890s.

Those grand **Corinthian** pilasters give this simple tenement a noble façade.

[Y7] **Old P.S. 290**, 311 E.82nd St., bet. First and Second Aves. 1900s.

Forget the building, but there's a florid baroque entrance worthy of **Rome**.

Y9

[Y11a] **Formerly Mayo Ballrooms**, 1493 Third Ave., NE cor. E.84th St. ca. 1927.

Eclectic ballroom dancing? **Art Deco** at the penthouse, classically pilastered below, polychromatic terra-cotta bas-relief panels everywhere.

[Y11b] **Sidewalk clock**, in front of 1501 Third Ave., bet. E.84th and E.85th Sts. E side. 1898. *E. Howard Clock Company.* ⬤

A pocket watch for **Gargantua** that once advertised *Adolph Stern*, Jeweler.

[Y12a] **325 East 84th Street**, bet. First and Second Aves. N side. 1978. *W.P. Chin.*

Each floor, or pair of floors (for the duplexes), provides a different piece of the exterior elevation: strip, square, balcony, greenhouse; a functional attitude that gives some variety to a subdued façade.

[Y12b] **Zion St. Mark's Church**/earlier **Zion Lutheran Church**/originally **Deutsche**

Y7   Y12b

Y11a

[Y8] **St. Stephen of Hungary Church and School** (Roman Catholic), 408 E.82nd St., bet. First and York Aves. 1928. *Emil Szendy.*

Yellow ocher brick in timid neo-**Romanesque**, sporting a tile hip roof. There were boys and girls separate entry doors (both blue).

[Y9] **St. Elizabeth of Hungary Roman Catholic Church**, 211 E.83rd St., bet. Second and Third Aves. 1918.

A classy, spired neo-**Gothic** exterior, but the treat is within: ascend the stairs to view a just heavenly groin-vaulted ceiling painted in the colors of *Ravenna's* mosaics.

[Y10] **222 and 224 East 83rd Street**, bet. Second and Third Aves. 1850s.

The extraordinary bowed metal fence shielding the garden at **224** adds style to this pair (again set-back, but they were here first).

Evangelische Kirche von Yorkville, 339 E.84th St., bet. First and Second Aves. 1888.

A frothy reminder of the early days of German immigration to this precinct. A blessed **neo-Gothic** survivor, but think how rich the materials must be under all that white paint.

[Y13] **1578-1600 York Avenue**, bet. E.83th to E.84th Sts. E side. ca. 1870.

An almost original blockfront of "first-class flats." Looks like a Hollywood backlot setting for Manhattan in the 1870s, but it's genuine.

[Y14] **The Lucida**, 151 E.85th Street, along Lexington Ave, to 86th St. E side. 2009. *Cook + Fox.*

Sleek glass and mouthwatering promises of luxury living. Just one of the many modernist housing units that sprouted like wildflowers during the Bloomberg Boom, promoting chic transparency as a (private) civic virtue.

[Y15] Formerly **Manufacturers Hanover Trust Company**/now **The Gap** and **Equinox Health Club**, 1511 Third Ave., NE cor. E.85th St. ca. 1915. Remodeled, 1996, *HLW International*.

A bank of the old school in **neo-Renaissance**-tailored dress of stone now shelters commerce and health. Savor the bronze doors. The **Equinox** entry is a welcome hi-tech addition.

[Y16a] **The Brompton** (apartments), 205 E.85th St. through to Lexington Ave. and 86th St. 2009. *Robert A.M. Stern with Ismael Leyva*.

A side-street entry neck leads to another huge **neo-Collegiate** endeavor from *Stern*, this time with *Leyva* on board for the ride. 86th or Lexington: both sound less classy than East 85th, hence the neck to capture the address.

[Y16b] **City Cinemas**/originally **Annex, Musical Mutual Protection Union**, 215 E.85th St., bet. Second and Third Aves. 1919. *Levitan & Fischer*. Entrance to theater at 210 East 86th St.

Colossal **Classical** piers support the mod-

[Y18b] **412 East 85th Street**, bet. First and York Aves. ca. 1855. Restored, 1998, *Alfredo De Vido*.

A rare **clapboard** shingle house, set deep in the row from a time when country houses (yes, here in the country) provided front gardens. *De Vido* has lovingly restored it.

[Y19] **120 East 87th Street**/originally **Gimbel's East**, on Lexington Ave, W side, from 86th to 87th Sts. *Abbott, Merkt & Co.* Converted to apartments, 1989, *Skidmore, Owings & Merrill*.

Once a windowless, anonymous ten-story box: **Gimbel's East**. In 1986, following Gimbel's collapse, *SOM* tailored a neo-1920s apartment to the existing steel frame, crowning it with twinned wannabe towers that say "wish we were on Central Park West."

[Y20] **Papaya King**, 179 E. 86th St. NW cor. Third Ave.

New York is full of meaningful adjacencies, juxtapositions, and intersections. Here **The Brompton**, clad in dull brick, occupies the SE

Y15   Y16a   Y19

Y16b

est entablature bearing the original building's engraved name (not surprisingly, an early musician's union). The main entrance was through a magnificent neo-Renaissance brick and terra-cotta façade on 86th Street, now demolished.

[Y17] **220-222 East 85th Street**, bet. Second and Third Aves. 1890s.

Bold, sensuous arches and their battered bases form, seemingly, key holes that ground these unusual tenements.

[Y18a] **406, 408, 410 East 85th Street**, bet. First and York Aves. ca. 1865.

A charming, but **dour, mansarded** trio, where painted brick and lintels have taken away some of the original verve.

corner of busy East 86th Street, and **Papaya King**, a squat riot of color and Coney Island–style signs, sits opposite on the NW corner. While *Stern* and *Leyva* promote a "stylishly proper" city, the other city continues to walk and eat, slathering mustard on a cheap hot dog on the way out the door.

[Y21] **222 East 86th Street**, bet. Second and Third Aves. ca. 1888.

A bit of **Victorian** London, bearing gracefully curved fire escapes, and topped with double pediments. The Manhattan, at the corner of Second Avenue, is its blood brother.

[Y22] **The Manhattan**, 244 E.86th St., SW cor. Second Ave. 1878-1880. *Charles W. Clinton*.

A six-story mild **Queen Anne** apartment block that was home to Senator (1927-1949) *Robert F. Wagner, Sr.*, father of the late Mayor (1954-1965) *R.F.W., Jr.* Its developers were the *Rhinelander* family.

Y29a

[Y23] **Channel Club Condominiums**, 455 E.86th St., NW cor. E.86th St. 1987. *Wechsler, Grasso & Menziuso.*

Sleek strip windows and brown glazed brick band the 40 floors, a tower that manipulates the ground-floor forms gracefully.

[Y24] **420 East 86th Street**, bet. First and York Aves. ca. 1936.

A six-story apartment building that looks as out of place in these parts today as it must have when built (a rare example for this neighborhood of **Grand Concourse Art Moderne**). Refreshing, nevertheless, particularly the polychrome brick spandrels.

[Y25] **247 East 87th Street**, NW cor. Second Ave. to E.88th St. 1966. *Paul & Jarmul.*

The same economics, the same materials, the same zoning and building laws as its speculative apartment house peers, here in the hands of someone who cared. The bold massing of the balconies reads as a great richness

Y26

Y27

Y25

on the avenue. It was the setting for the film version of *Neil Simon's The Prisoner of Second Avenue* (1975).

[Y26] **337-339 East 87th Street**, bet. First and Second Aves. 1890s.

Two connected houses: a grand essay in brick, with limestone articulating the segmental arches: elegant.

[Y27] **St. Joseph's Catholic Church of Yorkville**, 408 E.87th St., bet. First and York Aves. 1895. *William Schickel & Co.*

A charming basilican church with a flat **neo-Romanesque** limestone façade that contrasts with a tower ending in a quartet of vigorous Palladian openings.

[Y28] **232 East 88th Street**, bet. Second and Third Aves. ca. 1888.

A lusty tenement of arched and corbeled brick.

[Y29a] **Church of the Holy Trinity Complex** (Episcopal) & **St. Christopher House/Rhinelander Memorial** (parish house) and Parsonage, 316-332 E.88th St., bet. First and Second Aves. 1896-1897. ● Addition, 1897-1899, *Barney & Chapman.* ● Cloister chapel stained glass, *Robert Sowers.*

A remarkable enclave and *Rhinelander* family memorial. With the romantic forms of the **French Renaissance** (*François I*) in golden brick and terra cotta, the architects created architecture redolent of the Loire Valley, surmounted by one of New York's great bell towers.

[Y29b] **Rhinelander Children's Center**, Children's Aid Society, 350 E.88th St., bet. First and Second Aves. 1891. *Vaux & Radford.* Remodeled, 1958.

Once a school for crippled children, another beneficence of the *Rhinelanders*. Unfortunately, *Vaux's* brick and brownstone façade has been blurred with an expedient "brownstone" stucco coating.

[Y30] **436, 438 East 88th Street**, bet. First and York Aves. 1860s.

Brick and limestone town houses from a gentler streetscape.

[Y31] **Hardenburgh/Rhinelander Historic District**, 1340-1350 Lexington, 121-123 E. 89th St., NW cor. Lexington Ave. 1888-1889. *Henry J. Hardenburgh.*

Six brick, brownstone, and terra-cotta row houses and one building of "French Flats,"

Y32

Y34

Y35

constructed for the estate of *William C. Rhinelander* in the "Northern Renaissance" Revival style.

[Y32] **146-156 East 89th Street**, bet. Lexington and Third Aves. 1886-1887. *Hubert, Pirsson & Co.*

Six spectacularly romantic **Queen Anne** remainders of a row of ten single-family houses, brick with stone and terra-cotta trim, slate mansard roofs, pierced by dormers. All except No.146 are 12 feet wide, half a city lot. Originally commissioned by developer *William Rhinelander*, whose family's philanthropy can be admired at the **Holy Trinity** complex on East 88th.

[Y33] **1716-1722 Second Avenue**, NE cor. E.89th St. ca. 1880.

A pair of apartment buildings with detail reminiscent of one of *Calvert Vaux's* model tenements. The twin grand third-floor arches unite the façade.

[Y34] **East River Tower**, 1725 York Ave., bet. E.89th and E.90th Sts. W side. 1970. *Horace Ginsbern & Assocs.*

Clever: 33 stories of alternating balconies that zig and zag between projected columns. Beyond the balconies the cleverness stops.

[Y35] **Ruppert and Yorkville Towers**, E.90th to E.92nd Sts. bet. Second and Third Aves. 1976. *Davis, Brody & Assocs.* **Ruppert Park**, E.89th St. NW cor. Second Ave. 1979. *Balsley & Kuhl,* landscape architects.

Bulky modeled form. Notches, slots, cut corners from the vocabulary initiated by this firm at Waterside. The density is immense and overwhelming. Given that millstone, the architects have handled an unfortunate program in a sophisticated manner.

[Y36] **Our Lady of Good Counsel Church D.O.M.** (Roman Catholic), 236 E.90th St., bet. Second and Third Aves.

Robust, undisciplined, deeply three-dimensional: a great side-street **Gothic** façade of

Y36

Y37

limestone and Manhattan schist, revealed when the Ruppert site opened space across the way.

[Y37] **160 East 91st Street**, bet. Lexington and Third Aves. ca. 1880.

A precocious apartment building with eight stories of softly bowed red-brick bays enhanced by strings of wrought-iron fire escapes fashioned in the curves of a violin.

[Y38] **Our Lady of Good Counsel School** (Roman Catholic), 325 E.91st St., bet. First and Second Aves.

The rose-colored pressed brick, limestone trim, and generous mansard roof overcome the unfortunate loss of detail and scale contributed by its original windows.

Cipolla Rossa (Red Onion), 1762 First Avenue between 91st and 92nd, is an unpretentious, snug (eight tables) nook with cheap, delicious Tuscan cooking. Pierluigi Sacchetti, the affable owner, waiter, and cook, specializes in game: spaghetti with wild boar meatballs, tagliatelle with venison. Take a break from looking up at buildings and go there for lunch on a cold winter afternoon.

[Y39] **River East Plaza**, 402 E.90th St., bet. First and York Aves. 1983.

High upon the east, lot-line wall is a palimpsest of a former life: very powerful neo-Baroque forms. This was a garage, now apartments. A puzzlement.

[Y40] **The 92nd Street Y**/also known as **YM-YWHA/Young Men's and Young Women's Hebrew Association**, 1395 Lexington Ave., SE cor. E.92nd St. 1930. *Necarsulmer & Lehlbach and Gehron, Ross & Alley*. Expanded and altered. *www.92Y.org*

A citywide center for cultural affairs, the Y's Kaufmann Auditorium holds readings from the resident Poetry Center in addition to concerts and lectures of more general interest.

[Y41] Originally **Richard Hibberd House,** 160 East 92nd Street, bet. Lexington and Third Aves. 1852-1853. Attributed to *Albro Howell*, carpenter.

Another rare wood-framed house, here embellished with a quartet of Corinthian-capitaled porch columns (replaced around 1930). Once the home of *Eartha Kitt,* its modern occupants have installed inappropriate windows and false shutters.

GRACIE SQUARE AND ENVIRONS

The corridor along East End Avenue's length (until 1890 called Avenue B), running from East 79th to East 92nd Streets.

[Y44] **1 East End Avenue,** bet. E.79th and E.80th Sts. E side to FDR Drive. 1929. *Pleasants Pennington and Albert W. Lewis.*

A 14-story apartment building shoehorned

Y42

Y43

Y44

[Y42] **153 East 92nd Street,** bet. Lexington and Third Aves. 1890s.

An entrance portal of terra cotta and marble, eroding. Once worthy of a Byzantine church.

[Y43] **176 East 93rd Street,** bet. Lexington and Third Aves. 1973. *Gueron & Lepp.*

A brick tour de force: apartments for three families. Arched... and arch.

The Marx Brothers: While best known for their raucous Hollywood comedies, Leonard "Chico" Marx (1891-1961), Adolph Arthur "Harpo" Marx (1893-1964), and Julius Henry "Groucho" Marx (1895-1977), plus the more elusive Zeppo and Gummo, were all Manhattan natives. Their boyhood home ("ancestral" was their term) was a three-bedroom apartment in the row house at **179 East 93rd Street** *(now a gentrified and refaced tenement).*

into a narrow, trapezoidal site, 29 feet wide at the south end, 51 feet at the north, 204 feet away. Its east façade once fronted on Marie Curie Avenue, the name of the marginal street widened to create the Drive.

[Y45] **CUNY (City University of New York) Administration**/formerly **N.Y.C. Board of Higher Education Headquarters**/originally **Welfare Island Dispensary,** N.Y.C. Department of Hospitals, 535 E.80th St., NW cor. East End Ave. 1940. *Louis E. Jallade.*

A Classical/Art Deco/Art Moderne composite that is a cousin—at least once removed—to the Brooklyn's Board of Transportation Building.

[Y46] **The Brearley School,** 612 E. 83rd St., bet. East End and FDR Drive. 1929. *Benjamin Wistar Morris.*

A sober industrial-gothic pile of brick, tall for a school, with those ten stories of stairs. Nice details. For spectacular *Morris*, visit 25 Broadway, the old 1921 **Cunard Building.**

[Y47] The Chapin School, 100 East End Ave., NW cor. 84th St. 1928. *Delano & Aldrich.* **Addition**, 2008, *Farewell Mills Gatsch Architects.*

Said the modernist addition to the neo-Georgian brick school: "Sorry! I landed on your roof! Pardon me! Now I seem to be stuck to your cornice! Oh, well..."

Gracie Square and Gracie Terrace
Robert Moses, Andre Kostelanetz, Gloria Vanderbilt, Benno Schmidt, Constantine Sidamon-Eristoff, Osborn Elliott, mayors since Fiorello La Guardia, and other well-connected New Yorkers have lived in these surrounds. Changes in the original low-scale and working-class demeanor were first made in the 1920s when Vincent Astor built the apartments at **520** *and* **530 East 86th Street***. The zoning change of 1928 permitted residential developments along East End Avenue below 84th Street, the easternmost block of which is called* **Gracie Square***; the corresponding block of 83rd is* **Gracie Terrace***.*

between cartoonist *Edwin Marcus* and architect *Harvey Stevenson.* The walk connects with **Carl Schurz Park's Esplanade.**

[Y49] 525 East 85th Street, bet. York and East End Aves. 1958. *Paul Mitarachi.*

This type of glassy modernist house has made a big comeback of late. Gardens both in front and rear allow the raised living room (from its balcony) to overview its own garden to the south.

[Y50] Henderson Place Historic District, 549-553 E.86th St., NW cor. East End Ave. 6-16 Henderson Place. E. side. 140-154 East End Ave., W side. 552-558 E.87th St. 1881-1882. All by *Lamb & Rich.* 🍎

A charming cul-de-sac provides the name for 24 (of the original 32) dwellings that survive: tiny, zesty **Queen Anne** row houses that transport unwary romantics to other climes and another era. Regrettably overwhelmed and vulgarized by monster apartments to the west and north.

Y50

Maria Bowen **Chapin** *erected a new school at East End Avenue and 84th.* **Brearley** *soon followed suit directly on the riverfront, a site since compromised by the construction of FDR Drive—but resulting in the deck built over* **Finley Walk** *to compensate the school for the loss.*

Walk eastward toward the river along Gracie Square (84th Street extended) and at the end you'll find Finley Walk:

[Y48] John H. Finley Walk, over FDR Drive, bet. E.81st St. and E.84th St./Gracie Sq. 1941.

Shortly after his death, this elevated promenade was named for *Finley* (1863-1940), one-time editor of *Harper's Weekly,* president of City College, associate editor of the *New York Times*, and inveterate walker. What makes it special are the memorable cutout identification signs that line the pathway, a collaboration

Cross East End Avenue into Carl Schurz Park:

[Y51] Carl Schurz Park/originally **East River Park**, E.84th St./Gracie Sq. to E.90th St., bet. East End Ave. and the East River. 1876. Acquired by the City, 1891. Named for *Carl Schurz*, 1910. Reconstructed, *Harvey Stevenson*, architect, *Cameron Clarke*, landscape architect.

A brilliant solution to the intersection of city, river, and highway. Suspended over FDR Drive is a sinuous expansive esplanade overlooking **Hell Gate's** churning waters. It is edged with a curved, user-friendly wrought-iron fence so effective that its form was appropriated for the Battery Park City Esplanade. "Imitation is the sincerest form of flattery," *Charles Caleb Colton*, 1780-1832.

Carl Schurz (1829-1906), general, minister, senator, secretary of the interior, and editor, was the most prominent German immigrant of the 19th century.

Y47

Y51

Y52

The park is dedicated: "*Nearly a thousand persons attended the exercises. A touch of excitement was added by a blaze among the branches of a tree near the speaker's platform. A lighted newspaper placed in the crotch set the dry bark on fire, but a park employee with a sprinkling can soon extinguished it without interrupting the exercises.*" — New York Times, *October 3, 1910.*

[Y52] **Gracie Mansion**, originally **Archibald Gracie House,** Carl Schurz Park, East End Ave. opp. E.88th St. 1799-1804. Attributed to *Ezra Weeks.* Expanded, 1804-1808. Restored, 1934-1936, *Aymar Embury II.* **Susan Wagner Wing,** added, 1965-1966, *Mott B. Schmidt.* Further restorations, 1985, *Charles A. Platt Partners and Robert E. Meadows.* Open to public on a restricted basis.

Official residence of the mayor since 1942. A remote country house in its day, built on the site of a British fort, **Gracie** has been through the mill of reconstruction and restoration. The 1966 addition permits the mayor to use the house while others think they are using it. The 1985 restoration makes it (particularly on the interior) a true executive mansion. Its country peers from the same era include the **Hamilton Grange** (1802), **Abigail Adams Smith House** (1799), **Jumel Mansion** (1765), and **Van Cortlandt Mansion** (1748). *Mayor Bloomberg*, with a cozy town house on E.79th Street, chose not to live here.

[Y53] Originally **Municipal Asphalt Plant/** now **Asphalt Green Sports and Arts Center,** 655 E.90th St., NW cor. York Ave./ Franklin Delano Roosevelt Drive, to E.91st St. 1941-1944. *Kahn & Jacobs.* Altered, 1982, *Hellmuth, Obata & Kassabaum,* associated architects. *Pasanella+Klein,* design architects.

Exposed concrete over a parabolic, arched steel frame that was once a single giant space containing the equipment for mixing the City's asphalt. Now divided into levels for neighborhood athletic activities. Exhibited in the pace-setting MoMA exhibition **"Built in U.S.A. 1932-1944."**

[Y54] **Asphalt Green Aquacenter,** 1750 York Ave., bet. E.90th and E.92nd Sts. 1993. *Richard Dattner.*

A sensuous construction in undulating brick, glass block, and bright green sash. An honor for the neighborhood.

NECROLOGY

Convent of the Little Sisters of the Assumption/originally Convent of the Sisters of Bon Secours, 1195 Lexington Ave., NE cor. E.81st St. 1889. *William Schickel.*

The picturesque four-story red-brick building was one of the City's last Victorian Gothic

Y54

structures of its type. A last-ditch effort to designate it an official landmark failed. One less fine reminder of days past.

306 and 306A East 82nd Street, bet. First and Second Aves. ca. 1855.

Demolished: A charming early residence (and carriage house) at village scale, replaced by larger but lesser things.

Four great neighborhood cinemas: The **RKO 86th Street Theater** (1927. *Thomas W. Lamb.* Demolished, 1986), a grand 3,160-seat movie palace, where one of the authors spent Saturday afternoons in the 1930s watching *Flash Gordon* serials, occupied Gimbel's whole footprint. Also gone from 86th Street are **Loew's 86th Street** and **Loew's Orpheum**, once opposite each other, between Lexington and Third, and the **86th Street Garden/Grande**, east of Third.

Group Residence for Young Adults, Jewish Board of Guardians, 217 E.87th St., bet. Second and Third Aves. 1968. *Horace Ginsbern & Assocs.*

Bold, plastic, New Brutalist (but not brutal). Classy, personal, distinguished; monumental modernist. Replaced by bland brickery.

Starting in the 1870s, Jacob Ruppert's Brewery, together with **Ehret**'s and **Ringler**'s, occupied three giant blocks between 90th and 93rd

Necrology: Group Residence for Young Adults

Streets, Second and Third Avenues, for the glory of the German beer hall (this is Yorkville). Thirty-four buildings were assembled in less than a hundred years. Where there were originally almost 100 breweries in New York, now there are only micro breweries, established in the 1980s, where quality and special tastes are the rule.

The abandoned blocks were re-developed with middle-income housing.

The Heights and the Harlems

M1, Cathedral of St. John the Divine

North of Cathedral Parkway, Central Park North, and 110th Street, for the most part, lie the areas of **Morningside** and **Hamilton Heights, Harlem,** and **East Harlem,** the last extending southward to 97th Street east of Park Avenue. The Heights precincts are known for their college complexes—Columbia, Barnard, Teachers, the seminaries below the 125th Street valley, and City College above it; the Harlems are the City's best-known African-American and Latino enclaves. All four areas offer relics of the past, much new construction, and a display of diverse lifestyles that reflect their varied populations. There is much to tempt the eye . . . and the mind.

THE HEIGHTS AND THE HARLEMS KEY MAP

Hamilton Heights

125th Street Corridor

Morningside Heights

Northern Fifth & Madison Aves

Northwest of Central Park

Frawley Circle to Mt. Morris Park

East Harlem

MORNINGSIDE HEIGHTS

From Cathedral Parkway north to West 125th Street, the western hilly side of Manhattan Island is Morningside Heights. Between the steep escarpment of the Park on the east and a gentle slope along the Hudson's shore, lie many of Manhattan's most impressive visual, architectural, and cultural delights. The site of a 1776 Revolutionary War skirmish, Morningside Heights became home to the **Bloomingdale Insane Asylum** in 1818, and the **Leake and Watts Orphan Asylum** 20 years later. The opening of Morningside Park in 1887, Riverside Drive in 1892, and the simultaneous settlement here of major cultural institutions permitted the development of several great complexes, each in a well-designed setting. High-density housing along Riverside and Morningside Drives provided people power for the institutions and an active community life.

anointed: *Ralph Adams Cram of Cram & Ferguson*. *Cram*'s style was French Gothic, though over the years other versions of Gothic (and other architects: *Henry Vaughan, Carrère & Hastings*) were employed, all working within *Cram's* grand scheme. By 1942, the year of *Cram's* death, only his great nave and west front (minus its towers) were complete. There the work stopped, halted by our entry into World War II.

Work temporarily resumed in 1979 under the surveillance of then *Bishop Paul Moore, Jr.,* and *Dean James Parks Morton*, the latter combining the happy interests of social activism, avant-garde art and music, and a heady interest in architecture. *James Bambridge*, a British master stonemason, came to New York on the bishop's invitation to train a cadre of youths in stonecutting. The first efforts raised the south Amsterdam Avenue tower. Unfortunately, the

M2

St. John the Divine to Columbia's East Campus:

[M1] **Cathedral Church of St. John the Divine,** Amsterdam Ave. at W.112th St. E side. 1892-1911. *Heins & La Farge.* Work continued, 1911-1942. *Cram & Ferguson.* Assorted supporting buildings, 1909-1914. *Heins & La Farge; Cram & Ferguson; Cook & Welch; Howells & Stokes.* [M1a] **Leake & Watts Orphan Asylum Building.** 1843. *Ithiel Town.* Cathedral open 7-5 daily. 212-316-7540.

Bishop Henry Codman Potter (1834-1908) initiated this grand architectural coronet crowning Morningside Heights. In 1891 he purchased the site of the **Leake and Watts Orphan Asylum** (whose 1843, *Ithiel Town*–designed Greek Revival building still remains) and, after an architectural competition, commissioned *Heins & La Farge.* Apse, choir, and crossing bear their **Byzantine-Romanesque** influence. By 1911 the bishop and *Heins* had died (*Potter's* tomb is in the church's St. James Chapel; *La Farge* had been fired in the meantime), and a new architect

work has been stopped and the stoneyard closed.

The goal was to build the lantern over the crossing in accordance with *Cram's* original design, replacing the "temporary" dome that has sheltered the worshipping flock for nearly a century. Built of Guastavino vaulting, a process developed by Spanish architect *Rafael Guastavino*, it required no interior support during the course of construction. Craftsmen worked from the completed vault (of three staggered laminations) as they laid the remaining swirls of tile using a special adhesive mortar. The resulting underside, handsomely patterned, is visible from within, although the plans had originally called for concealing it with mosaics.

Despite its incompleteness and mix of styles, it is an impressive interior, enormous not only in plan but also in volume, its side aisles built as high as the nave. Visit the baptistry and ambulatory chapels radiating from the apse.

On the landscaped grounds are a number of ancillary buildings, among them the **Synod**

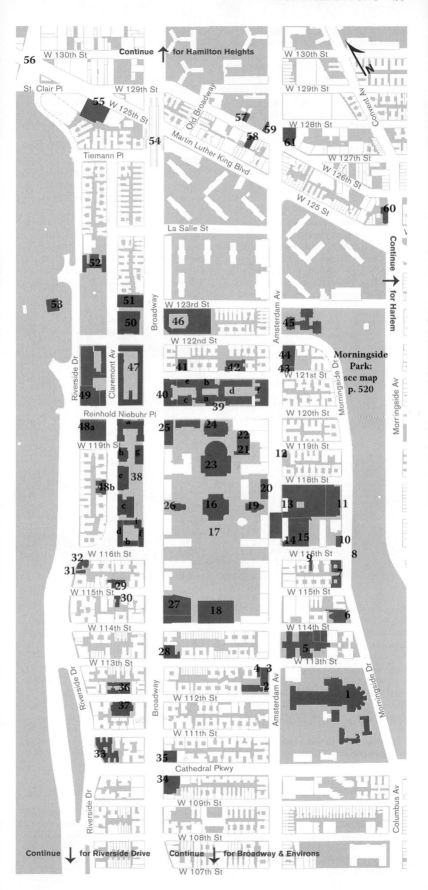

Continue ↑ for Hamilton Heights

W 130th St
56
St. Clair Pl
W 129th St

55 W 125th St
54
Tiemann Pl

Old Broadway
Martin Luther King Blvd
57
58 59
61

La Salle St

Continue → for Harlem

60

52
53

Broadway
W 123rd St
51
50
46

W 122nd St
Amsterdam Av
45
44
43

Morningside
Park:
see map
p. 520

Riverside Dr
Claremont Av
47
Reinhold Niebuhr Pl
49
48a
W 121st St

Morningside Dr

Morningside Av

41
42
e b
c a d f
40
39
W 120th St

25
24
22
21
12
W 119th St

h g
e 38
48b c
d i f
b a
23
W 118th St
20
13
11

26
16
19
14 15
10

17
W 116th St
9
8
32
31
7
29
30
W 115th St

27
18
6

28
W 114th St

5
W 113th St
36
37
4 3
2
W 112th St

33
35
W 111th St

34
Cathedral Pkwy
1

Riverside Dr
W 109th St

Columbus Av
Amsterdam Av

W 108th St
Continue ↓ for Riverside Drive   Continue ↓ for Broadway & Environs
W 107th St

House on Cathedral Parkway, whose Amsterdam Avenue portal is embellished with sculpture from *Alexius* to *Zinzendorf*.

The 2001 fire in the north transept ultimately resulted in restoration with an accompanying cleansing of the whole cathedral. *David Dunlap* in the *New York Times* said: "What we remembered as a gloomy expanse of gray now seems like a forest of lavender." His *Times* colleague remarked, nevertheless, that *Cram*'s work (compared to that of *Heins*) was "dry-toast archaeology." Understanding the English breakfast (cold) toast rack, it sounds like an Anglican evaluation. Strangely, the Cathedral is not an official landmark.

[M2] **Amsterdam House**, 1060 Amsterdam Ave., NW cor. W.112th St. 1976. *Kennerly, Slomanson & Smith*. **Amsterdam Avenue Wing**. 1997. *Geddes Partnership*.

The original building is an elegantly designed multistory slab for the care of the elderly, its use of naturally finished wood-

[M4] **Engine Co. No.47, New York City Fire Department**, 500 W.113th St., SW cor. Amsterdam Ave. 1889. *Napoleon LeBrun & Sons*. 🍎

Ubiquitous *LeBrun* fire houses are some of the City's great neighborhood treasures. Here rusticated brownstone supports a banded brick and terra-cotta façade, a row of **Romanesque Revival** arches and a Classical cornice. Polyglot, and nice.

[M5] **Plant and Scrymser Pavilions for Private Patients**, St. Luke's Hospital, Morningside Dr., 401 W. 113th St. and 400 W.114th St. 1904-1906, 1926-1928. *Ernest Flagg*. 🍎

The western pavilions have been replaced, and the handsome **Baroque** dome is gone, although its drum is still there; but the high mansard roofs and the profusion of **Classical** detail give the original buildings their dignity and charm. Still gorgeous.

M3

M5

M4

M6

framed windows a masterful touch. The "wing" thickly veneering this elegance aspires to the neo-Georgian, but is a heavy-handed **Disneyland** crowd-pleaser. What an insult to both Amsterdam House and the *Cram* cathedral façade across the street.

[M3] **Amsterdam House Adult Day Care Center**/originally **113th Street Gatehouse, New Croton Aqueduct**, W.113th St., SW cor. Amsterdam Ave. ca. 1890.

Construction labor was cheap in the 1880s when the **New Croton Aqueduct** was built, and manufactured items, such as cast-iron pipe, expensive. More economical, therefore, to build a masonry aqueduct here, where water pressure was low: horseshoe-shaped in cross section, it ran under Convent and Amsterdam from 119th to 113th Streets until 1987, when steel pipe replacements were installed. This finely crafted granite gatehouse and its mate at 119th Street (ca. 1880s) stand above shafts at each end of the aqueduct.

[M6] **Eglise de Notre Dame** (Roman Catholic), 40 Morningside Dr., NW cor. W.114th St. Apse, Sanctuary, 1909-1910. *Daus & Otto*. Nave and façade, 1914, *Cross & Cross*. Rectory, 1913-1914, *Cross & Cross*. 🍎

Like nearby St. John's, this "Grotto Church of Notre Dame" was never finished. The interior is lighted artificially because the oversized drum and dome, designed to bring skylight into the church, were never built. For a sense of what completion would bring, visit nearby **St. Paul's Chapel** at Columbia, where drum and dome are magnificent. Classical and cool within and without.

Columbia University

Columbia University campus, W.114th to W.120th Sts., bet. Broadway and Amsterdam Aves. Original design and buildings, *Charles McKim of McKim, Mead & White*. Construction begun, 1897. Additions and changes by others.

M9

Columbia is one of the nation's oldest, largest, and wealthiest institutions. Prior to relocating here on the Heights in 1897, Columbia occupied two previous campuses, the first southwest of current City Hall and later a site east of Rockefeller Center's buildings. (The university, up until 1987, owned the land under Rockefeller Center, from which it derived a substantial income.) Today's main campus occupies land bought from the **Bloomingdale Insane Asylum**.

The earliest buildings, north of 116th Street (now a pedestrian walkway), are situated on a high terrace, two flights of stairs above surrounding streets and separated from them by high, forbidding granite basements. The south campus, a later addition south of West 116th Street, is terraced below the level of the 116th Street pedestrian way.

Arranged along **Classical** lines, the campus is dominated by the great, domed, limestone Low Library. The Italian Renaissance–style instructional buildings, of red brick, limestone trim, and copper-green roofs, are arranged around the periphery of the campus and are augmented by planting, tasteful paving, statues, plaques, fountains, and a variety of Classical ornament and detail. All of this, however, fails to animate the campus into either a dramatic or picturesque composition. The old buildings, except for **Low Library** and **St. Paul's Chapel,** are bland.

McKim, Mead & White's original concept of a densely built-up campus, with a central quadrangle and intimate side courts, was never followed. Only the court between **Avery** and **Fayerweather** Halls was completed, and this is now changed by the subterranean extension of Avery Library. The abandonment of the compact plan, plus the university's explosive growth, resulted in the spread of Columbia's buildings to the remainder of Morningside Heights.

Newer Columbia buildings, except for *Tschumi's* **Lerner Student Center** and the **Northwest Corner Science Building** by *Rafael Moneo Valles,* are outside the McKim perimeter: *Polshek's* **Greene** and **Warren,** *Gruzen Samton's* **Kraft Center,** and *Gwathmey Siegel's* **East Campus Dormitory** have all brought much new life to that extended campus.

M8

Columbia east of the McKim superblock:

[M7] **Cathedral Court, La Touraine,** and **Mont Ceris,** 44-54 Morningside Dr., bet. W.114th and W.116th Sts. 1904-1905. *Schwartz & Gross.*

They look comfortable from the outside, and just imagine the views. The suave handling of the recessed fire escapes makes them a rich part of the façade. Many on the Columbia faculty call these home.

[M8] **Statue of Carl Schurz,** Morningside Dr. at W.116th St. E side. 1913. *Karl Bitter,* sculptor. *Henry Bacon,* architect.

A reformer, avid conservationist, and editor of the *New York Evening Post* and *The Nation,* Schurz (1829-1906) also has his own park, but you can't see that from here. But this is an excellent place to view Harlem from afar. Rising from the patchwork quilt roofscape below is a tall white building to the north, the **Harlem State Office Building**. To the north look down and enjoy massive buttresses supporting the Drive, flanking an entry into a cavernous world.

[M9] **William C. Warren Hall** (Columbia University Law Review), 410 W.116th St., bet. Amsterdam Ave. and Morningside Dr. 1995. *Polshek Partnership.*

A sleek glass and stainless steel canopy signals the narrow entry to a much more substantial volume behind. Elegant technology shelters blossoming lawyers.

[M10] **President's House, Columbia University,** 60 Morningside Dr., at W.116th

M10

M11

St. W side. 1912. *William Kendall of McKim, Mead & White.*

A stern **neo-Georgian** town house, built, as is much of Columbia, of Stony Creek granite, Indiana limestone, and overburned brick. In this 21st-century polarized political era, it's similar to having the White House, freestanding, facing Pennsylvania Avenue. Knock for the President?

[M11] **East Campus Complex,** SW cor. 118th St. and Morningside Drive. 1977-1981. *Gwathmey Siegel & Assocs.* Renovated, 1994, *Gruzen Samton.*

One swan song for the International Style, or perhaps a rooster crowing the neo-International 1930s Renaissance? In any categorization, it was handsome, but construction problems deemed a new façade necessary.

[M12] **Croton Aqueduct, 119th Street Gatehouse,** 424 W.119th St., SE cor. Amsterdam Ave. 1894-1895. *New York City Department of Public Works.* 🔾

One of the duet managing **Croton Aqueduct** water between 119th and 113th Streets. Formidable rockfaced granite.

[M13] **Casa Italiana,** 1151-1161 Amsterdam Ave., bet. W.116th and W.118th Sts. E side. 1926-1927. *William Kendall of McKim, Mead & White.* 🔾 Restored and east façade completed, 1996, *Buttrick, White & Burtis,* architects. *Italo Rota,* associate architect.

A **Renaissance** palazzo (rusticated, quoined, and grilled) seemingly appropriate for Ivy Leaguers seeking *la cultura Italiana.* There is wondrous Italian architecture throughout the City, derivatives drawn from the time of Julius Caesar to a recent year. Here is an excerpted package.

M12

Kent and Philosophy Halls

[M14] **Law School,** 435 W.116th St., NE cor. Amsterdam Ave. 1961. *Harrison & Abramovitz.*
[M15] **Jerome L. Greene Hall** (Street-level addition to the Law School), 435 W. 116th St., NE cor. Amsterdam Ave. 1996. *Polshek Partnership.*

Law's south façade on 116th Street provided that marvelous box where a dictator might posture to harangue the multitudes. Later (1977) an enormous sculpture by *Jacques Lipchitz* moved in. Now the new addition (and gracious point of entry) is the star, muting the 1961 building, and providing some 1990s verve.

Now to the central campus:

[M16] **Low Memorial Library,** N of W.116th St., bet. Amsterdam Ave. and Broadway. 1895-1897. *Charles McKim of McKim, Mead & White.* 🔾 Interior 🔾 Exhibition space open to the public, Mo-Fr 9-5:30.

Columbia University's most noteworthy visual symbol is the monumental, domed, and colonnaded **Low Library,** named not for its height but for *Abiel Abbot Low,* the father of its

M16

M14

donor. Donor *Seth Low* (1850-1916) was alternately **Mayor** of Brooklyn, **President** of Columbia, and **Mayor** of New York. Set atop three tiers of graciously proportioned steps, this dignified centerpiece for the campus is no longer the university library, its interior spaces more suited to ceremonial and administrative uses than to shelf space and reading rooms. Off the rotunda to the east is a small display of Columbiana, with items of interest to those who wish to trace the university's march northward through Manhattan from its 18th-century beginnings downtown as **King's College**.

[M17] **Alma Mater**. 1903. *Daniel Chester French*, sculptor.

Centered on the formal stair one tier below **Low** is **Alma Mater**, the once-gilded bronze statue that forms the background of nearly every university graduation ceremony. An evocative sculpture, the enthroned figure extends her hand in welcome as she looks up from the mighty tome of knowledge lying open in her lap. As a symbol, **Alma Mater** has under-

standably elicited both love (a protest in 1962 caused a newly applied gilding to be removed in favor of the more familiar green patina; now **debased to statuary bronze** popular with metal maintenance experts, but with the loss of the rich green matte surface so appropriate to the march of history) and hate (in 1968 she survived a bomb blast during that period of student unrest).

Charles Follen McKim: Despite the sometime-held belief to the contrary, not all buildings produced by the architectural firm of McKim, Mead & White were by its most notorius partner, Stanford White. Chief architect for the Columbia campus was Charles Follen McKim (1847-1909), commemorated in a bronze plaque set into the pavement in front of Alrna Mater. The Latin inscription can be translated as "An artist's monuments look down upon us throughout the ages." Pennsylvania Station (1910-1963) was the other great McKim work in Manhattan.

[M18] **Butler Library**/originally **South Hall**, W.114th St. bet. Amsterdam Ave. and Broadway. 1931-1934. *James Gamble Rogers.*

Columbia's principal library (named for *Nicholas Murray Butler,* Columbia's president from 1902 to 1945), its notable collections overshadowed architecturally by Low across 116th Street. The sturdy Ionic colonnade is impressive close up, but becomes diminished within an overall bland form at a distance.

[M19] **St. Paul's Chapel** (Episcopal), N campus, E of Low Library. 1903-1907. *Howells & Stokes.* ✪

The beginning Morningside Heights campus was generally, in both planning and building design, a *McKim, Mead & White* monopoly. One of two exceptions is this magnificent chapel (the other was *Arnold W. Brunner's* **School of Mines**), the **best of all** Columbia's buildings, a gift of *Olivia Egleston Phelps Stokes* and *Caroline Phelps Stokes*, sisters of wealthy financier and philanthropist *Anson Phelps Stokes*

*The last surviving building of the **Bloomingdale Insane Asylum**, on whose site Columbia was built, is East Hall (1878), just south of St. Paul's. As part of the asylum it was called the Macy Villa. It now serves as the home of the Temple Hoyne Buell Center for the Study of American Architecture.*

[M20] **Avery Hall**, N campus, N of St. Paul's Chapel. 1911-1912. *McKim, Mead & White.* Underground addition and courtyard to E, 1977, *Alexander Kouzmanoff & Assocs.* Exhibitions open to the public.

One of nine similar instructional buildings, Avery houses the **School of Architecture** and **Avery Library**, the nation's largest architectural library. The glazed conning towers are skylights for the undercourt addition.

[M21] **Sherman Fairchild Center for the Life Sciences**, NE campus, 1977-1997. *Mitchell/Giurgola Assocs.*

This radical building shields the campus from the banal façade of Seeley W. Mudd Hall. *Fairchild's* volume is layered with a screen wall that reveals a second skin through deeply modeled slots and openings. The tile (a thin material) floats and picks up the color of terra-cotta pavers on Columbia's walkways (a heavy material). Gorgeous modernism that enlivens its neighbors.

M17

M19

(1838-1913). The beautifully executed work was the design of *Howells & Stokes*, one of whose partners, *Isaac Newton Phelps Stokes* (author of *The Iconography of Manhattan Island*) was their nephew.

The interior is filled with exquisite *Guastavino* vaulting; magnificent light pours down from above. A visit during a performance of antique works by one of Columbia's musical groups will also reveal its sonorous acoustics. *Pro Ecclesia Dei.*

And in the basement, the long-running **Postcrypt Coffeehouse**, with weekend concerts during the fall and spring semesters, might be the most haunting (not haunted) performance space in the City: a tiny vault, lit by candles. The acoustics are so good that microphones aren't used. A great place to find yourself during a blackout. *www.postcrypt.org*

[M22] **Computer Science Building**, NE campus, partially under **Fairchild Center for the Life Sciences**, sharing terrace with Mudd Engineering and facing Amsterdam Ave. 1983. *R.M. Kliment & Frances Halsband.*

An interstitial weaving of three buildings, a plaza, and a street, this small, subtle architectural and urbanistic coup makes this campus extension a better precinct.

[M23] **Uris Hall Extension**, N campus, N of Low Library. 1983-1984. *Peter L. Gluck & Partners.*

Anything that could mask Uris would be a plus, and here is a shallow (in depth, not character) and handsome **postmodern** building to do the job.

[M24] **Shapiro Center for Engineering and Physical Science Research**, N end of Campus, abutting W.120th St. 1989-1992. *Hellmuth, Obata & Kassebaum.*

M21

Postmodernism with a heavy hand. Neither historicist nor modernist, it fails to subdue its bulk gracefully, its monumental colonnade and top floor terrace giving it an overweening stance.

[M25] **Northwest Corner Science Building**, NW cor. Broadway and W. 120th St., W of Pupin. 2009. *Rafael Moneo Valles & Davis Brody Bond Aedas.*

A new link between community and cam-

M24

pus, it opens the raised campus to the street, simultaneously completing *McKim, Mead & White's* master plan and Northwest Courtyard.

[M26] **Earl Hall,** N Campus, W of Low Library. 1900-1902. *McKim, Mead & White.*

Symmetrically modeled with *Howells and Stokes's* **St. Paul's**, **Earl** looks like, but is not, a neo-Georgian house of worship.

[M27] **Alfred Lerner Hall**, Columbia University, 2920 Broadway, NE cor. W.115th St. 1999. *Bernard Tschumi/Gruzen Samton, associated architects.*

Tschumi had said "quiet on the outside, dynamic on the inside," with an inner, six-story atrium "that will be at the cutting edge of technology with glass ramps, steel, and translucent glass." He's right. It works, elegantly: dour to Broadway, exuberant on the inner campus.

[M28] **Broadway Residence Hall**, Columbia University, NE cor. 113th St. and Broadway. 2000. *Robert A.M. Stern.*

364 Columbia seniors fill most of the bulk over a **New York Public Library** branch below. "Tawny" brick and limestone clad an almost anonymous façade.

[M29] **Morris A. Schapiro Hall**, 615 W.115th St., bet. Broadway and Riverside Dr. 1988. *Gruzen Samton Steinglass.*

M27

An infill building in the city streetscape, outside the formal boundaries of *McKim, Mead & White's* **Renaissance University**. A good neighbor to those next door, with architectural remembrances of the main campus in the color and texture of its brickwork. Dynamic bay windows peer back at the campus.

[M30] **Robert K. Kraft Center for Jewish Student Life**, W.115th St., bet. Broadway and Riverside Dr. 1999. *Gruzen Samton.*

Jerusalem stone clads facilities for Columbia's Jewish students.

[M31] Originally **The Alpha Club**, 434 Riverside Dr., bet. W.115th and W.116th Sts. 1898. *Wood, Palmer & Hornbostel.*

An elaborate fraternity house in the **Beaux Art** mode, so stylish as the 19th century turned into the 20th.

M38g

M29

M33

[M34] **Columbia University School for Children and Faculty Housing**, Broadway, SE cor. 110th St. (Cathedral Parkway). 2003. *Beyer Blinder Belle.*

Columbia gave up on the City's public schools and built this private school for the children of its faculty. An inoffensive background building in banded brick and limestone.

M35

M36

[M32] **The Colosseum**, 435 Riverside Dr., SE cor. W.116th St. 1910. *Schwartz & Gross.*

Like a heavily embroidered tapestry, this unusual curved façade, together with its opposite-handed sibling across West 116th Street, frames the main entrance of the Columbia campus atop the hill—best seen from the Drive.

An aside to the south, west of Broadway:

[M33] **The Hendrik Hudson**, 380 Riverside Dr., bet. Cathedral Pkwy. and W.111th St. 1907. Broadway addition/now College Residence Hotel, 601 Cathedral Pkwy., NW cor. Broadway. 1908. Both by *William L. Rouse of Rouse & Sloan.*

A grandiose apartment building in Tuscan villa style, pumped up to fit its Riverside Drive site. Many of its embellishments, as well as its both interior and exterior elegance, have been reduced by time, economics, and the elements.

[M35] **110+ Broadway Apartments**, NE cor. Broadway. 2007. *Platt Byard Dovell White.*

A background building: but bring us more of these, please! *PBDW* excels with their incisive detailing, raising the level of quality from good to elegant neighbor. The stacked glass hat (three floors) might better have been handled in masonry, as their masonry below just floats.

[M36] **625 West 112th Street**, bet. Broadway and Riverside Dr. 1900s.

A luscious stack of civilized **French Flats**: French doors set within a recessed bay window, contained by elegant ironwork. *Mrs. Manson Mingott* (from *Edith Wharton's The Age of Innocence*), move over.

[M37] **Bank Street College of Education**, 610 W.112th St., bet. Broadway and Riverside Dr. 1970. *Harry Weese & Assocs.*

A tall, heavy-handed, but reserved composition. This teachers' training school had its beginnings on **Bank Street** in Greenwich Village, hence its name.

Back to 116th Street and Broadway:

Barnard College

[M38] **Barnard College campus**, W.116th to W.120th (Reinhold Niebuhr Place) Sts., bet. Broadway and Claremont Ave. [M38a] **Milbank Hall**, comprising Milbank, Brinckerhoff, and Fiske Halls, 606 W.120th St., N end of campus. 1896-1897. *Lamb & Rich.* [M38b] **Brooks Hall** (dormitory). 1906-1907. *Charles A. Rich.* [M38c]

F38e

F38c

Barnard Hall, originally Students' Hall. 1916-1917. *Arnold W. Brunner.* [M38d] **Hewitt Hall** (dormitory). 1924-1925. *McKim, Mead & White.* [M38e] **Lehman Hall/Wollman Library.** 1957-1959. *O'Connor & Kilham.* [M38f] **Helen Reid Hall** (dormitory). 1957-1959. *O'Connor & Kilham.* [M38g] **Nexus Hall** (library and student center). 2009. *Weiss Manfredi,* architects. [M38h] **Helen Goodhart Altschul Hall.** 1966-1969. *Vincent G. Kling & Assocs.* [M38i] **Iphigene Ochs Sulzberger Hall** (dormitory). 1986-1989. *James Stewart Polshek & Partners.*

 Barnard was established as the undergraduate women's equivalent of Columbia in memory of *Frederick A. P. Barnard* (1809-1889), the Columbia president who had championed the cause of equal rights for women in higher education. Since Columbia itself has been coeducational since 1983, a "women's college" (with some male students) is somewhat of an anachronism within a world of unisexism.

 In its original *Lamb & Rich* quadrangle, crowned with *Arnold Brunner's* 1917 **Barnard Hall**, Barnard architecture aped Columbia's.

Later and lesser architects added **Lehman, Reid, McIntosh,** and **Altschul,** modern in their stance, but without reference to the context of street or campus. Quality control has now been reestablished with the construction of **Sulzberger Hall.**

 Lehman Library's grilled façade is the work of solar consultants *Victor and Aladar Olgyay,* Hungarian émigrés who somehow got their north arrow confused: the grillage faces slightly south of east, where there is negligible sun loading. They were, however, concerned more

M39d

with architectural imagery than with its reality.

 Weiss Manfredi's **Nexus Hall** is full of syncopated panels and light, and materials that give considerable warmth to the space.

North of the Columbia Campus:

[M39] **Teachers College**, Columbia University, 525 W.120th St., bet. Amsterdam Ave. and Broadway, to 121st St. [M39a] **Main Hall.** 1892-1894. *William A. Potter.* [M39b] **Macy Hall**/originally **Macy Manual Arts Building**, N of Main Hall. 1893-1899. *William A. Potter.*
[M39c] **Frederick Ferris Thompson Memorial Hall,** W of Main Hall. 1902-1904. *Parish & Schroeder.* [M39d] **Russell Hall,** E of Main Hall. 1922-1924. *Allen & Collens.*
[M39e] **Thorndike Hall,** NW of Main Hall. 1969-1973. *Hugh Stubbins & Assocs.*
[M39f] **Whittier Hall** (dormitories), Amsterdam Ave. bet. W.120th and W.121st Sts. W side. 1900-1919. *Bruce Price and M.A. Darragh.*

M38i

Tightly squeezed into a full city block, this semiautonomous branch of Columbia offers a rich range of red brick architecture largely from the turn of the 20th century. Peeking above the composition from West 121st Street—it is entered through a court from West 120th Street—is *Stubbins'* awkward Thorndike Hall, which doesn't even try to fit in.

[M40] Originally **Horace Mann School**/now **Horace Mann Hall**, Teachers College, Broadway bet. W.120th and W.121st Sts. E side. 1899-1901. *Howells & Stokes and Edgar H. Josselyn.*

Horace Mann was founded in 1887 as the laboratory school for Teachers College, but those activities are now conducted in the suburban Riverdale campus. Its vigorous forms, however, continue to enliven the Broadway blockfront it commands, as it now serves **TC** in other capacities. Dour brownstones.

[M41] **Corpus Christi Church** (Roman Catholic), 533 W.121st Street, bet. Broadway and Amsterdam Aves. 1935. *Wilfred E. Anthony.*

Nothing much outside, but the interior seems that of an eccentric *Wren* disciple's London church. Go in. Early (classical) music is played here.

[M42] **Bancroft Hall** (apartments), Teachers College, 509 W.121st St., bet. Amsterdam Ave. and Broadway. 1910-1911. *Emery Roth.*

The Dark Side: In the shadow of Teachers College is this ebullient eclectic warhorse of a façade: aggressive, bold, charming, mysterious.

M44

An altogether wonderful discovery, with verdigris copper-clad bay windows and a timber Italianate Tuscan roof.

[M43] **Lenfest Hall** (residence), Columbia Law School, 425 W. 121st St. 2003. *Gruzen Samton.*

Crisp brickwork for another of seemingly endless Columbia dormitories.

[M44] **Columbia School of Social Work**, Amsterdam Ave., bet. 121st and 122nd Sts. 2004. *Cooper Robertson.*

A classic understated contextual building. Glassy.

[M45] **Public School 36**, Manhattan, **The Morningside School**, 123 Morningside Dr., NE cor. Amsterdam Ave. 1967. *Frederick G. Frost, Jr., & Assocs.,* architects. *William Tarr,* sculptor.

An ensemble atop rock outcroppings on a demapped piece of Morningside Park. Simple brick stair towers, cast concrete construction, and large rectangular windows mark the earliest arrival of the **New Brutalism** in upper Manhattan. A photo in the First Edition of this Guide (1967) showed a gleaming new building, but the passage of time has been **brutal**.

[M46] **Jewish Theological Seminary**, 3080 Broadway, bet. W.122nd and W.123rd Sts. E side. 1928-1930. *Gehron, Ross & Alley*, architects. *David Levy*, associate architect. **Expansion and Library**, 1980-1983, *The Gruzen Partnership.*

This clunky, oversized neo-Georgian building is the central institution of the Conservative movement in American Judaism. A corner tower, used as library stacks, houses the gateway to the inner courtyard. The *Gruzen* addition, a low-

M47

key brick and limestone extension, manages to be both understated and appropriate.

Rabbi Mordecai Kaplan (1881-1983), founder of the Jewish Reconstructionist movement, taught at the Jewish Theological Seminary from 1909 to 1963 and established the Society for the Advancement of Judaism in 1922. He defined Judaism as a "civilization," embracing language, custom, and culture beyond the conventional limitations of religious belief.

An early champion of equal rights for women, Rabbi Kaplan is credited with having created the bat mitzvah, the rite marking a girl's arrival at the age of Jewish duty and responsibility. In 1922 Rabbi Kaplan's daughter, Judith, became the first bat mitzvah.

[M47] Union Theological Seminary, James Memorial Chapel, Brown Memorial Tower and James Tower. W.120th (Reinhold Niebuhr Place) to W.122nd Sts., bet. Broadway and Claremont Aves. 1906-1910. *Allen & Collens*. Altered, 1952, *Collens, Willis & Beckonert*. **Burke Library** renovations, 1982, *Mitchell/Giurgola*. ◉

A stronghold of theological modernism and social consciousness is housed in a Collegiate Gothic quadrangle of rock-face granite with limestone trim. Two handsome perpendicular towers, an exquisite chapel, library, refectory, and dormitories recall medieval Oxbridge, or perhaps F. Scott Fitzgerald's Princeton.

[M48a] Interchurch Center, 475 Riverside Dr., bet. W.119th and W.120th Sts. 1956-1958. *Voorhees, Walker, Smith, Smith & Haines and Collens, Willis & Beckonert*.

A bulky work that attempts to harmonize with—but only detracts from—lyrical Riverside Church to the north. Lots of good and welcome

Both carillon and bell are the world's largest. Commanding an imposing site along Riverside Drive, the church was criticized upon completion for its opulence, as "a late example of bewildered eclecticism." Nevertheless, despite problems of scale that seem to make it smaller than it is (particularly when seen up close), it is easily the most prominent architectural work along the Hudson from midtown to the George Washington Bridge. Within the church is the lovely Christ Chapel.

Once one could take an elevator to the carillon and climb the open stairway past the bells to the lofty windblown observation deck. But 9/11 intervened.

[M50] Manhattan School of Music/onetime **Juilliard School of Music**/originally **Institute of Musical Art**, 120 Claremont Ave., NE cor. W.122nd St. 1910. *Donn Barber*. Additions, 1930-1931, *Arthur L. Harmon of Shreve, Lamb & Harmon*. **Mitzi Newhouse Pavilion**. 1969-1970. *MacFadyen & Knowles*.

Innocuous limestone with a neat concrete and glass cafeteria.

M53

space for Christian religious and social activities and activists, but in banal architecture.

[M48b] Eton and Rugby Hall Apartments, 29-35 Claremont Avenue, bet. W. 116th and W. 119th Sts., W side. 1910. *Gaetan Ajello*.

Two Renaissance Revival apartment buildings side by side. Their decorations have vaguely Muslim undertones; one resident calls them his "Mosque of Cordoba."

[M49] Riverside Church, 490 Riverside Dr., bet. W.120th and W.122nd Sts. 1926-1930. *Allen & Collens and Henry C. Pelton*. Parish House, 1955-1959. *Collens, Willis & Beckonert*. ◉ 212-870-6700. *www.theriversidechurchny.org*

The ornament of **Chartres** adapted to a 21-story high-rise steel-framed church. Funded by *John D. Rockefeller, Jr.*, this church enjoyed the finest in available materials, stone carving, and stained glass of its era. Its 392-foot-high tower (largely an office building disguised as a place of bells) is surmounted by the 74-bell *Laura Spelman Rockefeller Memorial Carillon*, with its 20-ton tuned bass bell.

[M51] Andersen Residence Hall, Manhattan School of Music, Claremont Ave., bet. 122nd and 123rd Sts. 2001. *Beyer Blinder Belle*.

The missing campus component for musicians: Andersen's occupants can practice music where they live. (But does an oboist live next to a percussionist?)

[M52] International House, 500 Riverside Dr., N of Sakura Park, N of W.122nd St. 1924. *Lindsay & Warren; Louis Jallade*, partner-in-charge.

The multistory residence and garden for foreign (and other) students who attend the nearby centers of higher learning. Large without being imposing.

[M53] Grant's Tomb/General Grant National Memorial, Riverside Dr. at W.122nd St. 1891-1897. *John H. Duncan*. ◉ Mosaic benches, 1973. *Pedro Silva, Cityarts Workshop*. Interior. ◉ Restoration, 1997. Open to the public daily, 9-5. 212-666-1640.

This pompous sepulcher, its design chosen in an architectural competition, is, externally, a free copy of Mausoleus' tomb at Halicarnassus (present-day Turkey) of 350 B.C.—one of the **Seven Wonders of the Ancient World**: hence here titled a mausoleum. Though monumental seen from Riverside Drive (here parted to create its spacious greensward), it's far better within. There, through massive bronze doors, housed in austere white marble, President *Ulysses Simpson* and *Julia Boggs Dent Grant* rest side by side in identical polished black sarcophagi, an interior reminiscent of Napoleon's tomb in the Dome Church of the Invalides, Paris.

The sinuous mosaicked benches embracing the plaza bring shades of Gaudí and the Parque Güell—a populist huzzah for the solemn Grants.

To the memory of an amiable child: Almost lost at the edge of the monumental space commanded by Grant's Tomb is a tiny fenced area a bit to the north, across southbound Riverside Drive, and down a few steps. Here stands a modest stone urn "Erected to the Memory of an Amiable Child, St. Clair Pollock," a five-year-old who fell to his death from these rocks on July 15, 1797. When the property was sold, the child's uncle asked that the grave remain inviolate; and despite the bureaucratic problems involved, the request has been honored through the years. The views of the Hudson Valley are particularly beautiful from this tranquil spot.

NECROLOGY

Millicent Mcintosh Center, Barnard College. 1966-1969. *Vincent G. Kling & Assocs.*
Heavy-handed modernism replaced by Nexus Hall [M38g].

MANHATTANVILLE

Along the west end of the valley that cleaves Morningside Heights (on the south) and Hamilton Heights (on the north) grew the village of Manhattanville. It straddled both sides of today's West 125th Street, which leads to the former landing of the ferry to Fort Lee. A bustling village more in the New England mill town tradition than that of New York City, the settlement supported a pigment factory, D. F. Tiemann & Company (below 125th Street), a worsted mill (on 129th Street west of Broadway), Yuengling Brewery (128th Street east of Amsterdam), as well as a grammar school, post office, and a sprinkling of churches. Manhattan College began in 1853 along Broadway at 131st Street before relocating to Riverdale. The area still retains in its structures vestiges of its 19th-century industrial beginnings.

M54

[M54] **IRT Broadway Line viaduct,** along Broadway spanning W.125th St. 1904. *William Barclay Parsons*, engineer.
The sweeping latticed arch and its abutments are worthy of Eiffel. The masking billboard that for many years sullied this graceful engineering is, happily, gone.

[M55] **Prentis Hall** (Department of Chemical Engineering), Columbia University/originally **Sheffield Farms Bottling Plant**, 632 W.125th St., bet. Broadway and St. Clair Place. 1906. *Edgar I. Moeller.*
Milky-white glazed terra cotta, now somewhat pock-marked and crazed, is this ex-dairy's face to the world. How appropriate (poetically, at least) that it is now a chemical engineering laboratory.

*Columbia's Manhattanville campus expansion: the 17-acre site of a possible future campus includes four blocks from 129th to 133rd streets between Broadway and 12th Avenue, as well as property on the north side of 125th Street and east of Broadway from 131st to 134th streets. The Empire State Development Corporation invoked **eminent domain** on private commercial properties in the project area. A battle rages in the courts.*

125th Street did not always turn. The diagonal street in the valley between Morningside and Hamilton Heights was called Manhattan Street. running obliquely to the street grid only because topography made the valley the natural route for a wide thoroughfare—along it ran the streetcars to the Fort Lee Ferry. In 1920, however, it was decided that Manhattan Street should be renamed West 125th Street, and the old part of the original West 125th Street, west of Morningside Avenue, was renamed LaSalle Street. Now 125th Street has vanished entirely—at least on official maps, supplanted by Martin Luther King, Jr., Boulevard. But the A train will still take you to 125th. The City fathers also bestowed other new names: Moylan Place for West 126th Street (now eradicated by General Grant Houses), Tiemann Place (after the old color works) for 127th Street, and St. Clair Place for 129th Street. Incidentally, the oblique route of 125th follows a geological fault line similar to California's San Andreas but happily not nearly so active.

[M58] **Manhattanville Neighborhood Center**/originally **The Speyer School,** 516 W.126th St., bet. Amsterdam Ave. and Old Broadway. 1902. *Edgar H. Josselyn.*

A demonstration school for Teachers College and a neighborhood settlement, it serves the community more informally. Note the **Flemish Renaissance** silhouette of its parapet.

[M59] **Templo Biblico**/originally **Engine Company No.37**, N.Y.C. Fire Department, 503 W.126th St., bet. Amsterdam Ave. and Old Broadway. 1881. *Napoleon LeBrun.*

Old firehouses are sturdy and sought out for reuse. This one stands on a block originally devoted to a sprawling charitable institution called Sheltering Arms, today a city park and swimming pool. West on West 126th Street are other community-oriented buildings.

[M60] **St. Joseph of the Holy Family Church** (Roman Catholic), 401 W.125th St., NW cor. Morningside Ave. 1889. *Herter Brothers.*

M58

M56

[M56] **Riverside Drive Viaduct,** bet. W.124th and W.135th Sts. 1901. *F. Stewart Williamson, engineer.* Totally rebuilt, 1987.

From **Morningside Heights** to **Hamilton Heights** this lacy (from below) steel viaduct steps off 26 bays of filigreed steel arches across the 125th Street valley. One of the original arches was retained. The most northern one?

[M57] **St. Mary's Church** (Episcopal), 521 W.126th St., bet. Amsterdam Ave. and Old Broadway. 1908-1909. *T.E. Blake and Carrère & Hastings.* **Sunday School.** 1890. *George Keister.* **Parish House** (former Rectory). 1851. 🖤

Its name, cut into stone in Old English characters, and its archaic **English Gothic** form, preserve the image of **Manhattanville** as a remote 19th-century village.

The Parish House, tucked behind a garden, is in sprightly yellow clapboard!

An unpretentious church of modest scale and detail. The north end features a fascinating intersection of four gables; and note the blind oculi at the rear doors.

[M61] Originally **Bernheimer & Schwartz Pilsener Brewing Company,** W end of block bounded by W.126th and W.128th Sts. E side of Amsterdam Ave. 1905. *Louis Oberlein.*

A phalanx of 19th-century red brick brewery buildings (descendants of the earlier occupant of this site, Yuengling Brewery), now with a myriad cast of tenants.

The Met's tin shed: The grimy shed sheathed in corrugated iron occupying some two-thirds of an acre at 495 West 129th Street, east of Amsterdam Avenue, shelters all manner of bulky sets for the Metropolitan Opera House at Lincoln Center. It was built around 1895 as a storage shed for Amsterdam Avenue streetcars. The expanse of sloping roof, unusual for Manhattan, is best seen from the hill behind, along 130th Street.

T2

HAMILTON HEIGHTS

This neighborhood, west of St. Nicholas and Jackie Robinson Parks, ranging from Manhattanville north to Trinity Cemetery, includes once-famous **Sugar Hill** and the **City College Campus**. It takes its name from the country estate of *Alexander Hamilton*. That house (newly relocated for the second time in its life) and legions of 19th-century houses, churches, and institutional buildings survive, many distinguished, many charming, many landmarked. The apartment houses and tenements date from the arrival of the Broadway-Seventh Avenue IRT subway, in 1904.

[T1] **Riverside Drive retaining wall and viewing platforms**, W.135th to W.153rd Sts. 1873-1910. *Frederick Law Olmsted, Jr.*

T4

Smooth granite retains the Drive, crowned with a neo-Classical balustrade (between 141st and 147th Streets). Once the face of a seemingly fortified city, it is masked by the Henry Hudson Parkway, the old Hudson River Railroad freight line, and the North River Water Pollution Control Plant. The best view is from the plant's roof: **Riverbank State Park** (1991) by *Richard Dattner & Assocs.*

[T2] **North River Water Pollution Control Plant City of New York**, W.137th to W.145th Sts. W of the Henry Hudson Pkwy. to the Hudson River. 1986 (partial service) to 1991. *Theodore Long*, architect at *Tippetts-Abbett-McCarthy-Stratton*. **Riverbank State Park** on top, 1978-1993. *Richard Dattner & Assocs.*

Various designers attempted to assuage the Harlem community in return for positioning this 22-acre monster facility on their doorstep. In effect, this is the processing plant for all sewage on the West Side from Morton Street to

the Spuyten Duyvil, the effluents of more than a million people.

Richard Dattner succeeded. His handsome ensemble of facilities was built to provide community facilities. In return for the plant's intrusion, all of the **Riverbank State Park** is connected to the Riverside Drive bluff by two umbilical bridges.

[T3] **Riverside Park** (apartments), 3333 Broadway, bet. W.133rd and W.135th Sts. W side. 1976.
[T4] **Intermediate School 195, The Roberto Clemente School**, 625 W.133rd St., bet. Broadway and Twelfth Ave. 1976. Both by *Richard Dattner & Assocs., Henri A. LeGendre & Assocs., and Max Wechsler Assocs.*

T6

The local leviathan: a great slab-sided half octagon that embraces river views and the sun. A N.Y.C. Educational Construction Fund project, this oyster has, as its pearl, the local intermediate school.

[T5] **Claremont Theater Building**, 3320-3338 Broadway, SE cor. 135th St. 1913-1914. *Gaetano Ajello.* ✍

Thomas Edison produced a 1915 film in which the entrance is prominently featured. The second floor accommodated the Royal Palms Ballroom and Roof Garden. Until the early years of the Depression, area residents gathered here to eat, drink, and dance.

[T6] Originally **Academy of the Holy Child** (Roman Catholic)/then **St. Walburgas Academy**, 630 Riverside Dr., NE cor. W.140th St. ca. 1910.

A dark forbidding building with a rock-face random ashlar raiment. But the tower with its terra-cotta detail is charming.

T12

City College

[T7] **The City College North Campus, City University of New York**/originally the **Free Academy**, W.138th to W.141st Sts., St. Nicholas Terr. to Amsterdam Ave. 1902-1907. ●⚲ Including [T8] **Baskerville Hall**/originally Chemistry Building; [T9] **Compton Hall**/originally Mechanical Arts Building; [T10] **Goethals Hall**/originally Technology Building; [T11] **Wingate Hall**/originally Gymnasium, and [T12] **Shepard Hall.** All but Goethals by *George B. Post.* 1903-1907. **Goethals,** 1930. *George B. Post & Sons.* Renovation of **Shepard Hall,** interior, 1982-1989, *William Hall & Assocs.;* exterior, ongoing, *The Stein Partnership.*

This, the second campus of what is still referred to as **CCNY,** is clad with the by-product of the City's transit system. Manhattan schist, excavated during construction of the IRT Broadway subway, adorns the original quadrangle, trimmed with white glazed terra cotta. Its cathedral is **Shepard Hall,** a towered, skewed,

ed. Plagued by structural and environmental problems in recent years.

[T15] **North Academic Center,** W.135th to W.138th Sts., bet. Convent and Amsterdam Aves. 1983. *Bill Pederson of John Carl Warnecke & Assocs.*

A megastructure on the site of **Lewisohn Stadium,** the winter sport's field and onetime summer mecca for outdoor concertgoers, where symphony orchestras held sway until the overbearing noise of planes circling LaGuardia Airport squelched its acoustic usefulness.

"The NAC" crowns Hamilton Heights like a stranded aircraft carrier, out of scale with its surrounding town house blocks. *Pederson,* the designer, went on to be the *P* of *KPF* (*Kohn Pederson Fox*).

[T16] **South Campus**/formerly site of **Manhattanville College of the Sacred Heart,** W.130th to W.135th Sts. bet. Convent Ave. and St. Nicholas Terr. ca. 1840-1865.

T7

T14

Gothic bulk encrusted with terra-cotta quoins, finials, voussoirs, and other details. Shepard's satellites to the west, across Convent Avenue, also in Gothic fancy dress, are party however to a formal neo-Renaissance plan and courtyard.

[T13] **Grove School of Engineering, Steinman Hall,** Convent Ave. bet. St. Nicholas Terr. and W.141st St. E side. 1962. *Lorimer & Rose.* Reclad, 1996.

Once glass-block modern with the inescapable white glazed brick of the 1960s. Now grossly reclad in aluminum, a packaging that makes the original seem lyrical in retrospect.

[T14] **Marshak Science Building,** Convent Ave. S of 138th St. E side. 1971. *Skidmore, Owings & Merrill.*

Exposed concrete grillage on a battered rocky precast concrete base; an unfriendly place to the pedestrian. Its elevated terrace and bridge were intended to be the first link in a total campus plan that, fortunately, was abort-

[T17] **Schiff House**/onetime **President's House**/originally **Gatehouse, Manhattanville College,** Convent Ave. NE cor. W.133rd St. 1912.

The Roman Catholic academy and convent for its teachers, the **Ladies of the Sacred Heart,** was established here in 1847, also giving name to adjacent Convent Avenue. In 1952 the college and the sisters moved to Westchester, and the City bought the complex for City College.

[T18] **Bernard and Anne Spitzer School of Architecture,** 141 Convent Ave. SE cor. W.135th St. 2009. *Rafael Viñoly,* architect. *Lee Weintraub,* landscape architect.

The work-around-the-clock architecture students of CCNY finally get their own space, a drastic rebuilding of the former "Y Building" (only its structural frame was retained). The studios congregate around a central atrium and a *Rube Goldberg*–like stair. Go in and look up.

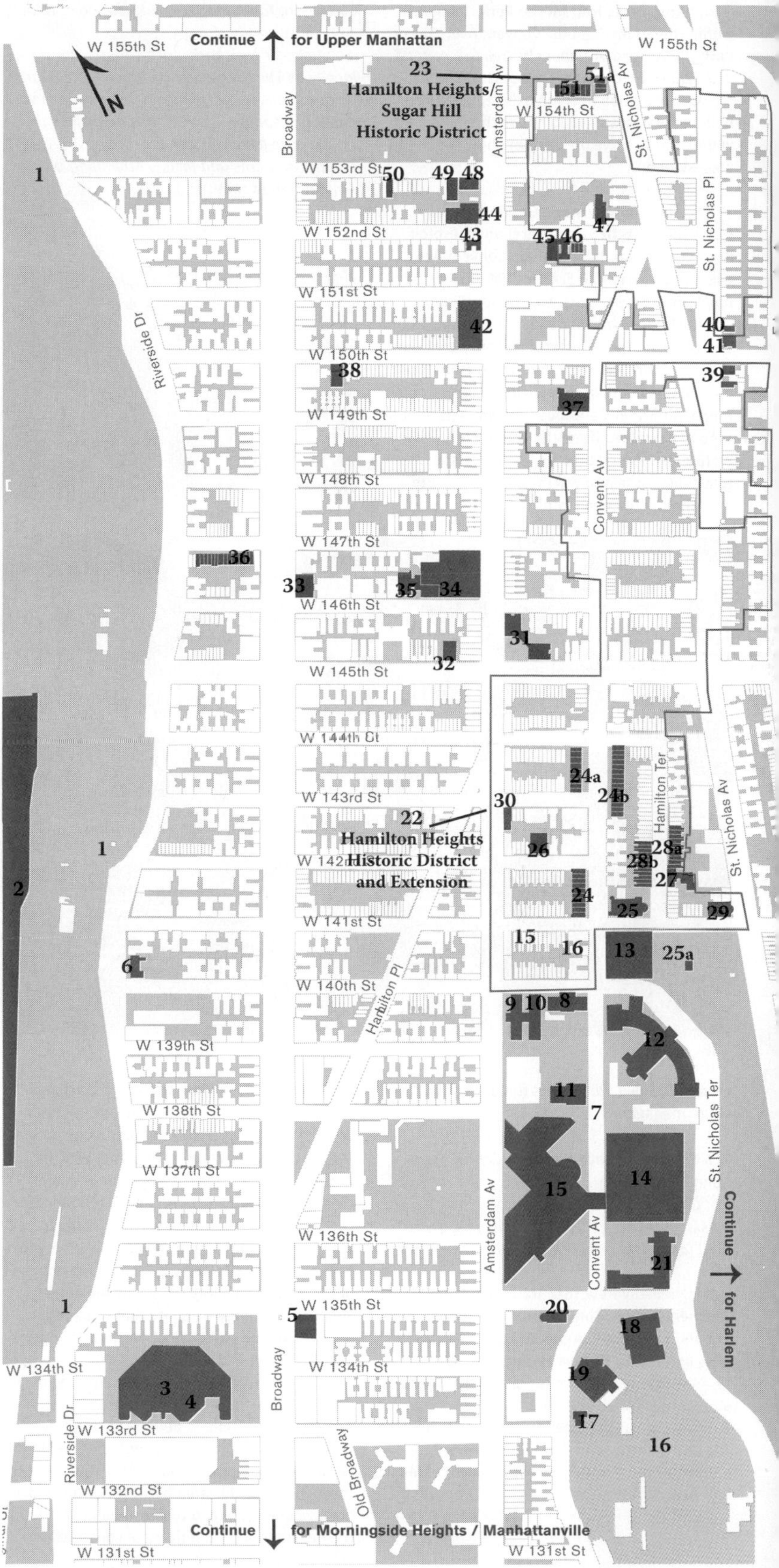

W 155th St

Continue ↑ for Upper Manhattan

N

Broadway

W 155th St

23
Hamilton Heights/
Sugar Hill
Historic District

Amsterdam Av

51a
51

St. Nicholas Av

W 154th St

St. Nicholas Pl

1

W 153rd St

50   **49 48**
44
43

45 46   **47**

Riverside Dr

W 152nd St

W 151st St

42

40
41

W 150th St

38

39

W 149th St

37

Convent Av

W 148th St

W 147th St

36

33   **35**   **34**

W 146th St

31

32

W 145th St

W 144th Ct

W 143rd St

30

22
Hamilton Heights
Historic District
and Extension

W 142nd St

24a

24b

Hamilton Ter

St. Nicholas Av

26

28a
28b   **27**

W 141st St

24

25   **29**

Hamilton Pl

15   **16**

13   **25a**

W 140th St

9 10   8

12

St. Nicholas Ter

W 139th St

11

7

W 138th St

15   **14**

W 137th St

Amsterdam Av

Convent Av

21

Continue → for Harlem

W 136th St

20

6

1

2

1

W 135th St

5

18

W 134th St

19

17

Riverside Dr

3   **4**

Broadway

16

W 133rd St

W 132nd St

Old Broadway

Continue ↓ for Morningside Heights / Manhattanville

W 131st St

[T19] **Aaron Davis Hall for the Performing Arts**, within the South Campus, Convent Ave., SE cor. W.135th St. 1979. *Abraham W. Geller & Assocs. and Ezra D. Ehrenkranz & Assocs.*

An expression of complexity, this intricate building was designed to house three theaters within and to serve one—an open-air amphitheater—without.

[T20] **Harlem Stage Gatehouse**/originally **135th Street Gatehouse, Croton Aqueduct**, W.135th St. SW cor. Convent Ave. 1884-1890. *Frederick S. Cook.* ● Converted for Harlem Stage, 2006, *Ohlhausen Dubois.*

Rock-faced brownstone and granite, it's the end of the 12-foot-diameter masonry aqueduct from **High Bridge**. From here water is distributed in a network of pipery whose next stop is the **119th Street Gatehouse**. Down in its subterranean chambers (formerly water works) the architects have created performance spaces that bring fantasy, a worthy counterpoint to the landmarked neo-Gothic conning tower

Collegiate Food Shop, 1600 Amsterdam Avenue, NW cor. W. 139th St.

A classic New York lunch counter, known locally as The Greeks, run by the affable George Kakomanolis for 30 years. There have been various lunch counter incarnations here since the 1940s, a de facto canteen for countless City College students and faculty streaming across Amsterdam Avenue.

T21

T18

entrance above. *Piranesi* is rumored to be the stage manager.

CCNY'S New Science Research Center. 2012. Kohn Pedersen Fox.

Glassy twins, sinuous in profile, rising side by side where once was City College's soccer field (and, before that, Manhattanville College).

[T21] Originally **New York Training School for Teachers**/now **A. Philip Randolph Campus High School**, 443-464 W.135th St., NE cor. Convent Ave. 1924-1926. *William H.Gompert.* ●

A glassy neo-Gothic complex, clad in limestone and mottled buff-to-brown ironspot brick, it has served as an experimental High School for the City College School of Education. But for almost 50 years it was the **High School of Music and Art.**

[T22] **Hamilton Heights Historic District and Extension**, generally along Convent Ave. bet. W.141st and W.145 Sts., including Hamilton Terrace, W.140th, W.141st, W.142nd, W.143rd, W.144th, and W.145th Sts.; and the E side of Amsterdam Ave. bet. 140th and 145th Sts. ●

Until the extension of elevated rapid transit up Columbus and Eighth Avenues in 1879, this was a rural area dotted with the country houses of the affluent. Among them was *Alexander Hamilton's* Grange on a site that was, until recently, on the east side of Convent Avenue between 141st and 142nd Streets.

The advent of the el brought a period of speculative expansion in the 1880s. Since Convent Avenue ended at West 145th Street (before its extension after 1900), and Hamilton Terrace formed a closed loop denying access to through traffic, this area became a protected enclave, ideally suited to high-quality residential development. That flurry of construction,

T20

T26

dating from 1886 to 1906, resulted in the pictur-
esque row houses that are the richness of these
blocks, designed by architects *William E.
Mowbray, Adolph Hoak, William Strom, Robert
Kelly, George Ebert, Henri Fouchaux, John
Hauser,* and the firm of *Neville & Bagge.*
Three historic churches, **Convent Avenue
Baptist, St. James Presbyterian,** and **St. Luke's,**
anchor the district. St. Luke's saved **Hamilton
Grange** and moved it in 1889 from its original
country setting to a site on Convent Avenue and
W.141st Street, where it was wedged, until 2008,
between the new church and subsequent apart-
ment blocks.

The romantic appearance of the district and
its varied row houses had a special appeal for
professors and staff from neighboring City
College who, after the campus opened in 1907,
began to take up residence here. The area's
popularity later waned, but brownstone revival
movements have caused a vigorous comeback.

[T23] **Hamilton Heights/Sugar Hill Historic
District and Extension** 🍎
Hamilton Heights/Sugar Hill Northeast, and
Hamilton Heights/Sugar Hill Northwest.

[T24] **280-298 Convent Avenue** (row houses),
bet. W.141st and W.142nd Sts. W side. 1899-
1902. *Henri Fouchaux.* [T24a] **320-336 Convent
Avenue,** bet. W.143rd and W.144th Sts. W side.
1890-1892. [T24b] **311-339 Convent Avenue,** bet.
W.142nd and W.144th Sts. E side. 1887-1890.
Adolph Hoak.

Picturesque houses all, with a profusion of
ornament and roots in a variety (and intermix) of
ancient styles: **Flemish, Tudor,** and
Romanesque. Those at the north end further
enhance the streetscape by being set back
behind gently raised front yards.

[T25] **St. Luke's Church** (Episcopal), Convent Ave., NE cor. W.141st St. 1892. *R.H. Robertson.*

Brownstone Romanesque Revival, massive in scale and volume, capitalizing on contrasts in texture by working the stone surfaces. It's sad that the monumental tower proposed (over the arched corner doorway) was not completed. But there's that stately arcade of arches across Convent Avenue's front. Next door was [T25a] **Hamilton Grange National Monument**/ originally **"The Grange,"** Alexander Hamilton Country House. ●ˇ

Has another National Monument ever been trundled off to greener pastures? It was lifted over St. Luke's, in 2008, and rolled down the hill to a new home in St. Nicholas Park.

[T26] **Our Lady of Lourdes Church** (Roman Catholic), 467 W.142nd St., bet. Convent and Amsterdam Aves. 1902-1904. *O'Reilly Brothers.* ●ˇ

A bizarre reincarnation made from parts of three important buildings. The gray and white

[T28a] **21-49 Hamilton Terrace,** bet. W.141st and W.143rd Sts. 1897-1898. *William Strom.*

Elegant town houses recycled for the millennium. These were advertised in the *New York Times* in 1898 as having "three styles," with ten rooms and two bathrooms, and a "rear view unsurpassed."

[T28b] **19-30 Hamilton Terrace,** bet. W. 141st and W. 143rd Sts. 1898. *Neville & Bagge.*

The *Times* 1898 ad described these as appealing "strongly to people of cultivated tastes and artistic perceptions."

[T29] **St. James Presbyterian Church and Community House**/formerly **St. Nicholas Avenue Presbyterian Church,** St. Nicholas Ave., NW cor. W.141st St. 1904. *Ludlow & Valentine.*

As the 19th century turned to the 20th, the richness of Gothic Revival church architecture ebbed. The shaft, however, of St. James's stark tower makes its finialed crest much richer by contrast.

T25

T27   T28a

T31

marble and bluestone façade on West 142nd Street includes elements salvaged from the Ruskinian Gothic-influenced **National Academy of Design** (1863-1865. *Peter B. Wight*), which stood at the northwest corner of East 23rd Street and Park Avenue South. The apse of the church and parts of its east wall are built from the segments of the Madison Avenue end of **St. Patrick's Cathedral,** removed to build the Lady Chapel there today. And the pedestals flanking the steps that lead up to the church are relics of department store magnate *A.T. Stewart's* **white marble mansion,** (1864-1869. *John Kellum*), which embellished the northwest corner of 34th Street and Fifth Avenue until 1901.

[T27] **Ivey Delph Apartments,** 19 Hamilton Terrace, bet. W.141st and W.143rd Sts., E side. 1951. *Vertner W. Tandy.*

Modestly scaled modernist apartments by the first African-American architect to be registered in New York State.

[T30] **434 West 143rd Street** (tenement), SE cor. Amsterdam Ave. 1900s.

The cool, flush façade on Amsterdam, and the symbolic architrave (windows and pilasters), frieze, and overhanging cornice, make this an American Renaissance marvel for the masses.

Vintage street lamp: ●ˇ *The lazily meandering route of old Bloomingdale Road is marked today by the diagonal of Hamilton Place. Where this street meets Amsterdam Avenue, creating the triangle of space known officially as* **Alexander Hamilton Square,** *stands an early cast-iron street lamp. It is not of the bishop's crook variety, but a more monumental version with a baronial base and two lamps rather than one. These relics can still be found infrequently throughout Manhattan. Long may they shine.*

[T31] **Jackson Center of Ophthalmology**/origi-nally **Lower Washington Heights Neighborhood Family Care Center**, 1727 Amsterdam Ave., NE cor. W.145th St. 1975. *Abraham W. Geller & Assocs.*

An understated civic building; its corner plaza is the main contribution of this wide-win-dowed salmon brick clinic.

[T32] **Hamilton Grange Branch, The New York Public Library**, 503 W.145th St., bet.

T32

T33

Amsterdam Ave. and Broadway. 1905-1906. *Charles McKim of McKim, Mead & White.* 🍎

All the ruffles and flourishes of a **Florentine** palazzo transferred to a New York street. *MM&W's* later 115th Street Branch may be bet-ter, but this is a lush resident for this spartan block. One of myriad New York City libraries contributed by *Andrew Carnegie's* 1901 $5 mil-lion contribution ($123 million in 2010 dollars!).

[T33] Former **Hamilton Theater**, 3560-3568 Broadway, NE cor. W.146th St. 1913. *Thomas W. Lamb.* 🍎

An early theater by the prolific *Lamb*, archi-tect of many of the City's fabled old movie palaces, including **Loew's Pitkin** (in Browns-ville) and the **RKO 81st Street Theatre**, among many others. Desecrated at the ground level and cornice, but the midsection retains *Lamb's* whimsical details: note the cast-iron figures "holding up" the third floor. Wonderful. Restoration, anyone?

[T34] **Public School 153, The Adam Clayton Powell, Jr., School**, 1750 Amsterdam Ave., bet. W.146th and W.147th Sts. W side. 1975. *Bureau of Design, N.Y.C. Board of Education.*

[T35] **Addition** on a former playground along 146th St., 1990s. *David Smotrich & Partners.*

A modest school, but the new *Smotrich* addi-tion is a rich and elegant complement to its par-ent building. It rests in the former playground, and replaces that activity on its own roof.

T37

T40

[T36] **Row Houses**, W.147th St., bet. Broadway and Riverside Dr. S side. ca. 1900-1905.

These houses are not extraordinary, but perched on this steep hill they make it a special street: San Francisco in New York.

[T37] **Church of the Crucifixion** (Anglican), Convent Ave., NW cor. W.149th St. 1967. *Costas Machlouzarides.*

An airfoil roof is the hat on these curved concrete forms. One can only wish the luxuriant ivy well as it encloses this tour de force: a kind of hallucinogenic version of *Le Corbusier's* **Ronchamp**.

[T38] **City Tabernacle, Seventh-Day Adventists' Church**/originally **Mt. Neboh Temple** (syna-gogue), 564 W.150th St., bet. Amsterdam Ave. and Broadway. 1917. *Berlinger & Moscowitz.*

From temple (Jewish) to temple (Christian) in two generations. A Spanish tile roof tops this adventure in clinker brick masonry and intricate dark brown terra cotta. Sober but proud.

T41

[T39a] **Dawn Hotel**/originally **John W. Fink House**, 8 St. Nicholas Place. 1886. *Richard S. Rosenstock.*

[T39b] **Jacob P. Baiter House**, 6 St. Nicholas Place, SE cor. W.150th St. 1895. *Theodore Stein.*

A neglected, but grand, brick and terra-cotta row house (No.6) is now married to the ravaged onetime Shingle Style extravaganza on the corner (No.8). Jointly in use as an emergency homeless shelter. The most notable neighbor is across West 150th Street:

[T40] **M. Marshall Blake Funeral Home**/originally **James Anthony and Ruth M. Bailey House**, 10 St. Nicholas Place, NE cor. W.150th St. 1886-1888. *Samuel B. Reed.* 🖊️

Rock-face granite, stylishly Dutch-gabled and corner-towered. Once it was a major mansion owned by circus entrepreneur Bailey, who joined with showman *Phineas T. Barnum* in 1881 to form the Barnum & Bailey Circus.

[T41] **14 St. Nicholas Place** (house), bet. W.150th and W.151st Sts. E side. ca. 1890.

The ogee-coned tower caps a neighborhood survivor: reshingled in cedar, curved at its edges, and bent to follow skirted form, it brings back some of the essence of Harlem's Gilded Age.

[T42] Originally **Joseph Loth & Company Silk Ribbon Factory**, 1828 Amsterdam Ave., bet. W.150th and W.151st Sts. W side. 1885-1886. *Hugo Kafka.* 🖊️

The 1893 **King's Handbook of New York** praised this local version of a New England textile mill: "Good taste and a degree of public spirit were shown by the firm in so designing the outward aspect of their establishment as to avoid the prosiness of business, and keep in harmony with the surroundings." Six hundred workers produced the ribbons known to seamstresses across the country in 15 widths, 200 colors, and up to 90 styles. Note the radiating wings visible from the side streets.

T45

[T43] Originally **32nd Precinct Station House**, 1854 Amsterdam Ave., SW cor. W.152nd St. 1871-1872. *Nathaniel D. Bush.* 🍎

A wondrous Victorian survivor. Brick with brownstone quoins, with a dignified mansard roof cresting in cast iron against the sky, it's straight from a *Charles Addams* cartoon.

[T44] **P.S./I.S. 210**, 501-503 W. 152nd St., NW cor. Amsterdam Ave. 2007. *Michael Fieldman Architects.*

A well-detailed modern school holding the corner: another exciting entry in a recent renaissance in the design of the City's new

T49

T51a

schools. See also *Peter Gluck's* **Bronx Prep Charter School** and *John Ciardullo's* **Bathgate Educational Campus** (pp. 835-836).

[T45] **Everett Center, Dance Theatre of Harlem**, 1994. *Hardy Holzman Pfeiffer.* **Dance Theatre of Harlem**/originally garage, 466 W.152nd St., bet. St. Nicholas and Amsterdam Aves. ca. 1920. Altered, 1971, *Hardy Holzman Pfeiffer Assocs.*

Through 1971: An early adaptive-reuse effort by a firm of architects who champion the ordinary, both in what they begin with and what they add. Pipes, ducts, bare lighting fixtures, old walls—all are used and, miraculously, become much more in the process.

The 1994 **Everett Center**: polychromatic, with robust volumes serving the dance community. An outpost of sophisticated modernism (a little Post-) in this neighborhood. Goodie.

[T46] **456, 458, and 460 West 152nd Street** (row houses), bet. St. Nicholas and Amsterdam Aves. ca. 1890.

A brick and brownstone trio framed by bayed projections, cylindrical on the west, hexagonal on the east. **Romanesque Revival.**

[T47] **Wilson Major Morris Community Center of St. John's Baptist Church**, 459 W.152nd St., bet. St. Nicholas and Amsterdam Aves. 1970. *Ifill & Johnson.*

A modest modernist study in beige brick, precast exposed aggregate, and glass with a particularly neat parapet treatment. *Morris* was founder of **St. John's Church** across the street at No.448 (with wondrous cornices).

[T48] **St. Luke A.M.E. Church** (African Methodist Episcopal)/originally **Washington Heights Methodist Episcopal Church**, 1872 Amsterdam Ave., SW cor. W.153rd St.

This neatly restored church (once painted barn-red) is one of a trio along the block of West

T48

153rd Street opposite the stillness of Trinity Cemetery. The other two:

[T49] Church of St. Catherine of Genoa (Roman Catholic) and Rectory, 504-506 W.153rd St., bet. Amsterdam Ave. and Broadway. 1890.

St. Catherine's, a unique star of this neighborhood: golden-hued brick crested with a many-stepped gable; a deep porch sheltered by a bracketed entryway.

[T50] Russian Holy Fathers Church (Russian Orthodox), 526 W.153rd St. ca. 1925.

Set back ten feet from adjacent housing, **Holy Fathers** seems reticent to reveal its lovely blue onion dome surmounted by a golden three-armed cross.

[T51] 411-423 West 154th Street (row houses), bet. St. Nicholas and Amsterdam Aves.
[T51a] 883-887 St. Nicholas Avenue, bet. W.154th and W.155th Sts. W side. ca. 1890.

Survivors: these mansard-roofed row houses sit high above the street, a robust addition to the community. The magnificent elms reinforce their stance. Enjoy!

NECROLOGY

Y Building, City College/originally **Morris Raphael Cohen Library**, within the South Campus, Convent Ave. SE cor. W.135th St. 1957. *Lorimer & Rose.*

A glass-block modern encore (to the original Steinman, which has been re-wrapped, but not by *Christo*). In this era of postmodern reconsideration of history, including various phases of "modern" architecture, such works pique the attention of young architects. Its designation as merely **Y** suggested that the University Powers didn't know what to do with it, and marked it for terminal leave. Its skeleton is still there, within the new School of Architecture. Perhaps it will haunt the students.

For Harlem Tour #'s 62-100, see map pp. 538-539.

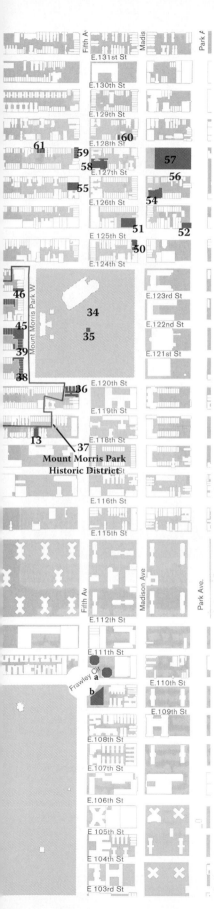

HARLEM

"...there is so much to see in Harlem."
—*Langston Hughes*

The village of **Nieuw Haarlem** was established by *Peter Stuyvesant* in 1658 in what is now East Harlem and was connected with New Amsterdam, ten miles to the south, by a road built by the Dutch West India Company's black slaves. Eight years later the British governor, *Richard Nicolls,* drew a diagonal across Manhattan, from the East River at 74th Street to the Hudson River at 129th Street, to separate New York from **Harlem**, which was henceforth to be known as Lancaster. Early in the 19th century *James Roosevelt* cultivated a large estate along the East River before moving to Hyde Park. A country village existed at 125th Street and First Avenue.

The opening of the New York and Harlem Railroad in 1837 marks the beginning of Harlem's development as a suburb for the well-to-do. The extension of the elevated to Harlem in 1879 was followed by the construction of tenement houses along the routes of the Els and apartment houses—some on a lavish scale—along the better avenues. These were augmented by schools, clubs, theaters, and commercial buildings.

Completion of the IRT Lenox Avenue Subway in 1904 encouraged a real estate boom in Harlem, but many more apartments were built than could be rented, and entire buildings adjacent to Lenox Avenue near 135th Street remained unoccupied. Just at this time the blocks west of Herald Square, where a large part of the City's African-American population was living, were being redeveloped. The construction of Pennsylvania Station, Macy's department store, large hotels, offices, and loft buildings was forcing African-Americans to seek living space elsewhere. But in no other parts of the City were they welcome.

Their settlement in the high-prestige neighborhood of **Harlem** was made possible by *Philip A. Payton, Jr.* (1876-1917), a remarkable realtor who founded the Afro-American Realty Company in 1904. Alert to both the opportunity in **Harlem** and the desperate housing situation in the Tenderloin, he was able to open Harlem's many vacant apartment buildings to African-Americans by assuming the management of individual buildings and guaranteeing premium rents to their landlords. The availability of good housing was unprecedented; the African-American community flocked to *Payton's* buildings, often paying exorbitant rents but, for a short while at least, enjoying good housing.

The great influx of African-Americans during the 1920s, instead of being allowed to spread, was bottled up in this one area. The privations of the Great Depression, the inadequacy of public and private measures to deal with poverty, and the failures of urban renewal further burdened **Harlem** and its people. As recently as the late 1990s **Harlem** was marked by burned-out shells and acres of vacant land where demolished housing had once stood. Around that same time yuppies began moving in. Whereas

Arthur A. Schomburg Plaza

every housing boom since World War II always seemed to just miss **Harlem**, the **Bloomberg Boom** caught it head-on, and rents and housing prices soared right along with the rest of the City. By 2006 it was difficult to find anything, burned-out shell or otherwise, for less than $1,000,000. On the positive side, previously neglected town houses have been meticulously restored, and new in-fill housing built. On the negative side, many see the lessening of Harlem's unique — largely African-American, East-Indian, and Latino — culture.

Renaming city streets: In the olden days, sur-names of dignitaries became the official titles of city thoroughfares. In this fashion Sixth Avenue above Central Park became Lenox Avenue after James Lenox, philanthropist, bibliophile, and founder of what became the New York Public Library's Lenox Collection. Later, however, the style changed, to include longer names. That same Sixth Avenue below Central Park is official-ly Avenue of the Americas, though few use that title. And above Central Park Lenox has officially given way to Malcolm X (Boulevard, not Avenue). To honor Harlem civil rights champion, provoca-tive preacher, and flamboyant congressman Adam Clayton Powell, Jr., Seventh Avenue north of Central Park was officially renamed and redubbed with all of Powell's names, thus creat-ing a particularly unwieldy mouthful for address-es or directions. Similarly, Central Park West—or Eighth Avenue, if you will—is officially Frederick Douglass Boulevard as it progresses northward to the Harlem River; and 125th Street both East and West is Martin Luther King, Jr., Boulevard. The first governor of Puerto Rico is honored by Luis Munoz Marin Boulevard, as 116th Street east of Lexington is officially known.

At the Northeast Corner of Central Park:

Frawley Circle:

[a] **The Museum for African Art**, Fifth Ave. at 110th St. 2011. *Robert A.M. Stern*.

A great chance for *Stern* to stretch out a bit, freed from the constraints of the retro "Between the Wars" style he often champions. Obviously inspired here, he goes modern (almost), with trapezoidal windows and an airy, light-filled lobby defined by a soaring, curving expanse of wood, like the hull of a ship. Beautiful, but the 19-story tower of luxury housing on top? It's business as usual.

[b] **Arthur A. Schomburg Plaza**, E.110th to E.111th Sts., bet. Fifth and Madison Aves. 1975. *Gruzen & Partners and Castro-Blanco, Piscioneri & Feder*.

Two vigorous 35-story octagonal prisms mark the northeast corner of Central Park— **Frawley Circle**. A landmark in a literal sense, it visually holds the park's corner from within the Park and along Central Park North (110th Street).

**Central Park North to
Marcus Garvey/Mt. Morris Park:**

On Central Park North a leisurely meander northward:

[H1] **Semiramis**, 137 Central Park N., bet. St. Nicholas Ave. and Adam Clayton Powell, Jr., Blvd. 1901. *Henry Anderson*. Renovated into condominiums, 1987.

Queen of Central Park North: rough-cut stone and maroon brick combine to produce a vigorous façade that lives up to its name: *Semiramis*, a mythical Assyrian queen known for her beauty (and to whom is ascribed the building of Babylon). Unfortunately the cornice is no more.

Amble west on Central Park North to:

[H2] **Towers on the Park** (apartment complex), Cathedral Pkwy. and Frederick Douglass Circle, bet. Manhattan Ave. and Frederick Douglass Blvd. N side. 1987. *Bond Ryder & James*.

Condominium apartments anchor this northwest corner of Central Park, as do the **Schomburg Towers** to the northeast. Crisp but bland. They bow, however, to the circle and consciously make a corner for the park.

A peek behind gives a glimpse of the forest primeval shared by Harlem and the Heights:

[H3] **Morningside Park**, bet. Cathedral Pkwy. and W.123rd St., Manhattan and Morningside Aves. and Morningside Dr. Preliminary plan, 1873. Revised plan, 1887. Both by *Frederick Law Olmsted and Calvert Vaux*. Western retaining wall and bays, 1882, *J. Wrey Mould*. Waterfall, 1988, *Quennell Rothschild*, landscape architects. 👁

This narrow strip contains the high and

H1

rocky cliff that separates **Harlem**, below and to the east, from **Morningside Heights**, above and to the west. It preserves a bit of primeval Manhattan as a dramatic foreground to the Cathedral of St. John the Divine, visible at its crest. Public School 36 ate away the northwest corner, and a proposed Columbia University gym would have usurped two additional acres. Instead, a *Quennell Rothschild* pond and waterfall first fills the aborted excavation, then cascades to the flats below: for **Harlem** it's **Yosemite in Manhattan**.

Back to Adam Clayton Powell, Jr., Boulevard, moving north through a thicket of Harlem architecture:

[H4] **Mt. Nebo Baptist Church**, NE cor. Adam Clayton Powell, Jr., Blvd. and W.114th St. 1900s.

A grand sextet of **Composite Ionic** columns forms a formidable Roman temple façade. Arcaded bell towers surmount mini temples (from afar they seem posh finialed howdahs on a touring elephant).

[H5] **Wadleigh School,** Junior High School 88, Manhattan/originally **The Lydia F. Wadleigh High School for Girls**, 215 W.114th St., bet. Adam Clayton Powell, Jr., Blvd. and Frederick Douglass Blvd. 1901-1902. *C.B.J. Snyder.* ✚

A prestigious high school for girls, Wadleigh later was Harlem's *only* high school (but co-ed). The stately brick and limestone dormer windows and tower are a distant reminder of the Loire Valley.

[H6] **115th Street Branch, The New York Public Library**, 203 W.115th St., bet. Adam Clayton Powell, Jr., Blvd. and Frederick Douglass Blvd. 1907-1909. *Charles F. McKim of McKim, Mead & White.* ✚

Horizontally and radially rusticated limestone, with arched windows and a carved seal of the City, is guarded by a pair of angels, and recalls the Strozzi Palace in Florence. One of New York's handsomest branch libraries.

Another former firehouse, one of many designed by the architects of the **Metropolitan Life** tower. The renovation to a health center is both seamless and elegant.

[H10] **First Corinthian Baptist Church**/originally **Regent Theatre**, 1910 Adam Clayton Powell, Jr., Blvd., SW cor. W.116th St. 1912-1913. *Thomas W. Lamb.* ✚

Vaguely inspired by Venice's **Doge's Palace** and adapted to the needs of the early motion

H4   H6   H5

H7   H9

[H7] **Memorial Canaan Baptist Church**/originally **Northminster Presbyterian Church**, 141 W.115th St., bet. Lenox (Malcolm X Blvd.) and St. Nicholas Aves. 1905.

A robust façade. Powerful circular and arched openings framed in limestone are set into a field of dark red and black tapestry brickwork. The architect made a compelling, creative statement.

[H8] **Community Center and Charter School**, 125 W.115th St. bet. Lenox and St. Nicholas Aves. 1998. *Beckhard Richlan Szerbaty & Associates, (BRS+A).*

A trim modern brick and limestone community center and charter school. The entry posts a stylish **postmodern** oculus above and glass block (popular in the 1930s and 40s) within its enframement.

[H9] **Helen B. Atkinson Health Center**/originally **Engine Company No.58**, N.Y.C. Fire Department, 81 W.115th St., bet. Fifth and Lenox (Malcolm X Blvd.) Aves. 1892. *Napoleon LeBrun & Sons.* Remodeled, 1998, *David W. Prendergast.*

picture. *S.L. Rothafel* (1882-1936), later famous as **"Roxy,"** began his career here as a picture palace impresario, successfully steering the theater out of its initial, catastrophic management failings. It is now a flamboyant Hollywood set for religion. Consult the index for more great *Lamb.*

[H11] **Graham Court Apartments**, 1923-1937 Adam Clayton Powell, Jr., Blvd., bet. W.116th and W.117th Sts. E side. 1899-1901. *Clinton & Russell.* ✚

Commissioned by *William Waldorf Astor*, this, the most luxurious apartment house in Harlem (not open to African-Americans until 1928), surrounds a court, entered through a splendid two-story *Guastavino* vaulted passageway. *Clinton & Russell* later designed the **Apthorp,** another vast courtyarded luxury apartment block at 79th Street and Broadway.

[H12] **Malcolm Shabazz Mosque No.7**/formerly **Muhammad's Temple of Islam**/originally **Lenox Casino**, 102 W.116th St., SW cor. Lenox Ave. (Malcolm X Blvd.) Converted to temple, 1965, *Sabbath Brown*.

An innocent translation of the forms of a **Middle Eastern mosque** into the vernacular materials of 20th-century shopping centers. The aluminum pumpkin-shaped dome is a parody of those found in the Middle East. Sorry to see it so.

[H13] **Bethel Way of the Cross Church of Christ**/ originally **Congregation Shaari Zadek of Harlem**, 25 W.118th St., bet. Fifth and Lenox (Malcolm X Blvd.) Aves. 1900. *Michael Bernstein*.

Fanciful forms borrowed from **Islamic** architecture grace the façade of what, in another culture, might have been a harem. Here its beginnings were as a synagogue, later converted to church uses when demographic tides shifted. Painted, but is it a painted lady?

Hyperactive, like many children it serves, this community sports and crafts center is literally a bright spot (of both color and form) in the Harlem landscape.

Back to ACP Boulevard:

[H17] **1971-1973 and 1975-1977 Adam Clayton Powell, Jr., Boulevard** (tenements), bet. W.119th and W.120th Sts. E side. 1890s.

H14   H19

H11   H16   H15

[H14] **105-137 West 118th Street** (row houses), bet. Adam Clayton Powell, Jr., and Malcolm X (Lenox) Blvds. 1890s.

A terrace of 17 houses, their bow-fronts modulating the long block, each with a variant supporting form under the bow: tooled brownstone, bracketed sub-cornice ... a civilized place to live.

[H15] **St. Thomas the Apostle Church** (Roman Catholic), 260 W.118th St., SW cor. St. Nicholas Ave. 1907. *Thomas H. Poole & Co.*

Berserk eclecticism reminiscent of the filigrees of **Milan's Cathedral** or of many Flemish or Venetian fantasies. It is unnameable but wonderful.

Off on its own to the west:

[H16] **Police Athletic League Harlem Community Center**, 441 Manhattan Ave., SW cor. 119th St. 1999. *Kevin Hom + Andrew Goldman*.

Sturdy, stubby, clustered Romanesque columns flank these monumental entrances.

[H18] **Washington Apartments**, 2034-2040 Adam Clayton Powell, Jr., Blvd., SW cor. W.122nd St. 1883-1884. *Mortimer C. Merritt*. Renovated, 1992. 💣

Queen Anne for the middle class seeking the new French Flats (*Edith Wharton's The Age of Innocence* revealed the rude shocks stylish New Yorkers felt about apartment housing). The **Victorian Baroque** "pediment" gives a simple façade vigorous identity.

[H19] **236 West 122nd Street** (tenement), bet. Adam Clayton Powell, Jr., and Frederick Douglass Blvds. S side. 1890s.

Those rounded corners and deep reveals make this ordinary tenement an exceptional building, articulating its presence, and allowing angled street views from its edges.

H18

[H20] **Church of the Master** (United Presbyterian), 86 Morningside Ave., bet. W.121st and W.122nd Sts. E side. 1972. *Victor Christ-Janer and Roger Glasgow.*

A dour modern concrete house of worship

H20

H26

H23

[H23] **28th Precinct, N.Y.C. Police Department,** 2271 Frederick Douglass Blvd., bet. W.122nd and W.123rd Sts. to St. Nicholas Ave. E side. 1974. *Lehrecke & Tonetti.*

The early 1970s were the heyday, and

H21

for parishioners following the steps of dour **Scottish** Protestants. Also see Necrology, p. 547.

[H21] **529-533 Manhattan Avenue** (row houses), NW cor. W.122nd St. 1890s.

A trio of stately brownstones, well-preserved and well-corniced, displaying a long brick flank (the brownstone, of course, as usual in row house New York, is merely a veneer).

[H22] **The Dwyer,** 264 St. Nicholas Ave., NE cor. W.123rd St. 2007. *James McCullar & Assocs.*

Condominium apartments that replace the demolished **Dwyer Warehouse**. Give credit to *McCullar* for rebuilding with touches of Dwyer's character, from its scale and materials to a ribbon of bay windows holding the corner.

sometimes neyday, of City-sponsored poured-in-place concrete buildings. Because this is a difficult technique, requiring much planning and patience, few agencies or architects bother these days.

Between Fifth and St. Nicholas Avenues to the 125th Street Corridor:

[H24] **Greater Metropolitan Baptist Church**/originally **Saint Paul's German Evangelical Lutheran Church,** 147 W.123rd St., bet. Malcolm X and Adam Clayton Powell, Jr., Blvds. N side. 1897-1898. *Schneider & Herter.* ●

Multifinialed as if with rockets ready to pierce the heavens. Smooth and rockface Vermont marble surfaces contrast sharply, enriching the forms.

[H25] **123 House,** 133 W.123rd St., bet. Malcolm X and Adam Clayton Powell, Jr., Blvds. 2005. *Keith Strand.*

A humble little modernist dwelling and office, wedged between bigger brothers.

H24

[H26] **Refuge Temple of the Church of Our Lord Jesus Christ**/formerly **Harlem Casino**, 2081 Adam Clayton Powell, Jr., Blvd., NE cor. W.124th St. Interior renovated, 1966, *Costas Machlouzarides.*

   Refuge Temple, founded in 1919 by the *Reverend Robert C. Lawson*, who criticized the lack of emotionalism in Harlem's more established churches and offered recent migrants the fire, brimstone, and personal Christianity with which they were familiar down South. The façade signals this story as if in a *retardataire* Hollywood.

H29

H27

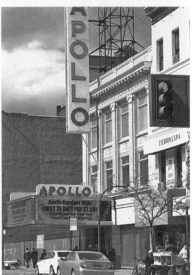

H30

[H27] Originally **Pabst Concert Hall**, 243-251 W.124th St., bet. Adam Clayton Powell, Jr., Blvd. and Frederick Douglass Blvd. N side. ca. 1900.

   Though the entrance to this concert hall was originally on bustling 125th Street, the fantastic vaulted roof is best seen from the rear on 124th. The curve of the roof is elegantly expressed in 124th's brick façade.

Along the 125th Street corridor:

[H28] **North General Hospital**, Paul Robeson Center/originally **Koch & Company Store**, 132-140 W.125th St., bet. Lenox Ave and Adam Clayton Powell, Jr., Blvd. 1893. *William H. Hume & Son.* Altered.

   The first established dry goods merchant from lower Sixth Avenue's grand stores to move northward. It moved too far; its success as Harlem's chief department store lasted only some 30 years. Brick, limestone, and terra-cotta eclectic (see the **Ladies Mile** for a host of its peers), the quintet of grand arches with foliated spandrels contribute to a lush façade.

[H29] **Theresa Towers**/originally **Hotel Theresa**, 2090 Adam Clayton Powell, Jr., Blvd., bet. W.124th and W.125th Sts. W side. 1912-1913. *George & Edward Blum.* Altered, 1971. 🖋

   Long a favored meeting spot in Harlem, the **Theresa** attracted Cuba's Prime Minister *Fidel Castro* as his New York hotel when he visited the U.N. in 1960. Russian Prime Minister *Khrushchev* came to Harlem to visit him. It has since been converted to office use.

[H30] **Apollo Theatre**/originally **Hurtig & Seamon's New Burlesque Theater**, 253 W.125th St., bet. Adam Clayton Powell, Jr., Blvd. and Frederick Douglass Blvd. 1913-1914. *George Keister.* Interior restoration, 2001, *Beyer Blinder Belle* and *Davis Brody Bond.* 🖋

   Opened in 1914, this became a hot spot only in 1934. That year the **Hurtig & Seamon** theatre (white-only admissions), was bought by *Leo Brecher* and *Frank Schiffman*, who renamed it the **Apollo** and opened its doors to the black community. Since then it has been the Harlem showplace for black entertainers. *Bessie Smith,*

America's "Empress of the Blues," appeared that first year, followed by other blues singers including *Billie Holiday* and *Dinah Washington*. *Huddie (Leadbelly) Ledbette*r sang from its stage in the 1930s shortly after doing time for intent to murder. *Duke Ellington's* sophisticated style and *Count Basie's* raw-edged rhythms filled the house later. Following World War II, bebop had its fling: the names of *Charlie (Bird) Parker, Dizzy Gillespie, Thelonius Monk*, and, later, such entertainers as *Gladys Knight* and

H31   H36

H32

Aretha Franklin have glittered on its marquee. **Amateur Night** remains the big attraction.

 [H31] **Sydenham Hospital Clinic**/originally **Commonwealth Building**, 215 W.125th St., bet. Adam Clayton Powell, Jr., Blvd. and Frederick Douglass Blvd. 1971. *Hausman & Rosenberg*.

Developed jointly by a local community group (black and Puerto Rican) and a suburban real estate company (white), this crisp, white concrete, precast façade is a happy addition to West 125th Street. The rear façade, on West 126th, is less pretentious but equally handsome.

[H32] **Harlem State Office Building**, 163 W.125th St., NE cor. Adam Clayton Powell, Jr., Blvd. 1973. *Ifill Johnson Hanchard*.

Built to provide a state resource and symbol within the Harlem community, this monumental work and its complementary plaza were a tangible outgrowth of 1960s racial unrest: a second cousin to Albany's **Empire State Plaza** edifice complex (1965-1978. *Harrison & Abramovitz*),

both architecturally and politically (*Nelson Rockefeller*, patron of *H & A*, was Governor of New York).

[H33] **Baptist House of Prayer**/originally **Methodist Third Church of Christ**, 80 W.126th St., bet. Fifth and Lenox (Malcolm X Blvd.) Aves. 1889.

Offbeat Romanesque Revival. The colonettes, ribbed elliptical arch, and contained bay window combine for a marvelous eccentricity.

Then back to Mount Morris Park and a Historic District, its streetscape lining the blocks between the Park and Lenox Avenues in a rich array of 19th-century finery:

[H34] **Marcus Garvey Memorial Park**/formerly **Mount Morris Park**/originally **Mount Morris Square**, interrupting Fifth Ave. bet. 120th and 124th Sts., Madison Ave. to Mount Morris Park W. Land purchased by the City, 1839.

Truly a mount springing out of the flat plain

H33

of central Harlem, a logical platform for the fire watchtower, which still remains. The park's unruly rocky terrain caused it to be largely left alone by park planners until the 1960s, when two major buildings were inserted. In 1973 the park was renamed in honor of black leader **Marcus Garvey** (1887-1940).

[H35] **Fire Watchtower**, in Marcus Garvey Memorial Park, SW of Madison Ave. and E.121st St. 1855. *Julius B. Kroehl*, engineer. 🌶

The lone survivor of many fire towers that once surveyed New York for signs of conflagration. The structure employs a post-and-lime cast-iron frame similar to that used by the early cast- and wrought-iron builder *John Bogardus*.

[H36] **2 West 120th Street**, SW cor. Fifth Ave. 1890s.

A stately brick and terra-cotta super-tenement, crowned with a magnificent dentiled cornice. The neo-Baroque broken pediments at the fifth floor are luscious.

[H37] **Mount Morris Park Historic District**, Mt. Morris Park W. to W of Lenox Ave. (Malcolm X Blvd.), bet. W.119th and W.124th Sts. 👞 For its inclusions, see the map.

Stately houses along the Park's west flank, others along side streets, reflect the varied **Victorian** styles of the late 19th century that characterize the fabric of this district. Interrupting the warp and woof are a sprinkling of fine churches and other institutional build-

[H40] **200-218 Lenox Ave. (Malcolm X Blvd.)** (row houses), bet. W.120th and W.121st Sts. E side. 1887-1888. *Demeuron & Smith.*

A Victorian nonet with mansard roofs worthy of *Napoleon III.* Of an original ten, one tooth, **No.204**, is missing. Music publisher *Carl Fischer* lived at **No.202** from 1894 to 1910.

H35

H38

H41

ings that date from the area's urbanization as a fashionable community. Fortunately the area has retained its architectural character. Among the architectural firms represented in the district, in addition to those responsible for the buildings listed below, are *Thom & Wilson, James E. Ware,* and *George F. Pelham.*

[H38] **1-10 Mount Morris Park West**, bet. W.120th and W.121st Sts. **Nos.1-5**, 1893. *Gilbert A. Schellenger.* **Nos.6-10**, 1891. *Edward L. Angell.*

Ghostly ruins in 2000, when the Fourth Edition of this Guide compared them to **Tintern Abbey**. Happily, renewal and restoration have brought these back to vibrant life.

[H39] **11-14 Mount Morris Park West and 1 West 121st Street**. 1887-1889. *James E. Ware.*

Gabled to the park, with bay windowed brick and elegant smooth cut limestone voussoirs; a corner tourelle has, unhappily, doffed its hat.

[H41] **Mt. Olivet Baptist Church/** originally **Temple Israel**, 201 Lenox Ave. (Malcolm X Blvd.), NW cor. W.120th St. 1906-1907. *Arnold W. Brunner.*

Once one of the City's most prestigious synagogues, this cool **neo-Roman** structure with a grand Ionic columned portico dates from the period when German Jewish families were taking up residence in town houses formerly occupied by families of Dutch, English, and Irish descent.

[H42] **Ebenezer Gospel Tabernacle/**one-time **Congregation and Chebra Ukadisha B'nai Israel Mikalwarie/**originally **Lenox Avenue Unitarian Church**, 225 Lenox Ave., NW cor. W.121st St. 1889-1891. *Charles Atwood.*

Romanesque Revival by *Atwood,* who became the design partner of Chicago's *D.H. Burnham* the year this church was completed and who executed Chicago's amazing avant-garde **Reliance Building**. The Unitarians were replaced by Jews in 1919, and an African-American congregation took over in 1942.

H39

[H43a] **220-228 Lenox Avenue** (Malcolm X Blvd.) (row houses), bet. W.121st and W.122nd Sts. E side. 1888-1889. *F. Carles Merry.*

No.226 is a particular delight: raise your eyes to rockface brownstone voussoirs at the third floor; **neo-Romanesque** arches and columns in brownstone and terra cotta at the fourth.

[H43b] **St. Martin's Episcopal Church and Rectory**/originally **Holy Trinity Episcopal Church**, 18 W.122nd St., SE cor. Lenox Ave., or

H43b

230 Lenox Ave. (Malcolm X Blvd.) 1887-1889. *William A. Potter.*

Rugged **Richardsonian Romanesque**, monumentally arched brownstone openings framing stained glass, its soaring tower a fortress of brownstone and light granite. The tower houses one of America's finest carillons: a group of 40 bells, which places it second in size in the City to the 74 at Riverside Church. Steep gables add to what Classical Architecture exponent *Henry Hope Reed* described as "picturesque eclecticism."

[H43c] **4-16 West 122nd Street**, bet. Lenox Ave. (Malcolm X Blvd.) and Mt. Morris Pk. W. 1888-1889. *William B. Tuthill.*

The architect of **Carnegie Hall** here presents imposing stoops and both bellying and polygonal bay windows to the street.

H43c

H44a, No.103

[H44a] **103-111, 131, 133-143 West 122nd Street** (row houses), bet. Lenox Ave. (Malcolm X Blvd.) and Adam Clayton Powell, Jr., Blvd. **Nos.103-111**, 1887-1888. *Thom & Wilson.* **No.131**, 1890. *Julius Franke.* **Nos.133-143**, 1885-1887. *Francis H. Kimball.* **101-111,** varied brownstones.

131, Stately gray granite **Richardsonian Romanesque.**

133-143, Rich **Queen Anne** for an English terrace. The brick and terra cotta blend almost as a monolith (even the shingle face is in the same palette).

[H44b] **241 and 243-259 Lenox Avenue** (Malcolm X Blvd.), bet. W.122nd and W.123rd Sts. **No.241**, 1883-1885. *A.B. Van Dusen.* **Nos.243-259**, 1885-1886. *Charles H. Beer.*

An intact blockfront of early brownstones. Corinthian-columned porticoes provide a counterpoint rhythm to the block. Imagine the whole neighborhood (both sides of the street) like this.

[H44c] **110 West 123rd Street** (row houses), bet. Malcolm X and Adam Clayton Powell, Jr., Blvds. 1880s.

Orphaned: once part of a trio of well-kept columned brownstones next door to Ephesus, it recently lost its siblings.

[H45] **Mount Morris Ascension Presbyterian Church**/originally **Harlem Presbyterian Church**, 16-20 Mt. Morris Park W. at SW cor. W.122nd St. 1905-1906. *Thomas H. Poole.*

By the time this Eclectic church was built, the effects of the 1893 **Chicago World's Fair's neo-Classicalism** were being felt: the Classical dome on a drum seems alien (and too small) on this Romanesque cum Moorish arched brownstone and ashlar body. It's just silly.

[H46] **Commandment Keepers Ethiopian Hebrew Congregation**/originally **John and Nancy Dwight House**, 31 Mt. Morris Pk. W., or 1 W.123rd St., NW cor. Mt. Morris Park W. 1889-1890. *Frank H. Smith.*

[H47c] **Greater Bethel A.M.E. Church** (African Methodist Episcopal)/originally **Harlem Free Library**, 32 W.123rd St., bet. Mt. Morris Park W. and Lenox Ave. (Malcolm X Blvd.) 1892. *Edgar K. Bourne.*

Originally built to serve as one of the City's many free libraries. In 1901 it joined the **New York Public Library** system, and a new branch building for the area was built in 1909 at 9-11 West 124th Street, with Carnegie funds.

 [H47d] **Bethelite Community Baptist Church**/originally **Harlem Club**, 36 W. 123rdSt., SE cor. Lenox Ave. (Malcolm X Blvd.) 1888-1889. *Lamb & Rich.*

Monumental. Once a private club for wealthy Harlem whites, it now serves as the monumental house of an African-American congregation. Splendid **Romanesque Revival** in rough brownstone and cut limestone, with brick flat and radial, boasting of craftsmanship in the 19th century's penultimate years.

H44b

H46

H47a

H47d

H48

A neo-Renaissance mansion for *John Dwight*, creator of **Arm and Hammer** baking soda. The body is dull, the portico magnificent. Now occupied by a congregation of black Jews who believe people of African descent to be one of the Lost Tribes of Israel.

[H47a] **4-26 West 123rd Street**, bet. Mt. Morris Park W. and Lenox Ave. (Malcolm X Blvd.). 1880-1882. *Charles Baxter.*

A dozen well-preserved brownstones: the whole, frequently, is greater than the sum of the parts. And **No.4's** bay window adds a touch of elegant independence.

[H47b] **28-30 West 123rd Street** (houses), bet. Mt. Morris Park W. and Lenox Ave. (Malcolm X Blvd.). 1884-1885. *John E. Terhune.*

Compact and ornately tooled brownstone and brick Queen Anne, each 13 feet wide.

[H48] **Ephesus Seventh-Day Adventist Church**/formerly **Second Collegiate Church**/originally **Reformed Low Dutch Church of Harlem**, 267 Lenox Ave. (Malcolm X Blvd.), NW cor. W.123rd St. 1885-1887. *John Rochester Thomas.* Church hall at rear, 1894-1895.

Stern random ashlar coursing and a very lofty spire for a **neo-Gothic** Lenox Avenue landmark. The Boys Choir of Harlem was founded here.

[H49] **The Lenox Lounge**, 288 Lenox Ave. between 124th & 125th Sts.

Legendary. *Billie Holiday, John Coltrane, Miles Davis,* and many others have gigged here. The Art Deco façade and interior are wonderful. Check out that great sign. Restored in 1999.

H51

North from the Mount Morris Park area to 125th Street and beyond:

[H50] **1944 Madison Avenue** (tenement), SW cor. W.125th St. 1890s.

An eclectic pleasantry: brick with limestone elliptical and round voussoirs and a pair of bay windows. A limestone oculus with radial voussoirs provides tenement fun.

[H51] **Harlem Children's Zone**, 35 E.125th St. NW cor. Madison Ave. 2005. *Davis Brody Bond.*

The **Promise Academy Charter School**, a medical clinic, and community center. Late modernist styling mixes sleek limestone and brick with metal and glass curtain walling, more in the character of an aspiring corporate headquarters than a surrogate land of children.

[H52] Originally **The Morris** (apartments and ground floor bank)/then **Mount Morris Bank and Safety Deposit Vaults**, 81-85 E.125th St., NW cor. Park Ave. 1883-1884. Enlarged, 1889-1890. *Lamb & Rich.* 🍎 🗡

This formerly elegant **Richardsonian Romanesque** building, on the way to restoration, lost its way. Partially demolished in 2010: only the first floor remains.

[H53] **Studio Museum in Harlem**, 144 W.125th St., bet. Lenox Ave. (Malcolm X Blvd.) and Adam Clayton Powell, Jr., Blvd. New entrance and garden sculpture terrace, 2001-2006, *Rogers Marvel Architects.* Open to the public: We-Fr 10-5; Sa & Su 1-6; closed Mo & Tu. 212-864-4500.

An inviting stylish new entry for a museum and cultural center for local and national black art.

[H54] **Metropolitan Community Methodist Church**/originally **St. James Methodist Episcopal Church**, 1975 Madison Ave., NE cor. E.126th St. 1871. **Rectory**, 1981 Madison Ave., 1871.

Somber Victorian brownstone clads this muted (faint buttresses, shallow arches) **Gothic**

H53

Revival edifice. In charming contrast is the prim, mansarded minister's house to the north, where cast-iron cresting still remains.

[H55] **Mt. Moriah Baptist Church**/originally **Mt. Morris Baptist Church**, 2050 Fifth Ave., bet. E.126th and E.127th Sts. W side. 1888. *Henry F. Kilburn.*

A midblock green-gray ashlar and brownstone church. Boxed in by neighbors, it lacks the sculptural vigor of so many Harlem churches but is graced with an array of gentle Romanesque Revival arches.

[H56] **Langston Hughes House**, 20 E.127th St., bet. Park and Madison Aves. 1869. *Alexander Wilson.* 🗡

An ivied brownstone's fourth floor for *Hughes.* Nice house, better poet.

[H57] **Intermediate School 201, Manhattan, The Arthur A. Schomburg School**, 2005 Madison Ave., bet. W.127th and W.128th Sts. 1966. *Curtis & Davis.*

A windowless masonry doughnut raised on concrete stilts offers no glassy temptations for vandals. Despite the rich brick and concrete textures on the school's exterior, and though a pleasing composition in the abstract, the public space under the building is dark, oppressive, and uninviting.

[H58] **St. Andrew's Church** (Episcopal), 2067 Fifth Ave., NE cor. E.127th St. 1872-1873. Enlargement, 1889-1890. *Henry M. Congdon.* 🔲

A dour, rugged rock-face granite church, its looming clock tower set not at the corner of the intersection, but in a more dynamic location, against the south transept along East 127th Street. The corner, therefore, is available for a picturesque, south-facing side entrance.

H56

H59b

H61

H62

[H61] **26, 28A, 30, 34, 58, 79, 81, 83 W. 128th Street** row houses, bet. Fifth and Lenox Aves. 2002. *Hirsch & Danois.*

David Hirsch, a prolific professional architectural photographer, became an architect. Here (with partner *Danois*) he has filled eight vacant lots with high stoops, trim cornices, and rather quaint oriel windows in a yellow brick matrix. For more austere *Hirsch,* see Columbia Terrace in Carroll Gardens, Brooklyn (p. 627).

H58

[H59a] **2064 Fifth Avenue** (town house), bet. W.127th and W.128th St. W side. 1880s.

The gable bears a sextet (chamber music?) of Composite pilasters with an extravagant **neo–Dutch Renaissance** silhouette. The elliptical and round arches at grade level are nice, but look up.

[H59b] **2068-2076 Fifth Avenue** (row houses), SW cor. W.128th St. 1890s.

Brick with brownstone both rockface and rusticated, sullied by horrendous cheap aluminum windows.

[H60] **17 East 128th Street** (house), bet. Fifth and Madison Aves. ca. 1864. 🔲

A Second Empire mansarded delight once decked out as a Painted Lady, now dourly dressed in what must be **Landmark green**.

[H62] **12 West 129th Street** (house), bet. Fifth and Lenox (Malcolm X Blvd.) Aves. ca. 1863. Alterations and additions, 1882-1883. *Edward Gustaveson*, builder. More work, 1886, *Asbury Baker, Tinkerer.* 🔲

A **Moorish** porch (1882 jigsaw work) and the nuns' protective stucco. Exoticism for the nuns.

Wretched refuse: On the morning of March 21, 1947, police converged on 2078 Fifth Avenue at East 128th Street in Harlem, summoned by a phone tip. There was a dead body, the caller said, in the once fashionable but now decaying brownstone row house in which the strange and reclusive Collyer brothers—Homer and Langley—had been living for 38 years. Though the search was balked by barricades of refuse, Homer's emaciated body, dressed in a tattered gray bathrobe, was soon found. In a massive manhunt for Langley, police plowed through the junk-crammed mansion, while tons of debris were carted off. Buried in the mountains of garbage were five pianos, several guns, thousands of empty bottles and cans, some 1910 pinup pictures, dressmaker's dummies, and a Model T Ford. Finally, Langley's body—smothered by debris rigged to boobytrap burglars—was extracted. It had taken almost three weeks to find it.

[H63] **17-25 West 129th Street** (row houses), bet. Fifth and Lenox (Malcolm X Blvd.) Aves. ca. 1885.

Tudor Gothic in red brick and red and white unglazed terra cotta. No.17 is the best survivor, bowing out to the street.

[H64a] **All Saints' Church** (Roman Catholic), 47 E.129th St. NE cor. Madison Ave. 1883-1886. *Renwick, Aspinwall & Russell.* [H64b] **Parish House**, 47 E.129th St. 1886-1889. *Renwick, Aspinwall & Russell.* [H64c] **All Saints' School**, 52 E.130th St. 1902-1904. *W.W. Renwick.* 🍎

The star of Harlem's ecclesiastical group-

H65

ings. **Gothic** tracery and the terra-cotta ribboning of buff, honey-colored, and brown brick wall surfaces make a confection of these related buildings designed by the successor firms of *James Renwick, Jr.* The patterned brickwork is reminiscent of Siena's cathedral.

[H65] **Astor Row** (row houses), 8-62 W.130th St., bet. Fifth and Lenox (Malcolm X Blvd.) Aves. S side. 1880-1883. *Charles Buek.* 🍎 Restoration, 1997, *Roberta Washington. Li/Saltzman*, preservation consultants.

Three-story brick, single-family row houses with wooden porches and large front and side yards. Their renaissance from years of neglect restores their understated elegance. **Landmark green** has taken hold of the painted porches. Opposite stands an almost intact terrace of brownstones.

[H66] **St. Ambrose Church** (Episcopal)/ originally **Church of the Puritans** (Presbyterian), 15 W.130th St., bet. Fifth and Lenox (Malcolm X Blvd.) Aves. 1875.

The original name of this rock-face granite Gothic Revival structure was the price of its construction: a gift proffered with the condition that the congregation (then the **Second Presbyterian Church of Harlem**) become the Church of the Puritans, which had just sold its lease on Union Square.

H67

And several blocks north:

[H67] **Strivers Gardens,** 300 W. 135th St. at Frederick Douglas Blvd. 2005. *Davis Brody Bond.*

Luxury housing, borrowing its nickname from the King Model Houses of the 1890s designed by *Stanford White, Bruce Price, and James Brown Lord.* Marketing by association? A stretch.

[H68] **Riverbend Houses** (apartments), Fifth Ave. bet. E.138th and E.142nd Sts. E side. 1967. *Davis, Brody & Assocs.*

Co-op housing that attracted middle-class black families when it opened in 1968; there were four buildings in total, with towers on the ends and smaller-scale buildings in between, with outdoor passages that afforded river views. As with most projects of this era, the windows are tiny. Groundbreaking, but **aging prematurely**: its concrete and brick façade is pocked with patches.

H68

H64a

A revolution in brick began at Riverbend Houses as a result of the skyrocketing costs of laying brick following World War II. To achieve economy and to introduce a new scale in exterior masonry units, architects Davis, Brody & Assocs. developed the giant brick (5-1/2" high X 8" wide) first used at Riverbend.

[H69] **369th Regiment Armory, N.Y. National Guard,** 2366 Fifth Ave., bet. W.142nd and W.143rd Sts. W side. Drill shed, 1921-1924. *Tachau & Vought.* Administration building, 1930-1933. *Van Wart & Wein.* 🍎

A superb example of the bricklayer's art. In this case the mason's efforts are in deep purpley-red and exhibit an **Art Deco/Moderne** style rather than an attempt to reconstruct a medieval fortress.

Sylvia's, 328 Lenox Ave. between 126th & 127th Streets, has been serving up great soul food since 1962. A neighborhood institution, and required dining for every campaigner who comes through, from Bill to Hillary.

[H70] **Metropolitan Baptist Church**/originally **New York Presbyterian Church,** 151 W.128th St., NE cor. Adam Clayton Powell, Jr., Blvd. 1884-1885. Auditorium, 1889-1890. *John Rochester Thomas and Richard R. Davis.* 🍎

The sheltering form of its majestic steep and rounded roof makes this handsome church monumental. Below, all is rock-faced granite, enlivened at the entrance by polished orange granite columns bearing Romanesque "Afro"

H69

capitals and, facing **ACP, Jr., Boulevard,** slender finialed towers flanking the west façade.

[H71] **Salem United Methodist Church**/originally **Calvary Methodist Episcopal Church,** Adam Clayton Powell, Jr., Blvd. NW cor. W.129th St. 1887. Enlarged, 1890.

It once housed the City's largest Protestant church auditorium and membership, but then came **Riverside Church.** The grand street and avenue arches and their myriad of ancillary supporters contribute to powerful façades, complementing a tall, slender tower (**Romanesque oriel**).

[H72] **Row houses, W.130th St.** bet. Lenox Ave and Adam Clayton Powell, Jr., Blvd. N and S sides. ca. 1885-1890.

Two rows of stately brownstones flank this street, many displaying their original stoops and cast-iron balustrades.

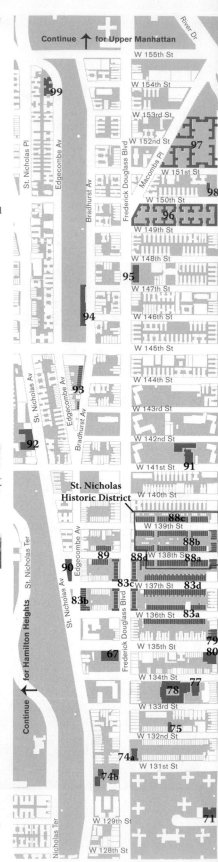

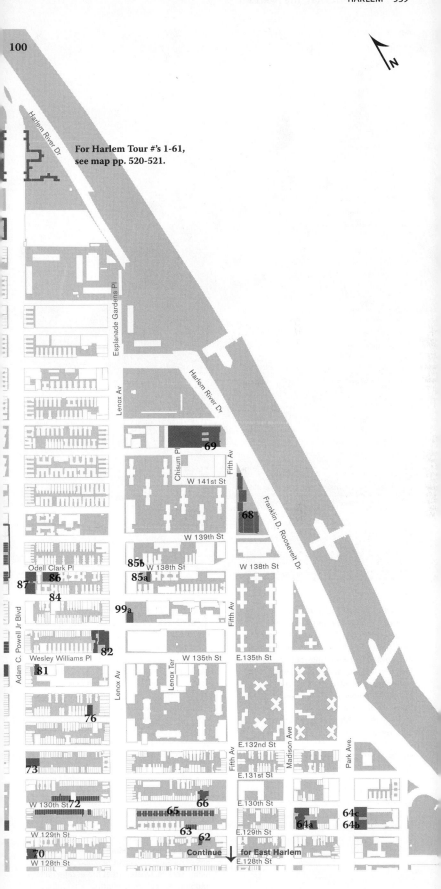

100

For Harlem Tour #'s 1-61,
see map pp. 520-521.

Harlem River Dr

Esplanade Gardens Pl

Lenox Av

Harlem River Dr

Chisum Pl

69

Fifth Av

W 141st St

68

Franklin D. Roosevelt Dr

W 139th St

85b W 138th St

W 138th St

Odell Clark Pl

86

85a

87

84

Fifth Av

99a

Adam C. Powell Jr Blvd

82

Lenox Av

Wesley Williams Pl

81

Lenox Ter

W 135th St

E.135th St

76

73

Fifth Av

E.132nd St

Madison Ave

Park Ave.

E.131st St

W 130th St 72

66

E.130th St

65

64c

63

62

64a

64b

W 129th St

E.129th St

70

Continue ↓ for East Harlem

W 128th St

E.128th St

H70

[H73] **Williams Christian Methodist Episcopal Church**/formerly **Lafayette Theatre**, 2225 Adam Clayton Powell, Jr., Blvd., bet. W.131st St. and W.132nd St. E side. 1912. *V. Hugo Koehler.*

Ravaged by alterations but fraught with history. For three decades the **Lafayette** was the nation's leading black theater. The critically acclaimed production of *Darktown Follies* (1913) started the vogue of midtowners coming to Harlem for entertainment. A place of history, not architecture.

[H74a] **Lionel Hampton Houses**, 273 W.131st St., NE cor. Frederick Douglass Blvd., 201 W.130th St., NW cor. Frederick Douglass Blvd.
[H74b] **410 St. Nicholas Ave.**, bet. W.130th and W.131st Sts. 1974. *Bond Ryder Assocs.*

A careful assembly of handsome modern housing on irregular sites.

[H75] **St. Aloysius Roman Catholic Church**, 209-217 W. 132nd St., bet. Adam Clayton Powell, Jr., Blvd. and Frederick Douglass Blvd. 1902-1904. *W.W. Renwick.*

Deep purple brickwork and pale green glazed-brick trim harmonize with terra cotta that recalls the texture and complexity of Belgian lace. An evocative and delicate façade, redolent of the exuberant Certosa at Pavia. *W.W. Renwick*, nephew of noted architect *James Renwick, Jr.,* had joined his uncle's firm in 1885 and became a junior partner in 1890. This may recall his earlier Italian travels.

[H76] **Engine Company No.59, Ladder Company, No.30**, N.Y.C. Fire Department, 111 W.133rd St., bet. Lenox Ave and Adam Clayton Powell, Jr., Blvd. 1962. *Giorgio Cavaglieri.*

Fashionable in its time, this bright red glazed brick-plus-*Miesian* framed firehouse conflicts with the more enduring architectural values of its older tenement neighbors, with their richly worked, twisted steel fire-escape railings and intricate cut stone plinths.

New York's Beale Street: Life in Harlem stimulated the curiosity of outsiders for the forbidden, particularly during the Roaring Twenties. Exploiters arranged specially trumped-up visits (for those who could pay) to see what was ballyhooed as "the primitive essence of Harlem Life." The night spots along West 133rd Street between Lenox Ave. (Malcolm X Blvd.) and Adam Clayton Powell, Jr., Blvd., such as Dickie Wells', Mexico's, Pod's and Jerry's, and the Nest, were in the center of such activity. A similarity to Beale Street in Memphis, made famous by black composer and blues compiler W. C. Handy, caused the name to be popularly applied to the street in Harlem. The Depression curtailed most of these goings-on.

[H77] **St. Philip's Church** (Protestant Episcopal), 214 W.134th St., bet. Adam Clayton Powell, Jr., Blvd. and Frederick Douglass Blvd. 1910-1911. *Vertner W. Tandy and George Washington Foster.* ●

This spare, northern Gothic church in salmon-colored Roman brick was founded in the

H74a

notorious **Five Points** section of the Lower East Side in 1809. A century later it was able to sell its properties in the **Tenderloin** for almost $600,000. With this windfall the church purchased its present site, as well as a row of ten apartment houses on West 135th Street previously restricted to whites.

Foster was among the first African-Americans to practice within the architectural profession in America. *Tandy* was the first African-American to be granted an architectural registration in New York State.

[H78] **Public School 92**, Manhattan, **The Mary McCleod Bethune School**, 222 W.134th St., bet. Adam Clayton Powell, Jr., Blvd. and Frederick Douglass Blvd. 1965. *Percival Goodman.*

A gentle blend: a creamy cast-in-place concrete frame infilled with Hudson River red brick creates a thoughtful, but dated, design where there were never architectural fireworks.

[H79] **2300-2306 Adam Clayton Powell, Jr., Boulevard**, NW cor. W.135th St. 1887-1888. *Richard Davis & Son.*

A stately brick tenement quartet. The breaking cornices (into triangles) modulates the group.

[H80] **Thurgood Marshall Academy**, 200-214 W. 135th St., SW cor. Adam Clayton Powell, Jr., Blvd. 2004. *Gruzen Samton.*

Six stories of academic brickwork emerging

H75

above an existing three-story 1924 building shell, the latter once home of legendary **Small's Paradise**, a Harlem jazz club: teaching emerging from a carapace of Harlem cultural history.

Small's Paradise: on the southwest corner of 135th Street and Adam Clayton Powell, Jr., Boulevard. A jazz club, "The Hottest Spot in Harlem," served up to 1,500 on its opening in the 1920s and 1930s. It was revived in the 1960s as Wilt Chamberlain's "Big Wilt's Small's Paradise." It finally closed in 1986.

[H81] **Harlem Branch, YMCA,** 180 W.135th St., bet. Lenox Ave. (Malcolm X Blvd.) and Adam Clayton Powell, Jr., Blvd. 1931-1932. *James C. Mackenzie, Jr.* ●

A stately red-brown brick Y not to be confused with its 1919 vintage predecessor across the street. Note the pair of broken pediments molded from the same brick.

[H82a] **135th Street Branch**, later **Schomburg Center**, New York Public Library, 103 W.135th St., bet. Lenox Ave. (Malcolm X Blvd.) and Adam Clayton Powell, Jr., Blvd. 1903-1905. *Charles F. McKim of McKim, Mead & White.* ● Open to the public Mo-We 12-8; Th-Sa 10-6; closed Su. 212-491-2200.

[H82b] **Schomburg Center for Research in Black Culture**, The New York Public Library, 515 Lenox Ave. (Malcolm X Blvd.), bet. W.135th and W.136th Sts. W side. 1969-1980. *Bond Ryder Assocs. Link, 1991, Davis Brody Bond.* Renovation, 2007, *Dattner Associates.*

The **135th Street** library building was, from 1926 to 1978, the unofficial headquarters of the black literary renaissance. *Arthur A. Schomburg* (1874-1938), a Puerto Rican, privately undertook the task of collecting raw materials of black American history, then in danger of loss through neglect by the academic community. In 1926 the Carnegie Corporation of New York purchased the collection and had it deposited here with *Schomburg* himself as curator. In 1972 the

Madame C. J. Walker: Born to freed slaves shortly after the Civil War, this enterprising promoter rose from washerwoman to become reputedly the richest black woman in New York, through the development and sale of hair-straightening products. Her home and adjacent hair parlor occupied the site on which the Countee Cullen Branch Library was built. She died in 1919 in Irvington, N.Y., where she had built a house (Vertner W. Tandy, architect) on the main street— to the consternation of her white neighbors.

[H83a] **202-266 and 203-267 West 136th Street**, bet. Adam Clayton Powell, Jr., Blvd. and Frederick Douglass Blvd. **Nos.202-266**, 1889-1890. *Frederick G. Butcher.* **Nos.203-267**, 1891-1895. *Thomas C. Van Brunt.*

Two facing blockfronts of row houses provide a flock of town house architecture equal to any of the Upper West Side's park blocks, doubly important as these are in Harlem. Architect/developer *Van Brunt* mixed sandstone in varied colors and brick.

H82a

H80 H82b

Schomburg Collection was formally renamed as a research center. The building is in *McKim's* consistent Italian Renaissance palazzo mode.

In 1978 the long-awaited **Schomburg Center** opened with proper facilities for storing, conserving, and disseminating the archive's treasures.

The 2007 renovation provided a new glass façade complete with video wall viewable at night from Malcolm X Boulevard, a new street level gallery, and a new **Center for Scholars.**

[H82c] **Countee Cullen Branch, The New York Public Library**, 104 W.136th St., bet. Lenox Ave. (Malcolm X Blvd.) and Adam Clayton Powell, Jr., Blvd. 1942. *Louis Allen Abramson.* Restored, 1988.

This **Art Moderne** library, named for a poet of the Harlem Renaissance, *Countee Cullen*, was built as an extension to the **135th St. Library**, original home of the Schomburg Center.

The Brotherhood of Sleeping Car Porters, the first African-American union, maintained headquarters at 239 West 136th from 1929 into the thirties. Its founder, A. Philip Randolph, waved a powerful political hand in both the Roosevelt and Truman administrations; he was the catalyst for desegregation in both World War II defense industries and the military itself.

[H83b] **26-46 Edgecombe Avenue**, bet. W.136th and W.137th Sts. E side, and 321 W.136th St., bet. Edgecombe and Frederick Douglass Blvd. ca. 1885.

Mansarded Victorians along a triangular intersection (Dorrence Brooks Square), behind which St. Nicholas Park forms a backdrop. Before the park's wild greenery was slashed, the contrast between nature and architecture must have been vivid. **No.26** at the corner of West 136th Street is special, but bay windows enliven the whole blockfront.

[H83c] **St. Charles Condominiums**, E and W sides of Frederick Douglass Blvd., bet. W.136th and W.138th Sts. 1997. *The Stephen Jacobs Group.*

120 units of affordable housing. A near miss: this could have been a modern re-interpretation of Strivers' Row.

[H83d] **203-231 and 202-252 West 137th Street**, Adam Clayton Powell, Jr., Blvd. to Frederick Douglass Blvd. 1897-1903. *John Hauser.*

Powerful, intact stoops guard these 41 houses, some **bowfronted** and incised with floral banding, some **flat-fronted** with strong Composite columns and pediments. Rich variations on a theme.

[H84] **Mother African Methodist Episcopal Zion Church**, 140-148 W.137th St., bet. Lenox Ave. (Malcolm X Blvd.) and Adam Clayton Powell, Jr., Blvd. 1923-1925. *George W. Foster, Jr.* 🅟

Random ashlar and terra cotta present a great stained-glass window to the street. Atop,

[H86] **Abyssinian Baptist Church and Community House**, 136-142 W.138th St., bet. Lenox and Adam Clayton Powell, Jr., Blvd. 1922-1923. *Charles W. Bolton and Son.* 🅟 212-862-7474. *info@abyssinian.org*

Random ashlar **"Collegiate Gothic"** (the building would be at home at Princeton or Yale), doubly a landmark in Harlem due to the charisma, power, and notoriety of its spellbinding preacher, *Adam Clayton Powell, Jr.* (1908-1972), 14-term member of the **House of Representatives.** The church has established a memorial room, open to the public, containing artifacts from his life. **Call before you visit.**

[H87] **Renaissance Theater and Renaissance Ballroom and Casino**, 2341-2359 Adam Clayton Powell, Jr., Blvd., bet. W.137th and W.138th St. 1920-1923. *Harry Creighton Ingalls.*

Abandoned. This Guide has been complaining about the condition of these handsome masonry twins since 1988. We hope a restoration finally happens. In the meantime, check out

H83d   H85a

encrusted finials enrich the simple façade. *George Foster* was an early **African-American** architect.

[H85a] **Union Congregational Church**/originally **Rush Memorial A.M.E. Zion Church** (African Methodist Episcopal), 60 W.138th St., bet. Fifth and Lenox (Malcolm X Blvd.) Aves. ca. 1910.
[H85b] **St. Mark's Roman Catholic Church**/originally **Church of St. Mark the Evangelist**, 65 W.138th St. 1908.

St. Mark's has stripped its sometime paint and restored the brick and terra-cotta façade to its original crispness. **Union** is still clad in the dour paint they originally shared.

the rusty sign left from a long-vanished Chinese restaurant: *"Chow Mein."*

[H88] **St. Nicholas Historic District (The King Model Houses/"Strivers' Row")**, generally W.138th to W.139th Sts., bet. Adam Clayton Powell, Jr., Blvd. and Frederick Douglass Blvd. 🅟 including [H88a] **202-250 W.138th St. and 2350-2354 Adam Clayton Powell, Jr., Blvd.** 1891-1893. *James Brown Lord.* 🅟
[H88b] **203-271 W.138th St., 202-272 W.139th St., and 2360-2378 Adam Clayton Powell, Jr., Blvd.** 1891-1893. *Bruce Price and Clarence S. Luce.* 🅟
[H88c] **203-267 W.139th St. and 2380-2390 Adam Clayton Powell, Jr., Blvd.** 1891-1893. *Stanford White of McKim, Mead & White.* 🅟

By the time *David H. King, Jr.,* built these distinguished row houses and apartments, he had been widely recognized as the builder responsible for the old **Times Building** of 1889

H86

on Park Row, *Stanford White's* **Madison Square Garden**, and the base of the **Statue of Liberty**. Displaying rare vision, *King* commissioned the services of three architects at one time to develop this group of contiguous blocks for the well-to-do. The results are an urbane grouping reflecting the differing tastes of the architects: all with similar scale, varied but harmonious materials, and related styles—Georgian-inspired in the two southern blocks, neo-Italian Renaissance in *Stanford White's* northern group. In addition, they share rear alleys entered from the side streets.

Despite Harlem's ups and downs, the homes and apartments retained their prestige and attracted (by 1919) many successful blacks in medicine, dentistry, law, and the arts such as *W.C. Handy* [232 W.139], *Noble Sissle, Fletcher Henderson* [228 W.139], *Eubie Blake*, and architect *Vertner Tandy* [221 W.139]. As a result, **Strivers' Row** became a popular term for the district in the 1920s and 1930s.

[H91] **St. Charles Borromeo Church** (Roman Catholic), 211 W.141st St., bet. Adam Clayton Powell, Jr., Blvd. and Frederick Douglass Blvd. 1888. Altered, 1973, *L. E. Tuckett & Thompson*. Rectory, 1880s.

The destruction of the nave by fire provided the opportunity for contemporary reuse by building a modern miniature sanctuary within the walls of the original. Limestone and brick neo-Gothic.

 [H92] **Harlem School of the Arts**, 645 St. Nicholas Ave., N of W.141st St. W side. 1977. *Ulrich Franzen & Assocs.*

A distinguished Harlem institution, once housed next door at St. James' Presbyterian Church Community House. Founded by the great operatic soprano in 1963, *Dorothy Maynor*, it first operated in the church proper, where *Shelby Rooks, Maynor's* husband, was rector. It now occupies its own building, nuzzled against the craggy hillside of Hamilton Terrace's backyards.

H88d   H89

H88   H91

[H88d] **Victory Tabernacle Seventh Day Christian Church**/formerly **Coachmen's Union League Society of New York City**, 252 W. 138th St., bet. Adam Clayton Powell, Jr., Blvd. and Frederick Douglass Blvd. 1895-1896. *Jardine, Kent & Jardine.*

Moorish-Venetian? **Limestone frippery**? It was built to sell life insurance to residents of this newly opened "suburb" of Harlem, particularly to those living in the King Model Houses.

[H89] **309-325 and 304-318 West 138th Street**. Nos.309-325, 1889-1890. *Edwin R. Will.* Nos.304-318, 1896. *J. Averit Webster.*

Gabled, bowed, and bayed **Queen Anne** on the north, neo-Renaissance corniced, a **Palladian** trio over bay windows on the south.

[H90] **St. Mark's Methodist Church**, Edgecombe Ave. SW cor. W.138th St. 1921-1926. *Sibley & Fetherston.*

Neo-Gothic, but heavy-handed: too much wall, too little glass, the neo-Gothic detail merely decoration added to the bulky body.

[H93] **Row houses, Bradhurst Ave.**, bet. W.143rd and W.145th Sts. W side. ca. 1888.

Stoop removal and general lack of maintenance have hurt this inventive row of Victorian houses. Nevertheless, their wit prevails.

[H94] **Jackie Robinson Play Center**/originally **Colonial Play Center** (swimming pool and bathhouse), in Jackie Robinson (formerly Colonial) Park, Bradhurst Ave. bet. W.145th and W.153rd Sts. W side. 1935-1937. *N.Y.C. Parks Department. Aymar Embury II*, consulting architect. ◐ Interior. ◐

The most dramatic of the City's **WPA**-built pools. Cylindrical volumes squeeze the abutting sidewalk and alternate with an assortment of half-round arches. These spring from varied **Romanesque**-inspired capitals to create a powerful statement in bold, red-brick masonry worthy of its **Roman** aqueduct (hence "Romanesque") forbears. The confident design of this outdoor natatorium overcomes the shortcomings of its unskilled masons: bricks in some archways bunch up as they reach their crests, giving them almost the shape of a pointed arch.

[H95] **PSA (Police Services Area) No.6**, 2770 Frederick Douglass Blvd., bet. W.147th and W.148th Sts. E side. 1998. Design, *NYC Housing Authority*. Production, *Gruzen Samton*.

Well-detailed brick corbels decorate the two lower floors, but a faux **United Nations General Assembly** sits on the roof. More cohesion needed between upper and lower.

[H96] **Dunbar Apartments**, 2588 Adam Clayton Powell, Jr., Blvd. to Frederick Douglass Blvd., bet. W.149th and W.150th Sts. 1926-1928. *Andrew J. Thomas*. 🐾

Named for black poet *Paul Laurence Dunbar* (1872-1906), these six apartment buildings, grouped around a landscaped inner court, have been home to such notables as *Countee Cullen, W.E.B. DuBois, A. Philip Randolph, Bill "Bojangles" Robinson—and Matt Henson*, who,

courts embellished with sculpture, *Lewis Mumford* exuberantly stated that the project offers "the equipment for decent living that every modern neighborhood needs: sunlight, air, safety, play space, meeting space, and living space. The families in the Harlem Houses have higher standards of housing, measured in tangible benefits, than most of those on Park Avenue." Perhaps he was being too exuberant. Design staff architect *John L. Wilson*, was the first **African-American architect** to graduate from Columbia's School of Architecture.

[H98] **Nicholas C. and Agnes Benziger House**, 345 Edgecombe Ave. 1890-1891. *William Schickel*.
A picturesque many-gabled survivor.

[H99] **409 Edgecombe Avenue Apartments**/ originally **Colonial Park Apartments**, bet. W.150th and W.155th Sts. 1916-1917. *Schwartz & Gross*. 🐾

A landmark more for who lived here than what it is: in its infancy, home to *Babe Ruth*.

H96

H97

as part of the *Peary* expedition, was the first westerner to set foot upon the North Pole in 1909. Financier *John D. Rockefeller, Jr.,* conceived the project as a model for solving Harlem's housing problem; under the pressures of the Depression, however, he finally foreclosed his mortgages and sold the property. It has been a rental development ever since.

[H97] **Harlem River Houses**, NYC Housing Authority, bet. W.151st and W.153rd Sts., Macombs Place and Harlem River Dr. 1936-1937. *Archibald Manning Brown,* chief architect in association with *Charles F. Fuller, Horace Ginsbern, Frank J. Forster, Will Rice Amon, Richard W. Buckley, John L. Wilson. Michael Rapuano,* landscape architect. *Heinz Warnecke,* assisted by *T. Barbarossa, R. Barthe, F. Steinberger,* sculptors. 🐾

The City's first federally funded, federally owned, and federally built housing project. Writing in 1938 of the four-story apartment buildings, grouped around open landscaped

Later, home to the elite of **black Harlem,** ranging from activist and NAACP founder, *W.E.B. Du Bois* to future Supreme Court Judge *Thurgood Marshall*.

*Sugar Hill: The model of the sweet life in Harlem was identified, between the 1920s and 1950s, with a stretch of Edgecombe Avenue west of (and overlooking) the escarpment of Colonial Park and the Harlem Valley below. The multiple dwellings which line Edgecombe above West 145th Street as it ascends **Coogan's Bluff** were accommodations to which upwardly mobile blacks aspired and in which those who had achieved fame lived: Cab Calloway, Duke Ellington, Walter White, Roy Wilkins, Thurgood Marshall, W.E.B. DuBois, Langston Hughes. Down by the Harlem River, the Flats below the Hill, were the old **Polo Grounds**, where the New York Giants once played; now it is a housing project.*

H100

H98

[H99a] **Harlem Hospital Modernization and Patient Pavilion**, 506 Lenox Ave. (Malcolm X Blvd.) bet. 136th and 137th Sts. E side. 2012 (predicted). *HOK (Hellmuth, Obata + Kassabaum) with Studio JTA.*

Harlem Hospital, founded in 1887, is known for its terrific collection of **WPA murals** by *Alfred Crimi, Georgette Seabrooke, Charles Alston,* and *Vertis Hayes.* The murals will be saved and have a new home in *HOK's* spiffy new building. No one ever wants to visit a hospital, but give *HOK* credit for turning the façade into a kind of community billboard, writ large: a five-story translucent wall featuring a blow-up of one of *Hayes'* murals.

[H100] **Macomb's Dam Bridge and 155th Street Viaduct**, across the Harlem River bet. W.155th St. Manhattan and Jerome Ave., The Bronx. 1890-1895. *Alfred Pancoast Boller,* consulting engineer. 🍎

A glorious rotating truss, with supporting viaducts, that connects Harlem to the West Bronx. Don't wait for it to move; cross it.

NECROLOGY

Originally **Morningside Avenue Presbyterian Church**, 360 W.122nd St., SE cor. Morningside Ave. 1893. *William C. Haskell.*

Another nice old church bites the dust. Still standing next door is the modernist Church of the Master.

Former **Dwyer Warehouse**/originally **O'Reilly Storage Warehouse**, 258-264 St. Nicholas Ave., NE cor. W.123rd St. 1892. *Cornelius O'Reilly.*

In 1915, three storage warehouses occupied this block of St. Nicholas Avenue; the last survived until 2002.

EAST HARLEM

East Harlem, once **Italian** Harlem, is today
Spanish Harlem. Unlike Central Harlem, it was
never a prestigious residential district: its
remaining older housing stock reveals its working-class beginnings. For over a century it has
been the home of laborer immigrants and their
families, including large German, Irish, Jewish,
and Scandinavian populations. The sizable
Italian community, now virtually gone, sank its
roots here prior to 1890. Today, East Harlem is **El
Barrio,** "the neighborhood," overwhelmingly
Puerto Rican in population, heritage, and culture, whose first settlers came here around the
time of World War I.

From the ubiquitous family-owned bodegas,
or grocery stores, found on practically every
street, to **El Museo del Barrio,** the sophisticated
local museum on Fifth Avenue, East Harlem is an
important link to the unique traditions of a vast
and still growing number of Latino residents.

E4

E2

▌ **[E1] Baum-Rothschild Staff Pavilion,** Mt.
Sinai Medical Center, 1249 Park Ave., SE
cor. E.97th St. 1968. *Pomerance & Breines.*

A snappy, slender tower with balconies that
presides over the **Park Avenue Tunnel** portal,
through which passengers travel 50 blocks to
Grand Central Terminal.

▌ **[E2] Long-Term Care Facility, Florence
Nightingale Nursing Home,** 1760 Third
Ave., bet. E.97th and E.98th Sts. 1974. *William
N. Breger Assocs.*

A flamboyant massing of brick gives memorable form to this nursing home. A modest program acquired a strong identity.

**[E3] Electrical substation, N.Y.C. Transit
Authority**/originally **Manhattan Railway Company,**
1782 Third Ave., SW cor. E.99th St. ca. 1902.

Not till 1901 did electric power come to the
City's elevated trains (Els). Until then trains were
powered by smoke-belching miniature steam
locomotives. Power distribution required substa-
tions like this sturdy block of brick and granite.

▌ **[E4] Metro North Plaza/Riverview
Apartments,** bet. E.100th and E.102nd
Sts., First Ave. and FDR Drive. 1976.
[E5] Public School 50, Manhattan, **The Vito
Marcantonio School.** 1975. Both by *Conklin &
Rossant.*

Exposed cast-concrete frames with ribbed-
block infill form high-rise and low-rise housing,
here arranged in a chaste, symmetrical pattern.
The school, approached on a ramp at the far
east end of the complex, makes a dramatic
statement within the discipline of the same
materials.

▌ **[E6] The East Harlem School at Exodus
House,** 309 E.103rd St. bet. First and
Second Aves. 2008. *Peter Gluck and Partners.*

More excellent school architecture from
Gluck (see his **Bronx Prep Charter School** in the
Crotona Park, South Bronx section of the
Guide). Here the façade alternates between
metal panels and windows; especially impres-
sive at night.

E5

[E7] **23rd Precinct, N.Y.C. Police Department**, and Engine Company No.53, Ladder Company No.43, 4th Division, N.Y.C. Fire Department, 1834 Third Ave., SW cor. E.102nd St. 1974. *Milton F. Kirchman.*

A powerful three-dimensional cubist composition, a strongly stated presence of the security apparatus; but how graceful is it for the firemen and police within or on their way in or out?

[E8a] **The Church of the Living Hope**, 161 E.104th St., bet. Lexington and Third Aves. Altered, ca. 1969. [E8b] Originally **Engine Company No.53**, N.Y.C. Fire Department, 179 E.104th St. ca. 1898. [E8c] **Hope Community Hall**/originally **28th Precinct, N.Y.C. Police Department**, 177 E.104th St. 1892-1893. *Nathaniel D. Bush.* 🍎

A curious trio. The somber **Italianate** brick and granite ex-police station bears contrasting elegant light bowed-steel fire escapes; the steel and cast-iron Corinthian post and beams that frame the ex-fire engine entry are enriched with cast bas-reliefs. Above **Romanesque** arches crown a field of textured brickwork.

[E9] **Park East High School**/originally **Manhattan School of Music**, 230-240 E.105th St., bet. Second and Third Aves. 1928. *Donn Barber.* Additions, *Francis L. Mayer.*

Sober and understated façades for the former Manhattan School of Music. **Manhattan** moved to Morningside Heights in a game of musical chairs with **Juilliard** (School of Music); **Juilliard** had moved to Lincoln Center.

[E10] **St. Cecilia's Church** (Roman Catholic) and Regina Angelorum, 112-120 E.106th St., bet. Park and Lexington Aves. Church, 1883-1887, *Napoleon LeBrun & Sons.* **Regina Angelorum** (unified façade), 1907. *Neville & Bagge.* 🍎

This ornate brick and terra-cotta façade is one of East Harlem's special treasures. **Neo-Italian Romanesque**, it has an exuberance that evaded most of Northern Europe.

E7

E8

E11

[E11] **Julia de Burgos Latino Cultural Center**/originally **Public School 72**, Manhattan/then Public School 107, 1674-1686 Lexington Ave., bet. E.105th and E.106th Sts. W side. 1879-1882. *David I. Stagg.* Addition, 1911-1913, *C.B.J. Snyder.* ● Converted to cultural center, 1995, *Lee Borrero and Raymond Plumey* with *Miguel Angel Baltierra.*

Patterned brickwork and a powerful tower give authority to this venerable onetime schoolhouse. Articulated in what some call the **Neo-Grec**, its restoration has been as if the building had passed through the fountain of youth.

[E12] **Franklin Plaza Cooperative**/originally **Franklin Houses**, N.Y.C. Housing Authority, bet. E.106th St. and E.108th St., First and Third Aves. 1959. *Holden, Egan, Wilson & Corser.* Plaza and play areas altered, 1961, *Mayer & Whittlesey.*

Typical housing of its era, when European-influenced urban planning meant lots of towers arranged like chess pieces on a board. Both **groundbreaking** and **heartbreaking**. A slender plan, corner windows, staggered massing, water towers on top.

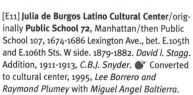 [E13] **East River Landing**/originally **1199 Plaza**, bet. E.107th and E.110th Sts., First Ave. and FDR Drive, plus extension to E.111th St. along the Drive. 1975. *The Hodne/Stageberg Partners*, architects. *Herb Baldwin*, landscape architect.

Sixteen hundred units of cooperative housing built by **District 1199** of the AFL-CIO's National Union of Hospital and Health Care Employees. A massive project whose planners thought construction of a Second Avenue subway line would spur the economic development of East Harlem. The subway line still hasn't happened, and this vast riverside **cliff of brick** has gone through the same periods of trauma (crime, negligence) experienced by many similar projects in the City.

There were good intentions here, as at **Franklin Plaza**, but the idea of efficiency as the highest aspiration in urban design has, thankfully, been outlived by small-scaled, stoop-lined neighborhoods that grow over time, naturally.

[E16] **"La Marqueta,"** under Park Ave. railroad viaduct bet. E.111th and E.115th Sts.

A hothouse of small merchants. Under rumbling commuter trains teems one of the most colorful, fast-moving, fragrant, and boisterous of New York's commercial pageants. A mecca for both bargain hunters and those who love to bargain.

[E17] **James Weldon Johnson Houses**, N.Y.C. Housing Authority, bet. E.112th and E.115th Sts., Third to Park Aves. 1948. *Julian Whittlesey, Harry M. Prince, and Robert J. Reiley.*

The Second Edition of this Guide (1978) proclaimed, **"Within the genre** of publicly assisted housing projects of the 1940s and 1950s ... this is one of the best." Perhaps, but the **whole genre was flawed**.

[E18] **Public School 57**, Manhattan, **The James Weldon Johnson School**, 176 E.115th St., SW cor. Third Ave. 1964. *Ballard, Todd & Snibbe.*

An overhanging cornice, generous small-

E20a

E13

[E14] **Thomas Jefferson Play Center**, First Ave., E side, bet. E.111th St. and E.114th Sts. 1935-1936. *Stanley C. Brogren, Aymar Embury, Harry Ahrens, and others.* 🖤

Almost forgotten by architects are the wonders of **WPA** mid-Depression construction of social and recreational facilities, here in high style Art Deco. Graceful, well worn, and wearing well in both style and substance.

[E15] **Aguilar Branch, The New York Public Library**, 174 E.110th St., bet. Lexington and Third Aves. 1898-1899. Expanded and new façade added, 1904-1905. Both by *Herts & Tallant*. Renovated, 1993-1996, *Gruzen Samton.* 🖤

A triumphal gateway to knowledge, three stories high, replaces an earlier and better one, half as wide, by the same architects. Founded in 1886 as an independent library to serve immigrant Jews (*Grace Aguilar* was an English novelist of Sephardic descent), it was brought into the **New York Public Library** system and expanded by a *Carnegie* gift. It now serves a newer, Latino population.

paned windows, and molded bricks make this school a warm, safe, and friendly place. The scale of this building would enhance and respect a block of row houses; but in its present setting, amid large housing projects, its attention to detail is less telling.

[E19] **Little Sisters of the Assumption Family Health Services,** 333 East 115th Street bet. First and Second Aves. 2003. *Peter Gluck and Partners.*

A crisp modern addition to the block. While other New York architects made bigger splashes in the 21st century's first decade, *Gluck* was quietly working on first-rate civic projects with a deeper social purpose in East Harlem and the South Bronx.

E14

E22

humble functions. A rich array of forms (gables, archways, the imposing corner tower) and materials (water-struck red brick, bluestone, granite, terra cotta, and copper) are worth a special visit.

[E23a] **1-7 Sylvan Court,** E.121st St. N of Sylvan Place, bet. Lexington and Third Aves. ca. 1885.

Seven brick town houses grouped around a charming pedestrian off-street walkway. Ain't landmarked; should be.

E24a   E24b

[E20a] **St. Paul's Church** (Roman Catholic), 121 E.117th St., bet. Park and Lexington Aves. [E20b] **Rectory,** 113 E.117th St. Both 1908. *Neville & Bagge.*

Sturdy limestone towers flank this late **Romanesque Revival** façade at the moment in history that revived pure Gothic for most Christian churches and many college campuses as well.

[E21] **Assemblea de Iglesia Pentecostal de Jesucristo**/originally **First German Baptist Church of Harlem,** 220 E.118th St., bet. Second and Third Aves. ca. 1895.

An ebullient and singular façade with a wide, inviting half-round arch entrance now painted off-white and pale blue.

[E22] **Harlem Courthouse,** 170 E.121st St., SE cor. Sylvan Place, bet. Lexington and Third Aves. 1891-1893. *Thom & Wilson.* ✒

Bold brick and brownstone, a spectacular 1890s palace of justice, now used for far more

[E23b] **Elmendorf Reformed Church,** 171 E.121st St., bet. Sylvan Place and Third Ave. ca. 1910.

A painted neo-Georgian limestone façade for the oldest congregation in Harlem, successor to the Dutch church founded here in 1660.

[E24a] **Chambers Memorial Baptist Church**/ originally **Carmel Baptist Church**/then **Harlem Baptist Church,** 219 E.123rd St., bet. Second and Third Aves. 1891.

A gabled smooth and stolid two-toned brick façade is modulated by an elegant array of Romanesque Revival arched windows and trabeated doors.

[E24b] **Police Services Area (PSA) No.5,** New York City Police Department, 221-235 E.123rd St., bet. Second and Third Aves. 1998. *Herbert Beckhard and Frank Richlan.*

A brick and limestone field office for what used to be the New York City Housing Police. A nice recent neighbor for **Chambers Memorial** next door.

[E24c] **Iglesia Adventista del Septimo Dia**/originally **Our Saviour Lutheran Church** (Norwegian), 237 E.123rd St., bet. Second and Third Aves. ca. 1912.

A humble façade enriched by an entrance arch, an oculus of stained glass, and an arched corble-table running under the sheltering roof.

[E25] **Taino Towers**, bet. E.122nd and E.123rd Sts., Second and Third Aves. 1979. *Silverman & Cika.*

Unlike most government-subsidized housing, this project was sponsored by a persistent coalition of local residents, politicians, and community leaders in concert with the project's architects. The results are an implant from **Miami Beach**: crisp 35-story towers reflecting the sky in floor-to-ceiling glass (without shading or thermal qualities later necessitated by energy-saving requirements). A bizarre, out-of-context neighbor.

[E26] Originally **Hook and Ladder Co. No.14**/now **Engine Co. No.36**, New York City Fire Dept., 120 E.125th St. 1888. *Napoleon LeBrun.*

Fire laddies and fire horses erupted from this Harlem landmark in the neighborhood's not-so-gay nineties. Clad in red brick and brownstone, an original dragon-head hoist above delivered hay for the resident horses (in the manner that old Dutch-gabled New York faced its pediments to the street, allowing similar transfer from street, or canal, to attic storage).

[E27] **125th Street Branch, The New York Public Library**, 224 E.125th Street. 1904. *McKim, Mead & White.*

Renaissance Revival in the manner of a Florentine palazzo. Clad in rusticated Indiana limestone, three stories high and three bays wide.

NECROLOGY

MaBSTOA Bus Garage/once **Metropolitan Street Railway Company** (trolley barn), E.99th to E.100th Sts., Lexington to Park Aves. ca. 1885.

In 1907 the Metropolitan Street Railway Company controlled 47 streetcar lines and 300 miles of track. That year its 3,280 cars handled 571 million passengers—not all from this barn, thank goodness—which limited its activities only to the Lexington Avenue and Lenox Avenue lines. The acronym is for Manhattan and Bronx Surface Transit Operating Authority. The replacement facility is functional, up-to-date, and banal.

Church of the Resurrection, East Harlem Protestant Parish, 325 E.101st St., bet. First and Second Aves. 1965. *Victor A. Lundy.*

A cocked hat among vacant lots. Economy dictated the substitution of a built-up roof for the intended brick-paved surface, and economics provided poor maintenance. The interior was more inviting. Obliterated.

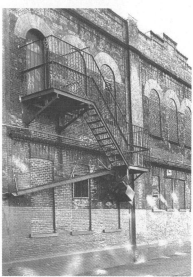

Necrology: MaBSTOA Bus Garage

Iglesia Luterana Sion/originally **St. Johannes Kirche** (Lutheran), 217 E.119th St., bet. Second and Third Aves. 1873.

An early brick church for this community, then remote from the City's center. The church began as a home for a German-speaking congregation. An unobtrusive little fellow, demolished for better (?) things.

Upper Manhattan

U2, Church of the Intercession

Upper Manhattan is the **finger pointing north-ward** toward the Bronx, a slender finial on this otherwise fat island. The district's southern boundary is marked by Trinity Cemetery at 155th Street, that northern ending of the 1811 commissioners plan beyond which New York "could never grow."

Indian cave dwellers once lived in Inwood Hill Park. The father of our country not only gave part of this area its name—Washington Heights—but also slept here (and headquartered) in what is now referred to as the **Morris-Jumel Mansion**. Once a country preserve of the wealthy, some estates have remained intact, although the rich live elsewhere. Museums, a park, a medical center, a bus terminal, and a university now occupy such land; and, in addition, other sacred and profane institutions ornament the district. Filled mainly with apartment houses, it is one of the City's most densely pop-

ulated sectors; its parks, institutions, and dramatic river views make it one of the most livable. The IRT Broadway-Seventh Avenue subway, which reached Dyckman Street and Fort George Hill in 1906, was the major impetus for development of the eastern section. The IND Eighth Avenue subway arrived in 1932, encouraging still more apartment house construction.

Within Upper Manhattan, and particularly in the sector called **Washington Heights**, there has been a maze of ethnic subcommunities. The long-departed Irish have been replaced by blacks, Latinos, and, surprisingly, yuppies, who are rediscovering the virtues of this enclave. Greek and Armenian populations were once large; and in the 1930s, after Hitler's accession to power, so many German-Jewish refugees settled here that the area was termed the **Fourth Reich**.

UPPER MANHATTAN KEY MAP

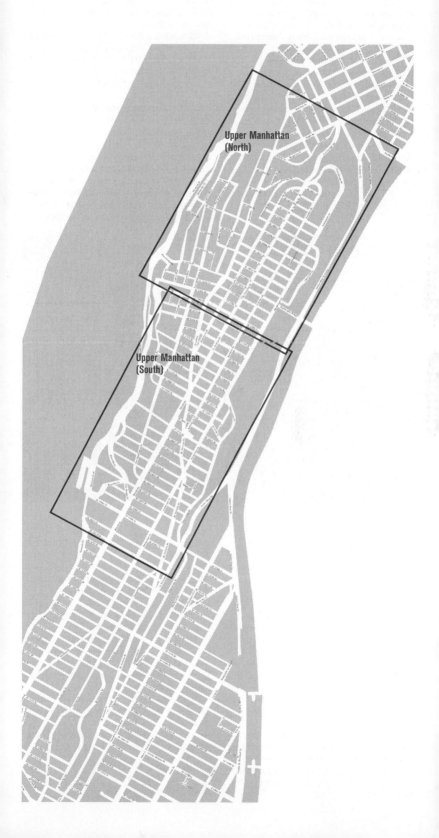

Upper Manhattan
(North)

Upper Manhattan
(South)

WASHINGTON HEIGHTS

[U1] **Trinity Cemetery**, Amsterdam Ave. to Riverside Dr., W.153rd to W.155th Sts. Boundary walls and gates, 1876. Gatehouse and keeper's lodge, 1883. *Vaux & Radford*. Grounds, 1881. *Vaux & Co.*, landscape architects. Open to the public.

Once part of the farm of *John James Audubon* (1785-1851), the great artist-naturalist (he is buried here), this farmland became the rural cemetery of Wall Street's Trinity Church. Here is bucolic topography: the cemetery climbs the hill from the river to Amsterdam Avenue, affording some idea of the topography of Manhattan Island before man cut, molded, and veneered it with brick, concrete, and asphalt. *Audubon's* home, **Minniesland**, was near the river at 155th Street. On Christmas Eve carolers visit the grave of *Clement Clarke Moore*, author of "A Visit from Saint Nicholas."

The memorial to the church's architect, *Bertram Grosvenor Goodhue* (*Lee Lawrie,* sculptor. 1929.) gives a Protestant interpretation to the royal tombs of St. Denis:

THIS TOMB IS A TOKEN OF THE AFFECTION OF
HIS FRIENDS
HIS GREAT ARCHITECTURAL CREATIONS THAT
BEAUTIFY THE LAND AND ENRICH CIVILIZATION
ARE HIS MONUMENTS.

[U3] **Audubon Terrace Historic District**, Broadway bet. W.155th and W.156th Sts. W side. Master plan, 1908. *Charles Pratt Huntington*. ♦

Three small museums, a church, and the National Institute of Arts and Letters once joined in this awkwardly proportioned court, part of the **Beaux Arts/American Renaissance** of the early 20th century. Enlivened in recent years by the conversion of the old American

U1

U3

Sadly missing today is the suspension bridge over Broadway (*Vaux, Withers & Co.,* architects, *George K. Radford,* engineer), which linked the cemetery's halves. It was demolished in 1911 to build:

[U2] **Church of the Intercession** (Episcopal)/originally **Chapel of the Intercession, and Vicarage**, 550 W.155th St., SE cor. Broadway. 1910-1914. *Bertram Goodhue of Cram, Goodhue & Ferguson*. ♦

Set at the edge of Trinity Cemetery, the largest chapel of Trinity Parish, now an independent church. Here dreams of **Gothic Revival** came true: a large "country" church, tower and cloister, parish house, and vicarage—all mounted on a bucolic bluff overlooking the Hudson. Inside, stone piers support a wood hammer-beam roof, washed in light from glass that is seemingly from **13th-century France**. Loose chairs, rather than pews, make it even more French. A charming cloister at the 155th Street entry.

Geographical Society building into **Boricua College,** and the (temporary) residency of the **Dia Center.**

[U3a] **Hispanic Society of America, East Building**/originally **Museum of the American Indian**, Heye Foundation, Audubon Terr., 3745 Broadway, NW cor. W.155th St. 1915-1922. *Charles Pratt Huntington*.

Originally the private collection of *George Heye*, this comprehensive museum was concerned with the prehistory of the Western Hemisphere and with the contemporary Native American, continent-wide.

The Museum collection relocated to new quarters on the Mall in Washington, while a boutique collection remains in the old **Custom House** at Bowling Green. The architecture of the building, flanked on 155th Street with a powerful

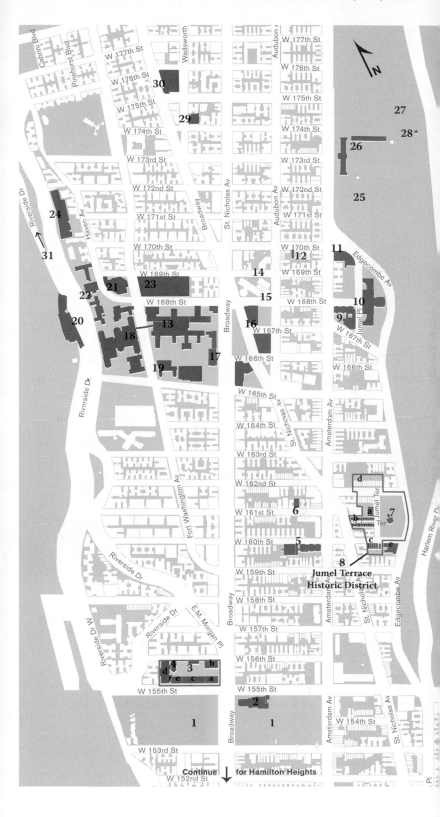

Ionic colonnade, is generic museum architecture of its time, Classical and pompous. The **Native Americans** (Indians) had no say in the matter.

🏛 [U3b] **Boricua College**/originally **American Geographical Society,** Audubon Terr., 3755 Broadway, SW cor. W.156th St. 1911. *Charles Pratt Huntington.*

A physically central place for information storage is less vital in the Internet Age: therefore, the Society's map collection, the largest in the Western Hemisphere, was lured to Milwaukee,

U3f

where the University provides better quarters and financial support. The replacement tenant, **Boricua College,** caters to Puerto Rican students, vital for the surrounding community. For maps that were here: *www.uwm.edu/Library/AGSL*

🏛 [U3c] **Hispanic Society of America, Museum & Library,** Audubon Terr., Broadway, bet. W.155th and W.156th Sts. W side. W Building, 1904-1908, *Charles Pratt Huntington.* E Building and additions to W Building, 1910-1926, *Charles Pratt Huntington, Erik Strindberg, and H. Brooks Price.* Museum open: Tu-Sa 10-4:30; Su 1-4; closed Mo. North Building open: Tu-Sa 10:15-4; closed Su. East Building open: Tu-Sa 10-4:30; Su 1-4; closed Mo. 212-926-2234.

A happy irony: the **Hispanics** in question were mostly those from Iberia and, sometimes, equidistant **South America**. Another Hispanic group now surrounds this symbolic site, making it an appropriate centerpiece to a newly arrived population.

The richly appointed storehouse of Hispanic painting, sculpture, and decorative arts confronts a pompous neo-Baroque sunken court (part of this unfortunate cul-de-sac) filled with lots of dull and academic bronze sculpture (by donor *Archer Huntington's* wife, *Anna Hyatt Huntington*). Would you believe *El Cid* plus a deer, a doe, a fawn, and four heroes?

Recently sharing its home with the **Dia Center for the Arts,** before and after a fixture in West Chelsea.

🏛 [U3d] **American Academy of Arts and Letters,** Audubon Terr. Administration Building, 633 W.155th St. 1921-1923. *William M. Kendall of McKim, Mead & White.* Auditorium and Gallery, 632 W.156th St. 1928-1930. *Cass Gilbert.* Museum open to the public when exhibitions are mounted: 212-368-5900. Tu-Su 1-4; closed Mo. *www.artsandletters.org*

The **Anglo-Italian Renaissance** clubhouse of an academy honoring distinguished persons in literature and the fine arts. The administration

U4

building contains a permanent exhibition of the works of the American impressionist *Childe Hassam,* a library, and a museum of manuscripts of past and present members.

On high the cornice is emblazoned:

ALL ARTS ARE ONE, ALL BRANCHES ON ONE TREE...
HOLD HIGH THE FLAMING TORCH FROM AGE TO AGE.

Chuck Close, Don DeLillo, Joan Didion, Peter Eisenman, E.L. Doctorow, Frank Gehry, Michael Graves, Red Grooms, Steven Holl, Hugh Hardy, John Irving, Garrison Keillor, Harper Lee, Maya Lin, John McPhee, Richard Meier, Cesar Pelli, I.M. Pei, Wallace Shawn, Calvin Trillin, Billie Tsien, and *Robert Venturi* are all among the many current members who like to write things, say things, and build things. **Fun parties?**

[U3e] **American Academy of Arts and Letters Annex**/formerly the **American Numismatic Society**, Audubon Terr., Broadway, bet. W.155th and W.156th Sts. W side. S side of courtyard. 1907. *Charles Pratt Huntington.*

Originally the museum of money and decorations: paper, coins, medals, and whatever, until moving downtown in 2005. The **Academy of Arts and Letters** has moved in (art collections have a way of constantly expanding).

[U3f] **New Entrance Link**, between the **American Academy of Arts and Letters** and the former **Numismatic Society**. 2009. *James Vincent Czajka with Pei Cobb Freed & Partners.*

Virtually invisible, this transparent link between two **Beaux Arts** monoliths is constructed with only seven pieces of glass! The floor, also glass, glows with light from below. Very simple. Richly elegant.

infilled with brick in the manner of **Henri IV**. Look up, and the illusion vanishes: a very American eagle, assisted by bundled Roman fasces.

[U7] Originally **Roger and Mary Phillipse House**/often known as the **Morris-Jumel Mansion**, 1765 Jumel Terr., bet. W.160th and W.162nd Sts. 1765. Remodeled, ca. 1810. ☀ Interior. ☀ Open to the public: We-Su 10-4; closed Mo & Tu. 212-923-8008. *www.morrisjumel.org*

U7

U5

[U4] **Church of Our Lady of Esperanza** (Roman Catholic), 624 W.156th St., bet. Broadway and Riverside Dr. 1912. *Charles Pratt Huntington.* Remodeled, 1925, *Lawrence G. White of McKim, Mead & White.*

By *Lawrence*, son of *Stanford*. The green and gold interior contains stained glass windows, a skylight, and a lamp—all given by *King Alfonso XIII* of Spain at its opening in 1912.

[U5] **The Duke Ellington School**, 500 W.160th St., SW cor. Amsterdam Ave. 1996. *Gruzen Samton.*

A refreshing variation from the minimal boxes of the 1950s, 1960s and 1970s. Here the *Duke* is honored by thoughtful architecture.

[U6] **Engine Company No.384, Hook & Ladder No.34**, N.Y.C. Fire Department, 515 W.161st St., bet. Amsterdam Ave. and Broadway. N side. 1906. *Francis H. Kimball.* ☀

A wishful *hôtel particulier* (Parisian town house) in Beaux Arts rusticated limestone,

Built by *Roger Morris* as a summer residence for his family, it served during the Revolution as *Washington*'s headquarters. But for most of that war the house was in British hands (as was all of Manhattan and, therefore, all of New York of that day). After the war it served as a farmhouse and tavern until 1810, when *Stephen Jumel* purchased it and partially renovated the house in the then-modern **Federal** style. Since then the finest view in Manhattan has been blocked by bulky apartment buildings to the south.

Tuscan-columned, **Georgian-Federal** style, with a façade of wood boards and quoins simulating stone, and a shingled behind. The hipped roofs to balustraded captain's walks are admirable cornices to this classic square linked to an octagon. A mile marker in the north lawn cites the distance from New York as 11 miles!

Morris's 115 surrounding acres were developed by the *Jumel* heirs after 1882 into 1,058 auctioned lots!

[U7a] **10-18 Jumel Terrace**, bet. W.160th and W.162nd Sts. W side. 1896. *Henri Fouchaux.*
    Lime- and brownstone stalwarts worthy of the best Upper West Side park blocks.

[U7b] **1-19, 2-20 Sylvan Terrace**, bet. Jumel Terr. and St. Nicholas Ave. 1882-1883. *Gilbert R. Robinson, Jr.*
    Two-story wood houses: savor the wooden canopies and the doors at No.5. Here are green shutters, brown hoods, and cream clapboards: a revived memory of very old New York. The streetbed of Sylvan Terrace is the path of the *Morrises'* original driveway.

[U7c] **West 160th Street** (row houses), bet. Edgecombe and St. Nicholas Aves. S side. No.418, 1890. *Walgrove & Israels.* **Nos.420-430**, 1891. *Richard R. Davis.*
    Brick and brownstone, with up-and-down picturesque profiles.

U7d

[U7d] **430-438 West 162nd Street**, bet. Jumel Terr. and St. Nicholas Ave. 1896. *Henri Fouchaux.*
    A phalanx of bow-fronts in limestone, carefully cared-for survivors. Bas reliefs, modest pier capitals, and substantial cornices enrich the façades.

[U7e] Originally **The Roger Morris**, 555 Edgecombe Ave., bet. W.159th and W.160th Sts. 1914-1916. *Schwartz & Gross.* ●✋
    Count Basie, Paul Robeson, Joe Louis, and Kenneth Clark all passed some time here. Otherwise as innocuous as most Park Avenue apartment houses.

[U8] **Jumel Terrace Historic District**, around Jumel Terr. bet. W.160th and W.162nd Sts., Edgecombe Ave. and St. Nicholas Ave., including 50 row houses and one apartment house. ●✋ See its limits on the map.

[U9] **P.S. 8, The Luis Belliard School**, 465 W.167th St., bet. Jumel Pl. and Amsterdam Ave. N side. 1996. *Gruzen Samton.*
    An exuberant set of boxes containing a tight, very European-scaled entrance courtyard. All enlivened with rampant polychromy.

[U10] **I.S. 90**, Jumel Place and 168th St. 1999. *Richard Dattner & Assocs.*
    A staid neighbor for P.S. 8 next door. The curved cornice (reminiscent of ancient Egyptian cavetto cornices) soberly crowns the brick body.

[U11] **33rd Precinct Station House**, W.170th St., bet. Jumel Pl. and Amsterdam Ave. 1997-2002. *Dattner Architects.*
    "A curved façade recalling Castle Clinton is

U9

bisected by a playful canopied atrium, creating a 'friendly fortress' in keeping with the community policing initiatives of the NYPD." Thus said *Dattner.* Now complete, it seems a plausible description. A handsome neighbor.

[U12] **Engine Company No.67**, N.Y.C. Fire Department, 518 W.170th St., bet. Amsterdam and Audubon Aves. 1901. *Flagg & Chambers.* ●✋
    Those who brought you the great firehouse on **Great Jones Street** brought here two years later an economy model of its monumental façade.

IRT's Hoosick: Named after the Hoosick Tunnel near North Adams, Mass., which holds the record as the longest two-track tunnel in the U.S. The tunnel, for the IRT Broadway-Seventh Avenue Line, is cut through solid rock under Broadway and St. Nicholas Avenue between W.157th Street and Fort George.

U7b

U10

Columbia-Presbyterian complex:

[U13] **Columbia-Presbyterian Medical Center,**
W.165th to W.168th Sts., Broadway to Riverside
Dr. 1928-1947. *James Gamble Rogers.* 1947-1964,
Rogers & Butler. 1964-1974, *Rogers Butler &
Burgun.*

Situated on a bluff over the Hudson, the
original Center buildings of this vast teaching
hospital are bulky and banal, the streetscape a
bore. Inside, however, medical wonders are performed. Later buildings, cited below, show great
promise.

[U14] **Irving Cancer Research Center**,
E. side Broadway bet. 165th and 168th
Sts. 2005. *Davis Brody Bond.*
[U15] **Russ Berrie Medical Science Pavilion,**
SE cor. W.168th St. and St. Nicholas Ave. 1997.
Davis Brody Bond.

Sleek *DBB* creations in the expanding flock
of Medical Center satellite researchers: **Lasker**
and **Berrie Pavilions** were here first, now joined
by **Irving** and the **Milstein Heart Center.**

[U16] **Mary Woodard Lasker Biomedical
Research Building**/Audubon Research
Park/originally **Audubon Theatre and
Ballroom**/onetime **Beverly Hills Theatre**/later
San Juan Theatre, Broadway at W.165th St.
E side. 1912. *Thomas W. Lamb.* **Alterations and
new building**, 1996, *Davis Brody Bond.*
Preservation façade, *Jan Hird Pokorny.*

A former theater with terra-cotta glazed
polychromy along its Broadway façade:
corniced and encrusted, in counterpoint to
Babies' Hospital opposite, which is detail-less,
except for its babies. In 1965, Black Muslim
leader *Malcolm X* was assassinated during a
rally in the second-floor ballroom. Plans to
demolish the theater in 1992 led to this compromise: partial demolition, partial restoration.

U16

U14

U17

U18

U19

[U17] **Morgan Stanley Children's Hospital**, 3959 Broadway, NW cor. 165th St. 2003. *Davis Brody Bond*. Interior architecture, *Ewing Cole*.

Shades of *Rennie Mackintosh's* **Scotland Street School** (Glasgow, 1898) dress the corners of this sleek children's hospital. The architects have handled bulk elegantly, the detailing (pediments, recessed bay windows, et al) contributing to a scale appropriate for children (or for that matter, for anybody).

[U18] **Milstein Pavilion**, Presbyterian Hospital, W.165th to W.168th Sts., Broadway to Riverside Dr. 1989. *Skidmore, Owings & Merrill*.

A giant **postmodern/neo–Art Deco** behemoth overlooking the Hudson. It goes down almost as far as it goes up, with a grand terrace looking to, then stepping down to the west, as if a prime location to stage a *Busby Berkeley* extravaganza. The interconnecting bridges over Fort Washington Avenue interlace with adjacent hospital buildings and add a necessary and stimulating visual complexity to the urban scene.

[U19] **Vivian and Seymour Milstein Family Heart Center**, 165th St. and Fort Washington Ave. 2009. *Pei Cobb Freed & Partners*.

The bellying glass wall acts in counterpoint to existing masonry neighbors while providing panoramic views. Within, a four-story atrium organizes and lights the activities. The language is of cables and glass.

[U20] **The Psychiatric Institute, New York State Office of Mental Health**, Riverside Drive west of Milstein Pavilion. 1998. *Peter Pran of Ellerbe Becket*.

Designed in a computer-generated world similar to one used by *Zaha Hadid* and *Frank Gehry*. A serious medical building that vends its sinuous style as an independent event, unrelated to its fellow Medical Center partners.

Freud's library: In the Freud Memorial Room of the Neurological and Psychiatric Institutes is shelved part of Sigmund Freud's personal library.

[U21] Julius and Armand Hammer Health Sciences Center, 701 Fort Washington Ave., bet. W.168th and W.169th Sts. W side. 1976. *Warner, Burns, Toan & Lunde.*
[U22] Lawrence G. Kolb Research Building, 722 W.168th St., extended N along Haven Ave. W side. 1987. *Herbert W. Riemer.*

Hammer, a somber blockbuster in self-weathering steel and rose brick, takes after its cousin, Mt. Sinai's Annenberg Center (SOM. 1976), another medical center tower. The two appeared in the year of the U.S. bicentennial, showing that aging (through self-rusting) might be a sign of maturity.

U21

Next door is **Kolb,** a somber brick monolith with those sloping sills of the stylish 1970s.

[U23] Fort Washington Armory, bet. W.168th and W.169th Sts., Ft. Washington Ave. and Broadway. 1920s.
A Romanesque arch forms the monumental entrance to the only building to compete in scale with the giant Columbia-Presbyterian complex. The cavalry is no longer in residence, but for years this was one of the world's largest exam rooms (written) for those seeking architect's, engineer's, nurse's, et al., licensure.

[U24] Bard-Haven Towers, 100 Haven Ave., bet. W.169th and W.171st Sts. W side, overlooking Henry Hudson Pkwy. 1971. *Brown, Guenther, Battaglia & Galvin.*
Tall cliff-hangers (literally) that cling to the escarpment and enjoy Hudson views. The corbeled lower stories are a dramatic sight for drivers approaching the George Washington Bridge.

[U25] Highbridge Park, W.155th to Dyckman Sts., Edgecombe and Amsterdam Aves. to the Harlem River Dr. 1888. *Calvert Vaux and Samuel Parsons, Jr.* Altered.
Once the site of an amusement park, marina, and promenade, this park gains its beauty from a steep slope and rugged topography. An excellent vantage point to survey the Harlem River Valley.

[U26] Highbridge Park Play Center, Amsterdam Ave., bet. W.172nd and W.174th Sts. 1934-1936. *Aymar Embury II,* consulting architect. *Gilmore D.Clarke,* landscape architect. 🍎
Streamlined **Art Moderne,** as at the 1939-1940 **New York World's Fair.** Not surprising as *Clarke* was a major figure there as well.

[U27] High Bridge/originally **Aqueduct Bridge,** Highbridge Park at W.174th St. 1838-1848. *John B. Jervis and James Renwick, Jr.* Addition, 1860. Replacement of piers with new central span, 1923. 🍎

U23   U26

U27

The oldest remaining bridge connecting Manhattan to the mainland, built as an aqueduct, but also symbol of Croton water flowing to Manhattan (they could have piped it under the river). Originally consisting of closely spaced masonry piers and arches, the bridge's central bays were replaced by the present cast-iron arch to accomodate the **Harlem River Ship Canal.** The pedestrian walk, closed for many years, may re-open to the public in 2012.

[U28] Highbridge Water Tower, Highbridge Park at W.173rd St. 1866-1872. *John B. Jervis.* Reconstructed, 1989-1990, *William Hall Partnership.* 🍎
This landmark tower, originally used to equalize pressure in the **Croton Aqueduct,** now simply marks the Manhattan end of High Bridge. Damaged in a fire (arson), it has been carefully restored.

Riverside Dr Pa

53, 54

52

W 203rd St
Tenth Av
Ninth Av
W 202nd St
W 201st St
Academy St

Thayer St

Dongan Pl
Sherman Av
Arden St
Sickles St

Ellwood St
Nagle Av
Hillside Av
Fort George Hill
49
48
Dyckman St
Marginal Street Wharf

50
W 196th St

Bogardus Pl
Fort George Av

51

Hillside Av
Fort George Av

W 193rd St
W 193rd St
Broadway Ter
Fairview Av
W 192nd St
W 192nd St
St. Nicholas Av
Wadsworth Av
W 191st St

Amsterdam Av
47

W 190th St
W 100th St
Wadsworth Ter
W 190th St
W 189th St
Cabrini Blvd
Fort Washington Av
W 189th St
Audubon Av
Chittenden Av
W 188th St

Broadway
W 187th St
W 187th St
Washington Ter
44
43
W 186th St
Overlook Ter
W 186th St
46
40
W 185th St
Bennett Av
W 185th St
42
39
W 184th St
W 184th St
45
41
Laurel Hill Ter
W 183rd St
W 183rd St
Colonel Magaw Pl
W 182nd St
38
W 181st St
37   Washington Bridge
Plaza Lafayette
Cabrini Blvd
Pinehurst Blvd
Fort Washington Av
W 181st St
Wadsworth Av
W 180th St
St. Nicholas Av
Amsterdam Av
W 180th St
Haven Av
W 179th St
W 179th St
35
35
36   Alexander Hamilton Bridge
34
W 178th St
W 178th St
32,33
Cabrini Blvd
Pinehurst Blvd
W 177th St
Wadsworth Av
Audubon Av
W 177th St

U28

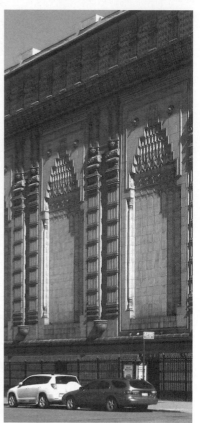

U30

[U31] **Henry Hudson Parkway**, from Van Cortlandt Park to and across Henry Hudson Bridge. Pavilion, in Fort Washington Park on Riverside Dr. at W.180th St. W side. 1913. *Jaros Kraus*.

Driving south into Manhattan on this Hudson-hugging parkway is one of New York's great gateway experiences. From Riverdale (the affluent West Bronx) one passes over the **Henry Hudson Bridge** (a dramatic object from the distance but a bore firsthand) before descending to

[U29] **Fort Washington Presbyterian Church**, 21 Wadsworth Ave., NE cor. W.174th St. 1914. *Thomas Hastings of Carrère & Hastings*. ●*

Brick and limestone **English Baroque**. **Tuscan** columns and pilasters downstairs, **Corinthian** columns and pilasters on the tower bring our minds back to *Christopher Wren's* (& *Nicholas Hawksmoor's*) 17th-century reconstruction of London's churches.

[U30] **United Church**/originally **Loew's 175th Street Theatre**, Broadway NE cor. W.175th St. 1930. *Thomas W. Lamb*. Altered.

Cambodian neo-Classical? The *Reverend Ike* holds forth here in splendor reminiscent of archaic **Miami Beach**. This terra-cotta place was at the apogee of movie palace glamour in those long-gone days when Hollywood ruled the world and free crockery on Wednesday nights was an added fillip. Compare with *Lamb's* **Loew's Pitkin Theater** in Brownsville, Brooklyn (p. 741).

the banks of the Hudson. Next, the **Cloisters**, romantically surmounting a hilltop, lonely and wondrous; through a wooded area; then under the majestic **George Washington Bridge**. All of a sudden the skyline of Manhattan materializes, and the rural-urban transition is complete.

[U32] **George Washington Bridge**, W.178th St. and Fort Washington Ave. over the Hudson River to Fort Lee, N.J. 1931. *O. H. Ammann*, engineer, & *Cass Gilbert*, architect. Lower level added, 1962.

"*The George Washington Bridge over the Hudson is the most beautiful bridge in the world. Made of cables and steel beams, it gleams in the sky like a reversed arch. It is blessed. It is the only seat of grace in the disordered city. It is painted an aluminum color and, between water and sky, you see nothing but the bent cord supported by two steel towers. When your car moves up the ramp the two towers rise so high that it brings you happiness; their structure is so pure, so resolute, so regular that here,*

U29

U34

U40

finally, steel architecture seems to laugh. The car reaches an unexpectedly wide apron; the second tower is very far away; innumerable vertical cables, gleaming against the sky, are suspended from the magisterial curve which swings down and then up. The rose-colored towers of New York appear, a vision whose harshness is mitigated by distance."
—Charles Edouard Jeanneret (Le Corbusier), *When the Cathedrals Were White*, 1947.

[U33] **Little Red Lighthouse**/originally **Jeffries Hook Lighthouse**, Fort Washington Park below the George Washington Bridge. Erected, Sandy Hook, New Jersey. 1880. Moved to present location, 1921. 🛥

Directly under the east tower of the Bridge, the lighthouse stood to steer grain barges away from the shoals of Jeffrey's Hook. When navigational lights were mounted on the bridge, it was no longer needed (1951) and put up for auction. A barrage of letters from children who had read

The Little Red Lighthouse and the Great Gray Bridge, by *Hildegarde Hoyt Swift* and *Lynd Ward*, saved it.

🚏 [U34] **George Washington Bridge Bus Station**, Fort Washington and Wadsworth Aves., W.178th to W.179th Sts. 1963. *Port Authority of New York* and *Pier Luigi Nervi.*

A concrete butterfly shelters a bus terminal at the end of the bridge, interlocking with the former IND Eighth Avenue subway. The shape is excused as a form for natural ventilation for the noxious buses, but also provides the opportunity for a formal tour de force for *Dr. Nervi*, an engineer more comfortable with Italian economics, where his skills provide the cheapest, as well as the most exciting, forms.

[U35] **Bridge Apartments**, bet. W.178th and W.179th Sts., Wadsworth and Audubon Aves. 1964. *Brown & Guenther.*

An early experiment in residential air rights over a highway, but fumes, dirt, and noise rise to the unfortunate dweller above. A lousy idea.

[U36] **Alexander Hamilton Bridge**, Highbridge Park bet. W.178th and W.179th Sts. over the Harlem River to the Bronx, 1964.

The bridge connecting the **Cross-Bronx Expressway** with the George Washington Bridge and New Jersey: serviceable but dull.

[U37] **Washington Bridge**, W.181st St. and Amsterdam Ave. over the Harlem River to University Avenue, The Bronx. 1886-1889. *Charles C. Schneider and Wilhelm Hildenbrand.* Modifications, Union Bridge Company, *William J. McAlpine, Theodore Cooper, DeLemos & Cordes,* with *Edward H.Kendall,* consulting architect. Reconstruction, 1989-1993.

A magnificent arched bridge **not to be confused** with the George Washington Bridge. A great filigree of steel is enjoyed by drivers on the Major Deegan or Harlem River Drive; but to those crossing on top it's just a flat plane.

[U38] **Fort Washington Collegiate Church,** Fort Washington Ave. NE cor. W.181st St. 1907.

This small country church dates from the time when Washington Heights was suburban; brick and timber **Gothic Revival.**

[U39] The highest point: In Bennett Park, along the west side of Fort Washington Avenue between 183rd and 185th Streets, is a rock outcropping that is the highest natural point in

U44

Manhattan, 267.75 feet above sea level. An added bonus is the outline of Revolutionary War Fort Washington, marked by stone pavers.

[U40] **Hebrew Tabernacle of Washington Heights,** 185th St., NW cor. Fort Washington Ave. 1930s.

From the time of Radio City Music Hall, limestone, stainless steel, and brass in the Art Moderne of the 1930s.

[U41] **Hudson View Gardens,** 116 Pinehurst Ave., bet. W.183rd and W.185th Sts. W side. 1924-1925. *George F. Pelham.*

Scarsdale Tudor once encrusted with Virginia creeper, and brick with simulated half-timbering. This romantic but urbane cluster of multiple dwellings embraces private gardens and enjoys, from many parts, romantic river views.

[U42] **Castle Village,** 120-200 Cabrini Blvd., bet. W.181st and W.186th Sts. W side. 1938-1939. *George F. Pelham II.*

At **Hudson View,** *Pelham père* embraced his public space; at Castle Village *Pelham fils* planted himself in it. Each floor of these cruciform buildings contains nine apartments, eight with river views. The site was formerly occupied by the *Charles Paterno* estate; massive walls retained the building site until a terrifying collapse in 2005 (now rebuilt in concrete).

[U43] **16 Chittenden Avenue,** at W.186th St. (Alex Rose Place). 1920s.

The guest house of the former *Paterno* estate perches on a great pier that drops to the parkway's edge below. Forget the house; enjoy the pier, and be jealous of the view.

Yeshiva University:

Yeshiva University Campus, W.183rd to W.187th Sts., along Amsterdam Ave.

U45

A mixed bag of architectural tricks, more a collection of separate opportunities than a whole that might have been greater than the sum of its parts.

[U44] **Main Building, Yeshiva University,** 2540 Amsterdam Ave., SW cor. W.187th St. 1928. *Charles B. Meyers Assocs.*

One of the great romantic structures of its time. Domes, towers, and turrets can be seen from miles away, and the architect's lavish use of orange stone, copper and brass, ceramic tile, and **Middle Eastern** eclectic architectural detail makes it a serious confection, this latter quality, perhaps, promoting a lust for learning.

[U45] **Science Center, Belter Graduate School of Science,** Yeshiva University, 2495 Amsterdam Ave., at W.184th St. E side. 1968. *Armand Bartos & Assocs.*

Monumental but hollow brick piers for a warehouse of science.

U46

U48

[U46] **Mendel Gottesman Library**, Yeshiva University, 2520 Amsterdam Ave., bet. W.185th and W.186th Sts. W side. 1967. *Armand Bartos & Assocs.* Museum (in the library) open to the public.

A rich tour de force of brick, terra cotta, and glass, highly articulated to make the best of sun, shadow, and view: in effect, super bay windows. *Bartos* was architect, with sometime partner, *Frederic Kiesler*, for the **Shrine of the Book** (housing the Dead Sea Scrolls) in Jerusalem.

[U47] **Isabella Neimath Home and Geriatric Center**, 525 Audubon Ave., bet. W.190th and W.191st Sts. E side. 1965. *Joseph D. Weiss.*

A home for the elderly, providing small apartments for their varied special needs. The pitched and folded roof was designed ostensibly in deference to its older neighbor (the original home), which no longer exists: it (the original home) was later replaced by an addition to this addition. Oh, well; so goes overdone contextualism.

[U48] **P.S. 5,** 3704 Tenth Ave., NE cor. Dyckman St. 1992. *Gruzen Samton.*

Colorful and playful, a departure from many years of somber schools. It is one of the **"systems schools,"** where a designed kit of parts, classrooms, cafeterias, and common spaces can be reused in different assemblies and configurations for a series of school buildings.

A flock of children from P.S. 5 could row next door:

[U49] **Peter Jay Sharp Boathouse,** Swindler Cove Park, Harlem River Drive at Dyckman Street, south of Sherman Creek. 2004. *Robert A.M. Stern Architects, Armand LeGardeur.*

The first serious, consciously created, floating architecture in the City (as opposed to the default floating architecture of the South Street Seaport ships). Less constrained than buildings founded on earth, here rides an exotic **neo-Victorian** pleasure craft.

U50

The New York Rowing Association introduces
local children and adults to the sport of rowing,
which once flourished on the **Harlem River**.

[U50] **Intermediate School 218**, The Salome
Ureña de Henriquez School, 4600 Broadway, NE
cor. W.196th St. 1990s. *Richard Dattner &
Associates.*

A grand exedra of banded brick, the center
stairway cylinder wrapped in glass block, providing a touch of **1930s** nostalgia.

De profundis: The two deepest subway stations
in the City are near here (why deepest? the land
merely gets higher and the tracks become, relatively, lower!). The IRT-Broadway Seventh
Avenue station at 191st Street and Saint
Nicholas Avenue (180 feet below the street, or
the street is 180 feet above the subway), and
the IND Eighth Avenue station at 190th Street
and Fort Washington Avenue (165 feet down). In
both cases elevators whisk passengers up and
down: level-equalizers.

[U51] **Fort Tryon Park Scenic Landmark**, W.192nd
to Dyckman Sts., Broadway to Riverside Dr.
1930-1935. *Frederick Law Olmsted, Jr.* Planting
plan, *James W. Dawson.* 🍎

A gift of the *Rockefeller* family to New York
City, this site was, in large part, the former
C.K.G. Billings estate (the triple-arched driveway from Riverside Drive was its entrance). The
park is famous for its Heather Garden.

The fort's grand site still remains; a plaque
states:

THE NORTHERN OUTWORK OF
FORT WASHINGTON, ITS GALLANT DEFENSE
AGAINST THE HESSIAN TROOPS BY THE
MARYLAND AND VIRGINIA REGIMENT,
16 NOVEMBER 1776, WAS SHARED BY
MARGARET CORBIN, THE FIRST AMERICAN
WOMAN TO TAKE A SOLDIER'S PART
IN THE WAR FOR LIBERTY.

U52

[U52] The Cloisters, Metropolitan Museum of Art, Fort Tryon Park. 1934-1939. *Charles Collens of Allen, Collens & Willis.* ✆ Alterations to receive the Fuentadueña Chapel, 1961, *Brown, Lawford & Forbes.* Open to the public: Mar-Oct: Tu-Su 9:30-5:15; closed Mo. Nov-Feb: Tu-Su 9:30-4:45; closed Mo. 212-923-3700. *www.metmuseum.org/cloisters/general*

Named for the French and Spanish monastic cloisters imported and reassembled here in concert with a 12th-century chapter house, the **Fuentadueña Chapel**, and Gothic and Romanesque chapels. Concept and reality are both romantic, and siting at this riverviewing crest an overwhelming confrontation between the City and a Hudson River School painter's view of—not surprisingly—the Hudson River.

The contents are the majority of the medieval art collection of the Metropolitan Museum of Art; most impressive are the **Unicorn tapestries**. A **Renaissance fair** is held here annually.

The tower, of course, is an office building.

U53

U54

Off the map to the north is the Dyckman House, don't miss it:

[U53] Dyckman House, 4881 Broadway NW cor. W.204th St. ca. 1785. Restoration, 1915-1916. *Alexander M. Welch.* ✆ Open to the public: We-Sa 11-4; Su 12-4; closed Mo-Tu. 212-304-9422. *www.dyckmanfarmhouse.org*

The site is monumental, the porch lovely. Rebuilt by *William Dyckman* after the British destroyed its predecessor, this is the only 18th-century farmhouse remaining in Manhattan. With its gambrel roof and brick and fieldstone lower walls, the house shows strong **Dutch** influence. The interior, with random-width chestnut floors and original family furnishings, is well worth a visit.

[U54] Columbia University Stadium, in Baker Field, W.218th St., NW cor. Broadway. 1986. *Richard Dattner & Associates.*

Cool concrete. A simple, graceful understated settee for **Ivy League** football watchers. It is said that college football in the northeast is a cultural pursuit (and in the west, entertainment; in the north, an allegory; in the south, religion).

BROOKLYN
Borough of Brooklyn / Kings County

 Colonial

 Georgian / Federal

 Greek Revival

 Gothic Revival

 Villa

 Romanesque Revival

 Renaissance Revival

 Roman Revival

 Art Deco / Art Moderne

 Modern / Postmodern

 Designated Landmark

Brooklyn *is* New York, but in ways that are proudly different from Manhattan. The most populous of the boroughs, Brooklyn has substantially more people than Manhattan and more people than Philadelphia, Baltimore, and Detroit *combined* (and yet it *still* has no major league baseball team!). Brooklyn is a matrix of **neighborhoods**: row houses, apartment blocks, and cottages marching from the steep slopes of its highest elevation at Cypress Hills south past Flatbush and Brownsville to the tidal flats of Gerritsen Beach, west to Coney Island and Bay Ridge, up the river to Red Hook and Brooklyn Heights, DUMBO, Williamsburg, and Greenpoint. At a smaller scale, those neighborhoods are defined by a seemingly endless, repeating sequence of stoops, rooftops, street trees (*London Plane, Honey Locust*), and backyard gardens.

The Town of Breukelen was established before 1658 and incorporated as a city in 1834. Brooklyn came into its own in the 19th century, when it began gobbling up adjacent villages: Williamsburgh and the Town of Bushwick in 1855, New Lots in 1886, Flatbush, Gravesend, and New Utrecht in 1894, Flatlands in 1896. The **Brooklyn Bridge**, Gothic Revival in style but modernist in spirit, largely shepherded to completion in 1883 by Brooklynites, provided a physical link to Manhattan and a new identity and confidence for the thriving young city. But Brooklyn itself was consolidated into greater New York City in 1898. The original Town, later City, of Brooklyn encompassed all the **brownstone** neighborhoods that have become fashionable in recent years, mostly atop the high ground left by the last glacier, the terminal moraine. Downtown, Brooklyn Heights, Fort Greene, Clinton Hill, Park Slope, Bedford-Stuyvesant, Crown Heights, Cobble Hill, Boerum Hill, Red Hook, Gowanus, and Sunset Park are all within the boundaries of the original town.

Brooklyn attained its identity and architectural cohesiveness largely because of its great 19th-century architects, including *Frank Freeman, William Tubby,* and *Rudolph L. Daus*, who were mostly forgotten once the modern movement gained a foothold in the 20th century. As modern architects succumbed to their passion for all things new and geometric, the glories of brownstone Brooklyn were rediscovered and preserved by young families, artists, and writers in the 1960s. But while Brooklyn Heights, followed by Park Slope and Cobble Hill, became more and more trendy (and expensive), much of the rest of the borough was unaffected by boom, bust, and fashion.

That all changed in the recent decade's pell-mell **Building Boom**, when neighborhoods like Carroll Gardens, Boerum Hill, Williamsburg, Fort Greene, and Red Hook *(Red Hook, for Pete's sake!)* were successfully marketed as the cool new places to be. The magazine *New*

BROOKLYN

·THE·BROOKLYN·APPROACH·

York suddenly seemed to have a reporter in every new restaurant, sampling fish tacos and inspecting mojitos, and even the staff of the *New Yorker* seemed to be finally (vaguely) aware of the borough's existence. Sunset Park, Gowanus, Bed-Stuy, Bushwick, and Greenpoint also became, at least partially, gentrified by incoming young families, Wallstreeters, and recent Ivy League grads. The Boom led to some egregious new buildings: cheaply constructed brick and glass boxes festooned with through-the-wall air conditioners, passed off as "luxury housing." The lifestyle, not the building, became the thing to sell. The marketing campaign for one *Robert Scarano*-designed condominium on Bond Street, only one block from the fetid Gowanus Canal, promised an "awakening of the senses" and claimed the building was "fueled by nature." Old Brooklynites could be seen sitting on their stoops and shaking their grey heads at the wonder of it all.

But the Boom also brought serious architects and architecture back to Brooklyn. *Richard Meier* built a huge glass contraption next to Grand Army Plaza. *James Stewart Polshek's* Newtown Creek Wastewater Treatment Plant was an architecturally bold, environmentally ambitious addition to Greenpoint. *Rafael Viñoly* and the late *Charles Gwathmey* both contributed whimsical children's museums in Crown Heights. *Sara Caples* and *Everardo Jefferson* completed substantial community-minded projects in Brownsville.

Trees, lots of them, do grow in Brooklyn, but since *Olmsted and Vaux's* Prospect Park, new parks have been few and far between. But critical new landscape projects have been undertaken in the last decade, including *Michael Van Valkenburgh's* long-awaited **Brooklyn Bridge Park** (in progress) and *Lee Weintraub's* **Erie Basin Park** in Red Hook.

West Central Brooklyn

Brooklyn is nothing if not vast. Much of Old Brooklyn is infinitely walkable, but for the farthest reaches (Spring Creek, Canarsie, Flatlands, New Lots) driving is easier. Before heading out to Greenpoint or Bushwick, though, it's best to start the tour in the heart of Old Brooklyn.

CIVIC CENTER / DOWNTOWN BROOKLYN

The independent City of Brooklyn moved quickly to give form to its identity by building a city hall, which still stands as its seat of borough affairs. As the 19th century progressed, Brooklyn's population and wealth grew, and so did its civic center. With city hall as the focus, there soon emerged a variety of richly embellished governmental and commercial buildings, hotels, and shopping emporia. But to a visitor to Downtown Brooklyn during this era of expansion, the most apparent features were not its richly ornamented buildings but the spindly iron trestles that inundated many of its major streets, throwing zebra-striped shadows. For this part of Brooklyn was to be not only the City's hub of government and shopping but of

D2

D1

transportation as well, and the elevated trains (els) crisscrossing overhead made their way down Fulton Street and Myrtle Avenue to their connections to Manhattan. It was not until after World War II that the elevated filigrees were demolished and today's Cadman Plaza Park built.

Civic Center/Downtown Brooklyn Walking Tour: From Borough Hall to the Flatbush Avenue-Fulton Street intersection, about a half-mile walk. (Subway to the Borough Hall Station of the IRT Lexington and Seventh Avenue Lines [Nos. 2, 3, 4, & 5 trains], or the BMT Court Street Station, Court Street exit [M, N, & R trains].)

The first buildings are gathered around Cadman Plaza. A walk, in general, north from Joralemon Street to Tillary Street and beyond:

[D1] **Brooklyn Borough Hall**/originally **Brooklyn City Hall**, 209 Joralemon St., at Cadman Plaza W. and Court St. N side. 1845-1848. *Gamaliel King*. Cupola, 1898, *Vincent C.*

Griffith and Stoughton & Stoughton. Statue of Justice installed and building restored, 1987-1989, *Conklin & Rossant*. ☙

A **Greek Revival** Palace, later crowned with a Victorian cupola, it presents a bold face to Cadman Plaza, particularly monumental due to the broad, steep mass of steps rising to its entrance colonnade. First intended to be a lesser copy of **New York's City Hall** (1802-1811) across the river, the project went through four designs. In the elapsed time aesthetic moods changed, and the Franco-Georgian design of 1802 became the Greek Revival world of the 1830s and 1840s. According to Brooklyn's city directory, *King* was a grocer until 1830, then a carpenter—not unusual in an era when *Thomas Jefferson* designed the University of Virginia, and the Capitol of the United States was built according to the competition-winning design of a physician, *William Thornton*.

[D2] **Brooklyn Municipal Building**, 210 Joralemon St., SE cor. Court St., opposite Borough Hall. 1926. *McKenzie, Voorhees & Gmelin.*

The background building where much of the municipal bureaucracy functions, as contrasted with the foreground building, **Borough Hall**, the ceremonial center. A grand set of Tuscan columns presents an entrance to the subway.

D3

[D3] **Brooklyn Law School Annex**, 250 Joralemon St., bet. Court St. and Boerum Pl. 1994. *Robert A.M. Stern.*

Postmodern in the free-wheeling neo-Renaissance sense, but blandly executed. But it is an architectural prizewinner compared to its earlier neighbor, the 1970s **Law School**.

[D4] **Borough Hall Station, IRT Lexington Avenue Line**, below Joralemon St., E of Court St. 1908. *Samuel B. Parsons,* chief engineer. *Heins & La Farge,* architects. Redesigned and restored, 1987, *Mayers & Schiff.*

Richly modeled, colored faience plaques display **BH**, with mosaic tesserae and pink marble further humanizing the straightforward engineers' works in this station, opened four years after completion of the first NYC subway, the original **IRT** Manhattan line. Ornate bronze dedication plaques located on the mezzanine's north wall (no fare required) explain the sequence further.

[D5] **Temple Bar Building**, 44 Court St., NW cor. Joralemon St. 1901. *George L. Morse.*

Three verdigris cupolas crown this office building, Brooklyn's tallest when built, heralding the arrival of the 20th century. Tacky at street level.

[D6] **Cadman Plaza** (officially S. Parkes Cadman Plaza), bounded by Cadman Plaza W., Court, Joralemon and Adams Sts., and the Brooklyn Bridge approaches. 1950-1960. *Designed by various city and borough agencies.* **Christopher Columbus** monument: statue, 1867, *Emma Stebbins,* sculptor; base and installation at this site, 1971, *A. Ottavino.* **Robert F. Kennedy**, 1972, *Anneta Duveen*, sculptor.

Scarcely a plaza, it's an amorphous park created by demolition of several blocks east of Brooklyn Heights. Principal goal was the creation of a graceful setting for new **Civic Center** buildings that would complement Borough Hall. Fringe benefits were the elimination of elevated trestles and the easing of automobile traffic

D5

through street-widening. *Stebbins'* statue of **Columbus** originally stood in Central Park. It was carved two years after she completed the **Angel of the Waters** and supporting cherubs for the Bethesda Fountain.

[D7] **N.Y.S. Supreme Court**, 360 Adams St., S part of Cadman Plaza opposite Montague St. 1957. *Shreve, Lamb & Harmon.*

Unlike the nation's **Supreme Court**, New York's Supreme Court is the lowest court, where legal action first commences. *Shreve, Lamb & Harmon* are best known for the **Empire State Building** (1931). A handsome set of architectural nostalgia is the pair of lamps from the now-demolished Hall of Records (1905. *R. L. Daus*).

[D8] **Statue of Henry Ward Beecher**, near Johnson St., S part of Cadman Plaza. 1891. *John Quincy Adams Ward,* sculptor; *Richard Morris Hunt,* architect of the base.

Mr. Beecher, the preacher and brother of *Harriet Beecher Stowe,* was relocated from his

perch confronting Borough Hall to decorate the
expanse of the new **Cadman Plaza**. The fence
and lawn surrounding the sculpture are unfortunate, for *Ward*'s strong concept should allow
people to join the figures already touching the
base at *Beecher's* feet. Large crowds, including
celebrities like *Ralph Waldo Emerson*, lined up
to hear him preach each Sunday at **Plymouth
Church**, on Orange Street between Henry and
Hicks, in Brooklyn Heights.

[D9a] **U.S. Post Office (Downtown
Brooklyn Station)** /originally **General
Post Office**, 271-301 Cadman Plaza E, NE cor.
Johnson St. 1885-1891. *Mifflin E. Bell* (original
design); *William A. Freret,* successor. 💠
[D9b] **U.S. Bankruptcy Court and United States
Attorney's Offices**/originally North addition,
Brooklyn General Post Office, 271-301 Cadman
Plaza E. 1930-1933. *James Wetmore.* Both remod-
eled, 2000, *R.M. Kliment & Frances Halsband.*

The original building on the south is in an
exuberant **Romanesque Revival.** Deep reveals
and strong modeling provide a rich play of light.
The taller addition is a humorless tail attempting to wag its lusty dog.

[D10] **Federal Courthouse**, 275 Washington St.,
NE cor. Tillary St., on Cadman Plaza. 2005. *Cesar
Pelli & Associates and HLW International.*

Another bow-bellied monster from the
scrapbooks of bigtime corporate architecture; 14
stories here tops out at 250 feet due to the
height of courtroom spaces.

D7

[D11] **Brooklyn War Memorial,** N part of Cadman
Plaza, opposite Orange St. 1951. *Eggers &
Higgins,* architects. *Charles Keck,* sculptor.

Though its innards contain a small museum
and other community facilities, its primary role
is as a wall, completing the plaza's formal composition of terrace, paths, shrubs, trees, and
lawn.

[D12] **New York City Office of Emergency
Management**, Cadman Plaza. 2007.
Swanke Hayden Connell.

Re-cladding and renovation of the former
Red Cross Building.

D9a

Return to Tillary Street and follow it east, turning left (north) on Jay for a block:

[D13] **St. James Cathedral** (Roman Catholic), Jay St., bet. Cathedral Place and Chapel St. E side. 1903. *George H. Streeton.*
   Neo-Georgian, with a handsome, verdigris copper-clad steeple. The first church on this site (1822) became the cathedral of Brooklyn in 1853; but in 1896, with the succession of Brooklyn's second bishop, it was officially renamed the pro-cathedral. Pro, in this instance, means in place of, for that bishop was planning an elaborate new cathedral of his own, the giant **Immaculate Conception Cathedral**, which never materialized. The pro-cathedral did not become the Cathedral once again until 1972. Within there hovers a baldachino, providing a rather plain American religious space with a touch of ceremonial wonder.

Back across Tillary:

[D14] **New York City Technical College**, CUNY, Tillary Street, bet. Jay and Adams Sts., S side. Expanded, 1987, *Edward Durrell Stone Assocs.*
   A vast greenhouse links the two earlier buildings that separately front on Adams and Jay. The resulting plaza is a welcome urban space. The Adams façade, peeling, is in serious need of restoration.

And entering an island of development:

MetroTech, roughly bet. Flatbush Ave., Tillary, Jay, and Willoughby Sts., excepting a NW quadrant including N.Y.C. Board of Education Channel 25 and Westinghouse High School; and a SW quadrant of commercial buildings largely facing Willoughby St. 1989 Master plan, *Haines Lundberg Waehler.*
   An unfortunate reprise of the "urban renewal" of the 1960s ("renewal" by obliteration, as on Manhattan's Upper West Side).

D12

Despite being the de facto campus for **New York University's Polytechnic Institute**, Metrotech feels decidedly more corporate than academic. The architecture is a mixed bag; some good 1990s additions by *Davis Brody Bond* haven't relieved an overall sense of sterility.
   Developed by *Bruce Ratner*, **MetroTech** commandeered eleven blocks of previously public streets and converted them to quasi-public spaces. Public or private? It's difficult to tell. MetroTech is full of vigilant security guards who will tell you to stop taking photos and might even ask you, out of the blue, where you're going. In a city renowned for freedom in its street life, it's a **disturbing development**.

[D15] **New York State Supreme Court and Kings County Family Court**, 320-330 Jay Street, SW cor. Johnson St. 2005. *Perkins Eastman.*
   Thirty-two stories, with 50 courtrooms for the Supreme Court, 34 for the Family Court. *That's a lot of gavels dropping!* Opened the same year as *Cesar Pelli's* **Federal Courthouse** around the corner on Tillary Street,

it's a soulmate: courthouse as corporate tower. The belle of the ball when compared to the dullsville Marriott Hotel next door.

[D16] Donald F. & Mildred Topp Othmer Hall, NYU Polytechnic Institute, 101 Tech Place, 85 Johnson St. 2002. *Davis Brody Bond.*

The first dormitory for Polytech students. Well-detailed, crisp modernism in concrete and glass, but it looks more like a research lab than a dorm.

[D20a] **Oro,** 306 Gold St., at Flatbush Ave. 2008. *Ismael Leyva Architects.*
[D20b] **Toren,** 150 Myrtle Ave., at Flatbush Ave. 2009. *Skidmore, Owings & Merrill.*
[D20c] **Avalon Fort Greene,** 343 Gold St., at Flatbush Ave. 2009. *Perkins Eastman.*

Three gleaming condos, tall and bulky, leading the pack in the unlikely development of a luxury Flatbush Avenue. A private conversation seems to be going on between them, joined by the even taller **111 Lawrence,** just to the west.

D13   D18

D16

D20b

[D17] New York City Fire Department Headquarters, 9 MetroTech Center, bet. Tech Pl. and Johnson St. 1997. *Swanke Hayden Connell.*

An understated background building appropriate for its tenants.

[D18] Bern Dibner Library of Science and Technology, NYU Polytechnic Institute, 5 MetroTech Center, bet. Tech Pl. and Myrtle Promenade. 1992. *Davis Brody Bond.*

An industrial elegance in precast concrete, articulated and connected with great panache. Its friendly scale dominates and humanizes the plaza.

[D19] Wunsch Hall (student center), NYU Polytechnic Institute/originally **First Free Congregational Church**/later **Bridge Street African Wesleyan Church,** 311 Bridge St., bet. Johnson St. and Myrtle Ave. E side. 1846-1847. 🍎

A **Greek Revival** temple in brick with a Doric-columned porch and entablature.

None of them seems to care a hoot about what happens at ground level.

[D21] 3 MetroTech Center, on Myrtle Promenade, bet. Duffield and Bridge Sts. S Side. 1997. *Skidmore, Owings & Merrill.*

Its detailing draws direct inspiration from the *Ralph Walker* **Telephone Building** next door.

[D22] Joseph J. & Violet J. Jacobs Building, NYU Polytechnic Institute, 305-315 Jay St., bet. Myrtle Ave. and Tillary St. 2002. *Davis Brody Bond.*

Six academic floors and a recreation/gymnasium complex with entry to a three-story atrium. A fun parlor game: try to say the name of this building five times fast!

[D23] **The Urban Assembly School for Law and Justice** and **The Urban Assembly Institute of Math and Science for Young Women**, 283 Adams St., SE cor. Johnson St. 2009. *GranKriegel.*

A former courthouse converted into a pair of high schools with very long names. The barrel-vaulted gym addition sprouting from the roof is deftly handled, and the entire building has been laboriously re-clad in limestone with red and blue **De Stijl** (early Dutch modern) highlights.

D23

D24

Part with MetroTech at Jay Street:

[D24] **N.Y.C. Transit Authority Headquarters**/ originally **N.Y.C. Board of Transportation Building**, 370 Jay St., NW cor. Willoughby St. 1950. *William E. Hauggard & Andrew J. Thomas.*

Home of the subway systems' managers... and bureaucracy. The two dingy lobbies to the subway, at north and south ends, are fringe benefits gained from a building contiguous to its subway lines. Windows here read as skin, rather than holes punctured in masonry, the glass flush with its limestone surrounds. Nightly money trains once brought the take from all boroughs directly to a spur in the building's bowels.

 [D25] **Brooklyn Friends School**/ originally **Brooklyn Law School**, Pearl St. N of Fulton St., E side. ca. 1930. *Thompson, Holmes & Converse.*

A curious **Art Moderne** building with a crowning of **Romanesque Revival** arches.

[D26] Originally **City of Brooklyn Fire Headquarters**, 365-367 Jay St., bet. Willoughby St. and Myrtle Ave. E side. 1892. *Frank Freeman.* 🍎

This is a building to write home about. A lusty Romanesque Revival monument with brick and terra-cotta details, supported by granite with sandstone trim. A grand arch, a sturdy tower, a fine example of the New York branch (with *Louis Sullivan's* **Condict Building**) of the Chicago School. *Freeman* learned much from

D26

afar by viewing *H.H. Richardson's* work, as did *Sullivan.*

Currently dilapidated and in need of immediate care. Scaffolding is a promising sign that help might be on the way.

[D27] Originally **New York & New Jersey Telephone Company Building**, 81 Willoughby St., NE cor. Lawrence St. 1897-1898. *Rudolph L. Daus.* 🍎

A grand **Beaux Arts-Renaissance Revival** palace, Brooklyn's first telephone headquarters. The carved entrance surrounds bear intertwined TC (for telephone company) over the door, adding to bells, earpieces, and ancient wall telephones worked into Classical Beaux Arts ornament. Hovering over it all is a grand copper-clad cornice.

[D28] **111 Lawrence Street**, bet. Willoughby St. and Myrtle Ave. 2010. *Gerner Kronick & Valcarcel.*

The nondescript slab fastened to the hip of *Daus'* **New York & New Jersey Telephone**

Company Building is (unfortunately) now Brooklyn's tallest building, surpassing the **Williamsburgh Savings Bank** by some two feet.

[D29] **BellTel Lofts**/originally **New York Telephone Company**, Long Island Headquarters, 365 Bridge St., NE cor. Willoughby St. 1929-1930. *Ralph Walker of Voorhees, Gmelin & Walker.* 🍎

Rippling brick with a graded palette, a delicate aesthetic. Note the equally elegant Art

The prolific *Keely* left this moment in history amongst the new **Gargantuas** of MetroTech.

A side trip up, down, and across the traffic stream on Flatbush Avenue:

[D32] **Long Island University, Brooklyn Center**, 385 Flatbush Ave. Ext., bet. DeKalb Ave. and Willoughby St. E. side. **Campus entry arch**, Long Island University, Flatbush Ave. Ext. N of DeKalb Ave. E side. 1985. Park, *Quennell-*

D27

D30

D32a

Deco grillages over the ground-floor windows. Now converted to condominiums.

[D30] **Duffield Street Houses**, bet. Willoughby St. and Myrtle Ave. 🍎

Not everything was obliterated in 1990 by MetroTech. These four houses were rescued and moved here from their original site on Johnson Street.

[D30a] **182 Duffield Street**, ca. 1839. Brick with **Greek Revival** features.

[D30b] **184 Duffield Street**, 1847. *Francis H. Chicester.* More **Greek Revival**.

[D30c] **186 and 188 Duffield Street**. ca. 1835. *Samuel R. Johnson.* Clapboard siding. No.186 has dormers and **Greek Revival** portico; No.188 has some Queen Anne frills.

And next door:

[D31] **St. Boniface Catholic Church**, 190 Duffield St. bet. Myrtle Ave. and Willoughby St. 1872. *Patrick Charles Keely.*

Rothschild Assocs., landscape architects. Arch design, *Nicholas Quennell.*

A latter-day, brightly colored triumphal arch fashioned from structural steel sections and a steel grid. A cheery welcome to the campus.

[D32a] **Humanities Building, Long Island University**/originally **Maltz Building**, 1967. *Davis, Brody & Assocs.* and *Horowitz & Chun.*

The structure of an existing warehouse was here re-clad and extended in brick. New guts and a new envelope on an existing skeleton, with fine materials, elegant detailing, and handsome spaces, make this extraordinary.

[D32b] **Library-Learning Center**, Long Island University, 1975. *Davis, Brody & Assocs.* and *Horowitz & Chun.*

Linked to the earlier Humanities Building by a bright red-painted, Vierendeel-trussed, glass-caged bridge, this crisp complex begins to knit together the disparate older buildings of the reworked Brooklyn Center campus.

[D32c] **Tristram W. Metcalf Hall,** formerly Arnold and Marie Schwartz Athletic Center, Long Island University, originally **Brooklyn Paramount Theater and offices,** NE corner Flatbush Ave. Ext. and De Kalb Ave. 1928. *Rapp & Rapp.*

Brooklyn's leading movie palace was converted in two phases to university use: the office block in 1950, the 4,400-seat auditorium in 1962. The intervening years witnessed the swan song of popcorn in these marble halls. LIU's **Blackbirds** played basketball games here until 2006, when they moved to a new building on Ashland Place (below).

 [D32d] **Zeckendorf Health Sciences Center,** Long Island University, 75 DeKalb Ave., bet. Hudson Ave. and Rockwell Pl. 1995. *Mitchell/Giurgola.*

An austere neighbor to **Metcalf Hall,** punctuated with a clock tower.

D32d   D34

D33   D37

[D33] **Recreation and Wellness Center, Long Island University**, 161 Ashland Place, NW cor. DeKalb Ave. 2006. *Arquitectonica.*

LIU's sleek new sports complex. Multi-colored logos splayed across the façade, fore and aft, make it look like a big surf shop. You can take the architects out of Miami, but you can't take Miami out of the architects.

An even longer stretch to the south along Flatbush to:

[D34] **Pioneer Warehouse,** 41 Flatbush Ave., opp. Livingston St. 1896-1914. *J. Graham Glover.*

Neo-Baroque columns flank the faded entry to this venerable warehouse. Look up: the prow of ships emerge from the cornice at four intervals, each with a different date inscribed above (left to right: 1910, 1896, 1902, 1914). Presumably the middle portion is oldest, with two additions (1910 and 1914) on either side. Recently added pink and blue racing stripes on the cornice are unfortunate.

Then back to DeKalb, turning left to see Roman Pomp in Brooklyn:

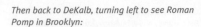 [D35] **The Dime Savings Bank of New York,** 9 DeKalb Ave., NE cor. Fleet St., off Fulton St. 1906-1908. *Mowbray & Uffinger.* Expanded, 1931-1932, *Halsey, McCormack & Helmer.* ◐ First floor interior. ◐

A comical, columned **Roman Revival** palace. The interior is remarkable; plan to visit it during banking hours. Gilded, monumental Liberty-head dimes are the predominant motif. Money must have been well managed by those who could afford such grandeur.

[D36] **Fulton Street Mall,** along Fulton St. and DeKalb Ave., bet. Flatbush Ave. Ext. and Adams St. 1985. *Seelye, Stevenson, Value & Knecht,* engineers. *Pomeroy, Lebduska Assocs.,* architects.

A thriving thoroughfare (100,000 shoppers per day) with **Macy's** as the anchor. Many of the buildings along Fulton Street are wondrous, but covered with layers of paint, neon, and billboards. Antiquated (1985) "mall" features (ungainly arches over the street, clunky bus shelters) fell out of fashion and were demolished in 2009, replaced by sleeker lights, benches, and glass bus kiosks by the now-ubiquitous Spanish street furniture specialists *Cemusa.* Best improvement: the planting of more desperately needed trees.

 [D37] Formerly **Offerman Building/** originally **S. Wechsler and Brother Store,** 503 Fulton St., bet. Bridge and Duffield Sts. N side. 1890-1893. *Peter J. Lauritzen of Lauritzen & Voss.* ◐

Grossly altered. The Duffield Street façade preserves some of the **Romanesque Revival** detail, even at ground level, that once embellished the whole body of the building. Look up at a great incised sign. The sleazy alteration of the Fulton Street façade has destroyed distinguished architecture that might well have been reinforced, rather than mutilated. But still, look up. *Gloriosky, Sandy, it must be Daddy Warbucks palace.*

[D38a] **A.I. Namm & Son Department Store**, 450-458 Fulton St., SE cor. Hoyt St. 1924-1925 and 1928-1929. *Robert D. Kohn and Charles Butler.* ◐

A modern rounded corner is the main attraction here, architecturally a very distant cousin to *Louis Sullivan's* **Carson Pirie Scott and Company** in Chicago (1899).

[D38b] Originally **Liebmann Brothers Building**, 446 Fulton St., SW cor. Hoyt St. 1885. *Parfitt Brothers.*

A four-story gem, with banality intruding at street level and creeping up the side. Look up to see the dynamic corner: Romanesque arches in brick and terra cotta punctured, like a rocket, by a black turret.

[D39] **Macy's**/originally **Abraham & Straus**, 420 Fulton St., bet. Gallatin Place and Hoyt St. Main

D39

building S side. 1929 and 1935. *Starrett & Van Vleck.* **Secondary building,** 177 Livingston St., NE cor. Gallatin Place. 1885.

Eight interconnected buildings jointly formed **A&S**, the great department store of Brooklyn, in a similar blockfilling manner to its Manhattan counterpart, Bloomingdale's. The main building is subdued **Art Deco**, but the small **Romanesque Revival** gem at Gallatin Place is distinguished in Roman brick, brown-stone, and granite. Some wondrous early cast-iron and brownstone façades commissioned by *Abraham Abraham* peek over later street and storefront modernizations aside the main block. All absorbed into the Macy's empire.

Take a left on old Red Hook Lane:
Originally an Indian trail that figured promi-nently in the Battle of Brooklyn (August 27, 1776), it was gradually built over and plowed under. But a remnant survives: a one-block long alley south of Fulton Street Mall, between Adams and Smith Streets. And two ghostly vestiges, in the form of property lines that don't conform to the city grid,

still exist just a few blocks to the south. Take a map of the neighborhood and draw a line with a ruler running southwest, and note how the remains of Red Hook Lane line up perfectly with two oddly-angled buildings: 234 State Street (across from Brooklyn Law School's Feil Hall) and 228 Atlantic Avenue (a tavern).

It was recently "de-mapped" by the City, meaning this last, tiny fragment may disappear underneath a future development.

[D40] **MTA (Metropolitan Transportation Authority) Building**, a block surrounded by Smith, Livingston, Schermerhorn Sts., and Boerum Place. 1989. *Murphy/Jahn.*

Black-and-white syncopation gave life to a onetime drab neighborhood, but this 1980s relic has been outpaced and jostled by a flurry of new construction.

[D41] **Central Court Building**, 120 Schermerhorn St., SW cor. Smith St. 1932. *Collins & Collins.*

D40

This **Renaissance Revival** hulk adds to the cityscape through its deep entrance porch, artic-ulated by three great neo-Renaissance arches.

[D42] **Brooklyn Friends Meetinghouse**, 110 Schermerhorn St., SE cor. Boerum Place. 1857. Attributed to *Charles T. Bunting.* 🍎

Once a freestanding structure in simple Quaker brick, it is overpowered by the Central Court Building adjacent to its contiguous former school.

[D43] **Brooklyn Men's House of Detention**, 275 Atlantic Ave., bet. Smith St. and Boerum Place. N side. ca. 1950. *LaPierre, Litchfield & Partners.*

Cheerfully described as the **Brooklyn Hilton**, this facility holds mostly those awaiting trial who cannot post bail, as well as those considered too dangerous to roam before trial. Recently there have been loud cries from the neighborhood to get rid of the jail once and for all. But where's a felon supposed to sleep? The jailbirds won, for now.

[D44] Former **N.Y.C. Board of Education Headquarters**/originally **Benevolent Protective Order of Elks**, 110 Livingston St., SW cor. Boerum Place. 1926. *McKim, Mead & White.* Conversion to apartments, 2007, *Beyer Blinder Belle.*

MM&W was deflated after *Stanford White* was shot to death by a jealous husband in 1906. The partnership's other powerful talent, *Charles Follen McKim*, died in 1909 (*Mead* was the business partner). The staff thereafter produced occasional wonders, as with Manhattan's Municipal Building of 1914. For the most part the production, as here, was pallid.

Glass and steel condos have been sutured, unceremoniously, to the roof, a relic of the **Great Condo Boom** (2003-08), when developers fell asleep each night dreaming of "air rights" and flat, endless roofs to build upon.

[D45] **Feil Hall, Brooklyn Law School**, 205 State Street, bet. Boerum Place and Court St. 2005. *Robert A.M. Stern Architects.*

Stern's second building for **Brooklyn Law**

D44

serves as residence for 239 students, part of the school's ongoing attempt to carve a campus of sorts out of Downtown/Boerum Hill. Massive, composed, and traditional, Stern has erected a veritable cliff of brick that can't quite live up to its **Monadnock dreams**.

[D46] **N.Y.C. Transit Museum**, Schermerhorn St., NW cor. Boerum Place. Downstairs, in the former IND Court Street subway station. Open to the public. Tu-Fr, 10-4; Sa-Su, 12-5; closed Mo and holidays. 718-694-1600. *mta.info/mta/museum*

A wonderful underground museum on an inactive spur of the subway system. Here are trains, turnstiles, and tesserae of varying vintages. Of special note is a rare 1949 Art Deco inspired, stainless steel "million dollar train" intended, but never used, for the still-unrealized Second Avenue line. Admission used to be by token, until tokens also became museum pieces.

[D47] **Court House Apartments**, 125 Court St., and **Dodge YMCA**, 225 Atlantic Ave., NE cor. Atlantic Avenue and Court St. 2007. *Beyer Blinder Belle.*

A keystone in the redevelopment of a previously shabby stretch of Court Street. This huge multi-use brick and glass cube is adeptly detailed, with crenellated brick that gives scale and casts pleasing shadows on its façade. The **YMCA** (*Dattner Architects*) is cramped but popular, turning the former site of a seedy concrete parking garage into a hub of family activity.

[D48] **Saints Constantine and Helen Cathedral** (Greek Orthodox), 64 Schermerhorn St. bet. Boerum Place and Court St. S side. 1916.

Squat brick with a shallow dome. A huge chandelier dominates the interior, with frescoes covering the walls and ceiling. Perforated windows let in an ethereal, amber glow. The last vestige of a tiny Greek district; there was, until the late 1990s, a fine Greek bakery at the corner of Court and Schermerhorn.

[D49] Originally **Brooklyn Public Library**, 67 Schermerhorn St., bet. Boerum Place and Court St. N side. 1887. *William Tubby.*

A bold moment at the height of Brooklyn's **Romanesque Revival**. The arched entry is a worthy but distant neighbor to that at *Frank Freeman's* **City of Brooklyn Fire Headquarters** on Jay Street.

[H50] **United Artists Cinema and Barnes & Noble Booksellers**, 106-108 Court Street

D45   D49

between State and Schermerhorn Sts. 2000. *Hugh Hardy of H3 Collaboration Architecture.*

Twelve movie theaters stacked atop and below **Barnes & Noble's** ranks of books. The theaters, *avec stadium seating*, are a welcome addition to a previously decaying site that had featured an abandoned adult movie house. The theater and bookstore draw huge crowds from the neighborhood, and their presence has enlivened the street life and economy on a prominent stretch of Court Street. The building is also overbearing, out of scale with its smaller neighbors, utterly blank, and clad in a fish-scale pattern more appropriate for the visual cacophony of Manhattan's Third Avenue.

***END** of Civic Center/Downtown Brooklyn Walking Tour: The subway station here at Nevins and Flatbush offers both the IRT Lexington and Seventh Avenue service (Nos.2, 3, 4, & 5 trains). The DeKalb Avenue Station, a block back along Flatbush Avenue Extension, provides connections to both BMT and IND subways (D, M, N, Q, and R trains).*

NECROLOGY

Brooklyn Fox Theater, 20 Flatbush Ave., bet. Nevins and Livingston Sts. *C. Howard Crane.* 1928.

Where the banal Con Ed Building (1974, *Skidmore, Owings & Merrill*) now stands once stood the **Fox**, an opulent movie and vaudeville showplace, demolished in 1971.

RKO Albee Theater. *1925. Thomas W. Lamb.*

On the site of **The Gallery at Metrotech** (1980, *Gruen Associates*) stood the **RKO Albee**, one of downtown Brooklyn's last great movie palaces, demolished in 1977. It was a neo-Renaissance fantasy of columns and star-twinkling ceilings, a vast place of 2,000 seats. *Edward F. Albee*, a vaudeville impresario, was the foster father of playwright *Edward Albee*. The theater's swan song included a screening of *Who's Afraid of Virginia Woolf?* based on the younger *Albee's* great play.

Necrology: Gage & Tollner's

Originally **German Evangelical Lutheran Church,** 63 Schermerhorn St., bet. Boerum Place and Court St. N side. 1888. *J. C. Cady.*

Replaced by a non-entity.

Gage & Tollner's Restaurant, 372 Fulton St., bet. Smith St. and Red Hook Lane. Building, ca. 1875. Interior, 1892. 👁️

The Victorian interior of plush velvet, cut glass, mirrors, gaslight, mahogany, and bentwood chairs was virtually unchanged until its unfortunate closing in 2004.

BROOKLYN HEIGHTS

Colonized by well-to-do merchants and bankers from the City across the river, Brooklyn Heights is the suburban product of a combined land and transit speculation; in this case the transit was the new steam-powered ferry. In 1814 *Robert Fulton's* invention, with financial backing from *Hezekiah Pierrepont*, first connected the newly renamed Fulton Streets of New York and Brooklyn by fast boats, giving occasion to *Pierrepont* and others (*Middagh, Hicks, Remsen, Livingston*) for profitable division and sale of their heights "farmland." With the new ferry it was quicker and easier to go by water from Fulton to Fulton than to travel by omnibus on Manhattan Island. This status continued until the New York and Harlem Railroad provided a route to the northern "frontier": in 1832 horse-cars linked the distant town of **Harlem**, and in 1837 steam trains crossed the Harlem River to Westchester. A surveyor's grid marked the Heights into 25 X 100-foot lots as the system for parcel sales. Although other subdivisions were made by speculators, those dimensions remain the basic module of the Heights.

That the oldest buildings (such as **155-159 Willow Street**) were built in the 1820s is not surprising. Lots did not come on the market until 1819, and even as late as 1807 there had been but seven houses on the Heights, with perhaps 20 more at or near the ferry landing at the river's edge below. By 1890 the infill was sub-

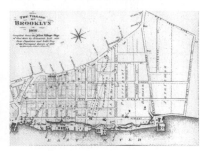

stantially complete, and the architectural history of the Heights primarily spans those 70 years. Occasional buildings were built much later in random locations, but the principal pre-1890 urban fabric was still intact in 1965, when the district was designated a historic district under the City's newly enacted Landmarks Preservation Law. Vacant lots on Willow Place afforded architects *Joseph and Mary Merz* a chance to add buildings in serious modern architectural terms, but within the scale of the surrounding environment. These, plus a few others, have extended (with the approval of the Landmarks Preservation Commission) a previously truncated architectural history to the present: the others include *Alfredo De Vido's* brown-brick at 222 Columbia Heights, *Ulrich Franzen's* building for the Jehovah's Witnesses on Columbia Heights, and a motley assortment of old and new residential buildings on Poplar Street by *Wids de la Cour, David Hirsch*, and *Charles Platt*.

H6

[H1] **Brooklyn Heights Historic District,** generally bounded on the W and N by the Brooklyn-Queens Expwy. and Cadman Plaza W.,—a logical choice, as the Heights was the City's foremost, discrete, and substantially intact enclave St., and an irregular line to Court St. and Atlantic Ave. ●

these fraternal architects. Rock-faced brownstone supports brick pilasters large and small. Sturdy granite piers articulately support the entrance archway.

H4

H7

The first district to be designated (1965) under the Landmarks Preservation Law—a logical choice, as the Heights was the City's foremost, discrete, and substantially intact enclave of architecture.

South Heights Walking Tour: A circuit that begins at Court and Remsen Streets (across from Borough Hall) and ends nearby at Livingston and Clinton Streets.

[H2] **St. Francis College Academic Center,** 180 Remsen St., bet. Court and Clinton Sts. 2005. *Helpern Architects.*

Replaced the demolished **McGarry Library** (see Necrology).

[H3] Originally **The Franklin Building,** 186 Remsen St., bet. Court and Clinton Sts. S. side. ca. 1890. *Parfitt Bros.*

One of four **Romanesque Revival-Queen Anne** red-brick extravaganzas in the vicinity by

[H4] **St. Francis College** /originally (1914-1962) **Brooklyn Union Gas Company Headquarters,** 176 Remsen St., bet. Court and Clinton Sts. S side. 1914. *Frank Freeman.*

A lesser work of *Freeman,* who graced Brooklyn with magnificence at the **City of Brooklyn Fire Headquarters** (endangered) and the **Brooklyn Democratic Club** (destroyed).

At this point you enter the Brooklyn Heights Historic District:

[H5] **Brooklyn Heights Synagogue**/formerly **The Brooklyn Club,** 131 Remsen St., bet. Clinton and Henry Sts. N side. ca. 1858. Converted to synagogue, 1996.

The paired Corinthian columns provide a strong portal to this bland brownstone.

[H6] **Brooklyn Bar Association**/formerly **Charles Condon House,** 123 Remsen St., bet. Clinton and Henry Sts. N side. ca. 1875.

The vibrant chromatics of white limestone

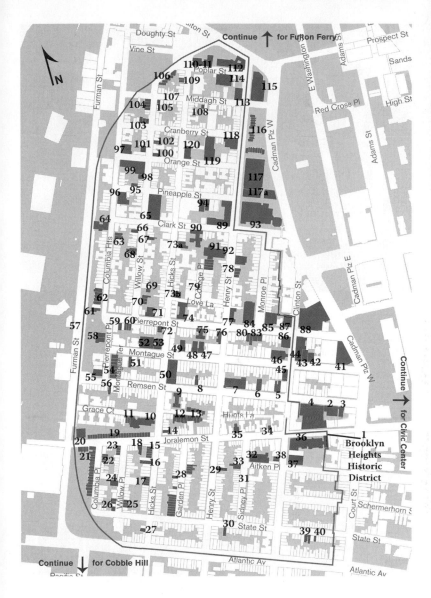

and dark red brick provide an exuberant note on Remsen Street. Atop, the **Second Empire** has provided a curved and slated mansard roof. The stone bears some incised *Eastlake* patterning.

[H7] **Our Lady of Lebanon Roman Catholic Church** (Maronite Rite)/originally **Church of the Pilgrims** (Congregational), 113 Remsen St., NE cor. Henry St. 1844-1846. *Richard Upjohn.* Rectory, 1869, *Leopold Eidlitz.*

Certainly, *Upjohn* was avant-garde: this has been called the nation's earliest example of Romanesque Revival, a bold massing of ashlar stonework, a solid, carven image. The spire was removed due to deterioration and the high cost of its replacement. Doors at both west and south portals were salvaged from the ill-fated liner **Normandie**, which burned and sank at its Hudson River berth in 1942. Note the images of Norman churches and Norman-built ocean liners.

The **Church of the Pilgrims** moved in with **Plymouth Church** in 1934, and its Tiffany windows were moved to an annex, Hillis Hall, of the combined congregation.

[H8] **70 Remsen Street,** bet. Henry and Hicks Sts. S side. 1929. *H.I. Feldman.*

Sturdy **neo-Romanesque** decorated arches over marble columns and spreading **neo-Byzantine** capitals give considerable style to a simple apartment block. *Feldman* similarly decorated the old **Pierrepont Hotel.**

[H9] **87 Remsen Street,** bet. Henry and Hicks Sts. N side. ca. 1890.

An exotic **Queen Anne** mansion with a melange of brownstone and terra-cotta detailing. Note the copper roof against the sky.

Turn left on Hicks Street:

[H10] **Grace Church,** 254 Hicks St., SW cor. Grace Court. 1847-1849. *Richard Upjohn.* Parish House to the west. 1931.

After his radical venture with the Church of the Pilgrims, *Upjohn* went "straight," back to a more academic brownstone **Gothic Revival.** A bit of urban charm is the entrance court, off Hicks

H15

Street at the south side, leading to the parish house. A backwater for pedestrians, it is crowned by the umbrella of a glorious elm some 80 feet tall. Benches are available.

[H11] **Grace Court**. W of Hicks St.

Its delight was the juxtaposition of Grace Church and the double-deep backyards of Remsen Street's houses. In the 1960s the construction of a banal six-story red-brick apartment building on some of those yards changed

H13

all that. The eastern half of this one-block cul-de-sac is still lovely.

[H12] **Grace Court Alley**. E of Hicks St.

A real mews (for Remsen Street and Joralemon Street mansions). A walk to its end and then a turnabout will reveal many delights not visible from Hicks Street. No.14's arched bearing wall of tooled brownstone is lusty. Many of these carriage houses still retain their iron hay cranes, some used today only for holding potted plants. Note the crisp contrasting brownstone quoins on **Nos.2** and **4**.

[H13] **21 Grace Court Alley**, at the far end. 1994. *Joseph Stella*.

Pas mal, but it suffers from a lack of the detail that its antecedents used to fill out their architectural vocabulary.

[H14] **263 Hicks Street**, bet. Joralemon St. and Grace Court Alley. E side. ca. 1860. Alterations ca. 1885.

An Italianate brownstone up-styled in the 1880s with a new stoop, replete with Norman zigzag ornamentation, a rock-face brownstone frieze, and a dormered tile roof.

[H15] **262-272 Hicks Street**, SW cor. Joralemon St. 1887. *William Tubby*.

A **Shingle Style** terrace, designed as a

H16

H17

group composition. The romantic corbeled brickwork, shingles, and picturesque profiles confer an identity on the various occupants. Each is different from its neighbor but part of an overall architectural composition.

[H16] **Engine Company 224**, N.Y.C. Fire Department, 274 Hicks St., bet. Joralemon and State Sts. W side. 1903. *Adams & Warren*.

A house for fire engines in scale with, but much grander than its house neighbors. **Renaissance Revival**, with copper-clad dormers.

[H17] **276-284 Hicks Street**, bet. Joralemon and State Sts. W side.

Five brick arches—two half-round, three half-ellipses—once swallowed carriages. Note the sculptured woman's head on the dormer of No.276. More carriages resided across the street at **Nos.291** and **293**.

🏛 [H18] **58 Joralemon Street,** bet. Hicks St. and Willow Place. S side. ca. 1847. Converted to present use, 1908.

The world's only **Greek Revival subway Ventilator**. It permits release of air pressure built up by IRT Lexington Avenue Line express trains rushing through the East River tunnel, deep beneath Joralemon Street. And it affords stranded passengers an emergency exit to the surface.

🏛 [H19] **29-75 Joralemon Street,** bet. Hicks and Furman Sts. N side. 1844-1848.

Twenty-five **Greek Revival** houses (several have been altered) step down Joralemon's hill. The row has a pleasant rhythm, with each pair stepping down roughly 30 inches from its neighbors.

[H20] **25 Joralemon Street**/formerly **High Pressure Fire Service**, Main Pumping Station, bet. Hicks and Furman Sts. N side.

Before superpumper fire trucks were available, this served to increase the pressure in fire

[H22] **7-13 Columbia Place**, bet. Joralemon and State Sts. E side.

Four charming modest clapboard houses, whose porches give a friendly scale to the block.

Now back a few steps to Willow Place and turn right:

[H23] **2-8 Willow Place**, bet. Joralemon and State Sts. W side. ca. 1847.

Gothic Revival detail decorates simple brick

H23   H26

H21

H25

mains to reach high-rise fires. Now it has joined the myriad building types converted to co-ops and condominiums.

[H21] **Riverside** (apartments), 4-30 Columbia Place, SW cor. Joralemon St. 1890. *William Field & Son*. Remodeled, 1988, *R.M. Kliment & Frances Halsband*.

On the river's side they stood, until truncated by the Brooklyn-Queens Expressway. The original contained a central garden, partially remaining between the extant units and the expressway's wall.

Alfred T. White, a prominent and paternalistic Brooklyn businessman, whose motto was "philanthropy plus 5 percent," commissioned these, as well as the Tower and Home buildings in Cobble Hill. They are the original limited-profit housing, predating the City and State's first "limited-dividend" projects (Stuyvesant Town) by 57 years. White also was a major participant in the creation of Forest Hills Gardens.

row houses. In the battle of the Revival styles, the basic plan and spatial arrangement of row houses were almost constant: their cornices, lintels, doorways, and portals are the variables that identify the **Federal** (1820s), **Greek Revival** (1830s), and **Gothic Revival** (1840s) styles. Many **Federal** houses were updated to the fashionable Greek Revival and, subsequently, from Greek to Gothic. The later **Renaissance Revival** houses had, however, both an extended plan and inflated volume.

[H24] **Willow Place Chapel**/originally a mission of the First Unitarian Church, 26 Willow Place, bet. Joralemon and State Sts. W side. 1875-1876. *Russell Sturgis*.

A retired chapel converted in 1962 to a theater by a small company, the Heights Players (*www.heightsplayers.org*). Ruskinian Gothic in the era of St. Ann's. *Sturgis* wrote a three-volume *Dictionary of Architecture and Building* (1901).

H27

[H25] **43-49 Willow Place**, bet. Joralemon and State Sts. N side. ca. 1846.

A Greek Revival wood colonnade joins four town houses, from an era when colonnades denoted class. And note **No.42**, directly across Willow Place: an identical vine-entwined fragment, sandwiched between the *Merz* creations.

[H26] **40, 44, and 48 Willow Place**, NW cor. State St. 1965-1966. *Joseph & Mary Merz.*

These four town houses (one is a double house) gave new life to Willow Place while respecting the scale and nature of their older

H32   H34

neighbors. Garages occupy ground-floor space; and cement block, in a special 8-inch-square size and used with sensitivity and imagination, assumes a dignity that most thoughtless users miss by a mile. Note the compact integration of garage, rear garden terrace, and handsome wood fence on the State Street side of **No.48**.

Turn left on State Street, with a quick peek down Hicks:

[H27] **322 Hicks Street Apartments**, bet. Atlantic Ave. and State Sts. 2003. *Smith-Miller + Hawkinson and Larsen Shein Ginsburg Snyder.*

Brooklyn Heights is so cohesive that any new architectural ideas usually prompt the Landmarks Commission to reach for their big rubber stamp marked "REJECTED!" Yet this apartment block passed the Commission's scrutiny and is a worthy attempt to break out (or rather, **stretch** out) of the **brownstone mold** by inflecting the brick façade and emphasizing the horizontal.

[H28] **Garden Place**, bet. Joralemon and State Sts.

A handsome urban space, one block long, contained on four sides. Note the terra-cotta, brick, and limestone **Queen Anne** at **No.26**, the Hansel and Gretel carriage house (**No.21**), the intruders from Queens (**Nos.17, 19, 19a.**), and the lush lintels at **No.34**. **Nos.40** through **56** form a handsome terrace.

Locals describe this as the Scarsdale of Brooklyn Heights, where the affluent nest in this cul-de-sac.

Left on Henry:

[H29] **269 Henry Street**, bet. State and Joralemon Sts. ca. 1920s.

A handsome apartment block, with stylish (and space-expanding) corner windows. But the special prize is the magnificent Art Deco entry: a bright red door with porthole, trimmed in a circle of stainless steel, under a curving steel-trimmed canopy!

[H30] **118 State Street**, bet. Henry St. and Sidney Place. S side. Converted, 1980s, *Eli Attia.*

A converted warehouse that displays a vast skylight in profile, when viewed from the west.

Turn left onto Sidney Place:

[H31] **Sidney Place**, bet. State and Joralemon Sts.

A more varied and interesting version of **Garden Place**. Its architecture includes everything that Garden Place offers, while adding a church, St. Charles Borromeo, and such specialties as a seven-story Greek Revival house! The front gardens on the east side between Aitken Place and State Street are unusual.

[H32] **St. Charles Borromeo Church** (Roman Catholic), 21 Sidney Place, NE cor. Aitken Place. 1869. *Patrick Charles Keely.*

A simplified brick **Gothic Revival** in maroon-painted brick. The interior is decorated with Carpenter Gothic arches and trim.

[H33] **Brooklyn Law School Residence Hall**, 18 Sidney Place, opposite Aitken Place. W side. ca. 1838. Altered and sur-elevated.

It seems, at first glance, that one has found the world's first seven-story Greek Revival town

H36

house (to match the world's only Greek Revival subway ventilator, around the corner). Alas, the lower floors are true to their 1838 history, but three stories were added in the late 19th century to expand the owners' good luck.

North to Joralemon Street:

[H34] **135 Joralemon Street**, bet. Henry and Clinton Sts. N side. ca. 1833.
Federal, with an opposite-hand plan from **24 Middagh Street.** Their similarities are concealed by a post–Civil War cast-iron porch, but the house is unfortunately dwarfed by two bulky later buildings.

[H35] **129 Joralemon Street**, bet. Henry and Clinton Sts. N side. ca. 1891. *C.P.H. Gilbert.*
A grandly scaled outpost of the **Chicago School** in Roman brick, sadly squeezed between a banal apartment building and a law office with pretensions, but inappropriate scale.

Turn right on Clinton Street:

[H36] **Packer Collegiate Institute**, 170 Joralemon St., bet. Court and Clinton Sts. S side. 1853-1856. *Minard Lafever.* Additions, 1884, 1886, *Napoleon Le Brun & Son.* Gym, 1957.
A parody of a British Victorian businessman's **Gothick** castle. The understated addition tries to remain a background neighbor. Collegiate only in the sense that it prepares students for college, not a college itself.

[H37] **Packer Collegiate Institute Middle School**/originally **St. Ann's Church** (Episcopal), Clinton St., NE cor. Livingston St. Chapel, 1866-1867. Church, 1867-1869, *Renwick & Sands.* Renovation and addition, 2003, *Hugh Hardy* of *H3 Collaboration Architecture.*
Brownstone and terra cotta of different colors and textures make an exuberant and unrestrained extravaganza. *Renwick* had produced more academically correct Gothic Revival churches at Manhattan's **Grace** and **St. Patrick's**—perhaps

by the time of St. Ann's his confidence had mush-roomed. The copybooks of the Pugins used at Grace were discarded in favor of current architectural events, particularly the "new" museum at Oxford by *Deane & Woodward,* designed and built with the eager assistance of theorist *John Ruskin*—hence "Ruskinian Gothic."

Hugh Hardy's middle school is a building within a building, a free-standing modernist glass-and-steel Jonah inserted into the belly of St. Ann's. *Hardy's* beautifully detailed, light-filled atrium (visible from Livingston Street) emerges from the rear of the church and links Packer's three disparate buildings.

[H38] **140-142 Clinton Street**, bet. Joralemon St. and Aitken Place. W side. ca. 1855.

Lintels and a cornice lush with volutes and garlands, both in cast iron. The detail and profiles survived well in comparison with those carved in erodible brownstone. It looks as if its many eyebrows were surveying St. Ann's Church across the street.

END of South Heights Walking Tour: To reach the Borough Hall/Court Street subway stations, return to Joralemon Street and walk one block east. If you are filled with energy, two other Brooklyn Heights walks follow. For a change of pace, respite, and refreshments, walk south to Atlantic Avenue [See Cobble Hill].

Central Heights Walking Tour: Starts and ends at Court and Montague Streets. Subways to Borough Hall Station of the IRT Seventh Avenue and Lexington Avenue Lines (Nos.2, 3, 4, & 5 trains), or east escalator of Court Street Station of the BMT local (M, N, & R trains).

Montague Street: Throughout the 19th century and until the end of World War II, this was the road to the Wall Street Ferry, dipping down the bluff to its wateredge terminal. Pier 4 now occupies that site. There were companion ferries to the north, the Fulton Ferry, and to the south at Atlantic Avenue, South Ferry. The latter is remembered in name only on its Manhattan end

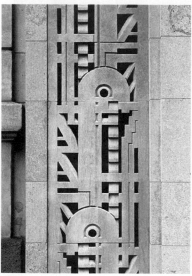

H42

H40

H44

H41

[H39] **168-170 State Street**, bet. Clinton and Court Sts. S side. ca. 1890.

Robust twin tenements with handsome bay windows from a time when architecture for the lower-income population was still architecture. The swooping cornice is phenomenal: beautifully restored with an ornate vine motif.

[H40] **174 State Street**, bet. Clinton and Court Sts. S side. ca. 1838.

An early 19th-century clapboard survivor, rare for this far south in the Heights. Maroon with black trim: always a winning color scheme for clapboard.

*Home of the Excelsiors: A plaque on the carefully groomed row house at **133 Clinton Street**, southeast corner of Livingston Street, identifies this building as the onetime clubhouse of the **Jolly Young Bachelors**. By 1854 this social club had evolved into the Excelsiors, an amateur baseball club with the distinction of having as their pitcher James Creighton, credited with having pitched the first curve ball!*

by the terminus of the IRT Seventh Avenue local.

A stone bridge by Minard Lafever (1855) and a later passerelle called the "Penny Bridge," both located between Pierrepont Place and Montague Terrace, once carried the brow of the Heights over Montague Street's steep incline, with its appropriate cable car line.

Only four blocks long, Montague is a chameleon in that short stretch: leafy, relatively quiet, full of handsome apartment buildings to the west; hectic, full of banks and restaurants catering to the crowds from the Civic Center to the east. Astronomically rising rents throughout the 1990s and 2000s squeezed out many of the local businesses and much of the old Brooklyn flavor, replaced by chain stores and yuppies. Still the main drag to grab lunch, buy a tie, or return a faulty cell phone, Montague isn't as hip as it once was, having been outpaced in the last decade by Smith Street to the south.

Walk west on Montague Street:

[H41] TD Bank/formerly **European American Bank** (EAB)/originally **Brooklyn Savings Bank**, 205 Montague St., NW cor. Cadman Plaza W. 1962. *Carson, Lundin & Shaw.*

Urban renewal swallowed the **Brooklyn Savings Bank's** great *Frank Freeman* edifice at the northeast corner of Pierrepont and Clinton Streets, his one exercise in Roman pomp. This neat replacement holds the three street lines it

H45

confronts, an important effort where Cadman Plaza Park tends to create an amorphous scene.

[H42] Originally **National Title Guaranty Building**, 185 Montague St., bet. Cadman Plaza W. and Clinton St. N side. 1930. *Corbett, Harrison & MacMurray.* Entrance altered.

A bold early **Art Deco** building from the team that immediately after shared the design responsibility for Rockefeller Center. The bold three-dimensional massing remains fresh to this day.

[H43] **Citibank**/originally **People's Trust Company**, 183 Montague St., bet. Cadman Plaza W. and Clinton St. N side. 1903. *Mowbray & Uffinger.* Pierrepont St. Rear addition, 1929, *Shreve, Lamb & Harmon.*

This is a *D.W. Griffith* version of a **Roman** temple. The bank, unfortunately, is neither staffed nor patronized by bacchanalian revelers, so that the total effect is a little wistful, like an abandoned movie set. Built of marble, not just wire lath and plaster, it provides a sense of secu-

rity to its depositors...and who is now around to drive the moneylenders from the temple?

The sculpture in the pediment is unconscious Pop Art, particularly when overlaid with antipigeon spikes.

[H44] **Chase Bank**/formerly **Manufacturers Hanover Trust Company**/originally **Brooklyn Trust Company**, 177 Montague St., NE cor. Clinton St. 1913-1916. *York & Sawyer.* Interior.

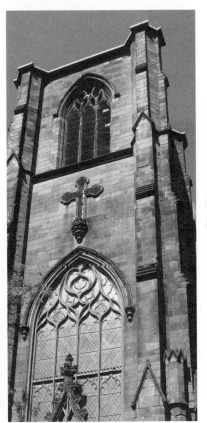

H46

The bottom and top of this rich Italian palace are copied from Verona's **Palazzo della Gran Guardia** (1610. *Domenico Curtoni*). In between, the model was stretched vertically to supply more floors for commerce. Corinthian engaged columns rest on rusticated tooled limestone. Free-standing "torcheres" guard the Montague Street entrance, aided by four mythological lions and an upper tier of tortoises.

At this point you enter the Brooklyn Heights Historic District:

[H45] **166 Montague Street Apartments**, originally **Franklin Trust Company**, SW cor. Clinton St. 1891. *George L. Morse.* Conversion to apartments, 2009, *Rothzied Kaiserman Thomson & Bee.*

A granite, rock-faced base, sunk within a moat, bears limestone arches and, in turn, brick and terra-cotta piers, columns, and arches. All are capped with a dormered red tile roof. A gem.

[H46] **St. Ann's and The Holy Trinity** (church)/ originally **Holy Trinity Protestant Episcopal Church**, 157 Montague St., NW cor. Clinton St. 1844-1847. *Minard Lafever*. Spire, 1866. Removed, 1905, *Patrick C. Keely*. Stained glass, *William Jay Bolton*. Restorations, 1979 to now, *Mendel Mesick Cohen Waite*.

Brownstone, unfortunately, weathers poorly. Here the New York Landmarks Conservancy has led the counterattack by citing this great neo-Gothic church as a cause célèbre. Concerts and theater of the avant-garde have aided its slow restoration, with a citywide constituency that gives heart to serious landmark preservation and restoration.

The interior is cast and painted plaster rather than carved stone, as it might appear at first glance. **Reredos** by *Frank Freeman*. The exterior is, unfortunately, minus its original brownstone spire.

[H47 & H48] **The Berkeley/The Grosvenor**, 111-113 and 115-117 Montague St., bet. Henry

H48

H49

and Hicks Sts. N side. 1885. *Parfitt Bros.*

Twin Queen Anne brownstone, terra-cotta, and brick apartment houses. Unsympathetic modern ground-floor shopfronts demean the wondrous architecture above; look up! There is a two-story Parisian-style mansard roof up there.

[H49] **The Montague**, 105 Montague St., bet. Henry and Hicks Sts. N side. 1885. *Parfitt Bros.*

Another **Queen Anne** extravaganza. Here a brooding face peers down from its terra-cotta pediment, leaning over a console bracket.

[H50] **Hotel Bossert**, 98 Montague St., SE cor. Hicks St. 1908-1913. *Helme & Huberty.*

Now a Jehovah's Witnesses hostel, this "modern" hotel was in the fashionable center of 1920s New York social life. The **Marine Roof** decorated in a yachting spirit by designer *Joseph Urban* (check his **New School** building in Greenwich Village), offered dining, dancing, and an unequaled view of the Manhattan skyline. The home of its founder, millwork manufacturer *Louis Bossert*, still stands.

[H51] **The Arlington**, 62 Montague St., bet. Hicks St. and Montague Terr. S side. 1887. *Montrose Morris.*

And yet another apartment house, modest housing of the middle class at a time when grand brownstones on adjacent Pierrepont and Remsen Streets housed single families and their servants. Shopkeepers, foremen, and others lived here next to the upper-income families of the Heights. The corner tower is undoubtedly for a resident *Rapunzel*.

[H52] **The Heights Casino**, 75 Montague St., bet. Hicks St. and Pierrepont Place. N side. 1905. *Boring & Tilton*. [H53a] **Casino Mansions Apartments**, 200 Hicks St., NW cor. Montague St. 1910. *William A. Boring*. [H53b] **24-32 Pierrepont Street**, bet. Hicks St. and Pierrepont Place. S side. ca. 1900. *Frank S. Lowe.*

Its founders described this indoor squash and tennis club as a "country club in the city." A handsome stepped gable dominates rich brickwork that was later mimicked in adjacent **200 Hicks**,

H50

H52

which stands on the site of the Casino's former outdoor tennis courts; the members required that architectural unity be retained as a condition for selling the land. **24-32 Pierrepont** is a handsome row of five houses that replaced the old **Martin House**, which had shared with the Casino (back-to-back) the footprint of the through-the-block site of an earlier and vaster mansion.

[H54] **1-13 Montague Terrace**, bet. Remsen and Montague Sts. E side. ca. 1886.
[H55] **8 Montague Terrace**, bet. Remsen and Montague Sts. W side. 1860s.

A complete terrace in the English sense, a set of row houses: another urbane remnant greater than the sum of its parts. Its cornice crowns the whole block, bonding it as if it were a grand single town house. Poet *W.H. Auden* lived at **No.1** from 1939-40, but missed having *Thomas Wolfe* as a neighbor by four years. *Wolfe* lived at **No.3** and wrote *Of Time and the River* here in 1933-1935.

No.8 is a particularly grand brownstone matron, broad in the beam, with sturdy Corinthian columns.

The view from the Esplanade

[H56] **24 Remsen Street**, bet. Montague Terrace and Hicks St. E side.
Roman yellow brick for a Renaissance Revival town house.

Take a detour to see the Manhattan skyline:

[H57] **The Esplanade**, W of Montague Terr., Pierrepont Place, and Columbia Heights, bet. Remsen and Orange Sts. 1950-1951. *Andrews, Clark & Buckley,* engineers. *Clarke & Rapuano,* landscape architects.

The most elegant brownstones remaining in New York: two out of an original trio; the third, (**No.1**, the **Henry E. Pierrepont House**. *Richard Upjohn*) was demolished in 1946 in favor of a playground at the time of the esplanade-expressway construction. *Alfred Tredway White*, Brooklyn philanthropist (**Tower and Home** and **Riverside Apartments** and the Botanical Garden's Japanese Garden), was born and brought up at No.2. *Abiel Low*, made a killing in the China trade, and his son, *Seth*, was mayor of Brooklyn, president of Columbia College, and

H58

The **Promenade**, as it's known locally, is a fringe benefit from the construction of this section of the Brooklyn-Queens Expressway, at first proposed by *Robert Moses* to bisect the Heights along Henry Street. A cantilevered esplanade—one of the few brilliant solutions for the relationship of auto, pedestrian, and city—was projected from the crest of the Heights to overlook the harbor on a fourth level, over two levels of highway and a service road (Furman Street) for the piers below. It's simple and successful: mostly hexagonal asphalt paving block, painted steel railings, hardy shrubbery, and honey locust trees. The lesson was most recently and happily repeated at the **Battery Park City Esplanade**.

Return to the street and turn left on Pierrepont Place:

[H58] Originally **Alexander M. White and Abiel Abbot Low Houses**, 2 and 3 Pierrepont Place, bet. Pierrepont and Montague Sts. W side. 1857. *Frederick A. Peterson.*

then mayor of a consolidated New York. He lived at No.3.

A peek at Pierrepont Street and then back onto Columbia Heights:

[H59] Originally **Mrs. Hattie I. James House**, 6 Pierrepont St., bet. Pierrepont Place and Willow St. S side. ca. 1890. *Parfitt Bros.*
Romanesque Revival with a strong, rock-face brownstone stair, elaborate foliate carved reliefs, and a bay window, not surprisingly, overlooking the bay.

[H60] **8-14 Pierrepont Street**, bet. Pierrepont Place and Hicks St. S side. ca. 1901.
Another terrace where the whole is greater than the sum of its parts. The bow windows form a gracious breast for these English town houses.

H60

[H61] **222 Columbia Heights**, NW cor. Pierrepont St. 1982. *Alfredo De Vido Assocs.*

Brown, glazed modern brick, with torii (rounded moldings) to assuage its Renaissance Revival flank. The bay window and garage door spoil this hearty attempt at landmark infill.

[H62] **210-220 Columbia Heights**, bet. Pierrepont and Clark Sts. W side. 1852-1860.

H61

H62

Two pairs and two singles. Altered, but the best remaining examples of group mansions in brownstone, although some have been painted light colors. Note No.210's rich **Corinthian** capitals and the varied neighboring mansard roofs and dormers, which create picturesque silhouettes.

[H63] **145 Columbia Heights**, bet. Pierrepont and Clark Sts. E side. ca. 1845.

Exquisite Corinthian columns on a simple brick volume.

[H64] **160 Columbia Heights** (apartments), SW cor. Clark St. 1937. *A. Rollin Caughey.*

An orange brick **Art Deco/Art Moderne** work with corner casement windows (not original, they were once in elegant slim steel) overlooking grand views of Manhattan. Shabby chic.

Turn right up Clark Street:

[H65] Originally **Leverich Towers Hotel**/now **Jehovah's Witnesses Residence Hall**, 25 Clark St., NE cor. Willow St. 1928. *Starrett & Van Vleck.*

Comfortably affluent materials borrowed from **Romanesque** architectural history: brick over random ashlar stonework over granite, with supporting molded terra-cotta decoration. The four arched and colonnaded towers were once spotlighted nightly after sunset.

H63

H66

Turn right again onto Willow Street:

[H66] **Dansk Sömandskirke**, 102 Willow St., bet. Clark and Pierrepont Sts. W side.

A brownstone happily converted into the Danish Seamen's Church.

Willow Street *offers a variety of buildings, all of which together form an urban allée of happy variations. Buildings of note other than those described below include **No.104,** a shingled remnant, gray and white, with a Federal fanlight; **No.106,** with interesting Eastlake incised lintels; **Nos.118, 120, 122,** with neo-Gothic window hoods and cast-iron railings; **No.124,** with a stepped neo-Amsterdam gable and weather vane; and **No.149,** a vigorous tenement, bay-windowed and reclaimed.*

[H67] Originally **S.E. Buchanan House**, 109 Willow St., bet. Clark and Pierrepont Sts. E side. 1905. *Kirby, Petit & Green.*

An awkward **neo-Federal** emulation of the original **Federal** style. There are many wonderful neo-Federal buildings in the City, especially on the Upper East Side, but few have the beautiful economy of the originals. Seek out the real things while they last.

[H69] **151 Willow Street**, bet. Clark and Pierrepont Sts. E side. ca. 1870.

Allegedly a link in the underground railroad, it is aligned with an earlier town plan, set back and skewed. Note the rare **dawn redwood** (*Metasequoia glyptostroboides*), from China, growing in the side garden.

[H70] **155-159 Willow Street**, bet. Clark and Pierrepont Sts. E side. ca. 1826.

Three elegant Federal houses equal to

H65

H72

[H68] **108, 110, and 112 Willow Street**, bet. Clark and Pierrepont Sts. W side. 1880. *William Halsey Wood.*

The **Shingle Style** in Brooklyn. Picturesque massing and profiles produce odd internal spaces and balconies for our contemporary fun. Terra-cotta reliefs, elaborate doorways, bay windows, towers, and dormers. The English architect *Richard Norman Shaw* (1831-1912) was group leader for these fantasies; in his bailiwick he produced what was strangely termed **Queen Anne**. This is arguably New York's finest example.

Queen Anne: *A style of English architecture introduced to this country in the British pavilion at the 1876 Philadelphia Centennial Exposition, it remained popular for some 20 years. Its name is deceiving. Queen Anne of England died in 1714, a century and a half before the style was so dubbed, but it was during her 12-year reign that some of the Gothic and Renaissance elements found in this romantic style were earlier revived.*

No.24 Middagh. but in brick. The glass pavers set into **No.157**'s sidewalk bear an apocryphal tale that they skylit a tunnel leading to **No.151**, which served the underground railroad leading slaves to northern freedom. The three houses are askew from Willow Street as they were built to the earlier geometry of Love Lane, which once extended this far west.

Take a left onto Pierrepont Street:

[H71] **35 Pierrepont Street**, bet. Willow and Hicks Sts. N side. 1929. *Mortimer E. Freehof.*

The roofscape and silhouette of this **Art Deco** apartment block have all stops pulled out. A pleasantly synthetic—or is it precocious—postmodern bag of tricks?

[H72] Originally **George Hastings House**, now apartments, 36 Pierrepont Street, bet. Willow and Hicks Sts. S side. 1846. *Richard Upjohn.*

A freestanding **neo-Gothic** house and garden. Its Pierrepont Street stoop, reincarnated in the 1990s, provides appropriate **ogees** and **trefoils**.

[H73a] **131 and 135 Hicks Street**, bet. Pierrepont and Clark Sts. E side. 1848.

Gothic Revival. 135 is where *Lewis Mumford* and his wife, *Sophia Wittenberg*, lived in 1925 when his critique on American architecture, "Sticks and Stones" was published. They occupied the basement garden apartment.

[H73b] **173-175 Hicks Street**, bet. Pierrepont and Clark Sts. E side.ca. 1848

Greek Revival flutes.

[H74] Originally **Hotel Pierrepont**, 55 Pierrepont St., bet. Hicks and Henry Sts. N side. 1928. *H.I. Feldman.*

From the days when even speculative hotels bore lion finials and griffin gargoyles. Now a neatly maintained home for the elderly. See **70 Remsen Street** for more Feldman neo-Romanesque.

[H75] **The Woodhull**, 62 Pierrepont St., bet. Hicks and Henry Sts. S side. 1911. *George Fred Pelham.*

The dowdy ground floor belies the extravagant Belle Epoque Parisian architecture above. Had it been built in London, it would be Edwardian.

[H76] **84 Pierrepont Street**/originally **Herman Behr House**/later **Palm Hotel**/ later **Franciscan House of Studies**/now a residential condominium. SW cor. Henry St. 1889. *Frank Freeman.*

After *Behr*, this mansion had a profane and then sacred existence prior to being converted

H73a

in 1977 into apartments. In the **Palm Hotel's** declining years it was said to have housed the local madam and her lovelies. It then served as a residence for Franciscan brothers. Despite the structure's social vagaries, *Freeman's* design remains a distinguished monument on the Heights streetscape. The façade, recently cleaned and restored, adds new sparkle to this prominent corner.

[H77] **161 Henry Street**, NE cor. Pierrepont St. 1906. *Schneider & Herter.*

This vigorous building's strong character shows that architecture was once part of a resident's basic needs. Here it bestows identity to the occupants in the process, as do **Central Park West's** grand apartment houses.

A short one-block detour to the left to Love Lane:

[H78] **137, 141, 143 Henry Street**, bet. Pierrepont and Clark Sts. E side. 1870s. No.143 restored, 1987, *Susan Podufaly.*

Three of a former quartet. Their restored painted clapboard splendor modulates the street, with bay windows and porches reinforcing the rhythm of the stoops.

[H79] **Love Lane and College Place**, both in the block bet. Henry and Hicks Sts. N of Pierrepont St.

The names of these two byways are more charming than their reality, but the mystery is worth a detour. Note that Love Lane is skewed from the grid's rectilinear geometry. **28-33 College Place** provide a memory of what the whole lane and place were about in the 19th century.

[H80] **104 Pierrepont Street**/originally **Thomas Clark House**, bet. Henry and Clinton Sts. S side. 1856.

H78

A brownstone row-mansion. A magnificent bronze railing, stolen in 1993, was mostly recouped and re-installed, but still missing are intricate strapwork panels. *Norval White* lived here for 30 years.

[H81] **106 Pierrepont Street**, bet. Henry and Clinton Sts. S side. 1890s.

Earlier brownstones on the block was cut without expertise, and from quarries of fragile stone. **106**, on the contrary, is of harder, firmer stone, and allowed the survival of delicate detail that failed in most earlier buildings—hence the proliferation of brownstone "restoration" in these parts.

[H82] Originally **P.C. Cornell House**, 108 Pierrepont Street at Monroe Place. S side. 1840.

The harried remains of a great **Greek Revival** double house; the only original part is the anthemlon-ornamented pediment over the front door. Once two stories and basement, it was raised to three, and a post–Civil War cornice was added.

H86

H82

H83

[H83] **114 Pierrepont Street**/originally **George Cornell House**, later Alfred C. Barnes House, at Monroe Place. S side. 1840. Totally altered, 1887. Further remodeled, 1912.

Once the siamese twin of No.108, this was "modernized" in 1887 for publisher *Barnes*, a transmogrification of staggering impact. A simple

[H84] **Appellate Division, N.Y.S. Supreme Court**, Monroe Place, NW cor. Pierrepont St. 1938. *Slee & Bryson.*

A prim and proper freestanding Classical Revival monument of the 1930s, with a pair of powerful Doric columns confronting Monroe Place.

brick building became a **Wagnerian** stage set: Romanesque Revival with some random eclectic tricks thrown in. Aside from its melodramatic architectural history, its social history includes use as a residence, as the Brooklyn Women's Club (after 1912), as a Christian Science Church, and, most recently, the fate of most if not all venerable buildings: condominiums.

*Monroe Place: A 700-foot-long, 80-foot-wide urban (and urbane) space, a quiet backwater on axis with the Cornell house described above. The proportions of the street and its containment at both ends are far more important than the buildings that line it; for this, like **Sidney, Garden**, and **Willow Places**, is the product of the staggered grid that fortuitously made this area so much richer than most of grid-planned Manhattan or Brooklyn. Do take a look at two houses at the north end: **No.3** (1849), with its later cast-iron planter and goldfish pond; and **No.12** (1847), where shutters have been returned to the façade.*

[H85] **First Unitarian Church**/properly **Church of the Saviour**, Pierrepont St. NE cor. Monroe Place. 1842-1844. *Minard Lafever.*

Country-Village neo-Gothic. *Lafever*, a carpenter by training, was a talented and prolific architect who practiced in many styles (including Egyptian Revival for a church in Sag Harbor). He wrote a well-known and well-used copybook for builders, The *Beauties of Modern Architecture*. The cast-iron fence is guarded by six crenellated castelets.

[H86] **Brooklyn Historical Society**/originally **Long Island Historical Society**, 128 Pierrepont St., SW cor. Clinton St. 1881. *George B. Post,* architect. *Olin Levi Warner*, façade sculptures. Restorations, 1998, *Jan Hird Pokorny*. Open to the public. Museum hours: We-Fr 12-5, Sa 10-5, Su 12-5; closed Mo-Tu. Library hours: We-Fr 1-5. 718-222-4111. *www.brooklynhistory.org*

Post used a bright but narrow range of Italian reds at a time when earth colors were popular, from the polychromy of *John Ruskin* to

H93

the near-monochromy of *Frank Freeman's* Richardsonian Romanesque City of Brooklyn Fire Headquarters on Jay Street. One of the City's great architectural treasures, both outside and in. There are usually small exhibits and always a great local history collection.

[H87] **St. Ann's School**/originally **Crescent Athletic Club,** 129 Pierrepont St., NW cor. Clinton St. 1906. *Frank Freeman.*
    Once one of Brooklyn's most prestigious men's clubs, it boasted a swimming pool, squash courts, gym, and three grand two-story spaces surrounded by mezzanines. After the club folded in 1940, it served as an office building until 1966, when St. Ann's School bought and converted it.

[H88] **One Pierrepont Place** also known as **Morgan Stanley Building,** Pierrepont St. bet. Clinton St. and Cadman Plaza W. N side. 1988. *Haines Lundberg Waehler.*

Brobdingnag comes to **Lilliput.** This behemoth not only looms over the Heights but has become an obese silhouette to much of Brooklyn. The mansarded crest gives a flashy cap to a dumpy body.

Within the Clinton Street flank, however:

[H88a] **Rotunda Gallery,** 33 Clinton St., bet. Pierrepont St. and Cadman Plaza W. 1991. *Smith-Miller & Hawkinson.* Tu-Sa, 12-6. 718-875-4047. *www.briconline.org/rotunda*
    A beautifully detailed space in poured concrete with movable partitions.

END of Central Heights Walking Tour: If you are hungry, Montague Street's eateries are only a block away, as is the BMT local Court Street subway station at Montague and Clinton Streets (M, N, and R trains). The IRT is a block further east, at Court (Nos.2, 3, 4, & 5 trains).

*North Heights Walking Tour: Of the three
walks through Brooklyn Heights this offers
the greatest contrasts: old and new, affluent
and modest, tiny and large, domestic and
institutional.*

*START on the southwest corner of Clark and
Hicks Streets, less than a block west of the IRT
Seventh Avenue Station turnstiles within the old
St. George Hotel arcade (Nos.2 and 3 trains).
Walk east along Clark Street across from the old
hotel, take a brief detour south into Henry Street,
and then return to Clark and continue east:*

[H89] Originally **St. George Hotel**, bet. Hicks and
Henry Sts., Clark and Pineapple Sts. 1885.
Augustus Hatfield. Additions, 1890-1923,
Montrose W. Morris & others. Tower Building,
1929-1930. *Emery Roth*.

The contrasts of the North Heights are
properly introduced by those of the old **St.
George,** a set of architectural accretions that
occupies a full city block and that once was the

*The route around Cadman Towers and through
Pineapple Walk takes you briefly outside the
Brooklyn Heights Historic District to the land of
the giants:*

[H93] **Cadman Towers**, 101 Clark St., bet. Henry
St. and Cadman Plaza W. N side; 10 Clinton St., at
Cadman Plaza W. W side; plus row housing along
Clark St., Monroe Place, and Cadman Plaza W.
1973. *Glass & Glass* and *Conklin & Rossant*.

Urban renewal, once a disastrous incision
into the City's fabric, was tempered here by a
1970s attempt at more sophisticated urban
design: low-rise town house elements form
façades that attempted to bridge the scale from
the towers proper to the contiguous 19th-
century Heights streetscape. The towers are
handsome but too big, and the town house
bridge is a joke, like doll houses confronting a
wall of four- and five-story brick and brownstone.

*Turn left at Cadman Plaza West and left again
into the pedestrian mall called Pineapple Walk.*

H87

H96

City's largest hotel (with 2,632 rooms). Now
separate properties.

[H90] **Clark Lane** (apartments), 52 Clark St., bet.
Hicks and Henry Sts. S side. ca. 1927. *Slee &
Bryson*.

Eclectic architects found a style for
every occasion. These, later designers of the
Appellate Courthouse, chose a Romanesque
arcade and Gothic gargoyles for this apartment
hotel.

[H91] **First Presbyterian Church**, 124
Henry St., S of Clark St. W side. 1846.
William B. Olmsted. Memorial doorway, 1921,
James Gamble Rogers.

[H92] **German Evangelical Lutheran Zion
Church**/originally **Second Reformed Dutch
Church**. 1840.

Two churches that occupy almost opposite
sites. The Presbyterian is solid, stolid, and dour;
the Lutheran is spare, prim, and denuded of its
northern spire.

*Continue west along Pineapple Street itself
(back into the Historic District), through the
dark backside of the St. George Hotel's original
block, its rear mysteriously more intriguing than
its bland Clark Street façade:*

[H94] **60** and **70 Pineapple Street** (condominiums), bet. Hicks and Henry Sts. S side.

A renovated segment of the old St. George
Hotel, cleaned of its dour gray paint down to the
roseate brick. Perks up this somber street.

[H95] **13 Pineapple Street** (house), bet. Willow
St. and Columbia Heights. N side. ca. 1830.

An unusually wide, gray-shingled, freestanding, white-trimmed, single house redolent of
these North Heights days before the masons took
over. Reminds us of Nantucket, of all places.

[H96] **Jehovah's Witnesses Dormitory
and Library Facility**, 119 Columbia
Heights, SE cor. Pineapple St. 1970. *Ulrich
Franzen & Assocs.*

An early design under the then new Landmarks Law. The three row-house façades south of this new building are integrated internally with the new structure. The stoops, with entries now closed off, are therefore no longer functional but still add to the rhythms of the block.

If you haven't savored the lower Manhattan skyline from these bluffs, cross Columbia Heights and walk to the right along the Promenade. The tour picks up one block north at:

[H97] **The Margaret** (apartments), 97 Columbia Heights, NE cor. Orange St. 1988. *The Ehrenkrantz Group & Eckstut.*

This apartment house (purchased by Jehovah's Witnesses) filled the site of the great **Hotel Margaret** by *Frank Freeman* (1889). Under extensive renovation as condominium apartments, that magnificent structure [see Necrology] burned disastrously in 1980.

[H98] **70 Willow Street**/originally **Adrian van Sinderen House**, bet. Orange and Pineapple Sts. W side. ca. 1839.

A wide **Greek Revival** house, originally free-standing, now cheek by jowl with Jehovah's Witnesses to the north. Former owners filled the southern gap with a set-back-from-the-street stair tower. Stage designer *Oliver Smith* rescued this from the Red Cross, to whom it had been bequeathed, restoring its multipaned windows and making other corrections.

[H102] **45 Willow Street**, bet. Orange and Cranberry Sts. E side. 1820.

A crisply restored Federal house.

[H103] **13, 15,** and **19 Cranberry Street** (houses), NW cor. Willow St. ca. 1829-1834.

Greek Revival houses modernized, most extravagantly at No.19. Here a mansard roof made this a fashionable grande dame when the spare classicism of the early 19th century gave way to elaboration. The Empire gown acquired a sturdy bodice and a bustle.

[H104] **20-26 Willow Street** (houses), SW cor. Middagh St. ca. 1846.

No-nonsense Greek Revival, this painted brick and brownstone terrace is straightforward, austere, yet elegant. The two-story porches at the rear look out upon the harbor, their views framed by projecting masonry walls. *Henry Ward Beecher* lived at No.22.

[H105] **24 Middagh Street**/formerly **Eugene Boisselet House**, SE cor. Willow St. ca. 1829.

The queen of Brooklyn Heights houses: a wood-painted, gambrel-roofed **Federal** house with a **garden cottage** connected by a garden wall. Note especially the exquisite Federal doorway with its Ionic colonnettes and the quarter-round attic windows. Proportion, rhythm, materials, and color are in concert throughout.

H100   H103   H104   H111

[H99] **54 Willow Street** (apartments), bet. Orange and Cranberry Sts. W side. 1987. *Alfredo De Vido Assocs.*

A simplistic infill of a vacant lot, here appearing neither old nor new—nor particularly noticeable. The columns are nice to have, but naive.

[H100] **57 Willow Street**/originally **Robert White House**, NE cor. Orange St. ca. 1824.

The Orange Street wall is a lusty composition of real and blind windows, chimneys, and pitched roofs.

[H101] **47-47A Willow Street** (houses), bet. Orange and Cranberry Sts. E side. ca. 1860.

The apocrypha here state that there were two daughters and one site, riven to create a half for each. The internal guts are complicated by the need for tucking a stair into each 12-foot-wide unit.

[H106] **1-9 Willow Street**, bet. Middagh and Old Fulton Sts. S side. 1990s. *Edwards Rullman and Herbert Kaufman.*

A serious attempt at new row housing, with serrated façades modulating the ensemble.

Having turned the corner into Middagh Street, continue east:

[H107] **Middagh Street,** bet. Willow and Hicks Sts. ca. 1817.

One of the earliest streets on the Heights, it contains most of the remaining wood houses. Aside from the glorious **No.24**, they are now a motley lot: **No.28**, 1829, mutilated beyond recognition; **No.30**, 1824, Federal entrance and pitched roof still recognizable in spite of the tawdry asphalt shingles; **No.25**, 1824, mutilated; **No.27**, 1829, early Italianate here in wood shingles with painted trim; **No.29**, similar to **No.27**; **Nos.31** and **33**, 1847, mutilated.

[H108] **56 Middagh Street** (house), bet. Hicks and Henry Sts. S side. 1829. Porch added, ca. 1845.

Bold Doric columns provide both guts and style, with a rather blatant blue body behind.

[H109a] Originally **Joseph Bennett House**, 38 Hicks St. ca. 1830. Restored, 1976.
[H109b] Originally **Michael Vanderhoef House**, 40 Hicks St. ca. 1831. Restored, 1976.
[H109c] **38A Hicks Street** (house), behind No.38. All bet. Middagh and Poplar Sts. W side.

An extraordinary trio restored in the 1970s. The alley leading to **No.38A** is effectively their common ground, as at Patchin and Milligan Places in Greenwich Village. Time for another restoration?

The block between Poplar, Hicks, and Henry Streets and the Expressway (referred to by technocrats as Block 207) contains an interesting new and reconditioned residential enclave comprising a tenement, an orphan asylum, a former

were the former branch of the **Bowery-in-Brooklyn**, a minimal overnight bunkhouse for the homeless (restored, 1987, *Wids de la Cour and David Hirsch*).

[H112a] **Poplar Hall**, 77 Poplar St., bet. Henry and Hicks Sts. ca. 1880.

Handsome brick with a grand, boasting cornice.

[H113] Former **Henry Street Studios**/originally **Mason Au & Magenheimer Candy Company**, 20 Henry St., NW cor. Middagh St. 1885. *Theobald Engelhardt*. Reconstructed, 1975, *Pomeroy, Lebduska Assocs.*, architects, *Martyn and Don Weston*, associate architects.

A light industrial building of mill construction. Its bold brick-bearing walls, timber columns, and heavy plank flooring provided loft space for real and would-be artists. The north façade was designer *Lee Pomeroy's* modern face where a blank wall formerly stood. Mouth-watering memories for older sweet teeth are

H105

flophouse, and modern infillings—all under one developer's sponsorship:

[H110] **55 Poplar Street**, bet. Hicks and Henry Sts. N side. 1987. *Wids de la Cour and David Hirsch*.
[H111] Originally **Brooklyn Children's Aid Society Orphanage**, 57 Poplar St., bet. Hicks and Henry Sts. N side. 1883. Restored, 1987, *Wids de la Cour and David Hirsch*.

Built as a **home for indigent newsboys**, this ornate Victorian pile was abandoned during the urban renewal craze of the 1960s—it was then being used as a machine works—before adaptive reuse tardily came to it in the late 1980s. The heavy hands that razed the blocks between Henry Street and Cadman Plaza, Poplar and Clark Streets, spared this odd gem and the candy factory (now Henry Street Studios) to the south.

[H112] **61-75 Poplar Street**, bet. Hicks and Henry Sts. N side. 1987. *Charles A. Platt Partners*.

A modern row recapturing some (but only some) of the scale and flavor of the Heights. Remodeled units at the corner of Henry Street

conjured by the faded lettering on the south façade: **Peaks and Mason Mints**. Now being converted to Swankdom.

[H114] Former **Police Precinct Station House**, 66-78 Poplar St., bet. Henry and Hicks Sts. 1920s.

A succinct precinct: a straight-forward Florentine palazzo with a dynamic cornice soaring from the façade on high. The cops are gone. Who will fix it up?

[H114a] **80 Poplar Street**, bet. Henry and Hicks Sts. ca. 1850.

Sagging clapboard, much mutilated, but with cornice intact.

[H115] **Cadman Plaza North** (apartments), 140 Cadman Plaza W., N of Middagh St. W side. 1967.
[H116] **Whitman Close** (town houses), 33-43, 47-53, 55-69 Cadman Plaza W., S of Middagh St. W side.

[H117] **Whitman Close** (apartments), 75 Henry St., at Orange St. E side.
[H 117a] **Pineapple Walk**, Pineapple Walk bet. Henry St. and Cadman Plaza W. N side only. 1968. All by *Morris Lapidus & Assocs.*

These early, ungainly urban renewal projects attempted to heal the wound left by the excision of Cadman Plaza from the cityscape. The removal of elevated lines was a civilized advance, but it was accompanied by the demolition of blocks of sturdy Heights-scaled buildings. Token row houses (Whitman Close) and a grilled garage (Cadman Plaza North) matching the height, if not the scale, of the other side of the street, were the prosthetics. They fail, however, to define the intervening streets as urban spaces (rather than simply surfaces on which autos navigate), one of the principal qualities of the Heights. They are as inappropriate as a Greek Revival house from Willow Street would be on an acre in Scarsdale.

[H118] **The Cranlyn** (apartments), 80 Cranberry St., SW cor. Henry St. 1931. *H.I. Feldman.*

Art Deco on the Heights. Here the style presents glazed terra-cotta bas-relief, a bronze-plaque fantasy over the entrance, and jazzy brickwork. *Feldman* contributed two other multiple dwellings of interest to the Heights, both with **Romanesque** detail: 55 Pierrepont and 70 Remsen.

[H119] **Plymouth Church of the Pilgrims**/originally **Plymouth Church**, Orange St. bet. Henry and Hicks Sts. N side. 1849-1850. *Joseph C. Wells.*

H116

[H120] **Parish House and connecting arcade**, 75 Hicks St., NE cor. Orange St. 1913-1914. *Woodruff Leeming.*

Henry Ward Beecher preached here from 1847 to 1887. Excepting the porch, his church was an austere brick box of a barn on the exterior, articulated by relieving arches. (The Tuscan porch was added long after *Beecher* left.) The parish house, in an eclectic Classical Revival, happily encloses—together with its connecting arcade—a handsome garden court. Here *Beecher*, as seen through the eyes and hands of sculptor *Gutzon Borglum*, holds forth—or perhaps holds court. Unfortunately in this era of vandalism, the churchyard, which could be a pleasant place of repose, is locked.

In 1934 the **Congregational Church of the Pilgrims** abandoned its own church building, now **Our Lady of Lebanon**, and merged with Plymouth Church, causing the combined renaming. The Pilgrims' Tiffany windows were relocated at that time to Hillis Hall, behind Plymouth.

END of North Heights Walking Tour: The nearest subways are the IRT Seventh Avenue Line in the St. George Hotel (2 and 3 trains) or, via the Whitman Close town houses at Cranberry Street, the IND Eighth Avenue Line High Street Station (A and C trains). If your legs are still nimble you may wish to visit the Fulton Ferry District, the waterfront, and the dramatic view of the Brooklyn Bridge as it leaps across the waters of the East River.

NECROLOGY

McGarry Library, St. Francis College (since 1962)/originally (1857-1895) **Brooklyn Gas Light Company Headquarters**/later (1895-1914) **Brooklyn Union Gas Company Headquarters**, 180 Remsen St., bet. Court and Clinton Sts. S side. 1857.

A Tuscan-columned Classical temple that saw a variety of uses. The gas company moved out in 1914. The library was first subsumed into St.

Necrology, Hotel Margaret

Francis and then replaced by a new, modern building in limestone and glass.

Hotel Margaret, 97 Columbia Hts., NE cor. Orange St. Brooklyn Heights. 1889. *Frank Freeman.*

In the dead of a raw winter night a fire began in the nearly completed apartment conversion of this once grand old hotel. Curiously, in a community where fire trucks get to the scene in seconds, here the fire had raged silently within its thick walls for hours. By the time the equipment arrived the flames were out of control, and the structure burned fiercely for more than a day. It took tremendous quantities of water to quell the fire, causing spectacular icicles to festoon the burned-out façades and turning the nearby streets into bumpy skating rinks. The building's exuberant nautical look, with ornate sheet metal panels trimmed in exposed rivet heads, was very appropriate to its harbor-view siting. **A great urban injury**.

FULTON FERRY

U1

This flat riverfront beneath the Heights might well be termed the Bottoms. The shore of tidal waters, it was the natural place for a ferry landing, bringing hardy New Yorkers to the rural wilds of Long Island and exporting the produce of lush, flat Long Island farms to the City. Rowers and sailors plied the narrow link at first, a tenuous connection because of shifting tides and winds. And in 1776 it became the unhappy port of embarkation for Washington's troops fleeing Long Island under cover of darkness and fog after their defeat in the Revolution's first major battle. The first steam-powered ferry came in 1814 and, with it, an ever-increasing flow of traffic that was honored by a grand Victorian terminal in 1865. After 1883, with the opening of the new New York and Brooklyn Bridge, which still looms over this edgewater, the area was doomed as a commercial center, losing its river commuters slowly until the ferry service was discontinued in 1924.

During much of the 19th century, Fulton Street's downward curving route to the river (now renamed Cadman Plaza West or, in places,

Old Fulton Street) was a bustling place, easily accessible by streetcar and elevated, lined with all manner of commercial structures, and graced by places to eat, drink, and rest one's weary bones. Some of these buildings—if not activities—remain today. Remember as you walk along Front Street that it received its name as the last thoroughfare above water. Landfill in the early 19th century pushed the bulkhead and beach further west. In retrospect, it seems strange that New York (that is, Manhattan today) was mapped to Brooklyn's high-water line, thereby assigning the water—and its islands—to Manhattan. Boaters, swimmers, divers, gulls, and garbage floating on the East River are in Manhattan.

Fulton Ferry Historic District, generally bounded by Water and Main Sts., the East River, Furman and Doughty Sts., and from Front St. to Water St. on a line in back of the buildings along Cadman Plaza West. (Old Fulton St.) 🍎

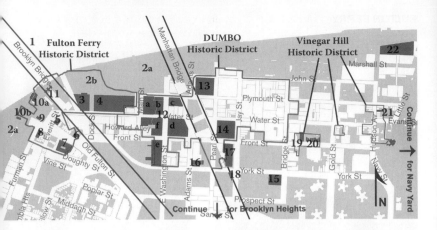

1 Fulton Ferry Historic District

DUMBO Historic District

Vinegar Hill Historic District

[U1] **The Brooklyn Bridge**, East River, bet. Adams St., Brooklyn, and Park Row, Manhattan. 1867-1883. *John A., Washington and Emily Roebling*. Reconstructed, 1955, *David Steinman*, consulting engineer. ☞

New York's supreme icon and most wondrous man-made object. The spider web of supporting and embracing cables richly enmeshes anyone strolling across its boardwalk, a highly recommended walk into the skyline of Manhattan. Start at the entrance stair on Washington Street where Cadman Plaza intersects the bridge. The current colors are reputed to be copies of the original subtle coffee and white, rather than the Public Works Gray that blunted lines and form in the 1930s through

U2b

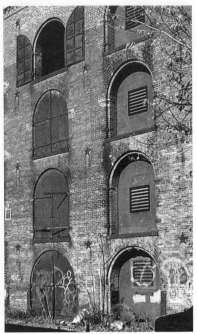

U4

1960s. New ramps for pedestrians and bicyclists opened in 1986, allowing (except for street crossings at each end) movement from island to island without stairs or steps.

[U2a] **Brooklyn Bridge Park.** 2011 (predicted). *Michael Van Valkenburgh,* landscape architect.
[U2b] **Empire Fulton Ferry State Park**, along Water Street between the bridges.

City dwellers meet the sea (the East River is a tidal connection between Long Island Sound and the Harbor, not a river) in a found park where one can sit on grassy lawns, under shady trees. The summer film series (*www.brooklynbridgepark.org*), with the Bridge as backdrop, is a lovely fringe benefit, with crowds lying on blankets watching, as boats churn lazily up the River.

Empire Fulton Ferry State Park was here first, still technically separate from **Brooklyn Bridge Park**, although the experience is of one continuous space. Within its bounds are grand arcaded historic brick warehouses:

[U3] **Tobacco Inspection Warehouse**, 25-39 Water St., bet. New Dock and Dock Sts. N side. ca. 1860.

Arched brickwork of the old Tobacco Warehouse, roofless: a magnificent contained plaza.

[U4] **Empire Stores**, 53-83 Water St., bet. Dock and Main Sts. N side. Western four-story group, 1869. Eastern five-story group, 1885. *Thomas Stone.*

A block of magnificent brick arched and some shuttered warehouses that once serviced the barks (square-masters), sailing freighters bearing goods to the Orient and Australia. The façades were brick, the expensive show material, the bearing walls within in rubble stone, the cheaper material paired with the then cheap labor. Forgotten by New Yorkers, they were rediscovered by photographer *Berenice Abbott* in the Federal Art Project of the WPA. Forgotten again, they were bought by Con Edison for a potential generating plant and then considered by the City as site for the Brooklyn meat market. Now recaptured for the people.

Norval White's uncle, Fred Taylor, embarked here on the Glasgow-based bark, Princess Margaret, in September 1905. He was 18, taken on as cabin boy in a voyage to Freemantle, Australia. The Brooklyn Bridge, then only 22 years old, and built to allow all ships to pass, didn't allow the bark through without its crew striking (folding down) the top section of its 164 foot tall masts. And so in turn did the U.S. Navy strike its masts in World War II, seeking the sea after works at Dry Dock #1 in the Navy Yard.

[U5] **Pete's** (restaurant)/originally **Franklin House** (hotel), 1 Old Fulton St., E cor. Water St. 1835. Altered, 1850s.

This simple relic of the ferry's balmy days and its neighbors recall the time before the Brooklyn Bridge, when the traffic of people and produce passed up Old Fulton Street.

[U6] Originally **Long Island Safe Deposit Company,** 1 Front St., N cor. Old Fulton St. 1868-1869. *William Mundell.*

A cast-iron Renaissance palazzo. This monumental bank overshadowed its older neighbors in the prosperous post–Civil War era. The Brooklyn Bridge's diversion of commuting traffic after 1883 forced the bank to close its doors in 1891.

[U7] **Eagle Warehouse**/originally **Eagle Warehouse and Storage Company of Brooklyn,** 28 Old Fulton St., SE cor. Elizabeth St. 1893. *Frank Freeman.* Condominium alteration, 1980, *Bernard Rothzeid.*

U6

U7

A stolid medieval revival warehouse, now recycled as condominiums. The **machicolations** (a word every cocktail party one-upman should know) are equaled only in a few remaining scattered Brooklyn armories. The bronze lettering, a lost art, articulates the grand Romanesque Revival arched entry, and the clock's glass face is the window of a spectacular studio loft. Note also the lusty ironwork at the entrance and over the streetside windows. *Freeman,* Brooklyn's greatest architect, designed two buildings tragically lost to fire: the **Bushwick Democratic Club** [see Bushwick Necrology] and the **Margaret Hotel** [see Brooklyn Heights Necrology].

[U8] **8 Old Fulton Street**/originally **Brooklyn City Railroad Company Building,** SE cor. Furman St. 1860-1861. Remodeled, 1975, *David Morton.* 🖉

When the ferryboat was queen, horsecars would line a row of gleaming tracks inlaid in the cobbled pavement, waiting to transport commuters into the heart of Brooklyn. What more appropriate place for the headquarters of that transit combine than here, overlooking the ebb and flow of both tide and passengers?

Now inevitable condominium apartments. Quieter, but much less lively.

[U9] Originally **Marine Company 7, N.Y.C. Fire Department** (fireboat)/onetime **Fulton Ferry Museum, National Maritime Historical Society,** foot of Old Fulton St. 1926.

This simple structure rears a tower for the traditional drying of fire hoses, a churchlike

U9

symbol on the site of the former ferry terminal. The latter expired in 1924. Now serving **homemade ice cream!**

[U10a] **Fulton Ferry Pier,** N.Y.C. Department of Ports & International Trade & Commerce, foot of Old Fulton Street, at the East River. 1976.

A sliver of river, and a popular gathering place for tourists and Brooklynites alike over the last 30 years, its role will now be as a link between north and south sections of Brooklyn Bridge Park.

[U10b] **Bargemusic,** foot of Old Fulton Street, moored to the Fulton Ferry Pier. 718-624-2083. *www.bargemusic.org*

Violinist *Olga Bloom* conceived the idea, renovated the barge, and founded this home to chamber music, opening in 1977.

[U11] **River Café**, 1 Water St., foot of Old Fulton Street, secretly sitting on piles.

A place to be in, not look at. Here the picture postcard of lower Manhattan is displayed live. Sit at the bar and savor the finial towers of the 1930s, the fat boxes of the 1950s, and the constant river traffic . . . for a price. Reservations are recommended at any pseudopopular moment. River-hopping celebrities can clutter the stage.

U12a

DUMBO

Largely the invention of developer *David Walentas*, DUMBO (Down Under the Manhattan Bridge Overpass!) has fast-tracked the usual gentrification trajectory (from industry to artists to small business to yuppies and chain stores) in just under ten years. As recently as the late 1990s Dumbo was a collection of deserted factories and loft buildings between the Brooklyn and Manhattan bridges, with no identity as a neighborhood. The actual neighborhood was the isolated enclave of Vinegar Hill, which remains in sleepy form just to the north, but Dumbo was desolate and often dangerous: a no man's land in the shadows of the bridges, perfect for *Robert DeNiro* films (fake) and mafia battles (real).

Dumbo is now just like any other expensive neighborhood in New York, but it has managed to preserve some of its uniqueness: its iconic and much photographed view down Washington Street of the Manhattan Bridge looming in the mist, the large rough-hewn cobbles that make up its streets,

and the endearing contrast in scale between the two massive bridges and the much smaller buildings below. Unfortunately, several new buildings would rather tower above the bridges than hunker in-between. "Down Under" now seems to be aspiring to "Rising Above." ("**RAMBO**," anyone?)

The location and views can't be beat, but Dumbo's popularity remains surprising considering the inescapable noise. The B, D, N, and Q trains thunder across the Manhattan Bridge continuously, drowning out conversation. Everywhere around the neighborhood are successful young people **RAISING THEIR VOICES** while yet another train rattles by overhead.

Dumbo Historic District, under the Manhattan Bridge, with varying edges, East to Bridge St., West to Main St., between John and York Sts. ✇

The Dumbo Historic District, located along the East River under and between the Manhattan and Brooklyn Bridges, with a projection to the East, is New York City's most significant extant industrial waterfront neighborhood.

U18

[U12a] **Walentas Building ("The Clock Tower")/ Gair Building No.7**, 1 Main St. ca. 1888. *William Higginson*. Converted to condominiums, 1999, *Beyer Blinder Belle*. [12b] **No.1,** 30 Washington St., bet. Plymouth and Water Sts., [12c] **No.2,** 25 Washington St., bet. Plymouth and Water Sts., [12d] **Nos.3 & 4,** 55 Washington St., bet. Front and Water Sts., [12e] **No.5,** 70 Washington St., bet. York and Front Sts., [12f] **No.6,** 45 Main St., bet. Front and Water Sts. 1904-1908. *William Higginson*.

A gaggle of reinforced-concrete loft buildings erected by *Robert Gair*, a pioneering entrepreneur in the corrugated box industry. They are some of the earliest concrete engineering in America. The Clock Tower's eponymous clocks surround a 3,500 square foot, 25 foot tall condominium volume.

[U13] **135 Plymouth Street/15 Adams Street**, NE cor. Adams St. 1901. *Rudolph L. Daus/William Tubby*.

A Romanesque Revival former factory, now with artist studios above and aromatic garbage compacting below.

[U14] Originally **Grand Union Tea Company,** 58-68 Jay St. and 57-67 Pearl St., bet. Front and Water Sts. 1896-1907. *Edward N. Stone.*

Built in two stages, with first the Pearl Street building, then Jay Street, with handsome brick and "jack-arched" windows. Grand Union segued into a huge grocery store chain (similarly the Great Atlantic and Pacific Tea Co. became the **A&P**). These buildings are the hub of the artist scene in Dumbo, with painters, photographers, furniture makers, theater groups, and rock bands all sharing studio spaces in a warren of twisting corridors. Lively.

[U15] Onetime **Eskimo Pie Building**/originally **Thomson Meter Company Building,** 100-110 Bridge St., bet. York and Prospect Sts. 1908-1909. *Louis E. Jallade.* 🖝

Glazed terra cotta swathes this lusty exposed-concrete building with lush foliage. *Jallade* may have seen *Auguste Perret's* **25 bis rue Franklin** in Paris, then recently completed, with an exposed concrete frame infilled with glazed tile by *Alexandre Bigot.*

U17

The new arrivals:

[U16] **Beacon Tower,** 85 Adams St., NE cor. York St. 2006. *CetraRuddy.*

Dumbo's tallest tower, trying to peek at *Gehry* (Beekman Tower) across the river. The lovable old **Between the Bridges** bar was demolished to make room.

[U17] **100 Jay Street,** SW cor. Front St. to York St. 2005. *Gruzen Samton.*

Another warehouse for burgeoning Dumbo, but for people. A glass bellied façade at odds with the Manhattan Bridge.

[U18] **110 York Street** (penthouse), bet. Jay St. and Manhattan Bridge overpass. 2004. *Robert Scarano.*

Scarano used every trick known to architects for this, his penthouse office atop a 19th-century warehouse. From below it's pleasantly ramshackle; from the bridge it's intrusive, its over-designed roof trusses garishly lighted.

VINEGAR HILL

A lost backwater of old Brooklyn, cut off to the east by the Navy Yard, and from the west by commerce and industry. Now that Dumbo is sprouting apartment towers, it assumes the status of a grand old, but seedy historic island among the hipsters.

Vinegar Hill Historic District, including 302-320 Plymouth St., 1-7 & 2-10 Evans St., 49-79, 50-54 & 70-74 Hudson Ave., all of Harrison Alley, 280-286 & 312-320 Water St., 202-204 & 225-249 Front Street. Extant buildings, 1805-1908. 🖝

[U19] Originally **Benjamin Moore & Co. Factory,** 231 Front Street. 1908. *William Tubby.*

Tubby's more elegant memories can be seen at the Charles Millard Pratt House. With a bit of imagination, one could see some Chicago style in this banded brick and limestone warehouse.

U22

🏛 [U20] **237-249 Front Street,** bet. Bridge and Gold Sts. 1840s.

A row of seven intact **Greek Revival** brick houses.

[U21] **51 Hudson Avenue,** bet. Plymouth and Evans Sts. E side. ca. 1845.

A bedraggled clapboard survivor, formerly with a bar on the ground floor, from the time before fire laws demanded non-combustible exterior materials.

[U22] **Consolidated Edison Stacks,** foot of Hudson Ave.

At the foot of Vinegar Hill the gaggle of stacks for Con Ed's generating plant form a triumphal punctuation to the local skyline.

*Hidden behind Hudson Avenue, south of Evans Street and nestled against the western edge of the Navy Yard, is mysterious **Harrison Alley**; from its locked gate several houses are visible amid thick vegetation.*

THE NAVY YARD

[N1] **Brooklyn Navy Yard Development Corporation**/formerly **Brooklyn Navy Yard**/officially **The New York Naval Shipyard**, Flushing Ave. to the East River, Hudson and Navy Sts. to Kent Ave.

Brooklyn's oldest industry, a shipyard founded here in the body of Wallabout Bay, purchased by the Navy in 1801 and abandoned in 1966. During World War II, 71,000 naval and civilian personnel toiled in this City within the City (24 hours per day, in three shifts). Many of its dry docks are still in use and its abandoned buildings are being refurbished, put to work in a variety of free-enterprise ways: manufacturing (windows, doors, pre-fab homes), stage sets for TV and movies, and artist's studios. Tours, in conjunction with the Brooklyn Historical Society, are available with an appointment. See *www.brooklynnavyyard.org* for more information.

[N2] Formerly **Commandant's House, Quarters A**, New York Naval Shipyard, S of Evans and Little Sts. (E of Hudson Ave.) 1805-1806. ❦ Apochryphally attributed to *Charles Bulfinch*, associated with *John McComb, Jr.*

Only a glimpse of the rear is possible, for the old Navy gates intervene. For most people—at least below the rank of admiral—a photograph had to suffice. But a rare Federal (style) wooden mansion surveys the working shipyard below.

[N3] **Dry Dock No.1** of the former New York Naval Shipyard, inside Navy Yard, Dock St. at the foot

N2

of 3rd St. 1840-1851. *William J. McAlpine*, engineer. *Thornton MacNess Niven*, architect and master of masonry. ❦

Considered one of the great feats of 19th-century American engineering, this granite-walled dry dock has serviced such ships as the **Niagara**, the vessel that laid the first transatlantic cable, and the **Monitor**, the Civil War's cheesebox on a raft. The **Niagara** was conceived and financed by a consortium headed by the painter-inventor *Samuel F. B. Morse* and the entrepreneur-philanthropist *Peter Cooper*. A tour of the Navy Yard is worth it just for a peak at this marvel, still in use!

[N4] **Paymaster's Building** (Building No.121), inside Navy Yard, SW cor. Chauncey Avenue and 3rd St. 1899.

The Navy Yard's bank, it's possibly the work of the great Philadelphia architect *Frank Furness*. If not *Furness*, it's the work of an admirer: the rich burgundy brick and decorative detail are certainly *Furnessian*.

[N5] **Perry Building**, inside Navy Yard, SE cor. Chauncey Avenue and 3rd St. 2008. *Stantec.* Interiors, *Steven Kratchman.*

A rare 21st-century New York industrial building, handsomely clad in taut corrugated steel, wind turbines on top. *Stantec* is a gargantuan "global design and engineering" firm that makes "big" offices like *Skidmore, Owings and Merrill* look puny; they could easily toss off Rome in a day.

[N6] **NYPD Tow Pound Operations Building**, inside Navy Yard, bet. Navy St. and First Ave. 2009. *Spacesmith.*

A simple box of stainless steel, its façade dominated by enormous letters: **NYPD**. The sign doubles as a sun screen. Architect *Robert Venturi* would call this shiny "vehicle redemption facility" a "decorated shed" (see his *Learning from Las Vegas*, 1972).

N3

[N7] **Marine Commandant's House (Building 92)**, inside Navy Yard, bet. Flushing Ave., 6th St. and Seventh Ave. 1857. *Thomas Ustick Walter.*

Walter was the fourth Architect of the Capitol and a founder of the AIA. Renovation into the **Brooklyn Navy Yard Center**, with a visitor's center addition (*Beyer Blinder Belle*) is planned.

[N8] **Steiner Studios**, inside Navy Yard, bet. Gee Ave., Market St., Assembly Rd., and Welding Rd., 2002-2006. *Dattner Architects.*

Sound stages for film production, precast concrete walls set between the stages (to dampen sound transmission), and a dutiful glass and steel façade. An important new presence in the Navy Yard, but dull compared to the dramatic sweep of great industrial buildings, docks, and cranes surrounding it.

N9

[N9] Originally **U.S. Marine Hospital**/later **U.S. Naval Hospital,** Flushing Ave., bet. Ryerson St. and Williamsburg Place. N side. 1830-1838. Wings, 1840. Alterations, 1862, *Martin E. Thompson.* 💣

N6

This austere Greek Revival hospice was built of Sing Sing marble quarried by those hapless prisoners. Later "Classical modernists" used similar spartan lines for simplistic public buildings of the 1930s and 1940s, culminating in the pompous buildings of *Albert Speer's* visions for *Hitler's* **Berlin** or *Mussolini's* **"Third Rome."** *Thompson* was a talented Greek Revivalist who muted his palette for such a functional program as this. Renovation is planned which will turn this magnificent ruin into an annex for Steiner Studios next door.

[N10] **Surgeon's House,** Quarters R1, 3rd Naval District, on grounds of U.S. Naval Hospital, opp. Ryerson St. 1863. *True W. Rollins and Charles Hastings,* builders. 💣

A spacious two-story brick house crowned with a French Empire concave-profiled mansard roof. Such was the privileged residence of the Naval Hospital's chief surgeon. Currently magnificent as a haunting (haunted?) overgrown relic.

ENDANGERED

[N11] **"Admiral's Row,"** along Flushing Avenue, NE cor. Navy St. ca. 1850-1900.

Slated for demolition to make way for a grocery store, these ten onetime handsome mansarded houses, now in ruin, were originally used as homes by high-ranking naval officials. The partial collapse of **Quarters C** in 2009 didn't help the cause of preservationists fending off demolition.

The long, low **Timber Shed** (ca. 1830) at the corner of Navy Street and Flushing Avenue, is also significantly historic, originally used to cure wood for ship's masts, but it too is gradually returning to the ground from whence it came. This is what happens when you leave buildings out in the rain.

N8

NECROLOGY

Formerly **U.S. Naval Receiving Station**/later **N.Y.C. Department of Correction facility,** 136 Flushing Ave., bet. Clermont and Vanderbilt Aves. to Park Ave. 1941.

A transient facility for naval personnel arriving, leaving, and/or tarrying at the old Naval Yard. It had that Art Moderne stylishness that went with the end of the depression and the beginning of World War II. The sailors were replaced by prisoners overflowing from other jails.

COBBLE HILL

South of Atlantic Avenue, just below fashionable Brooklyn Heights, lies the community of Cobble Hill with vast rows of distinguished housing, many institutions, and numerous fine churches, although many have given way to condominiums within their Gothic Revival guts. Overlooked by the urbane young middle class until the 1950s, when an enterprising real estate broker rediscovered the name *Cobles Hill* on the 1766 Ratzer map of New York and Brooklyn and updated its spelling. As the Heights filled with a new brownstone apartment-dwelling population, and rents soared, Cobble Hill became an attractive alternate, with equivalent housing just a bit further from the bridge and skyline. Coblehill, or **Ponkiesbergh**, referred to the steep conical hill (since removed) near the intersection of Court Street and Atlantic Avenue. Its peak, during the Revolution, was the site of an important Continental army fortification during the Battle of Brooklyn.

[C1] **Cobble Hill Historic District**, Atlantic Ave. to DeGraw St., Hicks to Court Sts., excepting the NW corner lands of Long Island College Hospital. ✸

Long Island College Hospital, the fun buildings (within the Historic District):

🏛 [C2] **Dudley Memorial**, formerly **Long Island College Hospital**, 110 Amity St., SE cor. Henry St. 1902. *William C. Hough.*

C2   C4

Richly adorned and in dark red brick, this latter-day miniature Henri IV "hôtel particulier" recalls the architecture of the **Place des Vosges** and the Hôpital St. Louis in Paris. It is a fitting neighbor to its adjoining bourgeois row houses. **Abandoned**. Are condominiums coming? Check our next edition for the outcome.

🏛 [C3] **Polhemus Memorial Clinic**, Long Island College Hospital, 100 Amity St., SW cor. Henry St. 1897. *Marshall Emery.*

An exuberant dollop of **French Mannerism**, where a ponderous stone base supports a brick mid-section, with as many quoins, brackets and broken pediments per square centimeter as Fontainebleau. The Amity Street entry verges on Proto-deconstructivist (the 20th century's neo-Baroque), the door flanked by four Corinthian-capped columns cut like sausages and reassembled with square blocks inserted between the slices.

Long Island College Hospital, the not-so-fun buildings (outside the Historic District):

[C4] **E. M. Fuller Pavilion**, 70 Atlantic Ave., SE cor. Hicks St. 1974. *Ferrenz & Taylor.*
[C5] **Joan Osborn Polak Pavilion**, Hicks St. bet. Atlantic Ave. and Amity St. 1984. *Ferrenz & Taylor.* Addition, 1988, *Ferrenz, Taylor, Clark & Assocs.*

Bulky monoliths at the heart of Long Island College's rebirth as a major medical institution.

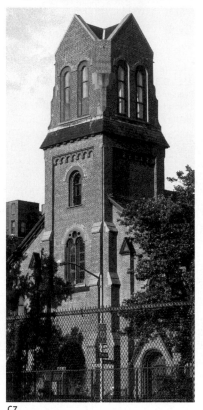

C7

Sited along Atlantic Avenue, they are in their own medical world, seemingly not part of either Brooklyn Heights to the north or Cobble Hill to the south. The hospital is a testament to the 19th-century German immigrants who lived here and established this institution to serve the community.

[C6] **Prospect Heights Pavilion**, Long Island College Hospital, 349 Henry St., NE cor. Amity St. 1963. *Beeston & Patterson.*

The earliest stroke in the hospital's renewal. Its exposed concrete frame was once considered stylish.

[C7] Originally **St. Peter's, Our Lady of Pilar Church** (Roman Catholic), Hicks St., NE cor. Warren St. 1860. *Patrick Charles Keely.*
[C8] Originally **St. Peter's Academy**. 1866.
[C9] **Cobble Hill Health Center**/originally **St. Peter's Hospital**, 274 Henry St., bet. Congress and Warren Sts. W side. 1888-1889. *William Schickel & Co.*

Once a full block to minister to the community's spiritual (church), educational (academy),

C3

social (home for working girls at Hicks and Congress Streets), and health (hospital) needs. The red painted brickwork held it all together. Things have changed: the church and school have both been converted to condos, and a banal brick medical building shoe-horned into the space between hospital and school. The church retains its sturdy, buttressed forms in brick, brownstone, and terra cotta, crowned with a squat tower.

[C10] **Tower Buildings**, 417-435 Hicks St., 136-142 Warren St., 129-135 Baltic St., E side of Hicks St. 1878.

[C11] **Workingmen's Cottages**, 1-25 and 2-26 Warren Place, bet. Hicks and Henry Sts., 146-154 Warren St. S side. 139-147 Baltic St. N side. 1879.

[C12] **Home Buildings**, 439-445 Hicks St. and 134-140 Baltic St., SE cor. Hicks St. 1876. All by *William Field & Son*. Restored, 1986, *Maitland, Strauss & Behr*.

Completion of the "sun-lighted tenements" in newly socially conscious late Victorian

Winnie's Mom didn't live here: At 426 Henry Street, just south of Kane, a plaque claims that Winston Churchill's mother, Jennie Jerome, was born in that house in 1850. Actually, she was born in 1854 in a house on Amity Street near Court. The confusion results from the fact that Jennie's folks had lived with her uncle, Addison G. Jerome, at 292 (now renumbered 426) Henry Street prior to her birth.

[C14] **143 Kane Street** (town house), opp. Cheever Pl. 1997. *Joseph and Mary Merz*.

A modest row house with an elegantly detailed balcony overlooking the length of Cheever Place.

[C15] Formerly **St. Francis Cabrini Chapel** (Roman Catholic)/originally **Strong Place Baptist Church**, DeGraw St., NW cor. Strong Place, 1851-1852. *Minard Lafever*. Converted to apartments, 2010.

A stolid brownstone **Gothic Revival** church, now completely gutted in anticipation of its con-

C10

C14

London inspired these 226 low-rent apartments and 34 cottages financed by businessman *Alfred Tredway White*. White's dictum, "philanthropy plus 5%," made him the first builder of limited-profit (and hence low-rent) housing in America. Innovations such as outside spiral stairs and open balconies that serve as access corridors achieved floor-through apartments with good ventilation. Common bathing facilities were originally provided in the basement. The tiny 11-foot-wide cottages line a wondrous private pedestrian mews, Warren Place. There are no rear gardens, but twin alleys provide rear access. The **Tower Buildings** embrace a garden courtyard.

[C13] **412-420 Henry Street** (row houses), bet. Kane and Baltic Sts. W side. 1888. *George B. Chappell*.

Upon completion, these modest Renaissance Revival houses were sold to *F.A.O. Schwarz*, the toy king. Nos.412, 414, and 416 retain their original doorways, low stoops, and some of the original ironwork.

version to condominiums. *Lafever* was one of Brooklyn's greatest architects.

[C16] **South Brooklyn Seventh-Day Adventist Church**/originally **Trinity German Lutheran Church**, 249 DeGraw St., bet. Clinton St. and Tompkins Place. N side. 1905. *Theobald Engelhardt*.

A simple brick church in the second Gothic Revival. The first flowered in the 1840s, the second at the turn of the century.

[C17] Formerly **Engine Company 204**, N.Y.C. Fire Department, 299 DeGraw St., bet. Court and Smith Sts. N side. ca. 1880.

A holdover from times when fires were fought by fire laddies stoking horsedrawn steam pumpers. This one began as Engine Company 4, Brooklyn Fire Department, as cast into the old terra-cotta shields. Brick-and-brownstone Gothic Revival, with an Italianate hat. Closed in 2003 despite loud neighborhood protests.

[C18] Originally **Dr. Joseph E. Clark House**, 340 Clinton St., bet. DeGraw and Kane Sts. W side. ca. 1860.

The widest single house in Cobble Hill, asymmetric and crowned with a slate mansard roof. Note the sinuous ironwork.

[C19] **334 Clinton Street** (house), bet. DeGraw and Kane Sts. W side. ca. 1850. Remodeled, 1888, *James W. Naughton*.

A kooky mansard-roofed Queen Anne miniature, the product of *Naughton's* remodeling of an originally simple body. Note particularly the corner tower and the lovely wrought-iron strapwork. As architect for the Brooklyn school system, *Naughton* later built the great **Boys' High School**.

[C20] **Christ Church and Holy Family** (Episcopal), 320 Clinton St., SW cor. Kane St. 1840-1841. *Richard Upjohn*. Altar, altar railings, reredos, pulpit, lectern, chairs, 1917, *Louis Comfort Tiffany*.

English Gothic in cut ashlar brownstone by the elder of the father-and-son architects, the *Upjohns*, who lived just down the street [at 296]. Four strong finials form an appropriate skyline apex in these low-rise blocks. A 1939 fire destroyed most but not all of the Tiffany windows.

[C21] **301-311 Clinton Street** (houses), 206-224 Kane Street and 10-12 Tompkins Place, 1849-1854.

Nine classy pairs of narrow Italianate houses developed by New York lawyer *Gerard W. Morris*. The street is pleasantly modulated by the rhythm of the projecting bays.

C20

C21

[C24] **Verandah Place**, S of Congress St., bet. Clinton and Henry Sts. ca. 1850.

A pleasant mews, long neglected but now reclaimed as charming residences. *Thomas Wolfe*, who lived at No.40, later described his apartment in *You Can't Go Home Again*.

*Church of the Holy Turtle was the affectionate nickname of the Second Unitarian Church, which stood for more than a century on the site of today's **Cobble Hill Park**. As built from designs of J. Wrey Mould in 1858, there was no denying*

C27

[C22] **Kane Street Synagogue**, Congregation **Beth Israel Anshei Emes**/formerly **Trinity German Lutheran Church**/originally **Middle Dutch Reformed Church**, 236 Kane St., SE cor. Tompkins Place. ca. 1856.

Originally a brick and brownstone Romanesque Revival, its present stuccoed exterior is bland but waterproof. The congregation is descended from a splinter group of Brooklyn's oldest synagogue, once located at State Street and Boerum Place.

[C23a] Originally **Richard Upjohn House**, 296 Clinton St., NW cor. Baltic St. 1843. *Richard Upjohn & Son*. [C23b] **Addition** to Upjohn House, 203 Baltic St., W of Clinton St. 1893. *Richard M. Upjohn*.

The younger *Upjohn's* **Romanesque Revival** addition retains some of the elegant detail obliterated in the older corner house on its conversion to a multiple dwelling. This is interesting more for the architects who lived here than its architecture.

*that the little edifice resembled a tortoise with a high carapace. (Mould's earlier, Manhattan work, the Unitarian Church of the Saviour, boasted a striped façade and was named the **Church of the Holy Zebra**. It too is gone.) With the Reverend Samuel Longfellow, the poet's brother, as its first minister, Second Unitarian quickly became known for the cultural interests and abolitionist views of both pastor and his transported New England flock. By the 1950s, however, the church had been abandoned, and the site was purchased for a new supermarket. Community intervention prevented this—and resulted in the creation of the park. A popular neighborhood hangout, but be warned: quiet bench-sitting after dusk can result in a summons and court appearance (as one of your authors can sadly attest).*

[C25] **166, 168, and 170 Congress Street**, bet. Clinton and Henry Sts. S side.

[C26] **159, 161, and 163 Congress Street**, bet. Clinton and Henry Sts. N side. ca. 1857.

Two triads of **Anglo-Italianate** row houses, each designed to read as a single unit. The southern group has segmental arched upper-floor windows; the northern group, square-headed ones.

[C27] **St. Paul's, St. Peter's, Our Lady of Pilar Church**, Court St., SW cor. Congress St. 1838. *Gamaliel King*. Steeple, early 1860s. Brownstone veneer, 1888. Additions of new sanctuary and sacristy, 1906.

[C28] **Rectory**, 234 Congress St., bet. Court and Clinton Sts. S side. 1936. *Henry J. McGill*.

Its copper-sheathed steeple is a giant finial along Court Street for blocks in both directions. It takes careful study to understand the Greek Revival form behind this later steeple. *King* was the carpenter who designed Brooklyn's City Hall, now Borough Hall. The steeple, repaired recently, has new copper sheathing not of the verdigris variety. Too bad. Green was nicer.

[C29] **223 Congress Street**, bet. Court and Clinton Sts. N side. 1851. Mansard roof, ca. 1880.

A large stuccoed Gothic Revival house origi-nally built as a rectory for St. Paul's opposite and the Free School for Boys. The mansard roof has been desecrated with—of all things—white aluminum clapboard.

C33   C34

[C30] **219-221 Congress Street**, bet. Court and Clinton Sts. N side. 1850s.

Ox-bow lintels bring a touch of exoticism.

[C31] **194-200 Court Street**, bet. Congress and Warren Sts. S side. 1898. *William B. Tubby*.

Two shades of brick articulate the façade, while FOSTER in its pediment names this turn-of-the-century tenement block. The storefronts are miraculously preserved in almost their origi-nal condition.

Across Court Street, east of the Historic District:

[C32a] **Annex, Brooklyn Heights Montessori School**, 185 Court St. , NE cor. Bergen St. 1998. *Gruzen Samton and De la Cour & Ferrara*.

A quiet modernist building that presents neighborly brick and windows to Bergen Street; crowned in blue seamed metal.

[32b] **271 Warren Street**, bet. Court and Smith Sts. ca. 1899.

Amid much masonry, this handsome clap-board **neo-Grec** house stands out. Painted blue with white trim and a proud, temple-like door-way.

[C33] **205 Warren Street**, originally **St. Paul's Parish School** (Roman Catholic), bet. Court and Clinton Sts. 1882.

An eclectic Victorian brick building with Corinthian-capped pilasters. Education seemed

C36b

more serious in such monumental and dignified surroundings.

[C34] **Formerly Ralph L. Cutter House**/originally **Abraham J. S. DeGraw House**, 219 Clinton St., SE cor. Amity St. 1845. Altered, 1891, *D'Oench & Simon*.

In the early and sparsely built development of Cobble Hill, most residents could view the harbor from their parlor windows. As the blocks infilled, the view was barred, inspiring here a tower for viewing the harbor over the rooftops beyond. Still freestanding, with a grand garden, it sports a rock-face brownstone stoop with both cast and wrought ironwork.

Winnie's Mom really did live here: Jennie Jerome was born January 9, 1854, at 197 Amity Street, near Court Street. She grew up to marry Lord Randolph Churchill and to give birth, in turn, to a son, Winston.

[C35] **214 Clinton Street** and **147 Pacific Street** (apartments), NW cor. Clinton St. 1892. *H.W. Billard*.

Queen Anne, in rock-face brownstone and rough brick, its sheet-metal bay windows ornamented with iron studs and sinuous Ionic colonnettes. See the face in the pediment at No.214.

[C36a] **172 Pacific Street**, bet. Clinton and Court Sts. S side. ca. 1840.

A lovely little whitewashed cottage in the Romanesque Revival style, formerly a stable, with red door. Dig the iron brackets holding up the cornice.

[C36b] **174 Pacific Street** (apartments)/formerly **Public School 78, Brooklyn**, bet. Clinton and Court Sts. S side. 1889.

A strong prim brick school building, looming over its row house neighbors.

the sealed, long-forgotten tunnel in 1980, leading tours down into the depths from the corner of Court Street and Atlantic Avenue. For tour info and reservations see www.brooklynrail.net

[C37] **191 Clinton Street**/originally **South Brooklyn Savings Bank**, SE cor. Atlantic Ave. 1871. *E. L. Roberts*. Restored, 1986.

A noble Eastlake commercial building in Tuckahoe marble. The bank's move to the east end of the Atlantic Avenue block in 1922 initiated years of decay. Happily, it has now been restored as apartments, a reborn and prominent citizen. Note the incised carvings in the lintels.

[C38] **164-168 Atlantic Avenue** (lofts), bet. Clinton and Court Sts. S side. 1859-1864.

Merchant princes of the 19th century were more concerned with the quality of their architecture than those of the 20th. Note the stone quoins and bracketed roof cornices. Recently restored, including the sign across the façade: *John Curtin Inc ^^^ Sailmakers Canvas Goods*.

C39

On Atlantic Avenue: A Near Eastern bazaar of exotic foods and gifts, cresting on the block between Court and Clinton Streets: halvah, dried fruit, nuts, pastries, dates, olives, copper and brass work, goatskin drums, inlaid chests. And Near Eastern restaurants too, serving hommus, babe ghannouj, kibbe, stuffed squash, cabbage, and grape leaves, and wonderful yogurt delicacies. Since the 1970s Atlantic Avenue has become a milelong bazaar for antique hunters, stretching from Hicks Street to Times Plaza at the LIRR Station.

Under Atlantic Avenue is an abandoned tunnel (1844), the world's first subway, that originally linked Times Plaza Station with the Ferry Terminal to Manhattan's South Ferry. The tunnel, 17 feet tall, 21 feet wide, and 1,611 feet long, is a grand brick barrel-vaulted space. Walt Whitman called the tunnel "a passage of solemnity and darkness." You may occasionally come upon Bob Diamond, a local rail enthusiast who discovered

The three peaks between "Inc" and "Sailmakers" must be stylized sails. Admirable, but painted signs are best left to fade; the shabby chic of the original is more convincing.

[C39] **180 Atlantic Avenue**, bet. Clinton and Court Sts. S side. 1873.

A rich, and unusual for these parts, cast-iron façade with wrought-iron railings modulating the window openings.

[C40] **Trader Joe's**/formerly **Independence Savings Bank**/ originally **South Brooklyn Savings Institution**, 130 Court St., SW cor. Atlantic Ave. 1922. *McKenzie, Voorhees & Gmelin*. Addition, 1936, *Charles A. Holmes*.

This Florentine Renaissance anchor marks the northeast corner of the Cobble Hill Historic District. A hundred eagles bear its cornice on their shoulders.

The plaque at the corner of Court and Atlantic Avenues cites this as the spot from which General Washington viewed the disastrous, but ultimately tide-turning, retreat at the Battle of Brooklyn in 1776.

And within, since 2008, a cavernous specialty grocery store. Would that it had been here for the good General to provision that retreat.

END of Cobble Hill Historic District.

NECROLOGY

Hoagland Laboratory, Long Island College Hospital, 335 Henry St., SE cor. Pacific St. Cobble Hill. 1888. *John Mumford.*

Devastated by fire and later demolished, this eclectic Romanesque Revival building was the first privately founded laboratory in the country devoted to bacteriological, histological, and pathological research. Its early Art Nouveau copper signs were glorious.

CARROLL GARDENS

Historically considered part of **Red Hook** or **South Brooklyn**, the area was renamed **Carroll Gardens** in the blooming gentrification of the 1960s. It has always been physically distinguished from its surrounding neighbors by its unique cityscape, created by land surveyor Richard Butts, whose 1846 map created unusually deep blocks on today's 1st through 4th Places, between Henry and Smith Streets: deep front yards as well as standard backyards were then extended eastward to Carroll, President, and Second Streets between Smith and Hoyt (Union Street is wider also, but without the gardens). Between row house façades and the narrow sidewalks are wonderful, lush front gardens, syncopated with front stoops, that gave the area its name.

Carroll Gardens Historic District, generally resembling a keystone on its side, including

C37

C41a

Smith Street, which unites Cobble Hill (to the west), Boerum Hill (to the north and east), and Carroll Gardens (to the south), was as recently as 1997 decidedly sketchy: seedy during the day, downright scary at night. The few businesses that held on tended to be long-running family-owned enterprises: bodegas, shoe stores, hardware, botanicas, furniture warehouses, even some light manufacturing (the Ecco cheese factory at Smith and Bergen).

Then trendy restaurants started moving in. Improbably, Smith Street became hip, with a built-in market of yuppies flowing to and from the F train stops at Bergen and Carroll Streets. The sudden success was a surprise, since Smith Street was never (and still isn' t) particularly scenic.

There is a place in the City for good, clean frivolity; many of the restaurants and shops on Smith Street are fun and have good, relatively affordable fare. But it all seems disposable, like a tent show come to town; even in the best of times the shops and eateries open and fold on a dime.

President and Carroll Sts., bet. Smith and Hoyt Sts., and Hoyt St. bet. President and 1st Sts. ●⛏

Only 2 of the 11 fine streets of Carroll Gardens were designated as the Landmark District, an unhappy oversight. Much of the district therefore lies outside the official boundaries.

[C41a] **358-366 Court Street**/formerly **South Congregational Church and Chapel,** NW cor. President St. Chapel, 1851. Church, 1857. ●⛏

[C41b] **257 President St.**, formerly **South Congregational Church**, originally **Ladies' Parlor,** to the W on President St. 1889. *F. Carles Merry.* ●⛏

[C41c] **255 President St.**, former **Rectory**, bet. Court and Clinton Sts. N side. 1893. *Woodruff Leeming.* ●⛏

One of several Brooklyn churches converted into condominium apartments by hook, crook, and the shrinking of the borough's Protestantism. The dour façade presents a series of stepped planes in brick, a counterpart in masonry to a theater proscenium's contoured

C46

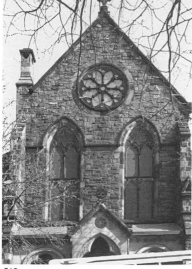

C42

C48

lone mansion amid farmland, it overlooked the Upper Bay in the same posture and prospect as the Litchfield Mansion in Prospect Park.

[C44] 450 Clinton Street/formerly **Den Norske Sjomannskirke**/originally **Westminster Presbyterian Church**, NW cor. 1st Place. ca. 1865.

Stolid and eclectic Romanesque Revival brownstone, converted to apartments. The air-conditioning units punctuating the clerestory spaces form a bizarre frieze. Whither the Norwegian seamen?

[C45] 98 First Place, SW cor. Court St. ca. 1860.

A brownstone bracketed Italianate corner villa.

[C46] 37-39 Third Place (houses), bet. Henry and Clinton Sts. N side. ca. 1875.

A Charles Addams mansarded outpost with cast-iron grillage in profile against the sky. Magnificent.

[C47] Sacred Hearts of Jesus and Mary and St. Stephen's Church (Roman Catholic)/originally **St. Stephen's Church**, Summit St., NE cor. Hicks St. ca. 1860. *Patrick Charles Keely*.

A lusty Gothick complex by the prolific *Keely*, who is believed to have designed 700 churches across the country. Unfortunately, he was no match for *Upjohn*.

velvet curtain. Its silhouette of verdigris-colored finials contrasts with the deep red masonry body. The former Ladies' Parlor is housed in sturdy sophisticated terra-cotta arches, quoins, and voussoirs, with a frieze worthy of *Louis Sullivan*; the former parish house next door is a brick and rockface limestone delight.

[C42] St. Paul's Episcopal Church of Brooklyn, 423 Clinton St., NE cor. Carroll St. 1867-1884. *Richard Upjohn & Son*.

A severe high Victorian Gothic work where light sandstone defines the Gothic openings, and serves as the architecture of a whole porch. Above is an incomplete steeple. Judging from the corner tower, it would have been enormous had it been finished. Grim Protestants.

[C43] F. G. Guido Funeral Home/originally **John Rankin House**, 440 Clinton St., SW cor. Carroll St. 1840. 🖼

A grand brick Greek Revival survivor. Somber gray granite supports rosy brick and articulates sills, lintels, and capitals. Once a

[C48] **Columbia Terrace**, 43-57 Carroll St. N side. 250-260 Columbia St. W side. 43-87 President St. S side. 46-90 President St. N side. 1987. *Wids de la Cour* and *Hirsch & Danois.*

Understated rows infilling the blocks of this neighborhood orphaned by the slashing separation of the Brooklyn-Queens Expressway's cut. Why not cover this moat and allow Cobble Hill to be sutured back to Red Hook?

[C49] Formerly **South Brooklyn Christian Assembly Parsonage**, 295 Carroll St., bet. Smith and Hoyt Sts. N side. 1878.

A modest Victorian Gothic manse.

[C50] **St. Agnes Church** (Roman Catholic), 417 Sackett St., NE cor. Hoyt St. 1905. *Thomas F. Houghton.*

The community's dominant structure is this quasi-cathedral soaring above low row-housed neighbors. Here is dressed Manhattan schist ashlar, with limestone detailing, pushing multi-finials to the sky.

C50

[C51] Formerly **Calvary Baptist Church of Red Hook**/originally **South Congregational Chapel**, 118 4th Place, bet. Court and Smith Sts.

This robust rotund chapel is *Friar Tuck* to its more restrained heroic *Robin Hood*, the former South Congregational Church.

Optical illusions? You can tell for sure only from a land book such as E. Belcher Hyde's of 1912, for example, but it is certain that the street façades of the Carroll Gardens row houses framing Carroll and President Streets are not parallel. As a matter of fact, the difference is considerable. At the Smith Street end they are 100 feet apart, at Hoyt Street the space increases to 129 feet. The surveyor's prestidigitation is concealed, however, by the length of these blocks and their lush greenery.

[C52] **191-193 Luquer Street** (apartments), bet. Court and Smith Sts. 2005. *Mark Dixon and Peter Guthrie.*

In three parts: a 19th-century row house in the grasp of flanking modernist glass-and-concrete twins. The effect is one of an elderly fellow at a cocktail party cornered by two chatty, well-dressed young gents.

[C53a] **St. Mary's Star of the Sea Church** (Roman Catholic), 471 Court St., bet. Nelson and Luquer Sts. E side. ca. 1870. *Patrick Charles Keely.* [C53b] **Girls' School**, 477 Court St., NE cor. Nelson St. **Rectory**, 467 Court St., SE cor. Luquer St.

Painted brick humility—a parish church trio for a 19th-century immigrant working-class parish. Compare it with other nearby Catholic churches by architect *Keely*. The raw, red-brick body behind the painted façade has a more pleasant texture.

Don't miss taking a peek at Dennett Place, just behind St. Mary's:

[C54] **Dennett Place**.

An atmospheric street that seems more like a stage set for *Maxwell Anderson's Winterset* than a brick-and-mortar reality. Lying between Court and Smith Streets, it connects Luquer with Nelson Street. It is more commonly termed a mews.

C53a   C54

NECROLOGY

Institutional Services, Roman Catholic Diocese of Brooklyn/originally **Catholic Seamen's Institute**, 653 Hicks St., NE cor. Rapelye St. 1943. *Henry V. Murphy.*

From the era of heavy maritime activity in this precinct. The faux Art Moderne lighthouse was intended as a moral beacon: "A challenge of the church to the barrooms of the river front."

Church of the South Brooklyn Christian Assembly/originally **Carroll Park Methodist Episcopal Church**/later **Norwegian Methodist Episcopal Church**, 297-299 Carroll St., bet. Smith and Hoyt Sts. 1873.

A memento of the large Scandinavian population that settled in South Brooklyn from the late 19th century until the mid-20th, when the Victorian Gothic structure was sold to the last occupant. The church, consumed by fire, was replaced by two town houses.

GOWANUS

For generations Gowanus encompassed everything south of Atlantic Avenue to Fifth Avenue and all the way south to Red Hook. The neighborhood still going by the name has shrunk in recent decades as developers successfully marketed large tracts as Cobble and Boerum Hills and Carroll Gardens. What is identifiable as Gowanus is the low-lying parts between Carroll Gardens and Park Slope, where the land gently slopes down to meet the Gowanus Canal and then rises again.

Legends about the canal have grown like weeds along its fetid banks, including one tale of two thieves who fled police by walking across the canal's Jell-O-like surface. An excursion by boat is always instructive (mysterious, viscous bubbles rising to the surface appear to be 1/4 inch thick), affording excellent views of the canal's most interesting features: its bridges and viaducts.

Before 1911 the Canal was known derisively

03

as **Lavender Lake**. At that time the Butler Street pumping station at its northern terminus began delivering the stale waters into New York Harbor's Buttermilk Channel, inviting freshwater to enter by hydraulic action. A new facility finally is increasing the flow (this time vice versa, drawing Buttermilk's waters into the Canal) and thus reducing stagnation.

It is a sign of just how booming the economy was circa 2003-2008 that developers drafted ambitious plans for turning the canal into a kind of faux-Venice, with high-end housing and cafes nodding on the banks instead of abandoned cars and trucks.

The Fed's recently announced plans to finally declare the canal a **Super Fund site** has generated controversy, but is a welcome sign that at long-last the canal might be decontaminated. Some residents, and developers, would prefer that the City clean it up, according to its own schedule. It remains a picturesque wasteland, but something must be improving: a recent jaunt to the canal revealed a seemingly happy jellyfish, swimming south towards the harbor.

[O1] **Butler Street Pumping Station**, City of New York, Butler St. bet. Nevins and Bond Sts., S side. New facilities, 1987.

An elegant wall screens the hardware while giving it a sophisticated interface with the street.

[O2] **Brooklyn Lyceum**/originally **N.Y.C. Public Bath No.7**, 227-231 Fourth Ave., NE cor. President St. 1906-1910. *Raymond F. Almirall.* ☎ 718.857.4816 *www.brooklynlyceum.com*

New York's Public Baths once sought grandeur, modestly imitating those of ancient Rome (in spirit, not in size). If you lived in penury, perhaps you could bathe in symbolic luxury. Look up to the witty cornice, where carved vats of water (or is it oil?) symbolically pour from the ramparts. This magnificent glazed terra-cotta neo-Renaissance relic is now the

05

headquarters of the Brooklyn Lyceum, a theater and event space.

[O3] **Carroll Street Bridge**, over the Gowanus Canal. 1888-1889. *George Ingram*, engineer-in-charge; *Robert Van Buren*, chief engineer; both of the *Brooklyn Department of City Works.* ☎

A retractile bridge, one that slides askew to a berth on the west side of the canal to allow waterborne traffic to pass. The oldest of four such bridges extant in the country. A gritty relic from the era when Brooklyn's public works were designed by its own municipal government.

[O4] **Vechte-Cortelyou House**, in James J. Byrne Memorial Playground, 3rd St., SW cor. Fifth Ave. Originally built, 1699. Replica, 1935.

The **"Old Stone House,"** re-created by the City's Parks Department in 1935, using old sketches and what were believed to be old stones. The original house had long before fallen into total ruin. In its re-created state it serves as a playground office, gallery, and event space.

The most severe fighting in the Revolutionary War's **Battle of Long Island** (1776) took place here. *General Stirling's* Continental troops fought a delaying action against *Cornwallis'* superior number of redcoats, thus permitting Washington's successful retreat.

*Washington Park was the original home of Brooklyn's major league baseball team, then known variously as the **Trolley Dodgers** and the **Superbas**. There were three separate versions of the ballpark: the first bounded by Fourth Avenue, Fifth Avenue, and 3rd and 4th Streets (presently James J. Byrne Memorial Playground, named after the Dodgers owner). The second version was across Fourth Avenue, bounded by Third Avenue, 1st and 3rd Streets. After the Dodgers moved in 1914 to Ebbets Field, on Bedford Avenue, a third version of Washington Park was built on the same site as the second, and was home to the **Brooklyn Tip Tops,** members of the Federal League, a short-lived rival to the National and American*

circa 1890, with meticulous corbeling at the top and rows of robust arched windows, now all broken. Graffiti artists have taken over and placed a very clear, succinct message along the cornice (its language a bit too colorful for this generally G-rated Guide). The best view is from 3rd Street, looking north.

[06] **Smith-9th St. Station**, IND Subway high-level crossing, over the Gowanus Canal. 1933.

The land in these parts proved so uneconomical for tunnel construction that the IND subway emerges here, rising over 100 feet to meet the Canal's navigational clearance requirements. This leaves the Smith and 9th Street subway station high and dry, and embraced in a latticework of steel. A spectacular construction, it lacked an *Eiffel* to make it equally significant visually. On a sunny day, it's a delightful place to wait for the **F train**. You might even catch a fleeting glimpse of a rarer species, the **G train**, only four cars in length and the only line too shy to venture into Manhattan.

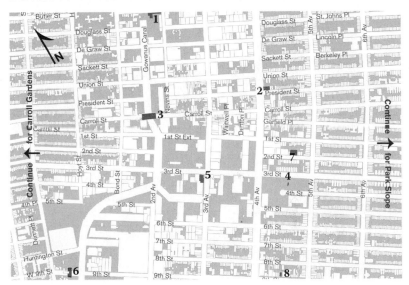

*Leagues. Intriguingly, much of the brick façade of that stadium is **still there**, along the site's entire Third Avenue side, and turning the corner at both 1st and 3rd Streets. Oh, to still hear the crack of the bat and smell the popcorn!*

[05] **New York & Long Island Coignet Stone Company Building**, 360 Third Ave., SW cor. 3rd St. 1872-73. *William Field & Son.*

The oldest known concrete building in the City, from the pioneering company that provided the arches and clerestory windows for St. Patrick's Cathedral. The brick on the façade is not original. Now in precarious condition, it is in need of **immediate architectural CPR**. Do plans for a Whole Foods supermarket on the site include saving this landmark?

Marooned and Mysterious: behind blocked-off 2nd Street, between Third Avenue and the Gowanus Canal, is a beautiful industrial relic, a Romanesque red-brick former power station,

[07] **Second Street Child Care Center**, 333 Second St., bet. Fourth and Fifth Aves. 1999. *Buttrick White & Burtis.*

Brick and limestone. Child sized, and playgrounded. An infill building, it drops the scale to two stories. Is that because modern city children have rarely used stairs?

[08] Originally **William B. Cronyn House**/later **Charles M. Higgins Ink Factory**, 271 Ninth St., bet. Fourth and Fifth Aves. N side to 8th St. 1856-1857. Altered, 1895, *Patrick Charles Keely.*

An extraordinary remnant of pre-brownstone Brooklyn: a freestanding **French Second Empire** stucco house crowned with a cupola, slate mansard roof, and cast-iron crests against the sky. India ink, that intense black fluid so misnamed (it should be Chinese ink) was made here for draftsmen, designers, artists, and calligraphers.

RED HOOK

The history of Red Hook is entwined with shipping. Railroad contractor *William Beard* transformed the marshes of Red Hook into the scythe-shaped Erie Basin, completed in 1864, and built long, low storehouses along its edge. Those handsome brick sheds are, happily, mostly intact along the water, between lanes of cottages and the open sea beyond. (*Beard* reportedly charged ships seeking to haul American cargoes 50¢ per cubic yard for the privilege of dumping the rock carried as ballast from overseas ports—thus, a free breakwater.)

Once the shipping industry began to fade, so did Red Hook. Construction of the Brooklyn-Queens Expressway in the 1950s severed the neighborhood and its docks from the rest of Brooklyn, the neighborhood falling into disrepair, looking very much like *Edward Hopper's* paintings. As recently as the late 1990s the area was beautiful but deserted, weedy, and forlorn.

of the present church was damaged by fire in 1949 when a nine-year-old boy accidentally dropped a hot taper into the creche in front of the altar. Way to go, kid.

[R2] Originally **Brooklyn Clay Retort & Firebrick Works**, 76-86 Van Dyke St., N side; 99-113 Van Dyke St. S side; 106-116 Beard St. all bet. Van Brunt and Richards Sts. ca. 1860. 🌺

Granite ashlar, powerful relics from an era of grand industrial architecture. This great enterprise brought clay from South Amboy, N.J., to the nearby Erie Basin, where it was converted to firebrick. Nos.76-86 was the firebrick storehouse, Nos.99-113 was the firebrick factory, Nos.106-116 the boiler house, carpentry shop, and engine room.

[R3] Originally **Beard & Robinson Stores**, 260 Beard St., along Erie Basin, SE cor. Van Brunt St. 1869.

R2

R3

R13a

Then young families, priced out of Carroll Gardens and Cobble Hill, began moving in, circa 2000. Many of the old storehouses have been transformed into housing, artist studios, and light manufacturing, and Red Hook is once again a vibrant, culturally diverse community. The recent arrival of "Big Box" retail giants (Ikea, Fairway) has taken away a bit of the backwater peace and quiet that made Red Hook unique, but the dearth of public transportation (the closest subway is the F and G lines at the Smith-9th Street station, 1.5 miles to the east) probably means Red Hook will never become the new SoHo, thank God.

[R1] **Visitation of the Blessed Virgin Mary Roman Catholic Church**, Richards St., bet. Verona St. and Visitation Pl. 1896. **Rectory**, 98 Richards St., NW cor. Visitation Pl. ca. 1878.

A monolithic church in Manhattan schist, and neighboring rectory, both convincingly neo-Gothic, fronting **Coffey Park**. The elegant bell tower includes four clocks, one on each face, framed in copper. An earlier church on the same site burned to the ground in 1896. The interior

[R4] **Van Brunt Stores**, 480 Van Brunt St., along Erie Basin, S of Reed St. ca. 1869. *William Beard*, builder.

[R5] **Merchant Stores**, 204-207 Van Dyke St., at Pier 41, bet. Conover and Ferris Sts. 1873. *Col. Daniel Richards*, builder.

Half-round arch openings and down-to-earth brickwork commend these and other nearby post-Civil War wharfside warehouses, the epitome of the functional tradition. Compare them with the better-known **Empire Stores**. A cut-stone marker modestly marks the streetside southernmost point of Beard & Robinson. Look up.

Much of the longer, lower **Beard & Robinson Stores** have been converted to artist studios, while the **Van Brunt Stores**, until recently abandoned and overgrown, are now beehives of activity, thanks to an endless **Fairway** grocery store on its ground floor, and rental apartments (with awkwardly designed new windows) above. **The Merchant Stores** were previously a bottling plant for the Morgan Soda (later White Rock Beverage) Company.

[R6] Waterfront Museum and Showboat Barge, 290 Conover St. at Pier 44, N of Reed St. Open to the public: Th 4-8; Sa 1-5. *www.waterfrontmuseum.org*

The red-painted, wooden barge (Lehigh Valley Railroad Barge No.79, ca. 1914) is the thing to see here.

Pier 44 Gardens, *Lynden Miller*, designer: A beautifully conceived waterfront garden connecting the barge to Pier 41 and the Merchant Stores. Open to the public.

[R7] Sunny's, 253 Conover, between Beard and Reed Streets, is a rare intact seafarer's tavern, virtually untouched since the early 20th century, presided over by the irrepressible Sunny Balzano. Open Wed., Fri., & Sat. 8 PM-4 AM.

[R8] 207, 209, 211, 213 Conover Street, bet. Coffey and Van Dyke Sts. ca. 1910.

A row of unusually diminutive clapboard cottages; one-story with a garden floor below street level.

food served on weekends from carts that ring the fields is cheap and unbelievably tasty!

[R12] Originally **Port of New York Grain Elevator Terminal N.Y.S. Barge Canal System**, Henry St. Basin. 1922.

Concrete silos dramatically aligned to receive grain shipments from the Midwest through the Great Lakes and the Erie Canal. The decline of grain traffic to New York Harbor led to their deactivation in 1955. The best view is from Columbia Street.

The longest dead-end street in New York is Columbia Street, at the Erie Basin, just to the east of IKEA. Driving its length is a quick and easy way to leave the City behind; a reminder that Brooklyn is a maritime city after all.

[R13] Erie Basin Park, 1 Beard Street, bet. Columbia and Otsego Sts., behind **IKEA**. 2008. *Lee Weintraub*, landscape architect.

"Big Box" stores like **IKEA** (and Walmart,

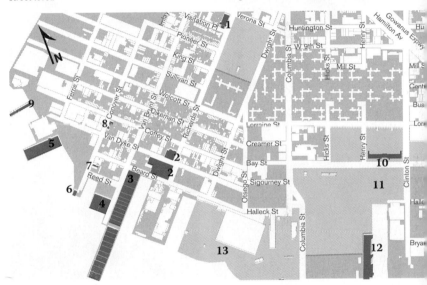

[R9] Louis Valentino, Jr., Park, Pier 39 at the end of Coffey St., W of Ferris St. 1997. *Weintraub & Di Domenico,* landscape architects.

A lance into the harbor, giving pedestrians dramatic views and allowing Red Hook residents to develop a better sense of place. Both fishing and a summer film series are popular here.

[R10] Sol Goldman Recreation Center and Pool, N.Y.C. Department of Parks & Recreation, Bay St., bet. Clinton and Henry Sts. N side, through to Lorraine St. 1936. *N.Y.C. Parks Department, Aymar Embury II*, consulting architect. Altered.

A WPA pool-bathhouse complex, now with added basketball and boxing. Savor the arches and massive piers. The giant Robert Moses-era pool is heavenly in summer.

[R11] Soccer and tacos: just across Bay Street from the pool, between Columbia and Clinton Streets, is the popular Red Hook Playground, a no-nonsense expanse of grass, mentioned here for this culinary tip: the Mexican and Caribbean

Home Depot, and Lowe's, to name a few) have a way of obliterating history, requiring that each store be exactly like the one in the next city. Here the Swedish retail giant has scraped the site clean, removing existing industrial buildings, covering over the charming, bumpy cobblestones on Beard Street, and filling in a historic dry dock (Graving Dock No.1*) that helped make Red Hook the center of the shipping industry in New York.

But not all is lost. Landscape architect *Weintraub* preserved four gigantic cranes from the former shipyard for his adjoining **Erie Basin Park.** Unfortunately, the filled-in dry dock is now a parking lot, and the cranes have been demoted to roles as imposing, but static, sculptures. The park is best at the water's edge; a welcome addition to the City's increasingly people-oriented waterfront.

*For a bird's eye view of the still very active dry dock (ca. 2006) see Google Maps, plan view. Note one ship in the dry dock, and one waiting patiently to get in. A flurry of industry, now replaced by a flurry of shopping.

BOERUM HILL

Boerum Hill is yet another previously forgotten neighborhood, like Cobble Hill and Carroll Gardens, that has become fashionable (and expensive), full of young families and occasional movie stars. Although the area claimed by the neighborhood association is larger, the most interesting blocks are on State, Pacific, Dean, and Bergen Streets, east of Court Street and

B1

west of 4th Avenue. The Historic District is but a small segment (see map). State Street in particular is delightful, lined with old London plane trees; its occupants zealously tend their small front stoop gardens.

Boerum Hill Historic District, irregular, generally lying bet. the Wyckoff St./Hoyt St. intersection on the SW, and the Pacific St./Nevins St. intersection on the NE, including sections of Pacific, Dean, and Bergen Sts. 🍎

The area chosen for designation includes some of the finest rows of housing as well as some of the precinct's architectural eccentricities, which enliven the streetscape. The row houses, single houses, and apartments listed below are among the many contained within the district's boundaries. Nevertheless, whole streets become a joint architectural ensemble and can be savored for their overall urban design, as well as in their separate parts. Buildings within the district are shown by the historic district map's boundary lines.

[B1] Primera Iglesia Bautista/aka **First Baptist Church**, 301-305 Pacific St., bet. Smith and Hoyt Sts. N side. 1860s.

Painted brick and brownstone make this a pastrymaker's powerful version of primitive Gothic Revival.

[B2a] 358 Pacific Street, bet. Hoyt and Bond Sts. S side. 1890s.

A retired chapel provides grand volumes for living and studio spaces.

[B2b] **360 Pacific Street**, bet. Hoyt and Bond Sts. S side. ca. 1861.

A lone and lovely painted clapboard house, presenting a Corinthian-columned porch to the street, bereft of its eastern garden, now consumed by **No.362**.

B4

B8

B5

[B3a] **372 and 372-1/2 Pacific Street**, bet. Hoyt and Bond Sts. S side.

A pair of small mansarded houses with double entrance doors. The slightly arched window openings are lissome.

[B3b] **374 Pacific Street**, bet. Hoyt and Bond Sts. S side. ca. 1850.

The neighborhood's unique Gothic Revival, stripped of much of its detail. Otherwise, the district is largely homogeneous, with earlier houses Greek Revival and those later Renaissance Revival. This Lone Ranger had ideas of his own. The ornate bronze balcony fronting the parlor floor was moved from a house in Fort Greene.

[B4] **245 Dean Street**, bet. Bond and Nevins Sts. N side. 1853. *John Dougherty and Michael Murray*, builders.

This house, one of 30 in a continuous row, remained in the ownership of one family for many generations, a typical history in this neighbor-

B2b

hood that explains the well-maintained façades. Note the intricately built-up entrance doors.

[B5] **240 and 244 Dean Street**, bet. Bond and Nevins Sts. S side. 1858. *Wilson & Thomas,* builders.

Two remaining of four original Victorian wood clapboard cottages that practiced another architectural theme than the adjacent blocks. Must have been immigrants from New England.

[B6] **87-89 Nevins Street**, bet. Atlantic Ave. and Pacific St. ca. 1860.

Boxy bay windows, added for commerce, glisten among their clinging vines, giving a third dimension to these sometimes flat (but for their stoops) façades.

[B7] **Hoyt Street** (group of single houses), bet. Bergen and Wyckoff Sts. E side. [B7a] **157 Hoyt Street.** ca. 1860. [B7b] **159, 161, 163 Hoyt Street.** 1871. [B7c] **163 and 165 Hoyt Street.** ca. 1854.

The north-south streets in this area tend to be through-traffic arteries, and therefore many

houses facing them have altered their ground floors as retail space. This grouping is an exception. **No.157** bears an Italianate gabled roof; **Nos.159-163** are mansarded, with vestiges of cast iron against the sky. **Nos.163** and **165** are innocuous, but their former deep-set front garden offers what might be euphemistically termed a tiny plaza.

[B8] **Brooklyn Inn** (tavern), 148 Hoyt Street, SW cor. Bergen St. 1851. *Thomas Maynard,* builder. Renovated, 1880s.

Two stories of carefully stripped and repointed brick, once the home of the chic Boerum Hill Café. The florid and magnificent sheet-metal work dates from the 1880s alterations. The dark, carved wooden interior, with gigantic mirror, is unique.

END *of Boerum Hill Historic District. All the Boerum Hill buildings that follow are outside the district.*

B13

[B9] **"The Mosaic House,"** 108 Wyckoff St. bet. Smith & Hoyt Sts. ca. 1860. Mosaics, ongoing.

Artist *Susan Gardner* has festooned her brick row house with shards of mosaic tile. A joyous, wonderfully personal work of art, gradually spreading across the façade. At last glance the tile had reached the second story.

Back houses: *More common in Greenwich Village, back houses are most often residential conversions of former stables, detached from the house in front and usually accessed through side alleys. There are two here, barely glimpsed from the street, at 57 1/2 and 59 1/2 Wyckoff, between Court and Smith Streets.*

B12b

B15

B20

B21

[B10] **Bishop Francis J. Mugavero Center for Geriatric Care**, Hoyt St., NE cor. Dean St. 1990s.

Five stories of geriatric care that, fortunately, fits into the neighborhood scale. Unfortunately the vast service and parking area toward Pacific Street spoils it all.

[B11] **212 Pacific Street**, bet. Court St. & Boerum Pl. ca. 1885.

A squat little tyke: brick, chubby with ornament. The carefully composed façade, twin entry doors, stable doors in the middle, large window above, tiny dormers in the cornice, are reminiscent of the great Philadelphia architect *Frank Furness*, but this is possibly the work of *Thomas Maynard* (see the **Brooklyn Inn** above). Note the tie-rod caps on the façade. Often star-shaped, here they are flowers.

[B12a] **"The State Street Houses,"** 291-299 State St., bet. Smith and Hoyt Sts. N side. 290-324 State Sts., bet. Smith and Hoyt Sts. S side. 1847-1874.

These 23 lovingly preserved **Renaissance Revival** brownstones have most of the original detail. Nos.**293-297** have their original cast-iron balustrades. Nos.**295-299** retain the original portals supported by console brackets. Outside the Historic District, they are landmarked as a separate group.

[B12b] **267-289 State Street**, bet. Smith and Hoyt Sts. N side. 2007. *Rogers Marvel*, architects.

Fourteen austere town houses approximating the rhythm, scale, and proportion — but not detail — of the older **neo-Grecs** in the neighborhood. As infill and definers of the street they work well; up close their lack of detail is unsettling, caught between innovation and replication.

[B13] **335 State Street**, bet. Hoyt and Bond Sts. N Side. 1890s.

A grand corner-towered, brick, and terra-cotta apartment house for late-in-the-century middle-class arrivals unable to afford a row house.

[B14] **St. Nicholas Antiochian Orthodox Cathedral**, 355 State St., bet. Hoyt and Bond Sts. N side.

Cut ashlar schist with sandstone trim enrich this English country church. The six dormer windows with curved eaves on each side of the nave roof add an elfic Victorian quality.

[B15] **371 and 375 State Street**, bet. Bond and Nevins Sts. N side. 1890.

The Albemarle and **The Devonshire** are spruce dowagers: brick and terra-cotta monoliths over rock-faced brownstone with a grand rock-faced granite entrance arch. Savor the regal bas-reliefs in the separate pediments.

[B16] **Engine Company 226, N.Y.C. Fire Department,** 409 State St., bet. Bond and Nevins Sts. N side. 1889.

A simple neighborhood civic building embellished with corbeled brick and a perfect cast-iron crest against the sky. Painted a garish red.

[B17] **443-451 State Street,** bet. Nevins St. and Third Ave. N side. ca. 1895.

Six sprightly tenements, with alternating round and polygonal bow/bayfronts and cor-

B19

nices. Carved brownstone enriches entries as do the cast- and wrought-iron balustrades.

[B18] **492-496 State Street,** bet. Nevins St. and Third Ave. S side. ca. 1900.

Stoopless "English" row houses. One enters the main floor directly, rather than walking up a stoop to the parlor floor, as in most of Brooklyn's brick and brownstone houses.

[B19] **Belarusan Autocephalic Orthodox Church,** 401-403 Atlantic Ave., NE cor. Bond St.

A simple Gothic brick church, its brickwork articulated with buttresses and bands.

[B20] **House of the Lord Pentecostal Church,** 415 Atlantic Ave., bet. Bond and Nevins Sts.

A late Romanesque Revival church, picturesque, with banded brick arches and a dour painted ocher brick body.

[B21] **Atlantic Gardens,** 525-535 Atlantic Ave., bet. Third and Fourth Aves. ca. 1890.

In the 1970s developer *Ted Hilles* gathered this cluster of simple brick buildings into a cooperative entered through a central portal into the gardens behind. The Victorian storefronts are happy remnants in wood, whose bayed fronts give modulation to the street.

[B22] **552-554 Atlantic Avenue,** bet. Third and Fourth Aves. S side.

An Arabian Nights building, fortunately now reclaimed by Arabs. Its spiral central column is a glazed candy cane, or **Hollywood Bernini,** with accompanying grand arches to each side.

[B23] **M.S. 449, Math and Science Exploratory School**/originally **Brooklyn Printing Plant, New York Times,** 59-75 Third Ave., bet. Dean and Pacific Sts. E side. 1929. *Albert Kahn.*

This monumental work in neo-Classical limestone hardly hints at the avantgarde indus-

B23

trial facilities that *Kahn* would soon create at the **Dodge Half-Ton Truck Plant** in Detroit (1938). The large windows along Third Avenue permitted the public to view the printing, collating, and folding of newspapers along a half-block-long printing press.

[B24] **Bethlehem Lutheran Church**/ originally **Swedish Evangelical Bethelem Lutheran Church,** SW cor. Third Ave. and Pacific Sts. 1894.

A North European brick church with a pair of marvelous verdigris copper-framed rose windows. It has a crisp hardness, like *Saarinen* père.

[B25] **Church of the Redeemer** (Episcopal), Fourth Ave., NW cor. Pacific St. 1870. *Patrick Charles Keely.*

Presiding over the chaotic intersection, this rock-face ashlar church offers polychromatic Ruskinian voussoirs and a sturdy tower set back from Fourth Avenue on Pacific.

B26

[B26] **Pacific Branch, Brooklyn Public Library**, 25 Fourth Ave., SE cor. Pacific St. 1903. *Raymond F. Almirall.*

If the Church of the Redeemer, across Fourth Avenue, is an architectural symphony, this branch library is a Sousa march—self-satisfied, robust, and stridently Beaux Arts. Note the cornice with torchères and swags, and the gargantuan consoles over the first floor.

B24

[B27] **St. Mark's Place**, bet. Third and Fourth Aves., both sides. ca. 1865.

An intact street of brownstones for lower middle incomes, three-story-and-basement "English" tenements marching up from Park Slope like a provincial brigade.

FORT GREENE

"To the rear of the boisterous city hall quarter was Brooklyn's other fine residential district, the Hill. Located in the center of the city and surrounded by diverse elements, its position was not unlike that of the Heights; but its elegant residences were fewer in number and their owners slightly further removed from the traditions of genteel respectability. It abounded in churches and middle class houses, the majority of whose owners worked in New York, but took pride in living in Brooklyn."
—*Harold C. Syrett,* The City of Brooklyn, *1865-1898.*

Clustering around Fort Greene Park and Pratt Institute are blocks of distinguished brownstones, many mansions, and a surprisingly rich inventory of churches and other institutions. The communities' edges at Fulton Street and Flatbush Avenue are roughened by cheap commercial areas, but the body is, for the most part, solid and handsome.

As to the local population, it dwells in a scale smaller than that of the Heights or Cobble Hill. Three-story row houses and a greater share of sky give the treed blocks a softer and homier aspect, rather than the urbane character of, say, Pierrepont Street. *Charles Hoyt* and his partner, *Russell Nevins*, acquired the area around their self-named streets in 1834. The oldest houses, from the mid 1840s, are in the **Greek Revival** style, with simple pediments and pilasters.

Fort Greene Walking Tour: Start at the Atlantic Avenue Station of the IRT (2, 3, 4, and 5 trains), IND (D and Q trains), and Long Island Railroad or the Pacific Street Station of the BMT (B, M, N, and R trains) (all at Times Plaza); or the Lafayette Avenue Station of the IND (A and C trains). The walk ends on Vanderbilt Avenue at Gates. Continue to Fulton Street and turn left to Clinton Avenue to reach the IND subway one stop farther away from Manhattan.

*Times Plaza: The five-way intersection of three major routes—Atlantic, Flatbush, and Fourth Avenues—together with secondary ones, Ashland Place and Hanson Place, forms **Times Plaza**, named for the **Brooklyn Daily Times**, once published nearby. Now dominated by the Williamsburgh Savings Bank tower, traditionally Brooklyn's tallest building (now edged out by two feet by the tower at 111 Lawrence Street), this chaotic starfish also serves the Long Island commuter, at the railroad's Atlantic Avenue Terminal.*

work for the subway system survives on these lines, mostly in the restored mosaic works. The restoration is heartwarming.

[F3] Originally **Williamsburgh Savings Bank Tower**, 1 Hanson Place, NE cor. Ashland Place. 1927-1929. *Halsey, McCormack & Helmer.* 🐿 Converted to apartments, 2007.

Inadvertently, this was New York's most exuberant phallic symbol (Manhattan's CitySpire is taking up the torch), its slender tower dominating the landscape of all Brooklyn. A crisp, clean tower, it is detailed in **Romanesque-Byzantine** arches, columns, and capitals. The 26th floor once included accessible outdoor viewing space, after a change of elevators. In these upper regions, all of Brooklyn's orthodontists once roosted. All in all, 512 feet of skyline. Inside, the basilican banking hall is described by the Landmarks Preservation Commission as a "cathedral of thrift." Too bad it's no longer a public space.

How tall is your antenna? *Neither the Williamsburgh Savings Bank nor the upstart Lawrence Street tower is Brooklyn's tallest structure. That honor goes to the Board of Education's lacy radio and television transmission tower for WNYE-FM and WNYE-TV atop nearby Brooklyn Technical High School, 29 Fort Greene Place (591 feet).*

[F4] **Hanson Place Central United Methodist Church**, 88 Hanson Place, NW cor. St. Felix St. 1929-1931.

F3   F2   F5

[F1] **Atlantic Avenue Terminal Complex**, Atlantic and Flatbush Aves. 2004. *Di Domenico/Parsons Brinckerhoff.*

The Flatbush Terminal, for arrival and departure of the Atlantic Branch of the LIRR, the IRT Atlantic Avenue station and a major underground circulation system that links the IRT Atlantic Avenue Station with the BMT Fourth Avenue line (Pacific Street station), and the BMT Brighton Line (Atlantic Avenue station).

[F2] Originally **IRT Atlantic Avenue subway kiosk**, in the triangle formed by Flatbush, Atlantic, and Fourth Aves. 1908. *Heins & La Farge.* Renovated, 2005, *Di Domenico/Parsons Brinckerhoff.*

A sorry fate overtook this anchor on the IRT subway lines. Constructed in 1908 to celebrate the new underground connection with Manhattan, it was abandoned as a working entrance and then buried within a filigree (now gone) intended to revitalize it visually and commercially. *Heins & La Farge's* distinguished

Gothic restyled in modern dress, an exercise in massing brick and tan terra cotta that might be termed cubistic Art Moderne. The street level contains stores, a surprising but intelligent adjunct to ecclesiastical economics. This building replaced its predecessor, on the site from 1847 to 1927.

[F5] **Baptist Temple**, 360 Schermerhorn St., SW cor. Third Ave. 1894. Rebuilt, 1917.

This Romanesque Revival fortress bears gables and a machicolated tower. Its lighted cross emblazons the fundamentalist preaching within. The intersection before it, officially Temple Square, understandably acquired the nickname Brimstone Square.

[F6] **Metropolitan Corporate Academy High School**/formerly **Public School 15**, Brooklyn/ originally **Brooklyn Boys' Boarding School**, 475 State St., NE cor. Third Ave. ca. 1840.

A dour red-painted institutional remnant that is the far-flung outpost of the bureaucracy centered at 110 Livingston Street.

[F7] Brooklyn Academy of Music Historic District, bet. Lafayette Ave., Ashland, Hanson, and Fort Greene Places, plus parts of the N side of Fort Greene Place and both sides of S. Elliott Place. 🍎

The row houses of St. Felix Street are a surprising and charming foil to the bulky neo-Renaissance Academy.

[F8] Brooklyn Academy of Music (BAM), 30 Lafayette Ave., bet. Ashland Place and St. Felix

F8

[F10] BAM Harvey Theater/formerly **Majestic Theater** of the Brooklyn Academy of Music (BAM). 651 Fulton St., NE cor. Rockwell St. 1903. Renovated, 1987, *Hardy Holzman Pfeiffer.*

Here the **avant-garde** holds sway. The small but monumental arch swallows you into the grand restored lobby, a palimpsest of real and simulated decay. Its consciously worn and reclaimed spaces are akin to old money in old clothes. *Ralph Lauren*, take note. Here is the real thing.

[F11] Hanson Place Seventh Day Adventist Church/originally **Hanson Place Baptist Church**, 88 Hanson Place, SE cor. S. Portland Ave. 1857-1860. *George Penchard.* 🍎

A glorious **Corinthian**-columned portico fronts on Hanson Place, with pilasters along the South Portland flanks. Cream columns, trim, and pediments over a dark red body. Victorian milk glass.

F12

F14

St. 1908. *Herts & Tallant.* 718-636-4100. **BAM Rose Cinemas**, 1998. New canopies, 2008, *Hugh Hardy/H3 Hardy Collaboration.* 🍎

Clad in cool Classical glazed terra cotta, and originally crowned with a great Renaissance Revival cornice, now gone: BAM's core building has regained panache at street level, where *Hugh Hardy's* sinuous undulating canopy provides classy shelter. BAM within is a multichambered performing arts center built two generations before Lincoln Center, now housing a symphony hall/opera house and multiplex movie theater. Culturally, New York's avant-garde experiments take place here, with a veritable Vesuvius of talent in dance, theater, and music.

[F9] Mark Morris Dance Group, 3 Lafayette Ave., NW cor. Flatbush Ave. 2001. *Beyer Blinder Belle.*

An awkward assembly of competing postmodern forms: faux-aircraft-hangar roof, terraces, white stucco and glass block walls. In need of choreography.

[F12] Oxford Nursing Home/originally **Lodge No.22**, Benevolent Protective Order of Elks, 144 S. Oxford St., bet. Hanson Place and Atlantic Ave. W side. 1912. *H. Van Buren Magonigle and A. W. Ross.* Altered, 1955, *Wechsler & Schimenti.*

The formidable bracketed cornice makes a wide-sweeping Catholic hat on this body, abused in alteration, but as austere as a **Tuscan** palazzo.

[F13] 143 and 145 South Oxford Street, bet. Hanson Place and Atlantic Ave. E side.

A handsome pair of Corinthian-columned porches, alive and loved, front these late **Greek Revival** houses.

[F14] 158 South Oxford Street, bet. Hanson Place and Atlantic Avenue. W side. ca. 1860.

A freestanding clapboard **Italianate** house with a jigsaw-Gothic porch set on a unique podium for these blocks: a raised lawn.

Continue ↑ for Bedford-Stuyvesant

Continue → for Prospect Heights

Continue → for Park Slope

Continue → for Boerum Hill

Continue ↓ for Civic Center

Fort Greene Historic District

Clinton Hill Historic District

BAM Historic District

[F15] *Cuyler Gore Park, a triangle of land between Fulton St., Green and Carlton Aves., was opened in 1901 in honor of Theodore L. Cuyler, noted abolitionist and minister of Lafayette Avenue Presbyterian Church. The park hosts the Fort Greene Juneteenth Festival (June 19) each summer.*

[F16] **Atlantic Commons**, in a subdivided block between Atlantic Ave. and Hanson Pl., So. Oxford and Cumberland Sts. 1990s.

An urban historicist was here, with an idea, but too much parking.

[F17] **170 South Portland Avenue** and **161 South Elliott Place**, bet. Hanson Place and Atlantic Ave. [F18] **455 and 475 Carlton Avenue**, bet. Fulton St. and Atlantic Ave. E side. **770 Fulton Street**, bet. Carlton Ave. and Adelphi St. S side. All buildings, 1976. *Bond Ryder Associates.*

Residential blocks urbanely designed and arranged for playgrounds and plazas.

F20

F26

[F19] **Atlantic Terminal Houses**, N.Y.C. Housing Authority, 487-495 Carlton Ave., NE cor. Atlantic Ave. 1976. *James Stewart Polshek & Assocs.*
Early, ungainly *Polshek.*

[F20] **98 South Oxford Street**, bet. Greene and Lafayette Aves. W side. ca. 1855.
A **Corinthian** columned porch is a welcome variant on the street. No.100 next door was its peer, but owners removed their porch and added a silly entry enframement.

Here we enter the Fort Greene Historic District:

[F21] **Fort Greene Historic District**, bounded by Willoughby and Vanderbilt Aves., S. Elliott Place, and an irregular line N of Fulton St., plus Fort Greene Park. 🍎

[F22] **Lafayette Avenue Presbyterian Church**, 85 S. Oxford St., SE cor. Lafayette Ave. 1862. *Grimshaw & Morrill.*
This **Romanesque Revival**, cut-ashlar brownstone church, with a sturdy tower (a poly-

gon over a square) bearing four finials, corners South Oxford and Lafayette. More notable, however, for its numerous *Tiffany* windows.

[F23] **The Griffin**, 101 Lafayette Ave., NW cor. S. Oxford Pl. 1920s.
Glazed polychromatic terra-cotta forms a rich arch for the main entry on South Oxford Street.

[F24] **The Roanoke**/onetime **The San Carlos Hotel**, 69 S. Oxford St., bet. Lafayette and DeKalb Aves. E side. ca. 1893. *Montrose W. Morris.*
A proud multiple dwelling, once gutted by fire. Its resurrection was a veritable Phoenix: a grand brick and rockface limestone **Romanesque Revival** dowager.

[F25] **South Oxford Street** and **South Portland Avenue**, bet. Lafayette and DeKalb Aves.
Two handsome, tree-shaded blocks of

F22

brownstones. South Oxford's offer a range from the early 1850s to the end of the 19th century. South Portland's are mostly Italianate from the later 1860s. This district sports not only these fashionable London street names but also **Adelphi, Carlton, Cumberland,** and **Waverly**.

At the end of these blocks rises Fort Greene Park, a later stop on the tour. Turn right on DeKalb Avenue, and left at the end of the park, with an aside to:

[F26] **252 Cumberland Avenue**, bet. Lafayette and Dekalb Aves. W side. 1870s.
Blue-gray clapboards and a cream porch give an elegant pause to these eclectic streets.

[F27] **Washington Park**, that portion of Cumberland St. facing Fort Greene Park. DeKalb to Myrtle Aves.
These two blocks of brownstone mansions once housed those equal in social stature to any in Brooklyn.

[F28] **192 and 198 Washington Park**, bet. DeKalb and Willoughby Aves. E side. ca. 1880. *Marshall J. Morrill.*

Italianate and **Queen Anne**, the former with a mansard roof that bears projecting bay windows, ending with a columned dormer at the crest.

[F29] **179-186 Washington Park**, bet. DeKalb and Willoughby Aves. E side. 1866. *Joseph H. Townsend,* builder.

A mansarded ensemble with paired dormer windows in each slated roof. Note the stained-glass fanlight at No.182 and the several wood-framed cut-glass doors. Publisher *Alfred C. Barnes* lived at 182.

[F30] **173-176 Washington Park**, bet. Willoughby and DeKalb Aves. E side. ca. 1867. *Thomas B. Jackson,* builder.

Less grand than 179-186 above, they housed, among others, *William C. Kingsley* at **No.176** and his partner, *Albert Keeney,* next door at **No.175.** *Kingsley* and *Keeney* were among

F24

F31

Brooklyn's most affluent contractors, builders of streets and sewers, a reservoir further out on Long Island, and much of Prospect Park. In 1867, when *Kingsley* bought his house, he was known to be the driving political force behind the **Brooklyn Bridge**; he later became its largest individual stockholder.

Enter Fort Greene Park and climb the hill to the base of the giant Doric column:

[F31] **Fort Greene Park**/originally **Washington Park**, DeKalb Ave. to Myrtle Ave., Washington Park St. to Edwards St. 1867. *Frederick Law Olmsted & Calvert Vaux.* Additions, 1908, *McKim, Mead & White.* Altered, 1972, *Berman, Roberts & Scofidio.*

The prospect of the harbor and Manhattan skyline from its summit suggests that this might better have been the park named **Prospect**.

[F32] **Prison Ship Martyrs Monument**, center of Fort Greene Park. 1906-1909. *Stanford White of McKim, Mead & White,* architects. *A.A. Weinman,* sculptor. (The stair within is not open to the public.)

A tall **Doric** column, crowned with a bronze brazier, remembers the 11,500 American patriots who died in the 11 British prison ships anchored in Wallabout Bay (1776-1783). The old Navy Yard infilled this former East River body of water. *Weinman's* brazier, 148 feet above the park summit, once held an eternal flame. Nearby the Doric temple (distyle in antis) is the park's visitors center.

[F33] **The Brooklyn Hospital,** DeKalb Ave. to Willoughby St., from Fort Greene Park to Ashland Place. 1920. *J.M. Hewlett.* Altered and expanded, 1967, *Rogers, Butler & Burgun.* 1985, *Rogers, Burgun, Shahine & Deschler.*
[F34] **Staff Residence,** NE cor. of site, Willoughby St., SW cor. St. Edwards St. 1976. *Walker O. Cain & Assocs.*

F32

The residential tower plays with some cubist carving at its crest, but the wing springing out to DeKalb Avenue is sleek and elegant in brown brick and glass.

[F35] **Walt Whitman Houses** and **Raymond V. Ingersoll Houses**/originally **Fort Greene Houses,** N.Y.C. Housing Authority, Myrtle to Park Aves., Carlton Ave. to Prince St. 1944. *Rosaria Candela, André Fouilhoux, Wallace K. Harrison, Albert Mayer, Ethan Allen Dennison, William I. Hohauser, Ely Jacques Kahn, Charles Butler, Henry Churchill, and Clarence Stein.*

Thirty-five hundred apartments (14,000 persons) on 38 acres, completed during World War II as high-priority housing for Brooklyn's wartime industrial labor force. Within its bounds are the **Church of St. Michael** and **St. Edward, Cumberland Hospital,** and **P.S. 67.** Its architects are a roster of New York's greatest talents in the 1930s and 1940s. Nevertheless, it's a bland place—perhaps another case of too many cooks.

[F36] **Church of St. Michael and St. Edward**/originally **Church of St. Edward,** within the bounds of Ingersoll Houses, 108 St. Edward's St., bet. Myrtle and Park Aves. W side. 1902. *John J. Deery.* Altar, 1972, *Carol Dykman O' Connor.* Cross, 1972, *Robert Zacharian.*

Twin conical-capped towers in the manner of a 16th-century Loire Valley château. The interior is **Pop Art** plaster, with huge sheets of pictorial stained glass (done by a *Norman Rockwell* of the medium). The altar and cross incorporate parts of the old Myrtle Avenue El, which once rumbled down the street next door.

For those who remember the dappled gloom of Myrtle Avenue as it suffocated under the El, a walk east on the wide, sunlit thoroughfare will be refreshing. Turn right at Clermont Avenue:

[F37] **171 Clermont Avenue**/formerly **3rd Battery, New York National Guard**/once **Encumbrance Warehouse, N.Y.C. Department of Sanitation,** bet. Myrtle and Willoughby Aves. E side. ca. 1890.

This vast carapace has been converted to, of all things, housing. Sorry about that.

Now reenter the Historic District:

[F38] **Eglise Baptiste d'Expression Française**/formerly **Jewish Center of Fort Greene**/originally **Simpson Methodist Church,** 209 Clermont Ave., SE cor. Willoughby Ave. 1870.

The capsule history of a neighborhood's demographic change is here illustrated: first WASP, then Jewish, now Haitian. The northern

[F41] **238 Adelphi Street,** bet. Willoughby and Dekalb Aves. W side. 1870s.

A gracious porch can make the difference for a whole block.

Return to Clermont Avenue:

[F42] **292 Clermont Avenue,** bet. Dekalb and Lafayette Sts. W side. ca. 1870s.

A vigorous bay window modulates the street.

[F43] **The Brooklyn Masonic Temple,** 317 Claremont Ave., NE cor. Lafayette Ave. 1906. *Lord & Hewlett and Pell & Corbett.*

They took the word "temple" literally in 1909. Some of the vigorous polychromy that archaeologists believe was painted onto 5th century B.C. Greek temples is recalled with the Ionic order in fired terra cotta.

[F44] **Our Lady Queen of All Saints School, Church** and **Rectory** (Roman Catholic), 300 Vanderbilt Ave., NW cor. Lafayette Ave. 1910-1913.

F38   F41

F39

Italian raiment of Lombardian Romanesque was adapted to the needs of a 19th-century Brooklyn church. Note the Star of David still ensconced above the portals.

Turn for a detour through the midblock playground to Adelphi Street:

[F39] **Institutional Church of God in Christ,** 164-174 Adelphi St., bet. Willoughby and Myrtle Aves. W side. 1890.

Terra cotta and brick for the *Reverend C.E. Williams,* crowned with steep pyramidal roofs: sharp punctuations against the sky over a bulky planar body below.

[F40] **Church of St. Michael and St. Mark** (Anglican), 230 Adelphi St., bet Willoughby and DeKalb Aves. W side. 1888.

While the "Institutional Church" above is in a sleek and sophisticated **Romanesque Revival,** this one is rockfaced and lusty.

Gustave Steinback of Reiley and Steinback.

George Mundelein, later cardinal at Chicago, commissioned this complex while of this local parish. A glassy church (stained) and a glassy school (clear) suggest on the one hand that stained-glass glory, the Sainte Chapelle in Paris and, on the other, the sunlit aspects of modern school buildings. Inside, the church's aisles are perhaps the world's narrowest. Outside, 24 saints stand guard over the façade. To enter the church one, in fact, tunnels through the school.

[F45] **La Salle Hall**/formerly **The Chancery**/formerly **Residence, Roman Catholic Bishop of Brooklyn,** 367 Clermont Ave., NE cor. Greene Ave. 1887. *Patrick Charles Keely.*

Dour. Hollywood would cast it as an orphan asylum in a *Charlotte Brontë* novel. The neatly dressed granite blocks and mansard roof may be austere, but they were meant to be subdued, in contrast to the unbuilt proposed neighboring cathedral. Its current use is a dormitory for boys from neighboring Bishop Loughlin Memorial High School.

[F46] **80 Greene Avenue**, SE cor. Clermont Ave. 1986. *Warren Gran & Assocs.*

A well-scaled modern infill building, with great balconies that happily corner this intersection. The beehive-crowned Church of the Messiah stood here until it burned.

[F47] **378-434 Vanderbilt Avenue**, bet. Greene and Gates Aves. W side. ca. 1880.

An almost perfectly preserved row of 29 Italianate brownstones steps down a gentle hill. At either end their march is stopped in a dignified way: Nos.378 and 434 return to the building line, embracing a long narrow space modulated with front stoops and front gardens. Note that the balustrades are cast iron painted to look like brownstone. Industrialization rears its head.

UNBUILT
Theater for a New Audience, Rockwell Place, bet. Lafayette and Fulton Sts. *Hugh Hardy/H3 Hardy Collaboration.*

Originally planned as a four-story glass expanse facing Ashland Place, the project, sans original collaborator *Frank Gehry*, now is scheduled to begin construction on a new site on Rockwell Place, north of BAM, sometime in 2010. Or 2011. Or 2012.

New BAM Theater, 321 Ashland Place, bet. Lafayette and Hanson Pl. *Hugh Hardy/H3 Hardy Collaboration.*

Hardy is also involved in plans for a new 263-seat theater on the site of a former Salvation Army building just behind BAM's main

F43

stages on Lafayette St. First performances are scheduled for 2012. Or 2013.

MEMORIES, THE UNBUILT
The entire block bounded by Vanderbilt, Clermont, Lafayette, and Greene Avenues was acquired in 1860 as the site for what was to be one of the world's largest churches, the **Cathedral of the Immaculate Conception**. *Patrick Charles Keely*, one of the 19th century's most prolific architects, was chosen to execute the commission. Foundations were laid and walls rose to heights of 10 to 12 feet. **The Chapel of St. John**, the largest of the cathedral's proposed six, was completed in 1878 and the Bishop of Brooklyn's residence, nine years later. Then funds dried up and all work stopped. The incomplete walls remained for decades, a challenging playground for imaginative neighborhood children. After *Keely's* death in 1896, *John Francis Bentley*, architect of Westminster Cathedral in London, was asked to draw new plans; but he too died,

and his plans remained incomplete. The walls stood until 1931, when they and the chapel were demolished to build **Bishop Loughlin Memorial High School**, a tribute to the prelate who had the original dream in 1860. The only relic is the bishop's residence, now used by the brothers who teach at the high school.

END of Fort Greene Walking Tour: The nearest subway is the IND, a block south and a block east, at Fulton Street and Clinton Avenue (A and C trains). If you're hungry or want a glimpse of adjacent Clinton Hill, walk north on Clinton Avenue.

NECROLOGY: FORT GREENE

New York & Brooklyn Casket Company, 187 S. Oxford St., bet. Hanson Place and Atlantic Ave. E side. 1927. *Vincent B. Fox.*

A lonely limestone neo-Georgian remnant now squeezed between tennis courts and devastation.

F47

Church of St. Simon the Cyrenian, 175 S. Oxford St., bet. Hanson Place and Atlantic Ave. E side. Fort Greene. ca. 1895.

A fine house that spent its last years as a church. A previous edition of the Guide called it "Black Forest Queen Anne": ornamented stucco, ornamented terra cotta, ornamented brick.

Church of the Messiah and Incarnation (Episcopal), 80 Greene Ave., SE cor. Clermont Ave. Fort Greene. 1865. *James H. Giles.* Redesigned, 1892, *R.H. Robertson.*

Until the church was engulfed by flames and then torn down, it was hard to miss its 130-foot-tall brick and terra-cotta beehive-capped spire, modeled after the 12th-century Byzantine Romanesque cathedral in Perigueux in southwest France.

460 Washington Avenue (house), bet. Greene and Gates Aves. W side. Clinton Hill. ca. 1890.

A Queen Anne porch enclosed this brick and terra-cotta mansion. Boarded up for some years, it was finally demolished.

CLINTON HILL

Clinton Hill Walking Tour: Start at Clinton Avenue and Fulton Street, at the Clinton-Washington Station (A and C trains), and end near the same station. In between pass what remains of the homes, many with monumental porches, built by the merchant and industrial kings of Brooklyn: the Pratts, Bedfords, Pfizers, and Underwoods.

Clinton Hill Historic District, generally bet. Willoughby Ave. at the N, Vanderbilt Ave. on the W, then a line N of Fulton St., and an eastern line on Downing St. N to Gates Ave., then Grand Ave. and Cambridge Pl. N to Lafayette Ave., then W to Hall St., then N to the Willoughby Ave. 🍎 *See map (p. 639) for exact boundaries.*

[F48] **Church of St. Luke & St. Matthew** (Episcopal)/originally St. Luke's Episcopal Church, 520 Clinton Ave., bet. Fulton St. and

F52

Atlantic Ave. W side. 1888-1891. *John Welch.* 🍎
Eclecticism gone berserk: battered greenish stone walls, Romanesque arches, and Ruskinian Gothic polychromy in three shades of brownstone. It all adds up to a great façade.

[F49] **487 Clinton Avenue**, bet. Gates Ave. and Fulton St. E side. 1892. *Langston & Dahlander.*
A sturdy Loire Valley château, towered, machicolated, and mated with a cut rock-faced brownstone **Richardsonian Romanesque** entry arch.

[F50] **Royal Castle Apartments**, 20-30 Gates Ave., SW cor. Clinton Ave. 1912. *Wortmann & Braun.* 🍎
An exuberant six-story structure, intended to rise to the high style of older Clinton Avenue residences. The ornament smacks of a familiarity with the **Sezession** movement, the Austrian variant of **Art Nouveau**. The skyline gables are Viennese. Croissants?

[F51] Originally **Morgan Bogart House**, 463 Clinton Ave., bet. Gates and Greene Aves. E side. 1902. *Mercein Thomas.*
Limestone Renaissance Revival unique on the Hill. Note the Ionic-columned bay window, quoins, and rustications. An exile from Manhattan's Upper East Side.

F54

[F52] **457 Clinton Avenue**, bet. Gates and Greene Aves. E side. ca. 1870.
This crisp building in gray and white wears a porch with four fluted Tuscan (Roman Doric) columns from an earlier era than most of Clinton Avenue, and a dormered mansard roof.

[F53] Onetime **Galilee Baptist Church**/originally **David Burdette House**, 447 Clinton Ave., bet. Gates and Greene Aves. E side. ca. 1850.
This Italianate brick villa wears sandstone quoins and two Tuscan columns at its front porch.

[F54] Originally **William H. Burger House**, 443 Clinton Ave., bet. Gates and Greene Aves. E side. 1902. *Hobart A. Walker.*
Bold Regency Revival, with fluted and banded Tuscan columns. A brace of gables fronting the mansard roof, one with a circle, one with a triangle, anticipates postmodernism's geometric abstractions.

F49

[F55] Originally built by **Frederick A. Platt,** 415 Clinton Ave., bet. Gates and Greene Aves. E side. ca. 1865.

A **General Grant** (or Second Empire) body in painted brick, mansarded with green slate; the generous porch is borne by sturdy wood Composite columns.

[F56] Originally **Charles A. Schieren House,** 405 Clinton Ave., bet. Gates and Greene Aves. E side. 1889. *William Tubby.*

A monumental Romanesque Revival/Queen Anne mansion in brick and stone. The sinuous gable was plucked from the best of Amsterdam's history. *Mr. Tubby* was one of Brooklyn's most prolific 19th-century architects (see **Pratt Institute**, coming up).

[F57] Originally **Cornelius N. Hoagland House,** 410 Clinton Ave. bet. Gates and Greene Aves. W side. 1882. *Parfitt Bros.*

An **Eclectic Queen Anne** brick, terra-cotta, and limestone mansion with picturesque dual chimneys. The brickwork dentils are elegant.

[F58] Originally **C. Walter Nichols** and **Henry L. Batterman Houses,** 404 and 406 Clinton Ave., bet. Gates and Greene Aves. E side. 1901. *Albert Ulrich.*

A **Renaissance Revival** pair, with a shared Tuscan-columned porch.

[F59] Originally **Liebman House,** 380 Clinton Ave., bet. Greene and Lafayette Aves. W side. 1907. *Herts & Tallant.*

One of the newcomers on these blocks, a product of the **Colonial Revival** that arrived in a backlash against **Romanesque Revival** and **Queen Anne.** A by-product of the Columbian Exposition of 1893, which had touted the Renaissance, but caused a more modest stylistic revival in houses.

[F60] Originally **John W. Shepard House,** 356 Clinton Ave., bet. Greene and Lafayette Aves. W side. 1905. *Theodore C. Visscher.*

A **stuccoed eccentricity,** articulated with brick and limestone, and a green tile roof. Some ladies wear funny hats; *Mr. Shepard* wore an eccentric house.

[F61] Originally **Joseph Steele House**, 200 Lafayette St., SE cor. Vanderbilt Ave. Before 1850. Altered. 👁️‍🗨️

A class act from the second quarter of the 19th century: **Greek Revival** with elegant narrow clapboards, a modillion-bracketed cornice with eyebrow windows, and an octagonal cupola that rises to view the harbor. It wears its age well, with dignity. The original Federal cottage is the eastern wing, the tail of the later Greek Revival dog.

F61

[F62] Originally **James H. Lounsberry House**, 321 Clinton Ave., bet. Lafayette and DeKalb Aves. E side. ca. 1875. *Ebenezer L. Roberts*.

A super-brownstone, in the same monumental class as **Nos.2** and **3 Pierrepont Place** in Brooklyn Heights. Here an Italianate cornice and roof hover on high.

[F63] Originally **John Arbuckle House**, 315 Clinton Ave., bet. Lafayette and DeKalb Aves. E side. 1888. *Montrose W. Morris*.

Robust red brick, brownstone, and terra cotta. Don't miss the intricately molded terra-cotta soffit below the bay window. *Arbuckle* was a coffee merchant who made his fortune from Yuban coffee.

[F64] Originally **William Harkness House**, 300 Clinton Ave., bet. Lafayette and DeKalb Aves. W side. 1889. *Mercein Thomas*.

Here are strong bay windows surmounted by a tiny **Queen Anne** balcony that gives stature to a child, or a would-be *Napoléon*, in the attic.

Take a short detour to the right along DeKalb Avenue and then resume your northern walk on Clinton:

[F65] **282-290 DeKalb Avenue**, SW cor. Waverly Ave. 1890. *Montrose W. Morris*.

Quintuplets unified by a pediment over the central trio and symmetrical cylindrical turrets at each end. A terrific tour de force, rare for both its design and its state of preservation.

[F66] **285-289 DeKalb Avenue**, NW cor. Waverly Ave. 1889. *Montrose W. Morris*.

This time a trio, with pyramidal and conical roofs connected by an intervening mansard. Brownstone, gray stone, terra cotta, and brick both flat and curved.

[F67] **Waverly Avenue**, bet. Gates and Myrtle Aves.

This narrow service street is sandwiched between the mansions of Clinton and Washington Avenues. Its many stables and carriage houses,

F63　　　　　　F65

F66

remnants of service facilities for those wealthy neighbors, have been recycled as apartments, restaurants, and other independent units.

Back to Clinton Avenue:

[F68] Originally **William W. Crane House**, 284 Clinton Ave., bet DeKalb and Willoughby Sts. W side. ca. 1854. *Field & Correja*.

A **Newport Stick and Shingle Style** house with wonderful serpentine jigsaw and carved work in its gables. The cut shingles give it a rich texture, and the varied picturesque gables provide a profile against the sky. Snazzy.

[F69] Originally **Behrend H. Huttman House**, 278 Clinton Ave., bet. DeKalb and Willoughby Sts. ca. 1884.

Bizarre columns mark a sturdy porch, with alternating smooth and rough drum segments. A **neo-Baroque oddity**.

[F70] Originally **Charles Pratt House**/now **St. Joseph's College Founders Hall,** 232 Clinton Ave., bet. DeKalb and Willoughby Aves. W side. 1874-1875. *Ebenezer L. Roberts.*

The original manor house and gardens of *Pratt* père: Italianate freestanding brownstone mansion. His sons across the street ventured into more daring architectural experiments.

Charles Pratt, refiner of kerosene at Greenpoint, joined his oil empire with that of John D. Rockefeller's Standard Oil Company in 1874. As legend has it, at the marriage of each of Pratt's first four sons, the couple was presented with a house opposite their father's place for a wedding present. Of these, three remain: those of **Charles M., Frederic,** *and* **George. Harold,** *succumbing to the changing fashion stimulated by the consolidation of Brooklyn and New York, built his nuptial palace on Park Avenue at 68th Street. Fifth son, John, also chose to live (more modestly than Harold) in Manhattan.*

F72

[F71] Originally **Frederic B. Pratt House**/now **Caroline Ladd Pratt House** (foreign students' residence of Pratt Institute), 229 Clinton Ave., bet. DeKalb and Willoughby Aves. E side. 1895. *Babb, Cook & Willard.*

Attached on one side and freestanding on the other, it forms a neat and handsome urban transition. The pergolaed entry supported by truncated caryatids and atlantides does the trick. The house proper is gray and white **Georgian/Renaissance Revival**. To the garden's rear, view another sturdy pergola borne by a dozen Tuscan fluted columns and, at the entry, a most venerable wisteria.

[F72] Originally **Charles Millard Pratt House**/now **Residence, Bishop of Brooklyn** (Roman Catholic), 241 Clinton Ave., bet. DeKalb and Willoughby Aves. E side. 1890. *William B. Tubby.*

A great **Richardsonian Romanesque** building. The detailing in smooth, rounded forms makes this place both powerful and sensuous.

Note particularly the spherical bronze lamp at the entrance and the semicircular conservatory high on the south wall.

[F73] Originally **George DuPont Pratt House**/now **St. Joseph's College**, 245 Clinton Ave. (N wing only), bet. DeKalb and Willoughby St. E side. 1901. *Babb, Cook & Willard.*

Red brick and limestone, quoined and corniced, this is **Georgian revival** (Edwardian division) that reeks of Englishness—it might well be

F71

the British embassy. The additions by the college to the south are properly unprepossessing.

[F74] **Clinton Hill Apartments,** Section 1, Clinton to Waverly Aves. Willoughby to Myrtle Aves. 1943. *Harrison, Fouilhoux & Abramovitz.*

World War II housing for the families of naval personnel (the old Navy Yard, now an industrial park, is a short walk away). Blue and white nautical motifs are included as ornament at the entrances, despite wartime restrictions on just about everything else. (Section 2 was completed by the same architects further south between Lafayette and Greene Avenues.)

[F75] **Lefferts Laidlaw House,** 136 Clinton Ave., bet. Myrtle and Park Aves. ca. 1836. S wing before 1855. ●´

A residential **Greek Revival** temple in wood, the roof supported by four Corinthian columns.

[F76] **St. Mary's Episcopal Roman Catholic Church**, 230 Classon Ave., bet. Myrtle and Willoughby Aves. ca. 1859. *Richard T. Auchmuty of Renwick & Auchmuty.* ☙

An especially beautiful brownstone **Gothic Revival** church, built to serve the community that grew around the Navy Yard, just to the north. A flying gothic arch leads to a close.

[F77a] **Convent of the Sisters of Mercy** (Roman Catholic), 273 Willoughby Ave., bet. Classon Ave. and Taaffe Pl. N side. 1862. *Patrick Charles Keely.*

A gloomy mansarded red-brick pile.

[F77b] Originally **St. Paul's School**, E side Taaffe Pl., bet. Willoughby and Myrtle Aves. ca. 1899.

Romanesque Revival in a ruddy palette of terra cotta, and brick. Note the basketweave brickwork surrounding the first floor arches.

Rope walks: Not for crossing jungle swamps or the River Kwai but long narrow buildings cre-

F81

F82

[F80] **Pratt Institute Campus**, Willoughby Ave. to DeKalb Ave., Classon Ave. to Hall St. 1887. Various architects. ☙

Originally five blocks and the streets that served them. Urban renewal gave the Institute opportunity to make a single, campus-style superblock. As the separate buildings were built to conform to the former street pattern, and the intervening buildings were removed, the result became surreal: **a kind of abstract chessboard**, where the pieces sit on a blank board without a grid.

A professional school of art and design, architecture, engineering and computer information, and library sciences. *Charles Pratt* ran it as his personal philanthropic fiefdom until his death in 1891. A similar case study to that of Cooper Union, with its patron, *Peter Cooper.*

[F81] **Pratt Row**, 220-234 Willoughby Ave., S side. 171-185 Steuben St. E. side. 172-186 Emerson Place. W side. 1907. *Hobart A. Walker.* ☙

These were preserved despite the mandates

F83a

ated for spinning rope. In 1803 one was erected in the two blocks north of the Convent of the Sisters of Mercy. It was so long (1,200 feet) that a tunnel was built for it to pass beneath intersecting Park Avenue.

[F78] **88th Precinct, N.Y.C. Police Department**, 300 Classon Ave., SW cor. DeKalb Ave. ca. 1890. South extension, 1924.

Mini-Romanesque Revival, it packs an arcuated castle into a tight site and at a small scale.

[F79] 220-232 **Taaffe Place Apartments**/ Originally **Warehouses**, bet. Willoughby and DeKalb Aves. W side. ca. 1885.

No-nonsense Romanesque Revival with virile, vigorous brickwork and arches that bound and abound; *H.H. Richardson* would have been pleased. Next door, to the south, are more sophisticated but less vigorous neo-Romanesquisms. But enjoy the ornate wrought-iron strapping for the tensile ties (stabilizing slender brick piers).

of the same federal urban renewal legislation that produced Willoughby Walk—mandates to declare a certain percentage of existing units substandard. The 27 that remain are faculty housing. Note the bay windows and alternating Dutch and triangular gables.

[F82] **Stabile Hall, Pratt Institute**, East side of Campus. 2000. *Pasanella + Klein, Stolzman + Berg.*

Three residential blocks are umbilically attached to their common services, providing a step into serious 21st-century architecture for dour Pratt.

[F83] **Pratt Activity/Resource Center**, E of Steuben St. 1975. Activity center (upper part), *Ezra D. Ehrenkrantz & Assocs.*

Tennis courts in a **hyperbolic paraboloidal** row, like a row of oversized pup tents. Unlike anything else on campus (or in the neighborhood), their style goes in and out of fashion.

[F83a] **Julia Curran Terian Pratt Pavilion**, bet. Steuben Hall & Pratt Studios. 2006. *Hanrahan/Meyers.*

Glass and steel suspended between two existing masonry buildings. Work from the Institute's arts programs is displayed here. It's a nice idea: the entire building acts as a frame for the artwork.

[F83b] **Children's Portico**, NW cor. of the Activity/Resource Center. 1912.

Here a much later appendage of the library was dismantled and relocated to the other side of Pratt Campus. It is said to be a copy of part of the King's School, Canterbury Cathedral: a **Norman Revival** Chevron-ornamented remnant.

[F84] **Memorial Hall**, Pratt Institute, S of Willoughby Ave. on Ryerson Walk. E side. 1926-1927. *John Mead Howells.*

Howells reversed history. Instead of grafting **Byzantine** capitals onto **Roman** columns to produce a **Romanesque** vocabulary, he grafted this

Looking backward: To enter the Pratt Institute engine room, located on the ground floor of the East Building (originally Machine Shop Building. 1887. William Windrim), is to pass through a time warp. Inside spin a gleaming trio of late 19th-century Ames Iron Works steam engines (actually installed in 1900), whose electrical generators still supply one third of the campus buildings with 120 volt D.C. service. These and other antique artifacts form a veritable museum of industrial archaeology. On display is a name plate of the DeLavergne Refrigerating Machine Company, chandeliers from the Singer Tower's boardroom, and a "No Loafing" sign from the Ruppert Brewery complex, among other industrial memorabilia.

To your right across the campus green is the library:

[F87] **Pratt Institute Library**/originally **Pratt Free Library**, Hall St., bet. Willoughby and DeKalb Aves. E side. 1896.

F85

whole building, a neo-Byzantine eclectically detailed hall, onto the adjacent Romanesque Revival Main Building.

[F85] **Main Building, Pratt Institute**, S of Memorial Hall on Ryerson Walk. E side. 1885-1887. *Lamb & Rich.* Porch added, 1894, *William B. Tubby.*

A gung-ho **Romanesque Revival**, where sturdy, squat columns bear a porch embellished with an organically ornamented frieze. At each side, wrought-iron cradles bear spherical iron lanterns.

[F86] **South Hall, Pratt Institute.** 1891. Porch, 1894. *William B. Tubby.*

Some modest *Tubby* in contrast to the old Charles Millard Pratt House, or his articulated library across the way.

William B. Tubby. North porch, 1936, *John Mead Howells.* Altered again, 1982, *Giorgio Cavaglieri & Warren Gran.*

Stubby *Tubby*: strongly articulated brick piers give a bold face to Hall Street and adjacent flanks. A free Romanesque Revival but with a Classical plan. Originally Brooklyn's first free public library, it was restricted to Pratt students in 1940. The south terrace is the roof of a mostly underground *Cavaglieri and Gran* addition.

[F88] **Thrift Hall, Pratt Institute**, Ryerson Walk, NE cor. DeKalb Ave. 1916. *Shampan & Shampan.*

The Thrift, as its Classical lettering proclaims atop a neo-Georgian limestone and brick body, was built to be a bank but now houses offices behind those Corinthian pilasters. *Charles Pratt, Sr.,* initiated the idea of student savings in 1889, shortly before his death (his original building was demolished to make way for Memorial Hall). The Thrift closed as a bank in the early 1940s.

F95

[F89] **St. James Towers**/originally **University Terrace**, DeKalb to Lafayette Aves., St. James Place to Classon Ave. 1963. *Kelly & Gruzen.*

The balconies are recessed within the body of these high-rise slabs rather than projecting. Their containment on three sides not only

[F92] **Independent United Order of Mechanics of the Western Hemisphere**/originally **Lincoln Club**, 67 Putnam Ave., bet. Irving Place and Classon Ave. N side. 1889. *Rudolph L. Daus.* ✪

Elegant Republicans left this florid structure, marking the memory of these streets with

F96

F98

solves a design problem but also reduces the possibilities for vertigo.

[F90] **361 Classon Avenue** and **386-396 Lafayette Avenue**, SE cor. of Classon and Lafayette Aves. ca. 1888.

A picturesque and romantic brick and brownstone Victorian "terrace." Compare this rich massing and detail with the high-rise public housing across the street: charm and personality confronted by tombstones.

[F91] **418-422 Classon Avenue**, bet. Gates Ave. and Quincy St. W side. ca. 1885.

An exuberant **Romanesque Revival** trio, posing for a group picture. Two brick- and brownstone-bowed façades flank an extraordinary terra-cotta arch at the center. A surviving fragment of a row that previously defined this block.

a remembrance of better times. The bracketed tower is in the Wagnerian idiom popularized by the fantastic 1850s Bavarian royal castle of *Ludwig II,* **Neuschwanstein.**

[F93] **James W. and Lucy S. Elwell House,** 70 Lefferts Pl., bet. Grand and Classon Aves. ca. 1854. ✪

An unusually fine **Italianate** clapboard villa, symmetrically organized around a temple-like second story, with cupola above. A riot of brackets holds up the majestic eaves. The wraparound porch at the main façade was enclosed around 1939, near the time of the sale of the house to the followers of *Father Divine.*

[F94] **Bethel Seventh-Day Adventist Church**/originally **Church of Our Father,** 457 Grand Ave., NE cor. Lefferts Place. ca. 1885.

The obtuse angle of this intersection suggested a stepped form to this architect. The brickwork is piered, arched, corbeled, and articulated, presenting pinnacles, finials, and oculi. A wonderful and vigorous brick monolith.

[F95] Originally **College of the Immaculate Conception,** Washington Ave., NE cor. Atlantic Ave. 1916. *Gustave Steinback.*

A neo-Gothic school building of great charm and elegance in brick and limestone.

[F96] Originally **Graham Home for Old Ladies,** 320 Washington Ave., bet. DeKalb and Lafayette Aves. W side. 1851. *J. G. Glover.*

A simple **Romanesque Revival** brick building with an industrial scale. The original patron was deftly titled *The Brooklyn Society for the Relief of Respectable, Aged, Indigent Females,* to whom paint manufacturer, *John B. Graham,* donated this building. Now restored to some of the splendor it had before falling into disrepair in the 1980s and 1990s. The current residents are, by no means, indigent.

[F97] **Underwood Park,** Lafayette Ave., bet. Washington and Waverly Aves. N side.

Site of the former *John T. Underwood* (of typewriter fame) mansion plus adjacent row

F100

houses, demolished at the direction of his widow, who saw **Clinton Hill** decline precipitously and did not want the grand house she shared with her husband to deteriorate in concert. Fortunately for the rest of the neighborhood, decline was checked and then reversed in the 1960s. Happy for the neighborhood, sad that we lost this one.

Her daughter, *Gladys Underwood James,* brought the preservation fight to Brooklyn Heights, buying **2 and 3 Pierrepont Street** (both significant 1857 mansions by *Frederic A. Peterson,* architect of the Cooper Union), plus a string of houses on Columbia Heights, spaced so that a developer could not assemble land for an apartment house. A quiet preservationist before there were landmark laws.

[F98] **Apostolic Faith Church**/originally **Orthodox Friends Meeting House,** 273 Lafayette Ave., NE cor. Washington Ave. 1868. Attributed to *Stephen C. Earle.*

A simple Lombardian Romanesque brick box, painted with vigor (white with red trim) by its current tenants. Not beautiful, but very handsome.

[F99] **Emmanuel Baptist Church,** 279 Lafayette Ave., NW cor. St. James Place. 1886-1887. *Francis H. Kimball.* Chapel. 1882-1883. *Ebenezer Roberts.* School. 1925-1927.

Yellow Ohio sandstone was carved here into an approximation of a 13th-century **French Gothic** façade. The interior, in startling contrast, is a Scottish Presbyterian preaching space, with radial seating fanning from the pulpit and baptismal font.

[F100] **Higgins Hall, Pratt Institute School of Architecture**/originally **Adelphi Academy,** 61 St. James Place, bet. Lafayette Ave. and Clifton Place. **North wing,** 1869. *Mundell & Teckritz.* **South wing,** 1887. *Charles C. Haight.* Reconstructed after fire, 1996, *Rogers Marvel Architects.* **Center wing,** 2005. *Steven Holl with Rogers Marvel Architects.*

Two 19th-century wings in **Richardsonian Romanesque,** with a 21st-century **modernist** wing as connector. The brickmasons were let loose first, with piers, buttresses, round arches, segmental arches, reveals, and corbel tables.

The minimalist **center wing,** replacing an earlier one destroyed by fire in 1996, is a jack-o-lantern in glass and steel that glows at night. The contrast between the styles and eras is deftly handled by *Holl.*

Henry Ward Beecher laid the cornerstone of the **North wing,** and *Charles Pratt* donated $160,000 for the **South wing.**

F101

[F101] **St. James Place,** the southerly extension of Hall St.
[F102] **Clifton Place,** running E from St. James Place.
[F103] **Cambridge Place,** starting S at Greene Ave. bet. St. James Place and Grand Ave.

Three Places that are really **places.** Each is a showpiece of urban row-house architecture built for the Brooklyn middle class between the 1870s and 1890s. When bored by the monotony of a uniform row, architects turned to picturesque variety, giving identity of detail and silhouette to each owner, as in Nos.202-210 St. James Place.

Nos.179-183 St. James Place are a Romanesque Revival trio built in 1892 by *William B. Tubby.* **Nos.127-135 Cambridge Place,** bet. Gates and Putnam Aves., are a quintet from 1894, also by *Tubby.*

F105

*If you wish a peek at **Cambridge Place**, turn left at Greene Avenue for a short block and then return. If not, turn right on Greene and right again at Washington Avenue, for a half-block excursion:*

[F104a] **357-359 Washington Avenue**, bet. Greene and Lafayette Aves. E side. ca. 1860. Attributed to *Ebenezer L. Roberts.*

Twin wood-clapboarded painted Victorians in pristine condition. Eyebrow windows peer out from under a strong cornice, echoed in the projecting hoods above windows below.

[F104b] Originally **Henry Offerman House**, 361 Washington Ave., bet. Greene and Lafayette Aves. E side. 1888.

Queen Anne brick body, with brownstone quoins and trim, a high mansard roof, and terra-cotta friezes. It boldly thrusts its bayed form into the streetscape.

F106b

[F104c] Originally **Van Glahn House**, 365 Washington Ave., bet. Greene and Lafayette Aves. 1921-1922. *Dwight James Baum.*

A bland Colonial Revival latecomer.

[F105] **The Mohawk**/onetime **Mohawk Hotel**, 379 Washington Ave., bet. Greene and Lafayette Sts. E side. 1904. *Neville & Bagge.*

A **Beaux Arts** latecomer to the Hill, festooned with limestone quoins and lintels, and a cornice with grand brackets and dentils. By the turn of the century, the idea of apartment living—they were termed French Flats—had begun to catch on.

[F106a] Originally **William H. Mairr** and **Raymond Hoagland Houses**, 396 and 398 Washington Ave., bet. Greene and Lafayette Aves. W side. 1887. *Adam E. Fischer.*

Bearded giants in the gables crown these vermilion terra-cotta **Queen Annes**.

[F106b] **400-404 Washington Avenue**, NW cor. Greene Ave. 1885. *Mercein Thomas.*

A trio of **Romanesque Revival** beauties, in

brick over brownstone, with picturesque silhouettes, and a glorious corner oriel tourette.

[F107] **163-175 Greene**, NE cor. Washington Ave. 1990s.

New infill housing.

[F108] **417 Washington Avenue**, bet. Greene and Gates Aves. E side. ca. 1860.

Expert carpenters (and shinglers and lathers and millworkers) created architecture in the

F108

center city until fire laws exiled wood to the suburbs. 417 is an elegant pre-law survivor, with a grand Second Empire cornice and a lovely bayed Ionic-columned porch.

[F109] **Brown Memorial Baptist Church**/originally **Washington Avenue Baptist Church**, 484 Washington Ave., SW cor. Gates Ave. 1860. *Ebenezer L. Roberts.*

A pinch of **Lombardian Romanesque** (arched corbel-tables) decorates a highly articulated square-turreted English Gothic body. The limestone water tables make lively counterpoint with the red brick.

END of Clinton Hill Walking Tour: The IND stops on Fulton Street at the Clinton-Washington Station (A and C trains). Make connections with the IRT (2, 3, 4, and 5 trains) or BMT (J, M, and Z trains) at Manhattan's Broadway-Nassau/Fulton Street Station.

PARK SLOPE

A somber-hued wonderland of finials, pinnacles, pediments, towers, turrets, bay windows, stoops, and porticoes: a smorgasbord of late Victoriana and the successor to the Heights and the Hill as the bedroom of the middle class and wealthy. These three districts are together the prominent topographical precincts of old brown-stone Brooklyn: **the Heights** sits atop a bluff over the harbor, **the Hill** is a major crest to the northeast, and **the Slope** slopes from Prospect Park down to the Gowanus Canal and the flat-lands beyond.

Despite its proximity to the park, the area was slow to develop. As late as 1884 it was still characterized as "fields and pasture." *Edwin C. Litchfield's* Italianate villa, completed in 1857, alone commanded the prospect of the harbor from its hill in present-day Prospect Park. By 1871 the first stage of the park had been constructed, yet the Slope lay quiet and tranquil,

[P1] **Park Slope Historic District**, generally along the S flank of Flatbush Ave. and Plaza St., and the W flank of Prospect Park W.; W to Sixth Ave., N of Union St., W to Seventh Ave., N of 3rd St., and W to Eighth Ave., N of 15th St. ☛

The first draft of the Historic District originally included only the park blocks. The Slope, emerging as the latest brownstone rediscovery of the upper middle class, was soon recognized as a precinct containing a rich fabric of row housing both within and beyond those initial arbitrary boundaries. The district finally designated reaches northwesterly from the park blocks to encompass part of the richness of Sixth Avenue between Berkeley and Sterling Places. And even with the expansion, good and great architecture thrives on the Slope outside district lines.

Park Slope Walking Tour A: From the newsstand where Flatbush Avenue joins Grand Army Plaza (at the surface of the IRT Grand Army Plaza Station, 2 and 3 trains) south into Park Slope and return.

P2

bypassed by thousands of persons making their way on the Flatbush Avenue horsecars to this newly created recreation area. By the mid 1880s, however, the potential of the Slope became apparent, and mansions began to appear on the newly laid out street grid.

The lavish homes clustered around Plaza Street and Prospect Park West eventually were christened the Gold Coast. Massive apartment buildings invaded the area after World War I, feeding upon the large, unutilized plots of land occupied by the first growth. These austere Park Avenue-like structures, concentrated at Grand Army Plaza are in contrast to the richly imaginative brick dwellings of Carroll Street and Montgomery Place, the mansions, churches, and clubs that still remain, and the remarkably varied row houses occupying the side streets as they descend toward the Manhattan skyline to the west.

Cross Plaza Street and admire:

[P2] **The Montauk Club**, 25 Eighth Avenue, NE cor. Lincoln Place. 1889-1891. *Francis H. Kimball.*

A Venetian Gothic palazzo, whose canal is the narrow lawn separating it from its cast-iron fence. Remember the Ça' d'Oro"? But here in brown-stone, brick, terra cotta, and verdigris copper. It bears the name of a local tribe, which explains the friezes at the third and fourth stories facing Eighth Avenue, honoring these onetime local natives.

Continue on Plaza Street and turn right into Berkeley Place:

[P3] Originally **George P. Tangeman House**, 276 Berkeley Place bet. Plaza St. and Eighth Ave. S side. 1891. *Lamb & Rich.*

Brick, granite, and terra-cotta **Romanesque Revival**, paid for by Cleveland Baking Powder. Cupid caryatids hold up the shingled pediment, with bulky Ionic columns supporting a frieze of scallop shells.

[P4] **64-66 Eighth Avenue**, bet. Berkeley Place and Union St. W side. 1889. *Parfitt Brothers*.

Two bold sandstone and granite residences by popular architects of that period. They bear carved foliate bas-relief friezes worthy of *Louis Sullivan*.

Take a peek to the right down Union Street:

[P5] **889-905 Union Street**, bet. Seventh and Eighth Aves. N side. 1889. *Albert E. White*.

More **Queen Anne**, a picturesque octet with eclectic medieval and Classical parts. Note the brownstone friezes, bay windows, and both elliptical and circular arches.

[P6] **905-913 Union Street**, bet 7th and 8th Aves. N side. 1895. *Thomas McMahon*.

A Queen Anne quintet in brick, brownstone, and shingles.

[P7] **70 Eighth Avenue**, NW cor. Union St. 1890s.

[P10] **944-946 President Street**, bet. Prospect Park W. and Eighth Ave. S side. 1886-1890. Attributed to *Charles T. Mott*.

An extravagant duet in brick and brownstone, with rich wrought iron, stained glass, and terra cotta. There is a picturesque profile against the sky.

[P11] **925 President Street**, bet. Prospect Park W. and Eighth Ave. N side. 1870s.

One of a magnificent and magnificently preserved phalanx of crisp brownstones, their bayed fronts modulating this wonderful block.

[P12] **Montessori School**, 105 Eighth Avenue, bet. President and Carroll Sts. E side. 1916. *Helmle & Huberty*.

A limestone English Regency Revival mansion with a bowed, Corinthian-columned entry.

[P13] **18 and 19 Prospect Park West**, SW cor. Carroll St. 1898. *Montrose W. Morris*.

An eclectic set in limestone Renaissance

P7

P8

A brick pepper pot anchors this corner mansion, scrubbed and slicked back to its Gay Nineties condition, showing off its picturesque silhouette of chimneys and gables. **Romantic Romanesque.**

[P8] **869 President Street**/originally **Stuart Woodford House**, bet. Seventh and Eighth Aves. N side. 1885. *Henry Ogden Avery*.

Two bracketed oriel windows punctuate the brick façade, articulated by *Viollet-le-Duc*-inspired struts. *Viollet-le-Duc* was a 19th-century French neo-Gothicist, fascinated with structure. *Woodford* was onetime ambassador to Spain. Eccentric and wonderful.

[P9] **876-878 President Street**, bet. Seventh and Eighth Aves. S side. 1889. *Albert E. White*.

Roman brick and brownstone in a bay-windowed **Queen Anne**. Note the elliptical brick archwork and remarkably lusty rock-face brownstone stoops.

Revival. Note the 2nd- and 3rd-floor Ionic pilasters and the hemispherical glass and bronze entrance canopy at No.18.

[P14] **Carroll Street**, bet. Prospect Park W. and Eighth Ave. 1887-1911. Various architects.

The north side of this street is as calm, orderly, and disciplined as the south side is picturesque. This block of Carroll Street is visual evidence of significant changing styles, viz.

North Side:

a. **No.863.** 1890. *Napoleon LeBrun & Sons*.

Roman Brick Renaissance, buried until recently behind the architecture of wild vines, but a renovation has revealed a house behind the growth. We preferred the Tarzan version.

b. **Nos.855-861.** *Stanley M. Holden*.

A quartet in yellow Roman brick and brownstone **Romanesque Revival.** There are stained glass, mock bay windows with ornamented pilasters, and beautifully articulated brick arches.

South Side:

c. **Nos.876-878**. 1911. *Chappell & Bosworth.*
   Park Avenue Georgian in ruddy brick and limestone-framed bay and double-hung windows.

d. **Nos.870-872**. 1887. *William B. Tubby.*
   Queen Anne/Shingle Style. The recessed bay window and rockface entry voussoirs are gratifying eccentricities.

e. **No.862**. 1889. *F.B. Langston.*
   Dour polychromed brick and sandstone.

f. **No.860.**
   Romantic in the spirit of Philadelphia's *Wilson Eyre.*

g. **Nos.856-858**. 1889.
   Brownstone underpinning orange Roman brick: flat, very flat, the arches seemingly incised from a plane. Up close the brick texture reveals impeccably crafted façades.

h. **No.848**. 1905. *William B. Greenman.*
   A narrow bay-windowed neo-Classical exile from the Upper East Side.

P14g

P17

i. **No.838**. 1887. *C.P.H. Gilbert.*
   Joined by two 40-foot-wide neighbors to the east: three brownstone and brick beauties. The clustered colonnettes at **No.838** support an arch of only three stone voussoirs.

[P15] Originally **Thomas Adams, Jr., House**, 119 Eighth Ave., NE cor. Carroll St. 1888. *C.P.H. Gilbert.*
   This, and the adjacent matching house at **115 Eighth Avenue**, are rock-face red sandstone and Roman brick. The Carroll Street arch is worthy of *H.H. Richardson*, incised with naturalistic bas-reliefs, and supported by clusters of Romanesque-capped columns.

[P16] **123 Eighth Avenue**, SE cor. Carroll St. 1894. *Montrose W. Morris.*
   Gray brick and terra cotta in a free version of the **Italian Renaissance**, complete with pilasters, columns, and an entrance tympanum; here are ornate foliage and a gloating satyr.

[P17] **747-789 Carroll Street**, bet. Seventh and Eighth Aves. N side. 1880s.
   Twenty-one brownstones step up this gentle hill, from just east of Seventh Avenue to a point opposite Polhemus Place.

[P18] **Old First Reformed Church**, 126 Seventh Ave., NW cor. Carroll St. 1893. *George L. Morse.*
   A somber granite and limestone neo-Gothic monolith, stolid, as if carved from a quarry, but with a soaring, slender needle-pointed spire

P18

[P19] **195 Garfield Place**, bet. Sixth and Seventh Aves. N side. Remodeled, 1986, *Saltini/Ferrara.*
   A quintet of renewed Eastlake brick tenements: moated, the renovation is a respectful understatement.

[P20] **12-16 Fiske Place**, bet. Carroll St. and Garfield Place. W side. 1896.
   A trio where mock bay windows are presented as an academic design exercise—a square, a semicircle, and a triangle—creating a picturesque ensemble. Back to back through the block, the same grouping occurs similarly at **11-17 Polhemus Place**. The voussoirs might be studied for their lively bas reliefs, particularly at **No.14.**

*Turn left onto **Garfield Place**, and left again onto Eighth Avenue. Note, as you pass, that James A. Farrell, elected president of the United States Steel Corporation in 1911, lived at 249 Garfield Place during his presidential tenure.*

*What shall we call it? Naming apartment buildings to give them panache may have begun with Manhattan's **Dakota**. At the northwest corner of Garfield Place and 8th Avenue are four more modest works: **the Serine, the Lillian,** and **the Belvedere**. But the Gallic influence determined number four: **the Ontrinue** (or was that **Entre Nous**?).*

[P21] **Congregation Beth Elohim**, NE cor. Eighth Ave. and Garfield Place. 1908-1910. *Simon Eisendrath & B. Horowitz.* **Temple House**, 1928. *Mortimer Freehof and David Levy.*

A domed Beaux Arts limestone extravaganza, its corner chamfered to receive the two resident Composite columns.

[P22] **Montgomery Place**, bet. 8th Avenue and Prospect Park W. 1888-1904.

One of the truly great blocks in the world of urbane row housing, built as a real estate development by *Harvey Murdock*. Seeking the picturesque, he commissioned noted architect *C.P.H.*

P21   P22v

P22j

Gilbert to create most of the scene. An **Art Moderne** amber brick apartment house closes the vista at 8th Avenue—an accidental and successful containment of the street's space. *Gilbert's* works are in a powerful **Romanesque Revival**, with rockface brownstone, brick, and terra cotta strongly arched and linteled. *Dixon* contributed a fussy neo-classicism. The ensemble, however, is a symphony of materials and textures.

a. **No.11.** 1898. *C.P.H. Gilbert.*
Brownstone and brick Romanesque Revival with a **Dutch** accent (a stepped gable: that northern European immigrant). **No.17** is also an 1898 *Gilbert*.

b. **No.19.** 1898. *C.P.H. Gilbert.*
Brick, rockface and rusticated brownstone with both semicircular and elliptical arches.

c. **No.21.** 1892. *C.P.H. Gilbert.*
Brownstone and tile roofed eclecticism. Dig those vegetative friezes. **No.25** is also an 1892 *Gilbert*.

d. **No.35.** 1889. *Hornium Brothers.*
Asymmetric and Classical, an oxymoron? The bearded entry keystone guards.

e. **Nos.37-43.** 1891. *George B. Chappell.*
Semi-dormer windows, masked by false gables, are the makings of timid, but fussy façades. It's hard to be on *Gilbert's* turf.

f. **No.45.** 1899. *Babb, Cook & Willard.*

P24

P25

g. **No.47.** 1890. *R.L. Daus.*
French Renaissance reincarnated in brownstone that would have been a shocking color in Paris.

h. **No.16.** 1888. *C.P.H. Gilbert.*
Look up to a great elliptically arched balcony in two shades of brickwork. **Nos.14** and **18** are part of this trio.

i. **Nos.30-34.** 1896. *Robert Dixon.*

j. **Nos.36-46.** 1889. *C.P.H. Gilbert.*
Roman brick, rockfaced brownstone, and terra-cotta modilions (under the roof eaves) all embrace a shingled center.

k. **Nos.48 & 50.** 1890. *C.P.H. Gilbert.*
Fraternal twins? Same womb, different looks.

l. **No.52,** 1890. *T. Williams.*
The rockface brownstone bay window is at the scale of a tower.

m. **Nos.54-60**. 1890. *C.P.H. Gilbert.*

The delicate terra-cotta ornament is in sharp contrast to the boldly scaled detail on much of the block.

Turn right on Prospect Park West, and proceed south:

[P23] **Poly Prep Lower School**/formerly **Woodward Park School**/onetime **Brooklyn Ethical Culture School**/originally **Henry Hulbert House**, 49 Prospect Park W., bet. 1st and 2nd Sts. W side. 1892. *Montrose W. Morris.*

A cadaverous rock-face and foliate-carved limestone Romanesque Revival. The polygonal and round corner towers compete for attention (their hats are different) amid arches and lintels, grimacing in their dour context.

[P23a] **Poly Prep Lower School Addition**. 2005. *Platt Byard Dovell White.*

A sleek, elegant and lively appendage to the historic main building, it has a subdued

P26

palette in black and white, crisply detailed. No historicism; lots of respect.

[P24] **Brooklyn Ethical Culture Society Meeting House**/originally **William H. Childs House**, 53 Prospect Park W., NW cor. 2nd St. 1901. *William B. Tubby.*

A **Jacobean** loner in these stolid stone precincts, erected by the inventor of Bon Ami. Here cleansing powder built this monument, as opposed to baking powder at the George P. Tangeman House on Berkeley Place.

[P25] **Brooklyn Headquarters, N.Y.C. Department of Parks and Recreation**/ originally **Edwin Clarke and Grace Hill Litchfield House**, Grace Hill, also known as **Litchfield Villa**, Prospect Park W., bet. 4th and 5th Sts. E side. 1854-1857. *Alexander Jackson Davis.* ☛ Annex, 1913, *Helmle & Huberty.* Stucco restoration, 1990s, *Hirsch/Danois.*

This was the villa of *Edwin C. Litchfield*, a lawyer whose fortune was made in midwestern railroad development. In the 1850s he acquired

a square mile of virtually vacant land extending from 1st through 9th Streets, and from the Gowanus Canal to the projected line of 10th Avenue, just east of his completed mansion, a territory that includes a major portion of today's Park Slope.

The mansion is the best surviving example of *Davis's* **Italianate** style (he also created **Greek Revival** temples and **Gothick** castles). More than 90 years of service as a public office have eroded much of its original richness: the

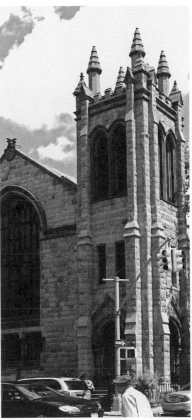

P29

original exterior stucco, simulating cut stone, had been stripped off, exposing common brick behind: now being restored. Note the **corncob capitals** on the glorious porch colonnades, an Americanization of things Roman—*Corinthian* or *Corn-inthian?* The bay window facing west contains a lush frieze of swags and goddesses.

Go in, look around, ye fellow citizen and part owner.

[P26] **108-117 Prospect Park West**, bet. 6th and 7th Sts. W side. 1896.

A Roman brick terrace, pristine and proud Renaissance Revival: greater than the sum of its parts.

[P27] **580-592 Seventh Street**, bet. Prospect Park W. and Eighth Ave. S side. **Dutch neo-Renaissance** gables give special syncopation to this handsome block.

END of Park Slope Walking Tour A. Walk north on Prospect Park West to the Grand Army Plaza subway station.

Park Slope Walking Tour B: From the newsstand where Flatbush Avenue joins Grand Army Plaza (at the surface of the IRT Grand Army Plaza Station, 2 and 3 trains) to the Bergen Street Station of the same lines (2 and 3 trains). Proceed south on St. John's Place. The silhouetted spires that you see on this lovely street are those of:

[P28] **Memorial Presbyterian Church**, 42-48 7th Ave., SW cor. St. John's Place. 1882-1883. *Pugin & Walter.*

P30

An ashlar brownstone sculpted monolith. Tiffany glass windows embellish both church and chapel. And which *Pugin* is this one? *Peter, Paul?*

[P29] **Grace United Methodist Church and Parsonage**, 29-35 7th Ave., NE cor. St. John's Place. 1882-1883. Parsonage, 1887. *Parfitt Brothers.*

Particularly intriguing is the **Moorish-Romanesque** façade along St. John's Place. The parsonage is a deft transition between the church and the Ward House cum town houses to the north.

[P30] Formerly **Lillian Ward House**, 21 7th Ave., SE cor. Sterling Place. 1887. *Lawrence B. Valk.*

A fanciful corner oriel worthy of the 16th-century French Renaissance guards this corner, all crowned with a slated and finialed roof. This special place (mansion to the locals) and its neighbors at Nos.23-27 were built by *Valk* for investor *Charles Pied*, a rare and rich group to be so well preserved.

Plane crash: In the morning mist of December 16, 1960, two airliners collided over Staten Island. The pilot of one attempted an emergency landing in Prospect Park but made it only to the intersection of 7th Avenue and Sterling Place. The plane sliced the cornice off a small apartment building west of 7th Avenue (the light-colored brick marks the spot) and came to a rest with its nose on the doorstep of the old Ward Mansion. A church on Sterling Place was destroyed by the resulting fire, but miraculously the mansion was untouched.

Retrace your steps on 7th Avenue south to St. John's Place. On your right, between Sixth and Seventh Avenues are St. John's Episcopal Church at No.139, and two robust Victorian town houses across the way at Nos.176 and 178:

[P31] **St. John's Episcopal Church**, 139 St. John's Place, bet. Sixth and Seventh Aves. N side. Chapel, 1889. *Edward Tuckerman Potter.* Church, 1885. *John Rochester Thomas.*

Victorian Gothic in varied hues and tones of

P31   P32

P36

brownstone, another English country gardened church for Brooklyn. Cut rock-face, random ashlar with, at the arched openings, alternating cream and brownstone Ruskinian voussoirs.

[P32] Originally **William M. Thallon and Edward Bunker Houses,** 176 and 178 St. John's Place, bet. Sixth and Seventh Aves. S side. 1888. *R.L. Daus.*

Wild **Hansel and Gretel** in brick, wood, brownstone, and terra cotta, some flavor from the Loire Valley, some from the Black Forest, all picturesque. The dour buildings adjacent must have trembled before their new neighbors.

[P33] **Brooklyn Conservatory of Music**/formerly **Park Slope Masonic Club**/originally **M. Brasher House,** 58 Seventh Avenue, NW cor. Lincoln Place. 1881. *S.F. Evelette.*

An austere brick and brownstone cornering.

[P34] **214 Lincoln Place**, bet. Seventh and Eighth Aves. S side. 1883. *Charles Werner.*

Brick and brownstone Queen Anne for *Charles Fletcher*, a gas company president.

P35

[P35] **Berkeley Carroll School,** 181 Lincoln Place, bet. Seventh and Eighth Aves. 1992. *Fox & Fowle.*

Conservative brick and limestone, gabled and bay-windowed, embraces a courtyard (with the original school building next door).

[P36] **The Lincoln**/formerly **F. L. Babbott House,** 153 Lincoln Place, bet. Sixth and Seventh Aves. N side. 1887. *Lamb & Rich.* Enlarged, 1896.

A sturdy but squat hexagonal tower corners this **Romanesque Revival** mansion, converted to 10 luxury condominiums. Brick and brownstone, but note the shingles on the faces of the tower's top level.

[P37] Originally **John Condon House,** 139 Lincoln Place, bet. Sixth and Seventh Aves. N side. 1881.

Another **Romanesque Revival,** with a lion's head corbel. *Condon* was a cemetery florist with his greenhouse opposite the 5th Avenue gate of Green-Wood Cemetery.

[P38] **Sixth Avenue Baptist Church,** Sixth Ave., NE cor. Lincoln Place. 1880. *Lawrence B. Valk.*

A small-scale many-gabled brick and limestone church, de-steepled in the 1938 hurricane.

[P39] **Helen Owen Carey Child Development Center,** 71 Lincoln Place, bet. Fifth and Sixth Aves. N side. 1974. *Beyer Blinder Belle.*

A strongly modeled brown brick modernist facility, happily in scale with the neighboring townscape.

[P40] **99-109 Berkeley Place,** bet. Sixth and Seventh Avenues. N side.

Three pairs of brick and rock-face brown- and limestone tenements with terra-cotta friezes and great entry arches. Here tenement is not a pejorative word.

[P41] St. Augustine's Roman Catholic Church, 116 Sixth Ave., bet. Sterling and Park Places. W side. 1897. *Parfitt Brothers.*

Sixth Avenue is one of Park Slope's grandest streets, block after block containing rows of amazingly preserved brownstones. St. Augustine's fills a role as a rich and monumental counterpoint to these streetscape neighbors. The crusty tower, with its mottled rock-face brownstone, anchors a nave with finials and flèche, presenting an elegant angel Gabriel. **Queen Victoria's** best (imported) awaits you within.

[P42] 182 Sixth Avenue, SW cor. St. Mark's Ave.

A magnificent commercial addition to a vernacular brownstone. A rare 19th-century commercial "improvement" that, in fact, enriches the street.

[P43] Cathedral Club of Brooklyn/originally **The Carleton Club**, 85 Sixth Ave., SE cor. St. Mark's Ave.

Built as an exclusive clubhouse, it was pro-

[P45] Brooklyn Public Library, Park Slope Branch, 431 Sixth Ave., bet. 8th and 9th Sts. 1906. *Raymond F. Almirall.*

Contemporary press described the library as "imposing" and "the most pretentious (of the Carnegie-donated libraries)."

[P46] 344 9th Street, bet. Fifth and Sixth Aves. S side. 1890s.

A towered sandstone bay provides grandeur for this ebullient brick town house. Terra cotta and sheet metal create the supporting details.

[P47] 466-480, 488-492, and 500-502 9th Street, bet. Seventh and Eighth Aves. 1890s.

Arches, gables, and oriels enliven these clusters of brick and limestone townhouses: **"townhouses"** because they each speak with personality, as opposed to the regimentation of **"row housing."**

P41

P47

gressively the **Monroe Club, the Royal Arcanum Club**, and in 1907, through the efforts of a young priest, the **Cathedral Club**, a Roman Catholic fraternal organization. The priest went on to become Cardinal Mundelein of Chicago.

***END** of Park Slope Walking Tour B: The Bergen Street Station of the IRT (2 or 3 train) is close by.*

Walking Tour C: Further afield into the southern reaches of Park Slope, in and out of the Historic District.

[P44] Public School 39, Brooklyn, The Henry Bristow School, 417 Sixth Ave., NE cor. 8th St. 1876-1877. *Samuel B. Leonard*, Superintendent of Buildings for the City of Brooklyn Board of Education.

A mansarded Victorian school house in painted brick and rusticated brownstone. The **Second Empire** (of *Napoleon III*) influenced the far reaches of Brooklyn (here) only five years after his downfall.

[P48] 519-543 9th Street, bet. Eighth Ave. and Prospect Park West. N side. 1908-09. *Thomas Bennett.*

[P49] 545-567 9th Street, bet. Eighth Ave. and Prospect Park West. N side. 1902-03. *Benjamin Driesler.*

The wide avenue of 9th Street has fine houses on either side, but the proud ranks on the north side leading to Prospect Park are exquisite: two storied Rennaissance Revival in rich limestone, with alternating curved and triangular bays. Nos.519-543 are virtually identical to a corresponding row, Nos.502-524 8th Street, by the same architect. Please note the *swags* in the *frieze.*

[P50] Public School 107, Brooklyn, The John W. Kimball School, 1301 Eighth Ave., SE cor. 13th St. 1894. *J. M. Naughton.*

A simple **Romanesque Revival** schoolhouse of orange-brown brick, terra cotta, and brownstone: a stern and stately building then serving a newly mushrooming Brooklyn population (consolidation with New York was still four years off).

[P51] Originally **14th Regiment Armory, N.Y. National Guard,** 1402 Eighth Ave., bet. 14th and 15th Sts. W side. 1895. *William A. Mundell.* 🖋

Picturesque massing, including battered walls, machicolations, and other heroic brick detailing, make this a special event among the rows of brownstones. Here stands a tower where boiling oil might be poured on mythical attackers. The statue of **The Doughboy** remembers World War I (1923, *Anton Scaaf*).

[P52] **Ansonia Court**/originally **Ansonia Clock Company Factory,** 420 12th St., bet. Seventh and Eighth Aves. 1881. Remodeled, 1982, *Hurley & Farinella,* architects. *Zion & Breen,* landscape architects.

Here 1,500 workers toiled in the **world's largest clock factory**. The brick functionalist tradition in 19th-century industrial building forms a handsome low-key envelope for apartments surrounding a central landscaped garden court.

PROSPECT HEIGHTS

Prospect Heights, a severed pizza slice (in plan), a bite missing from its side (at Grand Army Plaza; the southern half of the slice is Institute Park), is an ethnically diverse neighborhood just north of Park Slope, featuring leafy blocks of 19th-century brownstones designed by then leading architects, including *Rudolph Daus* and the *Parfitt Brothers.* Its western edge is marked by the hubbub of Flatbush Avenue; its eastern, less defined edge, blends at Washington Avenue into Crown Heights.

The Long Island Railroad yards and a swath of the neighborhood along Atlantic Avenue and Pacific Street is the site of the controversial proposed **Atlantic Yards** project. Partial demolition of buildings in the seven blocks of that project's "footprint" has created "developer's blight," a phenomenon in which a developer declares a neighborhood "blighted" in order to justify the use of eminent domain, then, by demolishing

P51

R1

[P53a] **Ladder Company 122,** N.Y.C. Fire Department, 532 11th St., bet. Seventh and Eighth Aves. S side. 1883.
[P53b] **Engine Company 220,** N.Y.C. Fire Department, 530 11th St. 1907.

The older **Italianate** firehouse once was adequate for the neighborhood's needs. As the row houses filled every vacant parcel up to Prospect Park's edge, the Classical adjunct to the west was added.

buildings, creates the very blight that didn't exist in the first place (a self-fulfilling prophesy). The result (for now) is a thriving neighborhood with incongruous blocks of contiguous wasteland, reduced to rubble, on its northern edge.

Begin the tour on Flatbush Avenue at the Bergen Street stop on the IRT, or walk south across the rail yards from Ft. Greene:

[R1] Formerly **Tiger Sign Company,** 245 Flatbush Ave., bet. Sixth Ave. and Bergen St.

A crisp triangular freestanding building that once housed a sign shop with apartments above: beige brick with a brownstone frieze. Here is the ultimate in streetfront architecture: an apartment dweller could conceivably view the City from three sides (but might go deaf from all the traffic noise).

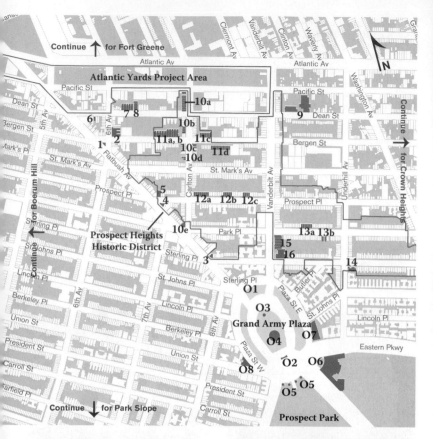

R2

R5

[R2] **78th Precinct, N.Y.C. Police Department,** NE cor. Bergen St. and Sixth Ave. 1925.

Another Anglo-Italianate neo-Renaissance limestone police palazzo. The rustication is modest, the cornice extravagant but wonderful; console-bracketed and dentiled.

[R3] **375-379 Flatbush Avenue,** NE cor. Sterling Place. 1885. *William Cook.*

A mansarded Second Empire tower tops this multi-use brownstone: commercial below, residential above, staunchly anchoring the hectic corner of Flatbush Avenue and Sterling Place.

[R4] **122-126 Prospect Place,** SE cor. Flatbush Ave. 1889. *John J. Keirst.*

A powerful sheet-metal turret hovers at this busy corner of Flatbush.

[R5] **115-117 Prospect Place,** bet. Flatbush and Carlton Aves. 1889. *Charles Hebberd.*

An exquisite example of Romanesque Revival, with wondrous details: rusticated

brownstone base and arches, terra-cotta plaques and capitals, rich dark red brick. A beloved and well cared-for survivor.

UNBUILT: Atlantic Yards (basketball arena and housing), Atlantic Ave. to Dean St., bet. Flatbush and Vanderbilt Aves., excluding a portion bet. Pacific and Dean Sts., from Sixth to Carlton Aves.

Ill-advised. A massive proposal by developer Forest City Ratner (of **MetroTech** fame: see Brooklyn Civic Center section) that, if built, would forever change the character of small-scale, tree-lined Prospect Heights. The plan calls for building over the rail yards between Atlantic Avenue and Pacific Street (good idea) and for demolishing blocks of homes and businesses in Prospect Heights, replacing them with modern residential towers and a basketball arena (bad idea). *Frank Gehry's* master plan (a swiveling cadre of towers) captivated many a City official and architecture critic, but opposition among community groups in Prospect Heights itself was fierce. As the downturn in the financial markets

R7

R8

R9

delayed the project, *Gehry's* designs were replaced by less flashy plans by the firms *SHoP* and *Ellerbe-Becket*. Now that *Gehry* isn't involved, more and more critics are coming out against the project. Where have they been?

The Empire State Development Corporation (ESDC), previously the New York State Urban Development Corporation (UDC), founded in 1968 and famous for its experiments in public housing (Coney Island, Twin Parks in the Bronx, Roosevelt Island), wields the power of **eminent domain** and can issue tax-exempt bonds without approval from the legislature or the public. So much power! The ESDC gave approval to Atlantic Yards, while an alternate plan by the developers Extell, designed by the firm *CetraRuddy* (*John Cetra* and *Nancy Ruddy*), was barely considered. *CetraRuddy's* subtle plan featured smaller-scale housing built over the railyards in such a way as to knit together Prospect Heights and Fort Greene, sans basketball arena and towers, and without resorting to eminent domain.

Along Dean Street, on the southern edge of the Atlantic Yards "footprint":

[R6] **474 Dean Street**, bet. Flatbush and Sixth Ave. S side. ca. 1870.
  An unpretentious yellow clapboard cottage amid bigger playmates.

[R7] **497-509 Dean Street**, bet. Sixth and Carlton Aves. N side. ca. 1890.
  Triangular bays enliven this handsome row.

[R8] **Temple of Restoration**, 515 Dean St. bet. Sixth and Carlton Aves. N side. ca. 1890.
  A strong Romanesque Revival church with expertly crafted brick details and powerful entrance archways.

[R9] **St. Joseph's Roman Catholic Church,** 856 Pacific St., bet. Vanderbilt and Underhill Aves. 1912. **Rectory**, 834 Pacific bet. Vanderbilt and Underhill Aves. ca. 1860. **School**, 683 Dean St. bet. Vanderbilt and Underhill Aves. ca. 1920.

A campus of buildings with a large garden on the eastern end of the site. The beige brick and stone church, in Spanish Colonial style, bears monumental twin bell towers, and a **majestic, barrel-vaulted interior**. The current church replaced an earlier brick church from 1861. The **rectory**, in neo-Gothic dark red brick, appears to be from the era of the first church. The **school** is now used as a senior center.

Prospect Heights Historic District, irregular boundaries roughly between Flatbush Avenue on the west, Bergen Street on the north (with extensions north to Pacific Street), Washington Avenue on the east (between Prospect and Sterling Places), and Sterling Place on the south. 🖝

The historic district includes many tree-lined streets fronted by generally intact rows of late 19th-century housing. Like much of brownstone Brooklyn (Park Slope, Fort Greene, Bed-Stuy) the architecture is a celebration of expressive comformity, where the whole is greater than the sum of its parts. Thankfully, the District

d. **Nos.578-580** bet. Bergen St. and St. Mark's Pl. ca. 1850.

The oldest extant houses in the area. Originally clapboard, their better days are concealed by current cladding in a variety of asphalt shingles, aluminum siding, and tar paper. What's underneath?

e. **No.634,** bet. Prospect Pl. and Park Pl. W side. ca. 1890.

A charming former carriage house, its hay loft doors still there. The main entry, originally carriage-width, has been bricked up and replaced by a human-width door.

[R11] **Bergen Street,** bet. Sixth and Vanderbilt Aves.:

a. **Nos.531-539,** bet. Sixth and Carlton Aves. N side. ca. 1894. *Isaac D. Reynolds*.

A **Romanesque Revival** row in brick and rock-faced brownstone: elliptical arches at the ground floor, half round arches below the protective sheet-metal cornice.

R10c

R12c

is free of large-scale housing projects.

A tour of the historic district should begin on Carlton Street, with forays back and forth along Bergen Street and Prospect, Park, and Sterling Places:

[R10] **Carlton Street**, bet. Pacific St. and Park Pl.

This main drag of the historic district is no drag architecturally. Delights abound:

a. **Nos.516-536,** bet. Pacific and Dean Sts. ca. 1869-80.

This genial row of houses is a finger poking into the Atlantic Yards site. The doors have lush, foliated console brackets.

b. **Nos.550-556,** bet. Dean and Bergen Sts. 1877. *Parfitt Bros.*

An understated row, with arched pedimented entries, by the prolific *Parfitts*.

c. **Nos.577-579,** SE cor. Bergen St. 1893. *Magnus Dahlander.*

Richardsonian Romanesque, with a conical-capped tower at the corner and arched entry on Bergen Street.

b. **Nos.541-549,** bet. Sixth and Carlton Aves. N side. 1904. *Henry Pohlman*.

Renaissance Revival, with gently bowed façades modulating the street.

c. **Nos.573-585,** bet. Carlton and Vanderbilt Aves. N side. 1889. *Walter M. Coots*.

Triangular bays enliven the façades, as on 497-509 Dean Street (p.665). *Coots* also designed the **Alice and Agate Courts Historic District** in Bed-Stuy.

d. **Nos.582-604,** bet. Carlton and Vanderbilt Aves. S side. 1886. *William H. Wirth*.

An intact row of diminutive Queen Annes, with terra-cotta inlays.

[R12] **Prospect Place**, bet. Carlton and Vanderbilt Aves. N side:

a. **Nos. 149-163.** 1871.

Nine **Italianate** brownstones, Nos.147 and 149 with mansard roofs and dormers.

R16

R13b

R15

b. **Nos.181-189.** ca. 1877. *F.B. Lincoln.*
Elegant **Greek Revival.**

c. **Nos.203-209.** ca. 1885. *Eastman & Daus.*
The prolific *Rudolph Daus*, like the *Parfitt Brothers*, knew how to let loose with flamboyant turrets, quoins, and cornices. Here he was willing to blend in with the brownstone crowd.

[R13] **Park Place,** bet. Carlton and Underhill Aves.:

a. **Nos.297-309,** bet. Vanderbilt and Underhill Aves. N side. ca. 1894. *William H. Reynolds.*
Rough-hewn **Romanesque** in brownstone and sandstone, with a decorative band above the first story, and stained-glass transoms.

b. **Nos.324 and 326,** bet. Vanderbilt and Underhill Aves. 1906. *Benjamin Driesler.*
Aliens in Prospect Heights: neo-**Classical** detached twin houses with generous front porches, serious cornices, and Doric columns.

[R14] **Duryea Presbyterian Church,** 185 Underhill Ave., SE cor. Sterling Pl. 1905. *W.O. Weaver & Son.*
Rock-faced stone, with a tower of power presiding at the corner.

[R15] **673-681 Vanderbilt Avenue,** SE cor. Park Pl. ca. 1895. *Dahlander & Hedman.*
A super-tenement with a conical tower at the corner and two towers along Vanderbilt. Only one tower has its original pyramidal hat.

[R16] **P.S. 9 condominiums**/formerly **Public School 340**/onetime Public School 111/originally **Public School 9, City of Brooklyn,** 249 Sterling Pl., NE cor. Vanderbilt Ave. 1867-1868. *Samuel B. Leonard.* Additions, 1887, *James W. Naughton.*
[R16b] Originally **Public School 9 Annex,** City of Brooklyn, 251 Sterling Pl., E of Vanderbilt Ave., 1895. *James W. Naughton.*
An exuberant eclectic brownstone, brick, and terra-cotta Renaissance Revival school, infused with **Romanesque Revival** detail; such was eclecticism in the 1890s. Grand Corinthian pilasters march around the third and fourth floors. Almost lost, its renaissance as condominiums is a joy. The annex across Vanderbilt is simpler but handsome as well.

GRAND ARMY PLAZA

[O1] **Grand Army Plaza**, within Plaza St. at the intersection of Flatbush Ave., Prospect Park W., Eastern Pkwy., and Vanderbilt Ave. 1870. *Frederick Law Olmsted & Calvert Vaux*. Scenic landmark.

Olmsted & Vaux designed this monumental oval traffic circle in the spirit of Paris's Etoile (now the Place Charles de Gaulle), that circular 12-spoked traffic rond point that bears on its central island the Arc de Triomphe, although they opposed an arch here. A masterstroke of city planning, this nexus joins their great **Eastern Parkway**, and **Prospect Park**, with the avenues that preceded it on other geometries. The triumphal arch did not arrive for 22 years: the [O2] **Soldiers' and Sailors' Memorial Arch** ●͏ by *John H. Duncan*, architect of Grant's Tomb, was built between 1889 and 1892, commemorating Union forces that perished in the Civil War. The arch provided, as in its Parisian inspiration, an excellent armature for sculpture,

O2

O4

O6

compromise, with *Kennedy's* bust bracketed from the side. Budget makers demeaned it all by causing the cube to be merely a box built of thin butted marble slabs. The [O4] **Bailey Fountain** (1932, *Egerton Swartwout,* architect; *Eugene Savage,* sculptor), a lush interweaving of athletic Tritons and Neptunes in verdigris bronze, is a delight when in action (unfortu-

O8

planned by *Stanford White (McKim, Mead & White*. 1894-1901), the most spectacular of which is *Frederick MacMonnies'* huge **Quadriga** on top (1898). Inside the arch itself is more subtle work, bas-reliefs of **Lincoln** (*Thomas Eakins*) and **Grant** (*William O' Donovan*), both installed in 1895. On the south pedestals are two bristling groups representing **The Army** and **The Navy** by *MacMonnies* (1901). A museum within the arch is open to the public.

The oval island to the north of the arch is of a more homely scale, with a double ring of formally trimmed London plane trees surrounding a generous complex of stairs and terraces, and a fountain. Around the [O3] **John F. Kennedy Memorial** at the north end (1965, *Morris Ketchum*, architect, *Neil Estern*, sculptor), the scale shrinks noticeably. This little memorial, the City's only official monument to *Kennedy*, was originally designed as a monolithic marble cube topped by a flame on top, but it was later abandoned as an unsuitable aping of the per petual flame at Arlington Cemetery's Tomb of the Unknown Soldier. This present form is a

nately rarely in this water-conscious city).

While the arch was being embellished, a necklace of Classical ornaments, designed by *Stanford White*, was strung across the park entrances facing it (completed in 1894) [O5]. Rising out of entangling fasces, four 50-foot Doric columns are topped with exuberant eagles (by *MacMonnies*), railings, bronze urns, and lamp standards; and two 12-sided templelike gazebos. Of the whole ensemble, the gazebos, with their polished granite Tuscan columns, Guastavino vaulting, and bronze finials, show *White's* talents most richly.

▦ [O6] **Main Library, Brooklyn Public Library** (Ingersoll Memorial), Grand Army Plaza at the intersection of Flatbush Ave. and Eastern Pkwy. 1941. *Alfred Morton Githens & Francis Keally*, architects; *Paul Jennewein*, sculptor of bas-reliefs; *Thomas H. Jones*, sculptor of the screen over the entry. ●͏

Streamlined Beaux Arts, or an example of how the École des Beaux Arts developed the **Art Moderne** of the Paris Exposition of 1937. In effect it is a formal participant in the geometry

07

of avenues radiating from the Soldiers' and
Sailors' Arch; but its Moderne/Beaux Arts idiom
allowed it to be stylishly modern in its costume
as well as Classical in its conformance to the
grand plan. Inside is lots of lavish space.

[O7] **On The Park** (apartments), Plaza St.,
Grand Army Plaza, cor. Eastern Pkwy.
2009. *Richard Meier.*
   A massive beached whale. *Meier* here tried
to replicate the success of his towers at **173-176
Perry** and **165 Charles Street** (see West Village)
with a similar vocabulary: boxy glass trimmed in
white mullions. The West Village condos, tall
slivers with small footprints, three crisp volumes
in a row facing the Hudson, worked. Here at
Prospect Park *Meier* has more land to sprawl
upon, but with less effect. Fortunately, it's not
actually o*n* the park; it just seems that way.

[08] **47 Plaza Street** (apartments), bet.
Union St. and Berkeley Pl. 1928. *Rosario
Candela.*
   A brick and terra-cotta apartment house
that curves evocatively around Grand Army
Plaza, narrowing to a thin sliver at Union Street.
Candela threw as much ornament as he possibly
could on the façade, but the way in which the
building swoops and embraces the Plaza was
precedent for a monumental circus (ring of
buildings enclosing a central space) on a scale
that would honor, American style, *John Wood's*
elegant **Circus** (Bath, England, 1754. *Wood* used
imperial grandeur for elegant row housing, a
cylinder of building that created a great moment
in the history of *urban design*). Building and
space in concert. Compare it with **On The Park**
across the way.

PROSPECT PARK

Once past *Stanford White's* grand entrance, one sees *Olmsted & Vaux's* park much as they conceived it. They considered it a better work than their first collaboration, Central Park, for several reasons, none of which reflects on that earlier work. Principally, as this commission did not result from a competition, with its inevitably fixed site and program, they could change the program first given—and they did. Delay of construction due to the Civil War aided their efforts. Almost half of the land set aside for a park by the City of Brooklyn in the 1850s lay to the northeast of Flatbush Avenue, the main artery to Flatbush, which was still a town in its own right: it centered around the reservoir on **Prospect Hill** (since filled in and used as a playground). *Olmsted & Vaux* rejected a scheme [Figure A] in which Flatbush Avenue completely bisected the proposed park, recommending instead that the allotted land be expanded to the south and west

Prospect Park Walking Tour: Grand Army Plaza (IRT subway to Grand Army Plaza Station) to southeast entrance at Parkside and Ocean Avenues (Parkside Avenue Station).

Enter between the east (left) pair of Doric columns. Note the statue of **James Stranahan** (1891, *Frederick MacMonnies*, sculptor), whose personal 24-year crusade is largely responsible for both Prospect Park and Olmsted & Vaux's other great contributions to Brooklyn: **Ocean** and **Eastern Parkways**. Note also the pine grove along the walk; it is replicated on the opposite corner, where the symmetrical entrance composition merges with the park's picturesque layout. Like all walks entering this park, this one quickly loses visual connection with the point of entrance, through its twisting route and the modeling of the terrain's topography.

Turn right at the first fork to **Endale Arch**

O8

[Figure B]. In severing the land to the northeast, they lost the hill that gave the park its name, but they also got rid of its reservoir (a major part of Central Park to this day) and provided, by default, a tract on which related institutions (the Library, the Brooklyn Museum, and the Brooklyn Botanic Garden) could be located without consuming park space (as the Metropolitan Museum of Art does in Manhattan). Another encumbrance considerably reduced here is the quantity of roads. With a more compact shape— and without transverse cuts—Prospect Park yielded much less area to wheeled traffic.

[A7] **Prospect Park**, Grand Army Plaza, Prospect Park W., Prospect Park SW., Parkside Ave., Ocean Ave., and Flatbush Ave. Designed 1865. Constructed 1866-1873. *Frederick Law Olmsted & Calvert Vaux*. Various alterations. Scenic landmark. 🛶

[A8], the first structure completed (1867); a dramatic tuned transition takes you into broad daylight and a 1/2-mile vista down the **Long Meadow**. The arch is a bucolic vault of Ruskinian Gothic in brick and sandstone, once festooned with crockets, bosses, and finials, and lined with a wooden interior (only traces of all this remain).

Once through the arch, note the corresponding but architecturally unique **Meadow Port Arch** [A9] to the right, at the west entrance to the meadow: it is a barrel vault rather than a Gothic one. Follow the path to the left along the edge of the meadow. The recreation on the meadow itself is deftly separated but still visible from the tree-dotted hillsides along the encircling walks. The undulations of the meadow, sculpted by Olmsted, offer a sense of place, and topographical variation allows participants to perceive the mass of people present—impossible on flat ground. This same trick is the basis of St. Peter's Square in the Vatican, a series of ups and downs within a vast dish that displays to each participant the scale of the whole crowd.

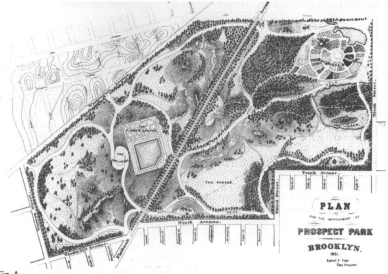

Fig. A

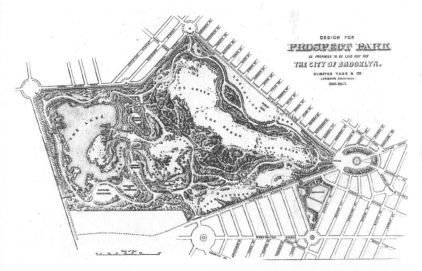

Fig. B

About 500 feet ahead a set of steps rises to the left. Go a bit beyond for a better view of the meadow, then back, up the steps, and across the road. On the other side go left, then right at the next fork down a curving walk to the **Rose Garden** [A10] (1895, designer unknown). This space is lovely even without any apparent rose-bushes these days. Turning right across the center of the circle, take the steps leading down to the **Vale of Cashmere** [A11]: meandering free-form pools with once-upon-a-time Classical balustrades, now fallen. Deep in a hollow facing due south, the Vale once supported a lush stand of bamboo (green year-round) and multitudes of birds, some uncommon in New York.

Follow the brick path along the east side of the Vale (left as you enter) straight out along the little meadow, from which there are glimpses of the Long Meadow across the road. Continue over a modest crest and down the wooded slope to **Battle Pass**. The park road at this point follows roughly the alignment of the original road from Flatbush to Brooklyn, and it was at this pass that Revolutionary volunteers

put up brief resistance against British troops advancing toward New York in 1776..

Prospect Park Zoo [A12]: An optional and recommended detour. The Zoo offers formal but intimate confrontations with animals, and those in need of services will find rest rooms and fast food. Its original neat semicircle of formally planned, understated brick buildings (1935, *Aymar Embury*) was decorated with bas-reliefs and murals by **WPA** artists, including *Hunt Diederich, F. G. R. Roth, and Emele Siebern*, representing scenes from *Rudyard Kipling's* Jungle Books. The takeover by the New York Zoological Society has led to a a different relationship between human and other animals, retaining the shells of the original buildings, removing most of the bars; it is an experience on paths, over a period of time, rather than a display of caged tenants. (1990s. *Goldstone & Hinz.*)

Of particular architectural interest is the central pavilion, an octagonal blue-tiled dome of *Guastavino* vaulting with 24 oculi windows. Once there were pachyderms under this pantheon—rhinoceroses, hippos, and heffalumps—but the heffalumps were removed to the Bronx Zoo. To the west along the park drive is a charming sculpture of a lioness and her cubs (1899, *Victor Peter*). See *www.prospectparkzoo.com* for more information.

At Battle Pass, cross the road and climb the stairs ahead to a plateau that was once the site of the **Dairy** [A13] (1869, *Calvert Vaux*). Turn left at the top of the stairs, and follow the brow of the plateau across the bridle path, past the red-brick service building, then right to cross the high boulder bridge (very romantic rocky rock), passing over a return loop of the bridle path. From the bridge, bear right, then left up the steps, and then left again at a T-intersection along a walk that skirts the knoll on which the **John Howard Payne monument** [A13] stands (1873, *Henry Baerer*, sculptor). Climb to the crest for a sweeping view of the Long Meadow. The red-brick **Picnic House** is directly across the meadow, the more elegant Palladian **Tennis House** [A14] (1910, *Helmle & Huberty*) is to its left. Return to the walk below, and take your first left on the walk along the slope's edge. At the next T-intersection

World War I Memorial

go right and then down the steps. Stop where the walk takes a sharp right for a view of the fantastic boulder bridge crossed earlier.

Continue your descent into a deep rocky glen, through which a brook gurgles happily. Turn left at the bottom, crossing a smaller boulder bridge, and follow the path along the brook. Turn right at the end of this walk, and pass through the triple [A15] **Nethermead Arches** (1870, *Calvert Vaux*), where walk, brook, and bridle path separately pass under the Central Drive. The arches are crowned with a trefoil sandstone balustrade; the bridge is supported by barrel vaults of brick, granite, and more sandstone. Continue along the brook, past some specimen trees and into the **Music Grove**. Here a **"music pagoda,"** a faintly Japanese bandstand, was the site for summer concerts. Cross Music Grove and bear right on the walk that crosses **Lullwater Bridge**. From the bridge there is a fine view of the white terra-cotta-faced **Boathouse** [A16] (1904, *Helmle & Huberty*). ☛ From the other side of the bridge there is a long view down the Lullwater, meandering toward the Lake. Note

that the sides of the Lullwater are hard-edged stone. At the end turn the bridge turn left for a closer look at the Boathouse; note particularly its elegant black iron lamp standards. The Boathouse is a pleasant terra-cotta remembrance of Palladian architecture. From the Boathouse take the path south past the **Camperdown Elm**, a weeping, drooping Japanese Brobningnagian bonsai of a tree, planted in 1872: aged, gnarled, arthritic, and eternal. Then turn left through the **Cleft Ridge Span** [A17] (1872, *Calvert Vaux*), with its two-toned incised-tile inner surface enriching this barrel vault.

Through this span is the formal **Garden Terrace** [A18] with the **Oriental Pavilion** (1874, Calvert Vaux), now happily restored after a disastrous fire. The view down this Beaux Arts-inspired garden to the Lake has suffered more than the Pavilion, for the semicircular cove at the foot of the Terrace is now filled by the **Kate Wollman Skating Rink**, a banal place, one of three that originally scarred this and Central Park. Recreational intrusions, particularly those which inflict buildings foreign to the spirit of the landscape, no matter how noble their intentions should be banned from the wondrous landscape art of such as *Olmsted & Vaux*. In this garden, on axis, is **Lincoln** (1869, *H. K. Brown*, sculptor). Follow Lincoln's gaze to the high wire fence and exposed refrigeration equipment at what was, until 1961, the edge of the lake. Lincoln seems to gesture with his right hand: "Take it away." To the left is the **Skating Shelter** [A19] (1960, *Hopf & Adler*).

Turn left around this unhappy intrusion, and then pass a **World War I Memorial** (1920, *A. D.*

Boathouse

Pickering). Continuing around the edge of the lake, you will find a landing shelter. This is a 1971 reconstruction of the original (1870, *Calvert Vaux*), the sole survivor of many rustic log-braced shelters that once bordered the lake, creating a kind of mini-Adirondacks image. From here follow the path along the lake's edge; then bear left across the drive, and continue straight out of the park through the Classical porticoes, crowned with **redwood trellises** (1904, *McKim, Mead & White*), to the intersection of Ocean and Parkside Avenues.

For further views of the lake and a look at some of the park's finest Classical structures, don't leave the park at this point, but instead follow the walk along the park's south side, between **Parkside Avenue and the drive, to the Croquet Shelter** [A20] (1906, *McKim, Mead & White*, restored, 1967). ☛ This Corinthian-columned pavilion of limestone, with terra-cotta capitals, frieze, and entablature, is supported within by Guastavino vaults. But there are no croquet mallets here; those Anglophile players have departed for Central Park.

INSTITUTE PARK

I2

The green triangle contained by Eastern Parkway and Flatbush and Washington Avenues, formerly known as Institute Park after the **Brooklyn Institute of Arts and Sciences** (land which *Olmsted & Vaux* rejected in their plan for Prospect Park), was reserved for related institutional uses. It now accommodates the Brooklyn Botanic Garden, the Brooklyn Museum, and the main branch of the Brooklyn Public Library. The garden and museum are contiguous and offer more than the expected horticultural specimens and works of art. The garden has some interesting examples of landscape architecture; and the museum houses extensive decorative craft collections, 25 period rooms, a whole Dutch Colonial house, one of the world's great Egyptian collections, and, in a garden behind, a collection of exterior architectural building parts (columns, friezes, sculptures, plaques) from demolished New York buildings.

Botanic Garden to Brooklyn Museum Walking Tour: From the BMT Prospect Park Station (D, Q and S trains) on Flatbush Avenue near Empire Boulevard (can also be reached from Grand Army Plaza Station by B41 bus) to the IRT Eastern Parkway Station (2 and 3 trains). Cross the street to the Lefferts Homestead, go back along Empire Boulevard to the Fire Department Bureau of Communications, and then enter the Botanic Gardens.

[I1] **Flatbush Turnpike Tollgate**, Empire Blvd. entrance road to Prospect Park. N side. ca. 1855.
A tiny, octagonal wooden guardhouse moved from its old position at Flatbush Turnpike (now Flatbush Avenue) is all that remains of the days when roads were privately built and tolls were charged for their use.

[I2] **Lefferts Homestead**/originally **Peter Lefferts House**, Flatbush Ave. N of Empire Blvd. W side. In Prospect Park. 1777-1783. ☛ 718-965-6505. Mar-July, Sep-Dec: Sa-Su, 12-4; closed Mo-Fr.
Six slender **Tuscan** colonnettes support a "Dutch" eave, the edge of a gambrel roof. Painted shingle body, stained shingle roof. The

English built many such copies of the basic Dutch house. Its predecessor, in 1776, was burned in the Battle of Long Island to prevent its use by the British. It was moved here in 1918 from a site on Flatbush Avenue between Midwood and Maple Streets.

[I3] **Brooklyn Central Office, Bureau of Fire Communications**, N.Y.C. Fire Department, 35 Empire Blvd., bet. Flatbush and Washington Aves. N side. 1913. *Frank J. Helmle.* ●☀
    Brunelleschi in Brooklyn: its arcades are those of his foundling hospital in Florence.

[I4] **Brooklyn Botanic Garden**, 1000 Washington Ave., bet. Empire Blvd. and S side of Brooklyn Museum, W to Flatbush Ave. Open to the public, 8-6; weekends 10-6. (Nov.-Mar. closes at 4:30.) 718-623-7200. *www.bbg.org*
    Enter the garden through the Palladian south gate at Flatbush Avenue and Empire Boulevard. Its 50 acres are intensively planted with almost every variety of tree and bush that

Laboratory), [I7] (1912-1917, *William Kendall* of *McKim, Mead & White*). ●☀ A new **Visitor's Center**, with shops and cafe, by the firm *Weiss/Manfredi*, is planned for the garden's northeast corner, and is already winning design awards before it's even built. 2011.
    Farther north is the **Japanese Garden** [I8] (1915. *Takeo Shiota*, designer), gift of philanthropist *Alfred Tredway White*. It resembles a stroll garden of the Momoyama period, but it is not copied from any one particular example. Around its small pond are examples of almost every traditional plant. This overcrowding fails to achieve the serenity of good Japanese prototypes. North of the Japanese Garden is the gate to Eastern Parkway, which leads to the Brooklyn Museum.

[I9] **Brooklyn Museum of Art**/formerly **Brooklyn Museum**/originally **Brooklyn Institute of Arts and Sciences**, 200 Eastern Pkwy., SW cor. Washington Ave. 1893-1915. *McKim, Mead & White*. ●☀ Alterations by WPA, 1935, *William Lescaze*. Addition, 1978, *Prentice*

19

will survive in this climate. The most popular attraction, and one that generates traffic jams at the end of April, is the grove of Japanese cherry trees, the finest in America. For a simple tour of the garden follow the east side, consistently staying to your right. For seasonal attractions (the cherry blossoms, roses, lilacs, azaleas) not on this route, ask the guard for directions.
    On the east edge of the garden are the greenhouses, facing a plaza with pools of specimen water lilies. The newer units [I6] are Hexagonal "icebergs" (1987, *Davis, Brody & Assocs.*) over sunken climatic gardens. This conservatory has a tropical jungle section and a desert section, but its prize exhibit is the collection of bonsai Japanese miniature trees unequaled in the Americas. North of the conservatory is another formal terrace planted with magnolias (a dazzling display in early to mid-April) in front of the garden's **Visitor's Center and Administration Building** (former School and

& *Chan, Ohlhausen*. Second Addition, 1987, *Joseph Tonetti*. Master plan competition winner, 1987, *Arata Isosaki/Polshek Partnership*, associate architects. 718-638-5000. We-Su, 10-5; closed Mo-Tu. *www.brooklynmuseum.org*
    One quarter of the grand plan envisioned for Brooklyn in the year before consolidation with New York. After the borough was incorporated in the larger metropolis, support for its museum waned. But what it lacks in sheer size, it makes up for in quality: inside is one of the world's greatest Egyptian collections.
    New Entry Pavilion and Plaza, 2004. *Arata Isosaki/Polshek Partnership,* architects. *Judith Heintz*, landscape architect.
    A spaceship has crashed-landed into the museum! *Isosaki* and *Polshek's* glass discus provides an entry sequence the museum has lacked since losing its grand stair in the 1930s. Fussily detailed, with more parts than a 20,000 piece Lego set, this is both a new entrance and a public amphitheater. It works best at what it was meant to do: provide a light-filled, spacious portal to the museum. Seen from Eastern

Parkway, it seems a collision of styles and eras; the new threatening to overwhelm the old. The new **fountain**, with programmed jets of water, is a great urban crowd pleaser.

The sculpted female figures on high represent Manhattan and Brooklyn (1916. *Daniel Chester French*, sculptor). They were moved to the Museum in 1963 when their seats at the Manhattan end of the Brooklyn Bridge were destroyed by a roadway improvement program.

Curios and antiquities: Just inside the south (parking area) entrance of the museum is the Gallery Shop, once the nation's largest museum shop, with an extensive stock of hand-crafted toys, jewelry, textiles, and ceramics from all over the world.

END *of Botanic Garden-Brooklyn Museum Walking Tour: The IRT Eastern Parkway subway stop (2 and 3 trains) is directly in front of the museum.*

I6

[I10] **Eastern Parkway**, designated a scenic landmark between Grand Army Plaza and Ralph Ave. 1870-1874. *Frederick Law Olmsted & Calvert Vaux.* ●✸

The first parkway in the nation, intended to bring open space into all areas of the City as part of a comprehensive park system, as yet unbuilt (and unplanned).

IN SUSPENDED ANIMATION

On the east edge of the Botanic Garden, a few hundred feet from the south entrance, was a reproduction of the garden from the **Ryoanji Temple**, Kyoto [I5]. Constructed with painstaking authenticity in 1963, this replica offered a unique opportunity to contemplate a Zen-inspired, virtually plantless landscape composition: rock islands in a sea of raked pebbles. Bring it back. We're stressed.

BEDFORD-STUYVESANT

Bed-Stuy, an amalgam of two middle-class communities of the old City of Brooklyn, combines **Bedford**, on the west, with **Stuyvesant Heights** to the east. Today's Bed-Stuy is one of the City's two major African-American enclaves; the other is **Harlem**. Like Harlem, Bed-Stuy's demographics and culture have changed in the last decade with the booming economy, with a significant influx of white middle-class families and artists, Latinos, West-Indians, and Africans. It's a handsome community, with block upon block of well-kept, often astonishingly distinguished town houses.

The southern and western portions comprise masonry row housing of high architectural quality and vigorous churches whose spires create the area's frequently lacy skyline. The northeastern reaches have considerable numbers of wooden tenements, but where Bedford-Stuyvesant has distinguished architecture, it is *very* good. Its façades of brownstones and brickfronts create a magnificent townscape as good—and sometimes better—than many fashionable areas of Brooklyn and Manhattan. Parts of Chauncey, Decatur, MacDonough, and Macon Streets, and the southern end of Stuyvesant Avenue, are superb. Hancock Street, between Nostrand and Tompkins Avenues, was considered a showplace in its time (late 1880s) and has been lovingly restored in recent years. The tiny **Alice and Agate Courts Historic District**, two short cul-de-sacs isolated from the macro-

Y3

cosm of the street system, are particularly special places in the seemingly endless, anonymous grid.

[Y1] **Friendship Baptist Church**, 92 Herkimer St., bet. Bedford and Nostrand Aves. S side. 1910.

"Hollywood Moorish" crowned with sheet-metal onion domes and a sturdy cornice over yellow patterned brickwork.

[Y2] **95 Herkimer Street**, bet. Bedford and Nostrand Aves. N side. 1860s.

Opposite Friendship Baptist, this wood and clapboard house speaks of another time in Bed-Stuy, long before the brownstones.

[Y3] **Brevoort Place**, S of Fulton St., bet. Franklin and Bedford Aves. 1860s.

A handsome block of brownstones in excellent condition, with much of their original detail undamaged by crass modernization closing in.

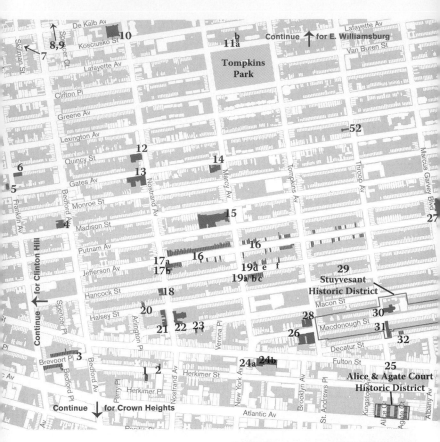

Y4

Y5

[Y4] **Miller Memorial Church of the Nazarene**/ formerly **Aurora-Grata Scottish Rite Cathedral**/ originally **East Reformed Church**, 1160 Bedford Ave., NW cor. Madison St. Rebuilt, 1888.

Bedford Avenue nearby is nondescript, and hence this brick and sandstone fantasy is a welcome relief. Its history dates back to 1877, when the Aurora-Grata Lodge of Perfection, a Masonic local, bought the old East Reformed Church on this site and rebuilt it for Masonic purposes. The Masons are gone, and the church is once again a church.

[Y5] **Evening Star Baptist Church**/originally **Latter Day Saints Chapel**, 265 Gates Ave., NW cor. Franklin Ave. 1917. *Eric Holmgren.*

Superficially reminiscent of *Frank Lloyd Wright's* Unity Temple in Oak Park (1904), this church is a unique cubist experiment for New York. Perhaps it could be termed "homespun Schindler" after *Richard Schindler*, the Austrian-born disciple of *Wright* who followed this idiom in southern California.

[Y6] **118 Quincy Street**, SE cor. Franklin Ave. ca. 1890.

A modest example of the lavish apartment buildings built in this community in the last decade of the 19th century. Battered stone walls support arched and rock-linteled brick. Note the fortuitously intact frieze and cornice.

[Y7] **St. Patrick's Roman Catholic Church and Rectory**, Kent Ave., NW cor. Willoughby Ave. Rectory, 285 Willoughby Ave. Academy, 918 Kent Ave., bet. Kent Ave. and Taaffe Place, N side. 1856. *Patrick Charles Keely.*

An austere **Gothic Revival**. Its rectory is an arch-windowed, mansarded, brick-and-brown-stone "New Yorker" cartoon by *Charles Addams*.

[Y8] **Wallabout Warehouse**/formerly **Franklin Brewery**/originally **Malcolm Brewery**, 394-412 Flushing Aves., bet. Franklin and Skillman Aves. S side. E section, 1869. W section, 1890. Both by *Otto Wolf.*

A truncated pyramid crowns this pile of many-arched brickwork, while below its façade

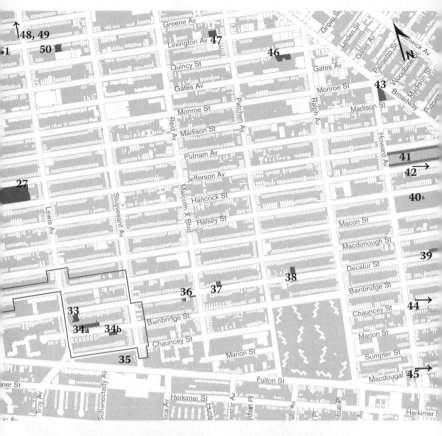

Y8

Y9

is enlivened with rock-face limestone segmental lintels. Its distinctive silhouette provides a landmark to thousands of motorists passing it daily on the nearby Brooklyn-Queens Expressway.

[Y9] **Engine Company 209**, Ladder Company 102, 34th Battalion, N.Y.C. Fire Department, 850 Bedford Ave., bet. Myrtle and Park Aves. W side. 1965. *Pedersen & Tilney.*

"Modernists" first enjoyed widespread commissions for New York's public buildings in the 1960s and 1970s. Their valiant attempts (including this one) now seem to pall in light of a new understanding of, and interest in, urban context. The **1869** station that this replaced, down the block between Myrtle and Willoughby Avenues, has unfortunately been demolished.

[Y10] **CABS (Community Action for Bedford-Stuyvesant) Nursing Home & Related Health Facility,** 270 Nostrand Ave., bet. Kosciusko and DeKalb Aves. W side. 1976. *William N. Breger & Assocs,* architects. *Leeds Assocs.,* interiors.

A stylish stacking of cubist brickwork crowned with a space-frame skylight. The atrium within is a delightful greenhouse filled with a "bamboo jungle."

[Y11a] **Magnolia Grandiflora,** in front of 679 Lafayette Ave., bet. Marcy and Tompkins Aves. N side., opp. Herbert Von King Park/formerly Tompkins Park. 1885. [Y11b] **677, 678, 679 Lafayette Avenue**/The Magnolia Tree Earth Center (row houses). 1880-1883. 🖍

One of two landmark trees in New York (the other is the **Weeping Beech** in Flushing). Here an expatriate southerner has survived many of its brownstone neighbors of the same vintage. A third wonder, the **Camperdown Elm,** still graces Prospect Park. The brownstones were designated landmarks to insure their continued service, shielding the tree from north winds.

Tree and brownstones face **Tompkins Park,** one of the 11 parks (or squares) included in Brooklyn's original 1839 city plan.

Y15

Y14

Y16

[Y12] **John Wesley United Methodist Church**/originally **Nostrand Avenue Methodist Episcopal Church**, Quincy St. SW cor. Nostrand Ave. 1880.

A brick body with milky **Tiffany**-style stained glass is crowned with timbered gables—part of the second Gothic Revival, Shingle, and Stick Style division. These were Romantic times, before a third round of Gothicism became Academic: that of the literalism of *Ralph Adams Cram* and the Collegiate Gothicists after 1900.

Governors: *Between Marcy and Stuyvesant Avenues, streets were named for New York governors: William L. Marcy, Daniel D. Tompkins, Enos T. Throop, Joseph C. Yates, Morgan Lewis, and the Dutch director general, Peter Stuyvesant. Yates Avenue became Sumner when confusion arose between it and Gates.*

[Y13] Onetime **IBM Systems Products Division**/formerly **Empire State Warehouse**/originally **Long Island Storage Warehouse and Jenkins Trust Company**, 390 Gates Ave., SW cor. Nostrand Ave. 1906. *Helmle, Huberty & Hudswell.*

Grand, paired Beaux Arts entry portals join the corner at this intersection. A rusticated base supports patterned brickwork above. Lost is a neo-Baroque tower that once was the crown of these brownstone blocks.

[Y14] **St. George's Episcopal Church**, 800 Marcy Ave., SW cor. Gates Ave. 1887-1888. **Sunday School**. 1887-1888. *Richard Michell Upjohn.*

An elegantly austere Ruskinian Gothic country church in the City, in brick, brownstone, and slate. The octagonal tower is both grand and lilliputian. The architect is the son of Trinity Church's *Upjohn*.

[Y15] Originally **Boys' High School**, 832 Marcy Ave., bet. Putnam Ave. and Madison St. W side. 1891-1892. *James W. Naughton*. Additions, 1905-1910, *C.B.J. Snyder.*

A splendid **Romanesque Revival** landmark, arched, quoined, and towered in the manner of *H.H. Richardson;* and lushly decorated in terra cotta in the manner of *Louis Sullivan.*

[Y16] **Brownstone Blocks**, Jefferson Ave., bet. Nostrand and Throop Aves. 1870s.

Merely three blocks out of dozens in the area with staid Renaissance Revival brownstones. *F.W. Woolworth* moved to **No.209** in

1890. Changing fashion, and vastly increasing wealth led him across the East River to 990 Fifth Avenue, where his later (1901) house was designed by *C. P. H. Gilbert*. Compare the similar migration of *Harold I. Pratt* from Clinton Hill to 68th Street and Park Avenue.

[Y17a] **Most Worshipful Enoch Grand Lodge/** originally **Reformed Episcopal Church of the Reconciliation**, Jefferson Ave., SE cor. Nostrand Ave. 1890. *Heins & La Farge.*

A stolid place, its octagonal corner tower rising above milky stained glass, brick, and terra cotta. Now a Masonic temple.

Y17a

[Y17b] **Clinton Apartments**, 425 Nostrand Ave., bet. Jefferson and Hancock Aves. E side. 1890s.

Roman brick and Roman arches crowned with a pressed metal garlanded cornice. Unfortunately, the bay windows are now clad with metal strip siding, and the ground floor defaced by an awkward concrete stair.

[Y18] **Renaissance Apartments**, 480-482 Nostrand Ave., SW cor. of Hancock St. 1892. *Montrose W. Morris.* 🖌

Cylindrical, conically capped towers, borrowed from Loire Valley châteaus, anchor a grand apartment house that has now regained its former splendor both inside and out. An address restored to distinction at the heart of Bed-Stuy.

[Y19a] **232 Hancock Street**, SE cor. Marcy Ave. 1886. *Montrose W. Morris.*

A mansarded extravaganza, replete with oriels, gables, dormers, and pediments—a **Queen Anne** wonder.

[Y19b] **236-244 Hancock Street** (house), bet. Marcy and Tompkins Aves. S side. 1886. *Montrose W. Morris.*

Pompeian-red terra cotta and brick form a rich tapestry in the manner of *George B. Post's* Brooklyn Historical Society. *Morris* designed most of this block himself, beginning with **No.238**, which he built as his own home, a model to spark interest in prospective neighborhood clients.

[Y19c] **246-252 Hancock Street** (house), bet. Marcy and Tompkins Aves. S side. 1880s. *Montrose W. Morris.*

Y17b   Y18

Y19a

Terra cotta, stained glass, elliptical arches, and Byzantine columns, mansarded and pedimented against the sky. **Shingle Style Richardsonian Romanesque**: a "terrace," in the English sense, that is greater than the sum of its parts.

[Y19d] Originally **John C. Kelley House**, 247 Hancock St., bet. Marcy and Tompkins Aves. N side. 1880s. *Montrose W. Morris.*

A formal freestanding **neo-Renaissance** town house (in Rome it would have been a palazzo, in Paris a hôtel particulier) on a triple-width site (81 feet) built for *Kelley*, an Irish immigrant who made his fortune in water meters. Legend claims that the brownstone was selected piece by piece to guarantee quality. Lovingly restored as a Bed and Breakfast.

[Y19e] **255-259 Hancock Street** (house), bet. Marcy and Tompkins Aves. N side. 1880s. *Montrose W. Morris.*

Arches with rugged rock-faced granite voussoirs bring vigorous shade and shadow to this trio. Bay windows project, terraces recede, adding more spatial play.

[Y19f] **273 Hancock Street** (house), bet. Marcy and Tompkins Aves. N side. 1890. *J.C. Reynolds & Son.*

Smooth and rock-faced brownstone, with a lion-faced keystone guarding the entry.

*Need lunch? **Trinidad Ali's Roti Shop**, 1267 ' Fulton St. bet. Nostrand Avenue & Arlington Place, serves wonderful roti, filled with chickpeas, potato, pumpkin, spinach, goat. Tasty, cheap, healthy. "Open 'til the food runs out!"*

[Y20] **74 Halsey Street**, bet. Nostrand Ave. and Arlington Place. N side. 1880s.

A wild Queen Anne place, with exuberant

Y19f

wrought-iron railings and canopy. Imagine bounding up those front steps.

[Y21] **Alhambra Apartments**, 500-518 Nostrand Ave., bet. Macon and Halsey Sts. W side. 1889-1890. *Montrose W. Morris.* Restored, 1998, *Anderson Associates.*

Morris did better here than for *Kelley*, with a richer collection of terra cotta and brick; arcaded, mansarded, chimneyed, and dormered. Shopfronts along Nostrand Avenue detract, however, from the grandeur overhead. *Morris* and *Frank Freeman* were Brooklyn's greatest architects.

[Y22] **N.Y.C. Board of Education Brooklyn Adult Training Center**/ formerly **Girls' High School**/ originally **Central Grammar School**, 475 Nostrand Ave., bet. Halsey and Macon Sts. E side. 1885-1886. Rear addition, 1891, *James W. Naughton.* Macon Street addition, 1912, *C.B.J. Snyder.*

A High Victorian painted Gothic Revival hulk.

[Y23] **64 and 68 Macon Street** (houses), bet. Nostrand and Marcy Aves. S side. 1880s.

The intervening "garden" gives status to these classy houses (and allows a view for **No.64**'s oriel). High up on **68** (**Romanesque Revival**) an overseeing face peers from the dormered roof. Below an incised second-story corner porch provides overview in counterpoint to the oriel across the garden.

[Y24a] **Restoration Plaza**, 1360 Fulton St., SE cor. New York Ave. 1976. *Arthur Cotton Moore.* **Planned renovation and expansion**, 2011, *James Garrison*, architect, with *Shawn Rickenbacker*; *Judith Heintz*, landscape architect.

A groundbreaking grassroots effort in the early 1970s yielded this modernist community center and plaza, which wisely incorporated, instead of demolishing, the majestic then-abandoned **Sheffield Farms Bottling Plant**.

A new plan by *Garrison* and his team will replace much of *Moore's* 1976 scheme, which

Y20

tied together disparate functions through liberal use of brown brick and glass. A previous edition of this Guide called it "Brooklyn's answer to San Francisco's Ghirardelli Square." *Garrison's* plan promises bells and whistles: fountains, plants, benches, a "wall of fame." It sounds like a potentially lively addition to an already bustling stretch of Fulton Street.

[Y24b] **Sheffield Farms Bottling Plant**, 1368 Fulton St., bet. Brooklyn and New York Aves. ca. 1900.

The rescued anchor for Restoration Plaza, and home to the **Billie Holiday Theatre**. A monumental cliff of glazed white terra cotta in a kind of **Bovine Renaissance Revival** style; note the busts of cattle in the cornice.

Compare with a virtually identical Sheffield Farms building in Morningside Heights, Manhattan, at 632 West 125th Street, between Broadway and Riverside Drive, now home to Columbia University's **Prentis Hall** (see p.506).

[Y25] Alice and Agate Courts Historic District, twin cul-de-sacs, N side of Atlantic Avenue, mid-block between Kingston and Albany Aves. 1888-89. *Walter M. Coots.* 👁

Thirty-six lovely Queen Anne rowhouses developed, designed, and built by architect *Coots* in red brick, brownstone, and terra cotta.

[Y25a] 1-17 Agate Court, W side. Two-story brick rowhouses, more ornate than Alice Court, with arches, bays, a dramatic turret at the end (**No.1**) and sunburst pediments (**Nos.9** and **11**) mid-row. **2-18 Agate Court,** E side. Mirror images of the west side, except **Nos.10** and **12** have lost their pediments. Agate Court has the original brick boundary wall at the rear of the site.

[Y25b] 1-17 Alice Court, W side. Slightly less decorative than Agate Court, but no less charming. **2-18 Agate Court,** E side. Again, a mirror of the other side of the street. The remains of an original fountain can be seen at the end of the cul-de-sac.

Y27

Y30

🏛 **[Y26] First African Methodist Episcopal Zion Church**/originally **Tompkins Avenue Congregational Church,** 480 Tompkins Ave., SW cor. MacDonough St. 1889. *George B. Chappell.*

The immense campanile is reminiscent of that of St. Mark's in Venice; brick is everywhere. Once the nation's largest Congregational congregation, it was often referred to as *Dr. Meredith's* church, after its well-known preacher.

🏛 **[Y27] Originally 13th Regiment Armory,** New York National Guard, now **Pamoja House** (social services), 357 Marcus Garvey Blvd. (Sumner Ave.), bet. Jefferson and Putnam Aves. E side. 1894. *Rudolph L. Daus.* Extended, 1906, *Parfitt Brothers.*

A grand granite arch gives support to twin battlemented towers: Gothic Revival (crenellations, machicolations, and a battered base) fit to defend against attackers armed with spears, arrows, rifles and an occasional war machine. But it gave symbolic shelter to the onetime modern National Guard warriors who marched within. Still a major neighborhood landmark.

[Y28] Stuyvesant Heights Christian Church, Tompkins Ave., NW cor. MacDonough St. 1880s.

Stocky Gothic Revival in brick and limestone. A modest form with grandly scaled windows.

[Y29] Stuyvesant Heights Historic District, an L-shaped area between Chauncey and Macon Sts., Stuyvesant to Tompkins Aves. 1870-1920. 👁

The wondrous row housing, particularly along Decatur, Bainbridge, and Chauncey Streets, is a cross section of Bedford-Stuyvesant vernacular architectural history. The locally designed buildings encompass attitudes from freestanding suburbia to the best of Victorian row housing, and present a sampling of modest apartment units.

Y31

Within the Historic District:

[Y30] **Our Lady of Victory Roman Catholic Church**, NE cor. Throop Ave. and MacDonough St. 1891-1895. *Thomas F. Houghton.*

Dark dressed rockfaced Manhattan schist

Y36a

with limestone enframements in a late, many-pinnacled Gothic Revival.

 [Y31] Office building/formerly **Fulton Storage Building**/originally **New York and New Jersey Telephone Company** (branch office), 613 Throop Ave., NE cor. Decatur St. ca. 1895.

Roman brick and **Renaissance** arches; the spandrels between are richly decorated in sculpted terra cotta. The façade now includes an unsightly garage door.

[Y32] **79-81 Decatur Street**/originally Clermont Apartments, bet. Marcus Garvey Blvd. (Sumner Ave.) and Throop Ave. N side. 1900.

A shrunken château: here **Roman** brick, limestone, and pressed metal produce a middle-class Azay-le-Rideau. Beautifully restored.

[Y33] **Mt. Lebanon Baptist Church**, 230 Decatur St., SE cor. Lewis Ave. 1894. *Parfitt Brothers.*

A superb **Richardsonian Romanesque** building in Roman brick and brownstone. Its grand

arch, bounding across the entry space, is embellished with a leafy bas-relief.

[Y34a] **113-137 Bainbridge Street** (row houses), bet. Lewis and Stuyvesant Aves. N side. ca. 1892. *Magnus Dahlander.*

Y38

Y43

The studied variegations of these 13 houses show pyramids, arches, and cones alternately punctuating the sky. Such a picturesque romance contrasts sharply with the normally sober regularity of mid–19th century Renaissance Revival brownstones.

[Y34b] **118-126 Bainbridge Street**, bet. Lewis and Stuyvesant Aves. S side. 1899. *D. Topping Atwood Company*, builders.

More individualistic stone town houses, with comically expressive figureheads "holding up" the bay windows.

Outside the Historic District:

[Y35] **Fulton Park**, Chauncey to Fulton Sts. at Stuyvesant Ave.

Along Chauncey Street just north of the park there remains a row of excellent small town houses with intact stoops. In the park's center is a statue of *Robert Fulton* holding his first steam ferryboat to Brooklyn, the Nassau. Originally sited in a niche at the Brooklyn ferry terminal, below the Brooklyn Bridge, the statue disappeared. It was later discovered and placed here in 1930 by the Society of Old Brooklyn.

City center: The geographical center of New York City lies within Bedford-Stuyvesant—to be exact, within the block bounded by Lafayette, Reid (Malcolm X Boulevard), Greene and Stuyvesant Avenues, the present site of a less than distinguished public school.

[Y36a] **352-356 Decatur Street** (row houses), bet. Stuyvesant Ave. and Malcolm X Blvd. 1880s.

Victorian Baroque, the cornices punctuating the streetfront with a jack-in-the-box routine.

[Y36b] **366 Decatur Street** (tenement), SW cor. Malcolm X Blvd. 1890s.

Triangular (in plan) bay windows extend like prows into Decatur Street, social observation points for those staying at home.

[Y37] **417-421 Decatur Street**, bet. Malcolm X Blvd. and Patchen Ave. 1880s.

Brick and brownstone, some painted, but all coiffed with cornices that surge forward, then hang back, a horizontal version of the Victorian Baroque acrobatics seen at 352-356 Decatur above.

[Y38] **Union Baptist Church**, 461 Decatur St., bet. Patchen and Ralph Aves. 1880s.

Yellow brick, limestone, terra cotta, and sheet metal (cornices) join in this local extravaganza, a Renaissance-Revival idea with exagger-

Y44   Y50

ated parts: rustication, Tuscan pilasters, great swags over the arched stained glass, and a Gargantuan frieze and cornice. Wonderful.

[Y39] **587-611 Decatur Street**, bet. Howard and Saratoga Aves. N side. 1891. *J. Mason Kirby.*

Pyramids and arches punctuate this picturesque group of low-scaled row houses built of assorted varieties of brick and stone.

[Y40] **Saratoga Park**, bet. Halsey and Macon Sts., Saratoga and Howard Aves.

A lovely Bloomsbury-scaled park surrounded by symbiotic row houses—none distinguished, but all pleasant.

[Y41] **Modern Row Housing**, bet. Hancock St., Jefferson, Saratoga and Howard Aves. 1990s.

An attempt at row housing in scale with Bed-Stuy's history: three stories, corniced, and with varying arched and pitched entry lobbies.

[Y42] **Saratoga Avenue Community Center**, 940 Hancock St., bet. Broadway and Saratoga Ave. 2008. *George Ranalli*, architect.

Ranalli, heavily influenced by *Frank Lloyd Wright* and the under-appreciated Italian genius *Carlo Scarpa*, here contributes a crisply detailed modernist cube in masonry, with wood trim.

While other architects were creating glass boxes for the wealthy in Chelsea and SoHo during the recent Building Boom, *Ranalli* and colleagues like *Sara Caples* and *Peter Gluck* were toiling away on people projects in the outer boroughs: Bed-Stuy, Brownsville, and the Bronx.

[Y43] Originally **RKO Bushwick Theater**, SE cor. Howard Ave. and Broadway. *William H. McElfatrick.* Altered, *Thomas W. Lamb.*

A ravaged warrior that has been through abandonment and fire; nevertheless Egyptian goddesses crown lavish and fantastic white-glazed terra-cotta oculi that are simultaneously embraced by giant cupids. The circular pediments abound with masks, swags, and festoons.

Y42

[Y44] **Engine Co. 233**, Ladder Co. 176, N.Y.C. Fire Department, Rockaway Ave., NE cor. Chauncey St. 1985. *Eisenman/Robertson.*

Contrapuntal geometry in gray and white block, tile and metal panels that might have been from the **1925 Paris Exposition**. The second-floor structural expression has been crudely filled in by others, and a lack of maintenance has taken a heavy toll.

[Y45] **Public School 73**, Brooklyn, 241 MacDougal St., NE cor. Rockaway Ave. 1888. Addition, 1895. Both by *James W. Naughton.*

Robust Romanesque Revival in brick, terra cotta, and limestone. A gem.

[Y46] **Junior Academy**/originally **Public School 26**, Brooklyn, 856 Quincy St., bet. Patchen and Ralph Aves. S side. 1891. *James W. Naughton.*

Romanesque Revival brick and terra cotta with a serrated silhouette of gables. Sturdy brick colonnettes at the second floor support rock-faced lintels; their third-floor companions bear arches.

[Y47] **St. Johns Bread and Life**, 795 Lexington Ave., bet. Reid (Malcolm X Blvd.) and Patchen Aves. N side. 2008. *Rogers Marvel.*

A social services facility (soup kitchen, food pantry, chapel, library) reusing an existing masonry structure with modest but lovely spaces inserted within. Old and new materials combine to provide interiors filled with natural light. The tiny chapel is extraordinary, simple and square, ethereal light (from a skylight above) bathing the existing brick wall.

[Y48] **Originally St. John the Baptist's College and Church**, Lewis Ave., bet. Hart St. and Willoughby Ave. E side. 1870. *Patrick Charles Keely.*

The church behind the college building is rough-cut brownstone ashlar, a vigorous Renaissance Revival hulk.

[Y49] **319 Broadway** (tenement), bet. Lewis and Stuyvesant Aves. 1890s.

Mildly bellying bays decorated with Gothic

NECROLOGY

St. Lucy's Roman Catholic Church, 780 Kent Ave., bet. Flushing and Park Aves. 1921.

A *John Soane* revival? Romanesque Baroque? Tucked away in this industrial precinct stood this striking architectural personality that resurrected Regency tricks and towers.

374-376 Franklin Avenue (double house), SW cor. Quincy St. Bedford-Stuyvesant. ca. 1865.

This looked as though it came right out of *A.J. Downing's* Victorian country house design manuals.

212 Gates Avenue (country house), bet. Franklin and Classon Aves. S side.

Board and battened **Carpenter Gothic** in three parts, with an inviting porch and extraordinary scrollsaw work in the eaves; it was the victim of fire and subsequent renovations.

Necrology: 212 Gates Avenue

detail over a Romano-Gothic base. A unique tenement.

[Y50] **Antioch Baptist Church**/originally **Greene Avenue Baptist Church** and Church House, 828 and 826 Greene Ave., bet. Stuyvesant and Lewis Aves. **Church**, 1887-1892. *Lansing C. Holden* and *Paul F. Higgs.* **Church House**, 1891-1893. *Langston & Dahlander.*

Romanesque Revival/Queen Anne that snuggles into the midblock cityscape, providing a compendium of exoticisms for its pastoral flock.

[Y51] **767-769 Greene Avenue**, bet. Marcus Garvey Blvd. and Lewis Ave. N side. 1890s.

Another lovely **Romanesque Revival** loner in these less explored blocks. Look around.

[Y52] **Ebenezer Gospel Tabernacle**, 470 Throop Ave., bet. Gates Ave. and Quincy St. W side. 1891.

A lusty and miniature Romanesque Revival gem.

Originally Temple Israel (synagogue)/then **Brooklyn Traffic Court**/ then **Bergen Tile** (store), 1005 Bedford Ave., NE cor. Lafayette Ave. Bedford-Stuyvesant. 1893. Parfitt Bros.

When this Byzantine Romanesque house of worship was dedicated by its affluent German-Jewish congregation, it rated front-page coverage in the *Brooklyn Daily Eagle.*

Originally Public School 19, Brooklyn, Kosciusko St., bet. Throop and Sumner Aves. N side. 1889.

A vast abandoned **Romanesque Revival** brick and terra-cotta wonder. We savored the bas-reliefs of the tympanums. This loner in the wilderness fell beyond the radar of preservationists.

CROWN HEIGHTS

W2

reinfusion of the Orthodox. Many West Indian immigrants reside in the area, with Haitian French and British English often heard in the streets.

Frank H. Taylor wrote early in the 20th century: "In the heart of the St. Mark's section are located many beautiful mansions, products of the master hand of the architect, the artist, and the modern mechanic. These beautiful homes are seldom offered for sale. They are cherished as homes and will probably pass from one generation to another, fine demonstrations of the great confidence our wealthy men have in the stability of Brooklyn."

[W1] **Crown Heights North Historic District**, from Rogers Ave. at Grant Sq., along a line between Pacific and Dean Sts. to Albany Ave.; then along a line down to St. John's Place, and back to Grant Sq.

This was an enclave of Brooklyn wealth equal to its peers in Brooklyn Heights, Clinton Hill, and Bedford. The vagaries of social change exiled many Brooklynites to Manhattan after the consolidation of 1898, but a vast reservoir of luscious architecture was left behind.

[W2] **23rd Regiment Armory**, New York National Guard, 1322 Bedford Ave., bet. Atlantic Ave. and Pacific St. W side. 1891-1895. *Fowler & Hough and Isaac Perry.*

With its eight great round towers, one soaring over its peers, and an arched entry complete

W3

The name **Crown Heights** covers the area east of Washington Avenue between Atlantic Avenue on the north, Empire Boulevard on the south, and East New York Avenue on the east. Included are the grand buildings surrounding Grant Square at Bedford Avenue and Bergen Street, originally the center of Bedford; that community's southern boundary is now considered Atlantic Avenue.

Crown Heights, the 19th-century Crow Hill, includes a succession of hills south of Eastern Parkway. The old designation derisively recalls the black colony of Weeksville along the former Hunterfly Road, with extant buildings now both preserved and restored (including a planned **Weeksville Heritage Center** by *Caples Jefferson*). Another old thoroughfare is Clove Road, once a two-mile, north-south link from the village of Bedford to Flatbush, dating from 1662. Only a block of Clove Road remains, above Empire Boulevard east of Nostrand Avenue.

The community has been in transition for a generation with, in sectors, an original Jewish population first declining, then reinforced, by a

with portcullis, this crenellated brick-and-brownstone "fortress" for the National Guard lacks only a moat to be out of King Arthur's realm.

[W3] Formerly **Medical Society of the County of Kings**, 1313 Bedford Ave., bet. Atlantic Ave. and Pacific St. E side. 1903. *D. Everett Waid* and *R.M. Cranford.*

A neo-Regency play written in a Georgian vocabulary. To a future archaeologist, its tiered Tuscan and Ionic columns could seem to be a 1980s postmodern arrangement of the 18th century.

[W4] **St. Bartholomew's Episcopal Church**, 1227 Pacific St., bet. Bedford and Nostrand Aves. N side. 1886-1890. *George P. Chappell.*

A charming, romantic place: squat and friendly, with stone and brick, and trimmed in terra cotta. The tower is crowned with "fish scales," imbricated tiles in a sinuous profile. All in a bosky bower with a Hansel and Gretel manse.

W11

 [W5] **Imperial Apartments**, 1198 Pacific St., SE cor. and 1327-1339 Bedford Ave. 1892. *Montrose W. Morris.*

Erected on an imperial scale, with great paired Corinthian terra-cotta columns and arches along both Pacific Street and Bedford Avenue. Advertised in their time as "elegant and well conducted" and "in the fashionable part of Bedford," the immense apartments have since been subdivided. It has many similarities with *Morris's* Alhambra Apartments on Nostrand Avenue.

[W6] **1164-1182 Dean Street**, bet. Bedford and Nostrand Aves. S side. 1890. *George P. Chappell.*

Ten lovingly maintained Queen Anne houses in a melange of brick, limestone, terra cotta, wooden shingles, and Spanish tile, with alternating stepped, peaked, and domed gables.

[W7] **Ulysses S. Grant Statue**, Grant Sq. at Dean St. and Bedford Ave. 1896. *William Ordway Partridge*, sculptor.

A youthful Grant bestrides his charger in this amorphous square.

[W8] **Bhraggs Grant Square Senior Citizens' Center**/ formerly **Union League Club of Brooklyn**, Bedford Ave., SE cor. Dean St. 1890. *P.J. Lauritzen.*

Once Brooklyn's most resplendent club, built to serve the social needs of Republican party stalwarts of Bedford, of which this area was considered a central part. Brownstone **Richardsonian Romanesque** arches support an eclectic body above; note *Lincoln* and *Grant* in the arches' spandrels and the monumental American eagle supporting the great bay window.

[W9a] **671 and 673 St. Mark's Avenue**, bet. Rogers and Nostrand Aves. N side. 1888. *E.G.W. Dietrick.*

Black Forest Queen Anne: an eccentric adventure that continues the experimental vital-

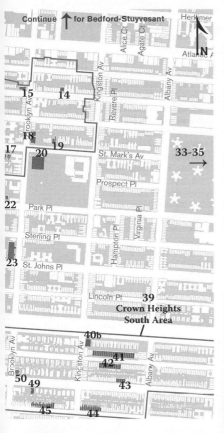

[W12] **919 Park Place**, NE cor. New York Ave. 1940s.

Two-tone brick and corner windows combine with the strong forms of solid parapeted balconies to create an elegant **Art Moderne/ modernist** apartment house.

[W13a] **Union United Methodist Church**/originally **New York Avenue Methodist Church**, 121 New York Ave., bet. Bergen and Dean Sts. E side. 1892. *J.C. Cady & Co.*

A powerful smooth and rounded **Romanesque Revival** red-brick and red sandstone monolith. The subtle transitions between brick and molded clay give it a special and powerful dignity.

[W13b] **Hebron French-Speaking Seventh-Day Adventist Church**/originally **First Church of Christ Scientist**, New York Ave. SW cor. Dean St., 1909. *Henry Ives Cobb.*

Eclectic, the old First Church is torn between **Romanesque** and the **Classical Revival** of the 1893 Chicago World's Fair. Note the rare, flat

W4

W13a

ity of St. Mark's Place, where a whole history of 19th-century experimentation will greet you. Paint stripping would reveal the brick and limestone reality masked with too much mascara.

[W9b] **675 and 677 St. Mark's Avenue**, bet. Rogers and Nostrand Aves. N side. ca. 1890.

Romanesque Revival in Roman brick from the **Chicago School.** The flush brick arches and lintels show a subtle hand.

[10] **Studebaker Building**, 1469 Bedford Ave., NE cor. Sterling Place. 1920. *Tooker and Marsh.*

White terra cotta, a crenellated parapet, and **neo-Gothic** ornament. It honors the corner with a gracious curve.

[W11] **MAHANAIM, Eglise Adventiste**/formerly **Ancient Divine Theological Baptist Church**, 814 Park Place, bet. Rogers and Nostrand Aves. S side. ca. 1890.

A neo-Flemish brick church with a stepped gable and a magnificent wheel window.

terra-cotta shingles (as opposed to Spanish or Roman terra-cotta tiles more commonly used).

[W14] **George B. and Susan Elkins House**, 1375 Dean St., bet. Brooklyn and Kingston Aves. N side. 1855-1869.

A freestanding sparsely decorated wood country house with **Greek Revival** and **Italianate** influence. See the copybooks of *Andrew Jackson Downing* and his peers. (cf. Downing's "Cottage Residences" 1850, in a 1968 reprint).

[W15] Originally **John and Elizabeth Truslow House**, 96 Brooklyn Ave., NW cor. Dean St. 1887-1888. *Parfitt Brothers.*

A freestanding mansion in red brick, sandstone, and granite, with grand rusticated arches on the ground floor, boxed oriel windows projecting to the side, gables and chimneys against the sky.

[W16] **Marcus Garvey Nursing Home**, 810 St. Mark's Ave., bet. New York and Brooklyn Aves. S side. 1977. *William N. Breger & Assocs.*

A simple building in terra-cotta-colored brick, well detailed, replacing three major mansions, including that of *Abraham Abraham*, cofounder of Abraham & Straus (A&S).

Abraham Abraham was first a partner in Wechsler and Abraham, the forerunner of Abraham & Straus, once Brooklyn's very own department store (the Fulton Mall main store is now a Macy's). Among his many philanthropic accomplishments was the founding of Brooklyn Jewish Hospital, built in 1894 as Memorial Hospital for Women and Children. His son-in-law Edward Blum and grand-son-in-law Robert A. M. Blum carried on both the business and philanthropic tradition. In the 1960s the latter Blum was board chairman of both Abraham & Straus and the Brooklyn Institute of Arts and Sciences.

[W17] **828-836 St. Marks Avenue**, bet. New York and Brooklyn Aves. S side. ca. 1914.

Five small fussy neo-Georgian houses. Their suburban front yards related to the ex-mansions that were replaced by the nursing home next door.

[W18] **St. Louis Senior Citizens' Center**/originally **Dean Sage House**, 839 St. Marks Ave., NE cor. Brooklyn Ave. 1869. *Russell Sturgis.*

Stolid rock-face brownstone Romanesque Revival. *Sturgis* was more noted as a critic and writer, and was author of the magnificent 1902 *Dictionary of Architecture.*

mounds. The structure is analagous to an iceberg: the pinnacle visible from outside gives few signals of the wonders within. Have a child bring you here.

 [W20b] **Brooklyn Children's Museum Expansion**, SE cor. of Brooklyn and St. Marks Aves. 2006. *Rafael Viñoly Architects.*

We all want to live in, or at least visit, a yellow submarine! Superimposed on the troglodytic *Hardy Holzman Pfeiffer* museum.

Lost mansions: The 1976 Brooklyn Children's Museum replaced the original, organized in 1899, which occupied two Victorian mansions on this site (see Necrology).

[W21] Originally **Brooklyn Methodist Church Home**, 920 Park Place, bet. Brooklyn and New York Aves. S side. 1889. *Mercein Thomas.*

It has the look of an asylum in its literal sense: a place of refuge for the indigent, a place of dread for the casual stroller, thinking how lucky he/she is to be able to stroll by....

[W22] **979 Park Place**, bet. Brooklyn and New York Aves. N side. 1888. *George P. Chappell.*

This could well be a prototypical model for *Vincent Scully's* great 1955 book *The Shingle Style*. With its projections, recessions, bay windows, and porches, it is an essay in American "neo-medievalism," although the Middle Ages never enjoyed such middle-class grandeur.

W20b

W23

[W19] **855 and 857 St. Marks Avenue**, bet. Brooklyn and Kingston Aves. N side. 1892. *Montrose W. Morris.*

Romanesque Revival brick and limestone twin-mansion, with an elegant corner tower capped by a belled cupola. The contrasting textures of rock-faced granite below and smooth, very smooth brick and limestone above, raises the design bar with architecture delivering both power and subtlety. Perhaps a Jesuit mind joins Protestant execution. Superb.

[W20a] **Brooklyn Children's Museum**, Brower Park, entrance at SE cor. of Brooklyn and St. Marks Aves. 1976. *Hardy Holzman Pfeiffer Assocs.* We-Fr, 2-5; Sa, Su, Hol, 12-5; closed Mo-Tu. *718-735-4400. www.brooklynkids.org*

Earth and metalworks worthy of a missile-launching station and festooned with the architecture of movement. Highway signs and an entrance through a transit kiosk lead into the bowels tunneled within the bermed earth

[W23] **St. Gregory's Roman Catholic Church**, 224 Brooklyn Ave., NW cor. St John's Place. 1915. *Frank J. Helmle.*

In brick, limestone, and terra cotta, this is Roman revival, remembering early Christian churches and the very idea of a basilica. Its inspiration might well have been San Paolo Fuori le Mura in Rome.

Further afield:

[W24] **Police Precinct**, NE cor. Park Place and Grand Ave. 1890s.

Much altered, but the arch at the entry springs from the original rock-faced granite.

[W25] Originally **Knox Hat Factory**, 369-413 St. Marks Ave., NE cor. Grand Ave. ca. 1890.

An increasingly hatless male population spelled the doom of one of Brooklyn's once flourishing industries. The grand Manhattan headquarters of Knox are incorporated into the **HSBC** office tower/complex across from the Public Library.

W19

[W26] **Public School 22**, NW cor. St. Marks and Classon Aves. 1993. *Perkins & Will.*

Some classy retro-**Art Moderne**; the yellow brick and black steel seem reminiscent of a 1940s World's Fair.

[W27] **Nursing Home, Jewish Hospital Medical Center of Brooklyn**, Classon Ave., bet. Prospect and Park Places. 1977. *Puchall & Assocs. and Herbert Cohen.*

An unabashed **modernist** in brown brick. Its cantilevered corners and sleek detailing bring back memories of the Bauhaus (the radical German school of architecture and the arts closed down by Hitler).

[W28] **St. Theresa Roman Catholic Church**, NE cor. Classon Ave. and Sterling Pl. 1890s.

Central European towers with bell-like caps anchor the west end of this neighborhood church.

[W29] **651-675 St. Marks Avenue**, bet. Franklin and Bedford Aves. N side. 1880s.

Simple two-story and basement, brick and limestone buildings, punctuated by a triangular and circular gables. Charming.

[W30] **49-57 Crown Street**, NW cor. Franklin Ave., near the Botanic Garden. 1976.

This slender tower is a dominant silhouette looming over the Botanic Garden.

[W31] **42nd Supply and Transport Battalion**, New York National Guard/originally **Troop C Armory**, 1579 Bedford Ave., bet. President and Union Sts. E side. 1908. *Pilcher, Thomas & Tachau.*

The last stand of the cavalry and a mighty fortress to this day. The great arched roof, sil-houetted on the outside, is a tribute to the prin-ciples of mid-Victorian train sheds, still prolific in European capitals.

[W32] **1035-1079 Carroll Street**, bet. Bedford and Rogers Aves. 1920s.

Hooded houses that might have been conceived as urban chalets.

[W33] **Weeksville Houses**/also known as **Hunterfly Road Houses**, along old Hunterfly Road, 1698-1708 Bergen St., near St. Mary's Place, bet. Buffalo and Rochester Aves. Restored, 1990s, *Li-Saltzman.* 🖑

Four simple wood houses occupied by *James Weeks* and friends (free black men) between 1830 and 1870. The architecture, in painted clapboard, is that of the 19th-century common man. It is the City's oldest black residential landmark.

[W33a] **Weeksville Heritage Center**, 158 Buffalo Ave., bet. St. Marks Ave. and Bergen St. 2011. *Caples Jefferson Architects.*

Much-needed exhibition and research space adjacent to the Weeksville houses, beautifully detailed in wood and glass, thoughtfully connected to the surrounding landscape. Terrific.

[W34] **Berea Baptist Church**, Bergen St., bet. Utica and Rochester Aves. N side. 1894.

A charming, castellated neo-Romanesque place.

[W35] **Intermediate School 55**, Brooklyn, The Ocean Hill Intermediate School, Bergen and Dean Sts., Hopkinson and Rockaway Aves. 1968. *Curtis & Davis.*

A grim, "fortified" place of brown brick with

W37

narrow slit windows. Its edge against the sky simulates crenellations.

[W36] **Crown Gardens**, Nostrand Ave., bet. President and Carroll Sts. E side. 1971. *Richard Kaplan. Stevens, Bertin, O' Connell & Harvey,* associate architects.

Stacked townhouses grouped around a courtyard. Brown brick and concrete present a rhythmic display of balconies and stair towers.

[W37] **Medgar Evers College New Academic Building**, 1632-1638 Bedford Ave., NW cor., Crown St. 2009. *Polshek Partnership.*

Sleek glass and angled brick; a nice addition to the college and neighborhood.

[W38] **Medgar Evers Preparatory School at Medgar Evers College**, 1186 Carroll St., SW cor. Nostrand Ave. 2005. *Davis Brody Bond.*

Medgar Evers Preparatory School, housed on the college campus in Crown Heights, began serving children in grades 6 in 2005 and now

has children in grades 6-12. Students may take the high school Regents exams for math and living environment as early as 7th grade.

Another closely packed precinct with many blocks of urbane interest:

[W39] **Crown Heights South** area, generally including President and Union Sts., bet. New York and Troy Aves., and Carroll St. from New York Ave. to Albany Ave. Mostly 1910-1930.

A **should-be historic district**, with tree-lined streets of bayed townhouses, as in Park Slope and Prospect Heights, along Carroll and Union Streets, and bigger suburban houses, with green lawns, along President Street.

[W40a] **1361-1381 Union Street**, bet. New York and Brooklyn Aves. N side. 1912. *Axel Hedman.*

An eccentric neo-Renaissance row of bowed and bayed limestone fronts. They are crowned with curious geometric parapets above their modillioned cornices: triangular, semicircular, rectilinear.

[W40b] **Jewish Children's Museum**, 792 Eastern Pkwy., SE cor. Kingston Ave. 2004. *Gwathmey Siegel.*

Tzivos Hashem, an international not-for-profit children's organization, commissioned *Gwathmey Siegel* to design an original, "wired" structure, versatile enough to act as both museum and community center. The result is way out there, but it is good to see star architects building in Crown Heights.

W40b

[W41] **1485-1529 Union Street**, bet. Kingston and Albany Aves. N side. 1909. *F.L. Hine.*

Alternating bow and bay windows modulate the streetfront. Note the friezes between the first and second floors and under the cornice.

[W42] **1476-1506 Union Street**, bet. Kingston and Albany Aves. S side. 1909. *Harry Albertson.*

A more exuberant set than those across the street, these are alternately crowned with conical and pyramidal hats, to match their bowed and bayed windows below.

[W43] **1483-1491 President Street**, bet. Kingston and Albany Aves. N side. 1913. *J. L. Brush.*

The whole façade presents a bow in these English basement (i.e., stoop-less) brownstone houses.

[W44] **1401-1425 Carroll Street**, bet. Kingston and Albany Aves. N side. 1913. *J. L. Brush.*

Similar to Nos.1483-1491 but with small stoops.

[W45] **1311A-1337 Carroll Street**, bet. Brooklyn and Kingston Aves. N side. 1913. *Slee & Bryson.*

A Federal Revival brick row with crisp white trim, strangely crowned with eclectic slate mansard roofs. The bay windows pleasantly modulate the street.

[W46] **1294 President Street**, bet. New York and Brooklyn Aves. S side. 1911. *William Debus.*

This double house is on the imposing scale of an English Renaissance palace.

[W47] **1281 President Street**, bet. New York and Brooklyn Aves. N side. ca. 1900.

A squat round tower with a conical tiled cupola makes this ordinary house into something special.

[W48] **1319 President Street**, bet. New York and Brooklyn Aves. N side. 1930. *H.T. Jeffrey.*

Mock Tudor, complete with small, leaded panes, an asymmetrical composition playing the gabled bay against a pair of decorated brick chimneys.

[W49] **1362 President Street**, bet. Brooklyn and Kingston Aves. S side. 1921. *Cohn Brothers.*

W44

A florid and showy intruder into these mostly modest and serene surroundings. The vocabulary comes from a smorgasbord of French Renaissance ingredients.

[W50] **1337 President Street**, NE cor. Brooklyn Ave. ca. 1900.

A neo-Georgian vocabulary clads an Italianate flat-roofed form in this turn-of-the-century eclecticism.

NECROLOGY

71st Precinct, N.Y.C. Police Department, 421 Empire Blvd., NE cor. New York Ave. Crown Heights.

A Florentine palace despite its un-Florentine brick, it was replaced by a modern police station.

Originally **Abraham Abraham House**, 800 St. Marks Ave., bet. New York and Brooklyn Aves. S side. Crown Heights. ca. 1890.

Built as a proper mansion for one of Brooklyn's most prominent philanthropists, the founder of A&S. It was demolished for a nursing home.

Originally **Ludwig Nissen House**, 814 St. Marks Ave., bet. New York and Brooklyn Aves. S side. Crown Heights. ca. 1905. *Arne Dehli.*

Also torn down for the nursing home. This Guide's 1968 edition called it "a miniature of the Potsdam Palace."

820 St. Marks Avenue (house), bet. New York and Brooklyn Aves. S side. Crown Heights. ca. 1890.

Another mansion removed for the nursing home.

Old Brooklyn Children's Museum, in Brower Park, Brooklyn Ave., bet. St. Marks Ave. and Park Place. Crown Heights. North Building:

W49

L.C. Smith House, ca. 1890. South Building: **William Newton Adams House**, 1867.

The museum's 1976 facility replaced its original buildings, two Victorian mansions that were familiar landmarks in Brower Park.

Loehmann's (women's apparel), 1476 Bedford Ave., NW cor. Sterling Place. Crown Heights.

Until it went out of business at this location, this chaotic store, wrapped in gilded Oriental detail, was filled with unbelievable bargains. Some Chinese dragons still lurk on Sterling Place.

St. Mary's Hospital, Division of Catholic Medical Center of Brooklyn and Queens, 1298 St. Mark's Ave., bet. Rochester and Buffalo Aves. S side. Crown Heights. 1882.

This picturesque brick edifice with mansard rooflets had been an outgrowth of St. Mary's Female Hospital, which also helped establish the Hospital of the Holy Family on Dean Street in Cobble Hill.

Northern Brooklyn

Town of Bushwick/Boswijck–"Wooded District"
Established as a town in 1660; Town of
Williamsburg became separate in 1840;
annexed to the **City of Brooklyn** in 1855.

This area, including the three communities
of Bushwick-Ridgewood, Williamsburg, and
Greenpoint, often was called the Eastern District
after the merger of 1855, to distinguish it from
the original area of the City of Brooklyn, the
"Western." In general the term has fallen into
disuse except in connection with the names of a
local high school and a freight terminal (with
some logic, as the Eastern District is now the
northern tip of Brooklyn, and South Brooklyn is,
in fact, at Greater Brooklyn's northwest corner).

B2

Much of this part of Brooklyn is devoted to
working-class residential areas clustered
between industrial concentrations strung along
the East River and Newtown Creek. It is in this
precinct that many fortunes were made in sugar,
oil, rope, lumber, shipbuilding, brewing, and glue.

BUSHWICK-RIDGEWOOD

Malt and hops, barley and barrels, beer and ale.
*Obermeyer and Liebmann, Ernest Ochs, Claus
Lipsius, Danenberg and Coles.* The history of
Bushwick has been the history of brewing. Beer
came to Bushwick in the middle of the 19th century when a large German population emigrated
here, some after unsuccessful uprisings in the
Fatherland in 1848 and 1849, most because of
poverty and lack of opportunity.

In its early years the community was noted
largely for farming, the produce being sold
locally as well as ferried to Manhattan's markets. By the 1840s *Peter Cooper* had moved his
glue factory here, since land values in
Manhattan's Murray Hill had risen so sharply
that an odoriferous glue factory was no longer
of economic sense there. Cooper, always a
shrewd businessman, chose this undeveloped
area of Brooklyn near main roads connecting
the ferries to New York with the farms on Long
Island. His site is that of Cooper Park Houses, a
low-rent housing project, named after the adjacent park given to the City of Brooklyn in 1895
by the Cooper family.

Bushwick Avenue once contained 20 blocks of
impeccable stolid mansions, freestanding town
palaces advertising the wealth and taste of local
industrial magnates. Originally a gloomy set of
Victorian buildings, they nevertheless revealed
the spirit of their times: wealth was a burden,
and the owners' moral duty to uplift the masses
was somberly fulfilled through dour stonework.
Several of the more glorious places have
burned, most tragically the old **Bushwick
Democratic Club** (see Necrology), at the northwest corner of Bushwick Avenue and Hart
Street, perhaps the greatest single piece of
architecture Bushwick ever knew.

[B1] Formerly **Vicelius & Ulmer's Continental
Lagerbier Brewery**/ later **William Ulmer
Brewery**, Beaver St., bet. Locust and Belvidere
Sts. 1872.

Although graffiti-covered at the ground
floor, scores of articulated arched brickwork
windows make an impressive façade. *Ulmer's*
mansion was on Bushwick Avenue a few
blocks east.

Continue ↑ for Williamsburg

Continue → for Ridgewood, Queens

Continue ← for Bedford-Stuyvesant

Continue ↓ for Highland Park / Cypress Hills

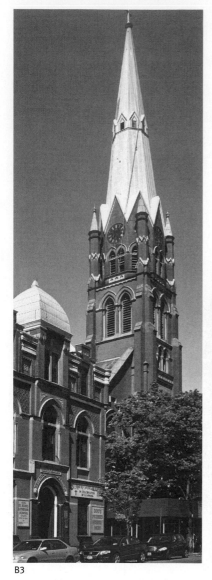

B3

B5   B7

B9   B10

[B4] Originally **William Ulmer House**, 670 Bushwick Ave., cor. Willoughby Ave. ca. 1885.

A stolid **Romanesque Revival** brick fortress, as befits a stolid brewer. Dr. *Frederick A. Cook*, a later owner, was a well- known but ill-heralded Arctic explorer. He claimed to have discovered the North Pole but lost in court to *Admiral Robert E. Peary*. Now renovated and inhabited after long abandonment.

[B5] **Brooklyn Public Library, DeKalb Branch**, 790 Bushwick Ave., SE cor. DeKalb Ave. 1905. *William B. Tubby.*

Squat **Renaissance Revival** in brick and limestone from *Tubby*, the architect of many buildings at **Pratt Institute** as well as the **Ethical Culture Center** in Park Slope. He was a virtuoso in style, ranging from the Renaissance Classicism of **St. Ann's School** (old Crescent Athletic Club) in Brooklyn Heights to the lusty Romanesque Revival of the **Charles Millard Pratt House** on Clinton Avenue.

[B2] **Arion Mansions**/originally **Arion Hall**, 13 Arion Place, bet. Beaver St. and Broadway. 1887.

Cleaned and powerful **Corinthian** pilasters and a strong newly painted cornice show that the booming real estate market has reached Bushwick. Rich embellishment once encrusted this hall, redolent of those days when the Arion Männerchor, the Eastern District's leading German singing society, met here.

[B3] **St. Mark's Lutheran Church and School**/originally **St. Mark's Evangelical Lutheran German Church**, 626 Bushwick Ave., cor. Jefferson St. 1892.

The verdigris-clad copper-sheathed spire dominates Bushwick Avenue for most of its length. Up close there are glorious **Victorian Gothic** brick and terra-cotta arches, tourettes, and bas-relief panels.

[B6] **South Bushwick Reformed Church**, 855-867 Bushwick Ave., cor. Himrod St. 1853. *Messrs. Morgan*. **Chapel and Sunday School**. 1881. *J.J. Buck.*

A New England outpost in these dour streets: late **Greek Revival** with imposing Ionic columns. The paint is peeling and the wood rotting, scarring this elegant anachronism with its delicate clapboard and purple and white milk glass. The street is the namesake of the first minister, *John Himrod*.

[B7] **1080 Greene Avenue**, cor. Goodwin Place. 1850s.

Italianate, with an exuberant bay window facing Goodwin Place. Lunettes in the frieze, Tuscan columns below. Purported to have belonged to the founder of the **Bohack's** grocery chain.

[B8] Originally **John F. Hylan House**, 959 Bushwick Ave., bet. Bleeker and Menahan Sts. 1885. *John E. Dwyer.*

One in a row of unpretentious brownstones (**Nos.945-965**), noted principally because it was the home of "Red Mike," mayor of New York from 1918 to 1925.

🏠 [B9] Originally **Gustav Doerschuck House**, 999 Bushwick Ave., cor. Grove St. ca. 1890.

A towered Romanesque Revival brewer's mansion, in brick and rock-faced granite. A ribbon of floriated terra cotta runs over the gable's arched corbel table. Take those metal awnings away.

[B10] Originally **Charles Lindemann House**, 1001 Bushwick Ave., cor. Grove St. ca. 1890.

A **Shingle Style** loner, turreted, porched, dormered, and recently restored to much of its original splendor. But how about the original natural materials instead of yellow stucco?

[B12] **1020 Bushwick Avenue**, SW cor. Linden St., and 37-53 Linden Street, bet. Bushwick Ave. and Broadway. W side ca. 1885.

Richly decorated **Queen Anne** brick and terra-cotta town houses. The corner house is special, enriched with a cast-iron crenellated mansard roof. These dark-red monoliths bear superb friezes: brow and waist. The wrought ironwork on the Linden Street stoops is magnificent.

🏛 [B13] **Bushwick Avenue Central Methodist Episcopal Church**, 1130 Bushwick Ave., cor. Madison St. 1886-1912.

The octagonal **Renaissance Revival** tower is a local landmark, in polytonal red sandstone and gray brick.

[B14] **Bethesda Baptist Church**/formerly **Bushwick Avenue Congregational Church**, 1160 Bushwick Ave., cor. Cornelia St. 1896. *Fowler & Hough.*

A powerful campanile corners this stolid brick church, but the open belfry has been bricked in, destroying its original elegance. Take

B13   B16   B17

[B11] Onetime **Arion Singing Society**/originally **Louis Bossert House**, 1002 Bushwick Ave., cor. Grove St. 1887. *Theobold Englehardt.*

This dour red-brick box crowned with a mansarded roof (downgraded from its original slate and stripped of its detail) once presented **Gothic-**bracketed dormers to the street (now gone). *Bossert* was a successful millwork manufacturer who later built Brooklyn Heights' **Bossert Hotel.** We need *Bossert's* millwork back.

Grove Street owes its name to Boulevard Grove, a park at the intersection of that street with Bushwick Avenue. Picnics were held there as early as 1863.

note of the Renaissance Revival brownstone and brick parish house next door.

[B15] **1278 Bushwick Avenue and neighbors**, bet. Halsey and Eldert Sts. S side. ca. 1880.

A group of simple, articulated brick row houses, corniced with a Renaissance profile in sheet metal.

🏛 [B16] **St. Barbara's Roman Catholic Church**, Central Ave., cor. Bleeker St. 1910. *Helme & Huberty.*

Built to serve a parish at first German, then Italian, and now largely Latino, it was named not only for the saint, but for *Barbara Eppig*, whose father, brewer *Leonard Eppig*, was a major contributor to its construction. Gleaming white and cream glazed terra-cotta Spanish Baroque. The towers are wedding-cake icing: edible.

[B17] **Engine Co.277/Ladder Co.112,** NYC Fire Department, 582 Knickerbocker Ave., bet. Gates Ave. and Palmetto St. 2009. *STV Architects.*

Two styles for the price of one. The front façade is crisp, orthogonal **modernism** in concrete block and glass; the sides are curvy **postmodernism** in the vein of *Zaha Hadid.*

[B18] **Public School 86**/also known as the **Irvington School,** 220 Irving Ave., bet. Harman St. and Greene Ave. 1892-1893. *James W. Naughton.*

B20

Romanesque Revival in painted brick and rock-faced granite.

[B19] **Engine Company 252**/originally Fire Engine Co. 52/later Engine Co. 152, 617 Central Ave. 1896-1897. *Parfitt Brothers.*

Whimsical **Flemish Revival,** the stepped and curling gable crowning a brick and terra-cotta façade.

[B20] Formerly **83rd Precinct, N.Y.C. Police Department and Stable**/originally 20th Precinct, Brooklyn Police, 179 Wilson Ave., cor. DeKalb Ave. 1894-1895. *William B. Tubby.* Restored, 1996. *Ehrenkrantz & Eckstut.*

The police precinct as defensive redoubt: powerful **Romanesque Revival,** crenellated, machicolated, with a columned porch bearing incised Sullivanesque ornament. Our older readers might appreciate that *Kojak* was filmed here, using the station as a backdrop.

NECROLOGY

696 Bushwick Ave. (house), SW cor. Suydam St.

This wonderfully elaborate Italianate frame mansion simply collapsed one day. Its replacement is a vacant lot.

Bushwick Democratic Club, later **Bethesda Pentacostal Church,** 719 Bushwick Ave., NW cor. Hart St. 1892. *Frank Freeman.*

One of the City's greatest buildings, by Brooklyn's greatest architect, featuring ornament worthy of *Louis Sullivan,* and unique structural forms including negative bay windows behind arches. Ravaged by seemingly endless fires, there was ultimately too little left to preserve.

Originally **Mrs. Catherine Lipsius House,** 680 Bushwick Ave., SE cor. Willoughby Ave. ca. 1886. *Theobaold Engelhardt.*

A brewer's widow commissioned this strangely proportioned Italianate Revival house. In 2000 this Guide noted that it was "fenced in

Necrology: Mrs. Catherine Lipsius House

and ravaged, the porch on the verge of collapsing." Correct prognostication.

Joseph Schlitz Brewing Company/originally Leonard Eppig's Germania Brewery/then Interboro Cereal Beverage Company (during Prohibition)/ then George Ehret's Brewery, 24-44 George St., SE cor. Central Ave. Bushwick. ca. 1877.

A richly worked brick behemoth gone to rest, together with the other once worldrenowned Brooklyn brewing industries.

HALF-DEAD

20 Bleecker Street (apartments), bet. Bushwick and Evergreen Aves. E side. Bushwick. ca. 1890.

A triumphant, magnificent Victorian wood and bay-windowed tenement. A survivor amid the surrounding devastation, the building is not in fact demolished but merely re-clad in aluminum, its façade and refined details totally concealed.

WILLIAMSBURG

Even though the **Williamsburgh Savings Bank** spells its name the old way (the "h" fell when it consolidated with the City of Brooklyn in 1855), and though it shares its current spelling with the well-known restoration in Virginia, the resemblance ends there. This Williamsburg, formerly part of the Town of Bushwick, later a village and city in its own right, was named after *Col. Jonathan Williams*, its surveyor and grandnephew of *Benjamin Franklin. Richard M. Woodhull* started the community when he purchased thirteen acres of land at the foot of today's South 2nd Street, in 1802. He commissioned *Williams* to survey it, established a ferry to **New York** (Manhattan), and quickly went bankrupt (1811).

Thomas Morrell and *James Hazard* picked up where *Woodhull* had left off. They also established a ferry, this time to the Grand Street Market at **Corlear's Hook,** providing an outlet for the farmers of Bushwick to sell their produce in

[W1] **667-677 Bedford Avenue**, bet. Heyward and Rutledge Sts. E side.

In 2000 there stood an entire blockfront of magnificent tenements encrusted with stone: rock-faced and smooth, brown, tan, and gray. New architecture has been inserted. In one case crisp steel balconies guard (and mask) the families of Orthodox Jewish families. Down the block another has been sheathed in bland brickwork. Nearby, Granite colonnettes with Byzantine capitals look on with dismay.

[W2] **Beth Jacob School**/formerly **Public School 71**, Brooklyn/sometime **United Talmudic Academy**, 125 Heyward St., bet. Lee and Bedford Aves. N side. 1888-1889. *James W. Naughton.* 👁

From *Napoléon III's* Second Empire: a mansarded central block over brick and brownstone by an admiring follower of *Lefuel* and *Visconti's* **Louvre.**

W1

W2

New York. The impetus to the area's growth, however, was the establishment of a distillery in 1819. The distillery is gone (as is the Schaefer brewery that followed it on the same site). Booze and beer helped build Williamsburg, but now are only drunk here, not distilled or brewed.

The most telling impact on the community came from the opening of the **Williamsburg Bridge** in 1903. Overnight the community changed from a fashionable resort with hotels catering to such sportsmen as *Commodore Vanderbilt, Jim Fisk,* and *William C. Whitney* to an immigrant district absorbing the overflow from New York's Lower East Side. (The *New York Tribune* of the period characterized the bridge as "The Jews' Highway.") Its elegant families moved away, and its mansions and handsome brownstones from the post-Civil War era fell into disuse and then were converted to multiple dwellings.

Bedford Avenue: The sequence is north, with the direction of traffic; the house numbers decrease as we proceed.

Hasidic community: Along Bedford Avenue are arrayed brownstones, mansions, and apartment houses such as described above: one of New York's most concentrated Hasidic (Jewish) communities. This unique settlement of the Satmarer Hasidim, recalling late medieval Jewish life in dress and customs, is a result of persecution of the Eastern European Jewish community during World War II. In 1946, Rebbe Joel Teitelbaum and several of his flock reached these shores and chose Williamsburg—even then a heavily Orthodox area—as their home. At the end of the war, the remaining survivors from Poland and Hungary migrated to the new settlement and reestablished their lives there. As the community grew parts of it split off and moved to other parts of Brooklyn and to the suburbs. Beards and uncut earlocks identify the men; shaved but wigged heads identify the women. Long frock coats and skullcaps are in evidence everywhere among its male population, young and old; and in the winter, the fur-trimmed hat, the shtreimel, is certain to make its appearance. Evidence of its residents' heritage is everywhere apparent, from

the proliferation of Hebrew signs on the mansions to the identification of small business establishments catering to them.

[W3] Bnos Yakov of Pupa/originally **Temple Beth Elohim**, 274 Keap St., bet. Marcy and Division Aves. S side. 1876.

This Hebrew congregation was the first in Brooklyn, dating from 1851. Ruskinian Gothic polychromy in brick and painted brownstone, terra cotta, stained glass, and tile. And lush ironwork gates.

[W4] *Rutledge Street*, bet. Lee and Marcy Aves. N side.

One of Williamsburg's loveliest streets. Williamsburg, a swampy, low-lying area, became the ideal spot for the culture of the ailanthus tree (a tree of fernlike leaves similar to those of the mimosa and locust). First imported from China about 1840, the tree was intended

for use as the grazing ground of the cynthia moth's caterpillar, a great, green, purpleheaded, horned monster (3/4 inch in diameter, three inches long) that spins a cocoon prized for its silk threads. The mills of Paterson, N.J., were to be its beneficiaries. Its grazing role proved uneconomical (the grazing still goes on, however, without cocoon collection), but the tree was believed to have another virtue for the locals: supposedly providing power to dispel the "disease-producing vapors" presumed to come from swampy lands. See Betty Smith's 1943 novel of Williamsburg life, A Tree Grows in Brooklyn.

[W5] 17th Corps Artillery Armory/formerly **47th Regiment Armory**/ originally **Union Grounds**, Marcy to Harrison Aves., Heyward to Lynch Sts. 1883.

The Harrison Avenue end is a squat fort: double clerestoried, with crenellated and machicolated corner towers. The Union Grounds were the site of early baseball games in the

W9

1860s, between the Cincinnati Red Stockings, the Philadelphia Athletics, the New York Mutuals, and the Brooklyn Eckfords.

[W6] **John Wayne Elementary School/P.S. 380**, Marcy Ave., bet. Lynch and Middleton Sts. 1977. *Richard Dattner & Assocs.*

A somber Pompeiian-red brick construction, formed from clustered polygons and happily appropriate for this dour and somber neighborhood. The painted skirt covers graffiti, but the upper body is the natural brick.

[W7] Formerly **Yeshiva Jesode Hatorah of Adas Yerem**, 571 Bedford Ave., bet. Keap and Rodney Sts. E side. ca. 1890.

Rock-faced brownstone dominates. But a powerful elliptical bay window bursts forth, and is crowned in copper with a frieze of cherubs; rising above, an ornate dormer window with round Baroque shell pediment, Classical pilasters and finials. Lush and seedy.

[W8] **Bais Yaskov of Adas Yereim**/formerly **Hanover Club**/originally **Hawley Mansion**, 563 Bedford Ave., SE cor. Rodney St. ca. 1875. Remodeled, 1891, *Lauritzen & Voss.*

Faded yellow painted brick with brownstone quoins—cast iron against the sky. But the cornice has been rudely ripped off, the window detailing denuded. The other *William Cullen Bryant* (1849-1905), publisher of the Brooklyn Times, was president of the **Hanover Club**.

[W9] **559 Bedford Avenue**, NE cor. Rodney St. ca. 1890.

An imposing terra-cotta castle, now minus the conical, Spanish tile crown over its round corner tower. The bay on Bedford Avenue modulates the basic body, and an owl is perched on Rodney's pediment.

[W10] Originally **Frederick Mollenhauer House**/now **Yeshiva Yesoda Hatora of K'Hal Adas Yereim**/onetime **Congress Club**, 505 Bedford Ave., NE cor. Taylor St. 1896. *Lauritzen & Voss.*

A neo-Renaissance, brick, and sandstone English clublike mansion drawn from Italian palazzo antecedents. *Frederick* was a son of *John Mollenhauer*, founder of the Mollenhauer Sugar Refinery (1867).

W15

[W11] Formerly the **Rebbe's House**, 500 Bedford Ave., NW cor. Clymer St.

Once the home of *Grand Rabbi Josel Teitelbaum* (the Rebbe), who led the bulk of the Hasidim from Europe to Williamsburg. Dilapidated, but scaffolding is a promising sign that a renovation may come. On closer examination, the scaffolding itself looks dilapidated.

[W12] **Saints Peter and Paul/Epiphany Roman Catholic Church**/originally **New England Congregational Church**, 96 S.9th St. bet. Bedford and Berry Aves. S side.

A Lombardian Romanesque brick church with arched corbeltables, a sturdy tower.

[W13] **Light of the World Church**/originally **New England Congregational Church**, 179 S. 9th St., bet. Driggs and Roebling Aves. N side. 1852-1853. *Thomas Little.* Destroyed by fire in 1893, rebuilt 1894.

A giant super-brownstone in wood, sheet metal, and stone, this Italianate church bears extraordinary console brackets. It was a remarkable architectural tack for **Congregational** immigrants from New England to take: theirs was for the most part the world of white clapboard and English steeples.

[W14] **396 Berry Street**, NW cor. S. 8th St. ca. 1885.

This smooth terra-cotta and brick warehouse is a monolith of narrow joints and virtuoso brickwork.

[W15] **Smith, Gray & Company Building**, 103 Broadway, bet. Bedford Ave. and Berry St. N side. 1870. Attributed to *William H. Gaylor*. Cast-iron façade by *George R. Jackson & Sons.* •'

An expatriate from SoHo! Graceful cast iron with glassy elliptical bays now contains studio lofts. Cast console brackets form visual keystones with grand Corinthian columns.

best, even the interior is carefully preserved, the gaslit chandeliers all present (but wired for electricity). Seek out the plaited Indian hut in the entry pediment.

[W19] **Williamsburgh Savings Bank**, 175 Broadway, NW cor. Driggs Ave. 1870-1875. *George B. Post*. Additions, 1906, 1925, *Helme, Huberty & Hudswell.* •' Restorations, 1990s, *Platt Byard Dovell*.

The eclectic Victorian crossbreeding of Renaissance and Roman parts produced one of Brooklyn's great landmarks, particularly to those who pass by train or car over the Williamsburg Bridge. It's a sharp, hard, gray place reminiscent of the work of Brooklyn's own great architect, *Frank Freeman*, at his old, long since demolished, Brooklyn Trust Company (below the dome).

Peter Luger's Steak House, 178 Broadway, bet. Driggs and Bedford Aves.

Alfred Hitchcock called its steak the "best in

W16

W18

[W16] Originally **Bedford Avenue Theater**/formerly **Fruitcrest Corporation**, 109 S. 6th St., bet. Berry St. and Wythe Ave. N side. 1891. *W.W. Cole,* builder.

Opened by actress *Fanny Rice* in a farce, "A Jolly Surprise." Its history as a theater was brief. Now a sleek health club, little of the old interior remains.

[W17] **H. Fink & Sons Building**/formerly **Nassau Trust Company,** 134-136 Broadway, SW cor. Bedford Ave. 1888. *Frank J. Helmle*.

Somber neo-Renaissance limestone and granite.

[W18] **Williamsburg Art and Historical Society**/originally **Kings County Savings Bank**, 135 Broadway, NE cor. Bedford Ave. 1868. *King & Wilcox. William H. Wilcox.* •'

Bands of smooth and vermiculated Dorchester stone and slender Ionic and Corinthian columns alternate to enliven the exterior of the banking floor of this splendid **Second Empire** masterpiece. Victorian at its

the universe." In this spartan outpost of polished oak and white aprons, far from the habitat of its elegant clientele, steak reigns supreme—all else being decoration or fodder for those who can't contend with greatness. It all began as Charles Luger's Café, Billiards, and Bowling Alley in 1876. Expensive. No credit cards. No vegetarians.

[W20] **195 Broadway**/originally **Sparrow Shoe Factory Warehouse**, bet. Driggs Ave. and New St. N side. 1882. *William B. Ditmars*.

Cast-iron, with exuberant console brackets and fluted, floral-decorated Composite pilasters.

[W21] **Holy Trinity Church of Ukrainian Autocephalic Orthodox Church in Exile**/formerly **Williamsburg Trust Company,** 117-185 S. 5th St., NW cor. New St. 1906. *Helmle & Huberty.*

Built as a bank, this opulent white terra-cotta Romanism is now a cathedral, the reverse of the common progression from religious to sectarian use; compare the various churches of Brooklyn Heights and Cobble Hill that are now condominiums. The architecture is the natural result of the World's Columbian Exhibition (1893), the inspiration for the American Renaissance.

[W22] **Washington Plaza**, S.4th St. to Broadway, New to Havemeyer Sts.

Cut into pieces by the elevated subway and the Brooklyn-Queens Expressway, which slice through it with abandon. The forecourt for the Ukrainian Cathedral, in the northwest corner is formally executed and the only part of the whole deserving of the title "plaza." It contains, among disintegrating Renaissance Revival ornaments, a fine verdigris equestrian statue, **George Washington at Valley Forge** (*Henry M. Shrady*, 1906).

[W23] **Nuestros Ninos/Community and Parents Day Care Center**, 243 S. 2nd St., bet. Roebling and Havemeyer Sts. 2009. *Beckhard Richland Szerbaty + Associates.* **Mi Casita**, sculpture, *Moses Ros.*

Neat glazed brick in interlocking primary colors, like a Lego set.

[W24] **Fillmore Place Historic District**, bet. Driggs and Roebling Sts., plus some buildings on Driggs St., W of Fillmore Pl. 🍎

The Landmarks Commission designates historic districts both small and large. This one is tiny: only one lane long.

[W25] **Northside Terrace** (row housing), North 3rd St., bet. Bedford and Berry Aves. 1992. *James McCullar & Associates.*

W20

Steel stoops for three-story brick row houses, corniced and linteled in limestone (or is it concrete?).

🍎 [W26] Formerly **Manufacturers Trust Company**/originally **North Side Bank**, 33-35 Grand St., bet. Kent and Wythe Aves. N side. 1889. *Theobald Engelhardt.*

Lusty, gutsy, rock face Romanesque, arched, cast-iron corniced, wrought iron. A super, lonely building. Don't miss it.

[W27] Originally **Havemeyers and Elder Filter, Pan and Finishing House**/formerly **Domino Sugar Refinery**/one time **American Sugar Refining Company**, 292-350 Kent Avenue, bet. S. 5th and S. 2nd Sts. W side. 1881-1884. *Theodore A. Havemeyer* and others, architect. 🍎

Bulky, bold Romanesque Revival behemoths, closed in 2004. Planned for conversion to housing, but initial designs by *Beyer Blinder Belle* (a glass chrysalis on the refinery's roof) met with resistance from the Landmarks

Preservation Commission. A scaled-down version looks like it will go ahead. An adjacent tower by *Cesar Pelli* is also in the works.

[W28] **Iglesia Bautista Calvario**/formerly **St. Matthew's First Evangelical Lutheran Church**, 197-199 N. 5th St., bet. Roebling St. and Driggs Ave. N side. 1864.

Battered buttresses flank this brick and glass-blocked church. The shell survives; the façade has had recent TLC, stripping away the old paint.

[W29] **56-64 Havemeyer Street**/originally **Convent of the Order of St. Dominic.** 1889. *P. J. Berlenbach.*

A hearty Romanesque Revival institution, now revived as a condominium.

[W30] **Church of the Annunciation** (Roman Catholic), 255 N. 5th St., NE cor. Havemeyer St. 1870. *F. J. Berlenbach, Jr.*

A crisply detailed and lovingly maintained

W29

Lombardian Romanesque basilica. Its related convent across the street, has been converted.

◼ [W31] **Hecla Iron Works**, 100-118 N. 11th St., bet. Berry and Wythe Sts. 1896-97. Attributed to *Niels Pouslon.* 🍎

The late-lamented cast-iron **IRT** subway kiosks (see the reconstruction at Cooper Union) were cast here, and many street clocks (including one landmarked, at 200 Fifth Avenue in Ladies Mile), as well as ornamentation for Grand Central Terminal. The building itself is an industrial precursor to the modern curtain wall.

[W32] **Bushwick Inlet Park and Community Facility,** Kent Avenue, bet. N. 9th and N. 10th Sts. Phase 1: 2010. Phase 2: 2011. *Kiss + Cathcart,* architects. *Starr Whitehouse,* landscape architects.

A riverfront park for sports (a soccer field dominates) and river edge contemplation. The real (potential) star here is the proposed Community Facility, a "green" building that literally peels up a section of the park along Kent

Street and tucks the building underneath. But will budget cuts derail the design? It's already won awards. Build it!

*Meanwhile, the adjoining **East River State Park** (2007), Kent Avenue bet. N. 7th and N. 9th Streets, is a pleasant but plain greensward. A competition in 2005 produced an ambitiously collaborative solution by **Gareth Mahon** and the firms **Fabrica 718** and **3 SAP**. But like many earnest design competitions, the winning plan hasn't been built (yet?).*

The Stalled Building District:

*Williamsburg was until recently an industrial backwater. Then, the usual trajectory: artists moved in, followed by hipsters wanting to be near artists, then stock brokers wanting to be near hipsters. The new arrivals spurred a **building boom** that transformed the neighborhood. Dozens of new apartment buildings were built from scratch or converted from existing industrial buildings.*

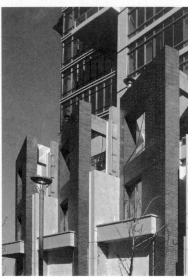

W33

*The **crash of 2008** resulted in the **stalling** of many of these projects, and left Williamsburg and Greenpoint littered with empty lots and incomplete buildings. Many have wistfully nostalgic names like the **Lucent** and the **Rialto**. Here are a few that were completed:*

[W33] Northside Piers, 4 N. 5th St., at Kent Ave. 2008-2010. *FxFowle.*

Three glass towers along the East River. This is Brooklyn?

[W34] The Edge, bet. N. 5th and N. 7th Sts, W of Kent Ave. 2010. *Stephen B. Jacobs Group* with interiors by *Andi Pepper.*

More towers along the water, just north of Northside Piers. Presumably named for its proximity to the water, not for the Irish guitarist. Again, this is Brooklyn?

South edge of McCarren Park:

[W35] 20, 30, 50 Bayard Street, bet. Lorimer and Union Sts. 2006. *Karl Fischer.*

Mr. Fischer, of Montreal, has been busy in Williamsburg. These three glass boxes, with a few curves thrown in here and there, stare down at the park. There are dozens of other similar projects in the neighborhood, and a stroll west and south will reveal them, but seeing these three is probably **more than enough**.

[W36] McCarren Park Play Center, N.Y.C. Department of Parks & Recreation, McCarren Park, Lorimer St., bet. Bayard St. and Driggs Ave. E side. 1934-1936. *Aymar Embury II,* lead architect, with *Joseph L.Hautman, Henry Ahrens* and others. *Gilmore Clarke*, landscape architect.

Piranesi would have loved swimming here. A monumental pool, featuring a fantastic brick-arched entry pavilion with an imposing clerestory and Art Moderne ticket booth. One of four WPA-

W36

built swimming pools erected in Brooklyn during the Depression (the others are Red Hook, Sunset Park, and Betsy Head). Gutted by fire in 1987, it became overgrown and abandoned, then was used for a summer concert series. Currently being restored to its rightful aquatic use.

Pete's Candy Store, 709 Lorimer Street between Frost and Richardson, one block south of McCarren Park, is interesting for its candlelit back room; long and narrow like a railroad car (or is it actually a railroad car?) where live music is performed, intimately, every night.

[W37] Russian Orthodox Cathedral of the Trans-figuration of Our Lord, 228 N. 12th St., SE cor. Driggs Ave. 1916-1921. *Louis Allmendinger.*

The Winter Palace at St. Petersburg is remembered in the yellow and beige tones of this magnificent cathedral, crowned with five onion-domed cupolas. The real treat, however, is within: the space is small (only 250 seats), and the central cupola is supported on four great columns painted to simulate richly veined

marble. The triple-altared eastern end is separated from the body of the church by the iconos-
tasis, a hand-carved wooden screen on which
icons were painted by the monks in the
Orthodox Monastery of the Caves in Kiev. A visit
should include the celebration of Divine Liturgy:
architecture, incense ritual, and sound, combined in many tongues, create a deeply moving
saturation of the senses.

[W38] **Iglesia Metodista Unida de Sur Tres**/
originally **South Third Street Methodist Church**,
411 S. 3rd St., bet. Union Ave. and Hewes St. N
side. 1855.
    Simple and painted **Lombardian Romanesque**.
The arched corbel table is its only embellishment.

[W39] **Iglesia Pentecostal Misionera**/originally
Deutsche Evangelische St. Peterskirche, 262
Union Ave., NE cor. Scholes St. 1881.
    That dour German brickwork now softened
in spirit by a Hispanic congregation.

[W40] **Formerly Public School 69**/origi-
nally **Colored School No.3**, 270 Union
Ave., bet. Scholes and Stagg Sts. E side. 1879-
1881. *Samuel B. Leonard.*
    An Italian Romanesque miniature for a
school in Williamsburg's rural days.

*The Fourteen Buildings: The turn Grand Street
takes at Union Avenue marks the beginning of
the site of the Fourteen Buildings. The street
was laid out between Union and Bushwick
Avenues so that it would pass through the prop-*

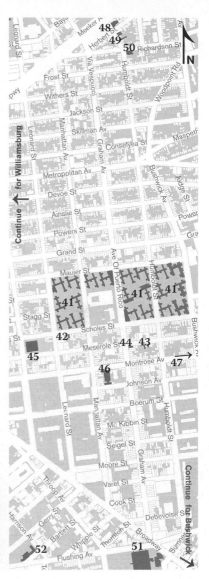

W38   W40

*erty of a group of men who then built for them-
selves a series of Greek Revival frame dwellings
in 1836. Each had a dome and a colonnaded
porch of fluted wood columns. The houses were
arranged one per block on both sides of Grand
Street, with two extras slipped in. By 1837 each
of the men had suffered the consequences of
that year's financial panic, and the houses
changed hands. In 1850 all fourteen still
remained, but by 1896 only one was left. Today
there is no sign on this busy shopping street of
that bygone elegance apart from the bend itself.*

EAST WILLIAMSBURG

[W41] **Williamsburg Houses**, N.Y.C. Housing
Authority, Maujer to Scholes St., Leonard St. to
Bushwick Ave. 1935-1938. Williamsburg Houses
Associated Architects: *Richmond H. Shreve,*
chief architect; *William Lescaze,* designer, with
*James F. Bly, Matthew W. Del Gaudio, Arthur C.
Holden, Samuel Gardstein, Paul Trapani,
G. Harmon Gurney, Harry Leslie Walker,* and *John
W. Ingle, Jr.* Restoration and reconstruction,
1999-2002.
    The first and most expensive (in adjusted
dollars) public housing project built in the City.
Its four-story buildings embrace semiprivate
spaces for both passive and active recreation.
Reinforced concrete and brick infill is punctuated by pedestrian ways that connect sequential courtyards through stepped and columned
portals. The apartments themselves are
reached without benefit of corridors by an entry
system that opens directly off the stair landings
(as in Princeton Collegiate Gothic, here in

serene modern dress). The aluminum double-hung windows are a clunky alteration, replacing elegant slender-mullioned, but unhappily deteriorated, steel casements. Stripped of its original brick, and articulated with blue tiles.

[W42] **Little Zion Baptist Church,** 98 Scholes St., bet. Leonard St. and Manhattan Ave. S side. 1890s.

Articulated arches with supporting colonnettes in the Romanesque manner; then topped off with a Second Empire hat.

[W43a] **174 Meserole Street House,** bet. Graham and Humboldt Aves. S side. 1887. *F.J. Berlenbach, Jr.* 🍎 [W43b] **178 Meserole Street House,** bet. Graham and Humboldt Aves. S side.

Exuberant, painted wood houses—**No.174,** Queen Anne, **No.178,** Renaissance Revival—two of the City's best. "Tenement" is a pejorative today; in fact it describes a walk-up apartment house that covers most of its building site. Here the light in the back rooms is minimal, but the visible architecture is magnificent.

[W47] **NYC Department of Sanitation Garages and Borough Offices,** 161 Varick St., bet. Stagg and Meserole Sts. 2002-2007. *Dattner Architects.*

A New York City Art Commission Award for Design Excellence: keeping the City clean by a sinuous, crisp, and shining example.

[W48] Originally **19th Police Precinct Station House and Stable,** 43 Herbert St. and 512-518 Humboldt St. 1891-1892. *George Ingram.* 🍎

Romanesque Revival by an architect with a superior sense of style. Check the ironwork overhead, but the arched entry in brick and brownstone is magnificent; the bracketed lighting elegant.

[W49] **492-494 Humboldt Street,** bet. Richardson and Herbert Sts. E side., and **201 Richardson Street** bet. Humboldt and N. Henry Sts. N side. ca. 1850.

These were slaughtered parts of one of several formerly great Brooklyn colonnade rows; only one still exists: on Willow Place in Brooklyn Heights. Here the decline is not one of abandon-

W43a

[W44] **182 Graham Avenue,** SE cor. Meserole Ave. ca. 1885.

Above a sullied ground floor rises a **Belle Epoque** confection with a curved Second Empire mansard roof and ornate and wondrous details. It's a parody of the elegantly dressed businessperson with scruffy unshined shoes.

[W45] **New York Telephone Company Communications Center,** 55 Meserole St., NE cor. Lorimer Ave. 1975. *John Carl Warnecke & Assocs.*

Stylish and expensive ironspotted brick with gargantuan hooded windows contributing to a powerful and inhuman place for telephone equipment.

[W46] **Holy Trinity Roman Catholic Church,** Montrose Ave. bet. Manhattan and Graham Aves. S side. 1882.

A huge twin-towered reprise of Manhattan's St. Patrick's Cathedral—or perhaps of the Abbaye-aux-Hommes in Caen, France.

ment but of cultural desecration: No.492 has been "improved" downhill, by cladding its natural columns with fluted sheet metal, false shutters, and turgid stone wainscoting. Good intentions have succeeded here only in destroying a bit of architectural heritage.

[W50] **St. Paul's Center,** 484 Humboldt Street, SE cor. Richardson St. ca. 1885.

Iron-spotted bricks and Romanesque Revival arches.

[W51] **Woodhull Medical and Mental Health Center,** SW cor. Broadway and Flushing Aves. 1977. *Kallman & McKinnell/Russo & Sonder,* associated architects.

A **space odyssey** that landed at this juncture of Williamsburg, Bedford-Stuyvesant, and Bushwick, this **machine for health** was the most technologically and architecturally up-to-date — and the most expensive — hospital of its time. The self-weathering steel has acquired a deep purple-brown patina on this bold, cubistic place. Great human-high trusses span 69 feet, within which workers can adjust the complex piping and tubing that serve the rooms and laboratories above and below these interleaved service levels. *Kallman* and *McKinnell's* first and major monument was the competition-winning Boston City Hall. A somewhat scary ode to health, dedicated more to the efficiency of health economics than to the serenity of its patients. Widely reviewed in architectural literature, it has won many prizes.

W51

[W52] **Beginning with Children School**, 11 Bartlett St., bet. Flushing and Harrison Aves. Renovations and additions, 2000, *Fox & Fowle*.

The original school, a former Pfizer industrial plant, has been remodeled and extended with a new gymnasium and classrooms.

NECROLOGY

Williamsburg Christian Church, Lee Ave., SE cor. Keap St., adjoining the Brooklyn-Queens Expressway. ca. 1885.

A superarched brick outpost, now just a vacant lot.

Smith Building, NE cor. Bedford Ave. and S. 8th St. 1860s. *Grosvenor Smith.*

Cast-iron elegance, far from the Manhattan districts that honor such construction. And it would be unique, even there; the great arch led to a department store.

Originally **Joseph F. Knapp House**/later a dancing academy/later Yeshiva Umesivta Torah V'Yirah D'Satmar, 554 Bedford Ave., NW cor Ross St. Williamsburg. 1894.

Built for the president of the Metropolitan Life Insurance Company, it was replaced for a "more modern" Williamsburg.

Originally **First Reformed Dutch Church of Williamsburg**/later Congregation Tifereth Israel (synagogue), 491 Bedford Ave., SE cor. Clymer St. Williamsburg. 1869.

The Gothic Revival structure was destroyed by fire and replaced by a matter-of-fact synagogue.

Originally **Dr. Charles A. Olcott House**/later Entre Nous Club, 489 Bedford Ave., NE cor. Clymer St. Williamsburg.

A relic of this area's more glorious upper-middle-class period.

Necrology: Williamsburg Christian Church

Originally **Williamsburg Gas Light Company**/ later Brooklyn Union Gas Company, 324 Bedford Ave., NW cor. S 2nd St. Williamsburg. ca. 1866.

A fine work of architecture, needlessly demolished—cast-iron façade and all. It stood on the site of the old Williamsburgh City Hall.

97 Broadway, bet. Bedford Ave. and Berry St. N side. Williamsburg. 1870.

The cast-iron Second Empire, mansard-roofed edifice once housed the Kings County Fire Insurance Company. A three-story Victorian Baroque porch was reminiscent of the porch on Alfred Mullett's State, War, and Navy Building in Washington—but in iron rather than stone.

GREENPOINT

Greenpoint is a quiet, ordered, and orderly community of discrete ethnic populations, with a central charming historic district all but unknown to outsiders, even those in neighboring sectors of Brooklyn. Its modern history began with the surveying of its lands in 1832 by *Dr. Eliphalet Nott*, president of Union College, in Schenectady (America's first architecturally planned campus), and *Neziah Bliss*. Much of it was purchased for development by *Ambrose C. Kingsland*, mayor of New York (1851-1853), and *Samuel J. Tilden*, who went on to fame in politics and who is happily remembered for leaving a bequest for the establishment of a free public library in New York, an act that triggered the merger of the Astor and Lenox Libraries, and the establishment of the New York Public Library.

The area soon became a great shipbuilding center. It was here, at the **Continental Iron Works** at West and Calyer Streets, that *Thomas F.*

Romanesque revivals. *Leonard* and *Naughton* were sequentially architects for Brooklyn's schools; *Leonard* from 1859-1879, *Naughton* following until 1898.

[G2] **Greenpoint Historic District,** roughly from Java to Calyer Sts., Franklin to Manhattan Aves.

A rich trove of intact churches with both row and free-standing housing. Pride of ownership here translates into buildings maintained (for the most part) in their original shape.

[G3] **Greenpoint Savings Bank,** 807 Manhattan Ave., SW cor. Calyer St. 1908. *Helmle & Huberty.*

Roman pomp under a pantheon dome, shingled delightfully in a fish-scaled pattern in slate. The Pantheon in Rome was similarly shingled but in bronze, stolen for valuable metal in medieval times. This grand Doric-columned bank wears limestone over a granite base.

G4

Rowland built the ironclad warship **Monitor** from plans created by *John Ericsson*. The "Yankee cheesebox on a raft" was launched on January 30, 1862, and battled the Confederate **Merrimack** at Hampton Roads, Va., two months later.

By 1860 the so-called five black arts (printing, pottery, gas, glass, and iron) were firmly established in Green Point, as it was first known. In 1867, *Charles Pratt* established his kerosene refinery (Astral Oil Works)—the first successful American oil well had flowed in 1859 at Titusville, Pa. *Pratt's* product later gave rise to the slogan, "The holy lamps of Tibet are primed with Astral Oil." Astral Oil provided the wealth that later made possible Pratt Institute, myriad Pratt family mansions, as well as Greenpoint's Astral Apartments.

[G1] **Public School 34,** Brooklyn, **The Oliver H. Perry School,** Norman Ave. bet. Eckford St. and McGuinness Blvd. N side. Central block, 1867. Additions, 1870, *Samuel B. Leonard.* Wings, 1887-1888, *James W. Naughton.*

An austere mixture of **Renaissance** and

[G4] **St. Elias Greek Rite Catholic Church**/formerly **Reformed Dutch Church of Greenpoin**t, 149 Kent St., bet. Manhattan Ave. and Franklin St. N side. Church, 1869-1970, *William B. Ditmars.* Sunday school, 1879, *W. Wheeler Smith.*

Bulky brick, brownstone, and whitestone, with Victorian Gothic polychromy (note the alternating red and gray voussoirs) promoted by writer-architectural historian *John Ruskin* and hence termed **Ruskinian Gothic.** Note the cast-iron fence with its Gothic crests, and the octagonal Sunday school.

[G5a] **Church of the Ascension** (Episcopal), 129 Kent St., bet. Manhattan Ave. and Franklin St. N side. 1865-1866. *Henry Dudley.*

Granite ashlar with brownstone trim, a double-pitched silhouette with red Episcopal doors. Its low and friendly scale is reminiscent of an English country church. Note the three oval oculi.

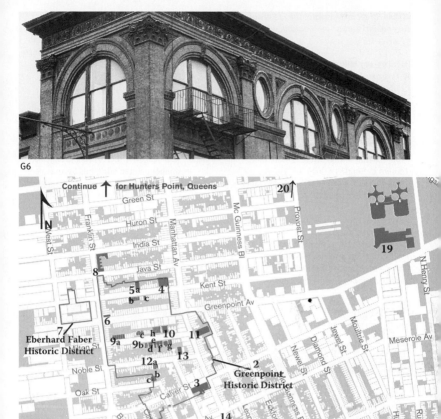

G6

[Map with numerous numbered labels. Visible text includes:]

Continue ↑ for Hunters Point, Queens

Green St

N

Huron St

India St

Java St

Kent St

Greenpoint Av

Eberhard Faber
Historic District

Noble St

Oak St

Quay St

Calyer St

Meserole Av

Guernsey St

Norman Av

N 15th St

N 14th St

N 13th St

Continue ↓ for Williamsburg

Franklin St
West St
Manhattan Av
Mc Guinness Bl
Provost St

Greenpoint
Historic District

N Henry St
Meserole Av
Diamond St
Jewel St
Moultrie St
Newel St
Eckford St
Leonard St
Lorimer St
Manhattan Av
Nassau Av
Driggs Av
Humboldt St
Russell St
Nassau A

20
19
17
16
15
18
14
1
2
3
13
11
10
8
6
7
5a
b c
4
9a 9b
12a
b
c

[G5b] **114-124 Kent Street Houses**, bet. Manhattan Ave. and Franklin St. S side. 1867-1868.

Cast-iron lintels and sheet metal cornices enliven plain brick façades.

[G5c] **130 Kent Street**, bet. Manhattan Ave. and Franklin St. S side. 1859. *Neziah Bliss*, builder.

A star on this handsome street of town houses. Here a bold Corinthian columned and capitaled porch (cast iron & sheet metal again) enlivens the streetscape.

[G6] Originally **Mechanics and Traders Bank**, 144 Franklin St., NE cor. Greenpoint Ave. ca. 1895.

Brooding but glorious **Renaissance Revival** in Pompeian red terra cotta, brick, and rock-faced brownstone, with grand pilasters crowned by fantastic Composite capitals. A terra-cotta frieze and console-bracketed cornice tame the exuberant bulk below.

[G7] **Eberhard Faber Company Historic District**, bounded by Greenpoint Ave. and West, Kent, and Franklin Sts., ca. 1885-1924. ●✴

An odd duck among historic districts: the remains of eight buildings used as a factory by the famed pencil makers. A **block**, rather than a **district**, of handsome brick buildings, some in better shape than others, but gentrification is predicted. For a view of the East River, stroll one block west on Greenpoint Avenue to **Transmitter Park**.

[G8] **The Astral Apartments**, 184 Franklin St., bet. Java and India Sts. E side. 1885-1886. *Lamb & Rich*. ●✴

Commissioned by *Charles Pratt* as housing for his kerosene refinery workers, designed by the team who created Pratt Institute's Main Building. *Alfred Tredway White* had initiated earlier housing experiments (1878-1879) in Brooklyn with the **Tower & Home** Apartments in Cobble Hill. Astral adds to the picturesque with dormers, grand chimneys, and a façade enlivened with oriels and polygonal bays; the structural steel storefronts use rivets themselves as decoration. A grand Protestant Baroque for the worker.

Milton Street encapsulates the history of Greenpoint's urban row housing, with a display of styles (1868-1909):

[G9a] **93-103 Milton Street**. N side. 1874. *James R. Sparrow, builder.*

Six brickfronted houses (Nos.105-109 were originally three more in a set of nine) that retain delicate archivolts over their entrance doors, curved Renaissance Revival window lintels, each façade once painted individually for identity.

[G9b] **118-120 Milton Street**. S side. 1868. *Thomas C. Smith.*

A sullied Second Empire pair, the roof & cornice bastardized at 120.

[G9c] **119-121, 123-125 Milton Street**. N side. 1876. *Thomas C. Smith.*

Eastlakian forms in cast iron & sheet metal embellish (lintels & cornices) plain brickwork. Some entries still bear the ubiquitous metal canopies vended to the Brooklyn innocent.

[G9g] **140-144 Milton Street**. S side. 1909. *Philemon Tillion.*

The streetscape here is enriched by grand neo-Classical porches at street level, grand neo-Classical cornices above.

[G9h] **141-149 Milton Street**. N side. 1894. *Thomas C. Smith.*

Arched and recessed loggias at the third floor enliven Milton Street's third dimension.

[G10] **St. John's Evangelical Lutheran Church**, 155 Milton St. N side. 1891-1892. *Theobold Engelhardt.*

In somber painted brick, this German neo-Gothic is a stolid place incised with its original name, Evangelische-Lutherische St. Johannes Kirche. Token flying buttresses and lancet windows enliven the façade.

[G11] **St. Anthony of Padua Church**, 862 Manhattan Ave., at the end of Milton St. E side. 1875. *Patrick Charles Keely.*

Attired in red brick and white limestone, a

G9a

G9c

G9e

G10

G9d

[G9d] **122-124 Milton Street**. S side. 1889. *Theobold Engelhardt.*

A profligate duet, here in luxurious brick and brownstone Queen Anne, in architecture of the 1880s labor-intensive society, where custom work was normal. The bracketed canopies over the entrances celebrate entry with elaborate doors and hardware.

[G9e] **128-134 Milton Street**. S side. 1909. *Philemon Tillion.*

Three cool, corniced, and bay-windowed tenements, well-kept and well loved, in brick and limestone.

[G9f] **Greenpoint Reformed Church**/originally **Thomas C. Smith House**, 138 Milton St. S side. 1867. *Thomas C. Smith.*

Italianate **Greek Revival** (those warring peoples could combine in style on occasion). Before 1891 this congregation resided at what is now St. Elias Church, two blocks north on Kent Street.

quasi-cathedral on this religious block offers fancy dress for this mostly dour neighborhood. Its 240-foot spire, at a bend in Manhattan Avenue, is a visual pivot not only for Milton Street and Manhattan Avenue but for all of Greenpoint.

[G12a] **128-132 Noble Street Houses**, bet. Manhattan Ave. and Franklin St. S side. 1867-1868.

Cast-iron lintels for this Italianate row.

[G12b] **Greenpoint Home for the Aged**, 137 Oak St., at the head of Guernsey St. N side. 1887. *Theobold Engelhardt.*

An eclectic brick mansion with Italianate massing and Romanesque Revival arches. But what a cornice!

[G12c] **133-135 Oak Street**, bet. Guernsey St. and Franklin Ave. N side. 1890s.

The rockfaced lintels in juxtaposition with brick arches make a special vocabulary.

[G13] **Union Baptist Church**/originally **First Baptist Church of Greenpoint,** 151 Noble St., bet. Manhattan Ave. and Franklin St. N side. 1863-1865.

An early Romanesque Revival Baptist dissenter from the English Gothic Revivalism of the Protestant Episcopal church—an independent architectural route for lusty Protestant congregations.

[G14] **Sidewalk Clock,** in front of 753 Manhattan Ave. E side. 🛈

One of the City's few remaining freestanding cast-iron clocks, now protected by landmark designation.

[G15] **St. Stanislaus Kostka Vincentian Fathers Church,** 607 Humboldt St., SW cor. Driggs Ave. ca. 1890.

Two complex, asymmetrical, octagonal spires of this, the largest Polish Catholic congregation in Brooklyn, dominate the local skyline. Humboldt Street and Driggs Avenue are here

G12a   G16

G19

Monitor and its designer, *John Ericsson*, and the Shelter Pavilion, reminiscent of the **Grand Trianon** at Versailles.

[G18] **Greenpoint EMS Station,** 332 Metropolitan Ave., bet. Roebling and Havemeyer Sts. 2011. *Michielli + Wyetzner Architects.*

A neat little shed with translucent façade that dips from the second story to form an exit stair that meets the street.

[G19] **Newtown Creek Wastewater Treatment Plant,** 3239 Greenpoint Ave., bet. Provost and N. Henry Sts. 2009. *Polshek Partnership.* Visitor's Center sculpture, *Vito Acconci.*

Bold industrial architecture from *Polshek.* This sprawling complex, the largest of 14 such facilities in New York, where city water is cleaned before being dumped back into the river, could have been merely utilitarian; instead *Polshek* has raised it to the level of great architecture. A series of modernist buildings with swooping roofs are scattered about the site, but

G20

renamed Lech Walesa Place and Pope John Paul II Plaza with the fervency that only a monolithic local ethnic population can supply. The spires' heavy encrustation of stone ornament is in rich contrast to the painted aluminum clapboard and asbestos shingles that line the local streets like exterior wallpaper, *Archie Bunker* style.

[G16] **650 Humboldt Street,** bet. Driggs and Nassau Aves. E side.

An unsullied remnant of wood housing: built for a single family. It demonstrates the texture and color of the community prior to the street's recladding in artificial aluminum, genuine asbestos, and real what-have-you.

[G17] **Monsignor McGolrick Park**/originally **Winthrop Park,** Driggs to Nassau Aves., Russell to Monitor Sts. **Shelter Pavilion,** 1910. *Helmle & Huberty.* 🛈

A park on the scale of London's Bloomsbury, with surrounding row houses too low to supply the same architectural containment. Within is a monument (*Antonio de Filippo,* sculptor), to the

the real stars here are the immense, stainless steel "digestors" where microbes do their work in cleaning the water. Shiny, roughly onion-shaped, they are visible for miles, and add to the beauty of Brooklyn's skyline.

[G20] **Newtown Creek Nature Walk,** foot of Paidge Ave. 2007. *George Trakas,* environmental sculptor.

Newtown Creek divides Brooklyn and Queens and is one of the most polluted bodies of water in the country, laden with toxins, raw sewage, and millions of gallons of spilled oil (which resides in the soil beneath Greenpoint and is slowly being sucked out with an industrial-grade straw). Such a **wasteland** seems a strange place for a **nature walk,** but *Trakas* has designed a meticulous loop of concrete and planting here, featuring all kinds of educational installations and native grasses and trees. Putting a little nature back into the creek is a good idea, but oddly the Nature Walk's most singular feature is the view it affords of *Polshek's* fantastic new Wastewater Treatment Plant.

Central Brooklyn

Town of Flatbush/Vlackebos—"Level Forest"

Established as a town in 1652; Town of New Lots separated from Flatlands in 1852. Annexed to the City of Brooklyn in 1894.

Until the 1880s Flatbush was a quiet place with a rural character. The introduction, in 1878, of the Brooklyn, Flatbush & Coney Island Railroad, now the Brighton Line, encouraged real estate speculation and development that transformed the farmland into a fashionable suburb by the turn of the century. The names of these subdivisions are still used in some cases, only dimly remembered in others: Prospect Park South (the most affluent of those extant),

(1862). These projects were never as successful as those in the quiet, lightly trafficked cul-de-sacs created by the railroad's cut on its way to Brighton Beach. Older names, such as Midwood, a corruption of the Dutch Midwout, are still used in areas that once constituted only a portion of that Dutch enclave.

Prospect-Lefferts Gardens Historic District, roughly bounded by Flatbush Ave., Fenimore St., Rogers Ave. (with a tail that loops almost to Nostrand Ave.), and Empire Blvd. beyond Bedford Ave. ●

A neighborhood of simple, early 20th-century houses in a variety of styles: Romanesque

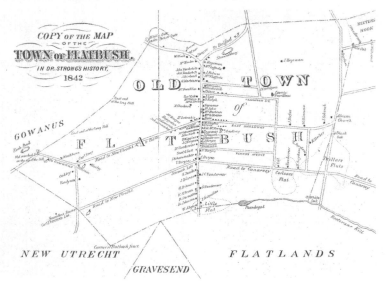

Vanderveer Park, Ditmas Park, Fiske and Manhattan Terraces, and a host of others like Matthews Park, Slocum Park, and Yale Park.

Earlier there had been a series of abortive attempts to impose grids of houses on the countryside, such as Parkville, the off-axis grid surrounding Parkville Avenue (1852); and Windsor Terrace, between Vanderbilt Street and Greenwood Avenue in the corridor separating Green-Wood Cemetery from Prospect Park

Revival, neo-Renaissance, neo-Georgian, neo-Federal, and neo-Tudor. Here is a classic case where the whole is greater than the sum of its parts, where the ensemble—rather than individual buildings—is the landmark. The product is best savored at the Renaissance Revival rows on Maple and Midwood (ca. 1910. *Alex Hedman*); and the Colonial Revival and neo-Medieval Rows on Fenimore and Midwood Streets and Rutland Road (1920s. *Slee & Bryson*).

CENTRAL FLATBUSH

[F1] **111 Clarkson Avenue** (house), bet. Bedford and Rogers Aves. N side. 1902. *Hugo von Wiedenfeld.*

A once fairyland place that might be termed **berserk eclecticism.** The onion domes were redolent of John Nash's Royal Pavilion at Brighton (England, not Beach). A continuing tragedy of neglect.

[F2] **Erasmus Hall Museum**/originally **Erasmus Hall Academy,** in the courtyard of **Erasmus Hall High School,** 899-925 Flatbush Ave., bet. Church and Snyder Aves. E side. 1786.

Established as a private academy by the Flatbush Reformed Dutch Church across the street. The site was previously occupied by the first public school in Midwout (Midwood), erected in 1658 by the New Netherlands Colony. The Academy building is **Georgian-Federal** with

F7

a hipped-gambrel roof and a Palladian window over a delicate Tuscan-columned porch.

Warning: Rule 9, Erasmus Hall Academy, 1797: "No student shall be permitted any species of gaming nor to drink any spiritous liquors nor to go into any tavern in Flat Bush without obtaining consent of a teacher."

[F3] **Erasmus Hall High School.** 1905-1911. *C.B.J. Snyder.* 1924-1925, *William Gompert.* 1939-1940. *Eric Kebbon.*

Snyder introduced the **Collegiate Gothic** style to New York public school architecture. The high school's buff brick façades (limestone and terra cotta) project oriel windows and crenellations at the sky.

[F4] Originally **Flatbush Town Hall,** 35 Snyder Ave., bet. Flatbush and Bedford Aves. N side. 1874-1875. *John Y. Culyer.*

Flatbush did not become part of Brooklyn until 1894. This lusty Ruskinian Gothic building is happily being preserved as a community center.

[F5] **P.S. 6,** Bedford Ave., NW cor. Snyder St. 1992. *Gruzen Samton.*

A busy place, both in the sense of resident children and the architecture that encloses them (fences, piers, towers, gables). They probably like it.

F3

[F6] **Flatbush District No.1 School**/later **P. S. 90,** 2274 Church Ave., SW cor. Bedford Ave. 1878. *John Y. Culyer.* Addition ca. 1890-1894.

Abandoned and neglected.

[F7] **Flatbush Dutch Reformed Church,** 866 Flatbush Ave., SW cor. Church Ave. 1793-1798. *Thomas Fardon.*

A rough, horizontally coursed-stone ashlar (Manhattan schist) church with Romanesque arched windows and doors. Crowning is a Georgian white-painted octagonal tower with Tuscan colonnettes surmounted by urns. The first of three churches built according to the mandate of *Governor Peter Stuyvesant* (the others were the **Flatland Dutch Reformed Church** and the **First Reformed Church);** this, however, is the third building to occupy the site.

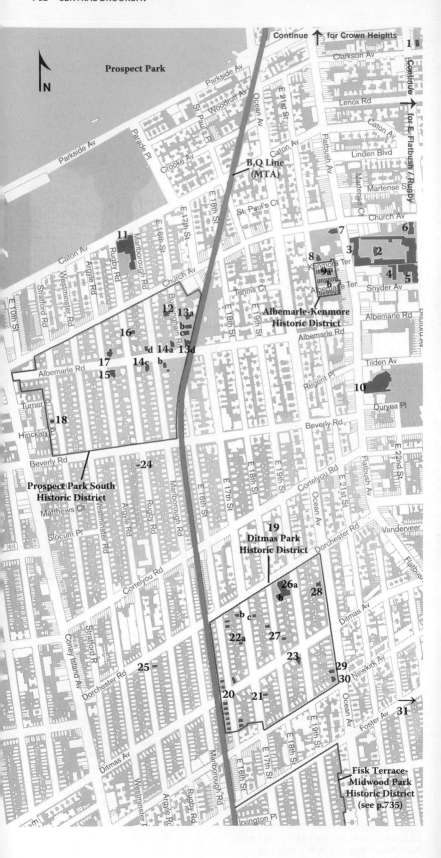

[F8] **Parsonage,** 2101-2103 Kenmore Terrace, NE cor. E. 21st St. Moved in 1918 from 900 Flatbush Ave. 1853. **Church House,** 1923-1924. *Meyer & Mathieu.*

Walk through the churchyard from Church Avenue, and you will pass delicately incised brownstone gravestones with elegant calligraphy. (Strangely, the limestone markers have eroded, washing off their graphics, while the brownstone survives.) Continue past the meetinghouse of the 1930s onto Kenmore Terrace. On the right is the **Parsonage,** a glorious late Greek Revival painted-shingled house with a gracious Corinthian-columned veranda, and a handsome cornice of dentils and Italianate modillions.

[F9] **Albemarle-Kenmore Terraces Historic District,** includes all row houses on the two streets listed below.

[F9a] **Kenmore Terrace,** E of E.21st St., bet. Church Ave. and Albemarle Rd. South houses, 1917-1920. *Slee & Bryson.*

F9a

F10

The Flatbush Reformed Church Parsonage forms one flank, and these pleasant English Arts and Crafts Revival row cottages, the other.

[F9b] **Albemarle Terrace,** E of E. 21st St., bet. Church Ave. and Albemarle Rd. 1916-1917. *Slee & Bryson.*

Charming **Georgian Revival** row houses in a cul-de-sac that says dead end but is far from dead. The simple brick architecture is enlivened by alternating bay and Palladian windows, entry porches, and dormers in the slate mansard roofs.

ENDANGERED

[F10] **Loew's Kings Theater,** Flatbush Ave., bet. Tilden Ave. and Beverly Rd. E side. 1929. *C.W. Rapp & George L. Rapp.*

With its ornate eclectic terra-cotta façade, this is one of the last movie palaces of that vibrant era when going to the movies was as much an adventure as watching the movie on the screen. Abandoned since 1977, a restoration is finally promised, with conversion to a live performance space by 2014.

PROSPECT PARK SOUTH

The streets between Church Avenue and Beverly Road, Coney Island Avenue and the Brighton Line subway's open cut, contain as unique a community as any in the City. The entrances to most of the streets are guarded by pairs of sturdy brick piers bearing cast-concrete plaques with the letters PPS in bas-relief. The area is Prospect Park South, characterized at the time of its initial development as *rus in urbe,* or "the country in the city," a description not inappropriate even today. Here is an environment that ranks with Forest Hills and Kew Gardens in Queens as an architecturally distinguished precinct of grand freestanding turn-of-the-century single-family houses.

PPS is a monument to the vision of the realtor *Dean Alvord.* What he conceived was a garden park within the confines of the grid, abandoning the row house urbanization that had infilled most of old Brooklyn, from the Heights

F12

to Bedford-Stuyvesant, from Greenpoint to Park Slope. To these ends he installed all the utilities and paved all the streets before selling one plot of land. Trees were planted not along the curb but at the building line, giving the streets a greater sense of breadth. Alternating every 20 feet were Norway maples for permanence, and Carolina poplars for immediate shade. The short-lived poplars, *Alvord* and his architect, *John Petit,* reasoned, would die out as the maples reached maturity.

[F11] **Addition, P.S.249, The Caton School,** 18 Marlborough Road, SW cor. Caton Ave. 2004. *GranKriegel.*

Not the Arc de Triomphe, but bold exposed steel bracing forms the **triumphant triangle** under which students enter. Arc de Caton.

Prospect Park South Historic District, generally bet. Church Ave. and Beverly Road, and from a line E of Coney Island Ave. to the Brighton Line's subway cut.

[F12] Originally **Russell Benedict House**, 104 Buckingham Rd., bet. Church Ave. and Albemarle Rd. W side. 1902. *Carroll H. Pratt.*

An architecture of columns, pilasters and cornices (Composite Ionic order, **Classical Revival**), where shingles (painted) are the incidental infill. A stylish place that has made a stylish recovery.

[F13a] Originally **William H. McEntee House**, 115 Buckingham Rd., bet. Church Ave. and Albemarle Rd. E side. 1900. *John J. Petit.*

A volumetric exercise in the **Shingle Style**: gambrel-roofed, incised for a porch and anchored by a corner "bell"-capped tower. The weathered shingles suggest a New England attitude (they were originally painted).

[F13b] Originally **George U. Tompers House**, 125 Buckingham Rd., bet. Church Ave. and Albemarle Rd. E side. 1911. *Brun & Hauser.*

F13d

F13a

F14a

Corinthian columns and finely scaled clapboard. An Americanized Roman temple as seen through Renaissance eyes.

[F13c] Originally **Frederick S. Kolle House**, 131 Buckingham Rd., bet. Church Ave. and Albemarle Rd. E side. 1902-1903. *Petit & Green.*

Japanese fancy dress on a stucco body. Sticks and struts, corbels and brackets, give a timber-structuralist look to what is a rather plain box underneath. *Alvord's* advertisement in Country Life described the interior as "a faithful reflection of the dainty Japanese art from which America is learning so much."

[F13d] Originally **William A. Norwood House**, 143 Buckingham Rd., NE cor. Albemarle Rd. 1906. Walter S. Cassin.

The **Italian Villa** style best exemplified in Brooklyn at Prospect Park's 1857 Litchfield Mansion. A sturdy tower overlooks the neighborhood.

Backyards: Today's four-track Brighton Line, which abuts the rear yards of the houses on the east side of Buckingham Road, was at the time of the original development only a two-track operation. In 1907 the Brooklyn Rapid Transit Company, successors to the original railroad and precursors of the later BMT, widened the cut, thus narrowing the backyards of these houses to the nominal amount visible today. Eminent domain is the villain.

[F14a] Originally **Louis McDonald House**, 1519 Albemarle Rd., NW cor. Buckingham Rd. 1902. *John J. Petit.*

To complement the adjacent Roman temple and Italian villa, *Petit* produced an all-American anti-Classical example (influenced by the Chicago School). The columns seem almost abstract caryatids: Ionic coiffures, tapered torsos with bas-relief.

[F14b] Originally **Maurice Minton House**, 1510 Albemarle Rd., SE cor. Marlborough Rd. 1900. *John J. Petit.*

A stately mansion with a grand conservatory and stable. Giant **Corinthian** columns and pilasters are enhanced by elegant narrow clapboarding.

[F14c] Originally **J. C. Woodhull House**, 1440 Albemarle Rd., SW cor. Marlborough Rd. 1905. *Robert Bryson and Carroll Pratt.*

Another **Queen Anne/Colonial Revival** hybrid, sullied by the bizarre asphalt sheeting simulating stone that replaced its original painted clapboarding. But what an entry with gallery above: break out the trumpets.

[F14d] Originally **Francis M. Crafts House**, 1423 Albemarle Rd., NW cor. Marlborough Rd. 1899. *John J. Petit.*

A veritable **Queen Anne** gem: shingled, gabled, with a bump here and a shimmy there. It reeks of romance.

F14c

[F15] Originally **John S. Eakins House**, 1306 Albemarle Rd., SE cor. Argyle Rd. 1905. *John J. Petit.*

The **Shingle Style** with a **Colonial Revival,** Tuscan-colonnaded porch. The house has been reclad with aluminum siding, a hideous mistake, obliterating the wood detailing, savaging the round corner tower.

[F16] **101 Rugby Road** (house), bet. Church Ave. and Albemarle Rd. 1890s.

The Shingle Style meets the French Renaissance, as seen through a Colonial Revival prism. **Electric eclectic.**

[F17] Originally **George E. Gale House**, 1305 Albemarle Rd., NE cor. Argyle Rd. 1905. *H. B. Moore.*

A well-preserved Classical Revival house, with eccentric second-story balconies behind the monumental two-story Ionic portico, shades of *Harry Truman's* efforts at that other White House. Those eyebrows peering from the roof bring a bit of the Shingle Style (shingles wrapping curving form) into this Classical equation.

[F18] Originally **Herman Goetze House**, 156 Stratford Rd., bet. Hinckley and Turner Places. 1905. *George Hitchings.*

Four-columned Roman temple with a Palladian-windowed bedroom in its pediment. Elegant Corinthian columns and pilasters, narrow clapboard, with stone quoins simulated in wood.

F15

F16

NECROLOGY

Knickerbocker Field Club, 114 E.18th St. at W end of Tennis Court. 1892-1893. *Parfitt Brothers.* 🖤

Until the 1980s concealed between apartment buildings on East 18th Street and the subway exit, this was a sprawling Shingle Style building: gambrel roofs and Tuscan-Columned porches.

DITMAS PARK

[F19] **Ditmas Park Historic District**, generally surrounded by Ocean, Dorchester, and Newkirk Aves., and the Brighton Line subway cut. 🖊️
Another significant but modest turn-of-the-century development in the spirit of Prospect Park South. Builder *Lewis Pounds* and architect *Arlington Isham*, in particular, created a district of **Bungalow Style**, **Colonial Revival**, and **neo-Tudor** houses.

[F20] **Bungalows**, East 16th Street, Newkirk to Ditmas Aves., and a stretch N of Ditmas Ave. Nos.511, 515, 519, 523, 549, E side, and Nos.490, 494, 500, 510, 514, 518, 522, 550, W side. 1908-1909. *Arlington Isham.*
Bungalows, in the **Shingle Style**, with steeply pitched roofs over front porches supported by columns frequently fat, sometimes polygonal, occasionally round. These are the brethren of myriad bungalows born in California

F20

and dotting the Midwest, which are supposedly Bengal style: sun-shielded and deeply sheltered from the sun. Brooklyn is milder, but, when leaving, please wear your topee.

[F21] Originally **Harry Grattan House**, 543 E.17th St., bet. Ditmas and Newkirk Aves. E side. 1906. *Arlington D. Isham.*
The blending of **Queen Anne** and **Colonial Revival**: dark stained shingles clad the volume, short Tuscan columns support brackets rather than a Classical abacus and frieze.

[F22a] Originally **Thomas A. Radcliffe House**, 484 E.17th St., bet. Dorchester Rd. and Ditmas Ave. W side. 1902. *Arlington Isham.*
A polygonal corner tower with a Classical swagged frieze bears a finialed hat, while multiple gables form picturesque profiles against the sky. Another blend of **Queen Anne** and **Colonial**.

[F22b] Originally **Paul Ames House**, 456 E.19th St., bet. Dorchester Rd. and Ditmas Ave. W side. 1910. *Arne Delhi.*
In **Spanish Mission** style with a bracketed tile roof, intersected by a third-story stepped and rounded (Dutch?) pediment. An exotic composition by a Norwegian architect practicing in Brooklyn.

[F22c] Originally **Arthur Ebinger House**, 445 E.19th St., bet. Dorchester Rd. and Ditmas Ave. E side. 1931. *Foster & Gallimore.*
Slate-roofed, tapestry-brick cottage, with a multifaceted chimney at the street—the fantasy of **England** brought to Brooklyn suburbia. Buried in foliage, its architecture doesn't wish to join the street.

[F23] Originally **George U. Tompers House**, 1890 Ditmas Ave., SW cor. E. 19th St. 1904. *Arlington Isham.*
Stately **Shingle Style/Colonial Revival**, steeply shingled roofs, and, best of all, a corner tower and vast porch. The latter hugs Classicism with a dentiled cornice and Tuscan columns. Seven years later *Tompers* purchased the Roman temple at 125 Buckingham Road.

[F24] **242 Rugby Road** (house), bet. Beverly and Cortelyou Rds. W side. ca. 1890.
Extraordinary **Shingle Style** volumes crowned with a polygonal onion-dome. Most

F22a   F23

Ditmas Park neighbors present columned projecting Colonial Revival porches. 242 harbors the porch within its volume.

[F25] **449 Argyle Road**, bet. Dorchester Rd. and Ditmas Ave. E side. ca. 1905. *Irving Farquharson.*
More near-perfect **Shingle Style**, this one with exaggerated geometries featuring an oversized double triangular upper story over a Doric-columned porch. The best Shingles anticipated the reductive abstraction of modernism.

[F26a] **Flatbush-Tompkins Congregational Church**, E. 18th St., SE cor. Dorchester Rd. 1910. *Allens & Collins, with Louis Jallade.*
A Georgian body with a **Greek Revival** Temple front, surmounted by a tower that *Christopher Wren* might have left behind. Mixed signals: an academic assemblage. Check the parish house for chutzpah.

[F26b] **Flatbush-Tompkins (originally Flatbush) Congregational Church Parish House**, 451 E.18th St., SE cor. Dorchester Rd. 1899. Whitfield & King.

A bold polygonal dark Shingle Style parish house that, if it were a complete form, would have 16 sides: a **hexadecagon**.

[F27] **499 East 18th Street** (house), bet. Dorchester Rd. and Ditmas Ave. 1890s.
Dour colors of the era combine with crisp architectural forms: a Queen Anne/Shingle Style/Colonial Revival interweave. The porch columns however, in dark green, belie the Classic spirit they represent.

F24

F26b

[F28] Originally **George Ramsey House**, 900 Ocean Ave., bet. Dorchester and Ditmas Aves. W side. 1910. *Charles G. Ramsey.*
A bland Colonial Revival house completed by an Ionic-columned porte-cochère. This is what happens when you get your brother to design your house.

[F29] Originally **George Van Ness House**, 1000 Ocean Ave., bet. Ditmas and Newkirk Aves. W side. 1899. *George Palliser.*
Once a gracious **Roman Revival** mansion, its Corinthian columns have vanished. The pediment survives, supported by crude square replacements. No.1010 next door shows what history has lost.

[F30] Originally **Thomas H. Brush House**, 1010 Ocean Ave., NW cor. Newkirk Ave. 1899. George Palliser.
A splendid **Georgian** mansion in red brick and white limestone, presenting Composite Ionic columns and pilasters to the street. The

Palladian window in the pediment is another bedroom, a trick that the Parthenon missed.

*The newly designated **Fiske Terrace-Midwood Park Historic District** begins only one block south of the Ditmas Park Historic District (can't we combine them?), from Foster Street to Avenue H. That district is covered in the Midwood section of this Guide (p. 735).*

A Shingle Style refugee to the southeast, not in either historic district:

[F31] **2693 Bedford Avenue** (house), bet. Foster Ave. and Farragut Rd. E side. ca. 1892.
Shingle Style: a powerful volumetric interplay results from the juxtaposition of deeply shadowed circular recesses and rectangular windows.

F29

EAST FLATBUSH/RUGBY

[E1] **SUNY Downstate Medical Center.**
Roughly bounded by Clarkson, New York and Albany Avenues and Winthrop Street, stepping down to Lenox Road, between New York and Brooklyn Avenues.

The various buildings listed next are within the rubric of this Center:

[E2] **Hospital and Intensive Care Unit**, 445 Lenox Rd. N side. 1966. *Max O. Urbahn.*
Concrete graph paper from a time when that meant Style. Certainly, the serious progeny of *Mies van der Rohe* should be honored for their austere discipline, but this one inspires only yawns.

[E2a] **SUNY Health Sciences Center**, Lenox Rd., bet. New York Ave. and E.34th St. 1992. *The Eggers Group.*

A sleek and monumental megabuilding for medical students. The *Eggers* have outdone themselves, but another staff member might have better designed the way in.

[E3] **Dormitories**, New York Ave., bet. Lenox Rd. and Linden Blvd. E side. 1966. *Max O. Urbahn.*

Nurses' and interns' dwellings with **Miami**

E2a

Beach styling, here seemingly stacked picture frames? An alien colony in these East Flatbush blocks.

[E4] **Kings County Hospital,** Clarkson Ave., bet. Brooklyn and Albany Aves. N side. 1931. *Leroy P. Ward,* architect. *S. S. Goldwater, M.D.,* consultant.

The **Bellevue** of **Brooklyn.** A high rise with bay windows, a brick body, and Spanish tile roofs, all crowned with marvelous towers and finials. This is rich architecture, reminding us that hospitals don't necessarily have to look like machines.

WINDSOR TERRACE

[W1] **Engine Company 240**, N.Y.C. Fire Department, 1309 Prospect Ave., bet. Greenwood Ave. and Ocean Pkwy. E side. 1896.

Brick, rock-faced limestone, and slate: castellated Romanesque Revival with a corner oriel (its turret has gone) and an arched corbel table. *Louis Sullivan* could have been here.

PARKVILLE

[K1] **Ocean Parkway**, designated a scenic landmark from Church to Seabreeze Aves. 1874-1876. *Frederick Law Olmsted and Calvert Vaux.* 🍎

Six miles of tree-planted malls linking Prospect Park to Coney Island. An addition to the system of parkways proposed by *Olmsted & Vaux* when planning Eastern Parkway.

W1

NECROLOGY

Parkville Congregational Church, 18th Ave., NW cor. E.5th St. 1895.

The stepped and shingled brackets of the gable, with its hipped-roof belfry, brought exotic detail to this lovely remnant, notable for its Victorian milk glass.

Southwestern Brooklyn

S1a

SUNSET PARK AND ENVIRONS

Named for its park, from which a sloping greensward provides sweeping views of the harbor. Once almost exclusively Scandinavian, the community shelters a broad ethnic mix, with a large Latino population. On the flats between the elevated Gowanus Expressway (over Third Avenue and a continuation of the Brooklyn-Queens Expressway) and the waterfront lie the Bush Terminal at the north and the old Brooklyn Army Terminal at the south. Beginning a few blocks north of Sunset Park's park is the magnificent, and enormous, Victorian burying ground, **Green-Wood Cemetery**.

[S1] **Green-Wood Cemetery,** Fifth Ave. to Macdonald Ave. and Fort Hamilton Pkwy., 20th to 37th Sts. 1840.

Brooklyn's first park by default (1840), long before **Prospect Park** was created. Here, on the highest points in Brooklyn, 478 acres of rolling landscape offered opportunities for Sunday strolling among the hills, ponds and plantings, with superb views of the harbor. Most of the more than half-million buried here (including *Henry Ward Beecher, Nathaniel Currier and James Ives, Peter Cooper, Samuel F. B. Morse, "Boss" Tweed,* and *Lola Montez*) are remembered by extraordinary mausoleums and monuments. A veritable history of New York Victoriana is indexed by the **gravestones, pyramids, obelisks, cairns, temples,** and lesser markers.

[S1a] **Main Green-Wood Entrance Gate and Gatehouse,** 5th Ave. opp.25th St. E side. 1861-1865. *Richard M. Upjohn of Richard Upjohn & Son.* Restored 2000. *Platt Byard Dovell White.* 🍃

At the main entrance, appropriately, stands a wondrous gatehouse, the **Gothic Revival** equivalent of a pair of **Roman** triumphal arches. Both a building and a gate, it was called the culmination of the Gothic Revival movement in New York by historian *Alan Burnham*.

[S1b] **Fort Hamilton Parkway Gate and Gatehouse,** 37th St. W of Ft. Hamilton Pkwy. 1875. *Richard M. Upjohn.* Restorations, 1996, *Platt Byard Dovell.* Open to the public. Inquire at gate.

At the **Fort Hamilton** parkway entrance, a

S4

Second Empire brownstone country château, happily preserved (and recently restored), from the era when Fifth Avenue was lined with many of its architectural cousins.

[S1c] **Green-Wood Hillside IV Mausoleum,** 2006. *Platt Byard Dovell White.*
[S1d] **Green-Wood Columbarium.** 2007. between the main gate and the chapel (1911. *Warren & Wetmore*). *Platt Byard Dovell White.*

Not a mournful place, but an elegance of glass and limestone, awash with light. Built into a steep hillside, it strews its skylight among the tombstones. Check the columbarium by the same architects.

[S2] **McGovern-Weir Florist**/formerly **Weir & Company Greenhouse,** Fifth Ave., SW cor. 25th St. 1895. *G. Curtis Gillespie.* 🍃

Sadly, this once-charming miniature crystal palace is sullied by inappropriate additions, alterations, and signs: once a garden showplace serving Green-Wood opposite. One apocryphal story says that it was moved to Brooklyn from the **St. Louis World's Fair** of 1904.

Continue ↑ for Park Slope

Continue ↓ for Bay Ridge

[S3] **Alku Toinen** (Finnish cooperative apartments), 826 43rd St., bet. Eighth and Ninth Aves. S side. 1916.

Reputedly the first non-profit cooperative dwelling in New York City. With understated architecture, it wears a palette of tan Scandinavian brick. Visit it more for its social history than any architectural revelations.

[S4] **Sunset Play Center**, N.Y.C. Department of Parks & Recreation, in Sunset Park at 7th Ave., bet. 41st and 44th Sts. W side. 1934-1936. *Herbert Magoon*, lead architect. *Aymar Embury II, Harry Ahrens and others*, consulting architects. ● First floor interior. ●

Sleek round forms dominate one of several similar sports and aquatic centers built during the depression by the WPA (Red Hook and McCarren are two others in Brooklyn).

[S5] **43rd Street Row Housing**, bet. Seventh and Eighth Aves. 1898-1904.

Bow-fronted yellow brick houses that are the staple of Sunset Park. Their cornices and brick-decorated belt courses are still intact.

[S6] **43rd Street Row Housing**, bet. Fourth and Fifth Aves. ca. 1885.

The topography gives these repetitive three-story brownstone units a chance to form character as a group, stepping merrily down the hill to Fourth.

[S7] **St. Michael's Roman Catholic Church**, 4200 Fourth Ave., SW cor. 42nd St. 1905. *Raymond F. Almirall.*

From his days at the École des Beaux Arts in Paris, *Almirall* recalls the shape of Sacré Coeur's domes (Paris, 1884. *Paul Abadie*). Marooned atop a spire, the "beehive" dominates the local skyline.

[S8] Formerly **68th Precinct Station House and Stable**/originally **18th Police Precinct House and Stable**, 4302 Fourth Ave., SW cor. 43rd St. 1890-1892. *Emile Gruwe.* ●

Although nearly a ruin, its Romanesque Revival architecture is so powerful that remnants express vigor even in their despair. We had hoped that the Sunset Park School of Music (who bought the building) would arrive with musicians soon. But rumor has it that a Chinese-American group might take charge. Someone, PLEASE. This is a major landmark.

[S9] **Bush Terminal**, 28th to 37th Sts., 3rd to 2nd Aves. (irregular). Buildings 1-4, 1911. 5-13 and 19-26, various years to 1926. *William Higginson.*

   Irving T. Bush introduced industrial buildings to these flatlands in 1890. Block after block of eight-story, white-painted buildings are the result of this mammoth industrial and warehousing enterprise, each building delivering three acres on any one floor.

In the neighborhood are older brick industrial structures around First Avenue and the 40s, such as:

[S10] Originally **National Metal Company**, 4201-4207 First Ave., SE cor. 42nd St. ca. 1890.

embellished his better-known buildings with ornament and sculpture —the Woolworth Building in Manhattan and Washington's Supreme Court, among many other confections. But when military functionalism was the order of the day, he could be as austere as *Gropius*, and almost as mum as *Mies.*

[S13] Originally **N.Y.S. Arsenal**/now **Keeper's Self-Storage Warehouse**, Second Ave., bet. 63rd and 64th Sts. E side. 1925.

   A grim, onetime ordnance and quartermaster facility, with limestone quoins and a battered base. Unhappily, its new owners have stripped the façade of the ivy that had once muted these bleak walls.

[S14] **Engine Company 201**, 5113 4th Ave., bet. 51st and 52nd Sts. 2009. *Rothzeid Kaiserman Thomson & Bee.*

   A firehouse built as part of the City's Department of Design and Construction **Design Excellence Program**, in which smaller firms are

S7   S8   S10

S12

A crenellated neo-Gothic tower is the local campanile. A wonderful mark in the landscape— and an enigma. But the enigma may not last if a lover cannot be found.

[S11] **68th Precinct, N.Y.C. Police Department**, 333 65th St., bet Third and Fourth Aves. N side. 1970. *Milton F. Kirchman.*

   An aggressive cubistic set of volumes and voids. In the loose civic commissions of the mid and late 1960s, architectural histrionics preempted any truly urbane attempts to blend into the scale and style of the neighborhood.

[S12] Originally **New York Port of Embarkation and Army Supply Base**, also known as **Brooklyn Army Terminal**/officially **Military Ocean Terminal**, Second Ave., bet. 58th and 65th Sts. W side. 1918. *Cass Gilbert.*

   These World War I exposed concrete embarkation warehouses are vast and appropriately devoid of extraneous ornament. The innards contain long skylit central galleries. *Gilbert*, not known for decorative restraint,

awarded civic projects they normally wouldn't stand a prayer of landing (community centers, police precincts, parks). This fine example shows that the program is succeeding.

NECROLOGY

Second Battalion Armory, N.Y. Naval Militia, 5100 First Ave., bet. 51st and 52nd Sts. W side. Sunset Park. 1904. *Lord & Hewlett.*

   A spectacular parabolic arched naval armory, visible from both land and harbor. No attempt was made here to conceal its structural form but, rather, to embellish it with a romantic façade of crenellated towers and battlements. Abandoned for years, it was demolished mercilessly in favor of a bland one-story post office.

Town of New Utrecht/Nieuw Utrecht
    Established as a town in 1662; annexed to the City of Brooklyn in 1894.
    The old Town of New Utrecht includes the present-day communities of Bay Ridge, Fort Hamilton, Dyker Heights, Borough Park, Bath Beach, and much of Bensonhurst. At various times in its past, other, barely remembered communities were identified within its boundaries —Blythebourne, Mapleton, Lefferts Park, and Van Pelt Manor— and the area was largely rural until the beginning of the 20th century.

B3

BAY RIDGE/FORT HAMILTON/DYKER HEIGHTS

Many of Brooklyn's most desirable residential sites lay along the high ground overlooking the Narrows and Gravesend Bay. Inevitably this best of topography became the site of magnificent mansions along Shore Road and the sometime higher ground behind, and along Eleventh Avenue in Dyker Heights. The ornate villa of *E.W. Bliss*, of Greenpoint fame; *Neils Poulson's* cast-iron fantasy, by the founder of Williamsburg's Iron Works; Fontbonne Hall, the home of *Tom L. Johnson*, the "three-cent mayor of Cleveland"; and many others lined the bluff overlooking the harbor. In the *Chandler* White House the group headed by *Cyrus Field* and *Peter Cooper* first gathered to discuss the laying of the Atlantic cable. The *Bliss* mansion was once the home of *Henry Cruse Murphy*, who, in 1865, met there with *William C. Kingsley* and *Alexander McCue* to formulate the original agreement for the construction of the Brooklyn

Bridge. Except for **Fontbonne Hall,** now a private school, all the mansions have been supplanted by endless ranks of elevator apartment buildings, forming a palisade of red brick along the edge of Shore Road.

[B1] **Gateway City Church & Academy**/onetime **Bay Ridge Masonic Temple**/originally **New Utrecht N. Y. Exempt Firemen's Association,** 257-259 Bay Ridge Ave., bet. Ridge Blvd. and 3rd Aves. N side. ca. 1890. Later additions & conversions.
    A fine exercise in above-ground archaeology. Look carefully at the entrance cornice and keystones over the windows. They bear the old volunteer fire company's seals and names (including the now disappeared community of **Blythebourne**). Once symmetrical around its ornate entrance, changes in brick color reveal the point of addition.

The Pier at the foot of Bay Ridge Avenue gives a promontory for viewers of the whole bay:

B6

tankers tug at anchors surrounding, and the distant views of the Verrazano Bridge, Staten Island, and the lower Manhattan skyline, make this a Brooklyn version of Battery Park.

[B2] **Madeline Court,** 68th St., bet. Ridge Blvd. and Third Ave. ca. 1940s.
    An urban space in this in-town suburbia, brick and slate-roofed where the whole is again serving as master of its architecturally undistinguished parts.

[B3] **Salem Evangelical Lutheran Church,** 355 Ovington St., bet. Third and Fourth Aves. N side. ca. 1940.
    A cascade of stepped gables enliven this north German-Swedish-Dutch brick vernacular church: handsome profiles crenellate the sky.

[B4] **Flagg Court,** 7200 Ridge Blvd., bet. 72nd and 73rd Sts. W side. 1933-1936. *Ernest Flagg.*
    Flagg Court, named for its architect (see the little **Singer Building** and his own Staten Island mansion), is a 422-unit housing development

B7

contained in six contiguous buildings. Among avant-garde features were reversible fans below the windows (long since gone), window shades on the outside of windows (the intelligent heat shield, also gone), concrete slabs serving as finished ceilings (commonplace in current architecture), and an auditorium of vaulted concrete. A prescient architect in his time.

[B5] **131 76th Street**, bet. Ridge Blvd. and Colonial Rd. N side. 1865.

A grand gray neo-Georgian stuccoed mansion, with a white Composite-columned porch. An aerie over the harbor.

[B6] **122 76th Street**, bet. Ridge Blvd. and Colonial Rd. S side. ca. 1900.

Neo-Gothic, the romantic return to Gothic shapes and details around 1900, here makes street theater: perhaps a set from the "Black Forest." Perched (with No.131 above) on a bluff rising 61 steps from Colonial Road.

[B7] **Howard E. and Jessie Jones House**, 8220 Narrows Avenue, NW cor.83rd St. 1916-1917. *J. Sarsfield Kennedy.*

Disguised as a witch's hideaway. Black Forest Art Nouveau. Bumpety stone and pseudo-thatchery make this Arts and Crafts revival one of Brooklyn's great private fantasies.

[B8] **163 and 175 81st Street**, bet. Ridge Blvd. and Colonial Road. N side. ca. 1880.

Shingle Style, conical capped, stepped gables. Note the round-cut shingles on the brick bodies. Vigorous. First prize to 163; 175 has muddied its image with an unsympathetic brick-piered porch.

[B9] **Visitation Academy**, Visitation Nuns (Roman Catholic), 91st to 93rd Sts., Colonial Rd. to Ridge Blvd. **Convent and Chapel**, 1913.

A fortification for virgins, with a 20-foot stone and concrete wall to protect first- through eighth-graders from sight. The attached chapel is brick Italian neo-Renaissance. Unwalled, it serves as the religious doorkeeper to the Academy.

[B10] Originally **James F. Farrell House**, 119 95th St., bet. Marine Ave. and Shore Rd. N side. ca. 1849.

A splendid **Greek Revival** wood house inundated but not drowned in an adjacent sea of red-brick apartment blocks. Painted cream and white, with a Tuscan-columned porch and green shutters (they work!), it's a distinguished architectural survivor miraculously preserved among bland multiple dwellings.

[B11] **St. John's Episcopal Church**, 9818 Fort Hamilton Pkwy., NW cor. 99th St. 1890. **Rectory**, 1910.

A homely cottage-scaled country church in the looming shadow of the Verrazano Bridge and its ramps. Stone and shingles clad a timbered body enriched with red, white, and gold polychromy. Popularly called **Church of the Generals**, it attracted the military from adjacent Fort Hamilton.

[B15] **National Shrine of St. Bernadette** (Roman Catholic), 8201 13th Ave., bet. 82nd and 83rd Sts. E side. 1937. *Henry V. Murphy.*

A polygonal exterior, with a verdigris copper roof, houses parabolic concrete arches within. The nave is awash with colored light and features a **kitsch** rock-piled shrine to St. Bernadette at its east end.

B9

B13

Off the map to the east:

[B12] **Fort Hamilton Veterans' Hospital**, 800 Poly Place, bet. Seventh and Fourteenth Aves. S side. 1950. *Skidmore, Owings & Merrill.*

A sleek slab with soothing views for veterans. Now 60, it's a modernist oldster.

[B13] **Poly Prep Country Day School**/ originally **Brooklyn Polytechnic Preparatory School**, 92nd St., bet. 7th and Dahlgreen Aves. 1924.

A neo-Georgian boys' school with spreading athletic fields on what is, for the City, a vast campus. Now coeducational.

And further afield:

[B14] **P.S. 69, Vincent D Grippo School**, 884 63rd St., bet. Eighth and Ninth Aves. 2007. *Hugh Hardy of Hardy3.*

A sprightly polychromatic brick and glass serrated façade, the first of two volumes linked by an open, light-filled atrium. Crisp.

NECROLOGY

Bay Ridge United Methodist Church, 7002 Fourth Ave., SW cor. Ovingston St. ca. 1895.

A green ashlar body with brownstone trim made this a lovely cared-for local confection, with its chocolate joints oozing. Demolished for an apartment building.

Pollio's Restaurant, 6925 Third Ave., near Bay Ridge Ave.

A real Italian mamma's restaurant, this hole-in-the-wall was authentic down to the chilled Chianti. You ate what she had just made. Too few left.

146 67th Street (house), bet. Sedgwick Place and Ridge Blvd. S side. ca. 1885.

A neo-Gothic Shingle Style villa, towered and with ogee arches sullied by asbestos shingles ... but it was a tree-hooded extravaganza, a loner among the philistines. Replaced with banal row houses.

The Ridge (house), 129 Bay Ridge Pkwy., bet. Ridge Blvd. and Colonial Rd. N side. Bay Ridge. 1900.

A Shingle Style mansion in the sky, perched high on a lawn retained by a giant rubble wall; its red cedar shingles were set off with crisp white trim. Demolished in favor of apartments.

8205 11th Avenue (house), SE cor. 82nd St. Dyker Heights. ca. 1870.

This clapboarded and towered Italianate

B14

country home sat high on the hill overlooking the bay. It was entered by a generous Tuscan-columned porch.

8756 21st Avenue (house), just N of Bath Ave. W side. Bath Beach. ca. 1888.

The Shingle Style House, with its white shingles and blue trim, formed a solid volume with sections cut away for porches and crowned with a bell-like tower. An adjacent gas station doomed it.

Cropsey House, 1740 84th St., SE cor. Bay 16th St. Bensonhurst. ca. 1860.

A Victorian frame house replaced by a mundane facility for the elderly.

BENSONHURST/BATH BEACH

This lower-middle-income residential area preserves the family name of *Charles Benson*, whose farm was subdivided into the gridiron we see today. At New Utrecht and 18th Avenues the original village of New Utrecht was settled in 1661, on a site now marked by the **New Utrecht Reformed Church.**

[B16] New Utrecht Reformed Church, 18th Ave., bet. 83rd and 84th Sts. E side. 1828. 🕊

A **Georgian Gothic** granite ashlar church, its brick-framed Gothic windows filled with Tiffany-like Victorian milk glass. Stone from an earlier church of 1699 was quarried for the present structure. The eneagled New Utrecht (gilt) liberty pole stands in front of the church; the pole's predecessors date back to 1783 (replaced six times since).

Liberty Poles: To harass British garrisons, or signify their defeat, Revolutionary patriots erected flagpoles, called liberty poles, on which to raise the flag of independence. Lightning and dry rot have taken their toll of the originals, but in some communities a tradition has developed to replace them.

[B17a] New Utrecht Reformed Church Parsonage, 83rd St. bet. 18th and 19th Aves. S side. ca. 1885.

A Shingle Style home for the pastor, with a generous Tuscan-columned porch.

B17b

[B17b] New Utrecht Reformed Church Parish House, 1827 84th St., bet. 18th and 19th Aves. N side. 1828. 1892. *Lawrence B. Valk.* 🕊

Robust **Romanesque Revival** in a class with *Frank Freeman's* City of Brooklyn Fire Headquarters (see p. 586).

And six long blocks to the east:

[B18] Engine Company 253/originally **Engine Company 53**, N.Y.C. Fire Department, 2425-2427 86th St., bet. 24th and 25th Aves. N side. 1895-1896. *Parfitt Brothers.* 🕊

The 1890s had nostalgia for forms they thought reminiscent of Dutch New Amsterdam (even though *Lady Moody's* English settlement at **Gravesend** is nearby): stepped gables and banded brick for fire engines.

Southern Brooklyn

GRAVESEND

Established as a town in 1645; annexed to the City of Brooklyn in 1894.

Of the six original towns that now constitute Brooklyn, Gravesend is unique: it was settled by English rather than Dutch colonists. Its list of patentees was headed by a woman, a precocious admission of the equality of the sexes. And Gravesend Village was organized using sophisticated town planning principles more recognized in New Haven, Philadelphia, or Savannah. Remnants of the plan survive in the neighborhood street layout.

In 1643 *Lady Deborah Moody* and her

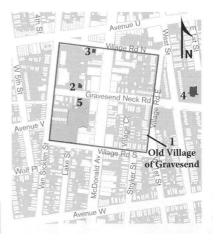

G2

G3

Anabaptist flock founded Gravesend after a bitter sojourn in New England, where they had encountered the same religious intolerance from which they had fled in "old" England. The free enjoyment of most religious beliefs, which characterized the New Netherlands colony, made Gravesend an obvious haven for them, an English social island in this Dutch-named place.

In the 19th century the territory of Gravesend became a great resort. No less than three racetracks were built within its bounds at various times, one northeast of Ocean and Jerome Avenues in Sheepshead Bay, another southeast of Ocean Parkway and Kings Highway, just north of the original village square. Before the development of Coney Island as a public beach and amusement area, Gravesend had fashionable hotels and piers, immense pinnacled wooden structures benefiting from the imagination and wit of Victorian elaboration. Regrettably, there is almost nothing left of its raucous spirit and lively architecture. Coney was revived after World War I

following the completion of subway connections to Manhattan and the Bronx; but it has lost its popularity as a recreation area, surpassed by more attractive suburban resorts accessible by automobile on *Robert Moses*–built highways. The streets, the beach, and the sea remain, but there is little of the physical and social vitality that once made this the daytime resort of the modest middle class.

[G1] The **Old Village of Gravesend**, Village Rd. N. to Village Rd. S., Van Sicklen St. to Village Rd. E., centered on the intersection of Gravesend Neck Rd. and McDonald (formerly Gravesend) Ave.

The bounds of *Lady Moody's* town plan, now remembered only in its streets and the turf on the cemetery.

[G2] **Hicks-Platt House**/also known as **Lady Moody House**, 17 Gravesend Neck Rd., bet. McDonald Ave. and Van Sicklen St. N side. 17th cent.

In the 1890s, *William E. Platt*, a real estate developer, publicized this as *Lady Moody's* own home, thereby becoming one of the earliest American hucksters of history. The fake stone veneer is ludicrous; bring back the clapboard! The fluted white columns are a later owner's do-it-yourself essay into the Colonial Revival.

[G3] **Ryder-Van Cleef House**, 38 Village Rd. N., bet. McDonald Ave. and Van Sicklen St., S side. ca. 1750.

The partial remnant of a narrow Dutch gambrel-roofed house, with later additions. Much more convincing than the Hicks-Platt collage of fake stone and dubious columns.

[G4] **Trinity Tabernacle of Gravesend**/formerly **Gravesend Reform Church,** 145 Gravesend Neck Rd., NW cor. E. 1st St. 1894. *J.G. Glover.*

This Gravesend Reform Congregation building replaced the congregation's original one (1655) at Neck Road and McDonald Ave. The

G4

neo-Gothic architecture is a far cry from plain white wooden Dutch Reform churches.

[G5] **Old Gravesend Cemetery** and **Van Sicklen Family Cemetery,** Gravesend Neck Rd., bet. McDonald Ave. and Van Sicklen St. S side. 1650s.

This shares history with the First Shearith Israel Graveyard as burial grounds for early religious exceptions to the mainstream Dutch Reform church. **Protestant Anabaptists** were interred here, whereas **Sephardic Jews** immigrating from Brazil were buried at Shearith Israel, starting in 1683. *Lady Moody's* own grave is somewhere within, but its location lost, although many stone markers from the eighteenth century remain. The cemetery is open four days a year.

SHEEPSHEAD BAY

[S1] **Henry and Abraham Wyckoff House**/also known as **Wyckoff-Bennett House,** 1669 E.22nd St., SE cor. Kings Highway. ca. 1766. Reoriented on the site.

A rural idyll: the most impressive of all the early Brooklyn houses in the Dutch style, and still in private ownership. This one is dated by a number cut into a wood beam. Used as quarters

S1a

by Hessian troops during the Revolutionary War, it contains this inscription scratched into a four- by seven-inch pane: *toepfer capt of regt de ditfurth mbach lieutenant v hessen hanau artilerie.*

[S1a] **1996 East 5th Street,** bet. Aves. S and T. W side. 1986. *Robert A.M. Stern.*

An exquisitely detailed postmodern detached house in a small enclave of others that date from the 1920s. Brick, stucco, and a green tile roof join in a collage of neighborly materials.

[S2] **Elias Hubbard Ryder House,** 1926 E.28th St., bet. Aves. S and T. W side. ca. 1834. Altered, 1929.

Dutch Colonialism squeezed between neighboring middle-class funk. The funkiness is compounded by specious shutters (non-working).

GERRITSEN BEACH

[S3] **Good Shepherd Roman Catholic Church,** Rectory, Convent, and School, Ave. S bet. Brown and Batchelder Sts. S side. School, 1932. McGill & Hamlin. Church, 1940. Rectory, 1950. Both by *Henry J. McGill.* Convent, 1956, *John B. O' Malley.*

McGill imported a modified California Mission Style church complex to this Marine Park section of Sheepshead Bay.

[S4] **Junior High School 43,** Brooklyn/**The James J. Reynolds School,** 1401 Emmons Ave., bet. E.14th and E.15th Sts. N side. 1965. *Pedersen & Tilney.*

A survivor from the exposed concrete mania of the 1960s. At 50 the cast-in-place concrete has weathered remarkably well.

Fishing and fish: A flotilla of fishing boats moored along Emmons Avenue from Ocean Avenue east to East 27th Street offers you the chance to catch blues, stripers, and miscellany— but you will have to rise early or go to bed late. Generations of compleat anglers have returned bearing far more fish than their extended families could eat. And at Ocean Avenue for several generations has stood a restaurant where the vast fruit of the sea was consumed:

[S5] Formerly **F.W.I.L. Lundy's Restaurant/** originally known as **Lundy's,** 1901-1929 Emmons Ave. at E.19th St. 1934. *Bloch & Hesse.* Reconstructed, 1996, *Van J. Brody.* 🖤

A big, brash, noisy place in a strangely appropriate **Spanish Mission** style building that served as many as 5,000 meals a day in its hey-

S2

day, was closed from 1979 until its reincarnation in 1996, then closed again in 2007.

Across the parkway:

[S6] **United Methodist Church of Sheepshead Bay,** 3087 Ocean Ave., bet. Voorhees Ave. and Shore Parkway service road.

Korean Methodists celebrate in this colorful, short and spiky, neo-Gothic wood building.

[S7] **Lighthouse,** 3165 Harkness, bet. Knapp St. and Shell Bank Creek.

A stubby local landmark on inland waterways, amidst local powerboat squadrons.

A low-lying peninsular community of approximately 1,600 lilliputian bungalows on lilliputian plots, with narrow streets barely wide enough for cars to pass. Originally marketed for summer settlement in the 1920s, its residents soon began insulating their vacation homes for year-round occupancy. In the late 1930s the community successfully fought the City's plan for a Belt Parkway exit down Gerritsen Avenue, and today residents still fight against the over-development and density that has plagued nearby Sheepshead Bay and Brighton Beach. Some homes remain below street level, from the time the streets were raised in the 1950s; others have risen to the occasion.

[B1] **St. James Lutheran Church,** 2776 Gerritsen Ave., bet. Gotham and Florence Aves. W side. 1925. *Fraser and Berau.*

Gothic Revival by the sea. A handsome wooden house of worship that would barely dent the skyline of most neighborhoods, but in **Lilliput** it's a towering landmark.

[B2] **Gerritsen Beach Branch Library**, 2808 Gerritsen Ave., bet. Bartlett Pl. and Gotham Ave., opp. a leg of Shell Bank Creek. W side. 1997. *John Ciardullo.*

An airy space structured by a timber frame and within a carapace of brick. It stands between the sailboats of Shell Bank and Gerritsen Creeks. Lilliput's major monument.

A sampling of authentic bungalows:

[B3] **105 Abbey Court**, bet. Bartlett Pl. and Cyrus Ave. W side. 1924. Altered, 1987.

A raised and renovated bungalow maintaining the original frame and gabled roof of yesteryear.

[B4] **5 Cyrus Avenue**, bet. Madoc Ave. and Shell Bank Creek. N side. ca. 1924.

A vernacular single-story bungalow on a sunken seaside lot. A test case for gradually rising sea levels if there ever was one.

B2

[B5] **8 Ivan Court**, bet. Seba Ave. and Kiddie Beach. E side. ca. 1924.

A glimpse back to the years of flappers and seaside bungalows. An almost perfect specimen, with its original wood frame, windows, moldings, and clapboard siding. In need of some TLC, or is it **Shabby Chic**?

[B6] **119 Garland Court**, S of Allen Ave. ca. 1928.

Its gabled roof is from the second wave of bungalows to be built in Gerritsen Beach, (bungalows north of the library are known as the "New Section") some five years after the original ("Old Section") bungalows.

MARINE PARK

[B7] **Salt Marsh Nature Center**, 3302 Ave U, across from Marine Park. 2006. *Mark Morrison Associates,* landscape architects.

A low-key protuberance upon a panoramic marshy backdrop. Here Brooklynites are welcomed to experience estuarine communities once vast across their borough's southern tier.

MANHATTAN AND BRIGHTON BEACHES

The eastern peninsula of what once was Coney Island is isolated, affluent, sometimes green, often dull. Its middle reaches harbor vast hordes of Russian Jewish immigrants; its tip houses the old World War II Naval Training Station, now infilled with the campus of Kingsborough Community College. Along the ocean sits the

M2

Brighton Beach Bath and **Racquet Club**, a privately owned enclave of summer fun in stylish contrast to the public sands of Coney Island proper to the west.

[M1] **Kingsborough Community College**, CUNY, main gate at the end of Oriental Blvd. bet. Sheepshead Bay and the Atlantic Ocean. Master Plan, 1968. *Katz, Waisman, Weber, Strauss.* Various buildings by *KWWS, James Stewart Polshek & Assocs., Lundquist & Stonehill; Warner, Burns, Toan & Lunde; Gruzen Samton Steinglass.*

A sprawlingly **complex complex**, with some stylish modern forms (particularly in profile when seen from the Belt Parkway).

[M2] **Leon H. Goldstein High School for the Sciences**, Kingsborough Community College. 2000. *Davis Brody Bond.*

Sleek modernist addition to the Kingsborough Community.

CONEY ISLAND

[C1] **Coney Island Hospital**, 2601 Ocean Pkwy., NE cor. Shore Pkwy. 1957. *Katz, Waisman, Blumenkranz, Stein & Weber.*

A landmark to motorists arriving at the Ocean Avenue gateway to Coney Island, even though it's on the other side of the road. Now a period piece of modern architecture, it displays the articulation of its functional parts, with sun-

C2

shades the major decoration permitted. It grew in the period when elimination of ornamentation was an almost holy mission, here well done by fervent acolytes of *Walter Gropius.*

[C2] **William E. Grady Vocational High School**, 25 Brighton 4th Rd., bet. Brighton 4th and Brighton 6th Sts. N side. 1956. *Katz, Waisman, Blumenkranz, Stein & Weber.*

Concrete is honored in the barrel vaults over the gymnasium and auditorium, but the effort is dated by its fervent modernism. Like its neighbor (by the same architects) across the parkway, it tells of that brief moment in the 1950s and 1960s when any token of architectural historicism was still rejected.

[C3] **New York Aquarium**, the Boardwalk at NE cor. W. 8th St. Exhibit Building, 1955. *Harrison & Abramovitz.* **Osborn Laboratories of Marine Sciences**, 1965. *Goldstone & Dearborn.*

To be visited for the contents rather than the envelope, although both are the pressured product of the conflicting needs of museum and

amusement park. The substantial things to see are the whales, penguins, octopi, and electric eels, but there are other natural and unconscious entertainments. Children, **please touch**—the horseshoe crabs can be fondled.

[C4] **Stillwell Avenue Station**, Surf Ave., bet. Stillwell Ave. and W.12th St. N side. 2004. *Kiss + Cathcart.*

A reconstruction of the old BMT and IND (D, F, N, and Q lines) station. As late as the Millenium the old station housed a remarkable time warp: old guys in fedoras killing time at the in-station lunch counter. The new version is spiffier, but retains some of the airy, shed-like splendor of its predecessor.

[C5] **Coney Island Amusement Area**, bet. W. 8th St. and W. 16th St., Surf Ave. and the Boardwalk.

Most of the great rides have become vacant land, fodder for new housing. **Luna Park** and **Steeplechase Park** are long gone, and **Astroland** closed in 2008. But some of old

C4

Coney Island remains: roller coasters, carousels, dodg'em cars, sideshows, corn dogs, cotton candy. **The Bowery**, a circus midway between the Boardwalk and Surf Avenue, provides some taste of the old charm and vulgarity of Coney's history. And don't overlook the great **Greek Revival** autoscooter rink between 12th and Stillwell. No Greek Revival autos?

Rides and buildings reveal myriad architectural styles and fantasia, many vernacular in origin, the work of creative local carpenters. New plans to redevelop the Boardwalk give pause: ghostly in winter, active in summer (especially during the annual Neptune Parade), funky old Coney Island definitely isn't Disneyland. Should it be?

Historic, surviving rides:

[C6] **Wonder Wheel**, 3059 W. 12th Street and the Boardwalk. 1918-1920. *Charles Herman*, inventor. *Eccentric Ferris Wheel Amusement Co.*, manufacturers. ●'

The iconic steel spider web survives from its

post–World War I inception, a glory to behold. Eight stationary and sixteen pivoting cars.

[C7] **Parachute Jump**, Boardwalk bet. W. 16th and W. 19th Sts. 1939. *Commander James H. Strong*, inventor. *Elvyn E. Seelye & Co.*, engineers. Moved from 1939-1940 World's Fair to present site, 1940-1941. *Michael Marlo*, architect. *Edwin W.Kleinert*, engineer. 🍎 New lighting program, 2006. *Leni Schwendiger*.

"Brooklyn's Eiffel Tower," the last fragment of the vanished **Steeplechase Park** (Steeplechase closed in 1964; the Last Jump was in 1968). Happily, after years of neglect, an on-going restoration commenced in 2002. Repainted and creatively lighted, plans have been tossed around for a "Parachute Pavilion" activities center at the tower's base. Look for news.

[C8] **Cyclone**, 834 Surf Ave., near W. 10th St. 1927. *Harry C. Baker*, inventor. *Vernon Keenan*, engineer. 🍎

Coney's **last roller coaster**. The wood struc-

C6

C8

C11   C10

C13

ture laced with its sinuous band of tracks stands as a powerful sculpture honouring the early days of American amusement parks.

[C9] **KeySpan Park**, 1904 Surf Ave., SW cor. W. 16th St. 2001. *Jack L. Gordon*, architect.

What a site for a ballpark! From the bleachers you can watch the game, the Parachute Jump, the Wonder Wheel, the Cyclone, and the ocean. Not the beloved, departed Dodgers, but the **Brooklyn Cyclones**, a minor league team, drawing people in droves to summer nights on Coney Island.

[C10] **Nathan's Famous** (the original), Surf Ave., SW cor. Stillwell Ave. Here since 1916.

After the demise of **Luna** and **Steeplechase**, Nathan's Famous remains as Coney Island's most venerable institution. Once upon a time it cost a nickel on the subway to reach Coney, and a nickel bought a hot dog at Nathan's. Open all year for stand-up treats: delicatessen sandwiches, clams on the half shell, and "shrimp boats" (shrimp cocktails in miniature plastic dinghies). We hope it lasts.

[C11] **Steeplechase Pier**, the Boardwalk at W. 17th St.

A retired monument, it is still a favored fishing dock. A walk along its 1,000 feet offers cool breezes and wonderful vantage points for summer fireworks or the setting sun. Try your hand at catching fluke, blues, flounder, or stripers.

[C12] **Abe Stark Center**, N.Y.C. Department of Parks & Recreation, W. 19th St. at the Boardwalk. 1969. *Daniel Chait*.

A would-be *Nervi* created these once-stylish structural forms to house a skating rink, where precocious figure-skating stars and promising hockey teams vie for space in the midnight hours.

[C13] Former **Childs Restaurant**, 2102 Boardwalk, at 21st St. 1923. *Dennison & Hirons*. 🍎

Incredible! A summer dream in **Spanish Colonial** (Revival Division), all in glazed terra cotta, with seaside details: galleons, fish, Neptune! If only the restaurant would re-incarnate in the spirit of this classy façade.

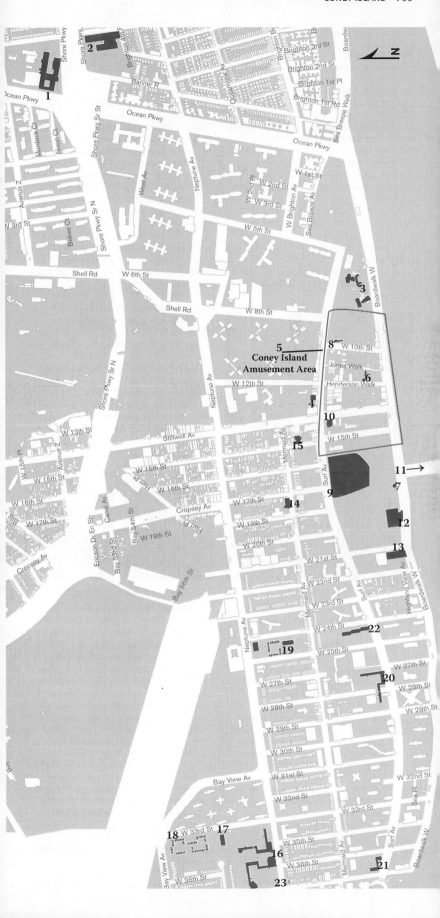

[C14] **Our Lady of Solace Church** (Roman Catholic), 2866 W. 17th St., NW cor. Mermaid Ave. 1925. *Robert J. Reiley.*

A plain brick **neo-Romanesque** church with a refreshingly austere exposed brick exterior and interior: arches, limestone columns, timbered roof. Go inside.

[C15] **Gargiulo's Restaurant**, 2911 W.15th St., bet. Mermaid and Surf Aves. Restaurant founded 1907; here since 1928.

A princely palace in plebian surroundings— vast and vulgar. Elsewhere it would be just another unimportant eatery; here it is an oasis. Expensive.

*Nelson Rockefeller's Urban Development Corporation's 1970s housing experiments implanted what seem now to be towering tombstones on a vast plain: blocks of buildings where the whole is **less** than the sum of the parts. And the parts are tragic. What were they thinking?*

C16

C19   C23

More of the same:

[C19] **Apartment tower and town houses**, Neptune Ave., bet. W. 24th and W. 25th Sts. S side. 1975. Tower, *Skidmore, Owings & Merrill*. Town houses, *Davis, Brody & Assocs.*
[C20a] **Sea Park East**, 2970 W.27th St., bet. Mer-maid and Surf Aves. 1975. Tower, *Skidmore, Owings & Merrill*. Town houses, *Davis, Brody & Assocs.* [C20b] **Sea Park East Apartments**, Surf Ave. bet. W. 27th and W. 29th Sts. N side. 1975. *Hoberman & Wasserman.*

The joyless parade continues.

[C21] **Housing for the Elderly,** Surf Ave. bet. W. 36th and W. 37th Sts. N side. 1975. *Hoberman & Wasserman.*

The stepped terraces are remarkably empty. Residents willfully cluster around the trafficked streets below, where the action is, not in their architect-assigned space. As *Jane Jacobs* articulated so strongly, streets are for people.

[C22] **Ocean Towers,** Surf Ave., bet. W. 24th and W. 25th Sts. N side. 1975. *Prentice & Chan, Ohlhausen.*

Unité d'Uninhabitable: grim.

[C23] **2837 West 37th Street**, bet. Neptune and Mermaid Aves. E side. ca. 1924.

Mykonos in Brooklyn, once a siamese twin, now severed. Its textured stucco and white-washed flanks bring Mediterranean memories to this remote spit of Coney Island. It's comic relief from massive UDC projects nearby. Thank God.

[C16] **Sea Rise I,** Neptune and Canal Aves., bet. W.33rd and W. 37th Sts. 1976. *Hoberman & Wasserman.*

Our grim tour of massive, inhumane public housing projects starts here and continues east, where more of the undead await. It's enough to make you go to Nathan's and get drunk on corn dogs.

[C17] **2730 West 33rd Street**, bet. Bayview and Neptune Aves. 1975. *Skidmore, Owings & Merrill.*
Stacked cubist balconies adorn this single tower. Soulless, but at least they have ocean views. The ground level is a wasteland.

[C18] **Town houses,** Bayview Ave. SW cor. W. 33rd St. 1975. *Davis, Brody & Assocs.*
Two-story brick and concrete town houses surrounding a garden court.

NECROLOGY

The Thunderbolt. Surf Ave., bet. W. 15th and W. 16th St. 1925. *John Miller*, designer.

A wooden roller coaster, older than and adjacent to the Cyclone. Closed in 1982, it sat majestically decaying until it was demolished in 2000. The Thunderbolt was memorably the childhood home of *Alvy Singer*, played by *Woody Allen* in his great film *Annie Hall*.

Fire Service Pumping Station, City of New York, 2301 Neptune Ave., bet. W. 23rd and W. 24th Sts. N side. 1937-1938. *Irwin S. Chanin.*

This streamlined but decayed remnant recalls the **Art Moderne** stimulated by the Paris Exposition of 1937. The entrance of this symmetrical modern palace was once guarded by two pairs of prancing steeds, now removed to the Brooklyn Museum sculpture garden. Too bad. Coney needed to keep this piece of architectural history.

Southeastern Brooklyn

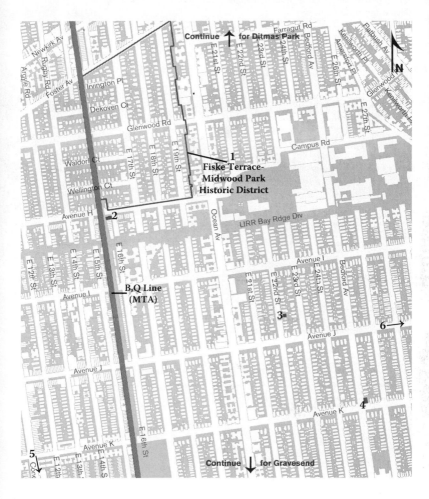

Continue ↑ for Ditmas Park

1
Fiske Terrace-
Midwood Park
Historic District

2

B,Q Line
(MTA)

3

6 →

4

5

Continue ↓ for Gravesend

Town of Flatlands/Nieuw Amersfoort

Established as a town in 1666, annexed to the
City of Brooklyn in 1896.

The name Flatlands aptly describes this bil-
liard table, much of it still marshy, a large part
bordering Jamaica Bay recaptured as landfill,
impossible under present-day environmental law.
The old town included much of what is now
Midwood to the north, and most inland area is
still termed Flatlands (in part an industrial park).
At its edges are the shorefront areas of old **Floyd
Bennett Field, Bergen Beach, Mill Basin,** and
Canarsie, tidal and aquatic edges now filled with
middle-class homeowners yearning to have a
powerboat at their bulkheaded edge of their
lawn. Boaters with sails dwell elsewhere.

MIDWOOD

[M1] **Fiske Terrace-Midwood Park Historic
District,** Foster Ave. south to Avenue H, bet.
the train tracks on the west and mid-block bet.
E.19th St. and Ocean Ave. on the west. ●

A tiny historic district, only one block south
of the Ditmas Park Historic District. Couldn't
they just combine them?

[M2] **Avenue H BMT Station House,** 802 E. 16th
St., at Ave. H. 1906.

If only every subway station were a charming cottage.

[M3] **Johannes Van Nuyse House**/also known
as **Van Nuyse-Magaw House,** 1041 E.22nd
St., bet. Aves. I and J. E side. 1800-1803. ●

Originally built in **Flatlands** at East 22nd Street
and Avenue M, moved here around 1916 and turned
perpendicular to the street to fit its new and narrow lot. The distinctive Dutch gambrel roof with
outsweeping curves is therefore the street façade.

[M4] Congregation Kol Israel, 3211 Bedford Ave., NE cor. Ave. K. Entrance on Ave. K. 1989. *Robert A.M. Stern*, architect. *Dominick Salvati & Son*, consulting architects.

A **postmodern** synagogue in banded brick successfully adapting to its semi-suburban residential setting. There is some flavor from *Frank Lloyd Wright* here.

[M5] Mesitva Yeshiva Chaim Berlin, 1605 Coney Island Ave., NE cor. Locust Ave. 1988. *Fox & Fowle*.

M3

M5

FLATLANDS

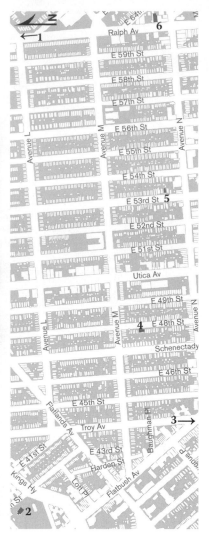

Polychromatic brick and granite swells out to Coney Island Avenue, the gridded windows a study hall for the resident bachurim (scholars). A stern (and learned?) place.

[M6] Joost and Elizabeth Van Nuyse House, sometimes called the **Coe House**, 1128 E.34th St., bet. Flatbush Ave. and Ave. J. W side. 1744, 1793, 1806.

A well-dressed neighbor in a tacky neighborhood, like a Harris tweed jacket among polyester leisure suits. Well maintained, it suffers from shutters and downspouts that were never part of its Dutch ancestry.

[F1] Originally **Pieter Claesen Wyckoff House**, 5902 Clarendon Rd., at intersection of Ralph and Ditmas Aves., SW cor. ca. 1652. Additions, 1740 and 1820. Restored, 1982, *Oppenheimer, Brady & Vogelstein.*
Open to the public. 718-629-5400.
May-Nov: Th-Sa, 12-5; closed Su-We;
Dec-Apr: Th-Fr, 12-4; closed Sa-We.

A lonely ancestor in a neat fenced park, marooned in these industrial precincts, remembering the New Netherlands with its handsome eaves and shingled body: a part is that of the oldest building in New York.

[F2] Flatlands Dutch Reformed Church, 3931 Kings Highway, bet. Flatbush Ave. and E.40th St. 1848. *Henry Eldert,* builder.

One of three Brooklyn churches established by order of *Peter Stuyvesant* (together with the Flatbush Reformed Dutch and the First

Reformed). Sited in a tree-filled park, this simple, but stately, **Greek Revival-Georgian** building rose where two earlier church buildings stood. The first, of 1663, was octagonal in plan. Note Brooklyn names in the adjacent cemetery: *Lott, Voorhees, Sprong, Kouwenhoven, Wyckoff.*

[F3] **Hendrick I. Lott House**, 1940 E.36th St., bet. Fillmore Ave. and Avenue S. W side. East Wing (Johannes Lott House), 1720. Main house and west wing, 1800.

Some elbow room allows this **Dutch Colonial** house to remember its rural beginnings. Modest owners have provided minimal maintenance, but it deserves serious care. The small wing *Lott's* grandfather's house of 1720; the main body built by *Hendrick Lott* himself in 1800. The projecting Dutch eaves, with a more than usual projection, are supported by columns square on one side and round on the other.

[F4] **John and Altje Baxter House**/originally **Stoothoff-Baxter-Kouwenhoven House**, 1640 E.48th St., bet. Aves. M and N. W side. Wing, ca. 1747. Main House, 1811.

The form of this lonely enfenced **Dutch** outpost remains, but its skin has been modernized . . . to its discredit. The older, smaller tail was married and moved to join its larger, later dog. And both were reoriented to the street around 1900.

[F5] **Donwe Stoothof House**/also known as **John Williamson House**, 1587 E.53rd St., bet. Aves. M and N. E side.

F1

Another poorly altered **Dutch Colonial**, veneered with asphalt-impressed false brick. Nevertheless the shape is there under that dowdy fabric.

[F6] **Mill Basin Branch, Brooklyn Public Library**, 2385 Ralph Ave., NE cor. Ave. N. 1974. *Arthur A. Unger & Assocs.*

A serene outpost of graceful modernism in brick carved and curved without overkill—in contrast to the Jamaica Bay Branch.

CANARSIE

What to see here are the adorable little seaside cottages that begin cropping up as you move south towards the ocean. But a few modernist projects stand out, too:

[C1] **Jamaica Bay Branch, Brooklyn Public Library**, 9727 Seaview Ave., NW cor. E.98th St. 1972. *Leibowitz, Bodouva & Assocs.*

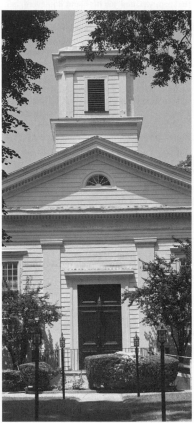

F2

Brutalism in Canarsie: ribbed concrete block, slots, notches, cantilevers, and splayed sills. A histrionic little building.

[C2] **Canarsie Pier**, Gateway National Recreation Area, S of Shore Pkwy. at the foot of Rockaway Pkwy.

Jutting into Jamaica Bay, the pier is a popular neighborhood hangout, where BBQ'ing, fishing, and flying kites is taken very seriously. One day, let's hope, pollution control will make it possible to gather clams and oysters once again.

Eastern Brooklyn

HIGHLAND PARK/ CYPRESS HILLS

[H1] **279, 341, and 361 Highland Boulevard**, bet. Miller Ave. and Barbey St. N side. ca. 1900.

Three gracious mansions survive from a precinct that originally had a myriad. Many were displaced by apartment houses seeking these spectacular views. **No.279**, in gray Roman brick and white limestone, presents a great composite Ionic-columned porte cochère. **Nos.341** and **361** were previously a Lithuanian cultural center (the reason for a wrap of out-of-place Brutalist concrete additions). Currently **No.341** is the **Pope John Paul II House of Discernment** (hous-

[H3] **130 Arlington Avenue, 69 Schenck Avenue**, SE cor. 1908-1912. Altered, 1977, *Rosemary Songer*.

Two grand Classical Revival houses of Roman brick with great Ionic-columned porches. Wealth was once here.

[H4] Originally **James Royal House**, 18 Ashford St., SW cor. Ridgewood Ave. 1904. *John Petit*.

A **Queen Anne/Shingle Style** gem, pedimented and towered, clad in abominable vinyl siding: note the joints in the round tower, and

H3

H4

ing for those considering the priesthood) while **No.391** is a Carmelite monastery, **Our Lady of Mt. Carmel and St. Joseph.** The Lithuanian's auditorium addition is now used as a chapel.

[H2] **101 Sunnyside Avenue**, bet. Hendrix St. and Miller Ave. N side. ca. 1930.

Nestled into the sharp precipice between Highland and Sunnyside Avenues, this apartment house presents a Classical Renaissance plan to the Sunnyside Avenue approach: a formal, symmetrical subplaza from which it rises to the view.

Sunnyside Avenue: A lovely, lively row of town houses, between Barbey and Miller Streets, with porches with paired Tuscan columns and supporting bracketed roofs sheathed in Spanish tile. Also pause to admire No.195 at the NW corner of Sunnyside and Barbey: Shingle Style minus the shingles, but with turret and wraparound porch still intact.

the loss of detail at eaves and windows. A shame.

[H5] **68 Ashford Street**, bet. Ridgewood and Arlington Aves. W side. ca. 1885.

Clapboard and fish-scale shingles, with a circle-in-the-square hooded oriel balcony of great charm. Torn and frayed.

[H6] **St. Joseph's Anglican Church**/originally **Trinity Episcopal Church**, 131 Arlington Ave., NE cor. Schenck Ave. 1886. *Richard M. Upjohn*.

Designed by the son of Manhattan Trinity Church's *Upjohn*, a bulky, vigorous, comforting, buttressed, brick and sandstone church with a friendly, squatting scale. It shows a Romanesque body, with Gothic finials.

[H7] **219-225 Arlington Avenue** (row houses), bet. Ashford and Cleveland Sts. ca. 1900.

The cornices that join these tan brick, bow-fronted, row houses are as prepossessing as some of the grandest of the **Italian Renaissance**. Recent restoration makes them new.

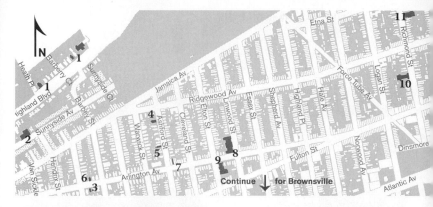

N

H8

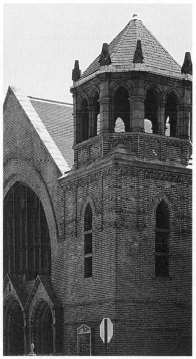

H9

[H8] **Public School 108**, Brooklyn, 200 Linwood St., NW cor. Arlington Ave. 1895. *James W. Naughton.*

Brownstone, sometimes rough, sometimes smooth, joins Roman brick: the flush voussoirs of the **Romanesque Revival** arches rise from foliated terra-cotta spring blocks. Sleek power.

[H9] **Presbyterian Church of the Crossroads**, SE cor. Elton St. and Arlington Ave. ca. 1890.

Stolid brick **Gothic Revival** with squat belfrys, terra cotta providing fine detail more economically than carved stone; brownstone is too porous a material to maintain such elegant profiles.

[H10] **Public School 65K**, Brooklyn, 158 Richmond St., bet. Ridgewood and Arlington Aves. W side. 1870. *Samuel Leonard*. Façade, 1889, *James W. Naughton.*

A somber brick outpost of education, that, if stripped of paint, might gain the same vigor and power as P.S. 108 above.

[H11] **Ghana Wesley United Methodist Church**/formerly **Andrews Methodist Church**/originally **Wesleyan Methodist Episcopal Church**, Richmond St. bet. Etna St. and Ridgewood Ave. E side. 1892. *George Kramer.*

Romanesque Revival/Shingle Style: a Methodist house of worship serving through changing demographics, from Irish builders to its current African-American congregation. A glorious rose window intersects both upper shingles and lower brick. A lovely, lonely "country" church.

B3

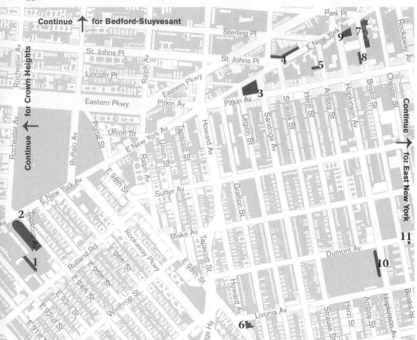

BROWNSVILLE

The neighborhood was first subdivided in 1865 by *Charles S. Brown*, to whom the community owes its name. A group of entrepreneurs purchased portions in 1887 and encouraged Jewish immigrants in the congested Lower East Side to move here. The arrival of the Fulton Street El in 1889 stimulated the influx, and the settlement became a great concentration of poor Eastern European Jews. The completion of the New Lots branch of the IRT subway in 1922 further improved rapid transit connections to Manhattan, and the area grew mildly prosperous. Following World War II the Jewish population moved to more middle-class precincts, and the area declined. Urban renewal efforts beginning in the 1960s were disastrous; good at demolition, not so good at building. By the 1980s the area was synonymous with urban decay. But crime has fallen here over the last decade, as it has all over the City, and the recent arrival of serious new architecture (see B5, B8) bodes well for Brownsville's resurgence.

[B1] **Rutland Plaza**, East New York Ave. and Rutland Rd., E.92nd to E.94th Sts. 1976. *Donald Stull & Assocs.*

One of the valiant, but misguided efforts in urban renewal, an island of concentrated poverty in a sleek superslab. What sometimes worked in Europe (*Le Corbusier's* **Unité d'Habitation** in Marseille, France) doesn't work here. Grim.

[B2] **Public School 398**, Brooklyn, The Walter Weaver School, East New York Ave., bet. E.93rd and E.94th Sts. S side. 1976. *Perkins & Will.*

In an era of open classrooms, when schools were conceived as shopping centers of education, this barrel-vaulted basilica could offer partitioning (or nonpartitioning) in the most flexible manner. Terra-cotta brick with bronze-anodized aluminum.

UNCLEAR FATE

[B3] Originally **Loew's Pitkin Theater**/later **Hudson Temple Cathedral**, 1501 Pitkin Ave., NW cor. Saratoga Ave. 1930. *Thomas W. Lamb.*

A neglected gem: its carefully ornate brick and terra-cotta exterior screened one of those fantasy, fairy-tale auditoriums conjured up by *Lamb* and his peers in the great picture palace era of the late 1920s, complete with twinkling stars and moving clouds across its ceiling-sky. Now vacant, its vertical sign and marquee missing, what are the plans? We hope not demolition. It should be a **landmark**.

[B4] **East New York House** (homeless shelter), 1381 East New York Avenue. 1990. *Skidmore, Owings & Merrill.*

SOM, to its credit, has designed several handsome shelters in the City over the last decade. This one has pleasant yellow brick, punctuated by communal spaces articulated by large expanses of glass.

[B7] **Crossroads Juvenile Center**, New York Department of Juvenile Justice, 17 Bristol St., bet. Pitkin and East New York Aves. 1998. *Kaplan, McLaughlin, Diaz*, architects.

A formidable detention facility, carefully detailed, its exaggerated cornice following the curving intersection of East New York Avenue and Bristol Street. The highly mannered façade supplies masonry gymnastics reminiscent of the City's armories: pleasant; the razor wire strung atop the walls is not.

B5

B10

[B5] **Marcus Garvey Houses Community Center**, 20 Amboy St., bet. E. New York and Pitkin Aves. 2009. *Caples Jefferson*, architects.

Marcus Garvey Houses acquired a much-needed community center from this talented, civic-minded partnership. Simply but crisply detailed, with an abundance of that rarest commodity in public housing: *natural light*. The building and its adjoining basketball court create a pleasant outdoor room for people, where once was a wasteland.

[B6] **Engine Company 238**, Squad Company 4, N.Y.C. Fire Department, 885 Howard Ave., SE cor. Livonia Ave. 1974. *Giovanni Pasanella.*

Red-brown square brick clads this simple, strong modern fire station, skylit at its rear. In need of maintenance, and a scrubbing of graffiti.

[B8] **The Beacon** (apartments), 54 Bristol St., bet. Pitkin and East New York Aves. 2009. *SLCE,* architects. *The RBA Group*, landscape architects.

Two seven-story buildings intended for mixed incomes, meaning (hopefully) **Brownsvillians** can live here. Handsome brick with large windows, it wouldn't receive notice in the condo-rich precincts of Manhattan, but here, after decades of desolation, it's a huge step in the right direction.

[B9] **73rd Precinct, N.Y.C. Police Department**, 1470 East New York Ave., bet. Bristol and Hopkinson Sts. S side. 1982. *Swanke Hayden Connell.*

A striking, serrated brick façade is a lively invader of the neighborhood, but shouldn't the police blend into their surrounds, rather than dominate them?

[B10] **Betsy Head Memorial Playground Bathhouse**, N.Y.C. Department of Parks & Recreation, Strauss St. to Hopkinson Ave., Dumont to Livonia Aves. 1940. *John Matthews Hatton*.

Liberal use of glass block and a parasol roof delicately balanced on parabolic ribs distinguish the WPA bathhouse that serves an immense swimming pool.

[B11] **Marcus Garvey Village** (row housing), Dumont Ave. to a point S of Riverdale Ave., from W of Bristol St. to Chester St. and including a portion of Rockaway Ave. 1976. Prototypical design, *Theodore Liebman* of the N.Y.S. Urban Development Corporation and *Kenneth Frampton* of the Institute for Architecture and Urban Studies. Construction documents by *David Todd & Assocs.*

A well-meaning experiment in low-rise, high-density housing: row houses with stoops, embracing paved and planted play and sitting areas. Austere and reminiscent of the fanatically regimented Amsterdam housing of the 1920s, it was a scholarly attempt at an urban redevelopment prototype by the British architect/theorist *Frampton*. Now almost 35 years old and frayed at the edges, it's no longer the brand-new neighbor.

[B12] **Van Dyke Community Center**, 392 Blake Ave., bet. Stone Ave. (Mother Gaston Blvd.) and Powell St. S side. 2004. *Ohlhausen Dubois*.

The Van Dyke center doesn't wear much glass outside. But inside are terraced common spaces, with glass walls showcasing the computer and photo labs, library, game and music rooms.

B11

NECROLOGY

Onetime **Banco de Ponce**/originally **The East New York Savings Bank**, Kings Highway and Rockaway Pkwy. E side. 1962. *Lester Tichy & Assocs.*

Some remember *Tichy's* equally violent intrusion into old Pennsylvania Station with a luminous canopy that blinded you to the glorious main waiting room surrounding it. Now this circular bank joins the ranks of the demolished.

EAST NEW YORK

[E1] **Grace Baptist Church**/originally **Deutsche Evangelische Lutherische St. Johannes Kirche**, 223 New Jersey Ave., bet. Liberty and Glenmore Aves. ca. 1885.

Gothic Revival in banded brown bricks, crowned with a slated pyramidal steeple.

[E2] **Holy Trinity Russian Orthodox Church**, Pennsylvania Ave., SE cor. Glenmore Ave. 1935.

One great and one minor onion dome sheathed in verdigris copper crown a salmon brick base. The porch on Glenmore Avenue, with its fat columns and steeply pitched pediment, is an eclectic fantasy.

[E3] **HELP/Genesis Houses**, 330 Hinsdale St., bet. Blake and Dumont Aves. 1992. *Cooper Robertson & Partners.*

This forbidding block embraces a lovely paved and planted courtyard providing gracious

E1

urban space and security for its residents (one entry point).

[E4] **Bradford Street**, bet. Sutter and Blake Aves.

This street preserves a sense of the early urbanization of East New York. Gaily painted, the block retains a charm that most of Eastern Brooklyn has lost to the ravages of blockbusting, poverty, and sleazy "modernizations."

[E5] **Bethelite Institutional Baptist Church**, 446 Elton St., bet. Belmont and Sutter Aves. 1990. *Theo. David.*

The stepped gable and columned portal lead to a light-filled white sanctuary; a wonderful renewal (there was a brick box to begin with) for East New York.

[E6] **New Life Baptist Church**, 931 Dumont Ave., near Elton St. 1992. *Theo. David.*

"Simple but stunning," said *Oculus* writers *Jayne Merkel* and *Philip Nobel*. And the spine, articulated on the façade by receding crosses, skylights the interior space.

NEW LOTS

Settled by farmers in the 1670s, the town of New Lots was incorporated in 1852 and annexed by Brooklyn in 1886. Today New Lots is indistinguishable from the rest of East New York to the north, but fragments of the old town remain, notably the lovely little **New Lots Reformed Dutch Church**, now New Lots Community Church.

E7

E5

E8

[E7] **New Lots Community Church/** formerly **New Lots Reformed Dutch Church**, 630 New Lots Ave., SE cor. Schenck Ave. 1823-1824. 🍎

Built by latter-day Dutch farmers of this area when weekly trips to the Flatbush church became too arduous. A painted wood-shingled body, with Gothic Revival openings.

[E8] **Essex Terrace** (apartments), bounded by Linden Blvd., Hegeman Ave., Linwood and Essex Sts. 1970. *Norval White.*

Crisp and well cared-for, this union-sponsored low-rise high-density project surrounds its own central private plaza. The corner gates allow residents to admit or restrict the neighborhood at their discretion. "Discretion" now means "permanently locked."

NECROLOGY

Parish House, New Lots Reformed Dutch Church, 620 New Lots Ave., SE cor. Schenck Ave. East New York. 1823.

The shingled parish house, a fitting complement to the church, was superseded by a new building.

SPRING CREEK

Spring Creek is the southern portion of East New York, south of New Lots, where the trees end and ocean breezes begin. A work in progress, Spring Creek is dominated by the super-project Starrett City, vast tracts of new low-income housing along Flatlands Avenue, and the huge Gateway Center shopping mall.

[E9] **Public School 306,** Brooklyn, 970 Vermont Ave., NW cor. Cozine Ave. 1966. *Pedersen & Tilney.*
   A no-nonsense, cast-in-place concrete school in an area whose flat monotony is being broken by towers sprouting everywhere.

[E10] **Starrett City,** bet. Flatlands Ave. and Shore Pkwy., Van Sicklen and Louisiana Aves. 1976. *Herman Jessor.*
   A surreal experience. Forty-six great building blocks housing 5,881 apartments, are placed in the manner of a supermodel in this boondock

E12

E10

landscape. *Jessor's* other giant anti-urban fantasies include Co-op City in the Bronx. The architecture of the building blocks is bland. Self-contained, the City has its own schools, churches, and synagogues and generates its own heat, light, and power. Attempts to sell the entire project to a private developer for **$1.3 billion** collapsed in 2007 because of community opposition.

[E11] **The Landings at Fresh Creek,** 556-630 Louisiana Ave., bet. Vandalia Ave. and Twin Pines Dr. 1995. *Herbert Mandel.*
   Brick row housing embracing parking lots. In this part of Brooklyn, this is architecture of great sophistication. Elsewhere (say Florida) it would be just another apartment complex.

[E12] **Spring Creek (Nehemiah housing),** SE cor. Elton Street and Flatlands Ave. south to Vandalia Ave. (both N and S sides). Phase 1: 2009; Phase 2: 2010. *Alexander Gorlin.*
   800 pre-fabricated low-income housing units on 45 acres of landfill. Perhaps no other architectural endeavor is as challenging as affordable housing, and *Gorlin* gets kudos for trying something new. Perhaps all that is needed is trees (lots of them), but without them the endless rows of brightly colored, flat façades are eerie and unsettling, like an abandoned movie set.

QUEENS

N

College Point

Whitestone /
Malba /
Beechurst

Ditmars /
Steinway

Hallets Point /
Ravenswood /
Astoria

Flushing

Jackson
Heights

Corona

South Astoria /
Sunnyside

Hunters Point /
Long Island City

Elmhurst

Ridgewood

Forest Hills /
Kew Gardens

Woodhaven /
Richmond Hill

QUEENS
Borough of Queens / Queens County

 Colonial

 Georgian / Federal

 Greek Revival

 Gothic Revival

 Villa

 Romanesque Revival

 Renaissance Revival

 Roman Revival

 Art Deco / Art Moderne

 Modern / Postmodern

 Designated Landmark

Queens is the home of two of the three metropolitan airports—LaGuardia and Kennedy International. Its residents are unable to forget that fact, the drone of jets and props ever reminding them as planes swoop out of the sky and into these all-weather aerodromes. Awareness of modern technology is balanced by contact with nature—postage-stamp-sized front lawns or the vastness of the Jamaica Bay Wildlife Refuge (now a part of the Gateway National Recreation Area), not to mention the borough's other parks: 16,397 acres in all. Queens is the largest borough: 114.7 square miles (126.6 including inland waters), constituting almost a third of the City's entire area, almost twice the area of Staten Island alone. In population it ranks second only to Brooklyn.

As a borough it is predominantly a bedroom community. The last great open spaces of New York were here until the late 1940s, allowing developers to meet the need for detached dwellings: suburbia within the City limits. However, a good deal of industry also thrives within its boundaries: in Long Island City and Maspeth and along the Long Island Rail Road are manufacturers of a wide variety of products.

Before Queens became a borough, it was a far larger county, encompassing its present-day area as well as that of Nassau (a new county created as a by-product of consolidation into Greater New York in 1898). The borough is named for Catherine of Braganza, Queen of Charles II.

The vastness of Queens and its relatively late development have encouraged the retention of the old town, village, and subdivision names for its various communities. From a strong sense of pride and identification with the outlying suburbs, residents never refer to themselves as "Queensites" but rather as living in Jamaica, or Flushing, or Forest Hills, or St. Albans. If pressed further, the response to "Where do you live?" becomes "Long Island."

W1

Western Queens

Greater Astoria

The peninsula projecting into Hell Gate's once turbulent waters is named for the family of *William Hallet*, who received it as a grant from *Governor Peter Stuyvesant* in 1652. From his family's early settlement and that of *Stephen Alling Halsey*, the Father of Astoria, the village of Astoria developed. As a Manhattan suburb its growth followed the introduction of steam-powered ferries in 1815. By 1839 the area had been incorporated, with friends of *John Jacob Astor* winning a bitter factional fight in naming Astoria for him.

W2

W3

1842 saw the completion of the turnpike to Greenpoint. Soon a shipping trade was established in lumber, particularly in exotic foreign woods. Just north of the cove on the mount called Hallets Point, lumber and shipping magnates built mansions, of which a few remain, but deprived of their former splendor and spacious view-laden grounds. Nearby, at the foot of Astoria Boulevard, the area's most significant ferry service to Manhattan, linking easily accessible East 92nd Street, plied the waters between 1867 and the advent of the Triborough Bridge.

The availability of fine lumber and cheap land persuaded piano manufacturer *William Steinway* in the early 1870s to extend his activities from Manhattan to a company town of some 400 acres, purchasing a superb stone house for his family at the foot of Steinway Street. The mansion, workers' housing, and both old and new factories all remain.

HALLETS POINT

[W1] Good Church of Deliverance, Pentecostal, and First Reformed Church of Astoria/originally **Reformed Dutch Church of Hallets Cove**, 27-26 12th St., bet. 27th Ave. and Astoria Blvd. W side. 1889. Steeple, 1900.

Squat church, worthy tower: a late **Victorian** terra cotta, brick, and verdigris copper Goth. Bold, monolithic, homely, and magnificent

[W2] Originally **Dr. Wayt House**, 9-29 27th Ave., NW cor. 12th St. ca. 1845.

An austere, elegantly proportioned brick **Italianate** mansion. The eyebrow windows are inherited from the Greek Revival.

[W3] Greek Orthodox Church of the Holy Protection of the Mother of God, 26-37 12th St., NE cor. 27th Ave. 1860s.

Lusty **Corinthian** columns carry a two-story porch spanning from a brick body to the street. The **Benner** house on 14th Street had porches far grander than this before the Vandals arrived. See Necrology.

W8

[W4] Astoria Branch, Queens Borough Public Library, 14-01 Astoria Blvd., NE cor. 14th St. 1904. *Tuthill & Higgins*.

One of many branch libraries donated by *Andrew Carnegie*: tan Roman brick and a steep hipped roof.

[W5] St. George's Church, SE cor. 14th St. and 27th Ave. ca. 1900.

Timber and stone join to suggest an English country church.

[W6] Bilquis Mansion/originally **Robert Benner House**, 25-37 14th St., bet. Astoria Park S. and 26th Ave. E side. 1852.

Once proudly presenting a two-story (balconied) **Doric** façade, this grand Southern mansion has been ravaged. Built by *James L. Stratton* and occupied by Manhattan lawyer *Robert Benner*, a fancier of flori- and arbori-culture, its deep front yard harbored a magnificent copper beech tree. The tree has given way to a parking lot; the **Doric** and **Corinthian** orders and balcony, to banality.

[W7] **25-38 14th Street** (house), bet. Astoria Park S. and 26th Ave. W side. 1880s.

A Shingle Style survivor, although clad in simulated brick (sheet asphalt siding).

[W8] **25-45, 25-47 14th Place** (two-family house), bet. 26th Ave. and Astoria Park S. E side. ca. 1910.

Both corniced, one columned, their adjoining two-story porches contribute to a strong bay-windowed composition. Who stole the missing **Roman Doric** column?

A venture to the north across Astoria Park South:

[W9a] **Astoria Park,** Shore Blvd. to 19th St., Ditmars Blvd. to Astoria Park S.

A tilted piece of greensward giving picnic views of the Triborough and Hell Gate Bridges and Manhattan skyline. And within its bounds, **Art Deco:**

[W9b] **Astoria Play Center and Swimming Pool,** N.Y.C. Department of Parks & Recreation, in Astoria Park. 1936. *J.M. Hatton.* 🖋

W12

W6

An expansive **Art Deco/Art Moderne** WPA-era pool complex and bathhouse.

[W10] **Triborough Bridge,** now **Robert F. Kennedy Bridge**. 1936. *O.H. Ammann,* engineer. *Aymar Embury II,* architect.

A whole highway system, trestled and bridged, of which this, the **Hell Gate** span, is the greatest part. Renamed in 2008.

🚋 [W11] **Hell Gate Bridge**/officially the **East River Arch Bridge of the New York Connecting Railroad**. 1917. *Gustav Lindenthal,* engineer. *Henry Hornbostel,* architect.

The through connection for the Penn Central (now **Amtrak**) on its way from Washington through New York to Boston (it tunnels under both the Hudson and East Rivers, rising in Queens to pass over and through these great over- and under-slung bowstring trusses). *Hornbostel* designed the massive Classical piers, but the glory of the bridge is in the forms of *Lindenthal*'s engineering.

RAVENSWOOD

Ravenswood, bordering the East River north of the Queensboro Bridge, is a low-density area with a mixture of waterside industry (cf. Con Ed's **Big Allis**) and public housing. Culture has moved in through the Noguchi Museum and the Socrates Sculpture Park.

[W12] **Piano Factory Apartments**/originally **Sohmer Piano Company** (factory), 31-01 Vernon Blvd., SE cor. 31st Ave. 1886-1887. *Berger & Baylies.* Top story and mansard added, 1910. 🖋

Steinway competitor *Sohmer* firmly established himself close to the piano king in this monumental **Romanesque Revival** factory-warehouse. Brick bearing walls, and segmentally-arched windows rise to a Second Empire clock tower, added, along with two more floors, as business flourished. Now a formidable condominium.

N

9b

Continue ↑ for Ditmars / Steinway

23rd Rd
23rd Dr
23rd Ter
24th Av

19th St
21st St
23rd St
24th Dr

24th Rd

10

Triborough Br

Hoyt Av North

9a

Hoyt Av South

Astoria Park South

25th Rd
25th Rd

26th St

Crescent St

29th St

7 6 8

Bayline St

26th Av
26th Rd

21st St

23rd St

Astoria Blvd South

26th Av

4th St

9th St

11th St

27th Av

26th Av

27th Av

Newtown Av

1st Av

2   3
5
1

Astoria Blvd

20

Crescent Av

27th Av

4

21st St

Crescent St

28th Av

Welling Ct

12th St

14th St

Main Av

30th Av

21

30th Rd

Astoria Blvd

Welling Ct

30th Rd

22
23

30th Rd

30th Dr

28th St

30th St

Hallets Cove

30th Dr

Alley

12

31st Av

31st Rd

Crescent St

16

31st Dr

13

27th St

29th St

31st St

Broadway

17 18

15

33rd Av

33rd Rd

14

33rd Rd

9th St

11th St

12th St

13th St

14th St

34th Av

Vernon Blvd

34th Av

21st St

22nd St

23rd St

24th St

Crescent St

27th St

28th St

29th St

35th Av

35th Av

36th Av

36th Av

14th St

37th Av

Vernon Blvd

9th St

11th St

38th Av

19

39th Av

40th Av

Continue ↑ for Hunters Point / Long Island City

[W13] **Socrates Sculpture Park,** 31-42 Vernon Blvd., bet. 31st Dr. and Broadway. W side on the bank of the East River. 1986. 718-956-1819. Open 365 days a year from 10am to sunset. Admission is free. *info@socratessculpturepark.org*

A fallow riverside site converted into an enormous outdoor sculpture garden through the combined efforts of the Athena Foundation, and the City's Departments of Parks & Recreation, and Cultural Affairs. On display can be found, from time to time, the lusty work of *Mark Di Suvero* (the foundation's founder), *Alice Aycock, Richard Serra*, and many others.

[W14] **Isamu Noguchi Garden Museum,** 32-37 Vernon Blvd., NE cor. 33rd Rd. (Entrance on 33rd Rd. bet. 9th and 10th Sts.) 1985. *Isamu Noguchi,* sculptor. *Shogi Sazao,* architect. 718-204-7088. Open to the public. April-October: We, Th, Fr 10-5; Sa, Su 11-6.

Sculptures in stone, metal, and wood grace this former *Noguchi* studio and its adjacent gar-

[W17] **Long Island City High School,** 1680 Broadway, bet. 14th St. and 21st St. S side. 1995. *Gruzen Samton.*

Bulky and largely no-nonsense, the School offers a strongly articulated, polychromatic entrance bay to its teenage horde. The more whimsical work of *Gruzen Samton* in public schools for the younger student is here muted for the hopefully serious challenge of high schooling.

W17

W14

W18

den. Stage designs for *Martha Graham* and *George Balanchine* as well as his astonishing rice paper and bamboo-shaded Akari lamps are also on display.

[W15] Originally **Lassie Coats (Barkin-Levin factory),** 12-12 33rd Ave., SW cor. 13th St. 1958. *Ulrich Franzen.*

Built for a clothing manufacturer **expatriate** from the overcrowded garment district of Manhattan. Incomparably crisp architecture, poorly maintained, and badly altered. Now a canvas for graffitti.

[W16] **12-15** and **12-17 31st Drive,** bet. 12th (one-way north) and 14th Sts. N side. 1920s and 1870s, respectively.

Two porticoes of finely crafted columns; well-proportioned columns can heal many architectural wounds.

[W18] **Community Church of Astoria,** 14-42 Broadway, bet. 14th St. and 21st St. S side. 1952. Total reconstruction, 1986, *Alfredo De Vido Assocs.*

A suave, subtle reconstruction and extension of a church serving a congregation of limited means.

[W19] **Ravenswood Plant, Consolidated Edison Company,** 36th to below 40th Aves., Vernon Blvd. to East River. 1961.

Towering candy-striped smokestacks, landmarks from all directions: two at 450 feet, one at 500 feet. Home of **Big Allis,** the enormous (and, for a time, quite cranky) electrical generator manufactured by Allis-Chalmers.

W20

W22

W23

ASTORIA

 [W20] **Our Lady of Mt. Carmel Roman Catholic Church**, 23-35 Newtown Ave., NW cor. Crescent St. Narthex, 1915. Nave, 1966.

A dignified **neo-Gothic** evocation in limestone, an architectural treat; Mt. Carmel Institute, the parish hall (across the avenue to the southwest), an intriguing Italian Renaissance foil.

[W21] **HANAC**/formerly **74th Precinct, N.Y.C. Police Department**, 23-16 30th Ave., bet. 23rd and Crescent Sts. ca. 1890.

A **Romanesque Revival** symphony. An important architectural-cultural anchor in a neighborhood showing many conflicting tides of development. (HANAC stands for Hellenic American Neighborhood Action Committee, a social-services agency for the area's large Greek community.)

[W22] **Episcopal Church of the Redeemer and Chapel**, 30-30 Crescent St., NW cor. 30th Rd. 1868. Consecrated, 1879.

A dark, brooding, ashlar stone church. Instead of a spire, the bell tower flaunts an illuminated cross.

[W23] **Good Shepherd United Methodist Church**/originally **First Methodist Episcopal Church of Astoria**, 30-40 Crescent St., SW cor. 30th Rd. 1908.

Naive **Gothic Revival** in light rock-faced granite ashlar, its stubby tower crudely crenellated.

DITMARS

Nearest trains: N, W to Astoria–Ditmars Blvd.

Con Edison Astoria: *Opened in 1906, covering hundreds of acres north of 20th Avenue and west of 37th Street, the enormous Con Ed power plant is an unsung landmark of Astoria. Built by the Consolidated Gas Company of New York, it was the world's largest cooking-gas generating plant*

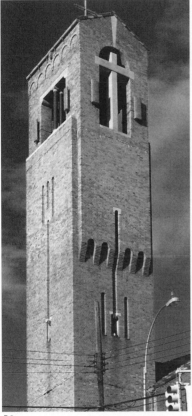

D2

when completed, serving both Manhattan and the Bronx via underwater tunnels. Both natural gas and electricity are now distributed from here.

[D1] Arleigh Realty Company row housing and apartments, 21-11 to 21-77, 21-12 to 21-72 28th St. Both sides. 21-12 to 21-72 29th St. W side, bet. 21st Ave. and Ditmars Blvd. ca. 1925.

Speculative mid-block terraces of mansarded row houses work with a gentle rise in topography, offering "the picturesque" despite repetition. Here, architecture enriches a neighborhood and gives it identity.

[D2] Church of the Immaculate Conception (Roman Catholic), 29-01 Ditmars Blvd., NE cor. 29th St. 1950. *Henry V. Murphy.*

Twentieth-century Italian **neo-Romanesque**. The powerful corbeled brick bell tower is a dramatic landmark.

[D3] Lawrence Family Graveyard, 20th Rd., SE cor. 35th St. 1703. ✺

A memorable location in history, one of two such landmarked *Lawrence* cemeteries. Here are 89 graves, the first in 1703, harboring *Major Thomas Lawrence*; the last, in 1956.

[D4] St. Irene Chrysovalantou (Greek Orthodox) **Church,** 36-25 23rd Ave., bet.36th and 37th Sts. N side. Altered from two former row houses, 1980.

A charming vernacular residential composition punctuated by the mid-block church. The delight is within: a folk art religious extravaganza, something like walking into a box by artist *Joseph Cornell*. Plan to visit when open.

D4

STEINWAY

William Steinway: *The individual from whom the community derives its name was a brilliant 19th-century entrepreneur. A manufacturer of pianos, Steinway was also a transit magnate (today's Steinway Transit Corporation), builder of an underwater tunnel (today's Flushing Line East River crossing), and developer, together with beer baron George Ehret, of a working-class resort, North Beach (site of today's LaGuardia Airport).*

[D5] Formerly **William Steinway House/** also known as the Steinway Mansion/ originally **Benjamin T. Pike, Jr., House**, 18-33 41st St., bet. Berrian Blvd. and 19th Ave. E side. ca. 1858. ✺

On a mini-mountain in a deciduous jungle inhabited by barking dogs, old cars, and trucks. *William Steinway's* dark gray granite house was a showplace in its time, a rough-hewn granite Italianate villa that served as this merchant's

D7

D8

[D7] **Steinway Reformed Church**/originally **Union Protestant Church**, 41-01 Ditmars Blvd., NE cor. 41st St. 1891.

In 1891 neighbor *William Steinway* contributed the pipe organ to this rural Gothic Revival gem (and no doubt thereby to its change of name and denomination). The many-finialed tower and strong **Shingle Style** volumes are a major monument in this neighborhood.

aerie, overlooking his piano factory and workers' housing to the southwest. His piano factory (1872) is still at the northwest corner of 19th Avenue and 38th Street.

[D6] Originally **Steinway workers' housing**, 41-17 to 41-25, 40-12 to 41-20 20th (Winthrop) Ave., bet. Steinway, 41st (Albert) St. and 42nd (Theodore) Sts. Both sides. 20-11 to 20-29, 20-12 to 20-34 41st St., bet. 20th Ave. and 20th Rd. Both sides. 1877-1879.

Trim, painted Victorian brick row houses, originally rented by the *Steinways* to their workers. Loved. Note the carved stone nameplates on the corner houses bearing the streets' original names, those of *Steinway* family members.

[D8] **St. Francis of Assisi Roman Catholic Church**, 45-04 21st Ave., SE cor. 45th St. 1930.

A modest wood and stucco **neo-Tudor** church.

To the east toward LaGuardia airport:

[D9] Originally **Abraham Lent House**/also known as **Lent Homestead**, 78-03 19th Rd., at 78th St. N side. ca. 1729.

Weathered shingled dormers and clapboard siding—a well-preserved "Dutch" farmhouse—nesting amid lush foliage that also embraces the family cemetery of the *Lent* and *Riker* families. Modern windows have lessened its 18th-century authority.

SOUTH ASTORIA

S3a

S5

Nearest trains: R, V to Steinway Street.

[S1] Sidewalk Clock, in front of 30-78 Steinway St., bet.30th and 31st Aves. W side. 1922. 🏮
One of a group of sidewalk clocks officially designated by the Landmarks Preservation Commission. An inspired decision.

[S2] Church of the Most Precious Blood (Roman Catholic), 32-30 37th St., bet. Broadway and 34th Ave. 1932. *McGill & Hamlin.* Stations of the cross, *D. Dunbar Beck.* St. Theresa and St. Anthony statues, *Hazel Clerc.* Stained glass, *Richard N. Spiers & Son.*
Henry J. McGill's masterpiece. Only the 37th Street façade is clad in stone, reflecting both medieval and modernistic influences in its boxy form. The interior, however, is a celebration of superior ecclesiastical decorative arts of the 1920s and 1930s. In 1934 partner *Talbot Hamlin* retired to become Avery (Architectural) Librarian at Columbia University.

[S3] Kaufman's Astoria Motion Picture and Television Center/formerly **U.S. Army Signal Corps Pictorial Center**/onetime **Eastern Service Studios**/originally **Famous Players Lasky Corporation (Paramount Pictures),** irregular site along 35th Ave. bet. 36th and 35th Sts. Both sides. 🏮
[S3a] Former Building No.1, 35-11 35th Ave., bet. 35th and 36th Sts. N side. 1919-1921. *Fleischman Construction Co.,* designer.
[S4] Museum of the Moving Image, 36-11 35th Ave., bet. 36th and 37th Sts. N side. Altered into museum, 1988, *Gwathmey Siegel & Assocs.* Tu-Fr, 12-4; Sa, Su, 12-6; closed Mo. 718-784-4520.
One of several venerable movie studios still to be found in New York, this sprawling complex is the largest. In the silent era, *Gloria Swanson, Rudolph Valentino, W.C. Fields,* and their peers performed here. After talkies arrived, "Beau Geste," "The Emperor Jones," and the W.P.A.'s "One Third of a Nation" were produced here. Its rebirth in the 1970s saw the making of "The Wiz" and other widely heralded films.
Futures: a new Museum of the Moving Image by *Leeser Associates* might appear around 2020.

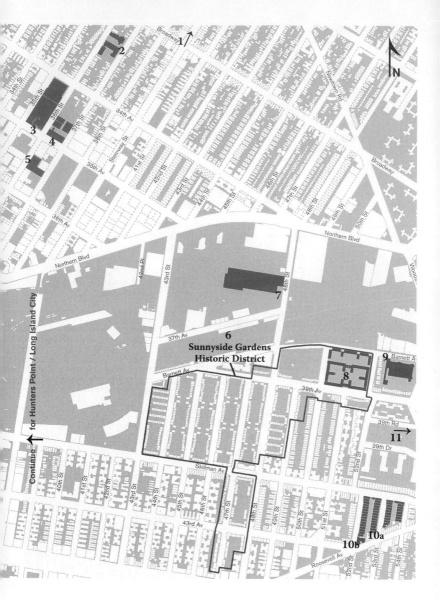

A constructivist steel building for welders
in training. Perhaps they will practice on the
building! See also *Goldner's* **163 Charles Street**
(in the West Village), hugging its *Richard
Meier*–designed neighbor.

SUNNYSIDE

A neighborhood triggered by the arrival of the
IRT Flushing Line nearby in 1917. Though surrounded by industry and cemeteries, its proximity and excellent access to Manhattan have
assured its stability. Its most noted feature is
Sunnyside Gardens.

Nearest trains: No.7 to 52nd Street.

[S6] **Sunnyside Gardens,** bet. 43rd and 48th
Sts., Skillman and Barnett Aves. to 39th Ave.,
plus parts of 49th and 52nd Sts. along Skillman
Ave. 1924-1928. *Clarence S. Stein and Henry
Wright; Frederick Ackerman.*

Seventy-seven acres of barren, mosquito-
infested land were transformed into a groundbreaking experiment in urban housing design by
the City Housing Corporation, headed by
Alexander M. Bing, a New York real estate mogul.
Forced into using the preordained street grid,
architects *Stein* and *Wright* arranged row housing

to face both the street and the interior garden spaces. Walk under **umbrellas of London plane trees** along the paths that penetrate each block, where the architecture is unimportant, but the urban arrangements a source of urbane delight. *Lewis Mumford* lived here from 1925 to 1936.

[S6a] **Sunnyside Gardens Historic District** 🍎
Designated area (see map) includes the **Phipps Gardens**, two courtyard apartment buildings constructed in 1931-32 and 1935, and Sunnyside Park.

[S7] **New York Presbyterian Church** (Korean)/partially the former **Naarden-UOP Fragrances**/originally **Knickerbocker Laundry Company,** 43-23 37th Ave., bet. 43rd and 48th Sts. N side. 1932. *Irving M. Fenichel.* Renovations, extensions, and surelevations, 1999, *Greg Lynn, Michael McInturf and Doug Garafalo.*
They started with Knickerbocker's sleek **Art Moderne** concrete, seemingly molded of stream-lined ice cream, a familiar monument to the

WOODSIDE

Just across the former Long Island City boundary.

[S9] **J. Sklar Manufacturing Company**/formerly **Lathan Lithography Company,** 38-04 Woodside Ave., bet. Barnett and 39th Aves. W side. 1923. *McDonnell and Pearl.*
A **Tudor** house on manicured lawns dis-guises this manufactory of surgical instruments. For once a factory becomes a visual amenity in the community.

[S10a] **Mathews & Company flats,** 52nd St. E side, 53rd St., both sides, 54th St., W side, bet. Skillman and Roosevelt Aves. 52-01 to 53-31 Skillman Ave., bet.52nd and 54th Sts. N side. 1924.
[S10b] **Mathews Apartment Building,** 41-45 52nd St., NE cor. Roosevelt Ave. 1924.
Three-story row-house apartments, with a single, corner apartment house, all of yellow

S7

hundreds of thousands of commuters who sped by on the adjacent LIRR into Manhattan. To this was added a gigantic steel-clad, computer-gen-erated nave that billows out (a rectilinear bal-loon) and down the grade behind.

[S8] **Phipps Gardens,** 51-01 39th Ave., bet. 50th and 52nd Sts. N side. 1931. 52-02 to 53-20 Barnett Ave., bet. 50th and 52nd Sts. S side. 1935. *Isador Rosenfeld,* office of *Clarence S. Stein.* 🍎
Four- to six-story architectural incunabula surrounding two square blocks of lush, green, private, courtyards. The architecture here is clearly secondary to a sense of place. (Look for a second grouping behind the first.)

Kreischerville (Staten Island) brick, by develop-ers who helped make early 20th-century Ridgewood a special place.

And off our map to the east, along Woodside Avenue:

[S11] **St. Paul's Episcopal Church of Woodside,** 39th Ave., SW cor. 61st St. ca. 1873.
An exquisite, rare, rural, board-and-batten **Gothic Revival** wooden church. Let there be a miracle: save this church as a living memorial to its motto, city church/country friendliness.

HUNTERS POINT

Hunters Point, approaching Newtown Creek, was formerly the center of borough government and recently the focus of major development projects by Citicorp, the Port Authority, and the **Queens West** housing.

Nearest trains: No.7 to Vernon Blvd/Jackson Ave. or Hunters Point Ave.; No.7, G to Long Island City/Court Square.

[H1] **Citicorp Building**, 44th Dr. to 45th Ave., W of Jackson Ave. Citicorp parking garage, S of courthouse. 1989. All by *Skidmore, Owings & Merrill.*

Forty-eight stories (some 663 feet), the City's tallest structure outside of Manhattan. The tower dominates Queens, orientating its residents as once the **Twin Towers** oriented Manhattanites.

H1

H3

[H2] **Court Square Place** (United Nations Federal Credit Union), 24-01 44th Rd., bet. 24th and Crescent Sts. 2006. *HLW (Haines Waehler Lundberg).*

A sleek and bulbous Jeff, this time for Citicorp's Mutt, brings a new wave of office workers to Hunters Point.

[H3] **New York State Supreme Court**, Long Island City Branch/originally Long Island City Courthouse, 25-10 Court Sq., at Jackson and Thomson Aves. 1872-1876. *George Hathorne.* Rebuilt, 1904-1908. *Peter M. Coco.* 🞄

Beaux Arts Baroque: limestone, brick, and three kinds of granite (smooth gray, rock-faced pink, and rock-faced slate gray). The present building was built upon the walls of its burned ancestor. It was in this courthouse that the famed 1927 murder trial of *Ruth Snyder* and her lover, *Henry Judd Gray,* took place and where *Willie ("the Actor") Sutton* was asked why he robbed banks. His reply: "Because that's where the money is."

[H4] **Vere26**, 20 Jackson Ave., SE cor. Purves St. 2009. *Robert Scarano.*

A sprightly frame of white-painted steel gives this multi-use building distinction compared to crude speculative building hereabouts in the Boom ending in 2008.

[H5] **Hunters Point Historic District**, 21-09 to 21-51, 21-12 to 21-48 45th Ave., bet.21st and 23rd Sts. Both sides. 44-70 23rd St., bet. 45th Ave. and 44th Dr. W side. Early 1870s. *Spencer B. Root, John P. Rust,* builders, and others. 🞄

A street of virgin row houses, complete with original stoops and cornices. Some are faced in Westchester (or Tuckahoe) marble, a material more resistant than brownstone to weathering.

[H6] **21-49 45th Road**, [H7] **21-33, 21-35, 21-37 45th Road**, bet. 21st and 23rd Sts. (45th Rd. one-way east). N side. ca. 1890. 🞄

The first, a grand symphony in **Romanesque Revival**; the others, a melodic Classical trio, two-story brownstones of a rare sort that can sometimes be found between here and Astoria.

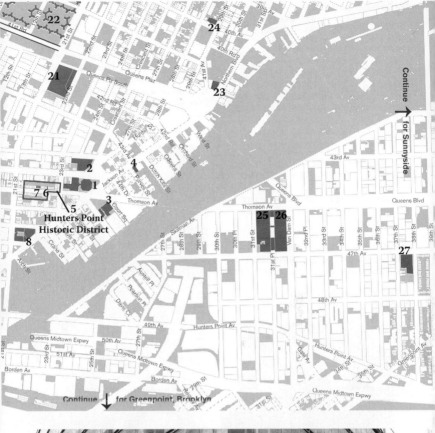

H2

[H8] **P.S.1 Contemporary Arts Center**/
onetime **P.S.1** artists' studios)/before that
Public School 1, originally **Ward 1 School**, 21st
St. bet. 46th Rd. and 46th Ave. 1890-1900.
Altered, 1976, *Shael Shapiro*. Expanded as the
Arts Center, 1997, *Frederick Fisher*.
We-Su, Noon-6; closed Mo-Tu. 718-784-2084.

Now converted to artists' studios, galleries
and supporting spaces in a continuing process
of adaptive reuse for the City's artist community,
this stolid **Romanesque Revival** building was
built when *"Battle Ax" Gleason* was mayor of
Long Island City. It once supported a clock
tower. Now affiliated with **MoMA** (Museum of
Modern Art), it offers the cutting edge that
MoMA's historical perspective lacks.

[H9] **Engine Company 258, Ladder
Company 115, N.Y.C.** Fire Department, 10-
40 47th Ave. (one- way west), bet. Vernon Blvd.
and 11th St. S side. 1903. *Bradford L. Gilbert.*
A robust multistory firehouse with stepped
super-Dutch gable. *Gilbert* was a nationally
recognized railroad architect.

[H10] **St. Mary's Roman Catholic Church**, 49-01
Vernon Blvd., SE cor. 49th Ave. 1887. *Patrick
Charles Keely.*

Brick and brownstone were revealed when
this local landmark was stripped of its many
coats of paint. *Keely's* modeling of the square
brick tower to meet its octagonal spire created
lovely undulating baroque surfaces.

[H11] **108th Precinct, N.Y.C. Police
Department**/originally 75th Precinct 5-47
50th Ave. (one-way east), bet. 5th St. and
Vernon Blvd. N side. 1903. *R. Thomas Short.*

Like the nearby firehouse, a bold municipal
presence, here **neo-Baroque** (or late Mannerist)
rather than the Fire House's Amsterdam revival.
Especially delightful are the extravagant bracketed torchères that frame the entrance. Short is
better known as partner in *Harde & Short.*

The Steinway Tunnels: The twin tubes of the Flushing Line under the East River were originally begun in 1892 by piano king William Steinway as a trolley car connection to Manhattan. A serious explosion, the Panic of 1893, and Steinway's death in 1896 interrupted the project until August Belmont, the IRT financier, revived it in 1902. The tunnel, with reversing loops at each end, became the first connection between Manhattan and Queens in 1907, though it was not put into regular use until converted to subway operation in 1915.

[H12] **Queens Ventilating Building, Queens Midtown Tunnel**, center of Borden Ave., bet. 2nd and 5th Sts. 1939.

A Brobdingnagian utilitarian event on the bed of Borden Avenue. Perhaps *Men in Black* is moving here.

[H13] **Power House Apartments**/originally **Pennsylvania Railroad generating plant**/later **N.Y. & Queens Electric Light & Power Company,**

H8

50-09 Second St., bet. 50th and 51st Aves. E side. 1909. *McKim, Mead & White*. Apartments, 2009. *Karl Fischer.*

Another *McKim, Mead & White* power house, that once bore four great stacks, rampant on the Queens skyline. In the condominium mania, the stacks went, and the powerful arcades that flanked the plant walls were subdued: what had been vigorous industrial architecture was reduced to this bland box.

[H14] **Pepsi-Cola sign**, Pepsi-Cola Bottling Company, 45-00 5th St. (one-way south), bet. 46th Ave. and 46th Rd. W side. Riverfront buildings, 1910-1920. Sign, 1936, *Artkraft Sign Co.*

The upland side of this great sign (**Pepsi-Cola** spelled in black letters backwards?) hardly compares with the colossal neon-lighted front along the East River opposite the UN and Beekman Place. Taken down and rebuilt in 2009.

QUEENS WEST

Adrift in the sea of Queens, this urban island stretches west from Fifth Street between 45th Road and 49th Avenue, then west of Second Street from 50th Avenue to Newtown Creek: lands developed under a Queens West Master Plan, with the Battery Park City model as its guidelines.

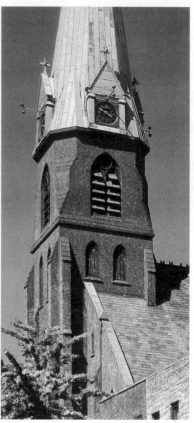

H10

[H15] **Citilights** (apartment building), 4-74 2nd St., bet. 48th and 49th Aves. E side. 1998. *Cesar Pelli & Associates.*

A high-style apartment building that lured needy yuppies with its magnificent views of Manhattan, and easy parking, in a backwater removed from the sounds of roaring traffic. BYOC: Bring Your Own Car.

[H16] **Gantry State Park**, opposite Citilights bet. 48th and 49th Aves., W of Center Blvd. 1998. *Weintraub & di Domenico* with *Thomas Balsley Associates and Sowinski Sullivan.*

The gantry cranes that served transfers of boxcars from rail barges to east-headed trains now serve as symbolic portals to this elegant park; an accessible edge to Queens that revels in the Manhattan skyline. See also *Weintraub's* more recent **Erie Basin Park** (Red Hook, Brooklyn).

[H17] **Trotwood Corporation Building** (apartments), bet. Center Blvd. and 2nd St., 49th and 50th Aves. E side. 2001. *Perkins Eastman.*
Yawn.

H14

H15

H19

[H18] **47-20 Center Boulevard** Apartments. 2007. *Arquitectonica.*

More blandness from the formerly flamboyant Miami-based firm.

*44th Drive: This unusually wide thoroughfare leading to nowhere is the footprint for the louvered IND subway tunnel below, whose tube to East 53rd Street in Manhattan begins under your feet. Both flanks of the Drive are host to a miscellany of municipal activities, including a subway ventilator dating from 1931. The **Water's Edge** restaurant (inside there's good food, clubby wood) at the end is said to specialize in matrimony (proposals and weddings).*

[H19] Originally **New York Architectural Terra-Cotta Company** (office), 42-10 to 42-16 Vernon Blvd., bet. Queens Plaza S. and 43rd Ave. W side. 1892. *Francis H. Kimball.*

Tudor Revival amber brick jewel with Sullivanesque terra-cotta trim. It stands proudly among the artifacts of industrial blight. Look at the chimney pots. Terra-cotta skins ordered through this home office clad such wonders as the **Ansonia** and **Carnegie Hall**, as well as *Kimball's* own **Montauk Club**.

[H20] **Queensboro Bridge**, from Queens Plaza to E.59th-E.60th Sts. in Manhattan. 1901-1908. *Gustav Lindenthal*, engineer. *Palmer & Hornbostel*, architects.

This ornate (note the *Hornbostel* finials) cantilevered bridge formed the backdrop for views from swank New York apartments in countless Hollywood films of the 1940s. Surprisingly, its completion did not lead to the migration across the river that the Williamsburg and Manhattan Bridges had caused. The last trolley car to see service in New York shuttled across the Queensboro, stopping at the (now demolished) elevator tower on Welfare (now Roosevelt) Island. The trolley and vehicular elevators were discontinued in 1955, when a bridge was completed between the island and Queens.

[H21] **Silvercup Studios**/originally **Gordon Baking Company**, Queens Plaza S. to 43rd Ave., bet. 21st and 22nd Sts. ca. 1939.

The old Silvercup bakery played a subsidiary role as pedestal for the magnificent giant neon sign advertising its product. Visible in Manhattan across the river, the refurbished sign now proclaims the bakery building's new role as a TV and movie studio.

[H22] **Queensbridge Houses**, N.Y.C. Housing Authority, Vernon Blvd. to 21st St., 40th Ave. to Bridge Plaza N. 1939. *William F.R. Ballard*, chief architect. *Henry Churchill, Frederick G. Frost, Burnett C. Turner*, associate architects.

One of the best City housing projects, its handsome light brown brick now minus its original red window frames. Once the nation's largest public housing complex: 3,149 units in 26 six-story buildings, occupying six superblocks.

H20

H21

[L24] **St. Patrick's Roman Catholic Church**, 39-38 29th St. (one-way north), NW cor. 40th Ave. 1898.

Squat and stuccoed **Renaissance Revival,** save for the neatly louvered boxes atop unfinished twin bell towers.

[L25] **LaGuardia Community College**, CUNY, Main Building/originally **White Motor Company Factory**, 31-10 Thomson Ave., bet. 31st St. and 31st Place. S side to 47th Ave. ca. 1920. Converted, 1977, *Stephen Lepp & Assocs.*
[L26] **East Building**/originally **Equitable Bag Company**, 31st Place to Van Dam St. S side, to 47th Ave. 1949. Addition, 1957. Conversion, 1990, *Warner, Burns, Toan & Lunde.*

The main building is a delicious, caramel-colored marvel with vermilion window frames and a similarly painted sculpted entry gate. Its eastern neighbor tries for monumentality, but seems an awkward cousin to the parent institution.

[L27] **Queens Vocational Technical High School**, 37-02 47th Ave., bet. 37th and 38th Sts. **Original School**, 1929. **Addition**, 2005, *Dattner Architects.*

The new addition adds technology laboratories and other supporting facilities, doubling the size of the original. Here is the school as factory, students punching the clock in a monumental brick container. Nice glass details at the corners.

LONG ISLAND CITY

Separated from the town of **Newtown** in 1870. Between 1870 and 1898, when consolidated into Greater New York, **Long Island City** was itself a city, encompassing not only the area we still identify with its name, but also adjacent communities to the north, northeast, and east.

What is currently called Long Island City includes the Queensboro bridge approaches, Queens Plaza, recycled factories, and railroad yards falling into disuse.

Nearest trains: 7, N, W to Queensboro Plaza; E, R, V to Queens Plaza; N, W to 39th Ave.

[L23] Formerly **Chase Manhattan Bank Building**/originally **Bank of the Manhattan Company**, 29-27 41st Ave., at Queens Plaza. 1927. *Morrell Smith.*

The crenellated clock tower commands this giant tangle of elevated train viaducts.

BLISSVILLE

Transport: car or the Greenpoint Avenue bus (No.24); there are no subways anywhere close to Blissville.

[B1] **N.Y.C. Fire Department Repair and Transportation Unit**, 48-58 35th St., NW cor. Hunters Point Ave., to 34th St. ca. 1935.

A tall radio-transmission tower and the series of exposed roof ribs identify this barrel-vaulted municipal garage where the City's fire trucks go for repairs—or to die.

[B2] **St. Raphael's Roman Catholic Church**, 35-20 Greenpoint Ave., SW cor. Hunters Point Ave. 1885.

A boldly modeled brick and sandstone church perched atop a hill abutting the Long Island Expressway and across from Calvary Cemetery, its steeple an orienting landmark in a widespread district.

[B3] Gatehouse, Old Calvary Cemetery (Roman Catholic), Greenpoint Ave. entrance opp. Gale Ave., off Borden Ave. S side. 1892.

A romantic, vernacular, spectacular **Queen Anne** gem. Others of its genre have almost all been confiscated by time. (By 1916, this first part of the accretive four-section cemetery had received 1,170,455 interments!)

H23

[B4] Chapel, Old Calvary Cemetery (Roman Catholic), in the center of the cemetery (drive in). ca. 1895.

A miniature **Sacré Coeur** beehive tower rises above a supporting cast of Spanish tile roofs, surrounded by huddled small Roman temple-mausoleums.

On axis with the chapel (cemetery section 3b) is the **Halloran Mausoleum**, an example of Victorian neo-Grecian: Philadelphia's *Frank Furness* and Berlin's *Karl Schinkel* could have been in partnership for this. The **Johnston Mausoleum**, a small domed neo-Baroque "chapel," crowns a hill 1,000 feet away.

*Cemetery within a cemetery: When the Roman Catholic Diocese of New York purchased the first lands for Calvary, in 1846, from the Alsop family, the deal depended upon the diocese permitting the existing **Alsop Burying Ground** to remain—which it still does—241 feet from the old Penny Bridge Entrance. It contains 34 monuments dating from 1743 to 1889.*

NECROLOGY

Remsen House, 9-26 27th Ave., SW cor. 12th St. ca. 1835.

Greek Revival stuccoed house, handsomely maintained with rural grounds, rubble garden walls, iron fence, slate sidewalk. Gone.

26-35 and 26-41 4th Street (houses), bet. 26th and 27th Aves. E side. ca. 1835.

Two of the last of Astoria's palatial Greek Revival mansions built by shipping and lumber entrepreneurs during the mid-19th century.

31-41 12th Street, SE cor. 31st Dr. (one-way east). ca. 1860.

Freestanding Italianate rural house inundated with brown-green composition asphalt-shingle siding that nevertheless allowed the window detail, the wood trim, and the house's basic form to carry the day.

Necrology, 26-22 12th Street

New York Daily News printing plant, 55-02 2nd St., SW cor. 55th Ave. at Newtown Creek. 1972. *Harrison & Abramovitz.*

A dated gray ghost on what for a while was called News Point. It occupied the former site, until World War II, of the National Sugar Refining Company, manufacturers of Jack Frost sugar. Demolished as part of an area-wide redevelopment by the Port Authority.

NECROLOGY (half-dead division)

12th Street, bet. Astoria Park S. and 26th Ave. 1860s.

Three Italianate houses (with Roman Tuscan columns) had survived until recently. Only one, **26-22,** is there now: **25-70** and **26-04** are gone.

Central Queens

Settled in 1642 and chartered by the Doughty Patent of 1640, the old Town of Newtown encompassed present-day communities that form central Queens. Its western reaches are filled with endless blocks of old frame buildings, whereas central and eastern parts have become dense apartment districts. **Jackson Heights** developed between the two world wars, and the trunk along Queens Boulevard in both Rego Park and Forest Hills branched out after World War II. **Forest Hills** was named (1901) by developer *Cord Meyer* and immortalized by Forest Hills Gardens, the magnificent town-

NORTH BEACH

North Beach is a community no more. But prior to World War I it was Queens County's Coney Island on the Sound, as Rockaway was the borough's resort on the ocean. North Beach was an outgrowth of the working-class resort named Bowery Bay Beach, which opened in 1887 through a joint investment of piano maker *William Steinway*, beer king *George Ehret*, and patent-medicine manufacturer *Henry Cassebeer*. Bad associations with the name Bowery resulted in its renaming in 1891 as **North Beach**. Located on Queens' north shore, between 81st

J5

planning/real estate scheme of the Russell Sage Foundation, to whom *Meyer* had sold vast land. **Rego Park** is named for the developing/building Rego (Real Good) Construction Company, which pioneered building in that area.

The center of "New Towne," occupied the winding stretch of Broadway north of Queens Boulevard. Vestiges of the community remained well into the 20th century, but only a single church building still stands. Newtown pippins, grown in the apple orchards of this area were prized by the English, to whom they were exported for the manufacture of cider! After consolidation with New York in 1898 the name Newtown quickly fell into disuse, and the local community became known as **Elmhurst**.

Street and Flushing Bay, it flourished until Prohibition. The picnic grounds and dance halls, the Ferris wheels and carrousels, the promenades and steamboat pier were emptied of their summer crowds with the banning of alcohol. In 1930 the site became **Glenn H. Curtiss Airfield**. The City rented it in 1935 to develop what was first dubbed **North Beach Airport** and, in 1939, renamed **LaGuardia Field**.

[N1] **LaGuardia Airport**/originally **North Beach Airport**, N of Grand Central Pkwy., bet. 81st St. and 27th Ave. (Entries at 94th St. and 23rd Ave.) **Original buildings**, 1939. *Delano & Aldrich*.

Built for the 1939-1940 New York World's Fair, it was New York's second (chronologically) municipal airport (after Floyd Bennett Field in Brooklyn).

[N1a] **Central Terminal**. 1965. *Harrison & Abramovitz*. Expanded, 2005. *William Nicholas Boudova + Associates*.

The main terminal, in a great glass arc, bears a parasol roof (with no function) as a symbol of flight. The new **Air Traffic Control Tower** stands 233 feet tall, dwarfing the ghost of its 150 foot predecessor.

J4

[N1b] **US Airways Terminal**. 1992. *William Nicholas Boudova + Associates*.

Typical of modern airline terminals: exposed trusses, concourses bathed in natural light, food courts, and lots and lots of retail to lure the nervous, impulsive, or delayed traveler.

[N2] **Marine Air Terminal, LaGuardia Airport**, entry at 82nd St. and Ditmars Blvd. 1939-1940. *Delano & Aldrich*. Restoration, 2005, *Beyer Blinder Belle*. 🍎 *Interior*.

This breathtaking **Art Deco** extravaganza lurks on the northwest edge of the field. Originally built to serve Pan American Airways flying boats of the 1930s (remember the Yankee Clipper?).

JACKSON HEIGHTS

Nearest trains: No.7 to 82nd St.-Jackson Heights.

Beginning in 1913 (on 82nd Street, between Roosevelt and Northern Boulevard), the Queensboro Corporation constructed residential Jackson Heights, named for *John C. Jackson*, who had laid out Northern Boulevard. Elevated transit service along Roosevelt Avenue would not arrive until 1917, and the lands, called "the cornfields of Queens," were still being tilled as market gardens, with some of them serving the special needs of the Chinatown community. At first, the Corporation's units were rental, but after 1919 they were also marketed as cooperatives.

[J1] **Jackson Heights Historic District**, mostly between Roosevelt Avenue and 34th Avenue, 78th and 88th Streets, with peninsulas north to Northern Boulevard and west to 76th Street. Mostly 1914 to 1939. 🍎

J7

A vast residential community whose livability remains high to this day, even though many avenue frontages originally intended as end-block parks were developed as lesser works of architecture ... and of habitability.

[J2] **37-46 to 37-60 83rd Street Apartments**. 1911. *Charles Peck*.

Brick and bay-windowed two-and-a-half-story row housing. Exceptional low rise housing in this central Heights location.

The core apartment houses:

[J3] **Laurel Court**, 33-01 to 33-21 82nd Street, SE cor. Northern Blvd. 1913-1914. *George Henry Wells*.

The northern anchor and **earliest entry** into what was to become the Historic District. Nice to think about.

[J4] **Towers Apartments,** 34th Ave., bet. 80th and 81st Sts. N side. 1923-1925. *Andrew J. Thomas.*

A brick apartment house morphs into romantic tile-capped **Romanesque Revival** towers at the sky.

[J5] **Chateau Apartments,** 34th Ave. bet. 80th and 81st Sts. S side. 1922. *Andrew J. Thomas.*

Again the skyline offers history; this time in high neo-*Mansart* roofs. Blois in Jackson Heights?

[J6] **Dunolly Gardens,** 78-11 35th Avenue, 78th to 79th Sts., bet. 34th and 35th Aves. 1939. *Andrew J. Thomas.*

Art Moderne with the very modern corner windows of the 1930s that did, in fact, expand the perceived apartment space.

[J7] **Greystone,** 35-15 to 35-51, 35-16 to 35-52 80th St., bet. 35th and 37th Aves. Both sides. 1917. *George Henry Wells.*

[J8] **Fillmore Hall,** 83-10 35th Ave., bet. 83rd and 84th Sts. S side. 1936. *Joshua Tabachnik.*

[J9] **Spanish Gardens,** midblock only, bet. 37th and Roosevelt Aves., 83rd to 84th Sts. 1923. *Andrew J. Thomas.*

[J10] **Linden Court,** midblock only, bet. 37th and Roosevelt Aves., 84th to 85th Sts. 1919-1921. *Andrew J. Thomas.*

Nice brickwork and leafy passages between save these vaguely neo-Gothic apartment blocks from being run of the mill.

[J11] **English Convertible Country Homes,** bet. 34th and 35th Aves., 84th to 88th Sts. 1920s. Various architects, including *Robert Tappan.*

Neo-Georgian cottages set amid lush lawns.

[J12] **34-19 to 34-47 90th Street, 34-20 to 34-48 91st Street**, bet. 34th and 35th Aves. 1931. *Henry Atterbury Smith.*

Two sets of three six-story apartments, similar in organization, but not appearance, to the same architect's **Shively Sanitary Apartments** on Manhattan's East 77th Street, turned diagonal to the street grid. Only the central structure of each group had an elevator; upper-floor tenants had to use roof bridges to reach adjacent buildings.

[J13] **87th to 90th Streets, 30th to 31st Avenues**, both sides. ca. 1939.

Latter-day "brownstones," in the sense that these too are embellished row houses, but in a simplified neo-Norman style.

[J14] **115th Precinct, N.Y.C. Police Department**, 92-15 Northern Blvd., bet. 92nd and 93rd Sts. N side. 1985. *Gruen Assocs.*

Dark brown brick and terra cotta make an unconvincing municipal fortress. What are they afraid of? The entrance doors recall those into a castle, but the brick arch that levitates around them gives it all away: architectural bravado masking the real bravery of police within.

[J15] **Blessed Sacrament Church complex** (Roman Catholic), 35th Ave. bet. 93rd and 94th Sts. N side. Auditorium, 1933, *McGill & Hamlin.* **Convent**, 1937, *Henry J. McGill.* **Church**, 1949, *Henry J. McGill.* Additions.

The 1930s work is the best here, influenced by *Lutyens, Dudok,* and *Sir Giles Gilbert Scott.* The church was built a decade after its design.

J14

J16

CORONA

Nearest trains: No.7 to 103rd St–Corona.

A Tribute to Satchmo: An exuberant mural to Louis Armstrong embellishes the otherwise ho-hum design of Intermediate School 227, which bears the trumpeter's name (32-02 Junction Boulevard, SW corner 32nd Avenue). Designer and team director, Lucinda Luvaas, of City Arts Workshop. 1981.

[J16] **Langston Hughes Community Library and Cultural Center,** Queens Public Library, NE cor. 100th St. and Northern Blvd. 2000. *Davis Brody Bond.* 718-651-1100.
Frozen poetry? Here is serious architecture dedicated to a great African-American poet.

[J17] **P.S. 92,** 99-01 34th Ave., bet. 99th and 100th Sts. 1993. *Gruzen Samton.*
Broken and bay-windowed forms, crowned with vaulted spaces, bring down the scale of this

J18

J23

polychromatic brick and copper-colored metal school. But where have the window washers gone?

[J18] **Shaw A.M.E. Zion Church** (African Methodist Episcopal)/originally **Northside Hebrew Congregation,** 100-05 34th Ave., bet. 100th and 101st Sts. N side. ca. 1910.
A generous pediment with four Ionic columns make a modest monument in the context of humility.

[J19] **Florence E. Smith Community Center,** Corona Congregational Church, 102-19 34th Ave., bet. 102nd and 103rd Sts. N side. 1981. *Medhat Abdel Salam.*
Strong, simple, necessary. The receding brick planes of the portico frame a dignified entry.

[J20] **Louis Armstrong House Museum**/formerly **Louis Armstrong House,** 34-56 107th St. (oneway north), bet. 34th and 37th Aves. W side. 1910. *Robert W. Johnson.* Later additions.

J17

J22

J25

Reconfigured for museum, 2000, *Rogers Marvel. & Platt Byard Dovell White.* ☎ 718-478-8274. *www.louisarmstronghouse.org*

No McMansion. As sensitive as this jazz great was to music, he was unconcerned with architectural pretensions. *Armstrong* lived here with his wife from 1943 until his death in 1971; his wife till hers, in 1983. Now elevated to museum status, it attracts hordes of dedicated followers. A svelte, glassy **Visitors Center**, by *Caples Jefferson*, is planned.

A one-way southbound trip down 104th Street:

🎵 [J21] **Our Lady of Sorrows Roman Catholic Church**, 104-01 37th Ave., NE cor. 104th St. 1899. Convent, ca. 1895.

No nonsense neo-Gothic; not as the French did it, nor the English, but stolid do-it-yourself Gothic, the arched nave stained glass window openings shielded with aluminum and clear glass by a heavy hand.

[J22] **Emanuel Lutheran (Evangelical) Church**, 37-53 104th St., SE cor. 37th Dr. Rectory, 37-57 104th St., bet. 37th Dr. and 38th Ave. W side. ca. 1910.

Church: spartan form and austere brick. Rectory: very lovely wood frame, set back deeply from the street.

🎵 [J23] **Iglesia Metodista**/originally **Corona Methodist Church**, 42-15 104th St., NE cor. 43rd Ave. ca. 1905.

Whitewashed rock-faced block composed as a squat primitive neo-Gothic tower and nave ensemble.

Along 47th Avenue, one-way westbound:

[J24] Originally **Edward E. Sanford House**, 102-45 47th Ave., bet. 102nd and 104th Sts. N side. ca. 1871. 🎵

A rare, largely intact survivor of the 19th-century village of Newtown, a freestanding rural house whose "fancifully carved elements...

transform a humble, domestic structure into an architectural delight," according to the Landmarks Preservation Commission.

Nicholas Coppola, Sr. At the headquarters of The Corona Community Ambulance Corps, at 104-38 47th Ave., between 104th and 108th Sts., one finds a humble front yard, an often used outdoor fireplace facing the street (and the community), and a large bronze marker dedicated in 1967 to the corps' founder, Mr.

J27

Coppola: *A Monumental Pillar Of Compassion And Benevolence For His Fellow Men.*

[J25] **Union Evangelical Church of Corona**, National St., NW cor. 42nd Ave. 1873.

Another modest country church from rural years, unfortunately clad in aluminum siding (the edge and framing details become crude and out of scale).

[J26] **Masjid Alfalah Mosque**, 42-12 National St., bet. 42nd and 43rd Aves. 1990s.

A mini-minaret towers over this outpost of Islam.

[J27] **Hook & Ladder Company 138/ Engine Company 289**, N.Y.C. Fire Department, 97-28 43rd Ave., bet. 97th Place and 99th St. S side. 🖐

Brick and limestone with a slated dormered mansard roof, this small French Renaissance château harbors the local fire company's equipment. Sapeurs et pompiers?

FLUSHING MEADOWS – CORONA PARK

"This is a valley of ashes . . ." In *The Great Gatsby*, F. Scott Fitzgerald wrote of the **Corona Dump**, the landfilled marshes that once straddled the Flushing River, navigational facility to the Village of Flushing. The Dumps, worked by the old Brooklyn Ash Company, achieved park status when selected as the site for the 1939-1940 New York World's Fair, with a repeat performance in 1964-1965. Remnants of both remain in Flushing Meadows-Corona Park. A sense of the area that *Fitzgerald* captured can still be gleaned in the scrap yards of Willets Point (no sidewalks, no sewers), east of Citi Field's parking lot.

[M1] **Citi Field**, bet. Northern Blvd. and Roosevelt Ave., Grand Central Pkwy. to 126th St. 2009. *HOK Sport*.

The Mets new home follows the trend that began in the early 1990s with the same firm's **Camden Yards** in Baltimore: faux-quirky. The old ballparks (Shibe, Wrigley, Fenway, Ebbets) were lovable and asymmetric, because of site constraints (neighboring buildings and railyards),

M1

and because of the way in which they were built: gradually. Then came the suburban, Astroturfed, multi-use stadia of the 1960s and 70s, of which **Shea Stadium** was a prime example. Citi Field evokes bygone days of flannel uniforms, peanuts, and bowler hats. But the ticket prices are pure 21st century.

[M2] **U.S.T.A. National Tennis Center.**
[M2a] **Louis Armstrong Stadium**/originally **Singer Bowl**, 1964-1965 World's Fair, Roosevelt Ave. opp. Willets Point Blvd. S side. 1964. Reconstructed, 1978, *David Kenneth Specter*. Refurbished, 1997, *Rossetti & Assocs.*
[M2b] **Arthur Ashe Stadium**, 1997. *Rossetti & Assocs.*

Two sleek, snappy, substitutes for the West Side Tennis Club's beloved but undersized stadium at Forest Hills (extant), necessary for an ever-expanding audience created by extensive TV promotion of tennis as a big-time spectator sport. The sequential upgrades and expansion of the U.S.T.A. facilities are partially due to the enthusiastic support of former mayor *David Dinkins*.

[M3] **The Unisphere**, 1964-1965 World's Fair. 1963-1964. *Peter Muller Munk, Inc.*, designer. *Gilmore D. Clarke*, landscape architect. ◉

Landscape architect *Gilmore D. Clarke* created the geometric, Beaux Arts–inspired plan for both the 1964-65 World's Fair and its 1939-40 predecessor. Here is his monument: a 380-ton, stainless-steel gridded globe representing the earth (together with orbiting satellites), 12 stories tall, perched on a 70-ton, 20-foot-high weathered-steel base. Weighty.

[M4] **New York Hall of Science**, Flushing Meadows-Corona Park at 111th St. opp. 48th Ave. 1964. *Harrison & Abramovitz*. Extended and remodeled, 1999. *Polshek Partnership and Beyer Blinder Belle*. Open to the public. 718-699-0005. *www.nyscience.org*. Check for opening times (they vary). **Preschool Park**, *Joan Krevlin* of *BKSK Architects*, *Lee Weintraub*, landscape architect, with *Ivan Chermayeff*.

An undulating tapestry of stained glass set in precast concrete, stylish in its time, but ill-suited for museum use. It adjoins its own space park, an array of secondhand American spacecraft. The new auditorium and streamlined retro moderne entrance hall (with shop and canteen), improve one's experience.

The adjacent **Preschool Park** is a festive set of concrete pipes, low plantings, bright colors, and tensile structures, sure to overstimulate even the most phlegmatic child.

[M5] **Queens Museum of Art**/originally 1939-1940 World Fair's **New York City Building**. 1939.

Fair. 60,000 structures were updated in 1992 and again beginning in 2009, this time by City College School of Architecture students.

[M6] **New York State Pavilion**, 1964-1965 World's Fair, Flushing Meadows-Corona Park. 1964. *Philip Johnson and Richard Foster,* architects. *Lev Zetlin*, structural engineer.
[M6a] **Queens Theater-in-the-Park**/originally **Theaterama**. 1964. *Philip Johnson and Richard Foster*. Reconstruction, 1993, *Alfredo De Vido*.

M2   M5   M6

Renovated, 1994, *Rafael Vinoly*. **Expanded,** 2011, *Grimshaw Architects/Amman & Whitney*. We-Su, 12-6; Fr, 12-8; closed Mo-Tu. 718-592-9700. *www.queensmuseum.org*

In 1994 the Queens Museum was the sophisticated hermit crab unleashed by *Vinoly* in this 1939 World's Fair **Art Moderne/Classical** shell. Exhibits of avant-garde art may eventually do for Queens what the radical presentations at **BAM** (Brooklyn Academy of Music) have done for Brooklyn. The *Grimshaw* alterations will more than double the size of the museum, creating seven new galleries organized around a central court. The exterior will be re-sheathed in glass, opening a visual interchange with the surrounding park.

The **Panorama** of New York City is a monumental model of the **whole city**—835,000 buildings—its streets, rivers, bridges, piers, and airports (with planes taking off and landing!), and is the prized centerpiece of the Museum, commissioned by *Robert Moses* for the 1964 World's

Expansion and reconstruction, 2008, *Caples Jefferson Architects*.

One of the few pavilions of 1964 that attempted to use fresh technology as generator of form. In this case tubular perimeter columns (as well as those supporting the observation deck) were slip-formed of concrete in a continuous casting operation that proceeded vertically. The roof, originally sheathed in translucent colored plastic, is a double diaphragm of radial cables separated by vertical pencil rods to dampen flutter. It was the architectural star of the fair: a happy park building working with park space.

The reconstructed **Queens Theater-in-the-Park** has brought sleek architecture and new vigor to this under-utilized complex.

ELMHURST

[E1] **Newtown High School,** 48-01 90th St., bet. 48th and 50th Aves. to 91st St. E side. 1920-1921. *C.B.J. Snyder.* Wings, 1930-1931. *Walter C. Martin.* 1958 Wing. *Maurice Salo.* ♂

Flemish Renaissance Revival with stepped gables and a dramatic 169-foot, central tower topped by a cupola and turrets. *Snyder's* choice of the style showed his awareness of New York

[Map of Elmhurst showing numbered locations 1-10]

as a Dutch colony, and his respect for *Boring & Tilton's* (demolished) turn-of-the-century Flemish Renaissance Revival-style design that his replaced.

[E2] **Reformed Church of Newtown,** and **Fellowship Hall,** 85-15 Broadway, SE cor. Corona Ave. Church, 1831. Hall, 1860. ♂

Magnificent and intact **Georgian-Greek Revival** in white clapboard, wearing Tuscan columns. The stained glass is Victorian.

[E3] **P.S.7, Louis Simeone School,** 80-55 Cornish Ave., at S. Railroad Ave. 2010. *Ehrenkrantz, Eckstut & Kuhn.*

A new prototype for a series of similar schools, built of the same parts (or modules). *E.E.& K.* had followed this route before with a similar program. See the index for examples.

[E4] **St. James Episcopal Hall**/originally St. James Episcopal Church, Broadway, SW cor. 51st Ave. 1734.

Carpenter Gothic additions updated this, the original St. James, built on land granted by the town. The steeple on the west end of this somber Colonial relic was removed at the turn of the century.

[E5] **Queens Long Island Medical Group**/originally **Queens Boulevard Medical Building,** 86-15 Queens Blvd., bet. Broadway and 55th Ave. N side. 1957. *Abraham Geller & Assocs.*

Atop the IND subway tunnel, this clinic required heating and air-conditioning equipment, normally placed in a basement, to be on the roof. The splendid resulting form, **a sophisticated cubist construction**, bears good materials and detailing. It suffers from poor maintenance and ugly signs. A cemetery, to its east, was a welcome forelawn until some enterprising exploiter bought the space, moved the bodies, and built a banal six-story apartment house.

E2

E5

[E6] **Queen's Place**/originally **Macy's Queens,** 88-01 Queens Blvd., bet. 55th and 56th Aves. N side. 1965. *Skidmore, Owings & Merrill.*

Ahh, the 1960s! Take a difficult site, consider that a department store requires exterior walls only as enclosure, calculate the parking problem, add the *SOM* touch, and you got **Macy's Queens**, a circular department store girded by a concentric parking garage. What could be more logical? Luckily, a recalcitrant property owner refused to part with the southwest parcel, forcing a notch to be cut into the squat cylinder of precast concrete panels; a welcome punctuation. The owner died in the early 1980s, and the intruding house was demolished in favor of a modern mediocrity.

[E7] **Citibank, Elmhurst Branch**/originally First National City Bank, 87-11 Queens Blvd. (next to Macy's). 1966. *Skidmore, Owings & Merrill.*

A smaller cylinder than Macy's, by the same architects, but this time in black aluminum and glass. Apparently, circles were a brief sixties' fashion.

| [E8] Originally **Jamaica Savings Bank**, 89-01 Queens Blvd., NE cor. 56th Ave. 1968. *William Cann.* 🖉

A prism of glass, more like an auto showroom than a bank. Designated as a landmark by the Landmarks Commission, but overturned by the City Council.

[E9] **First Presbyterian Church of Elmhurst**/originally First Presbyterian Church of Newtown, Queens Blvd., SE cor. 54th Ave. 1893.

E7

E8

E9

[E9a] **Manse**, 54-03 Seabury St., NE cor 54th Ave. [E9b] **Sunday School**, 54-05 Seabury St., bet. 54th and 55th Aves. ca. 1925.

The church, on a prominent Queens Boulevard corner, is a sober rock-faced granite composition with an 85-foot tower and brownstone trim. The manse behind it, however, is a domestic delight of Shingle Style architecture, currently displaying stylish olive-green garb.

| [E10] **Mathews Company row housing**, in the triangle formed by the embankments of the LIRR Main Line, the former New York Connecting Railway, N of Grand Ave., along Calamus and Ankener Aves., Elk Rd., and 82nd St. ca. 1930. *Louis Allmendinger.*

The same yellow and brown Kreischerville brick used in vast stretches of Ridgewood and Astoria here clads a brick Bauhaus: these could be forms from the experimental **Weissenhofsiedlung** in Stuttgardt (1927): casement windows, ocean liner railings, austere cubistic form. There the work was of *Le Corbusier, Gropius* and their peers. *Louis Allmendinger* didn't do so badly here either.

REGO PARK

[P1] **AT&T, Rego Park Communications Center**, Queens Blvd. bet. 62nd Ave. and 62nd Dr. N side. 1976. *Kahn & Jacobs.*

A bold, monumental brick mass set on a battered base of slab granite. Telephone equipment in fancy dress.

[P2] **Walden Terrace** (apartment complex), 98th to 99th Sts., bet. 63rd Dr. and 64th Rd. 1948. *Leo Stillman.*

Almost two full blocks of eight-story apartment structures whose exposed concrete frames gave them a precocious Continental look when they were erected right after World War II. The long, narrow, midblock courtyards are a green treat.

MASPETH

[P3] **59-37 55th Street** (house), bet. Flushing and Grand Aves. E side, N of LIRR. (55th St one-way south.)

The wood-clapboard frame house, together with its railroad crossing gate, makes an unusual vignette from the past. *"I heard that lonesome whistle blow."* - Hank Williams.

[P4] **St. Stanislaus Kostka Roman Catholic Church**, 57-01 61st St., SE cor. Maspeth Ave. 1913.

Neo-Romanesque, turned diagonally to

P1

the intersection. The inset decorative bricks, gilded and polychromed, subtly embellish the exterior walls.

🏠[P5] **Holy Cross Roman Catholic Church**, 61-21 56th Rd., bet. 61st and 64th Sts. N side. 1913.

The voluptuous curvilinear verdigris copper steeple makes this church extraordinary. *Disney* must be jealous.

[P6] **Church of the Transfiguration** (Roman Catholic), Rear, 64-10 Clinton Ave., bet. 64th St. and Remsen Place. S side. Front, 64-21 Perry Ave. E of 64th St. N side. 1962.

This Lithuanian congregation chose 1930s Art Moderne crossed with a Baltic A-frame. An inscription in Lithuanian recites: "mano namai maldos namai" translated as "my house is a house of prayer." The architecture, certainly fresh in its time, seems dated.

[P6a] **Replica, Lithuanian roadside shrine,** in front of 64-25 Perry Ave. 1981. N side. *Arthur Nelson*, designer and builder.

An exquisitely fashioned work of the master carpenter's traditional art/craft, contributed by the Knights of Lithuania, Council 110.

[P7] **Maspeth Town Hall, Inc.**/originally **Public School 73**, Queens/onetime **112th Precinct, N.Y.C. Police Department**, 53-35 72nd St., bet. 53rd Rd. and Grand Ave. E side.

Stockholm Street
Historic District

RIDGEWOOD

Around the turn into the 20th century Ridgewood was developed as a dense low-rise residential community for the growing German-immigrant population overflowing adjacent Bushwick. Electric streetcars came in 1894 and the Myrtle Avenue Line in 1906 (the elevated part extended in 1915). Members of many local families worked across the county border in the numerous breweries bearing German names.

[R1] **Adrian and Ann Wyckoff Onderdonk House**, 18-20 Flushing Ave., bet. Cypress and Onderdonck Aves. S side. 1731. Open to the public. 718-456-1776. Sat, 2-4:30. 🏠

Once a burned and mutilated hulk and the only remnant of the group of "Dutch" Colonial farmhouses in this area that had withstood the onslaught of heavy industry onto their farm-lands in the early part of this century. Restoration was accomplished by the Greater Ridgewood Historical Society.

The Yellow Brick Houses and Mathews Model Flats

Between 1895 and 1920 some 5,000 work-ing-class structures were built in Ridgewood's housing boom. Early ones were wood framed. But beginning in 1905 the expansion of fire lim-its forced the developers into brick construction, and a sea of two- and three-story yellow-brick row houses, tenements, and flats emerged.

One of the area's best-known builders was Gustave X. Mathews who, with his architect Louis Allmendinger, developed the Mathews Model Flats, considered so advanced in their planning that the City's Tenement House Department exhibited them at the 1915 Panama-Pacific Exposition, in San Francisco. The idiosyn-cratic yellow brick employed by three of the area's most prolific architects, Louis Berger & Company, Louis Allmendinger, and Charles Infanger, was speckled (or iron-spot) brick made in the kilns of the Kreischer Brick Manufacturing Company in what was then Kreischerville (now renamed Charleston), Staten Island. Block after

P5

(72nd St.: one-way south.) 1897.

The people saved this one. A municipal building from the time before Queens absorbed Maspeth and its neighbors: wood frame, wood clapboard siding, with large windows so that schoolchildren would have plenty of light.

NECROLOGY

Maspeth United Methodist Church/also United Methodist Korean Church of Central Queens, 66-39 58th Ave., bet.66th St. and Brown Place. N side. 1907.

A Gothic Revival country church, in its later years clad in wide white bogus clapboard. (The aesthetic problem was more in the detail where the boards meet, their edging and window trim, rather than the boards themselves.)

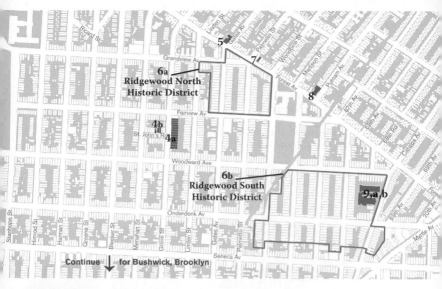

R2

golden block of these happy abodes remain, some of the best, urbanistically speaking, the setback Mathews Company rows along Bleecker and Menahan Streets, north of Cypress Avenue, across from Public School 81, Queens. Some 60 percent of the total number are recognized in what was, in 1983, the largest designation made to the **National Register of Historic Places**. *A few special examples:*

[R2] Stockholm Street, between Onderdonk and Woodward Avenues. 1862-1868, 1870-1894 Stockholm Street (row houses), W side. 1867 to 1893 Stockholm Street (row houses), E side. 376, 380 Woodward Avenue (apartments), SW cor. and SE cor. Stockholm St. ca. 1905. *Louis Berger & Co.*

Ridgewood's own **yellow brick road**. Here, Kreischerville brick not only clads the matching rows of narrow houses, peeking from behind their white-columned piazzas, but also makes up the street bed, which rises gently to meet the green ether of Linden Hill Cemetery.

[R2a] Stockholm Street Historic District, limited to the houses described above. 🍎

[R3] Roman Catholic Church of St. Aloysius, and Rectory, 382 Onderdonk Ave., SE cor. Stockholm St. 1907, 1917. *Francis J. Berlenbach*. **[R4] St. Aloysius Convent**, 1817 Stanhope St. ca. 1893.

Six five-globed cast-iron lampposts guard this **neo-Renaissance** church, with its 165-foot twin towers, and the adjacent rectory. But the true gem is the convent around the corner. When this parish began, the area was called **Old Germania Heights**.

[R4a] 1912-1936 Grove Street, bet. Woodward and Fairview Aves. E side.
[R4b] 11A, 15, 17 St. John's Road, bet. Grove and Menahan Sts. N side. 1908-1910. *Louis Berger*.

While many of Ridgewood's houses set off the yellow masonry with gray limestone trim, not all keystones bear carved human faces, as these groups do.

[R5] **J & C Platz, Inc.,** 65-25 Forest Ave., NW cor. Gates Ave.

A hardware and paint store whose wooden fixtures take one back at least 75 years: oiled floors, pressed-metal ceilings, a gold leaf sign lovingly applied to the glass transom. In this age of the Big Box Store (Home Depot, Lowe's) it's wonderful to find an old family-owned store soldiering on. And with a classy cornice.

[R6a] **Ridgewood North Historic District,** bounded by Forrest Avenue, Linden Street,

R7

[R8] **66-75 Forest Avenue,** NW cor. Putnam Ave. 1906. *Louis Berger & Co.*

Once the local major mansion: a Composite-columned porch fronting the Renaissance Revival body. Later it saw service as a knitting mill, a common "cottage industry" in modern-day Ridgewood, but now has been rescued by a religious community.

*Movie Set: To find a location to film Neil Simon's **Brighton Beach Memoirs** (1986), Hollywood came to the NW corner of Seneca Avenue and Palmetto Street, where the Metropolitan Avenue El structure and adjacent early 1900s buildings permitted the reincarnation of Brooklyn's BMT Brighton Beach elevated of an earlier day. With the right light it was possible to read the set decorator's addition to the outside of the station mezzanine: RIDE THE OPEN AIR ELEVATED.*

R8   R9

R5

Fairview Avenue, and Woodbine Street. Part of the original designation on the National Register of Historic Places. ☛

Bay-bellied yellow-brick workers housing and a 1920s Movie Theater.

[R6b] **Ridgewood South Historic District,** bounded by Woodward and Catalpa Avenues, Woodbine Street, and a midblock line running from Catalpa past Woodbine, between Onderdonk and Seneca Avenues. ☛

[R7] **66-45 Forest Avenue,** bet. Woodbine and Palmetto Sts. N side. ca. 1885.

Miraculous that this clapboard frame house has survived largely intact (meaning: it has not been entirely reclad with composition, asphalt, asbestos, aluminum, vinyl, Perma Stone, stucco, or "face" brick!) from the earliest days of Ridgewood's urbanization, before the stringent fire laws of the nearby City of Brooklyn dictated the use of masonry for densely spaced housing like this. A pure piece of history.

[R9] **St. Matthias Roman Catholic Church,** 58-25 Catalpa Ave., bet. Onderdonk and Woodward Aves. N side. 1926. [R9a,b] **Parish Hall, Rectory,** 1909. *Francis J. Berlenbach.*

Stacked Roman temples form the tower of this yellow brick and terra-cotta church. In its earlier years, the church published postcards that located it across the nearby Brooklyn border, no doubt the fulfillment of a wish by either the parish or the printer (or both).

MIDDLE VILLAGE

[M1] **Gatehouse, Mt. Olivet Cemetery**, Eliot Ave., NE cor. Mt. Olivet Crescent. ca. 1910.

The cemetery guarded by this picturesque gatehouse has not only originally interred remains but also the contents of other, discontinued burial places. For example, the remains from the vaults of the Bedford Street Methodist Episcopal Church, in Manhattan, were trans-

GLENDALE

[G1] **70-12 Cypress Hills Street** (house), opp. 62nd St. W side. ca. 1860.

Compromised by time, and shorn of its detail, this Italianate frame house is nevertheless important because its strong distinctive porched and corniced form is today a rare event for this neighborhood.

M1

ferred here in November 1913; the remains from the Hallet Family Cemetery in April and May 1905.

[M2] **Fresh Pond Crematory**/originally **United States Columbaria Company**, 61-40 Mt. Olivet Crescent, NW cor. 62nd Ave. 1901. *Otto L. Spannhake*. South addition, 1929. Chapel, 1937.

A pompous Ionic-pilastered pale brick and limestone crematory sited across from the undulating landscape of **Mt. Olivet Cemetery**. The neo-Gothic chapel to the north is actually a delightful (but recessive) composition, set back from the crescent as it is.

[M3] **Rentar Plaza**, Metropolitan Ave. at 65th Lane. S side. 1974. *Robert E. Levien Partners*.

An aircraft carrier gone astray that parks 1,200 cars on its flight deck. Glazed brown brick, rounded stair forms. One floor is equal in area to half the Empire State Building.

[G2] **Fourth Cemetery of the Spanish-Portuguese Synagogue**, Congregation Shearith Israel, Cypress Hills St. N of Cypress Ave./Interboro Pkwy. W side. Chapel and Gate, 1885, *Vaux & Radford*. Restoration, 1962, *Harmon Goldstone*.

High atop a gentle rise, amid cemeteries representing many faiths is this small burial ground, the latest of this Central Park West congregation whose three earlier ones are landmarks. The gate and chapel here are magnificent—though largely overlooked—works of *Calvert Vaux*.

FOREST HILLS

North of Queens Boulevard:

[F1] **Forest Hills South**, bet. Queens Blvd. and 1113th Pl., 76th Rd. and 78th Ave. 1941. *Philip Birnbaum*.

Neo-Georgian apartments subsidiary to the real joy of this complex: a grand mall that presents a lush park to the pedestrian in the spring, in the space 113th Street would have passed, here claimed for people. The southern view is axial with:

[F2] **Forest Hills Tower**, 118-35 Queens Blvd., NW cor. 78th Crescent. 1981. *Ulrich Franzen & Assocs.*

A prominent and carefully detailed 15-story office complex, the best large-scale architecture in these parts. Too tall, too prominent, too exquisitely detailed.

F2

F3

F4

[F3] **Civic Virtue**, NE cor. Queens Blvd. and Union Tpke. 1922. *Frederick MacMonnies*, sculptor.

Once directly in front of City Hall in Manhattan, this Nordic male chauvinist was banished to these boondocks by popular pressure (note that the writhing women are not being stepped upon, however). *MacMonnies*, Brooklyn's great sculptor (see **The Horse Tamers** at Prospect Park), was in his dotage when this was carved: a sorry reprise to a brilliant career.

[F4] **Queens Borough Hall**, Queens Blvd. bet. Union Tpke. and 82nd Ave. N side. 1941. *William Gehron & Andrew J. Thomas*.

A pompous neo-Classical building in red brick and limestone. *Thomas* was capable of much better. For that, see much of Jackson Heights.

[F5] **Queens Criminal Court**, 125-01 Queens Blvd., bet. Hoover and 82nd Aves. N Side. Remodeling and new additions. 1996. *Ehrenkrantz & Eckstut & Kuhn*.

At the east end new limestone and stainless steel sweep off the boulevard in a grand curve

shielding the public corridors that serve the courtrooms proper. A new entrance and lobby to the original court building adds understated style.

[F6] **Arbor Close and Forest Close**, from the back of Queens Blvd. storefronts to Austin St., 75th to 76th Aves. 1925-1926. *Robert Tappan*.

Picturesquely profiled row houses, clad in brick, slate, and half-timbering. The garden within offers privacy hedged at its edges. A charming, urbane place.

[F7] **Forest Hills Gardens**, 71st (Continental) Ave. to Union Tpke., Long Island Railroad right-of-way to an uneven line south of Greenway South. 1913-present. *Grosvenor Atterbury*, architect. *Frederick Law Olmsted, Jr.*, landscape architect. Other architects for some individual buildings.

F6

"Apart from its convenient location, within a quarter of an hour of the center of Manhattan Island, the Forest Hills Gardens enterprise differentiates itself … from other suburban development schemes most notably in that its size permits a unique layout of winding streets, open spaces and building lots and thus permits the development of an ideally attractive neighborhood, while its financial backing is such that the realization of the well studied plans is assured in advance beyond peradventure." *Alfred Tredway White* in a promotional booklet of 1911.

White, who had pioneered in housing for the working class, would not have been disappointed. This project, sponsored by the Russell Sage Foundation, has become one of Queens's most exclusive residential enclaves. It is also a splendid combination of good planning and of romantic, picturesque architecture.

KEW GARDENS

A community abounding in English allusions, not the least of which is its name, designed to echo—and to derive prestige from—its London suburb namesake. **Kew Gardens** was developed by a Manhattan lawyer, *Albon Platt Man* (and later by his son, *Alrick Hubbell Man*) for those who, in that placid era before World War I, were already wearying of city life and desirous of finding a garden spot only a short railroad trip from Manhattan. The *Mans* built some 300 houses and sold them, in the prices of those years, for between $8,000 and $20,000. Kew Gardens straddles the LIRR cut south of Forest Hills and is contained by major areas of greenery, Forest Park on the northwest and Maple Grove Cemetery on the east. The heavily trafficked Union Turnpike and Queens Boulevard mark its northern boundaries and 85th Avenue and 127th Street its southerly ones.

Murder in the night: Adjacent to the LIRR station on quiet Austin Street, near the location of the beloved Austin Book Store (now gone) is the site of the heavily publicized murder, in 1964, of Catherine (Kitty) Genovese, who was killed as neighbors ignored her screams for help.

[F8] **Mayfair Road**, bet. Park Lane So. and 116th St.

The most notable residences are **Nos.115-19** (Italian stucco with Spanish tile roof), **115-02**, **115-18**, and **115-27**.

[F9] **Grosvenor Lane**, bet. Park Lane So. and 116th St.

Particularly note **No.115-01**, at the Park Lane South corner, **No.115-19**, and **No.115-24**.

[F9a] **Ralph Bunche House**, 115-24 Grosvenor Road, bet. Park Lane So. and 116th St. 1927. *Koch & Wagner.* 🖤

From 1954 until his death in 1971, *Bunche* served the U.N. as Under Secretary-General, the highest post ever held by an American.

115-24 is a neo-Tudor romance faced in stucco pierced by random bricks and stones, half-timbering near the top of the gables; original (1927) wooden doors with iron strapping, original leaded glass windows and slate roof.

Abingdon Road:

▮ [F10] **Kew Gardens Jewish Center Anshe Sholom**, 82-52 Abingdon Rd., NW cor. 83rd Ave. 1970. *Laurence Werfel.*

The zeal to translate religious needs into new architecture here promotes an impassioned but awkward design solution: a copper-clad enclosure for the ark of the covenant slashes into a corner of the dark brick sanctuary. Too much zeal, too little serenity.

F11

[F11] **Abingdon Road**, bet. 83rd Ave. and Lefferts Blvd.

A street of wonderful freestanding homes of the early 20th century: **Nos.83-36**, comfortable and cozy with double gables; **83-42**, a modest Spanish Baroque silhouette; **83-48**, the Shingle Style desecrated by plastic siding and the associated ruin of corner and archway detailing; and **83-66** on the Boulevard's corner: a splendid Composite-columned portico.

▮ [F12] **Congregation Shaare Tova** (synagogue), 82-33 Lefferts Blvd., SE cor. Abingdon Rd. 1983. *Richard Foster.*

An alien on Abingdon, and a sophisticated design exercise: a rectangular volume with circular voids for the sanctuary of the **Mashhadi** community, Iranian Jews. *Foster* was *Philip Johnson's* partner for the Bobst and other N.Y.U. buildings.

[F13] **84-40, 84-50 Abingdon Road** (houses), bet. Lefferts Blvd. and Brevoort St. S side. ca. 1910.

Two of the finest **Colonial Revival** single houses in these parts. Stubby Tuscan columns articulate those wonderful porches!

[F14] **82-16, 82-18, 82-20, 82-22 Beverly Road** (residential grouping), bet. Onslow Pl. and Audley St. W side. ca. 1925.

Charming stucco and slate-roofed houses arranged around an intimate circular commons.

[F15] **80-55 Park Lane** (house), bet. 80th Rd. (Quentin St.) and Onslow Pl. E side. ca. 1925.

Perhaps a new style that might be termed **Tudor Moderne,** and over the top. The entrance portal seems to be a graft from the 1925 Paris Exposition des Arts Décoratifs.

[F16] **Grenfell Street**, bet. Quentin St. (80th Rd.) and Onslow Place. E side. ca. 1920.

Especially note **Nos.80-57, 80-63, 80-67, 80-83.**

F12

F14

[F17] **119-33** to **119-43 80th Road** (houses), bet. Austin St. and Queens Blvd. ca. 1920.

A cluster of four stuccoed houses with red tile roofs forming a welcome enclave on a tree-shaded street where other houses, each individually designed, are relatively bland.

[F18] **Austin Street** (house), 124-81 Austin St., NW cor. 81st Ave. 1920.

A second floor timber balcony gives this house a powerful posture on a prominent corner.

[F19] **Kew Hall Cooperative Apartments**, 83-09 Talbot St., bet. 83rd Dr. and Lefferts Blvd. ca. 1929.

Almost a block square, this structure surrounds an inner green space so large it admits car traffic (if you belong). The replacement in the 1980s of its original wood windows has cost it much of its original character.

F20

[F2o] **Maple Grove Cemetery,** entrance, 8315 Kew Gardens Rd., near 119th St. 1875.

The Center at Maple Grove. 2008. *Peter Gisolfi Associates.*

A trim concrete-vaulted building serves as gateway to the 65-acre landscape. *Gisolfi* has

Typical of the small private cemeteries of Long Island, few of which remain. A handful of very old tombstones cohabits with miniature World War I concrete doughboys. The adjacent family homesteads are long gone.

F18

Necrology, St. James Episcopal Church

perfected an economical postmodern style with industrial undertones.

[F21] **84-62 Austin Street,** near 84th Ave. W side. 1981. *Peter Casini.*

Radical façades along the LIRR Main Line in a structure built on a leftover sliver of land.

Off to one side (west on Metropolitan Avenue):

[F22] **North Forest Park Branch, Queensborough Public Library,** 98-27 Metropolitan Ave., bet. 69th Rd. and 70th Ave. N side. 1975. *Kaminsky & Shiffer.*

A modest branch library clad in a range of terra-cotta-colored, square brick, adding some character to a humdrum shopping street.

[F23] **Remsen Family Cemetery,** adjoining 69-43 Trotting Course Lane, NE cor. Alderton St. (N of Metropolitan Ave. Both the Lane and Street are one-way northish). ca. 1790 to mid 19th centuries. 🐝

NECROLOGY

Shea Stadium, bet. Northern Blvd. and Roosevelt Ave., Grand Central Pkwy. to 126th St. 1964. *Praeger-Kavanaugh-Waterbury.*

The simplicity and sheer bulk of this home for the Mets dominated the flat landscape for miles. The original arbitrary exterior appliqué of pastel panels (the "wire basket in a windstorm" look) gave way after the team's 1986 World Series victory to the equally inspired "douse everything with Mets blue" look. The Beatles played here in 1964 and again in 1965. Slowly, in 2008, it was demolished piece by piece.

St. James Episcopal Church, 87-07 Broadway, NE cor. Corona Ave. Elmhurst. 1849.

This mid–19th century church, destroyed by fire, was an outgrowth of the earlier one, which remains as the Parish Hall.

Northeastern Queens

N3

COLLEGE POINT

Named for a proposed (1836) Episcopal divinity school, it first had been Strattonsport, after *Eliphalet Stratton*, who purchased the land in 1790 from the *Lawrence* family, noted early settlers. At first, College Point was virtually an island separated from the Village of Flushing by creeks and flooded marshland, connected by the College Point Causeway (now Boulevard). Landfill and recent developments changed this, including the industrial and shopping development on the flat lands of the former Flushing Airport.

In the Civil War era the district was a lusty industrial community, attracting large German and Swiss populations whose beer gardens and picnic groves were the focus of Sunday outings by compatriot Manhattanites. Following the war the *Poppenhusen* family (*Conrad* was majority stockholder in the Long Island Rail Road) purchased large tracts of land and established the institute still bearing its name.

[N1] Poppenhusen Branch, Queensborough Public Library, 121-23 14th Ave., NW cor. College Point Blvd. 1904. *Heins & La Farge.* 🍎

N1

Town of Flushing/Vlissingen

Settled in 1642; chartered in 1645.

The town of Flushing is commonly associated with the growth of religious freedom in the New World. Founded by English settlers, it received its patent from *Dutch Governor Kieft*, who stipulated in its text that the freedom of conscience of its townspeople was to be guaranteed. *Kieft's* successor, *Peter Stuyvesant*, attempted to suppress the Quaker sect, a number of whose adherents had settled in Flushing. Quaker and non-Quaker residents banded together against *Stuyvesant* and were successful in having the patent's stipulation recognized and observed. Among these settlers was the *Bowne* family, whose house, dating from the 17th century, can still be seen. The old **Quaker Meeting House** of the same period also remains as a testament to this struggle for religious liberty.

One of the many public library branches in the City funded by *Andrew Carnegie*. A similar design vocabulary by *Heins & La Farge* appears, surprisingly, at the Bronx Zoo.

[N2] Beech Court (residential grouping), particularly **Nos.3** and **10** Beech Court (houses), N of 14th Ave. bet. College Point Blvd. and 121st St.

A handsome array of houses surrounds a grassy, treed, central green, including a rare **Art Moderne** intruder of stucco, glass block, and steel casement, at **No.10.**

[N3] First Reformed Church of College Point and Sunday School, 14th Ave., NW cor. 119th St. 1872.

Queen Anne meets **Eastlake**, and their style blooms. An exquisite and perfectly maintained excerpt from the most eclectic period of American Architecture. Gothic and Renaissance, Colonial and Romanesque—all had a share in this adventure.

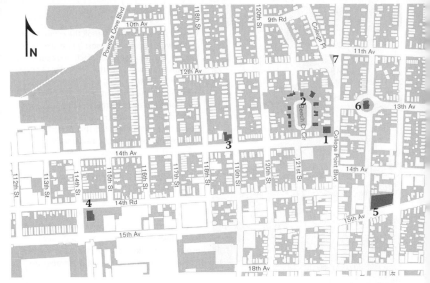

N2, 10 Beech Court

[N4] **Poppenhusen Institute**, 114-04 14th Rd., SE cor. 114th St. 1868. *Mundell & Teckritz.* ●

Cream and chocolate brown paint covers this somber mansarded **Second Empire** citizen. The Institute sheltered one of the nation's earliest free kindergartens, and also provided adult education for local workers. A philanthropy of *Conrad Poppenhusen*.

[N5] **St. Fidelis of Sigmaringen, Martyr, Roman Catholic Church**, 14-10 124th St., NW cor. 15th Ave. 1894.

Founded in 1856 for the 26 Catholic families then resident. A sweet memorial (carved in German and later in English) for its founder, the Reverend *Joseph Huber*, stands next to the octagonal baptistry. Inside, bold 1981-vintage wood sculptures float over the altar.

[N6] Originally **H.A. Schleicher House**/ later **Grand View Hotel**, 11-41 123rd St., on an island interrupting 13th Ave. E side. 1860.

A showplace of College Point that predates the street grid, hence its island setting. This stretch of 13th Avenue was once called **Schleicher Court**, perhaps giving rise to the neighborhood rumor that the mansion was the village courthouse. Actually, *Schleicher* was selling arms to the Confederates.

[N7] **Poppenhusen Memorial**, College Point Blvd., College Place, 11th Ave. 1884.

Set in an immaculate green triangle, this modest, bronze portrait bust atop a granite stele marks the area of *Conrad Poppenhusen's* home, a mansard-roofed structure that once commanded panoramic views from the top of this promontory.

MALBA, WHITESTONE, BEECHHURST

Though settled in 1645, it took the establishment of a tinware factory to convert it from a rural settlement into a thriving manufacturing center. A bit of industry survives, but the area is best known for its housing resources, such as the adjacent, formerly private, community of Malba, west of the Bronx-Whitestone Bridge; Beechhurst; and the Levitt House development, now known as Le Havre, in the shadow of the Throgs Neck Bridge: enclaves of special qualities and/or character.

MALBA

A small enclave, founded in 1908, of wide, sweeping, high-crowned residential streets that were private until recently. Few of the picturesque community-installed street signs remain, but the air of separateness still pervades the quiet scene.

N4

N5

And off the map:

[N8] Originally **India Rubber Company**/then **Hard Rubber Comb Company**/then **I.B. Kleinert Rubber Company,** intersection of 127th St. and 20th Ave. 1889, 1921.

Industrial archaeology. *Poppenhusen* founded this complex of rubber-products factories in 1877. They later became the home of **Kleinert Earmuffs.** At the sky the buildings still bear faded signs that reveal bits of their history. Look up!

[N9] **New York Times Printing Plant,** 26-50 Whitestone Expwy., bet. 20th Ave. and Linden Place. W side. 1997. *Polshek Partnership.*

Supergraphics enhance an elegant high-tech plant for the ubiquitous *New York Times.* Architectural color complements the color-printed papers within (the first *Times* color presses). But how long will the *Times* be printed on paper?

[W1] **Malba Lookout,** at the end of Malba Dr. next to the Whitestone Bridge.

A private fringe benefit for this upper-middle-class community. The view of the bridge is melodramatic.

WHITESTONE

W2

What little industry remains occupies newer, undistinguished buildings. Churches of every description today identify the community. Its older houses have largely been compromised, with only a few exceptions.

[W2] **Martin A. Gleason Funeral Home,** 10-25 150th St., NE cor. 11th Ave. ca. 1890.
The crucial corner of this generous house, now seeing reuse, is a wedding cake of conically capped **Ionic**-columned tiered porches.

[W3] **Whitestone Hebrew Center** (original sanctuary, now school), 12-41 Clintonville St., SE cor. 12th Rd. 1948. *John J. McNamara.* Addition, 1966. [W3a] **Whitestone Hebrew Center** (sanctuary), 12-25 Clintonville St., SE cor. 12th Rd. 1960.
The earliest part, now the school, is late **Art Moderne.** The cantilevered corners, steel sash windows, rounded wall intersections, and bold 1930s incised lettering suggest the architecture of the Grand Concourse in the Bronx, which congregants may have then viewed as a symbol of

middle-class arrival. By the time the new sanctuary had been commissioned, other concerns were evident: **center** had become **centre** and the quality of the architecture had deteriorated.

[W4] **Grace Episcopal Church and Sunday School,** 140-15 Clintonville St., bet. 14th Ave. and 14th Rd. E side. 1859. *Gervase Wheeler.* Additions, 1904, 1939, 1957.
The belfry is key here, an intriguing sculpture executed in fine red brickwork, with a single bronze bell and a simple rope to toll it. Damn those electronic carillons!

[W5] **Whitestone Branch, Queensborough Public Library,** 151-10 14th Rd., SE cor. Clintonville St. 1970. *Albert Barash.*
Trim institutional modern. The interior is standard-issue.

W4

BEECHHURST

A theatrical enclave: The 1920s saw the secluded location of Beechhurst on Long Island Sound become a favored location for Broadway theater people. Only minutes away from Manhattan via the LIRR branch whose terminal was Whitestone Landing, the area attracted actress-singer *Helen Kane, Thurston the Magician*, entertainer *Harry Richman*, and producers *Joseph Schenck* and *Arthur Hammerstein*.

[W7] **Le Havre Houses**/originally **Levitt House Development**, 162nd to Totten St., Powells Cove Blvd. to 12th Ave. 1958. *George G. Miller.*

Thirty-eight-story beige and henna apartment buildings built by *William Levitt's* (Levittown) brother, *Alfred*, an amateur architect, working with *Miller*, a pro. Actually, a very inviting housing estate, much in the style of modest–WWII British models.

W6

W8

[W6] **St. Nicholas Russian Orthodox Church of Whitestone**, 14-65 Clintonville St., bet. 14th Rd. and Cross Island Expwy. (North service road). E side. 1969. *Sergei Padukow.*

A psychedelic fantasy blending bizarre modern forms with the traditional onion dome of the **Eastern Orthodox Church**. Which would you rather have: this or the institutional modern library down the hill?

[W8] **Cryder House**, 166-25 Powells Cove Blvd., opp. 166th St. N side. 1963. *Hausman & Rosenberg.*

A lone apartment slab standing out dramatically from lesser construction. Its inhabitants enjoy great views. Its neighbors are overwhelmed.

[W9] **Wildflower Estate Condominiums**/surrounding **"Wildflower,"** originally **Arthur Hammerstein House**/ sometime **Ripples Restaurant**, 168-11 Powells Cove Blvd., E of 166th St. at Cryder's Point. 1924. *Dwight James Baum.* Additions, before 1930. 🐦

"Wildflower," somewhat tarted up, is now at the center of the sprawl of new condominiums. An asymmetrically massed, deeply shadowed, intricately detailed, **neo-Tudor** masterpiece designed for *Arthur, Oscar Hammerstein I's* second son. (*Oscar II*, the "King and I" *Hammerstein*, was *Arthur's* nephew.)

FLUSHING

Until the end of World War II, Flushing was a charming Victorian community laced with some six-story Tudor apartments constructed in the late 1920s and early 1930s. Many of its streets were lined with rambling white clapboard and shingle (Classical Revival and Shingle Style) houses dating from the last quarter of the 19th century. On its outskirts were vast reaches of undeveloped rolling land.

The construction of the Bronx-Whitestone Bridge, together with its connecting highways for the 1939-1940 New York World's Fair, set the stage for a change that was nipped in the bud by Pearl Harbor. After the war, the rush to build was on.

Two blocks of modest mansions:
    Bayside Avenue, east of Parsons Boulevard, and 146th Street to 29th Avenue.

F2

[F1] **Fitzgerald/Ginsberg House**, 145-15 Bayside Avenue (house), bet. Parsons Blvd. and 146th St. N side. 1924. *John Oakman.* 🔭
    Random granite ashlar, slate-roofed, brings a whiff of **Stockbroker Tudor** to the neighborhood.

[F2] **Buddhist Temple**, Han Ma Um Zen Center, 145-20 Bayside Ave. 2009.
    The swooping eaves display a rich, three-dimensional tapestry of authentic Asian wood work: rampant craftsmanship, lovely to see in Flushing's multi-cultural world of often arbitrary religious architecture.

[F3] **145-38 Bayside Avenue**, bet. Parsons Blvd. and 146th St. S side. ca. 1880.
    Napoleon III's extensions to the **Louvre** in the 1860s triggered the Second Empire style, with exaggerated mansard roofs (named for the works of the 17th-century architect *François Mansart*). Here is a charmer, with all the exuberance that the Louvre lacks.

[F4] **29-29 to 29-45 146th Street**, bet. Bayside and 29th Aves. Both sides. ca. 1925.
    A full, verdant, short block of 1920s **Tudor**, entered twixt a pair of low stone gateposts of a 19th-century estate. Check out 29-29 in particular: brick, timber, stucco, bay windows, high chimneys. Modern medieval?

[F5] **Flushing High School**, 35-01 Union St., cor. Northern Blvd. 1912-1915. *C.B.J. Snyder.* 🔭
    Collegiate Gothic set on a sweeping lawn. Does grass improve the intellect? Those neo-medieval bay windows must help.

Then, a taste of Flushing's oldest:

[F6] **Bowne House**, 37-01 Bowne St., bet. 37th and 38th Aves. E side. 1661. 🔭

F5

Additions, 1680, 1696, and ca. 1830. Open to the public. 718-359-0528. Tu, Sa, Su, 2:30-4:30.
    Quaker *John Bowne* built this simple wood house with its elegant sloping dormers. The forbidden Society of Friends met indoors here for the first time; earlier they had met clandestinely in nearby woods. *Bowne* was a central figure in the dispute with Governor *Peter Stuyvesant* over religious freedom.

The Weeping Beech Tree. 🔭
    *An immense canopy of weeping branches once hung from its broad trunk, creating a natural shelter. **Samuel Parsons**, who supplied much of the plant material for Central and Prospect Parks, planted this experimental Belgian shoot in 1847.*
    In decline, a funeral was held for the aged tree in 1998, and it was then cut down. But the venerable tree's offspring have sprouted around it.

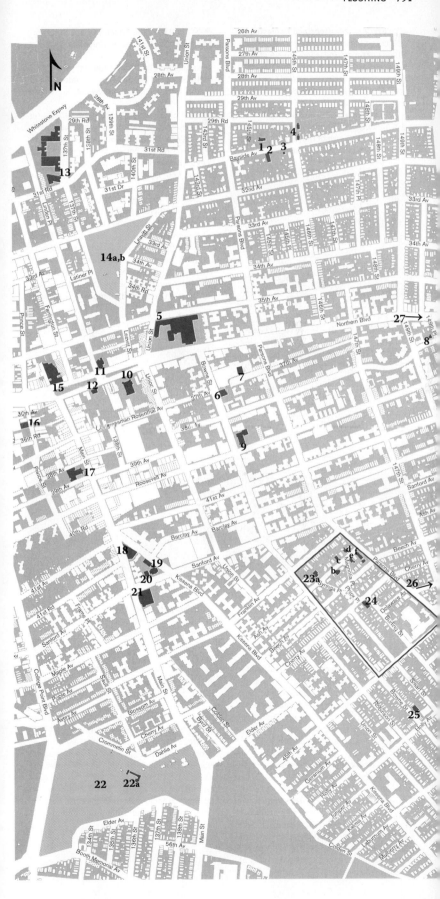

[F7] Originally **Kingsland Homestead/** once **Charles Doughty House**/later **William K. Murray House**/now home of **Queens Historical Society**, 143-35 37th Ave., W of Parsons Blvd. N side. 1785. Moved from 40-25 155th St. to current site in 1968. ●̀
Open to the public. 718-939-0647.
Tu, Sa, Su, 2:30-4:30; closed Mo, We, Fr.

A gambrel-roof, **English-Dutch** shingled house, once the home of the family for which Manhattan's Murray Hill was named.

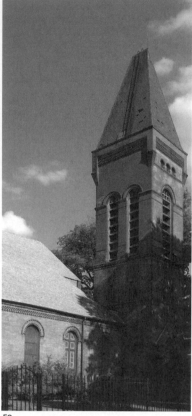

F9

[F8] **Voelker Orth Museum**, Bird Sanctuary & Victorian Garden, 149-19 38th Ave. ca. 1891. ●̀
A picturesque house, its garden and bird sanctuary.

[F9] **Bowne Street Community Church/** originally **Reformed Church of Flushing**, 143-11 Roosevelt Ave., NE cor. Bowne St. 1891.
Northern European brick **Romanesque Revival**, with a tower from Prague. The serrated brickwork at the arches and gables adds a level of elegance to the stolid volumes.

Next, move west along Northern Boulevard from Union Street:

The New Asia: *Beginning in the 1970s Flushing became the center of an enormous and diverse Asian community comprising Chinese, Japanese, Koreans, Vietnamese, and those from the Indian subcontinent. A visit to Union Street south of Northern Boulevard will reveal a vast array of signs in Eastern tongues.*

[F10] **Flushing Armory**, 137-58 Northern Blvd., bet. Main and Union Sts. S side. 1905.
A minifort: brick over brownstone, with a battered, crenellated and machicolated tower. Worthy background for **Hollywood** mini-epic.

[F11] Originally **Flushing Town Hall**/later **Municipal Courthouse**/now **Flushing Council on Culture and the Arts (FCCA)**, 137-35 Northern Blvd., NE cor. Linden Place. 1862-1864. Maybe *William Post*. Renovations, including second floor Great Hall, 1995-1999, *Platt Byard Dovell*. ●̀

Romanesque Revival brick from the Civil War era, its triple-arched portico crowned by a classical entablature, and Flushing's Town Hall until 1898, when Flushing became part of New York City. In its hey day, and on its second floor, its Great Hall once housed *Barnum and Bailey's Circus* (1897), and served as a concert hall for Swedish opera singer *Jenny Lind*. That Great Hall is now rejuvenated for modern uses, offer-

F10

F14a

ing a variety of concerts, exhibitions, educational programs, and plays. The renovation removed layers of white paint, revealing the original brick.

[F12] **Friends Meeting House**, 137-16 Northern Blvd., bet. Main and Union Sts. S side. 1694. Additions, 1716-1719. ●̀
Austere and brooding, this medieval relic looks out timidly upon the never-ending stream of cars on Northern Boulevard. On its rear façade, facing the quiet graveyard, are two doors, originally separate entrances for men and women. The wood-shingled, hip-roofed structure has been used continuously since the 17th century for religious activities by the **Society of Friends**, except for a hiatus as a British hospital prison and stable during the Revolution.

[F13] **Public School 242**, 29-66 137th St., bet. 29th and 31st Rds. 2006. *John Ciardullo Associates.*

An Early Childhood Center accommodating 400 pupils. Pre-kindergarten through third grade. Big, boxy in two-colored brick, it seems a friendly place for young children.

[F14a] **Latimer Gardens Community Center & Waveline Theater**, 34-30 137th St., bet. Leavitt St. and 32nd Ave. 2000.

F17

Hanrahan-Meyers and Castro Blanco Piscioneri and Assocs.

The sleek standing-seam metal-wrap gives a broken profile to this elegant community theater, a special architectural treat the Housing Authority commissioned (and similar ones at similar banal housing complexes).

[F14b] **Lewis H. Latimer House**, 34-41 137th St., bet. Leavitt St. and 32nd Ave. ca. 1887-1889.
Latimer, a noted **African-American** inventor, developed the long-lasting carbon filament in concert with *Thomas Edison*. The house was moved here to preserve it as a museum.

[F15] Formerly **RKO Keith's Flushing Theater**, 129-43 Northern Blvd. opp. Main St. N side. 1927-1928. *Thomas Lamb.* Partial interior. Altered, 1988, *Robert Meadows.*
A most obscure landmark; only the frame of the marquee is still visible, the landmarked interior walled away. "Designed by *Thomas Lamb* in a conventionally outlandish style...the interior...

is a procession of spaces in the Spanish Baroque style." *Christopher Gray.*

Prince's nursery: North of Northern Boulevard, from the site of the former RKO Keith's Theater, was a tree nursery, the first in the country, established by William Prince in 1737. The eight acres had, by 1750, become the Linnaean Botanic Garden. All traces of the site are erased, but not its produce. To this day, on its streets and in its parks, Flushing displays 140 genera, consisting of 2,000 species of trees that are, in large part, the progeny of Mr. Prince.

[F16] **Ebenezer Baptist Church**, 36-12 Prince St., bet. 36th Ave. and 36th Rd. W side. 1973. *Pedro Lopez.*

At the eastern outskirts of downtown Flushing is this ambitious, dramatically fashioned house of worship: striated concrete block and lots of amber stained glass—actually plastic—for an upwardly mobile black congregation.

[F17] **St. George's Episcopal Church**, Main St. bet. 38th and 39th Aves. W side. 1854. *Wills & Dudley.*
Miraculously, this stately **Gothic Revival** church has withstood the commercial, cacophonous onslaught on Main Street. *Francis Lewis*, a signer of the Declaration of Independence, was a church warden in the original building, completed in 1761. Manhattan schist ashlar and brownstone; it would be more convincing without the later wood-shingled steeple.

F18

[F18] **Flushing Regional Branch Library**, Main St., SE cor. Kissena Blvd. 1998. *Polshek Partnership.*

High style for a drab Main Street, it wears its skin of sleek sinuosity, punctuated with notable notches.

[F19] **The Free Synagogue of Flushing**, 41-60 Kissena Blvd., NW cor. Sanford Ave. 1927. *Maurice Courland.*

A stately **neo-Baroque** presence turned diagonally confronts a difficult intersection of streets.

[F20] **The Windsor School**, 136-23 Sanford Ave., bet. Main St. and Kissena Blvd. N side. ca. 1845.

Greek Revival mansion (the capitals have gone back to Corinth) with a mansarded, balustraded roof.

[F21] **U.S. Post Office, Flushing,** Main St., SE cor. Sanford Ave. 1932. *Dwight James Baum* and *William W. Knowles,* architects. *James A. Wetmore,* supervising architect, U.S. Treasury Dept.

A tasteful **neo-Georgian** building from an era when taste was all one had to hold on to;

F23c

F23f

[F22a] **Queens Botanical Garden Visitor and Administration Center.** 2007. *Joan Krevlin* of *BKSK Architects. Atelier Dreiseitl,* landscape architects.

A beautiful, environmentally sustainable building, with planting and photovoltaic panels on the roof, and channels and ponds to funnel and catch rain water for re-use. But the Center's real strength is its **organically modernist** design: a glass and concrete volume, shaped like a shoe box, emerges from the garden, as if it sprouted from the earth, and meets a hovering canopy supported by red columns.

[F23] **The Waldheim Neighborhood** (East Flushing Residential Blocks), bounded by Franklin Ave., Parsons Blvd., a line bet. Cherry and 45th Aves., and Bowne St. 1875-1900.

Porches, chimneys, mansards, and gambrels; **Shingle Style, Queen Anne,** and eclectic miscellany. A wonderful small district that, it is said, was preserved by a "conscious preservation" action in the late 1920s after completion of

a safe and comforting neighborhood monument. Check the beautiful WPA-era murals inside.

[F22] **Queens Botanical Garden,** 4350 Main Street, bounded by Dahlia and Blossom Aves. and Crommelin St. on the north, College Point Blvd. on the west, 133rd St., Peck and Elder Aves. on the south.

A wonderfully cohesive garden, every bit as magical as the City's better-known botanical gardens in the Bronx and Brooklyn. Delights abound here: the garden is full of contemplative spots, particularly the **Asian-influenced** fountain and brook bisecting the promenade at the Main Street entrance. Originally located in Flushing Meadows Corona Park (a version called "Gardens on Parade" was part of the 1939 World's Fair), it was relocated to its current home here in the Kissena Park Corridor in 1963 to make way for the 1964 World's Fair.

the apartment house at 42-66 Phlox Place—an anticipation of the Landmarks Preservation Commission 40 years later.

The original **Waldheim** area stretched from Sanford Avenue at the north to Rose Street on the South, Kissena Boulevard on the west to Murray and 156th Streets on the east. The Wallace-Appleton Company bought the 10 acres from the estate of *Allan MacDonald*; thick woods stretching across the site inspired the name Waldheim. The name disappeared for a time after 1916 (after the developer's bankruptcy, and anti-German feelings during the First World War).

Wander off Bowne St. and down Ash:

[F23a] **143-19 Ash Ave.** A **neo-Georgian** Buddhist temple. [F23b] **143-40 Ash Ave.** Early concrete block (1908). [F23c] **143-49 Ash Ave. Shingle Style** meets Colonial Revival. [F23d] **143-63 Ash Ave.** Awkward **Classical Revival.** [F23e] **143 64 Ash Ave.** Might as well be in *Frank Lloyd Wright's* Oak Park, Ill.

Where a junior Newport "cottage" once stood, at Ash Ave., SW cor. Parsons, is one of a group of oriental temples:

[F23f] **Nichiren Shoshu Temple**, Daihozan Myosetsu-Ji, 42-32 Parsons Blvd., SW cor. Ash Ave. 1984. *Ashihara Assocs.*

Constructed to serve the needs of a 13th-century form of **Japanese Buddhism**, this temple is composed of an austere stacking of rectilinear forms. We doubt that 13th-century Buddhists would understand.

[F24] **Won Buddhist Temple**, Song Eun Building, 43-02 Burling St., SW cor. Cherry Ave. 1986. *Bo Yoon & Assocs.*

A **Korean Buddhist** temple, with stylish, but awkward, stucco forms.

[F25] **Hindu Temple Society of North America**, 45-57 Bowne St., bet. 45th and Holly Aves. E side. 1977. *Baryn Basu Assocs.* architects. Sculpture by Department of Endowments, *Andhra Pradesh,*

F26

India. Expansion, *Parab Associates.*

As one wanders through the jungles of Flushing, the houses part and reveal this exquisitely ornate Indian sculpture totally overwhelming the temple's exterior.

MURRAY HILL

[F26] **149-19 Elm Avenue** (house), bet. 149th and Murray Sts. N side. 1895.

A midblock wonder, sporting a half-round second-story porch. Dig those finely spaced, square wood balusters betwixt Ionic columns.

BROADWAY-FLUSHING

[F27] **St. Andrew Avalino Roman Catholic Church**, 157-01 Northern Blvd., NE cor. 157th St. 1940. *Henry V. Murphy.*

A combination of **neo-Romanesque** and **Art Deco**, using materials so lovingly designed (inside and out) and finely crafted that the building itself could convert infidels to the faith.

[F28] **29-12** to **29-60, 29-01** to **29-61 167th Street** (row houses), bet. 29th and 32nd Aves. Both sides. ca. 1925.

A romantic composition in brick, stone, and stucco, with slate roof tiles; served by rear central driveways and garages for the then emerging motor car. Similar rows of houses define neighboring blocks; here's hoping they'll be spared from the invading rows of "Home Depot houses" that are destroying much of America's suburbs. Here, preservation of the leafy shade trees is as important as the preservation of the architecture.

F28

F22a

AUBURNDALE

[F29] **189-10** to **189-30, 189-11** to **189-29 37th Avenue** (houses), bet. Utopia Blvd. and 190th St. N and S sides. ca. 1925.

Clustered **Neo-Tudor** housing gives style and an urbane and friendly tenor to this otherwise prosaic steet.

[F30] **Joseph Cornell House**, 37-08 Utopia Parkway, bet. 37th and 39th Aves. ca. 1925.

Joseph Cornell (1903-1973), shy, reticent creator of exquisite and often mysterious works of art in the form of boxes, lived in this 1920s detached wood frame house.

[F31] **Temple Beth Sholom**, 42-50 172nd St., NW cor. Northern Blvd. to Auburndale Lane. 1954. *Unger & Unger.* South addition, 1964. *Stanley H. Klein.*

A bold brazen wall of green slate presents subdued monumentality to the visual cacophony of Northern Boulevard.

[F32] **St. Nicholas Greek Orthodox Church Chapel** and William Spyropoulos School, 196-10 Northern Blvd., SE cor. 196th St. 1974. *Raymond & Rado*.

A spartan octagonal auditorium is crowned with a spherical dome: bold concrete and brick. The chapel is a lilliputian version of the main church; both in what might be termed "romantic brutalism." A heavy hand was here.

M2a

M4b

FRESH MEADOWS

[M1] **Fresh Meadows Housing Development**, 186th to 197th Sts., Long Island Expwy. to 73rd Ave. (irregularly). 1949. *Voorhees, Walker, Foley & Smith*; 20-story addition, 1962. *Voorhees, Walker, Smith, Smith & Haines*.

This 166-acre development on the site of the old **Fresh Meadows Country Club** was a post–World War II project of the New York Life Insurance Company. Its (then) avant-garde site plan, including a mix of row housing, low- and high-rise apartments, regional shopping center, theater, schools, and other amenities, scores as excellent planning but dull architecture. Nevertheless, it is beautifully maintained.

[M2] **Long Island (Vanderbilt) Motor Parkway**: [M2a] **73rd Avenue overpass**, Cunningham Park W of Francis Lewis Blvd. [M2b] **Hollis Court Boulevard overpass**, N of Union Tpke and Richland Ave. [M2c] **Springfield Boulevard overpass**, N of Kingsbury Ave. 1924-1926.

These funky reinforced-concrete overpasses date from the construction of America's first "**super highway**." Built by race car enthusiast *William K. Vanderbilt* especially for automobiles, the road stretched a total of 45 "dustless" miles from a toll lodge at Hillside Avenue to Lake Ronkonkoma, in Suffolk County. Cars were narrower then: the road was only 16 feet wide, making it ideal for its current reuse (in Queens, at least) as a grade-separated bikeway.

[M3] **St. John's University, Queens Campus** (Roman Catholic), Union Tpke., SW cor. Utopia Pkwy., to Grand Central Pkwy. Relocated from Brooklyn, beginning 1955. [M3a] **Frumkes Hall**, 1971. *Carson, Lundin & Thorsen*. [M3b] **Sun Yat-sen Hall**, Center of Asian Studies. 1973. *Herman C. Knebel*.

In the vast 105 acres of this campus, mighty little architecture of note exists. **Sun Yat-Sen Hall**, however, a faux Chinese temple and polychromed gate, adds a brilliant splash of color to an otherwise drab setting.

[M4a] **Queens County Hospital**, 164th St., bet. Grand Central Pkwy. and 82nd Rd. W side. 2001. *Davis Brody Bond*.

Sleek. **Glass** is the new brick when it comes to building hospitals these days.

[M4b] **Ambulatory Care Pavilion**, Queens Hospital Center. 2007. *Perkins Eastman*.

Pre-cast concrete and a glass curtain wall, a two-story atrium and public entry plaza at the eastern end. The erector set details, steel I-beams, bolts, and glass, were put together with care.

M7   M8

[M5] Originally **Triborough Hospital for Tuberculosis** (now part of Queens Hospital Center), Parsons Blvd., NE cor. 82nd Dr. 1940. *Eggers & Higgins*.

A light, bright, softly modeled high-rise hospital turned to the sun and bedecked with south-facing tiers of balconies and solariums, designed when TB was still a scourge and sunlight was believed to be the salvation.

[M5a] **107th Precinct House**, N.Y.C. Police Dept., 71-01 Parsons Blvd., SE cor. 71st Ave. 1993. *Perkins Eastman*. Roof-top sculptures, 1988, *Alice Aycock*.

A **modernist** assembly of anodized aluminum and iron-spot brick. Fussy, and perhaps stylish, without enduring style.

[M6] **Queens College**, CUNY, 65-30 Kissena Blvd., bet. Long Island Expwy. and Melbourne Ave., to Main St.
[M7] **Main Building**/originally **New York Parental School**. 1908. Could well serve as a turn-of-the-century Central American capitol.

[M8] Science Building. 1987. *Davis Brody & Assocs*. Crisp, with glass block adding a touch of retro **Art Deco**.

[M9] Benjamin S. Rosenthal Library. 1988. *Gruzen Samton Steinglass*. The tower grabs campus attention. Hopefully it will lead students to the books.

[M10] Salick Center for Molecular & Cellular Biology. 2000. *Rafael Viñoly Architects*. The newest act on campus.

When opened in 1937, Queens College occupied nine Spanish Mission Style tile-roofed buildings built in 1908 for use as the **New York Parental School**, a special school for incorrigibles and truants. The current 52 acres contain a hodgepodge of architecture ranging from a few of the original structures to the sophisticated **Klapper, Science** and **Rosenthal** Library buildings.

Paul Klapper, for whom a college building and an adjacent elementary school are named, was the college's first president.

B2

BAYSIDE

Bayside is northeast of Flushing with an attractive suburban character maintained by an abundance of detached houses and low-rise apartments. Originally settled by *William Lawrence* in 1664, it remained largely rural until linked to Manhattan by the LIRR's East River tunnels in 1910.

Fort Totten Historic District: *in effect, a whole peninsula exploited by the Fort itself.* 🍎
This military reservation dates from 1857, but it wasn't until 1898 that it was designated Fort Totten by President McKinley in honor of General Joseph G. Totten (1788-1864), Director of the War Department's Bureau of Seacoast Defense. Entry from 212th Street, North of Bell Boulevard. Open to the public. Park in the public lot outside the gates and walk in. The old Officers Club and the ruins of the Battery are musts.

[B1] Bayside Historical Society/originally **Officers Club**, Murray and Totten Aves. opp. Weaver Ave. S side. ca. 1870. Enlarged, 1887. Restoration, 1990s. *Goldstone & Hinz*. 🍎

Castellated **Gothic Revival** in the spirit of *Alexander Jackson Davis* and *Andrew Jackson Downing*. Clapboard here simulates masonry grandeur in what began as **"the castle,"** a casino for officers.

[B2] Fort Totten Battery and Museum, Fort Totten. 1863-1864. *William Petit Trowbridge*, engineer. *Robert E. Lee*, designer. 🍎 Open to the public.

A monumental, tooled granite-block fortification reportedly designed by *Lee* when he was still a Yankee, just prior to the Civil War. Arched ways along its embrasured walls are arranged in a V-shape plan, with a bastion at its prow worthy of ancient Rome. It was built to protect, with Fort Schuyler across the strait, the east entry to New York Harbor. Enter through a 90-foot-long tunnel into the battery innards.

B5

And much to the south of the Fort:

[B3] 35-34 Bell Boulevard, NW cor. 36th Ave. 1905-1906. 🍎
Colonial Revival interpreted by Arts and Crafts? A unique example of random cobblestone construction in New York City (see Bergen County, N.J., for others). A **bumpy survivor** amidst commerce.

[B4] Crocheron Park, entry drive via 35th Ave. off Corbett Rd., at 216th St.
One of Queens's best-kept secrets: Golden Pond at the southeast corner of this park, literally only a few feet from the fast-moving traffic of Cross Island Parkway.

[B5] 217-17 Corbett Road, bet. 217th and 221st Sts. N side. ca. 1900.
A grand shingled "country" house that magically survived the 20th century, a symbol of the significant architecture that once thrived hereabouts.

[B6] Former **James J. Corbett House**, 221-04 Corbett Rd., SE cor. 221st St. ca. 1900.

The plaque on the boulder reveals that the world's heavyweight champion, *"Gentleman Jim" Corbett* lived here between 1902 and his death in 1933. He held the title from 1892 to 1897. He evidently also had taste in architecture. Wish he could KO the five aluminum-sided houses across the street (**Nos.217-63** through **217-79**).

Nearby:

[B7] **All Saints Episcopal Church**, 214-35 40th Ave. at 214th St. 1892.

A squat **neo-Gothic** fellow, its shingled tower roof swooping from square to octagonal spire with sumptuous curves that would make many Classical architects swoon. On recovery, a trip inside to view the Tiffany windows is in order.

South of the LIRR tracks:

[B8] **215-37 43rd Avenue**, NW cor. 216th St. 1931. *Benjamin Braunstein.*

Half-timbered, stucco and brick, slate-roofed: a **meandering medieval** close offers access, light, intimacy and privacy, and great charm. There are entries to the close on both streets.

[B9] **Lawrence Family Graveyard**, 216th St. bet. 42nd Ave. and LIRR. W side. 1830. ● Not open to the public.

One of two tiny private cemeteries of the ubiquitous Queens family, this one bordering the Long Island Railroad tracks. Sublime in its desolation.

Necrology:
Flessel Restaurant

Necrology:
Old Queens Hospital

NECROLOGY

Originally **Boker House**/then **College Point Clubhouse**, 12-29 120th St., NE cor. Boker Court (at N end of 120th St., N of 14th Ave.). 1870s.

A relic of the era when this part of College Point was a group of adjacent estates, such as *Herman Funke's*, next door. The rich bracketed porch colonnade preserved some of the flavor of the old neighborhood. Replaced with banal developer's multi-family eyesores.

H. Flessel Restaurant/originally **Witzel's Hotel**, 14-24 119th St., NW cor. 14th Rd. ca. 1890. Later additions.

The exterior of this accretive, village hotel-restaurant complex seemed totally untouched by time, save for a neon sign (clearly of the 1930s) that hung out over the corner. Founder *Witzel's* other enterprise was his nearby Point View Island.

Kempf/Ball House, 143-08 Malba Dr., at the East River. ca. 1937.

Rounded, stuccoed concrete block in the Art Moderne style of the Paris Exposition of 1937, first denuded of its **Art Deco** ornament and crassly marred by a glazed porch atop its north wing. A travesty. But then the travesty was demolished.

156-15 Cross Island Expressway (house), North service road (one-way west), bet. 156th and 157th Sts. N side. ca. 1860.

Finely proportioned, in the **Italianate** mode. Replaced by greed and fake brick.

144-85 Roosevelt Avenue, bet. Parsons Blvd. and 147th St. N side. 1885.

A well-preserved but (in inner Flushing, at least) rapidly disappearing breed: a Shingle Style single house. Perfection would have been possible with some modest shingle repairs and a new coat of paint. Gone.

23-27 College Point Boulevard, bet. 23rd and 25th Aves. E side. ca. 1870.

This well-kept **Victorian** country house on a large lot with blue mansard roof and cornice, was typical of fate 19th-century College Point. Demolished for a brick monster.

First Congregational Church of Flushing and Parish House, Bowne St., bet. 38th and Roosevelt Aves. W side.

Until destroyed by fire, these dignified 19th-century wood-frame structures enhanced the community, set as they were on a green carpet of grass.

143-43 and 143-46 Sanford Avenue (houses), bet. Bowne St. and Parsons Blvd. S side. Flushing. ca. 1860.

Two charming survivors from the mid 19th century. Until the 1960s central Flushing's gracious treelined streets were filled with amply proportioned, single-family **Victorian** frame homes. The number has been reduced to scarcely more than a handful.

St. Thomas Hall (school)/later St. Joseph's Academy (Roman Catholic), Kissena Blvd., NE cor. Sanford Ave. Flushing. 1839.

A dour **Victorian** institutional structure, today the site of a busy shopping complex.

Bell Homestead, 38-08 Bell Blvd., bet. 38th and 39th Aves. W side. Bayside. ca. 1845.

Imprudently replaced by Prudential.

Ash Avenue houses, bet. Bowne St. and Parsons Blvd: **No.143-10**, "Moorish" in glossy (!) stucco. Only the gate and garage remain; **No.143-13**, Shingle Style, well hedged, now history; **No.143-32 Ash Avenue**, an elegant bungalow featured bumpety stone and a squat Palladian window.

Old Queens Hospital Center, N.Y.C. Health & Hospitals Corporation/originally **Queens General Hospital**, 82-68 164th St., bet. Goethals Ave. and Grand Central Pkwy. 1937. *Sullivan W. Jones, John E. Kleist, Jacob Lust.*

Art Deco orange brick, built long before the post–World War II building boom in Queens, now replaced with *P&W/DBB's* new buildings.

Southern Queens

Town of Jamaica/Rustdrop

Settled in 1656; chartered in 1660.

The communities lying within the boundaries of the old **Town of Jamaica** contain, as a group, the widest contrasts of any section of Queens. Some, like Ozone Park, Richmond Hill, and Woodhaven, are quiet residential communities. Jamaica itself, on the other hand, is a bustling marketplace with department stores, specialty shops, and theaters. Affluence is everywhere visible in Jamaica Estates along Grand Central Parkway; poverty and squalor mark the black slums of South Jamaica; St. Albans, though, is a lovely, treelined, middle-

S1

S2

income black community. Parts of Jamaica date from the 17th and 18th centuries; Richmond Hill, Queens Village, from the 19th.

WOODHAVEN

[S1] **Fire Alarm Telegraph Station**, N.Y.C. Fire Department, 83-24 Woodhaven Blvd., NW cor. Park Lane S. ca. 1915.

A retardataire Classical container for 1920s high tech.

[S2] **Christ Church Congregational**, 85-27 91st St. (one-way north), SE cor 85th Rd. 1914. Addition, 1928.

Endangered. The imaginative carpentry at the belfry cornice (and the rooster weather vane) distinguish this grayed Italianate stucco edifice. That neon outlined crucifix is another matter. But it appears to be vacant. Can't some nice congregation move in? Or a family? Or a guide book author?

[S3] **St. Matthew's Episcopal-Anglican Church**. 1901. *R.F. Schirmer and J.A. Schmidt*. Parish Hall and Rectory, 85-36 96th St. (one-way southbound), bet. 85th Rd. and 86th Ave. E side.

The peaceful green compound formed by these three structures is a gift to 96th Street. The particularly lovely **neo-Gothic** church is built of an extremely handsome ashlar, whose joints have been deeply raked, giving the structure strong character in an otherwise softly configured neighborhood.

Midblock cemetery: Immediately behind St. Matthew's is the private Wyckoff-Snediker Cemetery, accessible to the families' descendants (Elderts included) by walking around the church, and via a lane that begins at 97-01 Jamaica Avenue.

[S4] Former **Lalance & Grosjean**/now the site of **Pathmark Shopping Center**, Atlantic Ave. bet. 89th and 92nd Sts. to 95th Ave. 1876. Shopping center, 1986, *Niego Assocs.* [S4a] Originally **Lalance & Grosjean, clock tower and factory**, Atlantic Ave., SW cor. 92nd St. 1876.

Once again, a shopping mall obliterates collective memory. Until most of the antique, red-painted brick structures were wasted in the mid 1980s to form yet another shopping center, this intricate array of 19th-century mill buildings was a remarkable relic of the era when the Village of Woodhaven claimed a nationally known tinware and agateware manufacture. Its products graced many an American kitchen for generations, and the Lalance & Grosjean factory employed hundreds.

In the end, saving the squat clock tower atop one factory building became a sop to those preservation interests which sought to save more of the historic building complex from destruction.

[S7] Originally **Lalance & Grosjean workers' housing**, 85-02 to 85-20 95th Ave. and 85-01 to 85-21 97th Ave., bet. 85th and 86th Sts. Both sides. 1884.

Modest wood-frame row houses built as a paternalistic gesture to its employees by the local company. Mostly altered and in poor repair, a favorite canvas for graffiti purveyors.

Mae West's early career: The brassy movie queen was born in nearby Brooklyn but is said to have begun her career performing in Louis Neir's Hotel, a combination tavern-hotel. The two-story structure still exists (in remarkably original shape) at 87-48 78th Street, at the northwest corner of 88th Avenue. (The streets here are all one-way, somehow always the wrong way: 78th runs northbound below Jamaica Avenue, where Neir's is now a bar.)

S4a

S8

S11

S6

[S5] Originally **The Wyckoff Building**, 93-02 95th Ave., SE cor. 93rd St. 1889.

Originally a real estate exchange and offices for the **Woodhaven Bank**. In this part of low-rise Queens, its four stories (plus the now missing corner egg-shaped dome) must have made it an imposing centerpiece when first opened.

[S6] **High School for Construction Trades, Engineering and Architecture**, 94-06 104th St., bet. 94th and 95th Aves. 2006. *Arquitectonica.*

Polychromatic polygonalism in concrete, stucco, steel and glass. This is the kind of project that put *Arquitectonica* on the map, not the more recent, more bland **Avalon** development along the Bowery in Manhattan.

RICHMOND HILL

West of **Jamaica** and south of **Forest Park's** hills lies the community of **Richmond Hill**. Its plan was evolved and its streets laid out by Manhattan lawyer *Albon P. Man* (also responsible for adjacent **Kew Gardens**) and his English landscape architect, *Edward Richmond,* from 1867 through 1872. Like Kew Gardens, Richmond Hill also owes its name to a London suburb.

Richmond Hill Driving Tour: A meandering drive through part of Richmond Hill's finest streets ending at The Triangle.

Begin with the former factories at the south flank of Forest Park at Park Lane South and 101st Street. Then scoot around and follow 86th Avenue (two-way) eastward as a rough spine for the trip. Take detours up and down the streets (mostly one-way) as you choose:

[S8] Formerly **William Demuth & Company-S.M. Frank & Company**, 84-10 101st St., SW cor. Park Lane So. ca. 1895. Converted to apartments, 1987.

Backing up to the old LIRR Rockaway Beach Line siding, a factory (now apartments) where briar was turned and polished to manufacture **Frank Medico** smoking pipes. Built at a time when every man could afford a pipe and conversations centered on which shape burned coolest to the taste. Brickwork is embellished with stepped corbels under the cornice and basketweave on the tower (the smoking room?).

[S9] **Public School 66, Queens, The Brooklyn Hills School**, 85-11 102nd St., bet. 85th Rd. and 85th Ave. E side. 1901. Additions. (102nd St is two-way.)

The **Romanesque Revival** bell tower has lost both its bell and its pyramidal cap sometime along its journey, but the **Art Nouveau** terracotta bas-relief pediments and frieze, once muffled with paint, now read loud and clear.

[S10] **85-58, 85-54 104th Street** (houses), bet. 85th and 86th Aves. W side. ca. 1900. (104th St is one-way north here.)

A pair of large gambrel-roof single houses, still wearing their original combination of shingle-and-stucco siding with diagonal wood muntins dividing the second-floor window sash.

[S11] **Trinity Methodist Church**, 107-14 86th Ave., bet. 107th and 108th Sts. S side. ca. 1910.

The church's florid neo-medieval column capitals are bulbous, provincial, yet charming. A strong, but inviting, entrance to a modest church.

[S12] **108-03 86th Avenue** (house), NE cor. 86th Ave. and 108th St. 1890s.

Shinglework and details are largely intact in this sturdy towered and double-pedimented survivor. A gracious, grandly porched mansion in these parts.

[S13] Richmond Hill War Memorial, edge of Forest Park, Park Lane S., NE cor. Memorial Drive, at Myrtle Ave. and 109th St. ca. 1925. *J.P. Pollia,* sculptor.

The poignant bronze sculpture of an innocent young lad caught up in a war not of his making sits atop a granite stele with an inscription that makes use of an uncommon gender for such memorials: *"erected by the people of richmond hill in memory of her men who served and died in the world war 1917-1918."*

S13

An exquisitely crafted bronze flagpole base is adjacent.

[S14] 85-12 110th Street, bet. 85th and 86th Aves. W side. ca. 1900. (110th St. is one-way north.)

A gambrel roof turned to the street, a broken pediment, much willful asymmetry, and fat bottle columns from the **Colonial Revival**. An Eclectic Shingle Style charmer.

[S15] 85-24 110th Street, bet. 85th and 86th Aves. W side. ca. 1900.

The porch lathework creates airy arches within the **Tuscan** column and beam ensemble. Upstairs plastic siding has taken hold.

[S16] 85-28 111th Street, bet. Myrtle and 86th Aves. W side. ca. 1900. (111th St. is two-way.)

A strong statement, its porch and upper balcony punctuated by a bevy of **Tuscan Doric** columns, still retains most of its original Shingle Style livery.

[S17] Church of the Holy Child Jesus (Roman Catholic), 111-11 86th Ave, NW cor. 112th St. 1931. *Henry V. Murphy.*

Neo-Romanesque cum **Art Moderne**, of orange brick and exquisitely carved limestone. Reminiscent, inside and out, of later *Bertram Goodhue* work. The bell tower is a gem.

[S18] 84-37 113th Street, NE cor. 85th Ave. (113th St. is one-way north.) ca. 1875.

Note the shy **Japanese** touches at the edge of the roof beams, from a time when some architects were flirting with oriental motifs.

114th Street (two-way) between 85th and 86th Avenues; one-way south below Myrtle Avenue:

[S19a] 85-04 114th Street (house), SW cor. 85th Ave. ca. 1900.

Exuberance in Victorian houses first caused them to fall from style (and be torn down in the 1950s) and, more recently, to regain it. Thank God!

S16

S17

[S19b] 85-10, 85-14, 85-20 114th Street (houses). W side. ca. 1900.

A once smashing group! But if, as *Mies* said, God is in the details, He's withdrawn support from these. The re-siders and re-windowers have gelded them.

[S19c] 85-03 114th Street (house), SE cor. 85th Ave. ca. 1900.

The original porch has been partly enclosed, but above it much architectural interest survives. This one is still a winner.

[S20] Union Congregational Church/ United Church of Christ, 86-02 115th St. (one-way north), SW cor. 86th Ave.

Built of black stone, with the mortar joints pointed in a projecting V-joint profile. A stolid grounded **neo-Gothic church**, with crenellations for its parishioners' protection when fending off imaginary pagans.

116th Street, south of Jamaica Avenue (one-way south):

[S21] Casa Latina/onetime **Landmark Tavern Building**/originally **Richmond Hill Branch, Bank of Jamaica,** 116-02 Jamaica Ave., SE cor. 116th St. ca. 1900.

Gentrification has given new life to this distinctive, turn-of-the-century corner commercial building. In the mid 1980s the prescription for real estate success in this locale was "call it a landmark." In this case, it is one (though still unofficial).

[S22] 87-72, 87-78 116th Street (houses), bet. 89th and Jamaica Aves. W side. ca. 1885.

Imagine when all the single homes on this block had basic forms like these. Some of the bones (columns) have been replaced, and a tan brick wall worthy of lesser architecture built in front of 87-78, but the old bodies are still there.

Returning to Jamaica Avenue:

The Triangle:

Actually, many triangles are formed where Lefferts Boulevard crosses the intersection of Myrtle and Jamaica Avenues, a special event in the otherwise ho-hum local street grid. The complex streetscape is further enriched by the route of the old LIRR Montauk Division viaduct, which—using its own geometry—passes over the streets but under the old BMT Jamaica Line's elevated struc-

S23

S19c

S20

S26

[S23] P.S.51, Early Childhood Development Center, 87-45 117th St., bet. Jamaica Ave. and 89th Ave. E side. 1994. *Gruzen Samton.*

High style in the neighborhood that may give support to those repairing and restoring the neighboring 19th-century architecture. Two colors of brick, limestone, and glass block make for a children's delight.

An aside to the south:

[S24] Arthur Ashe School, P.S. 161, 101-33 124th St., bet. 101st and 103rd Aves. 2000. *Gruzen Samton.*

The seventh in a *Gruzen Samton* series built from their prototype design for the Board of Education. Variations of site and neighborhood produced seven different configurations.

ture. A block west sees the northbound birth of Hillside Avenue, which swings around a quarter turn, dips beneath the LIRR viaduct, and merrily spins its way east to the Nassau County line.

The immediate area is filled with curiosities:

[S25] Richmond Hill Republican Club, 86-15 Lefferts Blvd., bet. Hillside and Jamaica Aves. E side. 1908. *Henry E. Haugaard.* Renovated, 2010. 🍎

A battered temple to the party of President *Abraham Lincoln* (archery range in basement). Richmond Hill was even more heavily Republican before the 1930s Depression.

[S26] Richmond Hill Branch, Queens Borough Public Library, 118-14 Hillside Ave., SW cor. Lefferts Blvd. 1905. *Tuthill & Higgins.*

One of many yellow brick *Carnegie* gifts, this on a green triangle of its own, originally called Library Square.

END *of Richmond Hill Driving Tour.*

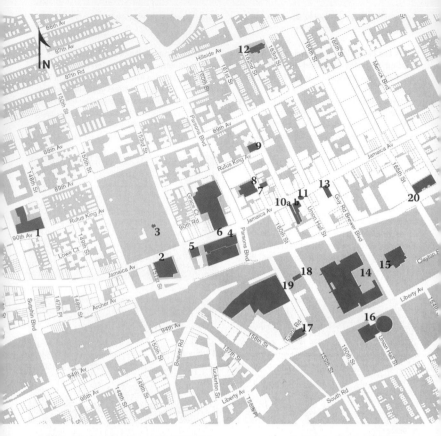

J1

J3

JAMAICA

Nearest trains: F to Parsons Blvd; E, J, Z to Jamaica Center-Parsons/Archer, LIRR to Jamaica Station.

[J1] Queens Civil and Housing Court Building, 89-17 Sutphin Blvd., SE cor. 89th Ave. 1997. *Perkins Eastman.*

Monumental within the tight cityscape, relating to surrounding buildings rather than setting itself apart, this Civil Court is a civil citizen. A five-story atrium provides a grand spatial adventure inside.

[J2] Queens Family Court and City Agency Facility, 151-20 Jamaica Ave. bet. 151st and 152nd Sts. 2001. *Henry H. Cobb, Pei Cobb Freed & Partners/Gruzen Samton,* Associated Architects.

A prize from the Art Commission honored this crisp courthouse before the excavators had broken ground. The result confirms that judgment: understated, beautifully detailed, a serene place for a Family Court.

[J3] King Manor Museum/originally **Rufus King House,** King Park, Jamaica Ave. bet. 150th and 153rd Sts. N side. North section, 1730; west section, 1755; east section, 1806. Additions, 1810 and ca. 1830s. Interior open by appointment. 718-523-0029. 🐾

A rambling, cream-colored clapboard number, bound to inspire square-footage lust in any city apartment dweller. Set on a greensward that also contains a wonderful Victorian pergola once used for band concerts.

[J4] U.S. Region II Social Security Administration Headquarters, Jamaica Ave., SW cor. Twombly Place (Parsons Blvd.) to Archer Ave. 1987. *Gruzen Samton* and *Ehrenkrantz Ekstut.*

This big, bulky, brick, bureaucratic block proves there was big government, even during the conservative *Reagan* administration, whose legions built it. Mammon, here government's version, overwhelms a pair of spiritual neighbors:

[J5] First Reformed Church of Jamaica, 153-10 Jamaica Ave., SE cor. 153rd St. S side. 1858-1859. *Sidney J. Young.* Addition, 1902, *Tuthill & Higgins.* ●

Red-brick **Romanesque Revival** arches, doorways, windows, corbel tables, with a Gothic tower. Neo-Medieval eclecticism.

[J6] Grace Episcopal Church and Graveyard, 155-15 Jamaica Ave., bet. 153rd St. and Parsons Blvd. 1861-1862. *Dudley Field.* **Chancel,** 1901-1902. *Cady, Berg & See.* Graveyard, ca. 1734. ●

A brownstone monolith from grass to finial. English country Gothic, appropriately, for the official church of the British Colonial government.

Along 160th Street, between Jamaica and 90th Avenues (one-way north):

[J7] Jamaica Business Resource Center/ originally **La Casina** or **Casino**/onetime

J5

Roxanne Swimsuits, 90-33 160th St. E side. ca. 1936. Renovated, 1995, *Li-Saltzman.* ●

A sophisticated mastaba of **Art Deco/Moderne** origins rescued by the JBRC. That sleek stainless steel is on a par with the Chrysler Building.

[J8] Farmers Market, 90-40 160th St., bet. Jamaica and 90th (Rufus King Ave.) Aves. W side. 1997. *James McCullar & Associates.*

A clerestoried steel portico leads to adaptive reuse and new construction: markets for fresh food and prepared food, dining, and office space.

Beyond:

[J9] Title Guarantee Company/formerly **Suffolk Title & Guarantee Building,** 90-04 161st St., NW cor. Rufus King Ave. 1929. *Dennison & Hirons.* ●

The decoration here is more important than the building: **Art Moderne** at the third-floor spandrels and the sky: blue, beige, orange, and black.

[J10a] Originally **Jamaica Savings Bank,** 161-02 Jamaica Ave., bet. 161st and 162nd Sts. S side. 1898. *Hough & Dewell.*

Second Empire/Beaux Arts flamboyance cheek by jowl with the Renaissance Revival "club" below.

[J10b] Jamaica Arts Center/originally **Jamaica Register Building,** 161-04 Jamaica Ave., bet. 161st and 162nd Sts. S side. 1898. *A.S. Macgregor.* ● 718-658-7400. Tu-Sa, 10-5; closed Su-Mo.

J10b

J8

In the style of a Pall Mall London clubhouse (**Italian Renaissance Revival**), now happily preserved as an arts center.

[J11] Sidewalk clock, in front of 161-11 Jamaica Ave., bet. 161st and 162nd Sts. S side. 1900. ●

A timely Classical landmark.

The Revolution: In the closing days of August 1776, the Battle of Long Island, there were skirmishes in Jamaica as well as Brooklyn. Boulder Crest, at the terminal moraine's summit overlooking the outwash plain on which the Jamaica business district was built, held the rifle pits of the retreating Continental soldiers. A commemorative glacial boulder and plaque can be found on the lawn at the southwest corner of 150th Street and 85th Drive.

J12

J13

tecture of this campus. The Union Hall Street arched pedestrian underpass (1913) through the LIRR embankment from Archer Avenue is an intriguing way to reuse the former path of a now discontinued street.

[J15] **York College Auditorium and Theater,** 94-45 Guy R. Brewer Blvd. 1990. *Polshek Partnership.*
   Polychromatic brick and a great glass wall greet the audience across a great entrance lawn.

[J16] **York College Health and Physical Education Facility,** 160-02 Liberty Ave. bet. 160th St. and Guy R. Brewer Blvd. 1987. *Cain, Farrell & Bell.*
   Simple and austere volumes for sports activities, with an adjacent greensward of playing fields.

J15

[J12] **Auxiliary Services for High Schools**/formerly **Hillcrest High School Annex**/formerly Jamaica Vocational High School/originally Jamaica Training School, 162-10 Hillside Ave., bet. 162nd and 163rd Sts. S side.
   Understated brick and brownstone, with witch-hatted dormers at the sky.

[J13] Originally **J. Kurtz & Sons** (furniture store), 162-24 Jamaica Ave., SW cor. Guy R. Brewer Blvd. 1931. *Allmendinger & Schlendorf.* 🖤
   Six spectacular stories of **Art Deco** commercial architecture, only minimally compromised since the *Kurtzes* left in 1978. Look up at ziggurats and pylons in a world of glazed tile, terra cotta, brick, and cast aluminum.

South of the LIRR embankment:

[J14] **York College, CUNY,** 94-20 Guy R. Brewer Blvd., S of LIRR to Liberty Ave. W side. 1983. *The Gruzen Partnership.*
   The cascade of steps at the boulevard entry leads to the neat, low, carefully controlled archi-

[J17] **Food and Drug Administration Laboratories & Offices,** 158-15 Liberty Ave., NE cor. 158th St. 2000. *Gruzen Samton/ HLW International,* Associated Architects.
   Black, gray, red, and white combine in a stylish ensemble. The FDA is concerned with the viability of prescription and non-prescription drugs, and may yet take on the nicotine in tobacco.

[J18] Originally **St. Monica's Roman Catholic Church,** 94-20 160th St., S of LIRR. 1856-1857. *Anders Peterson,* master mason. 🖤
   On the campus of York College, itself in monolithic brick, but demolished save for its tower, a haunting reminder of a different and lively neighborhood that once surrounded it.

[J19] **Prospect Cemetery,** 159th St., SW cor. Beaver Rd. 1668 onward. 🖤
   The first public burial ground of Jamaica. In the early years of this community the wealthy

were mostly buried in church—laymen under their pews, clergymen in the chapel or beneath the pulpit. Less affluent parishioners were interred in the churchyard. The rest were buried in Prospect Cemetery.

[J20] **Tabernacle of Prayer**/originally **Loew's Valencia Theater**, 165-11 Jamaica Ave., bet. 165th St. and Merrick Blvd. N side. 1929. *John Eberson.*

One of the City's great motion picture palaces, now a church. The fantastic **Churrigueresque** (late Spanish Renaissance) terra-cotta façade is the creation of *Eberson* the most theatrical of movie theater architects.

*America's first supermarket: It all began in June 1930 when **King Kullen** opened a large self-service grocery store, complete with "unlimited parking," at 171-06 Jamaica Avenue. It later became the machine shops of Thomas Edison Vocational High School.*

J19

J24

Somewhat to the north:

[J21] **Jamaica High School**, 16701 Gothic Drive, bet. 188th St. and Chapin Pkwy. 1925-27. *William H. Gompert.*

Sited in a park like a vast neo-Georgian country house, Jamaica High comes from an era where form trumped function, where symmetrical disciplines were placed before academic teaching needs. But we bet it works.

And considerably south:

[J22] **South Jamaica Branch, New York Public Library**, 108-41 Guy R. Brewer Blvd., bet. 108th and 109th Aves. 1999. *Carl Stein of Elemental Architecture.*

A modest but wonderful addition to this suburban street: three "saw tooths" in the roof allow natural light to pour into the reading room. The solar rays admitted through the windows also help heat the building.

Off to the east on Jamaica Avenue:

[J23] **Bethesda Missionary Baptist Church**/originally **Jamaica First German Presbyterian Church**, 179-09 Jamaica Ave., NW cor. 179th St., opp. 179th Place. 1900.

Neo-Gothic in a de-shingled **Shingle Style**, its white surfaces vivid planes where somber gray once reigned.

And to the south:

[J24] **Cathedral of Allen African Methodist Episcopal Church**, Merrick Blvd., SE cor. 110th Ave. 1998.

The vast church complex of the *Reverend Floyd H. Flake*, sometime congressman.

HOLLIS

[H1] **190-21 Hollis Avenue** (house), bet. 99th and 100th Aves. ca. 1875.

This large, freestanding, elaborately ornamented Italianate house is a remarkable throwback to the area's 19th-century roots. Good console brackets.

[H2] **First United Methodist Church of Hollis**, 91-31 191st St., bet. Jamaica and Woodhull Aves. E side. ca. 1885.

Abstract geometry of triangles, circles, and pyramids clad in shingles and slate. The modern windows don't help.

A1

ST. ALBANS

[A1] **Murdock Avenue**, bet. Linden Blvd. and LIRR. Addisleigh Park.

On either side of Murdock Avenue and on many streets nearby in greater St. Albans lies a superb suburban neighborhood, with well-kept homes and vast, immaculately manicured lawns. Here an affluent black community lives in architecture equal to Brooklyn's Prospect Park South.

SOUTH OZONE PARK

St. Teresa of Avila Roman Catholic Church, 109-71 130th St., bet. 109th and 111th Aves. W side. 1937.

A 1930s intermix of yellow brick and **Art Deco/Classical** styles.

Far Queens

Out beyond Cross Island Parkway and Springfield Boulevard, lying along the Nassau County border or abutting the northern shores of Jamaica Bay, is the area we call Far Queens. The northern parts, such as Douglaston Manor along the east side of Little Neck Bay, are among Queens's most exclusive neighborhoods. The areas to the southeast comprise an immense—largely unknown to residents of Manhattan—group of middle-class black suburban communities. To the south of this Queens "frontier" is the megaworld of Kennedy Airport and, to its west, the large community of Howard Beach and several smaller ones.

DOUGLASTON MANOR

[F1] **Douglaston Historic District**, including all of the peninsula north of 38th Drive and Cherry Street. 🍎

[F2] **Douglaston Club**/formerly **George Douglas House**/originally **Wynant Van Zandt House**, 32-03 Douglaston Pkwy. (West Drive), SE cor. Beverly Rd. Before 1835, with numerous additions.
   A large, homely country house with a Tuscan-columned porch; now a tennis club.

F5

DOUGLASTON MANOR, DOUGLASTON, LITTLE NECK, GLEN OAKS

Douglaston Manor, Douglaston, and Little Neck lie east of the Cross Island (Belt) Parkway, New York's circumferential highway, and, as a result, many assume they are part of adjacent Nassau County. The part above Northern Boulevard certainly lends credence to this belief, since the area resembles the prosperous commuter towns on the adjacent North Shore. Originally the peninsula was all Little Neck, but in 1876 the western part was renamed Douglaston after *William B. Douglas*, who had donated the LIRR station there. It is a rocky, treed knoll with sometimes narrow, winding streets chockablock with Victorian, stucco, shingled, myriad individual houses of romance, many with splendid views of water, sunsets, and sailboats.

[F3] **Benjamin Allen House**/sometimes called the **Allen-Beville House**, 29 Center Dr., SW cor. Forest Rd. 1848-1850. 🍎
   A **Greek Revival** snuggling up to the new **Italianate** style of the time. White shingles, Tuscan porch, octagonal widow's walk overlooking Little Neck Bay. Wide porches, front and back, are supported by elegant fluted Doric columns bearing a trim dentilled cornice.

[F4] **Cornelius Van Wyck House**, 37-04 Douglaston Pkwy. (126 West Drive), SW cor. Alston Place. 1735. Additions, 1735-1770. Kitchen wing, 1930. 🍎
   The original "Dutch" house is barely visible, engulfed as it is by later accretions. Rent a boat to enjoy it fully.

[F5] **233-26, 233-38, 233-50 Bay Street** (houses), bet. 233rd St. and Douglaston Pkwy. S side.
   A challenge: find these three **Shingle Style-Victorian** gems tucked away along this bosky lane. The last embraces an early gambrel-roof neighbor to its east wall.

1.
Douglaston
Historic District
& Proposed
Extension

2

4   **3**

5

5a
Douglaston Hill
Historic District

[F7] **Douglaston Manor Restaurant**/originally North Hills Golf Course Clubhouse, 63-20 Commonwealth Blvd., opp. Marathon Pkwy. W side. ca. 1925. Additions.

A romantic Spanish-tile-plus-beige-stucco confection occupying the high ground atop a city golf course.

GLEN OAKS

Long Island Jewish Hospital-Hillside Medical Center:

Like most hospitals this one just grew haphazardly. But amid the physical confusion a solo architectural work stands out:

[F8] **Ronald McDonald House** (residential facility), 76th Ave. opp. 267th St. N side. 1986. *Lee Harris Pomeroy Assocs.*

F4

F5a

F9

[F5a] **Douglaston Hill Historic District,** south of the Douglaston H.D., along Depew Ave., 240th St., 42nd and 43rd Aves.

Thirty-one more single-family homes, examples of many late nineteenth and early twentieth century architectural styles, including **Queen Anne, Colonial Revival, Shingle, Arts and Crafts and Tudor Revival.**

DOUGLASTON

[F6] **North Hills Branch, Queensborough Public Library,** 57-04 Marathon Pkwy., opp. 57th Ave. W side. 1987. *Abraham W. Geller & Assocs.*

Round and domed and bright blue and red, with a yellow canopy: a colorful but alien addition to the beige burbs.

A muted, dignified two-story structure, semicircular in plan welcoming visitors within its curvalinear embrace.

CREEDMOOR

[F9] **Queens County Farm Museum**/originally **Jacob Adriance Farmhouse**/also known as **Creedmoor Farmhouse,** 73-50 Little Neck Pkwy., bet.73rd Rd. and 74th Ave. W side. 1772. Additions, ca. 1835 and later. Open to the public.

An early farmhouse preserved by the happy accident of its location: protected by the lands of **Creedmoor Hospital,** the enveloping state institution (though now officially occupying City park property).

QUEENS VILLAGE

[F10] **Public School 34, Queens**, The John Harvest School, 104-12 Springfield Blvd., SW cor. Hollis Ave. ca. 1905. Addition, 1930.

Ornate limestone scrolls elevate this old elementary school's dark brick exterior to architecture. Beginning in 1844, the site of today's two-acre school playground was the potter's field for poorhouse inmates of Jamaica, Flushing, Newtown, Hempstead, North Hempstead, and Oyster Bay, all then part of Queens County. Nassau was severed in 1898, leaving the balance of Queens to join a Greater New York.

CAMBRIA HEIGHTS

THREATENED: [F11] Former **Martin's Garden Center**, 119-03 Springfield Blvd., SE cor. 119th Ave. at Francis Lewis Boulevard. ca. 1860.

F11

An **Italianate Villa Style** wood frame mansion, complete with cupola, once seemingly dipped in whitewash and given a new existence as a garden center. Poetic? It's on the edge of ruin, but could be glorious once more.

LAURELTON

[F12] **Springfield Cemetery Chapel**, 122-11 Springfield Blvd., opp. 122nd Ave. E side. 1849.

Venerable Springfield Cemetery is contained on three sides by newer Montefiore, but the old board-and-batten chapel remains.

[F13] **Laurelton Estates**, 224th St. E side; 225th St. Both sides; 226th St. Both sides, bet 130th and 133rd Aves. Also 229th St. bet. 130th and 131st Aves. Both sides. ca. 1925.

A display of what architectural imagination, builders' skills, and a reasonable budget can do to craft the repetitive façades of row housing

into a satisfying, memorable, picturesque composition. Is even this 20th-century skill forever lost to us?

JFK AIRPORT

[F14] **John F. Kennedy International Airport**/formerly **Idlewild Airport**/originally **Anderson Field**, Southern Pkwy., Rockaway Blvd., and Jamaica Bay. Entry via Van Wyck Expwy. 1942 to present.

With land claimed by fill in the swampy waters of Jamaica Bay, Kennedy's 4,900 acres are roughly equivalent in area to Manhattan Island south of 34th Street. It is so large that it's possible to run up several dollars' tariff on your taxi meter between the terminal and the airport's edge; Manhattan lies 15 miles further west. The fare will be well spent, however, for the trip will take you past every architectural cliché of the past four decades, some very hand-

F13

some works, and some less distinguished hangovers from earlier periods as well. A flurry of recent construction has returned JFK to its former glory, with some great new modern architecture, wrapped up neatly by the loop of the futuristic AirTrain.

[F14a] **Terminal One** (Japan Airlines; Air France; Korean Air, and Lufthansa). 1998. *William Nicholas Bodouva & Assocs.*

A sexy replacement for the the old Eastern Airlines. *Herbert Muschamp* in the *New York Times*: "...a trip back to an era before Kennedy became a theme park of life in modern Albania..." High tech and soaring spirits abound. Napoleon III, if resuscitated, might dub it a "parapluie de New York" (as he had described the great iron-and-glass railroad stations in Paris as the "umbrellas of Paris").

[F14b] **Terminal Two** (Delta Airlines). 1962. *White and Mariani.*

Originally home to long-gone airlines **Northeast, Northwest,** and **Braniff.** The lamented Braniff had the coolest design of any airline; everything from the stewardess' uniforms, dinnerware, and paint schemes on the actual airplanes, was the work of the great architect-designer *Alexander Girard (1907-1993).*

[F14c] **Terminal Three ("Worldport")**/originally **Pan Am** et al. 1960 with additions. *Tippetts-Abbett-McCarthy-Stratton; Ives, Turano & Gardner,* associate architects.

A tour de force produced a parasoled pavil-

years in limbo, its future uncertain. It was saved, and surrounded, by JetBlue's new Terminal Five.

[F14f] **Terminal Five (JetBlue).** 2005-2009. *Gensler,* architects, with *Arup.* Interiors, *The Rockwell Group.*

A large, functional shed embraces old TWA. Post–September 11 airport architecture, roomy and deft at sifting people through security to proper departure gates, it fails to delight. The

F14f

F14c, circa 1960

ion unfortunately marred from the beginning by gross details (i.e., the meandering drainpipes around the great piers). Now, expanded many-fold into a complex as large and confusing as the **Palace of Knossos** (the Minotaur's labyrinth), the parasol is but an entrance canopy to this depressing maze.

[F14d] **Terminal Four.** 2001. *Skidmore, Owings & Merrill.*
Replaces the 1957 Terminal Four, by the same firm (see Necrology). The new terminal presents swooping glass walls, appropriately spacey for airline architecture.

[F14e] Originally **Trans World Airlines (TWA) Terminal**/now part of **JetBlue's Terminal Five.** 1956-1962. *Eero Saarinen. Kevin Roche,* co-designer. Additions. Freestanding canopy addition, 1978, *Witthoeft & Rudolph.*
Romantic voluptuary: soaring, sinuous, sensuous, surreal, and for a long time, controversial. Well worth a visit to see for yourself what all the debate was about. The terminal spent

hanging wheel of video screens is interesting for approximately three minutes. The **food court,** however, is another matter: a sleekly designed cluster of restaurants (Italian, Spanish, Japanese, etc.) serves serious food, and in an airport! Arrive early and savor tiramisu, tapas and tempura.

[F14g] **Terminal Seven**/originally **British Airways Terminal.** 1970. *Gollins Melvin Ward & Partners.* Renovation, 1997, *Corgan Architects.* Addition, 2012, *William Nicholas Bodouva + Associates.*
Heavy-handed battered concrete over heavy-handed battered glass. An awkward attempt at a tour de force.

[F14h] **Terminal Eight.** 2007. *DMJM (AECOM),* architects.
Huge. JFK's largest terminal is festooned with curving white trusses. *Skyline of the World, a mural* (actually a digital print on vinyl panels) by *Matteo Pericoli,* introduces some modernist elegance to what is essentially a functional shed that replaced the old **Terminals Eight & Nine** (see Necrology).

▐ [F14i] **FAA Air Traffic Control Tower.** 1992. *Pei Cobb Freed & Partners, Leo A. Daly.*

This 320-foot concrete totem pole (with cantilevered glass control rooms) is the tallest in the world. Move over, Pocahontas.

▐ [F14j] **JetBlue Airways Aircraft Maintenance Hangar.** 2004. *HOK.*

A simple shed for airplanes, with clean lines and a dynamic swooping roof.

▐ [F14k] **Airport Power Plant.** 1996. *Hillier Group,* architects.

The simplest program can sometimes rise to the level of great architecture. Here is the power plant as a modernist creature, with glass walls revealing the innards, like a bisected bird. Classy. It replaced the 1957 plant by *SOM,* its inspiration, whose historic guts were equally on view.

▐ [F14l] **The AirTrain.** 2003. *STV,* architects. Automated trains (no driver!) smoothly riding an elevated monorail track in a loop con-

F14a, F14i

HOWARD BEACH

Spreading out east and west behind the false fronts of Cross Bay Boulevard's glitzy/tawdry fast-food and amusement strip intended to catch the eye of Rockaway Beach-bound motorists, Howard Beach lies south of Southern (Belt) Parkway and west of Kennedy Airport. It is the belated outgrowth of an early 20th-century Jamaica Bay shorefront resort developed by *William J. Howard.* (The LIRR first came to nearby onetime Ramblerville and Hamilton Beach in 1880.) The area is a flat, featureless, largely post–World War II development that, save for the strip that divides it in two, boasts few notable punctuations of its humdrum texture.

[F15] **Rockwood Park Jewish Center,** 156-45 84th St., bet. 157th Ave. and Shore Pkwy. E side. ca. 1972. *Hausman & Rosenberg.*

Described in a previous edition of this Guide as "dignified, if trendy," this hasn't been trendy since Nixon left office.

[F16] **St. Helen's Church** (Roman Catholic), 157th Ave., SW cor. 83rd St. 1979.

The yellow brick of the parish's earlier, conservatively designed buildings is here employed in a lively, asymmetrical, self-conscious bit of ecclesiastical expressionism.

West Hamilton Beach lies at the eastern flank of Howard Beach. Sandwiched between the banks of Hawtree Creek and Basin, a placid inland

F14l

necting the airline terminals to the Howard Beach subway station, various parking lots, and the Jamaica LIRR station. Beset with problems during its lengthy construction, the AirTrain has successfully smoothed out many of the panic-inducing traffic tie-ups that made getting to JFK a nightmare.

Architecturally, the **AirTrain** unites disparate terminals and ancillary buildings into one modernist steel and glass circuit. Each station, in shiny stainless steel, is a minor modernist tour de force, but take especially long ganders at the **Jamaica AirTrain Transit Hub** and the **Howard Beach-JFK Station.**

Warnerville: Squeezed between the eastern end of Kennedy Airport and the Nassau County town of Inwood is a waterbound settlement, many of whose houses are built on pilings, like those of Bangkok. Traffic along Rockaway Turnpike is rarely calm enough to allow a leisurely notice of the entrances to this curious community split between Queens and Nassau: at East Dock Street, 1st, or 3rd Streets. Picturesque.

waterway, and the speeding trains of the Transit Authority (once LIRR) Rockaway Division right-of-way, lies this little-known, isolated water-oriented community. Boats are everywhere. Car access is via Lenihan's Bridge (the neighborhood name) into one north-south street (103rd according to maps, 104th if you believe street signs); pedestrians can use the modern 163rd Avenue bridge. For local Tom Sawyers summers here are great—they can jump into the water whenever they feel like it. Sitting on damp, marshy soil or on pilings are hundreds of tiny homes along a string of threadbare lanes that dead end at water's edge. Most are barely one car-width wide, demarked by wooden telephone poles that sit in the gutter, rather than on sidewalks much too narrow to accommodate them. About the only way to determine the area's name is from reading it on the trucks of its volunteer fire company (before Kennedy Airport lopped off the eastern part, it was called Hamilton Beach).

Portion of Town of Hempstead/Hemstede
Settled and chartered in 1664.

This narrow spit of land, a barrier beach for Jamaica Bay (Floridians would term it a key), was so inaccessible prior to the coming of the railroads in 1868-1878 that it was an exclusive resort second only to Saratoga Springs. The accessibility afforded by rail connections by 1900 drove society leaders to more remote parts of Long Island's south shore in and around the Hamptons. Neponsit and Belle Harbor retain traces of this former splendor. (The IND subway, here not sub- but on grade or elevated, replaced the LIRR as the operator of the trestled connection to Long Island and the continent.)

After the departure of high society the area became a resort for the middle class. But in much of the peninsula, this too has changed: the Hammels and Arverne, both east of the terminus of the Cross Bay Bridge, became squalid slums.

R1

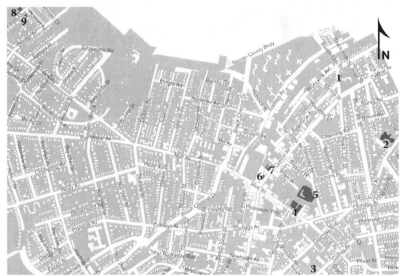

FAR ROCKAWAY

🏛 **[R1] Sage Memorial Church**, The First Presbyterian Church of Far Rockaway, 13-24 Beach 12th St. N side. 1909. *Cram, Goodhue, & Ferguson*.

Across an immaculate Central Avenue lawn is this exquisite memory of Far Rockaway in the first decade of the 20th century, in heavy (**Early English**?) **Gothic**. (The church remembers philanthropist *Russell Sage*, of Forest Hills Gardens fame.) On the lawn is a 1919 tablet to *Teddy Roosevelt* by the Village Beautiful Association.

[R2] Congregation Knesseth Israel, 728 Empire Ave., NW cor. Sage St. 1964. *Kelly & Gruzen*.

An octagonal sanctuary: a dated modernist monument that has survived the modern style wars.

[R3] Richard Cornell Graveyard, Caffrey Ave., bet. New Haven and Mott Aves. N side. 18th to 19th centuries. 🐾

To see this overgrown 67 x 75-foot tombstoneless midblock site where rest the remains of an ancestor of *Ezra Cornell (University)*, rent a helicopter. On second thought, don't bother.

🏛 **[R4] Beth El Temple** (church)/originally St. John's Episcopal Church, Mott Ave., NE cor. Scott Gadell Pl. ca. 1885.

Picturesque 19th-century wood chapel, up to its ears in 20th-century dissonance.

[R5] Intermediate School 53, Queens, The Brian Piccolo School, 1045 Nameoke St., bet. Cornaga Ave., Mott Ave., and Foam Place. 1972. *Victor Lundy*.

Its many-bay-windowed volume surrounds a central courtyard. The grand, monumentally staired entry—the intended main entrance—is now barred because of security problems. See it from both Nameoke and from Beach 18th/Foam Pl. (one-way north).

R4

BAYSWATER

A peninsula on a peninsula, located on Far Rockaway's north shore, in Jamaica Bay, between Norton and Mott Basins. Take Mott Avenue west, out of the business district.

[R8] **"Sunset Lodge,"** 1479 Point Breeze Ave., N of Mott Ave. W side. ca. 1910. [R9] **1478 Point Breeze Avenue**, N of Mott Ave. E side. ca. 1910.

R9

R6

[R6] **Tate Medical Center**/originally **National Bank of Far Rockaway**, 16-24 Central Ave., bet. Mott Ave. and Bayport Place N side. ca. 1900. *H. Gardner Sibell.*

Renaissance Revival in white glazed terra cotta with great Corinthian pilasters. The lattice of steel for its once prominent sign remains an element on the local skyline.

[R7] **1518 Central Avenue** (commercial structure)/originally **Masonic Hall**, bet. Mott Ave. and Bayport Place. N side. ca. 1890.

The ground floor, now broken up for crass commerce, soils the more distinguished history of its handsome symmetrical façade.

Two of Bayswater's venerable **Shingle Style/Colonial Revival** houses. Sunset Lodge is abandoned. Rescue it.

ARVERNE

[R10] **Ocean Village**, Rockaway Beach Blvd. to the Boardwalk, bet. Beach 56th Pl. and Beach 59th St. 1976. *Carl Koch & Assocs.*

Prefabricated, precast-concrete and brick slabs and towers surrounding a central courtyard at the edge of the sea: stark multi-family urban renewal in a sea of unrenewed weeds.

[R11] **Arverne-by-the-Sea**, 7303 Spinnaker Dr., bet. Beach 73rd and Beach 74th Sts. 2004. *Ehrenkrantz Eckstut & Kuhn*, architects. *Quennell Rothschild*, landscape architects.

Sophisticated row housing, in the style of Miami-based urban planners *Elizabeth Plater-Zyberk* and *Andres Duany*. The advance troops of a larger urbanization.

R13

BROAD CHANNEL

The community of Broad Channel occupies the southern end of Jamaica Bay's largest island, sharing it with Big Egg Marsh and, at the north, with Black Bank Marsh and Rulers Bar Hassock. Together these three constitute the Jamaica Bay Wildlife Refuge, one of *Robert Moses'* genuine achievements and now part of the National Park Service's Gateway National Recreation Area. This

R10

R4

[R12] Child Care Center, 4402 Beach Channel Dr., bet. Beach 44th and Beach 45th Sts. 1999. *The Edelman Partnership.*

A sprightly addition to the Rockaways. Brick in bright colors to stimulate this dour community.

[R13] Public School 43/Public School 256, bet. Beach 28th and Beach 29th Sts., S of Seagirt Ave. 1998. *Ehrenkrantz & Eckstut.*

One of the modular schools that offered each site a Chinese menu of parts: one from Group A, two from Group B. The result is handsome, and probably as good as almost any competing system of design.

is the bay's only island accessible by vehicles other than boats—it even has a subway station on the IND Line to the Rockaways. Broad Channel supports a devoted and proud, water-oriented community along narrow lanes that fan out from Cross Bay Boulevard like fishbones from a spine.

[R14] Visitors' Center, Jamaica Bay Wildlife Refuge, Gateway National Recreation Area, U.S. Department of the Interior, National Park Service/ originally N.Y.C. Department of Parks. Cross Bay Blvd. one mile N of Broad Channel settlement border. W side. 1971. *Fred L. Sommer & Assocs.* with *Elliot Willensky*. Altered and expanded, 2007, *Beyer Blinder Belle.* Open to the public.

The original 1971 building was serene concrete and fluted concrete block, appropriately noncompetitive with its surrounding vegetation. The 2007 expansion wraps the original concrete in brick and wood, providing much needed offices, library, and exhibition space. The refuge, sanctuary for thousands of our feathered friends, was largely the vision of *Herbert Johnson*, a sainted parkie.

RIIS PARK

[R15] **Jacob Riis Park**, Gateway National Recreation Area, U.S. Department of the Interior, National Park Service/originally N.Y.C. Department of Parks, Beach 149th to Beach 169th Sts., Atlantic Ocean to Rockaway Inlet. 1937. Frank Wallis, designer. *Aymar Embury II*, consulting architect.

A mile of sandy beach graced by simple, handsome, WPA-era buildings. In addition to swimming, there are other recreational possibilities, such as handball, paddle tennis, and shuffleboard, as well as a boardwalk for strolling.

NECROLOGY

Frappes and sundaes: **Frank Jahn's** was a neo-real 1890s ice cream parlor at 117-03 Hillside Avenue (near 117th Street and Jamaica Avenue), complete with marble countertops, leaded-glass Coca-Cola chandeliers, player piano, and wild—just wild—ice cream concoctions. *Jahn's* was a successful chain, well-known to generations of

Terminal Four (International Arrivals Building). 1957. *Skidmore, Owings & Merrill.*

The principal place of Customs, and hence a string of international airlines flanked a grand, vaulted central pavilion. Once a place of sumptuous lounges and bars where one could stroll past the glass arrivals hall to see and greet incoming passengers.

Terminal Eight (American Airlines). 1960. *Kahn & Jacobs.*

Notable for its stained glass mural, over 300 feet in length, by *Robert Sowers*. The terminal was demolished in 2007, the mural reportedly cut up for use as coffee tables and office partitions.

Terminal Nine. 1959. *Skidmore, Owings & Merrill.* Demolished in 2000.

JFK Control Tower. 1965. *Harrison & Abramovitz.*

Few airport control towers could be described as charming, but this one came close, festively punctured with round portholes. Its replacement is a brooding, inscrutable hulk. A

JFK's Terminal Six

outer-borough families. Only one remains, on 37th Avenue at 81st Street in Jackson Heights, but it doesn't have the original fixtures and ambience of the late, lamented Richmond Hill shop. Closed in 2007.

Hebrew Institute of Long Island, Seagirt Blvd., bet. Beach 17th and Beach 19th Sts. N side. ca. 1900.

The school occupied four Classical Revival white stucco and Spanish tile mansions, built when the Rockaways had been a classier area. In a decayed state for many years, they were replaced by an apartment complex.

JFK Airport's Terminated Terminals:

Terminal One. 1959. *Chester L. Churchill.*

The old home of Eastern Airlines ("if you had wings...").

fanciful, twisting pretzel of a tower proposed by *Voorsanger Associates* was never built. Too bad.

Congregation Derech Emunah (synagogue), 199 Beach 67th St., SE cor. Rockaway Blvd. 1903. *William A. Lambert.*

A neo-Georgian nave, clad in the Shingle Style. Plowed under by the massive Arverne-by-the-Sea development.

DEATH WATCH

Terminal Six/onetime **TWA Terminal B**/originally **National Airlines Sundrome.** 1972. *I.M. Pei & Partners.*

A classy, classic building, its rich travertine walls and floors under a great columned and corniced roof, but now slated for demolition. This serene temple to transport was, in its original corporate incarnation, the "portal to Florida" for many taking the bargain flights. Reinvigorated by JetBlue, then vacated when that airline flew the coop to their new nest at **Terminal Five.**

THE BRONX

THE BRONX
Borough of The Bronx / Bronx County

 Colonial

 Georgian / Federal

 Greek Revival

 Gothic Revival

 Villa

 Romanesque Revival

 Renaissance Revival

 Roman Revival

 Art Deco / Art Moderne

 Modern / Postmodern

 Designated Landmark

The northernmost of New York City's five boroughs, and the only one physically on the North American mainland; the others are either islands by themselves or parts of another (Long Island). The only wrinkle is where the borough of Manhattan became a smaller island upon the straightening of the Harlem River in 1895. That major earth-moving effort severed the community of Marble Hill from the northern tip of Manhattan Island and joined it instead, some 15 years later, to the Bronx, using as fill the earth dug out of the excavations for Grand Central Terminal.

Like the County of Westchester, of which it was a part for some 200 years, Bronx County's topography consists of hills and valleys in the west end and what was originally a marshy plain to the east. To this day are visible the rocky outcroppings and streets of steps which characterize many areas of the West Bronx. The east is, as a result of nonstop landfill and the post–World War II housing explosion, less identifiable as a marsh. But a drive or walk through Pelham Bay Park will reveal some of the borough's sylvan, preurbanized reeded landscapes along the peninsulas that extend into Long Island Sound.

In the 19th century the Bronx was covered with farms, market villages, embryo commuter towns, country estates, and a number of rambling charitable institutions: a place of rural delights. In 1874 the western portion of the Bronx (designated **Western, Riverdale, Central**, and **Southern Bronx** in this Guide) was annexed to the City. Bridgebuilding and the extension of elevated rapid transit lines from Manhattan, and then a growth of population, industry, and schools followed political union. The eastern Bronx (designated as **Eastern** and **Northern Bronx** in this Guide) became part of New York City in 1895.

Except for parts of Riverdale, the westernmost, hilliest, and least accessible part of the borough, the physical vestiges of the old villages with such names as **West Farms, Morrisania, Kingsbridge**, and **Middletown** were submerged by 20th-century development. The extension of the rapid transit lines along Jerome Avenue, Boston Road, White Plains Road, Westchester Avenue, and finally along Grand Concourse made the Bronx the next step in upward mobility for hundreds of thousands of families of average but improving means. But the post–World War II suburban exodus drained away many of their offspring. And governmental housing policy relocated many of the older generation who remained to Co-op City, a huge development of thirty-five-story apartment towers, bedding down, in aggregate, some 55,000 people.

The Bronx has become home to a population that is predominantly African-American and

S2

Latino. Stable communities continue to flourish with populations drawn from all racial and economic backgrounds, and much of the South, Central, and West Bronx that had approached the appearance of a burned-out wilderness by the mid-1980s, scenes not unlike those in war-ravaged cities, is now blooming with new housing, residential conversions of industrial buildings, and excellent new schools and community centers.

Green leafy camouflage flourishes in the borough's larger parks and the parkways that link them. They are the result of planning by local visionaries in 1883 and executed largely in the two decades that followed. The ability of nature to rejuvenate itself (fully one-fifth of the Bronx's area—5,861 acres—is parkland, although admittedly large amounts are not yet developed) is the ascending star of the Bronx's future.

Tips on touring: The Bronx, the smallest of New York's outer boroughs, is still quite **large**. The South and Western Bronx are readily accessible by a tangled knot of subway lines (B and D, Nos.1, 2, 4, 5, and 6) that straighten out into linear lines moving methodically north up the Grand Concourse (B, D) and Jerome Avenue (No.4) into the Central Bronx.

The farther reaches of the Northern Bronx may be reached by the No.5 line, although some walking or transfer to a bus may be required to visit all the buildings and parks described here. Meanwhile, **a car** is recommended for visits to the Eastern Bronx and to Riverdale. The tendrils of the MTA do not reach into those hinterlands.

Southern Bronx

Though their names persist into the present, the country villages that once existed in the South Bronx have long disappeared. Soon after the Civil War the farms that survived from colonial times began to give way to private homes and tenement rows. In more recent days these have, in turn, ceded space to arterial highways and public housing. The rapid growth of other parts of the Bronx in the 20th century eclipsed the South Bronx and shifted the focus of commerce, entertainment, and government to other parts of the borough. Successive waves of immigrants and industries have passed in and out of the South Bronx, but their footprints have been hard to find. Without money, power,

S3

or prestige, the area has been unable to cultivate its ornaments. Landmarks venerated in other places were, until recently, overlooked here. Some have completely disappeared; but some survivors are happily being rediscovered.

MOTT HAVEN

[S1] Formerly **Mott Iron Works**, Third Ave. bet. Harlem River and E.134th St., opp. Bruckner Blvd. to former Mott Haven Canal (filled-in). W side. 1828-1906.

Jordan L. Mott, inventor of a coal-burning stove, in 1828 established a factory west of Third Avenue, between East 134th Street and the Harlem River. The venture prospered and grew. Buildings of the ironworks were off the western walkway of the Third Avenue Bridge (but don't look too hard; architecture has vanished). It was *Mott* who founded the village of **Mott Haven**, whose monogram "MH" persists in the mosaics of the 138th and 149th Street Stations of the Jerome Avenue subway.

The Broncks: The first European settlers of this area were Jonas Bronck, a Dane from Amsterdam, and his family, whose farmhouse is believed to have been located east of the Third Avenue Bridge. Though some say the borough's official name, The Bronx, owes its initial article to friends of the settlers saying "Let's pay a visit to the Broncks," the less romantic but more

S5

accurate explanation lies elsewhere. As it was common to speak of the Army of the Potomac or the valley of the Hudson, each taking its name from a river, so it was with the lands along the banks of the local river here, The Bronx River.

Piano Town:
In the last decades of the 19th century, as an emerging urban middle class was able to amass enough surplus income to seek the finer things, pianos were in demand. In the Bronx they were player pianos, after the process for a "pianola" was patented in 1897. The local German immigrant population included skilled workers employed in these former piano factories, as others similarly skilled were employed across the East River at the Steinway and Sohmer factories in western Queens.

Nearest train: No.6 to Brook Ave.

[S2] Originally **Haines Piano Co.** (factory)/ later **Kroeger Piano Co.**, 26 Bruckner Blvd., bet. Alexander and Lincoln Aves. and 79 Alexander Ave., bet. Bruckner Blvd. and E. 132nd St. 1888. *Kreitler & Hebbard.*

A lovely **Romanesque Revival** loner, with forged iron strap-anchors, ornamented steel lintels, and subtle detailing of brick arches, their spring blocks, and brick and terra-cotta spandrels. L-shaped in plan, with two façades wearing the head of the horse costume (so it appears to be two separate buildings from street level).

[S3] **Warehouse, 82-96 Lincoln Ave.**, bet. E.132nd St. and Bruckner Blvd. E side. 1888. *C.C. Buck.*

Now a small business center, the former truck bays of its 132nd Street side present a formidable, but shallow, brick arcade (the glazing mutes the power of the original deeply recessed brickwork).

S6

[S4] Formerly **Estey Piano Company** (factory), E.132nd St., bet. Lincoln and Alexander Aves. N side. 1885. *A.B. Ogden & Son.*

Still the grande dame of the piano trade. Its grand clock tower joins façades elegantly detailed in terra cotta, textured brick, and contrasting stone. And on top machicolations!

[S5] **Branch, Chase Manhattan Bank/** originally **North Side Board of Trade Building**, 2514 Third Ave., SE cor. E.137th St. 1912. *Albert E.Davis.*

Giant Ionic attached columns and pilasters front a grand Venetian Renaissance white-terra-cotta palazzo for northern New York County business development. After the Bronx became part of the City of New York, but before it became a county of its own, it was the North Side of New York County. This served as headquarters of the board of trade.

[S6] **2602 Third Avenue** (warehouse), NE cor. E.140th St. ca. 1890.

Grand relieving arches, sturdy machicolations, and "decorative" iron lances elegantly stabilizing brick piers, combine to make this a superb fortress for wares in storage, and, perhaps, in need of defense.

[S7] **Mott Haven Historic District**, generally along both sides of Alexander Ave., bet. E.137th and E.141st Sts.

S7a

This district, named for *Jordan Mott*, owner of the Mott Iron Works at East 134th Street and the Harlem River, is the old Bronx at its best. Not only are there well-designed row houses and apartments—by such architects as *Carl A. Millner, Charles Romeyn,* and *Arthur Arctander*—but five fine institutional buildings as well, two of which, the churches, handsomely define the district at its south and north ends. 280 Alexander Avenue was the home of *Edward Willis,* a local land developer for whom nearby Willis Avenue is named.

The district includes:

[S7a] **St. Jerome's Roman Catholic Church**, 230 Alexander Ave., SE cor. E.138thSt. 1900. *Delhi & Howard.*

St. Jerome is remembered here by some vigorous late 19th-century neo-Baroque columns exuberantly breaking away from the body of the church, and of the church tower.

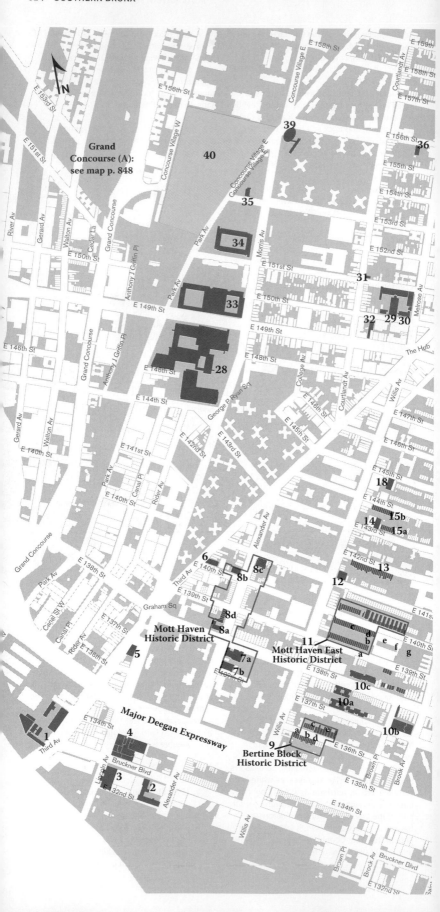

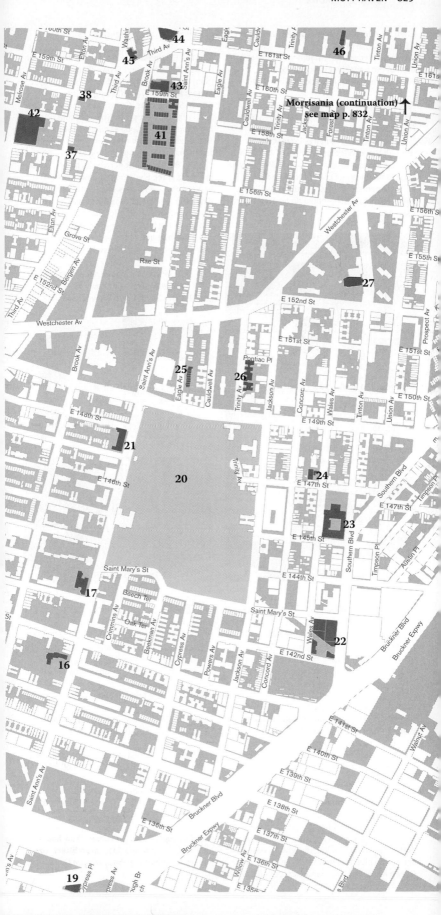

Morrisania (continuation)
see map p. 832

[S7b] **St. Jerome's School,** 222 Alexander Ave., NE cor. E.137th St.

An earlier, sterner St. Jerome for the children of the parishioners next door.

Flush and austere brick and limestone.

[S8a] **40th Precinct, N.Y.C. Police Department,** 257 Alexander Ave., NW cor. E.138th St. 1924. *Thomas E. O' Brien.*

A 16th-century Italian palazzo, filtered through the architectural history of 19th-century London clubs, now turns up in Mott Haven: brick with limestone quoins and window enframements, on a base of rusticated limestone, with a grand dentiled limestone cornice. Classy.

S8a

[S8b] **Mott Haven Branch, N.Y. Public Library,** 321 E.140th St., NW cor. Alexander Ave. 1905. *Babb, Cook & Willard.*

More neo-Renaissance, but the inflated quoins and white/black contrast of brick and limestone are an awkward American touch: bettering *Michelangelo*? We think not.

[S8c] **Tercera Iglesia Bautista** (Third Spanish Baptist Church)/originally **Alexander Avenue Baptist Church,** 322 Alexander Ave., SE cor. E.141st St. 1901. *Frank Ward of Ward & Davis.*

Baroque brickwork and broken cornices, for even the Baptists hereabouts could exult in architecture.

[S8d] **261-271 Alexander Avenue,** SW cor. 139th St. 1890s.

A somber, articulated brick terrace (of houses, in the English sense). Colonnettes support elliptical arches, giving Alexander Avenue serious architecture in what some would call **Queen Anne,** but historian *Vincent Scully* would term **The Stick Style.**

Mott Haven' s other "brownstones":

[S9] **The Bertine Block Historic District**, E.136th St. bet. Willis Ave. and Brown Place:
[S9a] **408-412 East 136th Street**. S side. 1877. *Rogers & Browne.* [S9b] **414-432 East 136th Street**. S side. 1891. *George Keister.* [S9c] **415-425 East 136th Street**. N side. 1892. *John Hauser.* [S9d] **434-440 East 136th Street**. S side. 1895. *Adolph Balschun, Jr.* [S9e] **Eight Tenements.** 1897-1899. *Harry T. Howell.*

The **Bertine Block** derives its name from a grouping of ten low-stooped, tawny brick and brownstone row houses erected by developer *Edward D. Bertine* in 1891 (**Nos.414-432**). The earlier houses precede *Bertine's* involvement and are in the less picturesque neo-Grec style. The later rows and tenements were added by *Bertine* in the subsequent eight years.

[S10] **Plaza Borinquen,** [10a] **E.137th St.,** bet. Willis Ave. and Brown Place. [10b] **E.137th St.,** NW cor. Brown Place.

S8b   S8c

S8d

[10c] **E.138th St. to E.139th St.,** bet. Willis and Brook Aves. 1974. *Ciardullo-Ehmann.*

Dated 1970s housing. The bright side: redbrown masonry with similarly toned mortar. The dim side: tiny windows and clumsy through-the-wall air conditioning units. *Borinquen* is the name given the island of Puerto Rico by its original settlers, the Taino people.

Between Willis and Brook Avenues (Brook Avenue is one-way south):

[S11] **Mott Haven East Historic District,** parts of East 139th and East 140th Streets, bet. Willis and Brook Aves.

Extant blocks encapsulating a slice of Bronx architectural life in the last quarter of the 19th century.

[S11a] **403-445 East 139th Street** (row houses). N side. [S11b] **406-450 East 140th Street** (row houses). S side. 1877-1892. *William O' Gorman.*

Neo-Grec, two-story, red-brick, mini-"brownstones" with powerful cast-iron railings defining the stoops.

[S11c] **407 East 140th Street.** 1890s. *O' Gorman and Hornum.*

The sinuous façade bows to receive the recessed line of adjacent row houses!

[S11d] **409-427 East 140th Street** (row houses). N side. 1897-1900. *William Hornum.*

S9b

Dutch/Flemish pediments make delightfully convoluted silhouettes against the sky!

[S11e] **St. Peter's German Evangelical Lutheran Church**, 435 East 140th St. 1911. *Louis Allmendinger.*

An austere and sturdy brick and limestone neo-Gothic.

[S11f] **441-461 East 140th Street** (tenements). 1902-1903. *George Pelham.* [S11g] **465-481 East 140th Street** (tenements). 1901-1902. *Neville & Bagge.*

The Corinthian-pilastered entrance portals at No.465 gave tenement life a certain outward grandeur.

[S12] Originally **Willis Avenue Methodist Episcopal Church**, 330 Willis Ave., NE cor. E.141st St. 1900. *George W. Kramer.*

A field of pointed glass-filled arches on its 141st Street façade brings a lightness to this somber building.

[S13] **404-450 East 142nd Street** (row houses). S side. 1897. *William O' Gorman.*

Again, **neo-Grec** returns: 24 three-story houses provide another turn-of-the-century streetscape.

[S14] Originally **Congregational Church of North New York**, 415 E.143rd St., bet. Willis and Brook Aves. N side. 1903. *Dodge & Morrison.*

Anchoring its small-scale row-house neighbors is this formidable late **Romanesque Revival**, creamy gray, rock-faced stone church.

[S15a] **419-437 East 143rd Street** (row houses). N side. 1887. H. S. Baker. [S15b] **404-446 East 144th Street** (row houses). S side. 1887. *H. S. Baker*

Another range of neo-Grec, some lovingly restored.

[S16] **St. Ann's Church** (Episcopal) and Graveyard, 295 St. Ann's Ave., bet. E.139th and E.141st Sts. W side. 1840-1841.

S11a

S17

St. Ann's, erected by *Gouverneur Morris, Jr.,* on his estate in memory of his mother, provides an echo from the Bronx's rural past. Mysterious hummocks in front of the edifice mark burial vaults in which early parishioners' remains are entombed. Built slightly askew to the street grid (or is it rather the street grid is slightly askew from St. Ann's?)

[S17] **Centro de Salud Segundo Ruiz Belvis** (neighborhood family-care center), E.142nd St., NW cor. St. Ann's Ave. 1972. *Frost Associates,* architects; *William Tarr,* sculptor.

An important step forward: not just a needed community health center but a physical symbol of hope in the cityscape.

[S18] **St. Pius V Roman Catholic Church**, 416 E.145th St., bet. Willis and Brook Aves. 1907. *Anthony F.A. Schmidt.*

Its strong silhouette suggests a 19th-century utilities building, but in fact this substantial red-brick church is an early 20th-century paean to God.

PORT MORRIS

East of the Bruckner Expressway and the Bronx approaches to the Triborough Bridge and south of East 141st Street lies a peninsula of industry largely forgotten by the wheels of progress: Port Morris.

[S19] **Bronx Grit Chamber** of Wards Island Water Pollution Control Plant, City of New York, 158 Bruckner Blvd., bet. St. Ann's and Cypress Aves. S side. 1936-1937. *McKim, Mead & White.* ☞

Appropriate grandeur for our public waters. Here *MM&W* remembered *Claude-Nicolas Ledoux's* many built and unbuilt works: the toll-gates of late 18th-century Paris and the Saltworks at Arc-en-Senans.

S21

MELROSE

Dominating this community is the traditional business and entertainment center of the borough, called **The Hub**, intersection of five busy streets: East 149th Street, Third, Willis, Melrose, and Westchester Avenues. Old-timers can recall the area as a bustling entertainment center, with fare ranging from silent flicks and burlesque to operatic performances, and with trolley lines converging from every direction. The Bronx stretch of the Third Avenue el, which once clattered overhead, was removed in the 1970s, but the pace on the street remains furious and chaotic, an expression of the coming together of the many Hispanic and black communities, of which Melrose and the rest of the South Bronx are today composed. If there is a word to sum up the Hub's purpose it is "buy!"

Closest trains: Nos.2 and 5 to 3rd Ave.-149th St. station / No.6 to E.143rd-St. Mary's station.

[S20] **St. Mary's Park**, St. Ann's to Jackson Aves., St. Mary's to E.149th Sts. Reconstructed, 1936.

Named for **St. Mary's Church**, a wooden country church that stood on Alexander Avenue and East 142nd Street until its demolition in 1959. The crest of the hill at the north end of the park is a good place from which to survey this neighborhood. It was once known as Janes' Hill and belonged to *Adrian Janes*, whose family's famous ironworks was located nearby.

The Capitol Dome: On the south side of Westchester Avenue between Brook and St. Ann's Avenues is the site of what was once the Janes, Kirtland & Company Iron Works. It was here, in one of America's largest foundries of its time, that were cast lowly devices such as iron furnaces and ele-

S24

*gant items of architectural ironwork such as Central Park's **Bow Bridge**. But literally crowning partners Janes' and Kirtland's many achievements was the casting and erection (using horse power) of the 8,909,200 pounds of iron composing the **Capitol Dome** in Washington, D.C., completed in 1863.*

West of St. Mary's Park:

[S21] **Public School 27**/also known as **St. Mary's Park School**/originally **Public School 154**, 519 St. Ann's Ave., bet. E.147th and E.148th Sts. W side. 1895-1897. *C.B.J. Snyder.* ☞

Eclectic **Renaissance-Revival**, built five stories tall for children with good legs and good lungs. Grand pedimented dormers provide a rich profile against the sky.

East of St. Mary's Park:

[S22] Former **Ward Bread Company** (bakery), 367 Southern Blvd., bet. E.142nd St. and St. Mary's St. to Wales Ave. W side. ca. 1900.

This six-story white, glazed terra-cotta former bakery abuts the old Port Morris Branch of the New York, New Haven & Hartford Railroad. The name once blazed in brick down the monumental stack was recently sheared off. Only the final "D" from "Bread" remains.

[S23] Originally **Samuel Gompers Industrial High School,** 455 Southern Blvd., along Tinton Ave., bet. E.145th and E.146th Sts. W side, to Wales Ave. 1932. *Walter C. Martin.*

A monumental symmetric and Classical plan dressed in stripped **neo-Romanesque/Art Deco.**

[S24] **St. Roch's Roman Catholic Church and Rectory,** 425 Wales Ave., bet. E.147th and E.149th Sts. W side. 1931. *DePace & Juster.*

Neo-Baroque, Spanish division, an exuberant style brought to Spanish America in the days of the Jesuit-led counter-Reformation, which sought to bring back the Protestants to Catholicism with a virtuoso and theatrical architectural display. Many descendants of the Latin Americans whom the Spanish sought to convert now live in this neighborhood.

North of St. Mary' s Park:

[S25] **560-584 Eagle Avenue** (2-family housing), bet. E.149th St. and Westchester Ave. E side. (Eagle Ave. one-way south.) ca. 1986.

Distinguished moderately priced housing. Three-dimensional in concept, it provides real backyards for its apartment dwellers. Much of the Bronx has been infilled with two-story hous-

S27

ing since the 1990s, most of it tacky, in spite of the lesson this elegant example provided.

[S26] 600, 610, 620 Trinity Avenue (apartments), bet. E.149th St. and Westchester Aves. ca. 1939.

Six-story Art Deco cream and brown brick, unusual for this area (they are more common in the West Bronx and the Grand Concourse).

[S27] **St. Anselm's Church** (Roman Catholic), 673 Tinton Ave., bet. E.152nd St. and Westchester Ave. W side. ca. 1907. *Anton Kloster.*

Bare-bones brick nearly everywhere except at the entrance, where poetically illustrated glazed tile plaques and neo-Romanesque ornament soften the bluntness of the masonry. Within a blue-green light washes the sanctuary from a circular, stained glass clerestory as though lighting a grotto. The walls shimmer with the brothers' ceramic tile tesserae. Moving.

THE HUB

Closest trains: Nos.2 or 5 to 3rd Ave.-149th St. station.

[S28] Lincoln Medical & Mental Health Center, N.Y.C. Health & Hospitals Corporation, Morris Ave., SW cor. E.149th St. 1976. *Max O. Urbahn Assocs.* Brick bas-relief mural, *Aleksandra Kasuba.*

S29, S30

The brickwork is too much of a good thing. An indescribably strident earth color, it aggressively grabs your attention. Nevertheless, swirled brick bas-reliefs on 149th Street are a handsome addition to the streetscape.

[S29] Immaculate Conception Church of the Blessed Virgin Mary (Roman Catholic) 389 E.150th St., NW cor. Melrose Ave. 1887. *Henry Bruns.* **[S30] School Hall,** 378 E.151st St., SW cor. Melrose Ave. 1901. *Anthony F.A. Schmitt.*

Romanesque Revival, this church boasts the highest steeple in the Bronx, its myriad white finials punctuating the skyline. Built in the days when Germans were the most populous ethnic group in the Bronx and their prominence in the building trades, brewing, and the manufacture of musical instruments was of central importance to the borough's prosperity.

[S31] **614 Courtlandt Avenue**, NE cor. E. 151st St. 1872. Altered, 1882, *Hewlett S. Baker.* ●⌐

The local tides of change seem never-ending, yet here is a miraculously intact three-story apartment house complete with an intricate mansard roof. Originally a saloon at street level, it was left here by *Jacob Ruppert*, who, not surprisingly, was promoting beer-drinking in this then **Germanic** neighborhood.

[S32] **Engine Company 41, N.Y.C. Fire Department**, 330 E.150th St., bet. Courtlandt and Morris Aves. S side. 1903.

Italian Renaissance Mannerist Revival, its cornice lost to erosion by time and the spartan budget for the maintenance of New York City buildings.

[S33] **Michelangelo Apartments**, E.149th to E.150th Sts., bet. Morris and Park Aves. 1976. *Weiner & Gran and Jarmul & Brizee.*

If this project's flat, modest façade on 149th Street was meant as a foil to the more colorful,

S31

S34

three-dimensional one of Lincoln Medical Center across the street, it succeeds. A project of the state Urban Development Corporation.

[S34] **Maria Lopez Plaza** (apartments), 635 Morris Ave., NW cor. E.151st St. 1975-1982. *John Ciardullo Assocs.*

White columns, half-cylindrical balconies, and thoughtful fenestration raise **Maria Lopez** to a level above the norm. And what only the residents see—in the block-square, green interior courtyard—is brilliant housing design united with enlightened urban living.

Humble churches:

[S35] **Greater Universal Baptist Church**/originally **Church of the Holy Trinity** (Italian Presbyterian), 253 E.153rd St., bet. Park and Morris Aves. N side. 1911.

A modest **Lombardian Romanesque** box (the arched corbel-table at the gable is a Lombard signature).

[S36] **Greater Victory Baptist Church**/originally **St. Matthew's Lutheran Church**, 374 E.156th St., bet. Courtlandt and Melrose Aves. S side. 1895.

Drab and dreary paint masks a handsome, but bedraggled, neo-Gothic building.

[S37] Originally **Reformed Church of Melrose**, 742 Elton Ave., NE cor. E.156th St. 1874. *Henry Piering.*

A longtime survivor of South Bronx desolation, but many a Phoenix has risen from the ashes.

[S38] Originally **Elton Avenue (German) Methodist Episcopal Church**, 790 Elton Ave., SE cor. E.158th St. 1879. *John Rogers or H. S. Baker.*

A sprightly neighbor to the Reformed Church, a block away. They are the architectural highlights in counterpoint to new infill housing.

[S39] **Bronx (Melrose) South Classic Center**, SE cor. 156th St. and Morris Ave. 2000. *Agrest & Gandelsonas.*

The institutional architecture of **Melrose Houses** receives an injection of shiny, sophisti-

S37

cated architecture. Don't miss it. The architects rightly said: "the gymnasium is a symbolic element of identification for the entire community."

[S40] Mott Haven Campus (Public Schools), Concourse Village W., bet. E. 156th St. (Thurman Munson Way) and E. 153rd St. 2011 (predicted). Perkins Eastman with Alexander Gorlin, architects.

Land is at such a premium these days, even in the South Bronx, that the City has begun building much-needed schools on contaminated sites, including this campus of four new middle and high schools grouped together on a site bordering the MetroNorth railroad tracks. The site was a railyard and home to leaky gas refining and dry-cleaning facilities and, not surprisingly, the ground is laced with dangerous chemicals, including numerous "SVOCs" (semi-volatile organic compounds). **A great idea** *(the schools will have separate entries and identities but share some facilities, including a performing arts center)* **on a questionable site** *has resulted in a costly decontamination effort (in 2007) by the City, and a lawsuit (in 2008) from worried parents. Construction, meanwhile, continues.*

MORRISANIA

S41

As the South Bronx was a German neighbor-hood in the 19th century, there was a continuing demand for lager beer. Before the advent of refrigeration, the brewing of lager (from the German liegen, to lie still) required a chilled place to age. Caves cut into hillsides made it possible to pack the beer kegs with naturally cut ice and then to seal the openings temporar-ily until the beer had aged. No surprise then that breweries backed up to the Eagle Avenue escarpment (it is so steep that Eagle Avenue negotiates East 161st Street over a high bridge). The caves are used today for less romantic man-ufacturing purposes. During Prohibition, both caves and breweries were converted into indoor mushroom farms. Here stood the former **Hupfel Brewery**, St. Ann's to Eagle Aves., bet. E.159th and E.161st Sts. Both ca. 1875. And the former **Eagle Brewery** to its south.

Trains: Nos.2 and 5 to Freeman Street station (at Northern Blvd). This will put you closest to the later entries in this section.

[S41] **Melrose Court**, bet. St. Ann's and Brook Aves., 156th to 158th Sts. 1998. *Magnus Magnusson.*

Magnusson's scheme surrounds courtyards with access stairs serving the individual units. Street façades are tacky (false gables), but inner workings are urbane.

[S42] **Via Verde Housing**, 156th St. and Melrose Ave. 2012. *The Phipps Houses, Jonathan Rose Companies, Dattner Architects, & Grimshaw.*

A widely touted coming attraction and win-ner of the New Housing New York competition with *The Phipps Houses*, developer *Rose*, and architecture firms *Dattner* and *Grimshaw*, collec-tively *PRDG.*

[S43] **Church of Sts. Peter and Paul** (Roman Catholic), 840 Brook Ave., NE cor. E.159th St. 1932. Rectory, 833 St. Ann's Ave., bet. E.159th St. and E.161st St./Third Ave. W side, 1900. *Michael J. Garvin.*

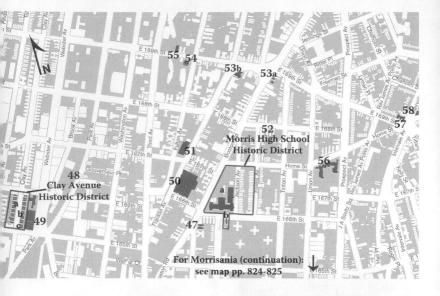

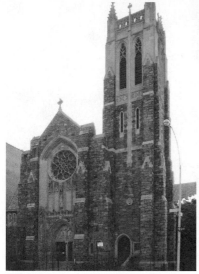

S43

S44

Collegiate Gothic (safe, solid, expensive) in granite ashlar, looking more as though it was commissioned by an Episcopal diocese than a Roman Catholic one. The rectory is a lustier reminder of the parish's earlier days.

[S44] Originally **Bronx Borough Courthouse**/then **Criminal Court of the City of New York,** Bronx County Branch/ now occupying triangle bet. E.161st St., Brook Ave., and Third Ave. 1905-1915. *Oscar Bluemner and Michael J. Garvin.* 🖤

Colossal Tuscan columns mount a rusticated base: an eloquent and abandoned **Beaux Arts** monument. In spite of many decades of smoke, grime, neglect, and the rattling of the long-gone Third Avenue el, it remains proud, even though windows are blocked up, metalwork tarnished, and walls covered with soot.

Promised by the City in 2008 to the "Bronx Academy of Promise Charter School." Bronx Academy remains in temporary quarters elsewhere.

[S45] **42nd Precinct, N.Y.C. Police Department**/originally **36th Precinct,** 3137 Third Ave. (entry on Washington Ave.), opp. E.160th St. at George Meade Plaza. 1904. *Charles Volz.*

This neo-Renaissance palazzo appeared in exterior shots of *Fort Apache, The Bronx,* a 1981 movie about life in an earlier and devastated South Bronx. The real Fort Apache was actually the **Simpson Street** station house.

[S46] **McKinney Community Center,** 751 E. 161st St., bet. Trinity and Tinton Aves. 2006. *Alexander Gorlin.*

One of several deftly detailed recent Housing Authority community centers (see the one on Saratoga Avenue in Bed-Stuy by *George Ranalli* and the one by *Caples Jefferson* in Brownsville). Amidst the recent obsession with luxury condominiums, it's good to see architects spending design time on architecture for social purposes.

[S47] **1074 Cauldwell Avenue**. 1887. *F. T. Camp;* and **1076 Cauldwell Avenue**. 1892. *Charles C. Churchill.* Both E cor. Boston Rd., S of E.166th St.

Two gleaming, well-maintained, expansive (for this outlying area) **Victorian** frame houses preside over a dusty intersection that has seen better days.

[S48] **Clay Avenue Historic District**, both sides of Clay Avenue between E.165th and E.166th Sts. 👁

A lovely group of Classically inspired row

S39

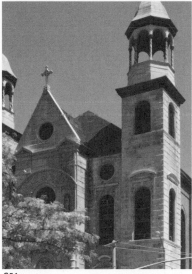

S51

[S49] Former **Sheffield Farms Company (Milk) Bottling Plant**, 1051 Webster Ave., bet. E.165th and E.166th Sts. W side. 1914-1921. *Frank Rooke.*

Though milk is no longer pasteurized or bottled behind this glazed terra-cotta façade, the cows and milk bottles are still visible—in the ornament. Now a **Tuck-it-Away** storage facility.

[S50] **Second Battery Armory**/also known as **105th Artillery Armory**, N.Y. National Guard, 1122 Franklin Ave., NE cor. E.166th St.

S48

houses on a site that had been the old Fleetwood Trotting Course until 1898. One of the richest row-house blocks in New York City. The apartment buildings that anchor three corners of Clay Avenue are by *Neville & Bagge* (1909-1910).

[S48a] **1041-1067 Clay Avenue** (row houses), bet. E.165th and E.166th Sts. W side. 1902. [S48b] **1040-1066 Clay Avenue** (row houses), bet. E.165th and E.166th Sts. E side. 1902. All by *Warren C. Dickerson.*

Both **neo-Renaissance** and **eclectic**, these lush row houses are crowned with stepped gables, bay-windowed and corniced below.

[S48c] Originally **Francis Keil House**, 1038 Clay Avenue, NE cor. E.165th St. 1906. *Charles S. Clark.*

In contrast to its Clay Avenue neighbors, this austere brick house, fronting on East 165th Street, seemed a penitent among the flamboyant. To compensate it has grown jungle vines, embracing and pendant from its cornice.

1906-1911. *Charles C. Haight.* Addition, 1926-1928, *Benjamin W. Levitan.*

A dark, red-brick fortress its slit windows overseeing a steep street of stairs. Together with **Hines Park** and the façade of **St. Augustine's Church**, the armory provides the backdrop for an exciting but forgotten urban space. It is the perfect stage for a medieval melodrama or a childhood game of knights in armor.

[S51] **St. Augustine's Church** (Roman Catholic), 1183 Franklin Ave., NW cor. E.167th St. 1894. *Louis C. Giele.* **St. Augustine's School**, 1176 Franklin Ave., bet. E.167th and E.168th Sts. E side. 1904.

Renaissance and **Baroque** elements combine in this somber but imposing façade. The parish school across the street to the north is distinguished by glazed blue and white terra-cotta sculpture set into the tympanum of its Classical pediment.

[S52] **Morris High School Historic District**, bet. Boston Rd. and Forest Ave. (incl. Jackson Ave.), bet. E.166th St. and Home St., plus Trinity Ave. SE cor. E.166th St. 🕭

[S52a] **Trinity Episcopal Church** of Morrisania, 690 E.166th St., SE cor. Trinity Ave. 1874.

A district of row houses primarily by architect *Warren C. Dickerson*, as well as others by *John H. Lavelle, Harry T. Howell*, and *Hugo Auden*. The modest brick church, Trinity Episcopal, shares its block with neighbors of the same scale. Crowning it all, however, is:

[S52b] **Morris High School**, 1110 Boston Rd., NE cor. E.166th St. 1904. *C.B.J. Snyder*. **Auditorium**, now Duncan Hall. 🕭

A powerful, turreted central tower, gabled green copper roof, buff brick, and terra-cotta trim make this a superior model of **Public School Gothic** and a centerpiece of the neighborhood.

[S55] **Morrisania Baptist Church**/originally **Temple Adath Israel**, 551 E.169th St., bet. Fulton and Third Aves. N side. ca. 1889. Altered later.

This modest edifice in banded and arched brickwork is thought by some to be the first synagogue built in the Bronx. It has since served the Puerto Rican community as a Baptist church.

[S56] **Lewis S. Davidson, Sr., Houses**, N.Y.C. Housing Authority, 810 Home St., bet. Union and Prospect Aves. S side. 1150, 1152 Union Ave., bet. E.167th and Home Sts. E side. 1221 Prospect Ave. W side. 1973. *Paul Rudolph*.

Exposed cast-in-place concrete frames with dark gray, ribbed block infill, these eight-story low-rent apartment buildings are a refreshing change from the monotonous red-brick towers typical of the Authority.

[S57] **Engine Company 82, Ladder Company 31,** N.Y.C. Fire Department, 1213 Intervale Ave., NW cor. E. 169th St.

This Roman brick firehouse figured promi-

S52b

S58

[S53a] **1266 and 1270 Boston Road**, bet. E.168th and E.169th Sts. at McKinley Sq. E side. ca. 1890.

Somewhat more humble structures than those on Cauldwell Avenue, these are in the **Grant Wood/American Gothic** mode, but, in the name of maintenance, much of the original detail has been shorn.

[S53b] **Morrisania Branch, New York Public Library**, 610 E. 169th St., SE cor. Franklin Ave. 1908. *Babb, Cook & Willard*. 🕭

Squat red brick and limestone classicism, wedged between two tenements.

[S54] Originally **Eichler Mansion**/now **Department of Mental Health**, Bronx-Lebanon Hospital Center, Fulton Division, 1285 Fulton Ave., SW cor. E. 169th St. 1890. *De Lemos & Cordes*.

A plethora of riches: yet another residential relic of the 19th century, this time in red brick and terra cotta. *Eichler* was a brewer; his mansion sits on the hill, a spot that once looked west to his brewery at Third Avenue south of East 169th Street.

nently in a 1972 fiction bestseller about fire fighting in the South Bronx, *Dennis Smith's Report from Engine Co. 82*.

[S58] **Walls A.M.E. Zion Church** (African Methodist Episcopal)/ formerly **Holy Trinity Lutheran Church**/originally **Free Magyar Reform Church**, 891 Home St., NE cor. Intervale Ave. 1909. *Thompson & Frohling*.

A charming tan and red brick church that exploits a triangular peninsula opposite Engine Company 82.

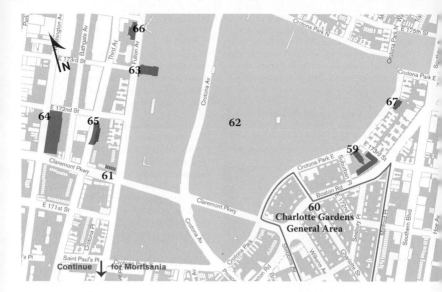

CROTONA PARK

Nearest trains: Nos.2 and 5 to 174th St. station.

[S59] Junior High School 98, The Herman Ridder Junior High School, 1619 Boston Rd., SW cor. E.173rd St. 1929-1931. *Walter C. Martin.* 🔑

Named for the philanthropist who was publisher of the New York Staats-Zeitung. On a difficult irregular site the architect has employed a monumental **Beaux Arts** tower in limestone **Art Deco** dress as the school's focal point.

[S60] **Charlotte Gardens,** along the spine of Charlotte St. and Louis Nine Blvd. (formerly Wilkins Ave.) radiating out toward Crotona Park, Minford Place, and E.170th St. *Edward J. Logue,* governmental developer.

President Carter made **Charlotte Street** a rallying point when, on a personal visit in October 1977 amid the burned-out hulks of five- and six-story apartments, he called for reconstruction. *President Clinton* returned in 1997 to a rebuilt neighborhood, transformed into suburbia.

[S61] 553-557 Claremont Parkway, NW cor. Fulton Ave. 1990s.

One of the more sophisticated examples of infill rowhousing. The checkerboard tile façade and arched parapets seem elegant in contrast to the tacky projects stuffed into the 1990s Bronx streetscape.

[S62] **Crotona Park,** Fulton, Third, E. Tremont, and Arthur Aves., Crotona Park North, East, and South, and a small jog to Southern Blvd. and E.175th St. Reconstructed, 1936.

Formerly the estate of the *Bathgate* family (for whom the nearby avenue was named—and you thought *Billy Bathgate, E.L. Doctorow's* eponymous hero, was a made-up name?) Crotona Park is one of six sites for parks selected by a citizens' committee in 1883.

S59

Named for Croton, an ancient Greek city renowned as the home of many Olympic champions, the park contains a vast array of sports facilities that are in sad disarray today.

[S63] Crotona Play Center, N.Y.C. Department of Parks & Recreation, in Crotona Park, Fulton Ave. at E.173th St. E side. 1934-1936. *Herbert Magoon & Others. Aymar Embury II,* consulting architect. 🔑 Interior. 🔑

A landmark in **Crotona Park,** the play center (actually a bathhouse and swimming pool) is one of the great red-brick WPA **Art Deco** structures of the 1930s. Its crowning clerestories give it a still avant-garde quality, but neglect in recent years has left it forlorn. Restoration may be on the way.

[S64] Bathgate Educational Campus, 1595 Bathgate Ave., between 172nd and Claremont Parkway. 2006. *John Ciardullo.*

Exciting things have occurred in city school design in the last decade. This one is **neo-**

Constructivist, with walls in startling colors sharply dividing the three separate high schools within. It would be instructive to see and compare this with the similarly cubist **High School for Construction Trades, Engineering and Architecture** in Woodhaven, Queens by *Arquitectonica* (see p. 800).

[S65] **Bronx Prep Charter School,** 3872 3rd Ave. bet. E. 172nd St. and Fairmont Parkway. 2006. *Peter Gluck and Partners.*
    Another wonderful new school, around the

S64

S67

corner from the Bathgate complex. Here *Gluck* employs his trademark everyday materials to great effect, with variously colored sheet metal siding expressing the various functions within. See also *Gluck's* **East Harlem School** (p. 548).

[S66] **Public School 171,** SW cor. 174th St. and Fulton Ave. 1990s.
    An elegantly detailed, but understated and thoughtful, school: appropriate as background architecture.

[S67] **Crotona Terrace** (apartments), 1714 Crotona Park E., bet. E.173rd and E.174th Sts. 1994. *Liebman Melting.*
    Polychromatic **neo–Art Deco.** A handsome reminiscence that fits in well with its venerable Art Deco neighbors.

LONGWOOD

Longwood is blessed with numerous subway lines. Take your pick: Nos.2 and 5 to Jackson, Prospect, or Intervale Avenue stations, or No.6 to E.149th St., Longwood Avenue, or Hunts Point Avenue stations.

[L1] **Longwood Historic District,** parts of Macy Place, Hewitt Place, Dawson, Kelly, Beck, and E.156th Sts., bet. Prospect Ave. and Fox St., from Leggett to Longwood Aves. 1898-1901. 🌶
Longwood Historic District Extension. 🌶
    An enclave of intact masonry row houses, complete with stoops, wrought-iron railings, and magnificent brownstone embellishments, developed by *George B. Johnson* and designed primarily by architect *Warren C. Dickerson.*

[L2] Formerly **The Martinique Club**/sometime **Longwood Club**/originally **Samuel B. White House,** 974 E.156th St., SE cor. Beck St. ca. 1850.
    Turned at an angle to today's street grid, this recently restored country house has seen a long series of adaptive reuses.

[L3] **United Church**/originally **Montefiore Hebrew Congregation,** 764 Hewitt Place, bet. 156th St. and Longwood Ave. E side. 1906. *Daumer & Co.*
    This sturdy **Romanesque**-arched sanctuary smiles down its one-block axis, Macy Place, toward busy, noisy Prospect Avenue, one of

L3

Hunts Point's main drags. Originally a synagogue patterned after the Eastern European model, it nevertheless was crowned with twin onion domes! Today, reflecting ethnic and religious shifts in the community, a crucifix occupies the space between the domes.

[L4] **Engine Company 73, N.Y.C. Fire Department,** 655 Prospect Ave., NW cor. E.152nd St. 1900. *Horgan & Slattery.*
    A mini-**Beaux Arts/Baroque** municipal outpost.

[L5] **711, 713, 715 Prospect Ave.** (houses), bet. E.155th and E.156th Sts. W side. ca. 1885.
    A once wonderful but bedraggled trio in a marvelously eclectic block.

[L6] **41st Precinct, N.Y.C. Police Department,** 1035 Longwood Ave., bet. Bruckner and Southern Blvds. N side. 1990s.
    A **postmodern** collage of gathered forms and arches.

[L7] Police Athletic League Bronx Community Center, 991 Longwood Ave., bet. Beck and Fox Sts. 1996. *Kevin Hom & Andrew Goldman.*

Gym/auditorium, boxing ring, fitness center, and game room: all conjoin to keep the young citizen off the street in a playful multicolored complex.

[L8] Hunts Point Branch, N.Y. Public Library, 877 Southern Blvd., NW cor. Tiffany St. 1928. *Carrère & Hastings.* ●
The architects of the public library in Manhattan here tried their hand on a modest branch with brilliant success. The arcade of brick arches is a memorable knockoff of *Brunelleschi's* **Ospedale degli Innocenti** in Florence.

L6

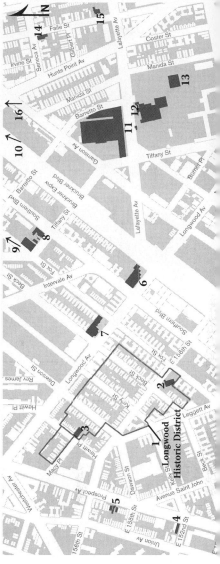

Off to the north, off the map:

[L9] Formerly **41st Precinct, N.Y.C. Police Department**/ originally **62nd Precinct**/also known as **The Simpson Street Station,** 1086 Simpson St., bet. Westchester Ave. and E.167th St. E side. 1914. *Hazzard, Erskine & Blagdon.* Restored, 1997, *Cabrera Barricklo Architects.*
An Italian palazzo—note those massive stone voussoirs radiating out from the entrance-way—once (and, happily, briefly) standing in not-so-splendid isolation, this was the real **Fort Apache.** New houses across the street now belie that bad reputation.

[L10] Longfellow Gardens, Longfellow Ave., bet. E.165th St. and Lowell St. E side. 1983. *Weintraub & di Domenico.*
A bottle-columned pergola, set within a handsomely fenced space, provides visual relief and material relaxation from everyday toil.

HUNTS POINT

The peninsular portion of the Hunts Point community is separated from the rest of the South Bronx not by a waterway but by a deep railroad cut, and by the massive elevated Bruckner Expressway. No subways venture here, but the closest train is the No.6 line, west of the Bruckner, with stops at E.149th St., Longwood Avenue, or Hunts Point Avenue stations.

[L11] The BankNote/originally **American Bank Note Company,** 1201 Lafayette Ave., NE cor. Tiffany St. 1910-1911. *Kirby, Petit & Green.* Converted to studio and residential use, 2009-2011, *Beyer Blinder Belle.* ●
Guarding a main entry to the "peninsula" is this dark, spare **Roman Revival** masonry fortress, which once served to guard its own valuable contents as well. Printed within were billions of pesos, cruzeiros, colóns, sucres, and gourdes for Mexico, Brazil, Costa Rica, Ecuador,

L13

L11

and Haiti, respectively, stock certificates, travelers' checks, and even lottery tickets.

[L12] **Corpus Christi Monastery,** 1230 Lafayette Ave., at Baretto St. E side. 1890. *William Schickel.*

The best time to visit this cloistered community of Dominican nuns is on Sunday afternoon, when they sing their office. The church, with its beautiful polished mosaic floor, bare walls, and scores of candles, is then fully lighted.

[L13] **Hunts Point Youth Center,** 765 Manida St., bet. Lafayette & Spotford Aves. 2004. *Hanrahan/Meyers.*

Another star in the recently stimulating architectural series of the City's expanding youth and community centers.

[L14] **Engine Company 94,** Hook & Ladder Company 48, N.Y.C. Fire Department, 1226 Seneca Ave., SW cor. Faile St. ca. 1925.

An open-air roof gallery and colorful terra-cotta shields embellish this **Renaissance Revival** firehouse.

[L15] **Bright Temple A.M.E. Church**/formerly **Temple Beth Elohim** (synagogue)/ originally **Peter A. Hoe House, "Sunnyslope,"** 812 Faile St., NE cor. Lafayette Ave. ca. 1860. Converted to synagogue, 1919. ●

This picturesque gray stone **Gothic Revival** mansion stands askew to today's street grid. It once shared a large estate with the now demolished "Brightside," the frame country house of *Col. Richard M. Hoe*, inventor of the rotary printing press.

[L16] **Bronx Charter School for the Arts,** 950 Longfellow Ave., bet. Garrison Ave. and Bruckner Expy. 2007. *Weisz + Yoes.*

Hooray! Another great new school. This one uses natural light and colored brick to transform an existing factory building.

NECROLOGY

Mott Haven Reformed Church, 350 E.146th St., bet. Third and College Aves. 1852.

Replaced by a modern edifice in a heavy-handed **Brutalist** style. Too much reform or not enough?

Old Bronx Borough Hall, in Crotona Park, E. Tremont Ave., SE cor. Third Ave. 1895, 1897. *George B. Post.*

Situated on a high bluff, the old local seat of government was irreparably damaged by fire while efforts were underway to find an adaptive reuse.

MIGHT AS WELL BE DEAD

Originally **Henry W. Boetteger Silk Finishing Factory**/later **Boetteger & Heintz Silk Manufacturing Company,** 401 Brook Ave., SW cor. 144th St. 1888. *Robert Otz and George Butz.*

Were the window openings to be reopened, this factory complex would rival the old mill buildings of New England. Check the stack for its new role as microwave transmission tower.

Central Bronx

The Central Bronx includes the **Bronx Zoo**, the **New York Botanical Garden, Fordham University, Belmont,** and the district encompassing the Webster Avenue corridor on the west and the Bronx River area on the east. Its south boundary is the gash of the Cross-Bronx Expressway. Within these limits can be found a great variety of flora, fauna, land uses, housing types, and building conditions. Institutions of world prominence are within sight of humble and exotic neighborhood establishments.

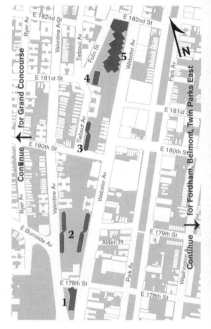

C2b

TWIN PARKS WEST/TREMONT

In the 1970s a group of architects created more than 20 low and middle income housing projects scattered over a mile-square area. They were the product of urban renewal theory, and the powers of New York State's Urban Development Corporation (UDC): a surgical strike by those believing the superblock to be the future of housing for the modest. It's fortunate that subsequent powers turned to low and medium rise housing, infilling the City's gaps, rather than continuing to erase existing city blocks to implant such as these. Some examples:

[C1] **1880 Valentine Avenue,** bet. Webster Ave. and E.178th St. E side. (Twin Parks project) 1973. *Giovanni Pasanella.*
Dark red, oversized-brick-clad UDC building for elderly tenants.

[C2a] **1985 Webster Avenue,** bet. E.178th and E.180th Sts. W side.
[C2b] **2000 Valentine Avenue,** bet. E.178th and E.180th Sts. E side. [C3] **2100 Tiebout Avenue,** NE cor. E.180th St. 1973. *Giovanni Pasanella.*
A prematurely aged (it's barely 40) cliff of brick, with split-level duplex apartments.

[C4] **333 East 181st Street,** at Crane Sq., Tiebout Ave., and Folin St. E side. 1973. *Prentice & Chan, Ohlhausen.*
Tall. Made of bricks.

[C5] **Intermediate School 137, The Angelo Patri School,** 2225 Webster Ave., bet. Folin St. and E.181st St. W side. 1975. *The Architects Collaborative.*
The Fourth Edition of this Guide called it an "exuberant concrete structure." Since surpassed by new ideas in school design by *Gluck, Weisz,* and others.

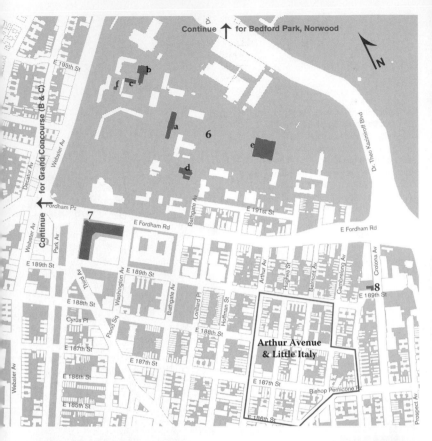

Continue ↑ for Bedford Park, Norwood

← Continue for Grand Concourse (B & C)

Arthur Avenue
& Little Italy

C6a

C6f

FORDHAM UNIVERSITY

A Jesuit institution since 1846, the university began as **St. John's College** in 1841, founded by the Right Reverend *John Hughes* (later New York's first Catholic archbishop) and guided initially by its first president, *John McCloskey* (later America's first cardinal). *Hughes* commissioned his brother-in-law, *William Rodrigue,* to design a residence hall and church for the fledgling institution to accompany the already existing **Rose Hill Manor House**—for which this campus is named. Later *Rodrigue* associated with *James Renwick, Jr.,* in the design of the new **St. Patrick's Cathedral**.

Fordham derived its present name in 1905 from that of the old manor, later village, of Fordham—not the other way around, as some well-meaning community people would have you believe. The campus's physical presence, along heavily traveled East Fordham Road, is very strong. Mature trees, dense shrubs, brilliantly green lawns, and a group of harmonious gray stone Collegiate Gothic buildings (built mostly from designs by architect *Emile G. Perrot* between 1911 and 1930) offer a distinguished contrast to the tacky commercial architecture adjacent to the campus. The best of Fordham's buildings, save the early **Manor House**, a rough-stone country-style Greek Revival masterpiece, is the last in the Collegiate Gothic style, **Keating Hall.**

Two literary tales relate to the campus. It is said that the 98 acres were the setting for *James Fenimore Cooper's* novel, *The Spy.* And it is also said that the bell in the University Church (appropriately dubbed "Old Edgar") was the inspiration for *Poe's* poem, "The Bell" (he lived nearby).

[C6] **Fordham University, Rose Hill Campus**, generally E of Webster Ave., N of E.Fordham Rd., S and W of Dr. Theo Kazimiroff Blvd.

[C6a] **Administration Building**/central part originally **Horatio Shepheard Moat House**, Rose Hill. 1836-1838. Perhaps *William Rodrigue*. Additions, 1907. 🍎

Random ashlar Greek Revival with a classy porch... fluted (a purist no-no) Ionic columns with an octagonal lantern lighting the stair within.

[C6b] **University Chapel**/originally **St. John's Church**/officially **Our Lady, Mediatrix of All Graces**, 1841-1845, *William Rodrigue*. Transept, chancel, crossing, and lantern added, 1928-1929. *Emile Perrot*. 🍎

Louis Philippe, of all persons, contributed the stained glass, but *Rodrigue* (later assisting *Renwick* at St. Patrick's Cathedral) contributed the shell and a cascade of buttresses, crockets, and finials.

BELMONT

The Bronx's Little Italy: The fork in the street grid where Crescent Avenue diverges from East 187th Street (just a few blocks southeast of Fordham University) provides a space which, straight out of the Mediterranean tradition, has fostered a great marketplace for the cohesive Italian-American community of Belmont. Along East 187th Street, past Belmont Avenue and the area's religious and social rallying point, Our Lady of Mt. Carmel Roman Catholic Church, and into busy, colorful Arthur Avenue, you will find a multitude of small retail shops resembling those which were once the mainstay of New York's streets. Long may they prosper here! Freshly baked Italian breads, salami, and olive oil. Latticini freschi, fresh fish, and clams on the half shell from a common plate served on a wooden sidewalk stand (with unlimited lemons). Drop into the European-feeling New York City Retail Market, a *Fiorello LaGuardia* morality gesture of

C6b

C7

[C6c] **St. John's Residence Hall**, Queen's Court, part of the **"Old Quad"**. 1841-1845. *William Rodrigue*. 🍎

Collegiate Gothic, of random ashlar (Fordham gneiss).

[C6d] **Thebaud Hall**/originally **Science Hall**. 1886. *Eugene Kelly*.

[C6e] **Keating Hall**. 1936. *Robert J. Reiley*.
Modern **Gothic**.

[C6f] **Alumni House**/now **Fordham University Housing** office. ca. 1840. *William Rodrigue*. 🍎

Greek Revival in dark fieldstone.

[C7] **Fordham Plaza**, 1 Fordham Plaza, E. Fordham Rd. SE cor. Third Ave. to Washington Ave. and E.189th St. 1986. *Skidmore, Owings & Merrill*.

Fordham Plaza, long an ill-defined **purgatory for pedestrians**, has now been graced with some thoughtful paraphernalia for bus travel cum shops. The glitzy ziggurat on the east corner is banal at street level, bizarre from afar.

1940 that removed Arthur Avenue's pushcart peddlers but, thankfully, not the street life. It's all worth an extra special good weather visit, every day but Sunday, of course.

Notable spots to nourish the itinerant architecture buff: Tra Di Noi, 622 E.187th St.; Borgatti's Ravioli and Egg Noodles, 632 E.187th St.; Egidio Pastry, E.187th St., SE cor. Hughes Ave.; Giovanni's, 2343 Arthur Ave.; Cosenza's Fish Market, 2354 Arthur Ave.; Randazzo's Seafood, 2327 Arthur Ave.

[C8] **2841 Crotona Avenue**, NW cor. E.189th St. ca. 1900.

A **stone ghost-house** from another era, with plywood for windows, with a parasitic one-story building attached to its hip. It could be brought back to life, but what would it say upon awakening from its long slumber? Probably *"Where's the old neighborhood?!"*

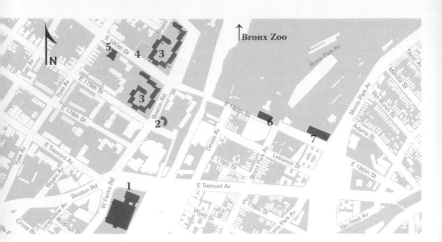

↑ Bronx Zoo

N

WEST FARMS

[W1] **Intermediate School 167,** The Lorraine Hansberry School, 1970 West Farms Rd., SE cor. E. Tremont Ave. 1973. *Max O. Urbahn Assocs.*

A cast-concrete structural frame and dark, rough-ribbed concrete block infill achieves their neat and dramatic geometry. Its site was once that of the **Bronx Bleachery**, an industry well-remembered because of its negative impact upon the purity of the adjacent Bronx River.

tombstones of soldiers from the War of 1812, the Civil War, the Spanish-American War, and World War I may be seen through the fence surrounding this tiny site.

[W5] **Beck Memorial Presbyterian Church**, 980 E.18oth St., bet. Vyse and Bryant Aves. S side. 1903.

A somber stone sentinel (capped with a terra-cotta-clad tower) overlooks the old cemetery across the street.

W6

[W2] Former **Peabody Home**, 2064 Boston Rd., NE cor. E.179th St. 1901. *E. A. Sargent.*

Across from the Lambert Houses and in the shadow of the IRT elevated lumbering overhead, this fine red-brick **Tudor Gothic** building adds note to the area.

[W3] **Lambert Houses**, Shopping Plaza, and Parking Garage, along Boston Rd., bet. Bronx Park S. and E.179th St. 1973. *Davis, Brody & Assocs.*,

These distinctive sawtooth-plan apartment, shopping, and parking structures south of Bronx Park were commissioned by **Phipps Houses**, a nonprofit foundation concerned with building better housing in the City.

[W4] **Old West Farms Soldiers' Cemetery**, 2103 Bryant Ave. (now a pedestrian walk), NE cor. E.18oth St. 1815 to now.

Forty veterans of four wars lie in repose amid trees and shrubs in this oasis of calm adjacent to the west edge of Lambert Houses:

Across the Bronx River to the east:

[W6] **Fire Alarm and Telegraph Bureau**, N.Y.C. Fire Department, 1129 E.18oth St., bet. Devoe and Bronx Park Aves. N side. 1923.

A buff-brick **Italian Renaissance** Revival structure dedicated to housing the high tech of the 1920s. The ghost of *Brunelleschi* strikes again.

[W7] Originally **New York, Westchester & Boston Railway Company**/now **IRT Dyre Avenue entry** to E.18oth Street Station of the Subway (Nos.2 and 5 trains), 481 Morris Park Ave., NW cor. E.18oth St. 1910-1912. *Fellheimer & Long, Allen H. Stem,* associated.

The **Italian Villa** style for a railroad that never made it. The N.Y., W. & B. was to have been a suburban line that would glamorously and swiftly transport commuters to the suburbs developing around White Plains and Port Chester prior to World War I; the picturesque architecture was to set the tone. It finally failed in 1937. The N.Y.C. Transit Authority still uses some of the City route.

BRONX ZOO

Closest trains: Nos.2 and 5 to West Farms Square-E. Tremont Ave. station.

[W8] **The Wildlife Conservation Society**/or **Bronx Zoo**/formerly **New York Zoological Park**, Bronx Park S of E. Fordham Rd. Founded, 1895. Opened in 1899. Original architects, *Heins &La Farge.* Open to the public. Apr-Nov: Mon-Fri, 10-

W8e

5; Sat, Sun, Hol, 10-5:30. Nov-Mar: 10-4:30. 718-220-5100. *www.bronxzoo.com*

The Bronx Zoo is the largest of the City's five zoos (privately run, it occupies city parkland and receives a municipal subsidy), and the most ambitious in both concept and execution. The area is divided into two contrasting parts. At the north is **Astor (once Baird) Court**, a large space around whose grassy plots and sea lion pool are formally arrayed many of the zoo's original buildings. This is a traditional zoological garden, with indoor and outdoor caged species and a pavilion housing animal heads and horns, trophies of some of the naturalist-hunter founders. The remainder of the zoo's acreage is more naturalistic, culminating in moated exhibitions, the **African Plains**, and the forest along the Bronx River displaying the wildlife of Asia. To shorten walking distances the Society introduced an aerial **"Skyfari"** and a monorail people-mover in the Asian area.

[W8a] **Jungle World/Tropical Asia Rain Forest**. 1985. *Herbert W. Riemer.*

An exotic structure that suggests the mysteries of the fauna of Asia and then helps to remove some of them, partly through a motorized outdoor trip, labeled Bengali Express, through the Wild Asia grounds. General Motors pioneered movement through display (then through the **City of Tomorrow**) at the 1939-1940 World's Fair.

[W8b] **The African Plains**, near the Boston Rd. zoo entrance. 1941. *Harrison & Fouilhoux*, architects. *Harry Sweeney*, designer.

Moats rather than bars protect the public from the lions, while other moats protect the other animals of the savannah from both lions and visitors. Full-size replicas of indigenous buildings attempt to re-create an African landscape in the Bronx. Notable as an early effort to make more natural the visual relationship between animals and visitors.

W8f

[W8c] **Carter Giraffe Building**. 1982. *Harold Buttrick & Assocs.*

Twenty-one feet high and a replacement for the original, which dated from 1908. When it opened, the *New York Times* said it looked "more like a Columbus Avenue bar than a zoo space." See for yourself. And giraffes are among nature's greatest wonders.

[W8d] **Aquatic Bird House**. 1964. *Goldstone & Dearborn.* [W8e] **The World of Birds**. 1972. *Morris Ketchum, Jr., & Assocs.*

Two works of modernist architecture from the 1960s-1970s can be found in the zoo: the Aquatic Bird House and the World of Birds. The display of some 550 birds in 25 different habitats is a plastic, flowing composition of rounded, roughfaced concrete-block forms dramatically illuminated within by skylights. Visitors walk in rooms with birds, not on the other side of grilles separated from them ... it makes a lot of difference.

W8g

upon an earlier, handsomely detailed Italian garden. In the center of the driveway's turnaround is an early 18th-century Italian fountain picked up near Lake Como by benefactor *William Rockefeller, John D. Sr.'s* brother.

[W8j] **Astor Court:** [W8k] **Lion House.** 1903. *Heins & La Farge.* Renovated, *FxFowle,* 2008. [W8l] **Primate House.** 1901. [W8m] **Administration Building.** 1910. [W8n] **Main Bird House.** 1905. [W8o] **Elephant House.** 1911. *Heins & La Farge.* [W8p] **Heads and Horns Building.** 1922. *Henry D. Whitfield.* All surround Astor Court. *Harold A. Caparn,* landscape architect. 🐾

The zoo's formal Astor Court was a direct outgrowth of the City Beautiful precepts of the **World's Columbian Exposition of 1893**. It was a controversial afterthought to what had been a desire to treat the zoo grounds as a naturalistic park. The elephant house, a Classical palace with a Byzantine interior, a high dome, and terra-cotta decoration, could serve as capitol of a banana republic.

W8i

W8k

[W8f] **Russell B. Aitken Seabird Aviary,** Wildlife Conservation Society. 1998. *FTL/Happold.*

Double-curved arches receive the almost invisible mesh drapery for this outdoor space for seabirds.

[W8g] **José E. Serrano Center for Global Conservation.** 2007. *FxFowle.*

Zesty modern architecture has arrived at the zoo: a research facility in bare concrete with an upper pavilion sided in wooden slats. Note the carefully crafted, thin steel corner details. Compare with *BKSK's* equally vibrant visitor's center at the **Queens Botanical Garden.**

[W8h] **Paul J. Rainey Memorial Gates.** 1929-1934. *Paul Manship,* sculptor; *Charles A. Platt,* architect of gate lodges and gateposts. 🐾
[W8i] **Rockefeller Fountain.** 1910. *Heins & Lafarge.* Both at E. Fordham Rd. entrance. 🐾

Manship's beautifully scaled **Art Deco–**inspired bronze gates, a gift of *Grace Rainey Rogers* (they are dedicated to her brother) open

NEW YORK BOTANICAL GARDEN

Closest trains: B or D to Kingsbridge Road or MetroNorth to Botanical Garden station.

[B1] **New York Botanical Garden,** Bronx Park, N of E. Fordham Rd. Site, 1895. *Calvert Vaux and Samuel Parsons, Jr.* Open to the public. 718-817-8500. Apr-Oct: Tues-Sun, 10-6; closed Mon. Nov-Mar: Tues-Sun, 10-4; closed Mon.

The Botanical Garden, incorporated in 1891 and patterned after the **Royal Botanical Gardens at Kew**, England, is one of the world's leading institutions of its kind. Its scientific facilities include a conservatory, museum, library, herbarium (a collection of dried plants), research laboratory, and a variety of groves and gardens. The selection of this site within Bronx Park, as recommended by *Vaux* and *Parsons,* enables the garden to perform a second valuable function: it contains and preserves the beautiful gorge of the Bronx River, a virgin hemlock forest, and some historic buildings that were here before the park was created.

[B2] Originally **Conservatory Range**/now **Enid Annenberg Haupt Conservatory**. 1896-1902. *William R. Cobb for Lord & Burnham*, greenhouse manufacturers. Altered, 1938, 1953. Restored, 1978, *Edward Larrabee Barnes & Assocs.*, architects. Reconstruction, 1997, *Beyer Blinder Belle.* 🍎

B2

A magnificent group of greenhouses in the tradition of *Decimus Burton's* **Great Palm House** at Kew and *Joseph Paxton's* Crystal Palace. In 1978, after many years of deterioration had threatened the glass fairyland and its wide-ranging plant species, restoration stemmed the decline. And in 1997 a complete reconstruction was accomplished, replacing the delicate wooden skeleton with one of aluminum. The *Lord & Burnham* image was, therefore, preserved.

[B3] **Garden Café and Terrace Room**. 1997. *Cooper Robertson & Assocs.*
A squatty neo-Georgian pavilion provides dining and catering facilities for the Garden's friends and patrons.

[B4] **Children's Adventure Garden Discovery Center**. 1998. *Richard Dattner*, architect. *Miceli Kulik Williams*, landscape architects.
Tree-trunk columns and an eyebrow-windowed, shingle roof shelter exposed ductwork serving exhibitions, laboratories, and offices.

[B5] **New York Botanical Garden Library Building**. 1896-1901. *Robert W. Gibson*. Addition, 1973.
Gibson created a grand English country house to serve the scale of the Garden.

[B6] **Pfizer Plant Study Center**. 2006. *Polshek Partnership.*
No nonsense modernist pavilion for the **Cullman Program for Molecular Systematics**. An elegant, low-key annex that is the external expression of a total renovation of the parent Museum building to which it's attached.

[B7] **Old Lorillard Snuff Mill**/now **Snuff Mill River Terrace Café**. ca. 1840. Restored, 1954. 🍎
This building, together with a later gatehouse and stables, is the only improvement that remains from the extensive local landholdings of the *Lorillards*, a family whose name is still associated with the tobacco industry. Built of local fieldstone, the mill once ground snuff, a tobacco product more popular in the 19th century than it is today. Fortunately the mill building, a fine example of local industrial architecture, is now maintained for Garden offices.

The Bronx River Gorge: Just north of the snuff mill is an arched stone footbridge, a great spot from which to view the gorge of the Bronx River and the turbulent waters that carved it over the millennia. The nearby hemlock forest is the last remaining part of a stand of trees that once covered much of New York City.

B5

NECROLOGY

Formerly **Biograph Company Studios**, 807 E. 175th St. and 790 E. 176 St., bet. Marmion and Prospect Aves. East Tremont. 1912.
Founded in 1895 to compete with *Thomas A. Edison*, the Biograph motion picture company was one of the studios centered in New York before the movie moguls folded their tents and stole away to Hollywood. In this building, built in what was once the wilds of the Bronx, *D.W. Griffith* shot his early films.
The building was destroyed by fire in 1980. The site is now occupied by a huge Department of Sanitation facility.

Western Bronx

The West Bronx

The West Bronx and Miami Beach maintain the largest arrays of Art Deco– and Art Moderne–inspired architecture in America. Miami's share, by no coincidence, is in part derived from New Yorkers' search for sun, many traveling from Arc Deco Bronx to Art Deco Miami Beach in seasonal migrations. An array of housing, schools, parks, hospitals, industries, and public works of social and architectural interest are all located here.

[W2] **Hostos Community College, CUNY,** Grand Concourse bet. W.144th and W.149th Sts. W side. East Academic Complex, 1994. *Gwathmey Siegel & Assocs. and Sanchez & Figueroa.* **Allied Health Complex,** 1991. *Voorsanger & Assocs.*
[W3] Originally **Security Mutual Insurance Company,** 500 Grand Concourse, SE cor. W.149th Sts. 1965. *Horace Ginsbern & Assocs.*

Elegant multicolored brick, a sleek bridge, and a serrated eastern façade participate in this community college jewel. The 1965 Security Mutual building adds a note of

W1

W2

THE GRAND CONCOURSE

The Grand Boulevard and Concourse (as it is officially named, but rarely called), one of the grand thoroughfares of New York, was designed in 1891 by *Louis Risse* as the **Speedway Concourse** to provide access from Manhattan to the large parks of the "annexed district" of the Bronx. The original design provided separate paths for horse-drawn vehicles, cyclists, and pedestrians, and for grade separation through underpasses at all major intersections.

[W1] **Public School 31, The William Lloyd Garrison School**/once temporarily **Theodore Roosevelt High School,** 425 Grand Concourse, bet. E.144th and E.146th Sts. to Walton Ave. W side. 1897-1899. *C.B.J. Snyder.* 🖉

Known locally as **The Castle on the Concourse** because of its Collegiate Gothic style. A runup for the same architect's later Morris High School.

history (short, but history) to an instant step into the 1990s.

[W4] **IRT subway junction,** beneath E.149th St. and Grand Concourse. Lower level, 1904. Upper level, 1917.

Here two subway stations have been built one below the other, separated by a mezzanine. (The trains on the upper level are marked Woodlawn Road, a nonexistent street.) The lower station, in the Parisian manner, is one large barrel vault. Despite uninspired decoration, poor lighting, and minimal maintenance, this station is one of the exciting spaces of the subway system.

[W5] **General Post Office,** The Bronx/originally **Bronx Central Annex,** U.S. Post Office Department, 558 Grand Concourse, NE cor. E. 149th St. 1935-1937. *Thomas Harlan Ellett,* architect; *Louis A. Simon,* supervising architect. 🖉

W5

Chaste gray brick and white marble articulate arches with glazing deeply revealed. A timid building, it has worn well, better than many modern aggressors. There are **WPA** murals by *Ben Shahn* in the lobby.

[W6] Cardinal Hayes Memorial High School (Roman Catholic), 650 Grand Concourse, SE cor. E.153rd St. 1941. *Eggers & Higgins.*

Reticent in sober buff brick, the school forms a quarter circle, therefore effectively creating an inviting green forecourt. Building embellishments are modest, but in the **Art Deco** mode.

Franz Sigel Park: Named for a Civil War general, this craggy park, on the west side of Grand Concourse north of East 153rd Street, is the repository of graffitied concrete "park furniture" installed by overzealous governmental bureaucrats in the early 1970s in the mistaken belief that physical amenities—any amenities—will cure acute social and economic ills.

The Concourse Style, a Driving Tour:

The Roaring Twenties gave many families the needed economic lift that allowed them to move from their relatively shabby Manhattan digs to spanking new quarters in outlying places like the Bronx. The IRT Jerome Avenue elevated, running parallel to the Concourse down the hill to the west, had been finished in 1918. By the late 1920s the City was digging a trench down the center of the Grand Concourse to install the northern leg of its own Independent subway, which would open on July 1, 1933, in the depths of the Great Depression. Nevertheless, the subway did connect to Manhattan's business districts, to the Garment Center, and to the reemerging Upper West Side. The convenience was unmistakable, and developers seized the opportunity to buy potential apartment sites along the Concourse deflated in price by the economic downturn.

During the 1930s, the golden age of the Concourse, two Paris expositions were having great effect upon American style. The **1925**

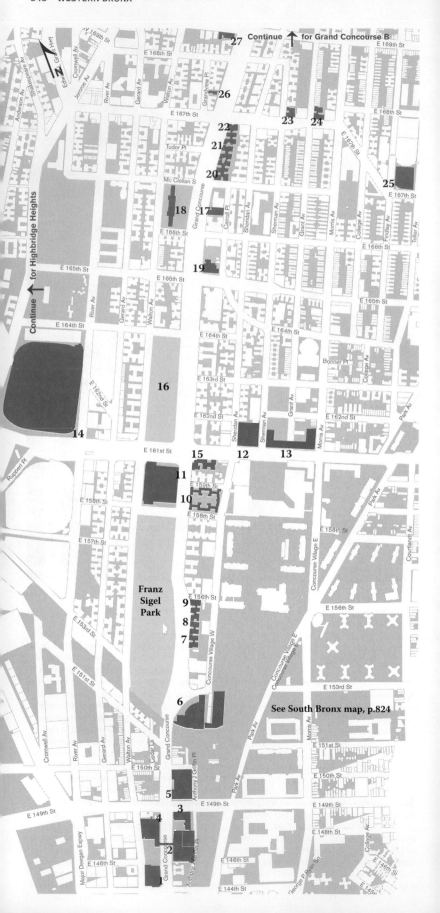

E 168th St

E 169th St

27 Continue ↑ for Grand Concourse B

26

E 167th St

23 24

22

21

Tudor Pl

20

Grandview Pl

Walton Av

Gerard Av

River Av

Jerome Av

Cromwell Av

Anderson Av

Shakespeare Av

Edwin J. Grant Hwy

N

Mc Clellan S

18 17

Continue ← for Highbridge Heights

E 166th St

E 165th St

E 164th St

19

E 167th St

E 168th St

25

Carroll Pl

Sheridan Av

Sherman Av

Grant Av

Morris Av

College Av

Findlay Av

Teller Av

E 167th St

E 166th St

E 165th St

Grand Concourse

River Av

Gerard Av

Walton Av

E 165th St

16

E 163rd St

E 162nd St

E 161st St

14

15

12

13

Bonner Pl

College Av

Park Av

E 164th St

E 162nd St

Sheridan Av

Sherman Av

Grant Av

Morris Av

Ruppert Pl

11

10

9

8

7

6

5

3

4

2

1

Franz
Sigel
Park

E 159th St

E 158th St

E 157th St

E 156th St

E 153rd St

E 151st St

E 150th St

E 149th St

E 146th St

E 144th St

Concourse Village W

Concourse Village E

Concourse Village E

E 158th St

E 156th St

E 153rd St

Courtlandt Av

Park Av

See South Bronx map, p.824

Grand Concourse

Anthony J Griffin Pl

Anthony Griffin Pl

Cedar La

Walton Av

Gerard Av

Cromwell Av

Major Deegan Expwy

E 149th St

E 148th St

E 146th St

George P Ryan St

Morris Av

Park Av

College Av

Exposition Internationale des Arts Décoratifs et Industriels Modernes had given birth to the ornamentalism of **Art Deco**; and the **1937 Exposition** Internationale des Arts et des Techniques Appliqués à la Vie Moderne evoked the streamlined forms of **Art Moderne**, which were paralleled in the **New York World's Fair of 1939-1940**. The former influenced the use of decorative terra cotta, mosaics, ironwork doors, and etched glass so rampant in the entry and lobbies of West Bronx apartments. The latter gave rise to the use of striped brick patterns, cantilevered corners, steel casement windows and particularly corner windows, and the use of highly stylized letter forms. The amalgam of these styles was concentrated along and near the Bronx's premier boulevard in dozens of six-story apartments; these and similar works of residential architecture could be characterized as the **Concourse Style**. Sprinkled between the older dour apartment blocks of the 1920s are the now somewhat grimy (sometimes happily scrubbed) gems.

ect, named for its architect, is one of two [see Manhattan's **Dunbar Apartments**] designed for *John D. Rockefeller, Jr.,* who hoped to solve the problems of the slums by investing in middle-income housing.

[W11] **The Bronx County Building**, 851 Grand Concourse, SW cor. E.161st St., at Lou Gehrig Plaza. 1931-1935. *Joseph H. Freedlander* and *Max L. Hausle,* architects. Sculpture at four entrances: *Adolph A. Weinman,*

W12

W13

W10

W11

START at Grand Concourse and East 153rd Street. The tour continues north along the entire length of the Concourse with a number of divergences along the way. While on the Concourse use service road except to make left turns, permitted only from center section.

[W7] **730 Grand Concourse**, bet. E.153rd and E.156th Sts. E side. 1939. [W8] **740 Grand Concourse**, bet. E.153rd and E.156th Sts. E side. 1939. [W9] **750 Grand Concourse** (apartments), SE cor. 156th Sts. E side. 1937. All by *Jacob M. Felson.*

No.750 is the best of the trio.

[W10] **Thomas Garden Apartments**, 840 Grand Concourse, bet. E.158th and E.159th Sts. E side. 1928. *Andrew J. Thomas.*

A block-square development of five-story **pre–Art Deco** walk-up buildings grouped about a westernized Japanese garden in a sunken central court. All of the units are reached through the court by walking past concrete lanterns, a water course, and charming bridges. This proj-

Edward F. Sanford, George Snowden, Joseph Kisselewski, associates. Frieze, *Charles Keck.* 🖝

An enormous, ten-story neo-**Classical/ Moderne** limestone pile whose ponderous form is, fortunately, relieved by sleek Moderne sculpture, both in the round and on friezes that beribbon its walls.

Divergences, east and west along E.161st Street:

[W12] **Criminal Court/Family Court**, City of New York, 215 E.161st St., bet. Sheridan and Concourse Village West. N side. (E of the Concourse.) 1977. *Harrison & Abramovitz.*

If architecture is expressive of the social order, then this formidable structure tells us that justice must be ponderous, rigid, and self-righteous.

[W13] **Bronx County Hall of Justice**, 265 E. 161st St., bet. Sherman and Morris Aves. 2008. *Rafael Viñoly.*

Thirty years after the overbearing courts above, *Viñoly's* glass cube arrived; gargantuan (two blocks long), yet much lighter than its dour

W15

W16

[W16] **The Lorelei Fountain**, Joyce Kilmer Park, Grand Concourse, NW cor. E.161st St. 1899. *Ernst Herter,* sculptor. Rebuilt and relocated, 1999.

It honors the author of "Die Lorelei," *Heinrich Heine*, his bas-relief portrait on the south side of the base. Presented to the City by a group of German-Americans, they hoped to place it at Manhattan's Grand Army Plaza, where *Saint-Gaudens'* horseback *Sherman* now stands. *Sherman* won this post-mortem battle.

[W17] **Bronx Family Court**, 1118 Grand Concourse, bet. E.166th St. and McClellan St. 1997. *Rafael Viñoly.*

A superb **modernist** building that, surprisingly, puts civic architecture in the forefront of this aging Art Deco/Art Moderne community. It flaunts high style, without being stylish.

[W18] **Andrew Freedman Home**, 1125 Grand Concourse, bet. E.166th and McClellan Sts. 1924. *Joseph H. Freedlander* and *Harry Allan Jacobs.* Wings, 1928-1931, *David Levy.* 🍎

A subdued **Italian Renaissance** palazzo, set in a garden that gives it the air of a large English country house. It is a home for the aged endowed by *Freedman*, a leading subway contractor and owner of the baseball team that became the N.Y. Giants.

[W19a] **Bronx Museum of the Arts**/originally **Young Israel Synagogue**, 1040 Grand Concourse, NE cor. E.165th St. 1961. *Simon B. Zelnik.* Expansion, 1988, *Castro-Blanco, Piscioneri & Feder.* Open to the public. Th, Sa, Su 11-6; Fr 11-8; closed Mo, Tu, We. 718-681-6000. *www.bronxmuseum.org*

Using a vacant 1960s synagogue building, this modest community museum has brought many intriguing displays of both art and history to the Bronx, utilizing a high level of curatorial skill. It began in the lobby of the Bronx County Building.

[W19b] **North Building, Bronx Museum of the Arts**, 1040 Grand Concourse, NE cor. E.165th St. 2003. *Arquitectonica.*

Folded vertical planes peek out at cars whizzing by on the Grand Concourse. Classy. For better and lesser *Arquitectonica*, see the index.

neighbor. The glass curtain sparkles, rippling like a folded screen, and the courtyard is public. See also *Viñoly's* **Bronx Family Court** [W17].

[W14] **New Yankee Stadium**, 1 E. 161st St., NW cor. River Ave. 2009. *HOK Sport.*

"The House That *Steinbrenner* Built." Its stone façade is ponderous, reminiscent of a mausoleum, but some of the decorative "victorian bandstand" details from the original ballpark (1923) have been recreated on the interior. In 2008, a construction worker, Red Sox fan *Gino Castignoli*, buried a Boston uniform under two feet of concrete, hoping to forever curse the new stadium. The Yankees dug it up.

Back to the Concourse:

[W15] **888 Grand Concourse**, SE cor. E.161st St. 1937. *Emery Roth.*

A modest effort for an important cornering by an architect whose earlier, more creative designs can still be found on Central Park West at the **San Remo** and the **Beresford.**

[W20] **1150 Grand Concourse**, NE cor. McClellan St. 1936. *Horace Ginsbern*.
[W21] **1166 Grand Concourse**, bet. McClellan St. and E.167th St. 1936. *Horace Ginsbern*.
[W22] **1188 Grand Concourse**, SE cor. E.167th St. 1937. *Jacob M. Felson*.

A full block of apartments stripped of their once elegant steel casement windows. No.1188 impressive with its sawtooth patterns; No.1150 adorned with mosaics and Moderne doors, rich

W17

with shade and shadow from its deeply revealed and canted windows.

More divergence from the Concourse, south on E.167th Street:

[W23] **1210 Sherman Avenue**, NE cor. E.167th St. 1937. *Charles Kreymborg*. 24
[W24] **1212 Grant Avenue**, NE cor. E.167th St. 1936. *Horace Ginsbern*.

Survivors, their polychromatic **Art Deco/Art Moderne** brickwork provides rich tapestries.

[W25a] **Daughters of Jacob Geriatric Center: Main Building**/ formerly **Home and Hospital of the Daughters of Jacob**, 321 E.167th St., bet. Findlay and Teller Aves. N side. 1920. *Louis Allen Abramson*. [25b] **Nursing and Rehabilitation Center**, 1160 Teller Ave. E side. 1973. *Blumenkranz & Bernhard*.

The ungainly, tall **Roman** portico provides symbolic entrance to the original building, added to give it a dignified appearance. But it is

the building behind the columns, built as eight radiating-spoked wings set at the end of a generous Italian garden, that is of interest. The radiating plan was common for hospitals (and penitentiaries) seeking centralized control.

[W26] **1227 Grand Concourse**, bet. E.167th and E.168th Sts. W side. ca. 1938.

A narrow **Art Moderne** orphan with a vane of masonry at its north end, looking like a movie house sign, but of brick.

W27

W20

W24

[W27] **Grand Concourse Seventh Day Adventist Temple**/originally **Temple Adath Israel**, 1275 Grand Concourse, SW cor. 169th St. 1927.

Predates the Concourse's **Deco-Moderne** heyday. Dignity here is achieved by restraint: smooth blank walls relieved by sparing use of ornamented neo-Classical columns and pilasters. The incised lettering of the original institution remains, as does the cornerstone.

[W28] Originally **Roosevelt Gardens**/later **Roosevelt Court**, 1455-1499 Grand Concourse, bet. E.171 stand E.172nd Sts. to Wythe Place. W side. 1924. Altered, ca. 1986.

Stripped of its original **Mission Style** details, this once-romantic giant is now a neat but barren visual remnant of the Concourse's discovery by an emerging middle class in the 1920s.

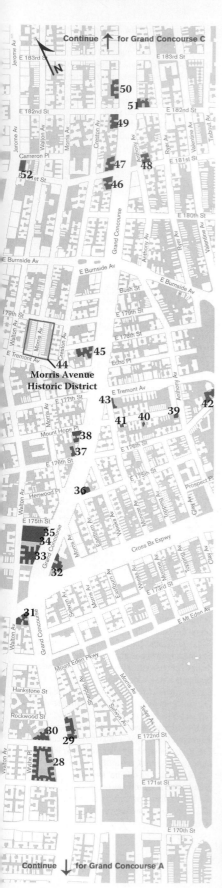

Continue ↑ for Grand Concourse C

Morris Avenue
Historic District

Continue ↓ for Grand Concourse A

[29] **1500 Grand Concourse**, NE cor.
E.172nd St. 1935. *Jacob M. Felson.*

The parapet limestone has been carved into
folds, like velvet. Here too the original windows
have been replaced, but the glass block and
stainless steel entry is wonderful.

[W30] **1505 Grand Concourse**, NW cor. E.172nd
St. 1930s.

This galaxy of cream brick is best appreciated
in its side-street series of bayed sub-façades.

[W31] **1675 Grand Concourse**, SW cor. E.174th St.
(street is below the Concourse) through to
Walton Ave. 1936. *Jacob M. Felson.*

Poetic, a graceful cornering, inlaid designs
in contrasting brick colors.

[W32] **1750 Grand Concourse**, NE cor. Cross-
Bronx Expwy. (below the Concourse). E side.
1937.

Geometric ornament, with steel casements
no longer in place.

W30

[W33] **Lewis Morris Apartments**, 1749 Grand
Concourse, NW cor. Clifford Place. (outdoor public stairway). 1923. *Edward Raldiris.*

A 13-story **West End Avenue** high rise. Once
the place to live on the Concourse.

[W34] **Bell Telephone Building**, 1775 Grand
Concourse, S of the SW cor. E.175th St. ca. 1923.
McKenzie, Voorhees & Gmelin.

A curious but bland **Florentine** palazzo in
cream brick and limestone, expanded upward as
telephones increased in number.

[W35] **1791 Grand Concourse**, SW cor.
E.175th St. 1936. *Edward W. Franklin.*

An eccentric site: the bend in the façade
gave opportunity for subtle massing that
enhanced the marvelous patterned brick spandrels and parapets.

[W36] **Pilgrim United Church of Christ**/
originally **Christ Congregational Church**,
1808 Grand Concourse, NE cor. E.175th St. 1910.
Hoppin & Koen.

A strong presence on the Concourse: **neo-Georgian** front and **Hagia Sophia** rear (don't miss that low-rise dome!). Torn and frayed, and in need of immediate architectural CPR.

[W37] **1835 Grand Concourse**, NW cor. E.176th St. 1939. H. *Herbert Lillien.*
Another eccentric site.

[W38] **1855 Grand Concourse**, SW cor. Mt. Hope Place. 1936. *Thomas Dunn.*

W31

W34

W36

Art Deco pilasters stand between strongly modeled bay windows. Very subtle, oblique, planar modeling.

A brief divergence, downhill to the east:

[W39] Originally **Edwin and Elizabeth M. Shuttleworth House**, 1857 Anthony Ave., SW cor. Mt. Hope Place. 1896. *Neville & Bagge.* ●
A miniature castle of rockfaced gray stone with finely carved limestone trim. Note particularly the modeling of the faces in the medallions near the roof. A mimosa tree and other verdant vegetation almost conceal this welcome relic. *Shuttleworth*, not surprisingly, was a dealer in stone, both plain and carved. **Needs love.**

[W40] **250 Mt. Hope Place**, bet. Anthony and Monroe Aves. ca. 1890.
A modest neighbor of the *Shuttleworths*, it still proudly displays Ionic columns on its porch.

[W41] **202-204 Mt. Hope Place**, SE cor. Monroe Ave. 1880s.
A pair of row house survivors that completes, on this one Mt. Hope block, the range of single-family house styles hereabouts in the late 19th century.

[W42] **Tremont Towers**, 333 E.176th St., NW cor. E. Tremont Ave., opp. Echo Park. 1937. *Jacob M. Felson.*
A grand curved façade slopes downhill from the Concourse.

Return to the Concourse:

[W43] **Mt. Hope Court**, 1882 Grand Concourse, SE cor. Monroe Ave., at E. Tremont Ave. 1914.

W39

Otto Schwarzler.
The Bronx's own **Flatiron Building**, built on a sharply acute-angled site and, for many years, the borough's tallest building, at ten stories. Predictions that residential elevators would make the Bronx a borough of ten-story structures didn't materialize until the advent of redbrick "projects," beginning with Parkchester.

[W44] **Morris Avenue Historic District**. 1969-1999 Morris Ave., bet. E.Tremont Ave. and E.179th St. W side. 1966-1998 Morris Ave., bet. E. Tremont Ave. and E.179th St. E side. 60 and 108 E.179th St., SW and SE cor. Morris Ave. 1906-1910. All by *John Hauser.* ●
A complete row of bowfront, three-story row houses with wrought-iron detail, stonework, stoops, and cornices largely intact. A refreshing look back at high-quality Bronx urbanism. *August Jacob* was the developer.

[W45] **1939 Grand Concourse**, SW cor. E.178th St. ca. 1940.

Art Moderne. One of the better zigzag fronts.

[W46] **2121 Grand Concourse**, SW cor. E.181st St. 1936. *Horace Ginsbern.*

The most stylish zig-zagger on the Concourse. **Art Deco** at its best, it needed to keep those original steel casement windows and to be delivered from those dreadful plastic store signs. Neither has happened. Note the richly molded gray cast-stone entry around the corner on East 181st.

[W47] **2155 Grand Concourse**, NW cor. E.181st St. to Creston Ave. 1939. *H. Herbert Lillien.*

Yet another zigzag façade.

[W48] **2186 Grand Concourse**, NE cor. Anthony Ave. ca. 1939.

A mediocre cousin to the group above.

W53

W44

W46

[W49] **2195 Grand Concourse**, SW cor. E.182 St. 1938.

Neo-Classical sashaying into Art Moderne.

[W50] **2255 Grand Concourse**, bet. E.182nd and E.183rd Sts. W side. 1936. *Horace Ginsbern.*

The windows are subtly bows, recessed within a flat façade. Note the three-dimensional, red-and-black granite entry surround. A tailored work.

[W51] **2230 Grand Concourse**, NE cor. E.182nd St. (Entry on E.182nd.) ca. 1937.

Pinstripe orange and brown brick spandrels. The banded, decorative fire escapes are an integral part of the design aesthetic.

[W52] **Engine Co. 75, Ladder Co. 33, Battalion 19**, 2175 Walton Ave., bet. 181st St. and Cameron Pl. 2000. *Dattner Architects.*

A fanciful firehouse in alternating bands of concrete block and brick that diverge to form a "mosaic" of a ladder truck. The playful "tower" at the corner springs open as if it's happy to see you.

[W53] **Intermediate School 115, The Elizabeth Browning School**/formerly **Bronx High School of Science**/earlier **Evander Childs, Walton, De Witt Clinton High Schools**/originally **Public School 9**, E.184th St., bet. Creston and Morris Aves. S side. 1915.

Physically, a very ordinary N.Y.C. public school, but this is where the Bronx High School of Science began in 1938 (and where its Nobel Prize-winning scientists were trained). **Bronx Science** is now in a custom-built structure opened in 1959 north of Lehman College.

[W54] Originally **Loew's Paradise Theater**/now **Utopia Paradise Theater**, 2417 Grand Concourse, bet. E.184th and E.188th Sts. W side. 1929. *John Eberson.*

Stars and clouds made the 4,000-seat Paradise special, but its terra-cotta façade on the Concourse is still a bit of neo-Renaissance Fantasy. Inside, it was an extravaganza of ornament, ornament, and more ornament, surmounted by a deep blue ceiling over the auditorium, twinkling stars, and projected moving

W55

W54

W57

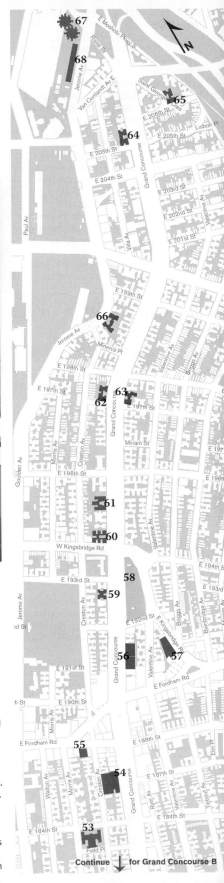

clouds. Considered by one connoisseur of such things the "most beautiful and elaborate" of *Eberson's* designs. *Christopher Gray* said it is "an architectural atomic pile with the control rods pulled all the way out."

[W55] **Creston Avenue Baptist Church**, 114 E.188th St., bet. Creston and Morris Aves. S side. 1905.

Limestone Gothic arches in a field of brick and a high-hatted stair-tower make this **neo-Gothic** church seem a castle... although crushed between retail shops reaching out for customers.

[W56] **Emigrant Savings Bank**/originally **Dollar Savings Bank**, 2516-2530 Grand Concourse, bet. Fordham Rd. and E.192nd St. W side. 1932-1933. *Adolf L. Muller of Halsey, McCormack & Helmer.* Additions: Tower, 1937-1938; 1949-1952. 🍎 Interior. 🍎

This sober **Classical/Art Deco** work (with its great clock) is by the team that designed two great Brooklyn banks: the Dime Savings' Roman palace (hedonistic?) and the Williamsburgh Savings Bank tower (phallic?).

[W57] **Bronx Library Center** (Former Fordham Branch Library), 310 E. Kingsbridge Rd., bet. E.Fordham Rd. and E. 192nd St. 2005. *Richard Dattner & Assocs.*

A whimsical parasol roof provides special interplay within. Sleek glass on the exterior, and uncompromising modernism.

[W58] **Poe Cottage, Poe Park,** 2640 Grand Concourse, SE cor. E. Kingsbridge Rd. ca. 1812. Moved in 1913 from its original site across Kingsbridge Road. ☙ **Visitor Center,** 2010. *Toshiko Mori.* Open to the public: Mo-Fr, 9-5; Sa, 10-4; Su, 1-5. 718-881-8900. *www. bronxhistoricalsociety.org/poecottage*

Edgar Allan Poe came in the hope that clear country air would aid his ailing young wife (she died during their first winter in this small house); he lived and worked here from 1846 until a few months before his death in 1849.

W58

And here he wrote "Annabel Lee."

Plagued by vandalism in the last decade, the cottage looks forward to a smoother future, with plans for a swooping visitor center by *Mori* (its shape inspired by "The Raven").

[W59] **2615 Grand Concourse**, bet. E.192nd and E.193rd Sts. W side. 1938. *Charles Kreymborg.*

Plain-Jane Moderne, but with a spirited patterned and red fire-escapes.

[W60] **2665 Grand Concourse**, NW cor. Kingsbridge Rd. E. 1922. *Margon & Glaser.* [W61] **Brockman Manor**, 2701 Grand Concourse, bet. Kingsbridge Rd. E. and E.196th St. W side. ca. 1927. *H.I. Feldman.* [W62] **McAlpin Court**, 2825 Grand Concourse, NW cor. E. 197th St. ca. 1927. *H.I. Feldman.*

An exile from West End Avenue, Renaissance Revival 2665 hulks over the Course, while the latter two, at only six stories, are crowned with intact handsome **Chicago School** cornices.

[W63] **Town Towers,** 2830 Grand Concourse, NE cor. E.197th St. 1931. *Horace Ginsbern.*

Its brick piers and crenellated parapet shimmer hello as thousands drive past it. Don't tell, for the pedestrian, there's a spectacular lobby.

[W64] **3155 Grand Concourse**, NW cor. E.205th St. 1936. *Jacob M. Felson.*

The vertically pinstriped spandrels proclaim its elegant understatement.

W63

[W65] **185 St. George's Crescent**, NE cor. 206th St. 1930s.

The streamlined rounding of the **Art Moderne** gives a sensuous series of curvaceous forms to the already curving Crescent.

[W66a] **Dornhage**, 2914 Jerome Ave. [W66b] **Edna** (apartments), 2928 Jerome Ave. Both bet. Minerva Place and 199th St. E side. 1936. *William I. Hohauser.*

Reverse the syllables of *Dornhage* and you have the client's name, *Hagedorn*. Art Deco with terrific polychromatic terra cotta.

END of Grand Concourse Driving Tour. But around the corner are:

[W67] **Tracey Towers,** 20 and 40 W. Mosholu Pkwy. S., SW cor. Jerome Ave. 1974. *Paul Rudolph.*

The tallest structures in the Bronx, these two residential towers offer residents phenomenal views in all directions. Similarly, the gray, ribbed-block towers are themselves visible from afar, resembling sand castles with overactive thyroids.

[W68] High Pumping Station, Jerome Reservoir, of the former N.Y.C. Department of Water Supply, Gas & Electricity, 3205 Jerome Ave., bet. Van Cortlandt Ave. E. and W. Mosholu Pkwy. S. W side. 1901-1906. *George W. Birdsall.*

Deceptively simple, this straightforward gabled masonry form in red brick is detailed with consummate skill. The result is a superb example of industrial architecture.

W68

HIGHBRIDGE HEIGHTS

These neighborhoods lie west of Grand Concourse and follow the University Avenue ridge and the Harlem River from Macombs Dam Park below West 161st Street northward to the vicinity of Kingsbridge Road. They contain hundreds of the familiar Bronx apartment houses, older one-family wooden homes, and a variety of institutions, public works, and landmarks, many of national fame and importance. Highbridge, the area south of the Cross-Bronx Expressway, was settled in the 1830s by Irish workers who built the Old Croton Aqueduct and High Bridge, as well as the railroad that soon appeared on the east bank of the Harlem River.

Nearest train: No.4 to 167th St. station.

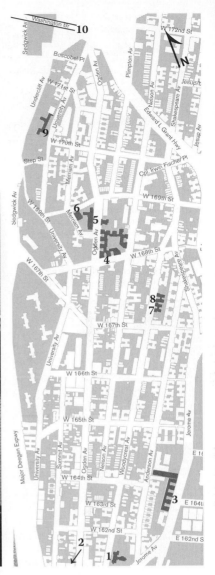

[H1] Highbridge Woodycrest Center/originally **American Female Guardian Society and Home for the Friendless,** 936 Woodycrest Ave., NE cor. Jerome Ave. 1901-1902. *William B. Tuthill.*

An eclectic limestone, terra-cotta, and brick mansion on a commanding precipice overlooking the valley of Macombs Dam Park and Yankee Stadium.

DEMOLISHED:

Macombs Dam Park, at Jerome Avenue and West 161st Street, together with Macombs Dam Bridge into Manhattan, recalled the nearby site of Robert Macomb's 1813 dam across the Harlem River. The dam used the waterway's tidal flow to power a mill until Macomb's neighbors demolished the dam in 1838, in order to open the river to shipping. The park was, regrettably, plowed under the new Yankee Stadium in 2009, a somewhat unfair trade: a private greensward replacing a public one.

H3

[H2] **Macombs Dam Bridge and 155th Street Viaduct**/also known as **Central Bridge**, over the Harlem River, bet. Jerome Ave., The Bronx, and W.155th St., Manhattan. 1895. *Alfred Pancoast Boller*, engineer. 👁‍🗨

   With the replacement of the original **University Heights Bridge** with a larger look-

H1

H8

alike, this stands out as the City's finest example of 19th-century swing bridges. While it may seem flimsy now, in 1895 it was one of the heaviest bridges ever built.

[H3] **Park Plaza Apartments**, 1005 Jerome Ave., bet. Anderson Ave. and E.165th St. W side. 1929-1931. *Horace Ginsbern and Marvin Fine*. 👁‍🗨

   One of the earliest (and best) **Art Deco**–inspired apartment buildings in the Bronx. Influenced both by the 1925 Exposition Internationale des Arts Décoratifs et Industriels Modernes in Paris, and motifs from Mayan architecture then fashionable. Note the elaborate polychromed terra-cotta ornament. The façade is *Fine's* work, the body *Ginsbern's*.

[H4] **Noonan Plaza**, 105- 145 W.168th St., NW cor. Nelson Ave. 1931. *Horace Ginsbern*.
   These seven-story apartments, arranged to form a quadrangle, are entered diagonally through a highly decorative masonry arcade that leads to a central court, the original splendors of which

can only be guessed at today. **Art Deco-cum-Mayan** was then the idiosyncratic style of the *Ginsbern* firm. A major West Bronx monument.

[H5] **Highbridge Community Church**/formerly **Union Reformed Church of Highbridge**, 1272 Ogden Ave., bet. W.168th and W.169th Sts. E side. 1889. *Alfred E. Barlow*.
   A bold ashlar and brownstone church contrasting magnificently with the **Moderne** decor of Noonan Plaza immediately adjacent.

[H6] **Public School 11**/formerly **Grammar School No.91**, 1257 Ogden Ave., bet. W.168th and W.169th Sts. W side. 1889. *George W. Debevoise*. Addition, 1905, *C.B.J. Snyder*. Addition, 1930, *Walter C. Martin*. 👁‍🗨
   A picturesque gem. Masonry craft like this is a lost art.

H10

[H7] **1182 Woodycrest Avenue**, bet. W.167th and W.168th Sts. E side. ca. 1875.
   A surviving cream and white, painted brick, **Victorian** country house.

[H8] **Woodycrest Gardens**, 1200 Woodycrest Avenue, bet. W.167th and W.168th Sts. E side. 1936. *Franklin, Bates & Heindsmann*.
   Art Moderne, neglected at the street level, still holds its own upstairs.

[H9] **Samaritan Village Highbridge**/originally **Carmelite Monastery**, 1381 University Ave. (Dr. Martin Luther King, Jr. Blvd.), opp. W.170th St. W side. 1940. *Maginnis & Walsh*.
   Seek (down below) **Highbridge** and from there a magnificent view of the old monastery, hugging the steep slope of the hill, tumbling down to the Harlem River valley; a latter-day, neo-medieval building—with its tower, cells, chapel, cloister, and gardens. Visible without revealing the life of contemplation within its walls.

[H10] **Washington Bridge**, over the Harlem
River, from University and Ogden Aves.,
The Bronx, to W.181st and Amsterdam Ave.,
Manhattan. 1888. *C. C. Schneider*, original
designer. *John McAlpine and William R. Hutton*,
successive chief engineers. ☛

Just plain Washington Bridge but, in its own
intricate way, superior to the more famous
George Washington Bridge. Two soaring sets of
arches: one spanning the water, the other the
river valley's flood plain. *Schneider* won the
design competition, but cost overruns forced the
substitution of steel latticework under the roadway. A happy compromise, particularly from the
deck of a leisurely **Circle Liner** below.

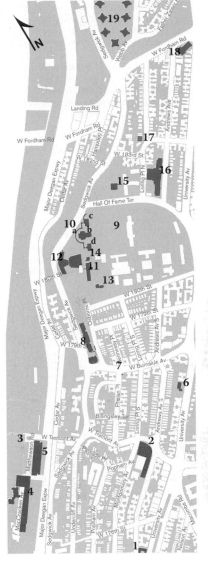

U2

UNIVERSITY HEIGHTS

Nearest train: No.4 to Burnside Avenue station.

[U1] **1660 Andrews Avenue** (NYCHA rehabilitated
apartments), bet. W.175th and W.176th Sts,
through to University Ave. E side. ca. 1925.
Altered, 1987, *Shelly Kroop and James McCullar.*

The balconies add oomph to tired but rehabilitated tenements and the stretch of street
that needs it.

[U2] **South Bronx Job Corps Center**/for-
merly **Salvation Army Training College**/
originally **Messiah Home for Children**, 1771
Andrews Ave., SW cor. W. Tremont Ave. 1908.
Charles E. Brigham. ☛

Princeton may have Collegiate Gothic nailed
down, but here is a neo-Jacobean complex
unique to these Heights. (*Brigham*, and partner,
Solon S. Bemau, designed the **Christian Science
Mother Church**, in Boston.)

*Along the banks of the Harlem River: Once a
decaying riverside frontage, this was the site of
coal unloading docks and the Consolidated Ship
Building Corporation, isolated by the tracks of
the Penn Central Railroad and the Major Deegan
Expressway. In the late 1960s these valuable
lands were brought to public use by the combined efforts of assorted City and State agencies.
The state park was named for Roberto Clemente,
a local baseball hero killed in a plane crash; the
housing, River Park Towers, to reflect its setting.*

[U3] **Roberto Clemente State Park**/originally
Harlem River Bronx State Park, Matthewson Rd.
off W. Tremont Ave. Bridge along Harlem River.
1973. *M. Paul Friedberg & Assocs.*, landscape
architects; *Dean McClure,* architect.

The first of the planned series of state parks
within the City, this recreation playland offers
swimming, diving, gymnasium events, and a
wonderful stroll along the seawall of the adjacent Harlem River. It may not have the verdancy
of an upstate park, but its lively forms animate
an otherwise isolated urban setting.

[U4] **River Park Towers**, 10, 20, 30, 40 Richman Plaza, off Cedar Ave. Bridge along Harlem River. 1975. *Davis, Brody & Assocs.*, architects; *M. Paul Friedberg & Assocs.*, landscape architects.

A bulky variation on *Davis Brody's* earlier **Waterside** project in Manhattan, these two joined towers form a dramatic landmark. To those who live in the towers (and those who visit) they are equally satisfying up close.

[U5] **Public School 229/Junior High School 229, The Roland N. Patterson School**, 225 Harlem River Park Bridge, NE cor. Richman Plaza. 1977. *Caudill Rowlett Scott.*

Built over the railroad tracks, it is unorthodox in appearance, with minimal windows but a dramatic exterior.

Old Croton Aqueduct: Completed in 1842, the Aqueduct was the first dependable supply system to bring drinking water to the growing city, running a 32-mile downhill course from Croton

[U7] **Gatehouse, New Croton Aqueduct**, W. Burnside Ave., SE cor. Phelan Place. ca. 1890. *Benjamin S. Church*, engineer.

One of a series of rock-faced granite buildings in the Bronx and Manhattan built to service the City's second water supply system, the New Croton Aqueduct (1885-1893).

[U8] **Public School 226, Nadia J. Pagan Primary School**, NE cor. W. Burnside and Sedgwick Aves. 1990s.

The public school as a village. The small and multiple forms create a minivillage for the lucky children who attend.

The Old N.Y.U. Uptown Campus:

[U9] **Bronx Community College, CUNY**/formerly **New York University, University Heights Campus**, University Ave. bet. W.180th St. and Hall of Fame Terr., W side, to Sedgwick Ave. and vicinity. Original grounds and Ohio Field, 1892-1912. *Vaux & Co.*, landscape architects.

U4

U8

Reservoir in Westchester County to High Bridge. In this area of the West Bronx it is particularly apparent, since much of its course is topped by a green walkway: open to the public for some fifteen blocks along a route which parallels University Avenue, the latter 30 yards to the east. Take a stroll.

Back along University Heights:

[U6] **Calvary Methodist Church**, 1885 University Ave., bet. Morton Pl. and W. Burnside Ave., W side. 1924.

Rough ashlar walls contrast with refined stained-glass windows. The small but strongly composed building appears a bastion against the changes that are sweeping the area. Built and physically endowed by a moneyed community in the 1920s, it now serves a congregation that must struggle to maintain its fine qualities.

This was the 50-plus-acre uptown campus of New York University until 1973, when sold to the City as a campus for Bronx Community College. The formerly resident **NYU College of Engineering** was absorbed into the newly renamed Polytechnic Institute of New York in downtown Brooklyn.

[U10a] **The Hall of Fame for Great Americans**, entrance on Hall of Fame Terr. 1892-1912. *Stanford White of McKim, Mead & White.* Open to the public: 10-5, daily. 718-289-5161. *www.bcc.cuny.edu/halloffame*

Not a hall at all but a semicircular **Classical** arcade between whose columns are arrayed bronze busts of great Americans. They are picked by a college of more than 100 electors chosen from the fields of higher education, science, jurisprudence, and business, plus others in public life. The colonnade was conceived by N.Y.U. Chancellor *MacCracken* to camouflage, from Sedgwick Avenue below, the unsightly high foundation walls underpinning *Stanford White's* Library, Philosophy Hall, and Language Hall.

U10a

[U10b] **Gould Memorial Library**, 1894-1899. 🔹 [U10c] **Cornelius Baker Hall of Philosophy**, 1892-1912. 🔹[U10d] **Hall of Languages** 1892-1895. All by *Stanford White of McKim, Mead & White.* 🔹

These three buildings—Gould is the domed one in the center— together with the Hall of Fame Arcade, are the pièce de résistance of this campus, all by *Stanford White* himself. Looked at in terms of their exquisitely detailed stone exteriors, they achieve a grand **Classical Revival** composition. A bit of Rome's Pantheon, coffered and columned, awaits within Gould.

[U11] **Gould Hall of Technology/ Begrisch Lecture Hall.** 1964. *Marcel Breuer & Assocs.* 🔹 [U12] **Colston Residence Hall and Cafeteria.** 1964. *Marcel Breuer & Assocs. Robert F. Gatje,* associate.

Modernist sculptural essays drawn from *Breuer's* sketchbooks: his ideas matured over the years in abstract forms. Here was an opportunity to install them in reality.

[U13] **South Hall**/formerly **Gustav H. Schwab House**. 1857.   [U14] **Butler Hall**/formerly **William Henry W. T. Mali House.** ca., 1859. [U15] **MacCracken Hall**/formerly **Henry Mitchell MacCracken House**/originally **Loring Andrews** House. ca. 1880. Hall of Fame Terr., bet. Loring Place and Sedgwick Ave. N side.

Mansions that predate the campus.

[U16] **Public School 15,** 2195 Andrews Ave., bet. Hall of Fame Terr. and W.183rd St., to Loring Pl. N. 1998. *Ehrenkrantz & Eckstut.*

A strong brick and limestone composition with a grand semi-cylindrical stair volume reminiscent of *Charles Rennie Mackintosh's* **Scotland Street School**, Glasgow.

[U17] **2253-2257 Loring Avenue,** N of W.183rd St. 1890s.

Copper-clad bay windows and stepped gables enrich these brick and limestone row houses.

KINGSBRIDGE HEIGHTS

U16

Nearest train: No. 4 to Kingsbridge Rd. station.

[U20] **Kingsbridge Veterans Hospital/** originally **U.S. Veterans Hospital No.81**, 130 W. Kingsbridge Rd., bet. Webb and Sedgwick Aves. S side. New Hospital, 1979. *Max O. Urbahn Assoc., Inc.*

This commanding green hillside site affords spectacular views across the Harlem Valley of upper Manhattan and has provided for needs of diverse occupants over the years. During the British occupation of New York it was the site of one of their forts. Later it was a private estate, then served as the Catholic Orphan Asylum before becoming a neo-Georgian veterans' hospital in the 1920s. The 1979 all aluminum-clad successor is as sleek as a resort hotel.

[U21] **The Jewish Home and Hospital for the Aged, Salzman Pavilion**, 100 W. Kingsbridge Rd., bet. Webb and University Aves. S side. 1975.

U18

Beyond the old N.Y.U. Campus:

[U18] **St. Nicholas of Tolentine Church** (Roman Catholic), University Ave., SW cor. Fordham Rd. 1928. *Delaney, O' Connor & Schultz.*

A conservative granite ashlar neo-Gothic church from a time when exuberance in neo-Gothic matters had given way to solemnity. Bring back *John Ruskin, Viollet-le-Duc,* and their combined polychromy and structuralism.

[U19] **Fordham Hill Cooperative Apartments/** originally **Fordham Hill Apartments**, Sedgwick Ave., NE cor. Webb Ave. 1950. *Leonard Schultze & Assocs.*

On the former site of the **Webb Academy & Home for Aged Ship Builders** are these nine pristine 16-story apartment towers developed for the Equitable Life Assurance Society by an architect of the Waldorf-Astoria. Bland.

[U22] **Greenwall Pavilion**, 2545 University Ave., at W.192nd St. W side. 1972. Both by *Weiss Whelan Edelbaum Webster.*

On the site of what was once the **Hebrew Infant Asylum** are two imposing additions to an institution for the elderly.

[U23] **2751 University Avenue** (apartments), NW cor. W.195th St. 1936. *Edward W. Franklin.*

Art Deco in cream, orange, and brown brick, its entry still intact.

[U24] **Rosenor Gables** (apartments), 2757 Claflin Ave., bet. W.195th and 197th Sts. W side. ca. 1928.

Deeply modeled **neo-Tudor**. Imposing except for the brown anodized aluminum windows.

[U25] **Rectory, Our Lady of Angels Roman Catholic Church**, 2860 Webb Ave., bet. W.197th St. and Reservoir Ave. ca. 1900.

Impressive and asymmetric, this romantic country house displays a ground floor of undressed fieldstone. Catch the porte cochère millwork.

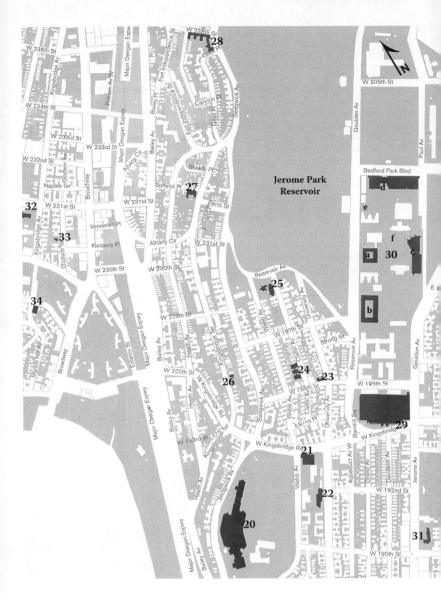

North along Kingsbridge Terrace:

[U26] **2744 Kingsbridge Terrace**, N of W. Kingsbridge Rd. E side. 1912.

Close to the vast veterans' hospital stands this tiny monument, a stucco castle with numerous gables, balconies, crenellated turrets, a weather vane, a TV antenna, and a tunnel reputedly leading from the "dungeon" to the street.

Nearest train: No.1 to 231st Street station.

[U27] **Kingsbridge Heights Community Center**/originally **50th Precinct, N.Y.C. Police Department**, 3101 Kingsbridge Terr., SW cor. Summit Place. 1900-1902. *Horgan & Slattery.*

Referring to the political connections of this structure's successful architects, *Seth Low* in 1902 called for the "dishorganizing and unslatterifying" of municipal architecture as one of his mayoral promises. A rich **Renaissance Revival-Eclectic** building.

[U28] **Sholom Aleichem Houses/Yiddish Cooperative Heim Geselshaft**, 3451 Giles Place, 3470 Cannon Place, 68 W.238th St., 3605 Sedgwick Ave. Entry via Giles Place (one-way north and east) from Kingsbridge Terr. 1927. *Springsteen & Goldhammer.*

Four unembellished red-brick apartments atop a hill overlooking the Harlem River valley. Built around a meandering courtyard by a Jewish community whose common goal was the preservation of Eastern European Yiddish culture (as contrasted with Hebrew religious culture) through membership in the **Arbeiter Ring** (Workmen's Circle).

The Old Jerome Park Reservoir, and its surrounding institutions:

Jerome Park Reservoir: First filled in 1905, this concrete-lined water basin holds 773 million gallons. Goulden Avenue, its eastern boundary, sits atop a combination of the Old Croton Aqueduct and a masonry dividing wall that was to separate it from the reservoir's second stage.

With a capacity twice that of the first, stage 2 was excavated to the east of the present reservoir, extending to Jerome Avenue between West Kingsbridge Road north to Mosholu Parkway. Abandoned in 1912, the pit was filled in and now serves as site for the Kingsbridge Armory, Lehman College, two subway yards, three high schools, a park, and a couple of publicly aided housing developments!

The reservoir and nearby Jerome Avenue take their name from the Jerome Park Racetrack, which occupied this site from 1876 until 1890. Leonard W. Jerome, Winston Churchill's grandfather, was a prime mover in sponsoring the American Jockey Club, which strived (with success) to elevate horse racing in this country to the status of an aristocratic sport.

[U29] **Kingsbridge Armory**/originally **Eighth Coastal Artillery Armory**/later **Eighth Regiment Armory**, 29 W. Kingsbridge Rd., bet. Jerome and Reservoir Aves. N side. 1912-1917. *Pilcher & Tachau.* 🍎

U26

Called the largest armory in the world, this picturesque 20th-century fortress, the **Pierrefonds of The Bronx**, is probably better known for peacetime activities such as indoor bicycle races than for suppressing civil insurrection. Whereas *Viollet-le-Duc's* medieval-revival "reconstructions" (read "imaginations") at **Pierrefonds** were banal, the Bronx, a younger, callower place, lives well with such fantasies.

Nearest train: No.4 to Bedford Park Blvd– Lehman College station.

[U30] **Lehman College, CUNY**/originally Hunter College Uptown, 250 Bedford Park Blvd, SE cor. Goulden Ave. Original buildings, 1932, *Thompson, Holmes, & Converse.*
[U30a] **Library and Shuster Hall**, 1960, *Marcel Breuer & Assocs.*; *Robert F. Gatje,* associate.
[U30b] **Carman Hall** (classrooms and cafeteria), 1970, *DeYoung & Moskowitz.*

[U30c] **New Library, Speech and Theater, and Auditorium Buildings**, along Paul Ave. 1980, *David Todd & Assocs. and Jan Hird Pokorny.*

[U30d] **Physical Education Facility**, 1994, *Rafael Viñoly Architects.*

[U30e] **Communication Center**, 2003, *FxFowle.*

[U30f] **Multimedia Center**, 2008, *FxFowle.*
The older buildings never had cohesion sufficient to create a context; and the ones along Paul Avenue are a mixed lot: *Breuer's,* an unassuming block with his trademark vertical windows. *DeYoung & Moskowitz* provide some unnecessary gold and limestone histrionics. The *Todd/Pokorny* buildings are modest background modern.

Viñoly's airy crustacean (oxymoron?) provides a north entry to the campus, and houses wondrous spaces for sport. *FxFowle's* Communications Center adds much pizzazz: a shiny cylinder acts as an observation post for security, while the Multimedia Center is underground but filled with light, courtesy of a skylight cut into the plaza.

U30e

[U31] **St. James Episcopal Church**, 2500 Jerome Ave., NE cor. E.190th St. 1864-1865. *Henry M. Dudley of Dudley & Diaper.* **Parish House**, 1891-1892. *Henry F. Kilburn.* 🍎
A stone Gothic Revival church in the shadow of the IRT Jerome Avenue elevated. The greenery of the churchyard and adjacent St. James Park (1901) seems to block out some of the clatter. What a serendipitous belfry...

KINGSBRIDGE

Kingsbridge, the flat area along Broadway below West 242nd Street, preserves the name of the earliest settlement (which grew up around the first bridge to Manhattan, built in 1693).

Nearest train: No.1 to 231st St. station.

[U32] **Church of the Mediator** (Episcopal), 3045 Kingsbridge Ave., SW cor. W.231st St. 1913. *Henry Vaughan.*
    Gray ashlar granite, this **neo-Gothic** sanctuary is neatly sited on a prominent corner by an architect of Washington's National Cathedral.

[U33] Originally **George H. Moller House**/formerly **Residence, Brothers of the Christian Schools**, 3029 Godwin Terr., bet. W.230th and W.231st Sts. W side. ca. 1875.
    Set back from adjacent 1920s brick multi-

U34

U33

ple-dwelling construction, atop a stone retaining wall, stands this mansard-roofed, stuccoed house, moved from its original site a few hundred feet west. "Remembrance of Things Past?"

MARBLE HILL (MANHATTAN)

Nearest train: No.1 to 225th St. station.

[U34] **St. Stephen's Methodist Episcopal Church**, 146 W.228th St., SE cor. Marble Hill Ave. 1897.
    A picturesque **Shingle Style** work with a commanding presence, a marker and sign of welcome to Manhattan's orphaned Marble Hill community, cut off from its mother island and physically connected to the Bronx by the technologies of canal digging and earth moving.

BEDFORD PARK

Nearest train: D to 205th St. station.

[B1] **Bedford Park Presbyterian Church**, 2933 Bainbridge Ave., NW cor. Bedford Park Blvd. 1900. *R. H. Robertson.* Addition, 1929.
    Now swathed in a jungle of vines like an over-furred matron, this granite ashlar and timber church recalls (underneath) critic *Osbert Lancaster's* term: **Stockbroker Tudor.**

[B2] **52nd Precinct Station House**/originally **41st Precinct, N.Y.C. Police Department**, 3016 Webster Ave., NE cor. Mosholu Pkwy. 1904-1906. *Stoughton & Stoughton.*
    In a quasi-rural setting at the turn of the century, the architects of Manhattan's Soldiers' and Sailors' Monument created a **Tuscan villa** for this precinct. The tower, a high point in such romantic design for the City, wears a polychromatic terra-cotta clock, a tapestry of brick, and deeply projecting eaves.

[B3] Police Officer George J. Werdann School, P.S./M.S. 20, 3020 Webster Ave., N of 52nd Precinct Station House. 1990s. *Ehrenkrantz & Eckstut.*

Cool limestone and brick, gabled to simulate row housing, this is another attempt to bring the scale of schools to the remembered scale of children's homes.

[B4] Bedford Park Congregational Church (United Church of Christ), E.201st St., NE cor. Bainbridge Ave. ca. 1890.

Tiny, but its ashlar and wood frame construction are special.

[B5] Ursuline Convent (Roman Catholic)/originally **Mount St. Ursula Convent,** 330 Bedford Park Blvd./2885 Marion Ave. ca. 1888. *Arthur Arctander.* **Chapel,** 1965, *George Murray.*

A venerable complex, bland (pre-Vatican II) on the outside, while the chapel shows off bursts of gleeful post–Vatican II modernity, notably in the extraordinary stained-glass windows.

NORWOOD

[B6] Mosholu Parkway, connecting Bronx and Van Cortlandt Parks.

One of the few completed links in the network of parkways proposed to connect the major parks of the Bronx. At the eastern entrance to the Parkway the **Victory Monument** serves to divide traffic.

B3   B8

[B7] St. Brendan's Church (Roman Catholic), Perry Ave., bet. E.206th and E.207th Sts. W side. 1966. *Belfatto & Pavarini.*

St. Brendan is the patron saint of navigators, so it should come as no surprise that this church was built to resemble the prow of a ship. Near the entrance of the upper church (there is a modest lower one), under the steeply sloping roof, the ceiling is low and the church dark; approaching the altar, space and light grow.

[B8] Valentine-Varian House/Museum of Bronx History/originally **Isaac Valentine House,** 3266 Bainbridge Ave., bet. Van Cortlandt Ave. E. and E.208th St. E side. 1758. ☛ Open to the public: Mo-Fr, 9-5; Sa, 10-4; Su, 1-5. 718-881-8900. *www.bronxhistoricalsociety.org*

A well-proportioned fieldstone farmhouse moved from its original location across the street. Today it is also the home of The Bronx County Historical Society and site of a museum of local history.

Williamsbridge Oval: The embankment behind the Valentine-Varian House continues to curve around to form an oval which today encloses an elaborate city playground. Between 1888 and 1923 the embankment formed a dam to contain the waters of the Williamsbridge Reservoir, part of the City' s water supply system. After its abandonment tunnels were cut through, and play equipment and benches were introduced. Appropriately named, the surrounding streets are called Reservoir Oval East and West.

[B9] Mosholu Preservation Organization Headquarters/former **Keeper's House,** Williamsbridge Reservoir, Reservoir Oval E., NE cor. Putnam Place. ca. 1890. *George W. Birdsall,* architect. *Benjamin S. Church,* engineer.

One of the many rock-faced stone buildings built for the City's water supply system. This one, however, was meant as a residence and office rather than as a gatehouse or service facility. It has outlived the effective life of the abandoned reservoir across the street.

[B10] Montefiore Hospital and Medical Center, E. Gun Hill Rd. bet. Kossuth and Tryon Aves. S side. Original buildings, 1913. *Arnold W. Brunner.* **[B11] Henry L. Moses Research Institute,** E. Gun Hill Rd., SE cor. Bainbridge Ave. 1966. *Philip Johnson & Assocs.* **[B12a] Edna and Monroe C. Gutman Center**/originally **Annie Lichtenhein Pavilion,** Kossuth Ave. bet. E. Gun Hill Rd. and E. 210th St. E side. 1970. *Gruzen & Partners and Westermann/Miller Assocs.* **[B12b] Loeb Pavilion,** E of Lichtenhein Pavilion.

B11

1966. *Kelly & Gruzen and Helge Westermann.*

Chaotic in appearance, Montefiore exhibits the result of a growing population and changing medical technology. It speaks well for administration and donors that newer additions are exemplary in their architecture beginning with *Philip Johnson' s* 1966 work. The **Montefiore II Apartments** is one of the tallest in the borough; its dark red-brown brick volume is impressive from afar.

[B12c] North Central Bronx Hospital, N.Y.C. Health & Hospitals Corporation, Kossuth Ave., NE cor. E.210th St. 1976. *Westermann/Miller Assocs.; Carl Pancaldo; Schuman, Lichtenstein & Claman.*

When viewed as architecture for the public, **North Central** is spectacularly successful. The internal medical workings are for others to judge. It is crisp, with neat, bold forms of brick and precast concrete that articulate the street façades with confidence.

[B13] **Montefiore Apartments II**, 3450 Wayne Ave., bet. E. Gun Hill Rd. and E.210th St. E side. 1972. *Schuman, Lichtenstein & Claman.*
Scale, but not human scale.

[B14] **Woodlawn Cemetery**, entrances at Jerome Ave. N of Bainbridge Ave. E side and at E.233rd St., SW cor. Webster Ave. Open to the public.
A lavish array of tombstones, mausoleums, and memorials in a richly planted setting. Many wealthy and distinguished people are buried

B12c

B13

here. Tombs and mausoleums are replicas and small-scale reproductions of well known European chapels and monuments. *Jay Gould, the Woolworths,* and Mayors *John Purroy Mitchel* and *Fiorello LaGuardia* are among the noted people interred at Woodlawn.

NECROLOGY

Formerly Bedford Park Casino, 390 Bedford Park Blvd., bet. Decatur and Webster Aves. S side. ca. 1880.
Although the ground floor was clearly 20th century, the upper portions of the wood façade revealed the original onetime center for neighborhood recreation. Before its demolition, the building was used by a violin bow manufacturer.

Bronx House of Detention for Men/originally **Bronx County Jail,** 653 River Ave., SW cor. E.151st St. (W of the Concourse.) 1931. *Joseph H. Freedlander.* Additions.

A curiously handsome high-rise penal institution by the architect of the nearby Bronx County Building. Replaced by a shopping mall.

Old Yankee Stadium, E.161st St., SW cor. River Ave. (W of the Concourse.) 1923. *Osborn Engineering Co.* Rebuilt, 1976, *Praeger-Kavanagh-Waterbury.*
Brewery magnate and team owner, *Colonel Jacob Ruppert,* built the original for his team and his most valuable player, *Babe Ruth* (the short right field helped him set his one-time home run record). In the 1970s the stadium (touted to be the "economic salvation of the Bronx") was rebuilt. Now it has just been replaced. There have been late-inning discussions about preserving at least parts of the old stadium (the site will become a park).
How about a nice ruin?

University Heights Bridge, over the Harlem River, bet. W. Fordham Rd., The Bronx, and W.207th St., Manhattan. 1893-1895. *William H. Burr,*

B14

consulting engineer, with *Alfred P. Boller and George W. Birdsall.* Relocated and extended, 1905-1908, *Othniel F. Nichols,* chief engineer. ☀️ Latticework superstructure demolished and underbridge reconstructed, 1987-1992.
The 1895 Tinkertoy bridge that occupied the 207th Street site once spanned the Harlem River at Broadway between West 220th and 225th Streets. When the IRT Broadway Line elevated came to the Bronx in 1907, that bridge was no longer purposeful. So, rather than waste a bridge, it was floated a mile or so down the Harlem to this West 207th Street site. But in the affluent 1980s, just years after the City faced bankruptcy, a second reuse to accommodate increased traffic couldn't be justified, and so the lacy, latticework structure was demolished (but only after a politically desirable landmark designation) so that a wider, stronger, modern bridge using some of the original ironwork could be erected in its place. A ghost of a landmark?

Riverdale

Riverdale (Broadway west to the banks of the Hudson) combines lush estates and lavish mansions with low-rent housing, and block after block of ordinary, middle-class apartments. The slopes of the old community of **Riverdale-on-Hudson**—house some of the borough's most affluent and influential people. Spuyten Duyvil is the hilly southwestern tip of this precinct, from which the graceful arch of the Henry Hudson Bridge springs to its opposite abutment in Manhattan.

R5

R1

SPUYTEN DUYVIL

Spuyten Duyvil, an early **Dutch** name for the region where the Harlem and Hudson Rivers meet, is also the name of the steeply sloped area of the Bronx that overlooks the confluence of the waters. It has been overbuilt with tall undistinguished apartments.

[R1] Edgehill Church of Spuyten Duyvil (United Church of Christ)/ originally **Riverdale Presbyterian Chapel,** 2570 Independence Ave., at Kappock St. S side. 1888-1889. *Francis H. Kimball.*

Occupying a spit of land between two roads that diverge at different grades stands this picturesque eclectic sanctuary: a medieval cocktail with a base of **random ashlar gneiss,** a body **Shingle Styled,** all in shades of neo-Gothic, Tudor division.

[R2] **Villa Charlotte Bronte,** 2501 Palisade Ave., NW cor. Independence Ave. 1926. *Robert Gardner.*

The Villa, with two romantic, intricate, visually intriguing wings containing 16 units, some partly above, some below street level. These charmers occupy the southwesternmost (and best) edge of the Spuyten Duyvil escarpment, overlooking the confluence of the Harlem and Hudson Rivers. A romantic pearl among apartment house swine.

[R3] **Henry Hudson Memorial Column,** Henry Hudson Park, Kappock St. NW cor. Independence Ave. 1912. *Walter Cook of Babb, Cook & Willard.* Sculpture of Hudson, 1938. *Karl Bitter* and *Karl Gruppe.*

The 100-foot Doric column was erected on this bluff through public subscription following the **Hudson-Fulton Celebration of 1909.** The 16-foot bronze explorer on top arrived later, hoping to oversee his river.

RIVERDALE

Riverdale, which slopes precipitously down to the Hudson, was once a name reserved for the area immediately around the onetime Riverdale New York Central R.R. station at West 254th Street: **Riverdale-on-Hudson**. Today, high-rise apartments hulking along Henry Hudson Parkway have diminished the exclusivity of both name and community. Fortunately, however, a cadre of tenacious residents, a couple of foreign governments, and some eleemosynary institutions still preserve the mansions, the lovely landscapes, and the tranquil beauty of the older community.

Caution: North of West 240th Street, and west of the Parkway, Riverdale is an obstacle course for the unwary. Narrow, winding, hilly streets are commonplace. Street signs are sometimes missing or misleading. The condition of the streets is sometimes abominable, partly because resi-

R6a

R2

dents wish to discourage idle visiting. Not only do potholes abound but in some areas asphalt bumps have been added to discourage reckless driving, as walking and cycling are popular. All this has probably helped to preserve this very special part of New York.

[R4] Delafield housing estate/originally "**Fieldston Hill,**" Edward C. Delafield House and estate/later **Delafield Botanical Estates**, Columbia University, 680 W.246th St., SW cor. Hadley Ave. ca. 1865. House altered, 1916, *Dwight James Baum*. Converted into housing estate, 1986, *James Stewart Polshek & Partners*.

The large fieldstone home of an old Riverdale family, the *Delafields*, with their lush overgrown estate, bequeathed to, and then sold by Columbia University: converted to condominiums within and without.

[R5] Eric J. Schmertz House, 4550 Palisade Ave., S of W.247th St. E side. 1971. *Vincent A. Claps.*

A leader in a short-lived modernist invasion, this stained-board sheathed house might be termmed "woodsy cubist." In comparison to its 1970s modernist peers in Riverdale, it shines.

[R6a] Originally **William E. and Melissa Phelps Dodge House, "Greyston"**/ later **Greyston Conference Center,** Teachers College, 690 W.247th St., SW cor. Independence Ave. 1863-1864. *James Renwick, Jr.*
[R6b] Gatehouse, ca. 1864. S of W.247th St.

When Riverdale became a country retreat in the 1860s, this was one of the earliest houses commissioned. The *Dodge* family was instrumental not only in the establishment of **Teachers College** in 1887 but also in the gift to TC in 1961 of this gray granite, many-gabled, many-chimneyed mansion.

The gatehouse, an asymmetric composition with jerkin head roofs, is in the style of *A. J. Downing* and *Calvert Vaux's* books on cottage design. It is once again a private house.

Riverdale's mansions and views: To call attention to every house worth mentioning in this architectural treasure chest of a community would require a tome in itself. Some of its narrow lanes (and the homes that border them) are particularly rewarding. Sycamore Avenue above West 252nd Street has buildings so picturesque that you won't believe you're in the City. Try Independence Avenue between West 248th and 254th Streets. The best view of Riverdale and the Hudson beyond is from a point just north of West 252nd Street.

R8

R12

[R9] Formerly **Anthony Campagna House**/now **Yeshiva of Telshe Alumni School**, 640 W.249th St., at Independence Ave. 1929-1930. *Dwight James Baum.* 🍎

A bit of **Tuscany** in New York: a stucco and tile villa at the end of a cobblestoned drive, complete with forecourt and fountain. The prolific *Baum* designed hundreds of houses in Riverdale while maintaining a second office in Sarasota, Florida, where his gargantuan 1924 home for *John Ringling* is now the **Ringling Museum of Art**. *Baum* was a distant relative of *L. Frank Baum*, author of *The Wizard of Oz*.

[R10] Coachman's House, Henry F. Spaulding estate, 4970 Independence Ave., NE cor. W.249th St. 1879. *Charles W. Clinton.* 🍎

A **Stick Style** picturesque cottage, moved from the west side of Independence Avenue in 1909. Glorious.

[R11] Wave Hill Garden and Cultural Center, 675 W.252nd St., parking at 249th St. and Independence Ave. W side.

[R11a] William Lewis Morris House, "Wave Hill" (northern building): center section, 1843-1844; north wing, late 19th century; armor hall, 1928, *Dwight James Baum*; south wings, after 1933; general renovation, 1975, *Stephen Lepp.* 🍎
[R11b] "Glyndor II" (southern building) ca. 1903. Both open to the public.
[R11c] Perkins Visitor Center, 2004, *Robert A.M. Stern Architects*. Open to the public.
718-549-3200. *www.wavehill.org*

[R7] "Alderbrook"/formerly **Percy Pyne House**/then Elie Nadelman House, 4715 Independence Ave., S of W.248th St. W side. ca. 1880.

An *Andrew Jackson Downing*-inspired neo-**Gothic** brick house sprouting gables and crockets, long the home and studio of sculptor *Elie Nadelman* (1882-1946). An adjacent private community snugly occupies a portion of Alderbrook's original lands and shares its name.

[R8] Riverdale Country School, River Campus, 1 Spaulding Lane, NW cor. Independence Ave. **Perkins Study Center**, 1967, *R. Marshall Christensen*. Originally **"Parkside,"** George H. Foster House, ca. 1871. Originally **"Oaklawn,"** Henry F. Spaulding House, ca. 1863. *Thomas S. Wall.*

Oaklawn's substantial mansard roof rises to a steeply shingled central pavilion crested in iron filigree. An American foretaste of the **Second Empire** Parisian roofs.

The original **Wave Hill** was begun in 1843 by *Morris* and was later the boyhood vacation home to *Teddy Roosevelt* (1870-71) and still later a retreat for *Mark Twain* (1901-03). Conservationist/financier *George Walbridge Perkins* bought the estate in 1903, and built **neo-Georgian** Glyndor soon after (his initials are on the metal downspouts).

Acquired by the City in 1960, the center features tours, concert series, workshops, weddings, conferences. *Stern's* subtle visitor center is a deft conversion of an existing garage with a new board-and-batten addition, all blended seamlessly into the existing fabric.

[R12] H. L. Abrons House, 5225 Independence Ave., NW cor. W.252nd St. 1980. *Harold Sussman, Horace Ginsbern & Assocs.*

A complex modernist form that, although it conflicts with the architecture of its neighbors, buffers them with dense landscaping.

[R13] **Riverdale Historic District,** between Independence Avenue and the Hudson River, 252nd to 254th Streets, including all of Sycamore Avenue. 🌑

In-city sub-urbia on the slopes of the Hudson, with many grand houses hiding amidst the shrubbery.

[R14] **5200 Sycamore Avenue**, bet. W.252nd and W.254th Sts. W side. 1922-1924. *Dwight James Baum.*

Gambreled nostalgia from the highly successful *Baum.*

[R15] Originally **William D. and Ann Cromwell House, "Stonehurst,"** 5225 Sycamore Ave., bet. W.252nd and W.254th Sts. W side. 1861. 🌑

Hidden by newer homes on Sycamore Avenue and by dense trees is another of the great stone mansions of Riverdale (such as **Greyston** or **Wave Hill**).

NORTH RIVERDALE

[R18] **Ladd Road**, off Palisade Ave. bet. W.254th St. and Sigma Place. E side.
[R19] **James Strain House**, 731 Ladd Rd. E side. 1970. *Keith Kroeger Assocs.*

A group of modern houses built 1957-1970, clustered along a cul-de-sac around a private swimming pool. The Strain House provides a geometrical clarity absent in its neighbors.

R15

R19

[R16] **5270 Sycamore Avenue**, bet. W.252nd and W.254th Sts. E side. ca. 1853.

🏠 [R16a] **William S. Duke barn**, 5286 Sycamore Ave., SE cor. W.254th St. ca. 1856-1858. Altered into carriage house, 1886, *Frederick Clarke Withers.*

These lovely **Shingle Style** barns, in various stages of reuse, once served country homes to the east (atop the hill along today's Independence Avenue).

🏠 [R17] **Salanter Akiba Riverdale Academy**, 655 W.254th St., bet. Independence and Palisade Aves. N side. 1974. *Caudill Rowlett Scott Assocs.*

Given a slope and the need to conjoin the educational activities of what were once three Hebrew day schools, what better solution than a a series of classroom floors stepping downhill (with a skylit roof providing all with transfluvial views). Shades of Harvard's **Gund Hall**—but here a result of the topography, not whim. A harsh statement in this placid suburbia.

[R20] **College of Mount Saint Vincent on Hudson**/originally **Convent and Academy of Mount Saint Vincent**, 6301 Riverdale Ave. at W.263rd St. W side. 🌑

🏠 [R20a] Original **College Building**/now **Administration Building**, central section, 1857-1859. *Henry Engelbert.* Additions: 1865, 1883, 1906-1908, *E. Wenz*, 1952. 🌑

🏠 [R20b] **Library**/formerly **"Fonthill,"** Edwin Forrest House, 1848-1852.
[R20c] **Louise LeGras Hall**/originally **St. Vincent's Free School**, W.261st St. opp. Netherland Ave. N side. 1875.
[R20d] **Marillac Hall**/originally in part **E.D. Randolph House**, ca. 1855. 🌑
[R20e] Originally **"Fonthill" cottage**. 🌑
[R20f] **"Fonthill" carriage house and stable**/now **Boyle Hall**, ca. 1848-1852.

The Sisters of Charity purchased this site from actor *Edwin Forrest* (his feud with *William Charles Macready* in 1849 touched off the Astor Place Riot) when their original quarters in

R22

Manhattan were to be destroyed by the construction of Central Park. *Forrest's* house,
Fonthill, is as eccentric a building for New York
as the "folly" it was patterned after was for
England: *William Beckford's* Fonthill Abbey.
Though this is the best-known building on the
campus, the old red-brick **College Building**
itself, four stories high and oh so long, is an
unfamiliar and more spectacular sight. Its 180-
foot tower rises some 400 feet above the level
of the Hudson. **LeGras Hall** was, between 1875
and 1910, the sparsely settled Riverdale's only
elementary school: a charming building, accessible directly from adjacent West 261st Street.

FIELDSTON

[R21] **Fieldston Historic District**, generally
bounded on the west by Henry Hudson Parkway
East, Tibbett Avenue on the east, Manhattan
College Parkway on the south, and lines north
of 250th Street on the north. 🌶️

A community of private streets and English-
inspired houses of the 1920s grouped along the
streets north of Manhattan College Parkway;
Fieldston Road, with its green central mall, is the
quiet main thoroughfare. Among the many charms
of the area is the oak tree preserved in the center
of the intersection of Delafield and Iselin Avenues.
If you are bicycling or driving, beware of the street
paving. Potholes can be the rule.

[R22] **Horace Mann High School**, 231 W.246th
St., NE cor. Tibbet Ave., [R22a] **Pforzheimer Hall**.
1956. *Victor Christ-Janer*. [R22b] **Prettyman
Gymnasium**. 1968. *Charles E. Hughes III*.
[R22c] **Gratwick Science Wing Addition and
Pforzheimer Hall renovation**. 1975. *Frost Assocs*.

[R22d] **Middle School and Arts/Dining Building**. 1999. *Gruzen Samton*.
Once located next to Teachers College in Manhattan (as was Horace Mann-Barnard Elementary School, across West 246th Street), the High School now occupies this more verdant campus. The new buildings by *Gruzen Samton* are full of natural light *and* knit the existing campus together.

[R23a] **Middle School and Athletic Building, Ethical Culture Fieldston School,** 3901 Fieldston Road, at Manhattan College Parkway (208th Pkwy). S side. 2007. *Cooper, Robertson & Partners*.
A neat modernist exercise in three cubist parts at the center of the school's campus, linking the existing Upper and Lower Schools and adjacent athletic fields. Rough stone bases rise to sleek glass, metal, and wood above. The indoor swimming pool is particularly swank: a **natty natatorium**.

[R24] Originally **C. E. Chambers House,** 4670 Waldo Ave., bet College Rd. and Livingston Ave. E side. ca. 1923. *Julius Gregory*.
A picturesque suburban house, reminiscent of the best in English country house design, by a master architect of such. *Gregory* did a number of similar fine houses in Fieldston.

[R25] **Conservative Synagogue Adath Israel of Riverdale,** 475 W. 250th St., NE cor. Henry Hudson Pkwy. 1962. *Percival Goodman*.
Conservative in its religious status, not in its

R26, rectory

architectural attitudes. Strong forms in concrete and dark red brick make this synagogue an unneighborly character.

[R26] **Christ Church,** 5030 Henry Hudson Pkwy E., SE cor. W.252nd St. 1865-1866. *Richard M. Upjohn of Richard Upjohn and Son.* 🍎
A small, picturesque romantic **Victorian Gothic Revival** church, of brick and local stone, with a simple pierced-wall belfry. Minimal alterations and careful maintenance have preserved it well. The mansarded parish house is its sprightly contemporary.

A detour west across the Parkway:

[R27] **Riverdale Presbyterian Church** and **Manse: The Duff House,** 4763 Henry Hudson Pkwy. W., at W.249th St. W side. 1863-1864. *James Renwick*. 🍎
A pair of late **Gothic Revival** *Renwick* designs (much altered: check that steeple) fortunately framed from distractions on either side by heavy greenery. The Duff House is curious in that

its original design called for both a mansard roof and Gothic Revival gables and dormers.

East across the Parkway and downhill to Broadway:

VAN CORTLANDT PARK

[R28] **Van Cortlandt Mansion Museum**/originally **Frederick and Frances Jay Van Cortlandt House,** Van Cortlandt Park, Broadway bet. W.242nd and W.246th Sts. E side. 1748-1749. Open to the public. 718-543-3344. Tues-Fri, 10-3; Sat-Sun, 11-4; closed Mon. *www.vancortlandthouse.org* 🍎
The carefully preserved fieldstone country house of a wealthy landed family, the austere exterior hiding a richly decorated interior. Its farmland, the Park to the north, now forms an enormous meadow used for a variety of sporting events, particularly cricket (enjoyed by the City's large West Indian population) and model airplane trials.

Vault Hill, *overlooking the Van Cortlandt Mansion, contains the Van Cortlandt family vault. When the British occupied New York in 1776 Augustus Van Cortlandt, the City clerk, hid the municipal records in the vault. In 1781, General Washington had campfires lit here to deceive the British, while he marched to Yorktown for the battle against Cornwallis.*

R28

NECROLOGY

Administration Building, Salanter Akiba Riverdale Academy/originally **Henry W. Boettger House,** 655 W. 254th St., bet. Independence and Palisade Aves. 1905.
This multistory orange brick neo-Tudor mansion was the last of conductor *Arturo Toscanini'* s sequential homes in Riverdale.

Barrymore's Inn/formerly **Riverdale Inn,** 6471 Broadway at Mosholu Ave. W side.
The closing of this restaurant marked the real end of an era. The colorful mayor *Jimmy Walker* was said to have tête-à-tête with dancer *Betty Compton* here back in the 1920s, when this spot was truly out of the way.

Eastern Bronx

Before World War II, the sleepy area of the Bronx. At its center was a large green space shaded by majestic trees, called the New York Catholic Protectory, an institute for destitute children. The neighborhoods around it were largely residential, with one-, two-, and four-family houses, stray apartment buildings, all kinds of minor commercial, industrial, and institutional establishments, and many empty lots. To the north, along Pelham Parkway, and to the west, down to the Bronx River, were groups of six-story apartment buildings. To the south and east were marshland and peninsulas jutting out into the East River and the Long Island Sound: **Clason Point**, a resort and amusement center with a ferry to **College Point**,

SOUNDVIEW

The community lying between the Bronx River and the parkway bearing the river's name. Cartoonist/playwright *Jules Feiffer* was raised here on Stratford Avenue when the area was predominantly Jewish (beginning with the arrival of the IRT Pelham Bay elevated in 1920). The population today is mostly Latino. Don't confuse it with adjacent Clason Point, the peninsula that really does have a view of Long Island Sound.

E2

Queens; **Ferry Point**; and **Throgs Neck**. To the east were the remnants of the old Village of Westchester, called Westchester Square, hardly recognizable. And beyond lay Pelham Bay Park, the borough's largest, stretching north to the Westchester County line, and City Island, an oasis in the Sound.

Then the New York Catholic Protectory grounds were purchased by the Metropolitan Life Insurance Company, and in February 1940 the first of the 40,000 tenants who were to populate red-brick, high-rise **Parkchester** moved in. The die was cast. Empty lots, cattail-filled swamp, even parts of Pelham Bay Park were to be decimated by the crush of a new population.

Today, the area south of Bruckner Boulevard is a phalanx of other red-brick housing projects. Hospital facilities occupy the marshy lands that fed Westchester Creek, now diminished by the construction of a behemoth high school only yards from Westchester Square. Two of the peninsulas are springboards for suspension bridges to Long Island. "Progress" came to the Eastern Bronx. Its effects are profound.

[E1] **Public School 152**, 1007 Evergreen Ave., NW cor. Bruckner Expwy. 1975. *Kahn & Jacobs.*

A composed earth-colored brick school that adds a whiff of gentle majesty to a physically humdrum neighborhood. Good view from the expressway.

CLASON POINT

A protuberance into either the Sound (or East River, depending on your geographical alliance). Labeled over the years by its successive occupants: Snakipins (the native American settlement), Cornell Point (after *Thomas Cornell*, 1642), and finally Clason Point (after *Isaac Clason*). Before the trolley came in 1910, access was via boat, launch, or steamer from Long Island, Mott Haven, and Manhattan. Attractions included dance halls and hotels, picnic grounds and a bathing pier, restaurants, a saltwater pool, and places with names like Gilligan's Pavilion,

Killian's Grove, and Kane's Casino. (Kane's Casino survived until a fire in 1942.) Prohibition, pollution, and competition (from filtered pools like easily accessible Starlight Park in nearby West Farms) finally doomed the resort area.

[E2] **Holy Cross Roman Catholic Church**, 600 Soundview Ave., NE cor. Taylor Ave. 1968. *Brother Cajetan J. B. Baumann, O.F.M.*

The 1960s confluence of **Vatican II** and wide acceptance of **modernism** unleashed many

E5

Catholic churches like this: swooping masonry walls, parabolic roofs, groovy stained glass.

[E3] **Bethlehem Evangelical Lutheran Church**, 327 Bolton Ave., bet. O'Brien and Soundview Aves. W side. ca. 1915.

White aluminum clapboard-sided church with neo-Federal trim. A bit of history for this history-starved community.

Harding Park, named for President Harding, was well described by the Times in 1981: "a folksy ramshackle village with an aura of another era. Its narrow macadam roads wander here and there, without benefit of sidewalks or street lamps, diverging off into muddy lanes and alleys. There are junked cars in driveways and wash drying on lines." Since then Puerto Ricans have moved in and transformed the neighborhood into a tight-knit, self-sufficient community, with paved streets and sewers. But ranks of endless, featureless row housing have taken over east of Bolton Avenue.

UNIONPORT

[E4] **White Plains Gardens** (apartments), 1221, 1223, 1225, 1227 White Plains Rd., bet. Gleason and Westchester Aves. W side. ca. 1929.

Enlightened middle-class housing: A privately sponsored for-profit miniproject: four six-story elevator apartment houses wrapped around a green center court entered through a **neo-Gothic** gateway.

VAN NEST

[E5] **Church of St. Dominic** (Roman Catholic), 1739 Unionport Rd., bet. Van Nest and Morris Park Aves. W side. 1926.

An asymmetrically placed Italian **Romanesque Revival** bell tower and a prominent spoked rose window brighten the narrow path of ancient Unionport Road.

E6

[E6] **1808-1814 Amethyst Street** (row houses), bet. Morris Park and Rhinelander Aves. E side. ca. 1895.

Common in **Mott Haven**, rare in Van Nest: brick, stone, and terra-cotta row houses, their stolid construction forms a healthy piece of history in this precinct of ephemeral materials.

PARKCHESTER

[E7] **Parkchester** (apartment development), E. Tremont Ave., Purdy St., McGraw Ave., Hugh J. Grant Circle, White Plains Rd. 1938-1942. Board of Design: *Richmond H. Shreve*, chairman; *Andrew J. Eken, George Gove, Gilmore D. Clarke, Robert W. Dowling, Irwin Clavan*, and *Henry C. Meyer, Jr.*

Called "a city within a city" in its early days, with direct subway access to Manhattan: included were a large movie theater, over 100 stores including Macy's first branch, a bowling alley and bar/restaurant, parking garages for 3,000 cars, and 40,000 residents at a density of 250,000 people per square mile! In planners' eyes, however, it was exceptionally thoughtful. Curving streets, well-kept lawn, shrubbery, and trees, carefully planned pedestrian routes and recreation areas, all calculated to inspire and delight whenever visual boredom set in. Metropolitan Life Insurance Company, its sponsor, maintained it for almost 30 years, until In 1968 it was sold to real estate giant Helmsley-Spear, Inc., who proceeded to co-op it, quadrant by quadrant.

Fantasia, a series of whimsical bronze sculptures set in and around the central pool, is worth a gander (*Raymond Granville Barger*, 1941).

[E8] **Parkchester Branch, N.Y. Public Library**, 1985 Westchester Ave., bet. Hugh J. Grant Circle and Pugsley Ave. N side. 1985. *Richard Dattner & Assocs.*, architects. *Marcia Dalby*, sculptor.

E8

A red-brick arch with inlaid white brick crosses defines a sturdily fenced semicircular forecourt that bids welcome to those strolling under the noisy Pelham Bay elevated. Apparently, the first to have entered the fenced enclosure were oversized plasticized beasties (thanks to the City's 1% for art program).

WESTCHESTER SQUARE

The now fractured green was the center of the old Village of Westchester, founded in 1653 and known as **Oostorp** under the Dutch. Between 1681 and 1759, while under British rule, the village was seat of the County of Westchester, of which the Bronx was then part. It is now the focus of neighborhood shopping and a stop on several bus lines.

[W1] **St. Peter's Church in the Village of Westchester** (Episcopal), 2500 Westchester Ave., opp. St. Peter's Ave. E side. 1853-1855. *Leopold Eidlitz*. Clerestory addition and restoration, 1879, *Cyrus L. W. Eidlitz*. ●
[W1a] Originally **St. Peter's Chapel and Sunday School**/now **Foster Hall**. 1867-1868. *Leopold Eidlitz*. ● [W1b] **St. Peter's Graveyard**. 1702+. ●

A tribute to the vitality of this dour **Gothic Revival** composition is that it has withstood the vibration and the visual pollution of passing trains on the adjacent IRT Pelham Bay elevated structure and has survived to be dubbed an official city landmark. Walk in the graveyard.

[W2] **Huntington Free Library and Reading Room**/originally **The Van Schaick Free Reading Room**, 9 Westchester Sq., bet. Westchester and Tratman Aves. W side. 1882-1883. *Frederick Clarke Withers*. **Addition** to rear, 1890-1892, *William Anderson*. ●

When advised of the cost of its upkeep, local taxpayers refused to accept this gift from a fellow resident, *Peter Van Schaick*. It was only opened in 1891 (together with an extension to the rear) through the efforts (and added funding) of railroad magnate *Collis P. Huntington*, who maintained a summer residence in nearby Throgs Neck.

[W3] **Owen Dolen Golden Age Center**, N.Y.C. Department of Parks & Recreation, Benson St., NW cor. Westchester Ave., Westchester Sq. Original park comfort station, 1927. Expanded and converted, New York Public Library, 1930s. Altered, 1983, *John Ciardullo Assocs.*

Dramatic use of concrete and brightly painted industrial forms gives life to a preexisting senior citizens' center marooned by asphalt and traffic.

[W4] **44-53 Westchester Square** (linked row houses), bet. Ponton and Roberts Aves. E side. ca. 1912.

Look carefully and your time invested reflecting on this structure's unified glazed surfaces will be well spent: glazed brick and glazed terra cotta wherever there are no windows or doors. A fascinating façade.

[W5] **Ferris Family Cemetery**, Commerce Ave. E of Westchester Sq., bet. Westchester Ave. and Butler Place. S side. 18th century.

As Woodlawn Cemetery is large, Ferris is small but surviving, considering that its once bucolic surroundings are now a grimy industrial area.

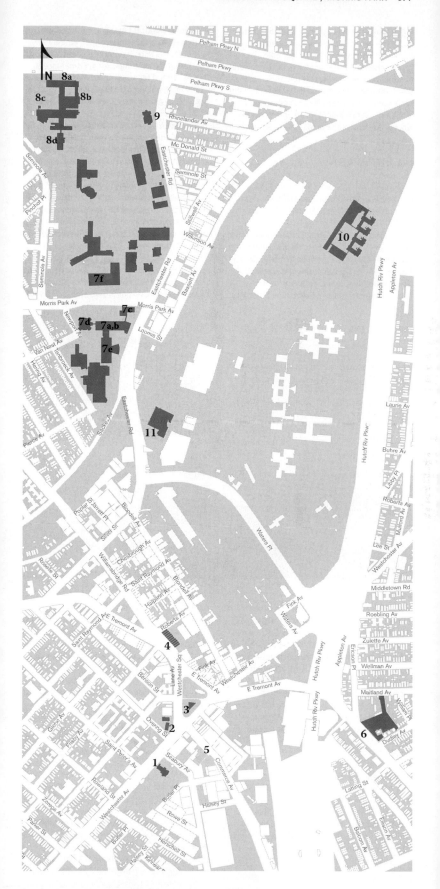

▥ [W6] **First Presbyterian Church in Throgs Neck**, 3051 E. Tremont Ave., bet. Ericson Place and Dudley Ave. N side. ca. 1880.

Perched comfortably on a hill above a series of stone retaining walls, this red brick, limestone-trimmed church (and its graveyard to the rear) seem oblivious to the changes evident along the avenue below. Its steeple is a noteworthy marking of the land.

MORRIS PARK

South of Pelham Parkway and West of Eastchester Road is a sprawling medical campus:

[W7] **Albert Einstein College of Medicine, Jack and Pearl Resnick Campus, Yeshiva University**, 1300 Morris Park Ave., bet. Eastchester Rd. and Seminole Ave. [W7a] **Forchheimer Medical Science Building**. 1955. *Kelly & Gruzen.* [W7b] **Friedman Lounge, Gottesman Library**

W7d

(within Forchheimer). 1958. *Kelly & Gruzen.* [W7c] **Ullman Research Center for Health Sciences**. 1963. *Kiesler & Bartos.* [W7d] Originally **Bassine**/now **Belfer Educational Center for Health Sciences**. 1971. *Armand Bartos & Assocs.* [W7e] **Chanin Institute Cancer Research Center**. 1976. *Schuman, Lichtenstein, Claman & Efron.* **Robbins Auditorium** (attached). 1958. *Kelly & Gruzen.*

▥ [W7f] **Price Center for Genetic and Translational Medicine/Harold and Muriel Block Pavilion**, Morris Park Ave., N side. 2008. *Payette Architects.*

Hospital complexes always grow (or seem to?), expanding and expanding. Here the Einstein campus has hurdled Morris Park Avenue to where a shapely, sharply glass research pavilion by *Payette Architects* gives *Pei Cobb Freed's* **Jacobi Medical Center Ambulatory Care Building**, just to the north, a run for its money. (If only geometry were currency.)

[W8] **Jacobi Medical Center**/originally **Bronx Municipal Hospital Center**, 1400 Pelham Pkwy. S., N of Morris Park Ave., W of Eastchester Rd. [W8a] **Original buildings**, 1955. *Pomerance & Breines.* [W8b] **Inpatient Building addition**, E side of main building. 2006. *Cannon Design.*

▥ [W8c] **Ambulatory Care addition**, W side of main building. 2009. *Pei Cobb Freed & Partners with daSilva Architects.* [W8d] **Rose F. Kennedy Center for Research in Mental Retardation and Human Development, Albert Einstein College of Medicine,** 1970. *Pomerance & Breines.*

Pomerance & Breines designed buildings for this complex for over 15 years. *Cannon's* 2006 addition is functional, with some half-hearted glass touches. *Pei's* sleek new addition, attached to the opposite side, has more convincing walls of glass, and atriums filled with natural light.

W8

W11

▥ [W9] **49th Precinct, N.Y.C. Police Department**, 2121 Eastchester Rd., opp. Rhinelander Ave. W side. 1985. *Smotrich & Platt,*

architects. *Ivan Chermayeff*, sculptor.

A geometric fantasy of a station house fronted by its own stand of—not trees—but blue-painted steel bulrushes.

The world's first air meets: On a 307-acre site, south of today's Pelham Parkway, between Bronxdale Avenue and Williamsbridge Road down to the former New Haven railroad right-of-way, some of the earliest public trials of powered aircraft were held in 1908 and 1909. Aviation pioneers Glenn H. Curtiss (and his partner Alexander Graham Bell) and Samuel P. Langley (of the Smithsonian) were drawn to the meets, as were as many as 20,000 spectators. The site had been, between 1889 and 1902, the Morris Park Racecourse, replacement for the earlier Jerome Park Racetrack, whose grounds in the West Bronx had been acquired to build the reservoir bearing the same name. Horse racing moved to Belmont Park in 1903; airplane meets moved too, and in 1910 a spectacular fire wiped out many of the remaining stables/hangars. Nary a trace of the course remains today save a blocked-up tunnel

W12

portal under Bronxdale Avenue, where crowded railroad coaches once deposited visitors to this onetime recreation mecca in the Bronx.

Bronx State Hospital campus:

[W10] **Bronx State Hospital Rehabilitation Center,** N.Y.S. Department of Mental Hygiene, 1500 Waters Place, bet. Eastchester Rd. and Hutchinson River Pkwy. N side. 1971. *Gruzen & Partners.*

Intricate in plan, an unassuming work.

[W11] **Bronx Children's Psychiatric Hospital, N.Y.S. Department of Mental Hygiene,** 1000 Waters Place, bet. Eastchester Rd. and Hutchinson River Pkwy. N side. 1969. *The Office of Max O. Urbahn.*

Domestically scaled interlinked units attempt to lessen the oppressive institutional quality of *Urbahn's* earlier Bronx State Hospital buildings.

PELHAM PARKWAY NEIGHBORHOOD

[W12] **Bronx Park Medical Pavilion**/former **Bronxdale Swimming Pool Facilities,** 2016 Bronxdale Ave. NE cor. Antin Place. ca. 1928.

Crowds of kids, mommas, and poppas no longer wait to plunge into the cool, chlorinated waters of this answer to the City's steamy summers. But the polychromed **Art Deco** terra-cotta ornament has been revived to house medical tenants.

[W13a] **2009 Cruger Avenue,** ca. 1930. **2039, 2055 Cruger Avenue,** ca. 1937. All bet. Bronxdale and Brady Aves. W side. [W13b] **2095, 2105 Cruger Avenue,** bet. Brady Ave. and Maran Place. W side. ca. 1938.

The West Bronx is **Art Deco/Art Moderne** heaven, but No.2009 (opposite the old Bronxdale Pool) is a special Deco work whose vermilion glazed terra cotta singles it out, although its owners thoughtlessly removed its

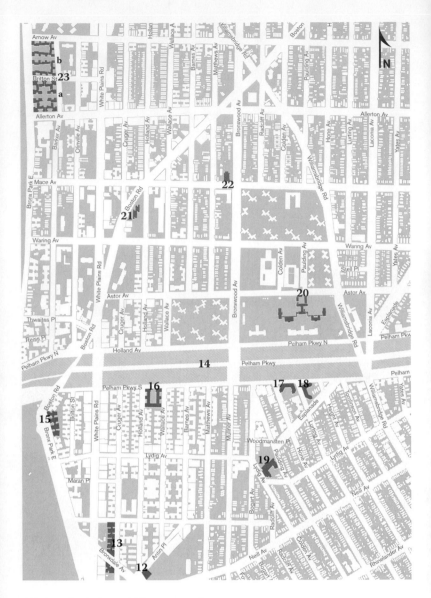

period metalwork after 1978. The casement windows of its Moderne neighbors up the block have been refenestrated, but the round-cornered fire escapes remain. Thank goodness!

[W14] Bronx and Pelham Parkway, connecting Bronx Park and Pelham Bay Park.

Usually referred to as Pelham Parkway, this wide and luxuriant greenway has not suffered from the widenings and removal of ancient trees that other thoroughfares in the City have undergone. Prior to World War II the center lanes were closed off on Sunday mornings for bicycle racing.

[W15] 2166 and 2180 Bronx Park East, bet. Lydig Ave. and Pelham Pkwy. S. E side. ca. 1937.

Six-story **Art Moderne** housing overlooking the lawns and trees of Bronx Park. The curse of the double-hung aluminum replacement sash has struck here as well.

[W16] Alhambra Gardens, 750-760 Pelham Pkwy., bet. Holland and Wallace Aves. S side. 1927. *Springsteen & Goldhammer.*

Unrepentantly romantic. The name **Alhambra** tells it all: Spanish tile, Spanish ironwork, Spanish detail all around a lush green courtyard. It's hard to accept that these are only well-planned six-story elevator apartments.

[W17] Morningside House (residence for the aged), **Reception Building,** 1000 Pelham Pkwy. S., bet. Lurting and Hone Aves. S side. **[W18] Administration and Medical Services Building,** bet. Lurting and Haight Aves. S side, through to Esplanade. All 1974. *Johnson Burgee.*

A rare architectural tribute to the dignity of our society's aged citizenry. An urbane pair of buildings with a carefully controlled, resortlike exterior, but without any reference to their Pelham Parkway context.

[W19] **Morris Park Station, IRT Dyre Avenue Line** (No.5 train)/originally on the former New York, Westchester & Boston Railway, The Esplanade at Paulding Ave. 1912. *Fellheimer & Long*, architects. *Allen H. Stem*, associated architect.

A **Spanish Colonial Revival** pavilion on axis of The Esplanade, a diagonal thoroughfare marking the 3,940-foot-long, cut-and-cover subway in which the defunct N.Y., W. & B. commuter line bypassed treelined Pelham Parkway.

BRONXDALE

[W20] **New York Institute for the Education of the Blind**, 999 Pelham Pkwy. N., bet. Bronxwood Ave. and Williamsbridge Rd. 1924. *McKim, Mead & White*.

An inoffensive campus of **neo-Georgian** buildings for the elementary and college-preparatory education of the blind and visually handicapped.

W13b

[W21] **2440 Boston Road**, N.Y.C. Housing Authority (apartments), bet. Waring and Mace Aves. E side. 1972. *Davis Brody & Assocs.*

1970s monumentalism: 20 stories of housing predominantly for the elderly. With a bit of visual sleight of hand, an otherwise bulky prism is made to look like three slender shafts offset slightly from one another. And to top off this architectural legerdemain, the tower is broader at the top (to accommodate larger apartments) than at the bottom, a technique that foreshadows more recent tall buildings (*Bernard Tschumi's* **Blue**, *Neil Denari's* **HL 23**) that swell at the top.

[W22] **Lourdes of America**, on grounds of St. Lucy's Roman Catholic Church, Bronxwood Ave., NW cor. Mace Ave. 1939. Open to the public.

Amazing. Outdoors a stone grotto rises high above the adjacent sidewalks as hundreds of **twinkling candles** in tiny red-glass containers, placed there by the devout who have come to share in the many cures claimed for this replica of the famous French shrine.

[W23] **Worker's Cooperative Colony/"The Coops"** (apartment development), Bronx Park E., bet. Allerton and Arnow Aves. to Barker Ave. [W23a] **First House**, 2700-2774 Bronx Park E., S of Britton St. 1925-1927. *Springsteen & Goldhammer.* [W23b] **Second House**, 2846-2870 Bronx Park E., N of Britton St. 1927-1929. *Herman J. Jessor of Springsteen & Goldhammer.*

The "Coops" (pronounced **COOPS**, not CO-ops). Walk-ups built under the sponsorship of the United Workers Cooperative Association, consisting largely of unionized Eastern European Jewish garment workers, a group with strong left-wing political attachments. That may explain the use of a hammer-and-sickle motif above an entry door of **First House** (otherwise designed in a neo-Tudor style quite commonly found in the Bronx in the 1920s). The later **Second House** dispensed with both the political symbolism and the picturesque stylizing.

W23

W23b

THROGS NECK

Spelled with one or two g's and sometimes with an apostrophe, the name once referred to the outermost peninsula of land beyond East Tremont Avenue's end. Its name is derived from *John Throckmorton*, who settled here in 1643 while New York was still under Dutch rule.

[T1a] **St. Joseph's School for the Deaf** (Roman Catholic)/originally **St. Joseph's Institute for the Improved Instruction of Deaf Mutes**, 1000 Hutchinson River Pkwy., SE cor. Bruckner Blvd. [T1b] **Msgr. Scanlan High School/St. Helena's Commercial High School** (Roman Catholic)/originally also **St. Joseph's School for the Deaf**, 55 Hutchinson River Pkwy., SW cor. Bruckner Blvd. Both ca. 1898. *Schickel & Ditmars.*

When the Hutchinson River Parkway was built in 1939 as the approach to the Bronx-Whitestone Bridge, it cut St. Joseph's campus in two. Later, when the children of Parkchester grew in numbers to be of high school age, the

W21

parish of St. Helena's established a new secondary school, using the west half of St. Joseph's holdings. From a distance at least, these seem the epitome of 19th-century gloom, now coming back into style.

[T2] **Preston High School** (Roman Catholic)/formerly **"Homestead,"** Collis P. Huntington (summer) House/originally **Frederick C. Havemeyer** House, 2780 Schurz Ave., SE cor. Brinsmade Ave. ca. 1870.

It's so rare that a summer house with a recorded history survives this long that one might forgive its lack of architectural distinction. A school since 1924, newer additions for high school use are unfortunate.

[T3] **Ferry Point Park**, bet. Westchester Creek and Hutchinson River Pkwy, and bet. Balcom Ave., Emerson Ave., and St. Raymonds Cemetery. Phase One: 2009. Phase Two: 2013. *Thomas Balsley Associates*, landscape architect, with *Karen Bausman*, architect.

A huge (222 acre) former landfill along the Sound, planned in 2000 as a PGA golf course that never happened. *Balsley* to the rescue! His projects (see **Riverside Park South** in Manhattan) work best when he keeps it simple (boardwalks and native grasses).

[T4] **Silver Beach Gardens Corporation**, Pennyfield and Schurz Aves. to Long Island Sound. (Entrance: Chaffee Ave. at Pennyfield Ave.)
[T5] Originally **Abijah Hammond House**/now Offices, Silver Beach Gardens Corporation, ca. 1800.

Originally summer cottages, now they are winterized. The *Hammond* house, with Federal detail, was built by a wealthy trader who moved here after serving the Revolution in Massachusetts. Later, sugar king *Frederick C. Havemeyer's* family occupied the house until 1914.

[T6] **Fort Schuyler**/now **SUNY Maritime College**, E end of Pennyfield Ave. ●✦

▦ [T7] **Fort Schuyler**. 1833-1856. *Capt. I. L. Smith.* Conversion to Maritime College 1934-1938. Conversion of fort's dining hall (gun galleries) to the **Adm. Stephen Bleecker Luce Library**, William A. Hall, 1967. [T8a] **Vander Clute Hall** (dormitory, dining). 1963. [T8b] **Riesenberg Hall** (health and physical education). 1965. [T8c] **Marvin-Tode Hall** (science and ocean engineering). 1967. 8a, b, & c by *Ballard Todd & Assocs.*

T1a

Second System, begun in 1807, was motivated by the potential danger from Great Britain that ended with the War of 1812. The Third System, unlike the first two (which had been responses to external threats), was initiated in a peaceful era in 1817 and continued until the time of the Civil War. Both Fort Schuyler and Fort Totten (1862-1864) were built as part of this Third System, to be able to rake with cannon fire any enemy approaching the port of New York via the Long Island Sound.

[T9] **St. Frances de Chantal Church** (Roman Catholic), 190 Hollywood Ave., SE cor. Harding Ave. 1971. *Paul W. Reilly.*

It's hard to miss this football-shaped church. Perhaps that's one of its faults. No faulting its stained glass, however—colorful chunks in the European style precast into concrete window panels.

[T10] **Modular House,** 3272 Tierney Place bet. Longstreet Ave. and Throgs Neck Expressway.

T11

Don't be put off by the gate: all are welcome; stop and drive on. A tour along the perimeter road (it changes names a number of times) of this narrow neck of land will reveal views of Long Island Sound that make looking at the college's architecture difficult. Old Fort Schuyler itself is well worth a stop to visit its interior court (called **St. Mary's Pentagon**) and to savor views from its ramparts, constructed of Connecticut granite, 5 to 11 feet thick. Another 19th-century fortress (and landmark), **Fort Totten**, across the Sound, is more easily seen from here than from its home borough of Queens. Abandoned between 1878 and 1934, then WPA funds enabled restoration for reuse.

Protecting our sea approaches: America's seacoast fortifications were developed in three stages. The First System was started in 1794 when it was feared that we might be drawn into wars that followed the French Revolution. The

2008. *Joseph Tanney and Robert Luntz of Resolution: 4 Architecture.*

Tanney and *Luntz's* small firm has done big things in recent years designing and building handsome modern housing using factory-assembled parts. Here they employ walls of cement panels and cedar in two modules, shipped to and installed on site.

All by itself to the northwest:

[T11] **714 Clarence Avenue** (house), bet. Randall and Philip Aves. NE side. ca. 1920.

The views over Long Island Sound make a drive along this part of Clarence Avenue unlike any other in the City. No.714 is encrusted with mosaics applied in a vernacular style. So is the garage—even the birdhouse.

PELHAM BAY

Named for the adjacent park, this community lies west of it, contained by the Hutchinson River Parkway, Bruckner Boulevard/Expressway, and on the south by St. Raymond's (Roman Catholic) Cemetery.

[P1] **Middletown Plaza** (apartments), N.Y.C. Housing Authority, 3033

P3

Middletown Rd., bet. Hobart and Jarvis Aves. NW side. 1973. *Paul Rudolph.*

Monumentally scaled housing for the elderly, the late *Rudolph's* best work in the borough: a tall, dramatic cast-concrete frame, gray, ribbed block infill, and gray window sashes. One of the Bronx's notable architectural apartment houses.

[P2] **Pelham Bay Branch, N.Y. Public Library,** 3060 Middletown Rd., SE cor. Jarvis Ave. 1976. *Alexander A. Gartner.*

A modest modern library with an inviting plaza.

[P3] **St. Theresa of the Infant Jesus** (Roman Catholic) Church, 2855 St. Theresa Ave., NW cor. Pilgrim Ave. 1970. *Anthony J. DePace.*

Heavily ornamented with robust stained glass and mosaic tile tesserae. The old church's bell is displayed across the street, and the inscription locates the original church at Pilgrim and Morris Park Avenues. (St. Theresa Avenue is the eastern extension of Morris Park Avenue; its name was changed in 1968.)

[P4] **Pelham Bay Park**

The largest of six parks purchased in the new Bronx parks program of 1883. It contains two golf courses, an archery range, bridle paths, the Police Department firing range (private), and ample facilities for hiking, cycling, horseback riding, and motoring. Shell racing is held in the North Lagoon. Between 1910 and 1913 a monorail traversed the park from the New Haven Railroad line to City Island.

[P5] **Pelham Bay Park World War Memorial,** Shore Rd. E of Bruckner Expwy. SE side. ca. 1925. *John J. Sheridan*, architect. *Belle Kinney*, sculptor.

A handsome, well-maintained monument.

[P6] **Bartow-Pell Mansion Museum**/originally **Robert and Marie Lorillard Bartow House**, Pelham Bay Park, Shore Rd. near Pelham-Split Rock Golf Course, S side. 1675. Alterations, 1836-1842, attributed to *Minard Lafever.* Restoration, 1914, *Delano & Aldrich.* Carriage House restoration, *Jan Hird Pokorny Assocs.* Interiors. Open to the public. 718-885-1461. We, Sa, Su, 12-4; closed Mo, Tu, Th, Fr.

Lords of the Manor of Pelham once owned this house. Its exterior is **Federal,** but *Pell* "modernized" the interior in **Greek Revival**. The mansion became the home of the International Garden Club in 1914. The *Pell* family plot, a magnificent formal garden, a view of Long Island Sound from the grounds, and rare and tasteful furnishings within combine to make a visit worthwhile.

P6

[P7] **Orchard Beach Bath House and Promenade,** E shore of Pelham Bay Park on Long Island Sound. 1934-1937. N.Y.C. Parks Department, *Aymar Embury II*, consulting architect; *Gilmore Clarke and Michael Rapuano*, consulting landscape architects.

A large, sandy, crescent beach reconstructed in 1936 after extensive remodeling by the WPA and the Department of Parks. The bathhouses, elegantly spartan in a **modern Classical** style, are enhanced by strong concrete colonnades that radiate outward from a raised central terrace; they are chastely decorated with blue terra-cotta tiles and yet are monumental without being overpowering. A beach cafeteria rests under the spacious entry terrace.

CITY ISLAND

A tight little island, part of New York City by law but with scarcely any other connections. Its first industry was the **Solar Salt Works** (1830), which made salt by evaporating seawater. Then came oystering and eventually yacht building. Filmmaking came to the island around 1900, together with *D. W. Griffith, Douglas Fairbanks, and the Keystone Kops*, who filmed a scene on

C2

Fordham Street. Fish and seafood fanciers are today's most important asset to the island's economy: City Island Avenue is filled with restaurants of every description.

On the streets that run perpendicular to the fishbone spine of City Island Avenue are more than a handful of distinguished older houses, now engulfed by latter-day lightweights. There is space to mention only a few:

[C1] **Samuel Pell House**, 586 City Island Avenue, bet. Bridge and Cross Sts. E side. ca. 1876. 🖤

A well-preserved **Second Empire** house, built by oysterman *Samuel Pell*. Note the vigorous mansarded roof, dormers, and original polychrome slate shingles.

[C2] **21 Tier Street** (house), W of City Island Ave. N side. ca. 1894.

A **Shingle Style** jewel. To own this would be reason enough to move to City Island. If only these venerable shingles would have proliferated.

[C3] **City Island Nautical Museum**/originally
Public School 17, Bronx, 190 Fordham St., E of
City Island Ave. S side. 1898. *C.B.J. Snyder.* Open
to the public (limited hours).

A stolid school, by the dean of New York
City's early school architects, that dates from
the very year of the City's consolidation. This
one, properly, is a modest work befitting a
remote outpost.

[C4] **284 City Island Avenue** (apartments), bet.
Fordham and Hawkins Sts. E side. ca. 1898.

C3

C4

C8

A 19th-century high (for City Island) rise. Its
gambrel roof and **Palladian** window add a bit of
dynamic scale to the Avenue.

Schofield Street, west of City Island Avenue:

[C5] **65 Schofield St.** (house). N side. ca.
1865. [C6] **62 Schofield St.** S side. ca. 1865.
No.65, serene and peeling, seems a candidate for a *Hopper* painting: austere, venerable,
self-confident with classic style.

[C7] **84-86 Schofield St.** (house). S side. ca. 1875.
Squat, sturdy and solitary, with a grand
mansard. Its monumental porch is enlivened by
French doors (instead of windows) opening onto
it. Check **No.90** next door as well.

[C8] **95 Pell Place** (house), W of City Island Ave.
N side. 1930.
It may be only an **Arts and Crafts** bungalow
from the Sears Roebuck catalog, but it's a
dynamic winner. The masonry-piered and tim-

ber-bracketed porch brings deeply shaded and
shadowed form to the street. Wonderful.

[C9] **Grace Church** (Episcopal), 104 City Island
Ave., SE cor. Pilot St. 1867. **Rectory**, ca. 1862.
A pair of gems that befits an off-the-beaten-
track seafaring community. The church is a
paragon of **Gothic Revival** wood craftsmanship.
The rectory is a modest frame structure derived
from the Italian Villa Style.

[C10] **141 Pilot Street** (house), NE cor. City
Island Ave. ca. 1862.
A flat-roofed **Italianate** delight, with lathe-
turned porch posts, stepped brackets, and eyebrow windows. The flush boards hoped to simulate stuccoed masonry.

[C11] **175 Belden Street House**, E of City
Island Ave. to the water. N side. ca. 1880.
(Down a single lane, dead-end street: walk.)
A most well preserved **picturesque** cottage,
rare in the City, located almost at the southern-

most tip of the island. A festival of jigsaw brackets, brackets, crossed stick-work, corbelled chimneys.

If you are in need of refreshment at this point, seafood is the logical option here. Johnny's Reef is a classic old Bronx clam shack, right on the water at the end of City Island Avenue. Smelts, red snapper, whiting, scallops, shrimp, cherrystones, little necks.

NECROLOGY

Bronx Developmental Center, N.Y.S. Department of Mental Hygiene, Waters Place bet. Eastchester Rd. and Hutchinson River Pkwy. N side. 1976. *Richard Meier & Assocs.*
   Dramatically located on a spacious, serene site along the Parkway's edge, its long, prismatic forms evoked the majesty of a rectilinear dirigible. Clad in a tightly stretched skin, it seemed fabricated by aircraft technicians, not by earthbound building contractors. A consummate work of architecture, it will be sorely missed.

Formerly Rectory, St. Peter's Church (Episcopal)/later **Westchester-Bronx YMCA**,

C9

C11

2244 Westchester Ave., bet. Castle Hill and Havemeyer Aves. S side. Parkchester. 1850.
   A neglected red-brick Victorian country House, one of the last of its type in New York, was replaced by a spanking new Y.

Monastery of St. Clare (Roman Catholic), 142 Hollywood Ave., bet. Schurz Ave. and Monsignor Halpin Place. N side. 1933. *Robert J. Riley.*
   An eclectic blend of north European medieval crossed with virtuoso bricklaying. The entrance gable signified a simplified Jesuitical façade. EGO • VOS • SEMPER • CUSTODIAM (let me always watch over you). But who was watching over the Monastery? The Little Sisters of the Poor, as it turns out, who demolished it in favor of an architecturally banal (forgive us, Sisters!) residence hall.

Museum of the American Indian, Heye Foundation Annex, Bruckner Blvd., SW cor. Middletown Rd.
   This was a warehouse and research center for the museum whose public galleries are in the old Custom House at Bowling Green in Manhattan. Totem poles, Indian houses, and concrete wigwams were displayed on the lawns, but you couldn't go inside because you weren't allowed. Now you can't go inside because it's gone.

Rice Memorial Stadium, Pelham Bay Park, NW of Middletown Rd. and Stadium Ave. 1922. *Herts & Robertson.*
   This concrete stadium was unusual because of the small Greek temple atop the bleachers that frames *Louis St. Lannes'* heroic statue *American Boy*. The stadium was given to the City by the widow of *Isaac L. Rice* as part of a complex of other athletic facilities, and a decorative 100-foot white marble Doric column. The stadium was demolished in 1989. *American Boy* was restored and reinstalled near its original position in 2004.

Northern Bronx

The **Northern Bronx** has been the site of settlement since the 17th century, and for two months in the 18th century the nation's executive mansion was here. But most of this area's modest homes and scattered groups of apartment houses (as well as gargantuan **Co-op City**) date from the 20th.

WILLIAMSBRIDGE

[N1] **Eastchester Heights**/originally **Hillside Homes**, almost five city blocks, W of Boston Rd. bet. Wilson Ave. and Eastchester Rd. through to

N5

N8

N2

Hicks St. bet. Wilson and Fenton Aves. 1935. *Clarence S. Stein.*

Is it not possible to duplicate this highly successful moderate-rental housing development? Most of the buildings here are only four stories high, and they occupy one-third of the land. A large central playground and community center are provided for school-age children, while sandboxes and tot lots are placed away from street traffic inside seven large sunken interior courts reached through tunnel passageways. The design builds upon *Stein's* earlier **Sunnyside Gardens**.

[N2] **Private Chapel** (Roman Catholic), 740 E.215th St. bet. Holland and Barnes Ave. S side. 1905. *Frank Lisanti.*

In contrast to public devotions at Lourdes of America, a place for private meditation: a humble chapel transposed from the slopes of southern Italy. Below the bell and the ornate wrought ironwork cross is carved:

F. LISANTI IN DEVOZIONE DELL' IMMACOLATA PER SE E FAMIGLIA ERESSE 1905
(*F. Lisanti erected [this] for himself and his family in devotion to the Blessed Virgin, 1905.*)

[N3] **Regent School**, Kindergarten and Primary Grades, 719 E.216th St., bet. White Plains Rd. and Barnes Ave. N side. ca. 1915.

Four economically spaced **Doric** columns carry a substantial pediment ornamenting a sprightly (if somewhat officious-appearing) structure in this modest, lower-middle-income community.

[N4] **Crawford Memorial United Methodist Church**, 3757 White Plains Rd., bet. E.217th and E.218th Sts., W side. ca. 1890.

Rockfaced random ashlar, with great arched openings and blind brownstone arches relieving the dour Fordham gneiss ashlar mass.

[N5] **Emmanuel Baptist Church**, 3711 White Plains Rd., bet. E.216th and E.217th Sts. W side. ca. 1895.

A powerful **Romanesque Revival** brick and terra-cotta church stands resplendent atop an earthen berm. The colonnettes at re-entrant tower corners are a late Victorian game in structural display. And what a nice hat.

[N6] Originally **St. Luke's Episcopal Church**, 661 E.219th St., bet. Carpenter Ave. and White Plains Rd. opp. Willett Ave. N side. ca. 1885.

A country church of shingles, stucco, and half timber, engulfed by an early, urbanizing Bronx. Its space has been shared, in an **ecumenical marathon**, by St. George's Episcopalians, St. Luke's Senior Center, the Emmanuel Seventh Day Adventists, and the Restoration Church of God!

[N7] **Peter Gillings Apartments**, 737 E.219th St., bet. White Plains Rd. and Barnes Ave. N side. ca. 1905.

The rock-faced stone and brick façade of this early (for this neighborhood) three-story multiple dwelling proudly proclaims its developer's name.

[N8] **St. Peter's Evangelical Lutheran Church**, 741 E.219th St., bet. White Plains Rd. and Barnes Ave. N side. ca. 1898.

A naive **Shingle Style** church with intact brown-stained shingles and white trim. Ever see wood-shingled buttresses before? Wonderful.

[N9] **First Presbyterian Church of Williamsbridge** and Rectory, 730 E.225th St., bet. White Plains Rd. and Barnes Ave. S side. 1903. *John Davidson.*

A provincial shingled masterpiece. Asymmetrical, its square belfry to one side bears a marvelous ogival roof atop four sets of paired pilasters. Worth a special visit.

[N10] **47th Precinct**, N.Y.C. Police Department, 4111 Laconia Ave., bet. E.229th and E.230th Sts. W side. 1974. *Davis, Brody & Assocs.*

It took the 1970s to encourage such overly contrived design. Handsomely done, but hell to maintain.

BAYCHESTER

[B1] **Junior High School 144, The Michelangelo School**, 2545 Gunther Ave., SW cor. Allerton Ave. 1968. *The Office of Max O. Urbahn.*

Entirely of cast-in-place concrete, in a 1960s strive for more advanced construction techniques. Raw concrete suffers from pollution and graffiti, and JHS 144 has weathered both.

[B2] **Co-op City**. Northern section: E of New England Thruway/ Baychester Ave. bet. Co-op City Blvd. and Bartow Ave. Southern section: E of Hutchinson River Pkwy. E., bet. Bartow and

B3

N9

Boller Aves. 1968-1970. *Herman J. Jessor*, architect. *Zion & Breen*, landscape architects.

Out in the middle of nowhere, on marshy land that was once the site of an ill-fated amusement park named Freedomland, a group of government officials, union representatives, and housing developers dreamed the impossible dream. Today the dream may better be described as a coma. From out of the pumped-sand fill rises a mountain range of 35-story residential towers, 35 of them, plus 236 clustered two-family houses and eight multistory parking garages. In addition, there are three shopping centers, a heating plant, a firehouse, and an educational park consisting of two public schools, two intermediate schools, and a high school. In this total non-environment, largely designed by bureaucrats with not a scintilla of wit, live some 55,000 souls, many of whom vacated sound accommodations in the West Bronx (in many cases Art Deco apartment blocks) to move here.

Let's be thankful for the landscaping. It's the best thing at Co-op City.

[B3] **Iglesia Evangelica de Co-op City Church**, 2350 Palmer Ave.. bet. Stilwell Ave. and the Hutchinson River Pkwy. 2005. *Gluckman Mayner.*

Church and community center, this modern church brings a breath of vitality to the dreary blocks of Co-op City.

EASTCHESTER

[B4] **Public School 15**, (Annex to P.S.68)/formerly **Public School 148**/originally **Village of Eastchester public school**, 4010 Dyre Ave., bet. Dark and Lustre Sts. E side. 1877. *Simon Williams.*

An architectural "pot of gold" at the end of the Dyre Avenue IRT. The wood bracketed eaves and sprightly tower of this brick schoolhouse bring a smile. P.S.15 wound up on New York City's side when Eastchester was split in two.

WAKEFIELD

▮ [B5] **St. Anthony's Church** (Roman
Catholic), 4501 Richardson Ave., NW cor.
E.239th St. 1975. *Belfatto & Pavarini.*
   Strong, serrated, and sinuous brick rise to a
tall slender pylon bearing a carefully detailed
cross.

[B6] **St. Paul's Slovak Evangelical Lutheran
Church**, 729 Cranford Ave., bet. White Plains Rd.
and Barnes Ave. N side. 1928. Altered, 1962.
   A small but singular ashlar stone church
distinguished by a trio of bronze bells embraced
by the crest of its façade.

NECROLOGY

**St. Valentine's Roman Catholic Church and
Parish Hall**, 809 E.220th St., bet. Barnes and
Bronxwood Aves. N side. ca. 1890.

Necrology, 4577 Carpenter Avenue

B2

The last edition of this Guide: "skip the
newer masonry church on East 221st Street, and
gaze upon the old wood-frame hall behind—
was it the original meeting place of the congregation?—before it falls to the march of
progress."
   As it happened, "progress" turned out to be
a parking lot.

4577 Carpenter Avenue (house), SW cor.
W.240th St. ca. 1880.
   A house in the Eastlake Style with imbricated shingles on the Carpenter Avenue
frontage and clapboard siding elsewhere.
Replaced by a row of boxes in the neo-Banal
style.

**Formerly Engine Company No.69, N.Y.C. Fire
Department**, 243 E. 233rd St., bet. E. 234th St.
and Katonah Ave. Woodlawn. ca. 1895.
   This lusty wood frame firehouse stood
almost in Westchester County. In this outpost of
New York, no wonder the structure looked more
like a barn than a municipal facility. Replaced by
a dull fireproof version.

24th Ward School/later **Evander Childs High
School Annex**/later **Resthaven Nursing Home**,
225 E.234th St., bet. Kepler and Katonah Aves.
N side. Woodlawn. 1893. *C.B.J. Snyder.*
   A fake white Colonial portico had obscured
a great Romanesque Revival façade. Fire eventually resulted in its demolition.

STATEN ISLAND
Borough of Staten Island / Richmond County

 Colonial

 Georgian / Federal

 Greek Revival

 Gothic Revival

 Villa

 Romanesque Revival

 Renaissance Revival

 Roman Revival

 Art Deco / Art Moderne

 Modern / Postmodern

 Designated Landmark

For most tourists, Staten Island is merely the terminus of a spectacular ferry ride. Few venture ashore to explore. From such thoroughfares as Bay Street or Hylan Boulevard the views are discouraging: drab brick houses, huge gasoline stations, and gaudy pizza parlors predominate. **Persevere.** Behind the listless dingy façades are hills as steep as San Francisco's, with breathtaking views of the New York harbor; mammoth, crumbling mansions surrounded by mimosa and rhododendron, rutted dirt roads, four-foot black snakes, and fat, wild pheasant. There are Dutch farmhouses, Greek temples, Victorian mansions beyond *Charles Addams'* wildest fantasies, and ridges where archaeologists still find Indian artifacts.

The roughly triangular island is 13.9 miles long and 7.5 miles wide, 2 1/2 times the size of Manhattan, and ranks third in area among the City's boroughs.

Hills and dales: one is frequently aware of being on an island. There is a slight salty dampness in the air, a brackish smell, a buoy braying forlornly in the distance, a feeling of isolation.

Down the backbone of the island, from St. George to Richmondtown, runs a range of hills formed by an outcropping of serpentine rock. These hills—**Fort, Ward, Grymes, Emerson, Todt,** and **Lighthouse**—are dotted with elegant mansions of the 19th and 20th centuries, many of them now occupied by private schools and charitable institutions. Todt Hill, often proclaimed the highest point on the Atlantic coast, is a dinky 409.2 feet compared with Cadillac Mountain at 1,532 on Maine's Mt. Desert Island. The views, however, are justly famous.

Links to the Mainland: In the north, the steel arch of the **Bayonne Bridge**, opened in 1931, connects Port Richmond and Bayonne. In the northwest, the **Goethals Bridge**, a cantilever structure built in 1928, joins Howland Hook and Elizabeth. In the southwest is the **Outerbridge Crossing**—named not for its remoteness from Manhattan but for *Eugenius H. Outerbridge*, first chairman of the Port of N.Y. Authority. It also opened in 1928 and spans the Arthur Kill between Charleston and Perth Amboy. The **Verrazano-Narrows Bridge**, completed in 1964, provides a crossing to Brooklyn and is responsible for the land (and people) boom that has swelled Staten Island's population ever since.

History books notwithstanding, Staten Island was first "discovered" by the Algonquin Indians. It was first seen by a European, *Giovanni da Verrazano*, in 1524, and was named Staaten Eylandt 85 years later by *Henry Hudson* while on a voyage for the Dutch East India Company. Following a number of unsuccessful attempts, the first permanent settlement, by 19 French and Dutch colonists, was established in 1661 near the present South Beach. The island was renamed Richmond (after *King Charles II's* illegitimate son, the *Duke of Richmond*) following the English capture of New Amsterdam in 1664.

STATEN ISLAND

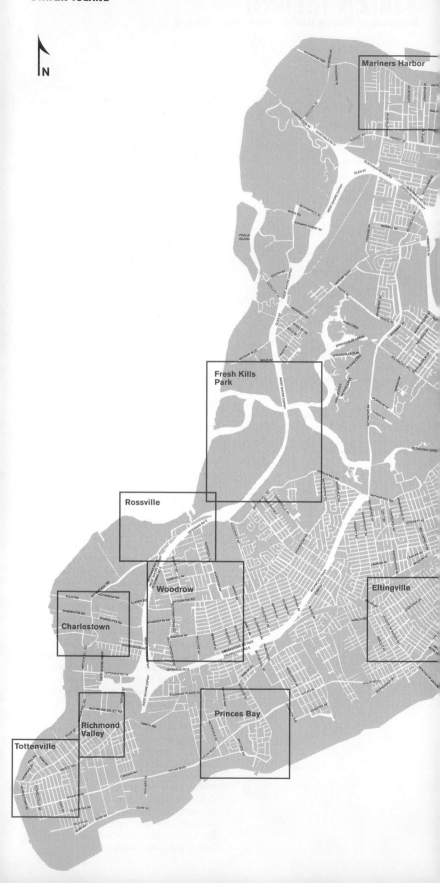

West Brighton / Port Richmond

New Brighton (West) / Livingston

St. George

New Brighton (East)

Tompkinsville / Stapleton / Stapleton Heights

Grymes Hill

Clifton / Rosebank

Westerleigh

Todt Hill

Arrochar

Richmond Town

New Dorp

REAR VIEW OF BOROUGH HALL,   ST. GEORGE, STATEN ISLAND, N. Y.

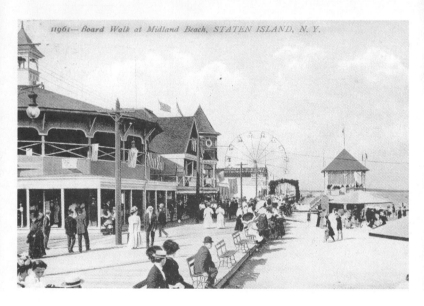

11961— Board Walk at Midland Beach, STATEN ISLAND, N. Y.

At the beginning of the 19th century a 16-year-old's $100 investment in a passenger-and-produce ferry across New York harbor marked the first successful business venture of a native-born islander, *Cornelius Vanderbilt*. As a result of such improved access across New York Bay the island began, in the 1830s, to develop into a summer retreat for wealthy, if not particularly prominent, families from New York and the South, who moved into the New Brighton area. A small literary colony sprang up around the eminent eye specialist *Dr. Samuel MacKenzie Elliott. James Russell Lowell, Henry Wadsworth Longfellow*, and *Francis Parkman* came to *Elliott* for treatment and stayed on the island to recuperate. Here Italy's patriot, *Giuseppe Garibaldi*, lived in exile, and *Frederick Law Olmsted* opened an experimental wheat farm. But Staten Island's connection with famous people has always been rather tenuous; more typical were gentleman farmers, shipbuilders, and oyster captains.

The rural nature of the island, however, did attract the sporting set from across the bay. Here the first lawn tennis court in America was built in 1880, and the first American canoe club founded. Lacrosse, cricket, rowing, fox hunting, fishing, bathing, and cycling engaged weekend enthusiasts. But by the beginning of the 20th century, the island's popularity had begun to wane. Fantastic schemes worthy of *Barnum and Bailey* were developed in a last-ditch attempt to lure the tourist trade. One promoter imported *Buffalo Bill's* Wild West Show, complete with sharpshooting *Annie Oakley*, "Fall of Rome" spectacles, and herds of girls and elephants.

Northern Staten Island

ST. GEORGE

[N1] St. George Ferry Terminal, Richmond Terrace bet. Bay and Wall Sts. 2005. *HOK.*
Both the Staten Island (**St. George**) and Manhattan (**Whitehall**) ferry terminals were finally rebuilt and opened in 2005. Thank God! Waiting for and disembarking from the ferry is no longer the most depressing experience known to humankind. At St. George, the terminal ceiling, supported by expressive structural steel, soars, with a wall of glass allowing riders to actually see the sea (harbor). An arch of tilted columns hovers above, the remnant of a

[N3] "Postcards" (Staten Island September 11 Memorial), North Shore Waterfront Esplanade, E of Hamilton Ave. 2004. *Masayuki Sono.*
270 victims of the **September 11** terrorist attacks were Staten Islanders; *Sono's* beautifully minimalist memorial resembles two unmailed envelopes gesturing towards the Manhattan skyline.

Richmond Terrace: between Borough Place and Hamilton Avenue. A grand (but incomplete)

N1

N3

more ambitious terminal/entertainment/museum complex intended for the site, designed by *HOK* and *Peter Eisenman* (ca. 2001), but never built.

[N2] Richmond County Bank Ballpark, 75 Richmond Terrace, bet. Wall St. and Hamilton Ave. 2001. *HOK Sport.*
Bland on the outside despite festive tensile steel here and there, but forget the exterior and go inside. Savor the brilliant green of the field set against the blue of the harbor, with the **Manhattan skyline** as backdrop beyond the outfield wall! Home to the **Staten Island Yankees,** a minor league affiliate of the Bronx Bombers. What a place to watch a game! What a place to just watch.

scheme of civic structures initiated by Staten Island's first borough president, George Cromwell.

[N4] Staten Island Borough Hall, Richmond Terr., NW cor. Nick La Porte Pl. 1904-1906. *Carrère & Hastings.* 🍎
Picturesque, this elegant brick structure, in the style of a **French hôtel de ville,** welcomes those arriving by ferry. And a nice greeting for architect *John Carrère* on his way home.

[N5] Richmond County Court House, 12-24 Richmond Terr., SW cor. Schuyler St. Designed, 1913. Completed, 1919. *Carrère & Hastings.* 🍎
A grand **Roman Corinthian**-columned portico and pediment provide pomp missing from the more people-friendly Borough Hall next door.

N5

[N6] **120th Precinct, N.Y.C. Police Department**/originally 66th Precinct/Borough Police Headquarters, 78 Richmond Terr., NW cor. Wall St. 1922. *James Whitford, Sr.* 🔹

A bland **Italian Renaissance** limestone palazzo, pale in comparison with *Whitford's* gutsy police station in Tottenville.

[N7] **Richmond County Family Courthouse**, 100 Richmond Terr., bet. Wall St. and Hamilton Ave. W side. 1933. *Sibley & Fetherston.* 🔹

It could be a *Robert Adam*–inspired country house, its terra-cotta façade presenting elegant Ionic columns to the visitor.

[N8] **N.Y.C. Department of Health Building**, 51 Stuyvesant Pl., bet. Wall St. and

N7

Hamilton Ave. E side. ca. 1935. *Henry C. Pelton.*

Modest Municipal mid-Depression **Art Deco**. Doesn't hold a candle to the Ambassador Apartments, on nearby Daniel Low Terrace.

[N9] **Staten Island Museum, Staten Island Institute of Arts and Sciences**, 75 Stuyvesant Pl., NE cor. Wall St. 1918, 1927, 1999 (addition). *Robert W. Gardner.* Open to the public.

A sleepy museum, bulging from its small **Georgian Revival** building. An ambitious new building by *Peter Eisenman* (2001), designed for a site next to the new ferry terminal, was never built. So the museum remains here, not there.

[N10] **St. George Branch, N.Y. Public Library**, 10 Hyatt St., SE cor. Central Ave. 1906. *Carrère & Hastings.* Altered, 1987, *David Paul Helpern.* Stained glass, *David Wilson.*

A bland hulk from these usually elegant architects: one of a group of four **Carnegie** gifts that began to bring a semblance of culture to the rural island early in the century. The other three are smaller, but with some style.

[N11] **St. George Apartments/Theater**, N side of Hyatt St., opposite Central Ave.

The height and bulk of the building, along with giant eagles that top it, announced the urban aspirations of St. George.

Behind the Bay Street wall:

[N12] **National Lighthouse Museum** (proposed): **Workshops**, 1864 and 1884; **Storage Vaults**, 1864; **Lampshops**, 1868 and 1902; **Foundry (Building 11)**, 1915. Restoration, 2005, *Jan Hird Pokorny Associates.*

[N13] Formerly **Administration Building, U.S. Coast Guard Base**, St. George/originally Office Building, U.S. Lighthouse Service, Third District Depot, 1 Bay St., S of Ferry Terminal. 1869.

N8

Alfred B. Mullett, Supervising Architect of the Treasury. Wings, 1901. 🔹

A group of historic but neglected waterfront structures, planned as a lighthouse museum, but not even in the pipeline. Locals are justifiably upset; with funding and city backing it could re-energize the St. George waterfront.

The central landmarked **Administration Building** is a crumbling ruin (gaping holes in the roof, broken windows, trees growing from dilapidated eaves): three mansard-roofed stories of granite and red brick, designed in the **French Second Empire** style by its American master *Mullett,* architect of those other (much larger) gems, Washington's old State, War, and Navy Department Building (saved as the Executive Office Building) and the old New York General Post Office in City Hall Park (demolished).

[N14] **Tower/Bridge**, Base of Bay St. 1996. *Siah Armajani*, artist. *Johansson & Walcavage*, landscape architects.

Staten Island takes a page here from the book of Battery Park City in an attempt to revi-

N13

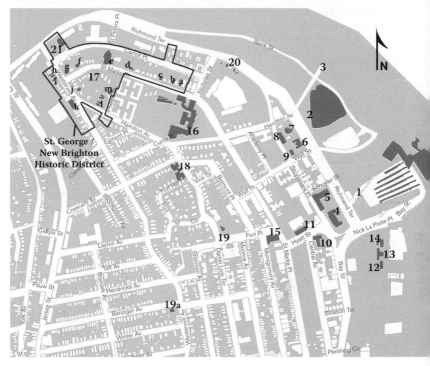

talize its waterfront: an artist's installation in the form of a symbolic bridge and lighthouse, poetry incorporated in its fence (the work of *Wallace Stevens*). Fussy.

Off to St. Mark's Place:
Between Fort Place and Westervelt Avenue, north side.

[N15] Brighton Heights Reformed Church, 320 St. Mark's Pl., SW cor. Fort Pl. 1999.
A fire in 1996 demolished the original landmark church (1866, *John Correja*). This less inspiring replacement has avoided any potential landmark status. Since we spoke in 2000 it has gained a spire.

[N16] Curtis High School, 105 Hamilton Ave, NW cor. St. Mark's Pl. 1902-1904. *C.B.J. Snyder*. Additions, 1922, 1925, 1937. Continued alterations. ●
Collegiate Gothic as applied to secondary-school education. Its lofty site and strong archi-

tectural forms add appropriately to its physical prominence as Staten Island's first municipal structure to be completed after Richmond County was absorbed into Greater New York in 1898.

Hotel Castleton was opened in 1889, in the days when Brighton Heights was a well-known resort. It was a 400-room wood-frame behemoth by architect C.P.H. Gilbert, just across St. Mark's Place from today's Curtis High School, where two large apartment towers now stand. The hotel was destroyed in 1907 in a spectacular fire, a depiction of which can be found among Borough Hall's lobby murals.

St. Mark's Place turns softly to the west at Nicholas Street:

[N17] St. George/New Brighton Historic District, 1-135 & 2-136 Carroll Place, 1-135 & 2-136 St. Mark's Place, 30-106 Westervelt Ave., 404-418 Richmond Terrace, 263-273 & 222-230 Hamilton Ave., and Phelps Place. ●

Seventy-eight buildings of an early planned suburban community, mostly from the 1880s and 1890s: **Queen Anne, Colonial Revival, Shingle Style** all are present.

Within the Historic District:

[N17a] Originally **Henry H. Cammann House**, 125 St. Mark's Pl., bet. Nicholas St. and Westervelt Ave. N side. 1895. *Edward Alfred Sargent.*

A squat conical-capped tower, its eyebrow windows peering outward, bellies to the street in this understated **Shingle Style** cottage. It was purchased in 1916 by silent film star *Mabel Normand* for her father, a stage carpenter.

[N17b] Originally **Vernon H. Brown House**, 119 St. Mark's Pl., bet. Nicholas St. and Westervelt Ave. N side. 1890. *Edward Alfred Sargent.*

More complex than **No.125**, but with less convincing volumes.

N17c

[N17c] Originally **Frederick L. Rodewald** House, 103 St. Mark's Pl., bet. Nicholas St. and Westervelt Ave. N side. 1890. *Edward Alfred Sargent.*

The powerful and fluid forms of the mature **Shingle Style** make this a monumental presence on the street. *Sargent* was not shy.

[N17d] **75 St. Mark's Place**, bet. Nicholas St. and Westervelt Ave. N side. ca. 1880.

Muted **Shingle Style** with delicate Doric columns. The rear boasts three tiers of porches peering out at Manhattan across the harbor.

[N17e] **St. Peter's Roman Catholic Church**, 49 St. Mark's Pl., N side. 1900-1903. **Cardinal's Tower**, 1919. Both by *Harding & Gooch.* **Rectory**, 1912, *George H. Streeton.*

Neo-Romanesque, with the **Cardinal's Tower** so named after its dedication by New York's *John Cardinal Farley.* (The complicated forms of the church complex are best seen from Richmond Terrace, below.)

[N17f] **17, 19 St. Mark's Place**, N side. ca. 1875.

Sumptuously mansarded wood shingled and sided double house.

[N17g] **1 St. Mark's Place** (double house), NE cor. Westervelt Ave. ca. 1860.

A craggy shingled structure that magnificently turns and holds the corner. And what an aerie space atop the tower.

[N17h] **36-38 Westervelt Avenue**, W side. ca. 1867.

Another double with, once more, mansard roofs from the French **Second Empire**.

[N17i] **42 Westervelt Avenue**, W side. ca. 1872.

Above, modest clapboard crowned with a monumental mansard. Below, a pretentious entrance in the volume of the original porch: heavy-handed.

[N17j] **65 Westervelt Avenue**, E side. 1908. *Thomas C. Perkins.*

N17a

N17g

A **Shingle Style** festival of turrets and dormers, with paired Tuscan Doric columns holding up a curving verandah.

[N17k] **St. George Gardens Stores**, 72-74 Westervelt Ave., W side. ca. 1910.

Before Staten Islanders discovered cars, malls, and highways, they shopped locally. This building, clad in delicately incised terra cotta, shows just how attractive the predecessors of strip malls could be.

Phelps Place: a time warp. Three frame 19th-century houses on one flank and, on the other, a large, raw-brick low-rise apartment complex— St. George Garden Apartments (on the site of the opulent Anson Phelps Stokes mansion). In the distance, ever in view, is St. Peter's slender tower and cross.

[N17l] **7, 8 and 9, 10 Phelps Place** (double houses), W side. 1891. *Douglas Smyth.*

Neo-Tudor, shingled, double-gabled houses abut the Shingle Style further within the enclave.

[N17m] **11 Phelps Place**, N end. ca. 1880.
A modest polygonal tower anchors this understated and convincing **Shingle Style** cottage.

Outside the Historic District:

[N18] **Ambassador Apartments**, 30 Daniel Low Terrace, bet. Crescent Ave. and Fort Hill Circle. W side. 1932. *Lucian Pisciatta.*
Art Deco at its Staten Island best. The metalwork on the entrance doors, done in a peacock pattern, is exquisite.

[N19] **117 Daniel Low Terrace**, NE cor. Fort Pl. ca. 1885.
An eclectic essay in reds: brick with matching terra-cotta ornament. The jerkin-head gable and dormers are an exotic touch.

[N19a] **Schoverling House**, 344 Westervelt Ave., bet. Benziger and Winter Aves., ca. 1880. 🍎
Dramatic **Second Empire** in brick, with angled bay windows and knee-braced wooden porch, set amid a lush lawn.

[N20] **198-202, 204 Richmond Terrace**, bet. Stuyvesant Pl. and Nicholas St. S side. ca. 1875.
Two lonely survivors from a group of mansarded frame houses in various states of repair, with their backs to the high ground and their fronts overlooking the Kill and New Jersey beyond. When built, theirs was a bucolic view. To the east are a number of stairs from the street that mark the former location of houses now vanished (see Necrology).

N21

[N21] **Pavilion on the Terrace** (restaurant)/ formerly **Columbia Hall, Knights of Columbus**/originally **Henry P. Robertson House**, 404 Richmond Terr., bet. St. Peter's Pl. and Westervelt Ave. S side. ca. 1835. Possibly *John Haviland.*
The last vestige of Temple Row, ten early 19th-century Greek Revival mansions built by wealthy New Yorkers and Southern planters along Richmond Terrace when the view across the Kill Van Kull was more pastoral. Sturdy Doric columns and a stately pediment recall more gracious times (for the elite) in these parts. A remarkable sinuous, petaled **fence** fronts the restaurant.

NEW BRIGHTON

A development begun in 1836 by *Thomas E. Davis,* a Manhattan speculator.

[B1] **St. Stanislaus Kostka Roman Catholic Church**, 109 York Ave., bet. Carlyle and Buchanan Sts. E side. 1925. *Paul R. Henkel.*
Lombardian (northern Italian) Romanesque Revival, used more for decor, appliqué, than the massive structure of original 11th-century sources.

[B2] **New York City Drinking Water Sampling Station**, NE cor. York and Pauw Sts.
These small silver boxes are sprinkled throughout the five boroughs; this one is a reminder that Staten Island is tied to the rest of the City by utilities as well as by ferries and bridges.

Hamilton Park: a number of suburban country dwellings of 12 to 14 rooms (nevertheless dubbed "cottages" at the time) are to be found

B4

*here, remnants of a 19th-century planned community. In 1853, the same year as West Orange, N.J.'s **Llewellyn Park,** developer Charles Kennedy Hamilton began a suburban development planned along the romantic precepts of landscape gardener Andrew Jackson Downing. The area even then was only a half hour by steam ferry from Manhattan's tip, much the same as today. The Hamilton lands lay on the heights between today's East Buchanan, Franklin, Prospect, and York Streets.*

[B3] **119 Harvard Avenue**, bet. Prospect Ave. and Park Pl., opp. Nassau St. ca. 1859.
A charming brick **Gothic Revival** cottage, deeply eaved and vigorously bracketed.

[B4] **32 Park Place**, SE cor. Harvard Ave. ca. 1864. Additions. *Carl Pfeiffer.*
Fronting on Harvard but bearing a Park Place address is this stolid brick house with a later ogee-curved mansard roof and segmental arched dormers, one of the 12 second-stage Hamilton Park cottages designed by *Pfeiffer.*

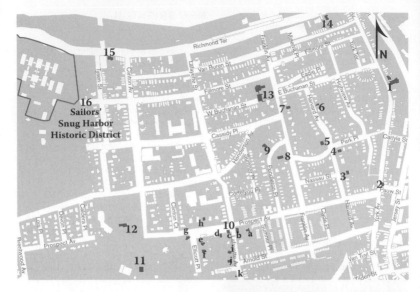

[B5] Originally **Pritchard House**, 66 Harvard Ave., NW cor. Park Pl. ca. 1853. *Carl Pfeiffer.* 🏵

Hidden behind privet hedge, birch trees, and wisteria stands this expansive, grand, eclectic (quoins, arches, and gingerbread) stucco house. Late **Greek Revival** with some **Italian Sauce.** Its front entrance was placed to command the downhill view to the west—today its large backyard. This is believed to be Hamilton Park's first speculative house.

B5

B7

[B6] **29 Harvard Avenue,** bet. Park Pl. and E. Buchanan St. E side. ca. 1864. *Carl Pfeiffer.*

Mansarded and urbane, another speculation of developer *Hamilton.*

[B7] **The Hamilton Park Cottage,** 105 Franklin Ave., bet. E. Buchanan St. and Cassidy Pl. E side. ca. 1864. *Carl Pfeiffer.* 🏵

Triple-arched, a stolid porticoed brick house. The term "cottage" is from a state of mind that in grander circumstances referred to Newport mansions (cf., **The Breakers**) as cottages.

🏠 [B8] Originally **William S. Pendleton House**/later **T.M. Rianhard House,** 1 Pendleton Pl., SW cor. Franklin Ave. 1861. *Charles Duggin.* 🏵

The "second" *Pendleton* house (for the first see below). A magnificent **Stick Style** silhouette and robust forms: jig-sawn brackets support a front porch and eaves. Note the cross-bracing in the gables.

[B9] Originally **William S. Pendleton House,** 22 Pendleton Pl., bet. Franklin and Prospect Aves. N side at the curve. ca. 1855. *Charles Duggin.* 🏵

After his business ventures prospered (he was president of the local ferryboat company and dabbled in real estate), *Pendleton* forsook this romantic wood-shingled **Gothic Revival** villa with criss-crossed muntin windows for the lustier confection across the street.

[B10a] **172 Prospect Avenue,** bet. Franklin and Lafayette Aves. S side. ca. 1870.

A stately slated mansard crowns this shingled Second Empire house.

[B10b] **180 Prospect Avenue,** SE cor. Lafayette St. ca. 1885.

Neo-Tudor: simulated half-timbering infilled with stuccoed brick. Lovely small-muntined glass porch solarium at the ground floor.

[B10c] **202 Prospect Avenue**, SW cor. Lafayette St. ca. 1885.

Brown shingles and a gambrel roof, a sloping dormer facing north (no doubt to illuminate an artist's studio in the attic).

[B10d] **212 Prospect Avenue**, bet. Lafayette Ave. and Ellicott Pl. S side. ca. 1895.

Three sunbursts over the three multipaned windows and doors.

[B10e] **232 Prospect Avenue**, SE cor. Ellicott Pl. ca. 1870.

Gawky **Shingle Style**, but unfortunately the shingles have been painted beige.

Ellicott Place: between Lafayette and Clinton Avenues. S side. Two brick gateposts and a green center island mark this one-block enclave, ever lovely in its entirety.

[B10f] **15 Ellicott Place**, S of Prospect Ave. E side. ca. 1870.

Shingle Style, enriched with ornate bargeboards and a salient bay under the gable.

[B10g] **254 Prospect Avenue**, SW cor. Ellicott Pl. ca. 1885.

Queen Anne Revival: complex and contradictory.

[B10h] **229 Prospect Avenue**, bet. Lafayette Ave. and Clinton Court. N side. ca. 1885.

A pale green (with yellow trim) stunner.

B12

B10i

[B10i] **270 Lafayette Avenue**, bet. Prospect Ave. and Arnold St. W side. ca. 1885.

Brown stained shingles, strongly chamfered corners, and a porch of turned columns with an ornate balustrade.

[B10j] **280 Lafayette Avenue**, NW cor. Arnold St. ca. 1870.

A grand mansard crowns this **Victorian** clapboard house, wrapped with an elegant bracket porch.

[B10k] **176 Arnold Street**, SW cor. Lafayette Ave. ca. 1900.

Not much to look at, but an example of cast-in-place concrete: an early and unusual use of the material in residential construction.

[B11] **"Woodbrook," Jonathan Goodhue House**/now **Goodhue Children's Center Recreation Building**, 304 Prospect Ave., at Clinton Ave. S side. ca. 1845. *B. Haynard and*

James Patterson, builders. [B11b] **William H. Wheelock Residence Facility, Goodhue Center**, 290 Prospect Ave., at Clinton Ave. S side. 1971. *Davis, Brody & Assocs.*

Woodbrook presents an image of a modest (but top-heavy) **Italianate** palazzo, its quoins simulated in wood, and a sober cornice. It shows its age, but still conveys some of the elegance it possessed when it was a villa commanding the vast acreage of the *Goodhue* estate. The **Wheelock Building**, named for a trustee of the center, is an experiment in group living for teenagers.

[B12] **Residence, St. Peter's Boys High School**/earlier **Nicholas Muller House**, 200 Clinton Ave., at Prospect Ave. W side. ca. 1857.

An eclectic mansion, double gables presented to the street, with a striking contrast of white detail against a deep red-painted brick body.

[B13] **Christ Church (Episcopal)**, 76 Franklin Ave., SW cor. Fillmore St. 1904. **Parish Hall**, 1906.

A gray ashlar complex featuring as its off-center centerpiece a comfortable **neo-Gothic** church that, together with the Parish Hall, forms a chaste green corner campus.

[B14] **536 Richmond Terrace**, bet. York Ave. and Franklin Sts. S side. ca. 1875.

Another stately mansard, this one hidden atop a black ashlar retaining wall behind dense, luxuriant hedges.

[B15] **Tysen-Neville House**, aka **Neville House**, 806 Richmond Terr., bet. Clinton Ave. and Tysen St. S side. ca. 1800. Verandah and cupola added 1890-1910. ☛

Identified by its slender-columned two-story veranda, it is said that the house reflects Bahamian architecture through the journeys of its retired owner, naval officer *Captain John Neville*. Its proximity to the old Sailors' Snug Harbor, just down the Terrace, gave it a period of

Building M, Maintenance, renovated into the **Staten Island Children's Museum**, 1987. *David Prendergast, Jeffrey Hannigan, James Sawyer. Keith Goddard/Works,* graphic design. **Music hall**, 1892. Restoration, 1987, *Rafael Viñoly.* Open to the public.

Five grand **Greek** temples serenely survey an immaculately groomed lawn.

The Harbor was founded by *Robert Richard Randall,* who converted his Revolutionary War privateer-father's bequest into a fund for the support of "aged, decrepit and worn-out sailors." For many years, the proceeds from *Randall's* property in Manhattan's Greenwich Village supported the Harbor.

The Harbor's trustees moved the institution to a new site on the North Carolina coast, paving the way, in 1976, for the reuse of the rich complex of **Greek Revival, Victorian,** and early 20th-century edifices, and 60 acres of romantic grounds to the south, as a cultural center.

B16

B14

B16, Building E

success as a local tavern, the **Old Stone Jug.** Today it could use some sprucing up.

[B16] **Snug Harbor Cultural Center**/originally **Sailors' Snug Harbor,** 914-1000 Richmond Terr., bet. Tysen St., Snug Harbor Rd., and Kissel Ave. S side to Henderson Ave. ☛ **Building A,** 1879. *Richard Smyth.* ☛ **Building B,** 1839-1840. *Minard Lafever.* ☛ **Building C** (central building facing Richmond Terr.), 1831-1833. *Minard Lafever.* Interior redecoration, 1884. ☛ **Building D,** 1831-1841. *Minard Lafever.* ☛ **Building E,** 1880. *Richard Smyth.* ☛ **Center (or north) Gatehouse,** 1873. *Richard P. Smyth.* **West Gatehouse,** 1880. ☛ **Chapel,** 1854-1856. *James Solomon.* Interior renovation, 1873. **Additions,** 1883. ☛ **Iron Fence,** 1841-1845. *Frederick Diaper.*

LIVINGSTON

[B17] **Walker Park Recreation Building**, N.Y.C. Department of Parks & Recreation, 50 Bard Ave., SW cor. Delafield Pl. 1934.

Full-timbered with brick infill, ashlar walls, a red slate roof, and charming casement windows, all built during the nadir of the Great Depression.

Walker Park: Mary Ewing Outerbridge brought lawn tennis to Staten Island from Bermuda in 1874 (vying with Nahant, Massachusetts, for the record of hosting the first sets played in this country). In 1880 the first national tennis tournament was played here, in what is now Walker Park. Ms. Outerbridge was the sister of Eugenius H. Outerbridge, for whom the Crossing is named, and the park is named for Mr. Outerbridge's good friend, Randolph St. George Walker, Jr., a casualty of World War I. Today tennis and cricket are played on the grounds.

B16, Building C

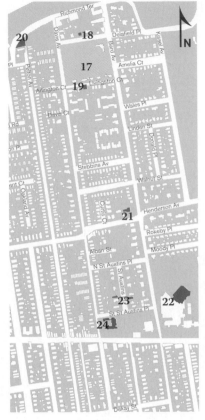

B22

B19

[B18] **Dr. Samuel MacKenzie Elliott House,** 69 Delafield Pl., bet. Bard and Davis Aves. N side. ca. 1850. 🖋

An eye surgeon of wide repute, *Dr. Elliott,* as a result of his distinguished patients, became the focal point of a small but far-flung literary colony: *James Russell Lowell, Henry Wadsworth Longfellow,* and *Francis Parkman,* among others. The house itself, one of some 15 he built in this area, is a straightforward ashlar granite box whose charm is enhanced by a serpentine verge-board along its gabled roof. (Another *Elliott*-built house in granite is at 557 Bard Avenue, south of Forrest Avenue/City Boulevard, E side.) It is unclear where *Elliott* himself lived.

[B19] Originally **Stewart Brown House,** 14-18 Livingston Court, bet. Bard and Davis Aves. S side. ca. 1860.

Bold of scale and originally rich in detail—note the many dormers. It squeezes **Livingston Court,** indicating that it predates the court. By default to its aluminum sheathers, it lost much of its rich detail (corners, window framing).

[B20] Originally **Cornelius Cruser House,** also known as **Kreuzer-Pelton House,** 1262 Richmond Terr., near Pelton Pl. S side. 1722. Additions, 1770 and 1836. 🖋

Typical of the area's **Colonial** residences. First a one-room structure, usually of local field-stone, with rooms later added as needed. The stone cottage on the right dates from 1722; the central clapboard section was added in 1770; the two-story brick section on the left was built in 1836. The man who was to become England's *King William IV* in 1830 was entertained here during the Revolution.

[B21] Originally **George W. Curtis House,** 234 Bard Ave., NW cor. Henderson Ave. 1850.

Curtis (an abolitionist and *Lincoln* supporter) hid *Horace Greeley* here from mobs of angry Staten Islanders, who generally supported the Southern cause. **Curtis High School** is his namesake.

[B22] **Convent, St. Vincent's Medical Center of Richmond**/originally **T.F. McCurdy House**/later **Henry M. Taber House**/later **William T. Garner House**/later **St. Austin's School,** 710 Castleton Ave., opp. Hoyt Ave. N side. ca. 1850. Rear addition, 1898, *Samuel R. Brick, Jr.* **Gatehouse,** Bard Ave., S of Moody Pl. E side. ca. 1850.

A huge granite mansarded **Victorian** mansion that proclaims by size, if not by beauty, the prodigious wealth garnered by 19th-century businessmen (*McCurdy* was a wholesaler, *Taber* a "cotton king," *Garner* a cotton mill owner). *Ulysses S. Grant* considered retiring here; but his wife, visiting the house on a warm damp day, was plagued by mosquitoes that still thrive in Staten Island's marshes and swamps.

St. Austin's Place, between North St. Austin's Place and South St. Austin's Place.

[B23] **Henderson Estate Company Houses,** 33 St. Austin's Pl. E side. 34 St. Austin's Pl. W side. Both, 1893. *McKim, Mead & White.*

B23

On opposite sides of this short street a pair of dark-brown **Shingle Style**-meets-**Colonial Revival** houses, designed by the *MM&W* staff as low-budget (for *MM&W*) houses.

[B24] **St. Mary's Episcopal Church,** 347 Davis Ave., NE cor. Castleton Ave. 1853. *Wills & Dudley.* Parish House, 1910-1914. Rectory, 1924. Both by *Ralph Adams Cram.*

An outgrowth of a then fashionable movement called **Ecclesiology,** the design of this small church is patterned after early 14th-century English precursors. (*Frank Wills* was the official architect of the New York Ecclesiological Society.) *Cram's* additions were skillfully related to the church building's unusual architecture.

WEST BRIGHTON

West *New* Brighton, officially, lying to the west of New Brighton. But the "New" has been dropped by all save fuddy-duddy mapmakers and government officials who advise them. One of the few official recognitions of the vernacular is in the foot-high lettering of the entrance sign of the West Brighton Pool.

Along Castleton Avenue:

[B25] **Engine Company 79, N.Y.C. Fire Department**/formerly Company 104/originally **Medora Hook & Ladder Company No.3** (volunteer), 1189 Castleton Ave., bet. Barker and Taylor Sts., opp. Roe St. N side. ca. 1885. Plaque, 1905, *Alexander Stevens,* Superintendent of Buildings.

The City inherited this eclectic firehouse from volunteer fire laddies when firemen became paid professionals (hence the plaque). Check the bizarre broken cornice!

B30

[B26] Formerly **Keypac Collaborative, Brooklyn Union Gas Company,** 1207 Castleton Ave., bet. Barker and Taylor Sts. N side. 1889.

A venerable commercial building rimmed in bluestone and sporting an Italianate cornice.

[B27] **Our Lady of Mt. Carmel-St. Benedicta Church and Rectory** (Roman Catholic), 1265 Castleton Ave., NE cor. Bodine St. 1969. *Genovese & Maddalene.*

A sophisticated modern church center in contrast to the commercial strip adjacent and opposite. The dramatic skylit altar and rich modern stained glass of the interior are effective.

[B28] Originally **Captain John T. Barker House,** 9-11 Trinity Pl., bet. Taylor and Barker Sts. N side. 1851.

An **Italianate** villa restored with restraint, but succumbing to a **"painted lady"** color scheme to emphasize its elegant details: bracketed roof eaves, center cupola, a porch supported by paired columns. *Barker,* a silk dyer by trade, was associated lastly with the New York Dyeing and Print Works.

[B29] **John De Groot House**, 1674 Richmond Terrace, SW cor. Alaska St. ca. 1870. Rear Wing, ca. 1810-1815. Additions and modifications, 1886-1898. 🖤

Second Empire from the period when the Terrace was lined with grand houses. The hex-slate-shingled mansard roof is a lovely reminder of both craftsmanship and grandeur.

[B30] **13 Dongan Street**, bet. Richmond Terr. and De Groot Pl. E side. ca. 1875.

Another **painted lady**, too made-up in sky blue for a lady with lace.

PORT RICHMOND

[B31] **Temple Emanu-El** (synagogue), 984 Post Ave., bet. Decker and Heberton Aves. S side. 1907. *Harry W. Pelcher.*

Classical Revival, its pediment, heavy columns, and tall octagonal domed cupola erased of detail. Only the shingles survived; a relic of this community's earlier days.

[B32] **Along Heberton Avenue:**

Port Richmond's prime residential thorough-fare, paralleling the business street two blocks west. Among its fine older homes, reflecting the onetime affluence of this important commercial community, are:

B32e

[B32a] **No.272**, a crisp pyramidal hat tops this interlocked form, traces of the original dyed fish-scale shingles still holding space. Sad plastic elsewhere.

[B32b] **No.253**, somewhat sullied by its siding and storm windows, the corner tower and gabled dormer remind us of its Shingle Style past.

[B32c] **No.252**, asymmetrical and mansarded, with a wrap-around porch that surveys the streetscape.

[B32d] **No.233**, the central tower gives this otherwise bland building a serious posture.

[B32e] **No.198**, stuccoed quoins and a Corinthian-columned portal enrich this grandly mansarded mansion.

[B32f] **Faith United Methodist Church**/originally **Grace Methodist Episcopal Church**, 221 Heberton Ave., NE cor. Castleton Ave. 1897. Addition, 1983. *George L. Smalle.*

An offshoot in 1867 of West Brighton's Trinity Methodist Church, this congregation's later **Gothic Revival** edifice, in dark brick with

terra-cotta trim, sits uncomfortably beside its modest addition.

[B33] **Northfield Township District School 6**/later Public School 20 Annex/ now Parkside Senior Housing, 160 Heberton Ave., NW cor. New St. 1891. Addition, Heberton Ave., SW cor. Vreeland St. 1897-1898. *James Warriner Moulton.* Converted to housing, 1993-1994, *Diffendale & Kubec.*

The original **neo-Romanesque** wing marks one of the island's last remaining school build-ings of its genre, in which a mandatory belfry and clock (now handless) made an important contribution to both the school's architecture and community life.

Across Veterans Park:

[B34] **Park Baptist Church**/originally **North Baptist Church** of Port Richmond, 130 Park Ave., NW cor. Vreeland St. 1843.

B33

[B35] **St. Philip's Baptist Church**, 77 Bennett St., bet. Heberton and Park Aves. N side. 1891. Altered, 1926, *George Conable.*

Park Baptist's congregation, overlooking the park's west edge, established a mission church in 1881 for the local black community. It became St. Philip's, much grander than its donor, with its brick neo-Gothic tower fronting the north side of the park. **Brick neo-Gothic**?

[B36] **121 Heberton Avenue House**, SE cor. Bennett St. ca. 1859-1861. *James C. Burger,* designer and builder. 🖤

A **Rustic** picturesque villa? Draw from the pattern books of *Calvert Vaux* and *Samuel Sloan*, and your design will feature the gables, brackets and simple ornament characteristic of the style.

[B37] **Port Richmond Branch, N.Y. Public Library**, 75 Bennett St., NW cor. Heberton Ave. 1905. *Carrère & Hastings.*

An *Andrew Carnegie* donation once again. Modest, perhaps prissy, it bares its twin Tuscan columns discreetly.

B40

B41

[B38] **Catholic Youth Organization**, 120 Anderson Ave., bet. Heberton and Port Richmond Aves., opp. Park Ave. S side. 1926. *James Whitford, Sr.*

A pompous Ionic-columned glazed terra-cotta **Roman Revival** temple façade, on the axis of Park Avenue.

[B39] **Staten Island Reformed Church**, 54 Port Richmond Ave., bet. old railroad viaduct and Richmond Terr., opp. Church St. W side. 1844. **Sunday School**, 1898, *Oscar S. Teale.*

Site of the first religious congregation on Staten Island, organized in 1663. The present **Georgian Revival** church (its steeple missing) replaced (in situ) three earlier ones. Read the plaques outside the church and walk through the old graveyard. Visit the Sunday School interior; it's incredible.

[B40] **Faber Pool, N.Y.C. Department of Parks & Recreation**, 2175 Richmond Terr., opp. Faber St. N side. 1932. *Sibley & Fetherston.* Open to the public.

A **Mission Style** public pool set behind a deep lawn and named for the pencil-manufacturing *Eberhard Faber* family, who lived nearby. California in New York?

Off maps to the west:

[B41] **Bayonne Bridge**, Willow Brook Expwy. and Hooker Pl. to Bayonne, N.J. over Kill Van Kull. 1931. *O.H. Ammann*, engineer. *Cass Gilbert, Inc.*, consulting architects.

A graceful soaring silver arch that rises from the water's edge and sweeps the mind away from the industrial slurbs at either anchorage.

[B42] **Standard Varnish Works Factory Office Building**, 2589 Richmond Terrace. 1892-1893. *Colin McLean*, builder. 📷

A variant on the German **Rundbogenstil**, with round-arched windows, brick pilasters, brick string courses, and bold corbelled brick ornament.

MARINERS HARBOR

Captains' Row, Richmond Terrace between Van Pelt and De Hart Aves. (and to the east) S side: In the 1840s and 1850s, before the waters became fouled, wealthy oyster captains lived in a row of two-story houses with columned two-story porches. The houses overlooked what was then called Shore Road, along which as many as 50 oystering sloops were moored in the Kill.

[B43] **2868 Richmond Terrace**, bet. Van Pelt and De Hart Aves. S Side. ca. 1875.

A mansarded mansion, built decades after its neighbors to the east, with walls now sheathed with vinyl clapboard.

 [B44] Originally **Stephen D. Barnes House**, 2876 Richmond Terr. bet. Van Pelt and De Hart Aves. S side. ca. 1853. ☙

A grand brick **Italianate** Captains' Row mansion with Gothic Revival detail: unusual for

[B47] **Summerfield United Methodist Church**/ originally **Summerfield Methodist Church**, 104 Harbor Rd. **Parsonage**, 100 Harbor Rd., both bet. Leyden Ave. and Richmond Terr. W side. 1869.

Some **Renaissance** gestures enliven this painted shingled church, with a tower that brought out the best in its Classical carpenter.

[B48] **74 Harbor Road**, bet. Leyden Ave. and Richmond Terr. W side. ca. 1845.

Sketchy, but proof that even fake brick siding cannot entirely defile the character of this **Greek Revival** "captain's house," with its four-columned double-height porch. Not entirely defiled, but in serious disrepair.

South Avenue, between Richmond Terrace and Arlington Place.

[B49] **95, 117, 131 South Avenue**, bet. Richmond Terr. and Arlington Pl., all E side. **116 South Avenue**, W side. ca. 1885.

These suburban houses are outstanding

B43

the bull's-eye windows in the attic below the deep cornice. Definitely a "fixer-upper." Come and get it.

[B45] **Staten Island Seventh-Day Adventist Church**/originally **Mariners Harbor Baptist Church,** 72 Union Ave., NW cor. Forest Court. 1858.

Such fine **Romanesque Revival** brickwork was unusual in this early Staten Island era. This church was founded by members of Port Richmond's North (now Park) Baptist Church. Sadly decrepit, with plywood covering its rose window.

[B46] **258 Harbor Road**, opp. Continental Pl. W side. ca. 1845, plus addition.

Columned and picket-fenced, but dead from an overdose of plastic at the dead end of Continental Place.

examples in the area. For two that didn't make it see Necrology.

*South of Arlington Place, **Things to Come:***

[B50] **Mariners Harbor Branch, New York Public Library**, 206 South Ave. bet. Arlington Pl. and Brabant St. 2012 (predicted). *Atelier Pagnamenta Torriani.*

If built, this spiffy, modern library will be a great addition to this down-and-out district. The architects claim the design is based on "a cracked open shell." An architectural omelet?

NECROLOGY

Public School 18, Staten Island, Broadway, NE cor. Market St. West Brighton. 1890. *Edward A. Sargent.* Addition, 1898.

A previous edition of this Guide advised the visitor to take "a leisurely walk around" the building to "savor its collection of richly configurated hip-roofed red-brick pavilions, which tilt

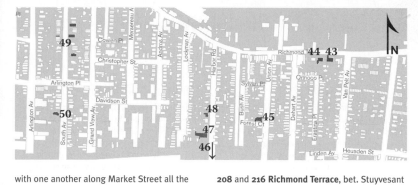

with one another along Market Street all the way back to Campbell Avenue." A visible loss to the community.

Brooks House, 414-418 Richmond Terr., SE cor. Westervelt Ave. New Brighton. 1835.

A common saga: a mansion allowed to deteriorate and then demolished. In this case, it was a porticoed Greek Revival temple.

208 and **216 Richmond Terrace,** bet. Stuyvesant Pl. and Nicholas St. S side. ca. 1875.

A long row of mansarded houses nestled into the hillside and gazed out to the ocean. Only two remain. **208** and **216** recently bit the dust.

Losses at Snug Harbor: a number of the Harbor's fine buildings succumbed to the high cost of maintenance long before its landmark

B47

B49

New Brighton Village Hall, 66 Lafayette Ave., SW cor. Fillmore St. 1868-1871. *James Whitford, Sr.* ✦

Promises of restoration failed to stem the decline into ruin of this mansarded brick, former civic building. Landmark status did not solve the problem. In a 1987 Streetscapes column in the *New York Times, Christopher Gray* said "The interior is like some ancient, ruined church. Floors and partitions are gone and high, bare brick walls support a patchwork roof. Pigeons swoop in and out, perching on surviving scraps of woodwork."

Brighton Heights Reformed Church, 320 St. Mark's Pl., SW cor. Fort Pl. 1863-1864. *John Correja.*

A delicate, 19th-century white wood-framed church, almost entirely overwhelmed by intrusive 20th-century competitors. It burned in 1996.

status was declared in the 1960s. Its most opulent structure was architect *R.W. Gibson's* 1892 **Randall Memorial Church,** with a dome that echoed London's St. Paul's Cathedral, but at a considerably smaller scale. (Five of its stained-glass windows are preserved at Calvary Presbyterian Church [1894], Castleton and Bement Avenues.) The other was the **Hospital,** a neo-Classical structure cruciform in plan (like 18th-century English prisons), with four long wings extending out from a domed central pavilion. It bit the dust in 1951.

109 and **113 South Avenue,** bet. Richmond Terr. and Arlington Pl., E side. ca. 1885.

Suburban houses, rich in Victorian detail, sacrificed for a banal complex of vinyl-sided boxes.

Eastern Staten Island

This area is, to most islanders' thinking, another part of the North Shore; no one in Staten Island refers to any area as "eastern." But for the purposes of isolating the communities along the right shoulder of the island, we've grouped them under this artificial rubric.

TOMPKINSVILLE

Established as a village around 1815 through the efforts of Governor *Daniel D. Tompkins*; hence its name. Some of its streets, Hannah and Minthorne (and Sarah and Griffin, since renamed), recall his children's names.

Along or near Bay Street:

[E1a] **Bay Street Landing**/originally American Dock Company, Piers 1-5, below Bay St. bet. U.S. Coast Guard Base and Victory Blvd. E side. Converted into apartments, 1982. [E1b] **Harbour Pointe**, 80 Bay Street Landing. Converted into apartments, 1987, *David Kenneth Specter & Assocs.*

Alfred J. Pouch (of Terminal fame) established the American Dock Company in 1872, but the

E1b

reinforced-concrete coffee and cocoa warehouses converted to residential use date from the early 20th century. Nice view. Klunky buildings.

A trip dockside via Hannah Street:

[E2] **Joseph H. Lyons Pool**, Murray Hulbert Ave., SW cor. Victory Blvd. 1936. N.Y.C. Department of Parks & Recreation, *Aymar Embury II*, consultant. 📷 Interior. 📷

Squat cylinders of economical red-brick masonry, helical concrete stairways, and **Art Deco** detailing identify this as one of eight city swimming pools built in the heyday of municipal construction, the Great Depression of the 1930s. The others: **Crotona Park** (Bronx), **Betsy Head Park, McCarren Park, Red Hook Park**, and **Sunset Park** (Brooklyn), **Colonial** (now **Jackie Robinson) Park** and **Highbridge Park** (Manhattan).

[E2a] **Horton's Row**, 411, 413, 415, 417 Westervelt Ave., bet. Scribner and Corson Aves. ca. 1882. *Harry L. Horton*, developer. 📷

Four landmarks in an original row of 12 attached houses with Greek Revival porches. Nos.419, 421, 429, 431, and 433 also survive, but have been altered too much for the Landmarks Preservation Commission's tastes. We see their point, and four landmarks out of the surviving nine isn't bad (Nos.423, 425, and 427 have been demolished). Perhaps the altered houses will be reverse-altered someday.

[E3a] **Richmond Chlorination Station**, N.Y.C. Department of Environmental Protection, Murray Hulbert Ave. at Hannah St. W side. 1974. *N.Y.C. Board of Water Supply.*
[E3b] **Tompkinsville Water Pollution Control Facility**, N.Y.C. Department of Environmental Protection, Murray Hulbert Ave. at Pier 7. W side. 1976. *Warren W. Gran & Assocs.*

The sophisticated and self-conscious control facility in **Brutalist** gray concrete is for society's waste products. The prim, well crafted neo-Georgian chlorination station of carefully laid brick and pink granite is for another vital need: pure water.

E3b

STAPLETON

Governor Tompkins' son, Minthorne, and William J. Staples purchased land south of Tompkinsville from Cornelius (later "Commodore") Vanderbilt, a native of Staten Island, and established the village of Stapleton (named after Mr. Staples) in 1833. Stapleton became the home of two large breweries in the 19th century: Bechtel's, at the foot of the cliff along Van Duzer Street (opposite Broad, where evidence still exists), and the Rubsam & Hohrmann Atlantic Brewery (1870-1953), later Piel's, which finally closed in 1963 and occupied the long blockfront along Canal Street's north side.

[E4] **Paramount Theater**, 560 Bay St., bet. Prospect St. and Union Pl. ca. 1935. *C.W. Rapp & George L. Rapp.*

The Paramount presents its wondrous **Art Deco** falsefront to a messy commercial street. Abandoned; an adaptive reuse would give a shot in the arm to its neighbors.

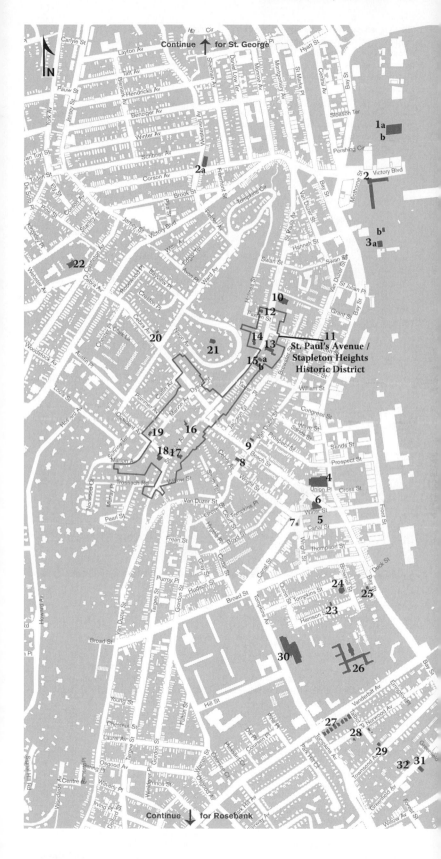

[E5a] **Tappen Park**/originally **Washington Park**, Bay to Wright Sts., Water to Canal Sts. Park reconstructed, gazebo added, 1982. *Quennell Rothschild Assocs.* [E5b] Originally **Edgewater Village Hall**, 111 Canal St., in Tappen Park. 1889. *Paul Kühne.* 🖊

Named for Edgewater, a 19th-century village all but forgotten today, this eccentric **Victorian** brick civic building is an anchor for Stapleton. Sitting in Tappen Park and shaded by stately old trees, it tempers the cacaphony of the many

E5b

E8

small businesses attempting on every side to invade its peaceful setting.

🏛 [E6] **Staten Island Savings Bank**, 81 Water St., cor. Beach St. 1924-1925. *Delano & Aldrich.* 🖊

Small-scaled **neo-Classicism**. Buildings anchoring the corner of diverging roads are often captivating, sometimes monumental (as in the seven-story pepper-pot corners that stand sentry at scores of Parisian streets). Here the architects placed a trim, round Doric-columned Greek temple where Water and Beach Streets split apart.

[E7] **Stapleton Branch, N.Y. Public Library**, 132 Canal St., SW cor. Wright St. 1907. *Carrère & Hastings.*

One of four *Carnegie* gift libraries that introduced a semblance of culture to the rural island.

Go Stapletons! *The Staten Island Stapletons played in the National Football League in its formative, leather helmet years, 1929-1932. They played at Thompson Stadium, on*

*Tompkins Avenue between Broad and Hill Streets, now the site of Stapleton Houses (1962), a vast public housing project known less for its architecture and more for its rap music; several members of the **Wu-Tang Clan** grew up there.*

Along Van Duzer Street:

🏛 [E8] Possibly **Richard G. and Susannah Tompkins Smith** House, 390 Van Duzer St., bet. Wright and Beach Sts. 18th and 19th centuries. 🖊

Diminutive in scale, four magnificent **Corinthian** columns camouflage the curving Dutch eaves. A valiant survivor between banal buildings adjacent.

🏛 [E9] **364 Van Duzer Street House**, bet. Beach and Prospect Sts. W side. ca. 1835. *Robert Hazard*, builder. 🖊

Moved from elsewhere, its **Greek Revival Doric** porch has been grafted onto a more ancient body.

E11

STAPLETON HEIGHTS

Along St. Paul's Avenue (one-way southbound):

⛪ [E10] Originally **Public School 15, Richmond (Daniel D. Tompkins School)**, 98 Grant St., SE cor. St. Paul's Ave. 1897-1898. *Edward A. Sargent.* 🖊

Eclectic, rugged **Queen Anne**, with a dramatic clock tower.

[E11] **St. Paul's Avenue-Stapleton Heights Historic District**, 168/169 to 447/458 St. Paul's Avenue, with peninsulas into Paxton St., Clinton St., Taxter Pl., Beach St., Willow St., Stone St., Trossach Rd., Marion Ave., Occident Ave., Cebra Ave., and Dyson St. 🖊

A more pleasant lane would be hard to find: St. Paul's Avenue's gently swelling topography reveals magnificent wood-frame Victorian-era stalwarts clustered around **St. Paul's Memorial Church**. And make sure to explore the side

E17

streets, too; especially Marion Avenue (one block west of, and parallel to, St. Paul's Avenue) and Occident and Cebra Avenues (intersecting St. Paul's Avenue).

Within the Historic District:

[E12] **172 St. Paul's Avenue**, bet. Grant and Clinton Sts., ca. 1830.
Greek Revival, originally the rectory for an earlier St. Paul's Church.

[E13] **St. Paul's Memorial Church** and **Rectory** (Episcopal), 217-225 St. Paul's Ave., bet. Clinton St. and Taxter Pl. E side. 1866-1870. *Edward T. Potter of Potter & Clinton.* 🌶
A lovingly crafted English country Gothic church whose traprock walls have weathered beautifully.

[E14] **218 St. Paul's Avenue**, bet. Clinton St. and Taxter Pl. W side. ca. 1845.
Perched on an embankment, proudly over-

E13

E23

E15a

looking **St. Paul's Church** across the street. The cornice, with bracketed eaves, is especially fine.

[E15a] **231 St. Paul's Avenue,** bet. Clinton St. and Taxter Pl. E side. 1888.
Singular and shingular: note the exaggerated triangular upper story with windows sheltered by an eye-lid roof, protruding octagonal bay window, and double **Dorics** holding up the porch.

[E15b] **239 St. Paul's Avenue**, bet. Clinton St. and Taxter Pl. E side. ca. 1887. 🌶
A confluence of exaggerated **Shingle Style** geometries and **Queen Anne** decoration.

[E16] **352, 356, and 364 St. Paul's Avenue**, bet. Beach St. and Occident Ave. W side. ca. 1856-61.
Three **Italianate** villas built for ship captains.

[E17] **387 St. Paul's Avenue**, bet. Cebra and Occident Aves. E side. 1886-1887. *Hugo Kafka.*

A **Queen Anne** extravaganza of balloon framing sheathed with shingles and clapboards; an interplay of powerful volumes bedecked with gingerbread. Built by brewer *George Bechtel* as a wedding present for his daughter *Annie Wiederer.*

[E18] **400 St. Paul's Avenue**, SW cor. Occident Ave. 1908-1909. *Otto Loeffler.*
A stucco **neo-Tudor** mansion clinging to the steeps of Occident Avenue (Ward's Hill).

[E19] **37 Occident Avenue**, NW cor. Marion Ave. ca. 1893. *Otto P. Loeffler.*
Extraordinary **Shingle Style**, here commanding a corner lot, with towering turret and flying triangular gables, one punctured by a Palladian window.

Outside the Historic District:

[E20] Originally **Gatehouse**/altered into **James Pietsch House**, 101 Cebra Ave., bet. Ward Ave. and Rosewood Pl. N side. 1927. *James Pietsch,* builder.

E22

Brooklynite *Pietsch* remodeled and then moved in to this existing stone estate gatehouse. The result would intrigue *Hansel and Gretel,* as it does us.

[E21] Originally **Caleb T. Ward House**/later Sally and Lewis Nixon House/called Ward-Nixon Mansion, 141 Nixon Ave. (loop), off Ward Ave. (Entrance driveway bet. Nos.135 and 143.) 1835. *Seth Geer.* 🌶
Grand **Ionics** greet you at the crest of Ward's Hill, amidst lesser 20th-century architecture, although from afar the house is seen better than on Nixon Avenue proper. This immense **Greek Revival** mansion once sat at the center of a 250-acre estate. It reflects the enormous wealth of its builder and the era when this and nearby areas of Staten Island were fashionable locations for the wealthy.

[E22] Originally **S.R. Smith Infirmary**/ later Frost Building, Outpatient Clinic, Staten Island Hospital, Castleton Ave. opp. Cebra Ave. N side. (Officially 101 Stanley Ave.)

E21

1889. *Alfred E. Barlow.* Additions, 1890, 1891, *Bradford L. Gilbert.*

Carcassonne on Staten Island? A medievel fantasy cornered with four conical-capped towers, abandoned and overgrown. It missed conversion to housing during the recent real estate boom. Now what?

Back to Bay Street, south of Tappen Park:

[E25] Originally **Dr. James R. and Matilde Boardman House**/ later Capt. Elvin E. Mitchell House, 710 Bay St., bet. Broad St. and Vanderbilt Ave. W side. 1848. ●*

A large **Italianate** villa atop steep Bay

E20

E26a

Back to Stapleton (Harrison Street and surrounds, between Quinn and Brownell Streets):

[E23] **53 Harrison Street**, bet. Quinn and Brownell Sts. ca. 1875-1895. *Charles Schmeiser* and others.

Mansarded, brick, and eclectic, this was home to the brewmaster of the nearby Rubsam & Hohrmann Brewery. It dominates this pleasant enclave where tightly packed individual homes of great variety and high quality stand on both sides of the street. Restored by its proud owner.

[E24] **First Presbyterian Church**, Brownell St., SW cor. Tompkins St. 1894.

Successor to an earlier First Presbyterian Church of Edgewater, the village's original name. The dark masonry, large rose window, and distinctive stepped gables, reminiscent of earlier **Dutch Colonial** architecture, make this a special event in this backwater of Stapleton.

Street, built for the resident physician of nearby Seaman's Retreat Hospital. It was purchased in 1894 by *Capt. Mitchell* with the proceeds of an award for saving all 176 persons aboard a Cunard liner that sank in Long Island Sound.

CLIFTON

[E26] **Bayley Seton Hospital** (Roman Catholic)/ formerly **U.S. Public Health Service Hospital**/ formerly **U.S. Marine Hospital**/originally **Seaman's Retreat**, 732-738 Bay St., NW cor. Vanderbilt Ave.

[E26a] Originally **Seaman's Retreat Main Building**, 731 Bay St. 1834-1837. *Abraham P. Maybie,* builder. ●* Additions, 1848, 1853, and 1911-1912. [E26b] Originally **Seaman's Retreat Physician-in-Chief's House**, 731 Bay St. 1842. *Staten Island Granite Co.,* builder. ●*
[E26c] **Later buildings**, 1933-1936, *Kenneth M. Murchison, William H. Gompert, Tachau &*

Vaught, associate architects; *J.H. de Sibou,* consultant; *James A. Wetmore, Louis A. Simon,* supervising architects, U.S. Treasury Dept.

Hard to spot through the trees from the exit driveway on Bay Street (but worth the effort) is the old hospital's imposing stone façade with two-story pierced galleries and pedimented pavilions. Originally operated successively by the state and federal governments—unlike the privately run Sailors' Snug Harbor on the island's North Shore—this early marine hospital building spawned the large complex of 1930s buildings that now dominates the site. The well-known **National Institutes of Health,** located in Bethesda, Maryland, had their modest beginnings here in a small laboratory of this old structure. In 1981, after the Feds left, locals established the Bayley Seton, named after *Dr. Richard Bayley* of the old quarantine station and his daughter, who later became *St. Elizabeth Ann Seton.* The 1930s additions manage to use **Art Deco** detailing effectively at dramatically different scales—from the attached houses flanking

E27

E33

the entrance to the massive central building that dominates the site.

[E27] **110 to 144 Vanderbilt Avenue,** bet. Talbot Pl. and Tompkins Ave. S side. 1900. *Carrère & Hastings.*

A blockfront of eight high-quality, matching, closely spaced, **neo-Tudor** suburban houses. *Carrère & Hastings* was responsible for other distinctive work on the island and later won the competition to design the **New York Public Library** at 42ndStreet. The developer was *George Washington Vanderbilt,* whose enormous estate Biltmore, in Asheville, N.C., was the work of *Richard Morris Hunt* and *Frederick Law Olmsted.*

[E28] **94, 112,** and **120 Norwood Ave.**
[E29] **241** and **242 Talbot Ave.,** S. of Norwood. All ca. 1900.

Less dressy family members allied to the *Carrère and Hastings* row on Vanderbilt.

[E30] Originally **Mariners' Family Asylum of the Port of New York**/now **Staten Island Reception Center, New York Foundling Hospital** (Roman Catholic), 119 Tompkins Ave., bet. Vanderbilt Ave. and Hill St. E side. 1855. *J. Graham Glauber.*

E32

Contiguous, at the rear of Bayley Seton site is this hostel constructed to care for the widows, wives, sisters, and daughters of the mariners of the port under care next door at the Seaman's Retreat.

[E31] **72 Greenfield Avenue,** bet. Bay St. and Tompkins Ave. viaduct. S side. 19th century.

An abandoned **Renaissance Revival** shell in need of attention. A distinguished loner on this lonely street, next to a lumber yard and concrete plant.

[E32] **73 Greenfield Avenue,** bet. Bay St. and Tompkins Ave. viaduct. N side. 19th century.

Crisp **Gothic Revival** wrapped with a porch, an unlikely moment of tidiness in the middle of what might just be the most backwater of backwater streets in the five boroughs. Greenfield Avenue terminates underneath the Tompkins Avenue overpass, making it seem more subterranean than suburban.

ROSEBANK

For much of its history a community of Italian Americans. Their presence is still very much felt, but many of the buildings and streets are lonesome beyond anything even *Edward Hopper* dreamed of. This is an authentic American working-class neighborhood, mixing housing and industry, immune to architectural fashion.

[E33] **Garibaldi-Meucci Memorial Museum,** 420 Tompkins Ave., SW cor. Chestnut Ave. ca. 1845. 🖝 Open to the public. 718-442-1608. Tu-Su, 1-5; closed Mo. *www.garibaldimeuccimuseum.org*

An unlikely refuge for fiery Italian patriot *Giuseppe Garibaldi*, who lived here with his friend *Antonio Meucci* beginning in 1850. Restlessly awaiting an opportunity to return to Italy, *Garibaldi* made candles in a nearby factory, killing time by fishing and "shooting thrushes." The museum has letters and photographs describing *Garibaldi' s* life and documenting

E36

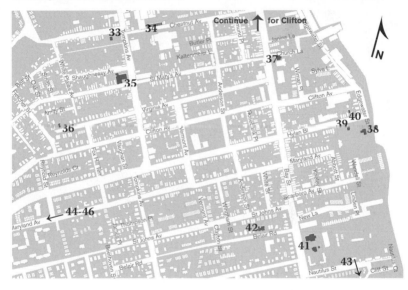

Meucci' s claim to invention of the telephone prior to *Alexander Graham Bell.*

[E34] Originally **Bachman Flats,** 103-125 Chestnut Ave., bet. Tompkins Ave. and Anderson St. N side. ca. 1865.

Workers' housing: a group of 10 brick row houses bracketed by "pavilions" at each end.

[E35] **Church of St. Joseph** (Roman Catholic), Tompkins Ave. bet. St. Mary's Ave. and Shaughnessy Lane. S side. 1957. *Neil J. Convery.*

A very orange **neo-Romanesque** church complemented by a sculptural freestanding bell tower with four bells. Unconvincing.

[E36] **Our Lady of Mount Carmel Society Shrine and Hall,** 36 Amity St., W of White Plains Ave. (Access via White Plains Ave. from St. Mary's Ave. Parking on Virginia Ave. bet. Fox Hill Terr. and Fletcher St.) Established, 1899. *Vito Louis Russo,* founder and builder.

A robust outdoor year-round folk art display, fervently honoring **Our Lady of Mount Carmel.**

The celebrations culminate here (and at other Mt. Carmel feasts all over the City) every summer, about the second week of July. Beat the crowds; visit another time. It's inspiring even on a bleak winter afternoon.

[E37] **St. Mary's Roman Catholic Church,** 1101 Bay St., opp. St. Mary's Ave. E side. 1857.

Tiers of round-arched triplet openings enliven the central bell tower, which identifies this church set on a berm astride Bay Street (once New York Avenue).

Toward the Narrows along Hylan Boulevard:

[E38] **The Alice Austen House, "Clear Comfort,"** 2 Hylan Blvd., bet. Bay and Edgewater Sts., S side, overlooking Upper New York Bay. ca. 1691-1750. North extension, porch, dormers added, 1846, probably *James Renwick, Jr.* Further changes, 1852-1878. Restored, 1985, *Beyer Blinder Belle.* Open to the public except

E43a

during Jan. and Feb; Th-Su, 12-5; closed Mo-We. 718-816-4506. *www.aliceausten.org*

The original one room frame house (1691-1710) was built by a Dutch merchant. Expanded over the next 134 years, it was ultimately purchased and altered in 1844 by *John Austen*, a wealthy and cultivated New Yorker, whose granddaughter, *Alice Austen* (1866-1952), came here at the age of two. She is remembered today for her pioneering work in photography.

E38

More than 7,000 of her glass-plate negatives are preserved at the Staten Island Historical Society. They depict, with consummate artistry, the world she knew between 1880 and 1930. The neat restoration somehow removes too many of the qualities that time had wrought, but the restored lawn is breathtaking.

[E39] **Originally Henry and Anne McFarlane House**/briefly New York Yacht Club/later Frederick Bredt House, 30 Hylan Blvd., bet. Bay and Edgewater Sts., inland of Austen House. ca. 1841-1845. Additions, ca. 1860, ca. 1870s, ca. 1890s.

Now a ruin, it once enjoyed a fantastic **Narrows** view. While the New York Yacht Club's second home, from 1868 to 1871, its members viewed, at the finish line (the Narrows), the first race in challenge for the America's Cup (originally secured by the club in 1851). It could be a marvelous annex to the Austen House next door (as a B & B?). But act quickly; it's returning to the earth. A shame.

[E40] **11 Hylan Boulevard**, bet. Bay and Edgewater Sts. ca. 1890.

Virginia Lee Burton's children's book *The Little House* comes to mind when viewing this adorable little **Shingle Style** bungalow squeezed on both sides by newer construction. Despite its small size, it's a perfect example of the style, with exaggerated triangular pediment above a bulging bay window.

[E41] **St. John's Episcopal Church**, 1331-1333 Bay St., bet. New Lane & Nautilus St. 1869-1871. *Arthur D. Gilman*. **Rectory**, ca. 1880.

Excellent **Victorian Gothic** in rose-colored granite with handsome stained-glass windows. Unfortunately, the original steeple has been altered. The first child baptized in the original frame building of this parish was *Cornelius Vanderbilt*, born in nearby Stapleton in 1794. The adjacent Rectory is a remarkably well-preserved **Stick Style** specimen: ground floor in rugged fieldstone, second story in shingles with neo-Tudor gables.

[E42] **33-37 Belair Road House**, bet. Bay and Clayton Streets. ca. 1845. then ca. 1900.

A picturesque Gothic cottage dubbed **Woodland Cottage** by its developer, the architect is unknown, but it is probably the work of an admirer of *Alexander Jackson Davis*. It was the rectory of St. John's Episcopal Church from 1858 to 1869.

[E43] **Fort Wadsworth Military Reservation**, S end of Bay St. [E43a] **Battery Weed**, originally Fort Richmond, 1845-1861. *Joseph G. Totten.* 👁 [E43b] **Fort Tompkins**, Hudson Road. 1858-1876. 👁 Military Museum open to the public.

The gate and guards look ominous, but visitors are welcome. Drive straight ahead; turn left beyond the bridge, follow signs to the Military Museum and the closeup view down to the landmarked **Battery Weed**, built at the water's edge before the Civil War. The three tiers of arched galleries make the interior of the polygonal fortress far less formidable in appearance than its severe exterior walls.

Romantic legend depicts Algonquin Indians standing here spellbound by the sight of *Hudson's* ship, the **Half Moon**, entering the Narrows in 1609. Since those sylvan times, Dutch, British, and Americans in times of war have stood watch here, scanning the horizon for enemy ships.

The fort was known well into the 1970s as the oldest continuously staffed military post in the United States. Parts of the site have been

E41, Church

added to the **Gateway National Recreation Area**. The National Park Service has created an inviting visitors center with displays locating and describing all of the military posts guarding New York Harbor and its approaches.

ARROCHAR

[E44] **St. Joseph's Hill Academy for Girls** (Roman Catholic)/originally "Clar Manor"/later William M. McFarland estate **"Arrochar,"** 850 Hylan Blvd., NE cor. Major Ave. ca. 1850.

The Scottish name of *McFarland's* estate is now the name of the **Arrochar** community radiating from the academy. The old Italianate villa itself has been compromised over the years, and the academy's newer architecture is uninspired.

🏛 [E45] **St. John's Villa Academy Convent**, Sisters of St. John the Baptist (Roman Catholic)/originally **"Hawkhurst," William H. Townsend House**, 57 Cleveland Pl., E of Landis

Ave./Chicago Ave. intersection. S side. ca. 1846. Additions.

A brick **Gothic Revival** fantasy attributed to architect *James Renwick, Jr.,* who had married a resident of Clifton.

[E46] **H.H. Richardson House**, 45 McClean Ave., bet. Duer and Lily Pond Aves. 1868-1869. *H.H. Richardson.* 👁

Early *Richardson*, before he hit his stride as the great purveyor of Romanesque Revival. Three years after the Civil War, he built this house on a gentle hill overlooking the harbor. *Richardson* died young; he was only 47 when he passed away in 1886. What would he think of his grand house now? The lawn is now a parking lot, the street in front is a traffic-choked intersection, the house is stripped of its detail and covered with white vinyl siding. A man of robust physique, he would probably sigh deeply and have a donut.

NECROLOGY

Planter's Hotel, 360 Bay St., NW cor. Grant St. Tompkinsville.

A fashionable hotel patronized by wealthy Southerners during the 19th century.

Free port to home port: In 1921 Mayor *John Hylan* (for whom Staten Island's Hylan Boulevard was named) ordered the building of a series of deepwater piers between Tompkinsville and Stapleton in an attempt to boost the island's maritime economy. The

E41, Rectory

scheme failed and was dubbed *Hylan's* Folly. In 1937 the area was designated Free Trade Zone No.1, where international cargo could be stored for transshipment without the payment of import duty. This scheme also failed; the truck and airplane had overtaken the ship. After years of neglect and vandalism, the facility was shut down. Taking its place in the 1990s: the home port for the battleship USS *Iowa* and its fearsome complement of nuclear missiles.

Demyan's Hofbrau, 742 Van Duzer St., W of Broad St. W side. Stapleton Heights.

Located in part of what had been a brewery on the hill overlooking Stapleton and the harbor, the restaurant was filled with local memorabilia. Destroyed by fire in 1980.

Nathaniel Marsh House, 30 Belair Rd., bet. Bay St. and Clayton St. S side. Rosebank. ca. 1860.

This pink brick, wisteria-covered mansion sat atop a shady hill enjoying superb harbor views. Removed to build a residence for the elderly.

Central Staten Island

C1

WESTERLEIGH

[C1] **Society of St. Paul Seminary** (Roman Catholic), 2187 Victory Blvd., NW cor. Ingram Ave. 1969. *Silverman & Cika.*

Staten Island's most bizarre building: a manic combination of architecture and monumentally scaled sculpture. Its large size and prominent location make it unescapable, even from a great distance.

Prohibition Park, a community occupying a wooded tract of 25 acres (bounded by today's Watchogue Road and Demorest, Maine, and

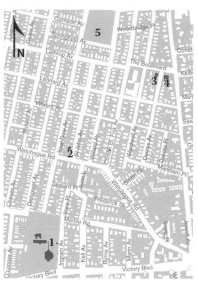

This area of the Guide stays clear of the shorefront communities of the North Shore, covered in Northern [N] and Eastern [E] Staten Island, and deals with the central belt of communities that stretches from the waters of Arthur Kill on the west to Lower New York Bay below South Beach on the east. It embraces the island's chain of inland hills like **Grymes** and **Todt** and **Emerson**, and the **Dongan Hills**, and the entire Staten Island Greenbelt. That verdant carpet stretches southwesterly from the never completed interchange of the Staten Island Expressway and the unbuilt northern leg of Richmond Parkway, to Historic Richmond Town.

Wardwell Avenues) was set up in 1887 for teetotalers; lots were sold to prohibitionists throughout the country. Some streets were named for dry states—Maine, Ohio, Virginia; others for Prohibition party presidential candidates— Bidwell, Wooley, Fiske. Another resident was Dr. Isaac Kauffman Funk, who with his associate Adam Willis Wagnalls was preparing A Standard Dictionary of the English Language (1890). The area today is known as Westerleigh, but the original street names remain to admonish the unwary of the evils of alcoholic beverages.

[C2] Originally **Peter Housman House**, 308 St. John Ave., NW cor. Watchogue Rd. ca. 1730-1760. ●

Long before this area became local focus for the national prohibition movement, this house was built in a position that is today off the street grid. *Housman* was a Loyalist during the Revolution. The tiny one-room stone unit on the right was undoubtedly built first, with the clapboard addition following 30 years afterward.

The Boulevard: this was Prohibition Park's pre-mier thoroughfare. Its 4,000-seat University Temple, a meeting hall similar to the Methodist facility in Ocean Grove, N.J., straddled the Fiske Avenue end with an arched entry spanning two bell towers; it burned in 1903. The Park Hotel, a large frame building, occupied the site of today's P.S.30, between Fiske and Wardwell Avenues, on the south side. A number of the Prohibition leaders' fine 19th-century homes also remain:

C4

[C3] Originally **Frank Burt House**, 42 The Boulevard, SW cor. Deems Ave. ca. 1893. *John H. Coxhead.*

Sitting atop a one-story cobblestone plinth, the most substantial house remaining on The Boulevard: **Palladian** window, fish-scale shingles, and sunburst-pattern ornament.

[C4] Originally **Isaac K. Funk House**, 6, 8 The Boulevard, SE cor. Deems Ave. ca. 1893. *Carr, Carlin & Coxhead.*

A baronial clapboard double house its twin projected bays on the second floor sandwiching an expansive solarium.

[C5] **Westerleigh Park**, N.Y.C. Department of Parks & Recreation, Neal Dow to Willard Aves., bet. Maine and Springfield Aves. 1887.

Today's 2.9 acres are all that remain of Prohibition Park's original green space where band concerts and outdoor lectures were given. The bandstand in the center is an echo of the early days.

SUNNYSIDE

[C6] **Swedish Home for Aged People**/ originally **L.B. La Bau House**, 20 Bristol Ave., bet. Cypress Ave. and Little Clove Rd. E side. ca. 1870.

The mansarded neo-Gothic home of *Commodore Cornelius Vanderbilt's* daughter *Alicia*, who married *La Bau*. **Jigsaw-Gothic** dormer bargeboards.

Clove Road:

[C7] Originally **John King Vanderbilt House**, 1197 Clove Rd., N of Victory Blvd. E side. ca. 1836. Expanded and restored.

A charming **Greek Revival** frame house built by one of "Commodore" *Vanderbilt's* cousins. Purchased in 1955, it was later restored by *Dorothy Valentine Smith.*

[C8] Formerly **Dorothy Valentine Smith House**/originally **John Frederick Smith House**, 1213 Clove Rd., N of Victory Blvd. E side. 1893-1895. Expanded and altered.

A **Queen Anne** late Victorian country house, the lifelong residence of *Dorothy Valentine Smith,* one of Staten Island's most devoted chroniclers.

[C9] **Julia Gardiner Tyler House**/also known as the **Gardiner-Tyler House**/originally **Elizabeth Racey House**, 27 Tyler St., bet. Clove Rd.-Broadway intersection and Bement

C9

Ave. N side. ca. 1835. Opposite St. Peter's Cemetery.

The elegant portico of this **Greek Revival** faces west toward a grand view. Note the crisply fluted columns with their florid capitals (unfortunately painted black) and the chunky console brackets that connect the portico to the house proper. *President John Tyler's* widow resided here after 1868, with her seven stepchildren.

[C10a] **Staten Island Zoo**, Clarence T. Barrett Park, 614 Broadway, at Colonial Court. W side. Rear entrance from Clove Rd. S of Martling Ave. 1936. *N.Y.C. Parks Department.*

Reptile Wing, renovated and extended, 2000, *Gruzen Samton.* Open to the public: Mon-Sun 10-5. *www.statenislandzoo.org*

A small zoo, specializing in snakes (the only zoo in America exhibiting all 32 species of rattlesnakes!), and an accompanying children's zoo. Snake lovers are reassured by the notice: *none of these snakes is fixed—all have full possession of fangs.*

from 1849, the arch-windowed front and tower from 1878. In the graveyard lies *Ichabod Crane*, whose name was used by his friend *Washington Irving* in the story of the headless horseman. The church itself was originally named for the circuit-riding *Reverend Francis Asbury*, the first American Methodist bishop, who made his first "circuit" on Staten Island in 1771.

C11

C12

[C10b] **Mark W. Allen House**, 665 Clove Rd., SE cor. West Raleigh Ave. 1920-1921. *Competent Home Building Company.*

A picturesque Craftsman-style bungalow, with wood shingles, stone chimney, and over-hanging eaves supported by brackets.

[C11] **Scott-Edwards House**, 752 Delafield Ave., bet. Clove Rd. and Raymond Pl. S side. ca. 1730. Altered, 1840.

A formal **Greek Revival** colonnaded porch was added a century after its original construction as a colonial farmhouse with a so-called **Dutch kick** roof. The original unwhitewashed fieldstone walls are still visible on the side. The addition of dormer and vents to the graceful roof line is unfortunate.

[C12] **Son-Rise Charismatic Interfaith Church**/ originally **Asbury Methodist Episcopal Church**, 1970 Richmond Ave., bet. Rivington Ave. and Amsterdam Pl. W side. 1849. Remodeling, 1878.

The side walls of this humble church date

WILLOWBROOK

[C13] **College of Staten Island**, CUNY, Central Campus/onetime **Halloran General Hospital**, U.S. Army/originally **Willowbrook State School**, Willowbrook Rd., SW cor. Forest Hill Rd. to Willowbrook Park. 1941. *William E. Haugaard*, N.Y. State Architect. Master plan for college, 1988, *Edward Durrell Stone Assocs.* [a] **Library**, 1992. *Mayers & Schiff.* [b] **Science Labs**, 1992. *Perry Dean Rogers.* [c] **Student Center**, 1992. [d] **Center For The Arts**, 1993. *Edward Durrell Stone Assocs.*

[e] **Sports & Recreation Facility**, 1996. *Conklin Constantin.*
[f] **N.Y.S. Institute for Basic Research in Developmental Disabilities**, 1050 Forest Hill Rd., on Willowbrook grounds, S of Willowbrook Rd. W side. 1967. *Fordyce & Hamby.*

Built by the State to care for retarded children, these late **Art Deco** facilities were commandeered by the army in 1941 (and renamed for *Col. Paul Stacey Halloran*, U.S. Army Medical Corps) to care for the wounded. In the 1980s it became the central campus of the City University's College of Staten Island. Among more recent campus construction, *Conklin Constantin's* **Sports & Recreation Facility** is a standout, with undulating glass block and lots of trusses.

GRYMES HILL

The hill that lies north of the **Clove**, the "cleft" that defines the route of the Staten Island Expressway. The main thoroughfare is Howard Avenue, which sinuously winds its way along the shoreward crest northward from Clove Road to Hero Park, at the edge of Stapleton Heights.

[C14] **Wagner College**, Howard Ave. bet. Campus Rd. and Stratford Rds. Both sides. 370 feet above sea level!

Founded in Rochester, N.Y., in 1883, Wagner Memorial Lutheran College moved to Staten Island

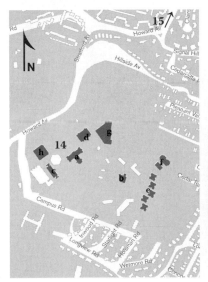

in 1918 after purchasing the *Cunard* property 370 feet above sea level on the brow of **Grymes Hill**. The *Cunards* were cousins of the English steamship family. The college today is coeducational and nonsectarian and boasts a great gathering of Victorian and modern architecture.

Drive up the steep hill to the college, and tour the campus on foot:

[C14a] **Main Building, Wagner College**, East Campus, 631 Howard Ave. E side. 1930. *Smith, Conable & Powley.*

Handsome **Collegiate-Gothic**, with asymmetrically crenellated towers (one with dome, one without).

[C14b] **Cunard Hall,** Wagner College, East Campus/originally **"Bellevue," Sir Edward Cunard House**, Howard Ave. E side. ca. 1851.

An Italianate mid-Victorian mansion, today used for college offices. Its name referred to the glorious view now diminished by new construction.

[C14c] **Mergerle Science and Dr. Donald and Dr. Evelyn Spiro Communications Center.** 1968. *Perkins & Will.* [C14d] **August Horrmann Library.** 1961. *Perkins & Will.* [C14e] **Towers Dormitory.** 1964. *Sherwood, Mills & Smith.*

[C14f] **Harbor View Dormitory.** 1968. *Sherwood, Mills & Smith.*

[C14g] **Student Union.** 1970. *Perkins & Will.*

[C14h] **Spiro Sports Center.** 1999.

An extraordinary collection of "organic mod-

C14a

ern" buildings that use the hilly site to full advantage, designed over a 30-year period by two firms. *Perkins & Will's* student union nestles into the top of the hill, while *Sherwood, Mills & Smith's* dormitory buildings stand proudly at the hill's edge, connected back to earth by bridges.

Organic modernism is a divergent strain of the more machined, glassy International Style of *Mies Van Der Rohe* and *Walter Gropius. Frank Lloyd Wright, Carlo Scarpa,* and *Louis Kahn* were all organic modernists, and their influence is obvious here in the celebration of the site's natural topography and in the use of rougher, "natural" materials (like unglazed brick).

[C15] **Louis A. and Laura Stirn House**, 79 Howard Ave., bet. Eddy and Louis Sts. 1908. *Kafka & Lindenmeyr.* ●

A sturdy **Renaissance Revival** villa with subtle terra-cotta detailing and red tile roof.

EMERSON HILL

Emerson Hill, marking the south side of the Clove opposite Grymes Hill, is named for Judge *William Emerson*, brother of poet *Ralph Waldo Emerson*, who regularly visited him here. The narrow roads and curious homes were largely developed in the 1920s by *Cornelius G. Kolff*, a local civic leader later remembered for a ferryboat named in his honor. **Nos.3, 93,** and **205 Douglas Road** are among the more interesting houses to be found here. (Don't be surprised if practically every lane you turn onto is called Douglas Road ... it just is that way.) Emerson Hill's quaintness results from the constricted yet rustic development patterns and a never ending feeling of closeness with nature, but don't miss the spectacular long-distance views between the houses and the dense foliage. A memorable spot.

its three-bell freestanding bell tower. Called "the church on the curve" since its forebear, "the church in the clove," was destroyed for the expressway.

[C17] The **Billiou-Stillwell-Perine House,** 1476 Richmond Rd., bet. Delaware and Cromwell Aves. SE side. ca. 1660s. Additions, ca. 1680-1830. Operated by Historic Richmond Town. Open to the public for private tours only; to schedule, call 718-351-1611.

Like the house that Jack built, this one grew additions sprawling in every direction. Looking at the building from the front and reading from left to right, you see rooms dating from 1790, 1680, 1662, and 1830. The original one-room fieldstone farmhouse with steep pitched roof, built in the 1660s, is best seen from the back. Inside is a magnificent open-hearth fireplace.

C17

DONGAN HILLS/CONCORD

Before good roads were cut through to the summit of **Todt Hill,** and its forested slopes were opened to high-end residential development, the hills south of the Clove (the cleft through which the Staten Island Expressway passes between Grymes Hill and Emerson Hill) carried the omnibus name: **Dongan Hills.** Since the opening of the Verrazano Bridge in 1964, every Staten Island hillock has been separately named to meet the marketing needs of the local real estate marketing. The area closer to the expressway is called Concord.

Along Richmond Road (between Staten Island Expressway and Four Corners Road/Flagg Place):

[C16] **St. Simon's Episcopal Church,** 1055 Richmond Rd., opp. Columbus Ave. W side. 1961. *James Whitford, Jr.*

A simple gabled brick church enhanced by

TODT HILL

Staten Island's most chic residential area. Its summit, 409.2 feet above sea level, is the highest point along the Atlantic coastline south of Cadillac Mountain on Mt. Desert Island, Maine.

Off and along Flagg Place:

[C18] **Richmond County Club**/originally **"Effingham," Junius Brutus Alexander House**/later **Meyers House,** 135 Flagg Pl. NW side. (Entrance on The Plaza, SE side.) ca. 1860. Many additions.

A much-altered **Renaissance Revival** house where Island *society* has played since 1897. *Alexander* was a wealthy Southern cotton grower who regularly voyaged north during the South's long hot summers.

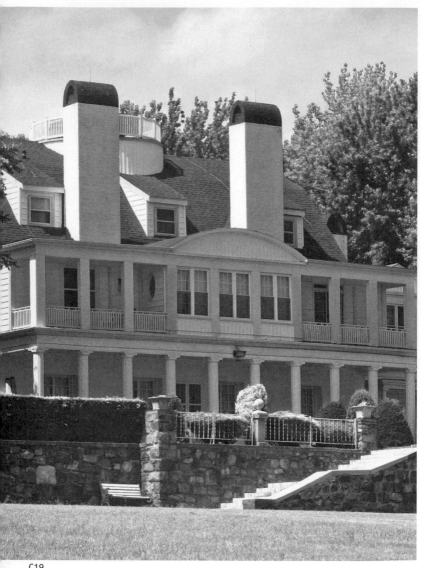

C19

[C19] Originally **"Stone Court," Ernest Flagg House,** gatehouse, gate, and site, currently (in part) **St. Charles Seminary,** Pious Society of St. Charles, Scalabrini Fathers (Roman Catholic), and (in part) **"Copper Flagg Estates"** (see below), 209 Flagg Pl., bet. W. Entry Rd. and Iron Mine Dr. NW side. 1898 to ca. 1917. *Ernest Flagg.* 👁 Additional structures include former **South Gatehouse,** 79 Flagg Court, NW side; former **Water Tower,** 96 Flagg Court, SE side; former **Stable,** 79 Flagg Court, NW side; former **Palmhouse,** 61 Flagg Court, NE side. All part of landmark site. 👁 Accessible from Coventry Rd.

Flagg (1857-1947) was once one of Staten Island's largest landowners as well as a prolific noted architect. Among his works were the **U.S. Naval Academy** in Annapolis and many of New York's finest buildings, such as the lamented **Singer Tower** and buildings for the **Scribner** publishing family. For decades Stone Court was his rural palatial residence, a grand house of unusual design which reflected *Flagg's* interest in, and permutations upon, the local French

Huguenot colonial tradition. (Disregard the insensitive later additions to the house itself.)

[C20] **"Copper Flagg Estates"** (residences on and adjacent to landmark site). Within the landmark site: altered **South Gatehouse, Stable, Palmhouse**. 1987. *Robert A.M. Stern.* New residences, **15, 16, 27, 39, 51, 71 Flagg Court.** 1987-1988. *Robert A.M. Stern.*

Outside landmark site: new residences, **60, 61, 81 Copperflagg Lane, 255 Flagg Place.** 1987. *Robert A.M. Stern.* **15, 25 Copperleaf Terrace, 24, 36, 48, 60, 76, 88, 100 Copperflagg Lane.** 1987-1988. *Calvanico Assocs., Charles M. Aquavella, Di Fiore & Giacobbe, Joseph Morace,* architects; *Robert A.M. Stern,* architectural design review.

In the early 1980s the City's Landmarks Preservation Commission added the rear of the site to its earlier designation, making a total of nine and a half acres, embracing a number of the estate's outbuildings such as the fieldstone **water tower,** the **stable,** and the **palmhouse,** and a generous lawn and pool. A developer, working with architect *Stern*, altered and expanded the existing small structures (the swimming pool, for example, was filled in and became a formal garden), and added new residences, to encircle the lawn. The ten altered and new units on the landmark site were regulated by the commission; the thirteen planned for neighboring lands were not, and there are discernibly clear differences. The entire enterprise is eerie, like a deserted stage set from the 1960s TV series *The Prisoner*; a recent visit revealed perfectly manicured lawns and trim houses, but no people.

Ernest Flagg's Todt Hill cottages: Flagg designed, built, and sold a number of picturesque cottages adjacent to **Stone Court** *on lands originally owned by his Flagg Estate Company.*

[C21] **Main cottage**, 45 West Entry Rd., W of Flagg Pl. N side. [C22] **"Bowcot,"** 95 West Entry Rd., W of Flagg Pl. N side. 1916-1918. ●✶ [C23] **"Wallcot,"** 285 Flagg Pl. NW side. 1918-

C20

C22

1921. ●✶ [C24] **"Hinkling Hollow,"** 309 Flagg Pl. NW side. 1927.

Each house is different in plan and elevation, but all of them share in the use of local stone, serpentine, as one of their principal exterior materials. That, combined with distinctive pitched roofs, a liberal use of traditional and inventive dormers, and hooded brick chimneys, gives them all a very special *Flagg* flavor. One of the group, the **Paul Revere Smith House**, was recently demolished (see Necrology).

[C25] Originally **The McCall's Demonstration House**, 1929 Richmond Rd., opp. and N of Hunter Ave. NW side. 1924-1925. *Ernest Flagg.* ●✶

In 1924-1925, **McCall's** (magazine) publicized (and sold plans for) eight house designs, ranging from four to seven rooms, responding to the needs of America's middle-class homemakers "by America's foremost architects." *Flagg* was one of the eight, but in his case he actually built his, on Richmond Road (a main drag even then), below his estate. Evidently an active self-

promoter, he installed a sign that once read: *this house cost less than the ordinary frame house of equal size.*

Along and off Todt Hill Road:

[C26] **St. Francis Novitiate, Franciscan Fathers** (Roman Catholic seminary), 500 Todt Hill Rd., opp. Whitwell Pl. W side. 1928.

A somber red-brick institution that began as a prep school for those planning a career in the church. Set amid a flowing green lawn, its 86-foot tower surmounts one of **Todt Hill's** highest elevations.

🏛 [C27] **Gillett-Tyler House**, 103 Circle Rd., a loop off of Benedict Rd. to Willow Pond Rd. ca. 1846. Reconstruction, 1931. Additions 1932, 1986-1993. ●✶

A **Greek Revival** manse with Ionic (not ironic) columns flanking the front door. Originally located in Enfield, Massachusetts, it would have been underwater had it not been

C27

moved here prior to construction in the Swift River Valley's Quabbin Reservoir.

[C28a] **New Dorp Moravian Church**, 1256 Todt Hill Rd., N of Richmond Rd. W side. 1844. **Parsonage**, ca. 1870. **Parish House**, 1913.

This "new" church is older than many of New York's "old" ones. The pretentious, gray stucco **Classical Revival** parish house was the gift of *William H. Vanderbilt*, son of *Cornelius*.

[C28b] **Moravian Cemetery**, Entrance, Richmond Rd. opp. Otis Ave. N side.

A large and fascinating cemetery in which some of the Island's most distinguished families are interred, including, in a separate, private area, the extended **Vanderbilt** family (see below). While the Vanderbilt area is not open to the public, the remainder of the cemetery's older parts offers beautiful landscapes, walks, and drives.

[C28c] **Old New Dorp Moravian Church**/now Church School and Cemetery Office, within Moravian Cemetery. 1763.

A good example of **Dutch Colonial**, the sweeping roof extending over eaves to form a porch.

[C28d] **Vanderbilt Mausoleum**, rear of Moravian Cemetery. 1866. *Richard Morris Hunt*, architect. *Frederick Law Olmsted*, landscape architect. Not open to the public.

C28c

[C30] **Gustave A. Mayer House**/originally **David R. Ryers House**, 24 St. Stephen's Pl., bet. Odin and New Dorp Lane. 1855-1856. ●

A stately villa atop the rise overlooking the New Dorp flats. In the basement *Gustave*, the inventor of the **Nabisco** wafer, compounded other savory confections.

EGBERTVILLE

Rockland Avenue, between Richmond Road and Brielle Avenue, hugs Egbertville Ravine, the proposed route of *Robert Moses'* Willowbrook Expressway. The route was chosen, naturally, because it required few relocations of residents and because the costs of acquiring the site would have been low. (The area between Manor Road and Brielle Avenue is part of Latourette Park and is known among devoted local naturalists as Buck's Hollow.) The fact that the ravine and forest south of Rockland Avenue in this

C30, mid-renovation

Seemingly carved out of the "living rock," with an ornate granite entrance and observation terrace added by *Hunt* and *Olmsted*. Buried within the 72 crypts are *"Commodore" Cornelius Vanderbilt* (who paid in advance for the tomb and was later reinterred there) and members of his family. In the remaining **14 acres** of the *Vanderbilt* plot (there had once been 22) are others of the extended family, including the *Sloans*.

[C29] Originally **New Dorp Light Station**/now private house, 25 Boyle St., N of Beacon Ave. 1854. ● Not open to the public.

A former Coast Guard navigation beacon, it guided ships entering New York harbor. Its clapboard tower is hardly reminiscent of the traditional lighthouse form. Now decommissioned, it sees adaptive reuse as a private house.

stretch are a remarkable natural area within the larger **Staten Island Greenbelt** was not—at least in *Moses'* time—much of a concern.

[C31] **High Rock Park Conservation Center,** 200 Nevada Ave., at summit of hill. Open to the public.

A primarily natural rather than built environment, this hardwood forest preserve is a rarity among New York City's protected green spaces. With about 100 acres it is only a small part of the 1,000-acre Staten Island Greenbelt. There are marked, self-guiding trails, a loose strife swamp, a pond, and a visitors' center where more information is available about this nationally recognized environmental-education center.

NEW DORP

Centered on either side of New Dorp Lane, between Richmond and Amboy Roads and Hylan Boulevard, New Dorp expanded easterly after the opening in 1964 of the Verrazano Bridge, and all the way to the ocean (an area earlier called New Dorp Beach). Miller Field, at New Dorp Beach, was once the home of the *Vanderbilts* and, later, of the U.S. Army Air Corps.

C32

[C32] Lane Theater, 168 New Dorp Lane, bet. 8th and 9th Sts. 1937-1938. *John Eberson.* Interior. 👁‍🗨

An **Art Moderne** former movie house hidden among the storefronts of New Dorp Lane. The rounded corners of the sign indicate a motif repeated throughout the building's exterior (look at the façades of the corner shops on the block) as well as inside. The projectors have stopped revolving, but here's hoping they'll start up again. The interior is a landmark; why not the exterior?

[C33] New York Public Library, 309 New Dorp Lane, bet. Clawson and 10th Sts. 2000. *Lepp Associates.*

A sleek glass and brick affair that fits well into the streetscape of New Dorp Lane. The interior is filled with natural light.

[C34] 248 Rose Avenue, SW cor. 10th St. ca. 1885.

A robust Victorian house that controls a suburban residential corner without crushing it to death. The house sports an octagonal corner cupola with an ogival roof, imbricated shingles, and a **Stick Style** railing on a balcony tucked beneath the jerkin-head roof.

[C35] Monsignor Farrell High School (Roman Catholic), 2900 Amboy Rd., S cor. Tysen's Lane. 1962. *Charles Luckman Assocs.*

California modern, in its day stylish and sophisticated (for Staten Island in the 1960s).

All by itself on the Ocean:

[C36] World War II Bunker, on the beach at former Miller Field/now Gateway National Recreation Area, NE of the foot of New Dorp Lane. ca. 1942.

All along the beaches of the east coast during **World War II** the military built observation

C34

posts to spot potential invaders by sea. Simple in conception and form, they were towers of reinforced concrete gashed near the top by a narrow horizontal slot facing oceanward. When hostilities ended, the priorities for their removal were less than those that had determined their rapid construction. And so, thankfully, this remains to remind us.

[C37] N.Y.C. Farm Colony/Seaview Hospital Historic District. 👁‍🗨

[C37a] Seaview Hospital, N.Y.C. Health and Hospitals Corporation, 480 Brielle Ave., bet. Manor Rd. and Rockland Ave. E and SE sides. 1914. *Raymond F. Almirall.* Open-air radial pavilions, auditorium, Group Building additions, 1917. *Edward F. Stevens and Renwick, Aspinwall & Tucker.* **Roman Catholic Chapel,** 1927. **Episcopal Chapel,** 1932.

The earliest buildings of **Seaview,** originally described as the world's largest tuberculosis hospital, are *Almirall*'s in the **Spanish Mission Style** with much inset decorative tile and Spanish tile

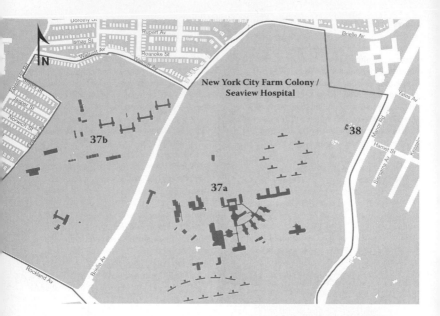

New York City Farm Colony /
Seaview Hospital

37b

38

37a

roofs. It now presents a split personality—many
of the early buildings are abandoned, overgrown,
and decaying, while the City continues to build
new buildings in their shadows.

[C37b] Originally **The N.Y.C. Farm Colony**, Brielle
Ave. bet. Walcott and Rockland Aves. W side.
1904+. *Renwick, Aspinwall & Owen.* Additional
buildings, 1930-1934. *Charles B. Meyers.*
    The **Farm Colony** ("poorhouse" in less

C38

euphemistic language) across Brielle Road consists of about a dozen structures in a range of
styles in which gambrel roofs and **Colonial
Revival** porticoes predominate. The extensive
Farm Colony site was once slated for private residential redevelopment under the auspices of
the City. Many of the buildings are roofless and
subsiding, and thick woods have reclaimed the
site. A ruin: sublimely beautiful.

[C38] **Joan & Alan Bernikow Jewish
Community Center,** 1466 Manor Rd. bet.
Brielle and Rockland Aves. 2006. *Dattner
Architects.*
    A gently sweeping arc of **Jerusalem lime-
stone** greets you on the parking lot side, while
the façade on Manor Road features more typically postmodern forms, including the obligatory round window.

C39

*Lighthouse Hill: west of Rockland Road (which
follows the Egbertville Ravine), north of
Richmond Road, and south and east of
Latourette Park.*

[C39] **Nathaniel J. and Ann C. Wyeth, Jr.,
House,** 190 Meisner Ave., bet. London Rd.
and Scheffelin Ave. S side. 1856. ☞
    Easy to miss if exploring by car, this unusual
two-story **Italianate** brick cube is topped by an
octagonal monitor, nestled amidst heavy shrubbery on this winding street. On the far side (private) it enjoys a panorama of the approaches to
New York harbor.

[C40] **Jacques Marchais Museum of Tibetan Art,**
338 Lighthouse Ave., W of Windsor Ave. S side.
1947. *Jacques Marchais,* designer. *Joseph
Primiano,* stonemason. Open to the public, Apr-
Nov: Wed-Sun, 1-5; closed Mon-Tues. 718-987-
3500. *www.tibetanmuseum.org*
    An improbable series of stone terraces,
designed by *Marchais* and built by local craftsman *Primiano,* winds its way up the steep face

of Lighthouse Hill, culminating in a museum (housing *Marchais'* art collection) and adjoining library (now offices and gift shop). Though she had no formal training, *Marchais* was nevertheless a pioneer, designing this spatially sophisticated complex (based on **Tibetan** mountain monasteries, with shades of *Frank Lloyd Wright*) at a time when few women were practicing architects. Listed on the *New York Register of Historic Places*.

[C41] **"Staten Island Lighthouse"** / **Richmond Light** or **Ambrose Channel Range Light**, Edinboro Rd. bet. Windsor and Rigby Aves. S side. 1912. Possibly *William E. Piatt.* ●́

Richmond Light is strangely distant from rocks and pounding waves but was built on this site because of its high elevation. Now captive to suburban backyards, a tiny circle of federal land amid private property. The tapered octagonal structure of yellow brick, with fanciful Gothic brackets supporting its upper-level wraparound walkway, is a pleasant change from

C42

pure white cylindrical lighthouses familiar to yachtsmen. Most dramatic looking up from Lighthouse Avenue.

[C42] **"Crimson Beech"** / originally **William and Catherine Cass House**, 48 Manor Court, W of Lighthouse Ave. S side. 1958-1959. *Frank Lloyd Wright.*

"Pre-Fab No.1" design (1956) by *Wright* for *Marshall Erdman & Associates*, Madison, Wisconsin. *Private residence; not open to the public.* ●́

Long and low, characteristic of *Wright's* "Usonian" period. A prime example of *Wright's* late obsession with **automatic** houses, this is one of the rare built versions of "Pre-Fab #1." *Wright's* automatics were planned as do-it-yourself projects for the homeowners, who were encouraged to actively participate in the construction, lifting concrete blocks, pouring grout, etc. This was *Wright's* only built house in New York City, and among his last projects (he intended to visit the construction site but died just before the trip).

In LaTourette Park, accessible from Edinboro Road, Lighthouse Hill and Richmond Hill Road:

[C43] Originally **David LaTourette House** / now **LaTourette Park Clubhouse**, LaTourette Park E of Richmond Hill Rd. ca. 1836. Altered, 1936. ●́

Either in silhouette on the brow of the hill or studied more carefully up close, this (minus its 1936 WPA porch addition) is a fine masonry **Greek Revival** mansion. As the clubhouse for a city-owned golf course, however, its interior is a great letdown: mostly barren, dim rooms used for snack bar purposes.

[C44] **The (Sylvanus) Decker Farmhouse**, Staten Island Historical Society, 435 Richmond Hill Rd., bet. Forest Hill Rd. and Bridgetown St. N side. ca. 1810. Porch addition, 1840. ●́ Operated by Historic Richmond Town.

A cozy clapboard **Dutch**-inspired farmhouse with barn-red outbuildings. Acquired by the Staten Island Historical Society in 1955, the farm is a private residence and retains its authentic character down to the stone walls bordering the site.

C44

RICHMOND TOWN

If you're arriving by car, the best approach is from the heights of LaTourette Park down the hairpin turns of Richmond Hill Road, from which **Richmond Town** appears to be a miniature village arranged under a celestial Christmas tree.

At its founding in 1685 Richmond Town was humbly known as "Cocclestown," presumably after oyster and clam shells found in streams nearby. Here, in 1695, the Dutch erected the **Voorlezer House**, their first meetinghouse, used for both church services and a teaching school. Subsequently a town hall and jail were built; by 1730 the town was thriving. It had a new courthouse, one tavern, about a dozen homes, and the **Church of St. Andrew**, and as the county seat of Richmond County was the largest and most important settlement on the island. As such, the name Cocclestown was considered inappropriate and was changed to the more staid Richmond Town. By the time of the American Revolution, when the British occupied it, Richmond Town had a blacksmith shop, a general store, a poorhouse, a tanner's shop, a Dutch Reformed Church, a gristmill, and several more private homes.

[C45] **Historic Richmond Town**, Staten Island Historical Society, Office and public parking, 411 Clarke Ave., SE of Arthur Kill Rd. N side. Begun 1939. Restored, *Wyeth & King,* and other architects; various landscape architects. Open to the public We-Su 1-5. 718-351-1611. *www.historicrichmondtown.org*

The efforts of interested members of the **Society**, combined with blessings (perhaps commandments) from *Robert Moses*, resulted in this "living historical museum" (a kind of intensive care unit for endangered landmarks) of 30 structures built around the physical nucleus of the county seat's remaining governmental buildings and other nearby survivors. To these have been added assorted endangered structures moved from various points on the island.

Walking Tour of Historic Richmond Town. Begin at the Visitor's Center (Third County Court House), on the north side of the parking lot, and proceed in a clockwise circle: west along Center Street, north on Arthur Kill Road, east on Richmond Road, and south on St. Patrick's Place back to Center Street.

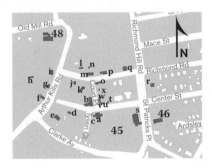

[C45a] **Third County Court House**/now **Visitor's Center**, Center St., opp. S end of Court Pl. 1837. S side. ☛

A grand **Greek Revival** portico succeeds in making clear that this is the architectural dean of this community.

[C45b] **Staten Island Historical Society Museum**/formerly **Richmond County Clerk's and Surrogate's Office**, 302 Center St., NW cor. Court Pl. 1848. Additions up to 1918. ☛

This charming **Federal** red brick building, once a governmental office, is today a museum. Odd bits of Americana of varying interest— china, lithographs, furniture, and toys—are on display, plus a marvelous collection of tools.

[C45c] **Rezeau-Van Pelt Cemetery**, SE cor. Center St. and Tysen Ct. ca. 1780s to 1860s. ☛

One of the City's few remaining private burial grounds, this one is tiny. Note the wrought-iron fence surrounding the plot, decorated with a familiar burial ground motif: winged hourglasses. Time has flown.

[C45d] **New Dorp Railroad Station**, Center Street bet. Tysen Ct. and Arthur Kill Rd. S side. ca. 1888.

Delightful clapboard, brackets, and stained glass in the **Queen Anne** style. Originally the depot, from 1888-1965, for the village of New Dorp.

[C45e] **Parsonage**, 74 Arthur Kill Rd., NE cor. Clarke Ave. ca. 1855. 🍎

A fine example, in clapboard, of **Gothic Revival**, with boisterous jig-sawed eaves and brackets. Still on its original site, it is thought to have been the parsonage of the Reformed Dutch Church of Richmond.

[C45f] **Voorlezer's House,** 59 Arthur Kill Rd. bet. Center St. and Clarke Ave. W side. ca. 1695. 🍎

An archetypical "little red schoolhouse." In Dutch communities unable to obtain a minister, a lay reader (**voorlezer**) was chosen by the congregation to teach school and conduct church services. It is the oldest-known elementary school building in the United States.

tavern, with pints of mead and a regular acoustic (there's no electricity) music series.

[C45k] **Edwards-Barton House**, 3742 Richmond Road, bet. Arthur Kill Rd. and Court Pl. S side. 1869. *Bedell & Hill,* builders. 🍎

A simplified **Gothic Revival** and **Italianate** smash-up.

[C45l] **Kruser-Finley House**, 3749 Richmond Road bet. Arthur Kill Rd. and Court Pl. N side. ca. 1790. Additions, ca. 1820 and ca. 1850-1860. 🍎

Rescued and moved here in 1965 before the **Willowbrook Parkway** sought to plow it under.

[C45m] **Britton Cottage**, 3741 Richmond Rd. N of Court Pl. (moved from New Dorp Beach). ca. 1670. Additions, ca. 1755, ca. 1765, ca. 1800. 🍎

The **oldest** structure in Historic Richmond Town.

[C45n] **Basketmaker's Shop (Morgan House)**, 3741 Richmond Rd., behind Britton Cottage (re-located from New Springville). ca. 1810-1820. 🍎

C45n

C45e

C45p

[C45g] **Boehm-Frost House**, 43 Arthur Kill Road (moved from Greenridge), ca. 1750. Addition, ca. 1840. 🍎

Whitewashed clapboard and fieldstone.

[C45h] **Christopher House**, behind Boehm-Frost House. Originally located at 819 Willowbrook Rd. (moved from Dongan Estate), ca. 1720. Addition ca. 1730. 🍎

A pre-revolutionary house in random fieldstone.

[C45i] **Treasure House**, 37 Arthur Kill Rd. ca. 1700. Additions, ca. 1740, ca. 1790, ca. 1860. 🍎

The oldest (middle) section was built by *Samuel Grosset* in 1700. A cache of gold coins was supposedly discovered during an 1860s renovation, hence its whimsical name.

[C45j] **Guyon Store**, Richmond Road bet. Arthur Kill Rd. and Court Pl. S side. ca. 1819. Addition ca. 1835.

Originally a shop, then a private house (1835). Now done up like a quaint old **candlelit**

[C45o] **Bennett House**, 3728 Richmond Rd., SE cor. Court Pl. ca. 1839. Addition, 1854. Restrained clapboard **Greek Revival** on its original site. 🍎

[C45p] **Lake-Tysen House,** 3711 Richmond Rd. bet. Court and St. Patrick's Pl. N side. ca. 1740. Additions, ca. 1820 and ca. 1840. 🍎

One of the best examples of **Dutch Colonial** remaining in the metropolitan area, saved at the last minute from destruction when moved in 1962 from its original site in New Dorp. It was, of course, built almost 80 years after the Dutch ceded New Amsterdam to the Duke of York.

[C45q] **Crocheron House**, Richmond Rd. bet. Court and St. Patrick's Pl. N side. ca. 1819.

Rambling **Federalist**. Built as a retirement home by *Jacob Crocheron*, it was moved here from Greenridge.

[C45r] **Stephens-Prier House**, 249 Center Street, NE cor. St. Patrick's Pl. ca. 1857. 🍎

A distinguished clapboard villa with both

Italianate and Greek Revival inclinations, sur-rounded by lush gardens.

 [C45s] **P.S. 28**/currently Staten Island Historical Society Archives and Library, 276 Center Street, SW cor. St. Patrick's Pl. 1907. *C.B.J. Snyder.* •

A sturdy old rural school in the **Picturesque style**. *Snyder* was clearly cribbing from *H.H. Richardson*: the mock-Tudor gables, towering chimney and "eye brow" dormers.

[C45t] **Seaman Cottage,** Center Street bet. Court and St. Patrick's Pls. N side. Formerly located at 218 Center St. 1836-1837. *Henry I. Seaman*, developer. •

Seaman built this clapboard **Greek Revival** cottage as part of a larger planned develop-ment, cut short by the Panic of 1837. This is the best preserved of the five houses *Seaman* man-aged to build.

[C45u] **Colon Store,** Center Street, west of Seaman Cottage. N side. ca. 1841. Addition, 1850.

Charming blue clapboard with green shut-ters. Once a grocery, it's now a **tinsmith shop**.

[C45v] **Stephens-Black House and General Store,** 297 Center St., NE cor. Court Pl. 1838-1840. Addition, ca. 1839-1853. ca. 1840. Store partially demolished, 1944. Reconstructed, 1964. •

Handsome **Greek Revival**, with a fascinating reconstruction of a 19th-century store attached to the rear. The musty smell of soap and candles delights a modern-day shopper used to CVS and Rite-Aid.

A brick church whose window openings carry **Romanesque Revival** half-round arches, but whose narrow proportions are more in keeping with Gothic Revival verticality.

[C47] **Reverend David Moore House,** also known as The **Moore-McMillen House**/formerly **Rectory of St. Andrew's Episcopal Church**, 3531 Richmond Rd., opposite Kensico St. N side. 1818. Restored, 2009. •

Excellence in the **Federal style**, countryside division, supported by a lovely doorway and neatly articulated cornice. Behind the house is a good view of the Staten Island Lighthouse. Meticulously restored.

Northwest of Historic Richmond Town:

[C48] **St. Andrew's Episcopal Church,** 4 Arthur Kill Rd., SE cor. Old Mill Rd. 1872. Attributed to *William H. Mersereau.* •

An "English" country church in a pictur-esque setting complete with a complementary graveyard. Borders the marshlands of LaTourette Park.

NECROLOGY

Horrmann Castle, 189 Howard Ave., opp. Greta Place. E side. Grymes Hill. ca. 1915.

A fantasy castle, it was Bavarian, French Renaissance, Flemish, Spanish, and English Queen Anne all heaped together and topped by a crow's nest with an onion-shaped cupola.

C45v   C46   C48

[C45w] **Eltingville Store,** Court. Pl. next to Gen-eral Store (moved from Eltingville). ca. 1860. •

Caution, nostalgists! The Colon Store wasn't originally a tinsmith shop, nor was this former grocery originally a **print shop**. Historic Richmond Town serves a vital service in the res-cue and restoration of truly unique architectural gems, but occasionally dips without apology into theme park territory. Now where *is* that Lionel train set?

[C45x] **Outhouse,** behind Eltingville Store. ca. 1860.

Historic Richmond Town has two such Civil War-era privies. Admire its simple clapboard form: floor, roof, door. Let the record show that this Guide honors noble structures no matter how humble!

East of Historic Richmond Town:

[C46] **St. Patrick's Roman Catholic Church,** 45 St. Patrick's Pl., bet. Center St. and Clarke Ave. E side. 1860-1862. •

Reverend William H. Boole House, 682 Jewett Ave., SW cor. Maine Ave. ca. 1890..

Boole was a well-known evangelist and a co-founder of Prohibition Park. His wife, *Ella Boole,* later became a leader of the Women's Christian Temperance Union, the W.C.T.U.

57 Butterworth Avenue (house), N of Ocean Terr., at end. E side. ca. 1925.

A romantic "gingerbread" house of stucco, stone, and sleek shingles, now replaced by a Disney World version of the same thing, on steroids. A crime!

Paul Revere Smith House, 143 Four Corners Rd., bet. Richmond and Benedict Rds. N side. 1924.

One of the "Flagg Cottages," most of which were either preserved or stuffed and displayed as trophies in the Copper Flagg Estates develop-ment. This one was replaced more recently by the banal. Another crime!

Southern Staten Island

THE SOUTH SHORE

Vast forested acres punctuated with farms, ancient burial grounds, and grand houses overlooking the sea have largely given way to runaway cookie-cutter tract housing. It's a shame, given that much of the south shore was substantially intact into the 1980s. A trip to the south shore is still intriguing, though, because fragments of the old shore still do exist, especially in **Tottenville** (still in every way a separate village) and along the **Arthur Kill Road**, which bends around the west tip of the south shore, following its many twists, turns and back roads. Tangents off the Arthur Kill reveal scenes straight from the 18th century: woods, chapels, mossy graveyards, magnificent old houses, salt marshes, deer, feral cats. *And in New York City!*

ELTINGVILLE

[S1] **St. Alban's Episcopal Church and Rectory**/originally **Church of the Holy Comforter**, 76 St. Alban's Pl. (one-way east, formerly Old Amboy Rd.), bet. Winchester and

S1

S2

Pacific Aves. S side. 1865. Moved with enlargements, 1872. *Richard M. Upjohn.* ● Restoration, 1990, *Li-Saltzman Architects.*

Extraordinary board-and-batten **Carpenter Gothic** with steeply pitched gables enriched by ornate scrollwork. The entrance is not opposite the apse area but from one side; an interesting variation. Formerly whitewashed, a 1990 restoration returned the church to its original colors (browns and tans).

[S2] **Public School 55,** Richmond, and playground, 54 Osborne St., SE cor. Woods of Arden Rd. to Koch Blvd. School, 1965. Playground, 1967. Both by *Richard G. Stein & Assocs.*

The school, a tame **New Brutalist** essay, was, nevertheless, more convincing than most public schools of the 1960s. Now restored with some of the crispness of its opening years.

[S3] Originally **Poillon House**/later **Frederick Law Olmsted House,** 4515 Hylan Blvd., bet. Woods of Arden Rd. and Hales Ave. N side. ca. 1720. Significantly altered, 1837. ● Not open to the public.

Before he became a landscape architect, *Frederick Law Olmsted* lived here, running a fruit farm, planting trees, and experimenting with landscape ideas. Later, when he began work on **Prospect Park,** he moved to Clifton, commuting daily to Brooklyn on the nearby ferry. There are plans to turn the house and site into a public park, but currently it is private (pay attention to NO TRESPASSING signs), and the house is mostly shielded from view by dense trees.

GREAT KILLS

[S4] Originally **Great Kills Masonic Lodge, No.912**, 4095 Amboy Rd., NW cor Lindenwood Rd. 1928.
Colonial Revival in **Greek Revival** dress, now mutilated beyond recognition. Before the stucco arrived, its entrance was graced with twin Corinthian columns flanked by walls in the true, 1830s Greek Revival Style (cf. Mariners Temple in Manhattan).

[S5] **Gatehouse, Ocean View Memorial Park** (cemetery)/formerly Valhalla Burial Park, Amboy Rd. opp. Hopkins Ave. ca. 1925.
A wonderfully romantic, asymmetric **neo-Gothic** composition in rough and dressed stone, with fine ironwork. A proper entrance to a place of repose.

[S6] *Fresh Kills Park:*
The largest dump in the world, Fresh Kills Landfill opened in 1948 and closed in 2001. Championed by Robert Moses as a way to fill in the vast salt marshes just north of Rossville (1940s-style wetlands management!) to provide a base for further development, it grew and grew, becoming a nightmarish mountain range of garbage (taller than the Statue of Liberty!) by the mid-1970s.
James Corner of Field Operations was chosen as landscape architect after a design competition in 2001. Corner, newly famous for his compelling linear park conversion of the abandoned

S9

High Line railroad viaduct (see Gansevoort Market section of this Guide), is the right man for the daunting job of turning a landfill three times the size of Central Park into public parkland. He is wisely taking the long view, de-emphasizing sexy design in favor of processes that will allow the park to grow naturally over time. (The site is essentially a slowly deflating balloon, with compressing, decaying garbage underneath a layer of soil, native trees, and grasses.)
*The ambitious plan is divided into five parts north of Arthur Kill Road and west of Richmond Road, with the West Shore Parkway (Route 440) cutting through it: **North Park** (230 acres), **South Park** (425 acres), **West Park** (545 acres), **East Park** (480 acres) and the **Confluence** (70 acres). Everything from hiking and cross-country skiing trails, bird sanctuaries, sports fields, golf courses, restaurants, and canoeing streams is promised, but patience is required: currently the site consists of lightly-planted arid mounds punctured by plastic tubes venting the combustible gasses (methane) that are the by-product of 150 tons of waste slowly decaying underfoot.*

ROSSVILLE

Rossville, once known as **Blazing Star**, was the site of the old Blazing Star Ferry to New Jersey, in service from 1757 to 1836. Stagecoaches between New York City and Philadelphia took the ferry, propelled by sail or oars, here and in Tottenville. Light industry is alive and well (scrap, auto body, garages) but the historic stuff next to it is mostly overgrown. The juxtaposition between active commerce, 17th-century remnants, and near-wilderness makes the place haunting and memorable.

[S7] **2286 Arthur Kill Road** (house), E of Rossville Ave. S side. ca. 1860.
A mansarded loner currently known, regrettably, as the **Lava Lounge**. It could be worse; at least it's still standing.

[S7a] **Sleight Family Graveyard**, also known as the **Rossville Burial Ground** or **Blazing Star Burial Ground**, Arthur Kill Rd. opp. and E of Rossville Ave. N side. 1750-1850. 🐦
This tiny graveyard is one of the island's earliest extant, sitting atop a concrete wall (an addition) that elevates it above the road and the dampness of the salt marshes beyond. Now overgrown, it is easy to miss. It is directly across the road from 2286 Arthur Kill Road (above).

[S7b] **Witte Marine Equipment Company**, 2453 Arthur Kill Road between Rossville Avenue and Zebra Place. 1964.

S10

A **graveyard** for ships. It is here, on dozens of mucky underwater acres, that rusting tugs, railroad floats, fireboats, and barges spend their last days prior to being liberated of their arcane spare parts for reuse on their still-operable cousins. *Witte's* collection is a sublime ad-hoc memorial to some truly historic craft. The parking lot is full of feral cats, and the proprietors frown on photography. Well worth a peek anyway!

[S8] **Old Bermuda Inn**/originally **Peter L. Cortelyou House**, 2512 Arthur Kill Road, NE cor. Hervey St. ca. 1855. Additions.
This resplendent and grandly scaled **Greek Revival** house sits on a rise inboard from the road. A 1980s front extension masks its stately two-story wood Doric columns (six round freestanding, two square engaged).

[S9] **2522 Arthur Kill Road** (house), SE cor. Hervey St. ca. 1840. Additions.
A lesser, but more visible, **Greek Revival** neighbor to the Bermuda Inn next door. Beautifully restored.

[S10] **St. Luke's Cemetery**/originally **Woglum Family Burying Ground**, Arthur Kill Rd. opp. Zebra Pl. N side. Established as St. Luke's, ca. 1847.

Another venerable cemetery, once the graveyard of the local Episcopal church established here in 1847, now in the shadow of the enormous (200 feet in diameter) steel cylinders built to contain liquefied natural gas (LNG). Among the family names: *Guyon, Winant, Disoway.* The grounds are administered by **All Saints Episcopal Church** in Westerleigh.

A side trip into the South Shore's heartland:

WOODROW

Sandy Ground:
The intersection of Bloomingdale and Woodrow Roads was known on maps as Bogardus Corners—after the Bogardus family's grocery, established in 1860—or, in modern times, as

[S11a] **Sandy Ground Historical Society Library and Museum**, 1538 Woodrow Rd., SE cor. Lynbrook Ave. Open to the public. July-Sept: Tu-Su, 1-4. Oct.-June: Tu, Th, Su, 1-4.

One of the few surviving houses from the Sandy Ground settlement, and the only repository of artifacts and memories of what should have been a meticulously cared-for historic site.

[S11b] **Rossville A.M.E. (African Methodist Episcopal) Zion Church Cemetery**, Crabtree Ave. 450 feet W of Bloomingdale Rd. S side. 1852-.

Established as the graveyard for the 1854 church on Crabtree Avenue, now gone. Its surviving gravestones help illuminate the history of **Sandy Ground**, a story richly told in *Joseph Mitchell's* "Mr. Hunter's Grave," collected in his 1960 book, *The Bottom of the Harbor.*

[S12] **Woodrow United Methodist Church**/originally Woodrow Methodist Episcopal Church, 1109 Woodrow Rd., bet. Rossville and Vernon Aves. N side. 1842. Tower, 1876. 🍎

S13

S15b

Woodrow. Part of the integrated community of Woodrow (on some maps, Wood Row) was Sandy Ground, a settlement of free African-American oystermen who migrated in the 19th century from the shores of Chesapeake Bay, drawn by the flourishing oyster industry of nearby Princes Bay.

A critical landmark in African-American history, little survives today beyond the burial ground and several old houses mixed with newer, banal tract housing. Surviving original houses include one at the corner of Crabtree Avenue and Bloomingdale Road, and one down a bumpy track called Turner Road, just west of the cemetery. A tragic fire in 1963 claimed many of the original houses. Runaway ticky-tacky housing has claimed even more.

This starkly simple **Greek Revival** temple is a step from being spoiled by the awkward arcaded bell tower added atop its roof in the late 19th century, when simplicity must have gone out of favor.

[S13] **Public School 25**, Annex D/once Public School 4/originally **Westfield Township School No.7, Richmond, "The Kreischer School,"** 4210-4212 Arthur Kill Rd., N of Storer Ave. E side. 1896. Enlarged, 1906-1907. *C.B.J. Snyder.* 🍎

Beautiful cream-colored brick with orange brick quoining, trim, and "pediment," constructed from the products of the onetime brick factory for whose founder the school is named. It overlooks tiny **Charleston Cemetery** and, since 1934, the fuel tanks of Port Socony, now renamed **Port Mobil.**

[S14] **Charleston Cemetery**, Arthur Kill Rd. N of Storer Ave. W side.

Another of the tiny community cemeteries that line Arthur Kill Road atop low retaining walls. The name *Storer* is evident on a number of the extant markers, as it is on the nearby street sign.

CHARLESTON

Charleston, formerly known as **Kreischerville** (*Balthazar Kreischer* started his brick factory in 1854), is an area rich in clay. Old clay pits can still be visited. Several brickmaking firms operated here during the 19th century. About as backwoods as you can be and still hold on to vague memories that you are in New York City, not West Virginia.

[S15a] Originally **Nicholas Killmeyer Store and House,** 4321 Arthur Kill Rd., NW cor. Winant Pl. ca. 1865.

A mansarded country store from the time when **Charleston** was a village in the deep rural countryside.

[S15b] **Free Magyar Reformed Church**/originally **St. Peter's German Evangelical Lutheran Church,** 19-25 Winant Pl., W of Arthur Kill Rd. N side. 1883. *Hugo Kafka.* **Parish Hall,** 1898. **Rectory,** 1926. *Royal Daggett.* ●

S17

Kreischer originally built the church for his **Lutheran** brethren. Its early character peeks through despite some unfortunate modernization.

[S16] Originally **Kreischerville Workers' Houses, B. Kreischer & Sons,** firebrick manufacturers, 71-73, 75-77, 81-83, 85-87 Kreischer St. S of Androvette St. E side. ca. 1890. ●

Some remaining examples of *Kreischer's* industrial paternalism. Shingled façades with Kreischer brick sidewalks.

[S17] Originally **Charles C. Kreischer House,** 4500 Arthur Kill Rd., opp. Kreischer St. (bet. Englewood Ave. and Veterans Rd. W.). SE side. ca. 1888. Attributed to *Palliser & Palliser.* ●

A hysterical **Stick Style** house with dramatic, rocketship turret, perched on a hill now overgrown with weeds. Deer congregate around the porch. It's a small miracle that the house is still here, and there are signs of a meticulous restoration in progress. An identical mirror-imaged house, owned by *Kreischer's* brother *Edward,* originally occupied the site just to the south.

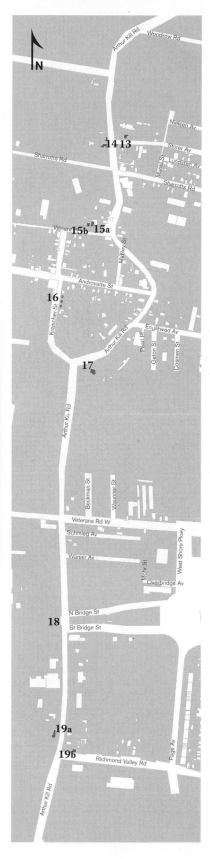

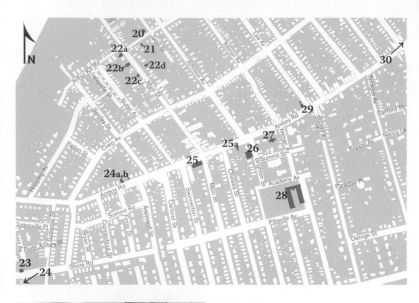

S21

[S18] **Outerbridge Crossing**, connecting Richmond Pkwy., Charleston, with Perth Amboy, N.J., over Arthur Kill. 1928. *Alexander Waddell*, engineer; *York & Sawyer*, architects.

With the decision to name this ungainly cantilever truss bridge after owner Port of New York Authority's first chairman, *Eugenius Outerbridge*, it became clear this would never be called the **Outerbridge Bridge.**

RICHMOND VALLEY

[S19a] Originally **Abraham Cole House**, 4927 Arthur Kill Road, NW cor. Richmond Valley Rd. ca. 1840, additions. [S19b] **4934 Arthur Kill Road,** N of Richmond Valley Rd. E side. ca. 1880.

Two grand houses, until recently a trio, that dignify a corner of remote Staten Island with stylistic idiosyncrasies decades apart, yet in harmony with one another.

TOTTENVILLE

Small-town America, unto itself, at the southernmost tip of the south shore, across the mouth of Arthur Kill from Perth Amboy, N.J. (Ferry service was available from the last stop of the SIRT train until October 1963.) Main Street features various taverns and shops, a shuttered movie house, and a Masonic Lodge.

[S20] **5403 Arthur Kill Road** (house), NW cor. Tyrell St. ca. 1855.

An embellished two-story cube. The flat roof and bracketed cornices of **Italianate** architecture join with **Tuscan** columns to form a delightful cross-cultural blend.

[S21] **5414 Arthur Kill Road** (house), bet. Tyrell and Main Sts. S side. ca. 1870.

A bracketed and dormered mansard roof is balanced by an intricately scrolled porch.

Along Main Street (one-way south):

[S22a] **104 Main Street**, opp. Arthur Kill Rd. W side. ca. 1890s.

The miles of twisting, turning, ever-surprising Arthur Kill Road end at this sprightly **Carpenter Gothic** cottage. (Actually Arthur Kill Road jogs a bit north here, but it seems to end.) It makes the trip worthwhile!

[S22b] **123rd Precinct, N.Y.C. Police Department**/originally 70th Precinct, 116 Main St., bet. Arthur Kill Rd. and Craig Ave. W side. 1924. *James Whitford, Sr.*

Italian Renaissance Revival, somewhat out of context with the small-scale village it inhabits, but elegantly conceived.

[S22c] **127 Main Street** (house), bet. Arthur Kill Rd. and Craig Ave. E side. 1890s.

A collection of ebullient **Shingle Style** volumes is enriched with turned columns, crossed lath, sprockets, and other décor of machined woodworking so popular in the late 19th century. Wonderful!

S22c

[S22d] **Theodore F. and Elizabeth J. De Hart House**, 134 Main St. bet. Arthur Kill Rd. and Craig Ave. W side. ca. 1850. Porch addition ca. 1870. 🍎

Vernacular clapboard with a squat second story. Elements of the **Greek Revival** style frame the handsome front door. Note the delicately jigsawed spandrels on the porch.

South of town, with a backdrop of boats plying the waters where the Arthur Kill meets the Harbor:

[S23] **The Conference House**, also known as Bentley Manor/originally **Captain Christopher Billopp House**, Conference House Park, Satterlee St. W side. ca. 1675. Open to the public. Apr 1-Dec 15: Fr-Su, 1-4. 718-984-6046. *www.conferencehouse.org* 🍎

A fieldstone manor house built by British naval captain *Christopher Billopp*, the gentleman mistakenly credited for Staten Island's inclusion in New York State. (Myth had it that he

Easterly, on and off Amboy Road:

[24a] **Rutan-Journeay House**, 7647 Amboy Road, bet. Bentley St. and Craig Ave. N side. ca. 1848. 🍎

Similar to the **DeHart House** (above), it presents similar Greek Revival columns and doorway, wide porch, and compressed upper story. Currently painted a cheery blue.

S23   S27

S22d

sailed around the island in less than the stipulated 24 hours, thereby winning the island from New Jersey.) The house was the site of a Revolutionary War conference (hence the name) during which the British representatives offered "clemency and full pardon to all repentent rebels" should they lay down their arms. *Benjamin Franklin*, *John Adams*, and *Edward Rutledge*, representing the unrepentant rebels, politely demurred ... and the war continued.

[S24] Originally **Captain Henry Hogg Biddle House**, 70 Satterlee St., opp. Shore Rd. W side. ca. 1840. (Satterlee is one-way north.) 🍎

A clapboard captain's house (like the ones on Captains' Row, in Mariners Harbor) but with a pair of matching tetra-style two-story porticoes, one facing Perth Amboy across the narrow Arthur Kill, the other facing inland. Private home, **not open to the public**, but visible from the street.

[24b] **7639 Amboy Road**, ca. 1850.

The **Rutan-Journeay House's** simpler neighbor to the east; a trim, neat cottage with Greek Revival trim and a compressed second story.

[S25] **St. Paul's Methodist Episcopal Church**, 7558 Amboy Rd., bet. Main and Swinnerton Sts. S side. 1883.

The stolid **Romanesque Revival** gabled brick sanctuary contrasts with and is enhanced by spare but frothy window framing and roof trim.

ENDANGERED

[S25a] **James L. and Lucinda Bedell House**, 7484 Amboy Rd. bet. Chelsea and Brighton Sts. S side. ca. 1869-1874. 🍎

At one time a well-preserved cousin of the **Second Empire**, with a flared mansard roof and jigsawn trim. Currently it's a plywood-covered ruin. Restoration, anyone?

[S26] **24 Brighton Street** (house and former stable), bet. Amboy Rd. and Pittsfield Ave. opp. Summit St. W side. ca. 1880.

A country house surrounded by the later town.

[S27] **Tottenville Branch, N.Y. Public Library,** 7430 Amboy Rd., bet. Brighton St. and Yetman Ave. S side. 1903-1904. *Carrère & Hastings.* Renovation, 1994, *Stephen D. Weinstein/John Ellis & Assocs.* 💰

One of four (and of three similar) *Carnegie* libraries for Staten Island, with knowledge announced by **Tuscan** columns and served by gracious new access for the disabled.

[S28] Originally **Westfield Township District School No.5**/now wing of Public School 1 Richmond, Yetman St., SW cor. Academy St. 1878. Enlarged, 1896-1897. *Pierce & Brun.* 💰

Vernacular brickwork crowned with an **Italianate** cornice forming a magnificent broken pediment. Powerful.

MOUNT LORETTO

[S31] **Church of St. Joachim and St. Anne** (Roman Catholic), Mt. Loretto Home for Children, Hylan Blvd. bet. Sharrott and Richard Aves. N side. 1891. *Benjamin E. Lowe.* New nave, 1976.

A disastrous fire in 1973 destroyed the church except for its main façade. In an imaginative architectural solution, the towering **Gothic**

S26

S28

S29

[S29] Formerly **Dr. Henry Litvak House and Office,** 7379 Amboy Rd., NW cor Lee Ave. ca. 1895. Altered to present form, 1941, *Eugene G. Megnin.*

White stucco and glass-block, perhaps inspired by *Le Corbusier*, but more a matter of exterior styling, as in the work of *Corbu's* contemporary, stage designer *Mallet-Stevens*. It is particularly startling to discover among (and out of context with) its Tottenville neighbors.

[S30] **Bethel Methodist Episcopal Church,** 7033 Amboy Rd., NE cor. Bethel Ave. 1886.

A bold brick and terra-cotta façade between regrettable ticky-tacky housing to the west and still-undeveloped woods to the east.

Revival front was preserved, and a simple A-frame nave was built against it. Economy, simplicity, harmony.

PRINCES BAY

Spelled variously Princes Bay, Prince's Bay, Prince Bay, Princess Bay.

Once a prosperous fishing and oystering village, with oysters so famous that fashionable restaurants in New York and London carried "Prince's Bays" on their menus. An area of run-down shacks with tar paper flapping, paint peeling, and curious developers seeking opportunities for profit.

[S32] Originally **John H. and Elizabeth J. Elsworth House,** 90 Bayview Ave., 400 feet S of SIRT. E side. ca. 1879. 💰

A delightful clapboard oysterman's house overlooking the Lemon Creek salt meadow. Beautifully restored.

[S33] Originally **Abraham J. Wood House**, 5910 Amboy Rd., bet. Bayview Ave. and Seguine Ave. S side. ca. 1840. 🍎

Another surviving example of the many unpretentious **Greek Revival** houses built for Princes Bay oystermen.

[S34] Originally **Joseph H. Seguine House**, 440 Seguine Ave., bet. Wilbur St. and Hank Pl. Set back on W side. 1837. Altered. 🍎

Modest Southern-style grandeur, with an awkwardly pedimented gable, but a commanding view of New York's lower bay. Squat **Greek Revival** columns support a second-story verandah.

ENDANGERED

[S35] **Manee-Seguine Homestead**/originally Abraham Manee House/later Henry Seguine House/later Homestead Hotel/later Purdy's Hotel, 509 Seguine Ave., NE cor. Purdy Pl. ca. 1690 to ca. 1820. 🍎

Two families of French Huguenot descent derived their income from harvesting the local oyster beds and farming the surrounding acres. The original house is the eastern part, built in two stages, of rubblestone walls. The additions to the west and north are of wood frame. *Henry Seguine's* oldest son, *Joseph*, built the larger house across Seguine Avenue. In 1874 the Manee-Seguine structure was purchased by *Stephen Purdy* for use as a hotel. Now a ruin in the middle of a dense thicket of trees. Will anyone save this landmark?

S30   S36

ANNADALE/HUGUENOT

The community of Annadale owes its name to the train station (since relocated to Historic Richmond Town) that honored *Anna S. Seguine*, of the nearby (Princes Bay) *Seguine* family. **Huguenot** honors the early French protestant settlers who came here fleeing persecution.

[S36] **Reformed Church of Huguenot Park**/originally **Memorial Church of the Huguenots**, 5475 Amboy Rd., NW cor. Huguenot Ave. **Library**, 1903-1905. **Church**, 1923-1924. *Ernest Flagg.* **Assembly Hall**, 1954-1955. *James Whitford, Jr.* 🍎

An offbeat design by one of America's most original architects. Built of native serpentinite, a stone quarried on the architect's estate in the Todt Hill section of the island, the church was dedicated as the national monument of the **Huguenot-Walloon Tercentenary** celebration in 1924. The library is the small framed structure of vaguely Classical style on the corner of the property up Amboy road.

NECROLOGY

Holmes-Cole House, 3425 Hylan Blvd., SW cor. Justin Ave. Great Kills. ca. 1730.

An early 18th-century house, overlooking Great Kills Harbor, bulldozed for a tacky subdivision.

S31

J. Winant House/formerly **Blazing Star Tavern**, 2930 Arthur Kill Rd., bet. St. Luke's and Engert Aves. S side. Rossville. ca. 1750.

One of the oldest buildings in New York City, it had been a cozy stopping place for **stage-coach** travelers to and from points south and weary from bouncing over the rutted roads.

Captain Cole House, 1065 Woodrow Rd., bet. Rossville and Vernon Aves. Woodrow. ca. 1836.

This venerable **Colonial** house was a nice complement to the nearby Woodrow United Methodist Church.

291 Richmond Valley Road (house), E of Arthur Kill Rd. N side. ca. 1870.

The third in a trio. Two survive; this one is now just a memory.

THE OTHER ISLANDS

 Colonial

 Georgian / Federal

 Greek Revival

 Gothic Revival

 Villa

 Romanesque Revival

 Renaissance Revival

 Roman Revival

 Art Deco / Art Moderne

 Modern / Postmodern

 Designated Landmark

Various islands, large, small, inhabited, uninhabited, once inhabited, open to the public, closed to the public; all within the City's waterways.

02

Manhattan and **Staten** are the obvious islands of New York City, but don't forget **Long**, the western part of which is occupied by the City's two largest boroughs (Queens and Brooklyn). And the City is festooned with yet other islands. Some are so small or low-lying that tides keep them under water most if not all of the time. Others appear in official documents but are in fact submerged by the City's offal in numerous landfill projects. Yet others are joined, either to each other or to some "mainland," so that they are no longer truly islands. Jamaica Bay, within the jurisdiction of both Brooklyn and Queens, has bits of mucky land that fall into all of the above categories. Luckily for municipal officials already overwhelmed by less arcane issues, the National Park Service now worries about most of Jamaica Bay's islands, pols, marshes, and hassocks as part of its Gateway National Recreation Area.

LIBERTY ISLAND

ELLIS ISLAND

Known until 1956 as **Bedloes Island,** after Isaac Bedlow, its English merchant owner in the 17th century.

[01] **Statue of Liberty** (National Monument), National Park Service, built atop Fort Wood. 1871- 1886. *Frédéric Auguste Bartholdi*, sculptor, *Alexandre Gustave Eiffel*, engineer; *Richard Morris Hunt*, architect of the base. Additions to the base, 1972. 📷 Refurbished, 1986, *Thierry Despont and Swanke Hayden Connell*. Open to the public. Stairway to the crown reopened July 4, 2009.

Bartholdi's sculpture **Liberty Enlightening the World** is indeed colossal: she stands 151 feet high, the tip of the flaming torch in her upraised hand rising some 395 feet above the harbor's waters: her index finger eight feet long, her eyes each two and a half feet wide. Journey to Liberty Island via the privately operated, regularly scheduled ferry, leaving from Castle Clinton in Battery

[02] Originally **U.S. Immigration Station**/ now **Ellis Island National Monument,** National Park Service and Ellis Island Historic District. [02a] **Main Building**/now **National Museum of Immigration.** 1897-1900. *Boring & Tilton.* Guastavino Tile Vaults, 1918. Reconstructed and restored, 1991, *Beyer Blinder Belle* and *Notter Finegold & Alexander*. Interior. 📷 Open to the public. [02b] **Kitchen and Laundry Building,** 1898-1901. *Boring & Tilton.* [02c] **Powerhouse,** 1900-1901. *Boring & Tilton.* [02d] **Old Hospital,** 1901-1909. *Boring & Tilton.* [02e] **Baggage and Dormitory Building,** 1907-1909. *James Knox Taylor,* Architect of the Treasury. [02f] **Assorted expansions and additional buildings,** early 1900s. *James Knox Taylor.* [02g] **New immigration building, ferry house, and recreation building,** 1934-1936. *Chester Aldrich of Delano & Aldrich.* Open 9-5 daily; last ferry at 3:30. 212-363-3200.

03f

Park, and ascend the 168-step helical stair through the verdigrised sheets of 3/32-inch-thick copper to the observation platform in the seven-spiked crown. There—if the crowd behind allows you enough time to gaze— you will see the City's great harbor spread before you.

The New Colossus: The symbolic relationship between Liberty's welcoming form and the millions of immigrants arriving in steerage in New York harbor was not formally established until 1903. It was then that a plaque was affixed to the base bearing the lines of a poem written in 1883 by Emma Lazarus as part of a fund-raising effort for the statue. Its last lines capture the cry of Liberty's silent lips: "Give me your tired, your poor, Your huddled masses yearning to breathe free, The wretched refuse of your teeming shore. Send these, the homeless, tempest-tost to me , I lift my lamp beside the golden door!" To the disappointment of many who climb the stair to the top, the poem is not inscribed on the tablet grasped in Liberty's left hand—that inscription reads july iv mdcclxxvi.

www.ellisisland.org; www.nps.gov/elis
 Successor to the old **Immigrant Landing Station** once housed in Castle Clinton, the Main Building, an extravagant eclectic reception structure, was created to greet (or is it process?) the hordes of, in particular, Eastern and Southern European immigrants arriving at the turn of the century: 1,285,349 entered in 1907 alone, the peak year.

Fanciful bulbous turrets must have brought to those immigrants remembrances of ornately detailed public buildings left behind. Restoration makes the main hall and its lesser companions a vast memorial to the principle that created America.

But will they ever get along? A 1998 Supreme Court decision settled a long-running boundary dispute between New York and New Jersey: New York now owns only the original, smaller island as it existed in 1834, and hence only parts of the buildings listed above. Be careful, lest ye wander unwittingly into the Garden State!

GOVERNORS ISLAND

The island's name derives from an act of the New York legislature in 1698, setting aside land "for the benefit and accommodation of **His Majesty's governors.**" Since then it has served as a sheep farm, quarantine station, racetrack, and game preserve. It is best known for use as a fortified army base, until 1966, and a Coast Guard station until 1996.

After the British evacuation of New York in 1783, Governors Island was owned by Columbia College. The first volunteers to work on the construction of **Fort Jay** included its students. (Columbia, then King's College, was located in Lower Manhattan at the time.) A few years later (1811), the island's major fort, **Castle Williams,** a more potent place, was added to guard the Battery of Manhattan.

While forts were created to protect the waterways, the island's inner land was used as a racetrack. The land was later infilled with the

O3a

O3b   O3i

[O3] **Governors Island Historic District. ☛**
Open to the public Fridays and weekends from May to October only, via a free ferry leaving Manhattan from the Battery Maritime Building, 10 South Street. *www.govisland.com*

The City's Landmarks Preservation Committee designated the northern half of the island an Historic District in 1996. Simultaneously, much of the same northern area of the island is a **National Historic Monument**. A visit is highly recommended. You can walk around or rent a bike. The forts are both highlights, of course, but so are the cluster of 19th-century buildings surrounding bucolic **Nolan Park**.

[O3a] **Fort Jay**/originally **Fort Columbus** (1808-1904), entrance to E of ferry landing on Andes Rd. 1806-1809. *Lt. Col. Jonathan Williams*, chief engineer, U.S. Army. **Officers' Barracks** within, 1834-1836. ☛

The officers' dwellings set within the walls of the fort add a note of domesticity that diminishes the fearsomeness of this now dry-moated

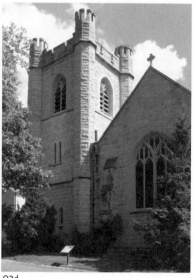

O3d

houses, housing, and barracks of the U.S. Army—a curious choice: the land-based military here at sea.

In 1934 Mayor *Fiorello La Guardia* proposed that Governors Island become a municipal airport. Fortunately, that idea did not succeed, for although the planes of 1934 could have landed on such a potentially short landing strip (and flying boats could use the harbor), it would be useless for modern jets.

Mayor *William O'Dwyer* had a better idea for the island in 1945: a home for the **United Nations**, where it could have been in "splendid isolation" from the commercial city.

New York State bought the island from the Feds in 2003 for **one dollar**. One prudent provision of the deal was that the island not be turned into a casino! Other recent ideas, some far-fetched, some not, have included a new campus for City College, a "World Park," an organic farm, and an artists colony. In the end some elegant and lusty 19th-century architecture has survived these various fantasies.

fortress, built in a pentagonal, star-shaped plan. The brownstone **Federal** entranceway is a felicitous effort bearing a handsome sculptural composition. It replaced an earth-bermed fortification of 1794-1796, parts of the new following the configuration of the original.

[O3b] **Castle Williams**, Andes Rd., W cor. Hay Rd., W of ferry landing. 1807-1811. *Lt. Col. Jonathan Williams,* chief engineer, U.S. Army. ☛ Converted to military prison, 1912.

Appearing from the harbor to be fully circular in shape (hence its onetime nickname, **The Cheesebox**), this 200-foot-diameter red sandstone fortification is actually chevron-shaped in plan on its inland side. Together with Castle Clinton at the Battery, it was built to crisscross the intervening waterway with cannonballs during the War of 1812. They were never used. *Williams*, its designer, was *Benjamin Franklin's* nephew and the individual for whom Williamsburg, Brooklyn, was named.

O4d

[O3c] Originally **The South Battery**, Comfort Rd., W cor. Barry Rd., SE of ferry landing. 1812.

Built to command **Buttermilk Channel**, the harbor's waterway between Governors Island and Brooklyn, this fort is now largely hidden by additions made to accommodate its later use as the island's officers club.

▥ [O3d] **Chapel of St. Cornelius the Centurion** (Episcopal), Barry Rd., W cor. Evans Rd., SE of ferry landing. 1905. *Charles C. Haight.*

Built by Trinity Parish during the period (1863-1924) when the War Department did not see fit to assign an official army chaplain to the military reservation. Inside the **Gothic Revival** chapel hang 87 battle flags and regimental colors from all periods of American history.

[O3e] **The Block House**/later **Post Hospital, Building 9**, Barry Rd., SE of ferry landing. 1839. Hipped roof, before 1863. *Martin E. Thompson.* 🍎

Two-story **Greek Revival**, minus its entrance steps.

▥ [O3f] **The Admiral's House**/Originally **Commanding General's Quarters, Building 1**, Barry Rd., S of Andes Rd., SE of ferry landing. 1843. *Martin E. Thompson.* South wing, 1886. Porch, ca. 1893-1918. Rear ironwork, 1936-1937, *Charles O. Cornelius.* 🍎

A grand brick manor house, porticoed front and rear with impressive (salute, sailor) slender white two-story **Doric** colonnades, served such illustrious generals as *Winfield Scott, John J. Pershing, Omar N. Bradley,* and *Walter Bedell Smith (salute, soldier).*

[O3g] **The Dutch House, Building 3**, Barry Rd., S of Andes Rd., SE of ferry landing. 1845.

Built to resemble the typical house of a New Amsterdam settler but used initially as a commissary storehouse, then as officers quarters.

O3f

[O3h] **The Governor's House**/originally a guard-house, cor. Andes and Barry Rds., SE of ferry landing. ca. 1805-1813. Roof slope altered, 1839. One-story addition and, perhaps, entrance portico, 1930s. 🍎

An unpretentious yet dignified Flemish-bonded brick manor house, the island's oldest structure (updated by historians in recent years from 1708 to 1805). Truly **Georgian** in style, since its official use as residence for the British governors required textbook adherence to the style of the motherland. The original two-story verandahs, fore and aft, were removed. Too bad.

[O3i] **Brooklyn-Battery Tunnel Ventilator Building**, Triborough Bridge and Tunnel Authority, off Governors Island, SE of ferry landing. 1950.

This prominent white octagonal prism contributes little to the harbor panorama but subtracts a lot with its bulk and unfriendly scale.

ROOSEVELT ISLAND

"Instant City" is what some people call Roosevelt Island but "New Town in Town" was the catch phrase preferred by the State's Urban Development Corporation. Back in 1971, the UDC planned a high-density residential community in the center of the two-mile-long, 600-foot-wide sliver of land in the East River then known as **Welfare Island**, a cordon sanitaire for the City's poor, destitute, and chronically ill. An ambitious master plan by *Philip Johnson* and *John Burgee* evoked a community for pedestrians arranged along a network of streets that flowed north from the island's subway stop on the 63rd Street Crosstown Line. Residents' and visitors' cars are stored in a mega-garage at the foot of the small bridge lift to Long Island City, and a bus system links the garage at the north with the tramway and subway at the south.

Logistical delays and the UDC's eventual bankruptcy contributed to changes in the mas-

O4c

ter plan and downsizing in the projected population, and only **Northtown** (dominated by housing towers on either side of Main Street) was built at first, in the 1970s. The 2003-2008 real estate boom finally brought new development to the island, with six new residential towers in **Southtown** adjacent to the tramway station, and the improbable restoration and conversion of the Lunatic Asylum ruins into high-end condominiums at the northern tip.

The silent but exhilarating aerial voyage via overhead tramcar (a subway fare each way) is the best way to reach Roosevelt Island. The silent ride is echoed by the curious silence on the island, a stone's throw from Manhattan's elegant east shore. The quiet is broken only by the buzz of auto tires along FDR Drive across the channel to the west and the hum of "Big Allis," Con Edison's turbine generator, on the opposite shore.

*Walk along the length of the gently zigzagging Main Street, and leave time for a saunter along the two perimeter walks, which offer entrancing views and open parkland on both north (**Lighthouse Park**) and south (the planned **Four Freedoms Park**) tips.*

[O4a] **Aerial Tramway Station**, N of Queensboro Bridge. 1976. *Prentice & Chan, Ohlhausen.* Renovated and expanded, 2010, *BL Companies.*

This was the main point of pedestrian arrival

O4b

at Roosevelt Island until completion of the subway (which can never compete successfully with the sensuous delights of this aerial voyage). The form of this tramway station conjures up images of Switzerland, its steep ski slope roof being very different from its Manhattan mate.

Southtown:

[O4b] **Riverwalk Crossing, Riverwalk Court,** and **Riverwalk Landing** (apartments), 405, 415, and 425 Main Street, N of tramway, W side. 2007-09. *Costas Kondylis.* **Riverwalk Place,** 455 Main St. 2006; **Weill Cornell Medical College Residences,** 465 Main St.; **Sloan-Kettering Cancer Center Residences,** 475 Main Street. 2003. *Gruzen Samton with SLCE,* architects. *Mathews Nielsen,* landscape architects.

Six gleaming housing towers in a row, architecturally part of the same glass-and-brick family tree that gave us recent additions to **Battery Park City** (Riverhouse, Verdesian, Solaire). Locals have been overheard calling it "Millionaires' Row," and while much of it is geared towards the luxury market, there are some mixed-income apartments, plus two towers reserved for Sloan-Kettering and Weill Cornell Medical College Staff. Riverwalk Court, at No.405, has the sharpest edges and coolest profile.

[O4c] **James Blackwell Farmhouse,** Blackwell Park, E side of Main St., S of Eastwood. 1796-1804. 🍎 Restored, 1973, *Giorgio Cavaglieri.* Blackwell Park. 1973. *Dan Kiley & Partners,* landscape architects.

Clapboard amidst the concrete! An early clue that something was here before the 1970s, this trim colonial house was built by the Blackwell family, who owned and farmed the island. Purchased by the City in 1828, it was then used as housing for the penitentiary's administrators.

Northtown:

[O4d] **Roosevelt Landings**/originally **Eastwood,** 510, 516, 536, 546, 556, 566, 576, and 580 Main St. E side, opp. "Big Allis," generator of Consolidated Edison. 1976. *Sert, Jackson & Assocs.*

Main Street is here defined on its east side **largely** by this mega-wall of undulating concrete block apartments, deftly detailed with red accents. Housing built for low-, middle-, and moderate income tenants, it feels less like New York City and more like Helsinki. Huge, it is the overlord to the little **Good Shepherd** across the street.

O4h

[O4e] **Good Shepherd Community Ecumenical Center**/originally **Chapel of the Good Shepherd** (Episcopal), 543 Main St. W side. 1888-1889. *Frederick Clarke Withers.* 🍎 Restored, 1975, *Giorgio Cavaglieri.* **Plaza,** 1975, *Johansen & Bhavnani,* architects. *Lawrence Halprin Assocs.,* landscape architects.

A lovely Gothic Revival country church, thankfully preserved and restored amid the flurry of mid-1970s construction, but adrift in a dreary sea of brick paving.

[O4f] **East and West Promenades.** 1975. *Zion & Breen,* landscape architects.

Both beautifully detailed: the west promenade, facing Manhattan, is the more complex, utilizing multilevels; the east promenade is modest, more subtle, and equally enjoyable.

[O4g] **Island House,** 551, 555, 575, and 595 Main St. W side, opp. Cornell-New York Medical Center. 1975. *Johansen & Bhavnani,* architects; *Lawrence Halprin Assocs.,* landscape architects.

This used to be the really ritzy digs on the island, now largely supplanted by the newer, glassier towers to the south (Riverwalk, etc.). A 1970s time warp, but still handsome.

[O4h] **P.S./I.S. 217,** 645 Main Street, near the Motorgate garage complex. 1992. *Michael Fieldman.*

Most of the Main Street architecture tends to blur together in the mind's eye after a while. But focus on this **tour de force**! Glass block and steel are set within a trim concrete frame that swells gently at the Main Street façade, animating that part of an otherwise banal sequence.

[O4i] **Motorgate (garage complex),** N of Roosevelt Island Bridge. 1974. *Kallmann & McKinnell.*

A mass of concrete, well-detailed. Parking for 1,000 cars.

O4i

The Southern Tip:

[O5a] **Coler Goldwater Specialty Hospital,** City of New York/originally Welfare Hospital for Chronic Diseases, S of Sports Park. 1939. *Isador Rosenfield,* senior architect, N.Y.C. Department of Hospitals; *Butler & Kohn; York & Sawyer.* Addition to south, 1971.

Low-rise chevron-shaped balconied wings extend from a central north-south spine, giving patients confronted with long confinements a maximum of sunlight and river views. Some **Art Deco** curves make this complex several cuts above its cousin to the north, the former Bird S. Coler Hospital (1952).

*The **City Hospital**/originally Island Hospital/ then Charity Hospital was a grim reminder of the 19th century's medical ministrations to the needy: built of stone quarried on the island by convicts from the adjacent penitentiary. It has since been demolished.*

[O5b] Originally **Strecker Memorial Laboratory**, overlooking E channel of the East River. 1892. *Withers & Dickson*. Third story added, 1905, *William Flanagan*. ◆ Converted to electric sub-station, 1999. *Page Ayres Cowley.*

A **neo-Renaissance** work that contrasts in both scale and style with its 19th-century neighbors to the north and south. In its day it was the City's most sophisticated medical research facility.

[O5c] **Smallpox Hospital**, SW of Strecker Memorial Laboratory. 1854-1856. *James Renwick, Jr*. S wing, 1903-1904. *York & Sawyer*. N wing, 1904-1905, *Renwick, Aspinwall & Owen*. ◆

Years of disuse and exposure to the elements have made this into a natural Gothick ruin. Its official landmark designation further encourages such a role in quoting architectural historian *Paul Zucker* on the qualities of ruins: "an expression of an eerie romantic mood . . . a palpable documentation of a period in the past .

The Northern Tip:

[O6a] **The Octagon** (condominiums)/origi-nally **Octagon Tower, N.Y.C. Lunatic Asylum**/later Metropolitan Hospital, 888 Main St. 1835-1839. *Alexander Jackson Davis*. Mansard roof and entry stair added, ca. 1880, *Joseph M. Dunn*. ◆ Conversion to apartments, 2006, *Becker & Becker and SLCE*. Lobby, *The Rockwell Group*.

It was only a matter of time until this happened: the ruins of an insane asylum converted to luxury housing. The mansarded dome has been nicely restored, and two rather bland wings that mimic what once was there have been added to either side of the tower. The afflicted patients, meanwhile, have been replaced by yuppies. Wisely, this project wasn't named **The Lunatic**.

[O6b] **Lighthouse**, in **Lighthouse Park**, N tip of island. 1872. *James Renwick, Jr.*, supervising architect, Commission of Charities and

O5c

. . something which recalls a specific concept of architectural space and proportion." The Commission Report suggests that the structure possesses all of these. It does.

[O5d] **Four Freedoms Park**, southern tip of island. 2011. Original design, 1974. *Louis Kahn. Mitchell/Giurgola,* project architects.

A memorial, the only one in New York, to *Franklin Delano Roosevelt*, designed in 1974 by *Kahn* shortly before his death, but budget cuts scuttled the project. *Kahn's* design is simple: rows of linden trees define a wedge-shaped lawn terminating at a granite enclosure at the water's edge. The park's name refers to a 1941 speech by *FDR*. This will be *Kahn's* **first built work** in New York City, almost 40 years after his death.

Correction. Lighthouse Park, 1979, *Quennell-Rothschild Assocs*. ◆

Built on a tiny island off the tip of today's Roosevelt Island (and since joined to it) under the direction of the Board of Governors of the City's Commission of Charities and Correction, whose supervising architect at the time was *Renwick*. The lamps for this "private" lighthouse were later furnished by the U.S. Lighthouse Service. An octagonal form of rock-faced Fordham gneiss—its crocketed cornice is sensuous. The park is a modest, green, ground-swelling place, with simple timber retaining walls.

*The legend of **John McCarthy**: An inscription carved on the local gray gneiss ashlar of the Lighthouse adds credence (of a sort) to the legend that a 19th-century patient at the nearby lunatic asylum was permitted to build this structure:*

   THIS IS THE WORK / WAS DONE BY / JOHN MCCARTHY / WHO BUILT THE LIGHT / HOUSE FROM THE BOTTOM TO THE / TOP ALL YE WHO DO PASS BY MAY / PRAY FOR HIS SOUL WHEN HE DIES

WARDS ISLAND / RANDALLS ISLAND

Located in the vicinity of turbulent Hell Gate at the junction of the East and Harlem Rivers, these formerly separate islands are now joined as a result of landfill operations. Randalls, the northernmost, houses the Triborough Bridge interchange as well as the administrative headquarters of the Triborough Bridge and Tunnel Authority. Wards Island, a recreation area joined to Manhattan by a pedestrian bridge at East 103rd Street, is the site of a number of City and State facilities, including:

[O7a] **Firefighters' Training Center**, N.Y.C. Fire Department/originally Firemen's Training Center, Wards Island, NE part of island opp. Astoria Park, Queens. 1975. *Hardy Holzman Pfeiffer Assocs.*

Built to substitute for the old firemen's training center demolished on Roosevelt Island, it's a

O6a

confident work of architecture and witty, too— shades of those wonderfully exuberant *Napoleon LeBrun & Sons'* firehouses of the 1890s!

[O7b] **Manhattan Children's Treatment Center, N.Y.S. Department of Mental Hygiene**, Wards Island, opp. E.107th St. recreation pier. 1972. *Richard G. Stein & Assocs.*

Campus style low-rise residence, teaching, and treatment facilities for mentally retarded and emotionally disturbed children. Vitreous block in variegated tones of brown enrich the appearance of this handsome grouping.

[O7c] **Randall's Island Tennis Center.** 2009. *Ricardo Zurita* with *Jerome Kerner/Bond Street Architecture & Design;* **Icahn Stadium.** 2005. *Ricardo Zurita* with *RMJM (The Hillier Group).*

Two first-rate sports facilities for Randall's Island Park. The Tennis Center, clad in blue and bright green metal panels, features 20 courts and a clubhouse, lounge, and café.

NORTH AND SOUTH BROTHER ISLANDS

Both are uninhabited and not open to the public. **North Brother** is home to both a population of nesting herons and the abandoned, overgrown ruins of Riverside Hospital, famous for confining *Typhoid Mary* until her death in 1938. *Phillip Lopate,* in his excellent collection *Waterfront: A Walk Around Manhattan* (2005), wrote a memo-

O6b

rable account of being stranded on the island during a heron-counting expedition. **South Brother**, meanwhile, is strictly for the birds.

OFF-LIMITS AND INACCESSIBLE

Other off-limits islands include **Rikers Island** and **Hart Island** (both technically parts of the Bronx). Rikers is, of course, home to the City's prison population, while Hart is the City's 45-acre potter's field, administered (strangely) by the prison system. To the north and west of Hart are spits of land hardly worth mentioning, except for their memorable names: **Goose** and **Rat Islands**, the **Chimney Sweeps**, and the **Blauzes**. Quite visible but inaccessible because the currents of the East River are tiny bits of land such as **Belmont Island**, south of Roosevelt Island opposite the United Nations; and **Mill Rock**, just east of 96th Street. No, you may not build your house on Mill Rock!

SUBJECT INDEX

Boldface names are the names of geographical entities, such as neighborhoods or historical districts.

Italicized names are the names of individuals or firms. They all include a qualifier in parentheses that specifies their role in relation to New York's architecture. The names of architects, landscape architects, sculptors, etc., are followed by a list of works whose evolution they participated in.

Plain text names are the names of buildings and other man-made structures. Some include a qualifier to identify the type of thing the name pertains to.

Boldface page numbers signify the location of an illustration pertaining to text describing a person, place, or thing. If the entry does not also have a plain text page number, the boldface number indicates the location of both the illustration and its corresponding text.

ADDRESS INDEX

Boldface page numbers signify the location of an illustration pertaining to text describing a person, place, or thing. If the entry does not also have a plain text page number, the boldface number indicates the location of both the illustration and its corresponding text.

PHOTOGRAPHY CREDITS

NW = Norval White. FL = Fran Leadon.
AB = Andrea Barley. CC = Cinthia Cedeno.
AC = Amanda Chen. GD = Glenn DeRoche.
MD = Mary Doumas. CD = Christopher Drobny.
KD = Katja Dubinsky. WE = William Eng.
JF = Jon Fouskaris. JG = Jaimee Gee.
AH = Adrian Hayes. CH = Calista Ho.
BK = Bradley Kaye. TL = Tiffany Liu.
AL = Adrian Lopez. DM = Douglas Moreno.
MO = Marina Ovtchinnikova.
RP = Ross Pechenyy. JP = Jason Prunty.

MANHATTAN:
Financial District: NW, FL, BK; Water St.
Corridor/South St. Seaport: NW, FL; Broadway-
Nassau: NW, FL, BK; Battery Park City: FL; World
Trade Center area: NW, FL; Tribeca: NW, FL, CD;
Civic Center: NW, FL, BK, CD; Chinatown/Little
Italy: FL, DM; Lower East Side: NW, FL, BK, AC;
SoHo: NW, FL, CD; Washington Square: NW, FL;
West Village: FL, IL, DM; Astor Place: NW, FL, IL;
South Village: FL; East Village: FL, DM;
Chelsea: NW, FL, MO, CH; Gansevoort Market/

The City College Research Team at the Jane Jacobs House, Greenwich Village, October 2009.
L to R: *Cinthia Cedeno, Andrea Barley, Bradley Kaye, Maria Olmedo, Douglas Moreno, Jason Prunty, Jon Fouskaris, Jaimee Gee, David Seto, Mary Doumas, Calista Ho, Adrian Hayes, Amanda Chen, Katja Dubinsky, Marina Ovtchinnikova, Billy Schaefer, William Eng, Adrian Lopez, Tiffany Liu. Not pictured: Glenn DeRoche, Christopher Drobny, Ross Pechenyy.*

BS = Billy Schaefer. DS = David Seto.
IL = Ian Leadon. KF = Ken Ficara.
JG = Jesse Goldstine.

Historic photographs and drawings are from the authors collections. All maps are original illustrations by Teresa Fox and Norval White, utilizing data derived from base maps copyrighted by the New York City Department of Information Technology and Telecommunications. All rights reserved. Photo of Greenhouse by ado (p. 186).

High Line: FL; W. Chelsea: FL, CH, JG; Hudson
River Park: FL; Ladies Mile: FL, MO, CH; Union
Square: BK; Stuyvesant Square: BK, JF; Rose Hill
and Kips Bay: JF; Madison Square/Bryant
Park/Javits: FL, GD; Murray Hill: AC; Clinton: FL,
KD; Times Square/Columbus Circle: NW, FL, KD,
CD, AH; Grand Central/Park Avenue: FL, AH, JF;
Fifth Avenue Swath: FL, JF, BK, AH; UN/Turtle
Bay: FL, JF, GD; Lincoln Center: FL, KD; Riverside
Drive: MO, CH; Broadway and Environs: FL, JF,
CD, AH; Central Park West/Park Blocks: NW, JF,
AC, JP; W. Side Urban Renewal/Manhattan
Valley: JP; Central Park: NW, KD, MO, CH; Gold
Coast: NW, CH, MO, JF, AH; Met Museum: AC,
AH; Carnegie Hill: KD, CD; East of Eden and
Yorkville/Hospitalia: FL, CD; Morningside
Heights: FL, GD, DM; Manhattanville: DM;
Hamilton Heights: FL, DM, AC; Harlem: JP;
Washington Heights: JP, GD.

THE AMERICAN INSTITUTE OF ARCHITECTS

BROOKLYN:
All by FL except Boerum Hill: FL, AC; Ft. Greene, Clinton Hill, Sunset Park: AC; Prospect Park and Institute Park: NW, FL, AC, AH; Park Slope: FL, BK; Bed-Stuy and Crown Heights: FL, KF; Williamsburg, Greenpoint, Prospect Park South, Bay Ridge/Ft. Hamilton/Dyker Heights, Bensonhurst/Bath Beach, Gravesend, Sheepshead Bay, Gerritsen Beach, Marine Park, Manhattan/Brighton Beach, Coney Island: JF.

QUEENS:
Hallets Pt., Ravenswood, South Astoria, Sunnyside, Woodside, Hunters Pt.: MD; Ditmars, Steinway, Long Island City, Jackson Heights: BS; Corona: JG, RP, BS; Blissville, Southern Queens, Far Queens, Rockaways: TL, WE; Elmhurst, Ridgewood, Middle Village, Glendale, Forest Hills, Kew Gardens, College Pt., Malba, Whitestone, Beechhurst, Broadway-Flushing, Flushing, Auburndale, Utopia, Fresh Meadows: JG, RP, Bayside, JFK Airport, Flushing Meadows/Corona Park, Queens Botanic Garden: FL.

BRONX:
Mott Haven, Port Morris, Melrose, The Hub, Morrisania: DS; Crotona Park, Longwood/Hunts Pt., Fordham, Belmont/Twin Parks East, West Farms, Riverdale, Westchester Square/Morris Park, Northern Bronx: AB, CC; Bronx Zoo, Botanical Garden, Grand Concourse, Highbridge, University, and Kingsbridge Heights, Marble Hill, Bedford Park/Norwood: JF; Soundview, Clason Pt., Unionport, Van Nest, Parkchester, Pelham Pkwy, Bronxdale, Throgs Neck, Pelham Bay, Country Club: TL, WE; City Island: FL.

STATEN ISLAND:
All by FL except St. George, New Brighton, Livingston: AL; Tompkinsville, Stapleton, Stapleton Heights: BS.

OTHER ISLANDS:
All by FL.

Since 1857 the American Institute of Architects has represented the professional interests of America's architects. As AIA members, more than 86,000 licensed architects, emerging professionals, and allied partners in design express their commitment to excellence and livability in our nation's buildings and communities. Membership in the AIA offers a vast pool of resources and keeps architects (and architecture students) informed of critical professional issues. The AIA New Chapter is headquartered at the Center for Architecture, a delightful space at 536 LaGuardia Place in Greenwich Village that features a regular series of events, including first-rate exhibitions and lectures. For information on membership, see *www.aiany.org* or call 212-683-0023. The AIA New York Chapter publishes a quarterly magazine, *Oculus*, that features the work of many of the architects mentioned in this Guide, and *e-Oculus*, a monthly online journal available at *www.aiany.org/eOCULUS/newsletter*.